Microsoft®
ENCARTA®
THESAURUS

Microsoft®
ENCARTA®
THESAURUS

GENERAL EDITOR

SUSAN JELLIS

St. Martin's Paperbacks

A BLOOMSBURY REFERENCE BOOK
Created from the Bloomsbury Database of World English

First published in the United States of America in 2002 by
St. Martin's Press
175 Fifth Avenue
New York, NY 10010

Library of Congress Cataloging-in-Publication Data is available on request.

ISBN 0-312-98363-8

10 9 8 7 6 5 4

Typeset by Selwood Systems, Midsomer Norton, Radstock, United Kingdom
Printed in the United States of America

Contents

Using the Microsoft® Encarta® Thesaurus

The *Microsoft® Encarta® Thesaurus* is arranged like a dictionary: you look up an entry word and immediately find alternatives for its common meanings. When there is more than one meaning of word, each meaning is numbered. The first alternative, printed in **bold**, tells you exactly which meaning is being illustrated. The lists of alternatives are arranged for ease of use, with the more general alternatives toward the beginning of the list.

Alternatives that can be used only in more specific contexts are shown toward the end, often with a label, e.g., *slang* or *literary*, to indicate the type of language they belong to. Words used in informal contexts are labeled *infml* and those used in formal contexts are labeled *fml*.

You will sometimes also be offered words with opposite or contrasting meaning, introduced by the term *Opposite:*

First alternative indicating the meaning

Entry word for which alternatives are given

masses *n* **common people**, crowd, multitude, commonality, hoi polloi *Opposite*: elite

Word with opposite meaning to entry word

massif *n* **mountain range**, chain, sierra, ridge, line

Part of speech of entry word

massive *adj* **1 bulky**, heavy, solid, weighty, hulking *Opposite*: slight **2 huge**, enormous, gigantic, immense, colossal *Opposite*: tiny

Each meaning distinguished by number

Phrases entered in their alphabetical place

make a hash of *(infml)* *v* **muddle**, confuse, jumble, spoil, mix up

Label indicating that entry word belongs to informal usage

make allowances *v* **take into account**, bear in mind, consider, take into consideration, cut somebody some slack *(slang)*

make amends *v* **compensate**, make reparations, make up for, pay back, recompense

Label indicating that alternative belongs to slang usage

At some entries there are also panels listing words that are not alternatives but *types of* the same thing, e.g., types of birds, or names for male or female animals.

gender *n* **sex**, sexual category, sexual characteristics, masculinity, femininity

WORD BANK
❑ **types of female animals** bitch, cow, dam, doe, ewe, filly, heifer, hind, jenny, lioness, mare, nanny goat, sow, tigress, vixen
❑ **types of male animals** billy goat, boar, buck, bull, bullock, colt, hart, jackass, ram, stag, stallion, steer, tom, tomcat, wether
❑ **types of male birds or female birds** capon, cob, cock, cockerel, drake, duck, gander, goose, hen, pen, rooster

Parts of objects, e.g., parts of an aircraft or the human body, are shown in the same way.

alimentary canal *n* **bowels**, guts, innards, insides, intestines

WORD BANK
❑ **parts of an alimentary canal** anus, appendix, bile duct, bladder, bowel, cecum, colon, duodenum, esophagus, gallbladder, gullet, gut, intestine, kidney, large intestine, liver, pancreas, rectum, small intestine, spleen, stomach, throat

The notes shown after some entries help to discriminate between the meanings of closely related words by giving brief definitions for them.

accomplish *v* **achieve**, attain, realize, carry out, pull off (*infml*)

COMPARE AND CONTRAST CORE MEANING: bring something to a successful conclusion
accomplish succeed in doing something; **achieve** succeed in something, usually with effort; **attain** reach a specific objective; **realize** fulfill a specific vision or plan; **carry out** perform or accomplish a task or activity; **pull off** (*infml*) to accomplish something, despite difficulties.

Test Your Word Power

Once – as a child – you were an expert, an accomplished virtuoso, at learning new words. Today, by comparison, you are a mere amateur.

Does this statement sound insulting? It may be – but if you are the average adult, it is a statement that is, unfortunately, only too true.

Educational testing indicates that children of ten who have grown up in families in which English is the mother tongue have recognition vocabularies of over twenty thousand words – *and that these same ten-year-olds have been learning new words at a rate of many hundreds a year since the age of four.* In astonishing contrast, studies show that adults who are no longer attending high school increase their vocabularies at a pace slower than twenty-five to fifty words annually.

So how do you assess your own vocabulary?

A Test of Vocabulary Range

Here are some brief phrases, each containing one word in *italics*; your task is to find the closest alternative definition for each italic word. To keep your score valid, avoid making wild guesses. The key to the correct answers will be found at the end of the test.

1. to *parry* a blow is to...
   - (a) fend it off
   - (b) fear it
   - (c) expect it
   - (d) invite it
   - (e) ignore it

2. a *prevalent* disease: is...
   - (a) dangerous
   - (b) catching
   - (c) childhood
   - (d) fatal
   - (e) widespread

3. an *erudite* person is...
   - (a) very wise
   - (b) very knowledgeable
   - (c) impolite
   - (d) serious
   - (e) wrong

4. to *supersede* something is to...
   - (a) enforce it
   - (b) specify penalties for it
   - (c) replace it
   - (d) repeal it
   - (e) continue it

5. an *indefatigable* worker is:
   - (a) well-paid
   - (b) tired
   - (c) skillful
   - (d) untiring
   - (e) pleasant

6. a *loquacious* person is...
   - (a) miserable
   - (b) easily annoyed
   - (c) indecisive
   - (d) good at public speaking
   - (e) talkative

7. an *incorrigible* optimist is...
   - (a) happy
   - (b) impossible to change or reform
   - (c) foolish
   - (d) hopeful
   - (e) unreasonable

8. a notorious *demagogue* is a...
   - (a) believer in democracy
   - (b) firebrand
   - (c) someone who commits fraud
   - (d) liar
   - (e) spendthrift

9. living in *affluence* involves...
   - (a) difficult circumstances
   - (b) countrified surroundings
   - (c) fear
   - (d) wealth
   - (e) poverty

10. a *gourmet* is a...
    - (a) seasoned traveler
    - (b) greedy eater
    - (c) vegetarian
    - (d) connoisseur of good food
    - (e) skillful chef

11. to *simulate* interest is to...
    - (a) fake it
    - (b) feel it
    - (c) lose it
    - (d) stir it up
    - (e) ask for it

12. a *magnanimous* action is...
    - (a) puzzling
    - (b) generous
    - (c) foolish
    - (d) unnecessary
    - (e) wise

13. a *clandestine* meeting is...
    - (a) prearranged
    - (b) hurried
    - (c) important
    - (d) secret
    - (e) public

14. to *vacillate* is to...
    - (a) avoid something
    - (b) act indecisively
    - (c) administer an injection
    - (d) treat somebody
    - (e) scold somebody

15. a *circumspect* person is...
    - (a) restrained
    - (b) confident
    - (c) cautious
    - (d) honest
    - (e) intelligent

16. *diaphanous* material is...
    - (a) strong
    - (b) sheer and gauzy
    - (c) colorful
    - (d) expensive
    - (e) synthetic

17. a *taciturn* host is...
   - (a) stingy
   - (b) generous
   - (c) disinclined to conversation
   - (d) charming
   - (e) gloomy

18. to *malign* somebody is to...
   - (a) accuse somebody
   - (b) help somebody
   - (c) disbelieve somebody
   - (d) denigrate somebody
   - (e) introduce somebody

19. a *tendentious* statement is...
   - (a) pompous
   - (b) biased
   - (c) misleading
   - (d) formal
   - (e) emotional

20. *vicarious* enjoyment is...
   - (a) complete
   - (b) unspoiled
   - (c) experienced by identifying with another person
   - (d) long-lasting
   - (e) short-lived

21. a *placebo* is...
   - (a) a calming drug
   - (b) a substance that counteracts a poison
   - (c) a drug that has no real effect
   - (d) a sleeping pill
   - (e) an anti-inflammatory drug

22. an *iconoclastic* attitude is...
   - (a) adoring
   - (b) sneering at tradition
   - (c) troubled
   - (d) difficult
   - (e) religious

23. a *tyro* is a...
   - (a) dominating personality
   - (b) beginner
   - (c) accomplished musician
   - (d) dabbler
   - (e) serious student

24. a *laconic* reply is...
   - (a) immediate
   - (b) assured
   - (c) brief
   - (d) unintelligible
   - (e) angry

25. an *anomalous* situation is...
   - (a) dangerous
   - (b) intriguing
   - (c) uncharacteristic
   - (d) pleasant
   - (e) unhappy

26. *perspicacity* is...
   - (a) sincerity
   - (b) astuteness
   - (c) love
   - (d) faithfulness
   - (e) longing

27. an unpopular *martinet* is a...
   - (a) candidate
   - (b) supervisor
   - (c) strict disciplinarian
   - (d) military leader
   - (e) discourteous snob

28. a *gregarious* person is...
   - (a) outwardly calm
   - (b) very sociable
   - (c) completely untrustworthy
   - (d) vicious
   - (e) self-effacing and timid

29. an *inveterate* gambler is...
   - (a) impoverished
   - (b) successful
   - (c) hardened
   - (d) occasional
   - (e) superstitious

Key:
1. parry = fend off
2. prevalent = widespread
3. erudite = very knowledgeable
4. supersede = replace
5. indefatigable = untiring
6. loquacious = talkative
7. incorrigible = impossible to change or reform
8. demagogue = firebrand
9. affluence = wealth
10. gourmet = connoisseur of good food
11. simulate = fake
12. magnanimous = generous
13. clandestine = secret
14. vacillate = act indecisively
15. circumspect = cautious
16. diaphanous = sheer and gauzy
17. taciturn = disinclined to conversation
18. malign = denigrate
19. tendentious = biased
20. vicarious = experienced by identifying with another person
21. placebo = drug with no real effect
22. iconoclastic = sneering at tradition
23. tyro = beginner
24. laconic = brief
25. anomalous = uncharacteristic
26. perspicacity = astuteness
27. martinet = strict disciplinarian
28. gregarious = very sociable
29. inveterate = hardened

Scoring:
Your score (one point for each correct choice): _____

The meaning of your score:
0–5:	below average
6–15:	average
16–24:	above average
25–29	excellent

A Test of Verbal Speed

Part 1
In no more than two minutes (time yourself, or have someone time you), decide whether the word in column B has the *same* (or *approximately the same*) meaning as the word in column A; the *opposite* (or *approximately opposite*) meaning; or whether the two words are merely *different*.
Circle S for *same*, O for *opposite*, and D for *different*.

Column A	Column B			
1. sweet	bitter	S	O	D
2. big	threatening	S	O	D
3. danger	peril	S	O	D
4. love	hate	S	O	D
5. stand	rise	S	O	D
6. tree	branch	S	O	D
7. doubtful	certain	S	O	D
8. begin	start	S	O	D
9. strange	familiar	S	O	D
10. male	female	S	O	D
11. powerful	weak	S	O	D
12. beyond	under	S	O	D
13. go	get	S	O	D
14. growl	cry	S	O	D
15. open	close	S	O	D
16. chair	table	S	O	D
17. want	desire	S	O	D
18. idle	working	S	O	D
19. rich	luxuriant	S	O	D
20. building	structure	S	O	D

Part 2
In no more than three minutes (again, time yourself or have someone time you), write down as many *different* words as you can think of starting with the letter D.
Do not use various forms of a word, such as *do, doing, does, done, doer,* etc.

Key: Part 1: 1 – O, 2 – D, 3 – S, 4 – O, 5 – S, 6 – D, 7 – O, 8 – S, 9 – O, 10 – O, 11 – O, 12 – D, 13 – D, 14 – D, 15 – O, 16 – D, 17 – S, 18 – O, 19 – S, 20 – S

Part 2: Any English word starting with D is correct unless it is merely another form of a previous word on the list.

Scoring:

Part 1
Score 5 points for each correct answer. Maximum score: 100 points.
Your score on Part 1: _____

Part 2
Score 1 point for each word.
Your score on Part 2: _____

Total score on verbal speed: _____

The meaning of your verbal speed score:

0–50:	below average
51–99:	average
100–149:	above average
150–200:	excellent

A Test of Verbal Responsiveness

Part 1

Write in the blank column B a word starting with the letter P that has the *same*, or *approximately the same*, meaning as the word given in column A:

Example:
look   peer

Remember: Every answer *must* start with the letter P.

Column A	Column B
1. fragrance	_____
2. faultless	_____
3. maybe	_____
4. forgive	_____
5. own	_____
6. likely	_____
7. annoy	_____
8. good-looking	_____
9. suggest	_____
10. choose	_____

Part 2

Write in the blank column B a word starting with the letter G that is *opposite*, or *approximately opposite*, or in *contrast to* the word given in column A.

Example:
stop   go

Remember: Every answer *must* start with the letter G.

Column A	Column B
1. lose	_____
2. innocent	_____
3. specific	_____
4. rough	_____
5. take	_____
6. host	_____
7. cheerful	_____
8. clean	_____
9. stingy	_____
10. clumsy	_____

Key:

Part 1: If more than one answer is given, count as correct any word you have written that is the same as any one of the answers.
1. fragrance = perfume
2. faultless = perfect
3. maybe = perhaps, possibly
4. forgive = pardon
5. own = possess
6. likely = probable, possible
7. annoy = pester
8. good-looking = pretty
9. suggest = propose
10. choose = pick

Part 2: If more than one answer is given, count as correct any word you have written that is the same as any one of the answers.

1.	lose	*Opposite*	gain, get
2.	innocent	*Opposite*	guilty
3.	specific	*Opposite*	general
4.	rough	*Opposite*	gentle
5.	take	*Opposite*	give
6.	host	*Opposite*	guest
7.	cheerful	*Opposite*	gloomy, glum
8.	clean	*Opposite*	grubby, grimy
9.	stingy	*Opposite*	generous
10.	clumsy	*Opposite*	graceful

Scoring:
Score Parts 1 and 2 together. Write in the blank the total number of correct responses you gave: ____

The meaning of your verbal responsiveness score:

0–5:	below average
6–10:	average
11–15	above average
16–20:	excellent

Vocabulary and Success

Now you know where you stand. If you are in the below average or average groups, you must consider, seriously, whether an inadequate vocabulary may be holding you back. If you scored above average or excellent, you have doubtless already discovered the unique and far-reaching value of a rich vocabulary, and you are eager to add still further to your knowledge of words. In either case, using the *Microsoft® Encarta® Thesaurus* regularly will help you to build up a mental library of alternative and opposite terms and vary the words you use to express yourself, whether in speech or writing.

A

A1 (infml) adj **excellent**, first-rate, first-class, perfect, flawless Opposite: inferior

abandon v 1 **dump**, discard, dispose of, throw out, throw away Opposite: keep 2 **desert**, leave, forsake, leave behind, walk out on (infml) 3 **end**, call off, cancel, give up, stop Opposite: continue ■ n **recklessness**, wildness, license, intemperance, unrestraint Opposite: restraint

abandoned adj 1 **discarded**, forsaken, dumped, neglected, cast off 2 **empty**, deserted, derelict, vacant 3 **wild**, uncontrolled, unrestricted, uninhibited, unrestrained Opposite: restrained

abandonment n **desertion**, leaving behind, leaving, rejection, neglect

abase (literary) v **lower**, demean, degrade, belittle, humiliate Opposite: respect

abasement (literary) n **degradation**, humiliation, effacement, belittlement, deprecation Opposite: aggrandizement

abase yourself (literary) v **grovel**, humble yourself, demean yourself, debase yourself, degrade yourself

abashed adj **embarrassed**, ashamed, mortified, disconcerted, dismayed Opposite: unabashed

abate (fml) v **decrease**, subside, grow less, decline, fade Opposite: rise

abatement (fml) n 1 **reduction**, decline, lessening, diminution, decrease Opposite: increase 2 **deduction**, discount, cut, reduction, decrease Opposite: increment

abbey n **religious foundation**, religious house, cloister, monastery, convent

abbreviate v **shorten**, cut, cut short, condense, abridge Opposite: lengthen

abbreviated adj **shortened**, condensed, abridged, truncated, curtailed Opposite: full-length

abbreviation n **short form**, contraction, ellipsis, acronym, shortening

ABCs n 1 **alphabet**, Roman alphabet, spelling system 2 **basics**, fundamentals, essentials, rudiments, nitty-gritty (infml)

abdicate v **renounce**, relinquish, resign, step down, hand over Opposite: accept

abdication n **resignation**, handing over, renunciation, abandonment, relinquishment

abdominal adj **stomach**, belly, front, intestinal, gut

abduct v **kidnap**, make off with, seize, hold somebody against his or her will, capture

abduction n **kidnap**, seizure, kidnapping, carrying off, capture

abductor n **kidnapper**, hostage taker, captor, hijacker, snatcher (infml)

aberrant adj **abnormal**, unusual, deviant, anomalous, peculiar Opposite: normal

aberration n **deviation**, abnormality, anomaly, irregularity, peculiarity

abet v 1 **assist**, help, support, aid, back Opposite: hinder 2 **encourage**, urge, connive, put up to, incite Opposite: deter

abhor v **detest**, hate, loathe, dislike, despise Opposite: adore

abhorrence n **hatred**, loathing, detestation, disgust, repugnance Opposite: adoration. See COMPARE AND CONTRAST at dislike.

abhorrent adj **repugnant**, objectionable, repulsive, detestable, hateful Opposite: desirable

abide v 1 **put up with**, stand for, stand, bear, stomach 2 (archaic) **withstand**, endure, survive, resist, bear 3 (archaic) **live**, have your home, stay, lodge (dated), dwell (literary)

abide by v **obey**, follow, keep to, conform to, stick to Opposite: defy

abiding adj **enduring**, remaining, surviving, long-lasting, unshakable Opposite: transient

ability n **aptitude**, skill, talent, competence, capacity

COMPARE AND CONTRAST CORE MEANING: the necessary skill, knowledge, or experience to do something

ability natural and acquired skills or knowledge; **skill** the ability to do something well gained through training or experience; **competence** ability measured against a standard; **aptitude** a natural tendency to do something well; **talent** an unusual natural ability to do something well; **capacity** mental or physical ability for something or to do something; **capability** the ability or potential to do something.

---

a bit (infml) adv **slightly**, rather, somewhat, a little, a tad (infml) Opposite: very

abject adj 1 **extreme**, utter, absolute, wretched, dismal 2 **humble**, servile, meek, submissive, subservient Opposite: confident

abjection n 1 **wretchedness**, misery, desolation, despair, despondence Opposite: cheerfulness 2 **humility**, humbleness, subservience, deference, servility Opposite: confidence

abjuration *n* renunciation, rejection, denial, repudiation, refrainment *Opposite*: affirmation

abjure *v* 1 renounce, reject, repudiate, deny, disavow 2 (*literary*) abstain, refrain, reject, deny yourself, shun

ablaze *adj* on fire, blazing, burning, in flames, alight

able *adj* 1 capable, competent, proficient, adept, skilled *Opposite*: incompetent 2 clever, talented, intelligent, bright, gifted *Opposite*: incapable. *See* COMPARE AND CONTRAST *at* intelligent.

able-bodied *adj* healthy, fit, well, active, strong *Opposite*: weak

ablutions (*fml*) *n* washing, bathing, wash, cleanup, toilette

ably *adv* capably, well, skillfully, competently, with ease *Opposite*: incompetently

abnegate (*fml*) *v* renounce, reject, deny, repudiate, abjure *Opposite*: accept

abnegation (*fml*) *n* rejection, renunciation, repudiation, denial, abstention *Opposite*: acceptance

abnormal *adj* irregular, nonstandard, uncharacteristic, atypical, anomalous *Opposite*: normal

abnormality *n* 1 irregularity, aberration, anomaly, deviation, oddity 2 defect, deformity, irregularity, malformation, malfunction

aboard *adv* 1 on board, on the ship, on the bus, on the train, on the plane 2 (*infml*) involved, participating, on the team, with us, on our side ■ *prep* onto, on, into, inside

abode (*literary*) *n* house, home, residence, place, dwelling (*fml*)

abolish *v* put an end to, eliminate, close down, bring to an end, stop *Opposite*: establish

abolition *n* elimination, ending, closing down, eradication, closure *Opposite*: establishment

abolitionist *n* opponent, objector, protester, eradicator, adversary *Opposite*: supporter

abominable *adj* dreadful, repulsive, offensive, detestable, monstrous

abominate (*fml*) *v* hate, loathe, detest, despise, dislike *Opposite*: love

abomination *n* 1 outrage, disgrace, scandal, eyesore, atrocity 2 (*literary*) hatred, dislike, repugnance, loathing, revulsion *Opposite*: love

aboriginal *adj* indigenous, original, native, local, autochthonous *Opposite*: foreign. *See* COMPARE AND CONTRAST *at* native.

abort *v* end, abandon, call off, call a halt, cancel *Opposite*: continue

abortive *adj* unsuccessful, failed, fruitless, unproductive, futile *Opposite*: successful

abound *v* 1 thrive, flourish, prosper, proliferate, be plentiful 2 brim, overflow, throng, teem, swarm

abounding *adj* many, varied, multifarious, plentiful, abundant *Opposite*: scarce

about *prep* concerning, regarding, in relation to, on the subject of, on ■ *adv* 1 approximately, roughly, in the region of, around, almost 2 around, close, nearby, near, in the vicinity

about-face *n* 1 turnaround, reversal, shift, transformation, sea change 2 turn, U-turn, 180° turn, revolution

about to *prep* ready to, on the verge of, on the point of, just going to, set to

above *prep* 1 more than, greater than, higher than, beyond, exceeding *Opposite*: below 2 on top of, over, higher than, atop *Opposite*: below

above all *adv* especially, in particular, primarily, principally, most of all

aboveboard *adj* open, fair, honest, forthright, straightforward *Opposite*: shady ■ *adv* openly, fairly, honestly, legally, lawfully *Opposite*: illegally

above-mentioned *adj* said, aforementioned (*fml*), aforesaid (*fml*)

abrade *v* graze, scrape, roughen, chafe, grind down *Opposite*: smooth

abrasion *n* scrape, scratch, scuff, graze

abrasive *adj* 1 rough, coarse, harsh, rasping, scratchy *Opposite*: smooth 2 rude, sharp, harsh, brusque, argumentative *Opposite*: gentle

abreast *adv* side by side, alongside, shoulder to shoulder, beside, level ■ *adj* well-informed, in touch, up-to-date, up on, up with *Opposite*: ignorant

abridge *v* shorten, edit, condense, abbreviate, reduce *Opposite*: expand

abridged *adj* shortened, edited, condensed, reduced, abbreviated *Opposite*: complete

abridgement *see* abridgment

abridgment *n* synopsis, digest, condensation, précis, abstract

abroad *adv* overseas, away, out of the country

abrogate (*fml*) *v* repeal, revoke, rescind, retract, nullify. *See* COMPARE AND CONTRAST *at* nullify.

abrogation (*fml*) *n* retraction, repeal, annulment, abolition, rescindment

abrupt *adj* 1 sudden, unexpected, unforeseen, rapid, hasty *Opposite*: gradual 2 curt, short, brusque, terse, rude *Opposite*: polite

abscess *n* boil, pustule, swelling, eruption, blister

abscond *v* run away, escape, break out, make off, elope

absconder *n* deserter, runaway, escapee, fugitive, truant

absence *n* 1 nonappearance, absenteeism,

time off *Opposite*: presence **2 lack**, deficiency, want, dearth, privation *Opposite*: surplus

absent *adj* **1 missing**, gone, out, away *Opposite*: present **2 inattentive**, absent-minded, far away, preoccupied, vague *Opposite*: alert **3 lacking**, deficient, nonexistent, in short supply *Opposite*: present

absentee *n* **truant**, defaulter, runaway, absconder

absenteeism *n* **absence**, nonattendance, nonappearance, truancy

absently *adv* **inattentively**, vaguely, dreamily, distractedly, abstractedly *Opposite*: attentively

absent-minded *adj* **forgetful**, distracted, scatterbrained, preoccupied, vague *Opposite*: attentive

absent yourself *v* **excuse yourself**, send your apologies, stay away *Opposite*: attend

absolute *adj* **1 total**, complete, utter, unqualified, out-and-out **2 unconditional**, unlimited, supreme, unmodified, unadulterated *Opposite*: provisional **3 conclusive**, resolved, firm, fixed, definite *Opposite*: unconfirmed ■ *n* **given**, rule, principle, truth, fundamental

absolution *n* **forgiveness**, pardon, release, freedom, liberty *Opposite*: condemnation

absolutism *n* **totalitarianism**, despotism, dictatorship, tyranny, autocracy

absolve *v* **pardon**, forgive, clear, release, free *Opposite*: punish

absorb *v* **1 soak up**, attract, take in, take up, suck up *Opposite*: exude **2 understand**, learn, grasp, admit, take in **3 engross**, fascinate, engage, captivate, grip *Opposite*: bore

absorbed *adj* **engrossed**, wrapped up, fascinated, captivated, immersed *Opposite*: detached

absorbency *n* **porosity**, sponginess, permeability, penetrability, perviousness

absorbent *adj* **porous**, spongy, permeable, penetrable, pervious

absorbing *adj* **fascinating**, engrossing, captivating, gripping, enthralling *Opposite*: boring

absorption *n* **1 preoccupation**, fascination, interest, captivation, engagement **2 amalgamation**, incorporation, assimilation, combination, inclusion *Opposite*: rejection

abstain *v* **1 desist**, refrain, withdraw, withhold, go without *Opposite*: indulge **2 sit on the fence**, stay neutral, not take sides, hedge *Opposite*: vote

abstainer *n* **1 avoider**, shunner, teetotaler, withholder, refrainer **2 nonvoter**, hedger, fence sitter

abstemious *adj* **self-denying**, self-disciplined, moderate, ascetic, sober *Opposite*: unrestrained

abstemiousness *n* **sobriety**, self-denial,

moderation, temperance, self-discipline *Opposite*: excess

abstention *n* **nonparticipation**, abstaining, refraining, holding back

abstinence *n* **self-denial**, self-restraint, self-discipline, moderation, asceticism *Opposite*: indulgence

abstinent *adj* **ascetic**, abstemious, sober, temperate, teetotal *Opposite*: indulgent

abstract *adj* **1 nonconcrete**, intellectual, mental, immaterial, intangible *Opposite*: concrete **2 theoretical**, conceptual, conjectural, hypothetical, speculative *Opposite*: practical ■ *n* **summary**, extract, précis, synopsis, abridgment ■ *v* **1 conceptualize**, theorize, hypothesize, intellectualize **2 summarize**, condense, shorten, précis, abridge *Opposite*: expand **3 extract**, take out, select, remove, separate

abstracted *adj* **inattentive**, preoccupied, vague, distant, distracted *Opposite*: alert

abstractedness *n* **preoccupation**, inattentiveness, inattention, pensiveness, distractedness *Opposite*: alertness

abstraction *n* **1 pensiveness**, preoccupation, dreaminess, vagueness, daydreaming *Opposite*: concentration **2 concept**, idea, thought, notion, construct *Opposite*: fact **3 removal**, extraction, withdrawal, deduction *Opposite*: inclusion

abstractly *adv* **theoretically**, conceptually, hypothetically, in theory *Opposite*: practically

abstruse *adj* **obscure**, perplexing, puzzling, complex, profound *Opposite*: simple. *See* COMPARE AND CONTRAST *at* obscure.

abstruseness *n* **complexity**, obscurity, difficulty, profundity, mysteriousness *Opposite*: simplicity

absurd *adj* **1 ridiculous**, ludicrous, farcical, nonsensical, illogical *Opposite*: reasonable **2 meaningless**, pointless, futile, empty, purposeless *Opposite*: meaningful

absurdity *n* **1 illogicality**, irrationality, silliness, ludicrousness, ridiculousness *Opposite*: logic **2 farce**, joke, nonsense, incongruity

absurdly *adv* **ridiculously**, ludicrously, farcically, nonsensically, preposterously *Opposite*: reasonably

absurdness *see* **absurdity**

abundance *n* **profusion**, plenty, richness, wealth, copiousness *Opposite*: scarcity

abundant *adj* **plentiful**, copious, rich, profuse, ample *Opposite*: scarce

a bundle of laughs *n* **a barrel of laughs**, a lot of fun, a barrel of monkeys, laugh *(infml)*, riot *(infml)*

abuse *n* **1 mistreatment**, cruelty, ill-treatment, violence, maltreatment **2 misuse**, exploitation, manipulation, taking advantage, mishandling **3 insults**, verbal abuse, swearing, name-calling, foul language ■

v **1 exploit**, take advantage, misuse, manipulate **2 treat badly**, ill-treat, mistreat, maltreat, molest *Opposite*: care for **3 insult**, swear, shout abuse, hurl abuse, shout insults *Opposite*: compliment. *See* COMPARE AND CONTRAST *at* misuse.

abused *adj* ill-treated, physically abused, battered, badly treated, injured *Opposite*: cared for

abusive *adj* **1 rude**, insulting, unmannerly, foul, offensive *Opposite*: polite **2 violent**, cruel, vicious, sadistic, rough *Opposite*: gentle

abusiveness *n* **rudeness**, unpleasantness, impoliteness, nastiness, vulgarity

abut *v* **be next to**, adjoin, border, be adjacent to, touch

abutment *n* **support**, buttress, prop, strut, brace

abutting *adj* **adjoining**, next to, bordering, adjacent to, against

abuzz *adj* **alive**, throbbing, humming, pulsating, busy *Opposite*: still

abysmal *adj* **terrible**, awful, dreadful, horrible, appalling *Opposite*: superb

abyss *n* **gulf**, chasm, gorge, hole, void

academia *n* **academic world**, academic circles, university, university circles, college circles

academic *adj* **1 educational**, school, college, university, scholastic **2 studious**, intellectual, scholarly, bookish, literary **3 theoretical**, speculative, abstract, moot, hypothetical *Opposite*: practical ■ *n* **researcher**, professor, college lecturer, scholar

academy *n* **school**, college, military school, conservatory, conservatoire

a case in point *n* **working example**, instance, case, paradigm, illustration

accede *v* **1 agree**, assent, consent, comply, grant *Opposite*: reject **2 come into**, inherit, succeed, take over, enter upon

accelerate *v* **go faster**, speed up, increase speed, gather speed, pick up the pace *Opposite*: slow down

accelerated *adj* **speeded up**, faster, quicker, speedier, advanced *Opposite*: slower

acceleration *n* **1 speeding up**, stepping up, hastening, hurrying, quickening *Opposite*: deceleration **2 increase of rate**, increase of velocity, spurt, burst of speed *Opposite*: deceleration

accent *n* **1 pronunciation**, inflection, intonation, tone of voice, enunciation **2 emphasis**, stress, beat, accentuation, inflection ■ *v* **emphasize**, stress, accentuate, put stress on, give weight to

accentuate *v* **emphasize**, highlight, put emphasis on, stress, draw attention to *Opposite*: play down

accentuation *n* **1 prominence**, highlighting, attention, notice, emphasis **2 accent**, rhythm, stress, inflection, beat

accept *v* **1 receive**, take, agree to take, admit *Opposite*: refuse **2 consent**, agree, say yes, say you will, give a positive response *Opposite*: turn down **3 take on**, undertake, acknowledge, assume, bear *Opposite*: reject **4 believe**, recognize, agree, admit, acknowledge *Opposite*: deny **5 put up with**, endure, tolerate, bow, take

acceptability *n* **suitability**, adequacy, appropriateness, tolerability

acceptable *adj* **1 satisfactory**, suitable, good enough, adequate, up to standard *Opposite*: unacceptable **2 welcome**, pleasing, gratifying, agreeable, enjoyable *Opposite*: annoying

acceptably *adv* **well enough**, adequately, sufficiently well, suitably, tolerably *Opposite*: unreasonably

acceptance *n* **1 agreement**, assent, acquiescence, concurrence, accession *Opposite*: refusal **2 receipt**, taking, getting, reception, receiving *Opposite*: rejection **3 belief**, acknowledgment, credence, currency, agreement **4 recognition**, approval, tolerance, acknowledgment, toleration *Opposite*: disapproval

accepted *adj* **conventional**, established, customary, acknowledged, usual *Opposite*: unconventional

accepting *adj* **tolerant**, compliant, patient, long-suffering, uncomplaining *Opposite*: intolerant

access *n* **1 way in**, entrance, entry, approach, gate *Opposite*: exit **2 right of entry**, admission, right to use, admittance, entrée ■ *v* **get into**, gain access to, retrieve, call up, log on

accessibility *n* **convenience**, user-friendliness, openness, availability, approachability

accessible *adj* **1 nearby**, available, reachable, easily reached, handy *Opposite*: inaccessible **2 comprehensible**, understandable, user-friendly, easy to use, clear *Opposite*: obscure **3 approachable**, affable, genial, friendly, welcoming *Opposite*: unapproachable

accessibly *adv* **1 conveniently**, handily, suitably, helpfully, usefully *Opposite*: inconveniently **2 clearly**, simply, understandably, comprehensibly, straightforwardly *Opposite*: obscurely

accession *n* **1 attainment**, succession, taking over, taking office, appointment **2 agreement**, consent, concurrence, accord, assent

accessorize *v* **ornament**, decorate, beautify, trim, embellish

accessory *n* **1 addition**, decoration, fixture, attachment, adjunct **2 accomplice**, partner, partner in crime, assistant, abettor

WORD BANK

❑ **types of accessories** ascot, bandanna, belt, bootlace, bow tie, corsage, cravat, cummerbund, earmuffs, glove, handkerchief, hat, jewelry, mitt, mitten, muff, muffler, neckerchief, necktie, pashmina, sash, scarf, shawl, stole, suspenders, tie, veil, wrap

accident n 1 **chance**, coincidence, fortune, fate Opposite: design 2 **crash**, collision, bump, smashup, pileup (infml) 3 **mishap**, misfortune, calamity, catastrophe, disaster

accidental adj **unintentional**, unintended, inadvertent, chance, unplanned Opposite: deliberate

accidentally adv **by chance**, by accident, by mistake, unintentionally, inadvertently Opposite: purposely

accident-prone adj **ill-fated**, unfortunate, unlucky, ill-starred, doomed

acclaim v **praise**, sing the praises of, give approval, hail, commend Opposite: criticize ■ n **approval**, praise, commendation, acclamation, approbation Opposite: disapproval

acclaimed adj **praised**, admired, commended, celebrated, applauded

acclamation n 1 **acclaim**, praise, commendation, approbation, approval 2 **applause**, clapping, cheering, ovation, roar Opposite: jeering

acclimate v **get used to**, become accustomed, accustom, adapt, adjust

acclimatization n **adaptation**, becoming accustomed, getting used to, adjustment, accommodation

acclimatize v **get used to**, become accustomed, accustom, adapt, adjust

accolade n **tribute**, honor, compliment, award, praise

accommodate v 1 **contain**, have room for, hold, seat, have capacity for 2 **house**, lodge, put up, billet, quarter 3 **get used to**, adapt, adjust, become accustomed to, familiarize 4 **assist**, help, oblige, be of service, find ways to help

accommodating adj **helpful**, willing, obliging, compliant, cooperative Opposite: uncooperative

accommodation n **adjustment**, adaptation, alteration, change, modification

accommodations n **housing**, lodging, room, space, place

accompaniment n **supplement**, accessory, garnish, adjunct, complement

accompanist n **pianist**, instrumentalist, musician, player

accompany v 1 **escort**, go with, go together with, go along with, attend 2 **go together with**, come with, be an adjunct to, supplement, complement

accompanying adj **supplementary**, associated, complementary, additional, addon

accomplice n **partner in crime**, assistant, accessory, collaborator, coconspirator

accomplish v **achieve**, attain, realize, carry out, pull off (infml)

COMPARE AND CONTRAST CORE MEANING: bring something to a successful conclusion
accomplish succeed in doing something; **achieve** succeed in something, usually with effort; **attain** reach a specific objective; **realize** fulfill a specific vision or plan; **carry out** perform or accomplish a task or activity; **pull off** (infml) to accomplish something, despite difficulties.

accomplished adj **talented**, skillful, gifted, skilled, proficient

accomplishment n 1 **completion**, execution, carrying out, finishing, realization 2 **feat**, achievement, triumph, success, deed 3 **talent**, skill, ability, expertise, capability

accord v 1 **give**, allow, permit, render (fml), confer (fml) 2 **agree**, concur, fit, match, correspond Opposite: clash ■ n 1 **agreement**, treaty, settlement, pact, deal 2 **consensus**, harmony, concurrence, unity, agreement Opposite: disagreement

accordance n **consensus**, agreement, accord, harmony, concord Opposite: disagreement

accordingly adv 1 **appropriately**, suitably, correspondingly, fittingly Opposite: inappropriately 2 **so**, for that reason, therefore, as a result, consequently

according to prep 1 **as said by**, as stated by, on the word of 2 **consistent with**, along with, in line with, in keeping with, in relation to Opposite: counter to

accost v **approach**, stop, confront, detain, hound

account n 1 **report**, description, story, relation, narrative 2 **explanation**, version, interpretation, justification, reason 3 **bank account**, checking account, savings account 4 **arrangement**, credit, tally, balance, bill

accountability n **answerability**, responsibility, liability, culpability

accountable adj **answerable**, responsible, liable, held responsible, blamed

accountant n **bookkeeper**, auditor, certified public accountant, cost accountant

account for v 1 **explain**, justify, give an explanation for, give a reason for, answer for 2 **comprise**, make up, total, represent, constitute

accounts n **books**, balance sheet, financial statement

accouterment n **accessory**, trapping, trimming, tool of the trade, equipment

accredit v **recognize**, sanction, endorse, authorize, certify

accreditation n **authorization**, endorsement, approval, certification, sanction

accredited adj **credited**, attributed, qualified, endorsed, official Opposite: unofficial

accretion n 1 **accumulation**, buildup,

increase, enlargement, addition *Opposite*: erosion **2 deposit**, layer, mass, lump, bump

accrual *n* **accumulation**, increase, buildup, accretion, addition *Opposite*: loss

accrue *v* **accumulate**, grow, mount up, build up, amass *Opposite*: dwindle

accumulate *v* **build up**, mount up, accrue, amass, collect *Opposite*: disperse. *See* COMPARE AND CONTRAST *at* **collect**.

accumulation *n* **1 buildup**, accretion, accrual, gathering, growth **2 collection**, stock, store, hoard, deposit

accumulative *adj* **1 acquisitive**, hoarding, materialistic, covetous, grasping **2 incremental**, increasing, rising, growing, mounting

accumulator *n* **collector**, saver, amasser, magpie *(infml)*, squirrel *(infml)*

accuracy *n* **correctness**, accurateness, exactness, precision, truth *Opposite*: inaccuracy

accurate *adj* **precise**, correct, exact, true, truthful *Opposite*: inaccurate

accursed *(literary) adj* **1 doomed**, ill-fated, fated, ill-starred, damned *Opposite*: blessed **2 awful**, horrible, terrible, appalling, hateful

accusation *n* **allegation**, indictment, claim, complaint, charge

accusatorial *(fml) adj* **1 critical**, judgmental, condemnatory, accusing, reproachful *Opposite*: complimentary **2 adversarial**, confrontational, argumentative, combative, antagonistic *Opposite*: amicable

accuse *v* **blame**, lay blame on, indict, point the finger, allege

accuser *n* **1 challenger**, confronter, criticizer, opponent, faultfinder **2 indicter**, litigant, petitioner, appellant, complainant **3 informer**, telltale, tattletale, talebearer, whistle-blower

accusing *adj* **reproachful**, condemning, reproving, critical, condemnatory

accustom *v* **get to know**, get used to, acclimatize, acclimate, become accustomed to

accustomed *adj* **1 familiarized**, inured, adapted, comfortable, habituated *(fml)* *Opposite*: unaccustomed **2 usual**, habitual, regular, familiar, customary *Opposite*: unusual

accustomed to *adj* **in the habit of**, given to, used to, apt to, prone to

ace *n* **champion**, star, expert, winner, victor ■ *adj (infml)* **first-rate**, top, world-class, wonderful, excellent *Opposite*: lousy *(infml)*

acerbic *adj* **cutting**, bitter, caustic, acid, sour *Opposite*: mild

acerbity *n* **sharpness**, bitterness, sourness, acidity, acrimony

ache *n* **pain**, throbbing, aching, twinge, headache ■ *v* **1 hurt**, throb, be painful, sting, smart **2** *(fml)* **long**, desire, yearn, want, wish

achievable *adj* **attainable**, realizable, possible, reachable, doable *Opposite*: unrealistic

achieve *v* **attain**, realize, accomplish, reach, complete *Opposite*: fail. *See* COMPARE AND CONTRAST *at* **accomplish**.

achievement *n* **attainment**, accomplishment, success, feat, triumph *Opposite*: failure

achiever *n* **high-flier**, doer, self-starter, success, go-getter *(infml)* *Opposite*: loser

Achilles heel *n* **weakness**, flaw, failing, weak point, chink in somebody's armor

aching *adj* **painful**, achy, sore, tender, throbbing ■ *n* **1 ache**, pain, painful feeling, throbbing, throb **2** *(fml)* **longing**, desire, yearning, pining, itch

achy *adj* **painful**, aching, sore, tender, throbbing

acid *adj* **1 acidic**, tart, sour, bitter, sharp *Opposite*: sweet **2 cutting**, biting, caustic, acerbic, mordant *Opposite*: mild

acidic *adj* **acid**, tart, sour, bitter, sharp *Opposite*: sweet

acidity *n* **sourness**, sharpness, tartness, bitterness *Opposite*: sweetness

acidly *adv* **sharply**, cuttingly, tartly, sourly, acerbically *Opposite*: sweetly

acid test *n* **litmus test**, touchstone, trial, indicator

acknowledge *v* **1 admit**, recognize, accept, concede, grant *Opposite*: deny **2 greet**, salute, wave, nod, hail *Opposite*: ignore **3 reply**, answer, respond, react, return *Opposite*: ignore

acknowledged *adj* **recognized**, approved, known, accredited, accepted *Opposite*: denied

acknowledgment *n* **1 greeting**, salutation, nod, wave, salute **2 response**, reply, reaction, answer, retort **3 recognition**, acceptance, admission, confession, appreciation

acme *n* **peak**, summit, top, zenith, pinnacle *Opposite*: nadir

acolyte *n* **1 attendant**, assistant, aide, helper **2 follower**, devotee, disciple, adherent, supporter

acoustic *adj* **audio**, aural, auditory, audile, sound

acoustics *n* **audibility**, auditory range, sound quality

acquaint *v* **make aware**, inform, let know, let in on, make familiar with *Opposite*: keep from

acquaintance *n* **1 associate**, friend, contact, colleague, consociate *(fml)* *Opposite*: stranger **2 knowledge**, familiarity, understanding, awareness, conversance *Opposite*: ignorance **3 relationship**, contact, association, friendship, relations

acquiesce *v* **agree**, comply, accept, consent, assent *Opposite*: resist. *See* COMPARE AND CONTRAST *at* **agree**.

acquiescence n **agreement**, consent, compliance, submission, acceptance Opposite: resistance

acquiescent adj **agreeable**, compliant, yielding, accepting, submissive Opposite: resistant

acquire v 1 **obtain**, get, get hold of, get your hands on, gain Opposite: lose 2 **develop**, learn, pick up, take up, assimilate Opposite: drop. See COMPARE AND CONTRAST at get.

acquisition n 1 **gaining**, attainment, achievement, getting hold of, procurement Opposite: loss 2 **purchase**, possession, asset, gain

acquisitive adj **greedy**, covetous, grasping, avaricious, materialistic Opposite: generous

acquisitiveness n **greed**, hoarding, avarice, covetousness, materialism Opposite: generosity

acquit v **find not guilty**, clear, set free, free, release Opposite: convict

acquittal n **release**, discharge, freeing, clearing, exoneration Opposite: conviction

acquit yourself (fml) v **conduct yourself**, act, behave, perform, work

acreage n **land**, estate, property, domain, acres

acres n 1 **land**, estate, domain, property, acreage 2 (infml) **expanse**, stretch, tracts, swathes, lots

acrid adj 1 **pungent**, harsh, unpleasant, choking, bitter Opposite: pleasant 2 **sharp**, cutting, caustic, bitter, vitriolic Opposite: mild

acrimonious adj **spiteful**, rancorous, discordant, hostile, unfriendly Opposite: amicable

acrimony n **bitterness**, spite, rancor, animosity, hostility Opposite: harmony

acrobat n **tumbler**, trapeze artist, circus performer, gymnast, funambulist

acrobatic adj **gymnastic**, athletic, lithe, supple, flexible

acrobatics n 1 **gymnastics**, aerobics, calisthenics 2 **agility**, skill, dexterity, nimbleness, quickness

acronym n **abbreviation**, short form, shortening, contraction, condensation

across adv **crossways**, crosswise, transversely, diagonally, from corner to corner

across-the-board adj **comprehensive**, sweeping, all-embracing, wide-ranging, far-reaching

act n 1 **action**, deed, doing, undertaking, exploit 2 **performance**, entertainment, turn, piece, item 3 **pretense**, show, sham, con, feint 4 **law**, piece of legislation, statute, decree, enactment ■ v 1 **take action**, take steps, proceed, be active, perform 2 **behave**, conduct yourself, perform, comport yourself (fml), acquit yourself (fml) 3 **pretend**, put on an act, put it on, play,

fake 4 **replace**, represent, act on behalf of, appear on behalf of, speak for 5 **function**, work, take effect, produce a result, produce an effect 6 **perform**, act out, be in, appear, play

acting n **drama**, the theater, performing, the stage, performing arts ■ adj **temporary**, substitute, stand-in, interim Opposite: permanent

action n 1 **act**, deed, exploit, achievement, accomplishment Opposite: inaction 2 **lawsuit**, suit, proceedings, charge, case 3 **battle**, fighting, combat, conflict, engagement

actionable adj **indictable**, litigious, suable, chargeable, imputable Opposite: legal

action-packed adj **exciting**, thrilling, gripping, enthralling, suspenseful Opposite: dull

activate v **make active**, set in motion, set off, turn on, trigger Opposite: stop

activation n **start**, beginning, initiation, instigation, stimulation

active adj 1 **lively**, vigorous, energetic, full of life, on the go Opposite: inactive 2 **in force**, functioning, effective, in action, operating Opposite: defunct 3 **working**, practicing, involved, committed, enthusiastic Opposite: half-hearted

actively adv **vigorously**, aggressively, energetically, enthusiastically, dynamically Opposite: half-heartedly

activeness n **liveliness**, animation, energy, vigor, vitality Opposite: passivity

activism n **direct action**, political action, social action, involvement, engagement

activist n **campaigner**, protester, objector, militant, advocate

activity n 1 **pursuit**, interest, hobby, occupation, leisure interest 2 **action**, movement, motion, bustle, commotion Opposite: inactivity

act on v 1 **follow up on**, tackle, start in on, take action 2 **have an effect on**, work, affect, perform

actor n **performer**, artist, thespian, artiste, player

act out v 1 **enact**, perform, portray, act, play 2 **work out**, work through, exorcize, express, purge

actress n **performer**, artist, thespian, artiste, player

actual adj **real**, genuine, authentic, concrete, tangible Opposite: imaginary

actuality n 1 **fact**, certainty, reality, practicality, actual fact 2 **real life**, the real world, here and now, reality

actually adv **in fact**, really, in point of fact, in reality, truly

actuate (fml) v **activate**, put into action, set in motion, trigger, start

act up v **cause trouble**, be difficult, misbehave, malfunction, go wrong Opposite: behave

acuity n **keenness**, acuteness, sharpness, alertness, awareness

acumen n **insight**, shrewdness, penetration, judgment, wisdom

acute adj 1 **severe**, serious, critical, grave, important Opposite: moderate 2 **perceptive**, shrewd, intelligent, canny, bright Opposite: obtuse 3 **sensitive**, sharp, keen, heightened, finely tuned Opposite: dull 4 **intense**, violent, strong, excruciating, piercing Opposite: mild

acutely adv **very**, intensely, highly, deeply, extremely Opposite: slightly

acuteness n 1 **intensity**, severity, gravity, seriousness 2 **sharpness**, keenness, sensitivity, perceptiveness Opposite: dullness

ad (infml) n **advertisement**, public notice, commercial, poster, flier

adage n **saying**, saw, proverb, maxim, axiom

adamant adj **obstinate**, obdurate, unyielding, unbending, inflexible Opposite: amenable

adapt v 1 **change**, alter, modify, adjust, vary Opposite: leave 2 **become accustomed**, familiarize, get a feel for, get used to, acclimatize

adaptability n **flexibility**, adaptableness, malleability, compliance Opposite: inflexibility

adaptable adj **flexible**, malleable, pliable, adjustable, compliant Opposite: inflexible

adaptation n 1 **alteration**, adjustment, acclimatization, modification, change 2 **version**, edition, revision, reworking, variation

adapter n **electric plug**, connector, converter, device

add v 1 **put in**, insert, adjoin, append, affix Opposite: delete 2 **add up**, add together, total, combine, tally Opposite: subtract 3 **enhance**, complement, improve, increase, supplement Opposite: detract

added adj **additional**, extra, supplementary, further, other

addendum n **addition**, supplement, appendix, postscript, P.S.

addict n **devotee**, fan, aficionado, aficionada, fanatic

addiction n **habit**, compulsion, dependence, need, obsession

addition n 1 **adding**, adding up, adding together, totaling, toting Opposite: subtraction 2 **supplement**, add-on, appendage, addendum, adjunct

additional adj **extra**, added, supplementary, other, further

additionally adv **as well**, in addition, moreover, furthermore, also

additive n **preservative**, stabilizer, improver, chemical, colorant

addle v **confuse**, befuddle, muddle, distract, bewilder

addled adj 1 **confused**, muddled, bewildered, befuddled, perplexed Opposite: clear 2 **spoiled**, rotten, decayed, off, putrid Opposite: fresh

addlepated (archaic) adj **confused**, muddled, bewildered, befuddled, perplexed Opposite: clear

add-on n **attachment**, addendum, adjunct, appendage, supplement ■ adj **supplementary**, accompanying, additional, extra, optional Opposite: essential

address n **speech**, talk, discourse, lecture, report ■ v 1 **direct**, deliver, dispatch, refer, forward 2 **speak**, lecture, talk, give a lecture, give a talk 3 **tackle**, deal with, take in hand, attend, concentrate Opposite: ignore

adduce (fml) v **offer**, present, put forward, bring forward, give

add up v 1 **add**, add together, total, combine, tally up Opposite: subtract 2 **make sense**, hang together, be consistent, ring true, come together

add up to v **come to**, number, total, amount to, mount up to

adenoidal adj **nasal**, thick, muffled, indistinct

adept adj **skillful**, skilled, expert, proficient, adroit Opposite: inept

adeptness n **expertise**, proficiency, skill, adroitness, aptitude Opposite: ineptitude

adequacy n 1 **sufficiency**, ampleness, abundance Opposite: insufficiency 2 **competence**, capability, suitability, tolerability, appropriateness Opposite: inadequacy

adequate adj 1 **sufficient**, ample, enough, plenty Opposite: insufficient 2 **passable**, satisfactory, tolerable, acceptable, suitable Opposite: inadequate

adequately adv **sufficiently**, passably, tolerably, effectively, satisfactorily Opposite: inadequately

adhere v 1 **stick to**, follow, keep to, stand by, abide by Opposite: abandon 2 **stick**, stick on, hold fast, hold, hold on

adherence n **devotion**, obedience, observance, loyalty, faithfulness Opposite: disobedience

adherent n **supporter**, believer, devotee, advocate, fanatic Opposite: opponent

adhesion n **union**, sticking power, hold, grip, linkage Opposite: separation

adhesive n **glue**, paste, gum, epoxy resin

ad hoc adj **unplanned**, informal, impromptu, improvised, off-the-cuff Opposite: planned

adieu (literary) n **farewell**, goodbye, sendoff, parting

ad infinitum adv **endlessly**, for ever, ceaselessly, repeatedly, infinitely

adjacent adj **neighboring**, nearby, bordering, next, next door Opposite: distant

adjoin v **connect**, link up, attach, affix, be close to

adjoining adj **touching**, attached, connecting, abutting, contiguous (fml) Opposite: detached

adjourn v 1 **suspend**, defer, delay, postpone, put off 2 (infml) **stop**, end, finish, break off, call it a day

adjournment n **suspension**, postponement, deferment, recess, break

adjudge v 1 **judge**, find, regard as, consider, decide 2 **pronounce**, rule, announce, declare, adjudicate

adjudicate v **arbitrate**, sit in judgment, pass judgment, referee, umpire

adjudication n 1 **judgment**, arbitration, mediation, negotiation, intercession 2 **settlement**, decision, judgment, decree, resolution

adjudicator n **judge**, arbitrator, referee, umpire, mediator

adjunct n 1 **addition**, attachment, add-on, appendage, accessory 2 **assistant**, aide, aide-de-camp, secretary, helper

adjure v 1 **command**, order, instruct, charge, demand 2 **appeal**, plead, beg, request, petition

adjust v **regulate**, alter, fiddle with, correct, fine-tune

adjustable adj **adaptable**, modifiable, changeable, variable, regulating Opposite: fixed

adjustment n **change**, alteration, modification, tuning, fine-tuning

adjutant n **assistant**, aide, aide-de-camp, secretary, personal assistant

ad-lib v **improvise**, do off the cuff, extemporize, make up on the spot, do cold ■ adj **off-the-cuff**, unplanned, informal, impromptu, improvised Opposite: rehearsed

administer v 1 **manage**, direct, run, order, control 2 **dispense**, give out, hand out, deal out, mete out

administrate v **control**, run, manage, direct, rule

administration n 1 **management**, direction, running, supervision, paperwork 2 **government**, executive, management, organization, presidency 3 **dispensation**, meting out, giving out, handing out, dealing out

administrative adj **managerial**, directorial, organizational, clerical, secretarial

administrator n **manager**, superintendent, commissioner, overseer, officer

admirable adj **estimable**, commendable, venerable, good, splendid Opposite: unworthy

admiration n **respect**, esteem, approbation, regard, approval Opposite: disapproval. See COMPARE AND CONTRAST at regard.

admire v **regard**, esteem, approve, think highly of, respect Opposite: disapprove

admired adj **respected**, venerated, esteemed, well-regarded, revered Opposite: despised

admirer n **fan**, devotee, follower, lover, aficionado

admiring adj **appreciative**, approving, complimentary, flattering, favorable Opposite: disapproving

admissibility n **acceptability**, tolerability, permissibility

admissible adj **allowable**, permissible, acceptable, tolerable Opposite: inadmissible

admission n 1 **admittance**, entrance, right of entry, access, permission Opposite: exclusion 2 **entrance fee**, entry fee, fee, charge, price 3 **confession**, declaration, profession, divulgence, disclosure Opposite: denial

admit v 1 **confess**, make a clean breast, acknowledge, own up, disclose Opposite: deny 2 **let in**, allow in, give access, permit, let pass Opposite: bar

admit defeat v **pull out**, withdraw, stop, call it a day, back out Opposite: persevere

admittance n **admission**, entry, access, right of entry, entrance Opposite: exclusion

admittedly adv **certainly**, definitely, indeed, undeniably, undoubtedly

admonish v **reprove**, caution, warn, reprimand, rebuke Opposite: praise

admonishment n **reprimand**, rebuke, reproach, caution, dressing-down Opposite: approval

admonition n **caution**, warning, reprimand, rebuke, reproach Opposite: approval

admonitory adj 1 **reproving**, reproachful, rebuking, condemnatory, critical Opposite: approving 2 **advisory**, cautionary, warning, deterrent, instructive

ad nauseam adv **on and on**, for ever, endlessly, interminably, ad infinitum

ado n **bustle**, activity, commotion, bother, excitement

adolescence n **teens**, youth, puberty, teenage years

adolescent n **teenager**, youth, youngster, juvenile, minor ■ adj **teenage**, young, youthful, juvenile, pubescent

adopt v **take on**, accept, assume, approve, take up Opposite: reject

adoption n **acceptance**, implementation, espousal, taking on, embracing Opposite: rejection

adoptive adj **legal**, step Opposite: natural

adorable adj **lovely**, gorgeous, delightful, lovable, delectable Opposite: detestable

adoration n 1 **esteem**, high regard, respect, admiration, adulation Opposite: hatred 2 **worship**, reverence, idolization, glorification, veneration

adore v 1 **love**, esteem, respect, admire, adulate Opposite: hate 2 **worship**, revere, idolize, glorify, venerate Opposite: revile

3 (*infml*) **like**, enjoy, love, be partial to, be crazy about (*infml*) *Opposite*: dislike

adored *adj* **revered**, venerated, worshipped, idolized, cherished *Opposite*: hated

adoring *adj* **affectionate**, loving, doting, admiring, indulgent *Opposite*: cold

adorn *v* **decorate**, embellish, ornament, beautify, prettify *Opposite*: strip

adornment *n* **decoration**, embellishment, ornamentation, beautification, prettification

adrift *adj* **drifting**, floating, loose, free *Opposite*: fixed ■ *adv* **aimless**, wandering, drifting, at loose ends, lost *Opposite*: focused

adroit *adj* **skillful**, nimble, practiced, able, dexterous *Opposite*: clumsy

adroitness *n* **skillfulness**, nimbleness, ability, dexterity, cleverness *Opposite*: clumsiness

adulate *v* **flatter**, put on a pedestal, elevate, praise, adore *Opposite*: disparage

adulation *n* **adoration**, praise, worship, hero worship, respect *Opposite*: disparagement

adulatory *adj* **praising**, flattering, fawning, sycophantic, obsequious *Opposite*: disparaging

adult *adj* **mature**, fully developed, grown-up, grown, full-grown *Opposite*: immature

adulterate *v* **contaminate**, taint, make impure, spoil, pollute *Opposite*: purify

adulteration *n* **contamination**, debasement, pollution, tarnishing, corruption *Opposite*: purification

adulthood *n* **maturity**, parenthood, middle age, old age, later life *Opposite*: childhood

advance *v* **1 go forward**, move forward, move ahead, press forward, move on *Opposite*: retreat **2 improve**, enhance, take forward, increase, expand *Opposite*: regress ■ *n* **1 development**, improvement, spread, progress, expansion *Opposite*: decline **2 loan**, early payment, down payment, fee, money up front

advanced *adj* **1 higher**, developed, sophisticated, complex, difficult *Opposite*: basic **2 later**, far along, well along, far ahead, well ahead *Opposite*: earlier **3 progressive**, forward-thinking, unconventional, cutting-edge, innovative *Opposite*: traditional

advancement *n* **progression**, progress, development, improvement, spread *Opposite*: decline

advantage *n* **benefit**, gain, lead, pro, improvement *Opposite*: disadvantage

advantageous *adj* **beneficial**, helpful, useful, to your advantage, valuable *Opposite*: disadvantageous

advent *n* **arrival**, start, beginning, coming on, dawn *Opposite*: departure

adventure *n* **escapade**, exploit, quest, venture, exploration

adventurer *n* **1 explorer**, traveler, voyager, buccaneer, swashbuckler **2 entrepreneur**, investor, speculator, trailblazer, pioneer

adventuresome *adj* **risk-taking**, carefree, daring, thrill-seeking, adventurous *Opposite*: unadventurous

adventurous *adj* **daring**, bold, audacious, brave, courageous *Opposite*: unadventurous

adversarial *adj* **confrontational**, argumentative, combative, antagonistic, oppositional *Opposite*: cooperative

adversary *n* **opponent**, challenger, rival, enemy, antagonist *Opposite*: supporter

adverse *adj* **1 opposing**, contrary, hostile, adversative, antagonistic *Opposite*: cooperative **2 unfavorable**, unpleasant, poor, difficult, unhelpful *Opposite*: favorable

adversity *n* **hardship**, difficulty, danger, misfortune, harsh conditions *Opposite*: privilege

advertise *v* **1 promote**, publicize, market, present, push **2 announce**, broadcast, make known, make public, shout from the rooftops *Opposite*: keep under wraps

advertisement *n* **commercial**, public notice, poster, billboard, announcement

advertiser *n* **publicist**, promoter, backer, supporter, advocate

advertising *n* **publicity**, promotion, marketing, publicizing, public relations

advice *n* **1 recommendation**, suggestion, guidance, opinion, counsel (*fml*) *Opposite*: warning **2 information**, guidance, instruction, assistance, intelligence

advisability *n* **wisdom**, prudence, sense, desirability, suitability *Opposite*: foolishness

advisable *adj* **sensible**, wise, prudent, worthwhile, desirable *Opposite*: unwise

advise *v* **1 recommend**, direct, guide, instruct, warn **2 inform**, let know, make aware, notify, instruct. *See* COMPARE AND CONTRAST *at* recommend.

advisedly *adv* **deliberately**, carefully, purposefully, on purpose, with intent *Opposite*: carelessly

adviser *n* **consultant**, counselor, advice-giver, guru

advisory *adj* **advice-giving**, consultative, counseling, review

advocacy *n* **support**, encouragement, backing, sponsorship, promotion *Opposite*: opposition

advocacy group *n* **alliance**, association, society, cartel, trade union

advocate *n* **supporter**, backer, promoter, believer, activist *Opposite*: opponent ■ *v* **support**, encourage, back, promote, recommend *Opposite*: discourage. *See* COMPARE AND CONTRAST *at* recommend.

aegis *n* auspices, sponsorship, guidance, protection, support

aerate *v* **ventilate**, let breathe, expose, freshen *Opposite*: close up

aeration *n* ventilation, airing, freshening

aerial *adj* **midair**, airborne, above ground, in-flight, floating *Opposite*: terrestrial

aerie *n* **sanctuary**, hideaway, refuge, stronghold

aerobatics *n* stunts, maneuvers, aerial tricks

aerobics *n* exercises, calisthenics, workout

aerodynamic *adj* **sleek**, smooth, slick, sweptback, clean

aerogram *n* **air letter**, airmail letter

aerogramme *see* aerogram

aerosol *n* **spray can**, spray, atomizer, mister

aerospace *n* **atmosphere**, upper atmosphere, space, troposphere, stratosphere

aesthete *n* **art lover**, aesthetician, connoisseur, cognoscente

aesthetic *adj* **artistic**, visual, appealing, beautiful

afar *(literary) adv* **far afield**, in the distance, far away, far and wide, far-off *Opposite*: nearby

a few *pron* **a small number**, some, one or two, not many, handful *Opposite*: many

affability *n* **friendliness**, sociability, cordiality, joviality, gregariousness *Opposite*: unfriendliness

affable *adj* **genial**, pleasant, friendly, sociable, jovial *Opposite*: unfriendly

affair *n* **matter**, issue, concern, business, situation

affairs *n* **business**, matters, dealings, activities, concerns

affect *v* **1 influence**, involve, shape, concern, change **2 touch**, move, disturb, mark, distress **3 assume**, put on, imitate, fake, adopt

affectation *n* **1 showing off**, pretension, exaggeration, artificiality, affectedness *Opposite*: naturalness **2 mannerism**, way, quirk, show, trait

affected *adj* **pretentious**, artificial, exaggerated, unnatural, precious *Opposite*: natural

affectedness *n* **exaggeration**, pretension, artificiality, affectation, showing off *Opposite*: naturalness

affecting *adj* **moving**, touching, upsetting, distressing, disturbing

affection *n* **liking**, fondness, regard, warmth, attachment *Opposite*: dislike. *See* COMPARE AND CONTRAST *at* love.

affectionate *adj* **loving**, demonstrative, warm, friendly, kind *Opposite*: cold

affective *adj* **emotional**, sentimental, moving, touching, affecting

affianced *(fml) adj* **engaged**, attached, promised, spoken for, involved *Opposite*: unattached

affidavit *n* **sworn statement**, official declaration, affirmation, confirmation, proclamation

affiliate *v* **link**, connect, join, associate, belong to ■ *n* **associate**, partner, colleague, member

affiliation *n* **association**, relationship, connection, attachment, membership

affinity *n* **1 empathy**, sympathy, fellow feeling, attraction, kinship *Opposite*: indifference **2 similarity**, resemblance, likeness, correspondence *Opposite*: difference

affirm *v* **1 assert**, insist, establish, state, verify **2 support**, confirm, encourage, sustain, uphold

affirmation *n* **assertion**, confirmation, pronouncement, declaration, announcement *Opposite*: denial

affirmative *adj* **assenting**, positive, confirmatory, agreeing, favorable *Opposite*: negative

affix *v* **attach**, fix, fasten, stick, pin *Opposite*: remove

afflict *v* **trouble**, bother, affect, worry, distress

afflicted *adj* **distressed**, aggrieved, stricken, plagued, tormented

affliction *n* **1 suffering**, difficulty, burden, problem, hardship **2 illness**, sickness, disease, condition, disorder

affluence *n* **riches**, prosperity, material comfort, privileged circumstances, wealth *Opposite*: poverty

affluent *adj* **rich**, wealthy, well-off, well-to-do, prosperous *Opposite*: poor

afford *v* **1 pay for**, have the funds for, manage to pay for, find the money for, come up with the money for **2** *(fml)* **give**, offer, present, allow, provide

affordable *adj* **reasonable**, within your means, inexpensive, cheap *Opposite*: expensive

afforest *v* **reforest**, tree-plant, plant *Opposite*: deforest

affray *n* **scuffle**, fight, brawl, disturbance, commotion *Opposite*: agreement

affront *n* **insult**, injury, slur, slight, outrage *Opposite*: compliment ■ *v* **offend**, insult, upset, outrage, slight *Opposite*: compliment

affronted *adj* **insulted**, injured, slighted, disrespected, upset *Opposite*: pleased

aficionada *n* **devotee**, enthusiast, adherent, fanatic, fan

aficionado *n* **devotee**, enthusiast, adherent, fanatic, fan

afire *see* aflame

aflame *adj* **1 on fire**, burning, in flames, ablaze, afire *Opposite*: extinguished **2 fired up**, enthusiastic, passionate, excited, fired *Opposite*: apathetic

afloat *adj* **flooded**, awash, inundated, under

water, submerged *Opposite*: dry

aflutter *adv* agitated, excited, trembling, aquiver, nervous *Opposite*: calm

afoot *adj* happening, going on, occurring, taking place, up

aforementioned *(fml)* *adj* above-mentioned, said, aforesaid *(fml)*

aforesaid *(fml)* *see* **aforementioned**

afraid *adj* frightened, fearful, terrified, petrified, scared *Opposite*: unafraid

afresh *adv* anew, again, once again, once more, over

after *prep* 1 later than, past, gone *Opposite*: before 2 behind, following, to the rear of, next to *Opposite*: ahead of 3 in pursuit of, in search of, in quest of, following, on the trail of 4 regarding, considering, taking into account, with, bearing in mind 5 following, subsequent to, later than *Opposite*: before 6 in the manner of, in imitation of, in the style of, similar to, like ■ *adv* afterward, subsequently, later, next *Opposite*: before ■ *conj* when, once, as soon as *Opposite*: before

after all *adv* on balance, finally, in the end, in spite of everything, nevertheless

aftercare *n* 1 postoperative care, posthospital care, home care, rehabilitation, rehab *(infml)* 2 support, assistance, help, upkeep, maintenance

aftereffect *n* repercussion, reverberation, aftermath, aftershock, final outcome *Opposite*: precursor

afterglow *n* warmth, glow, serenity, exhilaration, feel-good factor

afterlife *n* afterworld, next world, life after death, eternal life, spirit world

aftermath *n* result, consequences, outcome, upshot, repercussion

afternoon *n* after lunch, p.m., early afternoon, midafternoon, late afternoon *Opposite*: morning

afterthought *n* addition, postscript, extra, addendum, reflection *Opposite*: forethought

afterward *adv* next, after that, later, subsequently, then *Opposite*: before

afterworld *n* afterlife, next world, life after death, eternal life, spirit world

again *adv* once more, another time, yet again, over, over again

against *prep* 1 in opposition to, not in favor, hostile, critical, opposed 2 next to, alongside, beside, touching, adjacent to 3 in contradiction of, contrary to, counter to, in contrast to, compared to

agape *(literary) adj* 1 wide open, open, ajar *Opposite*: closed 2 astonished, amazed, open-mouthed, agog, surprised *Opposite*: unaffected

age *n* 1 era, period, time, times, epoch 2 time of life, stage, phase, stage of development ■ *v* mature, grow older, grow up, get on, advance in years

aged *adj* old, elderly, matured, ripened, hoary *Opposite*: young

age group *n* generation, cohort, age range, age bracket, contemporaries

ageless *adj* 1 youthful, fresh, unfading, unspoiled 2 timeless, endless, perpetual, everlasting, infinite

agency *n* 1 organization, bureau, society, charity, group 2 activity, action, work, intervention, help

agenda *n* program, schedule, plan, outline, memo

agent *n* 1 go-between, manager, negotiator, mediator, representative 2 cause, means, driving force, instrument, vehicle

age-old *adj* ancient, old, long-standing, venerable, hoary *Opposite*: recent

ages *(infml) n* days, weeks, months, years, eons *Opposite*: moment

agglomeration *n* accumulation, mass, collection, cluster, group

agglutinate *v* adhere, stick, clump, join, cling *Opposite*: separate

agglutination *n* accretion, cohesion, adhesion, clumping, joining

aggrandize *v* 1 increase, upgrade, expand, enlarge, develop *Opposite*: downgrade 2 *(fml)* exaggerate, overstate, puff up, build up, magnify *Opposite*: belittle

aggrandizement *n* 1 enhancement, enlargement, expansion, amelioration, improvement *Opposite*: deterioration 2 empowerment, enrichment, promotion, magnification, inflation *Opposite*: deflation 3 *(fml)* exaggeration, overstatement, braggadocio, glorification, embellishment *Opposite*: understatement

aggravate *v* 1 *(infml)* annoy, irritate, exasperate, provoke, make angry *Opposite*: soothe 2 worsen, exacerbate, exaggerate, heighten, intensify *Opposite*: alleviate

aggravated *adj* 1 serious, worse, intensified, heightened *Opposite*: alleviated 2 *(infml)* annoyed, angry, upset, put out, irritated *Opposite*: peaceful

aggravating *(infml) adj* annoying, irritating, infuriating, maddening, exasperating *Opposite*: pleasing

aggravation *n* worsening, exacerbation, intensification, magnification, augmentation *Opposite*: alleviation

aggregate *adj* *(fml)* collective, total, combined, cumulative, amassed ■ *n* *(fml)* total, collection, mass, sum, whole ■ *v* combine, amass, gather, collect, accumulate *Opposite*: separate

aggregation *n* combination, accumulation, collection, accretion, mass

aggression *n* 1 attack, assault, invasion, onslaught, offensive *Opposite*: defense 2 violence, hostility, anger, belligerence, antagonism *Opposite*: friendliness

aggressive *adj* 1 violent, hostile, destructive,

belligerent, antagonistic *Opposite*: peaceful **2 forceful**, insistent, assertive, hard-hitting, uncompromising *Opposite*: mild

aggressiveness *n* **1 violence**, belligerence, bellicosity, ferociousness, antagonism *Opposite*: friendliness **2 fierceness**, insistence, forcefulness, determination, assertiveness *Opposite*: mildness

aggressor *n* **attacker**, invader, assailant, provoker, antagonist *Opposite*: defender

aggrieve *(fml)* *v* **distress**, upset, hurt, injure, pain

aggrieved *adj* **1 hurt**, angry, upset, distressed, put out **2 wronged**, mistreated, persecuted, maltreated, victimized

aghast *adj* **horrified**, amazed, shocked, horror-struck, astonished *Opposite*: unaffected

agile *adj* **1 nimble**, supple, lithe, sprightly, alert *Opposite*: clumsy **2 quick-thinking**, alert, clear-headed, bright *Opposite*: dull

agility *n* **nimbleness**, suppleness, quickness, dexterity, liveliness *Opposite*: clumsiness

agitate *v* **1 disturb**, stir up, trouble, excite, rouse *Opposite*: calm **2 campaign**, stir up opinion, protest, advocate, raise a fuss **3 stir**, whisk, toss, shake up, disturb

agitated *adj* **restless**, disturbed, disconcerted, frantic, tense *Opposite*: calm

agitation *n* **1 anxiety**, worry, nervousness, tension, distress *Opposite*: calm **2 campaigning**, activism, demonstration, protest, stir

agitator *n* **campaigner**, protester, dissenter, activist

aglow *adj* **glowing**, shining, radiant, rosy, warm *Opposite*: pale

AGM *n* **annual general meeting**, annual meeting, open meeting, public meeting, meeting

agnostic *n* **doubter**, skeptic, doubting Thomas, questioner, nonbeliever *Opposite*: believer ■ *adj* **doubting**, uncertain, unsure, unconvinced, skeptical *Opposite*: believing

agnosticism *n* **doubt**, reservation, skepticism, uncertainty, dissent *Opposite*: certainty

ago *adv* **before**, previously, back, past, since *Opposite*: ahead

agog *adj* **eager**, excited, impatient, keen, avid *Opposite*: uninterested

agonize *v* **worry**, struggle, strive, vacillate, wrestle

agonized *adj* **anguished**, tormented, suffering, tortured, in pain

agonizing *adj* **excruciating**, unbearable, painful, distressing, worrying

agony *n* **anguish**, pain, torture, suffering, distress *Opposite*: ecstasy

agrarian *adj* **agricultural**, farm, farming, land, rural *Opposite*: urban

agree *v* **1 be in agreement**, be in accord, concur, see eye to eye, coincide *Opposite*: differ **2 consent**, say yes, assent, acquiesce, accede *Opposite*: refuse **3 decide**, reach agreement, come to an agreement, come to an understanding, settle *Opposite*: disagree **4 correspond**, match, be the same, tie in, harmonize *Opposite*: differ

---

COMPARE AND CONTRAST CORE MEANING: accept an idea, plan, or course of action that has been put forward

agree be in agreement with somebody else about a course of action; **concur** agree or reach agreement independently on a specified point; **acquiesce** agree to or comply with something passively; **consent** give formal permission for something to happen; **assent** agree to something formally.

---

agreeable *adj* **1 pleasant**, pleasing, pleasurable, enjoyable, delightful *Opposite*: unpleasant **2 friendly**, affable, pleasant, courteous, delightful *Opposite*: disagreeable **3 amenable**, willing, in accord, compliant, happy *Opposite*: unwilling

agreeably *adv* **pleasantly**, enjoyably, delightfully, pleasingly, pleasurably *Opposite*: unpleasantly

agreed *adj* **decided**, settled, arranged, approved, fixed

agreement *n* **1 contract**, arrangement, covenant, treaty, promise **2 accord**, concord, conformity, harmony, union *Opposite*: disagreement

agribusiness *n* **farming industry**, farming, agroindustry, agricultural business, business

agricultural *adj* **1 agrarian**, farming, agronomic, farmed, cultivated **2 unindustrialized**, pastoral, rural, bucolic, undeveloped *Opposite*: urban

agriculture *n* **cultivation**, husbandry, crop growing, food production, agronomy

aground *adj* **beached**, ashore, stranded, stuck, grounded *Opposite*: afloat

ahead *adv* **1 in front**, to the front, in the lead, in advance, further on *Opposite*: behind **2 into the future**, in the future, to come, yet to be, forward *Opposite*: ago **3 early**, in advance, prematurely, up front, ahead of *Opposite*: late

ahead of *prep* **1 in front of**, before, beyond, up ahead of, in advance of *Opposite*: behind **2 before**, in advance of, earlier than, in front of, just before *Opposite*: after

aid *v* **help**, assist, support, abet, give support to *Opposite*: thwart ■ *n* **assistance**, help, support, relief, encouragement

aid and abet *v* **conspire**, collaborate, collude, connive, be in league with

aide *n* **assistant**, adviser, helper, supporter, personal assistant. *See* COMPARE AND CONTRAST *at* **assistant**.

aide-de-camp *see* **aide**

aide-mémoire *(fml)* n **1 summary**, outline, résumé, synopsis, digest **2 memory aid**, mnemonic, note, reminder, memorandum

ail *(literary)* v **1 trouble**, pain, distress, be wrong with, affect **2 be ill**, be sick, feel unwell, suffer, be in pain

ailing adj **1 underperforming**, failing, deteriorating, inadequate *Opposite*: thriving **2** *(dated)* **unwell**, ill, sick, unfit, laid up *Opposite*: well

ailment n **illness**, sickness, disease, disorder, complaint

aim n **1 aspire**, plan, intend, try, mean **2 point toward**, point, take aim, direct, mark ∎ n **goal**, purpose, intention, object, objective

aimless adj **pointless**, meaningless, useless, worthless, purposeless *Opposite*: purposeful

aimlessness n **pointlessness**, purposelessness, senselessness *Opposite*: purposefulness

air n **1 atmosphere**, space, sky, heaven **2 appearance**, look, manner, tone, way of being **3 tune**, melody, song ∎ v **1 declare**, express, vent, make public, proclaim *Opposite*: suppress **2 ventilate**, aerate, expose

airborne adj **flying**, aerial, floating, midair, in-flight

airbrush v **blend in**, touch up, cover up, color, blend

air conditioner n **air cooler**, air exchanger, ventilator, dehumidifier, extractor *Opposite*: heater

air conditioning n **air-cooling system**, ventilation system, air-circulation system, air exchange system, climate control *Opposite*: heating

aircraft n **airplane**, plane, flying machine

WORD BANK
❑ **types of civil aircraft** airliner, airship, autogiro, biplane, blimp, dirigible, executive jet, glider, hang glider, helicopter, jet, light plane, monoplane, paraglider, seaplane, skiplane, STOL, ultralight, zeppelin
❑ **types of military aircraft** bomber, convertiplane, fighter, fighter-bomber, helicopter gunship, stealth bomber, transport, VTOL
❑ **parts of an aircraft** aileron, air brake, autopilot, cabin, cockpit, ejection seat, fin, flight deck, flight recorder, fuselage, jet engine, joystick, landing gear, nose cone, nose wheel, propeller, rotor, rudder, tail, tailplane, tail rotor, turbofan, turbojet, turboprop, undercarriage, wing

airdrop v **parachute in**, airlift, send in, parachute, drop

airfare n **fare**, tariff, charge, ticket price, seat rate

airfield n **airstrip**, landing field, landing strip, airdrome, airport

airily adv **lightheartedly**, lightly, carelessly, casually, easily *Opposite*: seriously

airiness n **1 lightheartedness**, buoyancy, animation, vivacity, cheerfulness *Opposite*: seriousness **2 spaciousness**, openness, freshness, lightness *Opposite*: closeness

airing n **1 ventilation**, aeration, exposure to air, drying, freshening **2 outing**, trip, excursion **3 exposure**, expression, disclosure, divulgence, ventilation

airless adj **stuffy**, close, muggy, unventilated, oppressive *Opposite*: airy

airlift v **fly**, transfer, winch, lift

airline n **air company**, commercial airline, scheduled carrier, carrier

airlock n **1 compartment**, cubicle, cell, chamber **2 blockage**, obstruction, air bubble, occlusion, block

airmail v **mail**, send, dispatch

airplane n **aircraft**, plane, flying machine, crate *(dated infml)*, bird *(slang)*

airplay n **airtime**, playing time, exposure, promotion, publicity

airport n **airfield**, airdrome, airstrip, landing field, landing strip

airpower n **air strength**, airborne army, air defense, air force

air raid n **aerial attack**, aerial bombardment, air attack, bombing, air strike

airship n **dirigible**, zeppelin, blimp, aircraft

airshow n **aerobatics**, flyover, stunts, show, exhibition

airsick adj **nauseous**, queasy, sick, ill, motion sick

airsickness n **motion sickness**, nausea, queasiness, sickness

airspace n **territory**, skies, boundaries, limits, flight exclusion zone

air strike n **aerial attack**, aerial bombardment, bombing, air raid, air offensive

airstrip n **runway**, landing strip, strip, landing field, airfield

airtight adj **1 sealed**, hermetically sealed, hermetic, impermeable **2 sound**, strong, unquestionable, unassailable, watertight *Opposite*: vulnerable

airwaves n **radio waves**, frequencies, frequency bands, radio frequencies, broadcasting frequencies

airway n **1 airline**, air transport company, air network **2 air route**, air corridor, flight lane, air lane, route

airworthiness n **safety**, soundness, reliability, working order

airworthy adj **flyable**, flightworthy, in working order, in good order, safe

airy adj **1 roomy**, ventilated, fresh, light, open *Opposite*: stuffy **2 unconcerned**, nonchalant, casual, light, carefree *Opposite*: serious

aisle n **passageway**, walkway, passage, corridor

ajar adj **half closed**, open, agape *(literary)*

a.k.a. adj **also known as**, better known as, otherwise known as, known to you and me as, alias

akin adj **similar**, of the same kind, parallel, like, analogous Opposite: unlike

alacrity n **promptness**, quickness, rapidity, speed, readiness Opposite: sluggishness

alarm n **1 fear**, apprehension, terror, fright, panic **2 alarm bell**, bell, warning, distress signal, siren ■ v **frighten**, terrify, panic, distress, startle Opposite: calm

alarmed adj **worried**, upset, distressed, shocked, frightened Opposite: untroubled

alarming adj **disturbing**, upsetting, frightening, distressing, shocking Opposite: soothing

alarmist adj **pessimistic**, gloomy, panicky, exaggerated, hysterical Opposite: down-to-earth

alas adv **unfortunately**, sadly, regrettably, unhappily, unluckily

albatross n **millstone**, shackle, encumbrance, burden, impediment

albeit conj **although**, though, even though, even if, notwithstanding (fml)

album n **1 book**, folder, photograph album, photo album, autograph album **2 record**, LP, CD, tape, cassette

albumen n **egg white**, white, white of egg

alchemy n **pseudoscience**, experimentation, transformation

alcoholic adj **intoxicating**, inebriating, fermented, distilled, strong Opposite: nonalcoholic

alcove n **recess**, niche, bay, cubicle, nook

alert adj **attentive**, watchful, prepared, aware, vigilant Opposite: unprepared ■ n **warning**, signal, alarm, siren, red alert ■ v **warn**, forewarn, notify, draw somebody's attention to, tell

alertness n **attentiveness**, watchfulness, awareness, preparedness, vigilance Opposite: inattentiveness

alfresco adv **out of doors**, outdoors, outside, in the open air, in the yard Opposite: indoors ■ adj **outdoor**, open-air, outside, yard, patio Opposite: indoor

algorithm n **procedure**, process, system, set of rules

alias adj **also known as**, also called, otherwise known as, under the name of, a.k.a. ■ n **assumed name**, pseudonym, pen name, nom de plume, stage name

alibi (infml) n **explanation**, excuse, defense, reason, account

alien n **1 extraterrestrial**, creature from outer space, space invader, Martian, intelligent life form **2 foreigner**, stranger, immigrant, resident alien ■ adj **unfamiliar**, unknown, strange, outlandish, unusual Opposite: familiar

alienate v **estrange**, make unfriendly, disaffect, set against, distance Opposite: involve

alienated adj **estranged**, disaffected, isolated, withdrawn, separate Opposite: involved

alienation n **estrangement**, disaffection, unfriendliness, hostility, isolation Opposite: closeness

alight v **1 get off**, get out, descend, dismount **2 land**, perch, rest, stop, settle ■ adj **burning**, on fire, in flames, blazing, ablaze

align v **1 bring into line**, line up, make straight, make parallel, make even Opposite: disarrange **2 side with**, support, ally, affiliate, associate Opposite: distance

aligned adj **allied**, united, associated, affiliated, ranged

alignment n **1 position**, arrangement, placement, configuration, orientation Opposite: disorder **2 alliance**, association, coalition, grouping, affiliation

alike adj **similar**, comparable, the same, identical, like Opposite: different

alimentary canal n **bowels**, guts, innards, insides, intestines

WORD BANK

❏ **parts of an alimentary canal** anus, appendix, bile duct, bladder, bowel, cecum, colon, duodenum, esophagus, gallbladder, gullet, gut, intestine, kidney, large intestine, liver, pancreas, rectum, small intestine, spleen, stomach, throat

alimony n **allowance**, maintenance, support, financial support, funding

alive adj **1 living**, animate, breathing Opposite: dead **2 energetic**, busy, active, perky, vibrant Opposite: inactive **3 thriving**, active, flourishing, successful, blooming Opposite: quiet **4 full**, packed, teeming, awash, swarming Opposite: dead **5 aware**, sensitive, tuned in, alert, interested Opposite: unaware. See COMPARE AND CONTRAST at **living**.

all adv (infml) **altogether**, completely, entirely, very, wholly ■ pron **1 every one**, each and every one, every single one, each Opposite: none **2 every part**, the entire, the complete, the whole, every bit Opposite: none

all along adv **from the start**, right from the start, from the very beginning, from the beginning, from the outset

all and sundry pron **everyone**, everybody, one and all, every person, the whole world Opposite: nobody

all-around adj **1 versatile**, exceptional, outstanding, talented, multitalented **2 all-inclusive**, grand, inclusive, sweeping, large-scale Opposite: restricted **3 on all sides**, in every direction, everywhere, in all directions

allay v **dispel**, alleviate, calm, assuage, relieve Opposite: stimulate

all clear *n* **green light**, all-clear signal, nod, signal, clear coast *Opposite*: thumbs down *(infml)*

allegation *n* **claim**, accusation, assertion, contention, charge

allege *v* **claim**, assert, contend, charge, declare

alleged *adj* **supposed**, unproven, suspected, so-called, assumed *Opposite*: confirmed

allegiance *n* **loyalty**, commitment, adherence, faithfulness, duty *Opposite*: disloyalty

allegorical *adj* **metaphorical**, symbolic, emblematic, figurative, allegoric *Opposite*: literal

allegory *n* **parable**, fable, metaphor, symbol, extended metaphor

all-embracing *adj* **comprehensive**, complete, extensive, catholic, wide-ranging *Opposite*: narrow

all-encompassing *see* **all-embracing**

allergic *adj* **sensitive**, affected, sensitized, hypersensitive, averse *(fml)*

allergy *n* **1 reaction**, allergic reaction, sensitivity, hypersensitivity **2** *(infml)* **dislike**, antipathy, distaste, hate, hatred *Opposite*: liking

alleviate *v* **ease**, lessen, assuage, improve, lighten *Opposite*: aggravate

alleviation *n* **mitigation**, lessening, improvement, easing, assuagement *Opposite*: aggravation

all for *prep* **in favor of**, pro, for, in support of *Opposite*: against

alliance *n* **1 coalition**, grouping, association, union, cooperation **2 relationship**, partnership, bond, link, tie

allied *adj* **1 joined**, united, combined, amalgamated, aligned *Opposite*: unilateral **2 related**, associated, connected, akin, linked *Opposite*: unrelated

all in *adj* **exhausted**, weary, tired, tired out, worn out *Opposite*: fresh

all in all *adv* **all things considered**, on the whole, in general, generally speaking, when all is said and done

all-inclusive *adj* **comprehensive**, grand, complete, broad, all-embracing *Opposite*: incomplete

alliteration *n* **assonance**, consonance, sound repetition, sound pattern, resonance

alliterative *adj* **repetitive**, echoing, assonant, poetic

allocate *v* **assign**, allot, apportion, distribute, deal

allocation *n* **1 distribution**, provision, sharing out, apportionment, division **2 share**, portion, allotment, allowance

all-or-nothing *adj* **win-or-lose**, uncompromising, winner-take-all, rigid, zerosum *Opposite*: flexible

allot *v* **assign**, designate, allocate, earmark, apportion

allotment *n* **share**, portion, part, allocation, allowance

all-out *adj* **maximum**, supreme, extreme, thoroughgoing, determined *Opposite*: half-hearted

allow *v* **1 let**, permit, agree, consent, tolerate *Opposite*: forbid **2 allocate**, set aside, make available, set a limit, allot **3** *(fml)* **accept**, admit, acknowledge, admit as true, grant *Opposite*: disallow

allowable *adj* **permissible**, acceptable, tolerable, admissible, suitable *Opposite*: unacceptable

allowance *n* **payment**, grant, stipend, pocket money, pin money

allowed *adj* **permitted**, allotted, authorized, approved, legitimate *Opposite*: prohibited

allow for *v* **take into account**, take into consideration, make allowance for, make allowances for, bear in mind

alloy *n* **1 blend**, amalgam, compound, mixture, composite **2 additive**, contaminant, adulterant, pollutant, ingredient. *See* COMPARE AND CONTRAST *at* mixture.

all-powerful *adj* **omnipotent**, invincible, supreme, almighty *Opposite*: weak

all-purpose *adj* **general purpose**, multipurpose, universal, overall, versatile *Opposite*: specialized

all-star *adj* **star-studded**, celebrity, famous, prestigious, well-known *Opposite*: unknown

all-time *adj* **unsurpassed**, record, unprecedented, unparalleled, best *Opposite*: insignificant

all told *adv* **altogether**, in total, all in all, in all, overall *Opposite*: in part

allude *v* **refer**, make reference, make allusion, mention, indicate

allure *n* **attraction**, appeal, draw, magnetism, charm

alluring *adj* **appealing**, attractive, tempting, interesting, fascinating *Opposite*: repulsive

allusion *n* **reference**, mention, hint, suggestion, insinuation

allusive *adj* **indirect**, oblique, hinting, referential, suggestive *Opposite*: direct

alluvial *adj* **sedimentary**, silty, deposited, muddy, sandy

all-weather *adj* **year-round**, all-season, rain-or-shine, all-purpose, four-season

ally *v* **associate**, join, affiliate, align, connect ■ *n* **friend**, helper, supporter, assistant, partner *Opposite*: enemy

alma mater *n* **old school**, college, university, school, institution

almanac *n* **directory**, calendar, yearbook, handbook, manual

almighty *adj* **1 omnipotent**, invincible, all-powerful, supreme, omnipresent **2** *(infml)* **enormous**, massive, huge, immense, gigantic

almost adv **nearly**, not quite, just about, virtually, practically Opposite: exactly

alms n **charity**, donation, contribution, gift, offering

aloft adv **in the air**, in flight, airborne, on the wing, high up Opposite: below

alone adv **unaccompanied**, by yourself, on your own, single-handedly, unaided Opposite: accompanied ■ adj **lonely**, lonesome, abandoned, deserted, isolated

along prep **next to**, beside, by the side of, by, adjacent to

alongside prep **next to**, beside, at the side of, flanking, near ■ adv **abreast**, nearby, cheek by jowl, shoulder to shoulder, at close quarters

along with prep **with**, together with, in company with, in conjunction with, as well as Opposite: without

aloof adj **1 remote**, standoffish, proud, reserved, indifferent Opposite: friendly **2 separate**, remote, distant, set apart, away Opposite: close

aloofness n **1 unfriendliness**, coldness, detachment, remoteness, reserve Opposite: friendliness **2 distance**, remoteness, separateness, independence Opposite: closeness

a lot adv **very much**, a great deal, a good deal, in a big way, enormously ■ **many**, plenty, a large number, lots, loads (infml) Opposite: a few

aloud adv **1 audibly**, out loud, distinctly, noticeably, clearly Opposite: silently **2 loudly**, noisily, riotously, blusteringly, boisterously Opposite: quietly

alpha adj **important**, dominant, chief, primary, leading

alphabet n **writing system**, script, character set, letters, symbols

---

WORD BANK

❏ **types of alphabets** Arabic, Braille, cuneiform, Cyrillic, Greek, Hebrew, hieroglyphics, hiragana, ideogram, kanji, katakana, phonetic, pictogram, Roman, runic

---

alphabetic see **alphabetical**

alphabetical adj **arranged**, in order, listed, in a list, sequential

alpine adj **mountainous**, mountain, high-altitude, hilly, high

already adv **by now**, previously, before now, even now, by this time

also adv **1 in addition**, and, what's more, moreover, furthermore **2 too**, as well, likewise, similarly, correspondingly

also-ran n **loser**, failure, flop (infml), dud (infml) Opposite: winner

altar n **table**, bench, slab, stand, platform

alter v **change**, modify, adjust, vary, amend Opposite: maintain. See COMPARE AND CONTRAST at **change**.

alteration n **modification**, adjustment, change, variation, amendment

altercate v **argue**, quarrel, disagree, dispute, squabble

altercation n **argument**, quarrel, disagreement, dispute, exchange

alter ego n **double**, shadow, doppelgänger, twin, clone

alternate v **1 interchange**, rotate, exchange, intersperse, substitute **2 fluctuate**, vary, swing, oscillate, vacillate ■ adj **1 every other**, alternating, every second **2 alternative**, substitute, different, another, other Opposite: same ■ n **substitute**, stand-in, alternative, fill-in, replacement

alternately adv **off and on**, in turn, by turns, one after the other, interchangeably Opposite: consecutively

alternation n **change**, interchange, repetition, rotation, fluctuation

alternative n **1 replacement**, substitute, substitution, change, another possibility **2 option**, choice, freedom of choice, discretion ■ adj **1 other**, another, substitute, alternate, different **2 unconventional**, unorthodox, nonstandard, complementary, unusual Opposite: conventional

alternatively adv **on the other hand**, otherwise, instead, then again

although conj **though**, even though, even if, while, granting

altitude n **height**, elevation, height above sea level, loftiness, highness

altogether adv **1 in total**, all in all, all told, overall, in sum **2 totally**, completely, wholly, thoroughly, entirely **3 on the whole**, when all's said and done, overall, in general, mostly

altruism n **unselfishness**, self-sacrifice, humanity, selflessness, philanthropy Opposite: selfishness

altruistic adj **unselfish**, humane, selfless, philanthropic, noble Opposite: selfish

alum (infml) n **graduate**, former student, ex-student, alumna, alumnus

alumna see **alum**

alumnus see **alum**

always adv **1 at all times**, continuously, all the time, continually, constantly Opposite: never **2 forever**, for all time, for eternity, until the end of time, for ever and a day Opposite: temporarily

a.m. adj **morning**, before noon, before lunch, prelunch Opposite: p.m.

amalgam n **mixture**, mix, combination, blend, fusion. See COMPARE AND CONTRAST at **mixture**.

amalgamate v **merge**, join, combine, unite, integrate Opposite: separate

amalgamated adj **combined**, merged, joined, incorporated, united Opposite: separated

amalgamation *n* **1 merger**, union, incorporation, consolidation, unification **2 combination**, mixture, mix, blend, fusion

amanuensis *n* **secretary**, scribe, writer, copier, copyist

amass *v* **accumulate**, collect, gather, stockpile, hoard *Opposite*: distribute. *See* COMPARE AND CONTRAST *at* collect.

amateur *adj* **1 unprofessional**, shoddy, slapdash, substandard, incompetent *Opposite*: skillful **2 part-time**, unpaid, nonprofessional, leisure, recreational *Opposite*: full-time ■ *n* **layperson**, nonprofessional, dilettante, dabbler *Opposite*: professional

amateurish *adj* **unprofessional**, shoddy, slapdash, clumsy, crude *Opposite*: skillful

amateurishness *n* **unskillfulness**, clumsiness, ineptness, incompetence, unprofessionalism *Opposite*: professionalism

amaze *v* **astonish**, astound, shock, stun, startle

amazed *adj* **astonished**, astounded, shocked, stunned, startled

amazement *n* **astonishment**, wonder, admiration, shock, incredulity

amazing *adj* **astonishing**, astounding, remarkable, wonderful, incredible *Opposite*: unremarkable

ambassador *n* **diplomat**, envoy, representative, emissary, legate

ambiance *n* **atmosphere**, feel, setting, environment, mood

ambience *see* **ambiance**

ambient *adj* **surrounding**, background, local, neighboring

ambiguity *n* **vagueness**, uncertainty, haziness, doubt, indistinctness *Opposite*: clarity

ambiguous *adj* **vague**, unclear, abstruse, equivocal, uncertain *Opposite*: clear

ambiguousness *n* **abstruseness**, opacity, obscurity, vagueness, uncertainty *Opposite*: clarity

ambit *n* **scope**, extent, range, realm, area

ambition *n* **1 drive**, determination, motivation, desire, spirit *Opposite*: apathy **2 goal**, aim, objective, aspiration, dream

ambitious *adj* **1 determined**, ruthless, striving, motivated, aspiring *Opposite*: unmotivated **2 grand**, impressive, bold, large-scale, elaborate *Opposite*: small-scale

ambitiously *adv* **1 determinedly**, ruthlessly, single-mindedly, energetically, pushily *(infml) Opposite*: unambitiously **2 optimistically**, overconfidently, unrealistically, idealistically, impractically *Opposite*: realistically

ambivalence *n* **uncertainty**, contradiction, unsureness, doubt, inconsistency *Opposite*: certainty

ambivalent *adj* **unsure**, undecided, hesitant, uncertain, indecisive *Opposite*: decisive

amble *v* **stroll**, saunter, wander, walk, mosey *(infml) Opposite*: dash

ambush *n* **trap**, surprise attack, ensnarement, ambuscade *(literary)* ■ *v* **trap**, ensnare, lie in wait, take by surprise, waylay

ameliorate *(fml) v* **better**, perfect, amend, upgrade, enrich *Opposite*: deteriorate

amelioration *n* **improvement**, enhancement, enrichment, upgrading, amendment *Opposite*: deterioration

amenability *n* **acquiescence**, docility, willingness, responsiveness, pliability *Opposite*: stubbornness

amenable *adj* **agreeable**, open, acquiescent, willing, docile *Opposite*: stubborn

amend *v* **alter**, adjust, modify, revise, change *Opposite*: maintain

amendment *n* **alteration**, adjustment, modification, revision, change

amends *n* **compensation**, recompense, replacement, restitution, return

amenity *n* **1 facility**, convenience, comfort, service, feature **2 pleasantness**, attractiveness, niceness, agreeableness, affability *Opposite*: discomfort

amiability *n* **friendliness**, amicability, sociability, cordiality, agreeableness *Opposite*: unfriendliness

amiable *adj* **friendly**, sociable, agreeable, affable, kind *Opposite*: unfriendly

amicable *adj* **friendly**, good-natured, harmonious, agreeable, good-humored *Opposite*: hostile

amid *prep* **1 in the middle of**, among, in the midst of, within, in **2 accompanied by**, along with, in the course of, during, at the same time as

amidst *see* **amid**

amiss *adv* **incorrectly**, inappropriately, mistakenly, wrongly, erroneously *Opposite*: correctly ■ *adj* **incorrect**, inappropriate, mistaken, wrong, erroneous *Opposite*: correct

amity *(fml) n* **friendship**, peace, good relations, goodwill, harmony *Opposite*: hostility

ammo *(infml) see* **ammunition**

ammunition *n* **bullets**, shells, missiles, bombs, grenades

amnesia *n* **loss of memory**, memory loss, forgetfulness, obliviousness, oblivion *Opposite*: recall

amnesty *n* **pardon**, reprieve, forgiveness, absolution, exoneration

among *prep* **1 in the middle of**, in the midst of, amid, amidst, amongst **2 with**, along with, amongst, amid, together with **3 as well as**, including, in addition to

amongst *see* **among**

amoral *adj* **unprincipled**, unethical, dishonorable, unscrupulous, immoral *Opposite*: principled

amorality *n* wickedness, sinfulness, unscrupulousness, immorality *Opposite*: morality

amorous *adj* ardent, passionate, affectionate, loving, romantic *Opposite*: dispassionate

amorphous *adj* formless, shapeless, nebulous, vague, unstructured *Opposite*: defined

amortization *n* repayment, paying back, payback, paying off, remuneration

amortize *v* pay back, repay, pay off, remunerate

amount *n* quantity, sum, total, volume, expanse

amount to *v* add up to, total, come to, make, be equal to

ampersand *n* and sign, and, symbol, character

amphitheater *n* 1 stadium, arena, bowl, ring, dome 2 lecture theater, theater, auditorium, lecture room

ample *adj* enough, sufficient, adequate, plenty, plentiful *Opposite*: insufficient

amplification *n* 1 intensification, strengthening, magnification, augmentation, extension *Opposite*: reduction 2 elaboration, clarification, development, expansion *Opposite*: obfuscation

amplify *v* 1 intensify, increase, strengthen, magnify, enlarge *Opposite*: reduce 2 enlarge on, go into detail, elaborate, add to, expand *Opposite*: abbreviate. *See* COMPARE AND CONTRAST *at* increase.

amplitude *n* largeness, scale, fullness, breadth, generosity

amply *adv* sufficiently, adequately, abundantly, thoroughly, fully *Opposite*: insufficiently

ampoule *n* container, vessel, bottle, flask

ampule *see* ampoule

amputate *v* cut off, chop off, remove, sever, separate

amulet *n* charm, good luck charm, talisman, lucky charm, juju

amuse *v* 1 make laugh, make smile, charm, please, divert *Opposite*: depress 2 entertain, keep busy, interest, absorb, engross *Opposite*: bore

amused *adj* smiling, laughing, pleased, tickled, entertained *Opposite*: annoyed

amusement *n* 1 laughter, enjoyment, delight, fun, pleasure *Opposite*: sadness 2 entertainment, pastime, hobby, distraction, diversion

amusing *adj* funny, humorous, entertaining, comical, witty *Opposite*: turgid

anachronism *n* relic, leftover, archaism, holdover, survival

anachronistic *adj* out-of-date, dated, old-fashioned, old, obsolete *Opposite*: contemporary

analgesia *n* 1 numbness, painlessness, insensibility, insensitivity, unawareness *Opposite*: pain 2 pain control, pain relief, pain management, pain killing, numbing

analgesic *adj* painkilling, palliative, pain-relieving, deadening, anodyne ■ *n* painkiller, palliative, pain reliever, anodyne, anesthetic

analogous *adj* similar, equivalent, parallel, corresponding, comparable *Opposite*: different

analogue *n* equivalent, similarity, referent, correspondent *(fml)*

analogy *n* similarity, likeness, equivalence, parallel, correspondence *Opposite*: contrast

analysis *n* 1 examination, study, investigation, scrutiny, breakdown 2 testing, examination, assay, assessment 3 psychoanalysis, psychotherapy, psychiatry

analyst *n* 1 forecaster, predictor, market analyst, expert, specialist 2 psychoanalyst, psychotherapist, psychiatrist

analytic *adj* logical, investigative, diagnostic, systematic, critical *Opposite*: illogical

analytical *see* analytic

analyze *v* examine, study, investigate, scrutinize, evaluate

anarchic *adj* 1 revolutionary, radical, anarchistic, rebellious, anarchical 2 lawless, chaotic, disordered, disorderly, out of control *Opposite*: orderly

anarchical *see* anarchic

anarchist *n* revolutionary, rebel, nihilist, radical

anarchistic *adj* revolutionary, anti-government, anarchic, anarchical, rebellious

anarchy *n* disorder, chaos, lawlessness, revolution, mob rule *Opposite*: order

an arm and a leg *(infml)* *n* king's ransom, small fortune, fortune, pretty penny *(infml)* *Opposite*: pittance

anathema *n* bane, scourge, canker, thorn in somebody's side, irritant

anatomical *adj* functional, structural, material, bodily, body

anatomy *n* 1 structure, composition, makeup, framework, frame 2 analysis, examination, investigation, review, study

ancestor *n* 1 forebear, antecedent, forefather, predecessor, progenitor *Opposite*: descendant 2 forerunner, precursor, antecedent, prototype, progenitor *Opposite*: successor

ancestral *adj* family, familial, inherited

ancestry *n* lineage, descent, origin, heritage, extraction

anchor *n* newscaster, commentator, announcer, broadcaster, journalist ■ *v* fasten, attach, fix, affix, secure *Opposite*: unfasten

anchorage *n* port, harbor, marina, dock, quay

anchorite *n* hermit, recluse, solitary

anchorman *see* **anchorperson**

anchorperson *n* newscaster, broadcaster, anchor, journalist, announcer

anchorwoman *see* **anchorperson**

ancient *adj* 1 antique, early, earliest, prehistoric, primeval *Opposite*: modern 2 old-fashioned, archaic, obsolete, outdated, antiquated *Opposite*: up-to-date

ancillary *adj* auxiliary, subsidiary, supplementary, additional, secondary *Opposite*: main

and *conj* 1 then, after that, next, as a consequence, afterward 2 in addition to, as well as, with, along with, coupled with 3 furthermore, moreover, also, what is more, in addition

and/or *conj* either/or, one or both, either or both

android *n* robot, automaton, bionic person, machine, humanoid

anecdotal *adj* subjective, circumstantial, hearsay, unreliable, untrustworthy *Opposite*: objective

anecdote *n* story, tale, sketch, narrative, narration

anemic *adj* weak, feeble, lackluster, insipid, pale *Opposite*: strong

anesthetic *n* painkiller, local anesthetic, general anesthetic, sedative, analgesic ■ *adj* painkilling, numbing, deadening, sedating

anesthetize *v* deaden, numb, sedate, freeze, put under

anesthetized *adj* knocked out, out cold, under, asleep, sedated

anew *adv* again, afresh, once again, once more, over

angel *n* 1 seraph, archangel, cherub, messenger, spirit *Opposite*: demon 2 backer, sponsor, guarantor, patron, benefactor. *See* COMPARE AND CONTRAST *at* **backer**.

angelic *adj* innocent, good, saintly, adorable, virtuous *Opposite*: wicked

anger *n* annoyance, irritation, fury, rage, wrath *Opposite*: calmness ■ *v* annoy, irritate, infuriate, incense, enrage *Opposite*: pacify

COMPARE AND CONTRAST CORE MEANING: a feeling of strong displeasure in response to an assumed injury
anger a strong feeling of grievance; **annoyance** mild anger and impatience; **irritation** impatience and exasperation; **resentment** aggrieved feelings caused by a sense of unfair treatment; **indignation** anger because something seems unfair or unreasonable; **fury** violent anger; **rage** sudden and extreme anger; **wrath** strong anger, often with a desire for revenge; **ire** (*literary*) strong anger.

angle *n* point of view, viewpoint, approach, position, slant ■ *v* slant, tilt, turn, twist, slope *Opposite*: level

angle for *v* fish for, seek, solicit, try for, try to get

angry *adj* annoyed, irritated, fuming, livid, irate *Opposite*: calm

angst *n* anguish, torment, anxiety, trouble, worry *Opposite*: happiness. *See* COMPARE AND CONTRAST *at* **worry**.

angst-ridden *adj* anguished, tormented, fearful, troubled, worried *Opposite*: content

anguish *n* suffering, torment, agony, torture, pain *Opposite*: contentment

anguished *adj* tormented, suffering, agonized, tortured, pained *Opposite*: content

angular *adj* bony, rawboned, rangy, lanky, gaunt *Opposite*: rounded

angularity *n* boniness, thinness, ranginess, lankiness, sharpness *Opposite*: roundness

animal *n* 1 creature, being, beast, mammal, organism 2 monster, beast, brute, swine ■ *adj* physical, bodily, visceral, instinctive, innate *Opposite*: spiritual

animate *v* liven up, enliven, rouse, bring to life, stir *Opposite*: put a damper on ■ *adj* living, alive, live, breathing, flesh-and-blood *Opposite*: inanimate. *See* COMPARE AND CONTRAST *at* **living**.

animated *adj* energetic, active, vibrant, vivacious, dynamic *Opposite*: lifeless

animation *n* 1 liveliness, energy, vibrancy, life, vigor *Opposite*: apathy 2 cartoon, moving picture, animatronics, computer graphics, simulation

animosity *n* hostility, hatred, loathing, ill feeling, ill will *Opposite*: goodwill. *See* COMPARE AND CONTRAST *at* **dislike**.

animus *n* 1 hostility, animosity, hatred, ill will, detestation *Opposite*: friendliness 2 temperament, personality, disposition, spirit, attitude

anklet *n* chain, bangle, band

annals *n* records, archives, chronicles, history, accounts

anneal *v* harden, strengthen, toughen, galvanize, forge

annex *v* take possession of, seize, take over, capture, invade *Opposite*: cede ■ *n* extension, new building, addition, ell, wing

annexation *n* capture, seizure, takeover, occupation, invasion *Opposite*: surrender

annihilate *v* 1 destroy, obliterate, extinguish, eradicate, exterminate *Opposite*: protect 2 (*infml*) defeat, rout, thrash, overwhelm, crush *Opposite*: lose

annihilation *n* total destruction, obliteration, extinction, eradication, extermination *Opposite*: protection

anniversary *n* birthday, centennial, bicentennial, wedding anniversary

annotate v **gloss**, add footnotes, interpret, explain, make notes on

annotated adj **glossed**, marked, marked up

annotation n **footnote**, gloss, marginal note, explanation, note

announce v **proclaim**, make known, publicize, broadcast, declare Opposite: keep secret

announcement n **statement**, declaration, message, notice, proclamation

announcer n **broadcaster**, telecaster, newscaster, anchor, reporter

annoy v **irritate**, exasperate, vex, irk, get on your nerves Opposite: please

---

COMPARE AND CONTRAST CORE MEANING: cause a mild degree of anger in somebody
annoy cause impatience or anger in somebody; **irritate** annoy somebody slightly; **exasperate** arouse anger or frustration in somebody; **vex** annoy somebody, especially causing upset or distress; **irk** annoy somebody by being tiresome or tedious.

---

annoyance n **irritation**, displeasure, exasperation, anger, infuriation Opposite: pleasure. See COMPARE AND CONTRAST at anger.

annoyed adj **angry**, irritated, infuriated, exasperated, aggravated Opposite: pleased

annoying adj **maddening**, irritating, infuriating, bothersome, exasperating Opposite: pleasing

annual adj **yearly**, twelve-monthly, once a year, once yearly, every twelve months

annuity n **pension**, allowance, income, grant, stipend

annul v **cancel**, call off, withdraw, end, dissolve Opposite: prolong. See COMPARE AND CONTRAST at nullify.

annulment n **cancellation**, withdrawal, dissolution, invalidation, deletion

anode n **terminal**, connection, contact

anodyne adj 1 **painkilling**, palliative, pain-relieving, deadening, analgesic 2 (literary) **soothing**, comforting, relaxing, settling, calming Opposite: stimulating 3 (literary) **insipid**, bland, tame, neutral, inoffensive Opposite: exciting

anoint v **smear**, daub, rub, smooth, massage

anomalous adj **irregular**, uncharacteristic, strange, abnormal, inconsistent Opposite: usual

anomaly n **irregularity**, incongruity, difference, variance, abnormality

anon (literary) adv **soon**, shortly, later, in a while, in a moment Opposite: now

anonymity n 1 **secrecy**, obscurity, concealment, inconspicuousness, namelessness 2 **indistinctness**, blandness, insignificance, ordinariness, dullness Opposite: distinctiveness

anonymous adj 1 **nameless**, unidentified,

unnamed, unsigned, unspecified Opposite: named 2 **undistinguished**, indistinctive, ordinary, everyday, run of the mill Opposite: distinctive

anonymously adv **incognito**, namelessly, in secret, secretly, in disguise

another adj **one more**, additional, a new, a different, a further

answer n 1 **response**, reply, riposte, retort, rejoinder (fml) Opposite: question 2 **solution**, key, way out, resolution, remedy Opposite: problem ■ v 1 **reply**, respond, react, come back with, counter Opposite: challenge 2 **solve**, satisfy, resolve, lay to rest, meet

---

COMPARE AND CONTRAST CORE MEANING: something said, written, or done in acknowledgment of a question or remark, or in reaction to a situation
answer an acknowledgment of a question, letter, or situation; **reply** or **response** a spoken or written answer, or a reaction to a situation; **rejoinder** (fml) a sharp, critical, angry, or clever reply, usually spoken; **retort** a sharp spoken reply, often to criticism; **riposte** a quick or witty reply, usually spoken.

---

answerable adj **responsible**, accountable, liable, chargeable, subject to blame Opposite: unaccountable

answer back v **retort**, argue, counter, respond, riposte

answer for v 1 **pay for**, suffer for, be punished for, make amends for, take the rap (slang) Opposite: get away with 2 **be responsible for**, be accountable for, vouch for, take the responsibility for, be to blame for

antagonism n 1 **resentment**, dislike, bitterness, hatred, antipathy Opposite: friendliness 2 **rivalry**, opposition, aggression, hostility, enmity Opposite: cooperation

antagonist n **rival**, adversary, opponent, enemy, contender Opposite: friend

antagonistic adj **aggressive**, hostile, argumentative, unfriendly, incompatible Opposite: friendly

antagonize v **provoke**, irritate, annoy, upset, get your back up Opposite: mollify

ante n **bet**, wager, stake, payment, raise

antebellum adj **early nineteenth-century**, eighteenth-century, colonial, historical, Federalist

antecedent n **precursor**, forerunner, ancestor, predecessor, forebear

antecedents n **past history**, background, record, previous circumstances, qualifications

antedate v **predate**, go before, be earlier than, date from before, occur before

antediluvian adj 1 **prehistoric**, ancient, old, primitive, primeval Opposite: modern 2 (infml) **antiquated**, out-of-date, obsolete, old-fashioned, archaic Opposite: up-to-date

antenna *n* **feeler**, projection, tentacle, probe, protuberance

anterior *adj* **1 fore**, front, leading, foremost *Opposite*: anterior **2** *(fml)* **before**, earlier, sooner *Opposite*: posterior *(fml)*

anthem *n* **song of praise**, national hymn, sacred song, psalm, hymn

anthology *n* **collection**, compilation, album, omnibus, compendium

anthropomorphize *v* **humanize**, personify, make human, give a human face to, sentimentalize

anti *(infml)* *adj* **opposed**, against, antagonistic, ill-disposed, hostile *Opposite*: pro

anticipate *v* **1 expect**, foresee, await, wait for, predict **2 do in advance**, think ahead, look forward, jump the gun

anticipated *adj* **expected**, predicted, projected, estimated, awaited *Opposite*: unexpected

anticipation *n* **expectation**, expectancy, hope, eagerness, keenness

anticlimax *n* **letdown**, disappointment, deflation, comedown *(infml)* *Opposite*: climax

antics *n* **clowning**, tricks, pranks, larks, frolics

antidote *n* **cure**, remedy, solution, answer, corrective *Opposite*: poison

antipathetic *adj* **opposed**, hostile, antagonistic, conflicting, anti *(infml)* *Opposite*: sympathetic

antipathy *n* **opposition**, hostility, antagonism, hatred, dislike *Opposite*: support. *See* COMPARE AND CONTRAST *at* **dislike**.

antiquated *adj* **out-of-date**, old-fashioned, old, obsolete, archaic *Opposite*: modern. *See* COMPARE AND CONTRAST *at* **old-fashioned**.

antique *adj* **old**, traditional, aged, historic, old-fashioned *Opposite*: new

antiquity *n* **1 ancient times**, the distant past, olden days, olden times, time immemorial **2 relic**, remains, archaeological find, antique, artifact

antiseptic *adj* **1 sterile**, antibacterial, uncontaminated, clean, pure *Opposite*: infected **2 bland**, insipid, tame, uninteresting, colorless *Opposite*: colorful

antisocial *adj* **1 disruptive**, rebellious, harmful, inconsiderate, belligerent *Opposite*: constructive **2 unsociable**, unfriendly, disagreeable, shy, reserved *Opposite*: sociable

antithesis *n* **opposite**, direct opposite, exact opposite, contrast, converse *Opposite*: epitome

antithetic *see* **antithetical**

antithetical *(fml)* *adj* **opposite**, differing, contradictory, opposed, contrary

anxiety *n* **nervousness**, worry, concern, unease, apprehension *Opposite*: calmness. *See* COMPARE AND CONTRAST *at* **worry**.

anxious *adj* **1 worried**, concerned, uneasy, apprehensive, restless *Opposite*: calm **2 eager**, keen, enthusiastic, impatient, itching *Opposite*: indifferent

any *adj* **1 some**, one, several, a few *Opposite*: none **2 every**, each, whichever, whatever ∎ *adv* **at all**, in the least, slightly, a little, somewhat

anybody *pron* **anyone**, any person, somebody, someone, everybody *Opposite*: nobody

anyhow *adv* **anyway**, in any case, at any rate, nevertheless, nonetheless

anyone *pron* **anybody**, any person, someone, somebody, everyone *Opposite*: no one

anyplace *(infml)* *adv* **anywhere**, wherever, where, somewhere, everywhere

anyway *adv* **anyhow**, at any rate, in any case, nevertheless, nonetheless

anywhere *adv* **wherever**, where, somewhere, everywhere, someplace *(infml)*

A-OK *(infml)* *adv* **excellent**, perfect, all right, just right, good

apace *adv* **quickly**, rapidly, swiftly, briskly, like lightning *Opposite*: slowly

apart *adv* **separately**, not together, at a distance, to one side, away from each other *Opposite*: together

apart from *prep* **1 aside from**, except for, with the exception of, not counting, excluding *Opposite*: including **2 as well as**, in addition to, on top of, besides

apathetic *adj* **indifferent**, uninterested, listless, dispirited, lethargic *Opposite*: enthusiastic. *See* COMPARE AND CONTRAST *at* **impassive**.

apathy *n* **indifference**, unconcern, lethargy, laziness, boredom *Opposite*: interest

ape *v* **imitate**, mimic, copy, reproduce, simulate. *See* COMPARE AND CONTRAST *at* **imitate**.

aperture *n* **opening**, hole, space, crack, slit

apex *n* **top**, peak, summit, climax, zenith *Opposite*: base

aphorism *n* **saying**, maxim, adage, cliché, saw

apiece *adv* **each**, respectively, to each, for each, individually *Opposite*: collectively

aplomb *n* **assurance**, self-confidence, self-possession, composure, style *Opposite*: awkwardness

apocalypse *n* **catastrophe**, disaster, destruction, cataclysm, Armageddon

Apocalypse *n* **end of the world**, day of reckoning, Judgment Day, Armageddon

apocryphal *adj* **mythical**, fictional, untrue, legendary, invented *Opposite*: true

apologetic *adj* **sorry**, remorseful, contrite, repentant, rueful *Opposite*: unrepentant

apologist *n* **defender**, supporter, ally, protector, champion

apologize *v* **make an apology**, ask for forgiveness, beg forgiveness, express regret, act contrite

apology n **1 admission of guilt**, request for forgiveness, expression of regret, confession, act of contrition **2 poor substitute**, pathetic excuse, poor example, pretense, stopgap **3 defense**, excuse, explanation, justification

apostate n **renouncer**, defector, deserter, renegade

apostle n **1 advocate**, supporter, promoter, champion, proponent Opposite: detractor **2 disciple**, follower, missionary, messenger, devotee Opposite: leader

apotheosis n **high point**, acme, apogee, climax, limit Opposite: nadir

appall v **horrify**, shock, disgust, dismay, upset Opposite: please

appalled adj **horrified**, shocked, outraged, disgusted, repelled Opposite: delighted

appalling adj **1 horrifying**, shocking, disgusting, sickening, outrageous Opposite: appealing **2 awful**, terrible, dreadful, horrendous, inexcusable Opposite: wonderful

appallingly adv **extremely**, very, utterly, awfully, terribly Opposite: wonderfully

apparatus n **1 device**, gadget, gear, tackle, kit **2 system**, method, mechanism, arrangement, operation

apparel n **clothing**, clothes, garb, wear, kit

apparent adj **1 obvious**, clear, evident, plain, noticeable Opposite: unclear **2 seeming**, ostensible, deceptive, superficial, specious Opposite: actual

apparently adv **1 it seems that**, it appears that, in fact, rumor has it that, evidently **2 seemingly**, deceptively, speciously, ostensibly, outwardly Opposite: actually

apparition n **ghost**, spirit, specter, phantom, ghoul

appeal n **1 plea**, petition, application, request, call **2 charm**, attractiveness, attraction, allure, influence Opposite: repulsion ■ v **1 request**, ask, plead, urge, petition **2 attract**, interest, fascinate, charm, tempt Opposite: repel

appealing adj **attractive**, tempting, interesting, pleasing, alluring Opposite: repulsive

appear v **1 come into view**, come into sight, become visible, emerge, come out Opposite: disappear **2 happen**, occur, be found, exist, surface **3 seem**, look, look as if, give the impression, give the idea **4 perform**, be seen, act, play, take part in **5 turn up**, show, be seen, arrive, roll up

appearance n **1 emergence**, development, arrival, growth, beginning Opposite: disappearance **2 look**, form, exterior, manifestation, outer shell **3 arrival**, entrance, advent, attendance, presence

appease v **1 mollify**, conciliate, pacify, placate, soothe Opposite: provoke **2 satisfy**, assuage, attenuate, calm, soothe Opposite: intensify

appeasement n **conciliation**, pacification, accession, mollification, placation Opposite: provocation

appeaser n **conciliator**, pacifier, gratifier, mollifier

appellation (fml) n **name**, designation, title, style, tag

append v **add**, add on, tag on, attach, affix Opposite: detach

appendage n **1 addition**, attachment, adjunct, add-on, accessory **2 extremity**, feeler, limb, member, projection

appendix n **adjunct**, add-on, supplement, appendage, P.S.

appertain (fml) v **relate**, belong, be associated with, be relevant to, have a bearing on

appetite n **1 hunger**, craving, taste, need to eat, desire for food **2 desire**, taste, enthusiasm, eagerness, keenness Opposite: aversion (fml)

appetizer n **sample**, introduction, sneak preview, taste, foretaste

appetizing adj **1 delicious**, tasty, mouthwatering, enticing, tempting Opposite: revolting **2 appealing**, inviting, attractive, desirable, enticing Opposite: unappealing

applaud v **1 clap**, give a round of applause, give a standing ovation, show your appreciation, congratulate Opposite: boo **2 approve**, support admire, celebrate, congratulate Opposite: condemn

applause n **1 clapping**, round of applause, ovation, hand, handclapping Opposite: jeering **2 praise**, appreciation, approval, approbation, support Opposite: condemnation

appliance n **1 domestic appliance**, labor-saving device, electrical equipment, machine, device **2 application**, use, employment, utilization, purpose

WORD BANK
❏ **types of appliances** blender, coffeemaker, dishwasher, food processor, garbage disposal, grill, iron, juicer, microwave, microwave oven, minibar, mixer, percolator, range, rotisserie, smoke alarm, smoke detector, stove, television, toaster, tumble dryer, washing machine

applicable adj **appropriate**, valid, related, pertinent, relevant Opposite: unrelated

applicant n **candidate**, interviewee, claimant hopeful, aspirant. See COMPARE AND CONTRAST at **candidate**.

application n **1 request**, claim, submission, bid, tender **2 use**, function, purpose, relevance, appliance **3 diligence**, concentration, hard work, effort, attention Opposite: negligence

applied adj **practical**, functional, useful, everyday, pragmatic Opposite: theoretical

apply v **1 submit an application**, request, ask, go in, put in **2 use**, operate, put into operation, employ, utilize **3 be relevant**, relate, pertain, affect, concern **4 put on**, rub on, spread over, smear, spread on *Opposite*: remove

apply yourself *v* **devote yourself**, work hard, concentrate, direct your efforts toward, attend to *Opposite*: neglect

appoint *v* **1 employ**, sign up, hire, assign, take on *Opposite*: dismiss **2** *(fml)* **select**, choose, settle on, agree, pick *Opposite*: reject

appointed *adj* **chosen**, selected, agreed, fixed, prearranged

appointment *n* **1 meeting**, date, scheduled time, engagement, rendezvous **2 selection**, choice, choosing, nomination *Opposite*: dismissal **3 job**, position, opening, office, post

apportion *v* **allocate**, allot, assign, divide up, distribute

apposite *adj* **appropriate**, apt, pertinent, relevant, suitable *Opposite*: inappropriate

appraisal *n* **assessment**, evaluation, judgment, review, consideration

appraise *v* **assess**, evaluate, judge, review, consider

appreciable *adj* **considerable**, substantial, significant, noticeable, palpable *Opposite*: insignificant

appreciate *v* **1 be grateful for**, be thankful for, be glad about, be pleased about, value **2 understand**, realize, be aware, recognize the value of, grasp **3 increase in value**, go up in price, rise, escalate, soar *Opposite*: depreciate

appreciation *n* **1 thanks**, gratitude, indebtedness, gratefulness, obligation *Opposite*: ingratitude **2 approval**, admiration, positive reception, enjoyment, pleasure *Opposite*: disapproval **3 understanding**, grasp, comprehension, perception, sense **4 rise**, increase, escalation, growth, inflation *Opposite*: depreciation

appreciative *adj* **1 grateful**, thankful, indebted, obliged, beholden *Opposite*: ungrateful **2 approving**, enthusiastic, admiring, positive, favorable *Opposite*: disapproving

apprehend *v* **catch**, arrest, detain, take in for questioning, take into custody *Opposite*: release

apprehension *n* **1 anxiety**, uneasiness, worry, trepidation, nervousness *Opposite*: confidence **2 capture**, arrest, detention, seizure, taking *Opposite*: discharge

apprehensive *adj* **uneasy**, worried, nervous, fearful, hesitant *Opposite*: confident

apprehensiveness *see* **apprehension**

apprentice *n* **trainee**, learner, beginner, novice, student *Opposite*: expert. *See* COMPARE AND CONTRAST *at* **beginner**.

apprenticeship *n* **traineeship**, internship, training, education, preparation

approach *v* **1 move toward**, come up to, come

near, draw near, come within reach of *Opposite*: retreat **2 speak to**, talk to, get in touch with, contact, make contact with **3 set about**, tackle, deal with, handle, manage **4 approximate**, come close to, be similar to, come near to, move toward ■ *n* **method**, line of attack, tactic, line, slant

approachability *n* **1 friendliness**, accessibility, openness, affability, cordiality *Opposite*: aloofness **2 user-friendliness**, accessibility, availability, ease of use, usability *Opposite*: inaccessibility

approachable *adj* **1 friendly**, amicable, sociable, open, open-minded *Opposite*: forbidding **2 user-friendly**, accessible, usable, useful, helpful *Opposite*: inaccessible

approaching *adj* **imminent**, impending, pending, future, forthcoming

approbation *n* **approval**, consent, praise, admiration, esteem *Opposite*: disapproval

appropriate *adj* **suitable**, fitting, apt, apposite, right *Opposite*: inappropriate ■ *v* **take**, take over, misappropriate, seize, assume

appropriateness *n* **suitability**, correctness, aptness, appositeness, relevance

appropriation *n* **seizure**, assumption, annexation, adoption, arrogation *(fml)*

approval *n* **1 appreciation**, admiration, liking, praise, esteem **2 endorsement**, support, sanction, consent, agreement *Opposite*: disdain

approve *v* **1 favor**, like, support, agree, accept *Opposite*: disapprove **2 grant**, consent, sanction, allow, pass *Opposite*: reject

approved *adj* **accepted**, permitted, official, agreed, sanctioned

approving *adj* **positive**, favorable, appreciative, sympathetic, complimentary *Opposite*: disapproving

approximate *adj* **estimated**, rough, loose, near, inexact *Opposite*: exact

approximation *n* **estimate**, guess, calculation, guesstimate *(infml)*

apron *n* **bib**, smock, pinafore, overall

apropos *(fml)* *prep* **regarding**, concerning, about, on the subject of, in relation to ■ *adj* **appropriate**, suitable, fitting, apt, apposite *Opposite*: inappropriate

apt *adj* **1 appropriate**, suitable, fitting, apposite, pertinent *Opposite*: inappropriate **2 prone**, likely, given to, inclined, tending **3 quick**, capable, competent, able, skilled *Opposite*: inept

aptitude *n* **ability**, skill, talent, gift, capacity *Opposite*: inability. *See* COMPARE AND CONTRAST *at* **ability, talent**.

aptly *adv* **appropriately**, fittingly, suitably, rightly, pertinently *Opposite*: inappropriately

aquatic *adj* **water**, marine, sea, river

aqueduct *n* **channel**, conduit, canal, watercourse, culvert

arbiter n 1 **arbitrator**, mediator, intermediary, negotiator, go-between 2 **authority**, influence, role model, leader, example

arbitrary adj **random**, chance, subjective, uninformed, illogical Opposite: systematic

arbitrate v **judge**, adjudicate, pass judgment, decide, settle

arbitration n **adjudication**, negotiation, mediation, settlement, intercession

arbitrator n **judge**, arbiter, mediator, go-between, intermediary

arbor n **bower**, retreat, nook, grove, dell (literary)

arc n **curve**, arch, semicircle, sweep, bow

arcade n 1 **walkway**, passageway, colonnade, cloister, loggia 2 **video arcade**, game parlor, amusement arcade

arcane adj **mysterious**, secret, esoteric, deep, hidden. See COMPARE AND CONTRAST at obscure.

arch n 1 **arc**, curve, semicircle, bend, bow 2 **archway**, doorway, portico ■ v **curve**, bend, bow, arc Opposite: straighten ■ adj **playful**, mischievous, roguish, knowing, cunning

archaic adj **old**, ancient, dated, outdated, out-of-date Opposite: modern

arched adj **curved**, rounded, round, high, bowed

archenemy n **opponent**, enemy, rival, challenger, foe (fml) Opposite: ally

archetypal adj **typical**, model, representative, standard, archetypical Opposite: unconventional

archetype n **model**, epitome, prototype, original, classic

archetypical see archetypal

architect n 1 **designer**, draftsman, draftswoman, planner, builder 2 **originator**, inventor, founder, creator, engineer

architecture n **design**, planning, building, construction

archive n **record**, file, documentation, document, library

archly adv **playfully**, mischievously, roguishly, knowingly, cunningly

archness n **playfulness**, mischievousness, roguishness, cunning, coyness

archway n **arch**, arcade, pergola, portico, doorway

arctic (infml) adj **freezing**, cold, chilly, wintry, frozen Opposite: tropical

ardent adj **passionate**, enthusiastic, keen, fervent, zealous Opposite: dispassionate

ardor n **passion**, love, enthusiasm, zeal, fervor Opposite: indifference

arduous adj **difficult**, hard, laborious, grueling, demanding Opposite: easy. See COMPARE AND CONTRAST at hard.

arduousness n **difficulty**, laboriousness, strenuousness, onerousness, rigorousness Opposite: ease

area n 1 **part**, zone, extent, expanse, range 2 **neighborhood**, locale, vicinity, part, quarter 3 **subject**, topic, field, question, matter

arena n **stadium**, grounds, showground, sports grounds, field

argot n **jargon**, slang, idiom, speech, dialect

arguable adj **debatable**, open to question, questionable, doubtful, dubious Opposite: certain

arguably adv **debatably**, questionably, perhaps, possibly, maybe Opposite: certainly

argue v 1 **quarrel**, dispute, fight, disagree, bicker Opposite: agree 2 **make a case**, contend, claim, say, maintain 3 **debate**, dispute, discuss, go over, explore. See COMPARE AND CONTRAST at disagree.

argument n 1 **quarrel**, fight, disagreement, dispute, row 2 **case**, line of reasoning, reason, contention, claim

argumentative adj **quarrelsome**, confrontational, contrary, belligerent, aggressive Opposite: peaceable

arid adj 1 **dry**, parched, bone dry, baked, waterless Opposite: humid 2 **boring**, dull, uninteresting, uninspiring, dry Opposite: exciting See COMPARE AND CONTRAST at dry.

aridity n **dryness**, drought, desiccation, parchedness, aridness Opposite: humidity

aridness see aridity

arise v 1 **happen**, occur, take place, come up, begin 2 **result from**, be the result of, arise from, arise out of, be caused by 3 (literary) **get up**, stand up, rise, get to your feet, ascend Opposite: sit down 4 (literary) **get out of bed**, get up, rise Opposite: retire

aristocracy n **nobility**, upper classes, landed gentry, gentry, upper crust (infml) Opposite: lower class

aristocrat n **noble**, lord, lady, peer, grandee

WORD BANK
❑ **types of aristocrats** baron, baroness, baronet, count, countess, crown prince, duchess, duke, earl, knight, marchioness, marquess, prince, princess, viscount, viscountess

aristocratic adj 1 **refined**, well-bred, patrician, noble Opposite: lowly 2 **titled**, blue-blooded, noble, patrician, upper-class Opposite: lower-class

arm n 1 **limb**, appendage, member 2 **support**, armrest, rest 3 **division**, wing, branch, subdivision, offshoot ■ v **equip**, provide, supply, prepare, ready Opposite: disarm

WORD BANK
❑ **parts of an arm or hand** ball, cuticle, elbow, finger, fingernail, fingerprint, fingertip, fist, forearm, forefinger, funny bone (infml), hand, hangnail, heel, index finger, knuckle, little finger, middle finger, palm, pinkie (infml), ring finger, thumb, thumbnail, wrist

armada *n* **fleet**, flotilla, navy, squadron, task force

Armageddon *n* **1 end of the world**, day of reckoning, Judgment Day, Apocalypse **2 disaster**, destruction, catastrophe, cataclysm, apocalypse

armament *n* **arming**, mobilization, rearmament, deployment, buildup *Opposite*: disarmament

armaments *n* **arms**, weapons, weaponry, guns, missiles

armed *adj* **equipped**, fortified, prepared *Opposite*: unarmed

armed forces *n* **military**, services, forces, defense force, militia

armhole *n* **opening**, slit, hole

armistice *n* **truce**, peace agreement, settlement, ceasefire, resolution

armor *n* **1 suit of armor**, chain mail, bulletproof vest, mail, breastplate **2 protection**, reinforcement, defense, covering, cover

armored *adj* **reinforced**, strengthened, steel-clad, bulletproof, protected *Opposite*: unprotected

armor-plated *adj* **reinforced**, steel-clad, armored, strengthened, bulletproof *Opposite*: unprotected

armory *n* **1 arsenal**, arms depot, ordnance depot, munitions store, weapon store **2 stock**, source, supply, array, range

armrest *n* **support**, arm, rest

arms *n* **weapons**, weaponry, armaments, guns, missiles

army *n* **1 military**, armed forces, defense force, militia, troops **2 crowd**, throng, mass, host, multitude

aroma *n* **smell**, perfume, fragrance, scent, odor. *See* COMPARE AND CONTRAST *at* **smell.**

aromatic *adj* **perfumed**, fragrant, sweet-smelling, scented, pungent *Opposite*: odorless

around *prep* **1 about**, all around, surrounding, covering, over **2 close to**, near, in the vicinity, in the environs, round **3 all over**, throughout, here and there, about, round **4 approximately**, about, in the region of, just about, roughly ■ *adv* **1 in**, here, round, about, present **2 from one place to another**, from place to place, about, everywhere, all over the place *(infml)* **3 near here**, nearby, about, round, in the area

arousal *n* **stimulation**, provocation, awakening, encouragement, excitement

arouse *v* **stimulate**, provoke, awaken, produce, stir *Opposite*: dampen

arraign *v* **accuse**, impeach, prosecute, bring before the court

arraignment *n* **charge**, prosecution, legal process, legal action, indictment *Opposite*: exculpation *(fml)*

arrange *v* **1 organize**, set up, coordinate, fix, fix up *Opposite*: cancel **2 position**, put in order, place, assemble, put together *Opposite*: disarrange

arranged *adj* **decided**, agreed, set, settled, organized

arrangement *n* **1 preparation**, plan, procedure, prearrangement, provision **2 agreement**, understanding, bargain, pact, deal **3 display**, array, composition, layout, assembly

arrant *adj* **complete**, total, outright, unmitigated, utter

array *n* **1 collection**, selection, display, range, arrangement **2 dress**, clothing, regalia, finery, garb ■ *v* **1** *(fml)* **arrange**, display, organize, set out, exhibit **2** *(literary)* **clothe**, dress, deck out, drape, attire *(fml)*

arrears *n* **amount overdue**, amount outstanding, debts, sum unpaid *Opposite*: credit

arrest *v* **1 take into custody**, seize, capture, detain, catch *Opposite*: release **2** *(fml)* **halt**, stop, block, prevent, obstruct **3** *(fml)* **attract**, engage, catch, hold, fix ■ *n* **capture**, seizure, detention, apprehension *Opposite*: release

arresting *adj* **impressive**, eye-catching, stunning, striking, interesting *Opposite*: uninteresting

arrival *n* **1 entrance**, entry, coming, appearance *Opposite*: departure **2 onset**, advent, occurrence, influx, coming *Opposite*: disappearance **3 newcomer**, visitor, guest, incomer, caller

arrive *v* **1 reach**, turn up, get there, land, disembark *Opposite*: depart **2 work out**, reach, come to, come up with, attain **3 succeed**, be successful, gain recognition, make your mark, make it *(infml)*

arrogance *n* **conceit**, haughtiness, egotism, pride, overconfidence *Opposite*: humility

arrogant *adj* **conceited**, haughty, egotistic, superior, proud *Opposite*: humble. *See* COMPARE AND CONTRAST *at* **proud.**

arrogate *(fml)* *v* **claim**, lay claim to, appropriate, misappropriate, assume *Opposite*: cede *(fml)*

arrogation *(fml)* *n* **appropriation**, misappropriation, assumption, takeover, annexation

arrow *n* **1 projectile**, missile, dart, barb, shaft **2 symbol**, sign, pointer, marker, indicator

arrowhead *n* **point**, tip, barb

arsenal *n* **1 weapon store**, munitions store, magazine, armory **2 store**, battery, fund, cache, collection

arson *n* **pyromania**, burning, incineration, ignition, firebombing

arsonist *n* **pyromaniac**, burner, firebomber, incendiary, firebug *(slang)*

art *n* **1 painting**, drawing, fine art, graphic arts, sculpture **2 skill**, talent, knack, ability, virtuosity

artefact *see* **artifact**

arterial *adj* **major**, main, principal, through *Opposite*: subsidiary

artery n route, road, highway, line, channel

artful adj **crafty**, devious, sly, deceitful, cunning Opposite: open

artfulness n **craftiness**, deviousness, slyness, cleverness, deceitfulness Opposite: straightforwardness

arthritic adj **stiff**, swollen, aching, sore, painful

article n 1 **piece of writing**, editorial, piece, item, commentary 2 **object**, item, piece, thing, artifact 3 **clause**, term, stipulation, condition, regulation

articulacy n **self-expression**, expressiveness, eloquence, fluency, articulateness

articulate adj **eloquent**, clear, coherent, fluent, lucid Opposite: inarticulate ■ v 1 **enunciate**, pronounce, speak clearly, speak, say Opposite: mumble 2 **speak about**, express, state, put into words, convey Opposite: suppress

articulated adj 1 **modular**, jointed, coupled, linked, connected Opposite: rigid 2 **spoken**, voiced, uttered, expressed, pronounced Opposite: unspoken

articulateness n **eloquence**, expressiveness, fluency, self-expression, coherence

articulation n 1 **enunciation**, pronunciation, speech, diction, delivery 2 **expression**, verbalization, communication, formulation

artifact n **object**, objet d'art, manufactured object, article, manufactured article

artifice (fml) n 1 **pretense**, ploy, trick, lie, sleight of hand 2 **deception**, deceit, cunning, trickery, artfulness

artificial adj 1 **false**, fake, mock, reproduction, synthetic Opposite: natural 2 **insincere**, false, put-on, pretend, fake Opposite: sincere

artificiality n **insincerity**, disingenuousness, affectedness, affectation, phoniness Opposite: sincerity

artillery n **weaponry**, arms, guns, armaments, weapons

artisan n **craftsperson**, skilled worker, handicrafts worker, craftworker, artist

artist n 1 **painter**, illustrator, drawer, sketcher, cartoonist 2 **performer**, entertainer, artiste

artiste n **performer**, entertainer, artist

artistic adj **creative**, imaginative, inventive, arty (infml)

artistry n **creativity**, originality, artistic ability, imagination, invention

artless adj **simple**, guileless, natural, unworldly, ingenuous Opposite: disingenuous

artlessness n **guilelessness**, naturalness, innocence, unaffectedness, inexperience Opposite: disingenuousness

artsy-craftsy (infml) adj **rustic**, artistic, creative, quaint, imaginative

artwork n 1 **work of art**, creation, representation, reproduction, painting 2 **illustrations**, pictures, photographs, diagrams, plates

arty (infml) adj **creative**, imaginative, inventive, artistic

as conj 1 **while**, when, during 2 **because**, since, seeing that, being as, considering that

as a result of prep **because of**, by, through, by means of, on account of

ascend v 1 **rise**, climb, soar, go up, come up Opposite: descend 2 **climb**, go up, come up, mount, scale Opposite: descend

ascendancy n **dominance**, domination, preeminence, predominance, power Opposite: subordination

ascendant adj 1 **rising**, dominant, ascending, prevailing, mounting Opposite: descendent 2 **dominant**, controlling, governing, ruling, influential Opposite: subordinate

ascendency see ascendancy

ascension (fml) n **rise**, ascent, climb, mounting, scaling Opposite: descent

ascent n 1 **climb**, rise, mounting, scaling, ascension (fml) Opposite: descent 2 **gradient**, slope, incline, rake, angle

ascertain v **determine**, discover, find out, learn, make certain

ascetic n **abstainer**, celibate, puritan, penitent Opposite: hedonist ■ adj **austere**, abstinent, frugal, abstemious, spartan Opposite: hedonistic

asceticism n **austerity**, self-discipline, abstemiousness, self-denial, self-restraint Opposite: hedonism

ascribe (fml) v 1 **assign**, credit, attribute, accredit, chalk up 2 **put down to**, attribute, blame on, lay at the door of, charge

aseptic adj **clean**, sterile, pure, sterilized, uninfected Opposite: septic

asexual adj 1 **genderless**, androgynous, neutral, sexless 2 **vegetative**, somatic, parthenogenetic, nonsexual

as far as conj **to the extent that**, to the degree that, insofar as, as much as, so far as

ash n **residue**, cinders, slag, embers, powder

ashamed adj 1 **embarrassed**, mortified, humiliated, abashed, humbled Opposite: proud 2 **unwilling**, reluctant, hesitant, unhappy, sorry Opposite: pleased

ashen adj **pallid**, wan, pasty, white as a sheet, drained of color Opposite: rosy

ashes n **ruins**, remains, vestiges, remnants, fragments

ashore adv **aground**, onto land, onto dry land, on shore

ashy see ashen

aside adv 1 **sideways**, away, to the side, sidewise, on the side 2 **disregarded**, ignored, excluded, set aside, apart 3 **in reserve**, separately, away, to one side, up your sleeve

■ *n* **1 digression**, departure, tangent, interposition, parenthesis **2 whisper**, mumbled comment, remark, undertone, by-play

aside from *prep* **1 as well as**, in addition to, on top of, besides, over and beyond **2 barring**, excluding, ignoring, except, except for *Opposite*: including

asinine *adj* **silly**, foolish, unintelligent *Opposite*: intelligent

ask *v* **1 request**, inquire, solicit, question, query *Opposite*: answer **2 invite**, ask over, have over, summon, request **3 count on**, expect, demand, look for, require

askance *adv* **doubtfully**, suspiciously, sideways, dubiously, distrustfully

askew *adv* **crookedly**, awry, out of kilter, off center, cockeyed *Opposite*: straight

ask for *v* **request**, provoke, solicit, inspire, demand *Opposite*: refuse

asking price *n* **price**, selling price, starting price, marked price, cost

aslant *adv* **obliquely**, at an angle, on a slope, diagonally, slantingly *Opposite*: straight ■ *adj* **slanting**, slant, slantwise, oblique, diagonal

asleep *adj* **1 sleeping**, slumbering, dead to the world, napping, sound asleep *Opposite*: awake **2 numb**, dead, benumbed, without feeling, lifeless

as long as *conj* **providing**, on condition that, given that, provided that, if

as of *(fml)* *prep* **from**, after, on or after, beginning, starting

aspect *n* **1 feature**, facet, characteristic, part, piece **2 position**, outlook, side, standpoint, viewpoint **3 appearance**, look, quality, bearing, air

as per *prep* **according to**, in accordance with, following, consistent with, in keeping with *Opposite*: counter

asperity *(fml)* *n* **severity**, brusqueness, gruffness, harshness, sharpness *Opposite*: affability

aspersion *n* **slander**, slur, slight, smear, accusation *Opposite*: praise

asphalt *n* **tar**, tarmac, bitumen, blacktop

asphyxia *n* **suffocation**, choking, lack of oxygen, oxygen deprivation, unconsciousness

asphyxiate *v* **suffocate**, smother, choke, stifle, strangle *Opposite*: resuscitate

asphyxiation *n* **suffocation**, choking, smothering, stifling, throttling

aspic *n* **jelly**, gel, mousseline

aspirant *n* **contender**, candidate, applicant, hopeful, seeker ■ *adj* **hopeful**, would-be, aspiring, wannabe *(infml)*. *See* COMPARE AND CONTRAST *at* **candidate**.

aspirate *v* **1 pronounce**, enunciate, articulate, sound, voice **2 remove**, extract, suck out, draw out, take out *Opposite*: inject

aspiration *n* **ambition**, goal, objective, aim, end

aspirational *adj* **ambitious**, self-improving, aspiring, hopeful, eager *Opposite*: unambitious

aspire *v* **seek**, aim, hope, desire, want

aspiring *adj* **hopeful**, would-be, ambitious, aspirant, wannabe *(infml)*

as regards *prep* **with regard to**, regarding, concerning, with reference to, as to

assail *v* **1 attack**, assault, set about, lay into, beset *Opposite*: defend **2 criticize**, attack, lay into, berate, revile *Opposite*: praise

assailant *n* **attacker**, mugger, accoster, goon, assaulter

assassin *n* **killer**, murderer, cutthroat, dispatcher, hired gun *(slang)*

assassinate *v* **kill**, murder, shoot, kill in cold blood, eliminate. *See* COMPARE AND CONTRAST *at* **kill**.

assassination *n* **foul play**, murder, killing, shooting, elimination

assault *n* **1 attack**, beating, stabbing, mugging, battering **2 offensive**, attack, onslaught, incursion, storming *Opposite*: retreat ■ *v* **attack**, mug, set about, assail, lay into *Opposite*: defend

assay *v* **1 examine**, assess, analyze, evaluate, test **2** *(literary)* **attempt**, try, undertake, take a shot at *(infml)*, take a stab at *(infml)*

assemblage *n* **1 accumulation**, grouping, assembly, collection, meeting **2 crowd**, throng, assembly, group, mass

assemble *v* **1 bring together**, collect, pull together, draw together, accumulate *Opposite*: disband **2 muster**, collect, meet, come together, convene *Opposite*: disperse **3 put together**, build, fit together, make, compile *Opposite*: take apart. *See* COMPARE AND CONTRAST *at* **collect**.

assembly *n* **1 gathering**, coming together, meeting, association, assemblage **2 meeting**, congress, assemblage, gathering, muster **3 legislative body**, legislature, council, government, representatives **4 construction**, building, compilation, putting together, fabrication *Opposite*: destruction

assembly point *n* **meeting point**, meeting place, rendezvous, rallying point

assent *v* **agree**, acquiesce, concur, go along with, subscribe to *Opposite*: disagree ■ *n* **agreement**, acquiescence, concurrence, acceptance, approval *Opposite*: disagreement. *See* COMPARE AND CONTRAST *at* **agree**.

assert *v* **1 declare**, state, insist on, proclaim, emphasize *Opposite*: deny **2 stand up for**, profess, defend, maintain, uphold *Opposite*: renounce

assertion *n* **declaration**, statement, proclamation, claim, allegation *Opposite*: denial

assertive *adj* **self-confident**, self-assured, confident, firm, forceful *Opposite*: shy

assertiveness *n* **confidence**, forcefulness,

insistence, decisiveness, boldness *Opposite*: shyness

assess v 1 review, consider, appraise, evaluate, judge 2 **calculate**, evaluate, value, rate, estimate

assessment n 1 **evaluation**, appraisal, judgment, review, consideration 2 **calculation**, estimation, valuation 3 **duty**, charge, impost, debt, bill

assessor n **evaluator**, appraiser, judge, inspector, revenuer (*infml*)

asset n 1 **advantage**, strength, benefit, positive feature, quality *Opposite*: drawback 2 **possession**, property, resource, holding

assets n **possessions**, property, resources, material goods, worldly goods

asset-stripping n **profit taking**, profitmaking, selling off, buying and selling, trading

assiduity n **diligence**, care, attention, application, industriousness *Opposite*: carelessness

assiduous adj **diligent**, persevering, industrious, painstaking, careful *Opposite*: lazy. *See* COMPARE AND CONTRAST *at* **careful**.

assiduousness n **diligence**, persistence, industriousness, attentiveness, tirelessness *Opposite*: laziness

assign v 1 **allocate**, allot, give, dispense, disperse 2 **appoint**, designate, delegate, send, transfer

assignation n **meeting**, tryst, rendezvous, appointment, date

assignment n 1 **task**, job, project, duty, obligation 2 **appointment**, duty, position, role, job 3 **transfer**, handing out, consignment, allocation, delegation

assimilate v 1 **integrate**, adapt, adjust, blend in, fit in 2 **incorporate**, take in, digest, absorb, understand *Opposite*: reject

assimilation n 1 **integration**, adjustment, acclimatization, accommodation, adaptation 2 **absorption**, incorporation, digestion, ingestion, inculcation

assist v help, aid, help out, lend a hand, give a hand *Opposite*: hinder ■ n **a helping hand**, a hand, assistance, help, support *Opposite*: hindrance

assistance n **help**, aid, support, backing, cooperation *Opposite*: hindrance

assistant n **helper**, aide, deputy, personal assistant, subordinate ■ adj **associate**, subordinate, secondary, junior

---

COMPARE AND CONTRAST CORE MEANING: somebody who helps another person in carrying out a task
assistant somebody who works to somebody else's instructions, often in a paid capacity; **helper** somebody who takes on an informal, often voluntary, role; **deputy** an officially designated chief assistant authorized to act on a superior's behalf; **aide** an assistant in military, political, or commercial contexts.

---

assisted adj **aided**, helped, abetted, supported, sponsored *Opposite*: unassisted

assize n **inquest**, court case, hearing, inquiry, examination

associate v 1 **connect**, relate, link, correlate, bracket *Opposite*: separate 2 **mix**, socialize, spend time with, see, be involved with *Opposite*: avoid 3 **unite**, combine, join together, group together, join *Opposite*: disband ■ n 1 **partner**, colleague, business partner, fellow worker, coworker 2 **companion**, comrade, acquaintance, friend, ally ■ adj **subordinate**, secondary, junior, assistant

associated adj **related**, allied, linked, connected, accompanying

association n 1 **organization**, union, alliance, society, company 2 **friendship**, relationship, connection, fellowship, involvement 3 **connotation**, overtone, suggestion, memory, reminder

assonance n **repetition**, recurrence, duplication, iteration, alliteration

as soon as *conj* **once**, the moment, the instant, the minute, immediately

assort v **classify**, separate, sort out, group, divide *Opposite*: disarrange

assorted adj **mixed**, various, miscellaneous, varied, multifarious *Opposite*: uniform

assortment n **variety**, collection, range, mixture, mixed bag

assort with v **associate**, mix with, socialize with, see, spend time with

assuage v **moderate**, ease, soften, lessen, appease *Opposite*: inflame

assume v 1 **take for granted**, suppose, presume, presuppose, deduce 2 **take up**, take responsibility, take on, take upon yourself, shoulder 3 **feign**, affect, fake, simulate, put on. *See* COMPARE AND CONTRAST *at* **deduce**.

assumed adj 1 **expected**, presumed, supposed, rumored, implicit 2 **false**, artificial, fake, phony, bogus

assumed name n **alias**, pseudonym, pen name, nom de plume, stage name

assuming adj **presumptuous**, pretentious, arrogant, haughty, high and mighty *Opposite*: humble

assumption n **supposition**, statement, postulation, hypothesis, guess

assurance n 1 **pledge**, declaration, word, guarantee, oath 2 **self-confidence**, self-possession, self-reliance, confidence, poise *Opposite*: timidity

assure v 1 **promise**, guarantee, give surety, pledge, swear 2 **make certain**, ensure, guarantee, nail down, know for certain

assured adj 1 **certain**, guaranteed, sure, confident, solid *Opposite*: uncertain 2 **confident**, self-confident, self-assured, self-possessed, poised *Opposite*: diffident

asterisk n **symbol**, sign, mark, character, star

■ *v* **mark**, identify, label, indicate, specify

astern *adv* **1 behind**, aft, at the back, in back of, at the rear *Opposite*: forward **2 to the rear**, backward, in reverse *Opposite*: ahead

astir *adj* **1 awake**, out of bed, up, up and about, aroused *Opposite*: asleep **2 active**, alive, moving, stirring, live *Opposite*: inactive

as to *prep* **with regard to**, as regards, regarding, concerning, with respect to

astonish *v* **surprise**, amaze, astound, dumbfound, overwhelm

astonished *adj* **surprised**, amazed, astounded, dumbfounded, incredulous

astonishing *adj* **amazing**, surprising, astounding, shocking, bewildering *Opposite*: predictable

astonishment *n* **surprise**, amazement, wonder, bewilderment, shock

astound *v* **amaze**, astonish, surprise, shock, dumbfound

astounded *adj* **astonished**, surprised, amazed, stunned, dazed

astounding *adj* **amazing**, astonishing, surprising, shocking, beyond belief *Opposite*: unsurprising

astral *adj* **1 stellar**, astronomical, astrophysical, cosmological, celestial **2 immaterial**, spiritual, psychical, otherworldly, transcendent *Opposite*: material

astray *adv* **off course**, lost, off track, off target, off beam

astride *prep* **on both sides of**, spanning, straddling, across

astringency *n* **acerbity**, acidity, causticity, mordancy, sharpness *Opposite*: blandness

astringent *adj* **harsh**, severe, biting, caustic, acerbic *Opposite*: bland

astrologer *n* **fortune-teller**, seer, soothsayer, prophet, forecaster

astrological *adj* **zodiacal**, horoscopic, fortune-telling, prophetic, forecasting

astrological sign *n* **sign of the zodiac**, birth sign, sun sign, constellation, house

WORD BANK
❏ **types of astrological signs** Aquarius, Aries, Cancer, Capricorn, Gemini, Leo, Libra, Pisces, Sagittarius, Scorpio, Taurus, Virgo

astrology *n* **fortune-telling**, clairvoyance, soothsaying, forecasting, prediction

astronaut *n* **space traveler**, space pilot, cosmonaut, rocket pilot, spaceman

astronomical *adj* **1 astral**, planetary, cosmological, astrophysical, lunar **2** (*infml*) **exorbitant**, excessive, sky-high, through the roof, huge *Opposite*: affordable

astronomically (*infml*) *adv* **exorbitantly**, exceedingly, excessively, inordinately, extremely

astute *adj* **shrewd**, smart, perceptive, judicious, incisive *Opposite*: credulous

astuteness *n* **shrewdness**, good judgment, smartness, intelligence, wisdom *Opposite*: credulity

asunder (*fml*) *adv* **apart**, open, in pieces, in bits, in halves *Opposite*: together

as well *adv* **too**, also, additionally, in addition, on top

as well as *conj* **in addition to**, on top of, over and above, with, and

as yet *adv* **at this time**, at present, up to now, so far, up to the present moment

asylum *n* **1 place of safety**, refuge, haven, safe haven, sanctuary **2 protection**, security, refuge, sanctuary, shelter

asymmetric *adj* **unequal**, uneven, lopsided, irregular, disproportionate *Opposite*: symmetrical

asymmetrical *see* asymmetric

asymmetry *n* **irregularity**, lopsidedness, unevenness, disproportionateness *Opposite*: symmetry

atavistic *adj* **primitive**, primeval, primal, ancient, ancestral

at fault *adj* **in the wrong**, to blame, guilty, wrong, responsible *Opposite*: in the right

at first *adv* **in the beginning**, at the start, originally, initially, at the outset

at hand *adv* **nearby**, just around the corner, within reach, near, close by *Opposite*: distant ■ *adj* **imminent**, approaching, impending, on the way, coming *Opposite*: far-off

atheism *n* **unbelief**, doubt, freethinking, skepticism, humanism *Opposite*: belief

atheist *n* **unbeliever**, doubter, nonbeliever, skeptic, agnostic *Opposite*: believer

atheistic *adj* **unbelieving**, nonbelieving, disbelieving, incredulous, irreligious *Opposite*: believing

athlete *n* **sportsperson**, contestant, participant, competitor, team member

athletic *adj* **fit**, sporty, healthy, in good shape, physical *Opposite*: unfit

athleticism *n* **fitness**, sportiness, litheness, agility, suppleness

at large *adj* **1 in general**, on the whole, overall, as a whole, all together **2 free**, at liberty, unconfined, on the loose, escaped *Opposite*: confined

at last *adv* **eventually**, finally, ultimately, in the end, at length *Opposite*: immediately

at least *adv* **1 as a minimum**, no less than *Opposite*: at best **2 at any rate**, in any case, however, nonetheless, nevertheless

at length *adv* **1** (*fml*) **long-windedly**, in detail, in depth, verbosely, wordily *Opposite*: in brief **2 eventually**, at last, at long last, finally, in the end *Opposite*: immediately

ATM *n* **cash machine**, automated teller machine, money machine

atmosphere *n* **1 air**, sky, heavens, ether (*literary*) **2 ambiance**, impression, feeling, feel, mood

WORD BANK

❑ **parts of the atmosphere** exosphere, ionosphere, mesosphere, ozone layer, stratosphere, thermosphere, tropopause, troposphere

atmospheric adj **impressive**, distinctive, moody, special, full of character

atmospherics n **interference**, disturbance, static, snow, hissing

at odds adj **1 in conflict**, at loggerheads, at variance, arguing, quarreling Opposite: in agreement **2 contradictory**, incompatible, conflicting, inconsistent, in disagreement Opposite: consistent

atoll n **island**, isle, islet, coral reef, coral island

atom n **particle**, bit, tiny part, iota, jot

atomic adj **1 nuclear**, thermonuclear, fissionable **2 microscopic**, submicroscopic, minute, infinitesimal, minuscule Opposite: gigantic

atomizer n **spray**, spray can, vaporizer, aerosol

atonal adj **twelve-note**, twelve-tone, discordant, dissonant, inharmonious

atonality n **twelve-note scale**, twelve-tone scale, serialism, discordance, dissonance Opposite: tonality

at once adv **1 immediately**, straightaway, right away, right now, now Opposite: later **2 simultaneously**, at the same time, in unison, in chorus, together Opposite: separately

atone (fml) v **compensate**, make up, make amends, redress, apologize

atonement n **compensation**, amends, penitence, penance, punishment

atop prep **on**, upon, on the top of, over, higher than Opposite: beneath

atrium n **hall**, foyer, entrance hall, entrance, vestibule

atrocious adj **1 bad**, terrible, dreadful, appalling, awful **2 brutal**, vicious, wicked, evil, cruel

atrociously adv **1 badly**, terribly, appallingly, fearfully, dreadfully Opposite: wonderfully **2 brutally**, viciously, wickedly, evilly, cruelly

atrociousness n **fearfulness**, dreadfulness, viciousness, wickedness, frightfulness

atrocity n **1 act of violence**, massacre, killing, outrage, brutality **2 violence**, cruelty, viciousness, barbarity

atrophy v **waste away**, waste, wither, weaken, shrivel

at stake adj **in the balance**, at risk, in danger, in jeopardy, at issue

attach v **1 fasten**, join, connect, fix, put together Opposite: detach **2 assign**, award, attribute, accord, ascribe (fml)

attaché n **diplomat**, public servant, civil servant, representative, envoy

attached adj **1 enclosed**, accompanying, supporting, supplementary **2** (infml) **emotionally involved**, devoted, fond of, close, friendly Opposite: uninvolved

attachment n **1 bond**, affection, connection, regard, friendship **2 add-on**, accessory, extra, addition, supplement

attack v **1 harm**, assault, harass, bother, molest Opposite: defend **2 criticize**, argue, confront, pounce on, disagree Opposite: support **3 infect**, occur, strike, hit, strike down **4 begin**, set to, deal with, tackle, pile in ■ n **1 violence**, assault, confrontation, act of violence, incident Opposite: defense **2 bout**, dose, spell, occurrence, outbreak **3 criticism**, condemnation, argument, disagreement Opposite: praise

attacker n **assailant**, aggressor, invader, enemy, foe (fml) Opposite: defender

attack the dignity of v **insult**, call names, abuse, give offense, offend

attain v **reach**, achieve, accomplish, conquer, manage Opposite: fall short. See COMPARE AND CONTRAST **at accomplish**.

attainable adj **within reach**, possible, achievable, realistic, reasonable Opposite: unattainable

attainment n **1 achievement**, accomplishment, realization, fulfillment, completion Opposite: failure **2 skill**, ability, talent, achievement, accomplishment

attar n **essence**, extract, essential oil, distillate, perfume

attempt v **make an effort**, try, bid, make an attempt, have a shot ■ n **effort**, try, go, shot, bid

attend v **1 be present**, go to, be there, grace with your presence, appear Opposite: miss **2 listen**, concentrate, focus, keep your mind on, pay attention Opposite: ignore

attendance n **1 presence**, attending, appearance, being present Opposite: nonattendance **2 turnout**, audience, number present, gate, crowd

attendant adj **associated**, linked, related, connected, consequent ■ n **1 assistant**, helper, aide, guide, employee **2 escort**, usher, bridesmaid, groomsman, pageboy

attend to v **deal with**, see to, tackle, turn your attention to, address Opposite: ignore

attention n **1 notice**, concentration, thought, awareness, consideration Opposite: inattention **2 care**, courtesy, consideration, kindness, devotion Opposite: neglect

attention-grabbing adj **eye-catching**, conspicuous, arresting, noticeable, striking Opposite: understated

attention to detail n **meticulousness**, thoroughness, care, carefulness, exactness Opposite: carelessness

attentive adj **1 considerate**, responsive, helpful, caring, thoughtful Opposite: inconsiderate **2 paying attention**, listening carefully, concentrating, observant, focused *Opposite*: inattentive

attentiveness *n* **1 care**, courtesy, thoughtfulness, consideration, kindness *Opposite*: neglect **2 concentration**, attention, focus, alertness *Opposite*: inattention

attenuate *v* **reduce**, decrease, lessen, diminish, dilute *Opposite*: intensify

attenuation *n* **reduction**, decrease, lessening, diminution, dilution *Opposite*: intensification

attest *v* **show**, bear out, prove, confirm, corroborate *Opposite*: refute

attestation *n* **confirmation**, corroboration, substantiation, verification, testimony *Opposite*: refutation

at the side of *prep* **beside**, next to, alongside, with, adjacent to

attic *n* **loft**, garret, roof space, upper floor *Opposite*: basement

at times *adv* **sometimes**, from time to time, on occasion, once in a while, now and then

attire *(fml)* *n* **clothing**, dress, clothes, outfit, garments

attitude *n* **1 view**, opinion, viewpoint, point of view, feeling **2 posture**, pose, position, bearing, stance **3** *(infml)* **boldness**, brashness, arrogance, insolence, defiance

attorney *n* **lawyer**, advocate, counsel, legal representative, attorney at law

attract *v* **1 draw**, bring together, pull, exert a pull on *Opposite*: repel **2 entice**, appeal, fascinate, charm, interest *Opposite*: put off

attraction *n* **magnetism**, lure, desirability, hold, charm *Opposite*: repulsion

attractive *adj* **1 appealing**, alluring, charming, pleasing, inviting *Opposite*: unattractive **2 good-looking**, beautiful, handsome, lovely, pretty *Opposite*: ugly. See COMPARE AND CONTRAST *at* **good-looking**.

attractively *adv* **nicely**, delightfully, charmingly, appealingly, prettily *Opposite*: unattractively

attractiveness *n* **1 good looks**, pleasant appearance, beauty, prettiness, charm *Opposite*: ugliness **2 magnetism**, charisma, draw, appeal, lure *Opposite*: repulsiveness

attribute *v* **ascribe**, put down to, lay at the door of, impute, blame on ■ *n* **quality**, characteristic, trait, property, feature

attribution *n* **credit**, acknowledgment, designation, ascription *(fml)*

attributive *adj* **prenominal**, preceding, modifying, qualifying

attrition *n* **abrasion**, erosion, slow destruction

attune *v* **adjust**, accustom, adapt, accommodate, acclimate

atypical *adj* **different**, unusual, uncommon, strange, odd *Opposite*: typical

auction *n* **sale**, mart, Dutch auction, silent auction

audacious *adj* **1 daring**, bold, brave, fearless, courageous *Opposite*: cowardly *(fml)* **2 impudent**, bold, disrespectful, overconfident, cheeky *(infml)* *Opposite*: courteous

audaciousness *see* **audacity**

audacity *n* **1 boldness**, daring, courage, bravery, fearlessness *Opposite*: cowardice **2 impudence**, disrespect, boldness, rudeness, discourtesy *Opposite*: courtesy

audibility *n* **loudness**, noise, distinctness, discernibility, perceptibility *Opposite*: inaudibility

audible *adj* **perceptible**, clear, distinct, noticeable, loud *Opposite*: inaudible

audience *n* **1 spectators**, viewers, addressees, listeners, onlookers **2 meeting**, interview, consultation, appointment, hearing

audio *adj* **acoustic**, auditory, aural, audial

audiovisual *adj* **video**, filmed, film, cinematic, movie

audit *n* **review**, check, inspection, examination, assessment ■ *v* **review**, inspect, examine, assess, appraise

audition *n* **test**, tryout, trial, interview ■ *v* **try out**, test, hear, interview

auditor *n* **1 examiner**, accountant, assessor, checker **2** *(fml)* **listener**, hearer, eavesdropper

auditorium *n* **hall**, lecture hall, theater, amphitheater

auditory *adj* **aural**, hearing, audio, acoustic

augment *(fml)* *v* **increase**, enlarge, expand, extend, amplify *Opposite*: diminish. See COMPARE AND CONTRAST *at* **increase**.

augmentation *n* **increase**, growth, rise, expansion, intensification *Opposite*: decrease

augur *v* **foretell**, predict, portend, promise, prophesy

augury *n* **1 divination**, prediction, prophecy, forecasting, prognostication **2 portent**, omen, auspice, indication, prediction

august *(fml)* *adj* **imposing**, impressive, grand, majestic, dignified *Opposite*: humble

aura *n* **air**, atmosphere, force, appearance, quality

aural *adj* **auditory**, hearing, acoustic, audio

auspice *n* **omen**, portent, augury, sign, indication

auspices *n* **sponsorship**, patronage, backing, support, help

auspicious *adj* **favorable**, fortunate, promising, propitious, lucky *Opposite*: inauspicious

austere *adj* **1 serious**, grim, severe, unsmiling, harsh *Opposite*: gentle **2 stark**, severe, simple, basic, sparse *Opposite*: comfortable **3 plain**, bare, simple, clean, undecorated *Opposite*: ornate

austerity *n* **1 severity**, strictness, sternness, gravity, soberness *Opposite*: levity **2 self-**

denial, shortage, scarcity, economy *Opposite*: abundance **3 plainness**, starkness, bareness, simplicity, cleanness *Opposite*: opulence

autarchy *n* autocracy, absolute power, absolutism, despotism, tyranny *Opposite*: democracy

authentic *adj* **1 genuine**, original, authenticated, valid *Opposite*: fake **2 true**, reliable, dependable, trustworthy, faithful *Opposite*: false

authenticate *v* **validate**, confirm, verify, substantiate, endorse

authentication *n* verification, confirmation, substantiation, validation, certification

authenticity *n* genuineness, legitimacy, validity, reality, truth

author *n* **1 writer**, novelist, playwright, dramatist, poet **2 creator**, originator, inventor, source

authoritarian *adj* strict, demanding, totalitarian, despotic, absolute *Opposite*: liberal

authoritarianism *n* totalitarianism, dictatorship, oppression, absolutism, tyranny *Opposite*: democracy

authoritative *adj* **1 reliable**, trustworthy, dependable, respected, convincing *Opposite*: unreliable **2 commanding**, imposing, firm, confident, convincing *Opposite*: weak

authoritatively *adv* with authority, confidently, firmly, commandingly, convincingly

authoritativeness *n* **1 reliability**, trustworthiness, dependability, validity, credibility *Opposite*: unreliability **2 authority**, command, standing, position, weight

authority *n* **1 power**, right, ability, influence, weight **2 citation**, source, evidence **3 agency**, group, government department, board, corporation **4 confidence**, conviction, knowledge, experience **5 expert**, specialist, consultant, buff, expert witness

authority figure *n* mentor, person of influence, leader, role model, example

authorization *n* approval, consent, endorsement, sanction, agreement

authorize *v* approve, allow, sanction, permit, give permission *Opposite*: forbid

authorized *adj* official, lawful, legal, sanctioned, approved *Opposite*: unauthorized

authorship *n* **1 writing**, composition, invention, production, output **2 origin**, source, provenance, derivation, genesis

autobiographical *adj* nonfictional, factual, first-person, real-life, true to life *Opposite*: fictional

autobiography *n* memoirs, life story, life history

autochthonous *adj* original, native, indigenous, aboriginal. *See* COMPARE AND CONTRAST *at* native.

autocracy *n* dictatorship, monocracy, despotism, tyranny, absolutism *Opposite*: democracy

autocrat *n* dictator, absolute ruler, tyrant, despot

autocratic *adj* **1 despotic**, tyrannical, repressive, oppressive, monocratic *Opposite*: democratic **2 dictatorial**, domineering, bossy, overbearing, imperious

autograph *n* signature, name, inscription, dedication

automated *adj* automatic, mechanical, programmed, preset, mechanized *Opposite*: manual

automatic *adj* **1 mechanized**, automated, mechanical, programmed, preset *Opposite*: manual **2 involuntary**, reflex, unconscious, instinctive, programmed *Opposite*: voluntary **3 routine**, habitual, mechanical, regular, repeated *Opposite*: spontaneous

automation *n* mechanization, computerization, robotics

automaton *n* robot, android, machine

autonomous *adj* self-governing, sovereign, free, independent, separate *Opposite*: dependent

autonomy *n* independence, self-government, self-rule, sovereignty *Opposite*: dependence

autopsy *n* postmortem, dissection, analysis, debriefing, examination

autosuggestion *n* self-suggestion, self-hypnosis, autohypnosis, power of suggestion, self-deception

autumn *n* end, conclusion, close, culmination, decline *Opposite*: beginning

autumnal *adj* fall, seasonal, equinoctial *Opposite*: spring

auxiliary *adj* supplementary, secondary, support, supporting, assisting *Opposite*: main

avail *n* benefit, advantage, reward, gain, purpose

availability *n* obtainability, handiness, convenience, readiness, accessibility *Opposite*: unavailability

available *adj* obtainable, accessible, on hand, to be had, existing *Opposite*: unavailable

avail yourself *v* make use of, use, benefit from, take, help yourself to

avalanche *n* **1 snow slip**, fall, slide **2 quantity**, increase, mass, flood, shower

avant-garde *adj* new, modern, experimental, unconventional, innovative *Opposite*: traditional

avarice *n* greed, greediness, materialism, covetousness, acquisitiveness *Opposite*: generosity

avaricious *adj* greedy, rapacious, grasping, acquisitive, covetous *Opposite*: generous

avariciousness *see* avarice

avenge *v* retaliate, punish, even the score, take vengeance, get even

avenger n **punisher**, retaliator, nemesis (*literary*)

avenue n **opportunity**, possibility, way, chance, opening

aver (*fml*) v **affirm**, state, claim, declare, assert *Opposite*: refute

average n **mean**, arithmetic mean, mode, median, norm ■ adj **regular**, normal, usual, typical, middling *Opposite*: extraordinary ■ v **be around**, be in the region of, be more or less, be close to

average down v **round down**, level down, bring down, lower, decrease

averagely adv **1 on average**, normally, typically, standardly, commonly *Opposite*: exceptionally **2 passably**, tolerably, adequately, unspectacularly, indifferently *Opposite*: exceptionally

average out v **equalize**, level out, balance out, even out

average up v **round up**, level up, bring up, raise, increase

averse (*fml*) adj **opposed**, antagonistic, loath, unenthusiastic, ill-disposed *Opposite*: favorable

aversion (*fml*) n **dislike**, hatred, loathing, repugnance, distaste *Opposite*: liking. *See* COMPARE AND CONTRAST *at* **dislike**.

avert v **1 prevent**, stop, ward off, avoid, forestall **2 turn away**, turn from, turn aside, divert, deflect

aviary n **birdcage**, coop, chicken coop, hen house, dovecote

aviation (*fml*) n **flying**, flight, aeronautics, air travel

aviator n **pilot**, flier, aeronaut, copilot

avid adj **keen**, enthusiastic, passionate, eager, devoted *Opposite*: indifferent

avidity n **greed**, eagerness, voracity, covetousness, greediness *Opposite*: indifference

avidly adv **keenly**, enthusiastically, passionately, eagerly, devotedly *Opposite*: indifferently

avocation (*fml*) n **1 occupation**, job, vocation, calling, profession **2 hobby**, pastime, diversion, amusement, sport

avoid v **1 keep away**, stay away from, shun, steer clear, let alone **2 evade**, circumvent, get around, get out of, dodge *Opposite*: face **3 prevent**, forestall, avert, preclude (*fml*) *Opposite*: promote

avoidable adj **preventable**, unnecessary, needless, stoppable *Opposite*: inevitable

avoidance n **1 evasion**, escaping, evading, dodging, circumvention **2 prevention**, anticipation, averting, forestalling, annulment *Opposite*: promotion **3 abstention**, refraining, refrainment, holding off, eschewal *Opposite*: indulgence

avow (*fml*) v **affirm**, state, declare, acknowledge, admit *Opposite*: deny

avowal (*fml*) n **affirmation**, statement, confirmation, declaration, acknowledgment *Opposite*: denial

avowed (*fml*) adj **affirmed**, stated, confirmed, declared, acknowledged *Opposite*: unspoken

avowedly (*fml*) adv **admittedly**, by your own admission, openly, self-confessedly, frankly

avuncular adj **kindly**, kind, kindhearted, benign, friendly *Opposite*: unkindly

await v **1 lie in wait for**, wait on, expect, look forward to, look out for **2 lie ahead**, be in store, be to come, loom, near

awaited adj **anticipated**, expected, presumed, waited for *Opposite*: unexpected

awake adj **wide-awake**, conscious, wakeful, up, up and around *Opposite*: asleep

awaken v **1 wake**, wake up, rouse, get up, stir **2 rouse**, arouse, set off, stir, promote *Opposite*: suppress

awakening adj **developing**, growing, emerging, emergent, new ■ n **1 arousal**, wakening, emergence, stirring **2 awareness**, attention, recognition, realization, revival

award n **1 prize**, honor, reward, gift, grant **2 verdict**, decision, determination, judgment, settlement ■ v **give**, present, grant, endow, bestow (*fml*)

aware adj **1 conscious**, mindful, alert, attentive, responsive *Opposite*: oblivious **2 knowledgeable**, interested, concerned, informed, experienced *Opposite*: ignorant

COMPARE AND CONTRAST CORE MEANING: having knowledge of the existence of something **aware** knowing something either intellectually or intuitively; **conscious** keenly aware of something and regarding it as important; **mindful** actively attentive, or deliberately keeping something in mind; **cognizant** (*fml*) having special knowledge about something; **sensible** (*fml*) keenly aware of something.

awareness n **1 consciousness**, mindfulness, alertness, responsiveness, attentiveness *Opposite*: oblivion **2 knowledge**, understanding, grasp, appreciation, familiarity *Opposite*: ignorance

awash adj **1 soaked**, flooded, drenched, waterlogged, saturated *Opposite*: dry **2 oversupplied**, full of, overflowing, packed, crammed *Opposite*: lacking

away adj **absent**, gone, left, missing, not here *Opposite*: present

awe n **1 wonder**, admiration, respect, amazement, surprise **2 fear**, terror, dread, fright, trepidation

awe-inspiring adj **overwhelming**, grand, breathtaking, splendid, tremendous

awesome *see* **awe-inspiring**

awestricken *see* **awestruck**

awestruck adj **impressed**, overwhelmed, stunned, enthralled, rapt *Opposite*: unimpressed

awful *adj* dreadful, terrible, appalling, unpleasant, horrible *Opposite*: wonderful

awfully *adv* **1 extremely**, very, really, terrifically, terribly **2 badly**, unpleasantly, dreadfully, terribly, appallingly *Opposite*: well

awfulness *n* dreadfulness, horror, misery, unpleasantness, terribleness

awhile (*literary*) *adv* a little, for a moment, a moment or two, a short time, for a while

awkward *adj* **1 embarrassing**, tricky, problematic, difficult, thorny *Opposite*: straightforward **2 unwieldy**, cumbersome, bulky *Opposite*: compact **3 clumsy**, inelegant, graceless, uncoordinated, ungainly *Opposite*: graceful **4 uncomfortable**, embarrassed, out of your depth, tongue-tied, self-conscious *Opposite*: comfortable

awkwardly *adv* **1 clumsily**, inelegantly, gracelessly, cumbersomely, gawkily (*infml*) *Opposite*: easily **2 uncomfortably**, uneasily, with embarrassment, self-consciously, gauchely *Opposite*: comfortably

awkwardness *n* **1 clumsiness**, ineptness, inelegance, gracelessness, ungainliness *Opposite*: ease **2 discomfort**, unease, embarrassment, uneasiness, self-consciousness *Opposite*: ease

awning *n* canopy, sunshade, sun shelter, blind

AWOL *adj* absent without leave, absent, missing, deserting, wanted *Opposite*: present

awry *adj* **1 crooked**, askew, skewed, off beam, out of kilter *Opposite*: straight **2 amiss**, wrong, muddled, incorrect, astray *Opposite*: right

ax *v* **1** (*infml*) **dismiss**, lay off, let go, fire (*infml*), sack (*infml*) *Opposite*: employ **2 reduce**, cut, cut back, scale down, slim down *Opposite*: increase **3 sever**, cleave, cut, hack, chop (*infml*)

axiom *n* maxim, adage, saying, saw, proverb

axiomatic *adj* self-evident, goes without saying, obvious, manifest, clear

axis *n* alliance, partnership, bloc, league, federation

B

babble *v* gabble, mutter, prattle, chatter, blather (*infml*)

baby *n* infant, child, newborn, babe in arms, little one ■ *v* pamper, coddle, mollycoddle, cosset, overprotect

baby-faced *adj* youthful, boyish, girlish, childlike, wide-eyed *Opposite*: wizened

babyhood *n* infancy, childhood, early years, youth

babyish *adj* childish, infantile, immature, puerile, adolescent *Opposite*: mature

baby-sit *v* look after, watch, take care of, protect, tend to

bachelor *n* unmarried man, single man, eligible male, unattached man, confirmed bachelor

back *n* backbone, spine, spinal column, vertebral column, vertebrae ■ *adv* behind, to the rear, toward the back, backward, rearward *Opposite*: forward ■ *v* **1 support**, provide for, finance, fund, help **2 go backward**, reverse, move backward, recede, back up *Opposite*: proceed

backache *n* back pain, back trouble, bad back, lumbago, sciatica

back away *v* recoil, shrink, draw back, shy away, back off *Opposite*: stay

backbiting *n* spitefulness, backstabbing, scandalmongering, cattiness, maliciousness

backbone *n* **1 spine**, spinal column, vertebral column, back, vertebrae **2 mainstay**, support, prop, spine, pillar **3 moral fiber**, strength of character, stamina, fortitude, courage

backbreaking *adj* strenuous, arduous, grueling, exhausting, taxing *Opposite*: easy

backcloth *n* backdrop, scenery, set, stage set, background

back country *n* wilderness, wilds, backwoods, rough country, sticks (*infml*)

back down *v* withdraw, concede defeat, accept defeat, yield, admit defeat *Opposite*: stand your ground

backdrop *n* **1 backcloth**, scenery, set, stage set, scene **2 background**, setting, milieu, environment, framework

backer *n* **1 sponsor**, patron, guarantor, benefactor, angel **2 supporter**, promoter, champion, advocate, ally

COMPARE AND CONTRAST CORE MEANING: somebody who provides financial support
backer a person who gives moral or financial support; **angel** a person who provides financial support for an enterprise, e.g., a theatrical venture; **guarantor** a person who gives a legal undertaking to be responsible for somebody else's debts or obligations; **patron** a person who gives financial or moral support to a person, institution, or charity, especially in the arts; **sponsor** a person or organization that contributes money to help fund an event, usually in return for publicity, or gives money to a

person taking part in a fundraising activity.

backfire *v* **go wrong**, boomerang, miscarry, fail, not go as planned

background *n* **1 upbringing**, circumstances, personal history, family, experience **2 backdrop**, setting, milieu, environment, surroundings *Opposite*: foreground

backhanded *adj* **indirect**, doubtful, oblique, insincere, snide

backing *n* **support**, help, assistance, sponsorship, patronage

backlash *n* **reaction**, repercussion, counterattack, criticism, hostile response

backlog *n* **accumulation**, buildup, excess, surfeit, logjam

back off *v* **1 retreat**, pull back, move away, go backward, recoil *Opposite*: advance **2 yield**, withdraw, admit you were wrong, backpedal, take back *Opposite*: insist

back out *v* **pull out**, withdraw, renege, go back on, cancel *Opposite*: continue

backpack *n* **rucksack**, knapsack, pack, bag, haversack

backpacker *n* **traveler**, hiker, walker, hitchhiker, tourist

back pain *n* **backache**, lumbago, back trouble, bad back, sciatica

backpedal *v* **backtrack**, back down, shift ground, go back on your word, recant

backroom *adj* **unobtrusive**, clandestine, secret, private, secretive *Opposite*: public

backside *(infml)* *n* **buttocks**, rump, behind, bottom, rear *(infml)*

backslide *v* **relapse**, go back to your old ways, lapse, revert, regress

backslider *n* **recidivist**, defaulter, transgressor, apostate, deserter

backstage *adv* **offstage**, behind the scenes, in the wings, in private, in secret

backstreet *n* **alley**, back alley, lane, side street *Opposite*: thoroughfare

back talk *n* **rudeness**, sassiness, cheekiness, impudence, impertinence *Opposite*: respect

back-to-back *adj* **consecutive**, end-to-end, nonstop, continuous, uninterrupted

backtrack *v* **1 retrace your steps**, go back over the same ground, turn back, begin again *Opposite*: move on **2 backpedal**, go into reverse, do a volte-face, do an about-face, do a U-turn

back up *v* **1 corroborate**, substantiate, authenticate, vouch for, reinforce *Opposite*: contradict **2 copy**, duplicate, make a backup, keep a backup, keep a copy **3 move backward**, reverse, go backward, recede *Opposite*: advance

backup *n* **1 support**, encouragement, help, moral support, assistance **2 holdup**, stoppage, gridlock, snarl, tie-up **3 standby**, reserve, substitute, replacement, reinforcement **4 copy**, duplicate, replica, substitute, alternate

backward *adj* **1 rearward**, to the rear, toward the back *Opposite*: forward **2 retrograde**, regressive, recessive *Opposite*: progressive **3 shy**, diffident, hesitant, reluctant, timid *Opposite*: confident ▪ *adv* **1 toward the back**, back, rearward, behind, toward the rear *Opposite*: forward **2 the wrong way**, in reverse, the wrong way around

backward-looking *adj* **retrospective**, nostalgic, retrograde, traditional, conservative *Opposite*: forward-looking

backwater *n* **backwoods**, the middle of nowhere, boondocks *(infml)*, sticks *(infml)*

backwoods *n* **1 wilderness**, wilds, rough country, back country **2 the middle of nowhere**, backwater, boondocks *(infml)*, sticks *(infml)*

backyard *n* **courtyard**, patio, deck, yard, terrace

bacterial *adj* **microbial**, bacteriological, infective, infectious, contagious

bacteriological *adj* **microbiological**, biological, bacterial, pathological

bad *adj* **1 poor**, inferior, deficient, flawed, faulty *Opposite*: good **2 awful**, terrible, dreadful, appalling, shocking *Opposite*: good **3 evil**, wicked, corrupt, immoral, depraved *Opposite*: good **4 naughty**, disobedient, troublesome, wayward, mischievous *Opposite*: good **5 harmful**, damaging, injurious, ruinous, dangerous *Opposite*: good **6 rotten**, off, decayed, decaying, decomposing *Opposite*: fresh **7 regretful**, penitent, remorseful, ashamed, apologetic *Opposite*: good **8 adverse**, difficult, unhappy, testing, unpleasant *Opposite*: good **9 serious**, severe, grave, critical, life-threatening *Opposite*: slight

COMPARE AND CONTRAST CORE MEANING: indicating wrongdoing

bad applies to a whole range of wrongdoing from the most trivial to the most immoral or evil; **criminal** punishable as a crime under the law; **delinquent** antisocial or unlawful, or *(fml)* neglecting a duty, commitment, or responsibility; **mischievous** playfully naughty or troublesome, or *(fml)* causing or meant to cause serious trouble, damage, or hurt; **naughty** badly behaved or disobedient, or *(infml)* mildly indecent or sinful.

bad blood *n* **bad feeling**, ill feeling, bitterness, acrimony, antagonism *Opposite*: affection

baddie *(infml)* *n* **bad character**, rogue, villain, scoundrel, outlaw *Opposite*: hero

bad feeling *n* **spite**, rancor, spitefulness, bad blood, bitterness *Opposite*: affection

badge *n* **1 brooch**, button, pin, clasp **2 insignia**, emblem, symbol, mark, device

badger *v* **pester**, press, harass, plague, harry

bad habit *n* **weakness**, failing, flaw, character defect, vice *Opposite*: virtue

badinage n banter, repartee, teasing, joking, mockery

bad language n swearing, swearwords, vulgar language, profanities, coarse language

bad luck n misfortune, hard luck, ill luck, unluckiness, ill fortune Opposite: luck

badly adv 1 poorly, deficiently, faultily, defectively, imperfectly Opposite: well 2 seriously, severely, gravely, critically, desperately Opposite: slightly 3 naughtily, disobediently, troublesomely, waywardly, mischievously

badly off adj poor, struggling, lacking, wanting, unfortunate Opposite: well-off

bad-mannered adj rude, ill-mannered, impolite, charmless, discourteous Opposite: well-mannered

bad manners n rudeness, impoliteness, incivility, discourtesy, discourteousness Opposite: courtesy

bad mood n bad humor, sulk, huff, bad temper, temper

badness n evilness, wickedness, immorality, evil, depravity Opposite: goodness

bad taste n tastelessness, vulgarity, showiness, crassness, crudeness Opposite: good taste

bad temper n irritability, petulance, sulkiness, ill temper, bad mood

bad-tempered adj cross, ill-tempered, ill-humored, irascible, short-tempered Opposite: good-tempered

baffle v confuse, perplex, puzzle, stump, nonplus

baffled adj puzzled, perplexed, mystified, lost, stumped

bafflement n bewilderment, perplexity, confusion, puzzlement, bemusement Opposite: understanding

baffling adj puzzling, perplexing, mystifying, confusing, bewildering Opposite: obvious

bag n container, receptacle, sack, paper bag, plastic bag ■ v 1 take possession of, grab, occupy, reserve, keep 2 catch, shoot, snare, take, capture

WORD BANK
❑ types of bags clutch purse, fanny pack, handbag, mailbag, nosebag, pocketbook, pouch, purse, reticule, satchel, shopping bag, shoulder bag, sporran, tote bag

bagatelle (fml) n trifle, trifling sum, nothing, a drop in the bucket, thing of no importance

baggage n luggage, bags, suitcases, cases, belongings

WORD BANK
❑ types of baggage attaché case, backpack, briefcase, carryall, carrycase, case, duffel bag, flight bag, haversack, kit bag, knapsack, luggage, overnight bag, pack, portmanteau, rucksack, suitcase, travel case, valise, vanity case, weekend bag

bagginess n looseness, formlessness, shapelessness, roominess, floppiness Opposite: tightness

baggy adj loose, loose-fitting, slack, shapeless, saggy Opposite: tight

bags n luggage, baggage, belongings, personal belongings, gear (infml)

bail n security, surety, payment, financial guarantee, bond

bailiff n sheriff's officer, law officer, legal officer, dispossessor, evictor

bail out v 1 post security, obtain somebody's release, put up bail 2 escape, run away, desert, flee, evacuate Opposite: stick out 3 help, rescue, save, assist, aid

bait n lure, attraction, enticement, temptation, inducement ■ v 1 entice, lure, tempt, attract, draw 2 taunt, tease, torment, harass, provoke

bake v 1 cook, heat, harden, dry out 2 (infml) swelter, overheat, scorch, burn, roast Opposite: freeze

baking adj sweltering, boiling, blazing, burning, blistering Opposite: freezing

baksheesh n bribe, handout, tip, gift, token

balance n 1 equilibrium, poise, sense of balance, stability, steadiness Opposite: unsteadiness 2 weighing machine, weighing scale, set of scales 3 remainder, surplus, rest, what's left, residue ■ v 1 maintain equilibrium, stay poised, keep upright, keep steady, poise Opposite: wobble 2 assess, weigh, consider, compare, evaluate 3 equalize, square, settle, even out, offset Opposite: weight

balanced adj 1 fair, impartial, unbiased, unprejudiced, disinterested Opposite: biased 2 stable, composed, well-adjusted, sensible, sane Opposite: unbalanced

balance out v even out, offset, compensate, make up, redress the balance Opposite: weight

balcony n 1 veranda, terrace, loggia, lanai, gallery 2 circle, upper circle, gallery

bald adj 1 hairless, balding, receding, thin on top, baldheaded Opposite: hirsute 2 bare, worn, threadbare, smooth, patchy 3 plain, blunt, frank, direct, straightforward Opposite: florid

balderdash n rubbish, nonsense, garbage, drivel, baloney (infml)

bald-faced adj barefaced, bold, brazen, shameless, unabashed Opposite: meek

baldheaded adj bald, hairless, balding, receding, thin on top Opposite: hirsute

balding adj bald, baldheaded, hairless, receding, thin on top Opposite: hirsute

baldly adv bluntly, plainly, flatly, frankly, directly

baldness n 1 hairlessness, hair loss, baldheadedness, lack of hair *Opposite*: hairiness **2 bluntness**, plainness, frankness, directness, straightforwardness *Opposite*: deviousness

bale *n* **bundle**, package, pack, roll, block

baleful *adj* **threatening**, menacing, malevolent, sinister, malignant *Opposite*: benevolent

balk *v* **recoil**, draw back, hesitate, refuse, pull back *Opposite*: leap at

ball *n* **sphere**, orb, globe, globule, blob

ballad *n* **poem**, song, narrative, folk song, traditional song

ballast *n* **weight**, bulk, makeweight, stabilizer, balance

ball cock *n* **regulator**, controller, control, device

ballistic *adj* **airborne**, air-to-air, surface-to-air, flying

balloon *n* **hot-air balloon**, helium balloon, inflatable, dirigible ■ *v* **swell**, distend, inflate, expand, puff out *Opposite*: deflate

ballot *n* **vote**, secret ballot, poll, election, survey ■ *v* **canvass**, consult, survey, poll, assess opinion

ballpark *adj* (*infml*) **approximate**, rough, estimated, inexact, imprecise *Opposite*: exact ■ *n* **stadium**, playing field, field, ground

ballyhoo *n* **uproar**, racket, hullabaloo, commotion, ruckus

balm *n* **1 ointment**, unguent, salve, oil, cream *Opposite*: irritant **2 comfort**, relief, solace, consolation, palliative

balmy *adj* **mild**, clement, pleasant, temperate, gentle *Opposite*: wintry

baloney (*infml*) *n* **drivel**, balderdash, nonsense, garbage, rubbish

baluster *n* **post**, support, leg, upright, pole

balustrade *n* **railing**, handrail, guardrail, rail, banister

bamboozle (*infml*) *v* **1 cheat**, deceive, con, trick, hoodwink **2 confuse**, bewilder, puzzle, bemuse, perplex

ban *v* **forbid**, outlaw, prohibit, veto, bar *Opposite*: allow ■ *n* **prohibition**, veto, bar, injunction, embargo

banal *adj* **commonplace**, hackneyed, prosaic, predictable, ordinary *Opposite*: original

banality *n* **triteness**, predictability, ordinariness, dullness, triviality *Opposite*: originality

band *n* **1 group**, combo, ensemble **2 gang**, crowd, mob, group, crew (*infml*) **3 stripe**, strip, belt, stretch, range

---

WORD BANK
❑ **types of bands** big band, brass band, chamber orchestra, choir, dance band, duo, ensemble, jazz band, mariachi, octet, orchestra, pipe band, pop group, quartet, quintet, septet, sextet, sinfonietta, steel band, string band, string quartet, symphony orchestra, trio

---

bandage *n* **dressing**, binding, strapping, compress ■ *v* **dress**, bind, tie up, cover, bind up

bandanna *n* **scarf**, neckerchief, headscarf, kerchief

bandit *n* **outlaw**, robber, thief, thug, gangster

banditry *n* **robbery**, theft, thieving, raiding, armed robbery

bandstand *n* **platform**, pavilion, stand, shelter, podium

band together *v* **join up**, unite, associate, get together, combine

bandwagon *n* **movement**, cause, trend, craze, fashion

bandy *v* **exchange**, toss around, throw around, mention, debate ■ *adj* **outward-curving**, bowed, bent, warped, convex *Opposite*: straight

bandy-legged *adj* **bowlegged**, bent, bowed, bandy

bandy words with *v* **argue**, dispute, bicker, wrangle, spar

bane *n* **nuisance**, curse, blight, bother, irritation *Opposite*: blessing

bang *n* **1 explosion**, boom, crash, knock, thud **2 knock**, hit, bump, blow, thump ■ *v* **1 hit**, knock, thump, hammer, pound **2 bump**, collide, crash, jolt, knock

banish *v* **1 expel**, send away, exile, deport, evict **2 get rid of**, remove, dismiss, eliminate, discard

banishment *n* **expulsion**, exile, deportation, eviction, exclusion

banister *n* **handrail**, balustrade, guardrail, bar, rail

bank *n* **1 set**, row, tier, series, group **2 store**, depository, reservoir, stock, collection **3 side**, edge, margin, embankment, border **4 pile**, heap, mound, stack, mass ■ *v* **1 deposit**, pay in, cash in, put in *Opposite*: withdraw **2 have an account**, save, deposit, invest **3 heap**, pile, mound, stack, mass *Opposite*: disperse **4 tilt**, pitch, turn, lean, veer *Opposite*: level off

bank account *n* **account**, deposit account, loan account, checking account, joint account

banker *n* **bank manager**, investment banker, banking executive, financier

banking *n* **investment**, lending, funding, financial transactions, online banking

banknote *n* **bill**, dollar bill, Federal Reserve note *Opposite*: coin

bank on *v* **count on**, depend on, rely on, trust, have confidence in *Opposite*: doubt

bankroll (*infml*) *v* **finance**, fund, back, pay, sponsor

bankrupt *adj* **insolvent**, penniless, ruined, broke (*infml*), bust (*infml*) *Opposite*: solvent ■ *v* **ruin**, destroy, liquidate, impoverish, make destitute

bankruptcy *n* **insolvency**, ruin, liquidation,

economic failure, impoverishment

banned adj 1 **barred**, disqualified, debarred, excluded, expelled Opposite: admitted 2 **forbidden**, proscribed, prohibited, illegal, illicit Opposite: permitted

banner n **sign**, poster, flag, placard, streamer ■ adj **excellent**, exceptional, notable, outstanding, marvelous

banquet n **feast**, dinner, meal, formal meal, ceremonial meal

banshee n **spirit**, supernatural being, ghost, ghoul, specter

banter n **teasing**, mockery, joking, repartee, wit ■ v **tease**, mock, joke, poke fun at, make fun of

baptism n **initiation**, introduction, debut, beginning, induction

baptize v **christen**, bless, immerse, sprinkle, initiate

bar n 1 **rod**, pole, stick, staff, shaft 2 **block**, slab, piece, ingot 3 **obstruction**, hindrance, block, barrier, impediment 4 **pub**, hostelry, drinking place, watering hole (infml) ■ v 1 **secure**, fasten, bolt, lock, barricade 2 **obstruct**, close off, hinder, get in the way, block 3 **ban**, exclude, keep out, debar, prohibit Opposite: admit ■ prep **excluding**, save, except, with the exception of, apart from

WORD BANK
❑ **types of bars or clubs** bodega, cantina, casino, country club, joint (slang), nightclub, nightspot, roadhouse (dated), saloon, shebeen, speakeasy, tavern, wine bar

barb n 1 **point**, hook, tip, spur, spike 2 **gibe**, insult, dig, taunt, cutting remark

barbaric adj **cruel**, brutal, vicious, ferocious, fierce Opposite: gentle

barbarism n **cruelty**, brutality, savagery, viciousness, ferociousness Opposite: gentleness

barbarity n 1 **cruelty**, brutality, savagery, viciousness, ferociousness Opposite: gentleness 2 **atrocity**, cruelty, outrage, assault, abuse

barbarous adj **cruel**, brutal, vicious, ferocious, fierce Opposite: gentle

barbecue v **grill**, sear, flame, chargrill, broil

barbed adj 1 **pointed**, hooked, spiky, spiny, thorny 2 **snide**, pointed, cutting, unkind, hurtful

barber n **men's hair stylist**, hair stylist, stylist, coiffeur (fml)

barbican n **tower**, keep, stronghold, turret, fortification

bard (literary) n **poet**, versifier, composer, wordsmith, songster

bare adj 1 **naked**, nude, exposed, uncovered, undressed Opposite: covered 2 **empty**, vacant, blank, clean, clear Opposite: full 3 **stark**, barren, austere, severe, hard Opposite: lush 4 **simple**, unadorned, plain,

basic, unembellished Opposite: ornate 5 **mere**, scant, meager, measly (infml) ■ v **expose**, reveal, display, show, uncover Opposite: cover. See COMPARE AND CONTRAST at naked.

barefaced adj **brazen**, blatant, unashamed, obvious, bald-faced

barefoot adj **unshod**, shoeless, barefooted

barely adv **hardly**, scarcely, only just, just about Opposite: easily

bareness n **emptiness**, nakedness, starkness, austerity, plainness

barf (infml) v **vomit**, spew, regurgitate, bring up, throw up (infml)

bargain n 1 **good deal**, good buy, steal (infml) 2 **deal**, agreement, accord, arrangement, pact ■ v **haggle**, barter, negotiate, make a deal, trade ■ adj **cheap**, low, reduced, inexpensive, rock-bottom

bargain-basement adj **cheap**, cut-rate, low-priced, reduced-price, bargain

bargain for v **expect**, count on, take into account, depend on, reckon with

bargain on see bargain for

barge v **rush**, push, elbow, burst, surge

barge in v 1 **walk in**, storm in, push in, rush in, breeze in 2 **interrupt**, butt in, cut in, break in, interject

barge into v **bump into**, collide with, clash with, smash into, knock into

bark v **howl**, yap, growl, yowl, snarl

barn n **outbuilding**, outhouse, shed, cowshed, store

barnyard n **farmyard**, yard, court, forecourt

barometer n **weatherglass**, indicator, gauge, aneroid barometer, barograph

barometric adj **atmospheric**, air, meteorological

baron n **tycoon**, magnate, mogul, industrialist, captain of industry

baronial adj **grand**, impressive, opulent, stately, imposing Opposite: humble

baroque adj 1 **ornate**, ornamental, decorative, elaborate, exaggerated Opposite: plain 2 **flamboyant**, exaggerated, overdone, over-the-top (infml) Opposite: restrained

barracks n **quarters**, garrison, station, billet

barrage n 1 **bombardment**, salvo, volley, fusillade 2 **onslaught**, outpouring, hail, storm, flood Opposite: trickle 3 **dam**, dike, bank, embankment

barred adj 1 **striped**, banded, lined, stripy, streaked 2 **grilled**, meshed, fenced, secure, solid 3 **banned**, excluded, disqualified, debarred, not allowed Opposite: admitted

barrel n **tub**, cask, vat, butt, rain barrel

barren adj 1 **infertile**, unproductive, sterile, unfruitful Opposite: fertile 2 **desolate**, bleak, inhospitable, stark, harsh

barrenness n 1 **emptiness**, bleakness, bareness, loneliness, inhospitableness 2 **infertility**, sterility, unfruitfulness, unproductiveness Opposite: fertility

barricade *n* **blockade**, barrier, cordon, obstruction, fortification ■ *v* **secure**, obstruct, bar, fortify, block

barrier *n* **1 obstacle**, difficulty, stumbling block, sticking point, impediment **2 fence**, wall, barricade, blockade, block

barring *prep* **except for**, without, excluding, apart from

barrow *n* **1 wheelbarrow**, cart, pushcart, transporter, trailer **2 burial mound**, mound, tumulus, long barrow, tomb

barter *v* **exchange**, trade, switch, negotiate, bargain

base *n* **1 foundation**, support, stand, pedestal, rest **2 source**, origin, center, heart, starting point **3 headquarters**, center, main office, seat, station ■ *v* **found**, ground, build, create, construct ■ *adj* **dishonorable**, sordid, disreputable, squalid, immoral *Opposite*: honorable

baseless *adj* **unfounded**, untrue, unjustified, unsubstantiated, groundless *Opposite*: well-founded

baseline *n* **1 starting point**, point of departure, reference point, reference line, starting position **2 standard**, model, criterion, starting point, quality check **3 reference**, control, check, set of data, set of values **4 boundary**, boundary line, line, periphery, white line

basement *n* **cellar**, vault, crypt, lower ground floor *Opposite*: attic

baseness *n* **wickedness**, sordidness, vileness, immorality, ignobility *Opposite*: nobility

bash *v* **1 thump**, punch, smash, whack, sock (*infml*) **2 criticize**, condemn, find fault with, attack, knock ■ *n* **1 punch**, hit, blow, thump, knock **2 dent**, bump, smash, knock **3** (*infml*) **party**, celebration, dance, ball, gala

bashful *adj* **shy**, timid, reserved, retiring, self-conscious *Opposite*: bold

bashfulness *n* **shyness**, modesty, self-consciousness, quietness, coyness *Opposite*: boldness

basic *adj* **1** *Opposite*: trivial, essential, central, key, principal, main **2 rudimentary**, straightforward, elementary, undeveloped, uncomplicated *Opposite*: complex

basics *n* **fundamentals**, essentials, necessities, nitty-gritty (*infml*), nuts and bolts (*infml*)

basin *n* **sink**, hand basin, washbasin, washbowl

basis *n* **foundation**, base, root, source, starting point

bask *v* **1 laze around**, lie, recline, lounge, stretch out **2 enjoy**, savor, relish, soak up, luxuriate

basket *n* **bag**, hamper, picnic basket, linen basket, wicker basket

WORD BANK
❑ **types of basket** breadbasket, bushel basket, creel, Easter basket, hamper, laundry basket,

picnic basket, shopping basket, wicker basket

bas-relief *n* **relief**, molding, basso-relievo, carving, paneling

bass *adj* **deep**, deep-toned, deep-voiced, low-pitched *Opposite*: high

baste *v* **1 moisten**, drizzle, grease, cover, saturate **2 thrash**, thump, clobber (*infml*), bash (*infml*), beat up (*infml*) **3 sew**, stitch, tack, hem, seam

bastion *n* **1 stronghold**, fortification, rampart, defense, bulwark **2 mainstay**, support, defender, upholder, supporter

bat *n* **1 racket**, paddle, willow, club **2 batter**, player, batsman ■ *v* **flutter**, wink, flicker, flap, blink

batch *n* **lot**, consignment, group, set, bunch

bath *n* **1 immersion**, soak, steam bath, bubble bath, sponge bath **2 tank**, basin, reservoir, container

bathe *v* **1 take a bath**, shower, wash, soak, immerse yourself **2 immerse**, dip, soak, rinse, dunk **3 swim**, go for a dip, paddle

bather *n* **swimmer**, diver, snorkeler, paddler, skinny-dipper (*infml*)

bathetic *adj* **1 anticlimactic**, disappointing, unsatisfying **2 trite**, sentimental, unsatisfying, commonplace

bathos *n* **anticlimax**, letdown, comedown (*infml*)

baths *n* **bathhouse**, Turkish bath, steam bath, sauna, Russian bath

baton *n* **stick**, rod, wand, cane, pointer

battalion *n* **throng**, crowd, mass, multitude, horde

batten *v* **fasten**, fix, close, secure, batten down *Opposite*: open

batter *v* **1 pound**, bang, thump, thrash, hit **2 assault**, maim, brutalize, attack, abuse ■ *n* **player**, bat, batsman

battered *adj* **1 maltreated**, assaulted, abused, beaten, injured **2 tattered**, decrepit, worn out, weather-beaten, damaged *Opposite*: pristine

battering *n* **pounding**, buffeting, hammering, beating, pummeling

battery *n* **series**, set, sequence, succession, run

battle *n* **1 fight**, clash, encounter, skirmish, engagement **2 struggle**, crusade, fight, war, campaign ■ *v* **1 fight**, go to war, attack, come to blows, engage **2 struggle**, wrestle, contend, fight, strive. *See* COMPARE AND CONTRAST *at* **fight**.

battleax *n* **ax**, hatchet, tomahawk, halberd

battle cry *n* **whoop**, war cry, yell, shout, cry

battlefield *n* **battleground**, combat zone, arena, theater of war, front line

battleground *see* **battlefield**

battlements *n* **ramparts**, fortifications, walls, parapet, bulwark

batty (*infml*) *adj* **irrational**, eccentric, crazy

(infml), around the bend *(slang)*, nuts *(slang)* Opposite: rational

bauble *n* trinket, trifle, gewgaw, decoration, ornament

baulk *see* balk

bawdy *adj* ribald, earthy, risqué, suggestive, indecent

bawl *v* 1 shout, yell, roar, shriek, screech Opposite: whisper 2 *(infml)* cry, howl, wail, sob, weep

bawl out *(infml)* *v* tell off *(infml)*, haul over the coals, read the riot act to, rap across the knuckles, chew out *(infml)*

bay *n* 1 inlet, cove, natural harbor, anchorage, haven *(literary)* 2 compartment, alcove, cubicle, recess, loading bay ■ *v* woof, bark, yap, yelp, howl

bay for *v* demand, insist on, be out for, cry for, shout for

bayonet *n* blade, knife, dagger, lance, spike ■ *v* stab, spear, impale, spike, knife

bayou *n* marsh, marshland, everglade, wetlands, bog

bazaar *n* market, marketplace, souk, open market, flea market

be *v* 1 exist, live, have being, be present, coexist 2 take place, happen, occur, transpire, come about 3 be situated, be located, remain, be there, be present

beach *n* seashore, seaside, coast, shore, coastline

beachcomber *n* scavenger, forager, explorer, collector, hoarder

beached *adj* stranded, aground, stuck, high and dry, run aground Opposite: afloat

beachhead *n* lodgment, foothold, base, strategic position, position

beachwear *n* swimwear, leisurewear, sportswear

WORD BANK

❏ **types of beachwear** bathing suit, bathing trunks, bikini, cover-up, one-piece, swimming trunks, swimsuit, swimwear, tank suit, trunks, two-piece

beacon *n* 1 signal, sign, alarm, warning, flare 2 bonfire, fire, flare 3 *(literary)* inspiration, guiding light, encouragement, example, shining example

bead *n* drop, droplet, drip, blob, globule

beaded *adj* 1 decorated, ornate, bead-trimmed, encrusted, sequined 2 wet, moist, dripping, soaked, drenched

beading *n* edging, border, trim, detail, molding

beady *adj* 1 small, round, shiny, bright, shining 2 beaded, decorated, ornate, bead-trimmed, sequined 3 *(infml)* watchful, unblinking, piercing, attentive, bright

beaked *adj* hooked, aquiline, Roman

beaker *n* cup, glass, mug, paper cup, plastic cup

beam *n* 1 girder, rafter, joist, timber, shaft 2 ray, shaft of light, sunbeam, stream of light 3 smile, grin, wide smile, big smile Opposite: scowl ■ *v* 1 smile, grin, look happy Opposite: scowl 2 shine, radiate, emit, send out, glow

beaming *adj* smiling, cheery, cheerful, sunny, genial Opposite: scowling

beanpole *n* support, stick, pole, post, cane

bear *v* 1 tolerate, stand, put up with, stomach, accept 2 support, take, stand, sustain, hold 3 assume, accept, shoulder, carry, take 4 show, display, exhibit, present, evince 5 carry, convey, bring, take, transport 6 produce, develop, yield, give birth to, bring forth

bearable *adj* manageable, tolerable, endurable, acceptable, sufferable Opposite: unbearable

bear a grudge *v* resent, begrudge, feel bitter about, have hard feelings about, feel aggrieved

beard *n* facial hair, whiskers, goatee, bush, stubble ■ *v* challenge, confront, accost, stand up to, face up to

bearded *adj* unshaven, hirsute, hairy, whiskery, bewhiskered Opposite: clean-shaven

bear down on *v* 1 advance on, close in on, converge on, march on, charge Opposite: retreat 2 push down, press down, thrust, press, lean on

bearer *n* 1 carrier, bringer, deliverer, conveyer, transporter 2 holder, possessor, owner, keeper, custodian

bear false witness *v* commit perjury, lie, equivocate, stretch the truth

bear fruit *v* succeed, be successful, show results, produce results, pay off Opposite: fail

bear hug *n* embrace, hug, cuddle, clinch, squeeze

bearing *n* 1 influence, effect, impact, connection, relevance 2 manner, behavior, attitude, deportment, demeanor 3 compass reading, direction, course, orientation, point of reference

bear in mind *v* remember, keep in mind, think of, consider, take into consideration Opposite: forget

bear out *v* support, verify, prove, substantiate, corroborate Opposite: undermine

bear the brunt *v* receive the impact, take the strain, receive the full force, bear the burden, bear the responsibility

bear up *v* hold up, hold out, cope, manage, get along Opposite: give in

bear with *v* be patient with, put up with, make allowance for, show forbearance, bear

beast *n* 1 creature, animal, being, living thing, quadruped 2 monster, fiend, ogre, animal, brute *(literary)*

beat *v* 1 **defeat**, overcome, overwhelm, thrash, trounce 2 **hit**, strike, bang, hammer, thump 3 **throb**, palpitate, thump, pound, pulsate 4 **whisk**, whip, blend, mix, combine 5 **surpass**, break, smash, do better than, go one better than ■ *n* 1 **stroke**, blow, hit, bang, thump 2 **rhythm**, pulse, pulsation, throb, thump. *See* COMPARE AND CONTRAST *at* defeat.

beat a hasty retreat *v* **depart**, leave, make off, run away, make a run for it

beat around the bush *v* **digress**, ramble, waffle, rabbit, bumble

beaten *adj* 1 **compressed**, packed down, trodden, flattened, crushed 2 **defeated**, conquered, crushed, vanquished

beaten-up *adj* **battered**, tattered, worn out, scruffy, tatty *Opposite*: pristine

beater *n* 1 **whisk**, blade, attachment, paddle, stick 2 *(infml)* **wreck**, rattletrap *(infml)*, jalopy *(dated infml)*, heap *(slang)*, junker *(slang)*

beatific *(literary) adj* **blissful**, radiant, sublime, heavenly, serene

beatification *n* **sanctification**, canonization, sainting, elevation, blessing

beatify *v* **sanctify**, bless, consecrate, canonize, saint

beating *n* 1 **thrashing**, whipping, thumping, pounding, hiding *(infml)* 2 **defeat**, setback, thrashing, trouncing, pasting *(infml)*

beat up *(infml) v* **attack**, assault, batter, mug, injure

beat-up *(infml) adj* **battered**, tattered, dilapidated, decrepit, shabby *Opposite*: pristine

beau *n* 1 **boyfriend**, admirer, steady *(infml)*, suitor *(fml)*, squire *(dated)* 2 *(archaic)* **fop**, peacock, poseur, dandy *(infml)*, swell *(dated infml)*

beaut *(infml) n* **beauty**, stunner *(infml)*, peach *(infml)*, knockout *(infml)*

beauteous *(literary) adj* **lovely**, beautiful, gorgeous, exquisite, elegant *Opposite*: ugly

beautification *n* **enhancement**, sprucing up, remodeling, prettification, embellishment

beautiful *adj* 1 **good-looking**, lovely, gorgeous, stunning, striking *Opposite*: ugly 2 **lovely**, picturesque, scenic, delightful, charming *Opposite*: unattractive. *See* COMPARE AND CONTRAST *at* good-looking.

beautifully *adv* 1 **attractively**, gorgeously, stunningly, handsomely, prettily *Opposite*: unattractively 2 **well**, excellently, superbly, brilliantly, magnificently *Opposite*: poorly

beautify *v* **prettify**, smarten, enhance, remodel, spruce up

beauty *n* 1 **loveliness**, attractiveness, good looks, prettiness, exquisiteness *Opposite*: unattractiveness 2 **advantage**, attraction, benefit, upside, plus *(infml) Opposite*: drawback

beaver *(infml) v* **work**, labor, toil, exert yourself, keep at *Opposite*: idle

becalmed *adj* **stuck**, at a standstill, stationary, at a halt, marooned *Opposite*: moving

because *conj* **since**, as, for

because of *prep* **owing to**, on account of, as a consequence of, due to, as a result of *Opposite*: despite

beckon *v* **signal**, sign, summon, gesture, indicate *Opposite*: dismiss

become *v* 1 **turn out to be**, turn into, develop, convert, grow into 2 **suit**, befit, flatter, enhance, show off

become acquainted *v* **meet**, meet for the first time, be introduced to, make the acquaintance of, get to know

become aware of *v* **notice**, detect, discern, make out, sense *Opposite*: miss

become of *v* **happen to**, occur, be the outcome of, befall *(literary)*

becoming *adj* 1 **flattering**, attractive, fetching, charming, pretty *Opposite*: unattractive 2 **suitable**, appropriate, apt, fitting, befitting *Opposite*: inappropriate

bed *n* 1 **plot**, flowerbed, patch, border 2 **layer**, band, base, strip, seam 3 **bottom**, floor, base, seabed, riverbed

---

WORD BANK
❏ **types of beds** bassinet, berth, bunk, bunk bed, cot, couchette, cradle, crib, day bed, divan, double bed, four-poster, futon, hammock, king-size bed, Murphy bed, queen-size bed, single bed, sofa bed, studio couch, trundle bed, twin bed, waterbed

---

bedazzle *(literary) v* **amaze**, stun, impress, bewilder, daze

bedazzled *(literary) adj* **bewildered**, dazed, bemused, amazed, confused *Opposite*: unimpressed

bedding *n* **bedclothes**, bed linen, covers

bedeck *(literary) v* **decorate**, festoon, adorn, ornament, deck out *Opposite*: strip

bedecked *(literary) adj* **decorated**, festooned, adorned, ornamented, decked out *Opposite*: stripped

bedevil *v* **beset**, assail, torment, harass, trouble

bedlam *n* **chaos**, pandemonium, confusion, anarchy, disorder *Opposite*: order

bed linen *see* bedding

bedpan *n* **chamber pot**, pot, potty, commode

bedraggled *adj* **unkempt**, disheveled, untidy, messy, scruffy *Opposite*: neat

bedridden *adj* **confined to bed**, flat on your back, laid up, incapacitated, disabled *Opposite*: active

bedrock *n* 1 **rock layer**, substratum, solid rock, base, foundation 2 **basis**, base, core, heart, root

bedroom *n* **dormitory**, sleeping quarters, boudoir, room, dorm *(infml)*

bedside manner *n* **rapport**, style, approach, relationship, behavior

bedsore *n* **ulcer**, pressure sore, ulceration, sore, bruise

bedspread *n* **coverlet**, cover, quilt, throw, eiderdown

bedstead *n* **bed**, frame, base

bedtime *n* **time for bed**, sleep time, time to turn in *(infml)*, time to hit the hay *(infml)*, time to hit the sack *(infml)*

beefiness *n* **muscularity**, sturdiness, burliness, brawniness, stockiness

beef up *(infml)* *v* **strengthen**, improve, enhance, boost, reinforce *Opposite:* weaken

beefy *adj* **muscular**, brawny, heavy, hefty, burly *Opposite:* puny

beep *v* **peep**, bleep, beep-beep, honk, hoot

beet *n* **sugar beet**, chard, Swiss chard, mangel-wurzel, mangel

befall *(literary)* *v* **happen**, occur, take place, come about, transpire

befit *v* **suit**, become, be fitting, be suitable for, be appropriate

befitting *adj* **becoming**, suitable, appropriate, apt, fitting *Opposite:* unsuitable

before *prep* **1 in front of**, facing, ahead of, afore *Opposite:* behind **2 previous to**, earlier than, sooner than, prior to, ahead of *Opposite:* after ▪ *adv* **beforehand**, previously, earlier, in advance, in the past *Opposite:* afterward

beforehand *adv* **earlier**, in advance, before, early, ahead of time *Opposite:* late

befriend *v* **make friends with**, take care of, look after, help, assist *Opposite:* shun

befuddle *v* **confuse**, muddle, mix up, bewilder, baffle *Opposite:* enlighten

befuddled *adj* **confused**, muddled, baffled, puzzled, perplexed *Opposite:* clearheaded

befuddlement *n* **confusion**, perplexity, bewilderment, bafflement, puzzlement *Opposite:* clarity

beg *v* **ask for**, request, plead, solicit, entreat

beget *v* **cause**, bring about, precipitate, create, bring

beg forgiveness *v* **apologize**, make an apology, express regret, say you're sorry

beggar *n* **mendicant**, homeless person, vagabond, vagrant, tramp ▪ *v* **defy**, be beyond, confound, surpass, exceed

begin *v* **1 start**, start on, commence, start in on, set in motion *Opposite:* finish **2 bring into being**, instigate, initiate, inaugurate, activate **3 start the ball rolling**, get down to, get to, get under way, set off *Opposite:* end

beginner *n* **novice**, learner, trainee, apprentice, student *Opposite:* old hand

---

COMPARE AND CONTRAST CORE MEANING: a person who has not acquired the necessary experience or skills to do something
beginner somebody who has just started to learn or do something; **apprentice** somebody who is being taught the skills of a trade over an agreed period of time by somebody fully trained; **greenhorn** somebody who lacks experience and may be naïve or gullible; **novice** somebody with no previous experience or skill in the activity undertaken; **tyro** somebody who is raw and inexperienced.

---

beginning *n* **start**, opening, launch, establishment, creation *Opposite:* end

beg off *v* **back out**, bow out, duck out, cry off *(infml)*, fink out *(slang)*

begrudge *v* **resent**, envy, be envious, be jealous, be resentful

beg to differ *v* **disagree**, take issue with, demur, dissent, object *Opposite:* agree

beguile *v* **entice**, lure, charm, captivate, mesmerize

beguiling *adj* **enticing**, charming, mesmeric, fascinating, captivating

behave *v* **1 act**, perform, conduct yourself, deport yourself, work **2 be good**, obey the rules, do the right thing, toe the line, keep out of mischief *Opposite:* misbehave

behavior *n* **actions**, deeds, activities, manners, conduct

behavioral *adj* **social**, interactive, communicative, negotiating, developmental

behead *v* **decapitate**, cut off somebody's head, guillotine, execute, put to death

behest *(literary)* *n* **request**, order, command, bidding, directive

behind *prep* **following**, after, in the wake of, at the back of, at the rear of ▪ *adv* **at the back**, at the rear, in the rear, after, following *Opposite:* in front ▪ *adj* **behindhand**, late, overdue, behind schedule, in arrears *Opposite:* early

behind closed doors *adv* **privately**, in private, in secret, secretly, confidentially *Opposite:* openly

behindhand *adj* **late**, behind, behind schedule, overdue, slow *Opposite:* early

behind schedule *adj* **behind**, late, slow, delayed, overdue *Opposite:* early

behind the scenes *adv* **out of sight**, surreptitiously, unobtrusively, unnoticed, in the background *Opposite:* openly

behind the times *adj* **old-fashioned**, dated, unfashionable, out-of-date, outmoded

behind your back *adv* **without your knowledge**, furtively, surreptitiously, on the sly, secretively *Opposite:* openly

behold *(literary)* *v* **look at**, look on, see, observe, witness

beholden *adj* **obliged**, grateful, in somebody's debt, indebted, obligated

behoove *(fml)* *v* **be somebody's duty**, fall to, befit, be fitting for, be incumbent upon *(fml)*

being *n* **1 existence**, life actuality, presence, animation *Opposite:* nothingness **2 self**, soul, mind, essence, spirit **3 life form**, organism, creature, living being, human being

belabor v 1 **overstate**, labor, stress, overemphasize, overdo 2 *(literary)* beat, hit, thrash, whip, cudgel

belated adj **late**, delayed, postponed, deferred, tardy *Opposite*: timely

belch v **bring up wind**, burp, hiccup, gulp, eruct ■ n **burp**, hiccup, eructation

beleaguer v 1 **harass**, annoy, pester, plague, badger 2 **besiege**, surround, lay siege to, threaten, menace

beleaguered adj **under pressure**, harassed, fraught, careworn, stressed *Opposite*: carefree

belfry n **bell tower**, campanile, tower, spire, steeple

belie v **contradict**, disprove, give the lie to, call into question, deny *Opposite*: confirm

belief n 1 **confidence**, trust, certainty, credence, acceptance *Opposite*: distrust 2 **faith**, conviction, principle, creed, idea

believability n **credibility**, plausibility, acceptability, trustworthiness, authenticity

believable adj **credible**, authentic, realistic, plausible, convincing *Opposite*: unbelievable

believe v 1 **trust**, have faith in, be certain of, have confidence in, accept as true *Opposite*: disbelieve 2 **consider**, think, suppose, judge, imagine *Opposite*: doubt

believer n **supporter**, advocate, fan, devotee, follower *Opposite*: skeptic

belittle v **disparage**, demean, decry, deride, depreciate *Opposite*: praise

belittlement n **depreciation**, disparagement, derision, disdain *Opposite*: praise

belittling adj **demeaning**, disparaging, depreciating, condescending, patronizing *Opposite*: supportive

bell n 1 **hand bell**, church bell, ship's bell, sleigh bell, school bell 2 **buzzer**, doorbell, chime, alarm, alarm bell

bellicose adj **belligerent**, aggressive, warlike, pugnacious, combative *Opposite*: compliant

belligerence n **hostility**, pugnaciousness, bellicosity, pugnacity, aggression

belligerency *see* belligerence

belligerent adj **aggressive**, argumentative, quarrelsome, confrontational, pugnacious *Opposite*: cooperative

bellow n **roar**, shout, yell, bawl, holler *(infml)* *Opposite*: whisper ■ v **shout**, roar, yell, bawl, thunder *Opposite*: whisper

belly *(infml)* n **stomach**, abdomen, middle, tummy *(infml)*, gut *(slang)*

bellyache *(infml)* n 1 **upset stomach**, stomach ache, stomach pains, tummy ache *(infml)* 2 **complaint**, grumble, moan *(infml)*, grouse *(infml)*, gripe *(infml)* ■ v **complain**, grumble, carp, whine, moan *(infml)*

belly flop n **fall**, flop, crash, dive

belly laugh n **guffaw**, laugh, chortle, horse-laugh, hoot

belong v **fit in**, fit, go, have its place, be in the right place

belongings n **possessions**, property, things, stuff, luggage

beloved adj **much-loved**, dearly loved, adored, favorite, darling *Opposite*: despised

below prep **less than**, under, beneath, not more than ■ adv 1 **underneath**, under, beneath, lower *Opposite*: above 2 **under**, underneath, beneath, lower than, further down *Opposite*: above

belt n 1 **girdle**, tie, sash, cummerbund, strap 2 **band**, ring, strip, ribbon, line ■ v 1 **fasten**, buckle, secure, attach, belt up *Opposite*: undo 2 *(infml)* **hit**, thump, thrash, beat, strike 3 *(infml)* **dash**, rush, speed, hurry, race *Opposite*: dawdle

belt up v **fasten your belt**, secure your belt, put on your belt, buckle up

bemoan v **lament**, regret, mourn, complain, grumble *Opposite*: applaud

bemuse v **confuse**, daze, puzzle, perplex, stun

bemused adj **confused**, dazed, puzzled, perplexed, mystified *Opposite*: clear-headed

bench n 1 **seat**, pew, stall, bleacher 2 **worktable**, counter, work surface, worktop, workbench

benchmark n **standard**, yardstick, level, target, point of reference

bend n **curve**, turn, crook, twist, curvature ■ v 1 **turn**, bow, twist, crook, change direction *Opposite*: straighten 2 **stoop**, bow, bend over, lean down, lean over *Opposite*: straighten up

bendable adj **flexible**, pliant, pliable, malleable, plastic *Opposite*: inflexible

bend over backward v **do all you can**, put yourself out, pull out all the stops, do your utmost, go all out

beneath prep **under**, underneath, below, lower than, less than *Opposite*: over ■ adv **underneath**, under, below, lower *Opposite*: above

benediction n **approval**, sanction, blessing *Opposite*: malediction *(fml)*

benefactor n **sponsor**, patron, supporter, backer

beneficence n **generosity**, charity, benevolence, big-heartedness, magnanimity *Opposite*: parsimony

beneficent adj 1 **charitable**, altruistic, generous, benevolent, humanitarian *Opposite*: self-seeking 2 **beneficial**, helpful, useful, advantageous, favorable *Opposite*: deleterious

beneficial adj **helpful**, useful, valuable, advantageous, positive *Opposite*: detrimental

beneficiary n **recipient**, receiver, heir, payee, legatee Opposite: benefactor

benefit n **1 advantage**, profit, help, assistance, use Opposite: detriment **2 subsidy**, allowance, payment, grant **3 fundraiser**, charity performance, charity event ■ v **help**, promote, profit, do good to, advance Opposite: harm

benefit from v **profit from**, enjoy, use, gain from, take advantage of

benevolence n **kindness**, compassion, generosity, munificence, goodwill Opposite: malevolence

benevolent adj **kind**, caring, compassionate, generous, giving Opposite: malevolent

benighted adj **ignorant**, unenlightened, unfortunate, disadvantaged Opposite: enlightened

benign adj **kind**, benevolent, caring, kindly, gentle Opposite: malignant

benignity n **kindliness**, gentleness, benevolence, compassion, warm-heartedness Opposite: malice

bent adj **1 twisted**, curved, bowed, crooked, turned Opposite: straight **2 determined**, set, fixed, resolved, decided ■ n **inclination**, gift, talent, flair. See COMPARE AND CONTRAST at **talent**.

bequeath v **leave**, give, donate, hand down, will Opposite: inherit

bequest n **inheritance**, legacy, gift, donation, settlement

berate v **rebuke**, shout at, harangue, criticize, scold Opposite: praise

bereaved adj **mourning**, bereft, in mourning, grieving, orphaned

bereavement n **loss**, grief, sorrow, mourning

bereft adj **1 bereaved**, mourning, in mourning, grieving, orphaned **2 empty**, starved, devoid, deprived, stripped

berserk adj **irrational**, mad, out of control, wild, off the deep end Opposite: rational

berth n **mooring**, dock, landing place, mooring place, wharf ■ v **dock**, moor, tie up, come in, land Opposite: put out

beseech (literary) v **beg**, request, ask, entreat, plead

beseeching (literary) adj **pleading**, begging, earnest, persuasive, imploring (fml) Opposite: diffident

beset adj **plagued**, tormented, overwhelmed, overcome, harassed Opposite: free ■ v **harass**, annoy, hamper, trouble, overwhelm Opposite: leave alone **2** (fml) **surround**, attack, overcome, overwhelm, assail

beside prep **next to**, at the side of, alongside, by, near

besides adv **1 as well**, in addition, also, above and beyond, too **2 moreover**, what's more, further, more to the point, anyway

besiege v **surround**, siege, lay siege to, encircle, blockade Opposite: defend

besieged adj **overwhelmed**, inundated, beleaguered, weighed down, plagued

besmirch v **sully**, defame, tarnish, damage, slander Opposite: praise

besotted adj **infatuated**, love-struck, head over heels in love, fanatical, obsessed Opposite: repelled

bespeak v **signify**, signal, indicate, convey, reveal

best adj **top**, finest, greatest, unsurpassed, paramount Opposite: worst ■ v **outdo**, overcome, top, surpass, defeat

bestial adj **inhuman**, foul, degrading, cruel, brutish Opposite: humane

bestiality n **cruelty**, inhumanity, savagery, brutality, depravity Opposite: humanity

bestir yourself (fml) v **motivate yourself**, stir yourself, busy yourself, rouse yourself, get going

bestow (fml) v **give**, bequeath, donate, grant, present Opposite: withdraw. See COMPARE AND CONTRAST at **give**.

bestride v **straddle**, span, sit astride, stand astride, be astride

bestseller n **record breaker**, hit, smash, success, winner Opposite: flop (infml)

bestselling adj **successful**, popular, blockbusting, hit, chart-topping

bet v **1 gamble**, stake, wager, put money on, lay a wager **2** (infml) **think**, expect, anticipate, consider, believe ■ n **1 wager**, gamble, stake, play, ante **2 option**, alternative, candidate, choice, plan

betoken (literary) v **represent**, indicate, signify, mean, connote

betray v **1 be disloyal**, give up, hand over, inform on, double cross Opposite: stand by **2 disclose**, leak, tell, give away, reveal

betrayal n **disloyalty**, unfaithfulness, bad faith, duplicity, infidelity Opposite: loyalty

betrothal (fml) n **engagement**, promise, pact, compact, troth (archaic)

betrothed (fml) n **fiancé**, fiancée, husband-to-be, wife-to-be, girlfriend

better adj **1 improved**, enhanced, superior Opposite: worse **2 healthier**, improved, well, recovering, in good health Opposite: worse ■ v **1** (fml) **improve on**, top, outdo, outstrip, outshine **2** (fml) **enhance**, improve, change for the better, advance, ameliorate (fml) Opposite: worsen

betterment (fml) n **furtherance**, improvement, advancement, benefit, progress Opposite: deterioration

better-off adj **rich**, wealthy, affluent, comfortable, prosperous Opposite: poor

between prep **1 flanked by**, sandwiched between, stuck between, amid, among **2 connecting**, linking, joining, involving, concerning

beveled *adj* **slanting**, oblique, chamfered, bias-cut, sloping

beverage *(fml)* *n* **drink**, hot drink, cold drink, liquid refreshment, brew *(infml)*

bewail *(fml)* *v* **lament**, bemoan, complain, regret, grumble *Opposite*: applaud

beware *v* **be careful**, be cautious, be wary, look out, watch out

bewilder *v* **confuse**, puzzle, baffle, perplex, confound

bewildered *adj* **confused**, puzzled, dazed, bemused, befuddled *Opposite*: clear-headed

bewildering *adj* **confusing**, puzzling, baffling, mystifying, incomprehensible *Opposite*: clear

bewilderment *n* **confusion**, incomprehension, bafflement, puzzlement, perplexity *Opposite*: clarity

bewitch *v* **enchant**, fascinate, captivate, charm, mesmerize, intrigue *Opposite*: repel

beyond *prep* **further than**, past, away from, clear of, ahead of

biannual *adj* **1 twice-yearly**, twice-a-year, six-monthly, semiannual **2 every other year**, biennial, two-yearly, regular, periodic

bias *n* **prejudice**, partiality, preference, unfairness, favoritism *Opposite*: impartiality

biased *adj* **prejudiced**, unfair, partial, influenced, predisposed *Opposite*: unbiased

biblical *adj* **scriptural**, holy, bible, sacred, theological

bibliography *n* **list**, index, appendix, checklist, catalog

bicameral *adj* **two-tier**, two-house, dual, bilateral, bipartite

bicentennial *n* **200th anniversary**, 200th birthday, anniversary

bicker *v* **argue**, dispute, quarrel, debate, squabble *Opposite*: agree

bicycle *n* **cycle**, two-wheeler, bike *(infml)*

bid *v* **1 tender**, offer, propose, submit, proffer **2 try**, attempt, undertake, seek, strive **3** *(archaic)* **order**, call on, command, direct, tell ■ *n* **1 offer**, proposal, proposition, tender, submission **2 attempt**, try, effort, undertaking, endeavor

biddable *adj* **compliant**, acquiescent, docile, obedient, amenable *Opposite*: intractable *(fml)*

bidder *n* **buyer**, collector, dealer, purchaser, customer

bidding *n* **request**, command, order, will, call

bide your time *v* **wait**, be patient, wait and see, play the waiting game, hold back

biennial *adj* **two-yearly**, biannual, regular, periodic

bier *n* **stand**, rest, base, pedestal, table

biff *(infml)* *v* **hit**, punch, thump, knock, clout

bifurcate *v* **divide**, branch, split, fork, diverge *Opposite*: converge

bifurcation *n* **fork**, junction, split, divergence, branching *Opposite*: convergence

big *adj* **1 large**, giant, immense, vast, great *Opposite*: small **2 spacious**, capacious, roomy, large, deep *Opposite*: cramped **3 significant**, considerable, substantial, sizable, large *Opposite*: insignificant **4 extensive**, vast, immense, wide, great *Opposite*: narrow **5 older**, elder, grown-up, adult, mature *Opposite*: little **6 bulky**, large, cumbersome, massive, outsize *Opposite*: petite **7 tall**, high, lofty, towering, soaring *Opposite*: short

bigamous *adj* **polygamous**, adulterous, two-timing *(infml)* *Opposite*: monogamous

bigamy *n* **polygamy**, adultery, two-timing *(infml)* *Opposite*: monogamy

big business *n* **trade**, commerce, industry, business sector, business world

big deal *(infml)* *n* **major concern**, federal case, matter of life and death, serious issue

biggie *(infml)* *n* **big one**, giant, colossus, monster, whopper *(infml)*

bighead *(infml)* *n* **boaster**, bragger, show-off *(infml)*, smart aleck *(infml)*, know-it-all *(infml)*

bigheaded *(infml)* *adj* **conceited**, egotistical, arrogant, vain, self-centered *Opposite*: modest

big-hearted *adj* **kind**, good-natured, supportive, helpful, kindly *Opposite*: mean-spirited

bigmouth *(infml)* *n* **1 gossip**, gossipmonger, telltale, tattletale, tattler **2 boaster**, bragger, braggart, blowhard, know-it-all *(infml)*

big name *n* **famous name**, celebrity, star, superstar, VIP *Opposite*: unknown

bigot *n* **extremist**, diehard, dogmatist, chauvinist, fanatic

bigoted *adj* **prejudiced**, dogmatic, opinionated, intolerant, narrow-minded *Opposite*: open-minded

bigotry *n* **prejudice**, intolerance, bias, narrow-mindedness, chauvinism *Opposite*: open-mindedness

big shot *(infml)* *n* **key player**, major player, VIP, big gun *(infml)*, bigwig *(infml)* *Opposite*: nobody

bigwig *(infml)* *see* **big shot**

bike *(infml)* *n* **bicycle**, cycle, motorbike, motorcycle

WORD BANK

❏ **types of bikes** boneshaker, dirt bike, exercise bike, moped, motor scooter, mountain bike, racing bike, rickshaw, scooter, snowbike, tandem bicycle, ten-speed, three-wheeler, trail bike, tricycle, two-wheeler, unicycle

❏ **parts of a bike** brake, chain, crossbar, derailleur, fender, fork, frame, handlebars, pedal, reflector, seat, spoke, tire, wheel

biker *n* motorcyclist, racer, rider, cyclist

bikini *n* swimsuit, two-piece, bathing suit

bilateral *adj* two-sided, two-pronged, joint, mutual, consensual *Opposite*: unilateral

bile *(literary) n* bitterness, irritability, vitriol, spleen, sourness *Opposite*: sweetness

bilge *n* 1 hull, keel, base, bottom 2 hold, tank, interior, recesses, bowels 3 sludge, mud, bilge water, silt, effluent 4 *(infml)* nonsense, garbage, rubbish, trash, drivel

bilingual *adj* fluent, multilingual, polyglot

bilious *adj* nauseous, sickly, queasy, sick, ill

bilk *(infml) v* cheat, trick, deceive, con, swindle

bill *n* 1 invoice, statement, demand, check, receipt 2 amount, total, sum, fee, price 3 proposal, measure, document, petition, proposition 4 poster, flyer, notice, advertisement, handbill 5 beak, mouth, mandible ■ *v* 1 charge, invoice, debit, send the bill to 2 promote, portray, publicize, hype, advertise

billboard *n* sign, poster, advertisement, panel, display

billet *n* accommodations, quarters, boarding house, guest house, lodgings *(dated)* ■ *v* accommodate, quarter, house, station, shelter

billet-doux *(literary) n* love letter, valentine, letter, missive, note

billionaire *n* multimillionaire, magnate, tycoon, moneybags *(infml)*, fat cat *(slang)*

billionth *n* tiny part, morsel, particle, modicum, touch

billow *v* 1 catch the wind, swell, bulge, balloon, fill *Opposite*: sag 2 waft, rise, curl, flow *Opposite*: fall ■ *n* puff, cloud, swell, swirl, rush

bin *n* 1 storage bin, basket, container, silo, holder 2 wastebasket, wastepaper basket, trash can, garbage can

binary *adj* two-part, dual, double, twin, twofold

bind *v* 1 attach, connect, join, combine, unite *Opposite*: undo 2 oblige, force, require, compel, coerce ■ *n* 1 quandary, tight situation, predicament, dilemma, muddle 2 nuisance, drag, bore, annoyance, pain *(infml)*

binder *n* 1 folder, file, ring binder, looseleaf folder, notebook 2 promise, pledge, vow, obligation, assurance

binding *n* 1 tie, band, attachment, fastening, truss 2 edging, cover, trim, stitching, strip ■ *adj* compulsory, obligatory, required, necessary, mandatory *Opposite*: voluntary

binge *n* spree, orgy, tear, rampage, splurge *(infml)* ■ *v* overdo, indulge, overindulge, gorge, pig out *(infml)* *Opposite*: diet

binoculars *n* field glasses, opera glasses, eyeglasses *(fml)*

biochemical *adj* chemical, biological, living, organic, natural

biodegradable *adj* recyclable, decomposable, ecological, environmental, green

biographer *n* writer, author, autobiographer, historian, profiler

biographical *adj* factual, nonfiction, true, fact-based, realistic *Opposite*: fictional

biography *n* life story, life history, profile, memoir, life

biological *adj* 1 organic, life, living, natural, biotic 2 natal, birth, natural, genetic, true *Opposite*: adoptive

bionic *adj* electronic, automatic, robotic, electromechanical

biopic *n* film, movie, biography, documentary, life story

biopsy *n* cell removal, operation, surgery, culture, tissue removal

biorhythm *n* cycle, change, cyclical change, rhythm

biosphere *n* environment, planet, earth, land, sea

bipartisan *adj* two-party, dual-party, cross-party, joint, combined

bipartite *adj* two-party, two-part, mutual, shared, in common

biped *n* two-legged animal, human, primate, humanoid

birch *n* cane, rod, stick, switch, whip ■ *v* whip, flog, punish, strike, thrash

birdbath *n* basin, bowl, receptacle

birdbrained *(infml) adj* silly, foolish, stupid, asinine, witless *Opposite*: sensible

birdcage *n* cage, coop, pen, aviary, enclosure

birdlike *adj* dainty, petite, small-boned, delicate, slight *Opposite*: heavyset

birdseed *n* seed, grain, mixture, feed, chicken feed

birdsong *n* call, cry, song, trill, whistle

birdwatcher *n* ornithologist, bird lover, birder

birth *n* 1 delivery, labor, childbirth, nativity, parturition *(fml)* *Opposite*: death 2 beginning, origin, dawn, start, onset *Opposite*: end ■ *adj* natal, natural, true, biological, genetic *Opposite*: adoptive

birthdate *see* birthday

birthday *n* date of birth, birthdate, anniversary

birthmark *n* mark, stain, discoloration, blemish, strawberry mark

birthplace *n* origin, source, home, hometown, place of birth

birthright *n* inheritance, legacy, bequest, heritage, patrimony

birth sign *n* sign of the Zodiac, astrological sign, sign

bisect *v* cut in half, intersect, divide, cut across, sever *Opposite*: join

bisection *n* halving, splitting, dissection, division, parting *Opposite*: union

bit *n* 1 **piece**, morsel, crumb, fragment, speck 2 **minute**, while, moment, second, a little while

bite *v* 1 **sink your teeth into**, nibble, gnaw, bite off, bite into 2 **wound**, nip, snap, attack, maul 3 **hurt**, sting, feel painful, nip, prick ▪ *n* 1 **taste**, mouthful, nibble, chew, piece 2 **wound**, sting, puncture, bite mark 3 **sharp taste**, spiciness, tartness, piquancy, tang

bite-sized *adj* **small**, little, minute, tiny, petite *Opposite*: big

bite the bullet *v* **take the bull by the horns**, do it, face up to, go for it *(slang) Opposite*: avoid

bite the dust *(infml) v* 1 **fall down**, fall flat, take a fall, tumble, tumble down 2 **die**, pass away, kick the bucket *(infml)*, croak *(infml)*, expire *(fml)* 3 **fail**, go under, die a death, be unsuccessful, go bankrupt *Opposite*: succeed

biting *adj* 1 **cold**, freezing, piercing, cutting, stinging *Opposite*: hot 2 **sarcastic**, scathing, acerbic, mordant, satirical *Opposite*: sympathetic

bitingly *adv* **acidly**, acerbically, tartly, woundingly, cruelly *Opposite*: sympathetically

bits and pieces *(infml) n* 1 **belongings**, things, odds and ends, stuff, personal possessions 2 **knickknacks**, leftovers, scraps, odds and ends, stuff

bitter *adj* 1 **sour**, acid, acidic, tart, astringent *Opposite*: sweet 2 **resentful**, embittered, sulky, cheated, angry *Opposite*: glad 3 **unpleasant**, acrimonious, antagonistic, nasty, hostile *Opposite*: amicable 4 **vicious**, rancorous, virulent, vehement *Opposite*: mild 5 **cold**, freezing, icy, biting, raw *Opposite*: hot

bitterly *adv* 1 **resentfully**, acrimoniously, sulkily, sullenly, cynically *Opposite*: gladly 2 **severely**, excessively, intensely, inordinately, desperately *Opposite*: slightly

bitterness *n* 1 **resentment**, acrimony, unpleasantness, sullenness, anger *Opposite*: friendliness 2 **sourness**, acidity, sour taste, astringency, bitter taste *Opposite*: sweetness

bittersweet *adj* **poignant**, nostalgic, affecting, touching, sentimental

bitty *(infml) adj* **tiny**, minute, itsy-bitsy *(infml)*, teeny *(infml)*, teeny-weeny *(infml) Opposite*: large

bitumen *n* **tar**, asphalt, tarmac, blacktop, paving

bivouac *n* 1 **camp**, encampment, temporary camp, mountaineering camp, military camp 2 **shelter**, awning, tent, pup tent, lean to ▪ *v* **camp**, set up camp, pitch a tent

biweekly *adv* 1 **once every two weeks**, every other week, twice a month 2 **twice a week**, semiweekly, every few days

bizarre *adj* **strange**, curious, inexplicable, out of the ordinary, unusual *Opposite*: ordinary

blab *(infml) v* **tell tales**, gossip, spread rumors, tattle, leak

blabber *v* **chatter**, babble, go on, drivel, jabber

blabbermouth *(infml) n* **gossip**, tattletale, chatterer, chatterbox *(infml)*, bigmouth *(infml)*

black *adj* **dark**, gloomy, obscure, dusky, murky *Opposite*: light

WORD BANK
❏ *types of black* blue-black, coal black, ebony, inky, jet black, pitch-black, raven, sable

black-and-blue *adj* **bruised**, aching, hurt, injured, battered

black-and-white *adj* **clear-cut**, straightforward, unambiguous, categorical, explicit *Opposite*: ambiguous

blackball *v* **exclude**, ban, keep out, reject, bar *Opposite*: invite

blackboard *n* **writing board**, board, chalkboard, slate

blacken *v* 1 **darken**, make black, dirty, turn black, besmirch *Opposite*: lighten 2 **slander**, libel, defame, vilify, malign *Opposite*: praise

blackguard *n* **scoundrel**, rascal, rogue, villain, wretch *(fml)*

blackhead *n* **blocked pore**, spot, pimple, blemish, zit *(slang)*

blacklist *v* **ban**, debar, bar, exclude, shut out

blackly *adv* 1 **angrily**, menacingly, threateningly, belligerently, aggressively *Opposite*: optimistically 2 **hopelessly**, gloomily, lugubriously, dismally, dolefully *Opposite*: sunnily

blackmail *n* **extortion**, intimidation, bribery, corruption, extraction ▪ *v* **extort**, extract, exact, hold to ransom, bribe

blackmailer *n* **extortionist**, coercer, criminal, crook *(infml)*

blackness *n* 1 **darkness**, duskiness, dimness, shadow, gloom *Opposite*: light 2 **hopelessness**, despondency, gloominess, depression, dolefulness *Opposite*: optimism 3 **anger**, fury, temper, aggression, belligerence *Opposite*: cheerfulness

black out *v* **faint**, pass out, lose consciousness, collapse, become unconscious *Opposite*: come to

blackout *n* 1 **fainting fit**, seizure, loss of consciousness, collapse 2 **power cut**, power outage, shutdown, power failure, brownout 3 **embargo**, veto, clampdown, suppression, censorship

black-tie *adj* **formal**, dressy, ceremonial, posh *Opposite*: casual

blacktop *n* **asphalt**, tar, bitumen, tarmac

blade *n* 1 **cutting edge**, knife-edge, edge,

razor blade, knife blade **2 vane**, fin, propeller, sail, oar

blame v **1 hold responsible**, censure, accuse, point the finger at, hold accountable Opposite: exculpate (fml) **2 criticize**, reproach, find fault with, condemn, think badly of Opposite: commend ■ n **responsibility**, guilt, culpability, fault, blameworthiness Opposite: commendation

blameless adj **innocent**, virtuous, righteous, faultless, irreproachable Opposite: guilty

blameworthy adj **responsible**, guilty, culpable, at fault, chargeable Opposite: innocent

blanch v **go pale**, grow pale, turn white, lighten, blench Opposite: redden

bland adj **1 insipid**, weak, tasteless, mild, plain Opposite: tasty **2 featureless**, ordinary, dull, lackluster, humdrum Opposite: exciting

blandishment n **flattery**, cajolery, praise, fawning, soft words

blandness n **1 tastelessness**, weakness, insipidness, mildness, plainness Opposite: tastiness **2 dullness**, banality, flatness, triteness, insipidness Opposite: interest

blank adj **1 empty**, vacant, bare, clean, clear Opposite: full **2 outright**, complete, total, absolute, unqualified Opposite: partial **3 uncomprehending**, impassive, vacant, empty, bemused Opposite: expressive ■ n **space**, void, gap, empty space, break

blanket n **coverlet**, cover, covering, afghan, throw ■ adj **comprehensive**, extensive, complete, total, wholesale Opposite: partial ■ v **cover**, obscure, encase, drape, carpet Opposite: uncover

blankness n **1 emptiness**, void, vacancy, bareness, barrenness **2 lack of expression**, vacancy, indifference, emotionlessness, vacuousness Opposite: animation **3 bewilderment**, confusion, obliviousness, incomprehension, lack of understanding Opposite: acuity

blank out v **block out**, blot out, suppress, wipe out, erase Opposite: acknowledge

blare v **ring out**, make a racket, boom, blast out, blare out

blare out see blare

blaring adj **deafening**, earsplitting, cacophonous, raucous, booming Opposite: quiet

blarney (infml) n **nonsense**, smooth talk, charm, drivel, flattery

blasé adj **nonchalant**, laid back, cool, relaxed, unmoved Opposite: concerned

blaspheme v **curse**, swear, issue oaths, use profanities, use foul language

blasphemer n **swearer**, curser, profaner, foul mouth, cusser

blasphemous adj **sacrilegious**, irreligious, offensive, improper, irreverent Opposite: pious

blasphemy n **1 profanity**, sacrilege, wickedness, irreverence, violation Opposite: piety **2 oath**, curse, profanity, swearword, cuss (infml)

blast n **explosion**, detonation, flash, flare, gust ■ v **1 blow up**, explode, detonate, demolish, blow away (slang) **2** (infml) **blare**, resound, boom, make a racket, ring out **3** (infml) **criticize**, attack, lambaste, vilify, censure **4 damage**, blight, disfigure, burn, blister. See COMPARE AND CONTRAST at criticize.

blast off v **take off**, lift off, launch Opposite: touch down

blastoff n **launch**, takeoff, liftoff Opposite: touchdown

blast out v **blare out**, ring out, make a racket, blare, boom

blatancy n **obviousness**, conspicuousness, ostentation, flagrancy, overtness Opposite: subtlety

blatant adj **obvious** unconcealed, barefaced, unashamed, deliberate Opposite: furtive

blather (infml) v **chatter**, go on, babble, blabber, jabber ■ n **drivel**, prattle, chatter, babble, blabber

blaze v **burn**, be on fire, burst into flames, rage, glow ■ n **1 fire**, inferno, conflagration, combustion **2 glare**, glow, flash, brightness, intensity

blazing adj **1 intense**, raging, mighty, heated, furious **2 burning** glowing, shining, radiating, blistering

blazon v **splash**, embellish, emblazon, display, show

bleach v **lighten**, peroxide, blanch, blench, whiten Opposite: color

bleached adj **lightened**, faded, sunbleached, washed-out, blanched

bleachers n **benches**, stands, stand seats, seating, seats

bleak adj **1 unwelcoming**, austere, miserable, bare, drab Opposite: welcoming **2 hopeless**, unpromising, gloomy, doubtful, futile Opposite: promising **3 cold**, harsh, wintry, cheerless, miserable Opposite: warm **4 forlorn**, miserable, dejected, disheartened, downhearted Opposite: cheerful

bleakly adv **forlornly**, dismally, hopelessly, drearily, despondently Opposite: cheerfully

bleakness n **1 hopelessness**, despondency, sorrow, misery, sadness Opposite: hopefulness **2 cheerlessness**, drabness, austerity, harshness, bareness Opposite: comfort

bleary adj **hazy**, watery, unfocused, fuzzy, blurry Opposite: clear

bleary-eyed adj **sleepy**, tired, half-awake, dozy, groggy Opposite: alert

bleat v **whine**, complain, nag, fuss, moan (infml)

bleed v **1 lose blood**, hemorrhage, shed blood

2 (infml) **extort**, exploit, drain, wring, deplete ■ n blood loss, hemorrhage, nose-bleed

bleed dry (infml) v drain, suck dry, deplete, bring to its knees, exploit Opposite: replenish

bleeding n blood loss, hemorrhage, flow of blood, flow

bleep n beep, tone, sound, noise

blemish n mark, defect, imperfection, flaw, fault ■ v damage, tarnish, spoil, ruin, stain Opposite: restore. See COMPARE AND CONTRAST at flaw.

blemished adj marked, stained, imperfect, flawed, tarnished Opposite: unblemished

blench v **1** go pale, grow pale, lighten, blanch, whiten Opposite: redden **2** draw back, hesitate, falter, recoil, flinch

blend v mix, merge, combine, bring together, unify Opposite: separate ■ n mixture, merger, combination, assortment, amalgam. See COMPARE AND CONTRAST at mixture.

blender n mixer, food processor, chopper

bless v **1** sanctify, consecrate, hallow, extol, laud Opposite: curse **2** approve, sanction, support, endorse, back Opposite: decry

blessed adj **1** holy, sacred, sanctified, hallowed, consecrated Opposite: profane (fml) **2** welcome, providential, lucky, fortunate, pleasant Opposite: unfortunate

blessing n **1** consecration, sanctification, benediction, dedication **2** approval, sanction, permission, consent, approbation Opposite: veto **3** lucky thing, good thing, miracle, piece of good fortune, stroke of luck Opposite: disaster

blight n disfigurement, stain, scar, blot, affliction ■ v ruin, disfigure, stain, scar, impair

blind adj sightless, unsighted, vision-impaired Opposite: sighted ■ n screen, window shade, canopy, awning, visor

blind alley n dead end, cul-de-sac, impasse

blind date n rendezvous, date, meeting, assignation, appointment

blindfold n bandage, cloth, covering, scarf, band

blinding adj **1** glaring, dazzling, bright, bedazzling, strong Opposite: soft **2** (infml) striking, extraordinary, outstanding, arresting, amazing Opposite: ordinary

blindness n **1** sightlessness, loss of sight, impaired vision Opposite: sight **2** thoughtlessness, carelessness, obliviousness, recklessness, rashness Opposite: thoughtfulness

blind spot n weakness, failing, failure, fault, flaw Opposite: strength

blink v **1** wink, bat an eyelid, flutter an eyelid, flicker an eyelid **2** flash, wink, flicker, twinkle, signal

blinkered adj inward-looking, insular, narrow-minded, narrow, limited

blip n problem, glitch, error, failure, breakdown

bliss n ecstasy, heaven, paradise, enjoyment, happiness Opposite: misery

blissful adj heavenly, wonderful, delightful, idyllic, perfect Opposite: miserable

blissfully adv supremely, wonderfully, ecstatically, delightfully, happily Opposite: miserably

blister n sore, swelling, eruption, burn, blood blister ■ v swell up, erupt, bubble, bulge, break out

blistering adj sweltering, baking, blazing, burning, searing Opposite: freezing

blithe adj **1** (literary) carefree, cheerful, happy, merry, happy-go-lucky Opposite: anxious **2** casual, unconcerned, indifferent, unthinking, uncaring Opposite: thoughtful

blitz n **1** bombardment, blitzkrieg, saturation bombing, onslaught, offensive **2** (infml) onslaught, attack, crackdown, concerted effort, cleanup ■ v **1** (infml) crack down on (infml), concentrate on, focus on, come down on, lower the boom (infml) **2** bombard, bomb, blast, barrage, hit **3** (infml) clean, clean up, tidy, clear away, clear up

blizzard n snowstorm, whiteout, winter storm, storm

bloat v swell, inflate, blow up, expand, distend Opposite: contract

bloated adj swollen, distended, overstuffed, full, overfed

blob n splotch, globule, spot, splash, dash ■ v splotch, dot, dab, daub, smudge

bloc n alliance, coalition, union, federation, league

block n **1** chunk, hunk, lump, slab, wedge **2** wing, extension, addition, unit, module **3** expanse, section, sector, zone, band ■ v obstruct, impede, hinder, jam, prevent Opposite: encourage. See COMPARE AND CONTRAST at hinder.

blockade n barrier, barricade, obstruction, line of defense, cordon ■ v deny access to, lay siege to, obstruct, defend, block

blockage n obstruction, impasse, jam, bottleneck, snarl

blockbuster (infml) n runaway success, hit, smash hit, chartbuster, bestseller Opposite: flop (infml)

blockbusting adj successful, sensational, outstanding, popular, record-breaking

blocked adj congested, impassable, choked up, plugged up, stopped up Opposite: clear

blocking adj obstructive, delaying, stalling, hindering, spoiling Opposite: cooperative

block off v **1** close off, block, close, cordon off, isolate Opposite: free **2** obstruct, obscure, hide, mask, cover Opposite: reveal

block out v blank out, blot out, suppress, wipe out, erase Opposite: acknowledge

block up v jam, fill, stop, obstruct, choke Opposite: free

blond adj fair-haired, towheaded, flaxen, golden, straw-colored Opposite: dark

blonde see blond

blood n 1 gore, body fluid, plasma, lifeblood 2 family, relations, kin, relatives, kinfolk 3 lineage, ancestry, extraction, heritage, stock

bloodbath n massacre, slaughter, atrocity, scene of carnage

blood brother n best friend, friend, ally, supporter, amigo Opposite: enemy

bloodcurdling adj terrifying, frightening, hair-raising, chilling, spine-tingling Opposite: comforting

bloodless adj 1 nonviolent, peaceful, nonaggressive, orderly, controlled Opposite: violent 2 pale, anemic, white, pallid, wan Opposite: ruddy

bloodletting n quarrel, fight, dispute, argument, fracas

bloodline n descent, heritage, lineage, ancestry, background

blood lust n bloodthirstiness, hatred, cruelty, inhumanity, revenge

blood money n compensation, money, recompense, retribution, atonement

bloodshed n carnage, killing, violence, slaughter, murder

bloodshot adj red, inflamed, sore, pink Opposite: clear

bloodstream n flow, circulation, blood, arteries, veins

bloodsucker n parasite, leech, tick, mosquito, vampire

bloodsucking adj parasitical, leechlike, vampiric, vampirish

bloodthirstiness n ferociousness, viciousness, cruelty, barbarism, brutality

bloodthirsty adj cruel, gory, murderous, ferocious, vicious

bloody adj gory, blood-spattered, bleeding, wounded, injured

bloom n 1 (literary) flower, flower head, blossom, posy, bud 2 coloration, tinge, tint, shadow, flush Opposite: pallor ■ v 1 blossom, flower, come into flower, come into bud Opposite: wither 2 (literary) thrive, prosper, blossom, flourish, do well Opposite: struggle 3 (literary) be a picture of health, glow, be radiant, thrive, flourish

blooming adj 1 flourishing, thriving, budding, up-and-coming, promising Opposite: struggling 2 blossoming, flowering, budding, in flower, in bloom

blooper (infml) n mistake, blunder, error, gaffe, misstep, faux pas (literary)

blossom n flower, flower head, bloom, posy, bud ■ v 1 bloom, flower, bud, come into flower, come into bud Opposite: wither 2 flourish, thrive, grow, bloom, prosper Opposite: struggle 3 develop, grow, come out of your shell, mature, come out of yourself

blossoming adj developing, growing, prospering, maturing, thriving

blossom out v develop, grow, come out of your shell, come out of yourself, blossom

blot n spot, blemish, stain, mark, imperfection ■ v stain, tarnish, spoil, ruin, disfigure

blotch n blot, mark, blemish, spot, stain

blotchy adj mottled, blemished, marked, spotty, spotted Opposite: plain

blot on the landscape n eyesore, scar, blemish, disfigurement, monstrosity

blot out v 1 conceal, hide, cover, eclipse, block Opposite: reveal 2 blank out, block out, forget, erase, put out of your mind Opposite: recall

blotter n logbook, notebook, log, record, journal

blow v 1 whoosh, gust, waft, puff, bluster 2 move, propel, drive, carry, waft ■ n 1 knock, crack, jolt, swipe, strike 2 setback, upset, disappointment, shock, misfortune Opposite: boost

blow away v distribute, disperse, scatter, dispel, spread

blowback (infml) n reaction, response, repercussion, feedback

blow-by-blow adj thorough, step by step, detailed, full, complete Opposite: sketchy

blower (infml) n boaster, egotist, show-off (infml), bigmouth (infml), loudmouth (infml)

blown-up adj 1 inflated, air-filled, hard, rigid, pumped-up Opposite: deflated 2 distended, swollen, bloated, enlarged, puffed-up Opposite: sunken 3 overdone, exaggerated, attention-grabbing, hyped, puffed-up Opposite: understated 4 bombed, wrecked, burned-out, ruined, demolished

blow out v extinguish, put out, snuff out, douse, dampen Opposite: ignite

blow somebody's cover v unmask, expose, uncover, make known, bring to light

blow the whistle v inform, report, turn in, expose, tell on

blow up v 1 destroy, explode, detonate, blast, demolish 2 inflate, pump up, fill, puff up, swell Opposite: deflate 3 enlarge, magnify, expand, increase, make larger Opposite: reduce 4 (infml) lose your temper, explode, be furious, flare up, hit the roof (infml) 5 (infml) exaggerate, overstress, embellish, embroider, make a mountain out of a molehill Opposite: play down

blowup n enlargement, magnification Opposite: reduction

blowy (infml) adj windy, breezy, blustery, gusty, squally Opposite: calm

blow your own horn *v* **brag**, boast, crow, show off, sing your own praises *Opposite*: deprecate

blow your top *(infml)* *v* **flare up**, lose your temper, fly into a rage, explode, hit the roof *(infml)* *Opposite*: calm down

blowzy *adj* **1** ruddy, red-faced, rubicund, coarse complexioned **2** unkempt, bedraggled, messy, tousled, disheveled *Opposite*: smart

blubber *(infml)* *v* **sob**, weep, cry, snivel, whimper

bludgeon *v* **1** beat, hit, slam, strike, batter **2** coerce, compel, bully, bulldoze, steamroller

blue *(infml)* *adj* **depressed**, down, sad, low, dejected *Opposite*: happy

---

WORD BANK
❑ **types of blue** azure, baby blue, cobalt blue, cornflower blue, cyan, electric blue, ice blue, indigo, lapis lazuli, midnight blue, navy blue, peacock blue, powder blue, Prussian blue, royal blue, sapphire, sky blue, slate blue, steel blue, turquoise, ultramarine

---

blue-blooded *adj* **aristocratic**, noble, high-class, well-bred, refined *Opposite*: common

blue-chip *adj* **top-class**, first-class, first-rate, top-grade, topnotch *(infml)* *Opposite*: second-rate

blue-collar *adj* **manual**, proletarian, working class, laboring *Opposite*: white-collar

blueprint *n* **plan**, drawing, design, proposal, outline

blues *(infml)* *n* **sadness**, melancholy, dejection, depression, despair *Opposite*: happiness

bluff *v* **trick**, con, fake, lie, pretend ■ *n* **1** sham, trick, con, pretense, fake **2** cliff, headland, hillside, hill, mound ■ *adj* plain-spoken, cheery, loud, hearty, forthright

bluffness *n* **cheeriness**, heartiness, directness, bluntness, plain-spokenness

blunder *n* **mistake**, gaffe, error, mix-up, misstep ■ *v* **1** make a mistake, get it wrong, err, slip up *(infml)*, goof *(infml)* **2** stumble, stagger, lurch, flounder, trip. *See* COMPARE AND CONTRAST *at* mistake.

blundering *adj* **clumsy**, careless, awkward, lumbering, ungainly *Opposite*: dexterous

blunt *adj* **1** dull, rounded, dulled, blunted *Opposite*: sharp **2** uncompromising, straightforward, direct, · frank, honest *Opposite*: indirect ■ *v* dampen, dull, put a damper on, take the edge off, diminish *Opposite*: heighten

bluntly *adv* **frankly**, straightforwardly, honestly, directly, candidly *Opposite*: indirectly

bluntness *n* **candor**, frankness, directness, straightforwardness, honesty *Opposite*: mendacity

blur *n* **distortion**, fuzziness, haze, impression, shape ■ *v* **1** obscure, cloud, make indistinct, hide, conceal *Opposite*: clarify **2** distort, confuse, shade *Opposite*: clear

blurred *adj* **blurry**, indistinct, unclear, hazy, distorted *Opposite*: distinct

blurry *see* blurred

blurt *v* **exclaim**, cry, utter, come out with, announce

blush *v* **go red**, flush, go red in the face, color, redden *Opposite*: blanch ■ *n* makeup, cosmetic, rouge *(dated)*

blushing *adj* **embarrassed**, self-conscious, red-faced, flushed, coy *Opposite*: bold

bluster *v* **1** harangue, threaten, bully, protest, rant **2** blow, gust, rage, puff, waft

blustery *adj* **windy**, gusty, stormy, squally, breezy *Opposite*: still

B movie *n* **supporting film**, short, B picture, support, supporting movie

BO *(infml)* *n* **body odor**, smell, sweatiness, rankness, reek

board *n* **1** plank, slat, floorboard, timber, beam **2** panel, sheet, boarding **3** committee, panel, commission, management team, advisory group **4** food, meal, sustenance, nourishment, rations ■ *v* **1** embark, enter, go on board, go aboard, go into *Opposite*: disembark **2** live, room, be accommodated, stay, lodge *(dated)*

boarder *n* **lodger**, paying guest, resident, tenant, occupant

board up *v* **close**, shutter, secure, cover up

boardwalk *n* **walkway**, footpath, path, causeway

boast *v* **1** brag, show off, crow, sing your own praises, blow your own horn **2** have, possess, pride yourself on, lay claim to, feature ■ *n* claim, assertion, brag, vaunt, pretension

boastful *adj* **arrogant**, proud, conceited, full of yourself, bragging *Opposite*: modest

boastfulness *n* **immodesty**, arrogance, conceit, self-importance, showing off *Opposite*: modesty

boasting *n* **boastfulness**, bragging, showing off, arrogance, self-aggrandizement *Opposite*: modesty ■ *adj* boastful, swaggering, arrogant, self-important, conceited *Opposite*: modest

boat *n* **craft**, ship, vessel

bob *v* **1** move up and down, nod, dip, bobble, jog **2** curtsy, bow, nod, duck, genuflect

bobbin *n* **reel**, spindle, spool, cylinder, roll

bobble *n* *(infml)* **mistake**, blunder, error, gaffe, slip ■ *v* move up and down, nod, bob, jog, dip

bode *v* **augur**, portend, promise, predict, divine

bodily *adj* **physical**, corporal, corporeal, fleshly, material *Opposite*: spiritual

body *n* **1** form, figure, frame, physique, build

2 corpse, dead body, cadaver, remains, carcass **3 organization**, group, association, federation, society **4 quantity**, corpus, amount, mass, area **5 bulk**, main part, essence, majority, mass

body blow n setback, blow, disappointment, upset, shock

body builder n athlete, weightlifter, muscle builder

body fluid n saliva, blood, urine, sweat, semen

bodyguard n guard, escort, attendant, guardian, protection officer

body language n mannerisms, stance, facial expression, movements, motion

bog n swamp, quagmire, mire, marsh, marshland

bogey n **1 worry**, problem, concern, bugaboo, bugbear **2 monster**, creature, beast, monstrosity, booger (infml)

bogeyman n monster, creative, beast, monstrosity, booger (infml)

boggle (infml) v confuse, baffle, perplex, astonish, overwhelm

boggy adj marshy, swampy, muddy, watery, wet Opposite: parched

bogus adj false, fake, counterfeit, phony, trick Opposite: genuine

bohemian n free spirit, freethinker, nonconformist, hippie, New Age traveler ■ adj unconventional, nonconformist, offbeat, alternative, carefree Opposite: conformist

boil v **1 rage**, fume, seethe, be angry, be irate **2 simmer**, bubble, poach, cook, stew ■ v (infml) **overheat**, swelter, stew, bake, burn Opposite: freeze ■ n ulcer, sore, spot, swelling, abscess

boil down to (infml) v amount to, come down to, end up as, add up to, wind up as

boiler suit n overalls, coveralls, protective clothing, dungarees

boiling adj hot, sweltering, baking, steaming, torrid Opposite: freezing

boiling point n crisis point, danger level, flashpoint, high point, peak

boil over v overflow, bubble up, overheat, spill over, blow

boisterous adj **1 energetic**, exuberant, active, animated, spirited Opposite: placid **2 wild**, turbulent, rough, stormy Opposite: calm

boisterousness n **1 high spirits**, unruliness, overexcitement, roughness, riotousness Opposite: placidity **2 wildness**, turbulence, roughness, storminess Opposite: calmness

bold adj **1 brave**, daring, courageous, audacious, valiant Opposite: cowardly **2 confident**, forward, brash, brazen, self-assured Opposite: timid **3 conspicuous**, bright, vivid, flashy, showy Opposite: muted **4 black**, heavy, boldface Opposite: light

boldface adj black, heavy, bold Opposite: lightface

bold-faced adj impudent, brash, brazen, unconcerned, shameless Opposite: unassuming

boldness n **1 courage**, daring, bravery, bravado, valor Opposite: cowardice **2 confidence**, self-assurance, brashness, nerve, impudence Opposite: timidity

bole n trunk, stem, stalk

bollard n post, marker, pillar, stake, pole

bolster v boost, strengthen, reinforce, encourage, shore up Opposite: undermine

bolt n bar, pin, rod, catch, latch ■ v **1 fasten**, secure, lock, lock up, attach Opposite: unlock **2 run off**, make a dash for it, run, make a run for it, disappear **3 gulp**, wolf, gobble, devour, down Opposite: nibble

bolt from the blue n surprise, shock, upset, jolt, blow

bolthole n hideaway, refuge, sanctuary, den, place of safety

bomb v **1 bombard**, shell, blast, barrage, blitz **2** (infml) **fail**, flop, fall flat, sink without trace, disappoint Opposite: succeed

bombard v **1 bomb**, shell, open fire on, blast, barrage **2 assail**, shower, flood, inundate, overrun

bombardment n **1 attack**, offensive, assault, salvo, bombing **2 barrage**, flood, onslaught, blitz, volley

bombast n pomposity, pretentiousness, verboseness, affectation, grandiloquence Opposite: directness

bombastic adj pompous, pretentious, verbose, long-winded, grandiloquent Opposite: direct

bombshell (infml) n shock, surprise, bolt from the blue, blow, upset

bomb site n area of devastation, crater, ruins, battlefield, wasteland

bona fide adj genuine, authentic, true, real, valid Opposite: bogus

bonanza n jackpot, crock of gold, gold mine, stroke of luck, bonus

bond n **1 tie**, link, connection, union, attachment **2 promise**, pledge, oath, word ■ v **1 adhere**, stick, glue, fix, join **2 connect**, get along, relate, become attached, hit it off (infml) Opposite: clash

bondage n slavery, enslavement, captivity, oppression, servitude Opposite: freedom

bonded adj fused together, fused, stuck, glued, attached Opposite: split

bonding n attachment, closeness, tie, connection, love

bone of contention n disagreement, sticking point, difficulty, problem, obstacle

boner (infml) n mistake, blunder, error, gaffe, misstep

bone up (infml) v find out about, research, look into, read up on, study

bonfire n fire, conflagration, blaze, beacon

bong n bang, blow, thud, crash, knock

bonhomie n **friendliness**, sociability, affability, geniality, amenability

bonk (infml) v **hit**, bang, knock, tap, slap ■ n **knock**, blow, slap, bang, tap

bon mot n **witticism**, quip, joke, epigram, clever remark

bonus n 1 **extra**, addition, advantage, windfall, benefit 2 **gratuity**, handout, pay supplement, reward

bon vivant n **pleasure-seeker**, lotus-eater, gourmet, epicure, gourmand Opposite: ascetic

bony adj **skinny**, scrawny, lanky, lean, thin Opposite: plump

boo n **catcall**, jeer, hoot, raspberry Opposite: cheer ■ v **jeer**, hoot, catcall, hiss Opposite: applaud

boob (infml) n **fool**, dupe, chump (infml), sucker (infml), fall guy (slang)

boo-boo (infml) n **blunder**, mistake, error, gaffe, slip-up (infml)

boob tube (infml) n **television**, TV (infml), tube (infml), small screen (infml)

booby trap n 1 **bomb**, tripwire, mine, explosive device 2 **snare**, trap, trick, ruse, con

boogie v (infml) **dance**, jig, jive, bop (infml), party (infml) ■ n **jig**, jive, bop (infml), party (infml)

book n **volume**, tome, manuscript, paperback, hardback ■ v **reserve**, order, engage, put your name down for, sign up for

booking n **reservation**, hold, option, deposit

bookish adj **studious**, serious, academic, scholarly, brainy

bookishness n **studiousness**, erudition, scholarliness, learning, learnedness

booklet n **brochure**, pamphlet, leaflet, flier

books n **records**, accounts, financial statements, balance sheet, profit and loss

bookworm (infml) n **avid reader**, book lover, bibliophile

boom v 1 **roar**, rumble, thunder, bellow, resound 2 **grow**, soar, rocket, increase, rise Opposite: collapse ■ n 1 **growth**, increase, rise, upsurge, expansion Opposite: collapse 2 **pole**, arm, bracket, beam ■ adj **prosperous**, flourishing, affluent, successful, thriving

boomerang v **rebound**, bounce back, return, ricochet, come back

booming adj 1 **thriving**, prosperous, wealthy, flourishing, successful Opposite: failing 2 **thunderous**, roaring, resounding, resonant, sonorous Opposite: quiet

boon n **advantage**, benefit, bonus, help, godsend Opposite: disadvantage

boondocks (infml) n **backwater**, middle of nowhere, country, provinces, sticks (infml)

boor n **lout**, oaf, loudmouth (infml)

boorish adj **rude**, ill-mannered, impolite, coarse, rough Opposite: well-mannered

boorishness n **crudeness**, loutishness, uncouthness, incivility, rudeness Opposite: courteousness

boost v 1 **increase**, improve, enhance, make better, further Opposite: reduce 2 **encourage**, support, lift, uplift, give a boost to Opposite: discourage ■ n **improvement**, increase, enhancement, lift, helping hand Opposite: blow

booster n 1 **promoter**, supporter, fan, advocate, admirer 2 **injection**, inoculation, vaccination, immunization, shot (infml)

boost up v 1 **increase**, improve, enhance, boost, add to Opposite: reduce 2 **encourage**, support, lift, uplift, give a boost to Opposite: discourage

booth n **cubicle**, stand, closet, compartment, sukkah

bootlace n **shoelace**, cord, lace, strap, tie

bootleg adj **illegal**, pirated, stolen, illicit, unlicensed Opposite: legal

bootless adj **useless**, scant, feeble, inadequate, unsuccessful Opposite: successful

boot out (infml) v **dismiss**, get rid of, eject, evict, bounce Opposite: appoint

booty n **loot**, spoils, plunder, ill-gotten gains, valuables

bop (infml) v 1 **dance**, jig, jive, boogie (infml) 2 **hit**, bang, knock, tap, thump ■ n 1 **jig**, dance, jive, boogie (infml) 2 **disco**, dance, party, ball, rave (slang)

border n 1 **frontier**, borderline, boundary, state line 2 **edge**, limit, boundary, margin, verge Opposite: center 3 **flowerbed**, bed, shrub border, herbaceous border ■ v **be next to**, touch, be bounded by, border on, run alongside

bordering adj **adjoining**, neighboring, adjacent, next door, nearby

borderland n **boundary**, edge, frontier, outer fringe, limits Opposite: heartland

borderline adj **marginal**, disputed, uncertain, doubtful, unclear Opposite: clear-cut ■ n **frontier**, boundary, state line, border

border on v 1 **approach**, be close to, resemble, be similar to, verge on 2 **be next to**, touch, be bounded by, border, adjoin

bore v 1 **turn off** (infml), weary, send to sleep, bore to death, bore to tears Opposite: interest 2 **drill**, perforate, penetrate, pierce, tunnel

bored adj **uninterested**, tired, bored rigid, bored stiff, bored to death Opposite: fascinated

boredom n **tedium**, monotony, dullness, tediousness, ennui Opposite: interest

borehole n **well**, hole, shaft

boring adj **uninteresting**, tedious, dull, dreary, mind-numbing Opposite: exciting

born adj **instinctive**, congenital, innate, intuitive, natural Opposite: trained

born-again adj **reinvigorated**, reborn, enthusiastic, avid, fervid

borough n **area**, district, municipality, division, township

borrow v 1 **use**, make use of, have access to, scrounge (infml), sponge (infml) Opposite: lend 2 **copy**, plagiarize, derive, pirate, steal

bosom adj (infml) **close**, best, dearest, special, firm Opposite: distant ■ n (literary) **heart**, center, midst, embrace, arms

boss n **manager**, supervisor, chief, head, person in charge Opposite: subordinate ■ v **give orders**, tell what to do, boss around, order around, command Opposite: obey

boss around v **give orders**, tell what to do, order around, boss, domineer Opposite: obey

bossiness n **imperiousness**, officiousness, high-handedness, authoritarianism, overbearingness Opposite: meekness

bossy adj **domineering**, officious, dominant, high-handed, dictatorial Opposite: meek

botanic see **botanical**

botanical adj **vegetal**, plant, botanic

botch n (infml) **fiasco**, failure, disaster, flop (infml) ■ v **spoil**, damage, ruin, do badly, make a mess of

botched adj **failed**, substandard, poor, ruined, inferior Opposite: first-rate

bother v 1 **make an effort**, take the trouble, put yourself out, go to the trouble of, extend yourself 2 **worry**, trouble, disturb, upset, unsettle 3 **interrupt**, disturb, distract, trouble, pester ■ n **trouble**, difficulty, problem, nuisance, inconvenience

COMPARE AND CONTRAST CORE MEANING: interfere with somebody's composure
bother cause to feel worried, anxious, or upset, or disturb or interrupt; **annoy** irritate or harass; **bug** (infml) persistently cause trouble and annoy; **disturb** interrupt or distract in the process of doing something, or to upset the peace of mind of; **trouble** cause distress or inconvenience to; **worry** cause to be anxious.

bothered adj **worried**, concerned, troubled, anxious, apprehensive Opposite: untroubled

bothersome adj **troublesome**, inconvenient, worrisome, niggling, difficult

bottle n **flask**, jug, carafe, flagon, decanter

bottleneck n **block**, blockage, restricted access, holdup, traffic jam

bottle up v **contain**, repress, suppress, keep in check, keep inside

bottom n 1 **base**, bed, foot, floor, substructure Opposite: top 2 **end**, far end, foot, extremity, limit Opposite: top 3 **underside**, underneath, bottom side, underbelly Opposite: top ■ adj **lowest**, bottommost, lowermost, nethermost (fml) Opposite: top

bottomless adj **unlimited**, unrestricted, endless, limitless, unending Opposite: restricted

bottom line n 1 **fundamental issue**, key issue,

fact of the matter, thing to bear in mind, crucial thing 2 **lower limit**, threshold, floor, cutoff point, limit

bottommost adj **lowest**, last, bottom, final Opposite: topmost

boudoir n **bedroom**, dressing room, chamber (literary), bedchamber (literary)

bouffant adj **backcombed**, fluffy, full, puffed up, voluminous

bough n **branch**, limb, spur

boulder n **rock**, stone, sarsen

bounce v 1 **rebound**, spring back, bound, spring up, recoil 2 **spring**, jump, bound, bob, bobble 3 **eject**, evict, throw out, remove, expel

bounce back v **recover**, improve, get better, pull through, perk up

bounciness n 1 **liveliness**, spirit, vivacity, friskiness, playfulness Opposite: lethargy 2 **elasticity**, springiness, resistance, resilience, pliability Opposite: firmness

bouncy adj 1 **effervescent**, energetic, playful, lively, vivacious Opposite: lethargic 2 **springy**, elastic, pliable Opposite: firm

bound adj 1 **certain**, sure, guaranteed, destined, assured Opposite: unlikely 2 **obliged**, compelled, forced, obligated, duty-bound Opposite: free ■ v **border**, border on, be next to, touch, be adjacent to ■ n **jump**, leap, spring, bounce, hop

boundary n **border**, frontier, borderline, state line, dividing line

bounded adj 1 **surrounded**, bordered, enclosed, encircled, delimited 2 **restricted**, hemmed in, limited, constrained, confined Opposite: free

boundless adj **unlimited**, endless, limitless, infinite, ceaseless Opposite: restricted

bounds n **limits**, boundaries, confines, restrictions, constraints

bounteous (literary) see **bountiful**

bountiful (literary) adj 1 **generous**, giving, munificent, openhanded, liberal Opposite: parsimonious 2 **plentiful**, generous, abundant, copious, profuse Opposite: scarce. See COMPARE AND CONTRAST at **generous**.

bounty n 1 **reward**, price, prize, payment, gift 2 (literary) **abundance**, plenty Opposite: scarcity

bouquet n 1 **bunch**, spray, posy, arrangement, nosegay 2 **smell**, aroma, scent, fragrance, perfume. See COMPARE AND CONTRAST at **smell**.

bourgeois adj **middle-class**, conventional, conformist, unadventurous, staid ■ n **conservative**, traditionalist, conformist, reactionary, conventional person

bout n **short period**, short time, session, spell, attack

bovine (literary) adj **stupid**, slow, unintelligent, dim, dense

bow n 1 **arc**, curve, arch, sweep, bend 2 **bob**,

bend, curtsy, obeisance (fml) ■ v 1 bend, bend over, lower, stoop, lean Opposite: straighten up 2 distort, deform, arch, droop, sag Opposite: straighten

WORD BANK
❏ types of bows crossbow, Cupid's bow, longbow

bowdlerize v censor, edit, abridge, clean up, expurgate

bowed adj curved, bent, deformed, convex, hooked Opposite: straight

bowels n guts, entrails, viscera, innards (infml), insides (infml)

bower n arbor, retreat, grove, copse, den

bowl n 1 container, vessel, dish, basin, mixing bowl 2 hollow, depression, crater, basin, valley 3 stadium, arena, amphitheater, ballpark, venue ■ v 1 careen, career, roll along, travel, speed 2 roll, pitch, throw, lob, hurl

bowlegged adj bandy-legged, bandy, bent, bowed

bowl over v 1 astonish, amaze, delight, overwhelm, take by surprise 2 knock down, knock over, scatter, upturn, overturn

bow out v back out, beg off, duck out, cry off (infml), fink out (slang)

bow tie n tie, cravat, necktie

bow to v accept, yield, resign yourself to, recognize, acknowledge Opposite: reject

box n 1 container, case, chest, package, carton 2 rectangle, square, frame, check box 3 cubicle, stall, booth, compartment, enclosure ■ v fight, spar, punch, hit, thump

box in v enclose, surround, contain, shut in, trap

boy n young man, lad, schoolboy, son, youngster

boycott v refuse, stay away from, impose sanctions, embargo, shun

boyfriend n male friend, date, escort, fiancé, partner Opposite: girlfriend

boyhood n childhood, youth, early years

boyish adj youthful, adolescent, childlike, gamine, young

brace n support, strut, prop, stay, bracket

brace yourself v prepare yourself, ready yourself, make preparations, get ready for, prime yourself

bracing adj invigorating, stimulating, brisk, healthy, cold Opposite: soporific

bracket n 1 support, strut, prop, stay, brace 2 group, set, range, cohort, band ■ v connect, link, join, relate, associate Opposite: separate

brackish adj salty, saline, salted, briny, salt Opposite: fresh

brag v boast, blow your own horn, crow, show off, swagger Opposite: underplay

braggart n boaster, egotist, show-off (infml), bigmouth (infml), loudmouth (infml)

bragging n boasting, boastfulness, showing

off, arrogance, self-aggrandizement Opposite: modesty ■ adj boastful, arrogant, self-important, conceited, swaggering Opposite: modest

braid v 1 plait, interweave, interlace, intertwine, weave Opposite: unravel 2 decorate, trim, edge, fringe, bind Opposite: strip

brain n 1 intelligence, mind, intellect, head, wits 2 (infml) mastermind, intellectual, genius, intellect, prodigy

brainchild n idea, invention, creation, innovation, breakthrough

brainless adj foolish, stupid, mindless, unintelligent, silly Opposite: sensible

brainpower n intellect, brains, capacity, ability, intellectual capacity

brains n intelligence, common sense, wits, intellect, brainpower Opposite: ignorance

brainstorm n 1 (infml) bright idea, inspiration, idea, breakthrough, innovation 2 aberration, fit, turn, disturbance, upset ■ v think, suggest, come up with, devise, dream up

brainteaser n problem, puzzle, riddle, challenge, conundrum

brainwash v persuade, indoctrinate, condition, program, convince

brainy (infml) adj intelligent, clever, bright, quick, academic Opposite: unintelligent

braise v cook, stew, casserole, steam, simmer

brake v decelerate, slow down, reduce speed, put on the brakes, lose speed Opposite: accelerate ■ n restraint, constraint, curb, control, limitation Opposite: incentive

bran n fiber, dietary fiber, cellulose, roughage, bulk

branch n 1 bough, limb, spur, twig 2 local office, division, area office, subdivision, outlet Opposite: headquarters 3 division, department, offshoot, wing, arm 4 area, field, topic, domain, sphere 5 turnoff, arm, tributary, fork, side road ■ v split, fork, divide, diverge, separate Opposite: converge

branch off v split, fork, divide, turn off, leave Opposite: merge

branch out v diversify, diverge, take a new direction, broaden, expand Opposite: consolidate

brand n 1 make, product, brand name, trade name, trademark 2 type, kind, sort, style, variety 3 identifying mark, mark, marker, identification, label ■ v 1 mark, imprint, stamp, label 2 call, classify, label, name, describe

brandish v wield, wave, flourish, handle, flaunt

brand name n trade name, brand, label, make, trademark

brand-new adj new, unused, pristine, fresh, mint Opposite: old

brash *adj* **1 aggressive**, arrogant, self-confident, brazen, presumptuous *Opposite*: self-effacing **2 hasty**, impetuous, rash, foolhardy, slapdash *Opposite*: measured

brashness *n* **boldness**, brazenness, forcefulness, insolence, assertiveness *Opposite*: shyness

brass (*infml*) *n* **nerve**, impudence, self-assurance, self-confidence, gall *Opposite*: bashfulness

brass tacks *n* **basics**, essentials, fundamentals, bare essentials, nuts and bolts (*infml*)

brassy *adj* **1 harsh**, loud, metallic, strident, grating *Opposite*: soft **2 brazen**, strident, overbearing, brash, arrogant *Opposite*: self-effacing

brat *n* **little monster**, imp, spoiled brat, terror (*infml*), holy terror (*infml*) *Opposite*: cherub

bratty *adj* **obnoxious**, spoiled, demanding, overindulged, selfish *Opposite*: well-behaved

bravado *n* **audacity**, boldness, daring, bluster, boasting *Opposite*: cowardice

brave *adj* **courageous**, valiant, heroic, bold, daring *Opposite*: cowardly ■ *v* **defy**, face, stand up to, confront, take on *Opposite*: shrink

brave out *v* **suffer**, face, bear, endure, stay the course *Opposite*: give up

bravery *n* **courage**, courageousness, valor, gallantry, daring *Opposite*: cowardice. *See* COMPARE AND CONTRAST *at* **courage**.

bravura *n* **boldness**, daring, spirit, nerve, guts (*slang*) *Opposite*: timidity ■ *adj* **brilliant**, magnificent, exceptional, dazzling, outstanding *Opposite*: nondescript

brawl *n* **scuffle**, fight, punch-up, clash, affray ■ *v* **fight**, scuffle, tussle, wrestle, clash

brawn *n* **strength**, muscle, brute force, power, burliness *Opposite*: weakness

brawny *adj* **muscular**, strong, powerfully built, hefty, burly *Opposite*: scrawny

bray *v* **1 whinny**, neigh, cry, call **2 grate**, rasp, bark, bellow, snort *Opposite*: murmur

braying *adj* **harsh**, loud, strident, jarring, grating *Opposite*: soft

brazen *adj* **bold**, barefaced, shameless, brash, unabashed *Opposite*: discreet

brazenness *n* **shamelessness**, boldness, barefacedness, flagrancy, impudence *Opposite*: discretion

brazen out *v* **face down**, stand your ground, face out, hold your own, stay the course *Opposite*: cave in

brazier *n* **stove**, barbecue, grill, hibachi, fire

breach *v* **1 get through**, break through, break, rupture, penetrate *Opposite*: block **2 break**, violate, contravene, infringe, flout *Opposite*: honor ■ *n* **1 opening**, break, hole, crack, fissure **2 violation**, contravention, infringement, defiance, betrayal *Opposite*: compliance **3 rift**, separation, division, rupture,

estrangement *Opposite*: reconciliation

breach of the peace *n* **public disturbance**, public nuisance, nuisance, riot, fracas *Opposite*: order

bread *n* **food**, daily bread, sustenance, nourishment, rations

---

WORD BANK

❏ **types of bread** baguette, black bread, brown bread, challah, chapati, ciabatta, corn bread, crouton, flat bread, focaccia, matzo, nan, pita, poppadom, pumpernickel, puri, roti, rye bread, soda bread, sourdough, spoon bread, toast, tortilla, white bread, whole-wheat

❏ **types of rolls or buns** bagel, brioche, bun, croissant, crumpet, English muffin, roll

---

bread and butter *n* **1 livelihood**, living, income, maintenance, upkeep **2 mainstay**, lifeblood, backbone, basis, core

bread-and-butter *adj* **basic**, primary, fundamental, essential, important *Opposite*: superfluous

breadth *n* **1 width**, span, wideness, extent, size *Opposite*: depth **2 extensiveness**, extent, range, scope, span *Opposite*: narrowness **3 latitude**, room, freedom, space, leeway *Opposite*: restriction

breadthwise *adj* **sideways**, side-to-side, widthways ■ *adv* **across**, from side to side, widthwise

breadwinner *n* **wage earner**, worker, employee *Opposite*: dependent

break *v* **1 smash**, fracture, rupture, shatter, split *Opposite*: mend **2 break down**, stop working, fail, collapse, crash **3 infringe**, violate, contravene, breach, disobey *Opposite*: uphold **4 stop**, end, interrupt, disturb, break into **5 take a break**, break into, have a break, rest, stop **6 beat**, surpass, exceed, top, better **7 destroy**, shatter, crush, overwhelm, defeat **8 become known**, make public, become public, disclose, get around **9 decipher**, crack, decode, solve, unravel ■ *n* **1 disruption**, breakdown, discontinuity, interruption, pause **2 rest**, respite, coffee break, pause, lunch break **3 time off**, trip, weekend trip, vacation **4 interruption**, pause, space, disruption, halt **5** (*infml*) **chance**, opportunity, opening, occasion, leg up

breakable *adj* **fragile**, delicate, brittle, frail, flimsy *Opposite*: sturdy

breakage *n* **breaking**, smashing, cracking, rupture, splintering *Opposite*: mending

break away *v* **secede**, separate, become independent, split, disaffiliate *Opposite*: join

breakaway *n* **separation**, rupture, severance, splitting up, breakup *Opposite*: fusion ■ *adj* **separate**, splinter, independent, autonomous, alternative *Opposite*: mainstream

break down v 1 **lose control**, cry, be overcome, collapse, burst into tears 2 **stop working**, break, fail, go down, crash 3 **overcome**, defeat, destroy, knock down, smash down Opposite: build 4 **analyze**, separate, dissect, break up, split 5 **divide**, classify, categorize, split, separate Opposite: lump 6 **decompose**, decay, putrefy, molder, disintegrate

breakdown n 1 **failure**, collapse, cessation, halt, interruption 2 **analysis**, rundown, classification, dissection, summary

breaker n **wave**, roller, whitecap

break free v **escape**, break away, break with, separate, get away

break in v 1 **tame**, train, discipline, domesticate, housetrain 2 **force an entry**, break into, burgle, break and enter, burglarize 3 **interrupt**, butt in, interject, interpose, cut in

break-in n **forced entry**, burglary, robbery, crime, felony

breaking n **contravention**, infringement, violation, breach, transgression Opposite: observance

breaking point n **verge of collapse**, limit, threshold, snapping point, crisis

break into v 1 **break in**, force an entry, burgle, break and enter, burglarize 2 **begin**, burst into, launch into, embark on, burst out Opposite: break off

breakneck adj **quick**, speedy, hurried, hasty, rapid Opposite: slow

break new ground v **be the first**, blaze a trail, lead the way, be in the vanguard, set a trend

break of day n **daybreak**, sunrise, daylight, first light, dawn Opposite: sundown

break off v 1 **detach**, come off, snap off, come away, separate Opposite: attach 2 **end**, terminate, stop, cease, finish Opposite: begin

breakoff n **discontinuation**, ending, interruption, suspension, stopping Opposite: continuation

break open v **open**, divide, come apart, burst, shatter

break out v 1 **begin**, start, erupt, burst into, embark on Opposite: end 2 **escape**, break loose, burst out, break free, emerge

breakout n **escape**, getaway, flight, running away, running off

break the ice v **get to know**, make friends, get acquainted, introduce yourself, set the ball rolling

break through v **burst through**, penetrate, come through, breach, wear down

breakthrough n **advance**, step forward, leap forward, new idea, innovation

break up v 1 **divide**, fragment, disintegrate, crumble, fall apart Opposite: fuse 2 **disperse**, separate, split up, keep apart, divide up Opposite: unite 3 **separate**, tell somebody it's over, split up, end, finish

breakup n 1 **disintegration**, fragmentation, division, crumbling, destruction Opposite: merger 2 **ending**, end, splitting up, finish, separation

breakwater n **offshore barrier**, mole, sea wall, harbor wall, causeway

break with v **separate**, split, leave, part company, escape Opposite: associate

breath n 1 **gasp**, sigh, pant, inhalation, exhalation 2 **puff**, waft, current, draft, gush

breathe v **respire**, take breaths, inhale, exhale, suck in air

breathe new life into v **revitalize**, reinvigorate, revive, resurrect, rejuvenate

breather (infml) n **rest**, break, respite, time out, sit-down (infml)

breathe your last (literary) v **die**, pass on, go to meet your maker, pass away, expire (fml)

breathing n **inhalation**, exhalation, panting, gasping, puffing ▪ adj **living**, alive, conscious, sentient, aware

breathing space n **respite**, relief, space, recovery time, time

breathless adj **out of breath**, panting, gasping, puffing, winded

breathlessly adv **eagerly**, excitedly, with bated breath, on tenterhooks, anxiously Opposite: nonchalantly

breathtaking adj **out of this world**, wonderful, magnificent, spectacular, incredible Opposite: banal

breathy adj **wheezy**, hissing, gasping, panting, husky

breed n **type**, strain, class, kind, variety ▪ v 1 **reproduce**, have babies, propagate, procreate, multiply 2 **raise**, rear, bring up, farm, produce 3 **cause**, create, generate, bring about, produce

breeding n **upbringing**, education, background, social standing, refinement

breeding ground n **environment**, conditions, source, medium, place

breeze n 1 **wind**, gust, gentle wind, light wind, waft Opposite: gale 2 (infml) **child's play**, cinch (infml), piece of cake (infml), walkaway (infml), walkover (infml)

breezily adv **brightly**, cheerfully, cheerily, happily, merrily Opposite: seriously

breezy adj 1 **blustery**, gusty, windy, brisk, windswept Opposite: still 2 **cheerful**, cheery, jolly, lighthearted, flippant Opposite: serious

breviary n **missal**, prayer book, hymnal, book of psalms

brevity n 1 **shortness**, briefness, quickness, swiftness, transience Opposite: length 2 **conciseness**, succinctness, concision, pithiness, terseness Opposite: verbosity

brew n 1 (infml) **drink**, potion, infusion, cocktail, beverage (fml) 2 **mixture**, mix, blend, combination, concoction ▪ v 1 **prepare**, make, infuse, steep, ferment **2 develop**, loom, threaten, grow, blow up

briar see **brier**

bribe n **inducement**, enticement, carrot, kickback, payola ■ v **induce**, corrupt, entice, suborn, persuade

bribery n **corruption**, inducement, enticement, subornation

bric-a-brac n **knickknacks**, curios, ornaments, stuff, junk (infml)

brick n **block**, slab, ingot, lump, piece

brickbat n **insult**, criticism, insinuation, suggestion, comment

brickwork n **fabric**, structure, bricks and mortar, masonry, stonework

bridal adj **wedding**, nuptial, marriage, honeymoon

bride n **wife**, wife-to-be, newlywed, spouse, partner

bridegroom n **husband**, husband-to-be, newlywed, spouse, partner

bridesmaid n **maid of honor**, attendant, matron of honor, flower girl

bridge n **bond**, tie, link, connection, conduit ■ v **link**, connect, join, span, tie together

WORD BANK
❏ **types of bridges** aqueduct, arch bridge, Bailey bridge, bascule bridge, beam bridge, cable-stayed bridge, cantilever bridge, drawbridge, footbridge, gangplank, overpass, pontoon bridge, suspension bridge, swing bridge, viaduct, walkway

bridgehead n **foothold**, position, stepping stone, jumping-off point, vantage point

bridle v **1 bristle**, get angry, become annoyed, become indignant, prickle **2 curb**, restrain, control, rein in, keep in check Opposite: let loose

bridle path n **ride**, horse trail, path, track, trail

brief adj **1 short-lived**, transitory, fleeting, ephemeral, short-term Opposite: lasting **2 short**, concise, succinct, to the point, pithy Opposite: lengthy ■ n **1 synopsis**, summary, digest, abstract, outline **2 briefing**, instructions, guidelines, preparation, orders ■ v **inform**, tell, give instructions, prepare, instruct

briefcase n **document case**, attaché case, case, portfolio, music case

briefing n **meeting**, conference, seminar, press conference, updating session

brigade n **group**, team, crew, contingent, gang

brigand (literary) n **lawbreaker**, bandit, thief, robber, thug

bright adj **1 brilliant**, vivid, intense, dazzling, light Opposite: dark **2 intelligent**, quick, sharp-witted, clever, smart Opposite: unintelligent **3 cheerful**, happy, lively, optimistic, positive Opposite: gloomy. See COMPARE AND CONTRAST at **intelligent**.

brighten v **1 feel better**, brighten up, look up, perk up, cheer up **2 make brighter**, lighten, make lighter, brighten up, illuminate Opposite: darken **3 improve**, make better, enhance, animate, revivify

brighten up v **raise the spirits**, make brighter, brighten, lighten, make lighter Opposite: cast down

brightly adv **1 luminously**, lustrously, radiantly, glossily, glowingly Opposite: dully **2 sunnily** perkily, cheerfully, cheerily, optimistically Opposite: gloomily

brightness n **1 illumination**, glare, intensity, brilliance, vividness Opposite: dullness **2 sunniness**, high spirits, cheerfulness, optimism, cheeriness Opposite: gloominess

brilliance n **1 brightness**, intensity, vividness, luminosity. radiance Opposite: dullness **2 cleverness**, wisdom, smartness, genius, talent Opposite: stupidity

brilliancy see **brilliance**

brilliant adj **1 luminous**, radiant, dazzling, sparkling, gleaming Opposite: dull **2 vivid**, bright, clear, intense, dazzling Opposite: faded **3 talented**, virtuoso, inspired, skillful, gifted Opposite: mediocre **4** (infml) **wonderful**, superb, marvelous, excellent, magnificent Opposite: awful

brim n **ridge**, edge, top, rim, lip

brimful adj **full to the top**, full, filled up, filled to the brim, overfull Opposite: empty

brimming adj **bursting**, teeming, overflowing, packed, filled

brine n **saline**, salt water, sea water

bring v **1 take along** carry, fetch, convey, transport Opposite: take away **2 cause**, bring about, produce, lead to, result in **3 command**, earn, produce, make, bring in

bring about v **generate**, cause, produce, result in, end in Opposite: prevent

bring alive v **awaken**, bring to life, make real, animate, enliven

bring around v **1 sway**, reason, convince, persuade, win over Opposite: deter **2 rouse**, bring to, revive, awaken, wake up Opposite: knock out

bring back v **1 evoke**, recall, bring to mind, summon up, reawaken **2 return**, replace, restore, reinstate, recapture Opposite: carry off

bring down v **1 overthrow**, topple, depose, defeat, dethrone Opposite: elect **2 fell**, floor, topple, demolish, knock over Opposite: raise

bring down a peg v **humble**, chasten, force to eat humble pie, cut down to size, put in their place

bring down to earth v **disillusion**, disappoint, disenchant, enlighten, disabuse

bring forth v **deliver**, bear, give birth to, produce, yield

bring forward v **1 speed**, advance, reschedule, move forward, change *Opposite*: delay **2 put on the table**, produce, present, offer, bring out *Opposite*: withdraw

bring home v **make clear**, clarify, illustrate, illuminate, underline

bring home the bacon *(infml)* v **provide**, keep a roof over your head, put food on the table, keep the wolf from the door, keep clothes on your back

bring in v 1 **introduce**, set up, establish, launch, start *Opposite*: end **2 recoup**, acquire, earn, make, take home *Opposite*: lose

bring into being v **create**, establish, found, institute, set up *Opposite*: destroy

bring into disrepute v **discredit**, dishonor, disgrace, shame, smear

bring into line v **standardize**, coordinate, synchronize, make uniform, harmonize

bring off v **succeed**, carry off, achieve, accomplish, engineer *Opposite*: fail

bring on v **cause**, create, produce, make, start

bring out v 1 **highlight**, spotlight, show up, reveal, bring to the surface *Opposite*: suppress **2 introduce**, produce, release, put on sale, launch *Opposite*: withdraw

bring shame on v **discredit**, sully, tarnish, smear, stain

bring to v **bring around**, rouse, awaken, wake up, revive *Opposite*: knock out

bring to a close *see* bring to an end

bring to an end v **conclude**, bring to a close, put a stop to, end, stop *Opposite*: start

bring together v 1 **combine**, mix, mix together, blend, pool *Opposite*: separate **2 gather**, amass, rally, compile, glean *Opposite*: distribute, scatter **3 reconcile**, integrate, unite, unify, link

bring to life v **make real**, animate, bring alive, anthropomorphize, give life to

bring to light v **expose**, unearth, disclose, uncover, publicize *Opposite*: hide

bring to mind v **summon up**, reawaken, rekindle, stir up, bring back

bring up v 1 **mention**, broach, raise, suggest, introduce *Opposite*: gloss over **2 raise**, care for, nurture, look after **3 vomit**, expel, spew, regurgitate, disgorge

bring up-to-date v **inform**, give the lowdown, look after, put in the picture, update *Opposite*: keep in the dark

brink n 1 **verge**, threshold, edge, point, precipice **2 edge**, rim, lip, brim, border *Opposite*: center

brinkmanship n **strategy**, tactics, politics, bluff, bluffing

briny adj **salty**, salt, saline, salted, brackish

brio *(literary)* n **energy**, vigor, enthusiasm, go, gusto

briquette n **block**, lump, brick, piece, cake

brisk adj 1 **energetic**, fast, quick, rapid,

hurried *Opposite*: slow **2 abrupt**, curt, impatient, brusque, hurried *Opposite*: measured **3 refreshing**, cool, cold, invigorating, stimulating *Opposite*: warm

briskness n 1 **speed**, rapidity, vigor, efficiency, urgency *Opposite*: tardiness **2 abruptness**, coldness, reserve, brusqueness, curtness *Opposite*: patience

bristle n **stubble**, hackle, hair, spine, spike ■ v 1 **stiffen**, become erect, stand up, rise, prickle **2 bridle**, be resentful, get your hackles up, object, get angry **3 brim**, be full, teem, overflow, be thick with

bristly adj **spiky**, coarse, wiry, stubbly, sharp *Opposite*: smooth

brittle adj **hard**, stiff, inelastic, fragile, breakable *Opposite*: robust

brittleness n **hardness**, stiffness, fragility, weakness, frailty *Opposite*: robustness

broach v **propose**, present, submit, mention, raise

broad adj 1 **spacious**, wide, large, big, extensive *Opposite*: narrow **2 comprehensive**, extensive, wide, far-reaching, wideranging *Opposite*: restricted **3 inexact**, rough, general, approximate, sketchy *Opposite*: precise **4 visible**, obvious, plain, clear, patent *Opposite*: subtle **5 distinctive**, distinct, thick, heavy, strong *Opposite*: slight

broad-brush adj **inclusive**, comprehensive, broad, across-the-board, all-embracing *Opposite*: narrow

broadcast v 1 **transmit**, air, show, televise, screen **2 air**, spread, disseminate, publicize, make known **3 scatter**, sow, distribute, disseminate, strew ■ n **transmission**, program, show, airing, newscast

WORD BANK
❑ **types of broadcasts** call-in, commercial, concert, current affairs, distance learning, docudrama, documentary, drama, game show, infomercial, infotainment, makeover program, miniseries, news, newscast, news flash, newsreel, play, quiz show, reality show, sitcom *(infml)*, soap *(infml)*, soap opera, sports, sportscast, talk show, telethon, travelogue

broadcaster n **newscaster**, anchor, announcer, reporter, journalist

broaden v **widen**, extend, increase, make wider, become wider *Opposite*: narrow

broadly adv **approximately**, sketchily, generally, largely, roughly

broadly-based adj **wide**, broad, wideranging, extensive, sweeping

broad-minded adj **tolerant**, progressive, liberal, permissive, open-minded *Opposite*: narrow-minded

broad-mindedness n **liberality**, open-mindedness, tolerance, progressiveness, permissiveness *Opposite*: narrow-mindedness

broadness n **1 width**, breadth, wideness **2 scope**, breadth, span, range, extensiveness

broadsheet n **paper**, newspaper, quality newspaper, serious newspaper, heavyweight (infml)

broadside n **attack**, diatribe, tirade, onslaught, volley

brochure n **booklet**, leaflet, pamphlet, catalog, information sheet

brogue n accent, burr, drawl

broil v **1 grill**, barbecue, roast, cook **2 swelter**, burn, roast, bake, boil Opposite: freeze **3** (archaic) **fight**, brawl, clash, tussle, scuffle

broke (infml) adj **bankrupt**, penniless, poor, in the red, overdrawn Opposite: wealthy

broken adj **1 wrecked**, imperfect, fragmented, fractured, shattered Opposite: intact **2 inoperative**, malfunctioning, faulty, defective, out of order Opposite: working **3 beaten**, licked, defeated, dejected, crushed Opposite: triumphant

broken-down adj **1 inoperative**, malfunctioning, not working, broken, out of order Opposite: working **2 in poor condition**, dilapidated, run-down, falling apart, ramshackle

brokenhearted adj **sad**, grief-stricken, disappointed, desolate, despairing Opposite: overjoyed

broker n **trader**, agent, dealer, negotiator, stockbroker

bronze n **sculpture**, figure, statue, statuette, effigy

bronzed adj **tanned**, brown, suntanned, golden-brown, coppery

brooch n **pin**, badge, ornament, trinket, accessory

brood n **1 young**, clutch, litter, issue, family **2 children**, offspring, family, progeny, kids (infml) ■ v **ruminate**, worry, mope, dwell on, fret

broodily adv **thoughtfully**, pensively, meditatively, fretfully, sullenly Opposite: cheerfully

broodiness n **pensiveness**, glumness, fretfulness, sullenness, moroseness

brooding adj **ominous**, menacing, threatening, gloomy, dark

broodingly adv **glumly**, fretfully, sullenly, morosely, moodily Opposite: cheerfully

broody adj **1 sullen**, thoughtful, pensive, moody, glum Opposite: cheerful **2 maternal**, motherly, tender, caring

brook n **stream**, rivulet, river, creek ■ v (literary) **tolerate**, allow, accept, put up with, suffer

broom n **brush**, sweeper, besom

broomstick n **handle**, broom handle, pole, stick, stave

brother n **comrade**, member, colleague, associate

brotherhood n **1 association**, society, union, guild, organization **2 comradeship**, friendship, companionship, unity, loyalty

brotherly adj **companionable**, fraternal, affectionate, kind, friendly

brouhaha n **commotion**, ruckus, brawl, rumpus, melee

brow n **summit**, top, crest, ridge, peak

browbeat v **intimidate**, badger, bully, dragoon, nag Opposite: coax

browbeaten adj **downtrodden**, oppressed, intimidated, bullied, subjugated Opposite: defiant

brown adj **tanned**, sunburned, bronzed ■ v **fry**, grill, sear, toast, char

---

WORD BANK

❏ **types of brown** auburn, bay, bronze, burnt sienna, burnt umber, caramel, chestnut, chocolate, copper, hazel, henna, khaki, liver, mahogany, mocha, mousy, nut-brown, roan, russet, sorrel, tan, tawny, umber, walnut

❏ **types of light brown** beige, biscuit, buff, butterscotch, café au lait, camel, coffee, dun, ecru, fawn, flesh color, honey, oatmeal

---

browse v **glance**, cruise, look, peruse, surf

bruise n **discoloration**, black eye, welt, bump, shiner (infml) ■ v **hurt**, damage, mark, injure, discolor

bruised adj **1 injured**, hurt, sore, black-and-blue, damaged Opposite: unhurt **2 wounded**, upset, hurt, offended, affected Opposite: unaffected

bruiser (infml) n **muscleman**, bodyguard, bouncer, tough, heavyweight

brunette adj **dark**, brown, raven (literary), Opposite: blond

brunt n **effect**, force, full force, impact, full impact

brush n **1 broom**, sweeper, besom **2 contact**, touch, stroke, graze, sweep **3 encounter**, meeting, confrontation, skirmish, disagreement ■ v **1 scrub**, clear, coat, groom, sweep **2 touch**, graze, scrape, sweep, stroke

brushed adj **fleecy**, fluffy, downy, furry, soft

brush off v **dismiss**, rebuff, snub, reject, give the cold shoulder to

brushoff (infml) n **turndown**, rebuff, snub, rejection, cold shoulder

brush up v **reread**, refresh, renew, revise, review

brushwood n **firewood**, twigs, branches, undergrowth, kindling

brusque adj **abrupt**, curt, offhand, rough, brisk Opposite: friendly

brusqueness n **roughness**, terseness, abruptness, offhandedness, lack of warmth Opposite: friendliness

brutal adj **1 ruthless**, cruel, vicious, fierce, pitiless Opposite: humane **2 harsh**, severe, rough, callous, insensitive Opposite: kind

brutality n cruelty, viciousness, violence, rough treatment, harshness Opposite: gentleness

brutalize v 1 coarsen, harden, dehumanize, desensitize Opposite: humanize 2 abuse, assault, maltreat, ill-treat

brute n 1 bully, thug, beast, swine, monster 2 (literary) animal, beast, creature, monster

brutish adj 1 animal, wild, violent, bestial 2 cruel, ruthless, insensitive, pitiless, harsh Opposite: humane 3 loutish, boorish, rough, unrefined, uncivilized Opposite: civilized

brutishly adv cruelly, harshly, unfeelingly, insensitively, callously Opposite: humanely

brutishness n cruelty, harshness, unkindness, unfeelingness, insensitivity Opposite: humanity

bubble v fizz, effervesce, boil, simmer

bubbly adj 1 effervescent, foamy, sparkling, fizzy, fizzing Opposite: still 2 cheerful, lively, sparkling, vivacious, bouncy Opposite: sad

buccaneer n pirate, adventurer, swashbuckler

buck n 1 (infml) dollar, money, cash, dough (slang) 2 (infml) responsibility, blame, liability, culpability, fault ■ v 1 jump, rear, kick, kick out, bound 2 resist, oppose, fly in the face of, go against, challenge ■ adj lowly, lowest, low-grade

bucket n pail, container, vessel

buckets (infml) n lots, scores, loads (infml), tons (infml), heaps (infml)

buckle n clasp, clip, fastener, catch, fastening ■ v 1 fasten, clip, clasp, secure, close Opposite: undo 2 collapse, crumple, cave in, bulge, fold Opposite: straighten

buckle down (infml) v put your shoulder to the wheel, set to, get down to, knuckle down (infml)

buck up v 1 (infml) raise the morale of, cheer up, raise the spirits of, hearten 2 improve, get better, look up, liven up, pick up (infml) Opposite: take a turn for the worse 3 (infml dated) hurry up, look lively, get going, get a move on (infml), get cracking (infml)

bucolic adj rural, pastoral, rustic, country, countrified Opposite: urban

bud n sprout, blossom, shoot, outgrowth ■ v blossom, flower, grow, bloom, open out

budding adj promising, potential, up-and-coming, nascent, burgeoning

buddy (infml) n friend, playmate, soul mate, companion, partner

budge v move, shift, dislodge, nudge, push

budget n financial plan, financial statement, accounts, finances, funds ■ adj cheap, economical, inexpensive, reasonable, low-priced Opposite: expensive ■ v plan, account, make financial arrangements, make provisions, cost

budgetary adj financial, economic, fiscal, commercial, monetary

buff v polish, rub, burnish, shine, clean ■ n fan, enthusiast, expert, connoisseur, aficionado ■ adj (infml) muscular, fit, healthy, toned, hard

buffalo (infml) v 1 confuse, baffle, deceive, hoodwink, bewilder 2 intimidate, coerce, threaten, inhibit, bully

buffer n shock absorber, bumper, cushion, barrier, shield ■ v cushion, shield, safeguard, defend, protect

buffet v rock, pound, batter, bang, knock

buffeting n battering, pounding, knocking, beating, pummeling

buffoon n clown, joker, comedian, fool, wag (infml)

buffoonery n horseplay, clowning, fooling around, frivolity, tomfoolery (infml)

bug n 1 insect, fly, pest, creature, creepy-crawly (infml) 2 (infml) germ, microbe, virus, bacterium, infection 3 (infml) fault, error, mistake, problem, gremlin (infml) 4 (infml) listening device, hidden microphone, surveillance device, wiretap ■ v 1 (infml) annoy, irritate, infuriate, bother, madden 2 tap, listen in on, keep under surveillance, spy on. See COMPARE AND CONTRAST at bother.

bugaboo see bugbear

bugbear n worry, problem, concern, bugaboo, bogey

bug-eyed (infml) adj popeyed, staring, big-eyed, wide-eyed, agog

buggy n 1 cart, vehicle, truck, transporter 2 baby carriage, stroller, perambulator (fml)

bugle v announce, herald, trumpet

build v 1 construct, put up, erect, make, put together Opposite: destroy 2 put together, create, make, join, assemble ■ n shape, size, figure, body, physique

build in v incorporate, include, integrate, add in Opposite: exclude

building n structure, construction, edifice, erection (fml)

WORD BANK
❑ parts of a building balcony, buttress, chimney, colonnade, deck, doorway, elevation, elevator, ell, escalator, exterior, façade, fire escape, frame, frontage, gable, gutter, landing, porch, roof, smokestack, soffit, stairwell, veranda, vestibule, wall, window, wing

build up v 1 increase, rise, develop, expand, enlarge Opposite: fall off 2 boost, bolster, pump up, inspire, encourage Opposite: discourage

buildup n 1 accumulation, backlog, accrual, collection, stockpile 2 hype, publicity, puff, praise, flattery

built-in adj 1 integral, fitted, fixed, en suite, in-built 2 natural, inherent, innate, intrinsic, ingrained Opposite: acquired

built-up *adj* **urbanized**, urban, developed, residential, industrial

bulb *n* **corm**, rhizome, tuber, storage organ, underground part

---

WORD BANK

❏ **types of flowers grown from bulbs** anemone, bluebell, crocus, cyclamen, daffodil, dahlia, freesia, gladiolus, hyacinth, iris, jonquil, lily, narcissus, snowdrop, tulip

---

bulbous *adj* **rounded**, spherical, bulging, globular, swollen

bulge *v* **stick out**, protrude, expand, be full to bursting, swell ■ *n* **protuberance**, swell, swelling, knot, lump

bulging *adj* **1 protruding**, protuberant, distended, swollen, swelling *Opposite*: flat **2** (*infml*) **full**, overfull, overfilled, overstuffed, crammed *Opposite*: empty

bulk *n* **1 size**, mass, volume, immensity, vastness **2 form**, body, weight, mass, hulk **3 greater part**, main part, largest part, majority, substance

bulkhead *n* **partition**, wall, dividing wall, screen, divider

bulkiness *n* **1 unwieldiness**, awkwardness, ungainliness, cumbersomeness, ponderousness **2 large size**, largeness, weight, bulk, mass *Opposite*: compactness

bulk large *v* **be prominent**, figure prominently, loom large, dominate, be important

bulk up (*infml*) *v* **build up**, increase, pad out, gain weight, gain muscle

bulky *adj* **1 unwieldy**, cumbersome, awkward, ungainly, ponderous *Opposite*: manageable **2 large**, huge, immense, massive, colossal *Opposite*: compact

bull *n* **papal decree**, decree, official statement, encyclical, instruction

bulldoze *v* **1 flatten**, raze, level, demolish, clear **2** (*infml*) **coerce**, bully, bludgeon, browbeat, steamroller

bulletin *n* **1 news report**, update, news item, news summary, press release **2 official statement**, communiqué, statement, announcement, press release **3 periodical**, journal, newsletter, newspaper, publication

bulletproof *adj* **1 toughened**, protective, armored, reinforced, shatterproof **2** (*infml*) **invulnerable**, secure, invincible, unassailable, untouchable *Opposite*: vulnerable

bullheaded (*infml*) *adj* **obstinate**, headstrong, stubborn, intransigent, uncooperative

bullheadedness (*infml*) *n* **obstinacy**, stubbornness, willfulness, intransigence, selfwill

bullion *n* **gold**, gold bars, gold ingots

bullish *adj* **1** (*infml*) **optimistic**, confident, buoyant, cheerful, enthusiastic *Opposite*: pessimistic **2 muscular**, strong, hulking, brawny

bullishness (*infml*) *n* **confidence**, optimism, buoyancy, hopefulness, self-confidence *Opposite*: diffidence

bullnecked *adj* **stocky**, bullish, brawny, beefy, muscular

bullring *n* **arena**, ring, stadium, amphitheater, sports stadium

bull's eye *n* **target**, center, mark, middle, middle point

bully *n* **tormentor**, aggressor, persecutor, tyrant, oppressor ■ *v* **intimidate**, terrorize, persecute, torment, frighten

bullyboy *n* **thug**, bully, hooligan (*infml*), heavy (*slang*) ■ *adj* **aggressive**, intimidating, bullying, rough, threatening

bullying *n* **intimidation**, mistreatment, oppression, harassment, victimization

bulwark *n* **1 fortification**, embankment, earthwork, barricade, rampart **2 safeguard**, protection, defense, buttress, buffer

bumble *v* **1 mumble**, murmur, hesitate, mutter, stutter **2 stumble**, lumber, blunder, stagger, lurch

bumbling (*infml*) *adj* **awkward**, clumsy, blundering, lumbering, ungainly *Opposite*: graceful

bump *v* **1 hit**, knock, bang, strike, wallop (*infml*) **2 jolt**, bounce, jounce, jar, jerk **3 collide**, slam into, crash into, knock, smash into ■ *n* **1 knock**, collision, smash, accident, crash **2 swelling**, lump, bruise, bulge, contusion (*fml*) **3 thud**, thump, bang, crash, blow

bumper *adj* **plentiful**, profuse, copious, extralarge, jumbo *Opposite*: meager

bumpiness *n* **unevenness**, roughness, lumpiness *Opposite*: smoothness

bump into *v* **1 collide**, slam into, crash into, knock into, smash into **2 meet by chance**, run into, happen upon, happen on, meet

bumptious *adj* **full of yourself**, pleased with yourself, self-satisfied, self-important, smug *Opposite*: modest

bumptiousness *n* **self-importance**, conceitedness, arrogance, pompousness, brashness *Opposite*: modesty

bump up (*infml*) *v* **increase**, put up, boost, enhance, add to *Opposite*: decrease

bumpy *adj* **1 uneven**, rough, rutted, potholed *Opposite*: smooth **2 uncomfortable**, rough, bouncy, jarring, jerky *Opposite*: smooth

bunch *n* **1 group**, set, lot, mixture, collection **2 bouquet**, posy, spray, corsage **3** (*infml*) **gang**, gathering, team, set, group ■ *v* **crowd together**, huddle, form a group, gather, cluster *Opposite*: disperse

bundle *n* **package**, pack, parcel, packet, bale ■ *v* (*infml*) **hustle**, hurry, rush, push, shove

bundle up *v* **1 package**, pack, wrap, parcel, tie up **2** (*infml*) **dress warmly**, wrap up, wrap up warmly

bung *n* **stopper**, plug, cork

bungle *(infml)* v **do badly**, make a mess of, mismanage, ruin, spoil *Opposite*: succeed

bungler *(infml)* n **blunderer**, incompetent, bumbler, botcher, muddler

bungling *(infml)* adj **clumsy**, unskillful, incompetent, inept, blundering *Opposite*: competent

bunion n **swelling**, lump, enlargement, distension, bulge

bunk n **bed**, single bed, berth, couchette, bunk bed

bunker n 1 **underground shelter**, shelter, dugout, foxhole, ditch 2 **bin**, chest, container, box, store

bunkum *(infml)* n **nonsense**, humbug, drivel, gibberish, garbage

bunting n **streamers**, decorations, flags, paper chains, ticker tape

buoy n **marker**, float, navigational aid ■ v **keep afloat**, hold up, sustain, maintain, prop up

buoyancy n 1 **lightness**, weightlessness *Opposite*: heaviness 2 **resilience**, resistance, flexibility, toughness 3 **optimism**, cheerfulness, good spirits, enthusiasm, jauntiness *Opposite*: pessimism

buoyant adj 1 **floating**, afloat, light 2 **cheerful**, optimistic, happy, jaunty, carefree *Opposite*: morose 3 **resilient**, resistant, flexible, tough

buoy up v **cheer**, uplift, encourage, boost, lift *Opposite*: depress

bur n **seed husk**, husk, seedpod, pod, pericarp

burble v 1 **bubble**, ripple, babble, splash, murmur 2 *(infml)* **gush**, babble, ramble, go on about, blather

burden n 1 **load**, weight, cargo 2 **problem**, drain, encumbrance, affliction, liability 3 *(literary)* **theme**, topic, subject, subject matter ■ v **weigh down**, saddle, encumber, trouble, yoke. *See* COMPARE AND CONTRAST *at* **subject**.

burdened adj **loaded**, fraught, weighed down, laden, held back

burdensome adj **onerous**, heavy, taxing, troublesome, arduous

bureau n 1 **government department**, agency, office, department, unit 2 **chest of drawers**, dresser, chest 3 **writing desk**, desk, writing table, escritoire

bureaucracy n 1 **system of government**, government, administration, civil service, establishment 2 **official procedure**, rules and regulations, formalities, paperwork, red tape *(infml)*

bureaucrat n **official**, public servant, civil servant, administrator, office holder

bureaucratic adj 1 **administrative**, official, governmental, civil service, organizational 2 **rigid**, inflexible, unbending, officious, involved

burgeon *(literary)* v 1 **mushroom**, multiply, prosper, proliferate, flourish *Opposite*: dwindle 2 **bud**, bloom, blossom, flower

burgeoning adj 1 **growing**, mushrooming, increasing, escalating, expanding *Opposite*: dwindling 2 **budding**, promising, up-and-coming, nascent *Opposite*: fading

burgher n **citizen**, resident, inhabitant, denizen, voter

burglar n **thief**, robber, intruder, cat burglar, housebreaker

burglarize v **rob**, steal, break into, break and enter, raid

burglary n 1 **break-in**, theft, robbery, crime, housebreak 2 **breaking and entering**, theft, robbery, aggravated burglary, stealing

burgle v **rob**, thieve, break in, burglarize, loot

burial n **interment**, committal, entombment, funeral

burial chamber n **sepulcher**, tomb, mausoleum, vault, crypt

burial ground n **cemetery**, graveyard, churchyard, necropolis, memorial park

burial place n **last resting place**, grave, tomb, crypt, mausoleum

buried adj 1 **underground**, concealed, hidden, covered, dug in *Opposite*: dug up 2 **suppressed**, hidden, covered up, repressed, forgotten *Opposite*: exposed

burlesque n 1 **parody**, caricature, travesty, lampoon, skit 2 **variety show**, vaudeville, revue, extravaganza, spectacular ■ v **spoof**, mock, make fun of, lampoon, caricature

burliness n **brawniness**, heftiness, broad shoulders, muscularity, robustness *Opposite*: slimness

burly adj **brawny**, hefty, broad-shouldered, husky, muscular *Opposite*: slim

burn v 1 **blaze**, be ablaze, flame, smolder, glow 2 **burn up**, burn down, gut, reduce to ashes, burn to a crisp 3 **scorch**, singe, sear, char, scald 4 **tingle**, sting, hurt, prickle, be on fire 5 **go red**, flush, blush, redden, color 6 **corrode**, eat away, eat into 7 **glow**, shine, twinkle, flare, glimmer 8 **use up**, use, expend, consume ■ n **injury**, blister, scald, scorch

burn down v **incinerate**, go up in flames, burn to the ground, burn to a crisp, reduce to ashes

burned-out adj 1 **exhausted**, worn out, tired out, drained, unwell 2 **gutted**, destroyed, reduced to ashes, incinerated, burned down

burner n **gas ring**, ring, heat, flame, gas jet

burning adj 1 **red-hot**, piping hot, boiling hot, fiery hot, sweltering *Opposite*: cold 2 **on fire**, ablaze, blazing, flaming, smoldering *Opposite*: extinguished 3 **strong**, ardent, fervent, all-consuming, passionate *Opposite*: weak 4 **important**, vital, crucial, urgent, significant *Opposite*: insignificant 5 **smarting**, stinging, tingly, prickly, painful 6 **feverish**, febrile, flushed, hot, red *Opposite*: cool

burnish v polish, shine, buff, rub, clean

burn out (infml) v **exhaust**, break down, wear out, tire, fatigue

burnout n **exhaustion**, stress, tension, weariness, poor health

burn the candle at both ends v **overdo things**, wear yourself out, do too much, exhaust yourself, burn the midnight oil

burn the midnight oil v **work late**, stay up, work day and night, work overtime, burn the candle at both ends Opposite: slack

burn up v **1 incinerate**, burn, burn down, reduce to ashes, burn to a crisp **2** (infml) **annoy**, irritate, vex, anger, obsess Opposite: please

burn your bridges v **pass the point of no return**, cross the Rubicon, nail your colors to the mast

burr n **accent**, twang, drawl, brogue, intonation

burrow n **hole**, warren, den, lair, hideaway ■ v **1 dig**, tunnel, excavate, channel, dig out **2 search**, dig, investigate, delve, scrabble **3 nestle**, snuggle, cuddle, nuzzle, cozy up

bursary n **scholarship**, grant, award, fund

burst v **1 rupture**, split open, disintegrate, break open, fracture **2 erupt**, spout, gush, rush, break out Opposite: trickle ■ n **spurt**, eruption, gust, torrent, rupture Opposite: trickle

bursting adj **overflowing**, teeming, full to bursting, packed Opposite: empty

bursting at the seams see **bursting**

burst in on v **1 interrupt**, intrude upon, intrude on, come upon, disturb **2 surprise**, take by surprise, catch unawares, take unawares, catch in the act

burst into tears v **break down**, dissolve in tears, break down and cry, burst out crying, lose control Opposite: laugh

burst out v **1 start**, begin, commence, burst into, break into **2 exclaim**, shout, cry, call out, say Opposite: whisper

bury v **1 inter**, put in the ground, lay to rest, entomb, put six feet under Opposite: exhume **2 hide**, conceal, cover, put out of sight, submerge Opposite: expose

bury the hatchet v **make up**, make peace, be reconciled, kiss and make up, resolve differences Opposite: fight

bus v **transport**, carry, take, convey, move

bush n **1 shrub**, plant, flowering shrub **2 scrubland**, wilds, outback, savanna, scrub

bushed (infml) adj **exhausted**, tired, worn-out, dead on your feet, all in Opposite: refreshed

bushes n **undergrowth**, scrub, underbrush, shrubbery, greenery

bushwhack (infml) v **ambush**, lie in wait for, hold up, surprise, attack

bushy adj **luxuriant**, abundant, profuse, shaggy, thick Opposite: sparse

busily adv **actively**, energetically, briskly, industriously, vigorously Opposite: lazily

business n **1 commerce**, trade, industry, selling, production **2 company**, corporation, conglomerate, establishment, partnership **3 custom**, trade, dealings, transactions, sales **4 concern**, affair, problem, responsibility, interest **5 matter**, affair, issue, situation, event ■ adj **commercial**, occupational, corporate, professional Opposite: private

businesslike adj **1 efficient**, practical, professional, competent, systematic Opposite: unprofessional **2 unemotional**, objective, professional, detached, uninvolved Opposite: emotional

businessperson n **business executive**, executive, executive director, director, manager

bust n **sculpture**, torso, statue, figure, model ■ v (infml) **break**, smash, shatter, burst, fracture Opposite: mend

busted (infml) adj **broken**, out of action, out of order, not working, smashed Opposite: fixed

bustle v **busy yourself**, be on the go, be busy, hurry, rush around ■ n **activity**, movement, stir, hustle and bustle, commotion Opposite: calm

bustling adj **busy**, active, full of go, full of life, hurried Opposite: still

busy adj **1 active**, on the go, hard-working, hard at it, diligent Opposite: idle **2 full**, full of activity, demanding, hard, tiring Opposite: empty **3 engaged**, occupied, unavailable, taken Opposite: free

busybody (infml) n **interferer**, meddler, nuisance, gossip, scandalmonger

but prep **1 however**, although, nevertheless, on the contrary **2 other than**, except, excluding, bar, save for ■ n (infml) **objection**, proviso, provision, rider, condition

butch adj **masculine**, tough, strong, muscular, beefy

butcher n **killer**, murderer, slaughterer, exterminator, slayer (fml or literary) ■ v **1 slaughter**, murder, kill, exterminate, massacre **2** (infml) **make a mess of**, ruin, spoil, botch (infml), make a hash of (infml)

butchery n **slaughter**, carnage, bloodshed, killing

butt v **ram**, hit, bump, strike, run into ■ n **1 object**, target, victim, scapegoat, stooge **2 handle**, stock, grip **3 end**, stub, stump, base, nub end **4 barrel**, tub, drum, cask, container

butte n **hill**, foothill, rise, mount, bluff

butterflies (infml) n **nervousness**, excitement, anxiety, tenseness, apprehension Opposite: confidence

butter up (infml) v **flatter**, curry favor, get on the right side of, sweet-talk (infml), suck up to (infml) Opposite: insult

butt in v **1 interrupt**, break in, cut in, interfere,

interject *Opposite*: mind your own business **2 jump the line**, squeeze in, barge in, shove in, skip the line

button n **1 push button**, switch, knob, key **2 badge**, pin, brooch ■ v **fasten**, do up, close *Opposite*: undo

buttoned-down (*infml*) *adj* **conservative**, traditional, stuffy, formal, strait-laced *Opposite*: easygoing

buttonhole (*infml*) v **accost**, waylay, corner, grab, confront

button up (*infml*) v **be quiet**, keep quiet, be silent, say nothing, stop talking *Opposite*: blather (*infml*)

buttress n **support**, prop, reinforcement, flying buttress, structure ■ v **strengthen**, support, prop, prop up, reinforce

buxom *adj* **plump**, rounded, ample, curvaceous, curvy

buy v **1 pay for**, purchase, acquire, procure, obtain *Opposite*: sell **2** (*infml*) **accept**, believe, fall for, credit, subscribe to *Opposite*: disbelieve ■ n **purchase**, acquisition, bargain, deal

buyer n **purchaser**, consumer, shopper, bargain hunter, customer *Opposite*: seller

buy off v **bribe**, induce, corrupt, suborn, pay off (*infml*)

buy out v **acquire**, take over, purchase, take control of

buyout n **takeover**, merger, acquisition, purchase

buzz n **1** (*infml*) **telephone call**, call, phone call, ring **2** (*infml*) **thrill**, high, kick, lift, jolt *Opposite*: downer (*infml*) **3** (*infml*) **gossip**, talk, word, rumor, whisper ■ v **hum**, drone, murmur, whine, whir

buzzer n **signal**, bell, beeper (*infml*)

buzzing *adj* **busy**, bustling, vibrant, full of life, lively *Opposite*: still

buzzword (*infml*) n **slogan**, catchword, saying, byword, catch phrase

by *prep* **1 through**, via, in, by means of, as a result of **2 with**, near, next to, beside **3 not later than**, before, sooner than

by accident *see* **by chance**

by and by (*literary*) *adv* **before long**, eventually, in a short time, in time, in a while *Opposite*: immediately

by and large *adv* **generally**, as a rule, normally, usually, in general *Opposite*: specifically

by chance *adv* **accidentally**, by accident, unintentionally, inadvertently, coincidentally *Opposite*: on purpose

by degrees *adv* **little by little**, bit by bit, gradually, slowly, a little at a time *Opposite*: at once

by design *adv* **intentionally**, knowingly, on purpose, purposely, deliberately *Opposite*: by coincidence

bygone *adj* **past**, former, previous, longgone, departed (*literary*) *Opposite*: future

by itself *adv* **of its own accord**, automatically, independently, without help

bylaw n **regulation**, rule, ruling, statute, guideline

byline n **acknowledgement**, credit, heading

by means of *adv* **by**, through, via, using, by way of

by mistake *adv* **accidentally**, mistakenly, inadvertently, wrongly, incorrectly *Opposite*: on purpose

by nature *adv* **characteristically**, naturally, innately, instinctively, normally

bypass v **go around**, avoid, get around, find a way around, sidestep

byproduct n **side effect**, spinoff, consequence, result, derivative

bystander n **onlooker**, passer-by, witness, eyewitness, spectator *Opposite*: participant

byword n **1 embodiment**, perfect example, epitome, shining example **2 catch phrase**, proverb, axiom, slogan, saying

byzantine *adj* **1 complex**, intricate, tortuous, convoluted, complicated *Opposite*: straightforward **2 devious**, scheming, underhand, deceitful, secretive *Opposite*: honest

C

cab n **1 taxi**, taxicab, yellow cab, hack **2 cabin**, compartment, cockpit

cabal n **1 faction**, section, unit, group, sect **2 plot**, scheme, conspiracy, connivance, collusion

cabana n **bathhouse**, shelter, change room

cabaret n **1 show**, floor show, live entertainment, burlesque **2 nightclub**, club, bar, nightspot

caber n **log**, beam, pole, stick

cabin n **1 lodge**, log cabin, cottage, bungalow, chalet **2 compartment**, cubicle, stateroom, room, berth

caboodle (*infml*) n **lot**, whole lot, entirety, totality, integrality

caboose n **car**, carriage, wagon

cache n **hoard**, store, accumulation, reserve,

collection ■ *v* **hide**, hoard, store, secrete, reserve *Opposite*: discard

cachet *n* **status**, prestige, distinction, respect, reputation

cackle *v* **laugh**, hoot, screech, crow, guffaw

cacophonous *adj* **discordant**, unmusical, unmelodious, dissonant, inharmonious *Opposite*: melodious

cacophony *n* **discord**, discordance, dissonance, disharmony, unmusicality *Opposite*: melodiousness

cad *(dated)* *n* **rogue**, scoundrel, rake, rascal, blackguard *Opposite*: gentleman

CAD *n* **computer-aided design**, computer graphics, graphics, product design, drafting

cadaver *n* **corpse**, dead body, remains, body

cadaverous *adj* **1 bony**, skeletal, emaciated, wasted, gaunt *Opposite*: healthy **2** *(literary)* **pale**, pallid, wan, ashen, sallow *Opposite*: rosy **3** *(fml or literary)* **corpse-like**, deathly, deathlike, skeletal, spectral

caddie *n* **assistant**, porter, carrier, transporter ■ *v* **transport**, assist, carry

caddish *(dated)* *adj* **dishonorable**, ungallant, rascally, rakish, ungentlemanly *Opposite*: gallant

caddy *n* **container**, tin, box, receptacle, carton

cadence *n* **1 tempo**, rhythm, pace, pulse, stroke **2 lilt**, intonation, accent, modulation, inflection

cadenza *n* **solo passage**, improvisation, solo, unaccompanied passage, showpiece

cadet *n* **trainee**, plebe, police cadet, army cadet

cadre *n* **1 squad**, corps, unit, team, band **2 faction**, group, core, hard core, band

cage *n* **enclosure**, coop, pen, birdcage, crate ■ *v* **confine**, enclose, pen, coop up, impound *Opposite*: release

WORD BANK

❏ **types of pens or cages** apiary, aquarium, aviary, beehive, birdcage, chicken coop, coop, corral, cowshed, doghouse, dovecote, henhouse, hutch, kennel, piggery, pig pen, pound, stable, stall, sty

caged *adj* **captive**, detained, confined, imprisoned, jailed *Opposite*: free

cagey *(infml)* *adj* **wary**, guarded, cautious, careful, reticent *Opposite*: reckless

caginess *(infml)* *n* **wariness**, caution, reticence, evasiveness, chariness *Opposite*: carelessness

cairn *n* **1 landmark**, marker, signpost, direction post, milestone **2 memorial**, monument, barrow, tomb, tombstone

cajole *v* **coax**, persuade, wheedle, entice, inveigle *Opposite*: compel

cake *n* **1 gateau**, pastry, fancy **2 bar**, block, slab, lump, tablet ■ *v* **cover**, coat, encrust, congeal, coagulate

WORD BANK

❏ **types of cakes** angel food cake, birthday cake, Black Forest cake, brownie, carrot cake, cheesecake, coffeecake, cruller, cupcake, Danish pastry, devil's food cake, doughnut, éclair, flapjack, fruitcake, gateau, gingerbread, jelly roll, key lime pie, macaroon, Madeira cake, madeleine, mince pie, muffin, pain au chocolat, petit four, seedcake, sponge cake, strudel, torte, turnover, wedding cake

caked *adj* **covered**, coated, encrusted, layered

calamitous *adj* **disastrous**, dreadful, catastrophic, ruinous, tragic *Opposite*: beneficial

calamity *n* **disaster**, catastrophe, mishap, misfortune, tragedy

calcify *v* **harden**, set, solidify, fossilize, turn into stone *Opposite*: soften

calculable *adj* **1 quantifiable**, countable, finite, assessable, measurable *Opposite*: incalculable **2 predictable**, anticipated, expected, foreseeable, likely *Opposite*: unpredictable

calculate *v* **work out**, compute, estimate, gauge, determine

calculated *adj* **intended**, designed, planned, considered, premeditated *Opposite*: spontaneous

calculating *adj* **scheming**, manipulative, devious, shrewd, conniving *Opposite*: candid

calculation *n* **1 computation**, estimate, reckoning, sum, result **2 control**, cunning, scheming, intention, design *Opposite*: candidness

caldron *n* **pan**, container, cooking pot, pot, vat

calendar *n* **datebook**, appointment book, schedule, year planner, timetable

caliber *n* **1 ability**, quality, capacity, talent, competence **2 size**, bore, diameter, gauge, measure

calibrate *v* **standardize**, adjust, regulate, tune, bring into line

calibration *n* **1 standardization**, correction, adjustment, tuning, setting **2 graduation**, gradation, mark, measurement, degree

calisthenics *n* **exercises**, aerobics, isometrics, training, work out

call *v* **1 shout**, cry out, scream, yell, call out **2 request**, summon, call on, invite, beckon **3 phone**, telephone, give a call, call up, call in **4 name**, describe, identify, entitle, label **5 visit**, call on, pay a visit, drop in, stop off **6 arrange**, convene, set up, organize, assemble ■ *n* **1 noise**, shout, cry, sound **2 song**, cry, birdsong **3 phone call**, telephone call, buzz *(infml)* **4 visit**, stop, halt **5 demand**, request, plea, appeal, bid **6 judgment**, verdict, decision, assessment, ruling

call a halt *v* **end**, stop, halt, bring to an end, close *Opposite*: start up

call a spade a spade v be direct, speak plainly, be blunt, speak your mind, lay it on the line (infml) Opposite: prevaricate

call attention to v make known, draw attention to, expose, publicize, highlight Opposite: conceal

call by v visit, stop by, come around, drop in, call in

call down v 1 invoke, invite, request, appeal, pray 2 **reprimand**, rebuke, reproach, admonish, scold Opposite: praise

caller n visitor, guest, friend

call for v 1 order, demand, claim, clamor, request 2 **need**, require, justify, necessitate, cry out for

call forth v produce, cause, inspire, provoke, stimulate

calligraphy n handwriting, hand, writing, script, print

call in v 1 recall, call back, pull in, take off the market 2 **summon**, invite in, call for, send for, bring in 3 **phone**, call, telephone, give a call, call up

calling n vocation, profession, occupation, business, line

call into question v query, question, dispute, challenge, doubt Opposite: accept

call it a day v stop, finish, end, give up, break off Opposite: start up

call names v insult, abuse, hurl insults at, taunt, bait Opposite: compliment

call off v cancel, stop, abandon, suspend, shelve

call on v 1 ask, request, appeal to, urge, entreat 2 **visit**, drop in on, go to see, look up, look in on

callous adj heartless, unfeeling, cold-hearted, hardhearted, uncaring Opposite: warm-hearted

calloused adj hard, hardened, hard-skinned, rough, rough-skinned Opposite: soft

callousness n heartlessness, insensitivity, cruelty, coldness, cold-heartedness Opposite: warm-heartedness

call out v 1 summon, send for, call for, get, page 2 **shout out**, exclaim, call, yell, make a noise

call out for v demand, clamor, be in dire need of, require, request

callow adj inexperienced, immature, naive, adolescent, green Opposite: mature

call together v summon, convene, gather, collect, round up Opposite: disperse

call to mind v evoke, recall, recollect, suggest, call up Opposite: forget

call up v phone, call, telephone, give a call

call upon v 1 ask, request, appeal to, urge, entreat 2 **make demands on**, demand, require, use, call for

callus n hard skin, corn, bump, lump, nodule

calm adj tranquil, peaceful, still, cool, composed Opposite: agitated ■ n **peace**, tranquillity, quietness, stillness, calmness Opposite: turbulence ■ v **pacify**, calm down, quiet, quiet down, soothe Opposite: excite

calmative adj calming, tranquilizing, soothing, pacifying, relaxing Opposite: disturbing

calm down v settle down, relax, soothe, quiet down, quiet Opposite: agitate

calming adj soothing, reassuring, comforting, restful, sedative Opposite: disturbing

calmness n serenity, tranquillity, quietness, stillness, peace Opposite: restlessness

calumny (fml) n slander, defamation, denigration, libel, lies

calve v give birth, drop, reproduce, produce

camaraderie n friendship, companionship, solidarity, company, comradeship Opposite: enmity

camelback adj arched, humped, curved, rounded Opposite: flat

cameo n character part, cameo role, appearance, role, part

camera-shy adj reclusive, retiring, reserved, private, aloof Opposite: extrovert

camouflage n concealment, disguise, smoke screen, cover-up, façade ■ v **disguise**, mask, hide, conceal, obscure

camp n 1 site, campground, encampment, base camp 2 **group**, faction, followers, clique, supporters ■ v **go camping**, camp out, sleep out

campaign n movement, crusade, operation, drive, fight ■ v 1 **fight**, work, push, struggle, battle 2 **electioneer**, canvass, drum up support, solicit votes, stump

campaigner n activist, crusader, fighter, supporter, champion

campsite n area, pitch, site, place

campus n grounds, precincts, site, property, estate

canal n 1 waterway, channel, seaway 2 **duct**, tube, passage, vessel

canalize (fml) v direct, channel, funnel, guide, convey Opposite: diffuse

cancel v 1 call off, stop, abandon, withdraw, scratch Opposite: arrange 2 **annul**, revoke, stop, rescind, repeal Opposite: reinstate

cancel out v nullify, efface, undo, contradict, neutralize

cancer n 1 growth, tumor, malignancy, disease, melanoma 2 **evil**, blight, scourge, canker, plague

cancerous adj 1 tumorous, malignant, carcinomatous, carcinogenic, oncogenic Opposite: benign 2 **harmful**, pernicious, malign, malignant, noxious Opposite: beneficent

candelabrum n candleholder, candlestick, chandelier, lamp holder, lamp

candid *adj* honest, frank, open, truthful, sincere *Opposite*: guarded

candidacy *n* application, contention, entry, submission, candidature

candidate *n* applicant, contender, entrant, runner, aspirant

COMPARE AND CONTRAST CORE MEANING: somebody who is seeking to be chosen for something or to win something
candidate somebody who is being considered for a job, grant, or prize, standing for election, or taking part in an examination; **contender** a competitor, especially somebody who has a good chance of winning; **contestant** somebody who takes part in a contest or competitive event; **aspirant** somebody aspiring to distinction or advancement; **applicant** somebody who has formally applied to be a candidate for something; **entrant** somebody who enters a competition or examination.

candidness *n* honesty, frankness, openness, truthfulness, bluntness

candied *adj* crystallized, glacé, preserved, sugar-coated, sugared

candle *n* taper, nightlight, rush light, rush candle, rush

candlelight *n* dim light, soft light, low light, glow, glimmer

candlestick *n* candleholder, candelabrum, chandelier, sconce

can-do *(infml) adj* positive, willing, confident, ambitious, eager *Opposite*: diffident

candor *n* frankness, forthrightness, directness, candidness, outspokenness

cane *n* 1 bamboo, wicker, rattan 2 stick, walking stick, staff ■ *v* beat, thrash, strike, hit, punish

canine *adj* doggy, dog-like, doggish ■ *n* dog, mongrel, cur, hound, pooch *(infml)*

WORD BANK
❏ **types of canines** coyote, dingo, dog, fox, jackal, wolf

canister *n* container, can, tin, flask, cylinder

canker *n* evil, cancer, scourge, blight, plague

canned *adj* 1 preserved, conserved *Opposite*: fresh 2 prerecorded, recorded, taped, reproduced, artificial *Opposite*: live

canniness *n* shrewdness, astuteness, sharpness, smartness, cleverness

cannonade *n* barrage, bombardment, hail, onslaught, pounding

cannonball *n* projectile, missile, ball, stone, grapeshot

canny *adj* shrewd, astute, sharp, smart, clever

canonical *adj* official, recognized, acknowledged, established, undisputed *Opposite*: apocryphal

canonization *n* 1 making into a saint, beatification, sanctification, consecration, hallowing 2 idolization, glorification, adoration, worship, adulation

canonize *v* 1 make into a saint, beatify, sanctify, consecrate, hallow 2 idolize, glorify, adore, worship, venerate

canoodle *(infml) v* carry on, kiss and cuddle, pet, smooch *(infml)*, neck *(infml)*

canopy *n* 1 awning, cover, covering, shelter, blind 2 top, crown, roof, covering, cover

cant *n* 1 clichés, platitudes, banalities, commonplaces, triteness 2 hypocrisy, insincerity, false piety, humbug, lip service *Opposite*: sincerity 3 jargon, slang, argot, patois, vernacular

cantankerous *adj* grumpy, irascible, irritable, crusty, quarrelsome

canter *n* trot, run, gallop, jog, sprint ■ *v* run, gallop, trot, jog, sprint

cantilever *n* beam, plank, girder

canto *n* stanza, verse, strophe, section, division

canton *n* region, district, area, borough, constituency

canvas *n* 1 painting, oil painting, picture, old master, work of art 2 background, backdrop, setting, context, scene

canvass *v* 1 campaign, electioneer, drum up support, solicit votes, stump 2 test, research, investigate, survey, poll

canvasser *n* 1 campaigner, supporter, party worker 2 researcher, investigator, examiner, pollster

canyon *n* ravine, gully, gorge, chasm, gulch

cap *n* 1 cover, lid, top, stopper, plug 2 restraint, limit, control, restriction, check ■ *v* 1 cover, top, stop, plug, stopper 2 surpass, top, improve, better, outdo 3 limit, regulate, control, restrain, restrict

capability *n* ability, capacity, competence, skill, resources. *See* COMPARE AND CONTRAST *at* ability.

capable *adj* 1 accomplished, talented, skilled, gifted, clever *Opposite*: inept 2 able, competent, proficient, efficient, qualified *Opposite*: incapable

capacious *adj* roomy, spacious, large, ample, big *Opposite*: cramped

capacity *n* 1 ability, capability, skill, talent, aptitude 2 volume, space, room, size, dimensions 3 role, position, responsibility, function, office. *See* COMPARE AND CONTRAST *at* ability.

cape *n* promontory, peninsula, headland, outcrop, point

caper *n* escapade, adventure, jaunt, lark, antics ■ *v* frolic, cavort, jump, leap, dance

capital *n* 1 assets, resources, funds, wealth, money 2 center, headquarters, hub

capitalist *n* entrepreneur, financier, industrialist, businessperson, investor ■ *adj* entrepreneurial, industrial, consumerist, consumer, commercial

capitalize v fund, finance, raise funding for, provide backing for

capitalize on v make the most of, maximize, take advantage of, use, utilize

capitation n 1 tax, poll tax, levy, toll, duty 2 fee, charge, payment, amount

capitulate v surrender, submit, yield, succumb, give way Opposite: resist. See COMPARE AND CONTRAST at yield.

capitulation n surrender, submission, defeat, retreat Opposite: resistance

caprice n whim, impulse, quirk, fancy, fad

capricious adj unpredictable, changeable, variable, impulsive, whimsical Opposite: predictable

capsize v overturn, turn over, roll over, keel over, turn turtle Opposite: right

capsule n 1 pill, tablet, lozenge 2 pod, container, case, casing, shell

captain n head, skipper, leader, chief, boss ■ v lead, skipper, manage, take charge, head

caption n slogan, subtitle, title, description, legend

captious adj 1 critical, pedantic, trivial, petty, nitpicking 2 confusing, misleading, devious, bewildering, disingenuous Opposite: clear

captivate v attract, charm, enchant, fascinate, entrance Opposite: repel

captivated adj enchanted, fascinated, charmed, entranced, spellbound Opposite: repulsed

captivating adj charming, attractive, appealing, fascinating, charismatic

captive n prisoner, detainee, internee, prisoner of war, hostage Opposite: escapee ■ adj 1 imprisoned, in prison, locked up, enslaved, confined Opposite: free 2 attentive, intent, fascinated, spellbound, rapt

captivity n imprisonment, custody, detention, confinement, internment Opposite: freedom

captor n abductor, imprisoner, kidnapper, hostage taker, jailer Opposite: liberator

capture v 1 take, seize, apprehend, arrest, pick up Opposite: release 2 imprison, detain, arrest, confine, take into custody Opposite: liberate 3 encapsulate, summarize, sum up, portray, describe 4 secure, attain, gain, acquire, obtain Opposite: lose 5 catch, seize, grab hold of, trap, ensnare ■ n imprisonment, detention, arrest, seizure, apprehension Opposite: release

capture your imagination v fascinate, excite, inspire, interest, enchant

car n cabin, carriage, coach, compartment, wagon

WORD BANK

❏ **types of cars** all-terrain vehicle, compact, convertible, coupe, dragster, four-by-four, hatchback, hot rod (slang), limo, limousine, minivan, off-roader (infml), racing car, roadster (dated), runabout, sedan, sports car, sport utility vehicle, station wagon, stock car, stretch limo, subcompact, SUV, three-wheeler, van

carafe n flask, decanter, bottle

caramelize v burn, heat, scorch, brown, broil

carapace n case, shell, covering, sheath, outside

caravan n convoy, group, procession, parade, motorcade

carbohydrate n biological compound, simple carbohydrate, complex carbohydrate, starch, sugar

carbon copy n replica, duplicate, copy, facsimile, exact likeness Opposite: original

carbuncle n blemish, boil, pustule, abscess, sore

carcass n corpse, remains, cadaver, body, skeleton

carcinogenic adj cancer-causing, oncogenic, hazardous, toxic, poisonous

card n 1 greeting card, birthday card, anniversary card, postcard, picture postcard 2 pass, identification card, membership card, business card, calling card

cardboard n board, paper, card, packaging, packing ■ adj insubstantial, unconvincing, phoney, plastic, wooden Opposite: substantial

card-carrying adj official, paid-up, bona fide, listed, genuine

cardinal adj basic, fundamental, key, prime, serious Opposite: secondary

cardiovascular adj circulatory, cardiac, vascular, heart, blood

cardsharp n cheat, gambler, hustler, swindler, pro (infml)

care v be concerned, be interested, feel a concern, take an interest Opposite: disregard ■ n 1 upkeep, maintenance, repair, overhaul Opposite: neglect 2 attention, caution, precaution, carefulness, watchfulness 3 worry, concern, anxiety, trouble, unease Opposite: nonchalance 4 treatment, provision, support, attention Opposite: illtreatment 5 supervision, guardianship, protection, custody, oversight (fml). See COMPARE AND CONTRAST at worry.

careen v swerve, sway, weave, lurch, swing

career n vocation, job, occupation, profession, calling ■ v rush, race, hurry, dash, speed

careerism n determination, single-mindedness, motivation, commitment, drive

careerist n professional, achiever, high flier, go-getter (infml) ■ adj single-minded, determined, motivated, focused, professional

care for v 1 like, feel affection for, love, have a soft spot for, cherish Opposite: dislike 2 look after, take care of, tend, supervise, oversee Opposite: ignore 3 (fml) want, desire, wish for, like to have, appreciate

carefree *adj* **untroubled**, happy-go-lucky, cheery, relaxed, cheerful *Opposite*: troubled

carefreeness *n* **lightheartedness**, cheerfulness, cheeriness, happiness, jollity *Opposite*: anxiety

careful *adj* **1 cautious**, wary, vigilant, watchful, alert *Opposite*: reckless **2 thorough**, meticulous, painstaking, particular, conscientious *Opposite*: careless **3 prudent**, sensible, judicious, cautious, well thought-out *Opposite*: foolish **4 protective**, sympathetic, sensitive, gentle, tender *Opposite*: rough

COMPARE AND CONTRAST CORE MEANING: exercising care and attention in doing something **careful** a wide-ranging term, suggesting attention to detail and implying cautiousness in avoiding errors or inaccuracies; **conscientious** showing great care, attention, and industriousness in carrying out a task; **scrupulous** having or showing careful regard for what is morally right; **thorough** extremely careful and accurate; **meticulous** extremely careful and precise; **painstaking** involving or showing great care and attention to detail; **assiduous** undevating in effort and care; **punctilious** very careful about the conventions of correct behavior and etiquette; **finicky** concentrating too much on unimportant details; **fussy** tending to worry over details or trivial things.

carefulness *n* **1 caution**, care, wariness, watchfulness, alertness *Opposite*: rashness **2 attention to detail**, thoroughness, precision, care, meticulousness *Opposite*: carelessness

careless *adj* **1 slapdash**, happy-go-lucky, devil-may-care, casual, slipshod *Opposite*: careful **2 uncaring**, thoughtless, offhand, inconsiderate, unthinking *Opposite*: considerate

carelessness *n* **sloppiness**, inattentiveness, inaccuracy, imprecision, negligence *Opposite*: care

caress *v* **stroke**, touch, pat, embrace, cuddle ■ *n* **touch**, stroke, pat, embrace, hug

caretaker *n* **caregiver**, attendant, nurse

careworn *adj* **haggard**, drawn, beleaguered, worried, burdened *Opposite*: carefree

cargo *n* **load**, freight, consignment, shipment, goods

caricature *n* **1 cartoon**, picture, drawing, sketch **2 travesty**, misrepresentation, false impression, distortion, falsification

caricaturist *n* **artist**, cartoonist, humorist, satirist

caring *adj* **kind**, thoughtful, gentle, helpful, considerate *Opposite*: uncaring

carnage *n* **killing**, bloodshed, slaughter, massacre, bloodbath

carnal *(fml) adj* **physical**, fleshy, sensual, sexual *Opposite*: spiritual

carnival *n* **1 festival**, celebration, street party, fair, fete **2 fair**, fairground, sideshow, midway, amusement park

carnivore *n* **flesh-eater**, meat-eater, predator, scavenger, insectivore

carnivorous *adj* **flesh-eating**, meat-eating, predatory, scavenging, insectivorous

carol *n* **song**, hymn, chant, chorus

carousal *(literary) n* **party**, celebration, binge, spree, bender *(infml)*

carouse *(literary) v* **revel**, celebrate, drink, get drunk, raise the roof

carousel *n* **container**, cassette, cartridge, drum, magazine

carousing *(literary) n* **festivities**, partying, revels, revelry celebrations

carp *v* **complain**, grumble, find fault, nag, go on. *See* COMPARE AND CONTRAST *at* **complain**.

carpentry *n* **joinery**, woodworking, turning, carving, cabinetmaking

carpet *n* **1 rug**, mat, runner, fitted carpet, carpet tiles **2 covering**, layer, blanket, mass, spread ■ *v* *(literary)* **cover**, swathe, coat, overlay, strew

carpeting *n* **floor covering**, flooring, matting

carping *adj* **critical**, nitpicking, complaining, dissatisfied, discontented ■ *n* **complaining**, nitpicking, faultfinding, dissatisfaction, whining

carport *n* **garage**, lean-to, shelter, porch, parking space

carriage *n* **1 horse-drawn carriage**, coach, horse and carriage **2** *(fml)* **bearing**, posture, deportment, air, presence **3 transportation**, delivery, carrying, haulage, conveyance

carried *adj* **approved**, accepted, passed, agreed, supported *Opposite*: rejected

carrier *n* **transporter**, hauler, delivery service, carter, shipper

carrion *n* **flesh**, meat, tissue

carrot *n* **incentive**, inducement, bribe, bait, lure

carroty *adj* **orange**, red, auburn, ginger

carry *v* **1 take**, bear, hold, support, clutch **2 transmit**, transport, convey, transfer, bring **3 contain**, include, involve, incorporate, hold **4 have in stock**, stock, store, keep, supply **5 approve**, accept, pass, agree, vote for

carrying *adj* **loud**, resonant, resounding, booming, ringing *Opposite*: quiet

carrying-on *(infml)* *n* **pranks**, goings-on *(infml)*, doings *(infml)*, high jinks *(infml)*

carry off *v* **1 take away**, take off, remove, steal, abduct *Opposite*: bring back **2 succeed**, manage, accomplish, achieve, do *Opposite*: fail

carry on *v* **1 continue**, keep, keep on, keep at, go on *Opposite*: stop **2 complain**, grumble, carp, nag, go on

carry out *v* **do**, perform, complete, achieve, succeed *Opposite*: neglect. *See* COMPARE AND CONTRAST *at* **accomplish**, **perform**.

carry over v postpone, defer, leave, reschedule, put back *Opposite*: expedite *(fml)*

carryover n leftover, legacy, inheritance, residue, remnant

carsick adj sick, nauseous, ill, unwell

cart n 1 **farm cart**, wagon, dray, tumbrel, wain *(literary)* 2 **handcart**, pushcart, barrow, wheelbarrow, trolley ■ v carry, lug, heave, haul, drag

carte blanche n free rein, blank check, complete freedom, full authority, complete discretion

cartel n interest group, lobby, alliance, association, union

cart off v remove, drag off, take away, haul off, carry off

carton n box, cardboard box, container, pack, sachet

cartoon n 1 animation, animated film, animated movie 2 drawing, caricature, picture, comic strip

cartoonist n artist, animator, caricaturist, satirist, humorist

cartridge n container, holder, casing, unit, cassette

cartwheel v turn, somersault, go head over heels, roll, flip

carve v 1 engrave, inscribe, etch, cut, notch 2 slice, pare, cut in slices, whittle, cut up

carve out v create, make, establish, build, set up

carve up *(infml)* v divide, allocate, share out, apportion, distribute

carve-up *(infml)* n division, allocation, distribution, partitioning, splitting up

carving n 1 model, statue, statuette, figure, figurine 2 cutting, engraving, etching, sculpting, fashioning

Casanova n libertine, Don Juan, gigolo, Romeo, ladies' man

cascade n waterfall, chute, cataract, falls, torrent ■ v flow, pour, fall, drop, gush

case n 1 circumstance, situation, instance, event, occasion 2 instance, item, example, illustration, paradigm 3 job, project, commission, assignment, task 4 court case, legal action, lawsuit, suit, indictment 5 argument, reason, defense, justification, rationale 6 container, holder, box, casing, cover 7 suitcase, overnight case, weekend case, briefcase, attaché case

casebook n record, log, diary, journal, notebook

casehardened adj unsympathetic, unfeeling, hard, hardened, toughened *Opposite*: sensitive

cash n money, hard cash, ready money, coins, currency

cashier n 1 treasurer, banker, bursar 2 bank clerk, clerk, teller, official, assistant ■ v dismiss, expel, drum out, court martial, boot out *(infml)*

cash in v redeem, trade in, sell, realize, bank

cash-in-hand adj in cash, cash, no questions asked, unofficially, off the record

cash in on v take advantage of, benefit from, do well from, exploit, make the most of

casing n covering, case, outside, exterior, skin

casino n gaming club, gambling den, nightclub, gaming house

cask n barrel, tub, drum, butt, vat

casket n coffin, sarcophagus, cist, box

casserole n cooking pot, deep dish, covered dish

cassette n 1 cartridge, tape, videotape 2 case, cartridge, holder, container, cover

cast v 1 throw, hurl, fling, toss, pitch 2 produce, generate, create, give rise to, engender 3 mold, form, shape, model ■ n company, troupe, dramatis personae, actors, players. *See* COMPARE AND CONTRAST *at* throw.

cast an eye over v scan, skim, skim through, dip into, pick through *Opposite*: study

cast around v search, look for, seek, seek out, hunt out

cast a shadow over v spoil, hang over, darken, loom over, eclipse *Opposite*: brighten

cast aside v get rid of, put aside, throw away, toss aside, forget *Opposite*: keep

cast away v give up, throw away, cast off, discard, jettison *Opposite*: keep

castaway n shipwrecked person, survivor, exile

cast down v discourage, dishearten, depress, demoralize, disparage *Opposite*: cheer up

caste n class, social group, standing, background, social order

castigate *(fml)* v criticize, reprimand, chastise, scold, rebuke *Opposite*: praise. *See* COMPARE AND CONTRAST *at* criticize.

castigation *(fml)* n criticism, rebuke, reprimand, scolding, telling-off *(infml) Opposite*: praise

casting n 1 molding, forming, manufacture 2 object, artifact, molding, cast 3 audition, selection, screen test, interview, test

cast-iron adj inflexible, rigid, unchangeable, immutable, fixed *Opposite*: flexible

castle n fortress, fort, citadel, stronghold, bastion

castles in Spain *see* castles in the air

castles in the air n flight of fancy, fancy, dream, fantasy, notion *Opposite*: reality

castles in the sky *see* castles in the air

cast off v discard, get rid of, reject, dispose of, abandon

castoff n reject, discard, hand-me-down, throwaway *Opposite*: purchase ■ adj discarded, rejected, unwanted, old, secondhand *Opposite*: new

cast out *(fml)* v **throw out**, evict, oust, eject, reject *Opposite*: install

castrate v **neuter**, sterilize, geld, spay

casual *adj* 1 **unpremeditated**, unplanned, chance, unintentional, unintended *Opposite*: premeditated 2 **seasonal**, informal, temporary, occasional, periodic *Opposite*: permanent 3 **informal**, nonchalant, relaxed, calm, cool *Opposite*: formal 4 **indifferent**, careless, offhand, blasé, cavalier *Opposite*: careful

casualness *n* 1 **informality**, nonchalance, calmness, coolness, insouciance *Opposite*: formality 2 **indifference**, carelessness, negligence, disregard, heedlessness *Opposite*: care

casualty *n* **injured person**, wounded person, dead person, fatality, loss

casuistry *n* **sophistry**, unsound reasoning, twisting the facts, rationalization, excuse

cat *n* **feline**, kitten, kitty, mouser, tom

WORD BANK
❑ **types of cats** Abyssinian, American shorthair, big cat, Birman, bobcat, British shorthair, Burmese cat, calico cat, cheetah, Egyptian mau, jaguar, leopard, lion, lynx, Maine coon, Manx cat, mountain lion, Norwegian forest cat, ocelot, panther, Persian cat, Siamese cat, tabby, tiger, tortoiseshell, wildcat

---

cataclysm *n* **catastrophe**, disaster, upheaval, calamity, debacle

cataclysmic *adj* **catastrophic**, disastrous, calamitous, dreadful, tragic

catacomb *n* 1 **underground cemetery**, crypt, vault, tomb, mausoleum 2 **tunnel network**, underground passage, labyrinth, warren, maze

catalog *n* 1 **list**, directory, file, index, register 2 **set**, collection, list, litany, series ■ v 1 **classify**, assemble, compile, arrange, categorize 2 **enter**, record, insert, include, document 3 **itemize**, list, enumerate, document, detail

cataloguing *n* **classification**, categorization, logging, sorting, taking down

catalyst *n* **promoter**, facilitator, stimulus, spur, incentive

cat-and-mouse *adj* **cruel**, sadistic, heartless, merciless, callous

catapult *v* **hurtle**, shoot, throw project, propel

cataract *n* **waterfall**, cascade, falls, chute, torrent

catarrh *n* **mucus**, phlegm, discharge

catastrophe *n* **disaster**, calamity, upheaval, devastation, ruin *Opposite*: good fortune

catastrophic *adj* **disastrous**, shattering, calamitous, appalling, terrible *Opposite*: fortunate

catatonic *adj* 1 **inert**, rigid, unresponsive, withdrawn, impassive 2 *(infml)* **unconscious**, asleep, comatose, inert, stupefied

catcall *n* **jeer**, hiss, boo, whistle, shout ■ v **taunt**, jeer, hiss, boo, shout

catch v 1 **grasp**, grab, hold, take, clutch *Opposite*: drop 2 **snare**, ensnare, entrap, hook, net 3 **capture**, arrest, apprehend, take prisoner, detain *Opposite*: release 4 **contract**, become infected with, fall victim to, pick up, go down with 5 **find**, discover, surprise, spot, notice 6 **hear**, perceive, notice, become aware of, grasp 7 **hit**, strike, knock, bump, bump into 8 **stick**, get trapped in, snag, cling, entangle *Opposite*: free 9 **hold**, hold on to, gather, grasp, receive ■ n 1 **fastening**, fastener, clasp, hook, latch 2 *(infml)* **snag**, drawback, problem, difficulty, hitch

Catch-22 *n* **predicament**, no-win situation, dilemma, quandary, impossibility

catch a glimpse of v **spot**, notice, spy, glimpse, catch sight of

catchall *adj* **general**, universal, all-encompassing, wide-ranging, blanket

catch hold of v **take**, grab, clutch, seize, grasp

catching *adj* **infectious**, contagious, communicable, transmittable, easily spread

catch napping v **surprise**, take by surprise, catch out, catch on the hop, catch in the act

catch on *(infml)* v 1 **become popular**, rise in popularity, become fashionable, be in fashion, take off *(infml) Opposite*: flop *(infml)* 2 **understand**, be with you, follow you, comprehend, grasp *Opposite*: misunderstand

catch out *(infml)* v **expose**, trip up, wrongfoot, discover, catch

catch phrase *n* **catchword**, motto, slogan, tag

catch sight of v **spot**, notice, spy, glimpse, catch a glimpse of *Opposite*: miss

catch unawares v **surprise**, startle, creep up on, give somebody a shock, ambush

catch up v **draw near**, draw level, get closer to, become equal, pull alongside *Opposite*: fall behind

catchword *n* **catch phrase**, byword, motto, watchword, slogan

catchy *adj* **memorable**, attractive, likable, beguiling, haunting *Opposite*: forgettable

catechesis *see* catechism

catechism *n* 1 **examination**, questioning, interrogation, dialectic 2 **religious instruction**, religious education, religious teaching 3 **dogma**, party line, mantra, article of faith, tenet

categorical *adj* **definite**, clear-cut, uncompromising, unconditional, unqualified *Opposite*: tentative

categorization *n* 1 **classification**, cataloging, labeling, tagging, grouping 2 **category**, class, group, set, grouping

categorize v **classify**, sort out, catalog, label, tag

category *n* **class**, sort, grouping, type, kind. *See* COMPARE AND CONTRAST *at* **type**.

cater *v* **provide**, supply, outfit, accommodate, gratify

cater-cornered *adv* **crossways**, catty-cornered, diagonally, across, corner to corner

caterwaul *v* **howl**, yowl, wail, squall, squeal

catgut *n* **cord**, line, thread, string, filament

catharsis *n* **release**, liberation, freeing up, cleansing, purification

cathartic *adj* **1** **therapeutic**, liberating, releasing, emotional, intense **2** **purifying**, cleansing, excretory, expulsive, purgative *(fml)*

catheter *n* **tube**, line, drip, drain, feed

catholic *adj* **wide-ranging**, broad, wide-reaching, all-embracing, extensive *Opposite*: narrow

catkin *n* **flower**, tassel, ament

catnap *n* **nap**, doze, rest, siesta, power nap ■ *v* **nap**, nod off, doze, sleep, catch some z's *(infml)*

cat-o'-nine-tails *n* **whip**, scourge, lash, birch

cattiness *n* **spitefulness**, nastiness, meanness, maliciousness, malevolence *Opposite*: kindness

cattle *n* **cows**, oxen, bulls, bullocks, steers

catty *adj* **spiteful**, nasty, venomous, mean, malicious *Opposite*: kind

catwalk *n* **1** **stage**, walkway, runway, ramp, gangplank **2** **bridge**, footbridge, walkway

caucus *n* **1** **conclave**, assembly, committee, conference, convention **2** **faction**, bloc, alliance, league, union

cauldron *see* **caldron**

caulk *v* **seal**, waterproof, fill, block, plug

causal *adj* **fundamental**, underlying, contributory, contributing, connecting

causality *n* **cause and effect**, connection, interconnection, connectedness, causation

causation *n* **action**, connection, interconnection, relationship, causality

causative *adj* **causal**, instrumental, contributing, contributory, connective

cause *n* **reason**, grounds, source, root, origin *Opposite*: effect ■ *v* **make happen**, bring about, produce, set off, instigate *Opposite*: impede

cause offense *v* **be offensive**, shock, hurt somebody's feelings, offend, antagonize

causeway *n* **walkway**, ramp, boardwalk, road, dike

caustic *adj* **1** **corrosive**, acid, acidic, corroding, burning **2** **sarcastic**, scathing, mordant, astringent, cutting *Opposite*: gentle. *See* COMPARE AND CONTRAST *at* **sarcastic**.

cauterize *v* **seal**, close, burn, sear, treat

caution *n* **1** **carefulness**, thoughtfulness, attentiveness, attention, risk avoidance *Opposite*: carelessness **2** **warning**, alert, notification, ultimatum, caveat ■ *v* **warn**, alert, notify, signal, give notice

cautionary *adj* **warning**, deterrent, admonitory, advisory, instructive

cautious *adj* **careful**, vigilant, guarded, wary, circumspect *Opposite*: reckless

---

COMPARE AND CONTRAST CORE MEANING: attentive to risk or danger

cautious aware of potential risk and behaving accordingly; **careful** taking reasonable care to avoid risks; **chary** cautiously reluctant to act; **circumspect** taking into consideration all possible circumstances and consequences before acting; **prudent** showing good judgment or shrewdness; **vigilant** alert and conscious of possible dangers; **wary** showing watchfulness or suspicion; **guarded** reluctant to share information with others; **cagey** *(infml)* secretive and guarded.

---

cautiousness *n* **caution**, carefulness, thoughtfulness, attentiveness, wariness *Opposite*: carelessness

cavalcade *n* **procession**, parade, column, line, convoy

cavalier *adj* **careless**, offhand, inconsiderate, high-handed, arrogant *Opposite*: polite

cavalry *n* **mounted troops**, horse regiment, horse soldiers

cave *n* **cavern**, grotto, hollow, pothole, fissure

caveat *n* **warning**, caution, admonition, qualification, stipulation

cave in *v* **1** **collapse**, subside, fall in, fall down, topple **2** **yield**, give in, surrender, give way, admit defeat *Opposite*: withstand

cave-in *n* **1** **collapse**, fall, drop, slide, demolition **2** **capitulation**, yielding, collapse, surrender, concession

cavern *n* **cave**, grotto, pothole, hollow, cavity

cavernous *adj* **1** **vast**, spacious, deep, yawning, gaping *Opposite*: cramped **2** **hollow**, echoing, resounding, sounding, resonant

caviar *n* **roe**, eggs, spawn

cavil *v* **quibble**, split hairs, be picky, complain, carp *Opposite*: accept

cavity *n* **hole**, space, hollow, crater, void

cavort *v* **frolic**, prance, caper, gambol, romp

caw *v* **call**, cry, croak, squawk

CB *n* **radio**, shortwave radio, citizens' band, telecommunication, walkie-talkie

CD player *n* **stereo**, personal stereo, hi-fi, CD, boom box

cease *v* **stop**, finish, end, come to an end, come to a close *Opposite*: start

ceasefire *n* **truce**, armistice, cessation of hostilities, end of hostilities, break in fighting

ceaseless *adj* **unending**, continual, constant, incessant, perpetual *Opposite*: sporadic

cease trading *v* **go out of business**, shut down, go bankrupt, close, fold

cede (fml) v **yield**, concede, give up, give, let go Opposite: resist

ceilidh n **dance**, barn dance, party, celebration, sing-along

ceiling n **limit**, threshold, cutoff point, cap, check

celebrate v **1 enjoy yourself**, have fun, have a good time, make merry, revel Opposite: lament **2 commemorate**, observe, mark, keep, remember **3 praise**, acclaim, commend, applaud, hail

celebrated adj **famous**, renowned, eminent, distinguished, illustrious Opposite: unknown

celebration n **1 festivity**, party, festival, gala, fete Opposite: lamentation **2 commemoration**, remembrance, observance, salutation, memorial

celebratory adj **festive**, triumphant, special, congratulatory, commemorative

celebrity n **1 superstar**, star, personality, name, figure Opposite: nobody **2 fame**, renown, notoriety, superstardom, prominence Opposite: obscurity

celerity (literary) n **speed**, rapidity, swiftness, alacrity, haste Opposite: slowness

celestial adj **1 heavenly**, holy, spiritual, godly, otherworldly **2 cosmic**, astronomic, planetary, galactic, solar

celibate adj **chaste**, abstinent, self-restrained

cell n **1 lockup**, prison cell, jail cell **2 group**, sect, faction, cabal, caucus

cellulite n **fat**, fatty deposits, lumpiness, dimpling

cement n **glue**, adhesive, paste, epoxy resin ■ v **1 join**, stick, fix, glue, fasten together Opposite: separate **2 strengthen**, reinforce, make stronger, prop up, fortify Opposite: undermine

cemetery n **graveyard**, burial ground, churchyard, garden of remembrance, mausoleum

cenotaph n **war memorial**, monument, memorial

censor v **1 edit**, cut, remove, expurgate, bowdlerize **2 stifle**, gag, repress, suppress, control

censored adj **cut**, expurgated, bowdlerized, blue-penciled, changed Opposite: complete

censorious adj **disapproving**, critical, severe, stern, hypercritical Opposite: approving

censorship n **restriction**, control, cutting, editing, bowdlerization

censure n **criticism**, disapproval, condemnation, denunciation, deprecation Opposite: approval ■ v **criticize**, fault, reprimand, condemn, reproach Opposite: praise. See COMPARE AND CONTRAST at **criticize, disapprove**.

census n **count**, survey, poll, registration, tally

center n **1 midpoint**, middle, halfway point, focal point, focus Opposite: edge **2 filling**, inside, middle, core, layer Opposite: coating **3 downtown**, inner city, heart **4 complex**, facility, development, building **5 cluster**, concentration, focus, magnet, hotbed **6 middle ground**, consensus, majority, middle course, happy medium Opposite: extreme **7 axis**, pivot, pivotal point, fulcrum **8 focus**, heart, core, nub, bottom Opposite: periphery ■ v **1 place**, position, arrange, balance, adjust **2 focus on**, turn on, concentrate on, home in on, revolve around Opposite: ignore

centerpiece n **center of attention**, focus, flagship, key feature, heart

center stage adv **in the limelight**, into the limelight, to the fore, at the fore, to the front

central adj **1 middle**, mid, inner, innermost Opposite: outer **2 vital**, dominant, essential, fundamental, chief Opposite: unimportant

centralism n **control**, concentration, monopolism, authoritarianism, centralization

centrality n **importance**, significance, criticality, supremacy, uniqueness Opposite: irrelevance

centralization n **unification**, integration, concentration, control, domination Opposite: decentralization

centralize v **unify**, consolidate, integrate, compact, concentrate Opposite: decentralize

centrist adj **middle-of-the-road**, moderate, mainstream, reasonable, uncontroversial Opposite: extreme

century n **period**, era, time, span, epoch

C.E.O. n **chief executive officer**, boss, head, manager, chief executive

ceramic adj **earthenware**, clay, pottery, terra cotta, ironstone china

cereal n **breakfast cereal**, porridge, grits, mush (dated)

WORD BANK
❑ **types of cereals** barley, corn, millet, oat, rice, rye, sorghum, wheat

---

cerebral adj **intellectual**, rational, highbrow, logical, analytical Opposite: intuitive

ceremonial adj **ritual**, traditional, ritualistic, formal, official Opposite: informal ■ n **rite**, ritual, ceremony, pomp, pageantry

ceremonious adj **formal**, solemn, dignified, grand, majestic Opposite: informal

ceremony n **rite**, ritual, formality, formal procedure, service

certain adj **1 sure**, convinced, positive, confident, firm Opposite: unsure **2 particular**, specific, individual, precise, specified **3 reliable**, dependable, undeniable, guaranteed, clear Opposite: uncertain **4 some**, a number of, a few, several, selected Opposite: all

certainly *adv* **1 surely**, positively, definitely, without doubt, undoubtedly *Opposite*: possibly **2 indeed**, absolutely, definitely, of course, sure *(infml)*

certainty *n* **1 foregone conclusion**, safe bet, inevitability **2 confidence**, conviction, faith, belief, assurance *Opposite*: uncertainty

certificate *n* **document**, license, diploma, credential, documentation

certification *n* **guarantee**, warranty, documentation, authorization, accreditation

certified *adj* **official**, licensed, approved, authorized, accredited

certify *v* **confirm**, state, verify, endorse, attest

certitude *n* **conviction**, certainty, sureness, assurance, confidence *Opposite*: uncertainty

cessation *n* **end**, termination, close, stop, ending *Opposite*: start

cesspit *n* **tank**, pit, sewer, drain, gutter

chafe *v* **1 rub**, scrape, irritate, scratch, abrade **2 annoy**, bother, provoke, vex, irritate

chaff *v* **tease**, mock, make fun of, josh *(infml)*, pull somebody's leg *(infml)* ■ *n* **joking**, banter, repartee, teasing

chagrin *n* **humiliation**, mortification, vexation, irritation, disappointment

chain *n* **1 cable**, hawser, line **2 restraint**, shackle, manacle, fetter **3 group**, string, franchise, series **4 sequence**, series, string, succession, procession ■ *v* **bind**, manacle, shackle, lock up, restrain *Opposite*: unchain

chain reaction *n* **series of events**, train of events, domino effect

chair *n* **chairperson**, presiding officer, president, head, leader ■ *v* **preside**, take the chair, lead, direct, oversee

chairperson *n* **presiding officer**, president, chair, head, leader

chalice *(literary)* *n* **cup**, goblet, vessel

chalk *v* **write**, draw, mark, doodle, scribble

chalk up *v* **score**, mark up, gain, win, obtain

chalky *adj* **1 crumbly**, dry, powdery, fine, dusty **2 white**, pale, pallid, anemic, ghostly

challenge *v* **1 confront**, defy, brave, face up to *Opposite*: shirk **2 dare**, defy, throw down the gauntlet, test **3 dispute**, contest, object to, question, argue *Opposite*: agree ■ *n* **test**, trial, task, contest, encounter

challenger *n* **contestant**, contender, competitor, opponent, pretender

challenging *adj* **1 demanding**, taxing, testing, difficult, tough *Opposite*: easy **2 stimulating**, thought-provoking, interesting, inspiring, exciting *Opposite*: routine **3 defiant**, disobedient, rebellious, insolent, impudent *Opposite*: compliant

chamber *n* **1 cavity**, hollow, compartment, space, slot **2 hall**, assembly room, meeting room, boardroom, legislative chamber

chamberlain *n* **official**, attendant, courtier, servant, manager

chameleon *n* **changeable person**, butterfly, trimmer, dilettante

champ *v* **chew**, munch, grind. masticate, chomp *(infml)* ■ *n* *(infml)* **champion**, winner, victor, title holder

champion *n* **1 winner**, victor, title holder, champ *(infml)* **2 defender**, supporter, backer, campaigner, advocate ■ *v* **defend**, support, back, campaign for, fight for

championship *n* **finals**, contest, challenge, title fight, battle

chance *n* **1 possibility**, probability, likelihood, prospect, risk **2 opening**, opportunity, option, occasion **3 luck**, fate, fortune, destiny, good fortune **4 gamble**, risk, hazard, venture, stake ■ *v* **risk**, hazard, gamble, try, attempt ■ *adj* **accidental**, coincidental, casual, fortuitous, unintended *Opposite*: planned

chancellor *n* **president**, leader, head of state, premier, prime minister

chance occurrence *n* **coincidence**, accident, twist of fate, quirk, happenstance

chance on *v* **stumble on**, happen on, strike on, hit on, come across

chancy *adj* **risky**, hazardous, dangerous, perilous, uncertain *Opposite*: safe

change *n* **1 alteration**, modification, variation, transformation, conversion **2 coins**, cash, loose change ■ *v* **1 alter**, modify, vary, adjust, amend **2 exchange**, replace, convert, substitute, transform

---

COMPARE AND CONTRAST CORE MEANING: make or become different

change make or become different in any way; **alter** change, especially to change an aspect of something; **modify** make minor changes or alterations, especially in order to improve something; **convert** change something from one form or function to another; **vary** change within a range of possibilities, or in connection with something else, with a suggestion of instability; **shift** change from one position or direction to another; **transform** make a radical change into a different form; **transmute** change into another form.

---

changeability *n* **1 unpredictability**, unsettledness, variableness, variability, irregularity *Opposite*: constancy **2 indecisiveness**, fickleness, unpredictability, flightiness, volatility *Opposite*: steadiness

changeable *adj* **variable**, unsettled, unpredictable, unreliable, unstable *Opposite*: constant

change around *v* **1 alter**, modify, amend, adjust. jiggle around *Opposite*: leave alone **2 reorganize**, move around, rethink, alter, change *Opposite*: leave alone **3 swap** *(infml)*, exchange, substitute, change, change over

changed adj altered, different, transformed, reformed, rehabilitated *Opposite*: unchanged

change direction v 1 veer off, swerve, turn, bend, curve around 2 start afresh, change course, change tack, have a rethink, turn over a new leaf

change for the better v improve, get better, look up, progress, pick up *(infml) Opposite*: deteriorate ■ n improvement, progress, development, upswing, upturn *Opposite*: deterioration

changeless adj unchanging, consistent, fixed, immutable, permanent *Opposite*: changing

changelessness n permanence, consistency, immutability, unalterability, invariability

change of heart n volte-face, second thoughts, rethink, change of attitude, change of opinion

change over v switch, substitute, convert, transfer, change around

changeover n move, reversal, conversion, alteration, substitution

change your mind v have second thoughts, come around, relent, back out, pull out

changing adj altering, varying, shifting, moving, fluctuating *Opposite*: changeless

channel n 1 station, network, frequency 2 canal, conduit, waterway, strait, passage 3 means, outlet, conduit, path, way 4 ditch, dike, groove, drain, trench ■ v direct, control, feed, conduct, route

chant n song, hymn, mantra, tune, carol ■ v sing, recite, repeat, vocalize, intone *(fml)*

chaos n disorder, confusion, bedlam, anarchy, pandemonium *Opposite*: order

chaotic adj disordered, muddled, confused, messy, untidy *Opposite*: orderly

chapel n sanctuary, oratory, chantry, side chapel, side altar

chaperon n supervisor, attendant, overseer, governess, escort ■ v supervise, oversee, escort, watch, look after

chaperone see chaperon

chaplain n minister, vicar, priest, pastor, rabbi

chapter n 1 section, part, subdivision, division, segment 2 period, episode, stage, phase, interval

char v burn, singe, scorch, carbonize, sear

character n 1 nature, quality, temperament, personality, disposition 2 charm, appeal, atmosphere, attractiveness, charisma 3 honor, integrity, strength, uprightness, rectitude 4 eccentric, personality, oddity, original 5 person, individual, creature, sort, type

character assassination n defamation, slander, libel, affront, verbal abuse

character-building adj challenging, demanding, instructive, educative, empowering

characterful adj individual, distinctive, strong, upright, inspiring

characteristic n trait, feature, quality, attribute, point ■ adj typical, distinguishing, distinctive, individual, representative *Opposite*: uncharacteristic

characteristically adv typically, usually, normally, naturally, routinely *Opposite*: unusually

characterization n description, classification, account, portrayal, depiction

characterize v 1 describe, portray, illustrate, depict, brand 2 typify, set apart, distinguish, differentiate, exemplify

characterless adj bland, dull, soulless, uninteresting, insipid *Opposite*: interesting

characterlessness n dullness, soullessness, insipidness

charade n pretense, farce, sham, fake, travesty

charge v 1 accuse, indict, allege, arraign, incriminate *Opposite*: absolve 2 attack, rush, storm, assault, assail *Opposite*: retreat 3 rush, dash, hurtle, stampede, hurry ■ n 1 cost, price, expense, rate, amount 2 custody, care, responsibility, control, trust 3 accusation, indictment, allegation, arraignment, imputation 4 assault, attack, advance, offensive, onslaught 5 order, command, direction, instruction, injunction

chargeable adj 1 punishable, criminal, indictable, imputable, actionable 2 taxable, liable to tax, declarable, dutiable

charged adj emotional, exciting, electric, thrilling, stimulating *Opposite*: calm

chariness n wariness, caution, circumspection

charisma n charm, personality, appeal, magnetism, allure

charismatic adj magnetic, compelling, alluring, fascinating, captivating

charitable adj 1 generous, giving, benevolent, altruistic, helpful *Opposite*: uncharitable 2 considerate, understanding, accepting, sympathetic, tolerant *Opposite*: unforgiving

charity n 1 aid, contributions, gifts, donations, help 2 aid organization, charitable trust, charitable foundation, aid agency 3 kindness, tolerance, humanity, compassion, generosity *Opposite*: unkindness

charlatan n fake, fraud, swindler, quack, counterfeit

charlatanism n quackery, trickery, pretense

charm n 1 attraction, appeal, allure, charisma, magic 2 ornament, keepsake, trinket, talisman, amulet ■ v captivate, enchant, beguile, hypnotize, mesmerize

charmed adj 1 lucky, fortunate, enchanted, magical, fairy-tale *Opposite*: unlucky 2 delighted, pleased, enchanted, thrilled, glad

charmer *n* **smooth talker**, enchanter, fascinator, smooth operator, ladies' man

charming *adj* **delightful**, amiable, attractive, appealing, charismatic *Opposite*: unattractive

charmless *adj* **unattractive**, unappealing, uninteresting, unsympathetic, unprepossessing *Opposite*: charming

chart *n* **diagram**, plan, graph, table, graphic representation ■ *v* **register**, record, project, plot, chronicle

charter *n* **contract**, deed, agreement, license, grant ■ *v* **rent**, lease, hire, take on, commission

chary *adj* **wary**, cautious, suspicious, guarded, careful *Opposite*: reckless. *See* COMPARE AND CONTRAST *at* cautious.

chase *v* **1** **pursue**, run after, hunt, hound, follow **2** **race**, dash, rush, career, hurtle ■ *n* **pursuit**, hunt, hunting. *See* COMPARE AND CONTRAST *at* follow.

chaser *n* **pursuer**, follower, hunter, shadow, tail

chasm *n* **crater**, gulf, gap, abyss, gorge

chaste *adj* **innocent**, uncorrupted, virtuous, unblemished, unsullied *Opposite*: impure

chasten *v* **1** **punish**, reprimand, discipline, censure, chastise **2** **subdue**, suppress, restrain, tame, humble

chasteness *n* **pureness**, innocence, purity, virtuousness, · faithfulness *Opposite*: immorality

chastise *v* **reprimand**, discipline, censure, punish, rebuke *Opposite*: praise

chastisement *(fml)* *n* **reprimand**, discipline, punishment, rebuke, scolding *Opposite*: praise

chastity *n* **purity**, innocence, virtue

chat *v* **talk**, converse, gossip, gab *(infml)*, chitchat *(infml)* ■ *n* **conversation**, one-on-one, heart-to-heart, tête-à-tête, talk

chattels *n* **possessions**, belongings, things, stuff, personal property

chatter *v* **babble**, prattle, rant, gossip, go on *Opposite*: shut up ■ *n* **talk**, gossip, chat, conversation *Opposite*: silence

chatterbox *(infml)* *n* **talker**, gossip, chatterer, tattler, blabbermouth *(infml)*

chatterer *see* chatterbox

chattily *adv* **conversationally**, informally, casually, easily

chattiness *n* **garrulity**, loquacity, communicativeness, informality

chatty *adj* **1** **talkative**, garrulous, loquacious, forthcoming, gossipy *Opposite*: quiet **2** **informal**, friendly, personal, casual, relaxed *Opposite*: formal. *See* COMPARE AND CONTRAST *at* talkative.

chauffeur *n* **driver**, motorist, valet

chauvinism *n* **bigotry**, sexism, prejudice, narrow-mindedness, dogmatism

chauvinist *n* **bigot**, sexist, racist, homophobe, jingoist

chauvinistic *adj* **bigoted**, prejudiced, opinionated, dogmatic, narrow-minded

cheap *adj* **1** **inexpensive**, economy, low-priced, economical, discounted *Opposite*: expensive **2** **shoddy**, inferior, second-rate, substandard, common *Opposite*: superior **3** **contemptible**, despicable, shameful, low, base *Opposite*: admirable **4** **stingy**, tight-fisted, miserly, parsimonious, close-fisted *(infml)* *Opposite*: generous

cheapen *v* **denigrate**, demean, belittle, lower, degrade *Opposite*: elevate

cheaply *adv* **inexpensively**, economically, reasonably, modestly, competitively *Opposite*: expensively

cheapness *n* **1** **tawdriness**, inferiority, shoddiness, tackiness *(infml)* *Opposite*: tastefulness **2** **tightfistedness**, miserliness, parsimony, stinginess *(infml)*, close-fistedness *(infml)* *Opposite*: generosity

cheapskate *(infml)* *n* **miser**, skinflint, killjoy, scrooge *(infml)*, tightwad *(infml)*

cheat *v* **deceive**, trick, con, swindle, defraud ■ *n* **double-dealer**, rogue, cheater, charlatan, double-crosser

cheating *adj* **duplicitous**, double-dealing, dishonest, unprincipled, deceitful *Opposite*: honest ■ *n* **dishonesty**, deceit, deception, duplicity, chicanery

check *v* **1** **test**, test out, prove, try, try out **2** **make sure**, ensure, verify, confirm, certify **3** **limit**, hold in, stop, impede, hold up *Opposite*: expedite *(fml)* ■ *n* **1** **inspection**, examination, test, assessment, trial **2** **safeguard**, curb, restraint, buttress, catch **3** **payment**, form, order, draft, instruction **4** **bill**, invoice, score, tab *(infml)*, damage *(infml)*

checked *adj* **check**, checkered, patterned, crisscross, plaid

checker *n* **inspector**, examiner, assessor, regulator, overseer

checkered *adj* **1** **uneven**, inconsistent, variable, changeable, volatile *Opposite*: even **2** **check**, checked, squared, patterned, crisscross

check in *v* **register**, sign in, sign up, sign on, enroll

check-in *n* **registration desk**, registration, reception desk, reception area, desk

checklist *n* **list**, specification, agenda, worksheet, spec *(infml)*

checkmate *n* **check**, mate, end, ending, victory *Opposite*: stalemate

check out *v* **1** **inspect**, investigate, look into, explore, examine **2** **leave**, depart, vacate, sign out, exit

check over *v* **look over**, reread, go through, go over, examine

checkpoint *n* **barrier**, turnpike, frontier, border, spot check

checkup *n* **examination**, looking over, physical, medical, inspection

check up on *v* keep an eye on, check on, spy on, watch, monitor *Opposite*: ignore

cheek by jowl *adv* side by side, on top of one another, close together, together, close

cheekiness *(infml) n* **impudence**, disrespect, effrontery, insolence, irreverence *Opposite*: respect

cheek-to-cheek *adv* close, close up, close together, together, intimately

cheeky *(infml) adj* **impudent**, bold, defiant, insolent, naughty *Opposite*: respectful

cheep *v* chirp, peep, tweet, twitter, sing

cheeping *n* chirping, tweeting, peeping, twittering, singing

cheer *n* **cheerfulness**, optimism, merriment, joyfulness, liveliness *Opposite*: gloom ■ *v* applaud, shout, root for, hail, praise *Opposite*: boo

cheerful *adj* happy, cheery, bright, smiling, joyful *Opposite*: sad

cheerfully *adv* **1** happily, optimistically, merrily, joyfully, gleefully *Opposite*: sadly **2** gladly, willingly, readily, with pleasure *Opposite*: grudgingly

cheerfulness *n* happiness, joyfulness, cheer, cheeriness, merriment *Opposite*: sadness

cheeriness *n* cheerfulness, happiness, joyfulness, liveliness, joviality *Opposite*: gloominess

cheering *adj* heartening, encouraging, positive, uplifting, promising *Opposite*: discouraging

cheerless *adj* gloomy, depressing, dismal, miserable, sad *Opposite*: bright

cheerlessness *n* **bleakness**, dreariness, gloominess, soullessness, wintriness *Opposite*: brightness

cheer on *v* encourage, root for, support, plump for, laud *Opposite*: discourage

cheer up *v* perk up, brighten, brighten up, liven, enliven *Opposite*: depress

cheery *adj* happy, joyful, smiling, cheerful, merry *Opposite*: gloomy

cheeseparing *adj* stingy, miserly, mean-spirited, avaricious, miserable *Opposite*: generous ■ *n* stinginess, miserliness, mean-spiritedness, avarice, cheapness *Opposite*: generosity

cheesy *(infml) adj* tasteless, cheap, tawdry, unpleasant, tacky *(infml) Opposite*: stylish

chemical *n* substance, element, compound

chemistry *n* **interaction**, attraction, understanding, empathy, sympathy

cherish *v* treasure, appreciate, relish, esteem, revere *Opposite*: neglect

cherished *adj* valued, precious, beloved, esteemed, appreciated *Opposite*: neglected

cherry-pick *v* select, choose, pick, hand-pick, pick and choose

cherub *n* angel, cupid, amoretto, putto

cherubic *adj* **1** angelic, cute, innocent,

attractive, lovable **2** holy, divine, spiritual, saintly, blessed

chest *n* upper body, torso, rib cage, ribs, trunk

chestnut *(infml) n* joke, tired joke, anecdote, cliché, old favorite *(infml)*

chevron *n* V-shape, V, stripe, badge, insignia

chew *v* masticate, chew up, gnaw, grind, crush ■ *n* portion, plug, wad

chew out *(infml) v* **scold**, reproach, reprimand, take to task, bawl out *(infml)*

chew over *v* meditate, ponder, think about, ruminate on, consider

chew up *v* **1** damage, crush, rip up, injure, destroy **2** chew, grind, masticate, champ, munch

chewy *adj* rubbery, stringy, fibrous, gristly, leathery *Opposite*: tender

chic *adj* stylish, fashionable, well-dressed, attractive, smart *Opposite*: unfashionable ■ *n* style, elegance, panache, stylishness, modishness

chicanery *n* deception, trickery, verbiage, smoke and mirrors, nonsense

chichi *adj* contrived, recherché, self-conscious, pretentious, affected

chicken *(infml) adj* **cowardly**, frightened, scared, reluctant, fearful *Opposite*: brave. *See* COMPARE AND CONTRAST *at* cowardly.

chicken feed *(infml) n* small change, next to nothing, small potatoes *(infml)*, small beer *(infml)*, chump change *(slang)*

chide *(literary) v* reproach, scold, reprimand, rebuke, blame *Opposite*: praise

chief *n* ruler, head, boss, captain, commander ■ *adj* principal, main, topmost, leading, foremost

chief executive *n* C.E.O., boss, leader, president

chiefly *adv* primarily, mainly, essentially, mostly, predominantly

chieftain *n* tribal chief, ruler, chief, overlord, lord

chieftainship *n* **leadership**, command, authority, rank, status

chilblain *n* swelling, inflammation, blister

child *n* **1** youngster, young person, adolescent, youth, juvenile **2** offspring, descendant, spawn, scion, son **3** baby, infant, newborn, toddler, preschooler **4** result, product, outcome, creation. *See* COMPARE AND CONTRAST *at* youth.

childbearing *n* reproduction, pregnancy, gestation, childbirth, motherhood

childbirth *n* giving birth, delivery, labor, contractions, childbearing

childhood *n* **babyhood**, infancy, youth, upbringing, infanthood *Opposite*: adulthood

childish *adj* **1** immature, irresponsible, silly, foolish, infantile *Opposite*: mature **2** childlike, juvenile, innocent, ingenuous

childishness *n* immaturity, silliness, irresponsibility, pettiness *Opposite*: maturity

childlike *adj* **innocent**, naive, candid, unsophisticated, trusting *Opposite*: jaded

childproof *adj* **safe**, tamper-proof, secure

child's play *n* **piece of cake** *(infml)*, picnic *(infml)*, walkover *(infml)*, pushover *(infml)*, cinch *(infml)*

chill *n* **1 coldness**, coolness, low temperature, chilliness, nippiness *Opposite*: warmth **2 sudden fear**, anxiety, apprehension, wariness, shudder **3 gloom**, depression, pall, shadow **4 unfriendliness**, aloofness, detachment, coolness, coldness *Opposite*: warmth ■ *adj* **1 biting**, freezing, wintry, nippy, chilly **2 remote**, uninvolved, aloof, indifferent, chilly *Opposite*: warm ■ *v* **1 cool**, freeze, make colder, put on ice, refrigerate *Opposite*: warm **2 discourage**, depress, deter, dispirit, cast a shadow over *Opposite*: encourage

chilled *adj* **ice-cold**, freezing, frozen, refrigerated, cooled *Opposite*: hot

chilliness *n* **1 coolness**, coldness, frostiness, nippiness, low temperature *Opposite*: warmth **2 unfriendliness**, aloofness, stiffness, detachment, formality *Opposite*: friendliness

chilling *adj* **frightening**, alarming, unsettling, distressing, terrifying *Opposite*: reassuring

chill out *(infml)* *v* **1 calm down**, take it easy, stop worrying, lighten up *(infml)* **2 relax**, loosen up, rest, unwind, kick back *(infml)*

chilly *adj* **1 cold**, cool, nippy, chill, frosty *Opposite*: warm **2 frigid**, formal, supercilious, aloof, detached *Opposite*: welcoming

chime *n* **clang**, ding, ding-dong, sound, peal ■ *v* **strike**, peal, ring, sound, ring out

chime in *v* **1 butt in**, interrupt, interject, voice your opinion, speak up **2 agree**, be compatible, be consistent, be in line, be in agreement *Opposite*: contradict

chimera *n* **fantasy**, fancy, whimsy, illusion, mirage

chimerical *adj* **imaginary**, fantastical, illusory, unreal

chimes *n* **bells**, glockenspiel, carillon

china *n* **1 tableware**, crockery, porcelain **2 collectables**, ornaments, figurines

chink *n* **narrow opening**, crack, crevice, slit, opening

chink in somebody's armor *n* **weak spot**, weakness, Achilles heel, flaw, failing

chinless *adj* **weak**, ineffectual, irresolute, inept, spineless *Opposite*: bold

chintzy *adj* **1 tightfisted**, cheap, miserly, stingy, parsimonious *Opposite*: generous **2 trashy**, cheap, inferior, shoddy, gaudy *Opposite*: superior

chip *n* **1 piece**, bit, crumb, flake, chunk **2 mark**, damage, imperfection, flaw, blemish **3 token**, counter, marker, playing piece, poker chip ■ *v* **1 break off**, fragment, hew, flake, pare **2 damage**, disfigure, mark, blemish, notch

chip away at *v* **weaken**, wear away, eat into, erode, diminish

chip in *(infml)* *v* **1 contribute**, help, participate, collaborate, take part **2 chime in**, butt in, interject, voice your opinion, say what you think

chip off the old block *(infml)* *n* **younger version**, mirror image, clone, living image, replica

chipper *(infml)* *adj* **cheerful**, high-spirited, lively, good-humored, exuberant *Opposite*: glum

chipping *n* **chip**, piece, fragment, bit, shaving

chirpy *(infml)* *adj* **lively**, vivacious, alert, bright, effervescent *Opposite*: gloomy

chiseled *adj* **regular**, clean-cut, strong, delicate, fine-boned

chit *(dated)* *n* **receipt**, bill, check, tally, account

chitchat *(infml)* *v* **talk**, discuss, have a chat, gossip, babble ■ *n* **chatter**, gossip, chat, conversation, talk

chivalrous *adj* **1 gallant**, courtly, brave, valiant, loyal *Opposite*: cowardly **2 courteous**, mannerly, gracious, polite, civil *Opposite*: discourteous

chivalry *n* **1 gallantry**, courtliness, loyalty, valor, courage *Opposite*: cowardice **2 courtesy**, courteousness, politeness, attentiveness, gentility *Opposite*: discourteousness

chivvy *v* **urge**, pester, harass, badger, pressure *Opposite*: discourage

chock *n* **wedge**, block, doorstop, chuck ■ *v* **brace**, steady, fix, block, stop *Opposite*: release

chock-a-block *(infml)* *see* **chock-full**

chock-full *(infml)* *adj* **packed**, jammed, crammed, full, crowded *Opposite*: empty

chocolate-box *adj* **pretty**, romanticized, picturesque, soft-focus, attractive

choice *n* **1 selection**, choosing, pick, election, adoption **2 range**, selection, variety, set, group ■ *adj* **excellent**, high-quality, superior, special, prime

choke *v* **1 strangle**, throttle, stifle, suffocate, asphyxiate **2 obstruct**, clog, block, stop up, congest *Opposite*: free up *(infml)* **3 fill with emotion**, freeze up, weep, well up, become teary-eyed

choke back *v* **suppress**, hold back, fight back, stifle, repress *Opposite*: let out

cholesterol *n* **fat**, saturated fat, saturated fatty acid, fatty acid, lipid

chomp *(infml)* *v* **chew**, munch, crunch, eat, masticate *Opposite*: nibble

choose *v* **1 select**, pick, take, pick out, point out *Opposite*: reject **2 decide**, want, prefer, desire, wish

choose up v **select team members**, choose sides, pick sides

choosy (infml) adj **particular**, hard to please, fussy, picky, fastidious Opposite: indifferent

chop v **cut**, slice, hack, ax, lop

chop down v **shorten**, decrease, cut back, cut down, lop off

choppy adj **stormy**, wild, tempestuous, rough Opposite: calm

chop up v **cut up**, chop, cut into pieces, slice, cube

choral adj **vocal**, harmonic, sung

chord n **harmony**, triad, arpeggio, major chord, minor chord

chore n **1 routine**, bore, hard work, imposition, inconvenience **2 task**, job, errand, odd job, assignment

choreograph v **1 create**, compose, design, arrange, put together **2 plan**, maneuver, direct, strategize, manage

choreography n **1 composition**, dance routine, step design, step sequence, step arrangement **2 maneuvering**, direction, management, manipulation, strategy

chorister n **singer**, musician, treble

chortle n **laugh**, chuckle, gurgle, giggle, snicker ■ v **chuckle**, laugh, gurgle, giggle, snicker

chorus n **refrain**, chorus line, response, repeat, repetition ■ v **speak at once**, speak together, speak in unison

chosen adj **selected**, select, elect, preferred, special

chow down (infml) v **eat**, dine, eat heartily, gulp, gobble

christen v **1 baptize**, name, bless, sanctify **2 name**, nickname, call, dub, label **3** (infml) **launch**, inaugurate, debut

christening n **1 baptism**, ceremony, rite, naming **2** (infml) **launch**, first use, inauguration, debut

Christian name n **first name**, given name, forename, personal name, praenomen

chronic adj **1 long-lasting**, lingering, persistent, continuing, enduring Opposite: fleeting **2 habitual**, persistent, ingrained, inveterate, established Opposite: occasional

chronicle n **record**, history, account, annals, journal ■ v **report**, record, recount, relate, narrate

chronological adj **sequential**, consecutive, linear

chronology n **1 sequence of events**, order of events, time line, timetable, train of events **2 account**, record, chronicle, narrative, history

chubbiness n **plumpness**, roundness, fleshiness, stoutness, fatness Opposite: slenderness

chubby adj **plump**, rotund, round, fleshy, stout Opposite: slender

chuck v **1** (infml) **throw**, hurl, toss, fling, pitch **2** (infml) **get rid of**, throw out, throw away, dispose of, discard Opposite: keep **3** (infml) **quit**, resign, walk off, leave, walk out **4 tap**, pat lightly, pat, tickle ■ n **1 chock**, wedge, block, clamp **2 food**, provisions, grub (infml), provender (literary). See COMPARE AND CONTRAST at **throw**.

chuckle v **laugh**, laugh to yourself, chortle, laugh inwardly, giggle ■ n **laughter**, chortle, inward laughter, giggle, snicker

chuck out (infml) v **get rid of**, toss out, dispose of, discard, throw away

chug (infml) v **continue**, keep going, keep at it, persist, plug away (infml) Opposite: stop

chum (infml) n **friend**, associate, acquaintance, companion, pal (infml) Opposite: stranger

chumminess (infml) n **friendliness**, sociability, closeness intimacy, friendship

chummy (infml) adj **friendly**, sociable, congenial, close, intimate

chunk n **piece**, hunk, mass, lump, portion

chunky adj **1 lumpy**, bumpy, coarse, rough Opposite: smooth **2 solid**, heavy, hefty, weighty, substantial Opposite: lightweight **3** (infml) **stocky**, stout, fat, chubby, plump Opposite: slender

churchgoer n **worshiper**, congregant, communicant

churchyard n **graveyard**, burial ground, cemetery, necropolis, boneyard (infml)

churlish adj **1 rude**, boorish, coarse, truculent, crass Opposite: polite **2 ill-natured**, irritable, unpleasant, grumpy, sullen Opposite: pleasant

churn v **mix**, roil, agitate, shake, whip

churn out v **mass-produce**, manufacture, turn out, roll out, issue

chute n **1 shaft**, slide, channel, sluice, raceway **2 waterfall**, cascade, cataract, descent, drop

chutzpah (infml) n **1 boldness**, self-confidence, self-assurance, assertiveness, bravado **2 gall**, boldness, nerve, impudence, effrontery

C in C n **commander in chief**, five-star general, generalissimo, commander, leader

cinch n **1** (infml) **snap**, child's play, piece of cake (infml), breeze (infml), walk in the park (infml) **2** (infml) **sure bet**, certainty, dead certainty, sure thing (infml) **3 girth**, restraint, belt, strap ■ v **1 bind**, restrain, fix, tighten, gird (literary) **2 dated** (infml) **guarantee**, assure, insure, settle, make certain

cinders n **embers**, ashes, residue, coals

cinema n **movies**, motion pictures, film, pictures (infml dated)

cinematic adj **filmic**, photographic, movie-like, filmmaking, moviemaking

cinematography n **photography**, shooting, film making, picture making, movie making

cipher *n* **1 code**, secret message, symbols, cryptograph, encryption **2 nobody**, nonentity, nothing, zero

circa *prep* **approximately**, about, around, roughly, round about *Opposite*: exactly

circadian *adj* **daily**, 24-hour, 24-hourly, diurnal, day by day

circle *n* **1 ring**, loop, round, sphere, disk **2 group**, gang, set, clique, crowd ▪ *v* **1 go around**, orbit, fly around, fly in a circle, circumnavigate **2 encircle**, surround, ring, enclose, bound

circlet *n* **band**, coronet, tiara, diadem, crown

circuit *n* **1 route**, track, trail, path **2 tour**, trip, journey, route, round

circuitous *adj* **1 indirect**, winding, meandering, roundabout, twisting *Opposite*: direct **2 complicated**, convoluted, discursive, tangential, long-winded *Opposite*: straightforward

circuitry *n* **electrical system**, electric circuit, circuit board, motherboard, printed circuit

circular *adj* **spherical**, rounded, globular, round ▪ *n* **leaflet**, flier, pamphlet, advertisement, handbill

circularity *n* **indirectness**, circuitousness, obliqueness, roundaboutness, convolutedness *Opposite*: directness

circulate *v* **1 pass around**, distribute, hand out, give out, send out *Opposite*: withhold **2 flow**, move, travel, pass **3** (*infml*) **mingle**, socialize, mix, meet people, be sociable

circulation *n* **1 flow**, movement, passage, motion, rotation **2 exchange**, flow, transmission, spread, dissemination **3 distribution**, readership, sales

circumference *n* **perimeter**, boundary, bounds, limits, edge *Opposite*: middle

circumlocution *n* **periphrasis**, indirectness, roundaboutness, long-windedness, convolutedness *Opposite*: directness

circumlocutory *adj* **periphrastic**, indirect, meandering, roundabout, long-winded *Opposite*: direct

circumnavigate *v* **orbit**, circle, travel around, fly around, go around

circumscribe (*fml*) *v* **limit**, restrict, define, demarcate, mark out

circumscription (*fml*) *n* **restriction**, limit, limitation, constraint, restraint *Opposite*: freedom

circumspect *adj* **cautious**, prudent, careful, guarded, wary *Opposite*: reckless. See COMPARE AND CONTRAST *at* **cautious**.

circumspection *n* **care**, carefulness, caution, cautiousness, judiciousness *Opposite*: rashness

circumstance *n* **1 condition**, situation, state of affairs, status quo, context **2** (*fml*) **event**, occurrence, incident, instance, happening

circumstantial *adj* **incidental**, contingent, indirect, inferred, conditional *Opposite*: concrete

circumvent *v* **avoid**, get around, evade, skirt, dodge

circumvention *n* **avoidance**, evasion, escape, sidestepping, dodging

circus (*infml*) *n* **show**, festival, spectacle, extravaganza, event

cirque *n* **combe**, hollow, valley, glaciated valley

cistern *n* **water tank**, storage tank, tank, reservoir, container

citadel *n* **fortress**, stronghold, bastion, fort, castle

citation *n* **quotation**, quote, mention, reference, excerpt

cite (*fml*) *v* **quote**, mention, refer to, allude to

citified *adj* **oversophisticated**, sophisticated, cosmopolitan, slick, suave *Opposite*: countrified

citizen *n* **inhabitant**, national, resident, legal resident, voter

citizenry *n* **people**, community, public, electorate, voters

citizenship *n* **social responsibility**, public spirit, social conscience, civic duty

city *n* **metropolis**, municipality, conurbation, capital, town *Opposite*: hamlet ▪ *adj* **urban**, metropolitan, town, municipal

---

COMPARE AND CONTRAST CORE MEANING: an urban area where a large number of people live **city** a large municipal center governed under a charter granted by the state; in the United Kingdom, a town having a cathedral or having such a status conferred on it by the Crown; in Canada, a large municipal unit incorporated by the provincial government, but now used generally for any large urban area; **conurbation** an urban region formed or enlarged by the merging of adjacent cities and towns through expansion or development; **metropolis** a large or important city, sometimes the capital of a country, state, or region; **town** a populated area smaller than a city and larger than a village; **municipality** a city, town, or area with some degree of self-government.

---

city dweller *n* **urbanite**, citizen, burgher, townie (*infml*)

civic *adj* **public**, municipal, local, community, town *Opposite*: private

civil *adj* **1 public**, political, municipal, civic, civilian **2 courteous**, polite, respectful, well-mannered, accommodating *Opposite*: rude

civilian *n* **noncombatant**, private citizen, citizen, member of the public, neutral *Opposite*: martial

civility *n* **politeness**, courtesy, good manners, courteousness, respect *Opposite*: rudeness

civilization *n* **1 society**, nation, culture, empire, polity **2 development**, evolution, progress, cultivation, refinement

civilize *v* **enlighten**, educate, cultivate, improve, advance

civilized adj **cultured**, educated, refined, enlightened, polite Opposite: barbarous

civilizing adj **humanizing**, taming, educating, cultivating, refining

civil liberties see **civil rights**

civilly adv **politely**, respectfully, courteously, amicably, considerately Opposite: rudely

civil rights n **human rights**, rights, constitutional rights, privileges, civil liberties

civil servant n **public servant**, government employee, bureaucrat, official, administrator

clack v **snap**, click, clap, bang, rap

clad adj **dressed**, clothed, covered, attired (fml), arrayed (literary)

cladding n **covering**, layer, facing, casing, shell

claim v **1 maintain**, assert, say, state, declare **2 ask for**, call for, demand, apply for, request Opposite: deny **3 receive**, obtain, take, pick up, retrieve ■ n **1 assertion**, statement, accusation, declaration, allegation **2 demand**, request, application, petition, call **3 right**, entitlement, prerogative, privilege, due

claimant n **applicant**, plaintiff, pretender, petitioner, appellant

clairvoyance n **psychic power**, telepathy, prophecy, fortune-telling, palm reading

clairvoyant n **psychic**, mystic, spiritualist, telepathist, diviner ■ adj **intuitive**, psychic, telepathic, second-sighted, perceptive

clamber v **climb**, scramble, crawl, scale

clamminess n **1 dampness**, wetness, moistness, dankness, sliminess Opposite: dryness **2 humidity**, mugginess, closeness, heat, airlessness Opposite: freshness

clammy adj **1 damp**, wet, moist, dank, slimy Opposite: dry **2 humid**, muggy, close, sticky, sweaty Opposite: fresh

clamor v **1 shout**, scream, yell, cry, screech Opposite: whisper **2 demand**, insist, appeal, cry out, bay ■ n **1 appeal**, demand, call, request, cry **2 uproar**, din, commotion, racket, noise Opposite: quiet

clamorous adj **noisy**, vociferous, loud, rowdy, boisterous Opposite: tranquil

clamp v **fasten**, hold, compress, fix, brace

clamp down v **shut down**, take tough action, come down hard, restrict, limit Opposite: relent

clampdown n **crackdown**, restriction, curb, suppression, embargo

clam up (infml) v **stop talking**, choke, refuse to speak, remain silent, be unforthcoming Opposite: rattle on

clan n **1 tribe**, family, relations, relatives, kinfolk **2** (infml) **clique**, fraternity, band, coterie, set

clandestine adj **secret**, underground, covert, concealed, stealthy Opposite: open. See COMPARE AND CONTRAST at **secret**.

clang v **clank**, sound, toll, ring, reverberate

clank n **clang**, clink, clatter, clash, bang

clannish adj **cliquey**, cliquish, unfriendly, unsociable, aloof Opposite: open

clap v **applaud**, give a standing ovation, put your hands together, give a round of applause, acclaim Opposite: boo ■ n **slap**, pat, tap, thrust, thwack

clapping n **applause**, appreciation, ovation, acclamation, acclaim Opposite: jeering

claptrap (infml) n **nonsense**, humbug, drivel, rubbish, hogwash (infml) Opposite: sense

clarification n **explanation**, amplification, illumination, clearing up, explaining Opposite: obfuscation

clarify v **1 elucidate**, make clear, explain, clear up, illuminate Opposite: confuse **2 refine**, purify, cleanse, filter, process Opposite: cloud

clarity n **clearness**, lucidity, simplicity, precision, intelligibility Opposite: ambiguity

clash v **1 fight**, conflict, disagree, quarrel, collide Opposite: agree **2 clatter**, clank, clang, crash, bang **3 conflict**, mismatch, jar, contravene Opposite: match ■ n **1 clank**, clatter, clang, crash, bang **2 battle**, encounter, brush, fight, skirmish **3 disagreement**, quarrel, argument, row, fight. See COMPARE AND CONTRAST at **fight**.

clashing adj **inharmonious**, conflicting, jarring, incompatible, nonmatching Opposite: compatible

clasp v **grasp**, hold, clutch, embrace, hug Opposite: release ■ n **fastener**, hook, catch, hook and eye, snap

class n **1 group**, set, tutorial group, course group **2 lesson**, period, session, lecture, seminar **3 category**, type, sort, kind, genre **4 refinement**, sophistication, elegance, style, flair Opposite: tackiness (infml) ■ v **categorize**, classify, rank, assign, group. See COMPARE AND CONTRAST at **type**.

class-conscious adj **snobbish**, classist, elitist, stuck-up (infml) Opposite: egalitarian

classic adj **1 timeless**, immortal, unforgettable, memorable, abiding **2 definitive**, typical, characteristic, standard, model Opposite: atypical **3 simple**, stylish, elegant, chic, understated ■ n **masterpiece**, landmark, benchmark, model, masterwork

classical adj **traditional**, conventional, orthodox, usual, typical Opposite: modern

classification n **1 organization**, cataloging, arrangement, sorting, ordering **2 category**, class, group, grouping, set

classified adj **secret**, confidential, top secret, off the record, hush-hush (infml) Opposite: open

classify v **categorize**, order, organize, pigeonhole, catalog

classiness (infml) n **refinement**, sophistication, elegance, stylishness, class *Opposite*: tackiness (*infml*)

classless *adj* **egalitarian**, meritocratic, equal, open, free *Opposite*: class-conscious

classmate *n* **fellow student**, fellow pupil, contemporary, peer

classroom *n* **schoolroom**, teaching space, seminar room, tutorial room, lecture theater

classy (*infml*) *adj* **refined**, sophisticated, elegant, stylish, chic *Opposite*: tacky (*infml*)

clatter *v* **rattle**, bang, clang, smash, clank

clause *n* **section**, article, part, division, passage

claustrophobic *adj* **enclosed**, confining, oppressive, suffocating, stifling

claw *v* **scrape**, scratch, scrabble, tear, graze ■ *n* **talon**, nail, hook

claw back *v* **recover**, regain, recoup, retrieve *Opposite*: lose

clay *n* **soil**, earth, dirt, mud

clean *adj* **1 spotless**, dirt-free, unsoiled, fresh, sparkling *Opposite*: dirty **2 pure**, wholesome, untainted, unadulterated, unpolluted *Opposite*: impure **3 neat**, tidy, orderly, shipshape, immaculate *Opposite*: slovenly ■ *v* **scrub**, scour, wipe, cleanse, dust *Opposite*: soil

clean-cut *adj* **neat**, well-groomed, tidy, smart, presentable *Opposite*: untidy

cleaner *n* **1 domestic**, domestic worker, help **2 cleaning product**, detergent, stain remover, cleanser, soap

cleaning *n* **housework**, spring-cleaning, scrubbing, dusting, washing

cleanliness *n* **hygiene**, sanitation, purity, spotlessness *Opposite*: dirtiness

clean-living *adj* **abstemious**, teetotal, moderate, wholesome

cleanly *adv* **easily**, efficiently, effectively, neatly, simply

cleanness *n* **purity**, freshness, simplicity, clearness *Opposite*: filthiness

clean out *v* **1** (*infml*) **bankrupt**, impoverish, reduce, drain, bleed dry (*infml*) **2 unclog**, flush, clear, clean, wash out *Opposite*: block up

cleanse *v* **rinse**, clean, rinse out, bathe, purify *Opposite*: soil

cleanser *n* **1 cleaner**, cleaning product, detergent, stain remover, soap **2 makeup remover**, cleansing cream, lotion, cream, cold cream

clean-shaven *adj* **shaved**, smooth, smooth-shaven, hairless *Opposite*: bearded

cleansing *n* **cleaning**, washing, scrubbing, bathing, rinsing

clean up *v* **1 smarten**, spruce up, tidy up, sanitize, clear up **2 wipe out**, eradicate, eliminate, get rid of, do away with

cleanup *n* **crackdown**, clampdown, elimination, onslaught, attack

clear *adj* **1 transparent**, translucent, see-through, sheer, filmy *Opposite*: opaque **2 strong**, rich, pure, vibrant *Opposite*: indistinct **3 unblemished**, perfect, pure, flawless, faultless **4 well-defined**, sharp, distinct, clear-cut *Opposite*: indistinct **5 ringing**, pure, bell-like, resounding *Opposite*: muffled **6 patent**, incontrovertible, out-and-out, obvious, evident *Opposite*: unclear **7 unambiguous**, understandable, comprehensible, lucid, self-evident *Opposite*: unclear **8 unobstructed**, empty, free, free-flowing, open *Opposite*: blocked **9 cloudless**, bright, sunny, fine, fair *Opposite*: cloudy ■ *v* **1 tidy**, clear out, empty, straighten, clean up **2 free**, vindicate, exonerate, absolve, acquit **3 evaporate**, dissipate, disperse, disappear, settle *Opposite*: form **4 unblock**, free, unclog, empty *Opposite*: block **5** (*infml*) **net**, earn, gain, take home, make *Opposite*: gross

clearance *n* **permission**, authorization, consent, approval, sanction *Opposite*: prohibition

clear-cut *adj* **precise**, distinct, definite, sharp, clear *Opposite*: ambiguous

clear-headed *adj* **lucid**, alert, coherent, perceptive, decisive *Opposite*: muddled

clearing *n* **glade**, clearance, clear-cut, dell (*literary*) *Opposite*: thicket

clearly *adv* **obviously**, evidently, undoubtedly, plainly, visibly *Opposite*: ambiguously

clearness *n* **1 translucency**, transparency, flawlessness, luminousness, limpidity *Opposite*: opacity **2 directness**, clarity, lucidity, comprehensibility, plainness *Opposite*: vagueness

clear out *v* **1 leave**, depart, get going, head off, be off **2 empty**, clear, clean up, turn out, throw out

clear-sighted *adj* **perceptive**, insightful, percipient, realistic, sensible *Opposite*: confused

clear up *v* **1 straighten**, clear, clean up, tidy, put away **2 resolve**, solve, clarify, explain, settle *Opposite*: complicate

cleave *v* **1 slice**, cut, slash, hew, chop *Opposite*: join **2** (*literary*) **stick**, hold on, stick like glue, cling, link *Opposite*: separate

cleft *n* **fissure**, crevice, crack, gap, split

clemency *n* **mercy**, leniency, forgiveness, pity, compassion *Opposite*: heartlessness

clement *adj* **mild**, moderate, temperate, balmy, pleasant *Opposite*: inclement

clench *v* **compress**, grit, tighten, clasp, scrunch *Opposite*: relax

clergy *n* **priesthood**, ministry, ordained priests, clerics *Opposite*: laity

cleric *n* **priest**, minister, ecclesiastic

clerical *adj* **1 secretarial**, office, bookkeeping, accounting **2 priestly**, religious, ecclesiastical, church

clerk n 1 **office worker**, counter clerk, bank clerk, accounts clerk, filing clerk 2 **administrator**, official, recorder, clerk to the council, court clerk

clever adj 1 **ingenious**, shrewd, astute, adroit, crafty Opposite: inept 2 **skillful**, talented, quick, adroit, gifted Opposite: clumsy 3 **bright**, intelligent, smart, knowledgeable, intellectual Opposite: foolish 4 **glib**, smart, slick, pert, flippant. See COMPARE AND CONTRAST at **intelligent**.

cleverness n skill, ingenuity, quickness, shrewdness, smartness Opposite: ineptness

cliché n truism, formula, line, platitude, prosaism

clichéd adj **corny**, hackneyed, trite, passé, old Opposite: original

click n **clack**, tick, snap, clunk ■ v 1 (infml) **make sense**, sink in, become clear, fall into place 2 (infml) **connect**, relate to, be on the same wavelength, hit it off (infml) Opposite: clash

client n **customer**, shopper, consumer, user, end user

clientele n **customers**, clients, regulars, patrons, custom

cliff n **precipice**, rock face, face, crag, overhang

cliffhanger n **crisis**, tiebreaker, knife-edge, nail-biter (infml)

climate n 1 **weather**, temperature, environment, microclimate, macroclimate 2 **atmosphere**, situation, ambiance, surroundings, environment

climax n **peak**, high point, pinnacle, culmination, height Opposite: low point

climb v 1 **scale**, go up, move up, mount, ascend Opposite: fall 2 **rise**, soar, go up, rocket, escalate Opposite: descend ■ n 1 **ascent**, scramble Opposite: descent 2 **increase**, rise, upswing, hike Opposite: fall

climb down v 1 **back down**, retreat, make concessions, give way, backpedal Opposite: stand your ground 2 **descend**, go down, get down, come down, dismount Opposite: ascend

climbdown n **change of mind**, concession, U-turn, shift, retreat

climber n 1 **mountaineer**, rock climber, alpinist 2 **climbing plant**, trailer, creeper, vine

WORD BANK
❏ **types of climbers** bougainvillea, bryony, clematis, convolvulus, grapevine, honeysuckle, ivy, jasmine, kudzu, liana, morning glory, passionflower, rattan, sarsaparilla, Virginia creeper, wisteria, woodbine

climbing n **mountaineering**, hiking, alpinism, rock climbing, artificial climbing

clime (literary) n **climate**, weather, zone, region, place

clinch v **settle** seal, close, tie up, decide ■ n **embrace**, hug, hold, bear hug, cuddle

cling v 1 **clutch**, grasp, hug, hang on to, hold Opposite: let go 2 **adhere**, grip, stick, hug, fit tightly 3 **retain**, maintain, hold to, keep to Opposite: give up 4 **be dependent on**, depend on, hang on, attach, latch onto (infml)

clingy adj 1 **dependent**, insecure, anxious, clinging Opposite: independent 2 (infml) **clinging**, tight-fitting, snug, close-fitting, form-fitting Opposite: baggy

clinic n 1 **hospital**, health center, consulting room, private clinic, treatment center 2 **workshop**, seminar, class, practicum, meeting

clinical adj 1 **scientific**, medical, experimental, quantifiable, proven 2 **detached**, disinterested, dispassionate, scientific, cold Opposite: personal

clink v **clank**, jingle, tinkle, chink, jangle

clip v 1 **cut**, trim, shorten, shear, cut off 2 **fasten**, attach, pin, staple, secure Opposite: undo ■ n 1 **excerpt**, passage, extract, quotation, quote 2 **fastener**, pin, staple, paperclip, clasp

clip-on adj **attachable**, fasten-on, hook-on, separable, removable

clipped adj 1 **trimmed**, neat, cut back, tidy, cut 2 **distinct**, short, brusque, concise, curt

clipping n **extract**, excerpt, article, feature, piece

clippings n **trimmings**, parings, ends, pieces

clique n **group**, in-group, faction, set, gang

cliquey adj **cliquish**, exclusive, clannish, unfriendly, unsociable Opposite: open

cloak n (literary) **screen**, cover, shroud, veil, façade ■ v **cover**, hide, conceal, shroud, veil Opposite: reveal

cloak-and-dagger adj **secret**, clandestine, undercover, covert, mysterious Opposite: aboveboard

clobber (infml) v **hit**, thump, beat, strike, punch

cloche n **cover**, cold frame, protection

clock n 1 **timepiece**, timer, chronometer 2 **regulator**, timer, device, control, meter

WORD BANK
❏ **types of clocks** alarm, alarm clock, clock radio, cuckoo clock, digital clock, grandfather clock, hourglass, pocket watch, quartz clock, stopwatch, sundial, watch, wristwatch

clock up v **achieve**, reach, score, attain, accomplish

clockwork n 1 **mechanism**, device, machinery 2 **regularity**, preciseness, accuracy, flawlessness, smoothness

clod n **lump**, clump, chunk, wad, hunk

clog v **block**, clog up, stop up, choke, obstruct Opposite: unblock

clogged adj **blocked**, obstructed, choked, congested

clog up v block, jam, obstruct, congest, stop up *Opposite*: unblock

cloister n 1 quadrangle, colonnade, arcade, portico, walkway 2 **monastery**, abbey, friary, convent, nunnery ■ v seclude, shelter, retreat, withdraw, closet

cloistered adj secluded, sheltered, confined, protected, insulated *Opposite*: accessible

clomp v clump, stomp, stamp, thump, bang *Opposite*: tiptoe

clone n replica, duplicate, genetic copy, twin, double ■ v duplicate, copy, make a replica of, replicate, emulate. *See* COMPARE AND CONTRAST *at* copy.

clonk v knock, bump, crash into, thump, bang

close adj 1 near, nearby, close by, adjacent, handy *Opposite*: distant 2 **intimate**, familiar, dear, devoted, loving *Opposite*: distant 3 **careful**, rigorous, particular, keen, meticulous *Opposite*: lax 4 **compact**, tight, concentrated, dense, packed *Opposite*: loose 5 **similar**, faithful, precise, exact, literal 6 **silent**, secretive, taciturn, uncommunicative, quiet *Opposite*: open 7 **oppressive**, muggy, airless, sultry, heavy *Opposite*: fresh 8 **stingy**, miserly, tight, tightfisted, grudging *Opposite*: generous ■ v 1 shut, lock, seal, close up, slam *Opposite*: open 2 **come together**, meet, join, unite, gather 3 **shut down**, close down, close up shop, go out of business, stop trading *Opposite*: open 4 **block**, bar, plug, obstruct, seal off *Opposite*: unblock 5 **conclude**, end, finish, complete, terminate *Opposite*: start ■ n end, conclusion, finale, completion, finish *Opposite*: start

close at hand *see* **close by**

close by adj nearby, near, round the corner, on hand, close at hand

close call n close thing, close shave, near miss, narrow escape, lucky escape

close-cropped adj short, close-cut, trimmed, close-trimmed

closed adj 1 shut, locked, bolted, padlocked, fastened *Opposite*: open 2 **impassable**, inaccessible, blocked, obstructed, impenetrable *Opposite*: open 3 **settled**, concluded, terminated, decided, ended *Opposite*: unfinished 4 **narrow-minded**, closed-minded, prejudiced, bigoted, intolerant *Opposite*: open 5 **exclusive**, restricted, private, limited, cliquish *Opposite*: open

closed book n mystery, puzzle, enigma, conundrum, riddle

closed-minded adj narrow-minded, intolerant, prejudiced, bigoted, closed *Opposite*: open-minded

close down v 1 end, shut down, pull the plug on, close, conclude *Opposite*: start 2 **shut**, go out of business, cease trading, come to an end, wind down *Opposite*: open

closedown n closure, closing down, shutting, shutting down, closing *Opposite*: inauguration

close-fisted (infml) adj miserly, tight, niggardly, parsimonious, tightfisted *Opposite*: generous

close-fitting adj body-hugging, tight-fitting, form-fitting, clinging, tight *Opposite*: baggy

close in v draw near, bear down, move in, approach, creep up *Opposite*: move away

close-knit adj close, supportive, strong, caring, cohesive *Opposite*: loose

close-lipped *see* **closemouthed**

closemouthed adj reticent, tight-lipped, reserved, silent, close-lipped *Opposite*: forthcoming

closeness n 1 nearness, proximity, propinquity (fml) *Opposite*: remoteness 2 **intimacy**, familiarity, friendship, nearness, understanding *Opposite*: distance 3 **airlessness**, stuffiness, mugginess, sultriness, oppressiveness *Opposite*: freshness

close-run adj near, close, closely contested, neck and neck, hard-fought

close shave *see* **close call**

closet v cloister, seclude, confine, shut up, lock up ■ adj secret, private, clandestine, undeclared, unprofessed *Opposite*: open

close thing *see* **close call**

close to prep 1 on the brink of, on the point of, near to, about to, on the verge of 2 **like**, similar to, resembling, akin to, bordering on ■ adv nearly, almost, near enough, not far off

close up v 1 shut, close, lock, lock up, secure *Opposite*: open 2 **huddle together**, squeeze up, squash up, bunch up, move up

close-up n detail, zoom, camera shot, shot, photo

close up shop v 1 stop, call it a day, turn in, close, shut *Opposite*: start up 2 **close down**, shut down, go out of business, go bankrupt, go to the wall *Opposite*: start up

close your eyes to v ignore, overlook, disregard, turn a blind eye to, pay no attention to *Opposite*: notice

closing adj final, concluding, last, finishing, ultimate *Opposite*: opening

closing stages n last part, final stages, conclusion, end, finale

closure n 1 end, conclusion, finish, closing, shutting *Opposite*: opening 2 **finality**, resolution, conclusiveness, definiteness, cloture

clot n mass, lump, accumulation, globule, blob ■ v coagulate, coalesce, thicken, congeal, set

cloth n 1 material, fabric, textile, stuff, dry goods 2 **rag**, tablecloth, handkerchief, napkin

clothe v dress, fit out, cover, garb, cloak *Opposite*: undress

clothes n dress, garments, outfit, wardrobe, apparel

clothing see clothes

cloud n mist, fog, haze, bank of cloud, cloud cover ■ v veil, blur, obscure, shadow, make unclear *Opposite*: clarify

WORD BANK
❑ **types of clouds** altocumulus, altostratus, cirrocumulus, cirrus, cumulonimbus, cumulus funnel cloud, mare's-tail, nimbus, rain cloud, storm cloud, stratocumulus, stratus, thundercloud, thunderhead

cloudburst n rainstorm, downpour, deluge, flood, shower

cloud-cuckoo-land n dream world, fantasy world, land of make-believe, dreamland, la-la land

clouded adj 1 troubled, anxious, concerned, worried, apprehensive *Opposite*: untroubled 2 **opaque**, cloudy, murky, misty, hazy *Opposite*: clear

cloudiness n 1 muddiness, murkiness, dirtiness, mistiness, opacity *Opposite*: transparency 2 **vagueness**, confusion, ambiguousness, uncertainness, imprecision *Opposite*: clarity 3 **darkness**, gloominess, dullness, grayness *Opposite*: brightness

cloudless adj clear, blue, sunny, bright, brilliant *Opposite*: cloudy

cloud nine n seventh heaven, raptures, bliss, nirvana, delight *Opposite*: despair

cloudy adj 1 overcast, gray, gloomy, dull, hazy *Opposite*: bright 2 **murky**, muddy, opaque, milky, churned up *Opposite*: transparent 3 **uncertain**, unclear, vague, confused, imprecise *Opposite*: clear

clout n 1 (infml) **influence**, power, authority, weight, sway 2 **thump**, whack, smack, blow, cuff ■ v hit, strike, thump, smack, slap

clove n piece, segment, section, portion, fragment

clover n ease, good life, high life

cloverleaf n highway interchange, junction, intersection, crossroads, crossing

clown n (infml) joker, tease, fool, buffoon, prankster ■ v clown around, fool around, horse around, play the fool, be silly

clowning n joking, buffoonery, horseplay, playing around, fooling around *Opposite*: seriousness

cloy v nauseate, sicken, be too much, satiate, pall

cloying adj 1 syrupy, sticky, sickly, sugary, saccharine 2 **sentimental**, nauseating, sickly-sweet, sickening, heavy

club n 1 **association**, society, guild, organization, union 2 **weapon**, blunt instrument, stick, cudgel 3 **nightclub**, disco, discotheque, casino, private club ■ v batter, hit, bludgeon, bang, strike

WORD BANK
❑ **types of clubs** baton, billy club, blackjack, bludgeon, cudgel, mace, nightstick, shillelagh, truncheon

cluck v 1 cackle, squawk, clack, make a commotion 2 **fuss**, coo, chuckle, tut

clue n sign, hint, evidence, inkling, suspicion

clued-in adj knowledgeable, well-informed, up to speed, au fait, on the ball (infml) *Opposite*: clueless (infml)

clueless (infml) adj naive, inexperienced, impractical, incompetent, ignorant *Opposite*: well-informed

clump n bunch, cluster, mass, tuft, thicket ■ v clomp, plod, stomp, clatter, tramp

clumpy adj ungainly, awkward, cumbersome, unwieldy, chunky *Opposite*: dainty

clumsiness n awkwardness, ungainliness, ineptness, gaucheness, gaucherie *Opposite*: gracefulness

clumsy adj awkward, inept, ungainly, maladroit, gauche *Opposite*: graceful

clunk n clang, clank, clink, thud

clunky adj chunky, heavy, solid, bulky, awkward

cluster n bunch, group, collection, band, gathering ■ v gather, come together, bunch, group, collect *Opposite*: disperse

clutch v grasp, hold, grab, grip, hang on to

clutter n mess, litter, disorder, confusion, untidiness *Opposite*: order ■ v encumber, litter, strew, fill, cover *Opposite*: free

cluttered adj untidy, messy, disordered, muddled, jumbled *Opposite*: orderly

coach n trainer, teacher, instructor, tutor ■ v teach, train, prepare, instruct, tutor. See COMPARE AND CONTRAST at teach.

coaching n training, education, schooling, teaching, tutoring

coachwork n bodywork, exterior, outside, paintwork

coagulate v clot, congeal, thicken, coalesce, set *Opposite*: thin

coagulation n 1 **clotting**, thickening, setting, congealing, gelling 2 **clot**, lump, ball, mass, cake

coalesce v merge, unite, combine, amalgamate, fuse *Opposite*: separate

coalescence n union, combination, amalgamation, meld, merger *Opposite*: separation

coalfield n coalmine, seam, mine, pit, colliery

coalition n alliance, union, partnership, combination, league

coalmine n colliery, mine, pit, coalface, quarry

coarse *adj* **1 rough**, uneven, abrasive, stiff, bristly *Opposite*: smooth **2 indelicate**, tasteless, vulgar, uncouth, crude *Opposite*: polite **3 unrefined**, crude, untreated, organic, unprocessed *Opposite*: refined

coarsen *v* **roughen**, harden, toughen, season, stiffen *Opposite*: soften

coast *n* **shore**, shoreline, coastline, beach, seashore *Opposite*: interior ■ *v* **glide**, cruise, drift, sail, freewheel *Opposite*: struggle

coastal *adj* **seaside**, littoral, sea, ocean, beach

coastline *n* **shoreline**, seashore, coast, shore, seaboard *Opposite*: interior

coast-to-coast *adj* **comprehensive**, extensive, complete, umbrella, blanket

coat *n* **1 fur**, wool, fleece, hide, skin **2 covering**, coating, layer, veneer, glaze ■ *v* **cover**, paint, smother, dip, smear

---

WORD BANK

❏ **types of jackets** anorak, blazer, blouson, bomber jacket, double-breasted jacket, flak jacket, fleece, jacket, Nehru jacket, reefer, safari jacket, single-breasted jacket, smoking jacket, sports jacket, tailcoat, tails, tux *(infml)*, tuxedo, waterproof jacket, windbreaker

❏ **types of overcoats** cape, cloak, duffle coat, frock coat, greatcoat, overcoat, parka, pea coat, poncho, raincoat, slicker, topcoat, trench coat

---

coated *adj* **covered**, caked, frosted, glazed, treated

coating *n* **covering**, veneer, varnish, glaze, layer

coat of arms *n* **crest**, emblem, badge, logo, design

coax *v* **wheedle**, persuade, cajole, charm, entice *Opposite*: browbeat

cobble *n* **cobblestone**, paving stone, paver, sett, stone ■ *v* **mend**, repair, patch, patch up, stitch

cobbled *adj* **paved**, cobblestoned, flagged

cobblestone *n* **cobble**, paving stone, paver, sett, stone

cobble together *v* **improvise**, rig, concoct, contrive, devise

cobwebs *n* **sluggishness**, tiredness, torpor, lethargy, listlessness *Opposite*: liveliness

cochineal *n* **coloring**, food dye, dye, food additive, additive

cock *v* **tilt**, lift, slant, angle, incline *Opposite*: lower

cock-a-doodle-doo *n* **crowing**, crow, cry, call

cock-a-hoop *adj* **elated**, delighted, thrilled, overjoyed, jubilant *Opposite*: dejected

cockcrow *(literary) n* **dawn**, sunrise, sunup, daybreak, the crack of dawn *Opposite*: sunset

cockeyed *adj* **1** *(infml)* **foolish**, absurd, madcap, ridiculous, silly *Opposite*: sensible **2 misaligned**, crooked, askew, awry, uneven *Opposite*: straight

cockpit *n* **arena**, battleground, fight arena, boxing ring, floor

cocksure *adj* **smug**, arrogant, conceited, confident, overconfident *Opposite*: modest

cocktail *n* **concoction**, mixture, brew, blend, combination

cocky *(infml) adj* **smug**, arrogant, boastful, brash, self-assured *Opposite*: modest

coconspirator *n* **collaborator**, partner in crime, accomplice, partner, associate

cocoon *n* **sheath**, covering, shell, case, bubble ■ *v* **wrap**, cover, envelop, insulate, protect *Opposite*: expose

coda *n* **1 conclusion**, ending, end, close, finale *Opposite*: introduction **2 addendum**, postscript, addition, afterthought, adjunct

coddle *v* **pamper**, mollycoddle, indulge, baby, overprotect

code *n* **1 cipher**, cryptogram, encryption, cryptograph, enigma **2 program**, programming, data, instructions, machine code **3 system**, policy, convention, regulations, rules

code-named *adj* **alias**, known as, dubbed, identified, named

code of conduct *n* **agreement**, rules, guidelines, regulations, protocol

code of practice *n* **regulations**, rules, guidelines, principles, protocol

codex *n* **manuscript**, scroll, papyrus, palimpsest, parchment

codicil *(fml) n* **appendix**, supplement, addition, rider, add-on

codification *n* **systematization**, organization, categorization, classification, collation

codify *v* **organize**, collect, collate, arrange, order

coefficient *n* **number**, constant, factor, amount, quantity

coerce *v* **force**, press, pressure, compel, bully

coercion *n* **pressure**, compulsion, force, intimidation, bullying *Opposite*: volition

coercive *adj* **forced**, forcible, intimidating, bullying, strong *Opposite*: gentle

coexist *v* **1 live**, exist, cohabit, live together, coincide **2 harmonize**, synchronize, collaborate, cooperate, reconcile

coexistence *n* **1 cohabitation**, living together, co-occurrence, symbiosis, concomitance **2 harmony**, accord, cohabitation, coevolution, synchronization

coexistent *adj* **concurrent**, simultaneous, contemporaneous, coincident, concomitant

coextensive *adj* **coincident**, equivalent, equal, parallel, corresponding

coffee break *n* **time off**, break, rest, time out, breather *(infml)*

coffeemaker *n* percolator, espresso machine, drip pot, coffeepot, filter

coffer *n* **strongbox**, chest, moneybox, cash box, treasure chest

coffers *n* **funds**, reserves, assets, capital, resources

coffin *n* **box**, casket, sarcophagus, cist

cog *n* **component**, part, gear, mechanism, cogwheel

cogency *n* **power**, strength, intensity, vigor, coherence

cogent *adj* **forceful**, convincing, persuasive, coherent, lucid *Opposite*: unconvincing. *See* COMPARE AND CONTRAST *at* **valid**.

cogitate *(fml)* *v* **think**, consider, reflect, deliberate, ponder

cogitation *(fml)* *n* **thought**, consideration, rumination, musing, reflection

cognate *adj* **similar**, alike, related, kindred, equivalent *Opposite*: different

cognition *n* **thought**, reasoning, understanding, perception, reason

cognitive *adj* **reasoning**, mental, intellectual, cerebral, perceptive

cognizance *(fml)* *n* **knowledge**, awareness, grasp, perception, understanding *Opposite*: ignorance

cognizant *(fml)* *adj* **knowing**, aware, conscious, acquainted, familiar *Opposite*: ignorant. *See* COMPARE AND CONTRAST *at* **aware**.

cognoscenti *n* **connoisseurs**, experts, specialists, authorities, pundits

cogwheel *n* **cog**, wheel, gearwheel, gear, flywheel

cohabit *v* **live together**, shack up *(infml)*, live in sin *(dated)*

cohabitation *n* **living together**, sharing, living in sin *(dated)*

cohabitee *n* **partner**, domestic partner, significant other, spousal equivalent

cohere *(fml)* *v* **1 adhere**, bind, stick, join together, stick together **2 conform**, match, tally, correspond, hang together *Opposite*: disagree

coherence *n* **consistency**, unity, rationality, logic, lucidity *Opposite*: inconsistency

coherent *adj* **1 consistent**, logical, sound, reasoned, reasonable *Opposite*: inconsistent **2 intelligible**, clear, comprehensible, articulate, lucid *Opposite*: unintelligible

cohesion *n* **sticking together**, unity, consistency, solidity, organization *Opposite*: disintegration

cohesive *adj* **unified**, consistent, solid, interconnected, organized *Opposite*: fragmented

cohort *n* **1 unit**, troop, regiment, legion, army **2 supporter**, accomplice, associate, partner, ally

coiffure *(fml)* *n* **hairstyle**, haircut, hairdo *(infml)* ■ *v* **style**, arrange, dress, cut, coif *(fml)*

coil *n* **loop**, curl, spiral, twist, twirl ■ *v* **wind**, convolute, twine, curl, loop

coin *n* **currency**, money, coinage, denomination, change ■ *v* **invent**, think up, make up, create, devise

coincide *v* **accord**, agree, match, correspond, concur *Opposite*: differ

coincidence *n* **1 accident**, chance, luck, twist of fate, quirk **2** *(fml)* **concurrence**, correspondence, correlation, agreement, relationship

coincidental *adj* **1 accidental**, chance, unplanned, spontaneous, unexpected *Opposite*: intentional **2 concurrent**, corresponding, simultaneous, synchronous, correlated *Opposite*: separate

coincidentally *adv* **accidentally**, by accident, by chance, unpredictably, unexpectedly *Opposite*: intentionally

col *n* **pass**, saddle, gap, dip, passage

cold *adj* **1 chilly**, freezing, icy, frosty, bitter *Opposite*: hot **2 emotionless**, unfriendly, unemotional, unsympathetic, unkind *Opposite*: friendly ■ *n* **1 coldness**, chill, chilliness, frost, iciness *Opposite*: heat **2 common cold**, head cold, flu, influenza, chill

cold-blooded *adj* **pitiless**, hardhearted, cold, cold-hearted, callous *Opposite*: compassionate

cold-bloodedness *n* **pitilessness**, coldness, hardheartedness, cold-heartedness, callousness *Opposite*: compassion

cold-hearted *adj* **cold-blooded**, cruel, callous, ruthless, unfeeling *Opposite*: compassionate

cold-heartedness *n* **cold-bloodedness**, cruelty, callousness, ruthlessness, unfeelingness *Opposite*: compassion

coldness *n* **1 cold**, chilliness, frostiness, iciness, wintriness *Opposite*: warmth **2 emotionlessness**, unkindness, unfriendliness, aloofness, distantness *Opposite*: friendliness

cold shoulder *n* **rebuff**, rejection, snub, slight, brushoff *(infml)* *Opposite*: welcome

cold snap *n* **freeze**, frost, iciness, wintriness, cold spell

colic *n* **stomachache**, cramp, indigestion, irritable bowel syndrome, stitch

collaborate *v* **work together**, join forces, team up, work in partnership, pool resources

collaboration *n* **cooperation**, teamwork, partnership, association, alliance

collaborative *adj* **cooperative**, concerted, collective, joint, combined

collaborator *n* **1 colleague**, coworker, partner, teammate, associate **2 traitor**, turncoat, spy, agent, double agent

collage *n* **collection**, combination, assortment, hodgepodge, medley

collapse *v* **1 fall down**, cave in, give way, crumple, subside **2 fail**, end, fold, break down, dissolve *Opposite*: boom **3 fold**, disassemble, fold up, put away, minimize *Opposite*: expand ■ *n* **1 failure**, ruin, downfall, breakdown, flop **2 illness**, breakdown, attack, crisis, crack-up *(infml)*

collapsible *adj* **folding**, foldup, stacking, foldaway, portable

collate *v* **order**, organize, collect, gather, assemble

collateral *n* **security**, surety, warranty, guarantee, insurance

collation *n* **1 ordering**, organization, collection, gathering, assembling **2 meal**, snack, buffet, spread *(infml)*, repast *(literary)*

colleague *n* **coworker**, associate, assistant, partner, collaborator

collect *v* **1 gather**, amass, assemble, accumulate, garner *Opposite*: disperse **2 store**, hoard, amass, stockpile, squirrel

COMPARE AND CONTRAST CORE MEANING: bring dispersed things together
collect bring things together, or to make a collection of similar things as a hobby; **accumulate** obtain things over a period of time; **gather** bring together things from various locations; **amass** obtain a large number of things over an extended period; **assemble** bring things together in an orderly way; **stockpile** collect and store things in large amounts for future use; **hoard** collect and store things in large amounts, often secretly.

collected *adj* **calm**, composed, poised, placid, serene *Opposite*: flustered

collection *n* **1 group**, gathering, assortment, assembly, assemblage **2 compendium**, compilation, set, corpus, anthology

collective *adj* **shared**, cooperative, communal, joint, united *Opposite*: individual ■ *n* **cooperative**, colony, kibbutz, commune, farm

collectively *adv* **en masse**, cooperatively, communally, jointly, together *Opposite*: individually

collectivism *n* **communism**, socialism, syndicalism, Marxism, Leninism

collectivist *adj* **communist**, socialist, syndicalist, Marxist, Leninist

collector *n* **gatherer**, amasser, gleaner, hoarder, accumulator

college *n* **school**, university, academy, seminary, institution

collegial *adj* **1 shared**, reciprocal, mutual, interconnected, communal **2 collegiate**, scholastic, academic, educational, institutional

collegiate *adj* **academic**, university, scholastic, educational, institutional

collide *v* **hit**, strike, crash, bump, bump into

colliery *n* **coalmine**, shaft, seam, pit, mine

collision *n* **1 crash**, smash, accident, impact, rear-ender **2 clash**, conflict, confrontation, disagreement, difficulty

colloquial *adj* **informal**, idiomatic, conversational, everyday, spoken *Opposite*: formal

colloquialism *n* **idiom**, popular expression, common term, vulgarism

colloquium *n* **seminar**, symposium, discussion, roundtable, conference

colloquy *(fml)* *n* **discussion**, meeting, conference, seminar, conversation

collude *v* **conspire**, plot, scheme, plan, connive

collusion *n* **conspiracy**, complicity, involvement, agreement, knowledge

cologne *n* **fragrance**, perfume, toilet water, scent, aftershave

colonial *adj* **foreign**, overseas, expatriate ■ *n* **expatriate**, settler, emigrant, émigré, migrant

colonialism *n* **expansionism**, colonization, imperialism, interventionism

colonialist *adj* **expansionist**, imperialist, interventionist, colonial

colonist *n* **settler**, immigrant, pioneer, migrant, explorer *Opposite*: native

colonization *n* **settlement**, establishment, foundation, occupation, annexation

colonize *v* **settle**, people, inhabit, take over, take possession of

colonizer *n* **settler**, immigrant, colonist, explorer, conqueror

colonnade *n* **arcade**, walkway, portico, porch, loggia

colony *n* **1 settlement**, outpost, dependency, protectorate, satellite **2 gathering**, group, collection, cluster, association

color *n* **hue**, tint, shade, dye, wash ■ *v* **1 tint**, dye, paint, shade, wash *Opposite*: bleach **2 blush**, go red, flush, redden *Opposite*: blanch **3 affect**, influence, incline, shade, modify

WORD BANK
❑ **types of colors** beige, black, blue, brown, gray, green, orange, pink, purple, red, white, yellow

colorant *n* **dye**, hair dye, hair color, pigment, stain

coloration *n* **pattern**, coloring, color, pigmentation, shade

colored *adj* **tinted**, dyed, painted, highlighted, stained

colorful *adj* **1 bright**, multicolored, multihued, polychrome, rich *Opposite*: dull **2 interesting**, full of character, flamboyant, intriguing, lively *Opposite*: uninteresting

coloring *n* **complexion**, skin tone, skin color, ruddiness, pallor

colorless *adj* **1 neutral**, monochrome, pale, pallid, dull *Opposite*: colorful **2 dull**, dreary, nondescript, monotonous, uninteresting *Opposite*: interesting

colors *n* **insignia**, flag, ensign, standard

colossal *adj* huge, massive, immense, gigantic, enormous *Opposite*: tiny

colossus *n* giant, titan, leviathan, behemoth, juggernaut

column *n* 1 pillar, post, support, pilaster, stake 2 line, file, string, procession, cavalcade 3 article, feature, editorial, piece, contribution

columnist *n* writer, journalist, newspaper columnist, magazine columnist, correspondent

coma *n* unconsciousness, blackout, stupor, oblivion, persistent vegetative state

comatose *adj* 1 unconscious, passed out, blacked out, out for the count (*infml*) 2 (*infml*) exhausted, tired, spent, used up, all in *Opposite*: energetic

comb *v* 1 untangle, unsnarl, disentangle, get knots out of, run through 2 search, examine, scrutinize, explore, rake

combat *n* battle, fight, war, contest, struggle ■ *v* 1 fight, battle, oppose, contest, contend 2 resist, prevent, check, reduce, stop

combatant *n* fighter, soldier, enemy, warrior, participant

combative *adj* argumentative, antagonistic, aggressive, belligerent, confrontational *Opposite*: peaceable

combat zone *n* battleground, battlefield, front line, theater of war, war zone

combination *n* 1 mixture, grouping, blend, amalgamation, recipe 2 arrangement, permutation, code, pattern, order. See COMPARE AND CONTRAST *at* mixture.

combine *v* 1 unite, join, merge, coalesce, mingle *Opposite*: divide 2 mix, blend, intermix, amalgamate, bring together *Opposite*: separate ■ *n* 1 syndicate, cartel, bloc, trust, association 2 harvester, thresher, reaper

combined *adj* joint, mutual, shared, collective, united *Opposite*: individual

combustible *adj* flammable, inflammable, explosive, burnable, ignitable *Opposite*: fireproof

combustion *n* ignition, fire, burning, incineration

come *v* 1 arrive, appear, turn up, get here, roll up *Opposite*: go 2 happen, occur, take place, fall, befall (*literary*) 3 approach, move toward, draw closer to, get nearer to, come up to *Opposite*: leave 4 originate, hail from, derive, come from, stem from 5 reach, extend, stretch, go, touch

come about *v* happen, occur, take place, transpire, fall out

come across *v* 1 come by, stumble across, meet, find, stumble upon 2 look, appear, seem, strike, impress

come alive *v* bloom, thrive, blossom, take off, enliven

come along *v* 1 appear, arrive, turn up, occur, materialize *Opposite*: disappear 2 progress, make headway, proceed, advance, unfold 3 accompany, chaperone, escort, tag along, follow

come apart *v* tear, fall apart, break, shatter, collapse

come around *v* 1 consent, acquiesce, comply, yield, compromise 2 revive, come to, wake up, awaken, regain consciousness 3 visit, call, stop by, come by, call by

come at *v* rush, pounce on, attack, threaten, fly at

come back *v* 1 return, reappear, flood back, rush back, revive *Opposite*: go away 2 reply, answer, retort, respond, talk back

comeback *n* 1 retaliation, reply, retort, response, riposte 2 return, revival, reappearance, recovery, reinstatement

come between *v* interfere, set against, meddle, alienate, disaffect *Opposite*: unite

come by *v* obtain, acquire, get, get hold of, get your hands on *Opposite*: lose

come clean (*infml*) *v* bare, reveal, confess, own up, tell the truth *Opposite*: keep secret

comedian *n* humorist, comic, standup, clown, wit

come down *v* decrease, drop, go down, dip, plunge *Opposite*: go up

comedown (*infml*) *n* disillusionment, blow, disappointment, letdown, reality check (*infml*) *Opposite*: boost

come down in favor of *v* approve, back, support, get behind, come down on the side of

come down in sheets (*infml*) *v* pour, sheet down, pelt down, come down in torrents

come down in torrents see come down in sheets

come down on *v* take to task, pick on, be hard on, scold, punish

come down on the side of *v* support, come down in favor of, favor, back, endorse *Opposite*: oppose

come down to *v* signify, amount to, mean, hinge on, boil down to (*infml*)

come down with *v* contract, sicken, incubate, take to your bed, catch *Opposite*: fight off

comedy *n* funniness, joking, amusement, entertainment, humor *Opposite*: tragedy

come first *v* 1 head, top, be at the top, be at the head, be in the lead *Opposite*: lose 2 be your priority, be your main concern, be the most important thing, be paramount, be the only thing that matters

come forward *v* volunteer, offer, put up your hand, step forward, step up to the plate *Opposite*: hold back

come from *v* 1 originate from, be from, hail from, live in, grow up in 2 descend, derive, issue, emanate, originate

come in *v* 1 finish, cross the line, be placed, finish up, end up 2 land, berth, enter, arrive, pull in *Opposite*: depart

come into v **inherit**, receive, be left, be bequeathed, take over

come into being v **come about**, begin life, develop, take form, take shape

come into bud v **blossom**, flower, bud, come to life, burgeon *(literary)*

come into contact with v **1 meet**, encounter, experience, come across, have dealings with **2 touch**, brush against, press against, rub up against, meet

come into flower v **blossom**, bloom, come into bloom, flower, come to life

come into sight v **appear**, emerge, come into view, become visible, heave into view *(literary)* *Opposite*: disappear

comeliness *(literary)* n **attractiveness**, beauty, good looks

comely *(literary)* adj **attractive**, beautiful, good-looking

come off *(infml)* v **happen**, occur, take place, come about, succeed *Opposite*: fail

come on v **start**, begin, go on, occur, kick in *(infml)* *Opposite*: stop

come out v **emerge**, materialize, appear, surface, come to light

come out of v **1 originate**, grow, develop, arise, have roots in **2 survive**, live through, escape, endure, come through

come out on top v **succeed**, triumph, win, emerge triumphant

come out with v **utter**, confess, admit, make known, blurt *Opposite*: conceal

come over v **affect**, engulf, flow over, sweep over

comestible *(fml)* adj **edible**, eatable, digestible

comestibles *(fml)* n **food**, provisions, fare, groceries

come through v **survive**, endure, last, prevail, get through

come to v **1 regain consciousness**, awaken, wake up, revive, come around *Opposite*: black out **2 amount to**, total, add up to, equal, make

come to a close v **end**, finish, conclude, come to an end, stop *Opposite*: begin

come to a decision v **make up your mind**, reach a verdict, decide, make a choice, reach an agreement *Opposite*: prevaricate

come to a halt v **stop**, come to rest, come to a stop, stop in your tracks, stop dead *Opposite*: continue

come to an end v **finish**, end, conclude, stop, cease *Opposite*: continue

come to a standstill *see* **come to a halt**

come to blows v **fight**, exchange blows, start fighting, raise your fists, go for each other

come together v **1 meet**, rendezvous, converge, gather together, congregate *Opposite*: disperse **2 combine**, mingle, meld, unite, take shape *Opposite*: separate

come to grief v **fall flat**, go up in smoke,

come to a bad end, collapse, fizzle *Opposite*: succeed

come to grips with v **cope with**, deal with, manage, handle, tackle

come to life v **awaken**, come to, revive, regenerate, breathe *Opposite*: flag

come to light v **leak out**, surface, emerge, come out, arise

come to nothing v **end in failure**, fail, end in tears, fall apart, fall through *Opposite*: succeed

come to pass *(literary)* v **happen**, occur, come about, take place, transpire

come to rest v **pause**, stop, come to a halt, come to a standstill, halt

come to terms with v **accept**, deal with, cope with, put behind you, get over

come up v **arise**, turn up, happen, occur, come about

come up against v **experience**, encounter, meet, run into, hit

come up for air v **take a break**, relax, break off, rest, take a breather *(infml)* *Opposite*: continue

come upon v **happen upon**, fall upon, come across, encounter, meet

comeuppance *(infml)* n **due**, punishment, just deserts, poetic justice, nemesis

come up to v **match**, meet, equal, satisfy, reach

come up with v **create**, produce, provide, supply, find

comfort n **1 well-being**, ease, relief, security, relaxation *Opposite*: discomfort **2 consolation**, reassurance, relief, cheer, solace *Opposite*: distress ■ v **1 cheer**, cheer up, encourage, gladden, hearten *Opposite*: depress **2 pacify**, soothe, console, reassure, calm *Opposite*: upset

comfortable adj **1 snug**, relaxing, restful, secure, cozy *Opposite*: uncomfortable **2 relaxed**, at ease, contented, happy, easy *Opposite*: nervous **3 well-to-do**, rich, wealthy, affluent, comfortably off *Opposite*: poor

comforted adj **consoled**, supported, reassured, cheered, heartened *Opposite*: distressed

comforter n **1 consoler**, reliever, comfort, support, ray of sunshine **2 quilt**, eiderdown, duvet

comforting adj **heartening**, uplifting, reassuring, cheering, encouraging *Opposite*: upsetting

comfy *(infml)* adj **comfortable**, secure, snug, cozy, relaxing *Opposite*: uncomfortable

comic adj **amusing**, funny, humorous, droll, sidesplitting *Opposite*: tragic ■ n **1 joker**, jester, comedian, standup, clown **2 comic book**, magazine, funny book, funny paper, comic strip. *See* COMPARE AND CONTRAST *at* **funny**.

comical adj **amusing**, funny, humorous,

droll, hilarious *Opposite*: tragic. *See* COMPARE AND CONTRAST *at* **funny**.

comicality *n* **funniness**, drollness, hilariousness, humor, comicalness

comics *n* **funnies**, comic books, comic strips, cartoons, cartoon strips

coming *adj* **forthcoming**, pending, impending, approaching, imminent *Opposite*: past ■ *n* **emergence**, launch, arrival, appearance, approach *Opposite*: departure

comings and goings *n* **activity**, movements, toing and froing, goings-on (*infml*)

coming up *adj* **imminent**, impending, forthcoming, about to happen, upcoming

command *n* 1 **order**, directive, commandment, demand, charge 2 **knowledge**, facility, knack, grasp, expertise 3 **authority**, control, rule, domination, power ■ *v* 1 **order**, direct, demand, charge, instruct *Opposite*: obey 2 **control**, dominate, rule, lead, be in charge

commandant *n* **superior**, chief, commander, chief officer, commanding officer

commandeer *v* **seize**, requisition, hijack, take, appropriate *Opposite*: request

commandeering *n* **appropriation**, acquisition, confiscation, seizure, sequestration

commander *n* **superior**, chief, commandant, chief officer, commanding officer

commanding *adj* **impressive**, forceful, strong, powerful, imposing *Opposite*: weak

commando *n* **SWAT team**, trooper, paratrooper

commemorate *v* **honor**, remember, celebrate, observe, venerate *Opposite*: ignore

commemoration *n* **memorial**, tribute, honor, remembrance, commemorative

commemorative *adj* **memorial**, celebratory, dedicatory, honoring ■ *n* **remembrance**, memorial, tribute, commemoration

commence *v* **begin**, start, originate, inaugurate, instigate *Opposite*: terminate

commencement (*fml*) *n* 1 **beginning**, start, origination, inauguration, instigation *Opposite*: end 2 **graduation**, graduation day, graduation ceremony

commend *v* 1 **praise**, speak well of, acclaim, extol, laud *Opposite*: denigrate 2 **entrust**, convey, hand over, consign, commit *Opposite*: keep

commendable *adj* **praiseworthy**, admirable, worthy, creditable, laudable *Opposite*: lamentable

commendation *n* 1 **praise**, approval, recommendation, acclamation, approbation *Opposite*: criticism 2 **award**, citation, certificate, honor, honorable mention

commensurate (*fml*) *adj* **equal**, proportionate, corresponding, appropriate, adequate *Opposite*: disproportionate

comment *n* 1 **remark**, observation, statement, aside, reference 2 **judgment**, observation, criticism, analysis, critique 3 **explanation**, interpretation, clarification, expansion, commentary ■ *v* **observe**, remark, mention, state, note

commentary *n* 1 **comment**, explanation, observation, note, annotation 2 **review**, essay, report, treatise, thesis

commentate *v* **describe**, explain, report, review, expound

commentator *n* **critic**, observer, reporter, analyst, reviewer

commerce *n* **trade**, business, market, buying, selling

commercial *adj* 1 **business**, business-related, trade, industrial, mercantile 2 **profitable**, salable, marketable, viable, moneymaking *Opposite*: unprofitable ■ *n* **advertisement**, infomercial, trailer, ad (*infml*), promo (*infml*)

commingle (*literary*) *v* **combine**, mix, mingle

commiserate *v* **sympathize**, pity, empathize, show compassion, offer condolences

commiseration *n* **sympathy**, condolences, compassion

commission *n* 1 **payment**, costs, percentage, cut (*infml*) 2 **task**, assignment, duty, job, charge 3 **committee**, authority, agency, administration, board 4 **formal order**, command, directive, instruction, charge 5 **authority**, power, responsibility, position, appointment ■ *v* **assign**, appoint, authorize, contract, order

commissioner *n* **official**, officer, representative, administrator

commit *v* 1 **obligate**, pledge, bind, promise, oblige 2 **earmark**, designate, dedicate, reserve, devote 3 **do**, perform, execute, carry out, perpetrate 4 **entrust**, give, consign, place, hand over

commit hara-kiri *see* **commit suicide**

commitment *n* 1 **promise**, pledge, vow, obligation, assurance 2 **dedication**, loyalty, devotion, steadfastness, allegiance *Opposite*: indifference 3 **obligation**, duty, responsibility, liability, charge

commit suicide *v* **kill yourself**, take your own life, end it all, fall on your sword, commit hara-kiri

committed *adj* **devoted**, dedicated, loyal, staunch, steadfast *Opposite*: uncommitted

committee *n* **group**, board, team, commission, working group

commit to memory *v* **learn**, memorize, learn by heart

commodious *adj* **spacious**, roomy, capacious, sizable, ample *Opposite*: cramped

commodity *n* **product**, service, goods, article of trade

common *adj* 1 **shared**, mutual, joint, public, communal *Opposite*: individual 2 **everyday**, usual, customary, familiar, normal

Opposite: extraordinary **3 widespread**, frequent, general, universal, familiar *Opposite*: rare **4 vulgar**, coarse, ill-mannered, rough, low-class *Opposite*: refined ■ *n* **green**, park, open space, playing field, playground

common denominator *n* **shared quality**, shared belief, commonality, common ground, unifying factor

commonly *adv* **usually**, normally, frequently, generally, regularly *Opposite*: unusually

commonness *n* **ordinariness**, normalness, frequency, prevalence, regularity

commonplace *adj* **1 ordinary**, everyday, usual, routine, common *Opposite*: extraordinary **2 dull**, pedestrian, hackneyed, trite, stale *Opposite*: original

common sense *n* **good judgment**, good sense, practicality, realism, judgment

commonsense *adj* **sensible**, practical, down-to-earth, realistic, commonsensical

commonsensical *see* **commonsense**

commonwealth *n* **nation**, people, nationality, state, country

commotion *n* **ruckus**, tumult, uproar, turmoil, hubbub *Opposite*: peace

communal *adj* **shared**, public, collective, joint, mutual *Opposite*: individual

commune *n* **community**, collective, collective farm, kibbutz, cooperative ■ *v* **communicate**, converse, empathize, connect, be in touch

communicable *adj* **infectious**, catching, transmissible, contagious, transmittable

communicant *n* **church member**, churchgoer, worshiper

communicate *v* **1 converse**, talk, speak, be in contact, be in touch **2 convey**, share, impart, transmit, reveal **3 connect**, interconnect, lead into, link, join

communication *n* **1 contact**, interaction, consultation, transfer, exchange **2 message**, communiqué, announcement, statement, letter

communications *n* **1 infrastructure**, public services, transportation, transport network, links **2 telecommunications**, broadcasting, postal system, data lines, network

communicative *adj* **talkative**, open, forthcoming, outgoing, chatty *Opposite*: reticent

communion *n* **unity**, spiritual union, empathy, closeness, relationship

communiqué *n* **announcement**, statement, communication, press release, bulletin

communism *n* **collectivism**, socialism, communalism, Marxism, Trotskyism

communist *n* **socialist**, collectivist, communalist, Marxist, Trotskyist *Opposite*: capitalist

community *n* **1 neighborhood**, area, village, hamlet, commune **2 kinship**, unity, identity, cooperation, convergence *Opposite*: isolation **3 society**, public, people, population, group

commute *v* **1 travel**, go back and forth, shuttle, car-pool **2 convert**, alter, exchange, transform, substitute

compact *adj* **1 dense**, solid, packed in, packed together, compressed *Opposite*: loose **2 small**, neat, trim, tiny, miniature *Opposite*: large ■ *v* **compress**, pack, squeeze, squash, tamp *Opposite*: loosen ■ *n* **contract**, pact, agreement, deal, treaty

compact disc player *n* **stereo**, personal stereo, hi-fi, CD, boom box

compact disk *see* **compact disc**

compactness *n* **1 density**, solidity, compression, firmness *Opposite*: looseness **2 smallness**, neatness, trimness, tininess, miniaturization *Opposite*: largeness

companion *n* **1 friend**, acquaintance, confidant, colleague, buddy (*infml*) **2 escort**, attendant, chaperon, fellow traveler, arm candy (*slang*)

companionability *n* **friendliness**, bonhomie, camaraderie, affability

companionable *adj* **friendly**, sociable, close, intimate, chummy (*infml*) *Opposite*: frosty

companionship *n* **company**, friendship, camaraderie, comradeship, esprit de corps *Opposite*: enmity

company *n* **1 business**, corporation, firm, concern, enterprise **2 companionship**, friendship, camaraderie, comradeship, esprit de corps *Opposite*: isolation **3 group**, crowd, circle, set, party *Opposite*: individual **4 visitors**, guests, friends, companions, invitees **5 theater company**, troupe, theater group, ballet, touring company

comparable *adj* **similar**, analogous, akin, equal, equivalent *Opposite*: dissimilar

comparative *adj* **relative**, reasonable, fair *Opposite*: absolute

compare *v* **1 evaluate**, contrast, assess, measure up, match up to **2 liken**, associate, link, relate, equate **3 equal**, match, measure up, parallel, compete

compare notes *v* **exchange information**, tell, relate, share, pass on

comparison *n* **1 contrast**, judgment, assessment, evaluation, appraisal **2 association**, link, relationship, similarity, likeness

compartment *n* **cubicle**, booth, partition, box, stall

compass *n* **scope**, range, area, extent, breadth

compassion *n* **sympathy**, empathy, concern, kindness, consideration *Opposite*: coldness

compassionate *adj* **sympathetic**, empathetic, feeling, concerned, kind *Opposite*: unfeeling

compassionless *adj* unsympathetic, unkind, unfeeling, uncaring, cold

compatible *adj* 1 well-matched, like-minded, well-suited, companionable, friendly *Opposite*: incompatible 2 **matching**, fitting, consistent, corresponding, harmonizing *Opposite*: incompatible

compatriot *n* national, fellow citizen, countryman, countrywoman *Opposite*: foreigner

compel *v* force, induce, require, coerce, oblige *Opposite*: cajole

compelling *adj* 1 **convincing**, persuasive, gripping, captivating, fascinating *Opposite*: unconvincing 2 **forceful**, powerful, urgent, undeniable, insistent

compendium *n* collection, anthology, digest

compensate *v* 1 recompense, reimburse, pay off, pay compensation, pay damages 2 **balance**, counterweigh, counteract, counterbalance, offset

compensation *n* 1 **recompense**, reimbursement, payment, damages, costs 2 **advantage**, reward, recompense, return, benefit

compete *v* 1 contest, contend, vie, strive, participate 2 **compare**, equal, measure up, rival, match

competence *n* ability, capability, skill, fitness, aptitude *Opposite*: ineptitude. *See* COMPARE AND CONTRAST *at* ability.

competent *adj* able, capable, skilled, proficient, adept *Opposite*: inept

competition *n* 1 **rivalry**, opposition, antagonism, war, struggle *Opposite*: cooperation 2 **contest**, match, race, struggle, battle

competitive *adj* 1 **spirited**, aggressive, rivalrous, adversarial, cutthroat *Opposite*: passive 2 **reasonable**, modest, good, inexpensive, cheap *Opposite*: expensive

competitor *n* contestant, participant, entrant, player, opponent

compilation *n* 1 **gathering**, compiling, collecting, assembling, composing *Opposite*: dispersal 2 **collection**, set, anthology, assemblage, edition

compile *v* 1 **amass**, accumulate, collect, bring together, assemble *Opposite*: disperse 2 **list**, draw up, compose, set down, register

complacency *n* satisfaction, smugness, self-satisfaction, contentment, gratification *Opposite*: anxiety

complacent *adj* satisfied, self-satisfied, smug, gratified, content *Opposite*: anxious

complain *v* 1 grumble, grouse, carp, whine, moan (*infml*) 2 **protest**, object, criticize, find fault, pick holes in *Opposite*: praise

COMPARE AND CONTRAST CORE MEANING: indicate dissatisfaction with something
complain express discontent or unhappiness

about a situation; **object** be opposed to something, or express opposition to it; **protest** express strong disapproval or disagreement; **grumble** disagree in a discontented way, possibly repeatedly or continually; **grouse** complain regularly and continually, often in a way that is not constructive; **carp** keep complaining or finding fault, especially about unimportant things; **gripe** (*infml*) to complain continually and irritatingly; **whine** complain in an unreasonable, repeated, or irritating way; **nag** find fault with somebody regularly and repeatedly.

complainer *n* whiner, objector, protester, grumbler, faultfinder

complaint *n* 1 **grievance**, criticism, protest, grumble, objection *Opposite*: praise 2 **illness**, condition, ailment, disorder

complaisant *adj* acquiescent, amenable, tractable, willing

complement *n* 1 **accompaniment**, foil, match, balance, counterpart 2 **quota**, set, allowance, quantity, number ■ *v* 1 **complete**, add, supplement, round out, make up for *Opposite*: detract 2 **balance**, set off, harmonize, match, be a foil for *Opposite*: clash

complementary *adj* balancing, opposite, matching, corresponding *Opposite*: clashing

complete *adj* 1 **finished**, completed, concluded, accomplished, fulfilled *Opposite*: unfinished 2 **whole**, comprehensive, wide-ranging, overall, thorough *Opposite*: partial 3 **absolute**, utter, downright, perfect, total ■ *v* 1 **finish**, finalize, conclude, end, bring to an end *Opposite*: start 2 **accomplish**, achieve, fulfill, carry out, realize

completed *adj* finished, accomplished, finalized, done, complete *Opposite*: unfinished

completely *adv* totally, wholly, entirely, fully, utterly *Opposite*: partially

completeness *n* wholeness, fullness, extensiveness, comprehensiveness, inclusiveness

completion *n* conclusion, close, achievement, accomplishment, end *Opposite*: start

complex *adj* 1 **complicated**, difficult, convoluted, involved, dense *Opposite*: simple 2 **multifaceted**, compound, composite, multipart, intricate *Opposite*: simple ■ *n* 1 **development**, center, campus, facility, multiuse building 2 (*infml*) **fixation**, psychosis, phobia, obsession, neurosis

complexion *n* 1 **skin**, face, coloring, appearance, features 2 **nature**, character, cast, tone, aspect

complexity *n* difficulty, intricacy, complication, complicatedness, density *Opposite*: simplicity

compliance *n* 1 **obedience**, acquiescence, agreement, submission, amenability *Opposite*: defiance 2 **conformity**, fulfillment, observance, accordance *Opposite*: noncompliance

compliant *adj* **1 acquiescent**, obedient, biddable, yielding, amenable *Opposite*: defiant **2 conforming**, in compliance, compatible *Opposite*: noncompliant

complicate *v* **make difficulties**, set hurdles, thwart, confound, confuse *Opposite*: simplify

complicated *adj* **complex**, difficult, intricate, byzantine, thorny *Opposite*: simple

complication *n* **difficulty**, snag, problem, impediment, obstacle *Opposite*: solution

complicity *n* **involvement**, collusion, collaboration, connivance, participation *Opposite*: detachment

compliment *n* **praise**, commendation, tribute, accolade, approval *Opposite*: criticism ■ *v* **flatter**, praise, admire, congratulate, approve *Opposite*: criticize

complimentary *adj* **1 flattering**, admiring, kind, gracious, civil *Opposite*: critical **2 free**, gratis, courtesy, on the house, free of charge

comply with *v* **obey**, fulfill, observe, conform, abide by *Opposite*: disobey

component *n* **constituent**, module, section, factor, element *Opposite*: whole

comportment *(fml)* *n* **conduct**, bearing, deportment, demeanor, manner

compose *v* **1 make up**, comprise, constitute, combine, unite **2 arrange**, order, set out, marshal, organize *Opposite*: disturb **3 create**, invent, make up, make, compile

composed *adj* **calm**, collected, self-possessed, serene, unruffled *Opposite*: flustered

composer *n* **creator**, originator, musician, writer, author

compose yourself *v* **calm yourself**, control yourself, calm down, get a hold of yourself, settle down *Opposite*: panic

composite *adj* **compound**, complex, multiple, multipart, multifactorial *Opposite*: simple ■ *n* **amalgam**, mixture, complex, compound, fusion

composition *n* **1 constitution**, makeup, structure, components, constituents **2 work of art**, creation, work, opus, masterpiece **3 arrangement**, configuration, conformation, structure, alignment

composure *n* **calm**, serenity, self-possession, tranquility, self-control *Opposite*: agitation

compound *n* **mix**, mixture, complex, amalgam, composite ■ *adj* **multiple**, complex, composite, multifaceted, multifarious *Opposite*: simple. *See* COMPARE AND CONTRAST *at* mixture.

comprehend *v* **1 understand**, know, realize, grasp, figure out **2** *(fml)* **include**, incorporate, bring in, add in, involve

comprehensible *adj* **understandable**, clear, logical, plain, coherent *Opposite*: unintelligible

comprehension *n* **understanding**, grasp, knowledge, command, conception

comprehensive *adj* **complete**, inclusive, full, all-inclusive, wide-ranging *Opposite*: incomplete

comprehensiveness *n* **inclusiveness**, completeness, all-inclusiveness, exhaustiveness, extensiveness

compress *v* **squeeze**, condense, pack together, squash, constrict *Opposite*: expand ■ *n* **pad**, wad, cold compress, ice pack, wrapping

comprise *v* **include**, encompass, contain, cover, consist of *Opposite*: exclude

compromise *n* **agreement**, settlement, arrangement, bargain, concession ■ *v* **cooperate**, bargain, negotiate, meet halfway, find the middle ground *Opposite*: confront

compulsion *n* **1 coercion**, force, pressure, obligation, duress **2 urge**, impulse, desire, craving, force

compulsive *adj* **1 obsessive**, neurotic, habitual, uncontrollable, irrational *Opposite*: rational **2 gripping**, compelling, mesmerizing, attention-grabbing, exciting *Opposite*: boring

compulsory *adj* **required**, obligatory, necessary, enforced, essential *Opposite*: optional

compunction *n* **regret**, scruple, reluctance, qualm, second thoughts

computation *n* **calculation**, reckoning, totaling, addition, subtraction *Opposite*: estimation

compute *v* **calculate**, work out, total, add, subtract *Opposite*: estimate

computer

WORD BANK

❏ **types of computers** adder, calculator, handheld computer, laptop, mainframe, microcomputer, minicomputer, notebook, palmtop, PC, PDA, personal computer, personal digital assistant, personal organizer, supercomputer, tablet computer, workstation

❏ **types of computer features** bit, bitmap, buffer, byte, cache, cursor, desktop, directory, emoticon, folder, pixel, platform, smiley, subdirectory, wallpaper, window, word

❏ **types of hardware** accelerator card, accumulator, backspace, bus, CD burner, CD writer, CD-ROM, central processing unit, chip, console, CPU, dataport, disk, disk drive, diskette, DVD, firmware, floppy disk, FPU, hard disk, integrated circuit, interface, joystick, keyboard, memory, microchip, microprocessor, modem, monitor, motherboard, mouse, network, numeric keypad, parallel, platform, port, printed circuit, printer, processor, RAM, readout, ROM, scanner, screen, serial, server, simulator, sound card, space bar, terminal, touch screen, trackball, VDT, video display terminal, visual display unit

❑ **types of software** application, CAD, codec, computer-aided design, database, emulator, firmware, freeware, GUI, interface, macro, OCR, operating system, OS, patch, program, screensaver, shareware, simulator, spell checker, spreadsheet, virus, word processor, worm

computer-aided design n **CAD**, computer graphics, graphics, product design, drafting

comrade n friend, companion, buddy (infml), pal (infml), chum (infml) Opposite: enemy

comradely adj **friendly**, companionable, brotherly

comradeship n camaraderie, brotherhood, friendship

con v **1 swindle**, defraud, cheat, trick, do (infml) **2** (infml) **deceive**, hoodwink, trick, mislead, dupe ■ n **1 negative**, disadvantage, minus, objection, downside Opposite: pro **2 confidence game**, fraud, ploy, rip-off (infml), scam (slang)

concave adj **curved in**, dished, hollow, sunken Opposite: convex

conceal v **1 hide**, cover, secrete, screen, obscure Opposite: reveal **2 suppress**, keep quiet, keep under wraps, sit on, censor Opposite: divulge

concealed adj **1 hidden**, covered, buried, obscured, masked Opposite: visible **2 secret**, cloaked, masked, veiled, disguised Opposite: open

concealment n **cover-up**, disguise, camouflage, suppression Opposite: revelation

concede v **1 acknowledge**, grant, admit, accept, allow (fml) Opposite: deny **2 yield**, give in, give up, admit defeat, compromise Opposite: stand firm

conceit n **self-importance**, pride, vanity, arrogance, superiority Opposite: modesty

conceited adj **self-important**, proud, vain, arrogant, high and mighty Opposite: modest. See COMPARE AND CONTRAST at **proud**.

conceitedness n self-importance, arrogance, narcissism, bigheadedness

conceivable adj **imaginable**, believable, possible, plausible, likely Opposite: implausible

conceive v **1 imagine**, visualize, envision, envisage, think up **2 create**, think up, dream up, make up, invent **3 consider**, regard, think of, look on, perceive

concentrate v **1 think**, focus, ponder, muse, deliberate Opposite: daydream **2 converge**, come together, assemble, collect, cluster Opposite: disperse **3 thicken**, strengthen, reduce, purify, distill Opposite: dilute ■ n **distillate**, essence, quintessence, reduction

concentrated adj **1 focused**, intense, concerted, rigorous, strenuous Opposite: half-hearted **2 strong**, thick, condensed, reduced Opposite: diluted

concentration n **1 attentiveness**, attention, absorption, awareness, focus Opposite: distraction **2 strength**, intensity, potency Opposite: dilution

concept n idea, notion, thought, impression, perception

conception n **1 comprehension**, understanding, grasp, command **2 idea**, notion, concept, thought, impression **3 beginning**, start, outset, origin, formation

concern v **1 worry**, trouble, disturb, bother, upset Opposite: reassure **2 relate to**, affect, be about, have to do with, be connected with ■ n **1 anxiety**, worry, apprehension, distress, alarm Opposite: reassurance **2 interest**, business, point, item, affair **3 company**, firm, business, enterprise, establishment

concerned adj **worried**, anxious, disturbed, alarmed, uneasy Opposite: carefree

concerning prep **about**, relating to, regarding, with reference to, as to

concert n **recital**, performance, show, gig (infml)

concerted adj **1 concentrated**, intensive, rigorous, strenuous, determined Opposite: half-hearted **2 combined**, collaborative, joint, mutual Opposite: solitary

concession n **1 privilege**, allowance, dispensation, indulgence, acknowledgment **2 yielding**, surrendering, granting, giving way, conceding **3 concession stand**, franchise, outlet, sublicense, business

concierge n **1 helper**, porter, agent, intermediary, booker **2 caretaker**, janitor, doorman, superintendent, doorkeeper

conciliate v **reconcile**, appease, placate, pacify, make peace Opposite: provoke

conciliation n **reconciliation**, appeasement, pacification, reunion, mollification Opposite: provocation

conciliator n **peacemaker**, mediator, intermediary, arbitrator, arbiter Opposite: troublemaker

conciliatory adj **appeasing**, peacemaking, placatory, pacifying, assuaging Opposite: provocative

concise adj **brief**, short, to the point, succinct, terse Opposite: verbose

conciseness see concision

concision n **succinctness**, terseness, brevity, shortness, curtness Opposite: wordiness

conclave n **meeting**, assembly, council, congress, gathering

conclude v **1 end**, close, finish, terminate, finish off Opposite: start **2 deduce**, assume, presume, decide, reckon Opposite: speculate **3 settle**, complete, close, clinch, arrange. See COMPARE AND CONTRAST at **deduce**.

concluded adj **decided**, settled, determined, resolved, clinched Opposite: unresolved

concluding adj **closing**, final, last, ultimate, ending Opposite: opening

conclusion n 1 deduction, assumption, inference, supposition, decision 2 **end**, close, finish, termination, finale *Opposite*: start

conclusive adj **decisive**, beyond question, definite, convincing, irrefutable *Opposite*: inconclusive

concoct v 1 **prepare**, cook, make, put together, mix up 2 **make up**, create, devise, invent, dream up

concoction n 1 **mixture**, brew, blend, potion, drink 2 **invention**, creation, fabrication, fantasy, fiction

concomitance n **accompaniment**, coexistence, conjunction, combination, association *Opposite*: independence

concomitant adj 1 **attendant**, associated, accompanying, connected, affiliated *Opposite*: unrelated 2 **simultaneous**, parallel, concurrent, coexistent, contemporaneous *Opposite*: independent

concord n 1 **agreement**, harmony, unity, accord, peace *Opposite*: conflict 2 **treaty**, pact, agreement, settlement, compact

concourse n 1 **open space**, public space, forecourt, courtyard, square 2 **crowd**, throng, horde, multitude, mass 3 **gathering**, assembly, meeting, rally, muster

concrete adj 1 **tangible**, existing, actual, material, solid *Opposite*: abstract 2 **specific**, particular, distinct, certain, definite *Opposite*: indeterminate

concubine n **mistress**, kept woman, hetaera, odalisque

concur v 1 **agree**, harmonize, be in accord, correspond, coincide *Opposite*: conflict 2 **coincide**, synchronize, fall together, coexist *Opposite*: diverge 3 **assent**, go along with, agree to, acquiesce, accept *Opposite*: resist. *See* COMPARE AND CONTRAST *at* agree.

concurrence n 1 **agreement**, accord, harmony, consensus, correspondence *Opposite*: conflict 2 **simultaneity**, coexistence, concomitance, coincidence, synchronism

concurrent adj **simultaneous**, synchronous, parallel, coexisting, contemporaneous *Opposite*: separate

condemn v 1 **censure**, denounce, deprecate, criticize, attack *Opposite*: commend 2 **rebuke**, reprove, reprimand, reproach, blame *Opposite*: commend 3 **convict**, sentence, find guilty, doom, judge *Opposite*: absolve. *See* COMPARE AND CONTRAST *at* criticize, disapprove.

condemnation n 1 **censure**, disapproval, blame, denunciation, criticism *Opposite*: commendation 2 **conviction**, sentence, judgment *Opposite*: absolution

condemnatory adj **disapproving**, critical, disparaging, reproving, denouncing *Opposite*: approving

condensation n 1 **wetness**, dampness, damp, humidity, water 2 **concentration**, compression, reduction 3 **abbreviation**, shortening, abridgment, summarization, cutting *Opposite*: expansion

condense v 1 **concentrate**, compress, compact, squeeze, pack *Opposite*: expand 2 **abbreviate**, shorten, abridge, summarize, reduce *Opposite*: expand

condensed adj 1 **shortened**, reduced, summarized, edited, abbreviated *Opposite*: expanded 2 **concentrated**, thickened, reduced, evaporated, thick *Opposite*: diluted

condescend v 1 **patronize**, humiliate, talk down, look down on, disdain *Opposite*: respect 2 **deign**, lower yourself, stoop, humble yourself, demean yourself

condescending adj **patronizing**, disdainful, superior, haughty, pompous *Opposite*: deferential

condescension n **disdain**, superciliousness, aloofness, haughtiness, arrogance *Opposite*: deference

condition n 1 **state**, form, order, repair, fitness 2 **stipulation**, clause, proviso, provision, requirement 3 **disorder**, illness, complaint, ailment ▪ v **acclimatize**, get used to, prepare, train, get ready

conditional adj **provisional**, restricted, restrictive, qualified, uncertain *Opposite*: unrestricted

conditioned adj **trained**, broken in, inured, hardened, accustomed *Opposite*: untrained

conditioning n **training**, breaking in, taming, habituation *(fml)*

conditions n **circumstances**, situation, surroundings, setting, environment

condolence n **sympathy**, commiseration, pity, comfort, concern

condolences n **commiserations**, words of comfort, deepest sympathy

condominium n **apartment building**, house, cooperative, condo *(infml)*, co-op *(infml)*

condone v **overlook**, excuse, disregard, forgive, ignore *Opposite*: oppose

conducive adj **favorable**, helpful, contributing, encouraging, advantageous

conduct v 1 **lead**, show, direct, accompany, guide 2 **manage**, run, control, direct, organize ▪ n 1 **behavior**, demeanor, way, manner, deportment 2 **management**, handling, organization, administration, running. *See* COMPARE AND CONTRAST *at* guide.

conduction n **transmission**, transference, transfer, conveyance, passage

conduct yourself v **behave**, act, behave yourself, carry yourself, comport yourself *(fml)*

conduit n **channel**, canal, duct, tube, pipe

confab *(infml)* n **chat**, tête-à-tête, heart to heart

confederacy n **union**, league, association, alliance, confederation

confederate n **partner**, associate, ally, colleague, accomplice Opposite: rival ■ adj **allied**, united, joined, associated, affiliated Opposite: rival ■ v **ally**, unite, join, affiliate, associate Opposite: disconnect

confederation n **association**, league, union, coalition, confederacy

confer v **1 discuss**, consider, talk over, go over, hash over **2** (fml) **award**, present, grant, give, bestow (fml) Opposite: withhold. See COMPARE AND CONTRAST at **give**.

conference n **1 session**, meeting, consultation, discussion, talks **2 symposium**, seminar, convention, forum, meeting **3 league**, association, alliance, union, federation

confess v **1 admit**, own up, acknowledge, make a clean breast, come clean (infml) Opposite: deny **2 declare**, profess, affirm, assert, make known Opposite: repress

confession n **1 admission**, concession, revelation, acknowledgment Opposite: denial **2 declaration**, affirmation, profession, assertion, statement

confidant n **friend**, soul mate, alter ego, sister, brother

confidante n **friend**, intimate, sister, soul mate

confide v unburden, disclose, reveal, divulge, tell Opposite: withhold

confidence n **1 self-assurance**, sureness, self-confidence, poise, assurance Opposite: timidity **2 certainty**, conviction, belief, faith, trust Opposite: doubt **3 secret**, intimacy, classified information

confidence game see **con game**

confident adj **1 self-assured**, poised, self-confident, self-possessed, cool Opposite: timid **2 definite**, sure, certain, positive, convinced Opposite: unsure

confidential adj **1 private**, secret, classified, off the record, restricted Opposite: unrestricted **2 intimate**, private, close, personal **3 sound**, stable, trusted, trustworthy, reliable Opposite: untrustworthy

confidentially adv **behind the scenes**, privately, in secret, just between you and me, one on one Opposite: openly

configuration n **shape**, outline, formation, conformation, arrangement

configure v **arrange**, design, set up, construct, align

confine v **1 restrain**, restrict, limit, narrow, keep Opposite: unleash **2 detain**, quarantine, imprison, jail, lock up Opposite: release

confined adj **1 limited**, restricted, curbed, restrained, hemmed in Opposite: free **2 constricted**, restricted, small, cramped, enclosed Opposite: open

confinement n **1** (dated) **childbirth**, giving birth, labor **2 imprisonment**, quarantine,

internment, detention, captivity Opposite: freedom **3 limitation**, scope, restriction, restraint, limit

confines n **limits**, boundaries, borders, limitations, margins

confirm v **1 corroborate**, verify, substantiate, bear out, prove Opposite: refute **2 settle**, check, authorize, approve, sanction **3** (fml) **strengthen**, firm up, fortify, reinforce, deepen Opposite: undermine

confirmation n **1 corroboration**, verification, substantiation, authentication, evidence Opposite: denial **2 validation**, authorization, approval, sanction, endorsement Opposite: refusal

confirmed adj **long-established**, established, dyed-in-the-wool, inveterate, deep-rooted

confiscate v **take away**, remove, sequester, seize, impound Opposite: restore

confiscation n **seizure**, repossession, appropriation, removal, sequestration Opposite: return

conflagration n **fire**, blaze, inferno, forest fire, brushfire

conflate v **combine**, amalgamate, consolidate, merge

conflation n **combination**, amalgamation, consolidation, merger

conflict n **1 battle**, fight, war, struggle, encounter Opposite: peace **2 opposition**, disagreement, difference, clash, argument Opposite: concord ■ v **1 disagree**, oppose, clash, differ, be at odds Opposite: concur **2 fight**, quarrel, struggle, argue, scrap Opposite: agree. See COMPARE AND CONTRAST at **fight**.

conflicting adj **contradictory**, incompatible, at odds, inconsistent, differing Opposite: consistent

confluence n **meeting**, convergence, union, joining together, coming together Opposite: divergence

conform v **1 fit in**, imitate, follow, toe the line, obey Opposite: rebel **2 agree**, match, correspond, fit, coincide Opposite: contradict

conformism n **conventionality**, toeing the line, conformity, orthodoxy, traditionalism Opposite: dissidence

conformist n **yes man**, traditionalist, follower, sheep Opposite: rebel ■ adj **conventional**, traditional, orthodox, obedient, unadventurous Opposite: rebellious

conformity n **1 toeing the line**, playing the game, conformism, conventionality, traditionalism Opposite: rebellion **2 agreement**, compliance, consistency, correspondence, accord Opposite: divergence

confound v **1 confuse**, muddle, mix up, mistake, misperceive Opposite: distinguish **2 stun**, amaze, puzzle, mystify, confuse

confounded adj **1** (infml) **annoying**, irritating,

wretched, blasted *(infml)*, darned *(infml)* **2 confused**, perplexed, mystified, baffled, puzzled

confrère *(fml)* n **colleague**, associate, collaborator, coworker

confront v **1 challenge**, oppose, antagonize, provoke, meet *Opposite*: appease **2 encounter**, handle, tackle, face up to, meet *Opposite*: duck

confrontation n **1 hostility**, war, battle, fight, clash **2 opposition**, argument, disagreement, quarrel, altercation *Opposite*: consensus

confrontational adj **argumentative**, quarrelsome, hostile, challenging, aggressive *Opposite*: amicable

confuse v **1 puzzle**, perplex, baffle, mystify, bewilder *Opposite*: enlighten **2 cloud**, muddy the waters, complicate, blur, muddy *Opposite*: clarify **3 muddle**, mix up, misperceive, mistake, confound *Opposite*: distinguish

confused adj **1 puzzled**, perplexed, baffled, mystified, bewildered *Opposite*: enlightened **2 disordered**, disorderly, muddled, mixed up, in disarray *Opposite*: orderly

confusing adj **unclear**, puzzling, perplexing, baffling, mystifying *Opposite*: clear

confusion n **1 bewilderment**, perplexity, puzzlement, mystification, uncertainty *Opposite*: understanding **2 misperception**, misunderstanding, mix-up, muddle, mistake *Opposite*: clarity **3 disorder**, chaos, turmoil, upheaval, commotion *Opposite*: order **4 embarrassment**, awkwardness, disorientation, uncertainty, self-consciousness *Opposite*: confidence

con game *(infml)* n **swindle**, confidence game, rip-off *(infml)*, snow job *(slang)*

congeal v **set**, clot, coagulate, thicken, solidify *Opposite*: liquefy

congealed adj **set**, dried, coagulated, clotted

congenial adj **agreeable**, friendly, affable, amiable, pleasant *Opposite*: hostile

congeniality n **affability**, bonhomie, geniality

congenital adj **1 inherited**, hereditary, inborn, inbred, genetic *Opposite*: acquired **2 ingrained**, established, long-established, habitual, inveterate

congest v **clog**, overfill, overcrowd, block, jam *Opposite*: clear

congested adj **1 overfilled**, jammed, choked, clogged, blocked *Opposite*: empty **2 obstructed**, clogged, mucous, stuffy, filled *Opposite*: clear

congestion n **1 overcrowding**, bottleneck, cramming, jamming, blocking *Opposite*: emptiness **2 blockage**, clogging, obstruction

conglomerate n **corporation**, multinational, company, firm, business

conglomeration n **1 assortment**, hodgepodge, potpourri, collection, accumulation **2 composite**, accumulation, mass, collection, assembly

congratulate v **commend**, toast, pat on the back, cheer, applaud *Opposite*: denigrate

congregate v **gather**, assemble, collect, meet, mass *Opposite*: disperse

congregation n **1 worshipers**, churchgoers, parishioners, flock **2 gathering**, crowd, throng, host, mass

congress n **assembly**, council, conference, meeting, convention

congressperson n **representative**, senator, legislator, lawmaker, deputy

congruent *(fml)* adj **corresponding**, consistent, matching, compatible, similar *Opposite*: disparate

conjectural adj **speculative**, tentative, unsubstantial, unsupported

conjecture n **guesswork**, estimation, guess, surmise, inference ■ v **estimate**, imagine, guess, speculate, infer

conjoin *(fml)* v **link**, join, connect, couple

conjugal adj **marital**, matrimonial, married, wedded, spousal *Opposite*: unmarried

conjunction n **combination**, union, unification, coincidence, concurrence

conjure v **1 raise**, summon, call up, invoke, conjure up **2 mesmerize**, charm, trick, voodoo, spellbind

conjure up v **1 evoke**, create, recall, call up, bring to mind **2 raise**, conjure, summon, call up, invoke

conjuring n **magic**, illusion, sleight of hand, trickery

conked-out *(infml)* adj **asleep**, dead to the world, crashed-out *(slang)*

conk out *(infml)* v **1 fail**, break, wear out, malfunction, stall *Opposite*: start up **2 collapse**, pass out, doze off, nod off, fall asleep *Opposite*: wake up

connect v **1 attach**, join, link, fix, fasten *Opposite*: disconnect **2 associate**, relate, link, tie, link up *Opposite*: separate **3 get along**, bond, click *(infml)*, hook up *(infml)*, hit it off *(infml)*

connected adj **1 joined**, attached, fixed, united, tied *Opposite*: separate **2 linked**, associated, related, allied, coupled *Opposite*: unrelated

connection n **1 joining**, fitting together, assembly, linking, piecing together **2 context**, association, relationship, correlation, relation **3 bond**, tie, union, link, join

connections n **1 influence**, network, associates, acquaintances, links **2 relations**, relatives, associations, links, family

connive v **plot**, scheme, conspire, collude, plan

conniver n **maneuverer**, manipulator, schemer, plotter, intriguer

conniving *adj* **devious**, scheming, conspiratorial, sly, crafty *Opposite*: ingenuous

connoisseur *n* **specialist**, authority, expert, enthusiast, aficionado

connotation *n* **implication**, association, suggestion, meaning, undertone

connote *v* **mean**, signify, suggest, intimate, imply

connubial *(literary) adj* **nuptial**, marital, matrimonial, wedded, conjugal *Opposite*: unmarried

conquer *v* **1 seize**, take, take over, take control of, capture *Opposite*: surrender **2 defeat**, beat, overpower, overthrow, subjugate *Opposite*: lose **3 overcome**, surmount, get the better of, triumph over, master *Opposite*: give in. *See* COMPARE AND CONTRAST *at* defeat.

conquered *adj* **defeated**, beaten, vanquished, overpowered

conqueror *n* **defeater**, vanquisher, subjugator, captor, victor *Opposite*: vanquished

conquest *n* **1 defeat**, subjugation, overthrow, takeover, rout *Opposite*: surrender **2 victory**, success, triumph, win *Opposite*: defeat

conscience *n* **scruples**, principles, ethics, integrity, sense of right and wrong

conscience-stricken *adj* **guilty**, sorry, remorseful, guilt-ridden, contrite

conscientious *adj* **1 careful**, thorough, meticulous, painstaking, punctilious *Opposite*: careless **2 dutiful**, responsible, honorable, upright, upstanding *Opposite*: dishonest. *See* COMPARE AND CONTRAST *at* careful.

conscientiousness *n* **scrupulousness**, thoroughness, assiduousness, meticulousness, carefulness *Opposite*: carelessness

conscious *adj* **1 awake**, wide awake, sleepless, insomniac *Opposite*: unconscious **2 aware**, mindful, sentient, sensible, cognizant *(fml) Opposite*: unaware **3 deliberate**, intentional, premeditated, willful, determined *Opposite*: unintentional. *See* COMPARE AND CONTRAST *at* aware.

consciously *adv* **deliberately**, intentionally, knowingly, determinedly, willfully *Opposite*: unintentionally

consciousness *n* **awareness**, realization, perception, mindfulness, notice *Opposite*: unconsciousness

conscript *v* **call up**, recruit, draft, enlist, enroll ■ *n* **recruit**, novice, draftee, rookie *(infml)*

conscription *n* **recruitment**, draft, mobilization, enlistment, enrollment

consecrate *v* **sanctify**, bless, set apart, hallow, dedicate *Opposite*: desecrate

consecrated *adj* **hallowed**, sanctified, sacred, holy, blessed *Opposite*: desecrated

consecration *n* **sanctification**, dedication, blessing, hallowing *Opposite*: desecration

consecutive *adj* **successive**, uninterrupted, following, repeated, serial *Opposite*: alternate

consensus *n* **agreement**, accord, harmony, compromise, consent *Opposite*: disagreement

consent *v* **1 permit**, allow, approve, accept, sanction *Opposite*: forbid **2 agree**, comply, assent, acquiesce, accede *Opposite*: refuse ■ *n* **1 agreement**, accord, consensus, harmony **2 permission**, approval, assent, blessing, sanction *Opposite*: refusal. *See* COMPARE AND CONTRAST *at* agree.

consequence *n* **1** *(fml)* **importance**, significance, value, concern, import **2 result**, effect, outcome, end result, corollary

consequent *adj* **resulting**, resultant, consequential, following, subsequent

consequential *adj* **1 important**, significant, momentous, far-reaching, substantial *Opposite*: inconsequential **2 resulting**, resultant, consequent, following, subsequent

consequently *adv* **as a result**, so, therefore, subsequently, accordingly

conservation *n* **preservation**, upkeep, maintenance, protection, management *Opposite*: destruction

conservative *adj* **1 traditional**, middle-of-the-road, conventional, conformist, reactionary *Opposite*: avant-garde **2 cautious**, moderate, careful *Opposite*: speculative ■ *n* **traditionalist**, conformist, reactionary, fundamentalist, purist *Opposite*: progressive

conservatory *n* **1 school of the arts**, music school, art school, school of dance, conservatoire **2 greenhouse**, hothouse, garden room, porch

conserve *v* **1 preserve**, save, keep, protect, safeguard *Opposite*: destroy **2 store**, save, keep, eke out, be careful with *Opposite*: expend ■ *n* **jam**, marmalade, preserve

consider *v* **1 think through**, mull over, chew over, reflect, deliberate **2 judge**, believe, think, regard, deem *(fml)* **3 respect**, bear in mind, care about, take into consideration, count *Opposite*: disregard

considerable *adj* **substantial**, significant, large, extensive, sizable *Opposite*: insignificant

considerably *adv* **significantly**, much, noticeably, by far, greatly *Opposite*: slightly

considerate *adj* **thoughtful**, kind, understanding, caring, sensitive *Opposite*: inconsiderate

consideration *n* **1 thought**, reflection, contemplation, attention, deliberation *(fml)* **2 respect**, concern, thoughtfulness, kindness, selflessness *Opposite*: thoughtlessness **3 matter**, factor, point, issue, fact **4 regard**, esteem, importance, significance, weight

considered *adj* **careful**, measured, well-thought-out, painstaking *Opposite*: rash

considering *prep* **bearing in mind**, allowing for, in view of, given, taking into account *Opposite*: excluding

consign *v* **1 entrust**, commit, hand over, give **2 relegate**, dispatch, condemn, banish, get rid of **3 deliver**, transfer, send, dispatch, ship

consignment *n* **batch**, delivery, shipment, load, package

consist *v* **1 contain**, be made up of, be made of, entail, involve **2 reside**, lie, be based on, depend on, be defined by

consistency *n* **1 constancy**, steadiness, reliability, uniformity, evenness *Opposite*: inconsistency **2 texture**, thickness, runniness, feel, makeup

consistent *adj* **1 reliable**, steady, dependable, constant, unswerving *Opposite*: inconsistent **2 coherent**, uniform, harmonious, even *Opposite*: contradictory

consistently *adv* **1 time after time**, time and again, again and again, repeatedly, every time *Opposite*: erratically **2 reliably**, steadily, dependably, constantly, unswervingly *Opposite*: inconsistently

consolation *n* **comfort**, solace, relief, support, succor *(literary)* *Opposite*: grief

consolatory *adj* **comforting**, consoling, cheering, soothing

console *v* **comfort**, cheer up, soothe, calm, relieve *Opposite*: depress

consolidate *v* **1 combine**, unite, join, fuse, merge *Opposite*: split up **2 strengthen**, firm up, establish, confirm, enhance *Opposite*: weaken

consolidation *n* **1 alliance**, merging, union, link, association *Opposite*: split **2 strengthening**, firming, establishment, solidification, firming up *Opposite*: weakening

consoling *adj* **comforting**, soothing, cheering, calming

consort *n* **1** *(fml)* **companion**, partner, associate, spouse, wife **2 ensemble**, group, orchestra, band

consortium *n* **group**, grouping, association, conglomerate, syndicate

consort with *(fml)* *v* **associate**, accompany, mix, mingle, hang around

conspicuous *adj* **1 visible**, noticeable, obvious, exposed, on show *Opposite*: inconspicuous **2 eye-catching**, striking, prominent, outstanding, notable *Opposite*: unremarkable

conspicuously *adv* **noticeably**, obviously, clearly, evidently, blatantly *Opposite*: inconspicuously

conspicuousness *n* **obviousness**, plainness, prominence, overtness

conspiracy *n* **plot**, scheme, plan, intrigue, collusion

conspirator *n* **schemer**, plotter, conniver, collaborator, accomplice

conspiratorial *adj* **private**, shared, confidential, complicit, collusive

conspire *v* **1 plot**, connive, plan, scheme, work against **2 combine**, work together, unite, collaborate, collude

constancy *n* **1 faithfulness**, loyalty, fidelity, dependability, reliability *Opposite*: unfaithfulness **2 steadiness**, firmness, consistency, steadfastness, endurance *Opposite*: inconsistency

constant *adj* **1 continuous**, endless, relentless, continual, persistent *Opposite*: intermittent **2 frequent**, persistent, recurrent, incessant, recurring *Opposite*: occasional **3 steady**, stable, even, invariable, unvarying *Opposite*: irregular **4 faithful**, loyal, trustworthy, devoted, staunch *Opposite*: disloyal

constantly *adv* **continually**, continuously, always, regularly, frequently *Opposite*: intermittently

constellation *n* **group**, gathering, collection, assemblage, pattern

consternation *n* **dismay**, disquiet, alarm, anxiety, worry *Opposite*: composure

constituency *n* **1 area**, borough, ward, region **2 electorate**, voters, population, public, community

constituent *n* **1 voter**, citizen, resident **2 ingredient**, element, component, part ■ *adj* **basic**, essential, integral, component, fundamental

constitute *v* **1 make up**, form, compose, represent **2 amount to**, represent, add up to, signify, total *Opposite*: fall short **3** *(fml)* **set up**, establish, found, create, institute *Opposite*: disband

constitution *n* **1 charter**, bill, statute **2 health**, makeup, disposition, nature, condition **3 establishment**, creation, formation, organization, foundation **4 composition**, structure, makeup, components, constituents

constitutional *adj* **legitimate**, legal, lawful, statutory *Opposite*: unconstitutional

constrain *v* **1 oblige**, compel, pressure, make, coerce **2 limit**, restrain, hold back, confine, restrict

constrained *adj* **forced**, unnatural, inhibited, unspontaneous, embarrassed *Opposite*: natural

constraint *n* **restriction**, limitation, restraint, constriction, limit *Opposite*: freedom

constrict *v* **1 tighten**, narrow, contract, compress, shrink *Opposite*: loosen **2 limit**, restrict, constrain, narrow, control *Opposite*: extend

constricted *adj* **limited**, restricted, restrained, bound, confined *Opposite*: free

constriction *n* **1 restriction**, constraint, limitation, limit, condition **2 tightening**, contraction, narrowing, compression, shrinking *Opposite*: loosening

construct *v* **1 build**, make, create, put up, erect *Opposite*: knock down **2 compose**, put together, create, structure, piece together *Opposite*: take apart ■ *n* **concept**, hypothesis, theory, paradigm, idea

construction *n* **1 creation**, assembly, manufacture, production, erection *Opposite*: destruction **2 building**, edifice, structure, creation, erection *(fml)* **3 interpretation**, understanding, comprehension, meaning, explanation

constructive *adj* **positive**, helpful, productive, useful, beneficial *Opposite*: unhelpful

construe *v* **interpret**, take, read, see, understand

consul *n* **diplomat**, ambassador, representative, emissary, envoy

consult *v* **1 ask**, check, discuss, talk to, confer **2 refer**, look up, turn to, check, access

consultant *n* **adviser**, expert, specialist, professional, authority

consultation *n* **discussion**, dialogue, talk, session, meeting

consume *v* **1 eat**, drink, devour, munch, feed on **2 use**, use up, expend, spend, utilize *Opposite*: conserve **3 destroy**, annihilate, burn up, incinerate, burn down

consumer *n* **buyer**, purchaser, shopper, customer, user

consummate *v* **complete**, carry out, achieve, accomplish, conclude ■ *adj* **1 skilled**, skillful, expert, accomplished, talented *Opposite*: inept **2 perfect**, excellent, complete, ideal, flawless *Opposite*: imperfect **3 utter**, out-and-out, total, complete, absolute

consumption *n* **1 ingesting**, feasting, feeding, eating, drinking **2 depletion**, use, expenditure, utilization, spending *Opposite*: conservation

contact *n* **1 interaction**, communication, touching base, dealings, connection **2 connection**, acquaintance, friend, link, associate ■ *v* **get in touch**, make contact, drop a line, communicate, write

contagious *adj* **transmissible**, transmittable, spreadable, infectious, catching

contain *v* **1 cover**, take in, comprise, encompass, hold *Opposite*: exclude **2 check**, control, restrain, hold back, inhibit *Opposite*: unleash **3 limit**, control, keep in check, delimit, restrict

contained *adj* **limited**, controlled, checked, confined, restricted *Opposite*: unbounded

contaminate *v* **soil**, pollute, foul, taint, infect *Opposite*: purify

contaminated *adj* **dirty**, dirtied, filthy, soiled, polluted *Opposite*: pure

contamination *n* **pollution**, adulteration, corruption, infection, uncleanness *Opposite*: decontamination

contemplate *v* **1 look**, gaze, stare, watch, examine **2 weigh**, muse, deliberate, consider, think **3 anticipate**, expect, plan, think of, consider **4 meditate**, muse, imagine, envisage, envision

contemplation *n* **1 inspection**, observation, survey, review, scrutiny **2 thought**, meditation, consideration, study, reflection

contemplative *adj* **thoughtful**, meditative, deep in thought, lost in thought, absorbed *Opposite*: unthinking

contemporaneity *n* **concurrence**, simultaneity, coexistence, contemporaneousness

contemporaneous *adj* **concurrent**, coexistent, concomitant, contemporary, simultaneous

contemporaneousness *see* **contemporaneity**

contemporaries *n* **age group**, generation, peers, coevals *(fml)*

contemporary *adj* **current**, modern, up-to-date, latest, present-day *Opposite*: old ■ *r* **peer**, colleague, classmate, coeval *(fml)*

contempt *n* **disdain**, dislike, disrespect, disapproval, scorn *Opposite*: admiration

contemptibility *n* **shamefulness**, reprehensibility, vileness, contemptibleness

contemptible *adj* **despicable**, disgraceful, shameful, detestable, distasteful *Opposite*: laudable

contemptibleness *see* **contemptibility**

contemptuous *adj* **scornful**, derisive, disdainful, disapproving, sneering *Opposite*: admiring

contemptuousness *n* **scornfulness**, disrespect, scorn, disdain, derision *Opposite*: admiration

contend *v* **1 argue**, assert, allege, insist, maintain **2 compete**, vie, challenge, run, put yourself forward **3 struggle**, resist, oppose, deal with, put up with

contender *n* **candidate**, nominee, competitor, contestant, challenger. *See* COMPARE AND CONTRAST *at* **candidate**.

contend with *v* **deal with**, cope with, face, experience

content *n* **substance**, matter, subject matter, theme, gist ■ *adj* **gratified**, happy, satisfied, contented, pleased *Opposite*: unhappy ■ *v* **gladden**, soothe, satisfy, please, make happy *Opposite*: dissatisfy

contented *adj* **happy**, satisfied, pleased, content, comfortable *Opposite*: unhappy

contention *n* **1 assertion**, position, argument, opinion, belief **2 argument**, disagreement, dispute, debate, conflict *Opposite*: harmony

contentious *adj* **1 controversial**, polemical, provocative, divisive, debatable *Opposite*: uncontroversial **2 argumentative**, combative, quarrelsome, antagonistic, disputatious *Opposite*: easygoing

contentment *n* **serenity**, gladness, satisfaction, happiness, pleasure *Opposite*: discontent

contest *n* **competition**, tournament, challenge, race, match ▪ *v* **challenge**, dispute, question, oppose, query *Opposite*: accept

contestant *n* **competitor**, contender, participant, participator, challenger *Opposite*: quiz master. *See* COMPARE AND CONTRAST *at* **candidate**.

context *n* **setting**, background, circumstances, situation, framework

contextual *adj* **background**, related, circumstantial, framing

contiguity *(fml) n* **proximity**, nearness, closeness, adjacency

contiguous *(fml) adj* **adjoining**, bordering, next to, adjacent, side by side

continent *n* **landmass**, mainland, land

contingency *n* **eventuality**, possibility, likelihood, exigency, emergency

contingent *adj* **depending**, liable, dependent, reliant, conditional ▪ *n* **commission**, legation, committee, party, group

continual *adj* **repeated**, frequent, recurrent, incessant, constant *Opposite*: intermittent

continuance *n* **extension**, protraction, extending, protracting, perpetuation *Opposite*: halting

continuation *n* **1 perpetuation**, progression, extension, drawing out, persistence *Opposite*: cessation **2 addition**, sequel, installment, extension, carryover

continue *v* **1 prolong**, maintain, sustain, perpetuate, carry on *Opposite*: stop **2 last**, endure, linger, remain, stay *Opposite*: end **3 renew**, restart, resume, reprise, revive

continuing *adj* **ongoing**, current, enduring, remaining, unending *Opposite*: finished

continuity *n* **steadiness**, endurance, continuousness, permanence, stability *Opposite*: interruption

continuous *adj* **incessant**, unceasing, nonstop, unremitting, constant *Opposite*: intermittent

continuousness *n* **continuity**, constancy, permanence

contort *v* **distort**, twist, screw, warp, deform

contour *n* **outline**, delineation, silhouette, relief, curve

contract *n* **agreement**, bond, indenture, pact, convention ▪ *v* **1 diminish**, grow smaller, shrink, tighten, narrow *Opposite*: expand **2 sign**, commission, sign up, commit, engage **3 become infected with**, catch, get, develop, be afflicted by *Opposite*: fight off

contraction *n* **1 reduction**, shrinkage, tightening, narrowing, retrenchment *Opposite*: expansion **2 tightening**, jerking, cramp, spasm, tic **3 shortening**, merging, combining, abbreviation, ellipsis

contractor *n* **worker**, independent, outside worker, freelancer, subcontractor

contract out *v* **delegate**, offer, subcontract, outsource, farm

contradict *v* **1 deny**, oppose, challenge, dispute, refute *Opposite*: confirm **2 disprove**, cancel, refute, dispute, undermine *Opposite*: support. *See* COMPARE AND CONTRAST *at* **disagree**.

contradiction *n* **1 illogicality**, flaw, inconsistency, incongruity, ambiguity **2 denial**, disagreement, challenge, negation, opposition *Opposite*: confirmation

contradictory *adj* **inconsistent**, self-contradictory, contrary, opposing, clashing *Opposite*: consistent

contraption *n* **gadget**, machine, device, apparatus, contrivance

contrarily *adv* **disobediently**, rebelliously, stubbornly, willfully, defiantly *Opposite*: cooperatively

contrariness *n* **disobedience**, uncooperativeness, perversity, rebelliousness, willfulness *Opposite*: cooperation

contrary *adj* **1 conflicting**, opposing, different, differing, divergent *Opposite*: similar **2 disobedient**, rebellious, obstinate, uncooperative, defiant *Opposite*: cooperative ▪ *n* **opposite**, inverse, other side of the coin, converse, reverse

contrast *n* **difference**, dissimilarity, distinction, disparity, gap *Opposite*: similarity ▪ *v* **1 compare**, juxtapose, analogize, weigh, distinguish **2 stand out**, stick out like a sore thumb, differ, diverge, conflict *Opposite*: agree

contrasting *adj* **conflicting**, opposing, complementary, different, distinct *Opposite*: similar

contravene *v* **break**, flout, breach, disobey, disregard *Opposite*: observe

contravention *n* **breaking**, flouting, breach, infringement, disobeying *Opposite*: observance

contribute *v* **1 donate**, pay, underwrite, subsidize, back **2 weigh in**, have a say, add, throw in, say **3 cause**, further, influence, impact, participate

contribution *n* **1 influence**, input, role, involvement, say **2 donation**, gift, giving, payment, subsidy

contributor *n* **donor**, sponsor, backer, giver, supplier

contributory *adj* **related**, influential, causal, causative, contributing

contrite *adj* **sorry**, repentant, remorseful, regretful, apologetic *Opposite*: impenitent

contriteness *see* **contrition**

contrition *n* **remorse**, repentance, penitence, regret, sorrow *Opposite*: shamelessness

contrivance *n* **1 gadget**, device, apparatus, machine, contraption **2 plot**, plan, plot, ruse, scheme

contrive v **design**, lay out, engineer, arrange, plan

contrived adj **forced**, artificial, unnatural, manufactured, affected Opposite: genuine

control v 1 **restrain**, limit, restrict, hold back, rein in Opposite: release 2 **operate**, work, run, use, utilize 3 **manage**, command, supervise, run, direct 4 **rule**, manipulate, influence, dominate, oppress 5 **oversee**, monitor, regulate, inspect, watch over ■ n 1 **switch**, regulator, controller, governor, circuit breaker 2 **power**, jurisdiction, rule, domination, hegemony 3 **skill**, manipulation, influence, handling, expertise 4 **limit**, limitation, constraint, restriction, restraint

controllable adj **manageable**, governable, malleable, tractable, easy to deal with Opposite: uncontrollable

controlled adj 1 **contained**, unflappable, under control, self-controlled, self-possessed Opposite: panicky 2 **accurate**, measured, precise, meticulous, exact Opposite: imprecise 3 **regulated**, structured, planned, measured, delimited Opposite: free

controller n 1 **supervisor**, manager, organizer, regulator, director 2 **regulator**, switch, control, device, governor

control panel n **instrument panel**, console, dashboard, dash, instrumentation

controls n **instrument panel**, wheel, helm

controversial adj **contentious**, provocative, hotly debated, debatable, divisive Opposite: uncontroversial

controversy n **disagreement**, argument, debate, storm, hullabaloo Opposite: agreement

contumacious (fml) adj **insubordinate**, rebellious, disobedient, defiant, noncompliant Opposite: conformist

contumely (literary) n **criticism**, disparagement, vilification, derision, scorn Opposite: praise

conundrum n **puzzle**, mystery, challenge, problem, riddle. See COMPARE AND CONTRAST at **problem**.

conurbation n **urban area**, built-up area, urban sprawl, city, metropolis. See COMPARE AND CONTRAST at **city**.

convalesce v **improve**, recover, recuperate, get better, rally Opposite: deteriorate

convalescence n **recuperation**, recovery, restoration, rehabilitation, R and R Opposite: deterioration

convalescent adj **convalescing**, recovering, recuperating, improving, getting better Opposite: deteriorating

convene v **call together**, assemble, summon, set up, organize Opposite: disband

convenience n **suitability**, expediency, ease, handiness, opportuneness Opposite: inconvenience

convenient adj 1 **suitable**, expedient, opportune, fitting, appropriate Opposite: inconvenient 2 **handy**, close at hand, adjacent, near, close Opposite: out-of-the-way

conveniently adv **suitably**, expediently, handily, opportunely, accessibly Opposite: inconveniently

convent n **nunnery**, religious foundation, religious community, cloister

convention n 1 **gathering**, meeting, conference, congress, assembly 2 **agreement**, pact, resolution, contract, settlement 3 **rule**, principle, custom, practice, habit

conventional adj 1 **conservative**, conformist, predictable, unadventurous, middle-of-the-road Opposite: adventurous 2 **usual**, established, standard, normal, regular Opposite: unusual

conventionality n **conformism**, conservatism, orthodoxy, predictability Opposite: unconventionality

converge v **meet**, join, touch, unite, congregate Opposite: diverge

convergence n **meeting**, junction, union, coming together, conjunction Opposite: divergence

conversance n **familiarity**, acquaintance, awareness, knowledge

conversant adj **familiar**, up-to-date, well-informed, up on (infml), knowledgeable Opposite: unfamiliar

conversation n **talk**, chat, discussion, tête-à-tête, dialogue Opposite: monologue

conversational adj 1 **informal**, chatty, relaxed, casual, familiar Opposite: formal 2 **colloquial**, spoken, everyday, vernacular, informal

conversationalist n **talker**, communicator, gossip, raconteur, speaker

converse v **natter** (infml), talk, speak, communicate, chat ■ n **contrary**, opposite, reverse, inverse, antithesis Opposite: same ■ adj **opposite**, contrary, opposing, reverse, inverse Opposite: same

conversely adv **on the other hand**, equally, by the same token, on the contrary, in opposition

conversion n 1 **change**, adaptation, alteration, translation, renovation 2 **switch**, change, changeover, transfer, move

convert v 1 **change**, adapt, alter, renovate, remodel 2 **switch**, change, change over, transfer, go over 3 **win over**, convince, induce, talk into, persuade Opposite: dissuade ■ n **recruit**, follower, disciple, supporter, proselyte. See COMPARE AND CONTRAST at **change**.

convertible adj **adaptable**, exchangeable, alterable, translatable, changeable

convex adj **curved**, curving, arched, rounded, bowed Opposite: concave

convey v 1 **take**, carry, transport, bear, send 2 **communicate**, express, suggest, put across, get across

conveyance n 1 **means of transport**, transport, vehicle 2 **transportation**, transport, carriage, transference, transmission

convict v **find guilty**, sentence, imprison, condemn, detain Opposite: acquit ■ n **criminal**, offender, prisoner, felon, lawbreaker

conviction n 1 **belief**, opinion, principle, faith, persuasion 2 **certainty**, certitude, confidence, assurance, sincerity Opposite: doubt 3 **sentence**, verdict, condemnation, imprisonment Opposite: acquittal

convince v **persuade**, prove, sway, influence, induce Opposite: dissuade

convinced adj 1. **persuaded**, influenced, swayed, won over, converted Opposite: doubtful 2 **certain**, sure, positive, persuaded, confident Opposite: unsure 3 **committed**, strong, firm, staunch, wholehearted Opposite: weak

convincing adj 1 **persuasive**, plausible, believable, credible, compelling Opposite: unconvincing 2 **authentic**, realistic, believable, credible, lifelike Opposite: implausible 3 **undoubted**, substantial, resounding, considerable, conclusive Opposite: dubious. See COMPARE AND CONTRAST at **valid**.

convincingly adv **believably**, credibly, plausibly, persuasively, winningly Opposite: unconvincingly

convivial adj **pleasant**, welcoming, warm, friendly, hospitable Opposite: unfriendly

conviviality n **pleasantness**, welcome, warmth, friendliness, hospitality Opposite: unfriendliness

convoluted adj **intricate**, complex, complicated, long-winded, elaborate Opposite: straightforward

convoy n 1 **group**, band, party, company, line 2 **motorcade**, cavalcade, cortege, caravan, flotilla

convulse v **shake**, jerk, tremble, shudder, quiver

convulsion n **seizure**, fit, spasm, paroxysm, tremor

convulsive adj **jerky**, sudden, abrupt, violent, uncontrollable

co-occur v **coexist**, coincide, concur

cook v **heat**, boil, prepare, fry, roast ■ n **chef**, caterer, kitchen worker

cooked adj **heated**, baked, prepared, broiled, roasted Opposite: raw

cookery see **cooking**

cookie (infml) n **person**, character, individual, sort (infml), type (infml)

cooking n **cuisine**, catering, food service, home economics, cookery

cook up v 1 **prepare**, concoct, make, throw together (infml), rustle up (infml) 2 (infml) **invent**, think up, concoct, devise, plan

cool adj 1 **cold**, chilly, chill, nippy, fresh Opposite: warm 2 **calm**, unruffled, nonchalant, casual, imperturbable Opposite: uptight (infml) 3 **unfriendly**, unenthusiastic, offhand, icy, distant Opposite: friendly 4 (infml) **fashionable**, sophisticated, stylish, trendy (infml), hip (slang) Opposite: unfashionable ■ v 1 **make cold**, freshen, refrigerate, chill, cool off Opposite: warm 2 **wane**, dampen down, dampen, cool off, decrease Opposite: increase

cool down v 1 **turn cold**, cool, cool off, freshen Opposite: warm up 2 **calm down**, compose yourself, settle down, simmer down, back off Opposite: flare up

coolness n 1 **cold**, coldness, chill, chilliness, freshness Opposite: warmth 2 **calmness**, level-headedness, detachment, aloofness, distance 3 **unfriendliness**, chill, chilliness, reserve, hostility Opposite: friendliness

cool off v 1 **turn cold**, cool, freshen, grow chilly Opposite: warm up 2 (infml) **calm down**, compose yourself, settle down, simmer down, cool down Opposite: flare up

coop n **pen**, cage, run, enclosure, hutch

co-op (infml) n 1 **cooperative**, collective, mutual society 2 **condominium**, apartment house, apartment building

cooperate v 1 **collaborate**, work together, unite, liaise, band Opposite: compete 2 **oblige**, accommodate, help, aid, assist Opposite: hinder

cooperation n **collaboration**, assistance, help, support, teamwork Opposite: hindrance

cooperative adj 1 **obliging**, helpful, supportive, accommodating, willing Opposite: difficult 2 **joint**, two-way, mutual, shared, collaborative Opposite: individual ■ n **collective**, company, organization, association, enterprise

co-opt v **appoint**, designate, choose, bring on board, draft Opposite: discharge

coop up v **cage**, enclose, pen, house, imprison Opposite: let out

coordinate v **organize**, direct, manage, synchronize, harmonize

coordination n 1 **organization**, direction, management, logistics, harmonization Opposite: disorganization 2 **dexterity**, skill, adroitness, grace, proficiency Opposite: clumsiness

cope v **manage**, handle, deal with, survive, get through Opposite: founder

copied adj **imitated**, imitative, counterfeit, mock, imitation Opposite: original

copious adj **abundant**, plentiful, profuse, many, numerous Opposite: scant

coppice see **copse**

copse n **wood**, coppice, thicket, grove, covert

copy n 1 **reproduction**, duplicate, replica, facsimile, print Opposite: original 2 **item**, book, disk, version, publication 3 **text**, words, manuscript, typescript, file ■ v 1 **reproduce**, duplicate, clone, replicate, recreate 2 **imitate**, mimic, emulate, ape, simulate Opposite: originate

COMPARE AND CONTRAST CORE MEANING: make something that resembles something else to a greater or lesser degree

copy make an identical version of something; **reproduce** make a copy of something by technical means; **duplicate** create an identical version of something two or more times; **clone** make a near or exact reproduction, especially of a piece of equipment or an organism; **replicate** create an identical version of something repeatedly and exactly; **re-create** make something that appears to be the same as something that no longer exists, or that exists in a different place.

coquettish (literary) adj **flirtatious**, flirty, teasing, coy

cord n **string**, twine, rope, cable, flex

cordial adj **pleasant**, affable, genial, friendly, affectionate Opposite: unfriendly

cordiality n **pleasantness**, geniality, affability, friendliness, affection Opposite: unfriendliness

cordless adj **battery**, battery-operated, freestyle, hand-held, mobile

cordon n **barrier**, barricade, obstruction, obstacle, line

cordon off v **close**, bar, isolate, block off, barricade Opposite: open

core n 1 **center**, heart, hub, nucleus, middle 2 **essence**, spirit, soul, heart, gist 3 **sample**, plug, extract ■ adj **essential**, central, fundamental, main, principal Opposite: peripheral

corner n 1 **angle**, crook, bend 2 **turn**, curve, junction, bend, intersection Opposite: straight 3 **place**, spot, area, location, locality ■ v **pin down**, surround, trap, restrict, confront

cornerstone n **foundation stone**, keystone, foundation, basis

corner the market v **dominate**, monopolize, control, command, predominate

cornucopia n **abundance**, profusion, wealth, copiousness, plethora Opposite: dearth

corny adj **unsophisticated**, trite, banal, clichéd, hackneyed Opposite: original

corollary n **consequence**, result, effect, outcome, upshot

coronet n **crown**, tiara, diadem, circlet, wreath

corporate adj 1 **business**, company, commercial, trade 2 **communal**, shared, group, community, mutual Opposite: individual

corporation n **company**, business, firm, establishment, concern

corps n 1 **force**, troop, group, company, cadre 2 **group**, body, company, organization, league

corpse n **dead body**, cadaver, carcass, stiff (slang)

corpulence n **obesity**, plumpness, fleshiness, heaviness, chubbiness

corpulent adj **obese**, fat, fleshy, rotund, plump Opposite: slim

correct v 1 **rectify**, fix, put right, sort out, mark 2 **modify**, amend, alter, adjust, revise ■ adj 1 **precise**, right, accurate, exact, truthful Opposite: inaccurate 2 **appropriate**, suitable, proper, acceptable, approved Opposite: unsuitable

correction n **alteration**, improvement, rectification, modification, amendment

correctness n 1 **precision**, rightness, truth, accuracy, exactness Opposite: inaccuracy 2 **appropriateness**, suitability, acceptability, fittingness, uprightness Opposite: unsuitability

correlate v **relate**, associate, compare, link, draw a parallel Opposite: dissociate

correlation n **association**, connection, relationship, link, parallel

correspond v 1 **agree**, resemble, parallel, match, match up Opposite: conflict 2 **communicate**, keep in touch, write, drop a line, fax

correspondence n 1 **letters**, mail, communication, messages, memos 2 **agreement**, similarity, resemblance, association, connection Opposite: clash

correspondent n 1 **communicator**, letter-writer, writer, pen pal 2 **foreign correspondent**, newspaperman, newspaperwoman, columnist, reporter

corresponding adj **consistent**, conforming, agreeing, matching, equivalent

corridor n 1 **passage**, passageway, hall, hallway, walkway 2 **strip**, access strip, air corridor, flight path

corroborate v **verify**, validate, document, support, agree Opposite: contradict

corrode v **rust**, disintegrate, destroy, decompose, decay

corroded adj **rusty**, discolored, rusted, tarnished, blemished Opposite: pristine

corrosion n **erosion**, weathering, decay, rust, deterioration

corrosive adj 1 **harsh**, scarring, eroding, destructive, acidic Opposite: gentle 2 **sarcastic**, acerbic, harsh, bitter, biting Opposite: kind

corrugated adj **ridged**, crenelated, ribbed, grooved, wavy Opposite: smooth

corrupt adj **immoral**, unethical, dishonest, shady, fraudulent Opposite: honest ■ v **debase**, degrade, taint, pervert, warp

corrupted adj **debased**, degraded, sullied, despoiled, spoiled Opposite: pure (literary)

corruption n 1 **dishonesty**, exploitation, bribery, sleaze, fraud Opposite: honesty 2 **depravity**, perversion, immorality, harm, debasement Opposite: purity (literary)

corruptness n **dishonesty**, immorality, sleaziness, degenerateness

corsage n **bouquet**, spray, posy, flowers, arrangement

cosmetic *adj* **1 ornamental**, decorative, aesthetic *Opposite*: substantive **2 superficial**, skin-deep, surface, token, outer *Opposite*: in-depth

WORD BANK
❏ **types of cosmetics** blush, blusher, concealer, eye shadow, eyeliner, face powder, foundation, kohl, lip gloss, lip pencil, lipstick, mascara, nail polish, powder, rouge *(dated)*

cosmetic surgery *n* **plastic surgery**, laser surgery, tuck, lift

WORD BANK
❏ **types of cosmetic surgery** Botox™ injection, breast enhancement, collagen injection, ear pinning, facelift, face peel, lipectomy, liposuction, nose job, rhinoplasty

cosmic *adj* **1 intergalactic**, interplanetary, interstellar, galactic, planetary *Opposite*: terrestrial **2 universal**, vast, enormous, huge, immense *Opposite*: tiny

cosmopolitan *adj* **multicultural**, multiethnic, pluralistic, diverse, international *Opposite*: provincial

cosmos *n* **universe**, space, outer space, ether, heaven

cosset *v* **shelter**, protect, spoil, coddle, indulge *Opposite*: neglect

cost *n* **1 price**, charge, rate, fee, price tag **2 budget**, amount, outlay, expenditure, expense **3 effort**, suffering, detriment, loss, expense

costar *n* **star**, movie star, actor, lead ■ *v* **1 perform**, collaborate, entertain, star, appear **2 feature**, showcase, spotlight, star

cost-cutting *n* **saving**, cutbacks, economizing, cutting back, belt-tightening

cost-effective *adj* **lucrative**, moneymaking, profitable, bankable, gainful *Opposite*: uneconomical

costly *adj* **1 expensive**, overpriced, inflated, highly priced, exorbitant *Opposite*: inexpensive **2 luxurious**, precious, valuable, lavish, rich *Opposite*: basic **3 damaging**, harmful, detrimental, disadvantageous, injurious *Opposite*: beneficial

costs *n* **price**, charges, budget, expenses, outlay

costume *n* **clothes**, clothing, regalia, dress, outfit

costume drama *n* **play**, spectacle, drama, historical drama, period piece

coterie *n* **clique**, circle, band

cotton on *(infml)* *v* **comprehend**, understand, follow, grasp, realize

couch *n* **sofa**, settee, divan, chaise lounge, chesterfield ■ *v* **express**, phrase, put, dress up, word

cough up *(infml)* *v* **pay up**, pay, give, fork out *(infml)*, fork up *(infml)*

council *n* **assembly**, meeting, board, congress, body

counsel *n* *(fml or literary)* **advice**, guidance, direction, warning, guidelines ■ *v* **1** *(fml or literary)* **advise**, recommend, advocate, suggest, propose **2 support**, help, guide, aid, encourage

counseling *n* **therapy**, psychotherapy, psychoanalysis, analysis, treatment

counselor *n* **therapist**, psychotherapist, psychoanalyst, analyst, social worker

count *v* **1 add up**, total, calculate, tot up, tote up **2 consider**, regard, view. hold, esteem **3 make your mark**, weigh, amount to something, matter, be important ■ *n* **1 calculation**, computation, reckoning, head count, bottom line **2 total**, sum total, sum, amount, tally

countable *adj* **calculable**, measurable, assessable, finite, quantifiable *Opposite*: incalculable

count against *v* **weigh against**, detract, diminish, hurt, backfire *Opposite*: help

countenance *n* **expression**, face, features, physiognomy, mien *(fml)* ■ *v* *(fml)* **tolerate**, stand for, put up with, allow, approve

counter *v* **1 contradict**, dispute, refute, oppose, answer **2 counteract**, offset, foil, frustrate, thwart

counteract *v* **counter**, offset, respond, frustrate, thwart

counterattack *n* **attack**, revenge, counteroffensive, defense, retaliation

counterbalance *v* **tip the scales**, offset, balance, correct, compensate ■ *n* **counterweight**, makeweight, ballast

counterfeit *adj* **fake**, forged, bootleg, phony, bogus *Opposite*: genuine ■ *v* **forge**, fake, copy, fabricate, imitate ■ *n* **forgery**, copy, fake, imitation, reproduction *Opposite*: original

counterfeiter *n* **forger**, criminal, fraudster, imitator, faker

countermand *v* **cancel**, revoke, stop, reverse, annul

counterpart *n* **opposite number**, equal, equivalent, colleague

counterrevolutionary *n* **rebel**, insurgent, insurrectionist, anarchist, radical ■ *adj* **antirevolutionary**, counterinsurgent, moderate, democratic, pacifist *Opposite*: revolutionary

counter to *prep* **against**, contrary to, in opposition to, at odds with, in conflict with *Opposite*: according to

countless *adj* **uncountable**, innumerable, myriad, limitless, immeasurable *Opposite*: few

count on *v* **depend on**, be sure of, rely on, trust, bank on

count out *v* **exclude**, weed out, leave out, omit, disregard *Opposite*: include

countrified *adj* **1 rustic**, rural, unspoiled *Opposite*: urban **2 unsophisticated**, unpolished, unfashionable, simple, rough *Opposite*: urbane

country n 1 republic, state, nation, realm, kingdom 2 farmland, woodland, grazing, pastures, wilderness Opposite: town 3 people, inhabitants, residents, nation, population

countryman n compatriot, national, fellow citizen, inhabitant, native

countrywoman n compatriot, national, fellow citizen, inhabitant, native

count up v total, add up, count, calculate, tot up

county n region, section, province, district, canton

coup n 1 coup d'état, overthrow, revolution, rebellion, putsch 2 feather in somebody's cap, achievement, accomplishment, triumph, feat

coup de grâce n deathblow, last nail in the coffin, knockout punch, killer punch

coup d'état n overthrow, coup, revolution, rebellion, putsch

couple n twosome, pair, duo, dyad ■ v combine, link, join, connect, pair Opposite: separate

coupled with prep together with, in addition to, on top of, as well as, besides

couplet n verse, distich, stanza, unit, rhyme

coupling n 1 link, join, connection, connector, coupler 2 combination, juxtaposition, pairing, blend, mixture

coupon n voucher, ticket, token, slip, form

courage n bravery, nerve, pluck, fearlessness, mettle Opposite: cowardice

---

COMPARE AND CONTRAST CORE MEANING: personal resoluteness in the face of danger or difficulties

courage the ability to show resoluteness and determination, whether physical, mental, or moral, against a wide range of difficulties or dangers; **bravery** extreme lack of fear; **fearlessness** resoluteness in the face of dangers or challenges; **nerve** coolness, steadiness, and self-assurance; **guts** (slang) strength of character and boldness; **pluck** resolution and willingness to continue struggling against the odds; **mettle** spirited determination.

---

courageous adj brave, daring, bold, spirited, plucky Opposite: cowardly

courageousness see courage

courier n messenger, carrier, biker, dispatch rider

course n 1 sequence, progression, development, passage 2 direction, route, path, track, road 3 option, choice, possibility, route, avenue 4 lesson, class, program, module, curriculum ■ v flow, pour, run, gush, stream Opposite: trickle

course of action n strategy, course, policy, plan, method

coursework n assignments, homework, reading, project

court n 1 law court, court of law, tribunal 2 courtyard, square, yard, patio, piazza ■ v 1 (dated) date, go out, see, pay court to (dated) 2 woo, cozy up to, curry favor with, pander to, flatter Opposite: shun 3 risk, invite, encourage, incite, attract Opposite: avoid

court case n lawsuit, suit, case, hearing, indictment

courteous adj polite, well-mannered, considerate, chivalrous, civil Opposite: rude

courteousness n politeness, good manners, courtesy, consideration, civility Opposite: rudeness

courtesy n politeness, good manners, courteousness, consideration, civility Opposite: rudeness

courthouse n court, courtroom, law court, court of law

courtier n flatterer, sycophant, self-seeker, creature, toady

courtly adj courteous, chivalrous, polite, civil, refined Opposite: rude

court order n legal ruling, order, sanction, interdict, veto

courtship n wooing, dating, relationship

courtyard n patio, yard, square, court, enclosure

cousin n friend, companion, colleague, partner, counterpart

cove n bay, inlet, harbor

covenant n agreement, contract, treaty, promise, pledge

cover v 1 conceal, hide, cover up, obscure, disguise Opposite: expose 2 protect, shield, guard, shelter, defend 3 wrap, coat, cover up, envelop, swathe Opposite: reveal 4 deal with, include, comprise, embrace, take in Opposite: overlook 5 travel, cross, traverse, pass through, go through ■ n 1 covering, wrapping, jacket, shell, case 2 shelter, concealment, protection, hiding place, refuge

coverage n attention, treatment, reporting, exposure, handling

covered adj enclosed, roofed, sheltered, protected, shielded Opposite: exposed

covering n cover, casing, top, lid, layer

coverlet n bedspread, cover, throw, counterpane Opposite: (dated)

covert adj secret, clandestine, underground, concealed, hidden Opposite: open ■ n copse, wood, thicket, coppice, undergrowth. See COMPARE AND CONTRAST at secret.

covertness n secrecy, stealth, concealment, surreptitiousness, underhandedness Opposite: openness

cover up v 1 conceal, hide, obscure, mask, disguise Opposite: expose 2 suppress, keep under wraps, keep secret, paper over, hide Opposite: divulge

cover-up n conspiracy, plot, scheme, smoke screen, fig leaf

covet v **want**, long for, yearn for, crave, hanker after. *See* COMPARE AND CONTRAST *at* **want**.

coveted adj **sought-after**, longed for, wanted, fashionable, desired *Opposite*: scorned

covetous adj **envious**, jealous, greedy, avaricious, acquisitive *Opposite*: generous

covetousness n **envy**, enviousness, jealousy, avarice, avariciousness *Opposite*: generosity

cow v **intimidate**, scare, frighten, bully, overawe

coward n **sissy**, deserter, runaway, weakling, chicken *(infml)*

cowardice n **weakness**, fearfulness, spinelessness, fear, timidity *Opposite*: courage

cowardly adj **gutless**, spineless, weak, craven, pusillanimous *Opposite*: brave

---

COMPARE AND CONTRAST CORE MEANING: lacking in courage

cowardly lacking in courage, or caused by a lack of courage; **faint-hearted** timid and lacking in resolve; **spineless** seriously lacking willpower or strength of character; **gutless** seriously lacking in courage and determination; **pusillanimous** showing a contemptible degree of cowardice; **craven** showing a contemptible degree of cowardice and weakness of will; **chicken** *(infml,* often used by children and young people) cowardly.

---

cowboy n **cowhand**, cowman, herdsman, stockman, rancher

cowboy movie n **western**, horse opera, oater *(slang)*

cowed adj **intimidated**, browbeaten, scared, frightened, submissive *Opposite*: defiant

cower v **shrink**, cringe, tremble, recoil, shy away *Opposite*: stand your ground

cowl n **hood**, cover, cloak, top

coworker n **colleague**, fellow worker, collaborator, associate, workmate

cowshed n **barn**, stable, corral, pen, stockyard

cox v **steer**, direct, pilot, navigate, coxswain

coy adj 1 **teasing**, playful, engaging, coquettish *(literary)* 2 **shy**, bashful, timid, modest, reserved *Opposite*: brazen

cozy adj 1 **snug**, warm, pleasant, comfortable, appealing *Opposite*: inhospitable 2 **familiar**, friendly, intimate, close, warm *Opposite*: cold 3 **expedient**, convenient, self-serving, cliquey, clannish

cozy up v **ingratiate yourself**, curry favor, make overtures, pander, insinuate

crabbed *see* **crabby**

crabbiness n **bad-temperedness**, bad temper, irritability, grumpiness, cantankerousness *Opposite*: equanimity *(fml)*

crabby adj **grumpy**, short-tempered, irritable, grouchy *(infml)*, tetchy *(infml)* *Opposite*: easygoing

crack v 1 **break**, fracture, split, splinter, snap

2 break down, go to pieces, lose control, collapse, crack up *(infml)* 3 **bang**, bump, hit, whack, bash *(infml)* 4 *(infml)* **solve**, work out, figure out, fathom, decipher ▪ n 1 **fissure**, flaw, break, fracture, chink 2 **weakness**, flaw, fault, imperfection, defect 3 *(infml)* **blow**, crash, bang, snap, pop 4 *(infml)* **gibe**, quip, dig, joke, aside ▪ adj **expert**, topflight, crackerjack, ace *(infml)*

crack a joke v **make a joke**, quip, joke, jest *(literary)*

crackbrained adj **eccentric**, irrational, foolish, stupid, crazed *Opposite*: rational

crack down *(infml)* v **clamp down**, tighten up, come down hard, get tough

cracked adj 1 **fractured**, broken, split, splintered, cleft *Opposite*: intact 2 *(infml)* **irrational**, eccentric, crazed, crackbrained, foolish *Opposite*: rational

cracker-barrel adj **straightforward**, unsophisticated, folksy, uncultivated, simple *Opposite*: sophisticated

crackle v **crunch**, snap, pop, sizzle, crack

crack of dawn n **daybreak**, dawn, daylight, sunrise, first light *Opposite*: dusk

crackpot *(infml)* adj **impractical**, unrealistic, eccentric, wild, outlandish *Opposite*: realistic

crack up *(infml)* v 1 **break down**, go to pieces, lose control, collapse, crack *(infml)* 2 **break up**, laugh, guffaw, giggle, titter

crack-up *(infml)* n 1 **breakdown**, collapse, crisis, meltdown, burnout 2 **crash**, accident, wreck, smash, collision

cradle n **support**, frame, structure, framework, underpinning ▪ v **hold**, embrace, support, cuddle, clasp *Opposite*: drop

craft n 1 **skill**, dexterity, expertise, ability, craftsmanship 2 **trade**, profession, art, job, calling 3 **vehicle**, vessel, boat, aircraft, spacecraft 4 **cunning**, deceit, slyness, wiliness, shrewdness *Opposite*: forthrightness ▪ v **make**, fashion, create, manufacture, construct

craftiness n **cunning**, slyness, shrewdness, wiliness, guile *Opposite*: forthrightness

craftsmanship n **skill**, artistry, workmanship, expertise, technique

craftsperson n **craftworker**, artisan, artist

crafty adj **cunning**, sneaky, sly, shrewd, devious *Opposite*: forthright

crag n **cliff**, rock face, precipice, peak, scarp

craggy adj 1 **rocky**, stony, rough, rugged, uneven *Opposite*: even 2 **lined**, rugged, wrinkled, wrinkly, weathered *Opposite*: smooth

cram v 1 **stuff**, pack, fill up, ram, shove *Opposite*: remove 2 *(infml)* **study**, review, go over, memorize, peruse *Opposite*: forget

crammed adj **full**, packed, filled, crowded, cramped *Opposite*: empty

cramp *n* spasm, pain, contraction, shooting pain, twinge ■ *v* restrict, hamper, limit, constrict, constrain

cramped *adj* **overcrowded**, confined, restricted, close, small *Opposite*: spacious

crane *n* hoist, derrick, winch, gantry

crank *v* turn, reel, wind, activate, move

crankiness *(infml)* *n* crabbiness, irritability, bad temper, touchiness, crossness *Opposite*: affability

crank up *v* start, turn on, wind up, activate, get going *Opposite*: turn off

cranky *(infml)* *adj* irritable, crabby, cantankerous, grouchy *(infml)*, ornery *(infml)* *Opposite*: good-humored

cranny *n* crevice, crack, fissure, chink, cleft

crash *n* **1** collision, accident, smash, smashup, pileup *(infml)* **2** failure, breakdown, collapse, shutdown **3** bang, smash, din, clatter, clang **4** bankruptcy, failure, collapse, liquidation ■ *v* **1** collide, run into, smash into, bump into, hurtle **2** break down, collapse, fizzle, fail **3** boom, bang, thunder, clash, clatter **4** go under, go bankrupt, fold, collapse, fail *Opposite*: thrive

crash course *n* training, orientation, workshop, immersion

crash-land *v* collide, crash, fall, smash, come down

crass *adj* insensitive, tactless, thoughtless, vulgar, obnoxious *Opposite*: sensitive

crassness *n* insensitivity, vulgarity, tactlessness, obnoxiousness, grossness *Opposite*: sensitivity

crater *n* pit, depression, hole, cavity, hollow *Opposite*: mound

crave *v* **1** desire, long for, need, want, yearn for *Opposite*: dislike **2** *(archaic)* ask, beg, pray, request, entreat *Opposite*: reject. See COMPARE AND CONTRAST at want.

craven *adj* cowardly, gutless, spineless, weak, timorous *Opposite*: bold. See COMPARE AND CONTRAST at cowardly.

craving *n* longing, desire, passion, hunger, thirst *Opposite*: dislike

crawl *v* **1** creep, edge, inch, wriggle, slither **2** skulk, scuttle, creep, sneak, slink **3** *(infml)* grovel, ingratiate yourself, flatter, fawn, suck up *(infml)* *Opposite*: alienate **4** apologize, eat humble pie, grovel, humiliate yourself, prostrate yourself

craze *n* fad, trend, fashion, enthusiasm, rage

crazed *adj* irrational, distraught, overwrought, wild, inflamed *Opposite*: rational

craziness *(infml)* *n* foolishness, stupidity, folly, idiocy, madness *Opposite*: reasonableness

crazy *(infml)* *adj* **1** foolish, unwise, silly, senseless, irrational *Opposite*: sensible **2** fond, keen, passionate, enthusiastic, devoted *Opposite*: lukewarm

creak *v* squeak, screech, scrape, grate, groan

creaky *adj* **1** squeaky, rusty, grating, rasping **2** *(infml)* stiff, rigid, inflexible, tight, arthritic *Opposite*: supple

cream *n* **1** ointment, salve, balm, unguent, emulsion **2** best, elite, finest, cream of the crop, pick of the bunch *Opposite*: dregs ■ *v* blend, soften, mash, emulsify, combine

cream off *v* skim off, handpick, select, choose, pick out *Opposite*: reject

crease *n* **1** pleat, fold, tuck, gather **2** crinkle, crumple, wrinkle, rumple, pucker **3** furrow, wrinkle, line, groove, crow's foot ■ *v* **1** fold, pleat, tuck, gather **2** crumple, wrinkle, scrunch, crinkle, rumple *Opposite*: smooth

creased *adj* wrinkled, wrinkly, crinkled, crinkly, lined *Opposite*: smooth

create *v* **1** make, produce, generate, fashion, form *Opposite*: destroy **2** invent, design, originate, initiate, give rise to **3** establish, set up, found, start, get going

creation *n* **1** formation, making, conception, construction, manufacture *Opposite*: destruction **2** nature, cosmos, universe, life, world **3** invention, handiwork, fabrication, innovation, concept

creative *adj* original, imaginative, inspired, artistic, inventive *Opposite*: unimaginative

creativeness *see* **creativity**

creativity *n* originality, imagination, inspiration, ingenuity, inventiveness

creator *n* maker, inventor, originator, architect, designer *Opposite*: destroyer

creature *n* **1** being, living being, person, man, woman **2** animal, beast, organism, insect, critter *(slang)*

crèche *n* Nativity, display, scene, tableau, spectacle

credence *n* credibility, authority, weight, belief, confidence

credential *n* qualification, diploma, recommendation, testimonial, certificate

credentialed *adj* qualified, certified, licensed, accredited

credentials *n* identification, authorization, ID, permit, pass

credibility *n* trustworthiness, reliability, authority, standing, sincerity

credible *adj* **1** believable, convincing, plausible, likely, probable *Opposite*: implausible **2** trustworthy, reliable, sincere, dependable, sound *Opposite*: unreliable

credit *n* **1** praise, recognition, thanks, acclaim, glory *Opposite*: blame **2** standing, position, status, esteem, prestige **3** belief, confidence, trust, faith *Opposite*: disbelief ■ *v* **1** believe, accept, trust, have faith in, have confidence in *Opposite*: disbelieve **2** acknowledge, recognize, acclaim, pay tribute, praise

creditable *adj* admirable, praiseworthy, good, worthy, laudable *Opposite*: shameful

credo n **creed**, doctrine, ideology, principle, view

credulity n **gullibility**, naiveté, innocence, trust, imprudence Opposite: astuteness

credulous adj **gullible**, naive, trusting, imprudent, unsuspecting Opposite: astute

credulousness see **credulity**

creed n **faith**, dogma, doctrine, credo, belief

creek n **1 stream**, rivulet, arroyo, brook, channel **2 cove**, bay, inlet, gulf

creep v **1 tiptoe**, skulk, steal, sneak, slink Opposite: stomp **2 crawl**, slither, inch, edge, worm

creeper n **climber**, trailer, vine, liana

creepiness (infml) n **eeriness**, scariness, weirdness, uncanniness, strangeness

creep up on v **sneak up on**, surprise, stalk, take by surprise

creepy (infml) adj **eerie**, disturbing, spine-chilling, uncanny, weird

creepy-crawly (infml) n **insect**, bug, beastie (infml)

cremate v **incinerate**, burn, consume, immolate (literary)

cremation n **burning**, incineration, immolation (fml)

crème de la crème n **best**, cream, pick, flower, elite

crescendo n **increase**, upsurge, swelling, buildup, climax

crescent adj **semicircular**, hemispheric, curved, arced, falcate

crest n **1 top**, peak, summit, crown, apex Opposite: base **2 tuft**, topknot, growth, cockscomb, comb **3 coat of arms**, blazon, emblem, symbol, heraldry

crestfallen adj **downcast**, dejected, disappointed, deflated, subdued Opposite: confident

crevasse n **fissure**, cleft, crack, split, fracture

crevice n **crack**, fissure, chink, split, cleft

crew n **1 team**, squad, staff, troop, company **2** (infml) **group**, gang, party, circle, crowd

crib (infml) v **cheat**, copy, plagiarize, steal, borrow

crick n **pain**, strain, discomfort, cramp, spasm ▪ v **strain**, hurt, pull, cramp, wrench

crime n **1 offense**, misdeed, felony, misdemeanor, transgression **2 corruption**, wrongdoing, misconduct, lawbreaking, delinquency **3 wrong**, sin, fault, transgression

crime novel n **detective story**, police procedural, whodunit, thriller

criminal n **offender**, convict, prisoner, felon, lawbreaker ▪ adj **1 illegal**, wrong, against the law, illicit, unlawful Opposite: legal **2 scandalous**, excessive, iniquitous, senseless, outrageous

criminality n **delinquency**, misconduct, wrongdoing, corruption, lawbreaking Opposite: honesty

criminalization n **1 outlawing**, illegalization, banning, interdiction, proscription (fml) Opposite: legalization **2 corruption**, delinquency, marginalization, alienation, deterioration Opposite: rehabilitation

criminalize v **1 outlaw**, ban, forbid, proscribe, interdict Opposite: legalize **2 corrupt**, marginalize, deprave, pervert Opposite: rehabilitate

criminal world n **underworld**, gangland, underbelly of society

crimp v **1 fold**, crumple, crinkle, press, rumple **2 pleat**, gather, fold, concertina, ruche Opposite: smooth **3 interfere**, hamper, hinder, constrain, curb

cringe v **1 recoil**, wince, flinch, shrink, shy away **2 squirm**, blush, wince, be embarrassed

crinkle v **crumple**, crease, rumple, wrinkle, ruffle Opposite: straighten out ▪ n **wrinkle**, fold, crease, line, pucker

crinkled adj **creased**, lined, wrinkled, crumpled, rumpled Opposite: straight

crinkly adj **wrinkled**, creased, furrowed, wavy, puckered Opposite: smooth

crippling adj **damaging**, debilitating, incapacitating, destabilizing

crisis n **1 disaster**, catastrophe, emergency, calamity, predicament **2 turning point**, head, watershed, crossroads, defining moment

crisis point n **critical stage**, flashpoint, breaking point, crunch time

crisp adj **1 crunchy**, brittle, hard, crusty, crispy Opposite: soggy **2 snappy**, brusque, terse, curt, sharp **3 cold**, cool, fresh, frosty, chilly Opposite: stuffy **4 incisive**, decisive, confident, businesslike, efficient Opposite: hesitant

crispy adj **crunchy**, brittle, hard, crusty, crisp Opposite: soggy

crisscross n **lattice**, network, grid ▪ v **cross**, traverse, intersect, overlap, cross over

criterion n **standard**, principle, measure, norm, condition

critic n **1 reviewer**, columnist, commentator, reporter, journalist **2 evaluator**, appraiser, judge, commentator **3 detractor**, opponent, enemy, censor, criticizer Opposite: supporter

critical adj **1 unfavorable**, disparaging, disapproving, nitpicking, judgmental Opposite: favorable **2 analytical**, judicious, diagnostic, serious, detailed **3 significant**, decisive, vital, important, essential Opposite: insignificant **4 dangerous**, serious, grave, life-threatening, perilous

critically adv **seriously**, gravely, dangerously, perilously, precariously Opposite: mildly

criticism n **1 censure**, disapproval, reproach, disparagement, condemnation Opposite: praise **2 analysis**, appreciation, assessment, evaluation, critique

criticize v 1 **disapprove**, censure, condemn, find fault with, castigate (fml) Opposite: praise 2 **assess**, analyze, dissect, evaluate, appraise

---

COMPARE AND CONTRAST CORE MEANING: express disapproval or dissatisfaction with somebody or something
criticize point out faults; **censure** make a formal, often public or official, statement of disapproval; **castigate** (fml) to criticize or rebuke severely; **blast** (infml) to criticize severely; **condemn** give an unfavorable judgment on somebody or something; **find fault with** criticize, often unfairly; **pick holes in** look for and find mistakes, particularly in an argument; **nitpick** find fault, often unjustifiably, with insignificant details.

---

critique n analysis, assessment, evaluation, account, review ■ v **assess**, evaluate, criticize, comment, review

croak n cry, caw, rasp, squawk ■ v 1 **call**, cry, squawk, caw, rasp 2 **grate**, gutturalize, rasp, growl 3 (infml) **grumble**, mutter, complain, moan, grouse (infml)

croaky adj **hoarse**, rasping, guttural

crockery n **tableware**, china, earthenware, plates, dishes

crony n **friend**, acquaintance, colleague, companion, comrade Opposite: enemy

cronyism n **favoritism**, nepotism, patronage

crook n 1 (infml) **criminal**, offender, felon, robber, lawbreaker 2 **staff**, rod, stick, crosier

crooked adj 1 **bent**, curved, warped, twisted, kinked Opposite: straight 2 (infml) **dishonest**, criminal, corrupt, fraudulent, illegal Opposite: honest 3 **uneven**, jagged, zigzag, oblique, askew Opposite: straight

crookedness n **dishonesty**, shadiness, corruption, illegality, fraudulence Opposite: honesty

croon v **sing**, serenade, murmur, hum, warble

crop n **harvest**, yield, produce, cash crop, catch crop ■ v 1 **collect**, harvest, gather, pick, bring in 2 **cut**, shorten, clip, trim, shear

cropped adj **short-haired**, close-cropped, clipped

crop up (infml) v **appear**, happen, turn up, arise, emerge

crosier n **staff**, rod, stick, crook

cross n **symbol**, mark, sign ■ v 1 **traverse**, go across, crisscross, cut across, span 2 **thwart**, frustrate, impede, oppose, obstruct Opposite: assist ■ adj **irritated**, angry, irritable, annoyed, snappy

---

WORD BANK
□ **types of crosses** Celtic cross, cross of Lorraine, Greek cross, Latin cross, Maltese cross, St.

Andrew's cross, St. Anthony's cross, St. George's cross, tau cross

crossbreed v **hybridize**, cross, interbreed, mongrelize

crosscheck v **check**, validate, substantiate, double-check, verify ■ n **validation**, substantiation, double-checking, verification

cross-country adj **off-road**, rough, outdoor, all-terrain

cross-cultural adj **multicultural**, multiracial, multiethnic, diverse, cosmopolitan

crosscurrent n **contrast**, divergence, deviation, rebellion, nonconformity

cross-examination n **questioning**, re-examination, interrogation, cross-questioning, probe

cross-examine v **question**, cross-question, interrogate, quiz, probe

cross-fertilization n 1 **pollination**, fertilization, cross-pollination Opposite: self-fertilization 2 **exchange**, interchange, interaction, synthesis, synergy

cross-fertilize v 1 **fertilize**, pollinate, cross-pollinate 2 **exchange**, interchange, interact, synthesize, share

crossfire n **clash**, disagreement, conflict, antagonism, flak

crossing n 1 **journey**, adventure, trip, voyage, passage 2 **intersection**, junction, overpass, grade crossing, crosswalk

cross cut v **score out**, score through, strike out, strike through, rub out

crossover n 1 **switch**, change, sea change, conversion, move 2 **overlap**, common ground, commonality

crosspatch (dated infml) n **curmudgeon**, malcontent, grouch (infml) grump (infml), pain (infml)

cross-purposes n **disagreement**, disparity, variance, contrast, frustration

cross-question v **cross-examine**, re-examine, interrogate, question, review

cross-questioning n **cross-examination**, re-examination, interrogation, review, double-checking

cross-reference n **citation**, reference, documentation, source, note

crossroads n 1 **junction**, intersection, crossing, crossway, traffic circle 2 **turning point**, landmark, decision, moment of truth, crisis

cross section n 1 **view**, section, slice, layer, plane 2 **sample**, example, range, representation

cross swords v **clash**, argue, disagree, do battle, fight Opposite: agree

crossways see crosswise

crosswise adv **sideways**, diagonally, kitty-corner, catty-corner, across

crossword n **acrostic**, mind-bender, game, puzzle, cryptic crossword

crotchetiness *(infml)* n **grumpiness**, grouchiness, tetchiness

crotchety *(infml)* adj **grumpy**, bad-tempered, irritable, difficult, cantankerous *Opposite*: good-humored

crouch v **squat**, bend, hunker, stoop, duck

crow v 1 **caw**, cry, call, squawk, screech 2 **gloat**, boast, brag, show off, swagger

crowd n 1 **troop**, throng, mass, multitude, swarm 2 **group**, set, gang, circle, clique ■ v 1 **throng**, flock, herd, assemble, gather 2 **overcrowd**, pack, cram, squeeze, squash

crowded adj **overcrowded**, packed, full, teeming, swarming *Opposite*: deserted

crown n 1 **circlet**, coronet, tiara, diadem 2 **trophy**, prize, garland, honor, laurels 3 **top**, peak, summit, pinnacle, head ■ v **cap**, top, round off, complete, finish off

crow's foot n **wrinkle**, line, laugh line

crucial adj **vital**, critical, central, decisive, key *Opposite*: trivial

crucible n 1 **container**, pot, receptacle, vat, kettle 2 **ordeal**, trial, test, baptism of fire 3 **hotbed**, hothouse, forcing ground, melting pot, ground zero

crucifixion n 1 **execution**, killing, punishment 2 **ordeal**, victimization, torment, agony, suffering

crucify v 1 **execute**, kill, hang, punish 2 **torment**, victimize, attack, savage, maul

crud *(infml)* n **nonsense**, gibberish, malarkey *(infml)*, twaddle *(infml)*, bunk *(slang)*

crude adj 1 **raw**, unrefined, unprocessed *Opposite*: refined 2 **approximate**, rough, inaccurate, inexact, loose *Opposite*: precise 3 **unpolished**, basic, simple, rudimentary, makeshift *Opposite*: sophisticated 4 **vulgar**, indecent, rude, coarse, obscene *Opposite*: delicate

crudeness n 1 **primitiveness**, roughness, rawness, coarseness, simplicity *Opposite*: sophistication 2 **vulgarity**, crudity, coarseness, rudeness, offensiveness *Opposite*: delicacy

crudity n 1 **rudeness**, crudeness, coarseness, vulgarity, offensiveness *Opposite*: delicacy 2 **roughness**, coarseness, rawness, simplicity, rusticity *Opposite*: sophistication

cruel adj 1 **unkind**, merciless, nasty, pitiless, brutal *Opposite*: kind 2 **painful**, punishing, devastating, harsh, hard *Opposite*: pleasant

cruelty n **unkindness**, nastiness, brutality, malice, spite *Opposite*: kindness

cruise v 1 **voyage**, sail, journey, travel, boat 2 **coast**, skim, spin, travel, glide ■ n **voyage**, vacation, trip, journey, tour

crumb n **morsel**, scrap, tidbit, bit, speck

crumble v 1 **smash**, beat, crush, grind, powder 2 **disintegrate**, dissolve, deteriorate, fall apart, fall down

crumbling adj **disintegrating**, decomposing, decaying, putrefying, caving in *Opposite*: solid

crumbly adj **brittle**, powdery, flaky, friable, crumbling *Opposite*: solid

crummy *(infml)* adj 1 **inferior**, shoddy, shabby, worthless, poor-quality *Opposite*: superior 2 **unwell**, sick, ill, sickly, miserable *Opposite*: healthy

crumple v **crease**, crinkle, rumple, crush, screw *Opposite*: smooth

crumpled adj **creased**, wrinkled, wrinkly, crinkly, lined *Opposite*: smooth

crunch v **munch**, chew, champ, chomp *(infml)* ■ n **crisis**, moment of truth, crunch time, critical situation, crux

crunchy adj **crispy**, crisp, brittle, crusty *Opposite*: soggy

crusade n **cause**, campaign, movement, battle, fight ■ v **campaign**, lobby, struggle, battle, apply yourself

crusader n **campaigner**, supporter, advocate, champion, activist

crush v 1 **squash**, squeeze, compress, press, mash 2 **quell**, suppress, put down, quash, subdue 3 **defeat**, rout, massacre, trounce, overwhelm 4 **humiliate**, devastate, mortify, put down, abash ■ n 1 *(infml)* **infatuation**, passion, affection, fondness, liking *Opposite*: dislike 2 **press**, squash, squeeze, crowd, throng. *See* COMPARE AND CONTRAST *at* **love**.

crushed adj **crumpled**, creased, wrinkled, crinkly, crinkled *Opposite*: smooth

crushing adj **devastating**, overwhelming, severe, draconian, humiliating *Opposite*: mild

crushingly adv **triumphantly**, exultantly, superciliously, haughtily, contemptuously

crust n **coating**, outside, outer layer, shell, top

crusted adj **encrusted**, caked, coated, covered, thick

crusty adj 1 **crispy**, crisp, hard, brittle, crunchy *Opposite*: soft 2 **grumpy**, bad-tempered, irritable, testy, cantankerous *Opposite*: good-humored

crutch n 1 **stick**, support, prop, walking aid, walker 2 **prop**, support, aid, help, buttress

crux n **root**, bottom, heart, core, nub

cry v 1 **weep**, sob, snivel, whimper, shed tears *Opposite*: laugh 2 **shout**, exclaim, shout out, call, call out *Opposite*: whisper ■ n **call**, shout, exclamation, yell, scream *Opposite*: whisper

crying adj 1 **desperate**, deplorable, awful, horrible, terrible 2 **in tears**, tearful, teary, sobbing, weeping

cry out v 1 **shout out**, shout, cry, call, call out *Opposite*: whisper 2 **need**, be in need of, require, demand, call for

crypt n **vault**, tomb, catacomb, sepulcher, burial chamber

cryptic adj **mysterious**, enigmatic, puzzling, obscure, ambiguous *Opposite*: obvious. *See* COMPARE AND CONTRAST *at* **obscure**.

crystal n mineral, rock crystal, quartz

crystalline adj 1 crystal-like, glassy, sparkling 2 clear, transparent, crystal clear, limpid, translucent Opposite: opaque

crystallization n manifestation, representation, outward expression, illustration, summation

crystallize v form, take shape, fall into place, come together, shape up Opposite: disintegrate

cry your eyes out v weep, sob, blubber (infml)

cub n novice, beginner, learner, apprentice, trainee Opposite: old hand

cubbyhole n compartment, nook, cranny, pigeonhole, cupboard

cubicle n compartment, booth, partition, stall, workspace

cubist adj abstract, geometric, modern

cuckoo (infml) adj eccentric, strange, weird, unusual, bizarre Opposite: ordinary

cuddle v hug, embrace, clasp, hold, nuzzle ■ n embrace, hug, clasp, hold, clinch

cuddle up v snuggle up, curl up, cozy up

cuddly adj soft, lovable, fluffy, warm, endearing

cudgel v hit, bludgeon, whack, pound, batter

cue n signal, prompt, sign, indication, reminder ■ v prompt, signal, show, indicate, remind

cuff v buffet, slap, strike, hit, rap

cuisine n food, fare, cooking, gastronomy, cookery

cul-de-sac n dead end, impasse, blind alley

culinary adj cooking, gastronomic, cookery, food

cull v 1 discard, reject, remove, scrap, get rid of Opposite: retain 2 pick, select, choose, gather, harvest ■ n reject, scrap, discard, castoff, second

culminate v end, conclude, finish, terminate, climax Opposite: start

culmination n conclusion, finale, peak, height, zenith Opposite: inception (fml)

culpability n blameworthiness, liability, blame, guilt, fault Opposite: innocence

culpable adj guilty, in the wrong, to blame, blameworthy, responsible Opposite: innocent

culprit n offender, criminal, guilty party, perpetrator, wrongdoer

cult n 1 sect, religious group, religious persuasion, movement 2 fad, craze, trend, adoration, veneration ■ adj alternative, offbeat, out of the ordinary, unusual, trendy (infml) Opposite: mainstream

cultivate v 1 farm, grow, plow, plant, tend 2 promote, encourage, nurture, work on, foster Opposite: neglect

cultivated adj refined, educated, cultured, sophisticated, urbane Opposite: uncouth

cultivation n 1 farming, agriculture, husbandry, crop growing, agronomy 2 development, promotion, encouragement, nurturing, fostering Opposite: neglect 3 refinement, education, culture, sophistication, urbanity Opposite: uncouthness

cultivator n grower, farmer, gardener, planter, agronomist

cultural adj 1 national, social, ethnic, folk, traditional 2 artistic, literary, intellectual, educational, edifying

culture n 1 sophistication, refinement, urbanity, civilization, cultivation Opposite: uncouthness 2 civilization, society, mores, traditions, customs 3 ethos, philosophy, values, principles, beliefs 4 art, music, and literature, arts, humanities, fine arts, performing arts

cultured adj refined, well-educated, learned, educated, erudite Opposite: uncouth

culvert n duct, channel, conduit, tunnel, main

cum (infml) prep with, together with, along with, in combination with, also used as

cumbersome adj unwieldy, awkward, weighty, bulky, clumsy Opposite: manageable

cumbersomeness n unwieldiness, awkwardness, weightiness, bulkiness

cumulative adj increasing, snowballing, swelling, accumulative, growing Opposite: diminishing

cunning adj 1 sly, wily, crafty, sneaky, shrewd Opposite: guileless 2 ingenious, inventive, resourceful, creative, innovative ■ n 1 slyness, wiliness, craftiness, sneakiness, shrewdness Opposite: ingenuousness 2 skill, cleverness, ingenuity, creativity, dexterity

cup n 1 mug, beaker, demitasse, teacup 2 trophy, chalice, goblet, prize

cupidity (fml) n greed, avarice, covetousness, materialism, conspicuous consumption Opposite: generosity

cupola n dome, vault, roof, ceiling

cur n mongrel, dog, hound, mutt (slang) Opposite: purebred

curable adj treatable, remediable, correctable, mendable, repairable Opposite: incurable

curate n priest, minister, cleric, ecclesiastic ■ v create, mount, install, stage

curative adj healing, remedial, restorative, therapeutic, palliative Opposite: injurious

curator n custodian, keeper, steward, guardian, overseer

curb n control, limit, restriction, restraint, check ■ v restrain, control, limit, hold back, rein in Opposite: promote

curdle v 1 coagulate, clot, thicken, congeal, gel Opposite: separate 2 (infml) go sour, go bad, turn, sour, spoil

cure v **heal**, treat, make well, restore to health, alleviate *Opposite*: exacerbate ■ n **treatment**, therapy, medicine, medication, remedy ■ v **preserve**, smoke, dry, salt, pickle

cure-all n **panacea**, universal remedy, magic potion, magic bullet, antidote

curfew n **restriction**, time limit, deadline, limitation, regulation

curio n **trinket**, antique, curiosity, souvenir, knickknack

curiosity n **1 inquisitiveness**, interest, prying, nosiness *(infml)*, snooping *(infml)* *Opposite*: disinterest **2 oddity**, rarity, novelty, curio, strange thing

curious adj **1 inquisitive**, inquiring, interested, questioning, probing *Opposite*: uninterested **2 peculiar**, odd, strange, unusual, intriguing *Opposite*: ordinary

curl v **1 swirl**, spiral, twirl, twist, curve **2 twist**, coil, bend, wave, crimp ■ n **1 coil**, twist, whorl, spiral, eddy **2 ringlet**, wave, lock, spit curl

curl up v **double up**, crouch, hug your knees, roll into a ball, go into a fetal position *Opposite*: straighten

curly adj **wavy**, coiled, twisted, frizzy, crimped *Opposite*: straight

curmudgeon n **malcontent**, grouch *(infml)*, grump *(infml)*, pain *(infml)*, crosspatch *(dated infml)*

curmudgeonly adj **bad-tempered**, crabby, cantankerous, grumpy, cranky *(infml)* *Opposite*: pleasant

currency n **1 money**, legal tender, coinage, coins, exchange **2 prevalence**, frequency, vogue, commonness, popularity

current adj **present**, existing, actual, in progress, recent *Opposite*: former ■ n **flow**, stream, undercurrent, tide, flux

curriculum n **course**, prospectus, program, syllabus, core curriculum

curry favor v **ingratiate yourself**, cozy up, get in good with, play up to, grovel

curse n **1 swearword**, oath, expletive, epithet, blasphemy **2 jinx**, spell, magic, setback, blow *Opposite*: blessing **3 scourge**, plague, blight, bane, misfortune ■ v **1 swear**, blaspheme, damn, use bad language, cuss *(infml)* *Opposite*: bless **2 plague**, afflict, trouble, blight, torment

cursed adj **1 damned**, afflicted, banned, anathematized, blighted *Opposite*: blessed **2** *(infml)* **annoying**, irritating, bothersome, vexatious, perturbing

cursor n **pointer**, arrow, marker, indicator

cursory adj **superficial**, hasty, brief, passing, quick *Opposite*: thorough

curt adj **abrupt**, brisk, brusque, rude, brief *Opposite*: civil

curtail v **limit**, restrain, restrict, hold back, cut back *Opposite*: extend

curtailment n **limitation**, restriction, curb, shortening, reduction *Opposite*: extension

curtain n **drape**, blind, screen, shutter, shade

curtain raiser n **prelude**, overture, prologue, preamble, lead-in

curtness n **brusqueness**, abruptness, shortness, briskness, snappiness *Opposite*: civility

curtsy v **genuflect**, bow, bob, kneel, stoop ■ n **bow**, genuflection, bob, obeisance *(fml)*

curvaceous adj **curvy**, rounded, curved, shapely, voluptuous

curvature n **curving**, bend, twist, warp, arc

curve n **arc**, bend, bow, arch, camber ■ v **bend**, bow, curl, coil, twist *Opposite*: straighten

curved adj **bent**, bowed, curled, coiled, rounded *Opposite*: straight

curvilinear *see* **curved**

curviness n **roundedness**, sinuousness, shapeliness, curvaceousness

curving adj **1 bent**, warped, twisted, bowed, crooked *Opposite*: straight **2 curved**, curvy, bending, sinuous, snaking *Opposite*: straight

curvy adj **undulating**, wavy, rounded, curved, curvilinear *Opposite*: straight

cushion n **pillow**, bolster, pad, headrest, beanbag ■ v **1 protect**, shield, guard, support, bolster *Opposite*: expose **2 mitigate**, moderate, lessen, stifle, soften *Opposite*: exacerbate

cushy *(infml)* adj **easy**, comfortable, undemanding, cozy, agreeable *Opposite*: difficult

cusp n **1 point**, tip, nib, end **2 crossover**, border, limit, edge, verge

cuss *(infml)* v **swear**, curse, blaspheme, profane, use bad language

cussed *(infml)* adj **annoying**, irritating, uncooperative, obstinate, stubborn *Opposite*: cooperative

cussedness *(infml)* n **pigheadedness**, stubbornness, obstinacy, willfulness, perversity *Opposite*: cooperation

custodial adj **1 protective**, safeguarding, safekeeping, sheltered, supervisory **2 prison**, jail, secure, penal, residential

custodian n **1 guardian**, curator, keeper, defender, upholder **2 caretaker**, janitor, concierge, night watchman, superintendent

custody n **1 protection**, keeping, safekeeping, care, charge **2 detention**, arrest, confinement, imprisonment, incarceration *(fml)* *Opposite*: liberty

custom n **1 tradition**, practice, convention, institution, ritual *Opposite*: novelty **2 habit**, practice, routine, pattern, way **3 trade**, business, patronage, clientele, market. *See* COMPARE AND CONTRAST *at* habit.

customary adj **1 usual**, normal, habitual,

expected, routine Opposite: exceptional **2 traditional**, conventional, time-honored, established, long-established Opposite: unconventional **3 typical**, characteristic, usual, habitual, normal Opposite: uncharacteristic. See COMPARE AND CONTRAST at usual.

custom-built adj **specially made**, commissioned, made-to-order, customized, personalized Opposite: off-the-rack

customer n **client**, buyer, shopper, purchaser, patron

customize v **modify**, tailor, adapt, alter, make to order

customized adj **modified**, tailored, adapted, made-to-order, personalized Opposite: mass-produced

custom-made see custom-built

customs n tax, duty, levy, impost, toll

cut v **1 chop**, slice, carve, saw, hack Opposite: join **2 pierce**, score, nick, incise, engrave Opposite: seal **3 reduce**, decrease, limit, curtail, cut down Opposite: increase **4 edit**, shorten, censor, condense, chop Opposite: restore **5 stop**, discontinue, bring to an end, bring to a halt, finish Opposite: continue ■ n **1 scratch**, wound, slash, graze, incision **2 reduction**, decrease, cutback, decline, drop Opposite: increase **3** (infml) **share**, commission, percentage, kickback, rake-off (infml)

cut-and-dried adj **1 decided**, finished, settled, fixed, agreed Opposite: undecided **2 predictable**, obvious, open-and-shut, anticipated, expected Opposite: anomalous

cut back v **reduce**, curtail, curb, decrease, restrain Opposite: develop

cutback n **reduction**, cut, decrease, decline, drop

cut dead v **snub**, coldshoulder, rebuff

cut down v **1 reduce**, decrease, cut back, ease up on, rein back Opposite: increase **2 fell**, chop down, bring down, hack down, lop **3** (infml) **kill**, strike down, slaughter, mow down, assassinate

cute adj **1 attractive**, pretty, delightful, charming, appealing Opposite: ugly **2 shrewd**, cunning, smart, sharp, quick

cuteness n **1 adorability**, lovability, attractiveness, appeal, charm Opposite: ugliness **2 shrewdness**, cunning, smartness, sharpness, quick-wittedness

cutesy adj **mawkish**, saccharine, sugary, chocolate-box, kitsch Opposite: austere

cut in v **interrupt**, break in, butt in, interject, move in

cut loose (infml) v **get free**, get away, escape, make a break, break away

cut off v **1 remove**, sever, amputate, excise, detach Opposite: reconnect **2 interrupt**, stop, cut short, cut in, butt in **3 stop**, disconnect, discontinue, bring to an end, halt Opposite: restore **4 isolate**, separate, keep apart, strand, detach Opposite: connect

cutoff n **1 limit**, end point, end date, deadline, expiry Opposite: start **2 stoppage**, end, finish, halt, freeze Opposite: continuation

cut out v **1 remove**, take away, excise, extract, take out Opposite: put in **2 give up**, stop, renounce, forgo, do without **3 exclude**, ignore, overlook, isolate, marginalize Opposite: include

cutout n **1 shape**, template, stencil, outline, silhouette **2 safety device**, kill switch, circuit breaker, safety switch, trip switch

cut-rate adj **reduced**, cheap, economy, budget, bargain

cut short v **break off**, discontinue, call a halt, suspend, stop in full flow Opposite: extend

cutthroat adj **merciless**, pitiless, ruthless, unsparing, fierce Opposite: merciful

cutting adj **1 hurtful**, wounding, unkind, acerbic, critical Opposite: kind **2 cold**, biting, icy, sharp, keen Opposite: mild ■ n **sprig**, offshoot, scion

cutting edge n **1 vanguard**, van, forefront, edge, leading edge Opposite: rearguard **2 sharp edge**, razor edge, knife edge, blade, razor blade

cutting-edge adj **leading-edge**, front-line, pioneering, trailblazing, radical Opposite: old-fashioned

cuttingly adv **harshly**, abrasively, hurtfully, sharply, severely Opposite: kindly

cut up v **chop**, mince, slice, chop up, dice

cutup (infml) n **joker**, clown, prankster, comic, comedian

cybernetics n **artificial intelligence**, information technology, AI, IT

cyberspace n **Internet**, World Wide Web, information superhighway, data superhighway, infobahn

cycle n **series**, sequence, set, round, rotation

cyclic see cyclical

cyclical adj **recurring**, returning, repeated, cyclical, recurrent Opposite: unique

cyclone n **storm**, windstorm, hurricane, typhoon, tornado

cylinder n **1 tube**, roll, pipe **2 container**, drum, canister, tank, bottle

cylindrical adj **tubular**, tube-shaped, cylinder-shaped, rod-shaped, rodlike

cynic n **skeptic**, doubter, detractor, disparager, misanthropist

cynical adj **1 distrustful**, skeptical, suspicious, disparaging, negative Opposite: naive **2 sarcastic**, mocking, scornful, sardonic, sneering Opposite: respectful

cynicism n **skepticism**, sarcasm, distrust, doubt, scorn Opposite: naiveté

cyst n **swelling**, lump, polyp, nodule, growth

czar see tsar

D

dab *v* pat, wipe, apply, touch, tap ■ *n* bit, blob, spot, dash, drop

dabble *v* **1** experiment, try your hand, dip into, play at, putter **2** dip, paddle, splash, immerse

dad *(infml)* *n* father, daddy *(infml)*, pa *(infml)*, pop *(infml)*, papa *(dated)*

daddy *(infml)* *see* **dad**

dado *n* panel, molding, frieze, feature

daemon *n* **1** demigod, supernatural being, spirit **2** guardian spirit, inspiration, guiding force, inner spirit, muse

daily *adv* every day, each day, on a daily basis, day by day, day after day ■ *adj* everyday, day-to-day, regular, diurnal, circadian

daintiness *n* delicacy, elegance, gracefulness, refinement, prettiness *Opposite*: clumsiness

dainty *adj* pretty, delicate, graceful, refined, exquisite *Opposite*: clumsy

dais *n* platform, podium, pulpit, stage, stand

dale *n* valley, glen, vale *(literary)* *Opposite*: hill

dalliance *(literary)* *n* flirtation, romance, relationship, liaison, involvement

dally *v* linger, dawdle, loiter, hang around, waste time *Opposite*: hurry

dam *n* barrier, barrage, weir, wall, boom ■ *v* block, block up, stem, hold back, control

damage *n* **1** injury, harm, hurt, impairment, destruction *Opposite*: reparation **2** *(infml)* cost, price, bill, total, amount ■ *v* injure, harm, spoil, hurt, smash up *Opposite*: repair. *See* COMPARE AND CONTRAST *at* harm.

damaged *adj* injured, hurt, spoiled, dented, scratched *Opposite*: pristine

damages *n* compensation, costs, reparation, reimbursement, recompense

damaging *adj* harmful, destructive, negative, detrimental, hurtful *Opposite*: harmless

damn *v* **1** condemn, sentence, doom, consign, punish **2** criticize, denounce, censure, lambaste, pan *(infml)*

damning *adj* critical, negative, disapproving, unfavorable, condemning *Opposite*: complimentary

damp *adj* **1** dank, moist, humid, soggy, clammy *Opposite*: dry **2** half-hearted, indifferent, insipid, unenthusiastic, weak *Opposite*: enthusiastic ■ *n* moisture, dampness, humidity, clamminess, wetness *Opposite*: dryness ■ *v* **1** dampen, moisten, humidify, wet *Opposite*: dry out **2** check, curb, restrain, hinder, hamper *Opposite*: encourage

damp down *v* dampen, diminish, check, dull, curb *Opposite*: increase

dampen *v* **1** damp, moisten, humidify, wet *Opposite*: dry out **2** damp down, reduce, diminish, check, dull *Opposite*: increase

damper *n* **1** discouragement, inhibition, hindrance, impediment, obstruction *Opposite*: spur **2** regulator, stopper, control, controller **3** mute, muffler, softener

dampness *n* humidity, moisture, moistness, clamminess, wetness *Opposite*: dryness

dance *v* **1** twirl, pirouette, sway, turn, bop *(infml)* **2** gambol, prance, skip, caper, frolic ■ *n* ball, disco, rave *(slang)*, hop *(dated infml)*

WORD BANK

❏ **types of dances** ballet, barn dance, belly dance, bop *(infml)*, bossa nova, breakdance, cancan, cha-cha, Charleston, fandango, flamenco, foxtrot, jig, jitterbug, jive, lambada, limbo, lindy hop, line dancing, macarena, mambo, merengue, minuet, polka, quadrille, quickstep, rumba, salsa, samba, square dance, step dancing, strathspey, tango, tap dance, waltz

---

dandified *(dated)* *adj* dressed up, dressed to kill, overdressed, fashionable, natty *Opposite*: scruffy

dandle *v* **1** jiggle, jog, bounce, dance, rock **2** pet, stroke, caress, fondle, pamper

dandruff *n* scurf, scale, skin flake

dandy *(dated)* *n* fop, fashion plate, clotheshorse *(infml)*, dude *(slang)*, beau *(archaic)*

danger *n* **1** hazard, risk, peril, threat, menace *Opposite*: safety **2** chance, possibility, likelihood, risk

dangerous *adj* **1** unsafe, hazardous, risky, treacherous, perilous *Opposite*: safe **2** grave, serious, critical, grievous, alarming *Opposite*: safe

dangle *v* hang, hang down, swing, sway, suspend *Opposite*: stick up

dank *adj* damp, moist, chilly, clammy, humid *Opposite*: warm

dankness *n* wetness, dampness, moistness, humidity, clamminess *Opposite*: warmth

dapper *adj* neat, elegant, smart, trim, well-dressed *Opposite*: scruffy

dappled *adj* speckled, spotted, mottled, stippled, piebald

dare *v* **1** venture, risk, gamble, face up to, have the courage **2** challenge, defy, taunt, provoke, goad **3** presume, venture, have the audacity, be so bold, take the liberty ■

n **taunt**, challenge, provocation, ultimatum, goad

daredevil *n* **risk-taker**, madcap, hothead, show-off *(infml)* *Opposite*: stick-in-the-mud *(infml)* ■ *adj* **reckless**, rash, madcap, hotheaded, bold *Opposite*: staid

daresay *v* **guess**, suppose, expect, assume, admit *Opposite*: deny

daring *adj* **1 bold**, brave, audacious, courageous, enterprising *Opposite*: cowardly **2 dangerous**, risky, unsafe, hazardous, treacherous *Opposite*: safe ■ *n* **bravery**, nerve, boldness, audacity, courage *Opposite*: cowardice

dark *adj* **1 dim**, shady, shadowy, murky, gloomy *Opposite*: bright **2 black**, brunette, brown, chestnut, sable *Opposite*: fair **3 gloomy**, depressing, bleak, sad, unhappy *Opposite*: cheery **4 sinister**, mysterious, threatening, evil, nefarious *Opposite*: good ■ *n* **darkness**, dusk, gloom, dimness, shadows *Opposite*: light

darken *v* **blacken**, dim, deepen, cast a shadow, grow dim *Opposite*: brighten

darkness *n* **dark**, night, dusk, gloom, dimness *Opposite*: light

darling *n* **1 sweetheart**, dear, love, dearest, honey *(infml)* **2 favorite**, firm favorite, pet, the apple of somebody's eye, fair-haired boy ■ *adj* **wonderful**, gorgeous, lovely, adorable, dear *Opposite*: horrible

darn *v* **sew**, stitch, repair, mend, sew up *Opposite*: tear ■ *adj (infml)* **very**, extremely, exceptionally, extraordinarily

dart *n* **arrow**, barb, shaft, missile, projectile ■ *v* **dash**, scurry, whiz, rush, run *Opposite*: saunter

dash *n* **1 sprint**, rush, run, race, surge **2 trace**, splash, drop, pinch, soupçon **3 verve**, vigor, spirit, flair, panache ■ *v* **1 rush**, hurry, hasten, tear, race *Opposite*: amble **2** *(fml)* **knock**, throw, hurl, slam, fling **3** *(fml)* **smash**, break, shatter, crash, splinter **4 frustrate**, confound, foil, shatter, discourage *Opposite*: encourage **5 shatter**, ruin, crush, blight, destroy *Opposite*: bolster

dashing *adj* **1** *(dated)* **spirited**, confident, jaunty, flamboyant, bold *Opposite*: staid **2 elegant**, stylish, chic, debonair, fashionable *Opposite*: dowdy

dastardly *adj* **low**, shameful, dishonorable, mean, reprehensible *Opposite*: honorable

data *n* **information**, statistics, facts, figures, numbers

database *n* **data bank**, store, folder, list, archive

data processing *n* **information retrieval**, data handling, number-crunching *(slang)*

date *n* **1 day**, day of the week, year, time **2 time**, point in time, period, era, day **3 meeting**, rendezvous, appointment, blind date, engagement

dated *adj* **old-fashioned**, old, behind the times, unfashionable, passé *Opposite*: up-to-date

dateline *n* **heading**, subheading, subhead, identification

daub *v* **smear**, spread, slap, spatter, slop ■ *n* **blot**, blotch, spot, splotch, stain

daunt *v* **put off**, deter, discourage, intimidate, scare *Opposite*: encourage

daunting *adj* **intimidating**, unnerving, discouraging, frightening, overwhelming *Opposite*: heartening

dauntless *(literary) adj* **resolute**, determined, confident, fearless, bold *Opposite*: timid

dawdle *v* **1 loiter**, delay, linger, plod, lag *Opposite*: hurry **2 waste time**, hang around, dally, linger, delay *Opposite*: hurry

dawdler *n* **1 straggler**, stroller, wanderer, laggard, dallier *Opposite*: leader **2 idler**, slacker, shirker, timewaster, shilly-shallier

dawdling *n* **dilly-dallying**, shilly-shallying, delaying, tarrying, loitering *Opposite*: haste ■ *adj* **slow**, sluggish, measured, leisurely, casual *Opposite*: hasty

dawn *n* **1 sunrise**, crack of dawn, daybreak, first light, daylight *Opposite*: dusk **2 beginning**, start, birth, emergence, dawning *Opposite*: end ■ *v* **1 begin**, start, be born, emerge, originate *Opposite*: end **2 occur**, cross your mind, register with, strike, become clear to

day *n* **1 daylight hours**, daylight, daytime, sunlight hours *Opposite*: night **2 date**, day of the week, calendar day **3 time**, era, period, generation, epoch

daybreak *n* **dawn**, crack of dawn, first light, daylight, morning *Opposite*: dusk

daydream *n* **reverie**, fantasy, musing, contemplation, dream ■ *v* **dream**, have your head in the clouds, be miles away, be inattentive, fantasize *Opposite*: concentrate

daydreamer *n* **idealist**, dreamer, fantasist, visionary, woolgatherer

daydreaming *n* **reverie**, woolgathering, fantasizing, pensiveness, dreaminess *Opposite*: concentration

daylight *n* **1 day**, daytime, sunshine, light of day, hours of daylight *Opposite*: nighttime **2 dawn**, crack of dawn, sunrise, daybreak, first light *Opposite*: dusk

day out *n* **outing**, trip, spree, jaunt, tour

day room *n* **lounge**, den, recreation room, seating area, reception room

days gone by *n* **former times**, earlier times, previous times, days of old, olden days *Opposite*: future

daytime *n* **day**, daylight, hours of daylight, morning, afternoon *Opposite*: nighttime

day-to-day *adj* **everyday**, commonplace, daily routine, usual *Opposite*: unusual

day trip *n* **excursion**, outing, day out, trip, field trip

day tripper *n* **tourist**, traveler, vacationer, sightseer

daze *n* **confused state**, stupor, trance, dream, daydream ■ *v* **stun**, shock, astonish, astound, surprise

dazzle *v* **1 amaze**, astonish, astound, impress, overwhelm *Opposite*: bore **2 blind**, daze, confuse, overwhelm, bedazzle (*literary*) ■ *n* **glare**, brightness, reflection, blaze, brilliance

dazzling *adj* **1 stunning**, amazing, astounding, incredible, alluring *Opposite*: unimpressive **2 bright**, glaring, glittering, blazing, luminous *Opposite*: dull

deactivate *v* **neutralize**, disable, switch off, turn off, disengage *Opposite*: activate

dead *adj* **1 lifeless**, late, defunct, deceased (*fml*), departed (*literary*) *Opposite*: alive **2 numb**, benumbed, stiff, insensitive, frozen *Opposite*: sensitive **3 boring**, quiet, dull, uninteresting, deadly *Opposite*: exciting **4 finished**, obsolete, over, ended, empty *Opposite*: current **5 silent**, blank, quiet, down, inactive *Opposite*: live

---

COMPARE AND CONTRAST CORE MEANING: no longer living, functioning, or in existence

dead describes organisms that are no longer alive, physical objects that no longer function or exist, and abstract entities that are no longer valid or relevant; **deceased** (*fml*, restricted to people, especially in legal or other technical contexts, or as a euphemism) no longer living; **departed** (*literary*, restricted to people) no longer living; **late** (restricted to people) having died recently or within living memory; **lifeless** not living, or apparently not living; **defunct** no longer operative, valid, or functional, or no longer in existence; **extinct** no longer in existence, or no longer active.

---

deaden *v* **soften**, dull, muffle, dampen, mute *Opposite*: amplify

dead end *n* **1 cul-de-sac**, blind alley, impasse, roadblock **2 block**, stalemate, standstill, impasse, deadlock

deadened *adj* **desensitized**, unfeeling, insensitive, insensible, numb *Opposite*: sensitive

deadhead *v* **take away**, cut off, remove

dead heat *n* **draw**, tie, photo finish, drawn game, stalemate

deadline *n* **time limit**, limit, goal, aim, target *Opposite*: extension

deadlock *n* **impasse**, stalemate, gridlock, standstill, logjam

deadly *adv* **completely**, absolutely, extremely, very, perfectly *Opposite*: slightly ■ *adj* **1 lethal**, fatal, terminal, mortal, poisonous *Opposite*: harmless **2** (*infml*) **boring**, tedious, tiresome, dull, dead *Opposite*: interesting **3 extreme**, implacable, mortal, sworn, absolute

---

COMPARE AND CONTRAST CORE MEANING: causing death

deadly likely or designed to cause death; **fatal** describes accidents or illnesses that result in death; **mortal** causing, continuing until, or relating to death; **lethal** certain to or intended to cause death; **terminal** describes illnesses that result in death.

---

deadpan *adj* **unsmiling**, straight-faced, poker-faced, expressionless, blank *Opposite*: expressive

dead ringer (*infml*) *n* **double**, doppelgänger, image, spitting image (*infml*), look-alike (*infml*) *Opposite*: opposite

deaf *adj* **1 hearing-impaired**, deafened, tone-deaf *Opposite*: hearing **2 unresponsive**, indifferent, oblivious, heedless, unmoved *Opposite*: mindful

deafening *adj* **loud**, earsplitting, ear-piercing, booming, thunderous *Opposite*: noiseless

deal *n* **transaction**, contract, agreement, arrangement, pact ■ *v* **1 distribute**, share out, give out, allocate, apportion *Opposite*: receive **2 trade**, do business, exchange, sell, transact business *Opposite*: buy

dealer *n* **trader**, merchant, seller, broker, supplier

dealership *n* **1 charter**, authorization, agreement, right, license **2 premises**, showroom, offices, workplace, workshop

dealings *n* **transactions**, contact, communication, business, connections

deal out *v* **give out**, issue, distribute, mete out, administer *Opposite*: collect

deal with *v* **cope with**, manage, handle, see to, take care of *Opposite*: evade

dear *adj* **beloved**, cherished, prized, valued, precious *Opposite*: hated ■ *n* **darling**, sweetheart, dearest, beloved, honey (*infml*) ■ *adj* **expensive**, costly, extortionate, valuable, exorbitant *Opposite*: cheap

dearest *n* **love**, sweetheart, precious, sugar (*infml*), honey (*infml*)

dearly *adv* **greatly**, extremely, exceedingly, profoundly, sincerely

dearth *n* **lack**, shortage, scarcity, drought, famine *Opposite*: glut. *See* COMPARE AND CONTRAST *at* lack.

death *n* **1 passing**, bereavement, loss, demise (*fml*), decease (*fml*) *Opposite*: birth **2 end**, fall, downfall, ruin, collapse *Opposite*: beginning **3 fatality**, casualty, loss of life, killing, murder *Opposite*: birth

deathblow *n* **body blow**, final blow, last straw, last nail in the coffin, end

death knell *n* **finish**, last nail in the coffin, end of the road, point of no return, last straw

deathless *adj* **eternal**, timeless, immortal, everlasting, undying *Opposite*: mortal

deathlike *adj* **skeletal**, gaunt, ashen, spectral, pallid

deathly *adj* **deadly**, deathlike, tomblike,

deep, stony ■ adv **extremely**, intensely, deadly, intensively, absolutely Opposite: slightly

death mask n **effigy**, cast, head, model, sculpture

death rattle n **gurgle**, rattle, rasp, wheeze, croak

death toll n **fatalities**, death rate, mortality rate, fatality rate, loss of life

deathtrap (infml) n **safety risk**, hazard, minefield, pitfall, health hazard

death warrant see **death knell**

debacle n **disaster**, catastrophe, fiasco, shambles, tragedy Opposite: success

debar v **exclude**, expel, bar, ban, prohibit Opposite: admit

debark v **disembark**, alight, go ashore, land, get off Opposite: embark

debarkation n **disembarkation**, alighting, going ashore, landing, getting off

debase v 1 **degrade**, impair, adulterate, sully corrupt Opposite: purify 2 **humiliate**, demean, degrade, shame, humble Opposite: glorify

debasement n 1 **humiliation**, degradation, disgrace, shame, disparagement Opposite: glorification 2 **ruination**, adulteration, corruption, defilement, tarnishing Opposite: purification

debatable adj **arguable**, dubious, controversial, doubtful, contentious Opposite: settled

debate v **discuss**, argue, dispute, deliberate, contest Opposite: conclude v **ponder**, wonder, deliberate, consider, contemplate Opposite: decide ■ n **discussion**, argument, dispute, examination, consideration Opposite: conclusion

debater n **speaker**, orator, public speaker, disputant, arguer

debauched adj **decadent**, dissolute, degenerate, dissipated, immoral Opposite: moral

debauchery n **decadence**, dissoluteness, immorality, self-indulgence Opposite: morality

debilitate v **weaken**, incapacitate, enervate, drain, hamper Opposite: fortify

debilitated adj **weakened**, incapacitated, enervated, drained, hampered Opposite: fortified. See COMPARE AND CONTRAST at **weak**.

debilitating adj **weakening**, incapacitating, enervating, draining, devastating Opposite: refreshing

debility n **weakness**, incapacity, frailty, ineffectiveness, enfeeblement Opposite: strength

debit v **deduct**, take out, withdraw, subtract, charge Opposite: credit ■ n **withdrawal**, subtraction, deduction, debt, charge Opposite: credit

debonair adj **suave**, elegant, refined, charming, well-groomed Opposite: graceless

debouch v **emerge**, move out, spread out, exit, come out Opposite: confine

debrief v **question**, interrogate, interview, examine, quiz

debriefing n **interrogation**, questioning, interview, examination, probing Opposite: briefing

debris n **wreckage**, remains, fragments, rubble, waste

debt n 1 **arrears**, liability, debit, balance, balance due Opposite: credit 2 **obligation**, duty, responsibility, dues, liability

debtor n **borrower**, mortgagor, insolvent, defaulter, pledger

debug v **clear up**, correct, sort out, repair, fix Opposite: corrupt

debunk v **expose**, show up, deflate, demystify, discredit Opposite: perpetuate

debut n **entrance**, introduction, unveiling, presentation, inauguration Opposite: retirement

decade n **period**, era, time, epoch

decadence n **corruption**, debauchery, depravity, dissolution, self-indulgence Opposite: temperance

decadent adj **debauched**, corrupt, depraved, dissolute, degenerate Opposite: innocent

decamp v **run away**, run off, escape, flee, abscond Opposite: turn up

decant v **pour**, pour out, transfer, empty, empty out Opposite: fill

decanter n **carafe**, flask, vessel, bottle, pitcher

decapitate v **behead**, guillotine, execute, amputate, truncate

decapitation n **beheading**, amputation, killing, guillotining, execution

decay v 1 **decompose**, rot, fester, grow moldy, molder 2 **decline**, degenerate, deteriorate, fall off, dwindle Opposite: flourish ■ n 1 **deterioration**, decline, degeneration, falling-off, falloff Opposite: growth 2 **decomposition**, rot, mold, rotting, putrefaction

decayed adj **decomposed**, rotten, rotting, putrefied, moldy Opposite: fresh

decaying adj **decomposing**, rotting, rotten, putrefying, moldy Opposite: fresh

decease (fml) n **death**, passing, departure, release, demise (fml) Opposite: birth

deceased (fml) n **corpse**, cadaver, body, decedent (fml), departed (fml or literary) ■ adj **dead**, late, lifeless, defunct, extinct Opposite: alive. See COMPARE AND CONTRAST at **dead**.

deceit n **dishonesty**, treachery, deceitfulness, deception, trickery Opposite: honesty

deceitful adj **dishonest**, deceiving, fraudulent, untrustworthy, cunning Opposite: honest

deceitfully *adv* **dishonestly**, cunningly, fraudulently, deviously, treacherously *Opposite*: honestly

deceitfulness *n* **dishonesty**, deceit, treachery, lies, falseness *Opposite*: honesty

deceive *v* **1 mislead**, betray, trick, take in, lie to **2 cheat**, two-time, betray, step out *(infml)*, cuckold *(literary)*

deceiver *n* **liar**, fraud, swindler, cheat, quack

deceiving *adj* **misleading**, lying, cheating, devious, deceptive *Opposite*: honest

decelerate *v* **slow down**, slow, slow up, brake, lose speed *Opposite*: accelerate

deceleration *n* **slowing down**, slowing up, slowing, braking, checking *Opposite*: acceleration

decency *n* **1 politeness**, decorum, decorousness, civility, courtesy *Opposite*: incivility **2 modesty**, respectability, uprightness, integrity, wholesomeness *Opposite*: decadence

decent *adj* **1 moral**, honest, virtuous, wholesome, demure *Opposite*: decadent **2 good**, right, proper, correct, suitable *Opposite*: inappropriate **3 reasonable**, respectable, adequate, sizable, generous *Opposite*: inadequate **4** *(infml)* **dressed**, clothed, clad, garbed, covered *Opposite*: undressed **5 respectable**, upright, polite, civilized, well-mannered

decentralization *n* **devolution**, subsidiarity, regionalization, delegation, reorganization *Opposite*: centralization

decentralize *v* **devolve**, regionalize, reorganize, disperse, distribute *Opposite*: centralize

deception *n* **1 dishonesty**, duplicity, deceptiveness, deceit, cheating *Opposite*: truthfulness **2 trick**, ruse, sham, fraud, con

deceptive *adj* **misleading**, illusory, deceiving, dishonest, false *Opposite*: reliable

deceptiveness *n* **falseness**, falsity, disingenuousness, deviousness, spuriousness *Opposite*: reliability

decide *v* **1 make a decision**, choose, come to a decision, make your mind up, settle on *Opposite*: equivocate **2 settle**, determine, conclude, resolve, decree *Opposite*: put off

decided *adj* **1 obvious**, definite, absolute, categorical, unquestionable *Opposite*: unclear **2 determined**, resolute, decisive, firm, sure *Opposite*: hesitant

decidedly *adv* **categorically**, definitely, absolutely, distinctly, particularly *Opposite*: possibly

deciding *adj* **determining**, decisive, conclusive, key, pivotal *Opposite*: insignificant

decimal *n* **number**, fraction, unit

decimate *v* **devastate**, destroy, annihilate, ruin, cut a swath through

decimation *n* **devastation**, destruction, slaughter, annihilation, ruin

decipher *v* **decode**, decrypt, interpret, translate, make out *Opposite*: encode

decipherable *adj* **readable**, legible, intelligible, comprehensible, understandable *Opposite*: unintelligible

decision *n* **1 choice**, result, conclusion, verdict, pronouncement **2 determination**, resolve, firmness, willpower, strength of mind *Opposite*: indecision

decisive *adj* **1 conclusive**, pivotal, key, critical, significant *Opposite*: insignificant **2 strong-minded**, resolute, determined, certain, clear-sighted *Opposite*: uncertain

decisiveness *n* **resoluteness**, determination, conclusiveness, authoritativeness, positiveness *Opposite*: indecisiveness

deck *n* **level**, floor, surface, area, sun deck ■ *v* **1** *(infml)* **hit**, knock down, knock over, floor, thump **2** *(literary)* **adorn**, decorate, hang, cover, wreathe *Opposite*: strip

declaim *v* **hold forth**, pronounce, proclaim, declare, utter *Opposite*: mutter

declamatory *adj* **dramatic**, formal, oratorical, rhetorical, theatrical *Opposite*: low-key

declaration *n* **statement**, announcement, assertion, speech, pronouncement

declare *v* **announce**, state, speak out, assert, affirm

declassification *n* **release**, publication, open access, derestriction, decontrol *Opposite*: restriction

declassify *v* **release**, publish, derestrict, open up, bring out *Opposite*: classify

decline *v* **1 refuse**, turn down, reject, pass up, beg off *Opposite*: accept **2 weaken**, fail, deteriorate, degenerate, fall off *Opposite*: improve ■ *n* **deterioration**, falling-off, falloff, decay, drop *Opposite*: improvement

declining *adj* **deteriorating**, decreasing, lessening, falling, diminishing *Opposite*: improving

decode *v* **decipher**, make out, make sense of, interpret, translate *Opposite*: encode

decoder *n* **cryptographer**, decipherer, interpreter, translator

décolleté *adj* **low-necked**, low-cut, plunging, low, revealing

decommission *v* **retire**, mothball, withdraw, take out, neutralize *Opposite*: introduce

decompose *v* **rot**, decay, crumble, get moldy, fester

decomposed *adj* **rotten**, disintegrated, decayed, putrid, putrefied *Opposite*: fresh

decomposing *adj* **rotting**, disintegrating, decaying, putrid, putrefying *Opposite*: fresh

decomposition *n* **decay**, rottenness, putrefaction, breakdown, disintegration *Opposite*: soundness

deconstruct *v* **analyze**, critique, criticize, decompose, review

decontaminate v **cleanse**, clean up, clean, purify, disinfect *Opposite*: contaminate

decontrol v **deregulate**, delimit, free, set free, loosen *Opposite*: control

decor n **decoration**, furnishings, interior decoration, scheme, design

decorate v **1 beautify**, adorn, ornament, embellish, trim *Opposite*: strip **2 honor**, award, garland, recognize, acknowledge

decorated adj **ornamented**, ornate, adorned, festooned, draped *Opposite*: plain

decoration n **1 beautification**, adornment, ornament, ornamentation, embellishment **2 feature**, festoon, beading, border, carving **3 honor**, medal, award, sash, ribbon

decorative adj **ornamental**, pretty, attractive, pleasing to the eye, enhancing *Opposite*: ugly

decorous adj **well-mannered**, well-behaved, good, correct, modest *Opposite*: improper

decorum n **dignity**, good behavior, propriety, sedateness, modesty *Opposite*: abandon

decoy n **lure**, trap, snare, trick, distraction ■ v **entice**, lure, lead astray, distract, entrap

decrease v **1 reduce**, cut, diminish, cut down, contract *Opposite*: increase **2 diminish**, decline, dwindle, subside, lessen ■ n **reduction**, cut, diminution, lessening, decline *Opposite*: increase

decreasing adj **diminishing**, declining, reducing, dwindling, shrinking *Opposite*: increasing

decree n **ruling**, verdict, announcement, pronouncement, declaration *Opposite*: request ■ v **command**, rule, pronounce, announce, dictate

decrepit adj **1 dilapidated**, crumbling, decaying, falling to pieces, falling apart *Opposite*: pristine **2** (*infml*) **old**, feeble, frail, weak, infirm *Opposite*: vigorous. See COMPARE AND CONTRAST *at* **weak**.

decrepitude n **1 decay**, dilapidation, ruin, shabbiness *Opposite*: soundness **2** (*infml*) **infirmity**, frailty, feebleness, weakness, debility

decriminalization n **legalization**, acceptance, allowance, toleration, sanction *Opposite*: criminalization

decriminalize v **make legal**, legalize, authorize, sanction, permit *Opposite*: outlaw

decry v **criticize**, complain, belittle, disparage, deprecate *Opposite*: praise

dedicate v **1 reserve**, devote, set aside, earmark, give over to **2 give**, commit, devote, consecrate, pledge

dedicated adj **committed**, devoted, steadfast, loyal, faithful *Opposite*: uncommitted

dedication n **devotion**, commitment, enthusiasm, keenness, perseverance

deduce v **1 conclude**, assume, presume, suppose, gather **2 infer**, reason, conclude, work out, figure out

COMPARE AND CONTRAST CORE MEANING: reach a logical conclusion on the basis of information **deduce** reach a conclusion using available knowledge; **infer** draw a conclusion from specific circumstances or evidence; **assume** take a premise or information as true without checking or confirming it; **reason** consider information and use it to reach a conclusion in a logical way; **conclude** form an opinion or make a judgment after much consideration; **work out** find a solution or explanation by careful thought or reasoning; **figure out** find a solution or reach a conclusion by careful thought or reasoning.

deduct v **subtract** take away, take, remove, abstract *Opposite*: add

deduction n **1 subtraction**, removal, withdrawal, abstraction, contribution *Opposite*: addition **2 inference**, assumption, conclusion, presumption, judgment

deductive adj **logical**, inferential, reasonable, empirical, rational *Opposite*: illogical

deed n **1 action**, feat, act, endeavor, exploit **2 document**, title deed, title, charter, record

deem (*fml*) v **think**, believe, consider, estimate, suppose

deep adj **1 bottomless**, profound, unfathomable, subterranean, cavernous *Opposite*: shallow **2 low**, rumbling, booming, sonorous, resonant *Opposite*: shrill **3 profound**, multifaceted, multilayered, mysterious, meaningful *Opposite*: transparent **4 deep-seated**, innate, inherent, entrenched, subconscious *Opposite*: superficial **5 intense**, profound, concentrated, potent, powerful *Opposite*: slight **6 hidden**, secret, arcane, mysterious, silent *Opposite*: open

deepen v **1 intensify**, extend, expand, concentrate, accumulate *Opposite*: weaken **2 dig out**, excavate, hollow out, scoop out, extend *Opposite*: fill in

deep in thought adj **contemplative**, thoughtful, pensive, lost in thought, mulling things over

deeply adv **intensely**, profoundly, seriously, extremely, greatly *Opposite*: mildly

deepness n **1 depth**, profundity, profoundness, bottomlessness, fathomlessness **2 lowness**, resonance, sonority, low pitch

deep-rooted see **deep-seated**

deep-sea adj **marine**, oceanic, ocean

deep-seated adj **innate**, inherent, entrenched, subconscious, ingrained *Opposite*: superficial

de-escalate v **scale down**, scale back, cut back, reduce, decrease *Opposite*: escalate

de-escalation n **reduction**, stepping down, scaling down, cutback, decrease *Opposite*: escalation

deface v **spoil**, ruin, mar, disfigure, mutilate *Opposite*: renovate

defacement n disfigurement, mutilation, vandalism, destruction, damage *Opposite*: restoration

defamation n insult, offense, slander, libel, slur *Opposite*: praise

defamatory adj insulting, offensive, slanderous, libelous, derogatory *Opposite*: complimentary

defame v insult, slander, libel, denigrate, malign *Opposite*: praise. *See* COMPARE AND CONTRAST *at* malign.

default v fail to pay, evade, dodge, shirk, duck (infml) *Opposite*: pay ■ n evasion, avoidance, nonpayment, defaulting, nonattendance

defaulter n 1 nonpayer, debtor, cheat 2 shirker, slacker, absentee, dodger (infml)

defeat n 1 overthrow, conquest, downfall, rout *Opposite*: victory 2 loss, reverse, setback, thrashing, shutout *Opposite*: victory ■ v 1 beat, overcome, conquer, vanquish, trounce *Opposite*: lose 2 baffle, confound, foil, frustrate, thwart

COMPARE AND CONTRAST CORE MEANING: win a victory

defeat win a victory over an enemy or competitor, or to cause failure; **beat** defeat somebody in a contest, or to overcome a difficulty; **conquer** defeat decisively in battle, or to overcome a difficulty; **vanquish** defeat decisively in battle or competition; **overcome** win or succeed after a struggle; **triumph over** succeed against an adversary or against difficult odds; **thrash** gain an easy decisive victory in a sporting contest; **trounce** defeat an opponent convincingly.

defeatism n pessimism, resignation, despondency, despair, negativity *Opposite*: optimism

defeatist adj pessimistic, negative, fatalistic, resigned, despondent *Opposite*: optimistic ■ n pessimist, loser, fatalist, doomsayer, doom-monger *Opposite*: optimist

defecate (fml) v excrete, eliminate waste, empty the bowels, have a bowel movement, evacuate

defecation n excretion, evacuation, elimination

defect n flaw, fault, imperfection, blemish, shortcoming ■ v desert, change sides, abscond, go over, turn traitor. *See* COMPARE AND CONTRAST *at* flaw.

defective adj faulty, imperfect, flawed, substandard, malfunctioning *Opposite*: perfect

defectiveness n faultiness, failure, inadequacy, unreliability, imperfection

defector n traitor, turncoat, renegade, convert, rebel *Opposite*: loyalist

defend v 1 protect, guard, shield, safeguard, preserve *Opposite*: attack 2 support, stand up for, stick up for, stand for, represent *Opposite*: oppose. *See* COMPARE AND CONTRAST *at* safeguard.

defendant n accused, respondent, suspect, corespondent *Opposite*: accuser

defender n 1 supporter, champion, advocate, sponsor, upholder *Opposite*: opponent 2 protector, guard, guardian, escort, bodyguard *Opposite*: attacker

defense n 1 protection, resistance, guard, security, cover *Opposite*: attack 2 justification, argument, vindication, plea, apology *Opposite*: accusation

defense force n army, armed forces, armed services, military, fighters

defenseless adj unprotected, unarmed, exposed, unguarded, vulnerable *Opposite*: protected

defenselessness n vulnerability, helplessness, powerlessness, weakness, frailty *Opposite*: strength

defenses n 1 fortifications, battlements, bunkers, ramparts, barricades 2 resistance, immunity, protection, shield, safeguard *Opposite*: vulnerability

defensible adj 1 defendable, impregnable, unassailable, invulnerable, secure *Opposite*: vulnerable 2 justifiable, valid, cast-iron, secure, rock-solid *Opposite*: indefensible

defensibly adv excusably, justifiably, explicably, forgivably, understandably *Opposite*: unjustifiably

defensive adj 1 self-justifying, self-protective, apologetic, touchy, distrustful *Opposite*: aggressive 2 protective, protecting, defending, shielding, fortified

defer v 1 put off, reschedule, put back, postpone, delay *Opposite*: bring forward 2 bow to, submit, be deferential, accede, comply

deference n respect, esteem, regard, reverence, admiration *Opposite*: disrespect

deferential adj respectful, admiring, reverent, polite, obsequious *Opposite*: disrespectful

deferment n adjournment, postponement, delay, stay, deferral

deferral n postponement, adjournment, delay, stay, deferment

defiance n insubordination, disobedience, insolence, rebelliousness, boldness *Opposite*: compliance

defiant adj disobedient, insolent, insubordinate, rebellious, bold *Opposite*: compliant

deficiency n 1 lack, shortage, absence, deficit, dearth *Opposite*: excess 2 inadequacy, defect, flaw, fault, imperfection. *See* COMPARE AND CONTRAST *at* lack.

deficient adj 1 lacking, poor, underprovided, undersupplied, short *Opposite*: abundant 2 inadequate, flawed, faulty, unsatisfactory, defective *Opposite*: perfect

deficiently adv inadequately, defectively, faultily, incorrectly, wrongly *Opposite*: perfectly

deficit *n* **shortfall**, shortage, arrears, discrepancy, debit *Opposite*: surplus. *See* COMPARE AND CONTRAST *at* lack.

defile *v* 1 *(fml)* **corrupt**, taint, besmirch, sully, spoil *Opposite*: purify 2 *(fml)* **dishonor**, desecrate, sully, violate, debase *Opposite*: respect ■ *n* **pass**, valley, gorge, gap

defiled *(fml) adj* 1 **corrupted**, tainted, besmirched, sullied, tarnished *Opposite*: untarnished 2 **dishonored**, desecrated, sullied, violated, debased *Opposite*: respected

define *v* 1 **describe**, outline, express, state, explain 2 **characterize**, classify, identify, distinguish, specify 3 **mark out**, outline, delimit, demarcate, mark

defined *adj* **clear**, distinct, definite, well-defined, sharp *Opposite*: indistinct

defining moment *n* **turning point**, landmark, watershed, crossroads, moment of truth

definite *adj* 1 **fixed**, settled, agreed, final, assured *Opposite*: indefinite 2 **sure**, certain, positive, set on, determined *Opposite*: uncertain 3 **exact**, specific, explicit, clear-cut, unambiguous *Opposite*: vague 4 **obvious**, recognized, significant, unquestionable, unmistakable *Opposite*: dubious

definitely *adv* **certainly**, absolutely, positively, unquestionably, without doubt *Opposite*: possibly

definiteness *n* **certainty**, assurance, assuredness, conviction, finality *Opposite*: uncertainty

definition *n* 1 **meaning**, description, explanation, classification, characterization 2 **clarity**, sharpness, distinctness, focus, clearness *Opposite*: haziness

definitive *adj* 1 **conclusive**, final, decisive, ultimate, absolute *Opposite*: tentative 2 **authoritative**, conclusive, perfect, best, classic

deflate *v* 1 **let the air out**, go down, let down, collapse, shrink *Opposite*: inflate 2 **belittle**, disappoint, flatten, squash, quash *Opposite*: boost 3 **devalue**, depress, decrease, reduce, lower *Opposite*: inflate

deflated *adj* 1 **emptied**, flattened, shrunk, collapsed, let down *Opposite*: inflated 2 **subdued**, humiliated, flattened, humbled, dispirited *Opposite*: exhilarated

deflation *n* **depression**, devaluation, depreciation, reduction, decrease *Opposite*: inflation

deflect *v* 1 **bounce**, glance, ricochet, rebound, bend 2 **turn aside**, ward off, repel, redirect, sidetrack *Opposite*: attract

deflection *n* **refraction**, ricochet, rebound, glance, bend

deforest *v* **log**, denude, strip, clear-cut, desolate

deform *v* **distort**, bend, warp, buckle, bow

deformation *n* **distortion**, twist, buckle, bend, warp

deformed *adj* 1 **misshapen**, distorted, bent, warped, malformed 2 **abnormal**, corrupted, perverted, spoiled, ruined

deformity *n* **disfigurement**, malformation, distortion, abnormality, misshapenness

defraud *v* **deceive**, swindle, cheat, trick, take advantage of

defray *v* **pay**, cover, meet, contribute, finance

defrock *v* **unfrock**, excommunicate, disqualify, drum out, expel

defrost *v* **melt**, thaw, thaw out, deice, unfreeze *Opposite*: freeze

deft *adj* **skillful**, adroit, neat, nimble, dexterous *Opposite*: clumsy

deftness *n* **skill**, dexterity, precision, handiness, swiftness *Opposite*: clumsiness

defunct *adj* 1 **obsolete**, invalid, redundant, outdated, out-of-date *Opposite*: current 2 **dead**, expired, extinct, gone *(infml)*, deceased *(fml) Opposite*: alive. *See* COMPARE AND CONTRAST *at* dead.

defuse *v* **resolve**, calm, soothe, smooth out, neutralize *Opposite*: aggravate

defy *v* **challenge**, confront, disobey, rebel, resist *Opposite*: obey

degeneracy *n* **depravity**, wickedness, corruption, dissoluteness, decadence *Opposite*: morality

degenerate *v* **deteriorate**, collapse, relapse, worsen, reduce *Opposite*: improve ■ *adj* **debased**, decadent, immoral, debauched, corrupt *Opposite*: moral

degeneration *n* **deterioration**, collapse, disintegration, falling apart, worsening *Opposite*: regeneration

degenerative *adj* **wasting**, worsening, deteriorating, progressive

degradation *n* 1 **humiliation**, disgrace, shame, mortification, misery 2 **squalor**, filth, dilapidation, deprivation, poverty

degrade *v* 1 **humiliate**, shame, disgrace, mortify, demean *Opposite*: exalt *(fml)* 2 **damage**, destroy, reduce, cut down, worsen *Opposite*: upgrade 3 **decay**, decompose, disintegrate, break down, rot

degrading *adj* **humiliating**, debasing, demeaning, undignified, corrupting *Opposite*: ennobling

degree *n* 1 **extent**, quantity, intensity, magnitude, level 2 **grade**, gradation, mark, notch, step

dehumanize *v* **desensitize**, brutalize, degrade, debase *Opposite*: humanize

dehydrate *v* **dry out**, dry up, become dry, desiccate, parch

dehydrated *adj* **dry**, dried out, arid, parched, desiccated. *See* COMPARE AND CONTRAST *at* dry.

dehydration *n* **dryness**, drying out, drying up, desiccation, thirst

deice *v* **unfreeze**, melt, thaw, thaw out *Opposite*: ice up

deification *n* **elevation**, veneration, adoration, beatification, exaltation *(fml)*

deify v **idolize**, worship, glorify, adore, venerate

deign v **condescend**, lower yourself, stoop, consent, agree

deity n **divinity**, god, goddess, godhead, immortal

dejected adj **sad**, disappointed, unhappy, miserable, depressed Opposite: cheerful

dejection n **sadness**, unhappiness, misery, gloom, depression Opposite: cheerfulness

delay n **1 postponement**, interruption, stay, suspension, adjournment **2 interval**, wait, pause, break, lull ■ v **1 postpone**, put off, suspend, adjourn, defer Opposite: bring forward **2 procrastinate**, hesitate, linger, dawdle, pause Opposite: hurry up **3 slow down**, slow up, hold up, set back, obstruct Opposite: speed up

delayed adj **late**, behind, behind schedule, overdue, tardy Opposite: early

delectable adj **1 delicious**, tasty, mouthwatering, appetizing, luscious Opposite: tasteless **2 delightful**, charming, adorable, appealing, heavenly Opposite: unappealing

delectation (fml) n **enjoyment**, delight, pleasure, appreciation, entertainment

delegate v **1 hand over**, farm out, pass on, give, assign Opposite: retain **2 designate**, assign, appoint, allocate, deputize ■ n **representative**, agent, envoy, ambassador, deputy

delegation n **1 commission**, deputation, mission, lobby **2 allocation**, assignment, handing over, giving out, passing on Opposite: retention

delete v **erase**, remove, strike out, cross out, obliterate Opposite: insert

deleterious adj **damaging**, harmful, injurious, destructive, adverse Opposite: beneficial

deletion n **removal**, obliteration, erasure, loss, omission Opposite: addition

deliberate adj **1 intentional**, purposeful, premeditated, conscious, calculated Opposite: accidental **2 careful**, thoughtful, slow, cautious, unhurried Opposite: hasty ■ v **think**, reflect, consider, mull over, ponder

deliberation n **1** (fml) **reflection**, thought, consideration, care, forethought Opposite: impulsiveness **2 discussion**, debate, negotiation, planning, pondering

deliberative (fml) adj **considered**, premeditated, planned, calculated, thought through Opposite: casual

delicacy n **1 tidbit**, treat, luxury, dainty, fancy **2 sensitivity**, tact, diplomacy, consideration, care Opposite: insensitivity **3 refinement**, fastidiousness, subtlety, elegance, fineness Opposite: vulgarity **4 gracefulness**, attractiveness, elegance, charm, grace Opposite: awkwardness **5 fragility**, flimsiness, slenderness, frailty,

weakness Opposite: sturdiness **6 precision**, skill, care, deftness, adroitness Opposite: inaccuracy

delicate adj **1 fragile**, frail, weak, slight, flimsy Opposite: robust **2 subtle**, faint, slight, gentle, mild Opposite: overpowering **3 sensitive**, refined, thoughtful, considerate, sympathetic Opposite: tactless **4 fine**, precise, detailed, accurate, skilled Opposite: rough **5 refined**, graceful, elegant, dainty, nice Opposite: inelegant **6 difficult**, tricky, complicated, sensitive, awkward Opposite: straightforward. See COMPARE AND CONTRAST at **fragile**.

delicateness n **fragility**, fragileness, frailty, vulnerability, feebleness Opposite: robustness

delicious adj **1 tasty**, appetizing, luscious, delectable, mouthwatering Opposite: tasteless **2 delightful**, lovely, wonderful, pleasant, enjoyable Opposite: unpleasant

deliciousness n **1 delectableness**, lusciousness, sweetness, tastiness, scrumptiousness (infml) Opposite: tastelessness **2 delightfulness**, charm, sweetness, attractiveness, pleasantness Opposite: unpleasantness

delight n **joy**, enjoyment, pleasure, happiness, glee Opposite: displeasure ■ v **1 please**, charm, amuse, thrill, gratify Opposite: disappoint **2 take pleasure in**, appreciate, revel in, relish, enjoy Opposite: dislike

delighted adj **pleased**, happy, charmed, enchanted, thrilled Opposite: unhappy

delightful adj **pleasant**, charming, lovely, wonderful, enjoyable Opposite: unpleasant

delimit (fml) v **set the limits of**, demarcate, define, restrict, mark out

delimitation (fml) n **demarcation**, definition, marking out, limitation, restriction

delineate v **1** (fml) **define**, describe, explain, portray, present **2 outline**, delimit, mark out, demarcate, define

delineation n **1** (fml) **description**, definition, explanation, setting down **2 demarcation**, definition, allocation, marking out, outlining

delinquency n **1 criminal behavior**, crime, felony, lawbreaking, misbehavior Opposite: uprightness **2** (fml) **negligence**, carelessness, recklessness, failure, irresponsibility Opposite: carefulness

delinquent adj **1 criminal**, aberrant, antisocial, offending, felonious Opposite: lawabiding **2** (fml) **negligent**, careless, reckless, irresponsible, neglectful Opposite: dutiful ■ n **criminal**, guilty party, felon, lawbreaker, wrongdoer

delirious adj **1 feverish**, fevered, hot, hallucinating, rambling Opposite: rational **2 elated**, ecstatic, thrilled, transported, in seventh heaven, beside yourself Opposite: dejected

delirium n 1 **fever**, hallucination, restlessness, confusion, frenzy Opposite: clarity 2 **ecstasy**, elation, fervor, euphoria, excitement Opposite: dejection

deliver v 1 **carry**, bring, transport, distribute, send Opposite: take away 2 **produce**, provide, supply, dispense, serve 3 (literary) **set free**, release, rescue, save, liberate Opposite: capture 4 **hand over**, give up, surrender, transfer, relinquish Opposite: keep

deliverance (fml) n **rescue**, release, liberation, relief, escape Opposite: capture

delivery n 1 **distribution**, transfer, transport, sending, conveyance 2 **manner of speaking**, presentation, approach, manner, technique 3 **rescue**, release, liberation, relief, escape Opposite: capture

dell (literary) n **small valley**, glade, hollow, clearing, basin

delta n **estuary**, outlet, mouth, channel

delude v **deceive**, take in, cheat, mislead, con

deluded adj **mistaken**, deceived, misled, duped, conned

deluge n 1 **torrent**, flood, downpour, cloudburst, rainstorm 2 **upsurge**, spate, flood, cascade, avalanche Opposite: trickle ■ v 1 **inundate**, flood, swamp, drown, soak Opposite: dry up 2 **overwhelm**, overload, overrun, swamp, bury

delusion n 1 **illusion**, hallucination, vision, mirage, figment of the imagination Opposite: reality 2 **misunderstanding**, misapprehension, misbelief, false impression, misconception

delusive adj **deceptive**, chimerical, misleading, specious, illusory Opposite: genuine

deluxe adj **sumptuous**, luxurious, luxury, exclusive, select Opposite: cheap

delve v 1 **look into**, investigate, research, probe, explore 2 (archaic) **dig**, burrow, tunnel, scrabble, scratch ■ n **rummage**, hunt, dig, search, dive

demagogic adj **rabble-rousing**, inflammatory, manipulative, declamatory, agitating

demagogical see demagogic

demagogue n **firebrand**, agitator, manipulator, crowd pleaser, haranguer

demand v 1 **insist**, command, order, require, stipulate Opposite: request 2 **ask**, inquire, question, query, want Opposite: answer 3 **require**, need, want, call for, necessitate ■ n 1 **request**, call, claim, petition, mandate Opposite: response 2 **requirement**, need, pressure, exigency, claim

demanding adj 1 **difficult**, hard, challenging, tough, severe Opposite: easy 2 **insistent**, self-centered, persistent, dissatisfied, discontented Opposite: satisfied

demarcate v 1 **define**, mark out, delineate,

draw, fix 2 **separate**, distinguish, differentiate, isolate, discriminate Opposite: unite

demarcation n **separation**, differentiation, distinction, discrimination, segregation

demean v **degrade**, debase, humiliate, disgrace, humble Opposite: uplift

demeanor n **manner**, conduct, behavior, character, deportment

demean yourself v **lower yourself**, swallow your pride, stoop low, go down on your knees, abase yourself (literary)

demented (infml) adj **irrational**, unreasonable, wild, frenzied, frantic Opposite: rational

demerit n **disadvantage**, failing, shortcoming, drawback, fault Opposite: merit

demijohn n **bottle**, flagon, magnum, jeroboam, rehoboam

demise (fml) n 1 **death**, passing, departure, decease (fml), expiry (fml or literary) Opposite: birth 2 **end**, termination, finish, failure, ruin Opposite: creation

demo (infml) n 1 **sample**, showpiece, example, specimen, demonstrator 2 **demonstration**, presentation, display, show, exhibition

demobilization n **discharge**, release, disbandment, dismissal, retirement Opposite: mobilization

demobilize v **discharge**, dismiss, disband, release, retire Opposite: mobilize

democracy n 1 **social equality**, equality, egalitarianism, classlessness, consensus Opposite: inequality 2 **democratic system**, democratic state, democratic organization, representative form of government, republic Opposite: dictatorship

democrat n **egalitarian**, populist, republican, social democrat, constitutionalist Opposite: totalitarian

democratic adj 1 **self-governing**, self-ruled, independent, autonomous, elected Opposite: autocratic 2 **egalitarian**, free, classless, equal, open Opposite: repressive

demolish v 1 **knock down**, tear down, pull down, bulldoze, blow up Opposite: build 2 **destroy**, ruin, flatten, smash, wreck Opposite: preserve 3 (infml) **beat**, annihilate, defeat, rout, thrash 4 (infml) **disprove**, tear to pieces, dismantle, undermine, take apart (infml) Opposite: support 5 (infml) **devour**, wolf, gobble, eat, consume Opposite: nibble

demolition n **destruction**, pulling down, knocking down, annihilation, devastation Opposite: construction

demon n 1 **fiend**, evil spirit, devil, monster Opposite: angel 2 **fear**, anxiety, terror, torment, trouble 3 (infml) **expert**, genius, fiend, whiz (infml), wizard (infml)

demonstrable adj 1 **obvious**, palpable, patent, evident, noticeable Opposite:

imperceptible **2 provable**, verifiable, self-evident, confirmable, comprehensible *Opposite*: doubtful

demonstrate *v* **1 explain**, expound, display, operate, instruct **2 prove**, validate, establish, reveal, make evident **3 protest**, march, rally, lobby, support

demonstration *n* **1 presentation**, display, illustration, explanation, exposition **2 proof**, evidence, validation, establishment, revelation

demonstrative *adj* **affectionate**, warm, loving, friendly, emotional *Opposite*: reserved

demonstrator *n* **1 protester**, supporter, activist, campaigner, lobbyist **2 presenter**, instructor, tutor, teacher, trainer

demoralization *n* **discouragement**, deflation, undermining, depression, dejection *Opposite*: encouragement

demoralize *v* **dishearten**, undermine, dispirit, deflate, discourage *Opposite*: encourage

demoralized *adj* **disheartened**, dispirited, downhearted, discouraged, deflated *Opposite*: optimistic

demoralizing *adj* **disheartening**, discouraging, depressing, dispiriting, crushing *Opposite*: encouraging

demote *v* **downgrade**, relegate, move down, devalue, reduce *Opposite*: promote

demotion *n* **relegation**, downgrading, devaluation, reduction, lowering *Opposite*: promotion

demotivate *v* **discourage**, demoralize, dishearten, dispirit, deter *Opposite*: motivate

demotivation *n* **demoralization**, discouragement, disheartenment, deterrence, dissuasion *Opposite*: motivation

demur *v* **object**, protest, raise objections, balk, express doubts *Opposite*: agree. See COMPARE AND CONTRAST *at* **object**.

demure *adj* **1 modest**, sedate, decorous, reserved, shy *Opposite*: bold **2 prim**, coy, prudish, strait-laced *Opposite*: pert

demystification *n* **clarification**, explanation, interpretation, revelation, decipherment *Opposite*: obfuscation

demystify *v* **clarify**, explain, elucidate, interpret, reveal *Opposite*: obscure

denial *n* **1 disavowal** *(fml)*, refutation, rejection, rebuttal, contradiction *Opposite*: confirmation **2 refusal**, deprivation, withholding, begrudging, turning down

denigrate *v* **1 disparage**, vilify, pour scorn on, degrade, belittle *Opposite*: glorify **2 defame**, slander, libel, abuse, stigmatize *Opposite*: praise

denigration *n* **1 disparagement**, vilification, scorn, depreciation, belittling *Opposite*: glorification **2 defamation**, slander, libel, abuse, stigmatization *Opposite*: commendation

denizen *n* **inhabitant**, resident, citizen, occupant, native

denotation *n* **meaning**, import, sense, signification, significance

denote *v* **1 mean**, signify, stand for, represent, symbolize **2 refer to**, allude to, imply, convey, express

denouement *n* **ending**, end, finale, conclusion, termination *Opposite*: opening

denounce *v* **1 criticize**, censure, deplore, deprecate, condemn *Opposite*: support **2 accuse**, point the finger at, blame, charge, inform. See COMPARE AND CONTRAST *at* **disapprove**.

dense *adj* **1 crowded**, packed, packed in, full, jam-packed *(infml)* **2 thick**, solid, impenetrable, compressed, condensed **3 complicated**, complex, difficult, obscure, deep

denseness *n* **1 crowdedness**, crowding, tightness, impenetrability, closeness **2 thickness**, opacity, solidity, impenetrability, darkness **3 complexity**, difficulty, complication, obscurity, opacity

density *n* **thickness**, compactness, mass, concentration, bulk

dent *v* **1 knock**, hit, bump, bang, indent **2 damage**, hurt, undermine, diminish, lessen ■ *n* **1 hollow**, indentation, depression, dimple, cavity *Opposite*: lump **2** *(infml)* **reduction**, hole, cut, dip, decrease **3** *(infml)* **blow**, knock, shock, setback, reversal *Opposite*: boost

denude *v* **strip**, uncover, bare, remove, shed *Opposite*: cover

denunciate *(fml)* *v* **condemn**, criticize, accuse, censure, reprove *Opposite*: commend

denunciation *n* **condemnation**, criticism, accusation, censure, reproof *Opposite*: commendation

deny *v* **1 repudiate**, refute, reject, contradict, disagree *Opposite*: agree **2 refuse**, disallow, block, forbid, prevent *Opposite*: permit **3 forgo**, renounce, disavow, reject, disown

deodorant *n* **roll-on**, deodorizer, spray

deodorize *v* **freshen**, scent, refresh, perfume, aromatize

depart *v* **1 start out**, set out, move off, set off, leave *Opposite*: return **2 pull out**, leave, go away, disappear, be off *Opposite*: arrive **3 deviate**, diverge, differ, vary, change *Opposite*: stick to **4** *(fml)* **die**, pass on, pass away, succumb, expire *(fml)*

departed *(fml or literary)* *adj* **dead**, late, defunct, lamented *Opposite*: living. See COMPARE AND CONTRAST *at* **dead**.

departing *n* **leaving**, going away, withdrawal, departure, retreat *Opposite*: arriving

department *n* **1 subdivision**, division, branch, sector, section **2** *(infml)* **responsibility**, area, specialty, realm, sphere

departure *n* **1 leaving**, going away, parting,

exit, exodus Opposite: arrival 2 change, deviation, divergence, digression, variation 3 **venture**, project, enterprise, endeavor, undertaking

depend v be contingent, hinge on, rest on, be subject to, hang on

dependability n reliability, steadiness, trustworthiness, loyalty, fidelity Opposite: unreliability

dependable adj reliable, trustworthy, loyal, faithful, steady Opposite: unreliable

dependence n 1 reliance, trust, confidence, belief, hope Opposite: independence 2 **need**, requirement, necessity, want 3 **addiction**, dependency, reliance, need, craving

dependency n 1 territory, colony, dependent state, dependent territory, adjunct 2 **dependence**, need, reliance, addiction, habit

dependent adj 1 reliant on, in need of, at the mercy of, hooked on (slang) 2 needy, reliant, helpless, supported Opposite: independent 3 **contingent**, conditional, determined, subject, related Opposite: independent

depend on v 1 need, require, rely on, be dependent on, lean on 2 **rely on**, count on, trust, be sure of, be certain of Opposite: mistrust

depict v portray, show, represent, describe, illustrate

depiction n representation, portrayal, description, illustration, delineation

deplete v use up, drain, exhaust, diminish, lessen Opposite: increase

depletion n reduction, exhaustion, diminution, lessening, running down Opposite: restoration

deplorable adj 1 disgraceful, terrible, awful, appalling, unacceptable Opposite: praiseworthy 2 **pitiful**, lamentable, woeful, appalling, shameful

deplore v 1 censure, condemn, criticize, deprecate, disapprove Opposite: praise 2 **lament**, bemoan, regret, be sorry, rue. See COMPARE AND CONTRAST at **disapprove**.

deploy v 1 position, arrange, set up, set out, install 2 **use**, employ, implement, utilize, adopt

deployment n 1 placement, disposition, positioning, distribution, arrangement 2 **utilization**, employment, implementation

depoliticize v humanize, personalize, socialize, neutralize Opposite: politicize

depopulate v clear, relocate, remove, clear out, evacuate Opposite: populate

depopulation n clearance, relocation, removal, evacuation, abandonment Opposite: settlement

deport v expel, extradite, banish, exile, transport

deportation n exile, banishment, extradition, repatriation, expulsion

deportee n exile, outcast, displaced person, refugee, evacuee

deportment n manner, gait, attitude, posture, bearing

depose v overthrow, oust, topple, throw out, remove Opposite: install

deposit v 1 pay in, credit, put in, bank, consign Opposite: withdraw 2 **put**, put down, set down, leave, place Opposite: remove 3 **accumulate**, lay down, leave behind, build up, pile up ■ n 1 credit, payment, sum Opposite: withdrawal 2 **security**, guarantee, pledge, surety 3 **sediment**, residue, accretion, layer, accumulation

deposition n 1 statement, testimony, admission, sworn testimony, confession 2 **removal**, overthrow, unseating, ousting, dethronement 3 **accumulation**, accretion, sedimentation, silting, buildup

depositor n saver, investor, account holder, creditor

depot n 1 train station, bus station, terminus 2 **yard**, maintenance yard, garage, workshop

deprave v lead astray, corrupt, degrade, ruin, debase

depraved adj debauched, immoral, corrupt, evil, wicked Opposite: righteous

depravity n debauchery, immorality, corruption, wickedness, evil Opposite: righteousness

deprecate v condemn, censure, denigrate, denounce, deplore Opposite: approve

deprecating adj condemnatory, disapproving, derogatory, deprecatory, pejorative (fml) Opposite: approving

deprecation n disapproval, denigration, condemnation, censure, criticism Opposite: praise

deprecatory adj 1 disapproving, derogatory, critical, denigrating, condemnatory Opposite: approving 2 **apologetic**, sorry, repentant, contrite, remorseful Opposite: unrepentant

depreciate v 1 lessen, devalue, deflate, decline, downgrade Opposite: appreciate 2 **denigrate**, belittle, disparage, run down, criticize Opposite: commend

depreciation n devaluation, reduction, decrease, decline, downgrading Opposite: rise

depreciatory adj belittling, deprecatory, critical, denigrating, derogatory Opposite: complimentary

depredation n plunder, destruction, pillage, despoliation, attack

depress v 1 sadden, dishearten, discourage, dispirit, demoralize Opposite: cheer up 2 **press down**, push down, press, push, lower Opposite: release

depressant n sedative, drug, narcotic, tranquilizer, downer (slang) ■ adj sedative, tranquilizing, sedating, calming, narcotic

depressed *adj* **1 unhappy**, miserable, dejected, low, disheartened *Opposite*: happy **2 rundown**, deprived, poor, underprivileged, neglected *Opposite*: affluent

depressing *adj* **sad**, miserable, disheartening, discouraging, gloomy *Opposite*: cheering

depression *n* **1 downheartedness**, unhappiness, despair, sadness, gloominess *Opposite*: happiness **2 slump**, recession, decline, downturn, slide *Opposite*: boom **3 hollow**, dip, dent, impression, dimple *Opposite*: hump

depressive *adj* **gloomy**, depressing, cheerless, miserable, bleak *Opposite*: uplifting

deprivation *n* **lack**, deficiency, scarcity, denial, withdrawal *Opposite*: plenty

deprive *v* **divest**, rob, deny, take away, remove *Opposite*: provide

deprived *adj* **disadvantaged**, underprivileged, poor, destitute, depressed *Opposite*: privileged

deprived of *adj* **without**, lacking, wanting, short of, starved of

depth *n* **1 deepness**, profundity, distance **2 intensity**, vigor, strength, power, concentration *Opposite*: weakness **3 complexity**, profundity, seriousness, gravity, wisdom *Opposite*: flippancy

deputation *n* **delegation**, commission, mission

depute *v* **delegate**, hand over, relinquish, allot, transfer

deputize *v* **stand in**, represent, fill in, act, replace

deputy *n* **second-in-command**, assistant, agent, delegate, representative. *See* COMPARE AND CONTRAST *at* **assistant**.

derail *v* **disrupt**, upset, wreck, ruin, spoil

derange *v* **1 distress**, unsettle, upset, unhinge, shake **2 disorganize**, disrupt, disturb, dislocate, upset

derangement *n* **1 imbalance**, irrationality, madness, insanity, instability *Opposite*: sanity **2 disorder**, confusion, muddle, disorganization, disturbance *Opposite*: order

derby *n* **contest**, race, match, clash, sporting event

deregulate *v* **free**, relax, liberalize, decontrol, derestrict *Opposite*: regulate

derelict *adj* **dilapidated**, in ruins, rundown, ruined, neglected

dereliction *n* **1 neglect**, negligence, disregard, recklessness, carelessness *Opposite*: assiduousness **2 abandonment**, desertion, neglect, dilapidation, default

deride *v* **ridicule**, scoff, disparage, mock, scorn *Opposite*: admire. *See* COMPARE AND CONTRAST *at* **ridicule**.

derision *n* **disparagement**, scorn, disdain, mockery, ridicule *Opposite*: admiration

derisive *adj* **mocking**, scathing, sarcastic, irreverent, contemptuous *Opposite*: admiring

derisory *adj* **pitiful**, laughable, insulting, ridiculous, contemptible *Opposite*: generous

derivation *n* **origin**, root, source, beginning, seed. *See* COMPARE AND CONTRAST *at* **origin**.

derivative *adj* **unoriginal**, imitative, plagiaristic, copied, derived *Opposite*: original ■ *n* **offshoot**, byproduct, spinoff, result, end product

derive *v* **1 originate**, stem, spring, arise, descend **2 get**, gain, obtain, draw, receive

derogatory *adj* **disparaging**, critical, insulting, offensive, depreciating *Opposite*: complimentary

derrick *n* **1 crane**, hoist, winch, elevator **2 wellhead**, rig, gantry, oil platform, frame

derring-do *(dated)* *n* **boldness**, bravery, courage, daring, bravado *Opposite*: cowardice

desalinate *v* **purify**, desalt, detoxify, distill, refine

desalination *n* **purification**, detoxification, distillation, salt removal

descale *v* **clean out**, scrape, scour, flush, clean

descant *n* **harmony**, part, line, tune, air

descend *v* **1 go down**, move down, come down, slide down, fall down *Opposite*: ascend **2 slope**, decline, fall away, go downhill, drop away *Opposite*: ascend **3 derive**, originate, come from, stem, spring **4 lower yourself**, stoop, sink, resort, fall *Opposite*: rise **5 arrive**, drop in, appear, turn up, show up *Opposite*: leave **6 fall**, fall on, affect, come over, come upon

descendant *n* **successor**, offspring, progeny, child, heir *Opposite*: ancestor

descendent *adj* **descending**, down, downward, plunging, sinking *Opposite*: ascendant

descent *n* **1 fall**, drop, dive, tumble, plunge *Opposite*: ascent **2 decline**, deterioration, depreciation, degeneration, drop *Opposite*: improvement **3 ancestry**, parentage, lineage, origin, succession

describe *v* **1 explain**, portray, depict, illustrate, express **2 label**, refer to, define, designate, pronounce

description *n* **1 account**, report, explanation, portrayal, picture **2 type**, sort, kind, class, variety

descriptive *adj* **1 explanatory**, illustrative, narrative, informative, factual *Opposite*: imaginative **2 evocative**, expressive, vivid, graphic, eloquent

desecrate *v* **defile**, vandalize, insult, violate, outrage *Opposite*: consecrate

desecration *n* **violation**, defilement, vandalism, sacrilege, despoliation *Opposite*: consecration

deseed v pit, stone, core

desegregate v integrate, unify, unite, bring together, merge Opposite: segregate

desegregation n integration, unification, reunion, reconciliation, merging Opposite: segregation

deselect v reject, abandon, discard, cast off, remove Opposite: select

desensitize v numb, deaden, dull, soothe, pacify Opposite: sensitize

desert n 1 wasteland, wilderness, barren region, arid region, waste 2 reward, return, recompense, wages, just reward ■ v 1 abandon, leave high and dry, leave, forsake, discard Opposite: support 2 abscond, leave, go AWOL, run away, take off (infml) Opposite: stay

deserted adj 1 empty, isolated, uninhabited, desolate, solitary Opposite: inhabited 2 abandoned, discarded, forsaken, cast off, ditched (infml)

deserter n absconder, runaway, fugitive, defector, traitor

desertion n absconding, abandonment, running away, disappearance, departure

deserve v merit, be worthy, earn, warrant, justify

deservedly adv justly, rightly, justifiably, reasonably, properly Opposite: unreasonably

deserving adj worthy, commendable, admirable, praiseworthy, justified Opposite: unworthy

desiccate v dry up, wither, dry out, dehydrate, parch

desiccated adj dry, dried, dried out, shriveled, dehydrated. Opposite: moist. See COMPARE AND CONTRAST at dry.

desiccation n dryness, dehydration, withering, shriveling, drying

design v 1 create, invent, conceive, originate, fabricate 2 plan, intend, aim, devise, propose ■ n 1 project, scheme, enterprise, plan, strategy 2 drawing, blueprint, plan, sketch, outline 3 pattern, motif, figure, shape, device 4 intention, purpose, scheme, plan, object Opposite: serendipity

designate v 1 call, label, title, entitle, term 2 specify, point out, indicate, choose, select 3 assign, select, choose, delegate, allocate ■ adj in waiting, elect, to be

designation n title, name, description, term, label

designedly adv intentionally, on purpose, purposely, deliberately, purposefully Opposite: accidentally

designer n creator, inventor, originator, engineer, stylist ■ adj fashionable, stylish, chic, expensive, exclusive Opposite: mass-produced

designing adj scheming, conniving, deceitful, wily, manipulative Opposite: ingenuous

desirability n 1 appropriateness, aptness, rightness, suitability, advantage 2 appeal, attractiveness, attraction, allure, prestige

desirable adj 1 wanted, needed, necessary, required, looked-for Opposite: undesirable 2 attractive, pleasing, enviable, pleasant, popular Opposite: undesirable

desire v 1 want, wish for, long for, covet, crave 2 (fml) request, ask, require, appeal, entreat ■ n wish, want, longing, craving, yearning. See COMPARE AND CONTRAST at want.

desired adj wanted, anticipated, sought after, looked-for, favorite Opposite: unwanted

desirous (fml) adj eager, hopeful, wishing for, longing for, hoping for

desist v cease, stop, discontinue, give up, end Opposite: continue

desolate adj 1 deserted, isolated, bleak, abandoned, forsaken Opposite: populous 2 unhappy, forlorn, miserable, depressed, inconsolable Opposite: happy 3 depressing, gloomy, dismal, austere, forbidding Opposite: cheerful

desolation n 1 unhappiness, misery, despair, anguish, sadness Opposite: happiness 2 barrenness, isolation, bleakness, emptiness, dereliction

despair n misery, desolation, hopelessness, anguish, gloom Opposite: joy ■ v lose hope, give up hope, have no hope, see no light at the end of the tunnel, lose heart Opposite: hope

despairing adj hopeless, desolate, miserable, pained, despondent Opposite: hopeful

desperado n criminal, outlaw, gangster, bandit, villain

desperate adj 1 frantic, anxious, worried, distressed, distracted Opposite: calm 2 eager, dying, raring, bursting, impatient Opposite: loath 3 reckless, careless, rash, impulsive, dangerous Opposite: safe 4 hopeless, wretched, irredeemable, deplorable, dreadful Opposite: hopeful 5 serious, grave, extreme, critical, threatening Opposite: harmless

desperately adv 1 frantically, anxiously, frenziedly, hastily, distractedly Opposite: calmly 2 very much, badly, to a great extent, dreadfully, urgently Opposite: hardly

desperation n 1 anxiety, worry, fear, distraction, nervousness Opposite: calmness 2 hopelessness, despair, despondency, misery, anguish Opposite: hopefulness

despicable adj appalling, dreadful, contemptible, wicked, shameful Opposite: admirable

despise v loathe, scorn, look down on, hate, spurn Opposite: admire

despised adj hated, reviled, loathed, shunned, scorned Opposite: beloved

despite prep in spite of, regardless of, in the face of, even with, notwithstanding (fml) Opposite: because of

despoil v **rob**, plunder, sack, pillage, loot

despoilment n **despoilation**, vandalism, defacement, destruction, desecration

despoliation n **plundering**, pillage, sack, theft, robbery

despondency n **hopelessness**, sadness, misery, dejection, depression *Opposite*: cheerfulness

despondent adj **hopeless**, low, dejected, despairing, downhearted *Opposite*: cheerful

despot n **dictator**, tyrant, autocrat, oppressor, authoritarian

despotic adj **tyrannical**, dictatorial, autocratic, authoritarian, repressive *Opposite*: democratic

despotism n **tyranny**, dictatorship, absolutism, autocracy, authoritarianism *Opposite*: democracy

destabilization n **weakening**, subversion, undermining, disruption, dislocation

destabilize v **undermine**, subvert, weaken, threaten, disrupt *Opposite*: strengthen

destination n 1 **journey's end**, terminus, last stop, end point, end of the road *Opposite*: starting point 2 **end**, purpose, target, aim, goal

destined adj **intended**, meant, fated, designed, certain

destiny n 1 **fate**, fortune, lot, luck, providence 2 **purpose**, vocation, intention, call, calling

destitute adj **poor**, penniless, impoverished, insolvent, needy *Opposite*: solvent

destitution n **poverty**, penury, hardship, need, insolvency *Opposite*: prosperity

destroy v 1 **obliterate**, annihilate, demolish, devastate, tear down *Opposite*: build 2 **ruin**, damage, break, break up, spoil *Opposite*: conserve 3 **abolish**, put an end to, get rid of, end, extinguish *Opposite*: sustain 4 **defeat**, crush, subdue, demolish, overcome

destroyed adj **demolished**, devastated, ruined, wrecked, smashed *Opposite*: intact

destroyer n **destructive force**, natural disaster, cause of death, killer, demolisher *Opposite*: creator

destruction n **obliteration**, annihilation, devastation, demolition, ruin *Opposite*: construction

destructive adj 1 **damaging**, devastating, harmful, detrimental, injurious 2 **unhelpful**, critical, negative, damaging, disparaging *Opposite*: constructive

destructiveness n 1 **harmfulness**, power, force, violence, ferocity 2 **criticism**, negativity, harshness, viciousness, hurtfulness *Opposite*: helpfulness

desultory adj **aimless**, casual, random, unfocused, haphazard *Opposite*: methodical

detach v **separate**, remove, disengage, disconnect, isolate *Opposite*: attach

detachable adj **removable**, separable, clip-on, hook-on, attachable *Opposite*: fixed

detached adj 1 **separate**, disconnected, standing apart, apart, removed *Opposite*: connected 2 **aloof**, indifferent, unemotional, unbiased, uninvolved *Opposite*: involved

detachment n 1 **aloofness**, remoteness, indifference, impassiveness, distance *Opposite*: involvement 2 **objectivity**, disinterest, disinterestedness, impartiality, fairness 3 **disconnection**, separation, disengagement, disentanglement, extrication *Opposite*: connection 4 **group**, unit, task force, detail, party

detail n 1 **part**, feature, aspect, point, element 2 **group**, unit, task force, detachment, party ■ v 1 **list**, specify, describe, itemize, particularize 2 **assign**, delegate, allocate, conscript, designate

detailed adj **full**, thorough, comprehensive, complete, exhaustive *Opposite*: sketchy

details n **particulars**, facts, information, minutiae, niceties

detain v 1 **delay**, hold up, keep, keep back, impede *Opposite*: let go 2 **arrest**, hold, keep in custody, capture, confine *Opposite*: release

detained adj **in custody**, in detention, under arrest, behind bars, in prison *Opposite*: free

detainee n **prisoner**, captive, internee, hostage, convict

detect v **notice**, sense, become aware of, perceive, spot

detectable adj **obvious**, visible, noticeable, measurable, demonstrable *Opposite*: undetectable

detection n **discovery**, uncovering, finding, recognition, exposure *Opposite*: concealment

detective n **investigator**, private detective, plain-clothes officer, operative, private eye (*infml*)

detector n **sensor**, indicator, gauge, finder

detente see **détente**

détente n **rapprochement**, agreement, cooperation, compromise, accommodation *Opposite*: hostility

detention n **custody**, imprisonment, confinement, arrest, locking up *Opposite*: release

deter v **discourage**, put off, daunt, dissuade, prevent *Opposite*: encourage

detergent n **cleaner**, cleansing agent, cleanser, shampoo, laundry detergent

deteriorate v **get worse**, worsen, decline, depreciate, go downhill *Opposite*: improve

deteriorating adj **worsening**, getting worse, falling, fading, waning *Opposite*: improving

deterioration n **worsening**, decline, weakening, drop, descent Opposite: improvement

determinant n **cause**, determining factor, factor, element, basis

determination n **strength of mind**, willpower, resolve, purpose, fortitude Opposite: weakness

determine v 1 **find out**, verify, clarify, uncover, establish 2 **decide**, settle, conclude, resolve, agree 3 **influence**, affect, shape, form, mold 4 **control**, regulate, govern, fix, limit

determined adj **strong-minded**, resolute, gritty, single-minded, unwavering Opposite: irresolute

determining adj **decisive**, causal, defining, influential, shaping Opposite: irrelevant

deterrence n **discouragement**, dissuasion, preemption, prevention, restriction Opposite: encouragement

deterrent adj **warning**, preventive, restrictive, restraining, limiting Opposite: encouraging ■ n **restraint**, disincentive, rein, curb, limit Opposite: incitement

detest v **hate**, loathe, despise, dislike, abhor Opposite: love

detestable adj **hateful**, despicable, repugnant, vile, revolting Opposite: lovable

detestation n **hatred**, hate, abhorrence, loathing, dislike Opposite: adoration

dethrone v **depose**, oust, unseat, overthrow, overwhelm Opposite: install

detonate v **explode**, blow up, set off, ignite, spark off

detonation n **explosion**, blast, ignition, report, bang

detour n **deviation**, diversion, roundabout route, alternative route, long way around

detoxication see **detoxification**

detoxification n **cleansing**, decontamination, purification, detoxication, reclamation Opposite: contamination

detoxify v **cleanse**, purify, clear, clean, depollute Opposite: contaminate

detract v **take away from**, diminish, lessen, reduce, weaken Opposite: bolster

detraction n 1 **lessening**, reduction, subtraction, taking away, deduction Opposite: addition 2 (fml) **slander**, abuse, disparagement, aspersion, denigration Opposite: praise

detractor n **critic**, disparager, cynic, heckler, attacker Opposite: supporter

detriment n **disadvantage**, loss, harm, damage, injury Opposite: advantage

detrimental adj **harmful**, damaging, disadvantageous, unfavorable, negative Opposite: beneficial

detritus n **debris**, litter, waste, trash, garbage

deuce n **tie**, draw, even-steven (infml)

devaluation n **deflation**, depreciation, reduction, depression, devaluing Opposite: appreciation

devalue v **diminish**, lessen, undervalue, bring down, cheapen Opposite: overvalue

devastate v 1 **destroy**, demolish, ravage, wreck, ruin Opposite: preserve 2 **overwhelm**, overcome, shock, distress, upset Opposite: comfort

devastated adj **overwhelmed**, overcome, shattered, confounded, shocked Opposite: comforted

devastating adj 1 **destructive**, harmful, damaging, ruinous, injurious 2 **overwhelming**, shocking, upsetting, disturbing, distressing Opposite: comforting

devastatingly adv **terribly**, dreadfully, overwhelmingly, extraordinarily, hugely

devastation n **destruction**, damage, ruin, desolation, waste Opposite: preservation

develop v 1 **grow**, mature, progress, advance, change 2 **arise**, result, happen, stem, come 3 **acquire**, pick up, foster, create, breed 4 **expand**, enlarge, extend, increase, widen Opposite: contract 5 **work out**, flesh out, expound, fill in, explain Opposite: outline 6 **build on**, exploit, utilize, build 7 **improve**, do up, renovate, refurbish, remodel

developed adj **technologically advanced**, industrialized, advanced, established, settled Opposite: developing

developer n 1 **designer**, creator, inventor, brains, maker 2 **buyer**, property developer, land developer, contractor, speculator

developing adj **emerging**, emergent, evolving Opposite: developed

development n 1 **event**, happening, occurrence, change, incident 2 **growth**, expansion, progress, advance, change Opposite: stasis 3 **enhancement**, expansion, advancement, training, education

developmental adj 1 **developing**, growing, evolving, changing, progressive Opposite: static 2 **age-related**, age-linked, growth-related, hormonal, child-development

deviance n **nonconformity**, unconventionality, eccentricity, unorthodoxy, aberration Opposite: conformity

deviant adj **different**, divergent, nonstandard, aberrant, irregular Opposite: standard

deviate v 1 **differ**, depart, diverge, stray, digress Opposite: conform 2 **diverge**, move away, stray, depart, swerve Opposite: keep to

deviation n 1 **difference**, departure, change, divergence, variation Opposite: normalization 2 **nonconformity**, unconventionality, eccentricity, unorthodoxy, aberration

device n 1 **machine**, tool, piece of equipment, mechanism, apparatus 2 **expedient**, maneuver, stratagem, ruse, dodge 3 **design**, emblem, logo, badge, crest

devious adj 1 deceitful, tricky, scheming, designing, wily Opposite: straightforward 2 circuitous, oblique, meandering, tortuous, winding Opposite: direct

deviousness n guile, cunning, artfulness, deceitfulness, untrustworthiness Opposite: straightforwardness

devise v think up, plan, figure out, work out, invent

devoid adj empty, barren, without, bereft, lacking Opposite: full

devolution n decentralization, delegation, transference, transfer Opposite: centralization

devolve v transfer, decentralize, give to, hand to, pass to Opposite: centralize

devote v dedicate, give, offer, apply, assign

devoted adj 1 committed, loving, caring, affectionate, kind Opposite: uncaring 2 dedicated, loyal, dutiful, faithful, staunch Opposite: uncommitted 3 keen, enthusiastic, dedicated, ardent, fervent Opposite: unenthusiastic

devotee n 1 fan, follower, supporter, aficionado, aficionada 2 disciple, follower, believer, votary

devotion n 1 commitment, attachment, love, fondness, affection Opposite: dislike 2 dedication, care, attentiveness, support, loyalty Opposite: neglect 3 enthusiasm, admiration, zeal, keenness, fervor Opposite: apathy 4 (fml) piety, devoutness, religious zeal, religious fervor, religious observance Opposite: impiety

devotional adj religious, worshipful, worshiping, prayerful, holy

devotions n prayers, holy rites, observances, supplications (fml)

devour v 1 consume, demolish, dispose of, gulp, wolf 2 (literary) overwhelm, overcome, engulf, consume, destroy

devout adj 1 religious, pious, spiritual, devoted, dedicated Opposite: uncommitted 2 (fml) sincere, heartfelt, deep, earnest, fervent Opposite: insincere 3 enthusiastic, keen, ardent, zealous, fanatical Opposite: casual

devoutly adv deeply, keenly, seriously, intensely, profoundly

devoutness n piety, spirituality, religious fervor, religious zeal, piousness Opposite: impiety

dew n droplets, precipitation, condensation, dewdrops

dewdrop n bead of moisture, droplet, drop, drip

dewy adj wet, dew-covered, heavy with dew, damp, moist Opposite: dry

dewy-eyed adj innocent, naive, trusting, unrealistic, idealistic Opposite: down-to-earth

dexterity n 1 deftness, skill, adroitness, handiness, legerdemain Opposite: clumsiness 2 ingenuity, acuity, sharpness, quickness, resourcefulness Opposite: dullness

dexterous adj 1 deft, adroit, handy, nimble-fingered, nimble Opposite: clumsy 2 quick-witted, sharp, acute, resourceful, clever Opposite: dull

dextrous see dexterous

diadem n crown, tiara, circlet, coronet, wreath

diagnose v make a diagnosis, identify, analyze, spot, detect

diagnosis n identification, analysis, judgment, finding, verdict

diagnostic adj analytic, analytical, indicative, investigative, problem-solving

diagonal adj slanting, oblique, sloping, crossways, crosswise

diagram n drawing, figure, illustration, plan, map

diagrammatic adj graphic, illustrative, pictorial, visual, drawn Opposite: verbal

dial n 1 knob, handle, control, button 2 face, gauge, indicator, disk, control panel ■ v call, telephone, phone, call up

dialect n vernacular, language, parlance, tongue, idiom

dialectic n 1 tension, conflict, interaction, clash, opposition Opposite: harmony 2 discussion, debate, investigation, examination, analysis

dialogue n 1 discussion, exchange of ideas, channel of communication, discourse, interchange Opposite: silence 2 (fml) conversation, interview, chat, discussion, discourse Opposite: monologue

diamanté adj glittery, sparkly, glittering, sparkling, diamantine Opposite: dull ■ n rhinestones, paste, strass

diameter n width, thickness, breadth, length, distance

diametrically adv absolutely, completely, utterly, totally, entirely Opposite: partially

diamond n rhombus, parallelogram, lozenge, equilateral

diaphanous adj transparent, delicate, gauzy, see-through, sheer Opposite: opaque

diarist n memoirist, writer, autobiographer, author, chronicler

diary n journal, record, log, chronicle, memoir

diaspora n dispersion, scattering, movement, displacement, migration Opposite: concentration

diatribe n criticism, attack, tirade, denunciation, harangue

dice v 1 cube, cut up, chop, cut into cubes 2 gamble, risk, stake, bet, wager

dice with death v face danger, sail close to the wind, play a dangerous game, cut it fine, play Russian roulette

dicey (infml) adj risky, dangerous, hazardous, chancy, uncertain Opposite: safe

dichotomy *n* contrast, opposition, irreconcilable difference, contradiction, gulf *Opposite*: harmony

dicker *(infml)* *v* bargain, haggle, argue, trade, wrangle

dictate *v* 1 speak, say, say aloud, read out, read aloud 2 order, state, command, decree, lay down 3 control, determine, have a bearing on, influence, shape ■ *n* 1 principle, rule, standard, tenet, precept *(fml)* 2 command, order, decree, prescription, injunction

dictation *n* transcription, notation, transcript

dictator *n* tyrant, ruler, despot, autocrat, authoritarian *Opposite*: democrat

dictatorial *adj* tyrannical, despotic, autocratic, authoritarian, overbearing *Opposite*: democratic

dictatorship *n* 1 despotism, autocracy, totalitarianism, authoritarianism, tyranny *Opposite*: democracy 2 regime, government, rule, era, reign

diction *n* 1 pronunciation, enunciation, articulation, delivery, elocution 2 wording, language, expression, phraseology, phrasing

dictionary *n* lexicon, vocabulary, glossary, phrase book, word list

dictum *(fml)* *n* pronouncement, dictate, saying, statement, maxim

didactic *adj* educational, instructive, informative, edifying, teaching

die *v* 1 pass away, pass on, kick the bucket *(slang)*, croak *(slang)*, expire *(fml)* *Opposite*: live 2 stop, give out, go dead, break down, fail *Opposite*: start

die away *v* fade, fade away, dwindle, fizzle, ebb *Opposite*: revive

die down *v* subside, decrease, lessen, diminish, decline *Opposite*: revive

diehard *adj* intransigent, reactionary, conservative, traditionalist, dyed-in-the-wool *Opposite*: progressive ■ *n* reactionary, conservative, traditionalist, fogy, conformist *Opposite*: progressive

die of *v* succumb, fall victim, surrender, yield, submit *Opposite*: survive

die off *v* die out, become extinct, pass away, pass on, disappear *Opposite*: survive

die out *v* become extinct, disappear, vanish, die off, pass away *Opposite*: survive

diet *n* 1 menu, food, fare, nourishment, nutrition 2 regime, intake, supply, regimen 3 parliament, legislature, assembly, council, congress ■ *v* slim, starve, fast, cut back, cut down *Opposite*: binge

dietary *adj* nutritional, dietetic, eating, alimentary, alimental

dieter *n* faster, starver, abstainer

differ *v* 1 be different, be unlike, be at variance, vary, fluctuate *Opposite*: match 2 disagree, argue, quarrel, fall out, wrangle *Opposite*: agree. *See* COMPARE AND CONTRAST *at* disagree.

difference *n* 1 change, alteration, variance, modification, transformation *Opposite*: consistency 2 dissimilarity, disparity, distinction, differentiation, divergence *Opposite*: similarity 3 argument, dispute, disagreement, quarrel, tiff

different *adj* 1 dissimilar, diverse, unlike, clashing, poles apart *Opposite*: similar 2 distinct, separate, discrete, another *Opposite*: same 3 unusual, special, singular, distinctive, atypical *Opposite*: run-of-the-mill

differential *n* difference, discrepancy, disparity, gap, variance

differentiate *v* distinguish, discriminate, tell apart, set apart, discern *Opposite*: blend

differentiation *n* 1 distinction, discrimination, delineation, demarcation, separation *Opposite*: assimilation 2 difference, diversity, variation, distinction, discrepancy *Opposite*: similarity

differently *adv* in a different way, another way, in your own way, otherwise, inversely *Opposite*: similarly

differing *adj* opposing, contradictory, contrary, divergent, different *Opposite*: similar

difficult *adj* 1 hard, tricky, complicated, thorny, complex *Opposite*: straightforward 2 challenging, hard, tough, trying, grim *Opposite*: easy 3 incomprehensible, unintelligible, impenetrable, involved, complicated *Opposite*: simple 4 obstinate, stubborn, recalcitrant, intractable, fractious *Opposite*: amenable. *See* COMPARE AND CONTRAST *at* hard.

difficulty *n* 1 complexity, complicatedness, intricacy, adversity, complication 2 problem, snag, obstacle, impediment, stumbling block 3 trouble, effort, struggle, exertion, strain *Opposite*: ease

diffidence *n* shyness, hesitancy, reserve, timidity, reticence *Opposite*: brashness

diffident *adj* shy, hesitant, insecure, timid, reticent *Opposite*: brash

diffract *v* bend, deflect, curve, divert, spread

diffraction *n* deflection, bending, curving, diversion, spreading

diffuse *v* disperse, spread, disseminate, distribute, circulate *Opposite*: concentrate ■ *adj* 1 dispersed, spread, disseminated, distributed, circulated *Opposite*: concentrated 2 wordy, verbose, prolix, longwinded, drawn-out *Opposite*: concise. *See* COMPARE AND CONTRAST *at* wordy.

diffusion *n* dispersal, dispersion, dissemination, distribution, circulation *Opposite*: concentration

dig *v* 1 break up, plow, turn, hoe, till 2 excavate, tunnel, hollow out, burrow, mine 3 prod, nudge, push, shove, jab ■ *n* 1 poke, prod, nudge, push, shove 2 gibe, taunt, jeer, crack, insult *Opposite*: compliment

digest *v* 1 process, assimilate, absorb, break

down, consume **2 assimilate**, absorb, take in, take on board, grasp *Opposite*: ignore ■ *n* **1 abridgment**, résumé, summary, condensation, abstract **2 publication**, journal, magazine, periodical, book

digestible *adj* **edible**, palatable, eatable, consumable, comestible *(fml) Opposite*: indigestible

digestion *n* **assimilation**, ingestion, absorption, incorporation, breakdown

digestive *adj* **peptic**, gastric, intestinal, gastrointestinal, duodenal

digestive tract *see* **alimentary canal**

digger *n* **1 miner**, excavator, gravedigger, gold digger, prospector **2 excavator**, bulldozer, earthmover, crawler, backhoe

diggings *n* **excavation**, mine, quarry, pit, dig

dig into *v* **1 stick into**, push into, sink into, stab, prod **2 examine**, look at, delve into, investigate, go into *Opposite*: ignore

dig in your heels *v* **stand firm**, hold your ground, stand your ground, hold out, resist *Opposite*: give in

digit *n* **number**, numeral, figure, cipher, character

digital *adj* **numerical**, numerary, numeral, alphanumeric, cardinal

dignified *adj* **distinguished**, honorable, decorous, stately, noble *Opposite*: undignified

dignify *v* **distinguish**, grace, glorify, venerate, honor *Opposite*: degrade

dignitary *n* **notable**, VIP, worthy, celebrity, luminary *Opposite*: nobody

dignity *n* **1 self-respect**, self-esteem, pride, self-possession, self-worth *Opposite*: ignominy **2 formality**, gravity, solemnity, grandeur, decorum *Opposite*: informality **3 worthiness**, worth, nobility, nobleness, goodness *Opposite*: unworthiness

dig out *v* **1 uncover**, excavate, dig up, unearth, expose *Opposite*: bury **2** *(infml)* **retrieve**, find, discover, locate, reveal

digress *v* **deviate**, depart, wander, go off on a tangent, stray *Opposite*: focus

digression *n* **deviation**, departure, aside, parenthesis, detour *Opposite*: focus

dig up *v* **1 unearth**, excavate, disinter, exhume, expose *Opposite*: bury **2** *(infml)* **bring to light**, dredge up, expose, reveal, find *Opposite*: hide

dike *n* **1 embankment**, dam, barrier, bank, wall **2 ditch**, watercourse, channel, drain, conduit

diktat *n* **command**, decree, edict, dictate, order

dilapidated *adj* **decrepit**, rundown, derelict, ramshackle, on its last legs *Opposite*: pristine

dilapidation *n* **disrepair**, dereliction, decrepitude, decay, ruin

dilate *v* **1 expand**, widen, open, enlarge, increase *Opposite*: contract **2 amplify**, expatiate, expand, dwell on, expound *Opposite*: abbreviate

dilation *n* **expansion**, opening, enlargement, increase, distension *Opposite*: contraction

dilatory *adj* **slow**, tardy, remiss, behindhand, slack *Opposite*: prompt

dilemma *n* **quandary**, tight spot, Catch-22, predicament, impasse

dilettante *n* **amateur**, dabbler, abecedarian, neophyte, novice *Opposite*: expert

diligence *n* **assiduousness**, meticulousness, conscientiousness, thoroughness, attentiveness *Opposite*: carelessness

diligent *adj* **industrious**, assiduous, painstaking, meticulous, conscientious *Opposite*: lazy

dilly-dally *v* **dawdle**, dally, delay, shilly-shally, drag your heels *Opposite*: hurry

dilute *v* **1 thin**, weaken, water down, adulterate *Opposite*: concentrate **2 reduce**, attenuate, temper, mitigate, water down *Opposite*: increase ■ *adj* **weak**, watered down, thinned, watery, insipid *Opposite*: concentrated

dilution *n* **1 thinning**, weakening, watering down, watering **2 reduction**, attenuation, enfeeblement, erosion, weakening *Opposite*: strengthening **3 concentration**, strength, intensity, potency

dim *adj* **1 badly lit**, murky, gloomy, shadowy, dusky *Opposite*: bright **2 soft**, faint, muted, weak, diffuse *Opposite*: strong **3 indistinct**, vague, blurred, blurry, hazy *Opposite*: clear ■ *v* **turn down**, lower, darken, reduce *Opposite*: turn up

dimension *n* **1 measurement**, length, height, width, breadth **2 aspect**, element, facet, feature, factor

dimensions *n* **size**, scope, extent, magnitude, proportions

diminish *v* **1 reduce**, lessen, make smaller, weaken, moderate *Opposite*: increase **2 shrink**, ebb, fade, fade away, fade out *Opposite*: grow

diminishing *adj* **lessening**, fading, waning, weakening, falling *Opposite*: increasing

diminution *n* **decrease**, reduction, lessening, attenuation, shrinking *Opposite*: growth

diminutive *adj* **small**, little, tiny, minuscule, miniature *Opposite*: huge

dimmer *n* **light switch**, dimmer switch, brightness control, regulator, rheostat

dimness *n* **1 murkiness**, gloom, gloominess, shadowiness, duskiness *Opposite*: brightness **2 softness**, faintness, weakness, diffuseness, dullness *Opposite*: brightness **3 indistinctness**, vagueness, blurriness, haziness, faintness *Opposite*: clearness

dimple *n* **hollow**, depression, pit, indentation, dent *Opposite*: bump

dimpled *adj* **1 dimply**, cleft, indented, dented, chubby *Opposite*: smooth **2 textured**, indented, dented, pocked, pockmarked *Opposite*: smooth

din n **noise**, hubbub, rumpus, racket, hullabaloo ■ v **drum into**, hammer, inculcate, instill, impress

dine v **eat**, feast, banquet, consume, ingest

diner n **patron**, customer, guest

ding n 1 **ringing**, ring, dong, ding-dong, ding-a-ling 2 (infml) **dent**, indentation, dint, hollow, dimple ■ v **ring**, tinkle, dong, ding-dong

dinge n **filth**, grime, mess, dirt, muck (infml) Opposite: cleanliness

dinginess n 1 **dirtiness**, discoloration, griminess, dullness, dreariness Opposite: brightness 2 **shabbiness**, drabness, squalidness, cheerlessness, seediness Opposite: neatness

dingy adj 1 **dirty**, grimy, soiled, grubby, dull Opposite: clean 2 **shabby**, drab, squalid, tatty, worn Opposite: bright

dinky (infml) adj 1 **small**, compact, neat, natty, cute Opposite: hefty 2 **small**, little, tiny, minute, insignificant Opposite: substantial

dinnertime n **mealtime**, suppertime, lunchtime, teatime

dinosaur n **relic**, museum piece, back number, fossil, has-been (infml)

WORD BANK

❏ **types of dinosaurs** allosaurus, ankylosaurus, apatosaurus, brachiosaurus, brontosaurus, cotylosaur, dicynodont, diplodocus, hadrosaur, ichthyosaur, iguanodon, megalosaur, mosasaur, oviraptor, pelycosaur, plesiosaur, pteranodon, pterodactyl, pterosaur, stegosaur, titanosaur, triceratops, tyrannosaur, velociraptor

dint n **indent**, dent, indentation, depression, hollow ■ v **dent**, damage, mark, spoil, blemish

dip v 1 **plunge**, immerse, dunk, douse, bathe 2 **drop**, drop down, descend, decline, sink Opposite: rise 3 **slope**, incline, slant, descend, fall away Opposite: level ■ n 1 **fall**, decline, drop, depression, falling off Opposite: rise 2 **swim**, plunge, bathe 3 **hollow**, depression, incline, slope, rise and fall

dip into v **skim**, flick through, flip through, glance, browse Opposite: study

diploma n **certificate**, qualification, credential

diplomacy n 1 **international relations**, mediation, negotiation, peacekeeping 2 **tact**, skill, subtlety, discretion, savoir-faire Opposite: tactlessness

diplomat n 1 **civil servant**, envoy, representative, attaché, ambassador 2 **tactician**, peacekeeper, negotiator, mediator, go-between

diplomatic adj 1 **political**, ambassadorial, consular, embassy 2 **tactful**, subtle, suave, discreet, sensitive Opposite: tactless

dipper n **ladle**, scoop, spoon

dire adj **terrible**, awful, dreadful, calamitous, horrible Opposite: wonderful

direct v 1 **manage**, control, regulate, rule, oversee 2 **aim**, point, turn, target, train 3 **show the way**, guide, lead, put on the right track, point in the right direction 4 (fml) **order**, give orders, instruct, give instructions, command Opposite: request ■ adj 1 **straight**, shortest, through, unswerving, undeviating Opposite: circuitous 2 **precise**, exact, absolute, complete, unequivocal Opposite: vague 3 **straightforward**, honest, open, candid, frank Opposite: devious ■ adv **directly**, straight, nonstop, right, in a straight line Opposite: indirectly. See COMPARE AND CONTRAST at **guide**.

direction n 1 **management**, control, government, guidance, leadership 2 **way**, course, track, route, path 3 **trend**, course, route, focus, aim

directional adj **maneuvering**, steering, turning, reversing, guiding

directions n **instructions**, information, orders, guidelines, commands

directive n **order**, command, instruction, direction, edict

directly adv 1 **in a straight line**, straight, right, unswervingly, nonstop Opposite: indirectly 2 **completely**, diametrically, absolutely, wholly, unequivocally 3 **openly**, honestly, frankly, straightforwardly, truthfully Opposite: ambiguously 4 (fml) **immediately**, quickly, at once, promptly, without delay

direct mail n **promotional mailing**, circular, junk mail, unsolicited mail, mailing

directness n **honesty**, openness, straightforwardness, truthfulness, sincerity Opposite: deviousness

director n **manager**, leader, executive, boss, administrator

directorate n **board of directors**, executive, executive board, executive committee, board

director-general n **president**, head, director, chairperson, chief executive

directorship n **director's post**, management post, executive post, managerial position, presidency

directory n **listing**, phone book, catalogue, inventory, register

dirge n **elegy**, requiem, funeral hymn, lament, chant

dirt n 1 **grime**, filth, mud, dust, muck (infml) 2 **soil**, earth, clay, loam, mud 3 **gossip**, scandal, filth, smut, lowdown (infml)

dirt-cheap (infml) adj **cheap**, reduced, cutrate, bargain, inexpensive Opposite: dear ■ adv **cheaply**, at a knockdown price, at bargain-basement prices, for a song, for next to nothing

dirtiness n **griminess**, filthiness, messiness,

muddiness, grubbiness *Opposite*: cleanliness

dirty *adj* **1** filthy, grimy, soiled, grubby, squalid *Opposite*: clean **2 dishonest**, illegal, corrupt, unfair, immoral *Opposite*: honest **3 dull**, muted, muddy, cloudy, murky *Opposite*: clear ■ *v* soil, stain, pollute, foul, defile *(fml) Opposite*: clean

COMPARE AND CONTRAST CORE MEANING: not clean

dirty stained or marked with dirt; **filthy** extremely or disgustingly dirty; **grubby** slightly dirty; **grimy** heavily ingrained with accumulated dirt; **soiled** stained or marked, especially during normal use; **squalid** insanitary and unpleasant; **unclean** dirty or impure, especially in moral or religious contexts.

dirty tricks *n* **unfair tactics**, foul play, deviousness, dishonesty, trickery

dirty word *n* **swear word**, expletive, four-letter word, obscenity, cussword *(infml)*

disability *n* **incapacity**, infirmity, frailty, debility, poor health

disable *v* **incapacitate**, restrict, inactivate, deactivate, put out of action

disablement *n* **impairment**, incapacitation, deactivation, spiking *(infml)*

disabuse *v* **persuade out of**, disillusion, enlighten, set straight, shatter the illusions of

disadvantage *n* **difficulty**, drawback, shortcoming, weakness, hindrance *Opposite*: advantage

disadvantaged *adj* **deprived**, underprivileged, needy, destitute, poor *Opposite*: privileged

disadvantageous *adj* **detrimental**, damaging, hurtful, harmful, injurious *Opposite*: advantageous

disaffect *v* **estrange**, disillusion, disenchant, dissatisfy, alienate

disaffected *adj* **disillusioned**, dissatisfied, disgruntled, cynical, alienated *Opposite*: enthusiastic

disaffection *n* **disillusionment**, alienation, estrangement, dissatisfaction, cynicism *Opposite*: enthusiasm

disagree *v* **1 take issue with**, differ, demur, agree to differ, be at odds *Opposite*: agree **2 differ**, vary, diverge, deviate, contradict *Opposite*: agree **3 argue**, quarrel, wrangle, dispute, bicker *Opposite*: agree

COMPARE AND CONTRAST CORE MEANING: have or express a difference of opinion with somebody

disagree have or put forward a different view or opinion; **differ** have different opinions about something; **argue** express disagreement, especially continuously or angrily; **dispute** have a heated argument; **take issue with** disagree strongly with; **contradict** argue against the truth or correctness of a statement or claim; **agree to**

differ stop arguing and accept that the opposing viewpoints are irreconcilable; **be at odds** be in disagreement, especially over a period of time or about a particular issue.

disagreeable *adj* **1 displeasing**, distasteful, offensive, nasty, unpleasant *Opposite*: agreeable **2 bad-tempered**, unfriendly, unhelpful, difficult, contrary *Opposite*: pleasant

disagreement *n* **1 dispute**, difference of opinion, quarrel, argument, misunderstanding *Opposite*: agreement **2 difference**, divergence, incongruity, discrepancy, dissimilarity *Opposite*: agreement

disallow *v* **1** *(fml)* **reject**, refuse, deny, throw, disapprove *Opposite*: pass **2 cancel**, prohibit, forbid, veto, bar *Opposite*: allow

disallowed *adj* **rejected**, forbidden, banned, excluded, vetoed *Opposite*: allowed

disappear *v* **1 vanish**, fade, fade away, go, evaporate *Opposite*: appear **2 cease to exist**, die out, die off, pass away, vanish *Opposite*: appear

disappearance *n* **vanishing**, evaporation, fading, loss, desertion *Opposite*: appearance

disappearing *adj* **vanishing**, waning, endangered, threatened, dying

disappoint *v* **let down**, disillusion, fail, dissatisfy, dishearten *Opposite*: please

disappointed *adj* **let down**, dissatisfied, disillusioned, upset, saddened *Opposite*: satisfied

disappointing *adj* **unsatisfactory**, unacceptable, second-rate, poor, below par *Opposite*: satisfactory

disappointment *n* **1 dissatisfaction**, displeasure, distress, discontent, disenchantment *Opposite*: satisfaction **2 setback**, failure, frustration, defeat, drawback

disapprobation *(fml) n* **disfavor**, condemnation, disapproval, dislike, displeasure *Opposite*: approval

disapproval *n* **condemnation**, displeasure, dissatisfaction, censure, discontentment *Opposite*: approval

disapprove *v* **1 condemn**, censure, criticize, deplore, frown on *Opposite*: approve **2** *(fml)* **reject**, refuse, veto, turn down, deny *Opposite*: approve

COMPARE AND CONTRAST CORE MEANING: have an unfavorable opinion of something or somebody

disapprove give a negative judgment based on personal standards; **frown on** express dislike or disapproval; **object** be opposed to something, or express opposition; **criticize** point out flaws or faults; **condemn** give an unfavorable judgment on somebody or something; **deplore** disapprove of something strongly; **denounce**

criticize or condemn publicly and harshly; **censure** make a formal, often public or official, statement of disapproval.

disapproving *adj* **critical**, judgmental, negative, censorious, stern *Opposite*: approving

disarm *v* 1 **deactivate**, defuse, make safe, neutralize *Opposite*: arm 2 **win over**, charm, enchant, beguile, win the affection of *Opposite*: annoy

disarmament *n* **arms reduction**, nuclear disarmament, unilateral disarmament, decommissioning, demilitarization *Opposite*: rearmament

disarming *adj* **charming**, enchanting, attractive, appealing, captivating *Opposite*: cold

disarrange *v* **disorder**, disturb, jumble, dishevel, mix up *Opposite*: order

disarranged *adj* **disordered**, untidy, rumpled, messy, jumbled

disarray *n* 1 **confusion**, dismay, panic, alarm, hysteria *Opposite*: order 2 **mess**, disorder, chaos, confusion, untidiness *Opposite*: order

disassemble *v* **take apart**, take to bits, undo, take down, take to pieces *Opposite*: assemble

disassociate *v* 1 **dissociate**, separate, split, set apart, disentangle *Opposite*: associate 2 **distance**, detach, set apart, dissociate, draw back *Opposite*: implicate

disaster *n* 1 **tragedy**, ruin, adversity, catastrophe, calamity 2 *(infml)* **failure**, debacle, fiasco, shambles, farce *Opposite*: success

disastrous *adj* 1 **calamitous**, catastrophic, tragic, terrible, devastating 2 **unsuccessful**, unfortunate, luckless, doomed, unlucky *Opposite*: successful

disavow *v* **disown**, deny, renounce, reject, recant

disavowal *(fml)* *n* **repudiation**, denial, negation, renunciation, abjuration *Opposite*: avowal *(fml)*

disband *v* **break up**, split up, scatter, separate, part

disbar *v* **expel**, throw out, dismiss, banish, exclude

disbarment *n* **expulsion**, dismissal, banishment, exclusion, removal

disbelief *n* **incredulity**, doubt, distrust, mistrust, suspicion *Opposite*: faith

disbelieve *v* **distrust**, doubt, mistrust, suspect, be suspicious of *Opposite*: believe

disbeliever *n* **doubter**, agnostic, atheist, nonbeliever, skeptic *Opposite*: believer

disbelieving *adj* **unconvinced**, incredulous, suspicious, doubtful, distrustful *Opposite*: believing

disburse *v* **pay out**, pay, spend, expend, lay out

disbursement *n* **payment**, expenditure, expense, costs, distribution

discard *v* **throw away**, abandon, dispose of, remove, get rid of *Opposite*: keep

discarded *adj* **cast off**, thrown away, thrown out, rejected, dispensed with *Opposite*: kept

discern *v* 1 **make out**, notice, see, perceive, discover *Opposite*: miss 2 **understand**, perceive, distinguish, fathom, be aware of *Opposite*: miss 3 **distinguish**, tell the difference, separate, discriminate, differentiate

discernible *adj* **visible**, apparent, obvious, perceptible, noticeable

discerning *adj* **discriminating**, sharp, astute, judicious, sensitive *Opposite*: indiscriminate

discernment *n* **judgment**, acumen, discrimination, perspicacity, taste

discharge *v* 1 **emit**, send out, excrete, expel, ooze 2 **dismiss**, relieve of duty, let go, lay off, give somebody their cards *Opposite*: retain 3 **free**, release, set free, emancipate, liberate 4 *(fml)* **pay off**, clear, settle, satisfy, liquidate ■ *n* 1 **emission**, flow, secretion, excretion, seepage 2 **release**, liberation, emancipation, expulsion, ejection

disciple *n* **follower**, believer, supporter, devotee, partisan

disciplinarian *n* **tyrant**, martinet, despot, authoritarian, stickler

disciplinary *adj* **punitive**, corrective, penal, penalizing

discipline *n* 1 **punishment**, correction, chastisement *(fml)*, castigation *(fml)* 2 **regulation**, order, control, restraint, authority *Opposite*: chaos 3 **self-control**, self-restraint, restraint, control, regulation 4 **subject**, branch of learning, field ■ *v* 1 **punish**, chastise, correct, chasten, castigate *(fml)* 2 **instruct**, educate, exercise, drill, prepare

disciplined *adj* **controlled**, self-controlled, orderly, well-ordered, methodical *Opposite*: undisciplined

disclaim *v* **deny**, disown, renounce, reject, repudiate

disclaimer *n* 1 **rider**, proviso, qualification, provision, condition 2 **repudiation**, denial, renunciation, negation, disassociation

disclose *v* **reveal**, unveil, divulge, make known, relate *Opposite*: conceal

disclosure *n* **revelation**, exposé, discovery, leak, confession

discolor *v* **fade**, stain, color, darken, tarnish

discoloration *n* **staining**, stain, tint, mark, streak

discolored *adj* **stained**, dirty, tarnished, faded, streaked

discomfit *(fml)* *v* **embarrass**, unsettle, disconcert, distress, rattle *Opposite*: relax

discomfiting *(fml)* *adj* **disconcerting**, embarrassing, unsettling, disturbing, distressing *Opposite*: reassuring

discomfiture *(fml)* n **embarrassment**, awkwardness, confusion, unease, disconcertment

discomfort n 1 **ache**, pain, soreness, tenderness, irritation 2 **uneasiness**, worry, distress, anxiety, embarrassment *Opposite*: calmness

discomposure n **agitation**, upset, uneasiness, embarrassment, discomfort

disconcert v **unsettle**, perturb, rattle, fluster, unnerve *Opposite*: relax

disconcerted *adj* **unsettled**, thrown off balance, confused, flustered, taken aback *Opposite*: calm

disconcerting *adj* **disturbing**, alarming, confusing, perplexing, bewildering *Opposite*: soothing

disconnect v **cut off**, detach, separate, divide, disengage *Opposite*: connect

disconnected *adj* **detached**, severed, disengaged, separated, divided *Opposite*: attached

disconnection n 1 **stoppage**, interruption, cessation, cutting off, discontinuation *Opposite*: connection 2 **separation**, severance, decoupling, disengagement, break *Opposite*: connection

disconsolate *adj* **unhappy**, dejected, gloomy, melancholy, sad *Opposite*: content

discontent n **dissatisfaction**, unhappiness, displeasure, disgruntlement, sadness *Opposite*: contentment

discontented *adj* **dissatisfied**, unhappy, disgruntled, malcontent, displeased *Opposite*: contented

discontentment n **dissatisfaction**, discontent, displeasure, unhappiness, irritation *Opposite*: contentment

discontinuation n **cessation**, termination, suspension, withdrawal, stoppage *Opposite*: continuation

discontinue v **stop**, cease, halt, end, suspend *Opposite*: continue

discontinued *adj* **obsolete**, finished, superseded, out-of-date, withdrawn

discontinuity n **break**, gap, cutoff, cutout, disjointedness *Opposite*: continuity

discontinuous *adj* **intermittent**, sporadic, broken, irregular, disjointed *Opposite*: continuous

discord n 1 **disagreement**, conflict, dispute, argument, friction *Opposite*: accord 2 **dissonance**, cacophony, disharmony, inharmoniousness, discordance *Opposite*: harmony

discordant *adj* 1 **disagreeing**, conflicting, frictional, dissenting, acrimonious *Opposite*: amicable 2 **dissonant**, jarring, harsh, inharmonious, cacophonous *Opposite*: harmonious

discount n **reduction**, money off, markdown, price cut, cut rate ■ v 1 **disregard**, overlook, ignore, disbelieve, pass over *Opposite*:

accept 2 **reduce**, mark down, lower, take off, deduct *Opposite*: mark up

discounted *adj* **reduced**, cut-rate, sale, cheap, promotional

discourage v 1 **dissuade**, oppose, hinder, inhibit, prevent *Opposite*: encourage 2 **dispirit**, dishearten, cast down, depress, dismay *Opposite*: cheer

discouraged *adj* **disheartened**, dispirited, downcast, depressed, dejected *Opposite*: positive

discouragement n 1 **disappointment**, dismay, despair, depression, low spirits *Opposite*: hopefulness 2 **dissuasion**, caution, warning, opposition, deterrence *Opposite*: encouragement 3 **deterrent**, hindrance, obstacle, impediment, damper *Opposite*: incentive

discouraging *adj* **disheartening**, depressing, dispiriting, gloomy, unpromising *Opposite*: encouraging

discourse n 1 **dissertation**, treatise, homily, sermon, address 2 **dialogue**, conversation, discussion, communication, speech ■ v *(fml)* **converse**, debate, compare notes, have a discussion, discuss

discourteous *adj* **rude**, ill-mannered, impolite, insolent, uncivil *Opposite*: polite

discourteousness *see* **discourtesy**

discourtesy n **rudeness**, impoliteness, disrespect, incivility, insolence *Opposite*: politeness

discover v 1 **find out**, learn, determine, notice, realize 2 **come across**, find, turn up, uncover, unearth

discoverer n **inventor**, originator, pioneer, innovator, creator

discovery n 1 **find**, innovation, breakthrough, invention, finding 2 **detection**, finding, unearthing, sighting, encounter

discredit v 1 **slur**, demean, smear, insult, humiliate 2 **question**, doubt, disbelieve, query, suspect

discreditable *adj* **shameful**, disreputable, ignominious, disgraceful, reprehensible *Opposite*: honorable

discreet *adj* 1 **tactful**, prudent, circumspect, cautious, careful *Opposite*: tactless 2 **inconspicuous**, subtle, unnoticeable, unobtrusive, understated *Opposite*: obvious

discrepancy n **inconsistency**, difference, incongruity, divergence, disagreement *Opposite*: correspondence

discrete *adj* **separate**, distinct, disconnected, detached, isolated

discretion n 1 **freedom of choice**, will, pleasure, option, choice 2 **carefulness**, prudence, caution, canniness, maturity *Opposite*: tactlessness

discretionary *adj* **optional**, flexible, open, elective, unrestricted *Opposite*: mandatory

discriminate v **distinguish**, tell apart, differentiate, separate, categorize

discriminating *adj* discerning, sharp, astute, selective, judicious

discrimination *n* **1** bias, prejudice, unfairness, inequity, bigotry *Opposite*: objectivity **2 taste**, judgment, good taste, discernment, insight **3 distinction**, difference, differential, contrast

discriminatory *adj* biased, prejudiced, unfair, bigoted, inequitable *Opposite*: nondiscriminatory

discursive *adj* expansive, lengthy, conversational, long-winded, circumlocutory *Opposite*: concise

discursiveness *n* expansiveness, long-windedness, roundaboutness, verbosity, circumlocution *Opposite*: concision

discuss *v* talk over, deliberate, debate, converse, confer

discussion *n* conversation, debate, argument, dialogue, chat

discussion group *n* class, seminar, tutorial, roundtable, committee

disdain *n* scorn, contempt, derision, condescension, disparagement *Opposite*: respect ■ *v* despise, scorn, spurn, hold in contempt, disparage *Opposite*: respect

disdainful *adj* sneering, scornful, derisive, condescending, aloof *Opposite*: respectful

disease *n* illness, sickness, ailment, infection, syndrome *Opposite*: health

diseased *adj* unhealthy, unwell, sickly, ill, sick *Opposite*: healthy

disembark *v* come ashore, go ashore, land, get off, arrive in port *Opposite*: embark

disembarkation *n* arrival, alighting, debarkation, landing, getting off

disembodied *adj* ghostly, spiritual, intangible, ethereal, immaterial *Opposite*: tangible

disembowel *v* eviscerate, gut, fillet, exenterate

disenchanted *adj* disillusioned, disappointed, dissatisfied, crestfallen, embittered *Opposite*: idealistic

disenchantment *n* disillusionment, disappointment, dissatisfaction, embitterment, bitterness *Opposite*: idealism

disenfranchise *v* marginalize, exclude, alienate, subjugate, disqualify *Opposite*: enfranchise

disenfranchisement *n* marginalization, exclusion, alienation, subjugation, disqualification *Opposite*: enfranchisement

disengage *v* undo, unfasten, unlock, untie, uncouple *Opposite*: fasten

disengagement *n* **1 withdrawal**, disentanglement, detachment, disconnection, extrication *Opposite*: engagement **2 release**, uncoupling, separation, extrication, withdrawal *Opposite*: attachment

disentangle *v* unravel, unscramble, untie, separate, straighten out *Opposite*: entangle

disequilibrium *n* imbalance, instability, uncertainty, flux, volatility *Opposite*: equilibrium

disestablish *v* reform, repudiate, renounce, reevaluate, disclaim *Opposite*: establish

disfavor *n* **1 disrepute**, unpopularity, discredit, disgrace, obscurity *Opposite*: favor **2 distaste**, disdain, disapproval, displeasure, scorn *Opposite*: favor

disfigure *v* mutilate, scar, deface, mar, spoil *Opposite*: enhance

disfigurement *n* scar, mutilation, defacement, deformity, blemish *Opposite*: enhancement

disgorge *v* expel, eject, empty, pour out, spew *Opposite*: retain

disgrace *n* shame, discredit, scandal, ignominy, humiliation ■ *v* bring shame on, discredit, bring into disrepute, shame, degrade

disgraced *adj* discredited, shamed, condemned, humiliated, fallen *Opposite*: popular

disgraceful *adj* shameful, shocking, outrageous, scandalous, discreditable

disgruntle *v* displease, irritate, anger, annoy, dissatisfy *Opposite*: satisfy

disgruntled *adj* discontented, dissatisfied, resentful, displeased, unhappy *Opposite*: contented

disguise *v* cover up, hide, conceal, mask, masquerade *Opposite*: reveal ■ *n* mask, costume, camouflage, masquerade, cover

disguised *adj* camouflaged, masked, masquerading, cloaked, veiled *Opposite*: overt

disgust *n* revulsion, repugnance, abhorrence, repulsion, antipathy *Opposite*: attraction ■ *v* sicken, repulse, revolt, repel, shock *Opposite*: please. *See* COMPARE AND CONTRAST *at* dislike.

disgusted *adj* sickened, revolted, repulsed, repelled, offended *Opposite*: charmed

disgusting *adj* revolting, repulsive, sickening, ghastly, filthy *Opposite*: attractive

dish *n* **1** plate, bowl, saucer **2 food item**, course, recipe

---

WORD BANK
❏ **types of cooked dishes** bruschetta, burritos, casserole, cassoulet, ceviche, chop suey, chow mein, couscous, curry, fajitas, falafel, fish cake, fondue, fricassee, frijoles, frittata, goulash, gruel, Irish stew, lasagna, meat loaf, moussaka, nachos, paella, pilaf, pirozkhi, pizza, quiche, ragout, ratatouille, risotto, satay, sauerkraut, stew, stir-fry, surf 'n' turf, tacos, tagine, tamale, tempura, teriyaki, tofu, yakitori

---

disharmonious *adj* conflicting, discordant, tense, uneasy, bitter *Opposite*: harmonious

disharmony *n* conflict, disagreement, discord, tension, unrest *Opposite*: harmony

dishcloth n dishrag, dish towel, kitchen towel, towel

dishearten v discourage, depress, sadden, cast down, dismay Opposite: buoy up

disheartened adj discouraged, depressed, saddened, dismayed, dejected Opposite: encouraged

disheartening adj intimidating, off-putting, daunting, dispiriting, depressing Opposite: encouraging

disheveled adj unkempt, wild, tousled, ruffled, untidy Opposite: well-groomed

dishevelment n messiness, scruffiness, untidiness, unruliness Opposite: tidiness

dishonest adj lying, deceitful, false, untruthful, fraudulent Opposite: honest

dishonesty n deceit, deceitfulness, fraudulence, lying, untruthfulness Opposite: honesty

dishonor n disgrace, shame, discredit, ignominy, disrepute Opposite: honor ■ v shame, disgrace, discredit, defame, bring into disrepute Opposite: honor

dishonorable adj disgraceful, disreputable, discreditable, shameful, ignominious Opposite: honorable

dish out (infml) v distribute, parcel out, allot, hand out, deal out

disillusion v disenchant, bring down to earth, disappoint, let down, dishearten Opposite: inspire

disillusioned adj disenchanted, disappointed, disheartened, cynical Opposite: starry-eyed

disillusionment n disenchantment, disappointment, cynicism, letdown, discouragement Opposite: gratification

disincentive n deterrent, discouragement, hindrance, impediment, encumbrance Opposite: incentive

disinclination n reluctance, unwillingness, opposition, hesitation, aversion (fml) Opposite: inclination

disincline v put off, deter, discourage, dissuade, prevent Opposite: encourage

disinclined adj reluctant, unwilling, opposed, unenthusiastic, loath Opposite: inclined. See COMPARE AND CONTRAST at unwilling.

disinfect v sterilize, sanitize, purify, fumigate, cleanse Opposite: contaminate

disinfectant n antiseptic, sterilizer, purifier, bleach, sanitizer

disinformation n deception, falsehood, propaganda, half-truth, misinformation Opposite: truth

disingenuous adj dishonest, insincere, untruthful, deceitful, hypocritical Opposite: honest

disingenuousness n dishonesty, insincerity, untruthfulness, deceit, hypocrisy Opposite: honesty

disinherit v cut off, disown, leave penniless, cut out, divest Opposite: bequeath

disintegrate v crumble, fragment, break, collapse, split Opposite: combine

disintegration n breakdown, breakup, collapse, fragmentation, crumbling

disinter v 1 exhume, dig up, unearth Opposite: bury 2 (fml) uncover, unearth, bring to light, expose, reveal Opposite: cover up

disinterest n indifference, unconcern, apathy, disregard, heedlessness Opposite: interest

disinterested adj fair-minded, unbiased, impartial, without prejudice, neutral Opposite: biased

disinterestedness n impartiality, objectivity, fair-mindedness, neutrality, distance Opposite: bias

disinterment n 1 exhumation, digging up, unearthing Opposite: interment 2 (fml) exposure, unearthing, discovery, revelation, uncovering Opposite: concealment

disjoint v 1 split, separate, come apart, sever, divide Opposite: join 2 dislocate, dislodge, move, relocate, separate Opposite: retain

disjointed adj rambling, fragmented, incoherent, disorganized, disorderly Opposite: coherent

disjointedness n disjunction, disjuncture, incoherence, dislocation, disconnection Opposite: coherence

dislikable adj disagreeable, unpleasant, offensive, repugnant, horrible Opposite: likable

dislike v hate, detest, loathe, frown on, disapprove Opposite: like ■ n distaste, antipathy, loathing, hatred, hate Opposite: liking

COMPARE AND CONTRAST CORE MEANING: a feeling of not liking somebody or something **dislike** a feeling or attitude of disapproval; **distaste** mild dislike, mainly of behavior and activities; **hatred** or **hate** intense dislike or hostility; **disgust** a feeling of horrified and sickened disapproval; **loathing** intense dislike; **repugnance** strong disgust, mainly of behavior and activities; **abhorrence** a feeling of aversion or intense disapproval, mainly of behavior and activities; **animosity** a feeling of hostility and resentment; **antipathy** a deep-seated dislike or hostility; **aversion** (fml) a strong feeling of dislike; **revulsion** a sudden violent feeling of disgust.

dislocate v 1 put out of place, displace, put out of joint, disjoint, dislodge Opposite: replace 2 disrupt, interrupt, disturb, upset, disorder Opposite: restore

dislocation n 1 displacement, disarticulation, dislodgment 2 disruption, interruption, disturbance, disorder, upset

dislodge v remove, get out, extricate, free, displace Opposite: wedge

disloyal adj unfaithful, treacherous, untrue, false, fickle Opposite: loyal

disloyalty *n* **unfaithfulness**, treachery, falseness, infidelity, betrayal *Opposite*: loyalty

dismal *adj* **miserable**, gloomy, depressing, dreary, dull *Opposite*: bright

dismay *v* **disappoint**, shock, sadden, depress, perturb *Opposite*: comfort ■ *n* **disappointment**, shock, consternation, apprehension, panic *Opposite*: comfort

dismayed *adj* **discouraged**, disheartened, demoralized, downcast, depressed *Opposite*: heartened

dismember *v* **tear limb from limb**, cut into pieces, cut up, dissect, tear apart

dismemberment *n* **taking apart**, mutilation, division, maiming, splitting off

dismiss *v* **1 discharge**, relieve of duty, let go, fire (*infml*), sack (*infml*) *Opposite*: retain **2 send away**, allow to go, release, send home *Opposite*: detain **3 reject**, set aside, think no more of, put out of your mind, shelve *Opposite*: dwell on

dismissal *n* **removal**, notice, discharge, release, firing (*infml*) *Opposite*: appointment

dismissive *adj* **flippant**, indifferent, unconcerned, trivializing, contemptuous *Opposite*: attentive

dismount *v* **get down**, get off, alight, climb down, descend *Opposite*: mount

disobedience *n* **defiance**, noncompliance, breaking the rules, insubordination, waywardness *Opposite*: obedience

disobedient *adj* **defiant**, noncompliant, rebellious, insubordinate, badly behaved *Opposite*: obedient

disobey *v* **defy**, refuse to comply, break the rules, contravene, violate *Opposite*: obey

disobliging *adj* **unhelpful**, uncooperative, unaccommodating, rude, unfriendly *Opposite*: obliging

disorder *n* **1 chaos**, disarray, confusion, mess, muddle *Opposite*: order **2 complaint**, illness, sickness, ailment, syndrome ■ *v* **disorganize**, disarrange, disturb, jumble, muddle *Opposite*: order

disordered *adj* **chaotic**, messy, muddled, topsy-turvy, higgledy-piggledy *Opposite*: well-ordered

disorderliness *n* **confusion**, messiness, muddle, chaos, disarray *Opposite*: orderliness

disorderly *adj* **1 muddled**, jumbled, confused, messy, unsystematic **2 unruly**, riotous, uncontrollable, rebellious, wild *Opposite*: orderly

disorganization *n* **inefficiency**, ineptitude, ineffectiveness, chaos, disorder *Opposite*: organization

disorganize *v* **muddle**, mix up, confuse, jumble, dislocate *Opposite*: organize

disorganized *adj* **muddled**, jumbled, confused, messy, unsystematic *Opposite*: organized

disorient *v* **confuse**, perplex, fox, befuddle, fuddle *Opposite*: orientate

disorientate *see* **disorient**

disorientation *n* **puzzlement**, bafflement, stupefaction, bewilderment, confusion

disoriented *adj* **confused**, unsettled, bewildered, perplexed, at a loss *Opposite*: clearheaded

disown *v* **renounce**, reject, wash your hands of, turn your back on, disclaim *Opposite*: acknowledge

disparage *v* **belittle**, laugh at, mock, ridicule, pour scorn on *Opposite*: praise

disparagement *n* **belittling**, mocking, ridicule, criticism, derision *Opposite*: praise

disparaging *adj* **critical**, unfavorable, disapproving, censorious, unsympathetic *Opposite*: approving

disparate *adj* **dissimilar**, unlike, different, incongruent, unrelated *Opposite*: similar

disparity *n* **difference**, inequality, discrepancy, disproportion, gap *Opposite*: parity

dispassion *n* **aloofness**, coolness, calmness, impassivity, serenity *Opposite*: enthusiasm

dispassionate *adj* **calm**, composed, unflustered, unemotional, detached *Opposite*: fiery

dispatch *v* **1 send off**, send out, post, mail, ship *Opposite*: keep **2 kill**, murder, assassinate, put to death, slaughter ■ *n* **message**, communication, notice, letter, report

dispatch rider *n* **courier**, messenger, deliverer

dispel *v* **dismiss**, chase away, drive out, disperse, scatter *Opposite*: attract

dispensable *adj* **expendable**, superfluous, unessential, unnecessary, replaceable *Opposite*: indispensable

dispensation *n* **indulgence**, allowance, special consideration, privilege, exemption

dispense *v* **give out**, hand out, distribute, allot, mete out *Opposite*: withhold

dispenser *n* **distributor**, slot machine, machine, vending machine

dispersal *n* **dispersion**, spreading, scattering, diffusion, distribution *Opposite*: concentration

disperse *v* **scatter**, go away, disband, break up, dissolve *Opposite*: concentrate

dispersion *n* **dispersal**, spreading, scattering, diffusion, distribution *Opposite*: concentration

dispirit *v* **dishearten**, discourage, dampen, depress, dismay *Opposite*: rouse

dispirited *adj* **disheartened**, discouraged, dejected, depressed, downhearted *Opposite*: cheerful

dispiriting *adj* **disheartening**, depressing, demoralizing, upsetting, saddening *Opposite*: uplifting

displace v 1 **move**, relocate, shift, transfer, put out of place *Opposite*: restore 2 **oust**, supplant, replace, supersede, succeed *Opposite*: restore

displacement n **movement**, dislocation, dislodgment, shift, supplanting

display v 1 **show**, exhibit, put on show, present, put on view *Opposite*: conceal 2 **flaunt**, parade, show off, strut, pose *Opposite*: conceal ■ n **show**, exhibition, presentation, demonstration, parade

displease v **anger**, annoy, irritate, upset, put out *Opposite*: please

displeased adj **annoyed**, dissatisfied, put out, irked, unhappy *Opposite*: pleased

displeasure n **anger**, annoyance, irritation, disapproval, discontentment *Opposite*: pleasure

disport (archaic) v **show off**, pose, swagger, strut, flaunt

disposable adj **throwaway**, one-use, nonrefundable *Opposite*: reusable

disposal n **removal**, discarding, clearance, dumping, throwing away *Opposite*: retention

dispose v 1 **incline**, influence, persuade, prompt, encourage 2 **settle**, resolve, fix, decide, determine 3 (fml) **position**, place, set out, arrange, set

disposed adj **willing**, likely, liable, inclined, of a mind *Opposite*: unwilling

dispose of v 1 **throw away**, throw out, dispense with, discard, get rid of *Opposite*: keep 2 **transfer**, pass on, divest yourself of, relieve yourself of, sell *Opposite*: keep 3 **kill**, murder, execute, assassinate, dispatch 4 (fml) **attend to**, determine, settle, sort out, sort 5 (fml) **consume**, demolish, get through, devour, use up

disposition n **nature**, character, temperament, temper, outlook

dispossess (archaic or fml) v **deprive**, divest, strip, rob, disinherit

dispossessed adj **evicted**, expelled, ejected, turned out, driven out

dispossession n **deprivation**, denial, withdrawal, removal

disproportion n **imbalance**, discrepancy, disparity, inequality, inconsistency *Opposite*: equality

disproportionate adj **uneven**, unequal, lopsided, inconsistent, top-heavy *Opposite*: corresponding

disproportionately adv **excessively**, unduly, unreasonably, extremely, too *Opposite*: slightly

disprove v **refute**, invalidate, contradict, challenge, negate (fml) *Opposite*: prove

disputable adj **arguable**, debatable, moot, questionable, uncertain *Opposite*: incontrovertible

disputation (fml) n **argument**, strife, conflict, debate, disagreement *Opposite*: agreement

disputatious (fml) adj **argumentative**, quarrelsome, awkward, difficult, contrary *Opposite*: conciliatory

disputative (fml) adj **argumentative**, quarrelsome, awkward, difficult, contrary *Opposite*: conciliatory

dispute v 1 **challenge**, question, contest, query, doubt *Opposite*: accept 2 **argue**, debate, discuss, quarrel, wrangle *Opposite*: agree ■ n **argument**, disagreement, quarrel, difference, clash *Opposite*: agreement. *See* COMPARE AND CONTRAST *at* disagree.

disqualification n **ineligibility**, banning, barring, disentitlement, debarment *Opposite*: entitlement

disqualified adj **ineligible**, banned, barred, debarred, prohibited *Opposite*: eligible

disqualify v **ban**, bar, debar, prohibit, exclude *Opposite*: allow

disquiet n **unrest**, uneasiness, concern, worry, anxiety *Opposite*: calmness ■ v (literary) **worry**, disturb, upset, disconcert, perturb

disquieting adj **worrying**, disturbing, alarming, unsettling, troubling *Opposite*: reassuring

disquisition (fml) n **essay**, tract, discussion, address, speech

disquisitional (fml) adj **verbose**, wordy, long-winded, rambling, digressive *Opposite*: concise

disregard v **ignore**, take no notice of, turn a blind eye to, discount, pay no attention to *Opposite*: heed ■ n **disrespect**, indifference, contempt, disdain, neglect *Opposite*: regard

disregarded adj 1 **ignored**, omitted, overlooked, unheeded, unnoticed *Opposite*: acknowledged 2 **snubbed**, slighted, marginalized, sidelined, dishonored *Opposite*: respected

disrepair n **poor shape**, bad shape, bad condition, poor order, disorder

disreputable adj **notorious**, infamous, scandalous, disgraceful, seedy *Opposite*: reputable

disrepute n **disgrace**, ill repute, disrespect, disregard, discredit *Opposite*: esteem

disrespect n **disregard**, contempt, insolence, impertinence, impudence *Opposite*: respect ■ v **insult**, affront, belittle, disparage, denigrate *Opposite*: respect

disrespectable adj **dishonorable**, frowned on, disreputable, unpopular, infamous *Opposite*: respectable

disrespectful adj **rude**, impolite, bad-mannered, discourteous, insolent *Opposite*: respectful

disrobe (fml) v **strip**, undress, unclothe, uncover, divest (fml) *Opposite*: dress

disrupt v **disturb**, upset, interrupt, dislocate, disorder

disruption n **disturbance**, commotion,

trouble, interruption, distraction

disruptive *adj* **troublesome**, unruly, disorderly, unsettling, disturbing

disruptiveness *n* **unruliness**, rowdiness, disorderliness, indiscipline, naughtiness

dissatisfaction *n* **displeasure**, discontent, disappointment, unhappiness, frustration *Opposite*: satisfaction

dissatisfied *adj* **disgruntled**, displeased, discontented, disappointed, unhappy *Opposite*: satisfied

dissatisfy *v* **displeasure**, displease, disappoint, put out, frustrate *Opposite*: satisfy

dissect *v* **1 cut up**, cut apart, divide, dismember, slice up **2 scrutinize**, break down, examine, study, explore

dissection *n* **1 cutting up**, partition, division, separation, segmentation **2 examination**, analysis, investigation, scrutiny, observation

dissemble *v* **1 pretend**, mislead, act, put on an act, dissimulate **2** *(fml)* **disguise**, conceal, hide, suppress, mask *Opposite*: disclose

disseminate *v* **distribute**, broadcast, circulate, spread, publicize. *See* COMPARE AND CONTRAST *at* scatter.

dissemination *n* **distribution**, broadcasting, diffusion, propagation, spreading

dissension *n* **opposition**, disagreement, dissent, discord, rebellion *Opposite*: consent

dissent *v* **disagree**, oppose, rebel, dispute, differ *Opposite*: agree ■ *n* **opposition**, disagreement, dissension, discord, rebellion *Opposite*: consent

dissenter *n* **rebel**, dissident, nonconformist, insurgent, mutineer

dissertation *n* **thesis**, paper, study, critique, essay

disservice *n* **damage**, harm, wrong, injury, difficulty *Opposite*: service

dissidence *n* **disagreement**, unorthodoxy, nonconformity, independence, rebellion *Opposite*: conformism

dissident *n* **dissenter**, rebel, nonconformist, protester, insurgent *Opposite*: conformist ■ *adj* **rebel**, rebellious, dissenting, unorthodox, nonconforming *Opposite*: conformist

dissimilar *adj* **unlike**, different, diverse, unrelated, disparate *Opposite*: similar

dissimilarity *n* **difference**, variation, distinction, contrast, divergence *Opposite*: similarity

dissimulate *v* **disguise**, conceal, hide, suppress, mask *Opposite*: disclose

dissimulation *(fml)* *n* **concealment**, suppression, disguise, camouflage, dishonesty *Opposite*: disclosure

dissipate *v* **1 dispel**, disperse, dissolve, scatter, drive away **2 squander**, waste, fritter away, throw away, blow *(slang)*

dissipated *adj* **dissolute**, degenerate, debauched, self-indulgent, immoral *Opposite*: upright

dissipation *n* **debauchery**, indulgence, rakishness, overindulgence, degeneracy *Opposite*: uprightness

dissociate *v* **distance**, detach, divorce, separate, disconnect *Opposite*: associate

dissociation *n* **detachment**, separation, disconnection, severance, alienation *Opposite*: association

dissolute *adj* **degenerate**, depraved, immoral, debauched, self-indulgent *Opposite*: upright

dissoluteness *n* **decadence**, overindulgence, extravagance, self-indulgence, degeneracy *Opposite*: temperance

dissolution *n* **closure**, disbanding, termination, ending, suspension *Opposite*: inauguration

dissolve *v* **1 melt**, soften, liquefy, thaw, run *Opposite*: solidify **2 disappear**, dissipate, dispel, disperse, melt away *Opposite*: appear **3 disband**, close, break up, suspend, end *Opposite*: inaugurate

dissonance *n* **discord**, disagreement, dissension, conflict, difference *Opposite*: harmony

dissonant *adj* **discordant**, unmusical, harsh, inharmonious, cacophonous *Opposite*: harmonious

dissuade *v* **deter**, put off, discourage, advise against, persuade against *Opposite*: persuade

dissuasion *n* **discouragement**, deterrence, persuasion, opposition, warning *Opposite*: encouragement

dissuasive *adj* **discouraging**, opposing, inhibitive, hindering *Opposite*: encouraging

distance *n* **1 space**, expanse, void, vastness, gap *Opposite*: closeness **2 coldness**, aloofness, detachment, reserve, remoteness *Opposite*: warmth ■ *v* **dissociate**, move away, detach, separate, avoid *Opposite*: associate

distant *adj* **1 faraway**, remote, far-off, far-flung, outlying *Opposite*: near **2 aloof**, cold, unfriendly, detached, reserved *Opposite*: warm **3 vague**, faint, indistinct, hazy, obscure *Opposite*: clear

distaste *n* **dislike**, antipathy, disgust, disfavor, aversion *(fml)* *Opposite*: love. *See* COMPARE AND CONTRAST *at* dislike.

distasteful *adj* **repugnant**, offensive, disgusting, repulsive, objectionable *Opposite*: pleasant

distastefulness *n* **unpleasantness**, offensiveness, nastiness, repulsiveness *Opposite*: pleasantness

distend *v* **swell**, bloat, balloon, inflate, swell up *Opposite*: deflate

distended *adj* **swollen**, bloated, inflated, enlarged, expanded

distension n **swelling**, expansion, enlargement, tumescence, dilation

distill v 1 **purify**, refine, condense, extract, concentrate Opposite: pollute 2 **extract**, glean, cull, garner, collect

distillate n **essence**, tincture, concentrate, extract, distillation

distillation n 1 **concentration**, condensation, refinement, purification, extraction Opposite: dilution 2 **essence**, epitome, embodiment, summation, condensation 3 **distillate**, tincture, extract, concentrate

distinct adj 1 **separate**, different, dissimilar, discrete, diverse Opposite: same 2 **clear**, definite, well-defined, noticeable, marked Opposite: unclear

distinction n 1 **difference**, division, dissimilarity, discrepancy, otherness Opposite: similarity 2 **merit**, excellence, note, worth, accolade Opposite: disgrace 3 **feature**, characteristic, idiosyncrasy, peculiarity, trait

distinctive adj **characteristic**, idiosyncratic, distinguishing, individual, typical Opposite: common

distinctiveness n **uniqueness**, individuality, particularity, individualism, singularity Opposite: sameness

distinctly adv **definitely**, clearly, noticeably, markedly, particularly Opposite: vaguely

distinguish v 1 **differentiate**, tell apart, tell between, discriminate, decide Opposite: homogenize 2 **set apart**, single out, characterize, mark, classify 3 **make out**, discern, see, recognize, perceive

distinguishable adj 1 **different**, unique, distinct, special, divergent 2 **discernible**, obvious, noticeable, clear, evident Opposite: indistinguishable

distinguished adj **illustrious**, eminent, famous, famed, well-known Opposite: undistinguished

distinguishing adj **unique**, individual, personal, distinctive, characteristic Opposite: typical

distort v 1 **misrepresent**, interfere with, twist, alter, garble 2 **deform**, disfigure, twist, warp, alter Opposite: straighten

distorted adj 1 **one-sided**, slanted, partial, inaccurate, partisan Opposite: accurate 2 **twisted**, malformed, warped, bent, contorted Opposite: straight 3 **unrecognizable**, grotesque, unnatural, monstrous, bizarre

distortion n 1 **misrepresentation**, alteration, lie, falsehood, falsification 2 **bend**, buckle, twist, deformation, warp

distract v 1 **sidetrack**, divert, confuse, addle, befuddle 2 **entertain**, amuse, divert, absorb, engross

distracted adj 1 **unfocused**, abstracted, preoccupied, sidetracked, diverted Opposite: attentive 2 **troubled**, agitated, anxious, perplexed, confused Opposite: calm

distracting adj **off-putting**, disturbing, diverting, disrupting

distraction n 1 **interruption**, disruption, commotion, disturbance, interference 2 **diversion**, entertainment, hobby, pastime, leisure activity 3 **agitation**, anxiety, bewilderment, confusion, desperation

distrait (literary) adj **inattentive**, distracted, unmindful, dreamy, vague Opposite: alert

distraught adj **distressed**, beside yourself, out of your mind, hysterical, upset Opposite: calm

distress n 1 **suffering**, pain, sorrow, anguish, agony Opposite: peace 2 **trouble**, danger, difficulty, misfortune, rigor ■ v **upset**, disturb, trouble, bother, afflict Opposite: soothe

distressed adj 1 **upset**, distraught, troubled, concerned, worried Opposite: content 2 **in pain**, suffering, anguished, tormented, miserable

distressing adj **upsetting**, worrying, difficult, stressful, painful

distress signal n **call for help**, cry for help, alarm bell, alarm, call

distribute v 1 **deal out**, hand out, share out, allocate, give out Opposite: amass 2 **deliver**, supply, circulate, spread out, spread Opposite: retain. See COMPARE AND CONTRAST at scatter.

distributer see distributor

distribution n 1 **sharing**, allocation, giving out, division, allotment 2 **delivery**, supply, circulation, transportation, dispersal 3 **spreading**, dispersal, dissemination, scattering

distributor n **supplier**, provider, wholesaler, broker, trader

district n **locality**, area, barrio, neighborhood, quarter

distrust n **suspicion**, disbelief, doubt, misgiving, cynicism Opposite: trust ■ v **disbelieve**, doubt, be suspicious of, mistrust, suspect Opposite: trust

distrustful adj **suspicious**, doubting, wary, nervous, disbelieving Opposite: trusting

disturb v 1 **interrupt**, distract, bother, disrupt, annoy 2 **upset**, worry, bother, concern, perturb 3 **move**, transfer, shift, dislocate, remove 4 **spoil**, unsettle, upset, meddle, tamper. See COMPARE AND CONTRAST at bother.

disturbance n 1 **trouble**, commotion, riot, uproar, fracas 2 **annoyance**, interruption, intrusion, bother, disruption

disturbed adj 1 **troubled**, bothered, concerned, worried, distressed Opposite: unconcerned 2 **unstable**, troubled, traumatized, unbalanced, unhinged Opposite: stable

disturbing adj **worrying**, troubling, alarming, upsetting, distressing Opposite: reassuring

disunite v **split**, divide, separate, undo, dissolve Opposite: unite

disunity n **disagreement**, discord, divergence, dissent, conflict *Opposite*: unity

disuse n **neglect**, abandonment, unemployment, dereliction *Opposite*: use

disused adj **empty**, abandoned, neglected, derelict, deserted *Opposite*: occupied

ditch n **channel**, trench, dike, drain, waterway ■ v (*infml*) **scrap**, get rid of, drop, split up with, discard

dither v **hesitate**, dally, dawdle, waste time, vacillate

ditherer n **vacillator**, dawdler, waverer, hesitater

dithering n **indecisiveness**, indecision, hesitation, irresolution, wavering *Opposite*: decisiveness

ditsy (*infml*) adj **empty-headed**, forgetful, absent-minded, scatterbrained, vague

ditty n **song**, poem, rhyme, limerick, nursery rhyme

diurnal adj 1 **day**, daytime, daylight *Opposite*: nocturnal 2 **daily**, 24-hour, 24-hourly, circadian, quotidian (*fml*)

diva n **prima donna**, singer, chanteuse, soprano

divan n **settee**, couch, sofa, davenport (*dated*)

dive v 1 **jump**, leap, drop, lunge, submerge *Opposite*: surface 2 **plummet**, plunge, fall, nose-dive, crash *Opposite*: shoot up ■ n 1 **lunge**, leap, drop, jump 2 **plunge**, fall, nosedive, crash, free fall 3 (*infml*) **dump** (*infml*), hole (*infml*), fleapit (*infml*)

diver n **swimmer**, deep-sea diver, snorkeler, frogman, scuba diver

diverge v 1 **deviate**, move away, wander, depart, swerve *Opposite*: converge 2 **differ**, disagree, vary, conflict *Opposite*: concur 3 **digress**, ramble, stray, deviate

divergence n 1 **deviation**, departure, discrepancy, disagreement, separation *Opposite*: convergence 2 **difference**, difference of opinion, disagreement, variance, conflict *Opposite*: agreement

divergent adj **different**, differing, deviating, conflicting, contradictory *Opposite*: similar

divers (*literary*) adj **various**, miscellaneous, assorted, sundry, several *Opposite*: similar

diverse adj 1 **varied**, miscellaneous, assorted, sundry 2 **different**, dissimilar, unlike, distinct, separate *Opposite*: similar

diversely adv **varyingly**, variously, distinctly, separately, dissimilarly *Opposite*: similarly

diversification n **change**, divergence, variation, modification, broadening *Opposite*: specialization

diversify v **branch out**, expand, spread, broaden your horizons, vary *Opposite*: specialize

diversion n 1 **distraction**, entertainment, pastime, hobby, leisure activity 2 **change**, alteration, departure, digression, deviation

diversionary adj **distracting**, diverting, misleading, deflecting, deceptive

diversity n **variety**, assortment, multiplicity, range, mixture *Opposite*: uniformity

divert v 1 **redirect**, deflect, reroute, switch 2 **distract**, sidetrack, turn away, avert, deter *Opposite*: focus 3 **entertain**, amuse, please, delight, gladden

divest v **strip**, rid, dissociate, separate, part from *Opposite*: give

divide v 1 **split**, separate, partition, segregate, break up *Opposite*: join 2 **share**, share out, divide up, deal out, distribute 3 **cause a rift**, split up, break up, split, come between *Opposite*: unite ■ n **gulf**, rift, division, split, gap

dividend n **bonus**, extra, payment, share, surplus

divider n **partition**, separator, screen

dividing line n **distinction**, margin, borderline, border, watershed

divination n **prophecy**, prediction, forecast, foretelling, insight

divine adj 1 **heavenly**, celestial, godly, godlike, deific (*fml*) *Opposite*: secular 2 (*infml*) **great**, exquisite, delightful, lovely, pleasing ■ v **discover**, guess, presume, deduce, discern

divinity n **religion**, theology, religious studies, spirituality, mysticism

divisible adj **isolatable**, detachable, separable, dividable *Opposite*: inseparable

division n 1 **separation**, splitting up, partition, dissection, detachment *Opposite*: union 2 **sharing out**, distribution, allotment, allocation, apportionment 3 **split**, rift, disagreement, discord, break *Opposite*: unity 4 **boundary**, partition, border, dividing line, demarcation 5 **category**, classification, type, class, grouping 6 **department**, section, group, branch, sector

divisive adj **discordant**, troublesome, disruptive, conflict-ridden, contentious

divisiveness n **disruptiveness**, dissension, disagreement, discord, disunity

divorce n **separation**, split, breakup, split-up, annulment *Opposite*: marriage ■ v **dissociate**, disconnect, separate, distance, detach *Opposite*: associate

divorced adj **separated**, removed, unconnected, split, detached *Opposite*: together

divot n **turf**, sod, clump, clod, piece

divulge v **reveal**, tell, make known, disclose, let drop

divvy (*infml*) v **divide up**, divide, share out, deal out, distribute

dizzily adv **dazedly**, woozily, lightheadedly, shakily, unsteadily *Opposite*: steadily

dizziness n **faintness**, wooziness, vertigo, shakiness, lightheadedness

dizzy *adj* **1 faint**, woozy, shaky, lightheaded, dazed **2** *(infml)* **playful**, frivolous, flippant, silly, lighthearted

DJ *n* **disc jockey**, MC, broadcaster, deejay *(infml)*, jock *(infml)*

do *v* **1 perform**, accomplish, act, carry out, complete **2 see to**, fix, prepare, sort out, look after **3 solve**, work out, resolve, figure out, puzzle out **4** *(infml)* **cheat**, trick, con, swindle, defraud. *See* COMPARE AND CONTRAST *at* **perform**.

doable *adj* **achievable**, possible, workable, feasible, attainable *Opposite*: impossible

do away with *v* **1 abolish**, dispense with, remove, dispose of, get rid of *Opposite*: retain **2** *(infml)* **kill**, murder, assassinate, finish off *(infml)*, do in *(infml)*

docile *adj* **quiet**, passive, unassuming, compliant, submissive *Opposite*: wild

docility *n* **quietness**, submissiveness, meekness, tameness, gentleness *Opposite*: fierceness

dock *n* **berth**, mooring, anchorage, wharf, quay ■ *v* **1 come in**, tie up, land, berth, moor **2 cut**, cut off, crop, stop, reduce *Opposite*: increase

docket *n* **1 tag**, sticker, label, marker, ticket **2 agenda**, program, schedule, calendar, timetable ■ *v* **label**, tag, identify, disclose, declare

dockside *n* **wharf**, jetty, dock, quayside, quay

dockyard *n* **shipyard**, boatyard, dry dock

doctor *n* **1 physician**, medical practitioner, healer, doc *(infml)*, medic *(infml)* **2 academic**, scholar, expert, specialist, Doctor of Philosophy ■ *v* **1 amend**, modify, adjust, meddle with, rework **2 treat**, care for, look after, cure, heal

doctorate *n* **higher degree**, research degree, university degree, Ph.D., Doctor of Philosophy

doctrinaire *adj* **rigid**, inflexible, stern, strict, unbending *Opposite*: liberal

doctrine *n* **policy**, principle, set of guidelines, canon, dogma

document *n* **text**, file, article, essay, paper ■ *v* **record**, keep a record, detail, write down, provide evidence

documentation *n* **certification**, papers, credentials, documents, citations

dodder *v* **1 tremble**, shake, waver, quake, quiver **2 totter**, reel, teeter, stagger, wobble *Opposite*: stride

doddering *adj* **tottering**, reeling, teetering, staggering, wobbling

doddery *adj* **shaky**, unsteady, tottery, feeble, frail *Opposite*: steady

dodge *v* **1 move**, cut, duck, move away, sidestep **2 avoid**, evade, shirk, elude, get out of

doer *n* **achiever**, dynamo, go-getter *(infml)*, live wire *(infml)*

doff *v* **take off**, lift, tip, tilt, remove *Opposite*: don

dog *n* **canine**, hound, doggy *(infml)*, mutt *(infml)*, pooch *(infml)* ■ *v* **1 follow**, pursue, chase, trail, track **2 bother**, beleaguer, harass, vex, plague

---

WORD BANK

❏ **types of large dogs** Afghan hound, Alsatian, bloodhound, borzoi, boxer, bulldog, collie, dalmatian, Doberman pinscher, German shepherd, Great Dane, greyhound, guide dog, husky, Labrador, mastiff, Newfoundland, Old English sheepdog, Pyrenean mountain dog, retriever, rottweiler, Saint Bernard, setter, sheepdog, wolfhound

❏ **types of small dogs** affenpinscher, airedale, basenji, basset, beagle, Border terrier, bull terrier, cairn terrier, chihuahua, chow, corgi, dachshund, fox terrier, foxhound, Jack Russell, Pekingese, pomeranian, poodle, pug, Scottie, Sealyham, shar-pei, shih tzu, spaniel, terrier, whippet, Yorkshire terrier

---

dog-eared *adj* **damaged**, tattered, battered, well-read, worn *Opposite*: pristine

dogfight *n* **fight**, conflict, combat, encounter, raid

dogged *adj* **determined**, single-minded, unwavering, indefatigable, steadfast *Opposite*: half-hearted

doggedness *n* **perseverance**, persistence, single-mindedness, tenacity, resolve *Opposite*: apathy

doggerel *n* **1 verse**, poetry, rhyme, limerick, ditty **2 gibberish**, nonsense, prattle, rubbish, garbage

dogleg *n* **sharp bend**, angle, corner, curve, bend ■ *v* **bend**, turn, curve, swerve

dogma *n* **creed**, doctrine, philosophy, canon, belief

dogmatic *adj* **rigid**, inflexible, unbending, strict, intransigent *Opposite*: flexible

dogmatism *n* **intransigence**, inflexibility, strictness, presumption, arrogance *Opposite*: openness

dog-tired *(infml)* *adj* **exhausted**, worn out, shattered, tired, all in *Opposite*: fresh

do in *(infml)* *v* **kill**, murder, assassinate, finish off *(infml)*, do away with *(infml)*

doings *(infml)* *n* **activities**, actions, events, happenings, deeds

doldrums *n* **1 stagnation**, sluggishness, boredom, lethargy, lassitude *Opposite*: energy **2 gloominess**, melancholy, dejection, despondency, pessimism *Opposite*: cheerfulness

doleful *adj* **unhappy**, miserable, sad, woeful, dejected *Opposite*: cheerful

dolefulness *n* **sadness**, unhappiness, misery, mournfulness, woefulness *Opposite*: cheerfulness

dole out *(infml)* *v* **share out**, dispense, distribute, allocate, allot *Opposite*: hoard

doll *n* toy, figurine, figure, model, puppet

dollar *n* dollar bill, buck (*infml*), big one (*infml*), greenback (*slang*)

dollop (*infml*) *n* blob, spoonful, spoon, squirt, drop

doll up (*infml*) *v* dress up, smarten up, spruce up, titivate, smarten Opposite: tone down

dolly (*infml*) *see* doll

dolmen *n* megalith, obelisk, trilithon, monument, standing stone

domain *n* area, field, sphere, sphere of influence, province

dome *n* vault, cupola, roof, ceiling

domed *adj* 1 vaulted, hemispheric, rounded, round

domestic *adj* 1 home, family, house, household, familial Opposite: public 2 national, local, internal, homeland, native Opposite: international

domesticate *v* tame, break, bring under control, control, housebreak

domesticated *adj* tame, pet, trained, tamed, housetrained Opposite: wild

domestication *n* taming, training, housetraining, housebreaking, subjugation

domesticity *n* home life, family life, home comforts, married life, creature comforts

domestic partner *n* cohabitee, partner, spousal equivalent, significant other

domicile (*fml*) *n* home, residence, house, apartment, quarters

dominance *n* supremacy, ascendancy, domination, power, authority Opposite: weakness

dominant *adj* 1 domineering, bossy, overbearing, officious, authoritarian Opposite: submissive 2 leading, main, central, foremost, prevailing Opposite: minor

dominate *v* 1 control, rule, lead, govern, direct 2 overlook, overshadow, tower above, tower over, dwarf

domination *n* power, control, command, authority, dominion

domineering *adj* bossy, dominant, overbearing, officious, authoritarian Opposite: meek

dominion *n* 1 power, authority, control, command, domination 2 territory, colony, province, region, protectorate

don *v* put on, throw on, get into, pull on, dress in Opposite: take off

donate *v* give, contribute, bequeath, provide, offer. *See* COMPARE AND CONTRAST *at* give.

donation *n* gift, contribution, payment, bequest, endowment

done *adj* complete, completed, ended, finished, through

donor *n* giver, contributor, benefactor, patron, supporter

doodle *v* draw, sketch, scribble, squiggle ■ *n* drawing, sketch, scribble, picture, squiggle

doohickey (*infml*) *n* gadget, widget, whatchamacallit (*infml*), thingamajig (*infml*), thingamabob (*infml*)

doom *n* 1 fate, destiny, lot, kismet, portion (*literary*) 2 disaster, trouble, end, death, tragedy

doomed *adj* 1 fated, destined, damned, condemned, predestined 2 hopeless, disaster-prone, ruined, lost, damned

doomsday *n* end of the world, end of time, Last Judgment, Judgment Day, Day of Judgment

door *n* entrance, gate, entry, exit, access

doorplate *n* name plate, sign, plaque, house sign, plate

doorstep *n* entrance, threshold, access, doorway, front doorstep

doorway *n* entrance, door, front entrance, entry, entryway

doppelgänger *n* double, mirror image, shadow, twin, clone

dormant *adj* 1 inactive, asleep, sleeping, quiescent, quiet Opposite: active 2 latent, undeveloped, hidden, unexpressed

dormitory *n* hall, residence, residence hall, student house, dorm (*infml*)

dosage *n* amount, quantity, dose, measure, prescription

dose *n* 1 amount, quantity, dosage, measure, prescription 2 (*infml*) bout, spell, period, attack, experience ■ *v* treat, give medicine to, dose up, medicate

dossier *n* file, record, report, folder, profile

dot *n* spot, point, mark, blotch, speck ■ *v* speckle, sprinkle, pepper, fleck, spot

doting *adj* fond, loving, devoted, affectionate, adoring

dotted *adj* scattered, sprinkled, spotted, speckled, spread

dotty *adj* 1 unconventional, odd, eccentric, idiosyncratic, strange Opposite: normal 2 absurd, impractical, illogical, foolish, nonsensical Opposite: practical 3 (*infml*) crazy (*infml*), fond, besotted, doting, infatuated

double *adj* dual, binary, twofold, duple, twin ■ *adv* twice, twofold, twice over, two times ■ *n* 1 duo, pair, duet, couple 2 doppelgänger, clone, alter ego, twin, stand-in ■ *v* 1 increase twofold, double up, amplify, magnify, expand Opposite: lessen 2 bend, fold, double up, bend over, fold up

double act *n* pair, twosome, duo, couple

double agent *n* spy, mole, infiltrator, inside agent, secret agent

double check *n* second check, reassessment, check, verification

double-check *v* make sure, ensure, reassure yourself, check, verify

double-cross *v* betray, con, let down, cheat, sell out ■ *n* betrayal, deception, swindle, trick, con

double-crosser n swindler, cheat, trickster, liar, fraudster

double-dealer n swindler, liar, cheat, fraudster, trickster

double-dealing n duplicity, betrayal, deceit, cheating, treachery Opposite: honesty ■ adj duplicitous, deceitful, double-faced, cheating, swindling Opposite: honest

double-edged adj ambiguous, two-edged, disingenuous, ironic, sly Opposite: ingenuous

double-faced adj insincere, deceitful, dishonest, two-faced, false Opposite: honest

double-jointed adj flexible, supple, agile, lithe

double-quick (infml) adv rapidly, swiftly, speedily, promptly, quickly Opposite: slowly

double talk n 1 gibberish, nonsense, trash, garbage, rubbish 2 sophistry, doublespeak, deceit, jargon, smoke and mirrors

double up v bend, fold, double, bend over, fold up

doubt v disbelieve, mistrust, suspect, have reservations, have doubts Opposite: believe ■ n hesitation, uncertainty, reservation, misgiving, distrust Opposite: certainty

doubter n nonbeliever, cynic, doubting Thomas, agnostic, pessimist Opposite: believer

doubtful adj 1 unsure, uncertain, hesitant, in doubt, dubious Opposite: certain 2 unlikely, unpromising, uncertain, insecure, shaky Opposite: probable 3 unreliable, dubious, suspect, questionable, untrustworthy Opposite: reliable

COMPARE AND CONTRAST CORE MEANING: feeling doubt or uncertainty
doubtful undecided or feeling hesitant; **uncertain** or **unsure** lacking certainty or confidence; **in doubt** still undecided and liable to change; **dubious** doubtful and, often, suspicious; **skeptical** questioning the truth or likelihood of something.

doubtfully adv uncertainly, hesitantly, distrustfully, doubtingly, suspiciously Opposite: confidently

doubtfulness n 1 uncertainty, hesitancy, indecision, doubt, distrust Opposite: certainty 2 unlikelihood, improbability, chance in a million, slim chance Opposite: likelihood

doubting adj hesitant, doubtful, distrustful, suspicious, unbelieving Opposite: trusting

doubtless adv no doubt, without a doubt, probably, almost certainly, without question Opposite: possibly

doughty (archaic) adj brave, determined, tough, spirited, indomitable Opposite: feeble

dour adj severe, unfriendly, sour, stern, hard-faced Opposite: kindly

dourness n severity, unfriendliness, sourness, sternness, grimness Opposite: kindness

douse v 1 drench, soak, wet, souse, cover 2 quench, extinguish, put out, smother, snuff Opposite: kindle

dovetail v fit together, slot in, join together, come together, unite Opposite: separate

dowdiness n drabness, plainness, dullness, dreariness, frumpiness

dowdy adj plain, frumpy, drab, unfashionable, dreary Opposite: fashionable

dowel n rod, pin, peg

do without v abstain, deny yourself, go without, keep off, forgo

down prep along, through, the length of ■ adj 1 depressed, unhappy, miserable, dejected, downhearted Opposite: happy 2 listed, nominated, scheduled, timetabled, tabled 3 out of action, inoperative, not working, out of order Opposite: working 4 behind, losing, short Opposite: winning ■ v 1 consume, eat, drink, gulp down, swallow 2 knock down, floor, overpower, overcome, defeat 3 put down, lay down, throw down, set down, lay aside Opposite: pick up

down-and-out adj destitute, penniless, homeless, on the streets, broke (infml) Opposite: well-heeled (infml)

downbeat adj pessimistic, gloomy, dark, bleak, negative Opposite: upbeat (infml)

downcast adj sad, pessimistic, dejected, depressed, down Opposite: cheerful

downer (infml) n disappointment, shame, pity, letdown, discouragement

downfall n failure, ruin, fall, end, demise (fml) Opposite: success

downgrade v demote, reduce, lower, relegate Opposite: upgrade

downhearted adj sad, pessimistic, dejected, disappointed, depressed Opposite: cheerful

downhill adj easy, simple, effortless, plain sailing, straightforward Opposite: uphill

download v transfer, copy, move, take

downmarket adj low quality, inferior, cheap, low cost, second-rate Opposite: superior

down payment n installment, payment, deposit, disbursement

downplay v tone down, moderate, restrain, soften, modulate Opposite: highlight

downpour n heavy shower, deluge, rainstorm, cloudburst, torrent

downright adv positively, undeniably, unquestionably, undoubtedly, totally Opposite: questionably

downscale adj inferior, cheap, low quality, shoddy, shabby Opposite: upscale

downside n negative aspect, shortcoming, weakness, snag, stumbling block Opposite: advantage

downsize v **slim down**, cut back, economize, rationalize, trim *Opposite*: expand

downstairs adv **below**, down the stairs, down, down below

downswing n **fall**, slump, decline, dip, downturn *Opposite*: upswing

downtime n **stoppage**, lost time, idle time, interruption

down-to-earth adj **practical**, realistic, sensible, matter-of-fact, pragmatic *Opposite*: fanciful

downtrodden adj **browbeaten**, subjugated, broken, oppressed, demoralized

downturn n **slump**, recession, dip, decline, depression *Opposite*: upturn

downward adj **descending**, down, downhill, sliding, descendent *Opposite*: upward

downy adj **silky**, soft, velvety, furry, feathery *Opposite*: rough

dowry n **wedding gift**, present, grant, settlement, portion

doyen n **leading figure**, senior member, leading light, notable, leader

doyenne n **leading figure**, senior member, leading light, notable, leader

do your homework (infml) v **prepare**, research, plan, find out

doze v **nap**, sleep, slumber, snooze (infml) ■ n **nap**, slumber, sleep, snooze (infml)

dozens (infml) n **lots**, tons (infml), stacks (infml), loads (infml), heaps (infml)

doze off v **fall asleep**, go to sleep, nod off, nod, drift off *Opposite*: wake up

dozily adv **sleepily**, tiredly, lethargically, sluggishly, drowsily *Opposite*: alertly

doziness n **sleepiness**, tiredness, lethargy, sluggishness, drowsiness *Opposite*: alertness

dozy adj **sleepy**, drowsy, tired, dozing, nodding *Opposite*: alert

drab adj **1 gloomy**, dull, dingy, dowdy, dreary *Opposite*: bright **2 uninteresting**, unexciting, monotonous, boring, dreary *Opposite*: interesting

drabness n **dullness**, plainness, dowdiness, dreariness, dinginess *Opposite*: brightness

Draconian n **harsh**, severe, strict, strong, austere *Opposite*: mild

draft n **1 current**, flow, waft, breeze, breath **2 recruitment**, mobilization, enlistment, enrollment **3 outline**, sketch, summary, plan, rough copy **4** (dated) **medicine**, concoction, tonic, mixture, brew ■ v **1 recruit**, conscript, sign up, enlist, enroll *Opposite*: discharge **2 draw up**, prepare, sketch out, outline, write

drag v **1 pull**, haul, draw, heave, lug **2 dawdle**, lag, crawl, creep, loiter *Opposite*: fly. See COMPARE AND CONTRAST *at* **pull**.

dragging adj **slow**, tedious, tiresome, wearisome, uninteresting *Opposite*: interesting

draggy (infml) adj **1 sluggish**, slow, slow-moving, snail-paced, dawdling *Opposite*: brisk **2 tiresome**, tedious, dragging, wearisome, uninteresting *Opposite*: interesting

drag in v **bring in**, involve, allude to, mention, implicate *Opposite*: exclude

dragnet n **1 search**, hunt, pursuit, tracking operation, quest **2 net**, mesh, trawl net, game net, trap

dragoon v **coerce**, press, bully, intimidate, browbeat

drag out v **extend**, prolong, draw out, lengthen, stretch *Opposite*: cut short

drag up v **return to**, bring up, dredge up, revive, mention

drag your feet v **hold back**, hang back, drag your heels, take your time, stall

drain v **use up**, exhaust, consume, deplete, sap *Opposite*: replenish ■ n **sewer**, ditch, channel, culvert, conduit

drained adj **exhausted**, weak, weary, tired, worn out *Opposite*: energetic

draining adj **exhausting**, trying, wearing, tiring, grueling

drama n **1 play**, stage show, performance, production, spectacle **2 excitement**, commotion, fuss, performance, crisis

dramatic adj **1 considerable**, significant, radical, noticeable, spectacular *Opposite*: modest **2 affected**, melodramatic, theatrical, histrionic, studied *Opposite*: natural

dramatics n **histrionics**, hysterics, excitement, commotion, fuss

dramatist n **playwright**, writer, author, scriptwriter

dramatization n **staging**, performance, production, adaptation

dramatize v **exaggerate**, sensationalize, play up, embellish, lay on *Opposite*: play down

drape v **swathe**, dress, wrap, cover, clothe

drapery n **curtains**, hangings, drapes, swags

drastic adj **radical**, severe, extreme, dire, sweeping *Opposite*: modest

draw v **1 sketch**, illustrate, copy, depict, describe **2 pull**, drag, haul, move, tow *Opposite*: push **3 get**, obtain, extract, derive, gain **4 pull out**, extract, withdraw, take out, unsheathe *Opposite*: put away **5 attract**, pull, lure, appeal, entice **6 finish equal**, tie, equal, square, even ■ n **1 attraction**, magnet, inducement, lure, enticement **2 dead heat**, tie, stalemate, deadlock, standoff. See COMPARE AND CONTRAST *at* **pull**.

draw a veil over v **conceal**, keep quiet about, ignore, forget, hush up (infml) *Opposite*: expose

draw back v **move away**, draw away, withdraw, retreat, recoil *Opposite*: approach

drawback n **disadvantage**, problem, downside, negative, weakness *Opposite*: advantage

draw in v **involve**, implicate, engage, ensnare, hook

drawing *n* **sketch**, picture, illustration, diagram, portrayal

drawl *n* **accent**, twang, brogue, tones, pronunciation

drawn *adj* **haggard**, strained, pinched, tired, wan *Opposite*: relaxed

draw near *v* **approach**, get closer, come nearer, come up, creep up *Opposite*: move away

drawn-out *adj* **protracted**, lengthy, long, convoluted, interminable *Opposite*: swift

draw off *v* **pour**, siphon off, pull, drain off, suck up

draw on *v* **use**, employ, be inspired by, resort to, fall back on

draw out *v* **prolong**, extend, make last, lengthen, stretch *Opposite*: cut short

drawstring *n* **tie**, string, lace, belt

draw the short straw *v* **get a raw deal**, do badly, be unlucky, come off worst, lose out

draw up *v* **draft**, put together, assemble, prepare, write

dray *n* **wagon**, cart, low-loader, transporter, truck

dread *v* **fear**, be afraid of, be terrified of, be frightened of, be worried about *Opposite*: look forward to ▪ *n* **terror**, fear, trepidation, anxiety, dismay *Opposite*: confidence

dreadful *adj* **terrible**, awful, horrible, frightful, alarming *Opposite*: lovely

dreadfully *adv* **extremely**, very, terribly, awfully, really

dreadfulness *n* **awfulness**, horror, misery, ghastliness, gruesomeness

dream *n* **1 vision**, daydream, reverie, nightmare, hallucination *Opposite*: reality **2 aspiration**, wish, goal, hope, ambition **3 delight**, joy, pleasure, marvel, ideal *Opposite*: nightmare ▪ *v* **fantasize**, visualize, imagine, fancy, daydream

dreamer *n* **visionary**, idealist, romantic, fantasist *Opposite*: realist

dreaminess *n* **1 pensiveness**, abstraction, vagueness, wistfulness, languor **2 perfection**, beauty, exquisiteness, loveliness, gorgeousness

dreamland *n* **paradise**, heaven, nirvana, fairyland, fantasy world *Opposite*: real world

dreamlike *adj* **unreal**, fantastic, surreal, weird, bizarre *Opposite*: real

dream up *v* **concoct**, think up, invent, imagine, come up with

dream world *n* **fantasy world**, land of make-believe, fairyland, never-never land, cloud-cuckoo-land *Opposite*: real world

dreamy *adj* **1 pensive**, vague, faraway, wistful, preoccupied *Opposite*: alert **2 wonderful**, beautiful, superb, out of this world, fantastic *Opposite*: ordinary

dreariness *n* **1 dullness**, monotony, tedium, boredom, routine *Opposite*: excitement **2 bleakness**, misery, cheerlessness, grimness, gloominess *Opposite*: cheerfulness

dreary *adj* **1 dull**, boring, monotonous, tedious, lifeless *Opposite*: interesting **2 bleak**, cheerless, dismal, miserable, grim *Opposite*: cheerful

dredge *v* **search**, scour, comb, ransack, rummage

dredge up *v* **unearth**, dig up, drag up, bring up, uncover *Opposite*: bury

dregs *n* **1 residue**, sediment, silt, lees, deposit **2** *(literary)* **last part**, end, tail end, remains, vestiges

drench *v* **soak**, wet, saturate, douse, steep *Opposite*: dry out

drenched *adj* **soaked**, sodden, wet, inundated, saturated *Opposite*: dry

dress *v* **1 wear**, put on, dress up, clothe, slip into *Opposite*: undress **2 adorn**, decorate, deck out, ornament, trim ▪ *n* **1 frock**, gown, robe **2 clothing**, clothes, costume, garb, wear

---

WORD BANK

❑ **types of dresses** ball gown, caftan, cheong-sam, cocktail dress, evening gown, jumper, kimono, muumuu, robe, sari, sheath, shift, shirtdress, sundress, wedding dress

---

dress down *v* **scold**, reprimand, lecture, rebuke, censure *Opposite*: praise

dressed *adj* **turned out**, robed, garbed, outfitted *Opposite*: undressed

dressing *n* **bandage**, covering, gauze

dressmaking *n* **couture**, tailoring, sewing

dress rehearsal *n* **practice**, run through, trial, rehearsal, preparation

dress sense *n* **flair**, stylishness, fashion sense, panache, chic

dress up *v* **disguise**, revamp, embellish, decorate, titivate

dressy *adj* **elegant**, fashionable, stylish, chic, classy *(infml)* *Opposite*: sloppy

dribble *v* **1 drool**, salivate, slobber, slaver, drivel **2 trickle**, ooze, drip, seep, leak *Opposite*: gush

dried *adj* **dehydrated**, dried out, dried up, desiccated, dry

drift *v* **float**, flow, glide, coast, waft ▪ *n* **gist**, meaning, point, sense, idea

drifter *n* **wanderer**, tramp, vagabond, rolling stone, vagrant

drifting *adj* **wandering**, nomadic, homeless, itinerant, traveling *Opposite*: settled

driftwood *n* **flotsam**, jetsam, wreckage, refuse, waste

drill *n* **practice**, exercise, discipline, training, instruction ▪ *v* **1 bore**, make a hole, pierce, puncture, penetrate **2 train**, coach, school, discipline, instruct. *See* COMPARE AND CONTRAST *at* **teach**.

drily *adv* **ironically**, humorously, wittily, subtly, wryly

drink v swallow, down, sip, gulp, slurp ■ n 1 thirst-quencher, liquid refreshment, soft drink, cold drink, hot drink 2 **mouthful**, taste, gulp, swallow, sip 3 **alcoholic drink**, alcohol, liquor, nip, tipple (infml)

drinkable adj fit to drink, safe to drink, filtered, potable

drinking fountain n water spout, jet, faucet

drip v dribble, trickle, drop, leak, seep Opposite: gush ■ n **drop**, trickle, dribble, leak Opposite: stream

drip-dry adj wash-and-wear, crease-resistant, permanent-press, easy-care, washable

dripping adj wet, soaked, drenched, sodden, saturated Opposite: dry

drive v 1 steer, handle, guide, direct, operate 2 take, run, chauffeur, transport 3 power, run, cause to move, set in motion 4 force, make, coerce, constrain, impel 5 **push**, propel, urge, goad, send 6 **hammer**, push, force, plunge, sink ■ n 1 **energy**, determination, ambition, initiative, motivation Opposite: lethargy 2 urge, desire, need, instinct, passion 3 **campaign**, crusade, push, fundraiser, appeal

drivel n nonsense, balderdash, gibberish, bunkum (infml), hokum (infml)

driven adj ambitious, determined, obsessed, motivated, compelled Opposite: apathetic

driver n chauffeur, motorist, operator, teamster

drive up the wall (infml) v exasperate, infuriate, make your blood boil, enrage, irritate

driving adj 1 heavy, pouring, lashing Opposite: light 2 powerful, dynamic, energetic, motivating, forceful

drizzle n light rain, trickle, shower, sprinkle Opposite: downpour ■ v **rain**, spot, shower, sprinkle, trickle Opposite: pour

drizzly adj damp, wet, rainy, misty

droll adj amusing, funny, comic, witty, humorous Opposite: dull

drone v hum, buzz, whine, murmur, whir

drool v dribble, salivate, slobber, slaver, drivel

droop v 1 sag, wilt, bow, hang down, flop 2 tire, tire out, wear out, flag, wilt Opposite: perk up

droopiness n 1 tiredness, fatigue, weariness, exhaustion, apathy Opposite: freshness 2 **floppiness**, limpness, lifelessness, slackness, bagginess Opposite: stiffness

droopy adj 1 tired, tired out, worn out, fatigued, weary Opposite: fresh 2 **hanging**, floppy, limp, dangling, sagging Opposite: upright

drop v 1 let fall, let go, release, throw down 2 **fall**, go down, plunge, plummet, crash Opposite: rise 3 drip, trickle, ooze, seep, dribble Opposite: pour 4 **abandon**, stop, shelve, give up, discontinue Opposite: maintain ■ n 1 **droplet**, drip, bead, globule, dewdrop 2 descent, fall, plunge, decline,

dip Opposite: ascent 3 **reduction**, decrease, decline, fall, cut Opposite: increase

drop a line v **write**, get in touch, correspond, contact, send a letter

drop back v **fall behind**, fall back, slow down, lag behind, straggle

drop behind see **drop back**

drop in v **call**, call by, call in, come around, drop by

droplet n **drop**, drip, bead, dewdrop, globule

drop off (infml) v 1 **go to sleep**, nod off, fall asleep, doze off, drift off Opposite: wake up 2 **deliver**, unload, deposit, leave Opposite: pick up

drop out v **leave**, give up, quit, withdraw, stop Opposite: carry on

dropper n **dispenser**, measurer, tube, glass dropper, eye dropper

droppings n **dung**, muck, stools, feces, manure

dross n **rubbish**, trash, garbage, scum, waste

drought n **lack**, dearth, deficiency, scarcity, famine Opposite: abundance

drove n **throng**, horde, crowd, gaggle, multitude Opposite: trickle

droves n **multitudes**, hordes, crowds, scores, flocks

drown v 1 **go down**, go under, sink, die Opposite: float 2 **drench**, soak, swamp, saturate, flood Opposite: dry 3 **cover**, mask, obscure, hide, overlie Opposite: amplify

drowse v **doze**, be sleepy, nap, have a nap, catnap Opposite: wake

drowsiness n **sleepiness**, lethargy, stupor, tiredness Opposite: wakefulness

drowsy adj **sleepy**, tired, dozy, lethargic, somnolent Opposite: awake

drub v **beat**, pound, thrash, defeat, hammer (infml)

drubbing n **beating**, thrashing, hammering (infml), pasting (infml), licking (infml)

drudge n **worker**, menial (fml), laborer Opposite: drone ■ v **work**, toil, labor, grind, plod

drudgery n **labor**, toil, work, chore, grind

drug n **medication**, medicine, painkiller

drum n **barrel**, cask, cylinder, container ■ v **pound**, beat, tap, thump, thud

drum into v **impress**, instill, drive into, teach, din in

drumming n **thudding**, pounding, beating, hammering, tapping

drumroll n **roll of drums**, tattoo, rattle, rumble, crescendo

drum up v **gather**, stimulate, rally, foster, encourage Opposite: suppress

drunk adj **inebriated**, intoxicated, plastered (infml), liquored up (infml), under the influence (infml) Opposite: sober

druthers (infml) n **preference**, free choice, first choice, fancy

dry adj 1 **dehydrated**, dried out, dried up,

arid, waterless *Opposite*: wet **2 thirsty**, dehydrated, parched, in need of a drink **3 deadpan**, wry, ironic, understated, droll *Opposite*: gushing **4 uninteresting**, dull, tedious, boring, monotonous *Opposite*: interesting **5 teetotal**, abstinent, abstemious, temperate, prohibitionist ■ *v* **1 make dry**, rub, rub down, towel, wipe *Opposite*: wet **2 desiccate**, become dry, dry out, dry up, dehydrate *Opposite*: swell

COMPARE AND CONTRAST CORE MEANING: lacking moisture

dry having little or no moisture; **dehydrated** experiencing fluid loss, or preserved by drying; **desiccated** (used of products, especially food) free from moisture, or preserved by drying; **arid** (used of land) dry from lack of rain; **parched** dry from excessive heat or lack of rain; **shriveled** dry, shrunken, and wrinkled; **sere** (*literary*) dry and withered.

dryad *n* **wood nymph**, fairy, naiad, pixie, nymph

dry-clean *v* **clean**, launder, wash, valet

dry-eyed *adj* **unemotional**, impassive, expressionless, unmoved, stoical *Opposite*: tearful

dry land *n* **solid ground**, shore, beach, terra firma *Opposite*: sea

dryness *n* **1 aridness**, aridity, dehydration, drought, desiccation *Opposite*: wetness **2 wryness**, irony, understatement, matter-of-factness, sarcasm

dry out *v* **1 air**, dry, dry off, tumble dry, tumble *Opposite*: damp **2 shrivel up**, curl up, dry up, wither, become dehydrated *Opposite*: soak

dry run *n* **rehearsal**, run-through, tryout, trial run, trial

dry up *v* **1 desiccate**, become dry, dry out, dry, dehydrate *Opposite*: swell **2** (*infml*) **falter**, lose the thread, stop midstream, forget your lines, come to a halt *Opposite*: continue **3 fail**, run out, be used up, come to an end, disappear *Opposite*: continue

dual *adj* **double**, twin, twofold

dualism *n* **symmetry**, contrast, dichotomy, opposition, polarity

duality *n* **dichotomy**, division, dyad, contrast, opposition

dub *v* **call**, nickname, christen, hail as; label

dubiety (*fml*) *n* **doubtfulness**, doubt, dubiousness, uncertainty, hesitancy *Opposite*: certitude

dubious *adj* **1 doubtful**, uncertain, unsure, undecided, unconvinced *Opposite*: certain **2 suspect**, untrustworthy, questionable, shady, unsavory *Opposite*: trustworthy **3 ambiguous**, doubtful, debatable, uncertain, questionable *Opposite*: unambiguous. *See* COMPARE AND CONTRAST *at* **doubtful**.

dubiousness *n* **1 doubt**, doubtfulness, uncertainty, hesitancy, suspicion *Opposite*: certainty **2 fallibility**, unreliability, improbability, ambiguity, vagueness *Opposite*: reliability

duchy *n* **dukedom**, estate, territory, barony, principality

duck *n* **water bird**, waterfowl, diver ■ *v* **1 stoop**, bend, bow, bob, nod *Opposite*: straighten **2 avoid**, evade, dodge, sidestep, circumvent *Opposite*: confront

duckboard *n* **walkway**, boardwalk, path, planking, catwalk

duck out *v* **back out**, pull out, drop out, withdraw, get out

duct *n* **channel**, canal, pipe, tube, vessel

ductile *adj* **pliable**, malleable, elastic, pliant, plastic. *See* COMPARE AND CONTRAST *at* **pliable**.

dud (*infml*) *n* **failure**, fiasco, letdown, disappointment, flop (*infml*) *Opposite*: success ■ *adj* **useless**, worthless, ineffective, broken, no good *Opposite*: usable

due *adj* **1 expected**, scheduled, appointed, anticipated, looked-for **2 appropriate**, fitting, suitable, proper, right and proper *Opposite*: undue **3 owing**, unpaid, outstanding, payable, owed *Opposite*: paid ■ *adv* **directly**, exactly, direct, dead, straight *Opposite*: indirectly

duel *n* **contest**, fight, battle, gunfight, combat ■ *v* **fight**, clash, battle, contest, struggle

duelist *n* **fighter**, combatant, opponent, gunfighter, contender

dues *n* **fees**, subscription, payment, charge, levy

duet *n* **duo**, double act, twosome, couple, pair

due to *prep* **because of**, owing to, by reason of, as a result of, attributable to

dugout *n* **bunker**, trench, foxhole, ditch, hollow

dulcet *adj* **melodious**, melodic, honeyed, soothing, pleasant *Opposite*: harsh

dull *adj* **1 boring**, uninteresting, tedious, monotonous, dreary *Opposite*: interesting **2 cloudy**, overcast, gloomy, gray, leaden *Opposite*: bright **3 dark**, dim, muted, faded, lackluster *Opposite*: bright **4 stupid**, obtuse, plodding, sluggish, unintelligent *Opposite*: bright ■ *v* **deaden**, dampen, stultify, cloud, blunt *Opposite*: accentuate

dullness *n* **1 tediousness**, tedium, monotony, dreariness, dryness *Opposite*: liveliness **2 cloudiness**, gloom, half-light, gloominess, grayness *Opposite*: brightness **3 darkness**, dimness, drabness, dowdiness, dinginess *Opposite*: brightness

duly *adv* **accordingly**, suitably, fittingly, appropriately, properly *Opposite*: unduly

dumbfound *v* **astonish**, amaze, astound, surprise, stagger

dumbfounded *adj* **astonished**, amazed, astounded, thunderstruck, staggered

dummy *n* **1 mannequin**, model, lay figure, figure, form **2 copy**, replica, imitation, fake, mock-up *Opposite*: original ■ *adj* **imitation**, fake, mock, pretend, replica *Opposite*: original

dummy run *n* **rehearsal**, run-through, dry run, trial run, trial

dump *v* 1 **put**, leave, abandon, tip, throw 2 **get rid of**, abandon, leave, dispose of, discard *Opposite*: keep 3 *(infml)* **abandon**, discard, leave, desert, walk out on *(infml) Opposite*: stand by ■ *n* 1 **landfill**, garbage dump, junkyard, scrapheap 2 *(infml)* **pigpen**, eyesore, mess, monstrosity, hovel

dune *n* **bank**, sandbank, hill, mound, ridge

dung *n* **manure**, droppings, slurry, muck, fertilizer

dungeon *n* **prison**, cell, jail, vault, oubliette

dunk *v* **dip**, submerge, immerse, soak, steep

duo *n* **pair**, twosome, couple, double act, two of a kind

dupe *v* **fool**, trick, deceive, con, take in ■ *n* **victim**, target, fool, sucker *(infml)*, fall guy *(slang)*

duplicate *v* 1 **replicate**, copy, photocopy, reproduce, make two of 2 **repeat**, replicate, reproduce, copy, do again ■ *n* **copy**, replacement, photocopy, spare, carbon copy *Opposite*: original ■ *adj* **identical**, matching, replica, replacement, spare *Opposite*: original. *See* COMPARE AND CONTRAST *at* copy.

duplication *n* 1 **repetition**, replication, doubling, copying, photocopying 2 **replica**, duplicate, copy, print, facsimile *Opposite*: original

duplicitous *adj* **double-dealing**, two-faced, tricky, deceitful, dishonest *Opposite*: honest

duplicity *n* **deceit**, deception, dishonesty, disloyalty, unfaithfulness *Opposite*: honesty

durability *n* **toughness**, sturdiness, strength, robustness, resilience *Opposite*: flimsiness

durable *adj* **tough**, sturdy, strong, robust, long-lasting *Opposite*: flimsy

duration *n* **length**, extent, period, time, interval

duress *n* **pressure**, force, threat, coercion, compulsion *Opposite*: persuasion

during *prep* **throughout**, through, in, in the course of

dusk *n* **twilight**, sunset, nightfall, sundown, evening *Opposite*: dawn

dusky *adj* **shadowy**, dark, darkish, gray, dim *Opposite*: bright

dust *n* **powder**, dirt, sand, earth, soil ■ *v* 1 **clean**, dust up, wipe, wipe down, wipe up 2 **sprinkle**, brush, cover, scatter, sift

dust bowl *n* **desert**, waste, wasteland, wilderness

dust jacket *n* **cover**, jacket, dust cover, paper cover

dustpan *n* **pan**, scoop, shovel, receptacle, container

dusty *adj* **dirty**, grimy, filthy, sandy, grubby *Opposite*: spotless

dutiful *adj* **obedient**, well-behaved, compliant, loyal, devoted *Opposite*: disobedient

duty *n* 1 **responsibility**, obligation, onus, burden, calling 2 **job**, task, function, responsibility, obligation 3 **tax**, payment, levy, due, impost

duty-bound *adj* **constrained**, compelled, obliged, forced, obligated

duty-free *(infml)* *adj* **tax-free**, tax-exempt, untaxed, nontaxable

duvet *n* **comforter**, quilt, eiderdown, coverlet

dwell *(literary)* *v* **reside**, live, have your home, stay, inhabit *Opposite*: leave

dweller *n* **inhabitant**, resident, occupant, occupier, tenant

dwelling *(fml)* *n* **house**, home, residence, place of abode, lodging

dwell on *v* **think about**, ponder, brood over, mull over, go on about *Opposite*: forget

dwindle *v* **decrease**, decline, diminish, fall off, drop *Opposite*: increase

dwindling *adj* **declining**, decreasing, diminishing, deteriorating, falling *Opposite*: burgeoning

dye *v* **color**, stain, tint, change the color of ■ *n* 1 **coloring**, color, colorant, stain, pigment 2 **hair dye**, color, colorant, tint, rinse

dyed-in-the-wool *adj* **long-established**, confirmed, committed, dedicated, incorrigible

dying *adj* 1 **last**, final, ultimate, closing, ending 2 **disappearing**, failing, fading, vanishing, becoming extinct *Opposite*: thriving

dying to *adj* **desperate to**, eager to, longing to, bursting to, impatient to

dynamic *adj* **active**, self-motivated, energetic, vibrant, forceful *Opposite*: lethargic

dynamics *n* 1 **changing aspects**, subtleties, forces at work, dynamic forces, underlying forces 2 **louds and softs**, dynamic range, changes in volume, dynamic contrast, crescendos

dynamism *n* **vitality**, vigor, energy, drive, enthusiasm *Opposite*: lethargy

dynamite *v* **blow up**, blast, explode, detonate, wreck

dynamo *n* 1 **electric generator**, generator, motor, turbine 2 *(infml)* **extrovert**, live wire *(infml)*, go-getter *(infml)*, live one *(infml)*

dynastic *adj* **hereditary**, successional, imperial, sovereign, ruling

dynasty *n* 1 **reign**, rule, empire, period, era 2 **family**, house, line

dyspepsia *n* **indigestion**, heartburn, acid stomach, upset stomach, unsettled stomach

dysphemism *n* 1 **offensiveness**, rudeness, vulgarity, obscenity, ribaldry *Opposite*:

euphemism **2 obscenity**, swear word, expletive, oath, profanity *Opposite*: euphemism

dysphemistic *adj* **vulgar**, lewd, offensive, obscene, rude *Opposite*: euphemistic

E

each *pron* **every one**, each one, all, both ■ *adj* **every**, all, both, every single

eager *adj* **keen**, enthusiastic, excited, raring to go, ready *Opposite*: unenthusiastic

eagerness *n* **keenness**, enthusiasm, excitement, readiness, willingness *Opposite*: apathy

eagle-eyed *adj* **observant**, hawk-eyed, sharp-sighted, sharp-eyed, alert *Opposite*: unobservant

ear *n* **1 external ear**, outer ear, earlobe, lobe **2 ability**, sensitivity, talent, knack, facility **3 attention**, hearing, heed, regard

---

WORD BANK
❑ **parts of an ear** anvil, auricle, cochlea, eardrum, hammer, incus, internal ear, malleus, middle ear, stapes, stirrup, tympanic membrane, tympanum, vestibule

---

earful *(infml)* *n* **scolding**, lecture, piece of your mind, reprimand, talking-to *(infml)*

earlier *adv* **before**, in advance, previously, formerly, beforehand *Opposite*: later ■ *adj* **previous**, former, past, prior *Opposite*: later

earliest *adj* **first**, initial, original *Opposite*: latest

early *adv* **1 early on**, at the beginning, before time, in advance, ahead of schedule *Opposite*: late **2 soon**, promptly, without delay, now, as soon as possible *Opposite*: later ■ *adj* **1 initial**, first, primary, premature *Opposite*: later **2 timely**, prompt, quick, speedy, immediate *Opposite*: tardy

early years *n* **babyhood**, infancy, childhood, youth, formative years *Opposite*: adulthood

earmark *v* **allocate**, assign, allot, set aside, put aside

earn *v* **1 make**, be paid, take home, receive, get **2 deserve**, work for, win, warrant, merit

earnest *adj* **1 serious**, solemn, grave, sober, intense *Opposite*: frivolous **2 sincere**, heartfelt, deep, intense, strong *Opposite*: superficial

earnestness *n* **sincerity**, seriousness, solemnity, intensity, feeling *Opposite*: facetiousness

earnings *n* **1 pay**, salary, wage, wages, income *Opposite*: expenditure **2 profit**, revenue, gain, return, dividend *Opposite*: loss

earphone *see* **earpiece**

earpiece *n* **receiver**, headset, headphones, earphone

earshot *n* **hearing range**, range, hearing distance, hearing

earsplitting *adj* **loud**, piercing, shrill, deafening, noisy *Opposite*: quiet

earth *n* **soil**, ground, dirt, mud, terrain

Earth *n* **world**, globe, planet

earthling *n* **human being**, human, earthly being, intelligent life-form, human life-form *Opposite*: extraterrestrial

earthly *adj* **1 worldly**, material, mortal, secular, everyday *Opposite*: heavenly **2 possible**, imaginable, conceivable

earthmover *n* **bulldozer**, digger, power shovel, excavator, steam shovel

earthquake *n* **tremor**, upheaval, trembling, shaking, seismic activity

earthshaking *see* **earthshattering**

earthshattering *adj* **momentous**, tremendous, remarkable, stunning, devastating *Opposite*: trivial

earthward *adv* **toward the earth**, toward the ground, downward, down, in a nose-dive *Opposite*: skyward

earthwork *n* **fortification**, rampart, bulwark, barrier

earthy *adj* **1 unpretentious**, down-to-earth, no-nonsense, simple, unsophisticated *Opposite*: refined **2 vulgar**, crude, gross, bawdy, rude

ease *n* **1 effortlessness**, simplicity, straightforwardness, facility, easiness *Opposite*: difficulty **2 comfort**, luxury, affluence, wealth, opulence *Opposite*: hardship ■ *v* **1 relieve**, alleviate, reduce, lessen, mitigate *Opposite*: worsen **2 slide**, slip, edge, push gently, draw out **3 make easier**, facilitate, help, aid, assist *Opposite*: hinder

easel *n* **stand**, frame, tripod, support, mount

ease up *v* **relax**, slow down, slacken off, calm down, ease off

easily *adv* **1 with no trouble**, without difficulty, without problems, effortlessly, simply **2 without doubt**, by far, by a long shot, by a long way, definitely

easy *adj* **1 simple**, trouble-free, straightforward, effortless, uncomplicated *Opposite*: difficult **2 informal**, relaxed, calm, cool, tranquil *Opposite*: tense **3 comfortable**, affluent, luxurious, undemanding, leisurely *Opposite*: hard

easygoing *adj* **relaxed**, casual, tolerant, even-tempered, calm *Opposite*: anxious

eat *v* 1 **consume**, have, gobble, wolf, munch *Opposite*: starve 2 **have a meal**, dine, lunch, breakfast, snack

eat away *v* **erode**, corrode, eat into, wear away, wear down

eat crow *(infml)* *v* **apologize**, retract, say you're sorry, take it all back, eat your words *(infml) Opposite*: stand firm

eater *n* **consumer**, feeder, diner, devourer, guzzler *(infml)*

eatery *(infml)* *n* **restaurant**, diner, cafeteria, bistro, eating place

eat into *v* 1 **use up**, eat up, gobble up, reduce, consume 2 **corrode**, rust, pockmark, attack, destroy

eat up *v* 1 **consume**, down, gobble, scarf *(infml)*, scarf down *(infml)* 2 **absorb**, obsess, take over, consume, dominate 3 *(infml)* **lap up**, love, applaud, enthuse about, rave about *(infml) Opposite*: hate

eat your heart out *(infml)* *v* **brood**, dwell on, grieve, pine

eat your words *(infml)* *v* **apologize**, retract, say you're sorry, eat humble pie, take it all back *Opposite*: stand firm

eau de cologne *n* **perfume**, cologne, fragrance, scent, toilet water

eavesdrop *v* **listen in**, overhear, tap, spy, pry

eavesdropper *n* **listener**, spy, observer

ebb *v* 1 **recede**, go out, flow away, retreat, fall away *Opposite*: come in 2 **fade**, diminish, recede, fail, disappear *Opposite*: surge ■ *n* **receding tide**, ebb tide, outgoing tide, falling tide *Opposite*: flow

ebb and flow *v* **fluctuate**, vacillate, vary ■ *n* **shift**, fluctuation, vacillation, variation, flux

ebullience *n* **joviality**, enthusiasm, liveliness, happiness, cheerfulness *Opposite*: lugubriousness

ebullient *adj* **jovial**, enthusiastic, lively, happy, bouncy *Opposite*: lugubrious

e-cash *n* **electronic cash**, digital cash, smart card

eccentric *adj* **odd**, unconventional, unorthodox, unusual, peculiar *Opposite*: conventional ■ *n* **oddity**, character, original, case *(infml)*

eccentricity *n* 1 **oddness**, unconventionality, peculiarity, strangeness, weirdness *Opposite*: conventionality 2 **quirk**, peculiarity, foible, idiosyncrasy, oddity

ecclesiastic *n* **clergyman**, clergywoman, priest, cleric, minister

ecclesiastical *adj* **church**, clerical, religious, apostolic, papal *Opposite*: secular

echelon *n* **level**, rank, grade, tier, class

echo *n* **reverberation**, resonance, repeat, boom, ricochet ■ *v* 1 **reverberate**, resonate, resound, boom, rebound 2 **repeat**, reiterate, copy, parrot, confirm

echoing *adj* **resounding**, reverberating, reflecting, ringing, resonant

eclectic *adj* **heterogeneous**, varied, wide-ranging, extensive, diverse *Opposite*: narrow

eclecticism *n* **extensiveness**, range, diversity, scope, variety

eclipse *v* 1 **hide**, conceal, obscure, cover, darken 2 **outdo**, overshadow, outshine, surpass, overwhelm

ecofriendly *adj* **biodegradable**, green, environmentally friendly, sustainable

ecological *adj* **environmental**, environmentally friendly, natural, biological, organic

ecologist *n* **environmentalist**, biologist, natural scientist, naturalist, conservationist

e-commerce *n* **e-business**, e-tailing, cybermarketing, electronic transactions

economic *adj* 1 **financial**, monetary, fiscal, pecuniary, commercial 2 **profitable**, cost-effective, moneymaking, lucrative, efficient *Opposite*: uneconomic

economical *adj* 1 **frugal**, parsimonious, thrifty, careful, sparing *Opposite*: wasteful 2 **inexpensive**, cheap, cost-effective, low-cost, budget *Opposite*: expensive

economize *v* **cut back**, cut down, retrench, save, scrimp and save *Opposite*: spend

economy *n* 1 **frugality**, thrift, cost-cutting, saving, parsimony *Opposite*: extravagance 2 **saving**, cutback, retrenchment, reduction, scaling-down ■ *adj* **cheap**, budget, reduced, family, low-cost *Opposite*: expensive

WORD BANK

❏ **types of economic conditions** austerity, boom, boom and bust, deflation, depression, downswing, downturn, hyperinflation, inflation, inflationary spiral, recession, recovery, reflation, slump, stagflation, upswing, upturn

❏ **types of economic systems** collectivism, command economy, free enterprise economy, free market economy, market economy, mixed economy, new economy, planned economy, private economy, service economy

ecosystem *n* **natural environment**, biome, biota, ecology, environment

ecstasy *n* 1 **joy**, delight, elation, bliss, rapture *Opposite*: misery 2 **trance**, high, frenzy, state *(infml) Opposite*: stupor

ecstatic *adj* 1 **overjoyed**, delighted, thrilled, elated, blissful *Opposite*: miserable 2 **elated**, high, overexcited, frenzied, in a frenzy *Opposite*: calm

eddy *n* **whirlpool**, swirl, vortex, whirl, maelstrom

edge *n* 1 **border**, rim, boundary, perimeter, periphery *Opposite*: center 2 **advantage**, upper hand, superiority, control, authority 3 **brink**, verge, threshold, point 4 **sharp-**

ness, bitterness, acidity, harshness, venom
■ *v* 1 **approach**, skirt, sidle, pick your way, creep 2 **border**, frame, trim, fringe, enclose

edgewise *adv* **sideways**, side-on, crossways, across, obliquely

edging *n* **border**, trim, fringe, hem, frill

edgy *adj* **nervous**, on edge, anxious, jumpy, jittery *Opposite*: relaxed

edible *adj* **eatable**, fit for human consumption, palatable, appetizing, comestible *(fml) Opposite*: poisonous

edict *n* **proclamation**, announcement, pronouncement, decree, statute

edification *n* **improvement**, education, enlightenment, instruction, elevation *Opposite*: obfuscation

edifice *n* 1 **building**, construction, pile, structure, mansion 2 **organization**, network, structure, association, group

edify *v* **enlighten**, inform, educate, instruct, improve *Opposite*: obfuscate

edifying *adj* **educational**, informative, illuminating, instructive, scholastic

edit *v* 1 **rewrite**, revise, amend, rework, correct 2 **oversee**, run, manage, be in charge of, direct

edited *adj* 1 **amended**, corrected, revised, rewritten, redrafted *Opposite*: unedited 2 **abridged**, concise, shortened, summarized, truncated *Opposite*: complete

edition *n* **version**, publication, copy, issue, impression

editor *n* 1 **publishing supervisor**, publishing manager, editor in chief, managing editor, executive editor 2 **line editor**, copy editor, copyreader, corrector, checker

editorial *n* **editorial column**, viewpoint, perspective, essay, commentary

editorialize *v* **expound**, pontificate, spout, preach, sermonize

edit out *v* **delete**, remove, cut, omit, abridge

educate *v* **teach**, instruct, edify, tutor, train. *See* COMPARE AND CONTRAST *at* **teach**.

educated *adj* 1 **well-informed**, well-read, learned, erudite, knowledgeable *Opposite*: uneducated 2 **cultured**, cultivated, tasteful, sophisticated, refined *Opposite*: boorish

educated guess *n* **guess**, estimation, estimate, guesstimate, approximation

education *n* **teaching**, learning, schooling, tutoring, instruction

educational *adj* **instructive**, enlightening, didactic, edifying, informative

educator *n* **teacher**, instructor, lecturer, professor

eerie *adj* **unnerving**, uncanny, weird, strange, peculiar

efface *v* **obliterate**, eradicate, destroy, wear away, rub out

effect *n* 1 **result**, consequence, outcome, upshot, end product 2 **influence**, weight,

force, power, validity 3 **impression**, meaning, sense, impact, purpose ■ *v (fml)* **achieve**, carry out, produce, bring about, realize

effective *adj* 1 **successful**, efficient, productive, useful, helpful *Opposite*: ineffective 2 **real**, actual, in effect, active, operative *Opposite*: nominal 3 **operational**, operative, in force, in operation, in effect *Opposite*: inoperative

---

COMPARE AND CONTRAST CORE MEANING: producing a result

effective causing the desired or intended result; **efficient** capable of achieving the desired result with the minimum use of resources, time, and effort; **effectual** *(fml)* potentially successful in producing a desired or intended result; **efficacious** *(fml)* having the power to achieve the desired result, especially an improvement in somebody's physical condition.

---

effectively *adv* 1 **efficiently**, successfully, productively, well, excellently *Opposite*: ineffectively 2 **in reality**, to all intents and purposes, in point of fact, in all but name

effectiveness *n* **efficiency**, productiveness, efficacy, success, use *Opposite*: ineffectiveness

effects *(fml) n* **belongings**, property, personal property, possessions, things

effectual *(fml) adj* **effective**, worthwhile, successful, productive, helpful *Opposite*: ineffectual

effervesce *v* **hiss**, fizz, bubble, sparkle, froth

effervescence *n* 1 **fizz**, bubbles, sparkle, froth, foam 2 **vivacity**, vibrancy, vitality, animation, sparkle *Opposite*: languor

effervescent *adj* 1 **fizzy**, sparkling, bubbly, aerated, bubbling *Opposite*: still 2 **lively**, vibrant, bubbly, bouncy, sparkling *Opposite*: dull

efficacious *(fml) adj* **effective**, efficient, successful, productive, useful *Opposite*: ineffective

efficacy *n* **effectiveness**, efficiency, usefulness, productiveness, worth *Opposite*: ineffectiveness

efficiency *n* **competence**, efficacy, effectiveness, productivity, proficiency *Opposite*: inefficiency

efficient *adj* 1 **well-organized**, effective, competent, capable, able *Opposite*: ineffective 2 **inexpensive**, timesaving, laborsaving, economical, cost-effective *Opposite*: wasteful. *See* COMPARE AND CONTRAST *at* **effective**.

effigy *n* **image**, statue, icon, figure, figurine

effluent *n* **waste**, sewage, bilge water, seepage, runoff

effort *n* 1 **exertion**, energy, determination, force, strength *Opposite*: ease 2 **attempt**, try, endeavor, go, shot

effortless *adj* **easy**, natural, unforced, graceful, unproblematic *Opposite*: strenuous

effortlessness n ease, naturalness, smoothness, simplicity, facility Opposite: difficulty

effrontery n impudence, nerve, boldness, gall, arrogance

effusion n outpouring, gush, rush, expression, declaration

effusive adj gushing, demonstrative, fulsome, vociferous, extravagant Opposite: reserved

e.g. adv for example, for instance, say, let's say, perhaps

egalitarian adj equal, classless, free, democratic, equal opportunity Opposite: class-conscious

egg n reproductive cell, ovum, egg cell, ovule ■ v urge, incite, spur, encourage, push Opposite: dissuade

egghead (infml) n intellectual, brain (infml), bookworm (infml), rocket scientist (infml)

egg on v encourage, urge, push, incite, spur Opposite: dissuade

eggshell n protective covering, shell, case, casing, covering

ego n personality, character, self, self-image, self-worth

egocentric see egotistical

egoism, egoist, egoistic see egotism, egotist, egotistical

egomaniac see egotist

egotism n self-centeredness, selfishness, conceit, vanity, arrogance Opposite: altruism

egotist n narcissist, self-seeker, individualist, self-publicist, self-aggrandizer

egotistical adj selfish, conceited, vain, self-centered, self-important Opposite: altruistic

eiderdown n quilt, comforter, continental quilt, duvet, bedspread

either adj 1 whichever, either one, one or the other, any 2 each, both Opposite: neither

eject v 1 expel, emit, get rid of, spew, spout 2 expel, banish, drive out, throw out, remove

eke out v 1 make something last, spin out, make a little go a long way, draw out, use sparingly Opposite: squander 2 supplement, complement, add to, pad out, make up Opposite: diminish 3 scrape, scratch, scrape together, scratch out, make

elaborate adj 1 complex, complicated, intricate, detailed, involved Opposite: straightforward 2 sumptuous, extravagant, ornate, decorative, rich Opposite: simple ■ v 1 expound, expand, enlarge, go into detail, explain Opposite: condense 2 complicate, work up, build on, develop, detail Opposite: simplify

elaboration n amplification, embellishment, explanation, expansion, development

élan (literary) n panache, verve, vivacity, flair, dash

elapse v pass, pass by, intervene, slip away, go by

elastic adj 1 stretchy, expandable, flexible, supple, resilient Opposite: rigid 2 flexible, adaptable, changeable, variable, mutable Opposite: inflexible. See COMPARE AND CONTRAST at pliable.

elasticized adj stretchy, elastic, expanding, expandable, stretchable Opposite: rigid

elate v exhilarate, thrill, excite, lift, uplift Opposite: dishearten

elated adj ecstatic, overjoyed, thrilled, delighted, euphoric Opposite: disheartened

elation n ecstasy, delight, euphoria, jubilation, excitement Opposite: despair

elbow v prod, jostle, nudge, shove, dig

elbowroom n 1 space, room, room to spare, room to maneuver 2 scope, freedom, room to maneuver, leeway, choice

elder n leader, head, chief

elderly adj senior, aging, old, aged, of advanced years Opposite: young

eldest adj oldest, first-born, first

elect v 1 vote for, return, vote into office, pick, select 2 choose, opt for, decide on, select, designate ■ adj designated, future, chosen, selected

elected adj chosen, designated, selected, voted, nominated

election n 1 vote, poll, ballot 2 selection, choice, appointment, designation, nomination

electioneer v campaign, whistle-stop, canvass, run, stump (infml)

elective adj 1 voting, chosen by election, filled by election, passed by vote Opposite: appointed 2 optional, voluntary, free, selective, discretionary Opposite: compulsory

elector n voter, member of the electorate, voting member, constituent

electoral adj democratic, voting, election, polling, balloting

electorate n people, voters, registered voters, voting public, constituency

electric adj 1 electronic, electrically powered, battery-operated, plug-in, rechargeable 2 absorbing, charged, exciting, thrilling, emotional Opposite: boring

electrical see electric

electricity n current, voltage, power, energy, electrical energy

electrified adj 1 excited, captivated, thrilled, transfixed, awestruck Opposite: bored 2 electric, electrically powered, wired-up, connected

electrify v captivate, transfix, thrill, excite, exhilarate Opposite: bore

electrifying adj exciting, stirring, thrilling, captivating, stimulating Opposite: boring

electrode n conductor, rod, anode, cathode, probe

electronic *adj* 1 **electric**, microelectronic, electrical, automated, computer-operated 2 **computerized**, high-tech, on-screen, online, computer

electronics *n* **microchip technology**, microelectronics, computer electronics, integrated circuit technology, semiconductor technology

elegance *n* **grace**, style, sophistication, chic, taste *Opposite*: inelegance

elegant *adj* **sophisticated**, stylish, graceful, chic, well-designed *Opposite*: inelegant

elegiac *(fml) adj* **mournful**, sad, melancholic, funereal, plaintive *Opposite*: cheerful

elegy *n* **funeral song**, dirge, requiem, poem, speech

element *n* 1 **component**, part, section, division, portion 2 **hint**, amount, quantity, touch, bit 3 **factor**, cause, feature, component, ingredient 4 **habitat**, environment, milieu, medium, domain

elemental *adj* **rudimentary**, basic, fundamental, essential, primary

elementary *adj* **basic**, simple, straightforward, uncomplicated, plain

elements *n* **rudiments**, basics, fundamentals, essentials, foundations

elephantine *adj* 1 **ponderous**, lumbering, clumsy, slow, heavy *Opposite*: dainty 2 **huge**, enormous, colossal, gigantic, massive *Opposite*: minute

elevate *v* 1 **lift**, lift up, raise, uplift, hoist *Opposite*: lower 2 **promote**, raise, advance, move up, further *Opposite*: demote

elevated *adj* 1 **raised**, raised up, lifted, high, higher 2 **preeminent**, eminent, important, prominent, high *Opposite*: lowly

elevation *n* 1 **height**, altitude, rise *Opposite*: depth 2 **raise**, promotion, advancement, boost *Opposite*: demotion

elevator *n* **storage plant**, silo, grain elevator

eleventh-hour *adj* **ultimate**, last-minute, last-ditch, final

elf *n* **pixie**, imp, sprite, fairy, gnome

elfin *adj* **sylphlike**, petite, dainty, tiny, waiflike

elicit *v* 1 **provoke**, cause, produce, bring about, occasion 2 **draw out**, draw, bring out, extract, obtain *Opposite*: repress

eligibility *n* **suitability**, aptness, entitlement, appropriateness, fitness *Opposite*: unsuitability

eligible *adj* 1 **qualified**, entitled, suitable, fit, appropriate *Opposite*: ineligible 2 **single**, unmarried, unattached, available

eliminate *v* 1 **remove**, eradicate, abolish, get rid of, do away with *Opposite*: retain 2 **destroy**, kill, exterminate, liquidate, wipe out *(infml) Opposite*: preserve 3 **defecate**, urinate, excrete, expel, pass

elimination *n* **removal**, abolition, exclusion, rejection, eradication *Opposite*: preservation

elite *n* **best**, cream, cream of the crop, elect, crème de la crème *Opposite*: hoi polloi ■ *adj* **choice**, best, select, selective, leading *Opposite*: run-of-the-mill

elitism *n* **exclusiveness**, exclusivity, superiority, selectivity, selectiveness *Opposite*: equality

elitist *adj* **exclusive**, discriminatory, selective, superior, snobbish *Opposite*: egalitarian

elixir *n* 1 **medicine**, tincture, solution, tonic, preparation 2 **potion**, restorative, tonic, cure-all, snake oil

ellipsis *n* **abbreviation**, contraction, elision, truncation, abridgment

elliptical *adj* 1 **oval**, ovoid, ovate, egg-shaped, elongated 2 **concise**, succinct, cryptic, indirect, oblique *Opposite*: verbose

elocution *n* **diction**, articulation, pronunciation, enunciation, delivery

elongate *v* **lengthen**, draw out, extend, stretch, prolong *Opposite*: shorten

elongated *adj* **lengthened**, stretched out, extended, drawn-out, prolonged *Opposite*: shortened

elope *v* **run away**, run off, escape, decamp, abscond *Opposite*: return

elopement *n* **flight**, escape, desertion, decampment, truancy *Opposite*: return

eloquence *n* **expressiveness**, articulateness, articulacy, persuasiveness, expression *Opposite*: inarticulacy

eloquent *adj* **expressive**, fluent, articulate, well-spoken, persuasive *Opposite*: inarticulate

else *adj* **different**, new, other, experimental ■ *adv* 1 **as well**, besides, in addition, other, more 2 **other**, otherwise, differently, different, new

elucidate *v* **explain**, clarify, explicate, expound, illuminate *Opposite*: confuse

elucidation *n* **clarification**, illumination, exposition, explanation, explication *Opposite*: obfuscation

elude *v* 1 **escape**, flee, evade, get away, dodge 2 **baffle**, confound, foil, puzzle, stump

elusive *adj* **indefinable**, subtle, intangible, vague, indescribable *Opposite*: obvious

elusiveness *n* **indefinability**, subtlety, intangibility, vagueness, tenuousness *Opposite*: accessibility

emaciated *adj* **thin**, wasted, skeletal, withered, shrunken *Opposite*: plump. *See* COMPARE AND CONTRAST *at* thin.

emaciation *n* **thinness**, skinniness, gauntness, scrawniness, scragginess *Opposite*: plumpness

e-mail *n* **electronic mail**, electronic message, communication, correspondence ■ *v* **send**, flame, spam, ping, chat

emanate v 1 originate, come, stem, spring, derive 2 (fml) radiate, emit, give off, give out, send out Opposite: absorb

emancipate v liberate, set free, free, release, unshackle Opposite: enslave

emancipation n liberation, freedom, release, deliverance (fml), manumission (fml)

emasculate (fml) v weaken, enfeeble, undermine, enervate, unnerve Opposite: empower

emasculated adj ineffectual, powerless, helpless, impotent, weak Opposite: strong

embalm v mummify, conserve, preserve, fix, keep

embankment n ridge, bank, mound, defenses, dam

embargo n ban, restriction, prohibition, restraint, stoppage Opposite: permission ■ v 1 forbid, prohibit, ban, stop, restrict Opposite: permit 2 confiscate, seize, take away, expropriate, snatch

embark v board, get on, go aboard Opposite: disembark

embark on v begin, start, commence, engage in, set off on Opposite: abandon

embarrass v humiliate, mortify, shame, abash, show up Opposite: honor

embarrassed adj uncomfortable, self-conscious, ill at ease, nervous, ashamed Opposite: proud

embarrassing adj awkward, uncomfortable, uneasy, disconcerting, trying

embarrassment n awkwardness, blushes, humiliation, mortification, shame Opposite: pride

embassy n consulate, legation, mission, delegation, deputation

embed v implant, set in, insert, drive in, push in

embellish v 1 decorate, adorn, embroider, beautify, ornament Opposite: simplify 2 exaggerate, elaborate, overdo, aggrandize, enhance Opposite: understate

embellishment n 1 decoration, adornment, ornamentation, embroidery, beautification 2 exaggeration, elaboration, aggrandizement, enhancement, enlargement Opposite: understatement

ember n cinder, ash, coal

embezzle v misappropriate, misuse, appropriate, steal, cheat. See COMPARE AND CONTRAST at steal.

embezzlement n misappropriation, misuse, appropriation, theft, larceny

embezzler n swindler, fraud, thief, larcenist, pilferer

embitter v disillusion, poison, sour, estrange, alienate

embittered adj disillusioned, bitter, resentful, sour, disaffected Opposite: mellow

emblazon v 1 decorate, adorn, embellish, ornament, illustrate 2 (literary) extol, celebrate, glorify, praise, honor

emblem n symbol, crest, logo, sign, badge

emblematic adj symbolic, representative, characteristic, illustrative, exemplary

emblematical see emblematic

embodiment n personification, example, quintessence, incarnation, epitome

embody v exemplify, symbolize, represent, personify, epitomize

embolden v encourage, hearten, buoy up, bolster, reassure Opposite: discourage

emboss v stamp, chase, tool, engrave, mark

embrace v 1 hug, hold, enfold, cuddle, clasp Opposite: release 2 accept, welcome, adopt, take up, support Opposite: reject 3 comprise, contain, include, incorporate, involve Opposite: exclude ■ n hold, hug, cuddle, clinch, clasp Opposite: release

embroider v 1 sew, stitch, cross-stitch, trim, decorate 2 elaborate, embellish, exaggerate, overstate, inflate Opposite: understate

embroil v involve, entangle, enmesh, ensnare, entrap

embryo n beginning, rudiment, germ, kernel, seed

embryonic adj developing, emergent, nascent, primary, early Opposite: advanced

emcee (infml) n MC, master of ceremonies, host ■ v host, present, introduce

emend v alter, correct, amend, revise, rewrite

emerge v 1 come out, appear, materialize, come into view, come into sight Opposite: disappear 2 come to light, transpire, leak out 3 arise, appear, occur, develop, begin

emergence n appearance, rise, advent, arrival, development Opposite: decline

emergency n crisis, disaster, tragedy, accident, danger ■ adj spare, extra, backup, alternative, reserve

emergent adj developing, up-and-coming, embryonic, growing, nascent Opposite: established

emigrant n expatriate, migrant, immigrant, settler, exile Opposite: native

emigrate v trek, migrate, travel, move away, leave Opposite: return

emigration n migration, expatriation, exile, relocation, exodus Opposite: return

eminence n distinction, renown, reputation, fame, importance Opposite: anonymity

eminent adj well-known, renowned, important, distinguished, famous Opposite: unknown

eminently adv very, highly, extremely, exceedingly, exceptionally

emir n ruler, commander, prince, leader, governor

emirate n principality, country, state, nation, land

emissary n representative, envoy, ambassador, messenger, agent

emission n release, production, discharge, emanation, secretion *Opposite*: absorption

emit v produce, release, give off, give out, send out *Opposite*: absorb

emollient adj soothing, palliative, placatory, calmative, calming *Opposite*: disruptive ■ n balm, lotion, moisturizer, ointment, salve *Opposite*: irritant

emolument (fml) n payment, remuneration, reward, fee, compensation. *See* COMPARE AND CONTRAST *at* wage.

emotion n feeling, sentiment, reaction, passion, excitement

emotional adj 1 moving, touching, poignant, affecting, bittersweet 2 expressive, open, demonstrative, emotive, sensitive *Opposite*: impassive

emotionless adj impassive, blank, unemotional, detached, cold *Opposite*: emotional

emotive adj sensitive, emotional, poignant, affecting, moving

empathize v identify with, understand, sympathize, commiserate, relate to *Opposite*: dismiss

empathy n understanding, sympathy, compassion, responsiveness, identification *Opposite*: indifference

emperor n ruler, tsar, sovereign, king, head of state *Opposite*: subject

emphasis n stress, importance, weight, accent, prominence

emphasize v highlight, stress, accentuate, call attention to, underline *Opposite*: understate

emphatic adj 1 forceful, categorical, vigorous, definite, unequivocal *Opposite*: hesitant 2 resounding, absolute, ringing, clear, evident *Opposite*: ambiguous

empire n territory, realm, kingdom, domain

empirical adj experiential, experimental, observed, pragmatic, practical *Opposite*: theoretical

empiricism n pragmatism, experimentation, observation, practicality

empiricist n pragmatist, observer, experimenter, realist, researcher *Opposite*: theorist

employ v 1 pay, retain, use, hire, take on *Opposite*: dismiss 2 use, utilize, make use of, occupy, spend *Opposite*: waste ■ n employment, service, pay, hire, engagement *Opposite*: unemployment. *See* COMPARE AND CONTRAST *at* use.

employed adj working, in a job, in employment, engaged, active *Opposite*: unemployed

employee n worker, operative, servant, wage earner, member *Opposite*: employer

employer n boss, company, manager, owner, proprietor *Opposite*: employee

employment n 1 service, pay, hire, engagement, occupation *Opposite*: unemployment 2 occupation, job, profession, trade, work

emporium n retail store, department store, warehouse, bazaar, superstore

empower v 1 authorize, allow, sanction, permit, vest *Opposite*: forbid 2 inspire, embolden, encourage, galvanize, rouse *Opposite*: discourage

empowerment n 1 authorization, enabling, permission, consent, dispensation *Opposite*: embargo 2 liberation, enfranchisement, emancipation, inspiration, encouragement

empress n ruler, tsarina, sovereign, queen, head of state *Opposite*: subject

emptiness n 1 bareness, barrenness, blankness, desolation, hollowness *Opposite*: fullness 2 meaninglessness, worthlessness, purposelessness, hollowness, futility *Opposite*: purpose

empty adj 1 unfilled, bare, blank, vacant, hollow *Opposite*: full 2 idle, futile, ineffectual, unproductive, insincere 3 meaningless, pointless, vain, hollow, futile *Opposite*: meaningful ■ v drain, clear, pour out, discharge, clear out *Opposite*: fill. *See* COMPARE AND CONTRAST *at* vacant, vain.

empty-handed adj unsuccessful, frustrated, thwarted, unrewarded, defeated *Opposite*: successful

empty-headed adj stupid, silly, vacuous, frivolous, inane *Opposite*: intelligent

emulate v 1 imitate, follow, copy, mimic, ape 2 compete with, vie with, contend with, rival, outdo. *See* COMPARE AND CONTRAST *at* imitate.

emulation n imitation, competition, rivalry, mimicry, simulation *Opposite*: originality

emulsify v blend, combine, beat together, stir together, mix *Opposite*: separate

emulsion n suspension, blend, mixture, cream, mix

enable v allow, permit, make possible, empower, qualify *Opposite*: prevent

enact v 1 pass, ratify, endorse, decree, sanction *Opposite*: reject 2 perform, act out, play, portray, represent

enactment n 1 performance, performing, acting out, portrayal, representation 2 passing, ratification, ratifying, endorsement, sanctioning

enamel n coating, varnish, veneer, glaze, lacquer ■ v coat, paint, varnish, lacquer, cover

enamored adj in love, charmed, captivated, taken with, besotted *Opposite*: repelled

en bloc adv all together, all at once, as one, collectively, en masse *Opposite*: separately

encamp v set up camp, set up, install, base, settle

encampment n camp, military camp, campground, base camp, army camp

encapsulate *v* **sum up**, summarize, put in a nutshell, epitomize, condense *Opposite*: expand

encase *v* **cover**, enclose, sheathe, coat, wrap *Opposite*: uncover

encased *adj* **covered**, enclosed, sheathed, coated, wrapped *Opposite*: uncovered

enchant *v* **charm**, captivate, fascinate, enthrall, entrance *Opposite*: disgust

enchanted *adj* **charmed**, enthralled, captivated, delighted, entranced *Opposite*: disgusted

enchanting *adj* **charming**, captivating, enthralling, alluring, delightful *Opposite*: disgusting

enchantment *n* **charm**, attraction, delight, fascination, allure

encircle *v* **surround**, enclose, ring, circle enfold

enclave *n* **1 region**, reserve, territory, commune, area **2 group**, community, class, clique, clan (*infml*)

enclose *v* **1 surround**, hem in, encircle, enfold, ring **2 wall**, fence, hedge, pen, seal off **3 include**, put in, attach, insert, add *Opposite*: leave out

enclosed *adj* **surrounded**, bounded, hemmed in, fenced, walled *Opposite*: open

enclosure *n* **1 inclusion**, attachment, insertion, addition, insert **2 field**, arena, stockade, pen, corral

encode *v* **encrypt**, code, put into code, scramble, convert *Opposite*: decode

encompass *v* **include**, cover, take in, incorporate, involve *Opposite*: exclude

encore *n* **repeat**, extra, impromptu item, curtain call, reprise

encounter *v* **1 meet**, come across, bump into, run into, come upon **2 face**, confront, contend with, grapple with, combat *Opposite*: avoid ■ *n* **1 meeting**, chance meeting, happenstance **2 confrontation**, engagement, contest, argument, skirmish

encourage *v* **1 inspire**, hearten, cheer, raise your spirits, buoy up *Opposite*: discourage **2 support**, egg on, urge, animate, incite *Opposite*: discourage **3 foster**, assist, help, aid, nurture *Opposite*: stifle

encouragement *n* **support**, backup, help, reassurance, inspiration *Opposite*: discouragement

encouraging *adj* **hopeful**, heartening, cheering, reassuring, promising *Opposite*: discouraging

encroach *v* **intrude**, infringe, invade, trespass, make inroads into *Opposite*: respect

encroachment *n* **infringement**, violation, advance, intrusion, invasion

encrusted *adj* **covered**, coated, thick, crusted, caked *Opposite*: bare

encrypt *v* **encode**, code, put into code, scramble, translate *Opposite*: decode

encumber *v* **burden**, hinder, hamper, impede, get in the way *Opposite*: facilitate

encumbrance *n* **burden**, hindrance, nuisance, impediment, handicap *Opposite*: help

encyclopedia *n* **reference work**, compendium, compilation, fact file, information database

encyclopedic *adj* **comprehensive**, full, complete, in-depth, thorough *Opposite*: narrow

end *n* **1 finish**, conclusion, ending, closing stages, last part *Opposite*: beginning **2 extremity**, edge, side, tip, top *Opposite*: middle **3 purpose**, aim, reason, objective, goal **4 remnant**, leftover, stub, scrap, remainder *Opposite*: whole **5 death**, downfall, decline, ruin, dissolution *Opposite*: birth **6 consequence**, outcome, upshot, result, end result *Opposite*: cause ■ *v* **1 stop**, finish, conclude, close, terminate *Opposite*: begin **2 result**, finish, conclude, culminate, end up

endanger *v* **put in danger**, jeopardize, risk, compromise, threaten *Opposite*: protect

endangered *adj* **rare**, in danger of extinction, dying out, scarce, threatened *Opposite*: common

endear *v* **commend**, recommend, ingratiate, make appealing, insinuate *Opposite*: alienate

endearing *adj* **appealing**, attractive, charming, engaging, winning *Opposite*: unappealing

endearment *n* **kind word**, sweet nothing, blandishment, loving word, flattery *Opposite*: insult

endeavor *v* (*fml*) **try**, strive, attempt, make every effort, do your utmost *Opposite*: neglect ■ *n* **1 attempt**, effort, try, exertion, best shot **2 enterprise**, undertaking, bid, venture, foray

endemic *adj* **widespread**, prevalent, common, rife, rampant *Opposite*: rare

ending *n* **end**, finish, finale, conclusion, culmination *Opposite*: beginning

end it all *v* **commit suicide**, kill yourself, take your own life, do away with yourself, die by your own hand

endless *adj* **1 boundless**, infinite, limitless, without end, interminable *Opposite*: finite **2 eternal**, continual, continuous, nonstop, perpetual *Opposite*: temporary

endorse *v* **1 sanction**, approve, ratify, recommend, countersign *Opposite*: reject **2 support**, back, advocate, subscribe to, favor *Opposite*: denounce

endorsed *adj* **permitted**, recognized, sanctioned, recommended, authorized *Opposite*: disallowed

endorsement *n* **1 authorization**, commendation, confirmation, countersignature, ratification **2 backing**, support, advocacy, sanction, encouragement

endow *v* award, donate, give, bequeath, provide

endowment *n* **1** donation, gift, bequest, legacy, award **2** natural gift, talent, ability, capability, aptitude

end product *n* outcome, end result, result, upshot, product

end result *n* outcome, end product, result, upshot, product

end up *v* finish up, finish off, transpire, turn out, result in *Opposite*: start out

endurable *adj* tolerable, manageable, bearable, passable, sufferable *Opposite*: intolerable

endurance *n* **1** staying power, strength, stamina, fortitude, resolution *Opposite*: weakness **2** stamina, fortitude, tolerance, grit, guts *(slang)* **3** persistence, perseverance, tenacity, continuance, survival

endure *v* **1** bear, tolerate, undergo, put up with, go through *Opposite*: succumb **2** last, continue, go on, persist, survive *Opposite*: perish

enduring *adj* lasting, continuing, durable, stable, long-term *Opposite*: short-lived

end user *n* user, purchaser, shopper, consumer, client *Opposite*: producer

endways *see* endwise

endwise *adv* endways on, jutting out, end foremost, end uppermost, endways

enemy *n* opponent, adversary, rival, opposition, competitor *Opposite*: friend

energetic *adj* **1** lively, active, vigorous, brisk, animated *Opposite*: lethargic **2** strenuous, vigorous, brisk, dynamic, challenging *Opposite*: easy

energize *v* invigorate, strengthen, boost, galvanize, electrify *Opposite*: enervate

energizing *adj* invigorating, stimulating, enlivening, revitalizing, reviving *Opposite*: draining

energy *n* **1** vigor, liveliness, dynamism, vitality, drive *Opposite*: lethargy **2** power, force, strength, momentum, resources

enervate *v* weaken, debilitate, sap the strength of, drain, fatigue *Opposite*: invigorate

enervating *adj* exhausting, weakening, enfeebling, fatiguing, draining *Opposite*: invigorating

enfeeble *v* weaken, debilitate, enervate, deplete, exhaust *Opposite*: strengthen

enfold *v* enclose, surround, wrap, wrap up, envelop

enforce *v* **1** apply, carry out, impose, implement, make compulsory **2** coerce, oblige, compel, require, insist on

enforced *adj* compulsory, obligatory, forced, imposed, required *Opposite*: optional

enforcement *n* implementation, application, execution, putting into practice, administration

enfranchise *v* give somebody the vote, empower, emancipate, liberate, naturalize *Opposite*: disenfranchise

enfranchisement *n* empowerment, naturalization, suffrage, manumission *(fml)* *Opposite*: disenfranchisement

engage *v* **1** involve, occupy, engross, absorb, take part **2** appoint, take on, employ, hire, contract *Opposite*: dismiss **3** battle, fight, combat, contest, encounter **4** hold, keep, absorb, charm, attract *Opposite*: repel **5** connect, slot in, fit into place, interlock, join *Opposite*: disengage

engaged *adj* **1** spoken for, involved, promised, tied up, betrothed *(fml)* *Opposite*: unattached **2** busy, occupied, unavailable, in use, being used *Opposite*: free

engagement *n* **1** appointment, meeting, rendezvous, assignation, visit **2** employment, job, position, situation, post **3** battle, fight, encounter, conflict, action. *See* COMPARE AND CONTRAST *at* fight.

engaging *adj* attractive, appealing, charming, winning, fetching *Opposite*: unattractive

engender *v* **1** produce, cause, create, bring about, stimulate **2** *(fml)* beget, give birth to, generate, propagate, spawn

engine *n* machine, motor, turbine, mechanism, generator

WORD BANK

❑ **parts of an engine** alternator, ball bearing, cam, camshaft, cog, cogwheel, coil, crank, crankshaft, cylinder, distributor, gasket, gear, gearbox, gearing, lever, manifold, oil pan, piston, pump, radiator, seal, shaft, solenoid, spark plug, starter, tappet, valve

engineer *v* bring about, cause, contrive, concoct, plot

engorge *v* swell up, swell, puff up, expand, blow up *Opposite*: deflate

engrave *v* etch, score, scratch, carve, incise

engraving *n* **1** etching, lithograph, print, reproduction, woodcut **2** engraved design, carving, etching, linocut, inscription

engross *v* absorb, captivate, hold your attention, hold, engage *Opposite*: bore

engrossed *adj* absorbed, captivated, enthralled, gripped, held *Opposite*: bored

engrossing *adj* absorbing, captivating, enthralling, gripping, interesting *Opposite*: uninteresting

engulf *v* swallow up, overcome, overwhelm, immerse, submerge

enhance *v* improve, add to, increase, boost, develop *Opposite*: impair

enhanced *adj* improved, greater, strengthened, heightened, boosted *Opposite*: diminished

enhancement *n* improvement, augmentation, development, enrichment, heightening *Opposite*: detraction

enigma n **paradox**, conundrum, problem, mystery, puzzle

enigmatic adj **mysterious**, inscrutable, puzzling, perplexing, obscure Opposite: straightforward. See COMPARE AND CONTRAST at **obscure**.

enjoin (fml) v **order**, command, instruct, direct, tell Opposite: forbid

enjoy v **1 like**, delight in, appreciate, revel in, relish Opposite: dislike **2 benefit from**, have, experience, be blessed with, possess Opposite: lack

enjoyable adj **pleasant**, agreeable, pleasing, entertaining, amusing Opposite: boring

enjoyment n **pleasure**, delight, satisfaction, gratification, fun Opposite: boredom

enjoy yourself v **be amused**, be delighted, let yourself go, play, party (infml)

enlarge v **1 increase**, expand, broaden, widen, lengthen Opposite: decrease **2 detail**, elaborate, expand, amplify, flesh out Opposite: compress. See COMPARE AND CONTRAST at **increase**.

enlargement n **expansion**, extension, amplification, increase, widening Opposite: decrease

enlighten v **tell**, inform, explain to, instruct, edify

enlightened adj **1 rational**, unprejudiced, reasonable, logical, open-minded Opposite: irrational **2 educated**, aware, informed, knowledgeable, wise Opposite: unaware

enlightening adj **informative**, instructive, edifying, helpful, educational Opposite: uninformative

enlightenment n **explanation**, illumination, clarification, insight, information Opposite: ignorance

enlist v **1 join**, join up, sign on, sign up, enroll **2 recruit**, conscript, procure, solicit, count on Opposite: reject

enliven v **liven up**, cheer up, invigorate, wake up, cheer Opposite: put a damper on

en masse see en bloc

enmesh v **entangle**, tangle, trap, catch, catch up Opposite: disentangle

enmity n **hostility**, hate, hatred, ill will, animosity Opposite: goodwill

ennui n **boredom**, languor, world-weariness, tedium, weariness Opposite: excitement

enormity n **1 atrociousness**, horror, monstrousness, wickedness, heinousness Opposite: goodness **2 atrocity**, abomination, outrage, evil, horror Opposite: kindness **3 size**, extent, vastness, scale, immensity

enormous adj **huge**, vast, massive, giant, mammoth Opposite: tiny

enormously adv **extremely**, very, a lot, a great deal, hugely Opposite: slightly

enough adj **sufficient**, adequate, ample, plenty, abundant Opposite: insufficient

enquire v **ask**, find out, query, investigate, probe Opposite: reply

enrage v **infuriate**, anger, make your blood boil, madden, incense Opposite: calm

enraged adj **furious**, infuriated, angry, beside yourself, fuming Opposite: calm

enrapture (fml) v **entrance**, delight, captivate, enchant, mesmerize Opposite: bore

enrich v **improve**, supplement, enhance, deepen, develop Opposite: diminish

enrichment n **enhancement**, improvement, augmentation, amelioration, upgrading Opposite: diminution

enroll v **register**, sign up, put your name down, join, join up

enrollment n **registration**, matriculation, signing up, admission, acceptance Opposite: resignation

ensconce (literary) v **entrench**, hide, hide away, conceal, screen Opposite: expose

ensemble n **1 band**, company, troupe, group, corps **2 suit**, costume, coordinates, outfit, getup (infml) **3 collection**, assembly, aggregate, set, combination ■ adj **collaborative**, collective, joint, group, cooperative Opposite: solo

enshrine v **protect**, treasure, hallow, preserve, cherish

enshroud v **obscure**, hide, mask, shield, cover Opposite: expose

ensign n **flag**, pennant, colors, banner, standard

enslave v **subjugate**, dominate, subject, bind, yoke Opposite: liberate

ensnare v **enmesh**, embroil, catch, trap, entrap Opposite: set free

ensue v **1 follow**, succeed, follow on, result, arise Opposite: precede **2 result**, follow, proceed, arise, derive Opposite: precede

ensuing adj **resultant**, subsequent, succeeding, resulting, following Opposite: preceding

ensure v **make sure**, make certain, safeguard, guarantee, confirm

entail v **involve**, require, demand, need, necessitate

entangle v **1 tangle**, twist, intertwine, snarl up, catch up Opposite: disentangle **2 snare**, trap, catch, snag, enmesh Opposite: free

entanglement n **predicament**, tangle, muddle, morass, mess

enter v **1 go in**, go into, come in, come into, cross the threshold Opposite: leave **2 input**, insert, put in, record, register Opposite: delete **3 submit**, put in, propose, hand in, state **4 compete**, participate, take part, take up, try **5 join**, sign up, agree to, enlist, enroll **6 walk on**, come on, appear, make an entrance Opposite: exit

enter into v **become involved in**, take part in, join in, throw yourself into, participate in Opposite: withdraw

enter on v start, begin, enter upon, move into, start out on *Opposite*: finish

enterprise n **1 initiative**, innovativeness, creativity, inventiveness, originality *Opposite*: apathy **2 venture**, project, activity, endeavor, undertaking **3 business**, company, firm, corporation, organization

enterprising adj **innovative**, inventive, imaginative, resourceful, adventurous *Opposite*: unadventurous

entertain v **1 amuse**, divert, distract, regale, interest *Opposite*: bore **2 accommodate**, wine and dine, feed, invite, regale *Opposite*: visit **3 consider**, think about, give thought to, contemplate, think over *Opposite*: reject

entertainer n **performer**, artiste, artist, talent, turn

WORD BANK

❏ **types of entertainers** actor, actress, clown, comedian, comic, conjurer, contortionist, costar, dancer, DJ, double act, emcee *(infml)*, impressionist, juggler, magician, mime, movie star, musician, popstar, rapper, singer, standup comedian, stooge, straight man, street entertainer, street musician, street performer, trapeze artist, ventriloquist

---

entertaining adj **amusing**, enjoyable, diverting, pleasurable, charming *Opposite*: dull

entertainment n **1 entertaining**, performing, acting, show business, theater **2 amusement**, fun, diversion, distraction, enjoyment *Opposite*: boredom **3 show**, production, concert, attraction, performance

enter upon v **start**, begin, enter on, move into, start out on *Opposite*: finish

enthrall v **captivate**, charm, mesmerize, beguile, fascinate *Opposite*: bored

enthralled adj **fascinated**, engrossed, gripped, captivated, absorbed *Opposite*: bored

enthralling adj **fascinating**, beguiling, engrossing, gripping, captivating *Opposite*: boring

enthrone *(fml)* v **crown**, instate, ordain, swear in, consecrate *Opposite*: dethrone

enthuse v **1 stimulate**, galvanize, excite, spur to action, impassion *Opposite*: bore **2 be enthusiastic**, be passionate, talk excitedly, show enthusiasm, rave

enthusiasm n **1 eagerness**, interest, passion, fervor, gusto *Opposite*: apathy **2 craze**, interest, hobby, passion, mania

enthusiast n **fan**, fanatic, buff, aficionado, aficionada

enthusiastic adj **eager**, keen, passionate, fervent, excited *Opposite*: apathetic

entice v **lure**, tempt, induce, seduce, bribe *Opposite*: put off

enticement n **lure**, temptation, incentive, inducement, bribery *Opposite*: deterrent

enticing adj **tempting**, alluring, inviting, attractive, appealing *Opposite*: uninviting

entire adj **1 whole**, complete, full, total, perfect *Opposite*: part **2 absolute**, complete, total, thorough, unqualified *Opposite*: partial

entirety n **sum**, whole, wholeness, totality, entireness *Opposite*: part

entitle v **1 enable**, allow, permit, sanction, authorize *Opposite*: debar **2 title**, call, name, dub, label

entitled adj **1 permitted**, in your own right, eligible, allowed, enabled *Opposite*: barred **2 titled**, called, named, dubbed, labeled

entitlement n **right**, power, prerogative, privilege, claim

entity n **object**, thing, article, being, unit *Opposite*: nonentity

entourage n **staff**, associates, following, followers, train

entrails n **guts**, intestines, bowels, viscera, innards *(infml)*

entrance n **1 entry**, way in, doorway, door, opening *Opposite*: exit **2 arrival**, entry, appearance, entering, ingress *(fml)* *Opposite*: departure **3 admission**, entry, ticket, pass, admittance ■ v **captivate**, engross, fascinate, charm, delight *Opposite*: bore

entrance hall n **lobby**, foyer, reception area, hallway, vestibule

entrancing adj **captivating**, enchanting, enthralling, spellbinding, fascinating *Opposite*: boring

entrant n **applicant**, contestant, candidate, participant, competitor. *See* COMPARE AND CONTRAST *at* candidate.

entrap v **trick**, deceive, ensnare, trap, lure

entrapment n **trap**, frame, snare, trick, setup *(infml)*

entreat v **plead**, beg, pray, ask, request *Opposite*: demand

entreaty n **appeal**, plea, petition, request, supplication *(fml)* *Opposite*: demand

entrée n **1 appetizer**, starter, hors d'oeuvre, first course, antipasto **2 introduction**, induction, entrance, access, admittance *Opposite*: exclusion

entrench v **embed**, ensconce, ingrain, root, establish

entrepreneur n **businessperson**, trader, organizer, impresario, financier

entrepreneurial adj **business**, small-business, commercial, risk-taking, empire-building

entrust v **trust**, commend, delegate, assign, deliver *Opposite*: deprive

entry n **1 admission**, entrance, access, pass, ticket **2 record**, item, note, account, statement **3 entrance**, doorway, door, opening, access *Opposite*: exit **4 application**, submission, attempt, effort, go *Opposite*: withdrawal

entwine v tangle, entangle, twist, interweave, interlace *Opposite*: undo

enumerate v 1 detail, list, spell out, itemize, catalog 2 **count**, number, tally, compute, reckon *Opposite*: estimate

enunciate v 1 **pronounce**, articulate, voice, utter, speak *Opposite*: mumble 2 **express**, spell out, detail, state, put forward *Opposite*: suppress

enunciation n 1 **pronunciation**, articulation, diction, speech 2 **expression**, assertion, declaration, proclamation, clarification *Opposite*: suppression

envelop v **enclose**, encircle, encase, engulf, swathe *Opposite*: unwrap

envelope n **cover**, wrapper, covering, wrapping, casing

enviable adj **desirable**, fortunate, lucky, privileged, to die for *Opposite*: unenviable

envious adj jealous, green with envy, resentful, spiteful, covetous

environment n 1 **nature**, ecosystem, earth, world, natural world 2 **surroundings**, setting, situation, atmosphere, scene 3 **background**, upbringing, circumstances, conditions, situation

environmental adj **ecological**, conservation, conservational, environmentally friendly, ecofriendly

environmentalist n **ecologist**, conservationist, preservationist, green

environs n **vicinity**, neighborhood, surroundings, locality, environment

envisage *see* envision

envision v **imagine**, foresee, predict, visualize, see

envoy n **representative**, diplomat, attaché, emissary, herald

envy n jealousy, greed, bitterness, resentment, spite *Opposite*: goodwill ■ v covet, desire, resent, begrudge, grudge

eons n a long time, years, ages (infml!), eternity (infml), forever (infml)

epaulet n **decoration**, insignia, strap, chevron

ephemeral adj short-lived, passing, fleeting, brief, momentary *Opposite*: lasting. *See* COMPARE AND CONTRAST *at* temporary.

ephemeralness n **brevity**, transitoriness, transience, fleetingness, temporariness *Opposite*: timelessness

epic n **classic**, historical fiction, costume drama, period piece, extravaganza *Opposite*: short story ■ adj **marathon**, heroic, classic, larger-than-life, impressive *Opposite*: minuscule

epicure n **gourmet**, gastronome, connoisseur, bon vivant, epicurean

epicurean adj 1 **hedonistic**, decadent, pleasure-seeking, pleasure-loving, sensualist *Opposite*: ascetic 2 **gastronomic**, gourmet, culinary ■ n **gourmet**, gastronome, connoisseur, bon vivant, epicure

epidemic n 1 **plague**, outbreak, endemic, scourge, contagion 2 **spate**, wave, rash, craze, increase *Opposite*: decrease ■ adj **widespread**, wide-ranging, prevalent, rampant, sweeping *Opposite*: restricted. *See* COMPARE AND CONTRAST *at* widespread.

epidermis n skin, hide, flesh, cuticle, integument

epigram n **witticism**, saying, axiom, ditty, rhyme

epilogue n **conclusion**, coda, speech, monologue *Opposite*: prologue

episode n 1 **incident**, affair, chapter, event, occurrence 2 **installment**, chapter, part, section, scene 3 **occurrence**, incidence, attack, outbreak, bout

episodic adj 1 **sporadic**, intermittent, periodic, discontinuous, irregular *Opposite*: regular 2 **serialized**, discontinuous, divided

epistle (fml) n **letter**, missive, communication, message, communiqué

epitaph n **inscription** legend, caption, epigraph

epithet n **nickname**, description, label, sobriquet, appellation (fml)

epitome n **essence**, personification, embodiment, model, quintessence *Opposite*: antithesis

epitomize v typify, characterize, exemplify, personify, embody

epoch n **era**, age, time, period, eon

epoch-making adj **historic**, crucial, important, momentous, earthshattering *Opposite*: insignificant

equable adj **composed**, calm, easygoing, unflappable, placid *Opposite*: jumpy

equal adj 1 **identical**, equivalent, like, alike, the same *Opposite*: unequal 2 **on a par**, even, uniform, level, on a plane *Opposite*: unequal ■ n **match**, equivalent, counterpart, parallel, peer ■ v 1 **come to**, amount to, equate, make, correspond 2 **match**, rival, keep pace with, copy, meet

equality n parity, fairness, equivalence, likeness, equal opportunity *Opposite*: inequality

equalize v **match**, level, even out, align, line up *Opposite*: differentiate

equally adv 1 **similarly**, likewise, in the same way, by the same token, alike *Opposite*: conversely 2 **evenly**, uniformly, regularly, equivalently, alike *Opposite*: unequally

equanimity n **composure**, calmness, levelheadedness, equability, self-control *Opposite*: volatility

equate v **associate**, liken, link, connect, parallel *Opposite*: contrast

equation n **reckoning**, calculation, comparison, equivalence, equality

equestrian adj **riding**, equine, show jumping, horsy, horseracing

equidistant *adj* **halfway between**, midway between, between, in between, intermediate

equilateral *adj* **symmetrical**, regular, square, rectangular, triangular

equilibrium *n* **balance**, symmetry, steadiness, stability, evenness *Opposite*: imbalance

equip *v* **1 provide**, endow, fit out, outfit, arm **2 prepare**, train, school, qualify, ground

equipment *n* **tools**, apparatus, tackle, utensils, paraphernalia

equitable *(fml) adj* **fair**, evenhanded, reasonable, justifiable, rightful *Opposite*: unfair

equity *n* **fairness**, impartiality, justice, evenhandedness, fair play *Opposite*: injustice

equivalence *n* **correspondence**, sameness, likeness, similarity, equality *Opposite*: difference

equivalent *adj* **equal**, corresponding, correspondent, alike, same *Opposite*: different ■ *n* **counterpart**, equal, opposite number, parallel, twin

equivocal *adj* **vague**, ambiguous, confusing, ambivalent, misleading *Opposite*: unambiguous

equivocate *v* **prevaricate**, beat around the bush, vacillate, be evasive, quibble *Opposite*: speak your mind

equivocation *n* **vagueness**, indirectness, ambiguity, prevarication, weasel words *(infml) Opposite*: directness

era *n* **age**, epoch, eon, time, period

eradicate *v* **eliminate**, get rid of, destroy, exterminate, do away with *Opposite*: introduce

eradication *n* **abolition**, purge, annihilation, extermination, obliteration *Opposite*: introduction

erase *v* **rub out**, remove, delete, expunge, obliterate

erasure *n* **removal**, destruction, eradication, elimination, deletion

erect *v* **1 build**, construct, assemble, set up, raise *Opposite*: demolish **2 create**, set up, found, initiate, establish ■ *adj* **straight**, upright, vertical, rigid, stiff *Opposite*: prone

erection *n* **1 construction**, building, assembly, creation, formation **2** *(fml)* **structure**, building, construction, edifice, pile

erode *v* **wear away**, wear down, corrode, eat away, eat into

eroded *adj* **weathered**, worn, weatherbeaten, corroded, eaten away

erosion *n* **corrosion**, attrition, destruction, loss *Opposite*: accretion

erotic *adj* **sexy**, sensual, stimulating, suggestive, arousing

err *v* **go wrong**, blunder, slip up *(infml)*, go astray, stumble

errand *n* **task**, duty, run, chore, job

errant *adj* **wayward**, sinful, naughty, misbehaving, delinquent *Opposite*: well-behaved

erratic *adj* **unpredictable**, unreliable, inconsistent, irregular, changeable *Opposite*: consistent

erroneous *adj* **mistaken**, flawed, wrong, specious, inaccurate *Opposite*: correct

error *n* **mistake**, fault, blunder, inaccuracy, miscalculation. *See* COMPARE AND CONTRAST *at* **mistake**.

ersatz *adj* **faux**, artificial, substitute, reproduction, imitation *Opposite*: genuine

erstwhile *adj* **former**, previous, past, old, earlier *Opposite*: current

erudite *adj* **scholarly**, knowledgeable, well-educated, well-read, cultured *Opposite*: uneducated

erudition *n* **knowledge**, learnedness, education, learning, culture *Opposite*: ignorance

erupt *v* **1 explode**, blow up, break out, flare up, go off *Opposite*: subside **2 explode**, lose your temper, hit the roof *(infml)*, blow your top *(infml)*, blow a fuse *(infml) Opposite*: hold back

eruption *n* **outbreak**, outburst, explosion, upsurge, epidemic

escalate *v* **intensify**, worsen, heighten, go from bad to worse, deteriorate *Opposite*: de-escalate

escalating *adj* **mounting**, rising, intensifying, ever-increasing, swelling *Opposite*: diminishing

escalation *n* **rise**, growth, boom, increase, climb *Opposite*: reduction

escalator *n* **moving staircase**, staircase, stairway, stairs

escapade *n* **adventure**, jaunt, antic, caper, spree

escape *v* **1 flee**, run away, get away, break out, run off *Opposite*: be captured **2 avoid**, evade, dodge, elude, shake off *Opposite*: face **3 leak out**, leak, drip, seep, flow ■ *n* **1 seepage**, leakage, leak, outflow, discharge **2 flight**, getaway, break, breakout, escaping *Opposite*: capture **3 diversion**, distraction, pastime, leisure activity, escapism

escapee *n* **runaway**, fugitive, absconder, deserter, fleer

escapism *n* **diversion**, distraction, entertainment, relaxation, daydreaming

escapist *adj* **diverting**, distracting, entertaining, relaxing, fantasy *Opposite*: realistic

escarpment *n* **cliff**, bluff, scarp, ridge, incline

eschew *v* **avoid**, shun, have nothing to do with, steer clear of, give a wide berth to *Opposite*: embrace

escort n **guide**, attendant, bodyguard, chaperon, aide ■ v **accompany**, guide, usher, lead, attend

esoteric adj **obscure**, mysterious, abstruse, impenetrable, cryptic *Opposite*: straightforward

ESP n **extra-sensory perception**, psychic powers, clairvoyance, second sight, telepathy

especial adj **special**, unusual, exceptional, extraordinary, outstanding *Opposite*: ordinary

especially adv 1 **exceptionally**, remarkably, notably, markedly, outstandingly 2 **particularly**, in particular, specially, above all, more than ever

espousal n **adoption**, backing, support, championship, promotion *Opposite*: opposition

espouse v 1 **take up**, adopt, support, back, advocate *Opposite*: oppose 2 *(archaic)* **marry**, wed, take your vows, walk down the aisle, get hitched *(infml)*

espy *(literary)* v **notice**, spy, catch sight of, spot, sight

essay n **paper**, thesis, dissertation, composition, article ■ v *(fml)* **try**, endeavor, strive, have a shot, attempt

essence n 1 **spirit**, core, heart, quintessence, crux 2 **concentrate**, extract, tincture, distillate, concentration

essential adj 1 **necessary**, vital, indispensable, important, crucial *Opposite*: unnecessary 2 **fundamental**, basic, elemental, key, central *Opposite*: secondary ■ n **necessity**, requisite, prerequisite, requirement, must *Opposite*: extravagance. *See* COMPARE AND CONTRAST *at* **necessary**.

essentially adv 1 **fundamentally**, basically, in essence, in effect, really 2 **effectively**, more or less, broadly, in the main, for the most part

essentials n **basics**, fundamentals, prerequisites, rudiments, necessities *Opposite*: frills

establish v 1 **set up**, found, institute, start, create *Opposite*: close down 2 **determine**, find out, prove, confirm, verify *Opposite*: disprove

established adj **recognized**, well-known, traditional, conventional, customary *Opposite*: new

establishment n 1 **founding**, formation, creation, setting up, institution *Opposite*: dissolution 2 **business**, firm, company, institution, concern 3 **authorities**, powers that be, the ruling classes, the established order, the system

estate n 1 **plantation**, land, park, lands, parkland 2 **area**, zone, business park, development, housing development 3 **assets**, property, holdings, worth, fortune

esteem v **appreciate**, cherish, hold dear, venerate, value *Opposite*: scorn ■ n **regard**, respect, admiration, high regard, honor *Opposite*: contempt. *See* COMPARE AND CONTRAST *at* **regard**.

esteemed adj **respected**, valued, honored, revered, admired *Opposite*: scorned

estimable adj **admirable**, worthy, deserving, laudable, venerable *Opposite*: unimpressive

estimate n 1 **quote**, price, estimation, valuation, costing *Opposite*: cost 2 **approximation**, estimation, guess, educated guess, evaluation ■ v **approximate**, guess, assess, reckon, value *Opposite*: calculate

estimated adj **projected**, assessed, valued, appraised, approximate

estimation n 1 **educated guess**, approximation, estimate, guesstimate, evaluation 2 **opinion**, assessment, inference, evaluation, view *Opposite*: fact

estop *(archaic)* v **prevent**, stop, thwart, prohibit, halt

estranged adj **alienated**, separated, apart, at odds, on bad terms

estrangement n **separation**, hostility, rupture, distancing, disaffection *Opposite*: reconciliation

estuary n **river mouth**, bay, inlet, sound, creek *Opposite*: source

etc. adv **et cetera**, and so on, and so forth, and the like, and the rest

etch v **engrave**, scratch, scrape, cut, incise

etching n **engraving**, drawing, print, design, impression

eternal adj **everlasting**, undying, unending, never-ending, perpetual *Opposite*: transient

eternity n 1 **time without end**, perpetuity, infinity, all time, ever and a day *(infml)* **a long time**, eons, forever *(infml)*, ages *(infml)*

ether *(literary)* n **air**, atmosphere, heaven, sky

ethereal adj 1 **ghostly**, otherworldly, unearthly, spectral, shadowy *Opposite*: earthly 2 **waiflike**, frail, delicate, airy, insubstantial *Opposite*: substantial

ethic n **moral belief**, ethos, idea, principle, code

ethical adj **moral**, principled, right, fair, decent *Opposite*: unethical

ethics n **principles**, morals, beliefs, moral code, moral principles

ethnic adj **cultural**, traditional, folkloric, racial, indigenous

ethnicity n **culture**, way of life, origin, background, traditions

ethos n **philosophy**, beliefs, principles, code, character

etiquette n **manners**, good manners, protocol, custom, propriety *Opposite*: bad manners

eulogize v **praise**, extol, laud, sing the praises of, praise to the skies *Opposite*: criticize

eulogy n tribute, acclamation, acclaim, praise, homage Opposite: criticism

euphemism n neutral term, understatement, rewording, bowdlerization, code word Opposite: dysphemism

euphemistic adj inoffensive, polite, bowdlerized, cleaned up, neutral Opposite: dysphemistic

euphoria n elation, ecstasy, jubilation, rapture, excitement Opposite: despair

euphoric adj overjoyed, elated, ecstatic, joyful, joyous Opposite: despairing

evacuate v 1 empty, abandon, withdraw from, leave, vacate Opposite: fill 2 send away, remove from, move out of, clear from Opposite: bring in

evacuation n removal, clearing, emptying, withdrawal, flight Opposite: influx

evacuee n refugee, émigré, emigrant, migrant

evade v 1 avoid, dodge, escape, elude, shirk Opposite: confront 2 equivocate, prevaricate, hedge, stonewall (infml), fudge (infml)

evaluate v assess, appraise, gauge, estimate, calculate

evaluation n assessment, appraisal, estimation, calculation, valuation

evaluator n assessor, surveyor, inspector, judge

evanescent adj short-lived, fleeting, momentary, ephemeral, passing Opposite: permanent

evangelical adj enthusiastic, fervent, eager, zealous, keen Opposite: apathetic

evaporate v vanish, fade away, fade, disappear, melt away Opposite: solidify

evaporation n vaporization, drying up, loss, vanishing, disappearance

evasion n 1 avoidance, dodging, elusion, circumvention, skirting 2 prevarication, equivocation, hedging, stonewalling (infml), fencing (infml)

evasive adj elusive, slippery, shifty, indirect, oblique Opposite: direct

evasiveness n indirectness, equivocation, shiftiness, elusiveness, ambiguousness Opposite: directness

eve n day before, evening before, night before

even adj 1 smooth, flat, level, straight, unfluctuating Opposite: uneven 2 equal, similar, level, on a par, just as Opposite: unequal 3 constant, steady, uniform, unvarying, unchanging Opposite: fluctuating ■ n (literary) evening, twilight, dusk, nightfall, sunset

evenhanded adj fair, impartial, unbiased, just, equal Opposite: biased

evenhandedness n fairness, impartiality, equity, justice, neutrality Opposite: partiality

even if conj though, albeit, although, even though, in spite of the fact that

evening n twilight, sunset, dusk, nightfall, late afternoon Opposite: morning

evenness n consistency, sameness, symmetry, uniformity, flatness Opposite: irregularity

even out v 1 flatten, level, smooth, square, align 2 balance out, balance, level out, balance up, equalize Opposite: unbalance

event n occasion, happening, occurrence, incident, affair

even-tempered adj calm, unflappable, equable, placid, imperturbable Opposite: temperamental

eventful adj exciting, action-packed, lively, busy, hectic Opposite: dull

eventual adj ultimate, final, last, ensuing, subsequent Opposite: immediate

eventuality (fml) n possibility, prospect, case, contingency, outcome

eventually adv finally, ultimately, sooner or later, in the end, in due course Opposite: immediately

even up v equalize, stabilize, even out, redress the balance, balance up Opposite: unbalance

ever adv always, forever, eternally, all the time, constantly Opposite: never

evergreen adj immortal, perennial, ever popular, classic, timeless Opposite: stale

---

WORD BANK

❏ **types of evergreen trees** bay, bo tree, boxwood, bunya, carob, cedar, cola, cypress, eucalyptus, fir, fir tree, gum tree, holly, juniper, kahikatea, kauri, larch, laurel, mahogany, mangrove, monkey puzzle, pine, redwood, sandalwood, sequoia, spruce, yew

---

everlasting adj eternal, endless, ceaseless, never-ending, perpetual Opposite: transient

evermore (literary) adv forever, for all time, always, eternally

ever-present adj ubiquitous, chronic, pervasive, omnipresent

every adj each, all, every single, every one

everyday adj ordinary, average, normal, unremarkable, common Opposite: extraordinary

everyone n everybody, all, one and all, each person, each one Opposite: no one

everything n all, the whole thing, the lot, the whole lot, the whole shebang (infml) Opposite: nothing

everywhere adv all over, ubiquitously, far and wide, the world over, universally

evict v throw out, expel, turn out, eject, remove Opposite: install

eviction n removal, expulsion, ejection, throwing out, exclusion

evidence n 1 indication, sign, signal, mark, suggestion 2 proof, confirmation, facts, data, substantiation ■ v show, demonstrate, evince, make clear, prove

evident *adj* **obvious**, plain, apparent, clear, manifest *Opposite*: obscure

evidently *adv* **1 obviously**, clearly, plainly, manifestly, palpably **2 apparently**, seemingly, as far as we know, it would seem, as far as one can tell

evil *adj* **1 wicked**, malevolent, sinful, malicious, criminal *Opposite*: good **2 foul**, vile, nasty, horrible, unpleasant *Opposite*: pleasant ■ *n* **wickedness**, malevolence, sin, iniquity, vice *Opposite*: good

evildoer *n* **wrongdoer**, sinner, criminal, offender, delinquent *Opposite*: benefactor

evilness *n* **wickedness**, badness, evil, immorality, sinfulness *Opposite*: goodness

evince *v* **show**, display, reveal, exhibit, manifest *Opposite*: conceal

evocation *n* **recreation**, elicitation, recall, air, hint

evocative *adj* **reminiscent**, suggestive, redolent, haunting

evoke *v* **call to mind**, bring to mind, suggest, call up, induce *Opposite*: suppress

evolution *n* **development**, fruition, growth, progress, progression *Opposite*: regression

evolve *v* **develop**, grow, progress, advance, go forward *Opposite*: regress

ewer *n* **jug**, pitcher, vessel, bottle, container

ex *adj* **former**, sometime, onetime, erstwhile, lapsed *Opposite*: future

exacerbate *v* **make worse**, worsen, aggravate, impair, intensify *Opposite*: soothe

exact *adj* **1 correct**, precise, accurate, strict, faithful *Opposite*: approximate **2 careful**, meticulous, precise, particular, thorough *Opposite*: careless ■ *v* **demand**, obtain, extort, extract, wrest

exacting *adj* **demanding**, testing, challenging, rigorous, tough *Opposite*: easy

exactitude *n* **precision**, correctness, accuracy, meticulousness, exactness *Opposite*: carelessness

exactly *adv* **precisely**, just, absolutely, quite, in every respect *Opposite*: approximately

exactness *n* **precision**, accuracy, exactitude, correctness, meticulousness *Opposite*: vagueness

exaggerate *v* **overstress**, embellish, embroider, make a mountain out of a molehill, inflate *Opposite*: understate

exaggerated *adj* **overstated**, inflated, embroidered, embellished, blown up *Opposite*: understated

exaggeration *n* **overstatement**, hyperbole, embellishment, embroidery, overemphasis *Opposite*: understatement

exalt *(fml)* *v* **1 promote**, raise, elevate, intensify, boost **2 praise**, laud, acclaim, applaud, pay tribute to *Opposite*: disparage

exaltation *(fml)* *n* **1 adulation**, adoration, acclaim, acclamation, praise *Opposite*: condemnation **2 excitement**, rapture, exhilaration, happiness, joy *Opposite*: despair

exalted *(fml)* *adj* **high**, lofty, glorious, dignified, illustrious *Opposite*: lowly

exam *see* **examination**

examination *n* **1 inspection**, scrutiny, checkup, investigation, analysis **2 test**, assessment, exam, paper, oral exam

examine *v* **1 look at**, inspect, scrutinize, observe, study **2 consider**, think about, look into, investigate, research **3 test**, assess, grade, judge, question

examiner *n* **inspector**, auditor, surveyor, superintendent, assessor

example *n* **1 sample**, instance, case, case in point, specimen **2 model**, pattern, paradigm, standard, paragon

exasperate *v* **infuriate**, madden, frustrate, annoy, irritate *Opposite*: placate. *See* COMPARE AND CONTRAST *at* **annoy**.

exasperating *adj* **infuriating**, maddening, frustrating, vexing, annoying *Opposite*: calming

exasperation *n* **frustration**, irritation, enragement, annoyance, vexation

excavate *v* **dig**, mine, quarry, dig out, exhume *Opposite*: bury

exceed *v* **go beyond**, surpass, go above, go over, top *Opposite*: fall short

exceedingly *adv* **very**, exceptionally, remarkably, extremely, extraordinarily *Opposite*: slightly

excel *v* **shine**, stand out, outshine, outclass, surpass *Opposite*: fall behind

excellence *n* **fineness**, brilliance, superiority, distinction, quality *Opposite*: mediocrity

excellent *adj* **outstanding**, brilliant, exceptional, admirable, superb *Opposite*: poor

except *prep* **apart from**, but, excluding, with the exception of, aside from *Opposite*: including

excepting *see* **except**

exception *n* **exclusion**, omission, exemption, concession, allowance

exceptionable *(fml)* *adj* **offensive**, obnoxious, rude, objectionable, repugnant *Opposite*: inoffensive

exceptional *adj* **excellent**, brilliant, special, extraordinary, incomparable *Opposite*: ordinary

exceptionality *n* **rarity**, infrequency, extraordinariness, uniqueness, remarkableness *Opposite*: normality

exceptionally *adv* **very**, remarkably, extremely, extraordinarily, outstandingly *Opposite*: slightly

excerpt *n* **extract**, passage, quote, quotation, selection

excess *n* **1 surplus**, glut, overload, surfeit, overabundance *Opposite*: shortage **2 over-**

indulgence, intemperance, dissipation, inordinateness, prodigality *Opposite*: moderation ■ *adj* **extra**, additional, surplus, spare, superfluous

excesses *n* extremes, dissipation, intemperance, overindulgence, prodigality

excessive *adj* extreme, too much, unnecessary, unwarranted, undue *Opposite*: moderate

excessively *adv* very, extremely, overly, exceptionally, markedly *Opposite*: moderately

excessiveness *n* extremeness, exorbitance, extravagance, immoderateness *(fml)*, immoderation *(fml) Opposite*: moderation

exchange *v* switch, replace, trade, barter, substitute *Opposite*: keep ■ *n* **1 conversation**, argument, talk, chat, discussion **2 trade**, switch, barter, replacement, substitute

exchangeable *adj* redeemable, transferable, negotiable, commutable, interchangeable

exchange blows *v* fight, scuffle, go for each other, trade punches, brawl

excise *v* delete, remove, edit, cut out, expunge *Opposite*: insert

excision *n* editing, deletion, removal, cutting out, erasure *Opposite*: insertion

excitability *n* nervousness, edginess, volatility, fieriness, temper *Opposite*: coolness

excitable *adj* nervous, emotional, edgy, impulsive, volatile *Opposite*: unflappable

excite *v* **1 stimulate**, enthuse, animate, motivate, enliven *Opposite*: bore **2 incite**, agitate, provoke, instigate, stir up *Opposite*: soothe

excited *adj* **1 happy**, enthusiastic, eager, animated, motivated *Opposite*: indifferent **2 agitated**, nervous, provoked, overwrought, hot and bothered *Opposite*: calm

excitement *n* **1 enthusiasm**, eagerness, anticipation, pleasure, exhilaration *Opposite*: indifference **2 agitation**, tension, unrest, ferment, restlessness *Opposite*: calm

exciting *adj* thrilling, exhilarating, stirring, stimulating, electrifying *Opposite*: boring

exclaim *v* cry out, cry, shout, call out, call *Opposite*: whisper

exclamation *n* shout, cry, yell, scream, howl *Opposite*: whisper

exclude *v* **1 keep out**, bar, reject, leave out, prevent *Opposite*: welcome **2 reject**, rule out, eliminate, discount, ignore *Opposite*: include

excluding *prep* exclusive of, not including, without, apart from *Opposite*: including

exclusion *n* **1 keeping out**, barring, rejection, leaving out, prohibiting *Opposite*: welcome **2 rejection**, elimination, marginalization, prohibition, veto *Opposite*: inclusion **3 ban**, refusal, sanction, embargo, prohibition

exclusive *adj* **1 high-class**, elite, select, restricted, limited *Opposite*: inclusive **2 sole**, complete, undivided, full, whole *Opposite*: partial

exclusiveness *n* **1 luxury**, sophistication, refinement, superiority, stylishness **2 selectiveness**, selectivity, exclusivity, elitism, snobbery

exclusive of *adj* not including, excluding, leaving out, without, except for *Opposite*: including

excommunicate *v* exclude, bar, debar, expel, eject *Opposite*: admit

excommunication *n* exclusion, barring, debarring, expulsion, ejection *Opposite*: admission

excoriate *v* **1 skin**, peel, pare, strip, flay **2** *(fml)* criticize, denounce, attack, berate, upbraid *Opposite*: commend

excrescence *n* monstrosity, eyesore, blot, growth, outgrowth

excruciating *adj* **1 agonizing**, painful, unbearable, awful, terrible *Opposite*: pleasant **2 embarrassing**, tedious, stultifying, irritating, infuriating *Opposite*: enthralling

exculpate *(fml) v* free, let off, excuse, clear, release *Opposite*: arraign

exculpation *(fml) n* acquittal, exoneration, discharge, pardon, clearing *Opposite*: arraignment

excursion *n* **1 trip**, jaunt, outing, junket, tour **2 group**, team, party, expedition **3** *(fml)* digression, departure, detour, deviation, tangent

excusable *adj* understandable, forgivable, justifiable, explicable, pardonable *Opposite*: inexcusable

excuse *v* **1 forgive**, pardon, let off, acquit, absolve *Opposite*: blame **2 overlook**, make allowances for, pass over, tolerate, justify **3 exempt**, release, let off, free, relieve *Opposite*: oblige ■ *n* **justification**, reason, explanation, pretext, defense

excused *adj* exempted, released, exempt, let off, relieved *Opposite*: required

execrable *(fml) adj* terrible, awful, appalling, disgusting, repulsive *Opposite*: excellent

execute *v* **1 carry out**, perform, implement, complete, accomplish **2 put to death**, kill, murder, hang, electrocute. *See* COMPARE AND CONTRAST *at* perform.

execution *n* **1 implementation**, performance, accomplishment, carrying out, completing **2 putting to death**, capital punishment, the death sentence, killing, hanging

executive *n* manager, senior manager, director, administrator, official ■ *adj* **1 decision-making**, policymaking, managerial, management, administrative **2 expensive**, exclusive, high class, superior, select

executor *n* doer, prime mover, initiator, originator, architect

exemplar *(literary)* *n* **ideal**, model, paradigm, example, archetype

exemplary *adj* **1 admirable**, praiseworthy, excellent, perfect, ideal *Opposite*: shameful **2** *(fml)* **model**, archetypal, textbook, typical, classic

exemplify *v* **demonstrate**, typify, represent, illustrate, show

exempt *adj* **excused**, exempted, released, relieved, discharged *Opposite*: required ■ *v* **excuse**, free, let off, let go, release *Opposite*: oblige

exemption *n* **exception**, immunity, release, indemnity, exclusion *Opposite*: obligation

exercise *n* **1 move**, movement, drill, step, calisthenics **2 physical activity**, working out, training, drill *Opposite*: inactivity **3** *(fml)* **implementation**, carrying out, use, application, employment *Opposite*: avoidance ■ *v* **1 work out**, train, do exercises, drill **2 use**, put into effect, implement, apply, employ *Opposite*: avoid

exercises *n* **military exercises**, maneuvers, drills, war games

exert *v* **bring to bear**, use, apply, exercise, make use of

exertion *n* **effort**, action, application, physical exertion, energy *Opposite*: ease

exert yourself *v* **make an effort**, try hard, push yourself, strive, labor

exhale *v* **breathe out**, blow out, puff out, let your breath out, respire *Opposite*: inhale

exhaust *v* **1 tire out**, wear out, drain, fatigue, weaken *Opposite*: refresh **2 use up**, use, wear out, consume, drain *Opposite*: renew

exhausted *adj* **tired**, worn out, fatigued, drained, wearied *Opposite*: refreshed

exhausting *adj* **tiring**, wearing, fatiguing, killing, grueling *Opposite*: refreshing

exhaustion *n* **tiredness**, fatigue, collapse, weariness, enervation *Opposite*: energy

exhaustive *adj* **thorough**, complete, comprehensive, in-depth, full *Opposite*: superficial

exhibit *v* **1 display**, show, unveil, put on a display, put on view *Opposite*: hide **2 show off**, parade, flaunt, expose, display ■ *n* **exhibition**, display, show, showcase, showing

exhibition *n* **display**, show, showing, demonstration, exposition

exhibitionist *n* **attention seeker**, grandstander, extrovert, braggart, show-off *(infml)*

exhilarate *v* **excite**, elate, thrill, enliven, invigorate *Opposite*: bore

exhilarated *adj* **elated**, ecstatic, euphoric, overjoyed, delighted *Opposite*: indifferent

exhilaration *n* **excitement**, elation, high spirits, animation, happiness

exhort *v* **urge**, press, push, pressure, insist *Opposite*: forbid

exhortation *(fml)* *n* **appeal**, call, encouragement, urging, incitement

exhume *v* **dig up**, disinter, unearth, disentomb, disclose *Opposite*: bury

exigency *(fml)* *n* **need**, demand, requirement, emergency, necessity

exigent *(fml)* *adj* **1 urgent**, pressing, crucial, vital, important *Opposite*: unimportant **2 demanding** tough, testing, challenging, taxing *Opposite*: easy

exile *n* **1 émigré**, tax exile, expatriate, deportee, refugee **2 banishment**, deportation, expulsion, separation, ostracism ■ *v* **banish**, send away, deport, expel, separate

exist *v* **1 be**, be real, be present, be existent, happen **2 live**, be, survive, continue living, stay alive

existence *n* **being**, life, reality, presence, survival

existent *(fml)* *adj* **existing**, current, present, extant, ongoing

existing *adj* **present**, current, in effect, prevailing, standing

exit *n* **1 way out**, door, outlet, egress *(fml)* *Opposite*: entrance **2 departure**, exodus, walking out, leaving, going away *Opposite*: arrival ■ *v* **go out**, leave, depart, go, walk out *Opposite*: enter

exodus *n* **mass departure**, departure, migration, emigration, flight *Opposite*: arrival

exonerate *v* **clear**, absolve, acquit, vindicate, forgive *Opposite*: blame

exoneration *n* **1 pardon**, absolution, acquittal, vindication, exculpation *(fml)* *Opposite*: blame **2 release**, freeing, liberation, exemption, discharge

exorbitant *adj* **excessive**, inflated, ridiculous, dear, overpriced *Opposite*: reasonable

exorcize *v* **get rid of**, get free of, banish, drive out, force out

exotic *adj* **1 unusual**, out of the ordinary, novel, striking, interesting *Opposite*: ordinary **2 foreign**, from abroad, tropical, alien, nonnative *Opposite*: familiar

expand *v* **make bigger**, get bigger, enlarge, increase, develop *Opposite*: contract. See COMPARE AND CONTRAST *at* **increase**.

expandable *adj* **stretchy**, elastic, foldup, foldout, pullout

expand upon *v* **enlarge on**, elaborate on, give details, embellish, amplify

expanse *n* **area**, breadth, stretch, span, region

expansion *n* **growth**, development, increase, extension, spreading out *Opposite*: contraction

expansive *adj* **1 communicative**, generous, magnanimous, friendly, open *Opposite*: reserved **2 extensive**, spread-out, spacious, roomy, sizable *Opposite*: cramped

expansively adv 1 **at length**, extensively, widely, comprehensively, broadly Opposite: briefly 2 **effusively**, lavishly, openly, generously, jovially

expansiveness n 1 **size**, large size, mass, extent, reach 2 **effusiveness**, lavishness, openness, generousness, enthusiasm Opposite: reserve

expat (infml) see expatriate

expatriate n émigré, tax exile, emigrant, refugee, colonial Opposite: native

expect v 1 **imagine**, suppose, guess, think, believe 2 **wait for**, anticipate, look forward to, await, look ahead 3 **demand**, require, insist on, count on, anticipate

expectancy n **anticipation**, expectation, hope, suspense, bated breath

expectant adj 1 **eager**, hopeful, in suspense, hoping, on tenterhooks 2 **pregnant**, expecting, in the family way (dated infml)

expectation n **hope**, anticipation, expectancy, belief, prospect

expected adj **likely**, probable, foreseeable, predictable, awaited Opposite: surprising

expecting adj **pregnant**, expectant, in the family way (dated infml)

expectorant n **cough medicine**, linctus, cough syrup, medicine

expediency n 1 **convenience**, practicality, pragmatism, usefulness, feasibility 2 **appropriateness**, suitability, fitness, advisability, convenience Opposite: unsuitability

expedient adj 1 **appropriate**, fitting, suitable, advisable, necessary Opposite: inappropriate 2 **advantageous**, convenient, practical, useful, beneficial Opposite: altruistic ■ n **measure**, means, method, maneuver, device

expedite (fml) v **speed up**, accelerate, hurry up, advance, further Opposite: impede

expedition n 1 **journey**, excursion, voyage, trip, outing 2 **team**, party, crew, group, company

expeditious adj **speedy**, prompt, quick, swift, hasty Opposite: slow

expel v 1 **dismiss**, fire, eject, oust, throw out 2 **drive out**, force out, push out, eject, flush out

expend v 1 **use up**, use, consume, spend, burn up Opposite: conserve 2 (fml) **spend**, disburse, pay out, lay out, pay Opposite: save

expendable adj 1 **dispensable**, disposable, superfluous, unessential, nonessential Opposite: indispensable 2 **consumable**, replaceable, throwaway, disposable, usable Opposite: durable

expenditure n **spending**, expenses, payments, outflow, costs Opposite: income

expense n 1 **cost**, expenditure, outlay, disbursement, outflow Opposite: income 2 **price**, rate, figure, amount, price tag 3 **sacrifice**, cost, detriment, disadvantage, loss

expenses n **expenditures**, outlay, payments, costs, overheads Opposite: income

expensive adj 1 **luxurious**, exclusive, affluent, lavish, classy (infml) Opposite: cheap 2 **costly**, dear, high-priced, steep (infml), pricey (infml) Opposite: cheap

experience n 1 **involvement**, knowledge, skill, practice, understanding Opposite: inexperience 2 **occurrence**, incident, episode, encounter, event ■ v **feel**, go through, face, live through, undergo

experienced adj **knowledgeable**, skilled, practiced, qualified, veteran Opposite: inexperienced

experiment n **trial**, test, investigation, research, experimentation ■ v **test**, try out, investigate, try

experimental adj **new**, tentative, untried, trial, speculative Opposite: proven

experimentation n **testing**, research, investigation

expert n **specialist**, authority, professional, connoisseur, maven Opposite: amateur ■ adj **skilled**, skillful, practiced, proficient, professional Opposite: inexperienced

expertise n **skill**, knowledge, proficiency, capability, know-how (infml)

expertness n **skillfulness**, dexterity, knowledge, expertise, proficiency Opposite: inexperience

expiate v **make amends**, compensate, make up for, recompense, redress

expire v 1 **end**, run out, finish, terminate, conclude 2 (fml) **die**, pass away, pass on, perish, breathe your last (literary)

expiry n 1 **end**, ending, running out, finish, finishing Opposite: beginning 2 (fml) **death**, passing, end, dying, demise (fml)

explain v 1 **make clear**, describe, put in plain words, elucidate, clarify 2 **justify**, account for, defend, rationalize, vindicate

explanation n 1 **description**, account, clarification, enlightenment, details 2 **reason**, justification, rationalization, vindication, account

explanatory adj **descriptive**, instructive, illustrative, illuminating, clarifying

expletive n **swearword**, curse, oath, exclamation, obscenity

explicable adj **explainable**, understandable, reasonable, justifiable, rational Opposite: inexplicable

explicate v **explain**, elucidate, spell out, clarify, expound

explicit adj 1 **clear**, obvious, open, overt, plain Opposite: implicit 2 **definite**, precise, exact, specific, unequivocal Opposite: vague 3 **frank**, uninhibited, candid, open, graphic

explode v 1 **blow up**, go off, burst, erupt, burst out Opposite: implode 2 **get angry**,

fly into a rage, hit the ceiling, hit the roof
(infml), blow up (infml) Opposite: calm
down **3 disprove**, prove wrong, discredit,
invalidate, nullify Opposite: prove

exploit v **1 use**, develop, make use of, take
advantage of, utilize Opposite: waste
2 take advantage of, abuse, misuse, ill-use,
manipulate ■ n **feat**, deed, adventure,
activity, heroic act

exploitable adj **1 usable**, utilizable, consumable, available **2 gullible**, credulous,
innocent, vulnerable Opposite: shrewd

exploitation n **1 misuse**, abuse, mistreatment, taking advantage, manipulation **2 use**, utilization, development,
management, operation

exploitative adj **unfair**, unequal, abusive,
manipulative Opposite: fair

exploration n **1 traveling**, discovery, jour-
neying, adventure, voyaging **2 examination**, investigation, survey, study,
consideration

exploratory adj **investigative**, examining,
probing, tentative, experimental

explore v **1 travel**, discover, reconnoiter, see
the sights, sightsee **2 investigate**, study,
search, look at, survey

explorer n **traveler**, voyager, surveyor,
pioneer, pathfinder

explosion n **1 bang**, blast, detonation, eruption, burst **2 outburst**, fit, eruption, paroxysm, burst **3 upsurge**, leap, flood,
outbreak, eruption Opposite: slump

explosive adj **1 volatile**, unstable, unpredictable, dangerous Opposite: stable
2 short-tempered, quick-tempered, hotheaded, volatile, fiery Opposite: placid

WORD BANK
❏ **types of explosive material** dynamite, gel-
ignite, gunpowder, napalm, nitroglycerin,
plastic explosive, propellant, Semtex™, TNT
❏ **types of explosive weapons** A-bomb, anti-
ballistic missile, atomic bomb, ballistic missile,
bomb, booby trap, bunker-buster, cruise
missile, daisycutter, depth charge, firebomb,
guided missile, hand grenade, hydrogen bomb,
mine, missile, Molotov cocktail, nail bomb,
neutron bomb, nuclear missile, nuclear
warhead, nuclear weapon, pipe bomb, smart
bomb, torpedo, smoke bomb, warhead, time
bomb, weapon of mass destruction

exponent n **1 advocate**, proponent, promoter, fan, champion **2 interpreter**,
explainer, performer, practitioner

export v **1 sell abroad**, sell overseas, send
abroad, send overseas, ship Opposite:
import **2 spread**, transfer, carry across, pass
on, disseminate

expose v **1 open up**, reveal, uncover, bare,
display Opposite: cover **2 subject**, lay open
to, put in danger, endanger, imperil (fml)
3 blow the whistle on, unmask, reveal, lay
bare, bring to light Opposite: cover up

exposé n **disclosure**, revelation, leak, exposure, discovery

exposed adj **unprotected**, visible, uncovered,
bare, out in the open Opposite: covered

exposition n **1 description**, discussion,
explanation, account, clarification **2 exhibition**, fair, show, trade fair, display

expostulate v **disagree**, protest, object,
reprove, remonstrate. See COMPARE AND CON-
TRAST at **object**.

exposure n **1 contact**, experience, introduction, acquaintance, dealings **2 revelation**, disclosure, revealing, unveiling,
publicity Opposite: whitewash

expound v **explain**, expand on, talk about,
develop, illustrate

express v **1 state**, articulate, utter, voice,
communicate **2 squeeze out**, extract, press
out, force out ■ adj **1 fast**, rapid, direct,
nonstop, prompt Opposite: slow **2 precise**,
explicit, definite, exact, specific Opposite:
vague

expression n **1 look**, face, air, appearance,
countenance **2 phrase**, idiom, turn of
phrase, term, saying **3 communication**,
manifestation, illustration, example, demonstration **4 extraction**, squeezing out, pressing out, forcing out

expressionless adj **straight-faced**, unresponsive, impassive, poker-faced, inexpressive Opposite: expressive

expressive adj **1 communicative**, sensitive,
open, easy-to-read, animated Opposite:
impassive **2 representative**, representing,
demonstrating, signifying, indicative

expressively adv **meaningfully**, dramatically,
emotionally, sensitively, vividly Opposite:
blandly

expressivity n **articulacy**, eloquence, self-
expression, fluency, clarity Opposite:
inarticulacy

expressly adv **specifically**, particularly,
explicitly, clearly, definitely

expropriate v **steal**, confiscate, seize, commandeer, appropriate

expulsion n **dismissal**, exclusion, throwing
out, eviction, removal Opposite: admittance

expunge v **obliterate**, purge, erase, delete,
rub out Opposite: insert

expurgated adj **cut down**, abridged, censored, edited, bowdlerized

exquisite adj **1 beautiful**, gorgeous, delicate,
attractive, superb Opposite: ugly **2 excellent**, perfect, delightful, flawless, wonderful Opposite: flawed **3 discriminating**,
discerning, sensitive, fastidious, refined
4 intense, touching, moving, excruciating,
poignant Opposite: dull

exquisiteness n **beauty**, delicacy, daintiness,
perfection, attractiveness Opposite: ugliness

extant adj **existing**, in existence, present,

living, surviving *Opposite*: lost. *See*
COMPARE AND CONTRAST *at* **living**.

extemporaneous *adj* **extemporary**, extemporal, unrehearsed, impromptu, ad-lib
Opposite: rehearsed

extempore *adj* **extemporaneous**, ad-lib, off-the-cuff, impromptu, unrehearsed *Opposite*: rehearsed ■ *adv* **extemporaneously**, ad-lib, off the cuff, impromptu, spontaneously *Opposite*: rehearsed

extemporize *v* ad-lib, improvise, speak off the cuff, play it by ear, make it up as you go along *Opposite*: prepare

extend *v* **1** spread, spread out, range, cover, encompass **2** **continue**, reach, stretch, go on, run **3** **make bigger**, expand, enlarge, make longer, lengthen *Opposite*: curtail **4** **prolong**, stretch out, drag out, lengthen, postpone *Opposite*: cut short **5** **increase**, expand; widen, broaden, add to *Opposite*: decrease **6** **offer**, give, hold out, proffer, tender *Opposite*: withdraw. *See* COMPARE AND CONTRAST *at* **increase**.

extended *adj* **lengthy**, protracted, long, prolonged, stretched *Opposite*: cut short

extension *n* **1** **additional room**, addition, lean-to, conservatory, annex **2** **expansion**, enlargement, lengthening, broadening, increase *Opposite*: contraction **3** **delay**, postponement, leeway, allowance, extra time

extensive *adj* **1** **big**, large, huge, vast, massive *Opposite*: restricted **2** **wide**, widespread, wide-ranging, general, all-embracing *Opposite*: narrow

extensively *adv* **1** **at length**, lengthily, widely, far, broadly *Opposite*: briefly **2** **significantly**, considerably, greatly, to a great extent, to a large extent *Opposite*: insignificantly

extensiveness *n* **breadth**, comprehensiveness, fullness, richness, vastness *Opposite*: narrowness

extent *n* **1** **degree**, amount, level, range, scope **2** **size**, area, coverage, limit, boundary

extenuating *adj* **mitigating**, explanatory, justifying, moderating, palliative

exterior *adj* **external**, outside, outdoor, peripheral, outward *Opposite*: interior ■ *n* **1** **outside**, façade, elevation, surface, shell *Opposite*: interior **2** **appearance**, look, aura, veneer, front

exterminate *v* **kill**, eliminate, annihilate, massacre, destroy

extermination *n* **extinction**, annihilation, execution, killing, slaughter *Opposite*: preservation

external *adj* **outside**, exterior, outdoor, peripheral, outward *Opposite*: internal

externalize *v* **express**, give voice to, utter, get off your chest, voice *Opposite*: internalize

externally *adv* **outwardly**, on the outside, on

the exterior, on the surface, superficially *Opposite*: inwardly

extinct *adj* **nonexistent**, inexistent, died out, destroyed, vanished *Opposite*: living. *See* COMPARE AND CONTRAST *at* **dead**.

extinction *n* **death**, extermination, destruction, loss, annihilation *Opposite*: survival

extinguish *v* **1** **douse**, quench, snuff, stub out, smother *Opposite*: light **2** **end**, take away, destroy, snuff out, do away with **3** **eclipse**, overshadow, outshine, obscure, show up

extol *(fml or literary)* *v* **praise**, commend, eulogize, admire, worship *Opposite*: deprecate

extort *v* **extract**, obtain under duress, obtain by threat, wrest, wring

extortion *n* **coercion**, threats, blackmail, squeezing, force

extortionate *adj* **expensive**, exorbitant, inflated, high, overpriced *Opposite*: reasonable

extra *adj* **additional**, further, added, spare, second ■ *adv* **1** **more**, in addition, further, on top, spare **2** **especially**, particularly, ultra, exceptionally, more ■ *n* **optional extra**, addition, add-on, supplement, bonus

extract *v* **1** **take out**, remove, haul out, pull out, dig out *Opposite*: put in **2** **obtain**, unearth, extricate, root out, dig out **3** **extort**, force, wrest, wring, drag ■ *n* **excerpt**, cutting, quotation, citation, abstract

extraction *n* **1** **removal**, taking out, withdrawal, pulling out, drawing out *Opposite*: insertion **2** **origin**, birth, descent, ancestry, family

extracurricular *adj* **1** **additional**, supplementary, optional, secondary, extramural *Opposite*: regular **2** *(infml)* **extramarital**, adulterous, clandestine, illicit, improper

extradite *v* **deport**, expel, banish, transfer, repatriate

extradition *n* **repatriation**, handing over, deportation, expulsion, return

extra-large *adj* **outsize**, outsized, giant, jumbo, oversized *Opposite*: undersized

extramarital *adj* **adulterous**, illicit, clandestine, improper, extracurricular *(infml)*

extramural *adj* **external**, extracurricular, additional, optional, vocational *Opposite*: intramural

extraneous *adj* **1** **irrelevant**, unrelated, unconnected, inappropriate, beside the point *Opposite*: pertinent **2** **inessential**, unimportant, unnecessary, superfluous, peripheral *Opposite*: essential

extraordinaire *adj* **excellent**, extraordinary, superb, exceptional, remarkable *Opposite*: ordinary

extraordinarily *adv* **1** **extremely**, very, unusually, particularly, amazingly

2 strangely, oddly, unusually, bizarrely, abnormally *Opposite*: normally

extraordinary *adj* **1 strange**, odd, unusual, unexpected, astonishing *Opposite*: ordinary **2 special**, particular, exceptional, remarkable, great *Opposite*: normal

extrapolate *v* **infer**, generalize, induce, deduce, conclude

extrasensory *adj* **telepathic**, psychic, clairvoyant, mystic, mystical

extraterrestrial *adj* **celestial**, interplanetary, Martian, alien, interstellar *Opposite*: terrestrial ■ *n* **alien**, creature, creature from outer space, space invader, ET *Opposite*: earthling

extravagance *n* **1 profligacy**, overspending, wastefulness, excessiveness, lavishness *Opposite*: prudence **2 luxury**, indulgence, folly, nonessential, overindulgence *Opposite*: essential

extravagant *adj* **1 profligate**, wasteful, excessive, spendthrift, overgenerous *Opposite*: thrifty **2 exaggerated**, overstated, profuse, excessive, elaborate *Opposite*: restrained

extravaganza *n* **show**, musical, variety performance, burlesque, gala

extreme *adj* **1 great**, tremendous, severe, intense, acute *Opposite*: insignificant **2 radical**, fanatical, immoderate, zealous, excessive *Opposite*: moderate **3 farthest**, furthest, outermost, ultimate, maximum **4 dangerous**, life-threatening, thrilling, risky, exciting *Opposite*: safe ■ *n* **limit**, boundary, edge, end, pole

extremely *adv* **very**, tremendously, enormously, awfully, really *Opposite*: somewhat

extreme sport *n* **adrenaline sport**, alternative sport, Xtreme sport

extremism *n* **radicalism**, fanaticism, zealotry, activism, intemperance *Opposite*: moderation

extremist *n* **radical**, fanatic, activist, revolutionary, rebel *Opposite*: moderate ■ *adj* **radical**, fanatical, revolutionary, rebel, terrorist *Opposite*: moderate

extremity *n* **1 edge**, limit, boundary, margin, extreme *Opposite*: center **2 limb**, hand, foot, arm, leg

extricate *v* **get out**, extract, remove, disentangle, detach *Opposite*: engage

extrication *n* **disconnection**, detachment, disentanglement, disengagement, release *Opposite*: engagement

extroversion *n* **sociability**, friendliness, self-confidence, socialness, conviviality *Opposite*: introversion

extrovert *n* **outgoing person**, gregarious person, assertive person, socializer, befriender *Opposite*: introvert ■ *adj* **sociable**, outgoing, gregarious, friendly, social *Opposite*: introverted

exuberance *n* **enthusiasm**, excitement, liveliness, energy, high spirits *Opposite*: apathy

exuberant *adj* **enthusiastic**, excited, lively, energetic, high-spirited *Opposite*: lethargic

exude *v* **1 radiate**, give out, give off, display, show *Opposite*: absorb **2 secrete**, release, ooze, leak, discharge

exult *v* **revel**, take pride, gloat, glory, triumph *Opposite*: lament

exultant *adj* **jubilant**, overjoyed, triumphant, joyful, thrilled *Opposite*: miserable

exultation *n* **happiness**, triumph, joy, rejoicing, jubilation *Opposite*: misery

eye *n* **appreciation**, sense, taste, discrimination, discernment ■ *v* **look at**, stare at, gaze at, watch, observe

WORD BANK
❏ **parts of an eye** aqueous humor, cone, conjunctiva, cornea, eyeball, iris, lens, macula, optic nerve, pupil, retina, rod, vitreous humor

eyeball (*infml*) *v* **stare at**, glare at, have a good look at, look at, gaze at

eye-catching *adj* **striking**, noticeable, attention-grabbing, startling, arresting *Opposite*: unremarkable

eyeful (*infml*) *n* **look**, view, glance, squint (*infml*), gander (*infml*)

eyelet *n* **hole**, grommet, eyehole, perforation, loophole

eye opener *n* **revelation**, discovery, realization, surprise, shock

eyesight *n* **vision**, sight, sightedness, eye, view

eyesore *n* **blot on the landscape**, blot, monstrosity, blemish, fright

eyewitness *n* **witness**, observer, bystander, onlooker, looker-on

F

fable *n* **tale**, legend, parable, myth, story

fabled *adj* **1 legendary**, wonderful, remarkable, extraordinary, famous *Opposite*: unknown **2 fictitious**, mythical, imaginary,

legendary, fairy-tale *Opposite*: factual

fabric *n* **1 cloth**, material, textile, stuff, yard goods **2 structure**, foundation, framework, basics, makeup **3 brickwork**, stonework, masonry, structure, superstructure

WORD BANK

❏ **types of fabrics from animals** alpaca, angora, astrakhan, baize, brocade, camel hair, cashmere, chenille, crepe de Chine, felt, flannel, fur, gabardine, horsehair, jersey, lambswool, leather, loden, mohair, pashmina, shahtoosh, silk, taffeta, tweed, vicuna, wool, worsted

❏ **types of fabrics from plants** burlap, calico, canvas, chambray, cheesecloth, chintz, corduroy, cotton, cretonne, damask, denim, drill, flannelette, gauze, gingham, grosgrain, hessian, lawn, linen, madras, moleskin, muslin, organdy, poplin, sacking, sailcloth, seersucker, tarpaulin, terry, terry cloth, ticking, twill, velour, velvet, voile

❏ **types of synthetic fabrics** acrylic, chiffon, crepe, fishnet, fleece, lamé, moquette, nylon, percale, polyester, PVC, rayon, sateen, satin, spandex, tulle, viscose

fabricate v 1 **construct**, make, manufacture, produce, engineer Opposite: destroy 2 **invent**, make up, concoct, dream up, trump up

fabricated adj **invented**, made-up, untrue, fictitious, fictional Opposite: genuine

fabrication n 1 **construction**, manufacture, production, assembly, creation 2 **untruth**, lie, invention, falsehood, cock-and-bull story Opposite: truth 3 **counterfeit**, forgery, fake, imitation. See COMPARE AND CONTRAST at lie.

fabulous adj 1 **excellent**, wonderful, tremendous, magnificent, marvelous Opposite: awful 2 **fictitious**, mythical, imaginary, legendary, fairy-tale Opposite: factual

façade n 1 **frontage**, portico, fascia, front 2 **pretense**, veneer, impression, front, face

face n 1 **countenance**, features, mug (slang), visage (literary) 2 (infml) **nerve**, gall, boldness, audacity, pluck 3 **expression**, look, appearance, air, aspect 4 **outside**, surface, aspect, façade, wall Opposite: back ■ v 1 **be opposite**, be in front of, stand in front of, stand facing, look toward 2 **confront**, tackle, meet, cope with, challenge Opposite: avoid 3 **accept**, admit, be realistic, realize, bite the bullet Opposite: deny

WORD BANK

❏ **parts of a face** brow, cheek, cheekbone, chin, chops (infml), eye, eyebrow, forehead, hairline, jaw, jawline, jowl, lips, mandible, mouth, nose, temple

faceless adj **impersonal**, featureless, unidentified, anonymous, nameless

facelift n 1 **plastic surgery**, cosmetic surgery, tuck 2 **renovation**, modernization, refurbishment, rehab (infml), redecoration

face-off n **confrontation**, conflict, argument, showdown, challenge

face pack n **face mask**, facial, beauty treatment, mudpack

face-saving adj **dignified**, diplomatic, tactical, tactful, restorative Opposite: humiliating

facet n 1 **aspect**, feature, part, component, factor 2 **surface**, face, side, plane, façade

face the music v **accept responsibility**, face the storm, face up to your actions, take the flak, bite the bullet

facetious adj 1 **flippant**, silly, ill-timed, ill-judged, inappropriate Opposite: earnest 2 **lighthearted**, playful, humorous, witty, droll Opposite: serious

facetiousness n 1 **flippancy**, frivolousness, inappropriateness, silliness, inanity Opposite: earnestness 2 **lightheartedness**, wittiness, wit, drollness, humorousness Opposite: seriousness

face to face adv 1 **in person**, in the flesh, personally, head-on, person to person 2 **head on**, opposite, in confrontation, nose to nose, head to head

face up to v **accept**, admit, come to terms with, realize, confront Opposite: deny

facial n **beauty treatment**, face mask, face pack, makeover, massage

facile adj **superficial**, simplistic, flippant, trite, inane Opposite: profound

facilitate v **make easy**, ease, make possible, enable, smooth Opposite: impede

facilitation n **assistance**, help, furtherance, advancement, easing Opposite: obstruction

facilitator n **organizer**, architect, originator, prime mover, initiator

facilities n **amenities**, services, conveniences, restroom, accommodations

facility n 1 **skill**, capability, capacity, talent, flair Opposite: inability 2 **service**, provision, resource, feature, advantage

facing prep **opposite**, in front of, fronting

facsimile n **copy**, duplicate, reproduction, replica, likeness

fact n 1 **truth**, reality, actuality, verity (fml) Opposite: fiction 2 **piece of information**, detail, point, circumstance, datum 3 **happening**, deed, occurrence, event, act

faction n 1 **section**, party, splinter group, bloc, division 2 **conflict**, division, disunity, schism, disharmony Opposite: agreement

factional adj 1 **sectarian**, dissenting, disaffected, separatist, schismatic Opposite: united 2 **dramatized**, fictionalized, drama-documentary, semirealistic, documentary

factious adj **divisive**, sectarian, schismatic, discordant, contentious Opposite: unifying

factitious adj **contrived**, artificial, simulated, affected, unnatural Opposite: genuine

fact of life n **reality**, practicality, fact, truth, actuality

factor n **influence**, thing, feature, aspect, reason

factory n plant, works, installation, industrial unit, manufacturing plant

WORD BANK

❏ **types of factories** assembly plant, brewery, cannery, distillery, forge, foundry, machine shop, mill, mint, pottery, sawmill, smithy, steelworks, sweatshop, water mill, workshop

facts n 1 particulars, details, specifics, essentials, data 2 **truth**, evidence, reality, actuality, proof

fact sheet n **information sheet**, information leaflet, booklet, brochure, handout

factual adj 1 **truthful**, accurate, realistic, honest, true-life Opposite: fictional 2 **objective**, hard, verifiable, bona fide, authentic Opposite: subjective

faculty n 1 **sense**, power, endowment, capability, function 2 **ability**, facility, gift, talent, knack Opposite: inability 3 **staff**, teaching body, teaching staff, teachers, professors

fad n **fashion**, craze, trend, whim, vogue

fade v 1 disappear, weaken, die away, diminish, fade away Opposite: grow 2 **become paler**, lighten, become lighter, lose color, bleach Opposite: darken 3 wane, wither, die, waste away, wilt Opposite: flourish

fade away v 1 disappear, vanish, fade, evaporate, dwindle Opposite: persist 2 **waste away**, shrivel, wane, wither, atrophy Opposite: thrive

fading adj **disappearing**, declining, dying, vanishing, diminishing Opposite: growing

fail v 1 **be unsuccessful**, nose-dive, miss the mark, go belly up, fall flat Opposite: succeed 2 **fall short**, not make the grade, not be up to scratch, flunk (infml) fluff (infml) Opposite: pass 3 **stop working**, break down, crash, go down, stop 4 **let down**, disappoint, neglect, forsake, desert Opposite: satisfy 5 **go out of business**, go bankrupt, crash, fold, go under Opposite: thrive 6 **weaken**, fade, diminish, dwindle, decline Opposite: rally

failed adj **unsuccessful**, botched, disastrous, futile, abortive Opposite: successful

failing n **shortcoming**, flaw, weakness, weak point, fault Opposite: forte ■ prep **without**, in the absence of, lacking ■ adj **deteriorating**, worsening, weakening, fading, waning Opposite: strengthening. See COMPARE AND CONTRAST at **flaw**.

fail-safe adj **foolproof**, guaranteed, dependable, reliable, unfailing Opposite: unreliable

failure n 1 **disappointment**, letdown, catastrophe, fiasco, disaster Opposite: success 2 **breakdown**, stoppage, malfunction, crash, collapse 3 **bankruptcy**, closure, crash, collapse, insolvency

faint adj 1 **dim**, weak, faded, indistinct, feeble Opposite: bright 2 **slight**, diminished, muffled, soft, low Opposite: loud 3 **dizzy**, giddy, woozy, unsteady, vertiginous ■ v **pass out**, collapse, black out, fall down, lose consciousness Opposite: come to

faint-hearted adj **fearful**, apprehensive, hesitant, cowardly shy Opposite: bold. See COMPARE AND CONTRAST at **cowardly**.

faintly adv 1 **dimly**, weakly, slightly, indistinctly, feebly Opposite: brightly 2 **slightly**, softly, barely, indistinctly, imperceptibly Opposite: loudly

faintness n 1 **dimness**, weakness, feebleness, indistinctness, haziness Opposite: brightness 2 **slightness**, quietness, weakness, feebleness, softness Opposite: loudness 3 **dizziness**, giddiness, wooziness, vertigo, lightheadedness

fair adj 1 **reasonable** just, fair-minded, open-minded, impartial Opposite: biased 2 **light**, blond, fair-haired, flaxen, tow-headed Opposite: dark 3 **adequate**, passable, average, reasonable, decent 4 **good**, bright, sunny, clear, cloudless Opposite: inclement 5 **pleasing**, attractive, good-looking, lovely, pretty Opposite: unattractive ■ n 1 **festival**, sale, exposition, bazaar, trade fair 2 **carnival**, fairground, midway, amusement park, theme park

fairground n **theme park**, amusement park, playground, park, midway

fair-haired adj **fair**, blond, flaxen, tow-headed Opposite: dark

fairly adv 1 **moderately**, rather, reasonably, somewhat, comparatively 2 **honestly**, justly, properly, without favoritism, legitimately Opposite: unfairly 3 **completely**, positively, literally, practically, absolutely

fair-minded adj **fair**, open-minded, even-handed, nondiscriminatory, impartial Opposite: prejudiced

fairness n **justice**, equality, even-handedness, impartiality, fair-mindedness Opposite: unfairness

fairy n **pixie**, brownie, sprite, elf, leprechaun

fairyland n **wonderland**, dreamland, dream world, seventh heaven, heaven

fairy tale n 1 **folktale**, folk story, myth, legend, fable 2 **invention**, fabrication, lie, untruth, falsehood

fairy-tale adj 1 **mythical**, enchanted, magic, magical, imaginary Opposite: real 2 **fortunate**, happy, storybook, perfect, romantic Opposite: unhappy 3 **fabricated**, unbelievable, make-believe, made-up, highly colored Opposite: truthful

faith n 1 **trust**, confidence, reliance, conviction, belief Opposite: disbelief 2 **loyalty**, devotion, faithfulness, commitment, dedication Opposite: disloyalty

faithful adj 1 **correct**, true, realistic, authentic, close Opposite: unrealistic 2 **loyal**, devoted, trusty, trustworthy, staunch Opposite: faithless

faithfulness n 1 **correctness**, closeness, realism, authenticity, accuracy Opposite: unreality 2 **loyalty**, devotion, staunchness, dependability, reliability Opposite: faithlessness

faithless adj **dishonest**, disloyal, untrustworthy, unfaithful, fickle Opposite: faithful

faithlessness n **dishonesty**, infidelity, inconstancy, fickleness, disloyalty Opposite: faithfulness

fake n **imitation**, copy, replica, simulation, mock-up Opposite: original ■ adj **false**, bogus, sham, counterfeit, phony Opposite: genuine ■ v 1 **falsify**, copy, counterfeit, forge, replicate 2 **simulate**, feign, pretend, act, dissemble

faker n **fraud**, fake, liar, pretender, impostor

fall v 1 **drop**, go down, descend, plunge, plummet Opposite: ascend 2 **tumble**, fall over, fall down, drop, trip over 3 **decrease**, reduce, sink, come down Opposite: increase ■ n 1 **season**, equinox, Indian summer, autumn 2 **reduction**, decrease, drop, tumble, descent Opposite: increase 3 **waterfall**, rapids, cataract, cascade, white water

fallacious adj **mistaken**, erroneous, misleading, deceptive, false Opposite: correct

fallacy n **misconception**, myth, error, mistake, delusion

fall apart v **disintegrate**, crumble, collapse, fall to pieces, break up Opposite: come together

fall asleep v **nod off**, doze off, go to sleep, drop off (infml) Opposite: wake up

fall back v 1 **retreat**, withdraw, draw back, run away, regroup Opposite: advance 2 **drop behind**, fall behind, drop back, lag, lag behind Opposite: catch up

fallback n **replacement**, contingency, alternative, stand-in, substitute

fall back on v **resort to**, rely on, turn to, depend on, have recourse to

fall behind v 1 **be delayed**, be late, be in arrears, default, fail to pay 2 **drop back**, drop behind, fall back, lag, lag behind Opposite: keep up

fall by the wayside v **come to nothing**, fold, collapse, fail, abandon

fall down v 1 **collapse**, fall over, tumble, trip over, trip 2 **fail**, be unsuccessful, disappoint, go wrong, flop (infml) Opposite: succeed

fall flat v **fail**, miss the target, be a disaster, flop (infml), bomb (infml) Opposite: succeed

fall for v 1 **fall in love with**, be attracted to, be taken with, be stuck on (infml), take a shine to (infml) Opposite: go off 2 **be duped by**, be deceived by, be tricked by, be taken in by, believe Opposite: see through

fall foul of v **come into conflict with**, tangle with, have a brush with, come up against

fallibility n **imperfection**, frailty, weakness, shortcoming, failure Opposite: infallibility

fallible adj **imperfect**, mortal, weak, frail, human Opposite: infallible

falling adj **dwindling**, dropping, deteriorating, tumbling, sinking Opposite: rising

falling-out n **quarrel**, fight, disagreement, misunderstanding, rift Opposite: reconciliation

fall into place v **work out**, shape up, make sense, come together, sort itself out

fall in with v 1 **meet**, come across, bump into, run into, get to know Opposite: avoid 2 **join**, join forces with, team up with, collaborate with, band together with 3 **agree with**, accept, support, go along with, comply with Opposite: reject

fall off v **decline**, go down, decrease, plunge, reduce Opposite: increase

falloff n **decrease**, decline, falling off, reduction, drop Opposite: increase

fall out v **quarrel**, argue, disagree, come to blows, row Opposite: make up

fallout n **consequence**, result, outcome, effect, upshot

fall over v **tumble**, fall down, collapse, trip, trip over

fallow adj 1 **uncultivated**, unplowed, unplanted, unseeded, unused Opposite: cultivated 2 **inactive**, unproductive, idle, sterile, infertile Opposite: creative

fall short v **be deficient**, be wanting, be lacking, prove inadequate, not make the grade Opposite: succeed

fall through v **fail**, go wrong, come to nothing, miscarry, misfire Opposite: succeed

fall to pieces v **disintegrate**, come apart, crumble, fall apart, break up

false adj 1 **incorrect**, untruthful, untrue, wrong, dishonest Opposite: true 2 **mistaken**, erroneous, fallacious, misleading, deceiving Opposite: correct 3 **artificial**, bogus, sham, phony, counterfeit Opposite: real

falsehood n 1 **lie**, untruth, tale, fiction, invention 2 **deception**, dishonesty, mendacity, deceit, deceitfulness. See COMPARE AND CONTRAST at lie.

false impression n **mistaken belief**, misconception, misreading, wrong idea, misapprehension

falseness n 1 **incorrectness**, dishonesty, deceit, deceitfulness, speciousness Opposite: honesty 2 **mistakenness**, erroneousness, wrongness, fallaciousness, deceptiveness Opposite: rightness

falsification n **fabrication**, distortion, forgery, misrepresentation, deception Opposite: correction

falsified adj **fabricated**, forged, untrue, counterfeit, false Opposite: true

falsify v **fabricate**, fake, forge, rig, misrepresent

falsity n **falseness**, spuriousness, hollowness, inaccuracy, deceptiveness *Opposite*: correctness

falter v 1 **hesitate**, pause, waver, stammer, stutter *Opposite*: continue 2 **fail**, weaken, fade, wane, abate *(fml or literary) Opposite*: rally 3 **stumble**, trip up, stagger, totter, sway. *See* COMPARE AND CONTRAST *at* **hesitate**.

faltering adj **hesitant**, tentative, halting, timid, uncertain *Opposite*: confident

fame n **renown**, celebrity, reputation, distinction, recognition *Opposite*: obscurity

famed adj **well-known**, famous, celebrated, renowned, eminent *Opposite*: unknown

familial adj **family**, ancestral, household, domestic, matrimonial

familiar adj 1 **well-known**, recognizable, common, customary, habitual *Opposite*: unfamiliar 2 **accustomed**, habitual, usual, recurring, everyday *Opposite*: unusual 3 **acquainted**, conversant, accustomed, used to, at home with 4 **friendly**, intimate, easy, informal, personal *Opposite*: formal

familiarity n 1 **knowledge**, understanding, acquaintance, awareness, ease *Opposite*: unfamiliarity 2 **intimacy**, informality, friendship, ease, closeness *Opposite*: formality

familiarization n **acquaintance**, getting used to, adjustment, adaptation, becoming accustomed

familiarize v **acquaint**, tell, explain, make clear, train

familiarize yourself v **get to know**, adapt, get used to, acclimatize yourself, acquaint yourself

familiarly adv **intimately**, closely, informally, cozily, casually *Opposite*: distantly

family n 1 **relations**, relatives, folks, children, family unit 2 **lineage**, descendants, dynasty, ancestors, line 3 **category**, genus, species, type, kind ■ adj **domestic**, household, everyday, intimate, private

family circle n **relatives**, relations, family, folks, people *(infml)*

family name n **surname**, last name, maternal name, paternal name, name

family tree n **ancestry**, pedigree, genealogy, ancestors, descendants

family unit n **family**, household, house, ménage *(fml)*

famine n **food shortage**, shortage, scarcity, dearth, want *Opposite*: abundance

famished adj **hungry**, ravenous, underfed, unfed, starving *(infml) Opposite*: sated

famous adj **well-known**, famed, celebrated, renowned, eminent *Opposite*: unknown

famously adv 1 **notably**, memorably, eminently, prominently, distinctively 2 **well**, excellently, superbly, like a house on fire, like nobody's business

fan n **admirer**, enthusiast, aficionado, aficionada, follower ■ v 1 **waft**, blow, cool, wave, percolate 2 **stir up**, stimulate, provoke, increase, fuel *Opposite*: defuse

fanatic n 1 **extremist**, zealot, radical, fundamentalist, crusader 2 **fan**, enthusiast, devotee, buff, follower ■ adj **fanatical**, obsessive, passionate, addicted, extreme *Opposite*: indifferent

fanatical adj **enthusiastic**, passionate, obsessive, dedicated, fervent *Opposite*: indifferent

fanaticism n **extremism**, radicalism, zeal, keenness, dedication *Opposite*: indifference

fanciful adj **imaginary**, fantastic, whimsical, unbelievable, out of this world *Opposite*: prosaic

fancy adj 1 **elaborate**, ornate, decorative, ornamental, intricate 2 **expensive**, upmarket, lavish, extravagant, upscale *Opposite*: plain ■ v **imagine**, picture, think, conjure, believe ■ n **notion**, dream, hope, desire, fantasy

fancy-free adj **free**, at liberty, unfettered, unconstrained, at leisure *Opposite*: tied

fanfare n **display**, trumpet blast, salute, elaboration, flourish

fan out v **spread out**, separate, expand, broaden, disperse *Opposite*: assemble

fantasize v **daydream**, imagine, dream, picture, visualize

fantastic adj 1 **excellent**, superb, great, marvelous, fabulous *Opposite*: awful 2 **bizarre**, eccentric, imaginary, strange, fanciful *Opposite*: normal 3 **incredible**, unbelievable, implausible, improbable, unlikely *Opposite*: plausible 4 **large**, big, enormous, huge, great *Opposite*: tiny

fantasy n 1 **dream**, daydream, image, fancy, hope 2 **imagination**, unreality, fancy, caprice, power of invention *Opposite*: reality

fan the flames v **exacerbate**, aggravate, inflame, make worse, worsen *Opposite*: calm

far adv 1 **far off**, far away, far afield, far and wide, distantly *Opposite*: close 2 **much**, greatly, considerably, a lot, significantly *Opposite*: barely ■ adj **distant**, remote, far-off, faraway, far-flung *Opposite*: near

faraway adj 1 **remote**, far-off, far-flung, outlying, distant *Opposite*: nearby 2 **dreamy**, preoccupied, bemused, distant, in a world of your own *Opposite*: alert

farce n **shambles**, travesty, absurdity, circus, sham

farcical adj **absurd**, ridiculous, ludicrous, silly, nonsensical *Opposite*: solemn

fare n 1 **price**, tariff, ticket, cost, fee 2 **passenger**, customer, client, payer, rider 3 **food**, menu, meal, dishes, provisions ■ v **do**, get on, manage, cope, get by

farewell *n* **goodbye**, sendoff, departure, valediction *(fml)*, leave-taking *(literary)* Opposite: greeting

far-fetched *adj* **unbelievable**, fantastic, implausible, incredible, fanciful Opposite: believable

far-flung *adj* **1 widespread**, extensive, sweeping, diffuse, wide-ranging Opposite: restricted **2 distant**, remote, far-off, faraway, outlying Opposite: nearby

far from *prep* **anything but**, unlike, different from, poles apart from Opposite: near

farm *n* **1 homestead**, ranch, spread **2 farmhouse**, farmstead, homestead, ranch ■ *v* **cultivate**, work, till, plow, grow

farmer *n* **agriculturalist**, grower, rancher, planter, sharecropper

farm hand *n* **farmworker**, laborer, seasonal worker, harvester, ranch hand

farming *n* **agribusiness**, agriculture, husbandry, cultivation, market gardening

farm out *v* **delegate**, subcontract, contract out, send out, hand out

farmstead *n* **homestead**, farm, ranch

farmyard *n* **yard**, barnyard, cattle yard, stable yard

far-off *adj* **distant**, remote, far, faraway, far-flung Opposite: nearby

farrago *n* **hodgepodge**, potpourri, mishmash, medley, mixture

far-reaching *adj* **extensive**, sweeping, broad, across-the-board, comprehensive Opposite: limited

farsighted *adj* **wise**, visionary, farseeing, provident, prophetic Opposite: shortsighted

farsightedness *n* **foresight**, providence, prescience, forethought, wisdom Opposite: short-sightedness

farthest *adj* **furthest**, utmost, uttermost, outermost, furthermost

fascinate *v* **captivate**, charm, enthrall, attract, mesmerize Opposite: repel

fascinated *adj* **captivated**, rapt, spellbound, charmed, involved Opposite: uninterested

fascinating *adj* **captivating**, charming, attractive, enthralling, mesmerizing Opposite: repellent

fascination *n* **captivation**, charm, attraction, appeal, allure

fashion *n* **1 style**, way, manner, mode, method **2 trend**, craze, fad, vogue, mode ■ *v* **shape**, mold, form, make, fit

fashionable *adj* **chic**, stylish, designer, up-to-the-minute, in Opposite: dated

fashion-conscious *adj* **chic**, stylish, fashionable, elegant, modish Opposite: old-fashioned

fast *adj* **1 quick**, speedy, rapid, swift, express Opposite: slow **2 ahead**, gaining, in advance Opposite: slow **3 sudden**, sharp, fleeting, momentary, short-lived Opposite:

long-lasting **4 firm**, steadfast, constant, unwavering, faithful Opposite: fickle **5** *(infml)* **debauched**, wild, reckless, dissolute, profligate ■ *adv* **1 quickly**, speedily, rapidly, swiftly, promptly Opposite: slowly **2 firmly**, firm, tightly, tight, stable Opposite: loosely ■ *v* **abstain**, starve yourself, go without Opposite: feast ■ *n* **diet**, abstention, starvation, cleansing, hunger strike

fasten *v* **1 secure**, attach, fix, clip, clasp Opposite: detach **2 shut**, close, tie, tie up, do up Opposite: undo

fastener *n* **clasp**, fastening, tie, closure, snap

fastening *n* **clasp**, tie, closure, fastener, clip

fastidious *adj* **1 demanding**, fussy, finicky, picky, particular Opposite: easygoing **2 delicate**, refined, particular, dainty, squeamish Opposite: slovenly

fastidiousness *n* **1 fussiness**, meticulousness, care, carefulness, neatness Opposite: carelessness **2 delicacy**, delicateness, daintiness, squeamishness Opposite: crudeness

fastness *n* **1** *(literary)* **stronghold**, fortress, castle, citadel, refuge **2 speediness**, swiftness, alacrity, speed, haste

fast track *n* **push**, boost, way forward, advancement, furthering

fast-track *v* **advance**, accelerate, forge ahead, progress, develop

fat *n* **1 oil**, lard, grease, shortening **2 flab**, adipose tissue, padding, insulation, blubber *(infml)* ■ *adj* **1 overweight**, plump, chubby, stout, portly Opposite: thin **2 fatty**, greasy, oily, oleaginous, blubbery *(infml)* Opposite: lean **3 thick**, hefty, sizable, big, large Opposite: slim **4 rich**, wealthy, affluent, well-off, prosperous Opposite: poor

fatal *adj* **1 deadly**, lethal, incurable, terminal, mortal **2 ruinous**, disastrous, destructive, serious, grave Opposite: beneficial **3 decisive**, critical, crucial, fateful, pivotal Opposite: unimportant. See COMPARE AND CONTRAST at **deadly**.

fatalism *n* **resignation**, passivity, acceptance, stoicism, pessimism

fatalistic *adj* **philosophical**, defeatist, resigned, stoic, stoical

fatality *n* **1 death**, accident, casualty, loss, decease *(fml)* **2 deadliness**, deathliness, lethalness, noxiousness, fatalness

fate *n* **1 destiny**, fortune, providence, luck, doom **2 outcome**, consequence, result, upshot, end

fated *adj* **predetermined**, destined, predestined, preordained, meant

fateful *adj* **1 critical**, important, momentous, significant, crucial Opposite: insignificant **2 ominous**, unfortunate, inauspicious, unlucky, ill-fated Opposite: lucky

father *n* **1 dad** *(infml)*, daddy *(infml)*, pa *(infml)*, pop *(infml)* **2 ancestor**, forefather, forebear, predecessor, progenitor *Opposite*: descendant **3 founder**, originator, initiator, contriver, architect **4 priest**, vicar, minister, padre, pastor ■ *v* **1 beget**, sire, engender, procreate, spawn **2 protect**, comfort, advise, look after, nurture

fatherhood *n* paternity, parenthood, kinship *Opposite*: motherhood

fatherland *n* homeland, native land, home, motherland, mother country

fatherliness *n* protectiveness, benevolence, affection, supportiveness, kindness

fatherly *adj* paternal, protective, concerned, caring, loving

fathom *v* **1 comprehend**, understand, work out, figure out, grasp **2 sound**, measure, plumb, gauge, probe

fathomable *adj* comprehensible, understandable, penetrable, graspable, intelligible *Opposite*: unfathomable

fathomless *adj* **1 incomprehensible**, immeasurable, unfathomable, obscure, incalculable *Opposite*: fathomable **2 deep**, immeasurable, unfathomable, bottomless, inestimable *Opposite*: shallow

fatigue *n* exhaustion, tiredness, weariness, weakness, lethargy *Opposite*: energy

fatigued *adj* exhausted, weary, tired, drained, worn-out *Opposite*: fresh

fatness *n* obesity, plumpness, chubbiness, stoutness, portliness *Opposite*: thinness

fatten *v* stuff, plump, build up, feed, fatten up *Opposite*: starve

fattening *adj* calorific, fatty, rich, greasy, oily *Opposite*: slimming

fatten up *v* stuff, build up, feed, fatten *Opposite*: starve

fatty *adj* greasy, fat, oily, blubbery (*infml*) *Opposite*: lean

fatuity (*fml*) *n* unintelligence, complacency, silliness, stupidity, childishness *Opposite*: sensibleness

fatuous *adj* unintelligent, complacent, unaware, silly, stupid *Opposite*: sensible

fatuousness *n* unintelligence, complacency, silliness, foolishness, stupidity *Opposite*: sensibleness

faucet *n* spout, spigot, nozzle, outlet, stopcock

fault *n* **1 responsibility**, liability, burden, culpability, accountability **2 mistake**, error, blunder, slip, omission **3 shortcoming**, failing, weakness, defect, flaw *Opposite*: strength **4 blemish**, defect, imperfection, flaw, mark *Opposite*: bonus ■ *v* **blame**, criticize, condemn, find fault with, question *Opposite*: praise. *See* COMPARE AND CONTRAST *at* **flaw**.

faultfinder *n* critic, carper, complainer, grumbler, nitpicker

faultfinding *n* criticism, grumbling, nitpicking ■ *adj* critical, reproachful, carping, damning, unfavorable *Opposite*: uncritical

faultless *adj* flawless, perfect, impeccable, immaculate, blameless *Opposite*: imperfect

faultlessness *n* flawlessness, perfection, purity, impeccability, immaculateness *Opposite*: imperfection

fault line *n* crack, rift, split, fissure, fault

faulty *adj* **1 out of order**, defective, broken-down, broken, on the blink (*infml*) *Opposite*: perfect **2 flawed**, imperfect, incorrect, incoherent, contradictory *Opposite*: coherent

fauna *n* animals, creatures, wildlife, beasts

faux *adj* fake, artificial, unreal, reproduction, false *Opposite*: genuine

faux pas (*literary*) *n* gaffe, blunder, mistake, indiscretion, misstep. *See* COMPARE AND CONTRAST *at* **mistake**.

favor *n* **1 good turn**, errand, kindness, courtesy, service *Opposite*: disservice **2 approval**, regard, kindness, esteem, sympathy *Opposite*: disfavor **3 gift**, trinket, token, present, keepsake ■ *v* **1 prefer**, choose, support, back, approve *Opposite*: reject **2 assist**, help, aid, advance, promote *Opposite*: hinder. *See* COMPARE AND CONTRAST *at* **regard**.

favorable *adj* **1 advantageous**, helpful, beneficial, opportune, convenient *Opposite*: unfavorable **2 promising**, auspicious, encouraging, propitious, bright *Opposite*: inauspicious **3 approving**, positive, constructive, good, sympathetic *Opposite*: negative

favorite *adj* chosen, beloved, pet, favored ■ *n* **1 pet**, darling, beloved **2 choice**, preference, pick

favoritism *n* preferential ism, preference, partiality, nepotism, bias *Opposite*: impartiality

fawn *v* flatter, grovel, toady, kowtow, crawl (*infml*)

fawning *adj* flattering, obsequious, smarmy, sycophantic, servile

fax *n* facsimile, message, document, transmission, copy ■ *v* send, transmit, convey, communicate, telex

faze *v* fluster, disconcert, disturb, put off, deter *Opposite*: encourage

fear *n* **1 fright**, alarm, trepidation, terror, dread *Opposite*: assurance **2 worry**, concern, anxiety, apprehension, misgiving ■ *v* dread, be afraid, be scared, be apprehensive, be frightened

fearful *adj* **1 worried**, afraid, scared, apprehensive, frightened *Opposite*: fearless **2** (*infml*) **terrible**, dreadful, appalling, awful, horrible *Opposite*: wonderful **3 frightening**, terrifying, terrible, frightful, horrific

fearfulness *n* **1 apprehension**, anxiety, awe, fear, dread *Opposite*: bravery **2 scariness**, terribleness, frightfulness, horror, terror **3** (*infml*) **terribleness**, atrociousness, dreadfulness, awfulness, horror

fearless *adj* **courageous**, brave, bold, unafraid, daring *Opposite*: cowardly

fearlessness *n* **courage**, bravery, boldness, heroism, valor *Opposite*: cowardice. *See* COMPARE AND CONTRAST *at* **courage**.

fearsome *adj* **1 frightening**, formidable, terrifying, alarming, awesome **2 impressive**, awesome, formidable, awe-inspiring, tremendous

feasibility *n* **viability**, possibility, probability, likelihood, practicability *Opposite*: impossibility

feasible *adj* **viable**, possible, practicable, achievable, reasonable *Opposite*: impossible

feast *n* **1 banquet**, dinner, meal, buffet, spread *(infml)* **2 celebration**, festival, holiday, feast day, holy day **3 delight**, treat, indulgence, pleasure, joy ◼ *v* **eat**, dine, indulge, partake, gobble *Opposite*: fast

feat *n* **achievement**, accomplishment, deed, exploit, act

feathery *adj* **downy**, fluffy, soft, light, plumy

feature *n* **1 characteristic**, trait, mark, attribute, quality **2 facial feature**, contour, lineament *(literary)* **3 article**, piece, report, item, story ◼ *v* **1 contain**, include, present, introduce, bring out **2 perform**, star, appear, act, turn up **3 highlight**, star, include, showcase, show **4 figure**, appear, participate, take part, play a part

featureless *adj* **dull**, drab, bland, uninspired, unremarkable *Opposite*: distinctive

febrile *adj* **feverish**, fevered, flushed, hot, delirious

feckless *adj* **good-for-nothing**, useless, hopeless, spineless, feeble *Opposite*: dynamic

fecklessness *n* **uselessness**, hopelessness, spinelessness, feebleness, irresponsibility *Opposite*: dynamism

fecund *adj* **1 productive**, creative, prolific, industrious, fruitful **2** *(fml)* **fertile**, prolific, productive, fruitful, rich *Opposite*: infertile

fecundity *n* **fertility**, productiveness, fruitfulness, richness, prolificacy *Opposite*: infertility

federal *adj* **central**, centralized, national, state, civic *Opposite*: regional

federate *v* **1 unite**, join, amalgamate, come together, merge *Opposite*: devolve **2 associate**, unite, combine, join, confederate *Opposite*: disassociate

federation *n* **1 alliance**, coalition, confederation, grouping, partnership **2 combination**, union, association, confederation, amalgamation

fee *n* **1 payment**, remuneration, salary, pay, stipend **2 charge**, subscription, toll, tariff, cost. *See* COMPARE AND CONTRAST *at* **wage**.

feeble *adj* **1 weak**, frail, delicate, shaky, thin *Opposite*: robust **2 unconvincing**, ineffectual, poor, half-hearted, ineffective *Opposite*: convincing. *See* COMPARE AND CONTRAST *at* **weak**.

feebleness *n* **1 weakness**, fragility, delicateness, frailty, shakiness *Opposite*: robustness **2 ineffectuality**, weakness, half-heartedness, ineffectiveness *Opposite*: effectiveness

feed *v* **1 nourish**, nurse, suckle, breast-feed, serve *Opposite*: starve **2 eat**, consume, partake, devour, swallow **3 support**, sustain, nourish, nurture, encourage ◼ *n* **feedstuff**, food, fodder, forage, provender

feedback *n* **response**, reaction, comment, criticism, advice

feed into *v* **1 contribute**, add to, supplement, enhance, add weight *Opposite*: draw on **2 connect**, join up, flow into, lead into, merge

feel *v* **1 touch**, finger, handle, sense, fondle **2 sense**, experience, undergo, be aware of, bear **3 think**, believe, consider, comprehend, understand ◼ *n* **1 sensation**, touch, texture, finish, sense **2 impression**, atmosphere, air, feeling, ambiance

feeler *n* **sensor**, antenna, whisker

feel for *v* **sympathize**, feel sorry for, pity, commiserate, empathize

feel-good *adj* **optimistic**, positive, satisfying, cheering, upbeat *(infml)*

feeling *n* **1 sensation**, sense, sensitivity, touch *Opposite*: numbness **2 emotion**, sentiment, mood, reaction, sense **3 opinion**, view, point of view, belief, impression **4 affection**, concern, regard, love, sympathy *Opposite*: antipathy **5 hunch**, instinct, suspicion, intuition, idea **6 air**, atmosphere, ambiance, feel, mood

feel like *v* **1 want**, desire, crave, wish, long for **2 seem**, appear, resemble, look like

feel sorry for *v* **pity**, empathize with, feel for, commiserate with, sympathize with

feign *v* **pretend**, put on, fake, simulate, make believe

feigned *adj* **put on**, artificial, insincere, pretend, fake *Opposite*: genuine

feint *n* **trick**, stratagem, ploy, maneuver, ruse

feisty *(infml) adj* **lively**, spirited, energetic, aggressive, hearty *Opposite*: feeble

felicitations *(fml) n* **congratulations**, compliments, best wishes, blessings, greetings

felicitous *adj* **1 appropriate**, apt, suitable, apposite, well-chosen *Opposite*: inapposite **2 fortunate**, lucky, fortuitous, timely, happy *Opposite*: unfortunate

felicity *n* **1 happiness**, contentment, joy, pleasure, luck *Opposite*: unhappiness **2 appropriateness**, aptness, suitability, appositeness, fittingness *Opposite*: inappropriateness

feline *adj* **graceful**, slinky, subtle, elegant, stealthy

fell v 1 **cut down**, chop down, hew 2 **knock down**, knock out, floor, demolish (infml), deck (infml) Opposite: set up

fellow n 1 **member**, associate, researcher, academic 2 **man**, boy, guy (infml) 3 (dated) **companion**, colleague, associate, partner, comrade

fellow feeling n **sympathy**, empathy, support, affinity, mutuality Opposite: hostility

fellowship n 1 **communion**, companionship, camaraderie, comradeship, friendship Opposite: enmity 2 **society**, association, college, affiliation, cooperative

felon n **criminal**, offender, lawbreaker, delinquent, villain (infml)

felony n **crime**, offense, misdemeanor, wrongdoing, lawbreaking

female adj **feminine**, womanly, ladylike, girlish Opposite: masculine ■ n **woman**, lady, girl Opposite: male

feminine adj **female**, womanly, ladylike, girlish Opposite: masculine

femininity n **femaleness**, feminineness, womanliness, girlishness Opposite: masculinity

feminism n **women's movement**, women's liberation, women's rights, women's suffrage, women's studies

feminist n **suffragist**, suffragette, activist, radical, campaigner

fence n **barrier**, boundary, hurdle, hedge, railing ■ v 1 **enclose**, hedge, shut in, restrict, confine Opposite: open up 2 **evade**, parry, feint, dodge, fight off

fencing n 1 **fence**, railing, paling, barrier, palisade 2 **repartee**, banter, wordplay, raillery, badinage

fender n **fireguard**, fire screen, guard, screen

fend for v **look after**, take care of, provide for, defend, support

fend for yourself v **take care of yourself**, look after yourself, support yourself, go on your own, manage on your own

fend off v **keep away**, repel, repulse, discourage, ward off Opposite: welcome

fenland n **marsh**, bog, fen, wetland, lowland Opposite: desert

feral adj **wild**, untamed, undomesticated, savage, uncontrollable Opposite: domesticated

ferment v **agitate**, inflame, stir up, incite, provoke ■ n **uproar**, tumult, confusion, excitement, commotion Opposite: peace

ferocious adj 1 **fierce**, vicious, violent, cruel, brutal Opposite: gentle 2 **intense**, strong, heated, raging, extreme Opposite: mild

ferociousness see ferocity

ferocity n 1 **fierceness**, aggressiveness, viciousness, violence, brutality Opposite: gentleness 2 **intensity**, strength, extremeness, severity Opposite: mildness

ferret v **hunt**, search, search out, rummage, dig out

ferret around v **look for**, search out, delve, search around, hunt around

ferret out v 1 **discover**, uncover, find, reveal, unveil Opposite: conceal 2 **track down**, flush out, uncover, hunt down, catch Opposite: hide

ferry v **transport**, carry, ship, convey, transmit

fertile adj 1 **lush**, productive, abundant, rich, fruitful Opposite: barren 2 **productive**, fruitful, prolific, generative, fecund (fml) Opposite: infertile

fertility n **fruitfulness**, richness, lushness, productiveness, fecundity Opposite: barrenness

fertilization n 1 **insemination**, impregnation, pollination, artificial insemination, donor insemination 2 **fertilizer application**, manuring, composting, top dressing, nourishment

fertilize v 1 **inseminate**, impregnate, pollinate 2 **manure**, feed, top-dress, compost, enrich Opposite: exhaust

fertilizer n **manure**, compost, top dressing, soil enricher, enricher

fervent adj **enthusiastic**, avid, ardent, eager, keen Opposite: indifferent

fervid adj **impassioned**, intense, heated, burning

fervor n **passion**, dedication, enthusiasm, eagerness, zeal Opposite: indifference

fester v **rankle**, irritate, gall, embitter, annoy

festival n **feast day**, holiday, celebration, anniversary, birthday

festive adj **celebratory**, cheerful, joyful, merry, happy Opposite: sad

festiveness n **merriness**, joyfulness, cheerfulness, happiness, jolliness Opposite: lugubriousness

festivities n **revels**, revelry, celebrations, merriment, partying

festivity n 1 **party**, event, gala, carnival, fete 2 **good cheer**, rejoicing, merriment, pleasure, enjoyment Opposite: sadness

festoon n **garland**, decoration, swag, ornament, chain ■ v **decorate**, adorn, swathe, hang, drape Opposite: strip

festooned adj **garlanded**, wreathed, hung, decorated, draped Opposite: unadorned

fetch v 1 **get**, obtain, bring, carry, bring back 2 **sell for**, make, raise, get, draw

fetching adj **attractive**, eye-catching, handsome, good-looking, stylish Opposite: unattractive

fete n **holiday**, anniversary, jubilee, centennial, feast day ■ v **honor**, commemorate, lionize, entertain, praise

fête see fete

fetid adj **rotten**, putrid, foul, rank, fusty Opposite: fresh

fetish n 1 **talisman**, charm, idol, image, totem

2 obsession, fixation, mania, craze, engrossment *Opposite*: aversion *(fml)*

fetishize v make a fetish of, worship, idolize, be obsessed by, get hung up on *(slang)*

fetter n shackle, bond, chain, yoke, handcuff ■ v tie, bind, chain, restrain, hamper *Opposite*: unfetter

feud n dispute, argument, row, quarrel, bad blood *Opposite*: friendship ■ v fight, argue, dispute, quarrel, disagree

feudal adj out-of-date, outdated, old-fashioned, medieval, primitive *Opposite*: modern

fever n **1 temperature**, infection, disease, illness, malaise **2 passion**, fervor, excitement, agitation, vehemence

fevered adj feverish, agitated, restless, frenzied, fanatical *Opposite*: calm

feverish adj excited, agitated, nervous, heated, intense *Opposite*: tranquil

few adj insufficient, a small number of, hardly any, not many, only some *Opposite*: many

fey adj whimsical, fanciful, otherworldly, unworldly, fantastical

fiasco n debacle, disaster, mess, shambles, failure *Opposite*: success

fiat n **1 official sanction**, sanction, authorization, permission, agreement **2 order**, command, decree, edict, instruction

fib *(infml)* n untruth, white lie, lie, tall tale, falsification *Opposite*: truth ■ v lie, not tell the truth, misrepresent, perjure yourself, tell stories *Opposite*: come clean *(infml). See* COMPARE AND CONTRAST *at* lie.

fibber *(infml)* n liar, deceiver, fabricator, prevaricator, perjurer

fibbing *(infml)* n lying, prevarication, falsification, evasion

fiber n **1 thread**, yarn, string, filament, twine **2 makeup**, composition, structure, character, stuff **3 grit**, strength, fortitude, backbone, character *Opposite*: weakness

WORD BANK
❑ types of fibers cane, coconut matting, coir, jute, kapok, matting, raffia, ramie, rattan, seagrass, sisal, straw, wicker

fibrous adj tough, leathery, stringy, rubbery, chewy *Opposite*: tender

fickle adj inconsistent, changeable, capricious, inconstant, indecisive *Opposite*: constant

fickleness n inconsistency, changeability, capriciousness, inconstancy, indecisiveness *Opposite*: constancy

fiction n **1 creative writing**, works of fiction, literature, narrative, novels *Opposite*: nonfiction **2 work of fiction**, novel, fantasy, story, short story **3 invention**, fantasy, imagination, nonsense, illusion *Opposite*: reality **4 falsehood**, fabrication, lie, untruth, misrepresentation *Opposite*: fact

fictional adj imaginary, imagined, illusory, unreal, false *Opposite*: real

fictionalization n fictional account, fictional version, account, narrative, story

fictionalize v dramatize, novelize, recount, adapt

fictitious adj untrue, fabricated, invented, made-up, false *Opposite*: factual

fiddle n *(infml)* swindle, fraud, cheat, hoax, con ■ v **1** *(infml)* defraud, swindle, cheat, con, hoax **2** *(infml)* falsify, doctor, tamper with, manipulate, fix **3 fidget**, play, play around, toy, pick at **4 meddle**, tamper, interfere, mess, play **5 tinker**, manipulate, adjust, tweak, jiggle *Opposite*: leave alone

fiddling adj petty, unimportant, trifling, trivial, insignificant *Opposite*: significant ■ n *(infml)* fraud, deception, cheating, fixing, swindling

fidelity n loyalty, faithfulness, reliability, trustworthiness, dependability *Opposite*: infidelity

fidget v **1 twitch**, squirm, fret, shuffle, jiggle *Opposite*: freeze **2 fiddle**, play, play around, toy, jiggle *Opposite*: leave alone

fidgetiness n twitchiness, fretfulness, restlessness, jitteriness, uneasiness *Opposite*: stillness

fidgety adj twitchy, fretful, restless, squirmy, uneasy *Opposite*: still

field n **1 meadow**, pasture, grassland, grazing, lea *(literary)* **2 sports grounds**, playing field, turf, arena, ground **3 subject**, area, topic, discipline, theme ■ v **1 catch**, retrieve, pick up, go after, fetch **2 deal with**, handle, tackle, take care of, see to *Opposite*: ignore

fielder n player, baseball player, sportsperson, outfielder, infielder *Opposite*: batter

field test n field trial, test, trial, clinical trial, experiment

field-test v test, try out, study, put through its paces, beta-test

fieldwork n research, information-gathering, investigation, fact-finding, exploration

fiend n villain, evil person, brute, beast, monster *Opposite*: angel

fiendish adj **1 cruel**, evil, brutal, monstrous, villainous *Opposite*: pleasant **2 cunning**, ingenious, clever, crafty, devilish **3 impossible**, tricky, difficult, hard, perplexing *Opposite*: straightforward

fiendishly adv **1 cruelly**, brutally, wickedly, inhumanly, maliciously *Opposite*: pleasantly **2 extremely**, excessively, extraordinarily, incredibly, impossibly

fierce adj **1 violent**, ferocious, aggressive, brutal, severe *Opposite*: gentle **2 intense**, violent, extreme, savage, ferocious *Opposite*: mild **3 strong**, powerful, profound, deep, turbulent *Opposite*: mild

fiercely adv **1 violently**, ferociously, aggressively, brutally, severely *Opposite*: gently **2 extremely**, exceedingly, very, passionately, resolutely *Opposite*: mildly **3 ferociously**, intensely, strongly, brightly, hotly *Opposite*: feebly

fierceness *n* **1 ferocity**, brutality, violence, aggressiveness, sternness *Opposite*: gentleness **2 intensity**, violence, strength, power, fury *Opposite*: mildness

fiery *adj* **1 burning**, blistering, sweltering, blazing, flaming *Opposite*: icy **2 fierce**, passionate, heated, angry, furious *Opposite*: mild

fiesta *n* feast, holiday, festival, carnival, celebration

fifth wheel *n* **supernumerary**, third wheel, ghost at the feast, hanger-on *(infml)*, wallflower *(infml)*

fifty-fifty *adv* **half and half**, half each, two ways, equally, halfway

fight *v* **1 brawl**, box, clash, scrap, wrestle **2 wage war**, clash, struggle, battle, skirmish **3 dispute**, oppose, struggle, contest, wrangle *Opposite*: accept ■ *n* **1 contest**, match, bout, competition, round **2 scrap**, tussle, brawl, fistfight, fisticuffs *(infml)* **3 argument**, dispute, wrangle, clash, row *Opposite*: reconciliation **4 conflict**, battle, engagement, skirmish, clash

---

COMPARE AND CONTRAST CORE MEANING: a struggle between opposing armed forces

fight a physical struggle between individuals or groups such as battalions or armies; **battle** a large-scale fight involving combat between opposing forces, warships, or aircraft as part of an ongoing war or campaign; **war** a state of hostilities between nations, states, or factions involving the use of arms and the occurrence of a series of battles; **conflict** warfare between opposing forces, especially a prolonged and bitter but sporadic struggle; **engagement** a hostile encounter involving military forces; **skirmish** a brief minor fight, usually one that is part of a larger conflict; **clash** a short fierce encounter, usually involving physical combat.

---

fight back *v* **1 retaliate**, defend yourself, put up a fight, riposte, resist *Opposite*: attack **2 repress**, control, hold back, suppress, push back *Opposite*: let out

fighter *n* **boxer**, wrestler, pugilist, prizefighter

fighting *adj* **aggressive**, belligerent, pugnacious, hostile, rebellious *Opposite*: pacifist ■ *n* **combat**, hostility, unrest, warfare, violence *Opposite*: peace

fight off *v* fend off, drive away, resist, repulse, repel *Opposite*: attack

fight shy of *v* **avoid**, evade, eschew, dodge *Opposite*: confront

figment *n* **fabrication**, creation, invention, illusion, fantasy

figurative *adj* **metaphorical**, symbolic, allegorical, nonliteral, emblematic *Opposite*: literal

figure *n* **1 shape**, form, outline, stature, build **2 number**, numeral, character, symbol, digit **3 amount**, cost, sum, quantity, total **4 diagram**, chart, picture, table, illustration **5 person**, dignitary, celebrity, notable, individual ■ *v* **1 play a part**, feature, appear, be included, be incorporated **2 reckon**, guess, believe, think, suppose *Opposite*: doubt

figure of speech *n* **expression**, symbol, idiom, image, rhetorical expression

---

WORD BANK

❏ types of **figures of speech** alliteration, antonomasia, assonance, chiasmus, hendiadys, hypallage, hyperbaton, hyperbole, litotes, meiosis, metaphor, metonymy, oxymoron, personification, prosopopoeia, simile, synecdoche, zeugma

---

figure out *v* **work out**, deduce, discover, fathom, decipher. *See* COMPARE AND CONTRAST *at* deduce.

figurine *n* statuette, figure, model, ornament, statue

filament *n* thread, strand, string, fiber, wire

filch *(infml)* *v* steal, rob, thieve, walk off with, snatch. *See* COMPARE AND CONTRAST *at* steal.

file *n* **1 folder**, sleeve, dossier, heading, box file **2 report**, dossier, profile, record, information **3 line** row, column, procession, lineup ■ *v* **1 record**, categorize, put on record, keep, file away **2 rub**, rasp, scrape, sand, smooth **3 march**, troop, parade, snake, walk in single file

filial *adj* **familial**, family, loving, devoted *Opposite*: parental

filigree *n* tracery, lacy pattern, lattice, latticework, lace

filing *n* **shaving**, particle, splinter, shard, shred

fill *v* **1 plug**, block, block up, seal, stop *Opposite*: clear **2 fill up**, pack, stuff, cram, jam *Opposite*: empty **3 pervade**, imbue, impart, permeate, saturate **4 satisfy**, fulfill, meet, satiate, provide for *Opposite*: fall short

filler *n* **1 plaster**, grout, putty, caulking, pitch **2 padding**, stuffing, wadding, filling, packing

fillet *v* bone, clean, prepare, gut, scale

fill in *v* **1 complete**, fill out, write out, answer **2 take somebody's place**, stand in, substitute, deputize, cover **3 bring up to date**, put in the picture, give the latest, give the lowdown **4 clog**, plug, choke, dam up, block

fill-in *n* substitute, stand-in, temp, replacement, temporary worker

filling *n* **1 inside**, contents, guts, innards *(infml)* **2 stuffing**, padding, bulk, wadding, packing ■ *adj* satisfying, substantial, big, heavy, rich *Opposite*: meager

filling station *n* **gas station**, garage, service station, services, service area

fillip *n* **boost**, tonic, spur, stimulus, impetus *Opposite*: knock

fill out v 1 **complete**, fill in, write out, answer 2 **put on weight**, fatten up, bulk up, grow, develop *Opposite*: waste away

fill up v 1 **refill**, fill, replenish, load, stock up *Opposite*: empty 2 **satisfy**, satiate, stuff, bloat, fill

film n 1 **picture**, big screen, silver screen, movie, motion picture 2 **layer**, coat, coating, covering, sheet ■ v **record**, tape, capture, shoot, take

film over v **mist over**, mist up, glaze over, steam up, cloud over *Opposite*: clear

filmy adj **light**, airy, translucent, transparent, diaphanous *Opposite*: solid

filter n **sieve**, strainer, colander, mesh, riddle ■ v 1 **sift**, sieve, strain, clean, clarify 2 **sort**, sort out, separate out, stream, categorize *Opposite*: mingle 3 **seep**, ooze, trickle, penetrate, permeate

filth n 1 **dirt**, grime, rubbish, refuse, soil 2 **smut**, rudeness, lewdness, immorality, obscenity

filthiness n 1 **dirtiness**, griminess, dirt, grubbiness, foulness *Opposite*: cleanliness 2 **lewdness**, rudeness, immorality, smut, obscenity *Opposite*: decency

filthy adj 1 **dirty**, grimy, muddy, soiled, grubby *Opposite*: clean 2 **rude**, indecent, lewd, obscene, offensive *Opposite*: decent. *See* COMPARE AND CONTRAST *at* **dirty**.

filtration n **percolation**, separation, purification, clarification, categorization

fin n 1 **appendage**, flipper, paddle, dorsal fin, organ 2 **projection**, stabilizer, blade, paddle, propeller

finagle (infml) v **trick**, cheat, manipulate, engineer, wheedle

final adj 1 **last**, concluding, closing, ending, finishing *Opposite*: first 2 **conclusive**, definitive, absolute, decisive, irrevocable *Opposite*: provisional ■ n **round**, match, game, decider, last leg

finale n **ending**, end, climax, culmination, finish *Opposite*: prelude

finalist n **qualifier**, contestant, challenger, runner-up, contender *Opposite*: also-ran

finality n **conclusiveness**, decisiveness, definiteness, inevitability, irrevocability *Opposite*: uncertainty

finalization n **completion**, conclusion, agreement, settlement, decision *Opposite*: commencement (fml)

finalize v **confirm**, settle, decide, firm up, complete *Opposite*: start

finally adv 1 **lastly**, in conclusion, to conclude, to finish, to end *Opposite*: firstly 2 **at last**, at length, at long last, ultimately, after all *Opposite*: initially 3 **conclusively**, completely, decisively, irrevocably, definitively *Opposite*: tentatively

finance n **money**, economics, business, investment, backing ■ v **back**, invest in, pay for, fund, support

finances n **money**, funds, assets, cash, capital

financial adj **monetary**, fiscal, economic, pecuniary, monetarist

financier n **banker**, investor, backer, sponsor, supporter

find v 1 **discover**, locate, come across, hit upon, unearth 2 **recover**, regain, get back, retrieve, discover *Opposite*: lose 3 **realize**, understand, get, obtain, attain ■ n **discovery**, bargain, treasure trove, treasure, novelty

find fault with v **criticize**, nitpick, pick holes in, take to task, badmouth (slang) *Opposite*: praise. *See* COMPARE AND CONTRAST *at* **criticize**.

finding n 1 **verdict**, ruling, result, sentence, decision 2 **discovery**, conclusion, result, verdict, outcome

find out v 1 **discover**, learn, realize, observe, note 2 **catch**, expose, uncover, reveal, unmask

fine adj 1 **tiny**, minute, light, delicate, small 2 **bright**, sunny, warm, beautiful, fair *Opposite*: dull 3 (infml) **acceptable**, satisfactory, good, all right, okay (infml) *Opposite*: unsatisfactory 4 **outstanding**, superb, excellent, superior, exceptional *Opposite*: poor 5 **light**, slight, faint, thin, tenuous *Opposite*: heavy 6 **delicate**, dainty, slender, refined, thin *Opposite*: coarse 7 **subtle**, keen, sharp, skilled, refined *Opposite*: dull ■ n **penalty**, punishment, payment, forfeit, levy ■ v **penalize**, punish, levy, charge

fineness n 1 **excellence**, greatness, superiority, quality, distinction *Opposite*: poorness 2 **delicacy**, sheerness, thinness, narrowness, slenderness *Opposite*: thickness

finer points n **details**, minutiae, nuances, fine print, nitty-gritty (infml)

finery n **regalia**, jewelry, evening dress, morning dress, dress uniform

finesse n 1 **skill**, flair, grace, poise, assurance *Opposite*: clumsiness 2 **subtlety**, delicacy, diplomacy, tact, discretion *Opposite*: tactlessness

finest adj **premium**, handpicked, optimum, best, supreme *Opposite*: worst

fine-tune v **adjust**, modify, tune, polish up, perfect

fine-tuning n **adjustment**, refinement, modification, perfection, tuning

finger n 1 **digit**, limb, member, extremity 2 **portion**, piece, sliver, slice, bit *Opposite*: hunk ■ v **handle**, touch, feel, manipulate, toy with

fingerprint n 1 **impression**, print, mark, pattern, thumbprint 2 **characteristic**, identification, evidence, pattern, diagnostic

fingertip adj **sensitive**, delicate, fine, sensitized, hair-trigger

finicky adj **fastidious**, fussy, picky, particular, choosy (infml) *Opposite*: sloppy. *See* COMPARE AND CONTRAST *at* **careful**.

finish v 1 **end**, stop, terminate, close, cease *Opposite*: start 2 *(infml)* **destroy**, ruin, annihilate, defeat, exhaust 3 **use up**, drain, exhaust, polish off, empty *Opposite*: stock up 4 **polish**, buff, rub, varnish, lacquer ■ n 1 **end**, ending, close, conclusion, completion *Opposite*: start 2 **surface**, texture, appearance, quality, varnish

finished adj 1 **over**, ended, broken down, broken up, broken off 2 **refined**, perfect, polished, elegant, professional *Opposite*: rough 3 **polished**, buffed, varnished, glossed, gilded *Opposite*: unfinished 4 **ruined**, wrecked, lost, destroyed, devastated

finish off v 1 **complete**, conclude, finalize, fulfill, wind up *Opposite*: start up 2 **use up**, eat up, exhaust, polish off, demolish *(infml)* *Opposite*: stock up 3 *(infml)* **eliminate**, kill, exterminate, dispatch, dispose of

finite adj **limited**, restricted, determinate, fixed, set *Opposite*: infinite

fire n 1 **blaze**, flames, bonfire, conflagration, inferno 2 **combustion**, conflagration, ignition 3 **passion**, ardor, fervor, excitement, enthusiasm *Opposite*: apathy ■ v 1 **shoot**, set off, detonate, trigger, launch 2 **excite**, arouse, inspire, enthuse, enliven 3 *(infml)* **dismiss**, let go, get rid of, lay off, throw out *Opposite*: take on

fire alarm n **bell**, siren, buzzer, warning, alarm

firearm n **gun**, weapon, handgun, pistol, rifle

fireball n **ball lightning**, ball of fire, flash, lightning

firebrand n **troublemaker**, agitator, hothead, revolutionary, demagogue

firebreak n **clearing**, opening, strip, break, barrier

fire drill n **fire practice**, drill, rehearsal, evacuation, exercise

fire escape n **stairway**, ladder, escape hatch, staircase, emergency exit

fireguard n 1 **fire screen**, screen, guard, fender, frame 2 **firebreak**, clearing, strip, glade, opening

firelight n **glow**, glimmer, flame, flare, blaze

fireplace n **hearth**, inglenook, fire, fireside

firepower n **weapons**, arms, guns, armaments, munitions

fire practice n **fire drill**, drill, practice, rehearsal, evacuation

fireproof adj **incombustible**, nonflammable, flame-retardant, fire-retardant, fire-resistant *Opposite*: combustible

fireside n **hearth**, inglenook, fireplace

firetrap n **fire hazard**, danger, deathtrap *(infml)*

fire up v 1 **get going**, initiate, start off, set off, launch 2 **ignite**, fire, light, kindle, set alight 3 **enthuse**, motivate, incite, stimulate, excite

firewood n **logs**, kindling, wood, fuel

firing n **gunfire**, fire, shooting, shots

firing line n 1 **front line**, front, battlefield, vanguard 2 **forefront**, vanguard, lead, cutting edge, leading edge

firm adj 1 **solid**, compact, hard, rigid, dense *Opposite*: soft 2 **secure**, stable, fixed, strong, safe *Opposite*: unstable 3 **determined**, certain, definite, fixed, resolved *Opposite*: uncertain ■ v **harden**, stiffen, solidify, set, press down *Opposite*: soften ■ n **company**, business, partnership, multinational, corporation

firmament *(literary)* n **sky**, heaven, vault, azure, space

firmly adv 1 **resolutely**, inflexibly, determinedly, decisively, definitely *Opposite*: irresolutely 2 **tightly**, securely, steadily, powerfully, strongly *Opposite*: loosely

firmness n 1 **hardness**, rigidity, compactness, density, stiffness *Opposite*: softness 2 **stability**, steadiness, strength, safety *Opposite*: instability 3 **determination**, steadfastness, resolve, resolution, decisiveness *Opposite*: uncertainty

firm up v 1 **settle**, conclude, tie up, confirm, establish 2 **stabilize**, balance, steady, settle *Opposite*: destabilize

first adj 1 **initial**, primary, original, opening, earliest *Opposite*: last 2 **chief**, head, principal, leading, major *Opposite*: minor 3 **fundamental**, basic, key, elementary, primary *Opposite*: advanced ■ adv **firstly**, initially, at the outset, in the beginning, to begin with *Opposite*: lastly

first aid n **emergency treatment**, medical treatment, medical care, resuscitation, mouth-to-mouth

first-class adj **best**, superb, unrivaled, first-rate, excellent *Opposite*: poor

firsthand adj **direct**, actual, immediate, personal *Opposite*: secondhand ■ adv **directly**, personally, from the horse's mouth, straight *Opposite*: indirectly

first light n **dawn**, daybreak, sunrise, daylight, sunup *Opposite*: dusk

firstly adv **to start with**, initially, first of all, at the outset, first *Opposite*: lastly

first name n **name**, Christian name, given name, moniker *(slang)* *Opposite*: surname

first-rate adj **best**, superb, first-class, unrivaled, excellent *Opposite*: poor

fish v 1 **catch fish**, angle, go fishing, trawl, cast a line 2 **search**, seek, trawl, probe, dig around

WORD BANK

❏ **types of flatfish** angelfish, brill, flounder, halibut, lemon sole, manta, plaice, pompano, ray, skate, sole, stingray, turbot

❏ **types of freshwater fish** bass, bream, carp, catfish, crappie, goldfish, grayling, guppy, loach, minnow, mullet, Nile perch, perch, pike, piranha, roach, stickleback, tench, tilapia, trout

❏ **types of ocean fish** anchovy, anglerfish, bluefish, cod, dogfish, eel, haddock, hake, herring, John Dory, ling, mackerel, monkfish, pilchard, salmon, sardine, sea bream, shark, sprat, sturgeon, whitebait, whiting

❏ **types of tropical fish** barracuda, flying fish, kingfish, mahi-mahi, marlin, pomfret, sailfish, sawfish, snapper, swordfish, tuna

❏ **parts of a fish** air bladder, anal fin, dorsal fin, fin, gill, pectoral fin, pelvic fin, roe, scale, tail

fish for v **search for**, angle for, be after, invite, hope for

fishing n **angling**, casting, trawling, harpooning, whaling

fishnet n **mesh**, netting, net, tulle, gauze

fish out (infml) v **pull out**, take out, haul out, drag out, dig out Opposite: put in

fishy (infml) adj **dubious**, suspicious, irregular, underhand, shady Opposite: aboveboard

fission n **breaking up**, separation, splitting, division, schism Opposite: fusion

fissure n **crack**, split, crevice, fracture, cleft

fist n 1 (infml) **hand**, knuckle, paw (infml), duke (slang), mitt (slang) 2 **fistful**, handful, bunch, wad

fistfight n **brawl**, scrap, scuffle, fisticuffs, skirmish

fistful n **handful**, bunch, fist, wad

fit v 1 **measure**, tailor, size, take in, take up 2 **match**, suit, correspond, tally 3 **install**, put in, mount, fix, provide with ∎ adj 1 **appropriate**, fitting, right, proper, acceptable Opposite: unfit 2 **healthy**, well, fine, in fine fettle, hale and hearty Opposite: unfit ∎ n **convulsion**, spasm, seizure, attack, turn

fitful adj **disturbed**, sporadic, broken, restless, irregular Opposite: undisturbed

fit in v 1 **conform**, blend in, integrate, go well with, assimilate 2 **find time for**, squeeze in, manage, cope with, take on

fitness n 1 **health**, strength, robustness, vigor, wellbeing Opposite: weakness 2 **suitability**, appropriateness, aptness, qualification, capability Opposite: inappropriateness

fit out v **equip**, supply, set up, outfit, fit up

fitted adj **tailored**, close-fitting, formfitting, trim, snug Opposite: baggy

fitting adj **suitable**, appropriate, right, correct, proper Opposite: inappropriate

fittingness n **suitability**, appropriateness, rightness, correctness, properness Opposite: inappropriateness

fit up v **equip**, supply, set up, outfit, fit out

five o'clock shadow n **beard**, stubble, bristles

fix v 1 **mend**, repair, correct, make right, patch up 2 **agree**, arrange, establish, organize, set up Opposite: cancel 3 (infml) **prepare**, make ready, make, get ready, cook 4 **fasten**,

attach, glue, stick, secure Opposite: detach 5 (infml) **rig**, manipulate, massage, arrange, fiddle (infml) ∎ n 1 (infml) **dilemma**, predicament, tight spot, quandary, corner 2 (infml) **solution**, answer, resolution, remedy 3 (infml) **con**, fraud, swindle, trick, setup (infml) 4 (slang) **dose**, injection, shot (infml), hit (slang)

fixated adj **obsessed**, absorbed, fanatical, engrossed, paranoid Opposite: indifferent

fixation n **obsession**, fascination, mania, passion, addiction

fixative n 1 **preservative**, preserver, spray, varnish, coating 2 **glue**, adhesive, cement, paste, gum

fixed adj 1 **secure**, immovable, immobile, static, motionless Opposite: fluid 2 **set**, unchanging, flat, preset, predetermined Opposite: variable 3 **rigid**, inflexible, hard-and-fast, cast-iron Opposite: flexible

fixedness n **secureness**, immovability, immobility, motionlessness, stability Opposite: fluidity

fixings n 1 **ingredients**, elements, constituents, components, parts 2 (infml) **trimmings**, accompaniments, accessories, dressing, extras

fixtures n **accessories**, decorations, equipment, furniture

WORD BANK

❏ **types of general fixtures** baseboard, ceiling rose, dado, fender, fireplace, looking glass, mantel, mantelpiece, mirror, picture molding, radiator, socket, wainscot

❏ **types of plumbing fixtures** ball cock, basin, bathtub, bidet, drinking fountain, faucet, hand basin, hot tub, nozzle, plumbing, rose, sauna, shower, sink, sitz bath, spa, spigot, spout, sprinkler, tank, toilet, towel rail, tub, vanity, washbasin, washbowl, wash-hand basin, whirlpool

fix up v 1 **arrange**, schedule, plan, make plans for, organize 2 **repair**, renew, refurbish, renovate, redecorate

fizz v **effervesce**, sparkle, bubble, froth, foam ∎ n **effervescence**, sparkle, bubbles, froth, foam

fizzle v 1 **fizz**, hiss, sizzle, spit, sputter 2 **fail**, fade away, peter out, tail off, disappear Opposite: flourish

fizzy adj **effervescent**, sparkling, bubbly, carbonated, foamy Opposite: still

fjord n **inlet**, sound, creek

flab n **fat**, chubbiness, plumpness, baby fat, corpulence

flabbergast (infml) v **amaze**, astonish, astound, dumbfound, stun

flabbergasted (infml) adj **amazed**, astonished, astounded, dumbfounded, dumbstruck

flabbiness (infml) n **flaccidity**, looseness, softness, slackness, floppiness Opposite: firmness

flabby *(infml) adj* **flaccid**, loose, soft, slack, saggy *Opposite*: firm

flaccid *adj* **limp**, soft, loose, drooping, sagging *Opposite*: firm

flag *n* **standard**, ensign, pennant, colors, pennon ▪ *v* 1 **weaken**, tire, weary, wane, fade *Opposite*: rally 2 **mark**, highlight, identify, label, signal

flagellate *v* **whip**, flog, scourge, lash, beat

flagellation *n* **whipping**, flogging, scourging, lashing, beating

flagging *adj* **weakening**, tiring, wearied, waning, fading *Opposite*: rallying

flagon *n* **bottle**, carafe, flask, canteen, carboy

flagpole *n* **flagstaff**, staff, pole, mast, post

flagrant *adj* **blatant**, scandalous, obvious, deliberate, brazen *Opposite*: covert

flagship *n* 1 **warship**, man-of-war, ship of the line, capital ship, battleship 2 **star**, leader, jewel, pearl, pièce de résistance ▪ *adj* **prize**, star, lead, top, leading

flagstaff *see* **flagpole**

flagstone *n* **paving stone**, slab, paver, block, cobblestone

flag-waving *n* **patriotism**, chauvinism, jingoism, nationalism, loyalism

flail *v* 1 **thrash**, wave, whirl, flap, flounder 2 **flog**, beat, batter, hit, strike

flail around *v* **flounder**, writhe, struggle, squirm, stagger

flair *n* 1 **talent**, skill, aptitude, feel, gift *Opposite*: ineptitude 2 **elegance**, stylishness, style, chic, panache *Opposite*: inelegance. *See* COMPARE AND CONTRAST *at* **talent**.

flak *(infml) n* **criticism**, condemnation, censure, disapproval, hostility *Opposite*: support

flake *n* **shaving**, fleck, sliver, chip, scale ▪ *v* **peel**, crumble, chip, come off, scale

flaky *adj* 1 **peeling**, crumbling, crumbly, chipped, scaly 2 *(infml)* **eccentric**, unconventional, irrational, weird, peculiar *Opposite*: conventional 3 *(infml)* **unreliable**, undependable, irresponsible, flighty, forgetful *Opposite*: reliable

flamboyance *n* **showiness**, ostentation, flashiness, gaudiness, splendor *Opposite*: modesty

flamboyant *adj* **showy**, ostentatious, colorful, flashy, gaudy *Opposite*: understated

flame *n* **fire**, blaze, flare, spark, flicker ▪ *v* **burn**, blaze, light up, glow, flare

flameproof *adj* **nonflammable**, noninflammable, incombustible, fireproof, fire-retardant *Opposite*: inflammable

flaming *adj* 1 **blazing**, burning, flaring, flickering, sparking *Opposite*: doused 2 **intense**, angry, passionate, blazing, heated *Opposite*: calm

flammable *adj* **inflammable**, combustible, incendiary, igneous *Opposite*: fireproof

flan *n* **quiche**, pie, tart, tartlet, pastry

flank *n* **side**, edge, verge, margin, border ▪ *v* **border**, edge, line, skirt, fringe

flap *n* 1 **tab**, fold, lappet, lap, tail 2 **flutter**, wave, flail, shake, wag

flare *v* 1 **burn**, blaze, flame, flicker, flash 2 **broaden**, splay, bell, widen, spread ▪ *n* **flash**, blaze, flicker, flame, burst

flared *adj* **widening**, wide, spreading, broadening, flaring *Opposite*: tapered

flare up *v* **erupt**, break out, explode, heat up, blaze *Opposite*: die down

flare-up *(infml) n* **outbreak**, eruption, flash, outburst, explosion

flaring *adj* **widening**, bell-shaped, broadening, spreading, splaying *Opposite*: tapering

flash *v* 1 **glint**, sparkle, twinkle, flare, flicker 2 **pass quickly**, rush, speed, race, zoom *Opposite*: crawl 3 *(infml)* **flaunt**, show, show off, display, exhibit ▪ *n* 1 **blaze**, spark, flare, flicker, sparkle 2 **moment**, instant, second, twinkling, minute 3 **news flash**, update, bulletin, announcement, report

flashback *n* **memory**, recurrence, remembrance, recollection, hallucination

flash flood *n* **deluge**, downpour, cloudburst, spate, surge

flashlight *n* **penlight**, light, lamp, lantern, flash *(infml)*

flashpoint *n* 1 **crisis**, breaking point, climax, turning point, crossroads 2 **trouble spot**, hot spot, minefield, inferno, hornet's nest

flashy *adj* **showy**, ostentatious, glitzy, gaudy, loud *Opposite*: understated

flask *n* **bottle**, flagon, carafe, hip flask, decanter

flat *adj* 1 **level**, even, smooth, plane, horizontal *Opposite*: uneven 2 **unexciting**, dull, monotonous, tedious, boring *Opposite*: exciting 3 **categorical**, downright, absolute, out-and-out, emphatic *Opposite*: equivocal 4 **fixed**, set, preset, invariable, nonnegotiable *Opposite*: variable ▪ *n* **surface**, plane, level, face, blade

flatly *adv* 1 **categorically**, flat, absolutely, unequivocally, emphatically *Opposite*: equivocally 2 **dully**, monotonously, lifelessly, blandly, tediously *Opposite*: animatedly

flatness *n* 1 **levelness**, evenness, smoothness, horizontalness, horizontality *Opposite*: unevenness 2 **dullness**, monotony, monotonousness, tedium, boringness *Opposite*: excitement

flatten *v* 1 **squash**, crush, level, even out, compress 2 **knock over**, knock down, poleax, fell, crush

flatter *v* **compliment**, praise, cajole, sweet-talk *(infml)*, butter up *(infml) Opposite*: insult

flatterer *n* **toady**, sycophant, fawner, bootlicker *(infml)*, apple-polisher *(infml) Opposite*: critic

flattering *adj* 1 **gratifying**, pleasing, satisfying, satisfactory, cheering *Opposite*: galling **2 obsequious**, smooth, toadyish, sycophantic, unctuous *Opposite*: uncomplimentary **3 becoming**, complimentary, kind, sympathetic, suitable *Opposite*: unbecoming

flattery *n* **sycophancy**, obsequiousness, toadyism, adulation, unctuousness *Opposite*: insult

flatulence *n* **pomposity**, pretentiousness, bombast, verbosity, grandiloquence *Opposite*: simplicity

flatulent *adj* **pompous**, pretentious, bombastic, verbose, grandiloquent *Opposite*: unpretentious

flatware *n* **knives and forks**, tableware, silverware, silver, silver plate

---

WORD BANK

❏ **types of flatware** butter knife, carving knife, chopstick, dessertspoon, fish knife, fork, knife, pastry fork, pastry slice, serving spoon, soupspoon, spoon, steak knife, tablespoon, teaspoon

---

flaunt *v* **show off**, exhibit, display, parade, flourish *Opposite*: hide

flavor *n* **1 taste**, savor, zest, tang, essence *Opposite*: tastelessness **2 additive**, seasoning, extract, spice, essence **3 hint**, sense, feeling, feel, suggestion ■ *v* **1 season**, spice, lace, salt, ginger **2 characterize**, distinguish, mark, pervade, run through

flavorful *adj* **tasty**, tangy, appetizing, palatable, toothsome *Opposite*: unappetizing

flavoring *n* **flavor**, additive, seasoning, extract, spice

flavorless *adj* **tasteless**, bland, insipid, flat, watery *Opposite*: tasty

flavorsome *adj* **tasty**, savory, delicious, appetizing, flavorful *Opposite*: tasteless

flaw *n* **fault**, defect, blemish, imperfection, failing

COMPARE AND CONTRAST CORE MEANING: something that detracts from perfection

flaw an unintended mark or crack that prevents something from being totally perfect and detracts from its value, or a weakness in somebody's character or in a plan, theory, or system; **imperfection** a fault that makes a person or thing less than perfect; **fault** something that detracts from the integrity, functioning, or perfection of a thing, or a weakness in somebody's character, usually more serious than a flaw; **defect** a fault in a machine, system, or plan, especially one that prevents it from functioning correctly, or a personal weakness; **failing** something that mars somebody or something in some way, especially an unfortunate feature of somebody's character; **blemish** a mark of some kind that detracts from the appearance of something, especially the complexion or skin, or a feature that detracts from somebody's otherwise undamaged reputation or record.

---

flawed *adj* **faulty**, defective, damaged, blemished, imperfect *Opposite*: perfect

flawless *adj* **perfect**, faultless, immaculate, impeccable, unblemished *Opposite*: imperfect

flawlessness *n* **perfection**, faultlessness, immaculateness, impeccability, spotlessness *Opposite*: imperfection

flaxen *adj* **fair-haired**, fair, blond, blonde, golden-haired

flay *v* **1 whip**, lash, thrash, flog, beat **2 criticize**, censure, condemn, pillory, lambaste *Opposite*: endorse

fleck *n* **speck**, spot, speckle, dot, flyspeck

flecked *adj* **marked**, speckled, dotted, streaked, splashed

fledgling *n* **novice**, beginner, learner, tyro, neophyte *Opposite*: expert ■ *adj* **inexperienced**, new, untried, young, inexpert *Opposite*: experienced

flee *v* **run away**, escape, fly, take flight, run off *Opposite*: remain

fleece (*infml*) *v* **swindle**, con, cheat, take for a ride, defraud

fleeciness *n* **woolliness**, downiness, fluffiness, fuzziness, flocculence

fleecy *adj* **woolly**, fluffy, flocculent, soft, shaggy

fleet *n* **navy**, flotilla, armada, convoy, task force

fleeting *adj* **brief**, transitory, short-lived, momentary, passing *Opposite*: permanent. *See* COMPARE AND CONTRAST *at* **temporary**.

fleetness (*literary*) *n* **speed**, haste, dispatch, alacrity, rapidity *Opposite*: sluggishness

flesh *n* **1 tissue**, soft tissue, muscle **2 skin**, surface, epithelium, epidermis, dermis **3 meat**, beef, lamb, pork, ham **4 pulp**, pulpiness, meat **5 relatives**, family, relations, blood relatives, kin **6 body**, flesh and blood, physicality, corporeality, corpus **7 substance**, details, information, reality, solidness

flesh and blood *n* **family**, relatives, kith and kin, flesh, family circle

flesh-and-blood *adj* **real live**, human, real, sentient, animate

fleshiness *n* **beefiness**, stoutness, portliness, heftiness, corpulence

fleshly *adj* **1 bodily**, corporeal, physical, corporal, human *Opposite*: psychological **2 carnal**, bodily, erotic, animal, voluptuous *Opposite*: ascetic **3 worldly**, secular, material, human, mundane *Opposite*: spiritual

flesh out *v* **amplify**, elaborate, pad, pad out, expand *Opposite*: condense

fleshy *adj* **plump**, ample, overweight, fat, corpulent *Opposite*: slender

flex *v* **1 bend**, loosen up, activate, move, warm up *Opposite*: straighten **2 contract**, tense, tighten, control *Opposite*: relax

flexibility n **suppleness**, litheness, elasticity, give, plasticity Opposite: rigidity

flexible adj 1 **supple**, lithe, elastic, plastic, stretchy Opposite: rigid 2 **adaptable**, accommodating, variable, compliant, open Opposite: intractable

flick n (infml) **movie**, motion picture, film, picture, big screen ■ v **brush**, tap, glance, flip, graze

flicker v **sparkle**, glimmer, flash, waver, sputter ■ n 1 **glimmer**, spark, sparkle, twinkle, glint Opposite: beam 2 **trace**, ghost, impression, flash, glimmer

flickering adj glimmering, shimmering, intermittent, irregular, flashing

flick through v **look through**, dip into, leaf through, flip through, riffle Opposite: scrutinize

flier n 1 **leaflet**, handout, advertisement, notice, insert 2 (infml) **venture**, undertaking, endeavor, risk, attempt

flight n 1 **trip**, journey, airlift, voyage, tour 2 **escape**, departure, getaway, breakout, evasion

flightiness n capriciousness, changeability, frivolity, volatility, erraticism Opposite: reliability

flight of fancy n fantasy, pipe dream, fancy, dream, daydream

flighty adj **unreliable**, capricious, changeable, erratic, undependable Opposite: dependable

flimsiness n fragility, weakness, delicacy, frailty, feebleness Opposite: sturdiness

flimsy adj 1 **fragile**, weak, delicate, insubstantial, slight Opposite: sturdy 2 **poor**, feeble, unconvincing, inadequate, weak Opposite: sound. See COMPARE AND CONTRAST at fragile.

flinch v recoil, start, cringe, shy away, balk Opposite: stand your ground. See COMPARE AND CONTRAST at recoil.

fling v **throw**, toss, hurl, pitch, lob ■ n (infml) **romance**, love affair, affair, involvement, relationship. See COMPARE AND CONTRAST at throw.

flinty adj **hard**, unemotional, stern, inflexible, pitiless Opposite: soft

flip v **turn over**, toss, flick, spin, overturn ■ adj (infml) **flippant**, casual, joking, jokey, dismissive Opposite: serious

flip over v **tip**, upset, upturn, flip, overturn

flippancy n **levity**, facetiousness, glibness, offhandedness, impertinence Opposite: seriousness

flippant adj **facetious**, offhand, glib, dismissive, frivolous Opposite: serious

flip through v **leaf through**, browse, flick through, skim through, scan

flirt v 1 **trifle**, toy, play, seduce, lead on 2 **flick**, jerk, toss, flip, propel

flirtation n **romance**, fling, love affair, entanglement, liaison

flirtatious adj **playful**, coy, seductive, suggestive, kittenish

flirt with v **consider**, toy with, entertain, think about, trifle with

flit v **fly**, flutter, dart, skim, flash

float v 1 **hover**, soar, drift, glide, hang Opposite: drop 2 **sail**, swim, drift, glide, tread water Opposite: sink 3 **propose**, suggest, put forward, promote, offer Opposite: reject

floating adj **fluctuating**, detached, variable, moving, free Opposite: fixed

flock n **group**, set, cluster ■ v **gather**, collect, congregate, assemble, cluster Opposite: disperse

WORD BANK

❑ types of flocks bevy (of quail/larks), brood (of chickens), cast (of hawks), charm (of finches), clutch (of chickens), colony (of gulls), covey (of partridges), exaltation (of larks) (literary), flight (of doves/swallows), gaggle (of geese), herd (of swans), kettle (of hawks), mob (of emus), murmuration (of starlings) (literary), muster (of peacocks), rookery (of penguins), siege (of herons), skein (of geese), watch (of nightingales) (literary), wedge (of swans in flight), wisp (of snipe)

floe n ice floe, iceberg, ice field, icecap, ice sheet

flog v **whip**, lash, beat, thrash, scourge

flood n 1 **deluge**, overflow, downpour, torrent, tidal wave Opposite: drought 2 **abundance**, glut, excess, stream, rush Opposite: shortage ■ v **inundate**, submerge, overflow, swamp, saturate Opposite: ebb

flooded adj **underwater**, swamped, waterlogged, inundated, drowned

floodgate n head gate, sluicegate, water gate, lock, weir

floodlight n **illumination**, lighting, stream, flood, searchlight ■ v **light up**, illuminate, light, irradiate, spotlight

floodlit adj **illuminated**, lit up, lit, illumined (literary)

floodplain n plain, valley, delta, water meadow, fen

flood tide n 1 **inflow**, high tide, current 2 **groundswell**, swell, surge, wave, upsurge

floor n 1 **story**, level, deck 2 **bottom**, base, level, surface, flat ■ v **astonish**, stupefy, astound, stagger, confound

flooring n parquet, floorboards, terrazzo, tiles, floor tiles

floor manager n **supervisor**, overseer, manager, duty officer, line manager

floor plan n **layout**, plan, design, arrangement, allocation

flop v 1 **collapse**, slump, fall down, slacken, sag Opposite: stand up 2 (infml) **fail**, fold, close, crash, nose-dive Opposite: succeed 3 (infml) **collapse**, slump, fall down, slacken, sag Opposite: stand up ■ n (infml)

failure, fiasco, dead loss, loser, dud (infml) Opposite: hit

floppiness n **limpness**, droopiness, looseness, slackness, softness Opposite: firmness

floppy adj **limp**, droopy, lank, loose, flappy Opposite: firm

flora n **plants**, flowers, vegetation, plant life

floral adj **flowery**, flowered, flower-patterned, floral-patterned

floral-patterned see floral

floret n **floweret**, bud, blossom, bloom, flower

florid adj **1 ornate**, baroque, elaborate, fancy, flowery Opposite: plain **2 ruddy**, red, sanguine, rosy, heightened Opposite: pallid

flotation n **launch**, initiation, debut, inauguration, introduction

flotilla n **fleet**, armada, convoy, task force, navy

flotsam n **debris**, refuse, driftwood, jetsam, wreckage

flounce v **prance**, storm, stomp, strut, swagger

flounder v **1 splash**, struggle, thrash, wallow, stumble **2 dither**, hesitate, falter, get into difficulties, waver

flour v **dust**, cover, coat, sprinkle, dredge

WORD BANK
❏ **types of flour** cornmeal, cornstarch, graham flour, meal, polenta, rice flour, self-rising flour, whole-wheat

flourish v **1 be successful**, succeed, thrive, grow, do well Opposite: decline **2 shake**, show, flaunt, display, wave ■ n **1 embellishment**, curl, curlicue, decoration, ornament **2 grand gesture**, display, fanfare, show, bravado

flourishing adj **doing well**, thriving, successful, booming, healthy Opposite: declining

floury adj **starchy**, crumbly, crumbling, farinaceous, floured

flout v **disobey**, break, ignore, defy, contravene Opposite: obey

flow v **1 run**, pour, flood, stream, gush **2 spring**, arise, emerge, emanate, issue ■ n **movement**, current, stream, course, drift

flower n **1 floret**, flower head, bud, blossom, bloom **2 best**, pick, height, choicest, elite Opposite: worst ■ v **1 bloom**, bud, blossom, open, come into bloom Opposite: fade **2 develop**, come to fruition, flourish, peak, blossom Opposite: wane

WORD BANK
❏ **types of annual flowers** aster, forget-me-not, lobelia, marigold, nasturtium, pansy, petunia, poppy, stock, sunflower, sweet pea
❏ **types of perennial flowers** African violet, begonia, buttercup, carnation, chrysanthemum, columbine, cowslip, daisy, del-

phinium, foxglove, fuchsia, geranium, lily of the valley, lotus, lupine, orchid, pelargonium, peony, pink, primrose, rose, snapdragon, sweet william, violet, wallflower
❏ **parts of a flower** androecium, anther, bract, calyx, carpel, corolla, fall, filament, floret, glume, gynoecium, involucre, lemma, lip, nectary, ovary, ovule, palea, pedicel, peduncle, perianth, petal, pistil, receptacle, sepal, spur, stamen, stigma, style, tepal

flowerbed n **plot**, garden plot, patch, border, herbaceous border

flowered adj **floral**, flowery, flower-patterned, floral-patterned

flowering n **peak**, high point, acme, blossoming, pinnacle Opposite: nadir

flower-patterned adj **floral**, flowery, flowered, floral-patterned

flowerpot n **plant pot**, planter, tub, jardinière, urn

flowery adj **1 ornate**, ornamental, baroque, embellished, florid Opposite: plain **2 floral**, flowered, flower-patterned, floriated

flowing adj **graceful**, smooth, curving, sinuous, elegant Opposite: jerky

flub (infml) v **blunder**, make a mess of, ruin, spoil, botch (infml)

fluctuate v **vary**, alter, ebb and flow, rise and fall, come and go

fluctuating adj **changing**, changeable, shifting, mutable, unstable Opposite: constant

fluctuation n **variation**, vacillation, rise and fall, oscillation, flux Opposite: steadiness

flue n **vent**, chimney, outlet, shaft, duct

fluency n **effortlessness**, eloquence, articulacy, ease, facility Opposite: hesitancy

fluent adj **1 easy**, flowing, confident, assured, smooth Opposite: halting **2 articulate**, eloquent, voluble, smooth-spoken, smooth-tongued Opposite: tongue-tied

fluff v (infml) **do badly**, make a mess of, ruin, spoil, botch (infml) ■ n **fuzz**, lint, hair ■ v **fluff up**, plump up, ruffle, shake, pat

fluffiness n **1 furriness**, fuzziness, hairiness, woolliness, fleeciness **2 lightness**, airiness, softness, flimsiness, frothiness Opposite: heaviness

fluffy adj **1 fleecy**, cottony, feathery, downy, furry **2 frothy**, foamy, bubbly, soft, light

fluid n **liquid**, solution, water Opposite: solid ■ adj **1 runny**, liquid, watery, liquefied, molten Opposite: solid **2 effortless**, flowing, smooth, graceful, elegant Opposite: jerky **3 changeable**, fluctuating, unstable, adaptable, flexible Opposite: constant

fluidity n **1 variability**, changeableness, changeability, flexibility, mutability Opposite: fixedness **2 smoothness**, gracefulness, grace, agility, flexibility Opposite: jerkiness

fluke (infml) n **stroke of luck**, accident, coincidence, lucky break, chance occurrence *Opposite*: mischance

flummox *(infml)* v **confuse**, perplex, baffle, stump, bewilder

flummoxed *(infml)* adj **confused**, perplexed, confounded, baffled, stumped

flunk *(infml)* v **fail**, be unsuccessful, not pass, do badly, bomb *(infml) Opposite*: ace *(infml)*

flunkey *(infml) see* **flunky**

flunky *(infml)* n **minion**, sidekick, assistant, helper, subordinate

fluorescent *adj* **glowing**, bright, shining, luminous, flaming

flurry n 1 **burst**, spell, outbreak, bout, flood 2 **wind**, gust, puff, squall, shower ■ v**fluster**, agitate, disturb, disconcert, perturb *Opposite*: soothe

flush v 1 **redden**, blush, go red, color, glow *Opposite*: pale 2 **clear**, wash out, cleanse, rinse, swill ■ n **blush**, high color, redness, rosiness, ruddiness *Opposite*: pallor ■ *adj* 1 **even**, level, flat, true *Opposite*: uneven 2 *(infml)* **well off**, rich, in the money, in funds, rolling in it *(infml)*

flushed *adj* **red-faced**, rosy, red, blushing, glowing *Opposite*: pale

fluster v **disconcert**, agitate, confuse, upset, bother *Opposite*: soothe

flustered *adj* **harassed**, agitated, nervous, disconcerted, rattled *Opposite*: calm

flute n **groove**, channel, indentation, line, furrow *Opposite*: ridge

fluted *adj* **grooved**, corrugated, furrowed, lined, indented *Opposite*: flat

flutter v **beat**, flap, wave, tremble, quiver ■ n **fluster**, excitement, flurry, agitation, confusion *Opposite*: composure

flux n **fluidity**, mutability, fluctuation, instability, unrest *Opposite*: stability

fly v 1 **hover**, soar, wing, take wing, take off 2 **zoom**, tear, dash, hurry, race *Opposite*: dawdle 3 **bolt**, run away, escape, flee, take flight *Opposite*: stand your ground

WORD BANK
❏ **types of flying insects** aphid, bee, blackfly, blowfly, bumblebee, cicada, crane fly, deer fly, dragonfly, firefly, fruit fly, gnat, grasshopper, greenfly, hornet, horsefly, locust, mayfly, midge, mosquito, no-see-um, punkie, tsetse fly, wasp, whitefly

flyaway *adj* **unmanageable**, unruly, uncontrollable, hard to handle, awkward *Opposite*: manageable

flyblown *adj* 1 **maggoty**, wormy, infested, worm-eaten, festering 2 **dirty**, filthy, contaminated, tainted, unclean *Opposite*: clean

fly-by-night *adj* **unscrupulous**, dubious, unreliable, shifty, questionable *Opposite*: reputable

flying *adj* 1 **hovering**, airborne, soaring, in the air, on the wing 2 **rapid**, brief, speedy, hurried, short

flying saucer n **UFO**, spaceship, spacecraft

fly in the face of v **challenge**, disagree with, go against, contradict, oppose *Opposite*: conform

fly in the ointment n **drawback**, complaint, impediment, snag, hitch

fly into a rage v **erupt**, explode, lose your temper, go wild *(infml)*, hit the ceiling *(infml) Opposite*: calm down

flyleaf n **front page**, first page, frontispiece, page, leaf

fly off the handle *(infml)* v **erupt**, explode, lose your temper, fly into a rage, hit the ceiling *(infml) Opposite*: calm down

flysheet n **flier**, handbill, handout, sheet, notice

fly the coop *(infml)* v **escape**, leave, run away, flee, bolt *Opposite*: remain

foal v **produce young**, produce offspring, breed, give birth, reproduce

foam n **bubbles**, froth, fizz, lather, suds ■ v **froth up**, effervesce, froth, bubble, fizz

foam at the mouth v **rage**, seethe, fume, boil, splutter

fob off v 1 **foist**, palm off, dump, pass on, offload 2 **mislead**, misinform, deceive, stall, pull the wool over somebody's eyes 3 **cheat**, con, palm off, rip off *(infml)*, do *(infml)*

focal *adj* **principal**, pivotal, central, crucial, important *Opposite*: peripheral

focal point n **central point**, pivot, core, center, focus *Opposite*: periphery

focus n 1 **nub**, central point, core, spotlight, center 2 **emphasis**, attention, effort, concentration, motivation 3 **focal point**, heart, hub, nucleus, meeting point ■ v **concentrate**, direct, converge, meet, come together

focused *adj* **motivated**, concentrated, fixated, attentive, absorbed

fodder n **food**, silage, hay, feed, feedstuff

foe *(fml)* n **adversary**, enemy, antagonist, rival, opponent *Opposite*: friend

foetid *see* **fetid**

fog n 1 **mist**, vapor, smog, haze, miasma 2 **muddle**, stupor, confusion, daze, haze *Opposite*: clarity ■ v **obscure**, cloud, bewilder, confuse, stupefy *Opposite*: sharpen

fogginess n 1 **mistiness**, murkiness, haziness, cloudiness, gloom *Opposite*: brightness 2 **obscurity**, confusion, doubtfulness, bewilderment, perplexity *Opposite*: clarity

foggy *adj* 1 **hazy**, misty, cloudy, murky, smoggy *Opposite*: clear 2 **unclear**, vague, confused, muddled, bewildered *Opposite*: precise

foghorn n **horn**, siren, hooter, Klaxon

foible n **weakness**, fault, shortcoming, quirk, idiosyncrasy *Opposite*: strength

foil v **stop**, frustrate, thwart, outwit, halt

foist v **force upon**, inflict upon, thrust upon, impose, palm off

fold v 1 **double over**, bend, fold up, fold over, double *Opposite*: straighten 2 **go out of business**, close, shut down, go bankrupt, collapse ■ n **crinkle**, crease, wrinkle, pleat, doubling

foldaway *see* **folding**

folded *adj* **doubled**, doubled over, doubled up, bent over, turned under *Opposite*: outspread

folding *adj* **portable**, foldup, traveling, foldaway, collapsible

fold up v **bend flat**, bend, collapse, double, fold over *Opposite*: unfold

foldup *see* **folding**

foliage n **leaves**, greenery, vegetation, undergrowth, shrubbery

foliage plant n **houseplant**, potted plant, greenery

folk *adj* **traditional**, popular, common, widespread, vernacular ■ n **people**, folks, the people, the population, everyone

folklore n **myth**, legend, oral tradition, mythology, tradition

folks n 1 (*infml*) **people**, folk, everyone, the silent majority, society 2 (*infml*) **everyone**, everybody, ladies and gentlemen, you guys, friends 3 **relatives**, nearest and dearest, family, kinfolk, kith and kin

folk singer n **singer**, folkie, balladeer, troubadour

folksy *adj* 1 **simple**, unsophisticated, unpretentious, wholesome, traditional 2 **friendly**, informal, relaxed, congenial, easygoing *Opposite*: restrained

folktale n **tale**, story, legend, myth, ballad

follicle n **sac**, cavity, gland, hair follicle

follow v 1 **pursue**, chase, stalk, trail, shadow *Opposite*: precede 2 **monitor**, check on, keep an eye on, track, chart 3 **keep on**, go along, stay on, keep to, stick to 4 **obey**, abide by, keep to, respect, adhere to *Opposite*: break 5 **understand**, see, comprehend, grasp, get the gist 6 **enjoy**, admire, support, keep up with 7 **come out of**, ensue, result, develop, arise

---

COMPARE AND CONTRAST CORE MEANING: go after

follow take the same route behind another person, for example by walking down the street or driving along the same road, deliberately or by chance, and not necessarily with the intention of closing the gap; **chase** try to reach, catch, or overtake another person who is in front; **pursue** make an effort to catch up with the person being followed; **tail** (*infml*) to follow secretly for purposes of surveillance; **shadow** follow secretly, used especially to talk about the activities of spies and detectives; **stalk** follow or try to get close to a person or hunted animal unobtrusively, especially obsessively to follow and criminally harass a person; **trail** follow tracks or traces left by a person or animal no longer in sight.

---

follower n **supporter**, fan, admirer, hanger-on, devotee

following *adj* **next**, subsequent, succeeding, ensuing, resulting *Opposite*: previous

follow-on *adj* **resulting**, consequent, resultant, ensuing, secondary ■ n **side effect**, continuation, consequence, result, repercussion

follow through v **complete**, see through, bring to completion, bring to the end, finish off *Opposite*: drop

follow-up n **continuation**, addition, supplement, complement, development

folly n **irrationality**, foolishness, madness, stupidity, idiocy *Opposite*: prudence

foment v **foster**, stir up, stimulate, incite, generate *Opposite*: dampen

fond *adj* **loving**, tender, affectionate, caring, warm *Opposite*: uncaring

fondle v **massage**, touch, stroke, caress, pet

fondness n **liking**, affection, weakness, soft spot, partiality *Opposite*: dislike. *See* COMPARE AND CONTRAST *at* **love**.

fond of *adj* **devoted to**, taken with, attached to, partial to, soft on *Opposite*: indifferent

font n 1 (*literary*) **source**, supply, wellspring, fount, basis 2 (*literary*) **fountain**, spring, water source, well, source 3 **typeface**, lettering, type style, type

food n 1 **nourishment**, nutrition, nutriment, diet, sustenance 2 **staple**, foodstuff, fare, provisions, groceries

foodie (*infml*) n **gourmet**, bon vivant, epicure, connoisseur, epicurean

food lover *see* **foodie**

foodstuff n **food**, staple, essential, ingredient, provisions

fool n **dolt** (*infml*), dope (*infml*), boob (*infml*), sucker (*infml*), ding-dong (*infml*) ■ v **mislead**, trick, deceive, take in, con

fool around v 1 **clown**, act the fool, play around, horse around, mess around (*infml*) 2 **putter**, idle, mess around (*infml*), fiddle around (*infml*), footle (*infml*)

foolhardiness n **recklessness**, imprudence, stupidity, idiocy, foolishness *Opposite*: prudence

foolhardy *adj* **reckless**, rash, imprudent, foolish, unwise *Opposite*: sensible

foolish *adj* 1 **stupid**, silly, unwise, imprudent, thoughtless *Opposite*: wise 2 **ridiculous**, laughable, silly, ludicrous, absurd

foolishness n **irrationality**, stupidity, idiocy, silliness, imprudence *Opposite*: wisdom

foolproof *adj* **secure**, safe, infallible, failsafe, perfect *Opposite*: risky

foot n **base**, bottom, end *Opposite*: top

footage n **film**, shots, tape, videotape, material

football n **matter**, point, problem, issue, hot potato

footer n **addendum**, title, footnote, note, text Opposite: header

footfall n **footstep**, step, tread, sound

foothill n **hill**, slope, base, foot, bottom Opposite: summit

foothold n **position**, base, purchase, grip, toehold

footing n **1 stability**, equilibrium, purchase, foothold, grip **2 basis**, position, foundation, base, support

footle (infml) v **1 fool around**, idle, putter, dawdle, fiddle around (infml) **2 chatter**, prattle, blabber, blather (infml), blab (infml) ■ n **nonsense**, rubbish, prattle, balderdash, bunkum (infml)

footlights n **acting**, the stage, the theater, the limelight

footling (infml) adj **trivial**, unimportant, insignificant, trifling, inconsequential Opposite: important

footloose adj **free**, unattached, uncommitted, unrestricted, single

footnote n **note**, annotation, cross-reference, appendix, addendum

footpath n **path**, trail, track, pathway, walkway

footprint n **footmark**, footstep, print, imprint, impression

footrest n **rail**, bar, stool, footstool, foot rail

footsore adj **tired**, weary, exhausted, aching, sore

footstep n **footfall**, sound, step, tread, pace

footstool n **footrest**, stool, support, ottoman

footway see footpath

footwork n **cunning**, skill, negotiation, horse-trading, deviousness

fop n **peacock**, narcissus, poseur, poser (infml), dandy (dated)

foppish adj **vain**, affected, preening, narcissistic, self-obsessed

for prep **1 aimed at**, intended for, designed for, meant for, used for **2 in favor of**, in support of, pro Opposite: against

forage n **1 food**, feed, fodder, silage **2 quest**, search for, hunt, exploration, foray ■ v **look for**, search, seek, scavenge, rummage

for all prep **despite**, in spite of, even with, notwithstanding (fml)

foray n **raid**, incursion, venture, sortie, expedition

forbear (fml) v **refrain**, restrain yourself, abstain, hold back, withhold

forbearance (fml) n **patience**, self-control, restraint, tolerance, moderation Opposite: impatience

forbearing (fml) adj **patient**, long-suffering, forgiving, tolerant, lenient Opposite: impatient

forbid v **prohibit**, ban, bar, prevent, outlaw Opposite: allow

forbidden adj **prohibited**, banned, outlawed, illegal, illicit Opposite: permissible

forbidding adj **1 hostile**, unfriendly, stern, harsh, unsympathetic Opposite: approachable **2 uninviting**, unpleasant, dismal, depressing, bleak Opposite: welcoming **3 threatening**, ominous, menacing, sinister, dangerous

force n **1 power**, strength, energy, might, vigor Opposite: weakness **2 influence**, weight, power, strength, intensity ■ v **1 compel**, oblige, make, impose, coerce **2 push**, shove, break down, break open, press

forced adj **1 strained**, unnatural, affected, put on, artificial Opposite: natural **2 involuntary**, compulsory, required, obligatory, enforced Opposite: voluntary

force-feed v **1 fatten**, fatten up, feed, nourish, sustain **2 teach**, brainwash, program, ram down somebody's throat, cram

forceful adj **1 powerful**, vigorous, strong, dynamic, potent Opposite: weak **2 persuasive**, convincing, compelling, valid, powerful Opposite: unconvincing

forcefulness n **1 strength**, power, vigor, dynamism, influence Opposite: weakness **2 persuasiveness**, validity, cogency, powerfulness, power

force out v **drive out**, expel, turn out, oust, evict

forces n **armed forces**, military, services, defense force

forcible adj **1 compulsory**, violent, aggressive, armed Opposite: peaceful **2 effective**, forceful, powerful, convincing, persuasive Opposite: weak

ford n **shallows**, crossing, passage, stepping stone ■ v **cross**, traverse, negotiate, cross over, wade

fore (literary) n **front**, forefront, forepart, bow, face Opposite: back

forearm v **prepare**, forewarn, prime, tip off (infml), alert

forebear n **ancestor**, forerunner, antecedent, predecessor, grandparent Opposite: descendant

foreboding n **premonition**, presentiment, feeling, fear, intuition ■ adj **ominous**, menacing, threatening, sinister, forbidding Opposite: encouraging

forecast v **predict**, estimate, calculate, project, anticipate ■ n **prediction**, estimate, guess, calculation, conjecture

forecaster n **forward planner**, interpreter, analyst, prophet

foreclose (fml) v **exclude**, shut out, close out, ban, exile

forecourt n **space**, area, courtyard, concourse, square

forefront *n* **1 front**, head, vanguard, lead, van *Opposite*: back **2 foreground**, forepart, front, frontage, face *Opposite*: background

forego *v* **1** *(fml)* **precede**, come first, go before, herald, pave the way

foregoing *adj* **previous**, prior, preceding, earlier, former

foregone *adj* **inevitable**, predetermined, inescapable, unavoidable, fated *Opposite*: uncertain

foreground *n* **forefront**, front, center, center stage, focus *Opposite*: background

foreign *adj* **1 alien**, external, extraneous, imported, overseas *Opposite*: indigenous **2 strange**, unfamiliar, unknown, alien, exotic *Opposite*: familiar **3 unrelated**, extraneous, irrelevant, external, unconnected *Opposite*: relevant

foreigner *n* **stranger**, foreign person, alien, immigrant, newcomer *Opposite*: national

foreknowledge *n* **premonition**, prescience, feeling, foresight, intuition *Opposite*: hindsight

foreleg *n* **front leg**, forelimb, limb, leg, appendage

foremost *adj* **chief**, leading, primary, prime, notable

forename *n* **first name**, given name, Christian name, nickname, pet name *Opposite*: surname

forerunner *n* **1 portent**, indication, omen, sign, harbinger **2 forebear**, ancestor, antecedent, precursor, predecessor

foresee *v* **expect**, foretell, prophesy, divine, predict *Opposite*: look back

foreseeable *adj* **1 predictable**, probable, likely, imaginable, conceivable *Opposite*: unforeseeable **2 near**, immediate, imminent, prospective, impending *Opposite*: far-off

foreshadow *v* **presage**, indicate, suggest, warn of, augur

foreshore *n* **shore**, beach, mudflat, sand, shingle

foresight *n* **1 forethought**, prudence, farsightedness, anticipation, sagacity *Opposite*: hindsight **2 premonition**, insight, prescience, intuition, foreknowledge *Opposite*: hindsight

forest *n* **woods**, woodland, forestry, plantation, jungle

forestall *v* **prevent**, avert, preempt, obviate, hinder

foretaste *n* **sample**, token, indication, example, taste *Opposite*: recollection

foretell *(literary)* *v* **predict**, prophesy, presage, portend, forecast *Opposite*: review

forethought *n* **anticipation**, consideration, foresight, prudence, planning *Opposite*: afterthought

forever *adv* **1 eternally**, for all time, in perpetuity, indefinitely, ad infinitum *Opposite*: momentarily **2** *(infml)* **incessantly**, persistently, repeatedly, continually, endlessly *Opposite*: never

forewarn *v* **warn**, caution, alert, prime, forearm

forewarning *n* **warning**, notice, notification, word of warning, signal

foreword *n* **preface**, introduction, prelude, preamble, prologue *Opposite*: conclusion

forfeit *n* **penalty**, forfeiture, loss, penalization, punishment ■ *v* **1 lose**, pay for, be deprived of, pay with, be stripped of **2 surrender**, sacrifice, give up, part with, go without

forfeiture *n* **penalty**, forfeit, loss, penalization, punishment

forge *n* **furnace**, hearth, oven ■ *v* **1 shape**, form, build, create, fashion **2 counterfeit**, fake, falsify, copy, imitate

forge ahead *v* **take the lead**, come to the fore, make progress, make headway, move forward *Opposite*: lag

forged *adj* **fake**, counterfeit, false, spurious, phony *Opposite*: genuine

forger *n* **counterfeiter**, falsifier, faker, coiner, imitator

forgery *n* **fake**, counterfeit, sham, phony, imitation *Opposite*: original

forget *v* **1 overlook**, disremember, fail to recall, be unable to remember, be unable to call to mind *Opposite*: remember **2 stop thinking about**, put out of your mind, disregard, put behind you, turn your back on *Opposite*: attend to. *See* COMPARE AND CONTRAST *at* neglect.

forgetful *adj* **1 absent-minded**, inclined to forget, vague, oblivious *Opposite*: mindful **2 inattentive**, neglectful, negligent, wandering, careless *Opposite*: attentive

forgetfulness *n* **absent-mindedness**, amnesia, obliviousness, insensibleness, vagueness

forgettable *adj* **unmemorable**, unremarkable, undistinguished, mediocre, ordinary *Opposite*: unforgettable

forgivable *adj* **pardonable**, excusable, allowable, defensible, justifiable *Opposite*: unforgivable

forgive *v* **pardon**, excuse, forgive and forget, let off, absolve *Opposite*: blame

forgiveness *n* **1 pardon**, absolution, amnesty, exoneration, reconciliation *Opposite*: blame **2 clemency**, pity, mercy, compassion, understanding *Opposite*: ruthlessness

forgiving *adj* **merciful**, lenient, magnanimous, sympathetic, compassionate *Opposite*: unforgiving

forgo *v* **do without**, sacrifice, pass by, waive, relinquish *Opposite*: take up

forgotten *adj* **lost**, gone, neglected, disregarded, buried *Opposite*: immortal

fork *n* **divide**, split, divergence, junction, branch

forked *adj* **split**, cleft, divided, branched, pronged *Opposite*: undivided

forlorn *adj* **1 miserable**, sad, dejected, despondent, unhappy *Opposite*: cheerful **2 desolate**, neglected, abandoned, lonely, lost *Opposite*: cherished

form *n* **1 structure**, state, condition, nature, status **2 procedure**, method, system, arrangement, formula **3 type**, variety, kind, mode, manner **4 shape**, configuration, appearance, outline, look **5 document**, paper, questionnaire, pro forma, blank ■ *v* **1 develop**, take shape, materialize, come into being, arise **2 fashion**, shape, mold, model, create **3 start**, found, create, bring into being, establish

formal *adj* **1 conventional**, reserved, stiff, prim, starched *Opposite*: relaxed **2 official**, proper, prescribed, recognized, strict *Opposite*: informal

formality *n* **1 conventionalism**, reserve, stiffness, primness, correctness *Opposite*: informality **2 procedure**, requirement, regulation, custom, ritual

formalization *n* **validation**, ratification, solemnization, reinforcement, celebration

formalize *v* **validate**, ratify, solemnize, reinforce, celebrate

format *n* **structure**, presentation, organization, arrangement, setup ■ *v* **arrange**, lay out, organize, configure, set up

formation *n* **1 creation**, development, construction, establishment, foundation **2 arrangement**, configuration, shape, structure, pattern

formative *adj* **influential**, determinative, seminal, decisive, developmental

formative years *n* **childhood**, early life, early years, early childhood, infancy *Opposite*: maturity

former *adj* **previous**, past, ex-, earlier, prior *Opposite*: current

formerly *adv* **previously**, before, in the past, once, earlier

formidable *adj* **1 difficult**, tough, daunting, arduous, challenging *Opposite*: easy **2 awe-inspiring**, impressive, remarkable, astounding, awesome *Opposite*: uninspiring **3 alarming**, frightening, dreadful, fearsome, redoubtable *Opposite*: encouraging

formless *adj* **shapeless**, amorphous, unformed, unshaped, unstructured *Opposite*: distinct

formula *n* **1 method**, plan, modus operandi, recipe, prescription **2 cliché**, stock phrase, expression, phrase, formulation

formulaic *adj* **1 prescribed**, standard, rigid, fixed, set **2 unoriginal**, imitative, clichéd, overused, cookie-cutter *Opposite*: original

formulate *v* **1 devise**, invent, prepare, put together, make **2 express**, represent, present, frame, put into words

formulation *n* **1 preparation**, design, construction, creation, invention **2 representation**, guise, form, presentation, manifestation

forsake *v* **1 abandon**, leave, disown, quit, desert *Opposite*: support **2 renounce**, relinquish, give up, turn your back on, sacrifice

forsaken *adj* **abandoned**, cast off, discarded, deserted, jilted *Opposite*: supported

forswear *(literary)* *v* **1 reject**, renounce, abjure, give up, disown *Opposite*: resort to **2 deny**, disavow, contradict, disclaim, swear *Opposite*: admit

fort *n* **fortification**, fortress, stronghold, citadel, castle

forte *n* **strong point**, specialty, strong suit, gift, strength *Opposite*: failing

forth *(fml)* *adv* **1 forward**, ahead, onward *Opposite*: back **2 out**, into view, into the open, into the world *Opposite*: back

forthcoming *adj* **1 approaching**, impending, imminent, upcoming, future *Opposite*: distant **2 available**, ready, offered, supplied, in the offing *Opposite*: unavailable **3 helpful**, open, obliging, cooperative, informative *Opposite*: reticent

forthright *adj* **straightforward**, direct, frank, outspoken, plain-spoken *Opposite*: timid

forthrightness *n* **frankness**, candor, directness, candidness, outspokenness *Opposite*: timidity

forthwith *adv* **immediately**, without delay, at once, right away, instantly *Opposite*: later

fortification *n* **1 strengthening**, reinforcement, defense, buttressing, building up *Opposite*: erosion **2 ramparts**, defenses, buttresses, walls, earthworks

fortified *adj* **1 encouraged**, heartened, invigorated, reinvigorated, stimulated *Opposite*: drained **2 defended**, protected, walled, garrisoned, secured *Opposite*: exposed **3 reinforced**, strengthened, hardened, buttressed, toughened *Opposite*: unsupported

fortify *v* **1 make stronger**, strengthen, reinforce, brace, support *Opposite*: weaken **2 defend**, protect, wall, garrison, secure *Opposite*: expose **3 give a boost to**, revive, refresh, reinvigorate, invigorate *Opposite*: drain **4 build up**, boost, bolster, support, sustain *Opposite*: weaken **5 enrich**, boost, enhance, improve, mix *Opposite*: deplete

fortitude *n* **strength**, courage, resilience, staying power, grit *Opposite*: weakness

fortress *n* **stronghold**, fort, citadel, fortification, castle

fortuitous *adj* **accidental**, chance, casual, unexpected, unplanned *Opposite*: planned

fortunate *adj* **1 lucky**, providential, happy, opportune, auspicious *Opposite*: unfortunate **2 privileged**, lucky, blessed, well-off, prosperous *Opposite*: unfortunate. *See* COMPARE AND CONTRAST *at* lucky.

fortunately *adv* 1 as luck would have it, by chance, luckily, providentially, opportunely *Opposite*: unfortunately 2 happily, luckily, mercifully, thank goodness, thank heavens *Opposite*: unfortunately

fortune *n* 1 wealth, riches, affluence, opulence, prosperity *Opposite*: poverty 2 luck, chance, providence, accident, fate *Opposite*: design 3 destiny, fate, kismet, karma, future *Opposite*: past 4 mint *(infml)*, pile *(infml)*, tidy sum *(infml)*, an arm and a leg *(infml)* *Opposite*: pittance

fortune-teller *n* clairvoyant, seer, soothsayer, psychic, medium

forty winks *(infml)* *n* nap, doze, sleep, siesta, catnap

forum *n* 1 opportunity, medium, environment, setting, scene 2 meeting, debate, discussion, conference, assembly

forward *adv* 1 onward, ahead, frontward, up, to the fore *Opposite*: backward 2 to the fore, into view, into the open, up *Opposite*: back ■ *adj* 1 onward, advancing, frontward, headlong, headfirst *Opposite*: backward 2 presumptuous, self-assured, bold, familiar, brazen *Opposite*: reticent ■ *v* 1 advance, promote, further, accelerate, progress *Opposite*: hold back 2 send, dispatch, mail, pass on, redirect

forward-looking *adj* progressive, modern, forward-thinking, avant-garde, open-minded *Opposite*: backward-looking

forwardness *n* boldness, directness, brazenness, forthrightness, self-assurance *Opposite*: reticence

forward-thinking *see* forward-looking

fossil *n* relic, remnant, vestige, remains

fossilization *n* petrification, preservation, calcification, hardening, solidification

fossilize *v* turn into stone, petrify, solidify, harden, calcify

foster *v* 1 take care of, care for, take in, bring up, raise 2 promote, further, advance, cultivate, forward *Opposite*: discourage ■ *adj* stand-in, substitute, adoptive, temporary, short-term *Opposite*: natural

foster child *n* child, dependant, adoptee, ward

foster parent *n* guardian, substitute parent, foster father, foster mother

foul *adj* 1 unpleasant, disgusting, offensive, distasteful, filthy *Opposite*: pleasant 2 vulgar, obscene, lewd, uncouth, unwholesome *Opposite*: decent 3 inclement, stormy, wet, unpleasant, rotten *Opposite*: fair 4 unclean, stinking, polluted, tainted, soiled *Opposite*: clean 5 dishonest, shady, criminal, treacherous, dishonorable *Opposite*: legitimate 6 *(infml)* horrible, rotten, unpleasant, nasty, dreadful *Opposite*: charming ■ *v* 1 entangle,

tangle up, catch, ensnarl, snarl *Opposite*: free 2 pollute, soil, make dirty, contaminate, taint

foul-mouthed *adj* blasphemous, crude, rude, dirty, vulgar *Opposite*: polite

foulness *n* 1 filth, filthiness, squalor, pollution, dirt *Opposite*: cleanness 2 vulgarity, obscenity, lewdness, profanity, uncouthness *Opposite*: decency

foul play *n* 1 criminal action, treachery, dishonesty, villainy, violence *Opposite*: honesty 2 deviousness, unfairness, cheating, trickery, monkey business *(infml)*

foul-smelling *adj* smelly, reeking, malodorous, fetid, rotten *Opposite*: sweet-smelling

foul-tasting *adj* nasty, disgusting, unpleasant, indigestible, revolting

foul-up *(infml)* *n* blunder, slip, mix-up, error, mistake *Opposite*: success

found *v* originate, set up, create, start, bring into being *Opposite*: close

foundation *n* 1 basis, grounds, substance, groundwork, underpinning *Opposite*: superstructure 2 establishment, institution, charity, institute, society

founder *n* creator, originator, initiator, organizer, forefather ■ *v* 1 sink, go down, plunge, wallow, submerge *Opposite*: float 2 fail, break down, come to nothing, fall through, miscarry *Opposite*: succeed

foundling *(dated)* *n* orphan, waif, stray, urchin, outcast

fount *(literary)* *n* source, fountain, well, spring, wellspring

fountain *n* 1 cascade, water feature, spout, jet, spring 2 source, origin, cause, beginning, fountainhead

fountainhead *see* fountain

four-letter word *n* swearword, vulgarity, vulgarism, obscenity, expletive *Opposite*: euphemism

foursome *n* group of four, quartet, group, ensemble

fourth *n* quarter, twenty-five percent, fourth part

fox *v* 1 deceive, trick, outwit, fool, con 2 confuse, baffle, muddle, puzzle, perplex *Opposite*: enlighten

foxy *adj* sly, cunning, crafty, sharp, wily *Opposite*: naive

foyer *n* lobby, vestibule, reception area, hall, entrance hall

fracas *n* quarrel, row, fight, brawl, melee *Opposite*: calm

fraction *n* 1 little bit, little, small part, tiny proportion, small percentage 2 part, portion, segment, section, division *Opposite*: whole

fractional *adj* slight, small, tiny, minuscule, insignificant *Opposite*: great

fractionally *adv* slightly, marginally, just, a

little, a fraction *Opposite*: greatly

fractious *adj* irritable, peevish, restless, complaining, grumpy *Opposite*: even-tempered

fracture *n* break, breakage, crack, rupture, fissure *Opposite*: repair ■ *v* **crack**, break, rupture, splinter, split *Opposite*: mend

fragile *adj* 1 **delicate**, brittle, flimsy, breakable, frail *Opposite*: sturdy 2 **tenuous**, unstable, delicate, precarious, shaky *Opposite*: stable 3 **frail**, weak, delicate, infirm, feeble *Opposite*: strong

COMPARE AND CONTRAST CORE MEANING: easily broken or damaged
fragile not having a strong structure or not made of robust materials, and therefore easily broken or damaged; **delicate** similar to *fragile*, used especially of things that are beautiful or remarkable because of their fragility; **frail** easily broken or damaged, or physically weak and vulnerable to injury; **flimsy** too easily broken, torn, or damaged, especially used of badly or cheaply made goods, or of light and insubstantial clothing; **frangible** capable of being broken or easily damaged; **friable** easily reduced to tiny particles.

fragility *n* 1 **brittleness**, flimsiness, delicateness, delicacy, breakability *Opposite*: solidity 2 **tenuousness**, instability, delicacy, delicateness, precariousness *Opposite*: stability 3 **frailty**, weakness, feebleness, ill health, infirmity *Opposite*: strength

fragment *n* piece, portion, bit, splinter, sliver *Opposite*: whole ■ *v* **break**, divide, break up, disintegrate, crumble *Opposite*: fuse

fragmentary *adj* incomplete, disconnected, scrappy, patchy, fragmented *Opposite*: entire

fragmentation *n* disintegration, destruction, shattering, breaking up, crumbling *Opposite*: fusion

fragmented *adj* disjointed, uneven, scrappy, patchy *Opposite*: continuous

fragrance *n* 1 **smell**, scent, perfume, bouquet, aroma 2 **cologne**, scent, perfume, toilet water, eau de toilette. *See* COMPARE AND CONTRAST *at* smell.

fragranced *adj* perfumed, scented, sweet-smelling, fragrant

fragrant *adj* perfumed, aromatic, scented, sweet-smelling, fragranced *Opposite*: smelly

frail *adj* 1 **weak**, infirm, delicate, feeble, puny *Opposite*: robust 2 **flimsy**, insubstantial, fragile, delicate, spindly *Opposite*: sturdy. *See* COMPARE AND CONTRAST *at* fragile, weak.

frailness *see* frailty

frailty *n* 1 **infirmity**, weakness, feebleness, fragility, ill health *Opposite*: robustness 2 **shortcoming**, weakness, imperfection, failing, defect *Opposite*: strength

frame *n* 1 **structure**, framework, scaffold, skeleton, support 2 **edge**, surround, border, mount, setting 3 **body**, form, build, physique, skeleton ■ *v* **enclose**, mount, border, edge, outline *Opposite*: inset

frame of mind *n* mood, mental state, mental condition, humor, temper

frame of reference *n* **context**, situation, standpoint, background, setting

framework *n* 1 **structure**, frame, scaffold, skeleton, support 2 **outline**, agenda, basis, context, background

franchise *n* permit, contract, authorization, charter, agreement ■ *v* license, permit, contract, contract out, grant

frangible *adj* breakable, fragile, brittle, easily broken. *See* COMPARE AND CONTRAST *at* fragile.

frank *adj* forthright, free, honest, guileless, open *Opposite*: insincere

frankfurter *n* hot dog, sausage, wiener, wienerwurst, frank *(infml)*

frankness *n* honesty, forthrightness, openness, bluntness, truthfulness *Opposite*: insincerity

frantic *adj* 1 **panicky**, hysterical, beside yourself, desperate, agitated *Opposite*: calm 2 **frenzied**, frenetic, hectic, feverish, wild *Opposite*: calm

fraternal *adj* 1 **sibling**, brotherly, brother's, familial, genealogical 2 **comradely**, brotherly, friendly, amicable, communal *Opposite*: hostile

fraternity *n* 1 **society**, frat, group, guild, association 2 **community**, network, group, world, clan *(infml)* 3 **brotherliness**, brotherhood, comradeship, mutual support, friendship *Opposite*: hostility

fraternization *n* mixing, socializing, intercourse, mingling, partying *Opposite*: avoidance

fraternize *v* associate, socialize, mix, hobnob, hang out *(infml)* *Opposite*: avoid

fraud *n* 1 **deception**, con, scheme, swindle, deceit 2 **dishonesty**, deceit, deception, double-dealing, trickery *Opposite*: honesty 3 **impostor** charlatan, hoaxer, swindler, cheat

fraudulence *n* deceit, duplicity, deceitfulness illegitimacy, dishonesty *Opposite*: honesty

fraudulent *adj* fake, deceitful, untrue, duplicitous, dishonest *Opposite*: genuine

fraught *adj* 1 **full**, charged, filled, weighed down, laden *Opposite*: free 2 **tense**, anxious, nervous, troubled, apprehensive *Opposite*: calm

fray *v* unravel, ravel, wear, wear out, tatter *Opposite*: mend ■ *n* fight, argument, quarrel, fracas, dispute

frayed *adj* threadbare, worn, tattered, ragged, unraveled

frazzled *(infml)* *adj* exhausted, weary, tired out, drained, fatigued *Opposite*: lively

freak n 1 **curiosity**, rarity, oddity, aberration, anomaly 2 **chance**, surprise, happenstance, accident, fluke (infml) 3 (infml) **enthusiast**, fanatic, fiend, buff, lover

freakish adj **variable**, volatile, changeable, unpredictable, inexplicable Opposite: stable

freaky adj **weird**, strange, amazing, grotesque, unexpected Opposite: commonplace

freckle n **spot**, mark, patch, speckle, speck

freckled adj **speckled**, freckly, dappled, spotted, stippled

free adj 1 **liberated**, unbound, released, emancipated, freed Opposite: imprisoned 2 **allowed**, at liberty, permitted, able, welcome Opposite: restricted 3 **open**, uninhibited, uncontrolled, spontaneous, honest Opposite: inhibited 4 **unrestricted**, unregimented, unconventional, loose, unstructured Opposite: conventional 5 **relaxing**, off, available, unoccupied, on vacation Opposite: working 6 **gratis**, free of charge, without charge, at no cost, complimentary ■ v 1 **release**, let go, set free, liberate, emancipate Opposite: imprison 2 **exempt**, rid, unburden, excuse, pardon

free-and-easy adj **indulgent**, overindulgent, lax, overfamiliar, relaxed Opposite: uptight (infml)

freebie (infml) n **free sample**, handout, perk, free gift, free offer

freedom n 1 **liberty**, autonomy, lack of restrictions, self-determination, independence Opposite: restriction 2 **frankness**, openness, abandon, free expression, ease Opposite: inhibition 3 **looseness**, inventiveness, nonconformity Opposite: conformity

free fall n 1 **skydive**, jump, descent, drop, fall 2 **decline**, descent, collapse, confusion, turmoil Opposite: upturn

free-fall v 1 **skydive**, drop, plummet, fall, descend Opposite: soar 2 **drop**, plummet, collapse, decline, fall apart

free-for-all (infml) n **brawl**, fight, brouhaha, riot, scuffle

free gift n **free sample**, free offer, giveaway (infml), freebie (infml)

freehand adj **without a pattern**, by eye, by hand, sketchy, free

freehanded adj **generous**, openhanded, unstinting, giving, liberal Opposite: stingy

freehold n 1 **tenure**, ownership, right, occupancy 2 **property**, estate, land, building, holding

freeholder n **property owner**, landowner, owner, holder, landlord

freeing n **release**, liberation, acquittal, emancipation, freedom Opposite: capture

freelance adj **self-employed**, temporary, irregular, casual, ad hoc Opposite: permanent

freeload (infml) v **live off others**, parasitize, take advantage, use others, sponge (infml)

freeloader (infml) n **slacker**, parasite, idler, hanger-on, user

freely adv 1 **liberally**, generously, unreservedly, without restraint, without stinting Opposite: parsimoniously 2 **without restrictions**, at will, at liberty easily, spontaneously

free-range adj **unconfined**, free, loose, at large, uncaged

free spirit n **individualist**, nonconformist, maverick, freethinker, rebel Opposite: conformist

freestanding adj **self-supporting**, unconnected, separate, detached, unattached Opposite: attached

freethinker n **individualist**, free spirit, nonconformist, nonbeliever, skeptic Opposite: conformist

freethinking adj **independent**, open-minded, enlightened, nonconformist, liberal Opposite: conformist

free time n **leisure**, leisure time, spare time, time off, recreation

free up v 1 **make available**, empty, make space for, clear, liberate Opposite: occupy 2 (infml) **loosen**, unjam, unblock, unsnarl, unclog Opposite: snarl

freewheel v 1 **take it easy**, drift, go with the flow, cruise Opposite: struggle 2 **coast**, sail, glide, cruise, roll along

freewheeling adj 1 **carefree**, free and easy, easygoing, unrestricted, self-indulgent 2 **wide-ranging**, open-ended, unstructured, unrestricted, with no holds barred Opposite: methodical

free will n **autonomy**, self-determination, choice, liberty, freedom Opposite: dependence

freeze v 1 **turn to ice**, freeze up, ice up, ice over, solidify Opposite: thaw 2 **hold**, fix, restrict, stop, control 3 **halt**, stop, stop in your tracks, stop dead, stiffen Opposite: relax 4 **refrigerate**, chill, cool, preserve Opposite: thaw 5 **suspend**, stop, halt, hold, break off Opposite: resume ■ n **restriction**, halt, embargo, check, stoppage Opposite: resumption

freeze out (infml) v **exclude**, ostracize, give the cold shoulder, ignore, neglect Opposite: welcome

freeze up v **ice over**, ice up, harden, solidify, freeze Opposite: thaw

freezing adj **cold**, subzero, icy, chilly, bitter Opposite: hot

freight n 1 **cargo**, goods, merchandise, consignment, load 2 **carriage**, shipping, conveyance, transport, transportation

frenetic adj **hectic**, bustling, busy, frantic, feverish Opposite: calm

frenzied adj **frantic**, hyperactive, hysterical, feverish, emotional Opposite: calm

frenzy n 1 **fury**, turmoil, fever, rage, passion

Opposite: calmness **2 whirl**, fit, tumult, rush, flurry

frequency *n* **incidence**, occurrence, regularity, rate of recurrence, rate

frequent *adj* **recurrent**, common, everyday, normal, numerous *Opposite*: infrequent ■ *v* **visit**, haunt, patronize, hang around, spend time at *Opposite*: avoid

fresco *n* **wall painting**, mural, frieze, wall, painting

fresh *adj* **1 new**, renewed, additional, replacement, other *Opposite*: old **2 clean**, bright, unmarked, unsullied, immaculate *Opposite*: soiled **3 wholesome**, crisp, pleasant, airy, refreshing *Opposite*: musty **4 at its best**, garden-fresh, crisp, moist, juicy *Opposite*: stale **5 novel**, original, new, inventive, innovative *Opposite*: hackneyed **6 alert**, energetic, lively, vigorous, active *Opposite*: tired. *See* COMPARE AND CONTRAST *at* NEW.

freshen *v* **tidy**, neaten, dust, clean, air

freshen up *v* **wash**, shower, change, wash up, clean up

fresh-faced *adj* **youthful**, young-looking, baby-faced, boyish, girlish

freshly *adv* **newly**, recently, just now, a moment ago, just this minute

freshness *n* **1 cleanness**, cleanliness, brightness, sparkle, brilliance *Opposite*: grubbiness **2 crispness**, juiciness, flavor, moistness *Opposite*: staleness **3 novelty**, originality, newness, inventiveness, innovation *Opposite*: tiredness

fret *v* **worry**, fuss, agonize, vex, trouble *Opposite*: calm down

fretful *adj* **worried**, restless, agitated, unsettled, distressed *Opposite*: calm

fretfulness *n* **anxiety**, restlessness, agitation, distress, unease *Opposite*: calmness

friable *adj* **crumbly**, powdery, workable, light *Opposite*: heavy. *See* COMPARE AND CONTRAST *at* FRAGILE.

friary *n* **religious community**, monastery, religious foundation, fraternity, brotherhood

friction *n* **1 rubbing**, abrasion, contact, chafing, rasping **2 hostility**, conflict, tension, antagonism, disagreement *Opposite*: accord

friend *n* **1 comrade**, companion, pal (*infml*), chum (*infml*), buddy (*infml*) *Opposite*: foe (*fml*) **2 acquaintance**, contact, colleague, associate, partner *Opposite*: stranger **3 ally**, helper, supporter, well-wisher, collaborator *Opposite*: rival

friendliness *n* **affability**, sociability, conviviality, amiability, approachability *Opposite*: reserve

friendly *adj* **1 affable**, sociable, approachable, outgoing, open *Opposite*: unfriendly **2 close**, familiar, intimate, congenial, amicable *Opposite*: frosty **3 beneficial**, helpful, favorable, welcoming, supportive *Opposite*: hostile

friendship *n* **1 companionship**, comradeship, camaraderie, closeness, familiarity *Opposite*: animosity **2 bond**, relationship, alliance, attachment, acquaintance

frieze *n* **decoration**, band, strip, panel, mural

fright *n* **1 fear**, terror, anxiety, foreboding, dread *Opposite*: composure **2 scare**, shock, start, turn, seizure

frighten *v* **scare**, terrify, alarm, startle, upset *Opposite*: soothe

frightened *adj* **scared**, afraid, terrified, alarmed, startled *Opposite*: calm

frightening *adj* **terrifying**, alarming, startling, fearsome, fearful *Opposite*: soothing

frightful *adj* **appalling**, horrible, unpleasant, dreadful, awful *Opposite*: pleasant

frightfully *adv* **terribly**, extremely, awfully, dreadfully, excessively

frightfulness *n* **awfulness**, atrociousness, severity, badness, hideousness *Opposite*: pleasantness

frigid *adj* **1 unfriendly**, standoffish, cold, distant, frosty *Opposite*: warm **2 cold**, frosty, chilly, icy, freezing *Opposite*: torrid

frigidity *n* **coldness**, frostiness, iciness, coldheartedness, aloofness *Opposite*: warmth

frigidly *adv* **coldly**, icily, frostily, unemotionally, unfeelingly *Opposite*: warmly

frill *n* **1 decoration**, flounce, trimming, ruffle, ruche **2 extra**, add-on, luxury, decoration, accompaniment

frills *n* **accompaniments**, trappings, added extras, embellishments, add-ons *Opposite*: essentials

frilly *adj* **lacy**, ruched, gathered, pleated, fancy *Opposite*: plain

fringe *n* **1 tassel**, edging, edge, border, trimming **2 periphery**, edge, extreme, perimeter, border *Opposite*: center ■ *adj* **1 peripheral**, outlying, marginal, far-flung, frontier *Opposite*: central **2 unconventional**, extreme, radical, marginal, extremist *Opposite*: mainstream

fringe benefit *n* **extra**, compensation, perk, privilege, reward

frisk *v* **1 play**, frolic, gambol, cavort, kick up your heels *Opposite*: plod **2 search**, pat down, body search, examine, inspect

friskiness *n* **playfulness**, excitability, excitement, liveliness, enthusiasm *Opposite*: lethargy

frisky *adj* **playful**, frolicsome, excitable, excited lighthearted *Opposite*: lethargic

fritter away *v* **dissipate**, waste, squander, misspend, gamble away *Opposite*: conserve

frivolity *n* **1 playfulness**, perkiness, lightheartedness, merriment, gaiety *Opposite*: seriousness **2 triviality**, frivolousness, unimportance, inconsequentiality, superficiality *Opposite*: seriousness

frivolous *adj* **1 playful**, frolicsome, perky,

lighthearted, silly *Opposite*: serious
2 trivial, silly, inconsequential, idle, shallow *Opposite*: serious

frizz v **curl**, crimp, frizzle, perm, kink *Opposite*: straighten

frizzle v **1 burn**, shrivel, scorch, sear, dry up **2 frizz**, curl, perm, crimp, kink *Opposite*: straighten **3 sizzle**, fry, pan-fry, sauté, grill

frizzy adj **curled**, wiry, curly, kinky, frizzed *Opposite*: straight

frolic v **play**, skip, cavort, frisk, gambol *Opposite*: plod

frolicsome adj **playful**, frisky, frivolous, lighthearted, spirited *Opposite*: solemn

frond n **leaf**, branch, palm leaf, fern leaf

front n **façade**, face, frontage, obverse, head *Opposite*: back

frontage n **front**, façade, face, outlook, front part *Opposite*: rear

frontal adj **forward**, anterior, front, fore *(literary)* *Opposite*: posterior *(fml)*

front door n **main entrance**, main door, door, entrance, entry *Opposite*: back door

frontier n **border**, boundary, limit, edge, border line

frontispiece n **illustration**, print, picture, photograph, drawing

front line n **1 front**, war zone, battle zone, combat zone, ground zero **2 forefront**, cutting edge, leading edge, sharp end, vanguard

front-page adj **headline**, important, significant, momentous, attention-grabbing

frontrunner *(infml)* n **leader**, head, favorite, prime candidate, number one *(infml)* *Opposite*: also-ran

frontward adv **ahead**, to the fore, forward *Opposite*: backward

frost n **1 ice**, rime, hoar frost **2 cold**, frostiness, iciness, coolness, frigidity *Opposite*: warmth

frosted adj **ice-covered**, frosty, iced, icy, snowy *Opposite*: thawed

frostily adv **coldly**, icily, coolly, frigidly, angrily *Opposite*: warmly

frostiness n **1 iciness**, coldness, cold, chill, rawness *Opposite*: warmth **2 coldness**, aloofness, frigidity, coolness, iciness *Opposite*: warmth

frosting n **1 icing**, cake coating, decoration, topping, ganache **2 dullness**, opaqueness, opacity, mat finish, mat surface

frosty adj **1 icy**, cold, chilly, freezing, frigid *Opposite*: warm **2 cold**, unfriendly, cool, icy, frigid *Opposite*: friendly

froth n **1 foam**, bubbles, lather, head, fizz **2 triviality**, trivia, frivolity, superficiality, shallowness *Opposite*: substance ■ v **to become foamy**, foam, bubble, lather, lather up

frothiness n **1 foaminess**, bubbliness, fizziness, fizz, soapiness **2 triviality**, insub-

stantiality, lightness, frivolity, pettiness *Opposite*: seriousness

frothy adj **1 foamy**, foam-covered, lathered, lathered up, bubbly **2 light**, inconsequential, superficial, trivial, shallow *Opposite*: serious

frown v **knit your brow**, scowl, glare, glower, lower *Opposite*: smile ■ n **scowl**, glare, glower, grimace, puckered brow *Opposite*: smile

frown on v **disapprove**, take a dim view of, frown upon, condemn, disfavor *Opposite*: favor. *See* COMPARE AND CONTRAST *at* **disapprove**.

frown upon *see* **frown on**

frowzy adj **unkempt**, disheveled, frayed, messy, shabby *Opposite*: neat

frozen adj **1 ice-covered**, cold, solid, freezing, iced up **2 immobile**, stationary, unmoving, still, motionless *Opposite*: mobile

frugal adj **thrifty**, prudent, economical, sparing, penny-wise *Opposite*: profligate

frugality n **thrift**, stinginess, parsimony, prudence, economy *Opposite*: profligacy

fruit n **1 ovary**, berry, pod, capsule, achene **2 produce**, bounty, harvest, crop, yield **3 product**, result, consequence, reward, fruition ■ v **produce fruit**, bear fruit, ripen, mature

WORD BANK

❑ **types of fruit** apple, apricot, avocado, banana, blackcurrant, cherry, citrus, damson, date, fig, grape, guava, kiwi fruit, kumquat, lychee, mango, melon, nectarine, olive, papaya, passion fruit, peach, pear, pineapple, plum, pomegranate, quince, raspberry, redcurrant, strawberry, watermelon

❑ **parts of a fruit** flesh, juice, kernel, peel, pip, pit, pith, pulp, rind, seed, skin

fruitful adj **productive**, fertile, rich, prolific, abundant *Opposite*: fruitless

fruitfulness n **productivity**, abundance, profitability, prosperity, fertility *Opposite*: fruitlessness

fruition n **completion**, maturity, readiness, realization, culmination

fruitless adj **unsuccessful**, futile, useless, unproductive, wasted *Opposite*: fruitful

fruitlessness n **uselessness**, futility, unproductiveness, failure, inadequacy *Opposite*: fruitfulness

fruity adj **1 rich**, sweet, tangy, zesty, lemony **2 mellow**, deep, rich, plummy, harmonious *Opposite*: shrill

frustrate v **1 thwart**, prevent, foil, stop, block *Opposite*: promote **2 discourage**, exasperate, irritate, upset, disturb *Opposite*: encourage

frustrated adj **1 unfulfilled**, unsatisfied, irritated, upset, angry *Opposite*: satisfied **2 foiled**, blocked, stymied, obstructed, hindered *Opposite*: successful

frustrating adj **annoying**, unsatisfying, exasperating, infuriating, maddening *Opposite*: satisfying

frustration *n* **1 prevention**, hindrance, blocking, foiling, defeat *Opposite*: success **2 dissatisfaction**, irritation, disturbance, annoyance, nuisance *Opposite*: satisfaction

fry *v* cook, sauté, stir-fry, fry up, deep-fry

frying pan *n* **pan**, skillet, spider *(dated)*

fuddle *v* **confuse**, bewilder, stupefy, muddle, dull *Opposite*: clarify ■ *n* **muddle**, dither, mess, state *(infml)*

fuddy-duddy *(infml)* *n* **fogy**, reactionary, stick-in-the-mud *(infml)*, stuffed shirt *(infml)*

fudge *(infml)* *n* **nonsense**, rubbish, garbage, verbiage, waffle *(infml)* ■ *v* **1 falsify**, doctor, alter, massage, fabricate **2 prevaricate**, beat around the bush, evade the issue, waffle *(infml)*

fuel *n* **energy source**, fossil fuel, alternative fuel, renewable fuel ■ *v* **1 power**, fire, run, drive, operate **2 stimulate**, increase, promote, fire, energize *Opposite*: quell

fug *n* **fog**, smog, haze, smoke, miasma

fugitive *n* **escapee**, deserter, absconder, outlaw, runaway ■ *adj* **brief**, fleeting, elusive, short, quick

fugue *n* **fugue state**, blackout, amnesia, memory loss

fulcrum *n* **pivot**, hinge, swivel, support, point

fulfill *v* **1 achieve**, accomplish, bear out, realize, live up to **2 carry out**, execute, follow, obey, complete *Opposite*: neglect **3 satisfy**, meet, conform to, be in conformity with, accord with *Opposite*: fall short **4 complete**, finish, see through, go through with, make it through *Opposite*: abandon **5 supply**, fill, deliver, provide, furnish *(fml)* *Opposite*: renege **6 succeed**, do proud, gain fulfillment, make good, fulfill your potential. *See* COMPARE AND CONTRAST *at* perform.

fulfilled *adj* **satisfied**, content, happy, pleased, rewarded *Opposite*: frustrated

fulfilling *adj* **satisfying**, rewarding, pleasing, gratifying, enjoyable *Opposite*: frustrating

fulfillment *n* **1 achievement**, realization, execution, completion, accomplishment *Opposite*: neglect **2 contentment**, serenity, inner peace, self-actualization, nirvana *Opposite*: dissatisfaction

full *adj* **1 occupied**, complete, bursting, packed, filled *Opposite*: empty **2 complete**, broad, extensive, comprehensive, detailed *Opposite*: sketchy **3 satiated**, satisfied, bursting, sated, replete *Opposite*: hungry **4 plump**, round, chubby, ample, broad *Opposite*: thin **5 sonorous**, resonant, rich, deep, plummy *Opposite*: shrill

full-blooded *adj* **vigorous**, hearty, thoroughgoing, forceful, robust *Opposite*: feeble

full-blown *adj* **complete**, full, full-scale, full-size, developed *Opposite*: incomplete

full-bodied *adj* **flavorful**, rich, intense, powerful, strong *Opposite*: insipid

full dress *n* **formal attire**, dress uniform, jacket and tie, evening dress, black tie

full-fashioned *adj* **shaped**, close-fitting, tailored, well-fitting, figure-hugging *Opposite*: loose-fitting

full-fledged *adj* **1 complete**, developed, mature, full-size, full-grown **2 qualified**, seasoned, genuine, real, actual

full-frontal *(infml)* *adj* **all-out**, unrestrained, wholehearted, uninhibited, concerted *Opposite*: half-hearted

full-grown *adj* **developed**, grown, matured, adult, full-size *Opposite*: immature

full-length *adj* **1 ankle-length**, floor-length, long *Opposite*: short **2 head-to-toe**, whole-body, full, long, tall **3 unabridged**, complete, uncut, unedited, unexpurgated *Opposite*: abridged

fullness *n* **1 completeness**, richness, abundance *Opposite*: emptiness **2 roundness**, plumpness, chubbiness, ampleness, pudginess *(infml)* *Opposite*: thinness

full of *adj* **alive with**, awash with, thick with, resplendent with, crammed with *Opposite*: lacking in

full-scale *adj* **1 life-size**, full-size, complete, full **2 total**, full-blown, unrestrained, all-out, unlimited *Opposite*: partial

full-size *adj* **normal**, standard, regular, ordinary

full-time *adj* **around-the-clock**, permanent, twenty-four-hour, day and night *Opposite*: part-time

full-timer *n* **full-time employee**, full-time worker, full-time member of staff *Opposite*: part-timer

fully *adv* **completely**, entirely, wholly, totally, altogether *Opposite*: partially

fulminate *v* **rail**, rant and rave, rage, rant, thunder *Opposite*: praise

fulsome *adj* **flattering**, excessive, immoderate, effusive, overgenerous

fumble *v* **1 grope**, scrabble, rummage, root, search **2 mishandle**, botch up, blunder, muddle, muddle up ■ *n* **mistake**, error, blunder, botched job, mess

fume *v* **seethe**, rage, bristle, be angry, be furious ■ *n* **1 emission**, vapor, miasma, smog, smoke **2 stench**, odor, smell, stink, reek

fumigate *v* **sterilize**, disinfect, decontaminate, delouse, smoke

fumigation *n* **disinfection**, decontamination, smoking, delousing, cleansing

fuming *adj* **furious**, irate, incensed, enraged, seething

fun *n* **amusement**, excitement, enjoyment, entertainment, merriment *Opposite*: boredom ■ *adj* *(infml)* **amusing**, entertaining, enjoyable, exciting, pleasurable *Opposite*: boring

function *n* 1 **purpose**, meaning, role, job, occupation 2 **event**, gathering, meeting, affair, party ■ *v* **work**, perform, operate, run, go *Opposite*: malfunction

functional *adj* 1 **practical**, useful, handy, purposeful, efficient *Opposite*: useless 2 **operational**, operative, running, going, working *Opposite*: inoperative

functionary *n* **official**, representative, bureaucrat, lackey, employee

fund *n* 1 **reserve**, account, supply, endowment, stock 2 **supply**, stock, store, source, collection ■ *v* **finance**, support, back, sponsor, subsidize

fundamental *adj* 1 **basic**, primary, original, essential, elementary *Opposite*: secondary 2 **central**, essential, vital, ultimate, major *Opposite*: superfluous

fundamentally *adv* **at heart**, at bottom, basically, essentially, primarily *Opposite*: superficially

fundamentals *n* **basics**, rudiments, essentials, ground rules, brass tacks

funding *n* **backing**, support, finance, subsidy, money

fundraiser *n* 1 **campaigner**, crusader, supporter, representative, moneymaker 2 **appeal**, campaign, crusade, push, drive

funeral *n* **service**, memorial, interment, burial, cremation

funereal *adj* **gloomy**, melancholy, sorrowful, mournful, sad *Opposite*: cheerful

fungal *adj* **fungiform**, mycological, fungoid, fungous

funky *(infml)* *adj* **up-to-date**, fashionable, trendy *(infml)*, cool *(infml)*, happening *(infml)*

fun-loving *adj* **playful**, joyful, high-spirited, frivolous, exuberant *Opposite*: staid

funnel *n* **chimney**, pipe, flue, smokestack, conduit ■ *v* **channel**, direct, focus, guide, concentrate

funnily *adv* 1 **strangely**, curiously, surprisingly, oddly, unusually 2 **comically**, humorously, amusingly, hilariously, wittily

funniness *n* **humor**, comedy, comicalness, wit, wittiness *Opposite*: solemnity

funny *adj* 1 **amusing**, humorous, comic, comical, hilarious *Opposite*: serious 2 **strange**, odd, weird, curious, peculiar *Opposite*: normal 3 **quaint**, unconventional, eccentric, quirky, odd 4 **unwell**, sick, nauseous, faint, giddy *(dated) Opposite*: well ■ *n* *(infml)* **joke**, pun, witticism, bon mot, gag *(infml)*

COMPARE AND CONTRAST CORE MEANING: causing or intended to cause amusement **funny** causing amusement or laughter, whether intentionally or not; **comic** used in the same way as *funny*, especially to describe books, poems, or plays; **comical** funny to the extent of being absurd, especially if this is unintentional; **droll** funny because it is whimsical or odd, or drily humorous; **facetious** supposed to be funny but ill-timed, inappropriate, or silly; **humorous** intended to make people laugh; **witty** using words in a clever, inventive, humorous way; **hilarious** extremely funny; **sidesplitting** very funny indeed, especially causing a great deal of uncontrollable laughter.

---

fur *n* **hair**, pelt, fleece, coat, fuzz

furious *adj* 1 **angry**, livid, fuming, irate, infuriated *Opposite*: calm 2 **energetic**, concerted, all-out, breakneck, violent

furiousness *n* 1 **anger**, rage, fury, wrath, crossness 2 **violence**, energy, vigor, ferocity, passion

furl *v* **roll up**, wrap up, curl, curl up, tie up *Opposite*: unfurl

furlough *n* 1 **leave of absence**, leave, absence, vacation, R & R 2 **layoff**, shutdown, unemployment

furnace *n* **heater**, oven, kiln, boiler, blast furnace

furnish *(fml)* *v* **supply**, provide, equip, give, deliver *Opposite*: strip

furnished *adj* **equipped**, fitted out, well-appointed, well-found *Opposite*: unfurnished

furnishings *n* **furniture**, tables, chairs, cabinets, beds

furniture *n* **tables**, chairs, cabinets, beds, furnishings

furor *n* 1 **uproar**, outcry, commotion, controversy, protest 2 **excitement**, hysteria, hype, frenzy, commotion

furore *see* furor

furred *see* furry

furriness *n* **hairiness**, fuzziness, woolliness, fleeciness, fluffiness *Opposite*: baldness

furrow *n* **channel**, groove, rut, undulation, gully ■ *v* **wrinkle**, crease, gather, draw, contract

furrowed *adj* **wrinkled**, crumply, creasy, wrinkly, crinkly *Opposite*: smooth

furry *adj* **hairy**, fuzzy, woolly, downy, furred

further *adj* **additional**, more, extra, added, supplementary ■ *v* **advance**, promote, foster, broaden, expand *Opposite*: prevent

furthermore *adv* **also**, in addition, besides, additionally, moreover

furthermost *adj* **farthest**, furthest, greatest, remotest, nethermost *(fml)*

furthest *adj* **farthest**, utmost, uttermost, outermost, furthermost

furtive *adj* **secretive**, stealthy, secret, sly, sneaky *Opposite*: open. *See* COMPARE AND CONTRAST *at* secret.

furtiveness *n* 1 **secrecy**, stealth, covertness, surreptitiousness, discreetness *Opposite*: openness 2 **sneakiness**, suspiciousness, guiltiness, slyness, craftiness *Opposite*: straightforwardness

fury *n* anger, rage, wrath, ferocity, ire *(fml)*. *See* COMPARE AND CONTRAST *at* anger.

fuse *v* combine, blend, mingle, meld, coalesce *Opposite*: fragment

fusion *n* synthesis, union, combination, mixture, blend *Opposite*: fission

fuss *n* 1 commotion, excitement, bother, bustle, activity 2 worry, concern, bother, trouble, hassle *(infml)* 3 protest, controversy, argument, complaint, reaction ■ *v* worry, fret, stew, bother, niggle

fussiness *n* 1 trivialness, pedantry, obsessiveness, prissiness, hairsplitting 2 meticulousness, dogmatism, inflexibility, fastidiousness, exactness 3 elaborateness, frilliness, ornateness, overstatement

fussy *adj* 1 trivial, pedantic, obsessive, prissy, assiduous 2 picky, particular, finicky, fastidious, selective *Opposite*: laid-back *(infml)* 3 elaborate, busy, frilly, ornate, overelaborate. *See* COMPARE AND CONTRAST *at* careful.

fusty *adj* 1 stale, moldy, damp, fetid, musty *Opposite*: fresh 2 stuffy, antiquated, dull,

boring, old-fashioned *Opposite*: trendy *(infml)*

futile *adj* useless, pointless, fruitless, unsuccessful, vain *Opposite*: useful

futility *n* uselessness, pointlessness, ineffectiveness, ineffectuality, vainness *Opposite*: usefulness

future *n* prospect, outlook, potential, time ahead, time to come *Opposite*: past ■ *adj* upcoming, forthcoming, coming, imminent, yet to come *Opposite*: past

futures *n* stocks, commodities, contracts, investments

futuristic *adj* innovative, revolutionary, ahead of its time, advanced, ultramodern *Opposite*: antiquated

fuzz *n* down, hair, fur, fluff

fuzziness *n* 1 hairiness, fluffiness, woolliness, down, wool 2 uncertainty, vagueness, incoherence, ambiguity, indistinctness *Opposite*: certainty 3 blurriness, nebulousness, haziness, vagueness, mistiness *Opposite*: clarity

fuzzy *adj* 1 hairy, furry, fluffy, downy, woolly 2 blurry, unclear, fluffy, hazy, vague *Opposite*: clear 3 unsure, ambiguous, vague, unclear, indistinct *Opposite*: clear

G

gab *(infml)* *v* chatter, chat, gossip, natter, prattle ■ *n* chat, chatter, talk, conversation, gossip

gabble *v* jabber, rattle on, blabber, gibber, talk a mile a minute ■ *n* gibberish, chatter, prattle, rubbish, nonsense

gabby *(infml)* *adj* talkative, chatty, garrulous, voluble, gushing *Opposite*: taciturn

gad *v* socialize, go partying, go clubbing, have a night on the town *(infml)*, gallivant *(infml)*

gadabout *n* pleasure-seeker, fun lover, social butterfly, partygoer, raver *(infml)*

gadfly *(dated)* *n* nuisance, pest, irritator, tormentor, meddler

gadget *n* 1 device, tool, appliance, implement, contraption 2 thingamajig *(infml)*, thingamabob *(infml)*, gizmo *(infml)*, doohickey *(infml)*, jigger *(infml)*

gaffe *n* blunder, solecism, mistake, error, boo-boo *(infml)*

gag *n* 1 restraint, curb, muzzle, tape, binding 2 *(infml)* joke, one-liner, funny, shaggy-dog story, quip 3 ban, gag order, injunction, restriction, interdiction ■ *v* 1 muzzle, stifle, muffle, restrain, curb 2 suppress, silence, interdict, prohibit, ban 3 choke, retch, suffocate, stifle, hyperventilate

gaggle *n* crowd, group, horde, throng, multitude

gag order *n* restraining order, injunction, gag, interdiction, prohibition

gaiety *n* joyfulness, lightheartedness, happiness, liveliness, merriment *Opposite*: misery

gaily *adv* happily, joyfully, cheerily, merrily, brightly *Opposite*: sadly

gain *v* 1 get, achieve, accuire, obtain, secure *Opposite*: lose 2 increase, add, put on, grow, expand *Opposite*: decrease ■ *n* 1 achievement, improvement, advantage, advance, increase *Opposite*: setback 2 advantage, profit, reward, benefit, return *Opposite*: loss. *See* COMPARE AND CONTRAST *at* get.

gain access *v* get into, enter, infiltrate, access, get permission

gainful *adj* profitable, advantageous, lucrative, rewarding, useful *Opposite*: unprofitable

gain ground *v* progress, advance, improve, expand, spread *Opposite*: fall back

gain on *v* near, close in on, approach, catch up on, close the gap

gainsay *(fml)* *v* oppose, contradict, argue, refute, deny *Opposite*: agree

gait n **walk**, step, pace, bearing, manner

gala n **festival**, celebration, party, ball, festivity

galactic adj 1 (infml) **huge**, enormous, immense, vast, extensive Opposite: infinitesimal 2 **celestial**, cosmic, planetary, astronomical, space Opposite: terrestrial

galaxy n **gathering**, assembly, meeting, cluster, collection

gale n **wind**, windstorm, storm, tempest, hurricane Opposite: breeze

gall n 1 **audacity**, impudence, boldness, nerve, effrontery 2 **sore**, irritation, lesion, wound, blister ■ v **irritate**, annoy, infuriate, anger, vex Opposite: please

gallant adj 1 (literary) **brave**, courageous, heroic, valiant, fearless Opposite: cowardly 2 **courteous**, chivalrous, polite, gentlemanly, thoughtful Opposite: rude

gallantry n 1 (literary) **courage**, bravery, heroism, valor, daring Opposite: cowardice 2 **courtesy**, thoughtfulness, chivalry, politeness, attentiveness Opposite: boorishness

gallery n 1 **colonnade**, portico, arcade, galleria, corridor 2 **balcony**, veranda, porch

galling adj **frustrating**, annoying, irritating, infuriating, exasperating Opposite: soothing

gallivant (infml) v **globetrot**, tour, travel around, gad, wander Opposite: stay put

gallop n **sprint**, dash, charge, bolt, mad dash ■ v **dash**, career, hurtle, run, fly

gallows n **scaffold**, gibbet, gallows tree, crossbeam, arm

galore adj **abundant**, plentiful, copious, aplenty, plenteous (literary) Opposite: scant

galvanize v **stimulate**, spur, rouse, electrify, fire up Opposite: dampen

gambit n **stratagem**, maneuver, ploy, scheme, strategy

gamble v 1 **bet**, wager, back, game, stake 2 **risk**, stake, venture, hazard, chance Opposite: play safe ■ n 1 **wager**, bet, stake 2 **chance**, risk, hazard, venture, speculation

gamble away v **squander**, lose, fritter away, waste, throw away

gambler n 1 **bettor**, high roller, wagerer, speculator, plunger (infml) 2 **risk-taker**, adventurer, speculator, risker

gambling n **betting**, gaming, bookmaking

gambol v **frolic**, skip, hop, spring, leap

game n 1 **pastime**, sport, diversion, amusement, entertainment 2 **match**, fixture, competition, contest, derby 3 **wild animals**, big game, game birds, game fish ■ adj 1 **willing**, ready, up for, disposed, inclined Opposite: unwilling 2 **brave**, spirited, plucky, resolute, determined Opposite: spiritless

WORD BANK

❑ **types of board games** backgammon, checkers, chess, Chinese checkers, dominoes, go, mahjongg, Monopoly™, pachisi, Scrabble™

❑ **types of card games** baccarat, blackjack, bridge, canasta, contract bridge, cribbage, euchre, gin rummy, hearts, pinochle, poker, rummy, solitaire

gamekeeper n **warden**, game warden, breeder, keeper, handler

gamely adv **bravely**, sportingly, spiritedly, stoically, determinedly Opposite: weakly

game plan n **plan**, strategy, scheme, stratagem, ploy

games n **sports**, competition, tournament, cup, sports event

gamut n **range**, scale, length, scope, extent

gander (infml) n **look**, peek, glimpse, glance

gang n 1 **mob**, band, ring, clique, posse (slang) 2 **team**, squad, group, lineup, crew (infml)

gangland n **underworld**, criminal world, organized crime, vice, racketeering

gangling adj **lanky**, gangly, tall, rangy, awkward Opposite: elegant

ganglion n **swelling**, tumor, lump, knot, concentration

gangly see **gangling**

gangplank n **bridge**, walkway, footway, footbridge, gangway

gangrene n **infection**, decay, rot, decomposition, putrefaction ■ v **fester**, putrefy, decompose, decay, molder

gangrenous adj **infected**, festering, diseased, decaying, rotting Opposite: healthy

gangster n **criminal**, thug, goon, hoodlum, racketeer

gang up on v **unite against**, join forces against, combine against, pick on, mob

gangway n **walkway**, footway, aisle, passage, passageway

gantry n **scaffold**, framework, support

gap n 1 **break**, opening, breach, slit, fissure 2 **interval**, hiatus, pause, break, interruption Opposite: continuity 3 **disparity**, difference, divergence, mismatch, inequality Opposite: parity 4 **chasm**, gorge, ravine, canyon, rift

gape v 1 **stare**, gaze, ogle, look hard, gawk (infml) 2 **part**, separate, divide, yawn, break open. See COMPARE AND CONTRAST at **gaze**.

gaping adj **wide**, wide open, huge, yawning, cavernous Opposite: narrow

garage n **carport**, shed, outbuilding, parking garage

garb n **clothing**, dress, costume, apparel, outfit ■ v **clothe**, dress, do up, dress up, attire (fml)

garbage n 1 **trash**, refuse, compost, debris, litter 2 **nonsense**, trivia, drivel, rubbish, hogwash (infml) Opposite: sense

garbage can n **wastebasket**, trash can, ash can

garbage dump n **junkyard**, landfill, scrapheap

garbed adj **arrayed**, clothed, dressed, robed, wearing

garble v **jumble**, confuse, muddle, mangle, distort

garbled adj **jumbled**, confused, muddled, distorted, mangled Opposite: clear

garden n 1 **yard**, back yard, plot, patch, bower 2 **park**, gardens, public park, green, common ■ v **plant**, cultivate, tend, work, grow

---

WORD BANK

❏ **types of gardens** bog garden, community garden, container garden, cottage garden, cutting garden, flower garden, herb garden, Japanese garden, kitchen garden, knot garden, orchard, raised bed garden, rock garden, rose garden, vegetable garden, vegetable plot, water garden

❏ **parts of a garden** arbor, arboretum, bed, border, container, flowerbed, lawn, patio, pergola, planter, rockery, shrubbery, water feature, window box

---

gardener n **horticulturist**, landscape gardener, grower, planter, landscaper

gargantuan adj **huge**, large, gigantic, enormous, vast Opposite: tiny

gargle v 1 **rinse**, wash out, disinfect, freshen, cleanse 2 **gurgle**, bubble, burble

gargoyle n **ornament**, decoration, carving, figurehead, effigy

garish adj **gaudy**, showy, lurid, vulgar, brash Opposite: tasteful

garland n 1 **wreath**, chaplet, coronet, circlet, crown 2 **festoon**, swag, drape, chain, lei

garment n **clothing**, vestment, costume, dress, coat

WORD BANK

❏ **parts of a garment** brim, buckle, button, buttonhole, coattail, collar, cuff, décolletage, drawstring, gusset, hem, lace, lapel, leg, lining, neck, neckband, neckline, pocket, sash, sleeve, strap, waistband, zipper

---

garner v 1 **gather**, bring in, save, lay down, store Opposite: scatter 2 **acquire**, get, gain, collect, bring together Opposite: squander

garnish v **enhance**, improve, set off, embellish, decorate ■ n 1 **accompaniment**, sauce, relish, side dish, gravy 2 **embellishment**, decoration, adornment, ornament, trimming

garret n **attic**, loft, gable, penthouse, top story

garrison n **barracks**, quarters, base, military base, casern

garrulous adj **talkative**, voluble, chatty, effusive, loquacious Opposite: taciturn. See COMPARE AND CONTRAST at **talkative**.

garrulousness n **verbosity**, volubility, chattiness, prattling, long-windedness Opposite: taciturnity

gas n **air**, vapor, fume, smoke ■ v (infml) **chat**, gossip, chitchat (infml), natter (infml), yak (infml)

gaseous adj 1 **vaporous**, gassy, steamy, smoky, fumy 2 **carbonated**, fizzy, bubbly, sparkling, effervescent Opposite: still 3 (infml) **talkative**, verbose, long-winded, chatty, chattering Opposite: tight-lipped

gash n **wound**, slash, cut, tear, laceration ■ v **cut**, slash, wound, tear, lacerate

gasket n **seal**, washer, ring, liner, lining

gasp n **wheeze**, pant, huff, puff, breath

gasping adj **out of breath**, winded, breathless, panting, wheezing

gas station n **service station**, service area, garage, gas pumps, filling station

gassy adj 1 **carbonated**, fizzy, bubbly, sparkling, effervescent Opposite: still 2 **vaporous**, gaseous, steamy, smoky, fumy 3 (infml) **talkative** verbose, long-winded, chatty, gossipy Opposite: tight-lipped

gastric adj **stomach**, abdominal, intestinal, digestive, gastrointestinal

gastrointestinal adj **stomach**, abdominal, intestinal, digestive, gastric

gastronome n **gourmet**, food lover, connoisseur, epicure, bon vivant Opposite: glutton

gastronomic adj **culinary**, cooking, food, gourmet, epicurean

gastronomy n **cookery**, cooking, cuisine, food, gourmandise

gasworks n **gas plant**, power station, installation, power plant

gate n 1 **entrance**, entry, door, gateway, opening 2 **attendance**, crowd, turnout, audience 3 **receipts** proceeds, revenue, take, takings

gatecrash v **sneak in**, barge in, invade, intrude, crash (infml)

gatepost n **support**, upright, post, frame, doorpost

gateway n 1 **entry**, doorway, entryway, entrance, opening 2 **opening**, first step, opportunity, access, way in

gather v 1 **meet**, get together, collect, congregate, assemble Opposite: disperse 2 **collect**, bring together, draw together, amass, pull together Opposite: distribute 3 **harvest**, pick, collect, garner, pluck Opposite: scatter 4 **understand**, conclude, assume, deduce, surmise 5 **pleat**, fold, pucker, ruche, shirr Opposite: smooth ■ n **fold**, pleat, pucker, wrinkle, ruck. See COMPARE AND CONTRAST at **collect**.

gathering n **meeting**, assembly, congregation, crowd, jamboree

gathering place n **meeting place**, center, assembly point, forum

gather up v **pick up**, take up, draw up, scoop up, dredge up Opposite: put down

gauche adj **awkward**, uncouth, tactless,

callow, graceless *Opposite*: poised

gaudiness *n* **showiness**, luridness, flamboyance, garishness, tawdriness *Opposite*: tastefulness

gaudy *adj* **garish**, flashy, kitschy, loud, showy *Opposite*: tasteful

gauge *v* **evaluate**, judge, assess, determine, measure ■ *n* **measurement**, estimate, assessment, measure, test

gaunt *adj* **thin**, skinny, lean, bony, emaciated *Opposite*: plump

gauntness *n* **thinness**, skinniness, leanness, boniness, scrawniness *Opposite*: plumpness

gauzy *adj* **thin**, delicate, filmy, see-through, gossamer *Opposite*: heavy

gawk *(infml)* *v* **stare**, gape, gaze, watch, rubberneck *(infml)*. *See* COMPARE AND CONTRAST *at* gaze.

gawkiness *(infml)* *n* **awkwardness**, clumsiness, inelegance, gracelessness, ungainliness *Opposite*: gracefulness

gawky *(infml)* *adj* **awkward**, clumsy, gangling, gangly, ungainly *Opposite*: graceful

gaze *v* **look**, stare, watch, contemplate, gape *Opposite*: ignore ■ *n* **stare**, look, contemplation, observation, scrutiny *Opposite*: glance

---

COMPARE AND CONTRAST CORE MEANING: look at somebody or something steadily or at length **gaze** look for a long time with unwavering attention; **gape** look at somebody or something in surprise or wonder, usually with an open mouth; **gawk** stare stupidly or rudely; **ogle** look steadily at somebody for sexual enjoyment or show sexual interest; **rubberneck** *(infml)* stare at somebody or something in an over-inquisitive or insensitive way; **stare** look at somebody or something directly and intently without moving the eyes away, as a result of curiosity or surprise, or express rudeness or defiance.

---

gazette *n* **newspaper**, paper, journal, periodical, newsletter

gear *(infml)* *n* **1** **kit**, stuff, things, paraphernalia, tackle **2** **clothes**, clothing, kit, outfit, togs *(infml)*

gear to *v* **adjust to**, align with, adapt to, tailor, modify

gear up *v* **get ready**, prepare, mobilize, ready yourself, prepare yourself *Opposite*: wind down

gel *n* **cream**, lotion, balm, ointment, salve ■ *v* **1** *(infml)* **come together**, take shape, crystallize, develop, form *Opposite*: fall apart **2** *(infml)* **see eye to eye**, relate, get along, get along like a house on fire, hit it off *(infml)* **3** **congeal**, thicken, coagulate, clot, harden *Opposite*: liquefy

gelatinous *adj* **viscous**, jellylike, gummy, gooey, sticky

geld *v* **castrate**, neuter, spay, sterilize, vasectomize

gem *n* **1** **jewel**, stone, precious stone, cut stone, gemstone **2** *(infml)* **treasure**, pearl, star, godsend, paragon

gemstone *n* **jewel**, stone, gem, precious stone, cut stone

WORD BANK

❏ **types of gemstones** agate, amethyst, aquamarine, beryl, bloodstone, carnelian, chalcedony, chrysoprase, diamond, emerald, garnet, jade, lapis lazuli, moonstone, mother-of-pearl, onyx, opal, pearl, ruby, sapphire, sard, topaz, tourmaline, turquoise

gender *n* **sex**, sexual category, sexual characteristics, masculinity, femininity

WORD BANK

❏ **types of female animals** bitch, cow, dam, doe, ewe, filly, heifer, hind, jenny, lioness, mare, nanny goat, sow, tigress, vixen
❏ **types of male animals** billy goat, boar, buck, bull, bullock, colt, hart, jackass, ram, stag, stallion, steer, tom, tomcat, wether
❏ **types of male birds or female birds** capon, cob, cock, cockerel, drake, duck, gander, goose, hen, pen, rooster

gene *n* **genetic factor**, inheritable factor, protein sequence, DNA segment

genealogical *adj* **hereditary**, ancestral, family, pedigree

genealogy *n* **family tree**, descent, lineage, pedigree, family

general *adj* **1** **overall**, universal, all-purpose, wide-ranging, broad *Opposite*: specific **2** **usual**, typical, conventional, customary, accustomed *Opposite*: unusual **3** **widespread**, common, blanket, across-the-board, sweeping *Opposite*: unique **4** **unspecific**, undefined, unclear, vague *Opposite*: specific

generality *n* **1** **generalization**, sweeping statement, simplification, oversimplification, overview *Opposite*: detail **2** **platitude**, cliché, banality, truism, axiom

generalization *n* **sweeping statement**, simplification, oversimplification, overview, generality *Opposite*: detail

generalize *v* **simplify**, oversimplify, take a broad view, make a sweeping statement *Opposite*: specify

generalized *adj* **widespread**, sweeping, comprehensive, general, global *Opposite*: isolated

generally *adv* **usually**, normally, in general, in the main, by and large *Opposite*: rarely

general public *n* **population**, populace, ordinary people, hoi polloi, rank and file *Opposite*: elite

generate *v* **make**, produce, create, cause, engender *Opposite*: prevent

generation *n* **1** **age group**, peer group, peers, cohort, group **2** **age**, era, epoch, period, eon **3** **production**, making, creation, invention, initiation *Opposite*: destruction

generator *n* producer, maker, creator, originator, initiator

generic *adj* general, broad, common, basic, nonspecific *Opposite*: specific

generosity *n* kindness, big-heartedness, openhandedness, liberality, munificence *Opposite*: miserliness

generous *adj* 1 kind, big-hearted, liberal, openhanded, charitable *Opposite*: stingy 2 substantial, large, lavish, liberal, plentiful *Opposite*: meager

---

COMPARE AND CONTRAST CORE MEANING: giving readily to others

generous willing to give money, help, or time freely; **liberal** free with money, time, or other assets; **magnanimous** very generous, kind, or forgiving; **munificent** very generous, especially on a grand scale; **bountiful** (*literary*) generous, particularly to less fortunate people.

---

genesis *n* origin, origins, beginning, start, birth

genetic *adj* hereditary, inherited, heritable, inherent, genomic *Opposite*: learned

genial *adj* friendly, amiable, warm, welcoming, hospitable *Opposite*: unfriendly

geniality *n* friendliness, warmth, cordiality, amiability, conviviality *Opposite*: hostility

genie *n* sprite, spirit, apparition, jinni, imp

genius *n* 1 mastermind, prodigy, intellect, virtuoso, whiz kid (*infml*) 2 brilliance, intellect, brains, virtuosity, intelligence *Opposite*: stupidity. See COMPARE AND CONTRAST at **talent**.

genocide *n* killing, slaughter, massacre, ethnic cleansing, liquidation

genre *n* type, sort, kind, category, field. See COMPARE AND CONTRAST at **type**.

gent (*infml*) *n* gentleman, man, fellow, guy (*infml*)

genteel *adj* 1 refined, proper, polite, courteous, discreet *Opposite*: vulgar 2 pretentious, snobbish, condescending, patronizing, affected *Opposite*: modest

gentility *n* refinement, propriety, manners, breeding, decorum *Opposite*: vulgarity

gentle *adj* 1 mild, calm, kind, tender, moderate *Opposite*: harsh 2 soft, light, soothing, mellow, restful *Opposite*: rough

gentleman *n* 1 man, male, guy (*infml*), fellow (*dated*) 2 nobleman, aristocrat, squire, grandee *Opposite*: cad

gentlemanly *adj* chivalrous, gallant, courteous, polite, civil *Opposite*: rude

gentleness *n* 1 mildness, calmness, kindness, tenderness, placidity *Opposite*: harshness 2 quietness, softness, lightness, smoothness, mellowness *Opposite*: harshness

gentrification *n* redevelopment, refurbishment, urban renewal, renovation, restoration *Opposite*: neglect

gentrify *v* redevelop, refurbish, renovate, restore, improve

gentry *n* upper class, nobility, aristocracy, elite, ruling class *Opposite*: working class

genuflect *v* 1 kneel, bow, curtsy, bend the knee, bob 2 bow to, defer to, kowtow, show respect for, grovel *Opposite*: disrespect

genuflection *n* kneeling, curtsy, bow, bob, dip

genuine *adj* 1 real, authentic, indisputable, true, unadulterated *Opposite*: fake 2 sincere, honest, frank, open, unaffected *Opposite*: false

genuineness *n* authenticity, realness, substance, legitimacy, validity

genus *n* type, kind, sort, species, class

geographic *adj* physical, topographical, terrestrial, earthly, environmental

geographical *see* geographic

geography *n* topography, natural features, characteristics, layout

geologic division *n* eon, era, epoch, period

WORD BANK

❑ **types of eons** (from oldest to most recent) pre-Archean, Archean, Proterozoic, Phanerozoic

❑ **types of epochs** (from oldest to most recent) Paleocene, Eocene, Oligocene, Miocene, Pliocene, Pleistocene, Holocene

❑ **types of eras** (from oldest to most recent) Paleozoic, Mesozoic, Cenozoic

❑ **types of periods** (from oldest to most recent) Cambrian, Ordovician, Silurian, Devonian, Carboniferous, Permian, Triassic, Jurassic Cretaceous, Tertiary, Quaternary

---

geometric *adj* regular, symmetrical, ordered, orderly, linear

geriatric *adj* elderly, aged, old, senior *Opposite*: young

germ *n* 1 microbe, microorganism, bacteria, virus, bug (*infml*) 2 origin, seed, embryo, rudiment, kernel

germane *adj* relevant, useful, connected, to the point, of interest *Opposite*: irrelevant

germ-free *adj* sterile, antiseptic, hygienic, sanitary, uninfected *Opposite*: contaminated

germinate *v* sprout, grow, develop, take root, evolve

germination *n* sprouting, propagation, incubation, growth, development

gestation *n* development, growth, incubation, maturation, pregnancy

gesticulate *v* gesture, wave, signal, motion, sign

gesticulation *n* sign, signal, gesture, wave, motion

gesture *n* 1 sign, signal, gesticulation, motion, wave 2 act, action, deed, token, intimation ■ *v* gesticulate signal, shrug, nod, wave

get *v* 1 become, grow, begin, have, attain

2 cause, make, induce, persuade, urge
3 catch, contract, acquire, develop, be
infected with **4 move**, step, progress, walk,
climb **5 obtain**, acquire, secure, procure,
gain **6** *(infml)* **understand**, comprehend,
grasp, follow, perceive

COMPARE AND CONTRAST CORE MEANING: come
into possession of something
get become the owner of something or succeed
in finding and possessing it; **acquire** get possession of something, sometimes suggesting
that time or effort was involved; **obtain** get something, especially by making an effort
or having the necessary qualifications; **gain** get
something through effort, skill, or merit; **procure**
get something, especially with effort or special
care; **secure** get something, especially after
using considerable effort to persuade somebody
to grant or allow it.

get across *v* put across, put over, convey,
impart, communicate

get a grip *(infml)* *v* **calm down**, get hold of
yourself, compose yourself, control yourself, chill out *(infml)*

get ahead *v* **advance**, climb the ladder, progress, make progress, prosper *Opposite*:
fail

get ahead of *v* **pass**, pass by, be in front of,
overtake *Opposite*: hold back

get ahold of *v* **grasp**, secure, grip, clutch,
snare

get along *v* **1 like**, be compatible with, work
well with, relate to, gel with *(infml) Opposite*: dislike **2 survive**, get by, manage,
cope, live

get a move on *(infml)* *v* **speed up**, hurry up,
get going, get moving, accelerate *Oppo-
site*: slow down

get angry *v* **bristle**, bridle, explode, lose your
cool, lose your temper

get a raw deal *v* **suffer**, draw the short straw,
get shafted, get the shaft, be hard done by

get around *v* **1 become known**, break out,
circulate, get out, be revealed **2 avoid**, go
around, bypass, sidestep, evade

get at *v* **1 reach**, find, contact, speak to, write
to **2 annoy**, tease, irritate, get to, rub the
wrong way

get away *v* **leave**, go away, escape, flee,
depart

getaway *n* **escape**, exit, retreat, breakout,
flight

get away from *v* **elude**, shake off, lose, escape
from, outrun

get away with *v* **get off**, get off scot-free,
escape, evade, elude *Opposite*: answer for

get a word in edgewise *v* **get a word in**,
have your say, voice your opinion, say
anything, speak

get back *v* **retrieve**, recoup, repossess,
regain, recuperate *Opposite*: lose

get back at *v* **get even**, turn the tables on,

take revenge, even the score, fight back

get behind *v* **support**, endorse, back, join
forces, put in a good word for *Opposite*:
oppose

get better *v* **recover**, recuperate, improve,
turn the corner, bounce back *Opposite*:
deteriorate

get bigger *v* **swell**, grow, inflate, mount,
expand *Opposite*: shrink

get by *v* **survive**, manage, cope, scrape by,
fare

get cracking *(infml)* *v* **get going**, make a start,
get moving, get a move on *(infml)*

get done *v* **accomplish**, achieve, complete,
finish, do

get down *v* **descend**, get off, dismount, come
down, climb down

get down to *v* **get to work**, begin, start, concentrate, focus *Opposite*: put off

get down to business *v* **get on with it**, get
down to it, get down to brass tacks, get
down to the nitty-gritty, stop beating about
the bush

get even *v* **get back at**, take revenge, turn the
tables, get you back, even the score

get free of *v* **get rid of**, exorcize, escape,
jettison, eliminate

get-go *(infml)* *n* **beginning**, start, outset,
genesis, commencement *(fml) Opposite*:
finish

get going *v* **1 start**, make a start, hurry up,
stir, push off **2 start up**, turn on, activate,
operate, power *Opposite*: turn off

get hitched *(infml)* *v* **get married**, marry, walk
down the aisle, tie the knot *(infml)*, wed
(fml or literary)

get hold of *v* **1 obtain**, find, acquire, search
out, lay hands on **2 contact**, reach, find,
get in touch with, talk to

get in *v* **1 arrive**, enter, appear, turn up
(infml), show up *(infml) Opposite*: depart
2 join, be accepted, be included, make the
cut, make the grade

get in on the act *(infml)* *v* **take part**, join
in, be included, be involved, jump on the
bandwagon

get in the way *v* **obstruct**, hinder, impede,
interfere, encumber

get into *v* **1 gain entry**, enter, open, access,
hack into *Opposite*: get out of **2 put on**, slip
into, don, change into, dress in *Opposite*:
take off

get in touch with *v* **call**, contact, reach,
speak to, write to

get into your stride *v* **get going**, get up to
speed, get the hang of something, get off
the ground

get involved *v* **interfere**, intervene, join in,
be drawn in, step in *Opposite*: hold back

get in with *v* **ingratiate yourself**, make friends
with, curry favor, gain the favor of, associate with

get it *(infml)* v understand, see, get the drift, follow, comprehend *Opposite*: misunderstand

get it off your chest v bare your soul, tell somebody, let it out, unburden yourself, share *Opposite*: bottle up

get it wrong v misunderstand, blunder, err, get the wrong idea, get the wrong end of the stick

get less v subside, die down, lessen, reduce, fall *Opposite*: grow

get longer v lengthen, elongate, grow, extend, spread out *Opposite*: shorten

get lost v lose your way, lose your bearings, go astray, go wrong, take a wrong turn

get married v marry, walk down the aisle, get hitched *(infml)*, tie the knot *(infml)*, wed *(fml or literary)*

get moving v hurry up, speed up, get going, make a move, get a move on *(infml)*

get off v 1 leave, depart, exit, go, embark *Opposite*: arrive 2 **dismount**, get down, descend, come down, climb off *Opposite*: get on

get on v 1 deal with, handle, manage, accept, progress *Opposite*: mismanage 2 **board**, climb on, mount, get on board, embark *Opposite*: get off

get on your high horse v give yourself airs, put on airs, lord it, get all high and mighty

get on your nerves v annoy, irritate, bother, put your back up, irk

get out v leave, depart, quit, evacuate, retreat *Opposite*: enter

get out of v evade, avoid, dodge, duck, get around *Opposite*: participate

get over v 1 recover, live through, endure, survive, get beyond *Opposite*: succumb 2 **come to terms with**, accept, surmount, overcome, conquer 3 **convey**, communicate, impart, pass on, get across

get ready v prepare, steel, prime, brace, organize

get rid of v dispose of, discard, throw away, throw out, jettison *Opposite*: keep

get smaller v shrink, shrivel up, narrow, deflate, recede *Opposite*: swell

get somewhere v make headway, make progress, make inroads, achieve something, make a breakthrough *Opposite*: fall behind

get the better of v defeat, beat, trounce, triumph over, get the upper hand

get the drift v understand, see, follow, get it *(infml)*, get the message *(infml)*

get the hang of v learn, pick up, understand, master

get the message *(infml)* v understand, get the drift, take the hint, grasp, follow

get the most out of v maximize, make the most of, get the full benefit, exploit, milk *(infml)*

get the picture *(infml)* v understand, follow, see, grasp, get it *(infml)*

get the wrong end of the stick v misconstrue, misinterpret, make a mistake, misunderstand, misread

get the wrong idea v misunderstand, misread, misinterpret, misconstrue, misjudge

get thinner v narrow, taper, slim down, lose weight, slenderize *(dated)*

get through v 1 survive, come through, endure, weather, ride out 2 **use**, consume, wear out, go through, expend 3 **breach**, break through, penetrate, cross, pass

get to v 1 annoy, irritate, bother, irk, affect 2 **reach**, make, arrive at, attain

get-together *(infml)* n meeting, gathering, social, assembly, rendezvous

get to know v become acquainted with, be introduced to, meet, become familiar with

get to your feet v stand up, rise, stand, get up, arise *(literary)*

get under way v begin, start, proceed, launch, commence *Opposite*: come to a halt

getup *(infml)* n outfit, clothes, costume, suit, dress

get-up-and-go *(infml)* n energy, vitality, verve, life, drive

get used to v become accustomed to, get into the habit, adjust, adapt, acclimatize

get your bearings v orient yourself, find your way, find your feet, adjust, adapt

geyser n hot spring, spring, natural spring, fountain, jet

ghastly adj 1 horrifying, shocking, upsetting, distressing, grisly *Opposite*: pleasant 2 **terrible**, horrible, appalling, dreadful, nasty *Opposite*: pleasant 3 *(infml)* **ill**, sick, unwell, dreadful, bad *Opposite*: well 4 *(literary)* **pale**, pallid, ashen, wan, deathly *Opposite*: rosy

gherkin n pickled cucumber, dill pickle, pickle

ghostlike adj eerie, spectral, ghostly, supernatural, ethereal

ghostly adj ethereal, spectral, indistinct, supernatural, eerie

ghostwrite v cowrite, write, compose, author, coauthor

ghostwriter n cowriter, writer, composer, author, coauthor

ghoulish adj 1 morbid, macabre, dark, chilling, ghastly 2 **cruel**, savage, brutal, fiendish, bloodthirsty *Opposite*: gentle

GI n soldier, private, enlisted person, draftee, volunteer

giant adj huge, enormous, vast, large, massive *Opposite*: tiny

gibber v babble, rant, prattle, jabber, gabble

gibberish n nonsense, prattle, babble, gabble, rubbish *Opposite*: sense

gibe n jeer, taunt, sneer, remark, joke ■ v taunt, mock, tease, jeer, ridicule

giblets *n* guts, offal, innards *(infml)*

giddiness *n* **1** dizziness, unsteadiness, light-headedness, wooziness, shakiness *Opposite:* steadiness **2** *(dated)* **frivolity,** capriciousness, volatility, overexcitement, flightiness *Opposite:* seriousness

giddy *adj* **1** dizzy, unsteady, off-balance, lightheaded, woozy *Opposite:* steady **2** *(dated)* **frivolous,** scatterbrained, capricious, volatile, excited *Opposite:* serious

gift *n* **1** present, donation, contribution, reward, bequest **2** talent, skill, ability, flair, knack. *See* COMPARE AND CONTRAST *at* **talent.**

gifted *adj* talented, skilled, bright, able, intelligent. *See* COMPARE AND CONTRAST *at* **intelligent.**

giftwrap *v* wrap up, wrap up, package

gigantic *adj* huge, enormous, massive, vast, gargantuan *Opposite:* tiny

giggle *v* titter, snicker, chuckle, laugh, chortle ■ *n* titter, chuckle, laugh, chortle, twitter

giggly *adj* silly, hysterical, immature, tittering, sniggering *Opposite:* serious

gilded *adj* golden, gold-plated, gilt, gold

gild the lily *v* overdo it, get carried away, go too far, lay it on thick, go over the top *(infml)*

gilt *n* gold, gold leaf, gold plate ■ *adj* golden, gold-plated, gilded, gold

gimmick *n* trick, ploy, stunt, device, promotion

gingerly *adv* cautiously, tentatively, warily, delicately, carefully *Opposite:* boldly

girder *n* beam, joist, bar, rafter, crossbeam

girdle *n* belt, sash, cummerbund, tie, drawstring

gird your loins *v* brace yourself, get ready, grit your teeth, prepare yourself, steel yourself

girlfriend *n* partner, lover, sweetheart, fiancée, lady friend *(infml) Opposite:* boyfriend

girlhood *n* childhood, youth, infancy, early years, adolescence

girlish *adj* youthful, adolescent, childlike, young

girth *n* circumference, breadth, width, span, thickness *Opposite:* height

gist *n* idea, essence, substance, general picture, point *Opposite:* minutiae

give *v* **1** provide, offer, hand over, present, donate *Opposite:* take **2** grant, award, accord, bestow *(fml),* confer *(fml) Opposite:* withhold **3** impart, convey, communicate, pass on, share *Opposite:* withhold **4** perform, put on, stage, produce, organize **5** devote, dedicate, give up, sacrifice, spend *Opposite:* withhold **6** yield, collapse, break, go, split *Opposite:* hold up

---

COMPARE AND CONTRAST CORE MEANING: hand over something to somebody

give hand over a possession to somebody else

to keep or use; **present** give something in a formal or ceremonial way; **confer** *(fml)* give somebody an honor, privilege, or award, often at a formal ceremony; **bestow** *(fml)* present somebody with something, especially something unexpected or undeserved; **donate** give a contribution to a charitable organization or another good cause, or, in a medical context, give blood for blood transfusions or organs for transplant; **grant** agree to allow a request, favor, or privilege, especially at the discretion of a person in authority, or formally or officially give money.

give a boost *v* strengthen, boost, lift, encourage, boost up *Opposite:* deflate

give a lift *v* encourage, boost, boost up, strengthen, fortify *Opposite:* deflate

give-and-take *(infml) n* cooperation, compromise, reciprocity, collaboration, teamwork *Opposite:* selfishness

give away *v* **1** get rid of, donate, offer, give, pass on *Opposite:* keep **2** disclose, reveal, let slip, betray, divulge *Opposite:* keep secret

giveaway *n* **1** telltale sign, clue, hint, indication, symptom **2** *(infml)* gift, special offer, free sample, trial offer, promotion ■ *adj (infml)* bargain, rock-bottom, low, introductory, special *Opposite:* exorbitant

give a wide berth *v* steer clear, avoid, avoid like the plague, shun, keep at arm's length *Opposite:* seek out

give back *v* return, restore, hand back, repay, refund *Opposite:* keep

give chase *(fml) v* pursue, follow in hot pursuit, follow, go after, chase

give in *v* lose, admit defeat, surrender, concede, submit *Opposite:* stand your ground

give instructions *v* direct, inform, brief, instruct, tell

given *adj* known, assumed, agreed, specified, prearranged ■ *prep* because of, in view of, as a result of, taking into consideration, taking into account

given name *n* first name, Christian name, forename, name, moniker *(slang)*

given that *conj* providing, provided that, as long as, only if, assuming that

give off *v* emit, radiate, send out, discharge, exude

give out *v* **1** hand out, distribute, provide, offer, allot *Opposite:* keep **2** declare, announce, proclaim, pronounce, reveal *Opposite:* withhold **3** emit, send out, transmit, give off, radiate **4** run out, dry up, fail, come to an end, end *Opposite:* hold out **5** fail, collapse, break, yield, go *Opposite:* hold

give over to *v* **1** dedicate, devote, allocate, reserve, allot **2** *(literary)* give up, relinquish, hand over, surrender, abandon

give permission *v* consent, agree, allow, let, authorize *Opposite:* forbid

give somebody the slip v **lose**, shake off, get away from, escape from, avoid

give the cold shoulder to v **ignore**, rebuff, exclude, look straight through, freeze out

give the lie to v **contradict**, belie, rebut, refute, conflict with

give the once-over (infml) v **examine**, inspect, check out, scrutinize, look at

give up v 1 **admit defeat**, give in, surrender, concede, submit Opposite: stand your ground 2 **hand over**, part with, surrender, relinquish, give away Opposite: keep 3 **despair**, abandon, lose hope, give up on 4 **stop**, quit, leave off, renounce, abstain from Opposite: stick with 5 **devote**, dedicate, give, surrender, sacrifice Opposite: withhold 6 **reveal**, disclose, divulge, tell, let slip Opposite: keep secret

give up on v 1 **stop**, give up, quit, abandon, leave off 2 **despair**, abandon, lose hope, give up

give your word v **promise**, vow, swear, pledge, assure

gizmo (infml) n **gadget**, device, contraption, appliance, thing

glacial adj 1 **icy**, ice-cold, freezing, biting, bitter Opposite: tropical 2 **hostile**, unfriendly, icy, cold, cool Opposite: warm

glacier n **ice field**, icecap, ice floe, iceberg, floe

glad adj 1 **delighted**, happy, pleased, content, grateful Opposite: sad 2 **willing**, ready, prepared, happy, eager Opposite: unwilling

gladden v **delight**, please, cheer, bring joy to, hearten Opposite: sadden

glade n **clearing**, opening, gap, open space, dell (literary)

gladiator n 1 **fighter**, fencer, sword fighter, warrior, battler 2 **campaigner**, lobbyist, supporter, advocate, champion

gladness n **happiness**, cheerfulness, delight, joy, pleasure Opposite: sadness

glad rags (infml) n **best clothes**, finery, black tie, Sunday best, best bib and tucker (infml)

glamor see **glamour**

glamorize v 1 **romanticize**, idealize, exaggerate, embellish, dress up Opposite: understate 2 **beautify**, decorate, adorn, do up, dress up

glamorous adj **stylish**, fashionable, glitzy, dazzling, splendid Opposite: drab

glamour n 1 **allure**, charm, appeal, fascination, attraction Opposite: dullness 2 **good looks**, beauty, glitz, glitziness, style Opposite: drabness

glance v 1 **look**, peep, peek, glimpse, squint Opposite: gaze 2 **glint**, shine, glimmer, gleam, glitter ■ n **peep**, look, glimpse, scan, squint (infml) Opposite: gaze

glance off v **bounce off**, ricochet, reflect, deflect, rebound

glancing adj **sideways**, sidelong, lateral, slanting, tangential

glare v 1 **scowl**, stare, glower, frown, look daggers 2 **dazzle**, flash, glimmer, glitter, shine 3 **stand out**, leap out, jump out, catch the eye, show ■ n 1 **dirty look**, stare, glower, scowl, frown 2 **shine**, brightness, dazzle, flash, shimmer Opposite: dullness

glaring adj 1 **conspicuous**, obvious, obtrusive, evident, blatant Opposite: inconspicuous 2 **dazzling**, brilliant, shimmering, bright, intense Opposite: dim 3 **garish**, brash, gaudy, loud, clashing Opposite: soft

glaringly adv **blatantly**, patently, flagrantly, clearly, extremely

glass n **beaker**, tumbler, wineglass, goblet, flute

glasses n **spectacles**, goggles, specs (infml)

WORD BANK

❑ types of glasses bifocals, dark glasses, eyeglasses (fml), monocle, pince-nez, shades (infml), sunglasses

---

glassy adj 1 **smooth**, slippery, shiny, glossy, slick Opposite: dull 2 **expressionless**, glazed, dazed, blank, vacant Opposite: alert

glaze v **varnish**, finish, seal, coat, cover ■ n **coating**, varnish, finish, seal, cover

glazed adj 1 **glassy**, blank, fixed, expressionless, dull Opposite: alert 2 **glossy**, shiny, smooth, lustrous, varnished Opposite: dull

gleam v 1 **shine**, glow, beam, burn, blaze 2 **flash**, flicker, twinkle, shimmer, sparkle ■ n 1 **glow**, shine, beam, ray, blaze 2 **flicker**, flash, twinkle, shimmer, sparkle

gleaming adj **shiny**, polished, luminous, lustrous, glossy Opposite: dull

glee n 1 **delight**, happiness, pleasure, joy, elation Opposite: sadness 2 **triumph**, jubilation, smugness, exultance Opposite: despondency

gleeful adj 1 **delighted**, happy, pleased, joyful, elated Opposite: sad 2 **triumphant**, jubilant, smug, gloating, exultant Opposite: despondent

glen n **valley**, gorge, ravine, dale, cleft

glib adj 1 **persuasive**, fluent, smooth, convincing, slick Opposite: hesitant 2 **superficial**, shallow, facile, casual, simplistic Opposite: profound

glibness n 1 **persuasiveness**, fluency, slickness, smoothness Opposite: hesitation 2 **superficiality**, shallowness, facileness, casualness Opposite: profoundness

glide v 1 **slither**, slide, slide along, slip, skate 2 **fly**, soar, wheel, drift, coast

glimmer v **twinkle**, shine, gleam, flicker, glow ■ n **shine**, twinkle, gleam, flicker, glow

glimpse n 1 **look**, glance, peep, sight, peek (infml) 2 **sight**, foretaste, indication, pointer ■ v **see**, catch sight of, glance at, peep at, look at

glint v **sparkle**, flash, wink, shine, twinkle ■ n **flash**, sparkle, shine, twinkle, spark

glisten v **gleam**, sparkle, glint, flash, reflect ■ n **sparkle**, gleam, glint, flash, shine

glistening adj **gleaming**, shining, sparkly, shiny, glittering

glitch n **hitch**, problem, malfunction, fault, anomaly

glitter v **gleam**, sparkle, shine, dazzle, shimmer ■ n **1 sparkle**, gleam, shimmer, flash, twinkle **2 tinsel**, sequins, spangles **3 dazzle**, splendor, flashiness, glamour, showiness

glittering adj **impressive**, sparkling, dazzling, splendid, scintillating

glittery adj **shiny**, sparkly, shimmering, brilliant, dazzling

glitz n **glamour**, style, stylishness, glitziness, showiness

glitziness n **1 glamour**, glitter, style, glitz, stylishness **2 showiness**, tawdriness, flashiness, extravagance, tastelessness

glitzy adj **showy**, ostentatious, flashy, extravagant, swanky (infml)

gloat v **revel**, wallow, exult, smirk, delight

glob (infml) n **blob**, gobbet, drop, globule, lump

global adj **1 worldwide**, international Opposite: local **2 universal**, comprehensive, total, inclusive, overall

globally adv **1 internationally**, worldwide, universally Opposite: locally **2 altogether**, as a whole, generally, universally, totally

globe n **1 sphere**, ball, orb **2 earth**, world, planet

globetrot v **travel**, journey, tour, shuttle, backpack

globetrotter n **tourist**, backpacker, journeyer, adventurer, explorer

globular adj **spherical**, round, circular, bulbous, rotund

globule n **drop**, blob, bead, bubble, gobbet

gloom n **1 darkness**, shade, murkiness, shadow, dimness Opposite: brightness **2 pessimism**, despair, sadness, dejection, unhappiness Opposite: happiness

gloominess n **1 dimness**, darkness, murkiness, shade, shadow Opposite: brightness **2 despondency**, pessimism, gloom, depression, despair Opposite: happiness

gloomy adj **1 dark**, depressing, dim, overcast, dull Opposite: bright **2 depressed**, low, low-spirited, melancholy, miserable Opposite: cheerful

glorification n **adoration**, veneration, elevation, deification, praise Opposite: belittlement

glorify v **worship**, adore, lionize, deify, elevate Opposite: belittle

glorious adj **magnificent**, wonderful, splendid, celebrated, superb Opposite: shameful

glory n **1 magnificence**, splendor, beauty, wonder, grandeur **2 credit**, fame, praise, laurels, triumph Opposite: criticism

glory in v **enjoy**, lap up, wallow in, make the most of, revel in Opposite: despise

gloss n **1 luster**, polish, shine, brightness, sheen **2 annotation**, commentary, footnote, explanation, comment **3 interpretation**, explanation, spin (slang)

glossary n **lexicon**, dictionary, word list, vocabulary, thesaurus

glossiness n **1 shininess**, smoothness, sheen, patina, luster **2** (infml) **veneer**, surface, façade

gloss over v **skim over**, pass over, dismiss, evade, dodge Opposite: dwell on

glossy adj **sleek**, silky, silken, lustrous, shiny Opposite: dull

glow n **radiance**, ruddiness, light, luminosity, glimmering ■ v **burn**, blaze, flame, shine, smolder

glower v **glare**, frown, scowl, look daggers, look hard

glowering adj **angry**, dark, scowling, sullen, surly

glowing adj **1 bright**, shimmering, radiant, lustrous, shining Opposite: dull **2 fulsome**, complimentary, flattering, appreciative, congratulatory Opposite: derogatory **3 healthy-looking**, tanned, rosy, shining, radiant Opposite: pale

glue n **adhesive**, paste, superglue, cement, gum ■ v **paste**, stick, fasten, attach, join

gluey adj **sticky**, gummy, tacky, glutinous, thick

glum adj **gloomy**, down, morose, sad, low Opposite: cheerful

glumness n **pessimism**, unhappiness, misery, depression, dejection Opposite: cheerfulness

glut n **excess**, surplus, superfluity, flood, overabundance Opposite: shortage

glutinous adj **sticky**, gluey, gooey, tacky, gummy

glutton n **overeater**, gourmand, greedy guts (infml), gannet (infml), pig (infml)

gluttonous adj **greedy**, voracious, insatiable, excessive, desirous (fml)

gluttony n **greed**, greediness, excess, piggishness, rapaciousness

gnarled adj **knotted**, twisted, bent, knotty, crooked Opposite: straight

gnash v **grind**, clench, grit, grate, rasp

gnash your teeth v **be fuming**, be upset, grind your teeth, be frustrated

gnat n **midge**, mosquito, fly, firefly, insect

gnaw v **worry**, trouble, bother, cause anxiety, concern Opposite: comfort

gnome n **elf**, sprite, goblin, troll, leprechaun

go v **1 leave**, go away, go off, depart, set off Opposite: come **2 move**, move on, proceed, progress, make for **3 work**, run, function, operate, move *Opposite*: stop **4 reach**, extend, stretch, spread **5 become**, get, grow, come to be **6 die**, pass away, pass on, depart *(fml)*, expire *(fml) Opposite*: live ■ **n 1 try**, attempt, turn, chance, shot **2 energy**, liveliness, enthusiasm, spirit, verve *Opposite*: lethargy **3** *(infml)* **energy**, life, zest, zip *(infml)*, oomph *(infml)*

go about v perform, carry out, accomplish, transact, set about

goad v provoke, prod, push, stir, stimulate *Opposite*: calm ■ **n 1 stick**, prod, poker, rod, whip **2 stimulus**, impetus, driving force, spur, stimulation. *See* COMPARE AND CONTRAST *at* motive.

go adrift v wander, drift, stray, go astray, deviate

go after v try for, aim for, target, go all-out for, do your utmost

go against v violate, disobey, fly in the face of, infringe, buck *(infml)*

go-ahead *(infml)* n permission, consent, approval, green light, support

goal n **1 objective**, aim, end, ambition, purpose **2 goalmouth**, penalty area, box, area, goal line

go along with v acquiesce, concur, agree, grant, accept *Opposite*: refuse

go around v **1 circulate**, spread, pass on, hand on, disseminate **2 travel**, go from place to place, ride, walk, move **3 revolve**, rotate, twirl, spin, twist

go-around *(infml)* n argument, disagreement, fight, tiff, quarrel *Opposite*: agreement

go around with *(infml)* v accompany, escort, tag along, spend time with, be together

go astray v stray, get lost, transgress, go off the rails, deviate

go away v **1 leave**, get away, move, depart, be off *Opposite*: stay **2 disappear**, vanish, fade, fade away, recede *Opposite*: stay

go back v return, turn back, revert, revisit, retrace your steps *Opposite*: advance

go back on v change your mind, backtrack, break your promise, have second thoughts, retract *Opposite*: keep your word

go back over v reconsider, reexamine, repeat, revise, return to

go backward v reverse, retreat, regress, lose ground, fall back *Opposite*: advance

go bad v decay, rot, go moldy, decompose, putrefy

go bankrupt v fail, collapse, fold, go to the wall, go bust *(infml)*

gobble v **1 devour**, bolt, wolf, guzzle *(infml)*, scoff *(infml) Opposite*: nibble **2** *(infml)* **use up**, go through, run through, consume, eat into *Opposite*: conserve

gobbledygook *(infml)* n nonsense, jargon, gibberish, drivel, rubbish

go berserk v lose control, lose your temper,

lose your cool, be beside yourself, be furious

go-between n mediator, intermediary, broker, arbitrator, messenger

go beyond v surpass, outdo, rise above, overtake, pass

goblet n glass, cup, chalice, wineglass

goblin n elf, sprite, imp, gnome, troll

go bust *(infml)* v go bankrupt, go under, shut down, fail, go to the wall

go by v pass, pass by, elapse, lapse

god n deity, divinity, idol, spirit, supernatural being

goddess n deity, divinity, idol, spirit, supernatural being

godlike adj divine, superhuman, transcendent, heavenly, holy

godliness n **1 religiousness**, holiness, devoutness, goodness, saintliness *Opposite*: wickedness **2 divinity**, holiness, heavenliness, transcendence, sacredness

godly *(fml)* adj **1 religious**, devout, holy, pious, saintly *Opposite*: wicked **2 divine**, holy, heavenly, transcendent, godlike

go down v **1 descend**, drop, sink, dive, plunge *Opposite*: go up **2 deteriorate**, decline, slip, go downhill, get worse *Opposite*: improve

go downhill v deteriorate, worsen, fail, get worse, go down *Opposite*: improve

go down with *(infml)* v catch, become ill with, contract, pick up, come down with

godsend n blessing, boon, stroke of luck, bonus, benefit *Opposite*: disaster

go easy on *(infml)* v **1 treat gently**, indulge, give somebody a break, sympathize, oblige *Opposite*: punish **2 take it easy**, slow down, avoid, stint, temper *Opposite*: overdo

gofer *(infml)* n runner, messenger, minion, assistant, lackey

go for v **1** *(infml)* **try for**, go after, target, aim for, set your sights on **2** *(infml)* **like**, enjoy, prefer, follow, love *Opposite*: dislike **3** *(infml)* **choose**, pick, select, prefer, opt for *Opposite*: refuse **4 attack**, lay into, set upon, assault, tear into

go forward v advance, progress, go on, move along, proceed *Opposite*: go back

go from bad to worse v worsen, take a turn for the worse, deteriorate, degenerate, go downhill *Opposite*: improve

go-getter *(infml)* n achiever, doer, self-starter, high-flier, live wire *(infml) Opposite*: layabout

go-getting *(infml)* adj ambitious, highpowered, determined, positive, singleminded

goggle v stare, gaze, gape, ogle, look

goggles n glasses, spectacles, specs *(infml)*

go in v enter, set foot in, gain admittance, step in, access *Opposite*: leave

go in for v **like**, prefer, follow, love, practice *Opposite*: dislike

going n 1 **departure**, exit, disappearance *Opposite*: arrival 2 **conditions**, circumstances, situation, case, setup ■ adj 1 **successful**, profitable, moneymaking, working *Opposite*: bankrupt 2 **accepted**, standard, valid, current, present 3 **available**, obtainable, ready, free, open *Opposite*: taken

going-over *(infml)* n 1 **examination**, inspection, check, investigation, analysis 2 **overhaul**, service, restoration, checkup, improvement 3 **rebuke**, reprimand, scolding, talking-to *(infml)*, telling-off *(infml)*

going rate n **market price**, standard price, usual price, average price, price

goings-on *(infml)* n **activity**, comings and goings, affairs, business, toing and froing

go into v 1 **discuss**, go over, talk about, look into, examine *Opposite*: ignore 2 **enter**, go in, set foot in, gain admittance, step in *Opposite*: leave

go into detail v **elaborate**, enlarge on, amplify, expand, explain

go in with v **partner**, join, cooperate, merge, combine

gold n 1 **treasure**, bullion, ingots, gold plate, sovereigns 2 **wealth**, money, assets, resources, riches 3 *(infml)* **first place**, first prize, title, medal, trophy ■ adj **gilded**, gilt, gold-leaf, gold-plated, golden

gold brick n **fake**, fraud, fool's gold, counterfeit, swindle

goldbrick *(infml)* v **shirk**, loaf, idle, slack, laze around ■ n **shirker**, loafer, idler, slacker, malingerer

golden adj 1 **excellent**, unique, first-rate, wonderful, superb 2 **gold**, gold-plated, gold-leaf, gilt, gilded 3 **idyllic**, best, peak, utopian, paradisaic 4 **superior**, special, elite, select, favored

golden age n **peak**, pinnacle, apex, summit, zenith

golden mean n **middle**, midway, mean *Opposite*: extreme

golden opportunity n **opportunity**, advantage, chance, chance of a lifetime, good fortune

golden rule n **standard**, belief, tenet, code, guide

gold mine n **moneymaker**, treasure-trove, treasure house

gold-plated adj **gilded**, gilt, gold-leaf, golden, gold

gold standard n **benchmark**, system, yardstick, touchstone, criterion

go missing v **disappear**, vanish, abscond, escape, go AWOL

gone adj 1 *(infml)* **dead**, passed away, passed on, no more, deceased *(fml)* *Opposite*: alive 2 **absent**, away, left, disappeared, moved out *Opposite*: present 3 **used up**, spent, finished, consumed, depleted *Opposite*: remaining

gonfalon n **pennant**, banner, flag, standard, ensign

goo *(infml)* n 1 **sludge**, slush, slop, sticky stuff, gook *(infml)* 2 **slush**, sentimentality, emotionalism, mush, corn *(infml)*

good adj 1 **high-quality**, first-class, superior, excellent, first-rate *Opposite*: poor 2 **skillful**, skilled, able, proficient, accomplished *Opposite*: bad 3 **virtuous**, decent, respectable, moral, upright *Opposite*: immoral 4 **enjoyable**, pleasant, nice, lovely, satisfactory *Opposite*: unpleasant 5 **suitable**, helpful, beneficial, sound, safe *Opposite*: useless 6 **nice**, lovely, clear, mild, pleasant *Opposite*: bad 7 **obedient**, well-behaved, well-mannered, polite, courteous *Opposite*: naughty 8 **effective**, useful, valuable, right, appropriate *Opposite*: ineffective ■ n **benefit**, help, advantage, usefulness, profit

good cause n **charitable organization**, voluntary organization, deserving cause, charity, benefit

good deed n **good turn**, favor, kindness, service *Opposite*: sin

good faith n **honesty**, lawfulness, sincerity, probity, integrity

good fortune n **luck**, good luck, chance, a stroke of luck, lucky break *Opposite*: misfortune

good guy *(infml)* n **hero**, winner *Opposite*: baddie *(infml)*

good health n **fitness**, strength, vigor, healthiness, robustness *Opposite*: illness

goodhearted adj **kindhearted**, kind, caring, generous, giving

good-humored adj **friendly**, good-natured, good-tempered, easygoing, genial *Opposite*: ill-tempered

good judgment n **judiciousness**, acumen, astuteness, wisdom, perspicacity

good life n **luxury**, comfort, ease, life of ease, life of Riley

good-looking adj **attractive**, handsome, beautiful, lovely, pretty *Opposite*: unattractive

---

COMPARE AND CONTRAST CORE MEANING: having a pleasing facial appearance

good-looking having a pleasant personal, especially facial, appearance; **attractive** pleasing in appearance or manner, or sexually desirable; **beautiful** pleasing to the senses, especially pleasing to look at, and often used to describe women whose appearance is generally considered ideal or perfect; **handsome** with good facial features or a pleasing general appearance, generally used of men, but also of women who have strong but attractive features; **lovely** pleasing to look at, most often used of women; **pretty** with an attractive, pleasant face that is appealing, rather than outstandingly beautiful, most often used of women.

good looks n beauty, attractiveness, prettiness, handsomeness, loveliness

goodly adj large, substantial, fair, considerable, reasonable

good manners n propriety, manners, courtesy, decorum, etiquette Opposite: bad manners

good name n reputation, credit, standing, status, prestige

good-natured adj pleasant, cheerful, friendly, kind, happy Opposite: disagreeable

goodness n virtuousness, decency, kindness, honesty, integrity Opposite: badness

good offices n intervention, intercession, support, mediation, help

goods n 1 wares, stock, articles, produce, supplies 2 property, personal property, belongings, goods and chattels, things 3 merchandise, imports, exports, cargo, freight

good sense n prudence, reason, intelligence, practicality, gumption (infml) Opposite: stupidity

good-sized adj sizable, generous, big, substantial, large Opposite: small

good taste n discernment, style, elegance, judgment, refinement Opposite: bad taste

good-tempered adj placid, good-natured, good-humored, easygoing, amicable Opposite: bad-tempered

good thing n advantage, blessing, boon, benefit, plus (infml)

good turn n favor, kindness, good deed, service

goodwill n kindness, friendliness, favor, helpfulness, benevolence Opposite: malice

good word n recommendation, defense, testimonial, reference, character

goody n 1 treat, perk, bonus, reward, extravagance 2 tidbit, candy, snack

goody-goody (infml) n teacher's pet, goody two-shoes (infml), bluenose (dated infml) ■ adj sanctimonious, smug, self-satisfied, self-righteous, prudish

gooey adj 1 sticky, viscous, thick, glutinous, gummy 2 (infml) slushy, corny, cloying, sentimental, mushy

goof (infml) n error, blunder, slip, gaffe, mistake ■ v 1 mistake, get it wrong, make a blunder, blunder, go wrong 2 mix up, muddle, botch (infml), mess up (infml), foul up (infml)

go off v 1 explode, blow up, go up, detonate 2 leave, go away, go, depart, set off Opposite: stay

go off the deep end v lose your temper, lose your cool, go berserk, lose control, be beside yourself Opposite: calm down

go on v 1 continue, last, keep on, keep up,

persist Opposite: stop 2 occur, happen, take place, come about 3 blabber, chatter, prattle, blather (infml), blab (infml)

goon n thug, gangster, attacker, assailant, hoodlum

go one better v surpass, outdo, top, crown, better

goop (infml) n slime, mess, goo (infml), gunk (infml), gook (infml)

goose step v strut, stride, tramp, pace, walk

go out v 1 socialize, meet friends, party (infml), go out on the town (infml), paint the town red (infml) 2 ebb, recede, flow out

go out of business v go bankrupt, fold, close down, shut down, go belly up

go over v discuss, go into, examine, look at, study Opposite: ignore

go over the top v overdo it, get carried away, gild the lily, go to town (infml), go mad (slang)

gore v wound, pierce, stab, spear, stick ■ n blood, violence, bloodletting, slaughter, killing

gorge n valley, ravine, canyon, defile, gap ■ v 1 devour, wolf, bolt, gobble, consume Opposite: nibble 2 overeat, stuff, binge, glut, sate

gorgeous adj beautiful, magnificent, stunning, elegant, attractive Opposite: unattractive

gorgeousness n elegance, magnificence, beauty, splendor, exquisiteness

gorilla (infml) n thug, brute, bully, hoodlum, goon

go-round see go-around

gory adj 1 bloody, bloodstained, blood-soaked 2 violent, gruesome, brutal, bloodthirsty, fierce Opposite: pleasant 3 disgusting, gruesome, grisly, unpleasant, ghastly Opposite: delightful

gossamer n threads, filaments, spider's web, cobwebs ■ adj delicate, flimsy, sheer, filmy, ethereal Opposite: robust

gossip n 1 chatter, chat, talk, conversation, blather (infml) 2 rumor, hearsay, tittle-tattle, scandal, chitchat (infml) 3 tattler, telltale, tattletale, rumormonger, gossipmonger ■ v chatter, talk, converse, chat, natter (infml)

gossipmonger n tattler, telltale, tattletale, gossip, rumormonger

go the distance v complete, finish, achieve, accomplish, carry out Opposite: give up

Gothic adj supernatural, melodramatic, eerie, grotesque, gloomy

go through v 1 experience, endure, undergo, bear, suffer 2 examine, look through, look over, go over, study 3 use, get through, run through, consume, utilize Opposite: keep

go through the roof v soar, rocket, rise, shoot up, spiral upward Opposite: plummet

go to bed v retire, turn in (infml), hit the hay (infml), hit the sack (infml)

go to pieces v **break down**, crack, lose control, collapse, crumple

go to pot (infml) v **deteriorate**, disintegrate, fall apart, go downhill, go from bad to worse *Opposite*: improve

go to rack and ruin (infml) see **go to pot**

go to sleep v **fall asleep**, nod off, doze off, drift off, drop off (infml) *Opposite*: wake up

go to the dogs (infml) v **go downhill**, deteriorate, degenerate, decline, go from bad to worse *Opposite*: improve

go to the wall v **go bankrupt**, fold, go under, fail, close down

go to waste v **be wasted**, go down the drain, fall by the wayside, go to seed, go down the tube (infml)

gouge v 1 **scratch**, score, scrape, mark, cut into 2 **extort**, extract, wring, wrest, squeeze ■ n **score**, scratch, gash, groove, hollow

gouge out v **dig out**, hollow out, press out, squeeze out, force out

go under v 1 **collapse**, go to the wall, fold, fail, go bust (infml) 2 **lose consciousness**, pass out, black out, faint

go up v **explode**, go off, detonate, blow up, ignite

go up in smoke v 1 **burn**, catch fire, burst into flames, burn to a crisp, burn to the ground 2 **fail**, fold, collapse, go wrong, go awry

gourmand n 1 **glutton**, overeater, gannet (infml), pig (infml) 2 **gastronome**, food lover, connoisseur, gourmet, epicure

gourmet n **gastronome**, food lover, connoisseur, gourmand, epicure

govern v **rule**, preside over, oversee, administer, administrate

governess n **tutor**, teacher, instructor, schoolteacher, educator

government n **administration**, rule, management, direction, regime

governmental adj **administrative**, parliamentary, legislative, executive, constitutional

governor n **director**, ruler, manager, administrator, chief

governorship n **administration**, leadership, stewardship, directorship, captaincy

go wild (infml) v **run riot**, rampage, run amok, go on the rampage, run wild

go with v 1 (infml) **date**, go out with, see, socialize, go steady 2 **adopt**, accept, follow, run with, support

go without v **do without**, be without, lack, want, be deprived *Opposite*: have

gown n **dress**, robe, evening dress, wedding dress, ball gown

go wrong v 1 **fail**, break down, not work, not succeed, go awry *Opposite*: succeed 2 **make a mistake**, misjudge, blunder, err, slip up (infml)

GP n **family doctor**, doctor, clinician, practitioner, medic (infml)

grab v 1 **grasp**, clutch, grip, take hold of, seize *Opposite*: let go 2 **steal**, snatch, take, seize, remove 3 (infml) **affect**, appeal, impress, attract, please

grab hold of v **grab**, grasp, grip, snatch, clutch

grace n 1 **elegance**, refinement, loveliness, beauty, polish *Opposite*: awkwardness 2 **kindness**, kindliness, decency, favor, mercy *Opposite*: unkindness 3 **blessing**, prayer, thanks, thanksgiving ■ v 1 **adorn**, embellish, enhance, decorate, ornament *Opposite*: deface 2 **dignify**, honor, favor, distinguish *Opposite*: demean

graceful adj 1 **elegant**, beautiful, supple, agile, nimble *Opposite*: graceless 2 **poised**, dignified, polished, refined, stylish *Opposite*: awkward 3 **flowing**, fluid, smooth, easy on the eyes, attractive *Opposite*: ugly

gracefulness n 1 **elegance**, grace, smoothness, fluidity, subtlety *Opposite*: inelegance 2 **poise**, dignity, refinement, grace, restraint *Opposite*: awkwardness

graceless adj 1 **clumsy**, ungainly, inelegant, awkward, maladroit *Opposite*: graceful 2 **rude**, impolite, ill-mannered, boorish, offensive *Opposite*: polite

gracelessness n 1 **inelegance**, awkwardness, clumsiness, ungainliness, unskillfulness *Opposite*: gracefulness 2 **rudeness**, impoliteness, mannerlessness, bad manners, boorishness *Opposite*: politeness

grace period n **extension**, overtime, overrun

gracious adj 1 **kind**, polite, tactful, courteous, civil *Opposite*: rude 2 **condescending**, haughty, superior, patronizing, high and mighty *Opposite*: genuine 3 **luxurious**, elegant, comfortable, well-appointed, plush (infml) *Opposite*: modest 4 **merciful**, compassionate, lenient, humane, charitable *Opposite*: harsh

graciousness n **kindness**, courteousness, politeness, civility, affability *Opposite*: rudeness

gradation n **nuance**, degree, stage, progression, shift

grade n 1 **score**, mark, rating, ranking, evaluation 2 **hill**, gradient, incline, slope, ascent 3 **rank**, position, status, standing, class ■ v **classify**, categorize, sort, arrange, order

gradient n **slope**, incline, ramp, hill, rise

gradual adj **slow**, measured, slow but sure, plodding, continuing *Opposite*: rapid

graduate v 1 **progress**, move up, advance, go forward, move on *Opposite*: fall back 2 **mark off**, measure off, divide up, regulate 3 **arrange**, order, categorize, classify, rank

graduation n 1 **matriculation**, qualification, completion, validation, attainment 2 **award ceremony**, graduation day, ceremony, commencement **3 mark**, division, line, unit, step **4 calibration**, divisior, measurement, marking up, marking out

graffiti *n* **drawing**, doodle, scrawl, scribble, writing

graft *n* **implant**, insert, transplant, scion, slip ■ *v* **splice**, attach, join, embed, implant

grain *n* **1 cereal**, wheat, corn, barley, maize **2 seed**, kernel, germ **3 particle**, speck, fragment, crumb, bit **4 pattern**, direction, configuration, arrangement, texture

grammar *n* **syntax**, sentence structure, language rules, parsing

grammatical *adj* **1 linguistic**, syntactic, structural **2 correct**, well-formed, right, proper, standard

gran *(infml) see* **grandmother**

granary *n* **warehouse**, barn, grain elevator, silo

grand *adj* **1 outstanding**, impressive, imposing, majestic, magnificent *Opposite*: humble **2 ambitious**, impressive, far-reaching, major, substantial *Opposite*: limited **3 distinguished**, illustrious, celebrated, well-known, famous *Opposite*: ordinary **4 wonderful**, fantastic, excellent, memorable, great *Opposite*: poor

granddad *(infml) see* **grandfather**

grandee *n* **dignitary**, notable, public figure, VIP, personage *(fml) Opposite*: upstart

grandeur *n* **splendor**, magnificence, sumptuousness, opulence, majesty *Opposite*: austerity

grandfather *n* **granddad** *(infml)*, grandpa *(infml)*, gramps *(infml)*

grandiloquence *n* **pomposity**, bombast, loftiness, fustian, rhetoric

grandiloquent *adj* **pompous**, lofty, haughty, bombastic, high-flown *Opposite*: plain

grandiose *adj* **1 pretentious**, pompous, flamboyant, ostentatious, extravagant *Opposite*: modest **2 magnificent**, lavish, splendid, impressive, stately *Opposite*: modest **3 elaborate**, ambitious, complex, impenetrable, unfathomable *Opposite*: simple

grandiosity *n* **1 pretentiousness**, pompousness, self-importance, affectedness, pomposity *Opposite*: unpretentiousness **2 magnificence**, lavishness, impressiveness, stateliness, imposingness *Opposite*: modesty **3 elaborateness**, ambitiousness, complexity, impenetrability *Opposite*: simplicity

grandma *(infml) see* **grandmother**

grandmother *n* **grandma** *(infml)*, nana *(infml)*, gran *(infml)*, granny *(infml)*, nanny *(infml)*

grandness *n* **magnificence**, splendor, majesty, dignity, stateliness *Opposite*: simplicity

grandpa *(infml) see* **grandfather**

grandstand *v* **show off**, play to the gallery, ham up, attract attention, impress

granny *(infml) see* **grandmother**

grant *v* **1 allow**, permit, agree to, consent to, approve of *Opposite*: prohibit **2 give**, accord, award, sign over, present ■ *n* **funding**, scholarship, endowment, contribution, donation. *See* COMPARE AND CONTRAST *at* **give**.

granular *adj* **gritty**, grainy, rough, coarse, granulated *Opposite*: smooth

granulated *adj* **ground**, coarse, grainy, gritty, rough

granule *n* **grain**, pellet, particle, morsel, crumb

grapevine *n* **rumor mill**, gossip, word of mouth, viral marketing, bush telegraph *(infml)*

graph *n* **chart**, diagram, grid, display

graphic *adj* **1 explicit**, realistic, vivid, striking, detailed *Opposite*: sketchy **2 illustrative**, pictorial, drawn, diagrammatic, decorative

grapple *v* **1 struggle**, wrestle, seize, grab, grasp **2 contend**, deal with, cope, face, hardle

grasp *v* **1 take hold of**, clutch, grab, seize, grip *Opposite*: let go **2 understand**, comprehend, see the point of, follow, get ■ *n* **1 grip**, hold, clutch, clasp, clench **2 understanding**, comprehension, knowledge, awareness, perception **3 reach**, scope, extent, range, capacity

grasping *adj* **greedy**, avaricious, covetous, selfish, acquisitive *Opposite*: generous

grass *n* **grassland**, meadow, pasture, prairie, sward

WORD BANK
❑ **types of grasses** bamboo, beach grass, bluegrass, bulrush, couch grass, crabgrass, esparto, fescue, Kentucky bluegrass, lyme grass, marram, meadow fescue, pampas grass, reed, rye grass, spinifex, sugar cane, sword grass, timothy

grassland *n* **plains**, prairie, savanna, steppe, heath

grassroots *n* **1 masses**, hoi polloi, rank and file, ranks, also-rans **2 basis**, origin, foundation, base, root ■ *adj* **popular**, proletarian, public, common, ordinary

grassy *adj* **green**, verdant, lush

grate *n* **grill**, lattice, grille, trellis, grid ■ *v* **1 shred**, scrape, rasp, file, grind **2 irritate**, annoy, exasperate, vex, chafe *Opposite*: please

grateful *adj* **1 thankful**, appreciative, obliged, indebted, glad *Opposite*: ungrateful **2** *(literary)* **comforting**, gratifying, satisfying, pleasing, pleasant *Opposite*: unwelcome

gratefulness *n* **thankfulness**, appreciativeness, appreciation, gratitude, thanks *Opposite*: ingratitude

gratification *n* **satisfaction**, fulfillment, indulgence, enjoyment, delight *Opposite*: displeasure

gratify v **please**, satisfy, indulge, fulfill, oblige *Opposite*: displease

gratifying adj **rewarding**, satisfying, agreeable, heartwarming, acceptable *Opposite*: humiliating

grating n **grille**, grate, lattice, grid, screen ▪ adj **1 rough**, harsh, raucous, strident, discordant *Opposite*: mellifluous **2 irritating**, annoying, infuriating, insensitive, vexing *Opposite*: pleasant

gratis adj **free**, free of charge, on the house, complimentary, for nothing

gratitude n **thanks**, thankfulness, appreciation, gratefulness, appreciativeness *Opposite*: ingratitude

gratuitous adj **1 unwarranted**, uncalled-for, wanton, unjustified, unnecessary *Opposite*: necessary **2 free**, gratis, complimentary, at no charge, on the house

gratuitously adv **unnecessarily**, pointlessly, unreasonably, needlessly, wantonly *Opposite*: necessarily

gratuity n **tip**, service charge, contribution, token of appreciation, reward

grave n **tomb**, crypt, vault, burial chamber, sepulcher ▪ adj **1 serious**, severe, weighty, momentous, crucial *Opposite*: minor **2 solemn**, serious, somber, grim, earnest *Opposite*: cheerful **3 ominous**, foreboding, forbidding, fateful, dire *Opposite*: favorable

gravel n **stones**, pebbles, shingle ▪ v (*infml*) **1 annoy**, irritate, grate, vex, chafe **2 bewilder**, puzzle, confuse, perplex, baffle

gravelly adj **1 croaky**, gruff, hoarse, rough, harsh *Opposite*: velvety **2 pebbly**, shingly, stony, rocky, gritty

gravely adv **1 grimly**, sternly, austerely, seriously, solemnly *Opposite*: cheerfully **2 fatally**, dangerously, critically, incurably, mortally

gravestone n **headstone**, marker, cenotaph, tombstone, memorial

graveyard n **cemetery**, churchyard, necropolis, burial ground, boneyard (*infml*)

gravitas n **seriousness**, gravity, sobriety, solemnness, somberness

gravitate v **1 sink**, settle, drop, fall, descend *Opposite*: rise **2 incline**, lean, move, drift, be attracted *Opposite*: repel

gravitation n **movement**, attraction, gravity

gravity n **1 gravitation**, gravitational force, pull, draw **2 seriousness**, importance, significance, severity, enormity *Opposite*: insignificance **3 solemnity**, grimness, sedateness, dignity, earnestness *Opposite*: cheerfulness

graze v **1 browse**, crop, nibble, forage, eat **2 glance**, brush, skim, sweep, touch **3 scrape**, scratch, scuff, rub, skin ▪ n **scratch**, scrape, abrasion, lesion, scuff mark

grease n **fat**, lard, oil ▪ v **lubricate**, oil, smear

greasiness n **fattiness**, griminess, sliminess, oiliness, oleaginousness

greasy adj **oily**, fatty, slippery, slimy, oleaginous

great adj **1 huge**, immense, enormous, vast, large *Opposite*: tiny **2 countless**, inordinate, prodigious, excessive, boundless *Opposite*: limited **3 important**, significant, momentous, critical, major *Opposite*: unimportant **4 absolute**, utter, complete, downright, intense *Opposite*: slight **5 famous**, illustrious, eminent, distinguished, celebrated *Opposite*: ordinary **6 noble**, elevated, lofty, imposing, stately *Opposite*: lowly **7 wonderful**, fantastic, magnificent, excellent, incredible *Opposite*: awful

greater adj **better**, superior, larger, bigger, more

greatest adj **most**, maximum, record, utmost, supreme

greatly adv **1 very much**, really, to a great extent, to the highest degree, deeply *Opposite*: hardly **2 importantly**, significantly, momentously, critically, seriously

greatness n **1 magnitude**, enormity, immensity, vastness, size **2 importance**, prominence, seriousness, significance, weightiness *Opposite*: insignificance **3 fame**, eminence, distinction, impressiveness, prominence *Opposite*: commonness

greed n **1 gluttony**, voracity, ravenousness, insatiability, hunger *Opposite*: moderation **2 avarice**, covetousness, materialism, acquisitiveness, greediness *Opposite*: generosity

greediness *see* greed

greedy adj **1 gluttonous**, voracious, ravenous, insatiable, hungry *Opposite*: moderate **2 avaricious**, covetous, grasping, materialistic, acquisitive *Opposite*: generous

greenery n **foliage**, vegetation, greens, plants, leaves

greenhorn n **novice**, recruit, initiate, beginner, neophyte. *See* compare and contrast *at* beginner.

greenhouse n **orangery**, hothouse, conservatory

green light n **permission**, clearance, consent, approval, stamp of approval *Opposite*: red light

greens *see* greenery

greet v **1 welcome**, meet, make the acquaintance of, receive **2 address**, speak to, acknowledge, hail, salute *Opposite*: ignore **3 respond to**, react to, receive, meet, hail

greeting n **salutation**, welcome, welcoming, reception, acknowledgment

gregarious adj **outgoing**, sociable, social, extrovert, expressive *Opposite*: shy

gregariousness n **sociability**, friendliness, openness, unreservedness, conviviality *Opposite*: shyness

gremlin *(infml)* n **jinx**, malfunction, blip, glitch, bug *(infml)*

grid n **network**, lattice, net, web, gridiron

griddle v **grill**, sear, barbecue, cook, broil

gridiron n **grid**, lattice, grating, framework, network

gridlock n 1 **traffic jam**, jam, holdup, backup, snarl 2 **deadlock**, stalemate, standstill, logjam, impasse

grief n **sorrow**, heartache, anguish, misery, unhappiness *Opposite*: joy

grief-stricken adj **grieving**, distraught, traumatized, inconsolable, heartbroken *Opposite*: happy

grievance n 1 **complaint**, protest, criticism, objection, grumble 2 **injustice**, wrong, cause of distress, ill-treatment, unfairness

grieve v 1 **mourn**, feel sad, be sad, lament, be distressed *Opposite*: rejoice *(literary)* 2 **hurt**, afflict, pain, distress, upset *Opposite*: cheer

grievous adj 1 **serious**, significant, critical, dangerous, grave *Opposite*: slight 2 **dreadful**, awful, terrible, shameful, painful

grill v 1 *(infml)* **question**, interrogate, examine, press, probe 2 **cook**, barbecue, toast, brown, frizzle ∎ n **griddle**, grate, barbecue, rotisserie. See COMPARE AND CONTRAST at **question**.

grille n **grating**, lattice, framework, grid, trellis

grim adj 1 **forbidding**, ugly, unattractive, uninviting, gray *Opposite*: attractive 2 **depressing**, bleak, dismal, gloomy, cheerless *Opposite*: hopeful 3 **stern**, serious, dour, severe, morose *Opposite*: kind 4 **shocking**, ghastly, horrible, horrific, gruesome *Opposite*: pleasant

grimace n **scowl**, frown, smirk, sneer, pout *Opposite*: smile ∎ v **frown**, scowl, smirk, sneer, pout *Opposite*: smile

grime n **filth**, dirt, stain, soot, dust

griminess n **dirtiness**, dinginess, filthiness, grubbiness, dustiness *Opposite*: cleanliness

grimness n 1 **bleakness**, cheerlessness, dismalness, ominousness, gloominess *Opposite*: brightness 2 **forbiddingness**, ugliness, unattractiveness, grayness, dinginess *Opposite*: attractiveness 3 **sternness**, seriousness, dourness, severity, moroseness *Opposite*: kindness 4 **gruesomeness**, horror, hideousness, grisliness, dreadfulness *Opposite*: pleasantness

grimy adj **dirty**, grubby, smudged, soiled, filthy *Opposite*: clean. See COMPARE AND CONTRAST at **dirty**.

grin v **smile**, beam, smirk, laugh, chortle *Opposite*: frown ∎ n **beam**, smile, smirk, laugh, chortle *Opposite*: frown

grin and bear it *(infml)* v **put up with**, take the bad with the good, weather, ride out, lump it *(infml)*

grind v 1 **crush**, break up, mill, pound, mince 2 **grate**, rasp, grash, scrape *Opposite*: glide 3 **sharpen**, file, whet, abrade, polish *Opposite*: blunt ∎ n *(infml)* **toil**, chore, slog, tedium, routine

grind down v 1 **wear**, erode, eat away, abrade, rub 2 **oppress**, tyrannize, persecute, harass, weaken *Opposite*: nurture

grinder n **mill**, mincer, crusher, pounder, pulverizer

grinding adj 1 **crushing**, oppressive, relentless, unending, never-ending 2 **grating**, crunching, earsplitting, screeching, squealing *Opposite*: pleasant

grip n 1 **grasp**, hold, clasp, clutch *Opposite*: release 2 **control**, rule, command, authority clutches 3 **understanding**, comprehension, grasp, command, appreciation *Opposite*: ignorance ∎ v 1 **grasp**, clasp, clutch, catch, seize *Opposite*: release 2 **stick**, adhere, cling, hang on, cleave to *(literary)* 3 **overwhelm**, fill, pervade, suffuse, swamp 4 **fascinate**, enthrall, spellbind, transfix, mesmerize *Opposite*: bore

gripe *(infml)* v **complain**, grumble, protest, object, moan *(infml)* ∎ n **complaint**, grumble, grievance, protest, objection *Opposite*: compliment. See COMPARE AND CONTRAST at **complain**.

gripped adj **absorbed**, engrossed, rapt, obsessed, enthralled *Opposite*: bored

gripping adj **fascinating**, spellbinding, enthralling, mesmerizing, transfixing *Opposite*: boring

grisliness n **gruesomeness**, ghastliness, grimness, hideousness, dreadfulness *Opposite*: pleasantness

grisly adj **gruesome**, ghastly, horrible, horrific, horrid *Opposite*: pleasant

gristle n **cartilage**, tendon, sinew

gristly adj **tough**, chewy, sinewy, stringy, leathery *Opposite*: tender

grit n 1 **gravel**, stones, pebbles, sand, shingle 2 **determination**, perseverance, tenacity, bravery, fortitude *Opposite*: cowardice ∎ v **clench**, grind, gnash, grate

gritty adj 1 **determined**, persistent, resolute, courageous, persevering *Opposite*: cowardly 2 **realistic**, graphic, harsh, stark, uncompromising *Opposite*: romantic 3 **grainy**, coarse, rough, granular, sandy *Opposite*: smooth

grit your teeth v **steel yourself**, nerve yourself, brace yourself, persevere, hold on tight *Opposite*: knuckle under

groan v 1 **creak**, squeak, squeal, screech, grind 2 **moan**, cry out, whimper, grunt, growl *Opposite*: laugh 3 *(infml)* **grumble**, complain, carp, moan, gripe *(infml)*

groceries n **food**, shopping, provisions, rations, victuals

grogginess *n* tiredness, fatigue, sleepiness, unsteadiness, bleariness *Opposite*: alertness

groggy *adj* tired, sleepy, slow, unsteady, bleary *Opposite*: alert

groin *n* breakwater, mole, barrier, bulwark, jetty

groom *v* 1 clean, clean up, brush, comb, tidy 2 prime, train, coach, prepare, tutor *Opposite*: hinder

groove *n* channel, furrow, rut, trench, indentation *Opposite*: ridge

grope *v* 1 fumble, feel, cast about, scrabble, flounder 2 *(infml)* fondle, touch, molest, caress, feel up *(infml)*

gross *adj* 1 aggregate, combined, whole, overall, total *Opposite*: net 2 flagrant, blatant, glaring, arrant, serious *Opposite*: minor 3 coarse, vulgar, crass, rude, crude *Opposite*: polite 4 uncultured, uncivilized, uncultivated, unsophisticated, unpolished *Opposite*: cultured 5 overweight, obese, fat, heavy, stout *Opposite*: slim ■ *v* earn, make, take in, receive, bring in

grossly *adv* 1 wholly, totally, completely, utterly, unacceptably *Opposite*: slightly 2 rudely, coarsely, uncouthly, crassly, crudely *Opposite*: politely

grotesque *adj* 1 distorted, bizarre, misshapen, monstrous, gross *(slang)* *Opposite*: attractive 2 incongruous, ridiculous, ludicrous, laughable, outrageous *Opposite*: fitting

grotto *n* cavern, pothole, hollow, cave

grouch *(infml)* *n* 1 complaint, grumble, whine, grouse *(infml)*, moan *(infml)* *Opposite*: praise 2 grumbler, complainer, malcontent, moaner *(infml)*, grouser *(infml)* ■ *v* complain, grumble, sulk, gripe *(infml)*, moan *(infml)*

grouchiness *(infml)* *n* peevishness, irritability, cantankerousness, crabbiness, bad temper *Opposite*: equanimity *(fml)*

grouchy *(infml)* *adj* bad-tempered, complaining, touchy, grumpy, crabby *Opposite*: even-tempered

ground *n* 1 earth, soil, land, field, dry land 2 playing field, field, arena, ballpark, stadium ■ *adj* crushed, pulverized, broken up, milled, minced ■ *v* 1 punish, deal with, chastise 2 base, substantiate, support, build, justify 3 initiate, prepare, coach, instruct, tutor

groundbreaking *adj* innovative, pioneering, revolutionary, radical, trailblazing *Opposite*: outdated

grounding *n* foundation, basis, preparation, training, instruction

groundless *adj* baseless, unsupported, unjustified, unwarranted, unfounded *Opposite*: sound

ground plan *n* 1 outline, sketch, blueprint, draft, preliminary design 2 floor plan, plan,

scale drawing, blueprint, diagram

ground rule *n* fundamental, axiom, stipulation, point of departure, modus operandi

grounds *n* 1 basis, foundation, reason, justification, argument 2 estate, land, park, parkland, gardens 3 dregs, lees, sediment, residue, deposit

groundswell *n* 1 upsurge, wave, outpouring, rise, swell 2 swell, wave, storm, squall, heavy sea

groundwork *n* foundation, basis, base, footing, underpinning

group *n* 1 collection, cluster, set, assemblage, assembly *Opposite*: individual 2 grouping, set, faction, crowd, company *Opposite*: individual 3 musical group, band, trio, duo, quartet *Opposite*: soloist 4 alliance, federation, consortium, amalgamation, confederation ■ *v* gather, assemble, congregate, convene, cluster *Opposite*: disperse 2 classify, categorize, arrange, sort, bracket

groupie *(infml)* *n* follower, fan, enthusiast, supporter, aficionado

grouping *n* 1 alliance, federation, consortium, assemblage, alignment 2 category, class, set, type, group

grouse *(infml)* *v* complain, grumble, moan, gripe *(infml)*, bellyache *(infml)* ■ *n* complaint, grumble, objection, protest, moan *(infml)*. *See* COMPARE AND CONTRAST *at* **complain**.

grout *n* mortar, filling, plaster, cement, putty ■ *v* fill, mortar, plaster, cement, render

grove *n* copse, coppice, orchard, wood, stand

grovel *v* 1 plead, beg, cringe, fawn, bow and scrape 2 crawl, crouch, stoop, kneel *Opposite*: stand up

grow *v* 1 produce, cultivate, nurture, breed, raise 2 develop, grow up, mature, shoot up, sprout 3 expand, enlarge, swell, extend, spread *Opposite*: shrink 4 increase, multiply, intensify, escalate, strengthen *Opposite*: decrease

growing *adj* rising, mounting, upward, budding, emergent *Opposite*: decreasing

growl *v* roar, snarl, bark, howl, rumble

grow less *v* weaken, wear off, fade, subside, decrease *Opposite*: increase

grown *adj* grown-up, full-fledged, adult, full-grown, developed *Opposite*: immature

grown-up *adj* adult, mature, developed, grown, responsible *Opposite*: immature

growth *n* 1 growing, development, evolution, progress, advance *Opposite*: decay 2 increase, enlargement, expansion, augmentation, development *Opposite*: reduction 3 tumor, cyst, lump, swelling, outgrowth

grow up *v* 1 grow, develop, mature, evolve, flourish 2 take shape, arise, be born, develop, come about

grub *v* 1 dig, burrow, root out, excavate, pull

up **2 search**, hunt, rummage, forage, scour ■ *n* **1 larva**, maggot, caterpillar, bug, creepy-crawly (*infml*) **2** (*infml*) **food**, victuals, sustenance, feed, nourishment

grubbiness *n* **1 dirtiness**, griminess, filthiness, muddiness, sloppiness *Opposite*: cleanness **2 sordidness**, squalidness, seediness, contemptibleness, despicableness *Opposite*: purity

grubby *adj* **1 dirty**, grimy, soiled, filthy, muddy *Opposite*: clean **2 sordid**, squalid, seedy, contemptible, despicable *Opposite*: honorable. *See* COMPARE AND CONTRAST *at* dirty

grudge *n* **complaint**, rancor, bitterness, resentment, dislike ■ *v* **resent**, hold against, begrudge, loathe, mind

grudging *adj* **reluctant**, unwilling, complaining, resentful, rancorous *Opposite*: willing

grueling *adj* **arduous**, demanding, exhausting, taxing, tough *Opposite*: easy

gruesome *adj* **grisly**, ghastly, horrible, horrific, horrid *Opposite*: pleasant

gruesomeness *n* **grisliness**, ghastliness, horror, dreadfulness, hideousness *Opposite*: pleasantness

gruff *adj* **1 bad-tempered**, grumpy, angry, impatient, brusque *Opposite*: friendly **2 hoarse**, husky, gravelly, rasping, harsh *Opposite*: soft

gruffness *n* **1 grumpiness**, crustiness, abruptness, curtness, sternness *Opposite*: pleasantness **2 hoarseness**, huskiness, thickness, throatiness, harshness *Opposite*: softness

grumble *v* **complain**, protest, mutter, object, moan (*infml*) ■ *n* **complaint**, protest, objection, moan (*infml*), grouse (*infml*). *See* COMPARE AND CONTRAST *at* complain.

grumbler *n* **complainer**, whiner, groaner, grouch (*infml*), moaner (*infml*)

grumpiness *n* **bad-temperedness**, irritability, cantankerousness, petulance, crabbiness *Opposite*: cheerfulness

grumpy *adj* **bad-tempered**, irritable, sullen, cantankerous, ill-tempered *Opposite*: cheerful

grunge (*infml*) *n* **filth**, grime, dirt, mess, muck (*infml*) *Opposite*: cleanliness

grungy (*infml*) *adj* **shabby**, dirty, scruffy, unkempt, dilapidated *Opposite*: clean

grunt *v* **speak indistinctly**, mumble, groan, snort

guarantee *n* **1 assurance**, promise, pledge, agreement, security **2 warranty**, certification, undertaking, contract, agreement ■ *v* **assure**, ensure, promise, pledge, warrant

guaranteed *adj* **certain**, definite, sure, cast-iron, fail-safe *Opposite*: uncertain

guarantor *n* **backer**, sponsor, underwriter, supporter, patron. *See* COMPARE AND CONTRAST *at* backer.

guard *v* **protect**, defend, safeguard, shield,

watch over ■ *n* **1 protector**, sentinel, sentry, picket, lookout **2 safeguard**, security, protection, shield, fortification. *See* COMPARE AND CONTRAST *at* safeguard.

guarded *adj* **1 protected**, secured, watched over, defended, safeguarded *Opposite*: unprotected **2 wary**, cautious, careful, circumspect, hesitant *Opposite*: open. *See* COMPARE AND CONTRAST *at* cautious.

guardhouse *n* **prison**, jail, lockup, cells, detention center

guardian *n* **1 guard**, sentinel, keeper, custodian **2 protector**, caretaker, godparent

guardianship *n* **protection**, custody, care, responsibility, supervision

guardrail *n* **handrail**, rail, banister, railing, paling

guerrilla *n* **freedom fighter**, rebel, insurgent, irregular, paramilitary

guess *v* **1 deduce**, presume, speculate, suppose, estimate **2 predict**, solve, fathom, work out, conjecture ■ *n* **deduction**, conjecture, supposition, presumption, speculation

guesstimate (*infml*) *n* **guess**, estimate, conjecture, projection, reckoning ■ *v* **estimate**, guess, reckon, conjecture, project

guesswork *n* **conjecture**, deduction, presumption, speculation, estimation

guest *n* **visitor**, caller, invitee, boarder, lodger *Opposite*: host

guestroom *n* **room**, bedroom, spare room

guff (*infml*) *n* **nonsense**, rubbish, rigmarole, stuff, stuff and nonsense *Opposite*: sense

guffaw *v* **laugh**, chuckle, chortle, roar, crack up (*infml*) ■ *n* **chuckle**, laugh, chortle, roar, belly laugh

guidance *n* **1 leadership**, direction, supervision, management, control **2 help**, assistance, advice, support, counseling

guidance counselor *n* **adviser**, therapist, mediator, counselor

guide *v* **1 direct**, steer, lead, conduct, escort **2 steer**, drive, pilot, direct, handle ■ *n* **1 leader**, director, attendant, chaperon, controller **2 tour guide**, leader, escort, conductor, director **3 influence**, standard, model, ideal, guiding light **4 guidebook**, handbook, manual, instructions, vade mecum

---

COMPARE AND CONTRAST CORE MEANING: show somebody the way to a place

guide take somebody the way in the right direction or give a tour of a particular place; **conduct** take somebody to or around a particular place, especially when the person showing the way has some kind of authority or specialized knowledge; **direct** show or indicate the way; **lead** show the way to others, usually by going ahead of them; **steer** encourage somebody to take a particular course; **usher** escort somebody to or from a place, especially a seat.

guidebook *n* travel guide, vade mecum, gazetteer, guide, manual

guideline *n* advice, recommendation, standard, guide, parameter

guild *n* club, union, society, association, league

guile *n* cunning, treachery, astuteness, slyness, wiliness *Opposite*: frankness

guileful *adj* cunning, treacherous, sly, astute, wily *Opposite*: naive

guileless *adj* naive, frank, candid, ingenuous, straightforward *Opposite*: guileful

guillotine *v* behead, decapitate, execute, kill

guilt *n* 1 fault, responsibility, blame, culpability, guiltiness *Opposite*: innocence 2 remorse, shame, self-reproach, conscience, contriteness

guiltless *adj* innocent, blameless, faultless, unimpeachable, irreproachable *Opposite*: guilty

guilt-ridden *adj* guilty, fearful, anguished, tormented, haunted *Opposite*: unashamed

guilty *adj* 1 culpable, responsible, at fault, blameworthy, in the wrong *Opposite*: innocent 2 shamefaced, remorseful, embarrassed, mortified, guilt-ridden *Opposite*: unashamed

guilty conscience *n* guilt complex, conscience, twinge, pang, guilt trip *(slang)*

guise *n* 1 appearance, semblance, show, pretext, excuse 2 form, appearance, shape, light 3 costume, disguise, dress, outfit, mask

gulch *n* ravine, gorge, gully, valley, gap

gulf *n* 1 bight, bay, inlet, sound, cove 2 hole, abyss, chasm, gap, hollow

gullet *n* crop, maw, throat, craw, esophagus

gullibility *n* trustfulness, innocence, credulity, unwariness, acceptance *Opposite*: shrewdness

gullible *adj* naive, susceptible, innocent, trusting, accepting *Opposite*: discerning

gully *n* 1 ravine, gorge, valley, gap, chasm 2 channel, ditch, furrow, rut, culvert

gulp *v* swallow, drink, toss down, guzzle *(infml)*, swig *(infml) Opposite*: sip ■ *n* swallow, drink, mouthful, swig *(infml)*, slug *(infml) Opposite*: sip

gulp back *v* stifle, suppress, restrain, hold back, fight back

gulp down *v* wolf, swill, swallow, down, gobble *Opposite*: sip

gum *n* 1 secretion, exudate, resin, latex, juice 2 glue, adhesive, paste, cement, epoxy resin ■ *v* stick, glue, paste, bond, cement *Opposite*: unstick

gummy *adj* sticky, gooey, gluey, tacky, adhesive

gumption *(infml) n* 1 courage, nerve, bravery, mettle, pluck 2 common sense, sense, shrewdness, practicality, presence of mind *Opposite*: stupidity

gumshoe *(dated infml) n* sleuth, detective, private detective, private eye, private investigator

gun *n* firearm, handgun, shooter *(infml)*, piece *(slang)*

WORD BANK
❑ **types of guns** air pistol, air rifle, antiaircraft gun, automatic, bazooka, blunderbuss, cannon, carbine, flamethrower, handgun, howitzer, machine gun, magnum, mortar musket, pistol, revolver, rifle, sawed-off shotgun, semi-automatic, shotgun, submachine gun, Tommy gun *(infml)*

---

gun down *(infml) v* kill, assassinate, shoot, shoot down, mow down

gunfight *n* gun battle, shootout, firefight, fight, duel

gunfire *n* firing, shooting, gunshot, shots, bombardment

gung ho *(infml) adj* 1 enthusiastic, eager, keen, zealous, ardent *Opposite*: reluctant 2 combative, belligerent, militaristic, bellicose, aggressive *Opposite*: peaceable

gunk *(infml) n* grease, mess, filth, dirt, slime

gunman *n* 1 sniper, murderer, assassin, killer, gangster 2 marksman, markswoman, shot, crack shot, good shot

gunner *n* soldier, shooter, artilleryman, fusilier, rifleman

guns *n* weapons, ordnance, firepower, artillery, arms

gunshot *see* gunfire

gurgle *v* 1 bubble, slosh, splash, ripple, murmur 2 babble, burble, coo, warble, crow

guru *n* 1 spiritual leader, religious teacher, maharishi, spiritual guide, spiritual adviser 2 leader, authority, leading light, expert, pundit

gush *v* 1 pour, flood, stream, surge, spurt *Opposite*: trickle 2 be effusive, prattle, flatter, ooze, admire *Opposite*: criticize ■ *n* flood, flow, spurt, jet, stream *Opposite*: trickle

gushing *adj* 1 pouring, flowing, overflowing, spouting, torrential *Opposite*: trickling 2 effusive, voluble, enthusiastic, emotional, sentimental *Opposite*: reserved

gusset *n* patch, insert, inset, reinforcement, support

gust *n* 1 squall, draft, flurry, breeze, blast *Opposite*: calm 2 burst, explosion, expulsion, eruption, outburst ■ *v* blow, bluster, squall

gusto *n* enjoyment, delight, enthusiasm, passion, zest *Opposite*: apathy

gusty *adj* windy, breezy, squally, stormy, blustery *Opposite*: calm

gut *v* 1 strip, clear out, empty, empty out, plunder 2 disembowel, eviscerate, clean, prepare, dress 3 ruin, damage, destroy, burn, raze *Opposite*: build up ■ *adj* instinctive, intuitive, emotional, automatic, unconscious *Opposite*: considered

gut feeling *n* **guess**, hunch, instinct, impression, intuition *Opposite*: fact

gutless *adj* **cowardly**, spineless, spiritless, weak, timid *Opposite*: plucky. *See* COMPARE AND CONTRAST *at* **cowardly.**

gut reaction *see* gut feeling

guts *n* **1 intestines**, bowels, stomach, viscera, entrails **2 interior**, recesses, bowels, inner workings, heart

gutsy *(infml) adj* **1 brave**, plucky, courageous, fearless, determined *Opposite*: cowardly **2 passionate**, impassioned, emotional, intense, fiery *Opposite*: insipid

gutted *adj* **cleaned**, disemboweled, eviscerated, prepared, dressed

gutter *n* **drain**, sewer, channel, trench, groove ■ *v* **flicker**, sputter, waver, drip, fade *Opposite*: flare

guttural *adj* **harsh**, rough, rasping, throaty, deep *Opposite*: melodious

guy *(infml) n* **man**, fellow, gentleman, boy, fella *(infml)*

guys *(infml) n* **people**, folks, gang, everybody

guywire *n* **rope**, lashing, string, halyard, hawser

guzzle *(infml) v* **1 gulp**, gobble, wolf, stuff, consume *Opposite*: nibble **2 consume**, use, devour, burn up, use up *Opposite*: conserve

gym *(infml) see* **gymnasium**

gymnasium *n* **exercise room**, sports club, health club, sports hall, aerobics studio

gymnastic *adj* **1 athletic**, acrobatic, sporty, sporting **2 energetic**, athletic, lithe, supple *Opposite*: stiff

gymnastics *n* **aerobics**, calisthenics, exercises, physical training

gypsy *n* **nomad**, traveler, drifter, wanderer

gyrate *v* **rotate**, whirl, spin, revolve, twirl

gyration *n* **whirling**, twirling, spinning, turning, revolving

gyratory *adj* **spiral**, rotating, revolving, spinning, whirling *Opposite*: still

H

habit *n* **1 custom**, routine, tradition, convention, practice **2 tendency**, inclination, leaning, preference, fondness **3 addiction**, problem, dependency, weakness, fixation **4 uniform**, garb, apparel, outfit, garment

COMPARE AND CONTRAST CORE MEANING: established pattern of behavior

habit an action or behavior pattern that is regular, repetitive, often unconscious, and sometimes compulsive; **custom** the way somebody normally or routinely behaves in a situation, or a traditional practice in a particular community or group of people; **tradition** a long-established action or pattern of behavior in a particular community or group of people, especially one that has been handed down from generation to generation; **practice** an established way of doing something, especially one that has developed through experience and knowledge; **routine** a typical pattern of behavior that is regularly followed on a day-to-day basis, sometimes with the suggestion that this is monotonous and tedious; **wont** *(fml)* something that somebody does regularly or habitually.

habitable *adj* **inhabitable**, livable, fit for human habitation, comfortable, fit to live in *Opposite*: uninhabitable

habitat *n* **home**, locale, environment, surroundings, territory

habitation *n* **1 occupancy**, occupation, tenancy, residence **2 house**, home, lodging, residence, place **3 building**, structure, housing, construction, architecture

habitual *adj* **1 regular**, usual, routine, customary, normal *Opposite*: unusual **2 persistent**, frequent, chronic, long-term, ongoing *Opposite*: occasional **3 characteristic**, usual, customary, typical, expected *Opposite*: uncharacteristic. *See* COMPARE AND CONTRAST *at* **usual.**

habituate *v* **familiarize**, adjust, accustom, inure, acclimatize *Opposite*: disorient

habituation *(fml) n* **familiarization**, adjustment, acclimatization, orientation, adaptation *Opposite*: disorientation

hack *v* **1 cut**, chop, slash, lacerate, scythe *Opposite*: splice **2** *(infml)* **cope**, manage, handle, deal with, succeed ■ *n* *(infml)* **1 drudge**, slave, factotum, flunky *(infml)*, menial *(fml) Opposite*: specialist **2 journalist**, reporter, scribbler, writer, stringer

hackneyed *adj* **trite**, clichéd, tired, stale, everyday *Opposite*: original

haggard *adj* **worn**, fatigued, tired, faded, exhausted *Opposite*: fresh

haggle *v* **bargain**, barter, quibble, negotiate, wrangle

hail *n* **storm**, volley, burst, flood, barrage ■ *v* **1 greet**, welcome, address, speak to, call to *Opposite*: ignore **2 acclaim**, acknowledge, salute, uphold, confirm *Opposite*: reject **3 summon**, call, call over, flag down, wave *Opposite*: dismiss

hair n 1 **tresses**, curls, mop, shock, mane (*literary or infml*) 2 **coat**, fur, wool, pelt, fleece

haircut n 1 **trim**, cut, clip, restyle 2 **hairstyle**, style, hairdo (*infml*), coiffure (*fml*)

hairdo (*infml*) n **haircut**, hairstyle, style, do (*slang*), coiffure (*fml*)

hairdresser n **stylist**, barber, hair stylist, cutter, coiffeur (*fml*)

hairdressing n **hair gel**, styling gel, mousse, hair cream, styling spray

hairiness n **furriness**, shagginess, fuzziness, hirsuteness, fluffiness *Opposite*: baldness

hairless adj **bald**, receding, thin on top, bald as a coot, shaved *Opposite*: hairy

hair-raising adj **terrifying**, horrifying, extraordinary, spine-tingling, frightening *Opposite*: calming

hairsplitting n **quibbling**, nitpicking, cavilling, pettifoggery, equivocation

hairstyle n **haircut**, style, cut, hairdo (*infml*), coiffure (*fml*)

WORD BANK
❏ **types of hairstyles** Afro, bangs, beehive, big hair (*infml*), bob, bouffant, braids, bun, buzz cut, chignon, cornrow, cowlick, crew cut, crop, dreadlocks, flat top, French twist, mohawk, mullet, pageboy, pigtail, plait, pompadour, ponytail, ringlet, topknot

hairy adj 1 **hirsute**, bearded, bushy, furry, shaggy *Opposite*: hairless 2 (*infml*) **dangerous**, hazardous, treacherous, risky, perilous *Opposite*: safe

halcyon (*literary*) adj **untroubled**, calm, peaceful, still, tranquil *Opposite*: turbulent

hale adj **healthy**, well, fit, robust, in good shape *Opposite*: unhealthy

half-baked (*infml*) adj 1 **unplanned**, ill-considered, impulsive, ill-conceived *Opposite*: considered 2 **impractical**, silly, unrealistic, idealistic, starry-eyed *Opposite*: sensible

half-hearted adj **unenthusiastic**, perfunctory, lukewarm, indifferent, lackadaisical *Opposite*: wholehearted

half-light n **twilight**, semi-darkness, dusk, gloom, gloominess

halfway adv 1 **midway**, centrally, in the middle, between, in-between 2 **almost**, nearly, mostly, partially, partly *Opposite*: completely ■ adj **middle**, central, intermediate, mid, midway

hall n 1 **corridor**, passageway, hallway, foyer, entrance 2 **gallery**, great hall, room, public room, ballroom 3 **mansion**, dormitory, manor, tower, castle

hallmark n 1 **seal**, stamp, trademark, symbol, logo 2 **characteristic**, feature, trait, property, quality

hallow v **consecrate**, sanctify, bless, deify, revere *Opposite*: desecrate

hallowed adj **sacred**, holy, sanctified, blessed, consecrated *Opposite*: profane (*fml*)

hallucinate v **see things**, have delusions, have visions, fantasize, be delirious

hallucination n **vision**, illusion, figment of the imagination, phantasm, mirage

hallway n **corridor**, passageway, hall, foyer, entrance

halo n **corona**, aureole, nimbus, aura, radiance

halt n **standstill**, stop, close, break, pause *Opposite*: start ■ v **stop**, pause, cease, freeze, come to an end *Opposite*: begin

halter n **bridle**, rein, strap, lead, noose

halting adj **hesitant**, uncertain, tentative, stumbling, faltering *Opposite*: firm

halve v 1 **bisect**, divide, cut in two, cut in half *Opposite*: double 2 **split**, split fifty-fifty, go halves on, share, share out 3 **decrease**, reduce, cut, slash, cut down *Opposite*: double

ham v **overact**, lay it on thick, overplay, overdo it, mug

ham-fisted (*infml*) see **ham-handed**

ham-fistedness (*infml*) see **ham-handedness**

ham-handed (*infml*) adj **clumsy**, inelegant, inept, blundering, awkward *Opposite*: dexterous

ham-handedness (*infml*) n **clumsiness**, ineptness, awkwardness, heavy-handedness

hamlet n **village**, settlement, homestead, community, colony *Opposite*: city

hammer v 1 **strike**, pound, hit, knock, beat 2 (*infml*) **batter**, beat, assault, attack, brutalize 3 (*infml*) **defeat**, beat, thrash, trounce, walk over (*infml*) 4 (*infml*) **criticize**, disparage, condemn, censure, put down (*infml*) *Opposite*: praise

hammering n 1 **pounding**, buffeting, battering, beating, lashing 2 (*infml*) **defeat**, beating, thrashing, trouncing, hiding (*infml*) *Opposite*: victory

hammer out v 1 **beat**, pound, forge, shape, craft 2 **accomplish**, establish, arrive at, reach, produce

hamper n **basket**, picnic basket, pannier ■ v **hinder**, obstruct, get in the way of, impede, slow down *Opposite*: facilitate. See COMPARE AND CONTRAST *at* hinder.

hamstrung adj **constrained**, restricted, thwarted, confined, cramped *Opposite*: liberated

hand n 1 **pointer**, needle, indicator, arrow, finger 2 **influence**, part, share, role, involvement 3 **clap**, ovation, standing ovation, round of applause, burst of applause *Opposite*: boo 4 **handwriting**, writing, script, scrawl, scribble ■ v **give**, hand over, offer, pass, tender *Opposite*: take

handbag n **bag**, shoulder bag, clutch bag, backpack, purse

handbill n leaflet, flier, pamphlet, advertisement, circular

handbook n manual, instruction manual, guide, guidebook, instruction book

handcuff n manacles, chains, shackles, fetters, irons ■ v chain, manacle, shackle, fasten, tie up Opposite: release

hand down v leave, bequeath, pass down, transmit, will

handful n 1 some, a few, one or two, not many, hardly any Opposite: many 2 (infml) test, trial, problem, nuisance, hard work

handicraft n craft, handcraft, handiwork, skill, art

WORD BANK

❑ **types of handicrafts** appliqué, basketry, crochet, embroidery, knitting, lacemaking, macramé, needlepoint, needlework, quilting, sewing, smocking, stitching, tapestry, tatting, weaving

handily adv 1 conveniently, closely, accessibly, nearby, in easy reach Opposite: inconveniently 2 skillfully, dexterously, cleverly, neatly, ably Opposite: awkwardly

hand in v 1 submit, give, give in, tender, offer Opposite: withhold 2 surrender, return, give up, give back, hand over Opposite: withhold

handiness n 1 convenience, proximity, closeness, accessibility Opposite: inconvenience 2 usefulness, utility, efficacy, helpfulness, practicality Opposite: uselessness 3 skillfulness, skill, dexterity, practicality, cleverness Opposite: awkwardness

handiwork n 1 deed, action, achievement, work, creation 2 handicraft, craft, skill, talent, art

handkerchief n tissue, paper handkerchief, facial tissue, hankie (infml)

handle n grip, holder, handgrip ■ v 1 touch, finger, feel, move, hold 2 control, deal with, run, cope with, conduct 3 manage, operate, conduct, supervise, take charge of 4 trade in, sell, buy, deal in, import

handler n trainer, coach, manager, supervisor

handling n treatment, management, conduct, supervision, control

hand-me-down adj secondhand, castoff, recycled, used, worn Opposite: brand-new

hand out v dispense, distribute, administer, give away, give out Opposite: take in

handout n 1 windfall, bonus, gift, donation, charity 2 document, leaflet, brochure, pamphlet, booklet

hand over v give up, tender, surrender, entrust, relinquish Opposite: withhold

handover n delivery, abdication, assignment, conferral, bestowal

handpicked adj select, elite, exclusive, finest, top-quality Opposite: run-of-the-mill

handrail n banister, rail, railing, guardrail, balustrade

hands down adv easily, decisively, unquestionably, safely, clearly Opposite: questionably

handset n receiver, earpiece, mouthpiece, phone, telephone

hands-off adj detached, remote, distant, non-interventionist, laissez-faire Opposite: hands-on

handsome adj 1 good-looking, fine, attractive, striking, beautiful Opposite: ugly 2 generous, substantial, sizable, attractive, liberal Opposite: ungenerous. See COMPARE AND CONTRAST at good-looking.

handsomely adv generously, substantially, sizably, attractively well

hands-on adj practical, active, applied, proactive, energetic Opposite: hands-off

handspring n somersault, cartwheel, flip, flip-flop, vault

hand-to-hand adj unarmed, close-range, face-to-face, direct, bareknuckle

handwork n handiwork, handicraft, skill, art, craft

handwriting n script, writing, calligraphy, penmanship, scrawl

handy adj 1 convenient, near, nearby, within reach, in easy reach Opposite: inconvenient 2 useful, helpful, practical, usable, well-designed Opposite: useless 3 skillful, dexterous, practical, clever, skilled Opposite: awkward

hang v 1 suspend, dangle, droop, drape, hang down Opposite: take down 2 lynch, suspend by the neck, execute, put to death, swing (infml) 3 droop, flop, drape, sag, trail Opposite: stick up 4 (infml) relax, hang around, hang loose, chill out (infml), hang out (infml)

hang back v hesitate, drag your feet, drag your heels, linger, drop behind Opposite: forge ahead

hangdog adj guilty, dejected, furtive, intimidated, sheepish Opposite: chirpy (infml)

hang down v sag, dangle, droop, swing, hang Opposite: stick up

hanger n coat hanger, hook, peg, support, nail

hanger-on n follower, sycophant, disciple, proselyte, associate

hanging n 1 execution, lynching, killing 2 wall hanging, tapestry, drape, drapery, swag

hang on v 1 grip, grasp, clutch, cling, hold on Opposite: let go 2 persevere, keep it up, stick with it, stick it out, hold on Opposite: give up 3 depend on, hinge on, follow from, turn on, rely on 4 wait, linger, stay, hold on, remain Opposite: leave

hang out v 1 suspend, dangle, drape, swing, hang up Opposite: take down 2 (infml) spend time, loiter, hang around, frequent, haunt **3** (infml) **relax**, hang around, loll around, mess around (infml), chill out (infml) **4** (infml) **associate**, mix, be friendly, hang around, interact

hangout (infml) n **haunt**, den, retreat, meeting place, lair (infml)

hangover n **relic**, leftover, remnant, aftermath, aftereffect

hang together v **make sense**, add up, hold up, tell the complete story, give the full picture Opposite: fall apart

hang up v **1 suspend**, dangle, droop, drape, swing Opposite: take down **2 put the phone down**, disconnect, get off the phone, replace the receiver, end the conversation Opposite: pick up

hang-up (infml) n **anxiety**, worry, complex, inhibition, fixation

hank n **coil**, length, reel, skein, ball

hanker v **yearn**, crave, desire, long, ache

hankering n **yearning**, craving, longing, desire, ache Opposite: dislike

haphazard adj **random**, chaotic, hit-or-miss, slapdash, disorganized Opposite: systematic

hapless adj **unfortunate**, unlucky, luckless, ill-fated, wretched Opposite: fortunate

haplessness n **misfortune**, bad luck, ill fortune, wretchedness, misery Opposite: luck

happen v **occur**, take place, go on, come about, ensue

happening n **occurrence**, event, incident, episode, phenomenon ■ adj (infml) **fashionable**, stylish, in, up-to-the-minute, edgy Opposite: old-fashioned

happenstance n **accident**, coincidence, chance, happenchance, fluke (infml)

happily adv **1 luckily**, fortunately, thankfully, as good luck would have it, opportunely Opposite: sadly **2 gladly**, willingly, cheerfully, freely, voluntarily Opposite: unwillingly **3 cheerfully**, contentedly, joyfully, gleefully, blissfully Opposite: sadly

happiness n **contentment**, pleasure, gladness, cheerfulness, joy Opposite: sadness

happy adj **1 content**, contented, pleased, glad, joyful Opposite: sad **2 lucky**, fortunate, favorable, opportune Opposite: unlucky

happy-go-lucky adj **carefree**, optimistic, easygoing, lighthearted, nonchalant Opposite: anxious

harangue v **berate**, lecture, criticize, rant, address ■ n **tirade**, diatribe, criticism, lecture, rant

harass v **annoy**, pester, bother, pursue, worry Opposite: leave alone

harassed adj **1 stressed**, under pressure, distraught, beleaguered, worried Opposite: relaxed **2 put upon**, pressured, persecuted, singled out, discriminated against

harassment n **pestering**, nuisance, annoyance, irritation, persecution

harbinger n **forerunner**, herald, portent, omen, indication

harbor n **port**, dock, anchorage, waterfront, wharf ■ v **1 believe**, embrace, entertain, hold, cherish **2 protect**, shelter, conceal, hide, give refuge to

hard adj **1 firm**, stiff, rigid, solid, tough Opposite: soft **2 difficult**, strenuous, laborious, tough, arduous Opposite: easy **3 problematical**, tricky, difficult, awkward, thorny Opposite: easy **4 intense**, fast, violent, brutal, fierce Opposite: gentle **5 cruel**, callous, harsh, severe, unkind Opposite: kind ■ adv **intensely**, fast, violently, fiercely, powerfully Opposite: gently

COMPARE AND CONTRAST CORE MEANING: requiring effort or exertion

hard requiring mental or physical effort or exertion to do or achieve; **difficult** requiring considerable planning or effort to accomplish; **strenuous** requiring physical effort, energy, stamina, or strength; **tough** needing a great deal of effort; **arduous** requiring hard work or continuous physical effort; **laborious** requiring unwelcome, often tedious, effort and exertion.

hard-bitten adj **tough**, hardened, cynical, stubborn, uncompromising

hard-boiled (infml) adj **unsentimental**, hardened, tough, cynical, unfeeling Opposite: sentimental

hard-core adj **uncompromising**, committed, dedicated, firm, staunch

harden v **1 solidify**, set, freeze, consolidate, settle Opposite: soften **2 toughen**, strengthen, reinforce, fortify, stabilize Opposite: weaken

hardened adj **hard-bitten**, toughened, tough, cynical, unsentimental

hardheaded adj **1 stubborn**, obstinate, willful, inflexible, obdurate **2 shrewd**, sharp, practical, no-nonsense, tough Opposite: impractical

hardhearted adj **callous**, cold, hard, insensitive, unfeeling Opposite: kind

hardheartedness n **callousness**, coldness, insensitivity, pitilessness, stoniness Opposite: kindness

hardiness n **toughness**, hardihood, stamina, durability, robustness Opposite: frailty

hardline adj **uncompromising**, inflexible, rigid, extreme, radical

hardly adv **barely**, only just, scarcely, by a hair's breadth, by the skin of your teeth

hardness n **rigidity**, stiffness, firmness, inflexibility, solidity Opposite: softness

hardship n **adversity**, privation, lack, poverty, destitution Opposite: comfort

hard up (infml) adj **short of money**, poor, impoverished, in a bad way, impecunious Opposite: well-off

hardware n equipment, apparatus, tackle, gear, kit

hard-wearing adj durable, strong, resilient, indestructible, heavy-duty

hardy adj robust, resilient, enduring, tough, strong Opposite: frail

hark (literary) v listen to, hear, pay attention to, heed

hark back v go back to, revisit, recall, relive, revive

harm n damage, hurt, injury, destruction maltreatment Opposite: help ■ v hurt, damage, spoil, injure, impair Opposite: help

---

COMPARE AND CONTRAST CORE MEANING: weaken or impair something or somebody **harm** cause physical or mental impairment or deterioration; **damage** cause physical deterioration that makes an object less useful, valuable, or able to function, or impair something abstract such as a chance or somebody's reputation; **hurt** cause physical or mental pain or harm to people and animals; **injure** cause physical harm to a person or animal, usually causing at least a temporary loss of function or use, or impair something abstract such as somebody's reputation or pride; **wound** inflict physical harm on somebody, especially as a result of the use of a weapon, a violent incident, or a serious accident, or upset or offend somebody.

---

harmed adj injured, damaged, hurt, wounded, impaired Opposite: untouched

harmful adj damaging, injurious, destructive, detrimental, dangerous Opposite: harmless

harmless adj 1 inoffensive, innocuous, innocent, meaningless, bland 2 safe, risk-free, nontoxic, nonhazardous, sound Opposite: harmful

harmlessness n 1 inoffensiveness, naiveté, innocence, wholesomeness, blandness Opposite: offensiveness 2 innocuousness, safety, mildness, nontoxicity

harmonious adj 1 musical, melodious, tuneful, pleasant-sounding, sweet Opposite: discordant 2 agreeable, congruous, balanced, matching, corresponding Opposite: discordant 3 friendly, cordial, affable, congenial, agreeable Opposite: hostile

harmonize v 1 go with, match, blend, complement, tone 2 bring into line, synchronize, standardize, make uniform, make conform

harmonized adj in line, consistent, coordinated, matched, in step Opposite: uncoordinated

harmonizing adj consistent, toning, matching, agreeing, coordinating Opposite: clashing

harmony n agreement, accord, concord, synchronization, congruence Opposite: discord

harness v 1 tie together, strap up, yoke, bind, attach Opposite: separate 2 control, exploit, employ, channel, utilize

harp on v complain, go on, keep on, whine, grumble

harried adj harassed, put upon, bothered, agitated, stressed Opposite: calm

harrowing adj disturbing, upsetting, traumatic, distressing, frightening Opposite: relaxing

harry v harass, bother, pester, badger, annoy

harsh adj 1 severe, bleak, austere, inhospitable, stark Opposite: mild 2 cruel, unkind, unsympathetic, insensitive, callous Opposite: kind 3 punitive, exacting, strict, stern, severe Opposite: lenient 4 discordant, loud, blaring, raucous, jangly Opposite: pleasant

harshness n 1 severity, austerity, ruggedness, bleakness, starkness Opposite: gentleness 2 callousness, cruelty, ruthlessness, strictness, severity Opposite: gentleness

harvest n crop, yield, produce, return, fruitage Opposite: sowing ■ v reap, gather, collect, bring in, pick Opposite: sow

hash v chop, cut up, grind, shred, mince

hassle (infml) n bother, annoyance, irritation, disturbance, stress ■ v harass, irritate, annoy, bother, get on your nerves Opposite: leave alone

haste n speed, swiftness, rapidity, alacrity, rush Opposite: slowness

hasten v hurry, make haste, rush, speed up, speed

hastiness n impulsiveness, impetuosity, rashness, thoughtlessness, carelessness Opposite: carefulness

hasty adj quick, speedy, hurried, swift, rapid Opposite: slow

hatch v 1 give forth, emerge, produce, break open, come out 2 devise, come up with, originate, formulate, plan 3 shade, mark, crisscross, crosshatch, highlight

hate v detest, loathe, despise, abhor, revile Opposite: love ■ n hatred, abhorrence, detestation, loathing, odium Opposite: love. See COMPARE AND CONTRAST at dislike.

hated adj loathed, detested, despicable, despised, unloved Opposite: loved

hateful adj horrible, detestable, vile, odious, unbearable Opposite: lovable

hatred n hate, abhorrence, detestation, loathing, odium Opposite: love. See COMPARE AND CONTRAST at dislike.

haughtiness n arrogance, conceit, pride, self-importance, overconfidence Opposite: modesty

haughty adj supercilious, proud, self-important, superior, high and mighty Opposite: humble

haul v drag, pull, tow, lug, tug Opposite: shove. See COMPARE AND CONTRAST at pull.

haul over the coals v rebuke, scold, reprimand, take to task, tell off *(infml)*

haunch n 1 upper leg, hip, buttock, thigh, loin 2 side, flank, hindquarter, thigh, rump

haunt v 1 trouble, disturb, worry, bother, preoccupy *Opposite*: soothe 2 walk, roam, frequent, prowl, inhabit *Opposite*: leave ■ n meeting place, stomping ground, rendezvous, stamping ground *(infml)*, hangout *(infml)*

haunted adj 1 eerie, ghostly, weird, sinister, spooky *(infml)* 2 troubled, preoccupied, worried, disturbed, anxious *Opposite*: relaxed

haunting adj lingering, melancholy, poignant, evocative, moving *Opposite*: forgettable

hauteur n haughtiness, arrogance, superiority, loftiness, snobbishness *Opposite*: humility

haut monde n elite, crème de la crème, high society, rich and famous, aristocracy *Opposite*: masses

have v 1 possess, own, boast, exhibit, enjoy *Opposite*: lack 2 must, need, ought to, should, require 3 receive, obtain, grasp, get, gain *Opposite*: lose 4 consume, take, partake, eat, drink *Opposite*: abstain 5 think of, come up with, devise, develop, entertain 6 experience, undergo, partake, engage in, take part in 7 be affected by, suffer from, suffer with, be afflicted with, be sick with 8 organize, carry out, arrange, hold, give 9 tolerate, put up with, allow, permit, endure 10 produce, bear, give birth to, bring forth

have a hand in v partake in, play a part in, play a role in, participate, be part of

have a horror of v fear, dread, be frightened of, be afraid of, be scared of

have in mind v propose, suggest, be thinking of, come up with, intend

have it in for v persecute, harass, bully, victimize, target *Opposite*: favor

haven n 1 refuge, safe place, place of safety, sanctuary, shelter 2 *(literary)* harbor, port, anchorage, dock, port of call

have-nots n disadvantaged, poor, deprived, underprivileged, underclass *Opposite*: privileged

have on v wear, be dressed in, be clothed in, show off, flaunt

haversack n rucksack, backpack, pack, knapsack, shoulder bag

have second thoughts v change your mind, go back on, reconsider, think better of, get cold feet

have to do with v relate to, concern, involve, be regarding, be in connection with

have your eye on v want, desire, aim for, be after, hanker

havoc n chaos, destruction, disorder, turmoil, disaster *Opposite*: order

hawk v sell, peddle, vend, deal, market *Opposite*: buy

hawker n dealer, vendor, seller, marketer, salesperson *Opposite*: client

hawk-eyed adj eagle-eyed, sharp-eyed, sharp-sighted, observant, perceptive *Opposite*: unobservant

hawkish adj aggressive, belligerent, warmongering, warlike, militant *Opposite*: peaceable

hawser n cable, rope, chain, towline, tow

hay n straw, feed, fodder, dry feed, winter feed

hayrack n rack, trough, manger, feeder

haywire *(infml)* adj wild, out of order, erratic, nonfunctional, confused *Opposite*: functional

hazard n danger, threat, risk, peril, menace *Opposite*: safeguard ■ v 1 suggest, proffer, put forward, propose 2 risk, take a chance, chance, gamble, venture *Opposite*: protect

hazardous adj dangerous, unsafe, harmful, risky, lethal *Opposite*: safe

haze n mist, fog, miasma, cloud, vapor ■ v become cloudy, mist over, cloud over, darken *Opposite*: clear

haziness n 1 mistiness, fogginess, cloudiness, obscurity, smokiness *Opposite*: clarity 2 confusion, muddle, uncertainty, indistinctness, vagueness *Opposite*: clarity

hazy adj 1 misty, foggy, cloudy, obscure, blurred *Opposite*: clear 2 unclear, indistinct, muddled, confused, obscure *Opposite*: distinct

head n 1 skull, cranium, dome, crown, nut *(infml)* 2 mind, intelligence, intellect, sense, brain 3 boss, leader, chief, president, controller 4 top, peak, crown, promontory, apex *Opposite*: base 5 introduction, beginning, start, opening, heading *Opposite*: end ■ v 1 come first, lead, be first, precede, be foremost *Opposite*: follow 2 control, rule, regulate, have control over, lead 3 go, move, journey, advance, proceed

headache *(infml)* n annoyance, pain, bother, bore, nuisance *Opposite*: relief

headband n hairband, sweatband, bandeau, circlet, headdress

header n 1 shot, pass, goal 2 heading, title, caption, slogan, legend *Opposite*: footer

headfirst adv headlong, head over heels, diving, pitching, plunging

headily adv 1 exhilaratingly, thrillingly, invigoratingly, excitingly, stimulatingly *Opposite*: dully 2 pungently, aromatically, strongly, richly, spicily *Opposite*: mildly 3 impetuously, impulsively, recklessly, rashly, hastily *Opposite*: cautiously

heading n 1 title, caption, headline, banner, header 2 direction, bearing, course, route, trajectory

headland n promontory, cape, peninsula, point, bluff

headline n caption, banner, title, heading, header ▪ v 1 feature, present, top, introduce, advertise 2 **top the bill**, feature, star, head, top

headlong adv 1 headfirst, head over heels, diving, pitching, plunging 2 impetuously, rashly, recklessly, hastily, hurriedly Opposite: carefully ▪ adj impetuous, rash, reckless, hasty, hurried Opposite: considered

head off v 1 divert, reroute, redirect, turn back, intercept 2 **forestall**, block, prevent, stop, avert Opposite: encourage 3 leave, go away, depart, take off, commence Opposite: remain

head office see **headquarters**

head of state n premier, president, leader, ruler, sovereign

head-on adv 1 straight on, straight ahead, frontally, directly, full steam ahead 2 **unflinchingly**, uncompromisingly, with guns blazing, confrontationally, bluntly Opposite: indirectly ▪ adj face-to-face, frontal, uncompromising, direct, confrontational Opposite: indirect

headpiece n header, heading, design, ornament, decoration

headquarters n HQ, control center, nerve center, head office, command center

headset n headphones, receiver, earpiece, earphones

headship n leadership, direction, management, control, regime

head start n advantage, edge, lead, helping hand, help Opposite: disadvantage

headstone n tombstone, gravestore, stone, slab, memorial

headstrong adj obstinate, willful, stubborn, inflexible, mulish Opposite: docile

head-to-head adv adjacent, next to, end-to-end, in line, together ▪ adj **one-on-one**, face-to-face, direct, intimate, personal ▪ n encounter, meeting, discussion, dialogue, confrontation

headway n progress, movement, advance, progression, improvement

headwind n breeze, wind, gale, gust

heady adj 1 exhilarating, thrilling, invigorating, exciting, stimulating Opposite: dull 2 **pungent**, aromatic, strong, rich, spicy Opposite: mild 3 **impetuous**, imprudent, impulsive, reckless, rash Opposite: cautious

heal v 1 cure, restore to health, make well, nurse, mend Opposite: worsen 2 **make good**, settle, patch up, reconcile, set right Opposite: damage

healer n doctor, faith healer, naturopath, homeopath, therapist

healing n recovery, restoration, recuperation, therapy, treatment ▪ adj curative, remedial, therapeutic, medicinal, restorative

health n fitness, condition, healthiness, well-being, strength

healthful adj healthy, good for your health, good for you, beneficial, wholesome Opposite: unhealthy

healthiness n health, good condition, robustness, well-being, fitness

healthy adj 1 fit, well, strong, vigorous, in good physical shape Opposite: sick 2 **healthful**, good for your health, good for you, beneficial, nourishing Opposite: unhealthy

heap n mound, pile, stack, mountain, bundle ▪ v pile up, pile, layer, mound, mass

heaps (infml) n lots, loads (infml), tons (infml), piles (infml), stacks (infml)

heap up v 1 pile up, pile, mound, mass, stack 2 **collect**, amass, gather, accumulate, stockpile

hear v 1 make out, catch, get, overhear, pick up 2 **gather**, learn, find out, understand, pick up 3 **understand**, pay attention to, attend to, heed, take notice of Opposite: miss 4 **listen to**, catch, get, pick up, receive 5 **sit in judgment**, try, judge, preside over, examine

hear from v have news of, have contact with, be in touch with, be contacted by, have a call from

hearing n 1 earshot, range, hearing distance, reach 2 **trial**, inquiry, investigation, examination, consideration

hear of v consider, conceive, tolerate, permit, admit

hearsay n rumor, gossip, tittle-tattle, idle talk, word of mouth Opposite: fact

heart n 1 core, heart of hearts, mind, sentiment, soul 2 **compassion**, sympathy, empathy, feeling, sensitivity Opposite: cruelty 3 **spirit**, courage, bravery, fortitude, pluck

heartache n sorrow, sadness, distress, anguish, despair Opposite: joy

heart attack n 1 cardiac arrest, coronary, seizure 2 (infml) shock, fright, scare, turn

heartbreak n grief, despair, anguish, sorrow, pain Opposite: joy

heartbreaking adj tragic, distressing, upsetting, sad, heartrending Opposite: uplifting

heartbroken adj inconsolable, forlorn, despairing, dejected, disconsolate Opposite: thrilled

heartburn n stomach pain, acid stomach, indigestion, colic, dyspepsia

hearten v encourage, inspire, raise your spirits, uplift, buoy Opposite: dishearten

heartening adj encouraging, promising, cheering, optimistic, reassuring Opposite: disheartening

heartfelt adj sincere, genuine, earnest, warm, cordial Opposite: superficial

hearth n 1 fireside, fireplace, inglenook,

grate **2 family life**, home sweet home, home, household

heartiness *n* vigor, enthusiasm, gusto, energy, fervor

heartland *n* **core**, hub, nucleus, focus, center *Opposite*: hinterland

heartless *adj* **callous**, cruel, unfeeling, cold-blooded, merciless *Opposite*: caring

heartlessness *n* **cruelty**, callousness, cold-bloodedness, mercilessness, unkindness *Opposite*: kindness

heartrending *adj* **heartbreaking**, tragic, distressing, pitiful, pathetic *Opposite*: uplifting. *See* COMPARE AND CONTRAST at **moving**.

heart-searching *n* **soul-searching**, self-examination, self-analysis, introspection, deep thought

heart-to-heart *adj* **frank**, honest, open, candid, forthright ■ *n* **talk**, tête-à-tête, one-on-one, chat, discussion

heartwarming *adj* **cheering**, positive, encouraging, heartening, pleasing *Opposite*: depressing

hearty *adj* **1 enthusiastic**, sincere, whole-hearted, emphatic, vigorous *Opposite*: half-hearted **2 jovial**, cheerful, warm, genial, welcoming **3 substantial**, nourishing, filling, plentiful, abundant *Opposite*: meager **4 strong**, sincere, abiding, deep, profound

heat *n* **1 warmth**, high temperature, temperature, hotness, warmness *Opposite*: coldness **2 passion**, emotion, fervor, intensity, ardor *Opposite*: indifference ■ *v* **warm**, heat up, warm up, reheat, roast *Opposite*: cool

heated *adj* **animated**, frenzied, impassioned, fiery, intense *Opposite*: calm

heater *n* **fire**, stove, radiator, electric fire, electric heater *Opposite*: air conditioner

heating *n* **1 central heating**, heating system, solar heating, space heating *Opposite*: air conditioning **2 warming**, warming up, heating up, reheating, microwaving

WORD BANK
❏ **types of heating appliances** boiler, electric fire, furnace, heater, heat pump, immersion heater, oil burner, quartz heater, radiator, space heater, storage heater

heat wave *n* **hot spell**, Indian summer, drought, scorcher *(infml)*, sizzler *(infml)*

heave *v* **1 haul**, drag, pull, yank, lug *Opposite*: push **2** *(infml)* **throw**, toss, pitch, fling, chuck *(infml)* **3 rise and fall**, throb, palpitate, swell, surge. *See* COMPARE AND CONTRAST at **throw**.

heaven *n* **1 bliss**, paradise, ecstasy, rapture, cloud nine *Opposite*: hell **2 air**, sky, cosmos, ether *(literary)*, firmament *(literary)*

heavenly *adj* **1 wonderful**, blissful, delightful, lovely, fantastic *Opposite*: dreadful **2 divine**, holy, angelic, cherubic, saintly

heavenward *adv* **upward**, skyward, up, into the air, into the sky *Opposite*: earthward

heaviness *n* **weight**, bulk, mass, substance, solidity *Opposite*: lightness

heavy *adj* **1 weighty**, hefty, substantial, heavyweight *Opposite*: light **2 thick**, dense, full, viscous, compact *Opposite*: thin **3 demanding**, onerous, burdensome, tiring, tedious *Opposite*: easy **4 busy**, packed, tight, hectic, frenetic *Opposite*: light **5 powerful**, forceful, violent, hard, jarring *Opposite*: weak

heavy-duty *adj* **forceful**, tough, durable, long-lasting, strong *Opposite*: lightweight

heavy-handed *adj* **1 clumsy**, rough, careless, awkward, uncoordinated *Opposite*: dexterous **2 oppressive**, harsh, forceful, hard, severe

heavy-handedness *n* **1 clumsiness**, roughness, carelessness, awkwardness, gaucheness **2 oppressiveness**, harshness, forcefulness, severity, brutality

heavy-hearted *(literary) adj* **unhappy**, sad, miserable, downcast, dispirited *Opposite*: cheerful

heavy-laden *(literary) adj* **burdened**, encumbered, weighed down, troubled, distraught *Opposite*: carefree

heavyset *adj* **stocky**, well-built, sturdy, solid, thickset *Opposite*: slight

heavyweight *n* **1** *(infml)* **leader**, big name, leading light, key player, colossus **2 muscleman**, bodyguard, bouncer, heavy *(slang)*

heckle *v* **jeer**, interrupt, butt in, boo, shout down *Opposite*: cheer

heckler *n* **critic**, jeerer, interrupter, protester, troublemaker *Opposite*: supporter

heckling *n* **criticism**, jeering, interruption, protest, repartee

hectic *adj* **frantic**, frenzied, excited, confused, chaotic *Opposite*: calm

hector *v* **bully**, intimidate, harass, badger, hassle *(infml)*

hedge *n* **hedgerow**, privet, border, verge, windbreak ■ *v* **1 ring**, fence, protect, encircle, surround **2 evade**, prevaricate, stall, beat around the bush, fudge *(infml)*

hedgerow *n* **hedge**, border, verge, windbreak, shrubbery

hedonism *n* **pleasure-seeking**, high-living, intemperance, self-indulgence, profligacy *Opposite*: asceticism

hedonist *n* **pleasure-seeker**, rake, degenerate, sybarite, epicure *Opposite*: ascetic

hedonistic *adj* **self-indulgent**, pleasure-seeking, profligate, debauched, sybaritic *Opposite*: ascetic

heed *v* **pay attention to**, listen to, take note of, observe, notice *Opposite*: ignore ■ *n* **attention**, notice, note, regard, mindfulness *Opposite*: disregard

heedful *adj* **mindful**, vigilant, watchful, thoughtful, careful *Opposite*: heedless

heedless *adj* **neglectful**, oblivious, without regard, rash, reckless *Opposite*: careful

heedlessness *n* **thoughtlessness**, recklessness, carelessness, neglectfulness, rashness *Opposite*: carefulness

heel *v* **repair**, resole, mend, fix, reinforce

heel in *v* **dig in**, put in, bury, cover

heft *v* **lift**, hoist, heave, raise, raise up ■ *n* **weight**, bulk, size, mass, immensity *Opposite*: lightness

heftiness *n* **robustness**, burliness, stoutness, heaviness, stockiness

hefty *adj* **1 bulky**, large, robust, sturdy, stocky *Opposite*: slight **2 heavy**, weighty, substantial, cumbersome, awkward

hegemony *n* **domination**, control, supremacy, dominion, power

height *n* **1 tallness**, stature, altitude, loftiness, elevation *Opposite*: depth **2 pinnacle**, summit, peak, top, apex *Opposite*: nadir

heighten *v* **intensify**, amplify, increase, enhance, add to

heinous *adj* **monstrous**, atrocious, odious, dreadful, shocking

heir *n* **successor**, inheritor, beneficiary, legatee, recipient

heirloom *n* **family treasure** inheritance, valuable, gift, bequest

helideck *see* helipad

helipad *n* **landing pad**, landing strip, helideck, heliport, helistop

heliport, helistop *see* helipad

helix *n* **spiral**, coil, corkscrew, spring, ringlet

hell *n* **1 Hades**, underworld, perdition, inferno, abyss *Opposite*: heaven **2 torture**, misery, torment, agony, anguish

help *v* **1 aid**, assist, help out, lend a hand, be of assistance *Opposite*: hinder **2 relieve**, improve, ease, alleviate, amend *Opposite*: worsen **3 avoid**, evade, dodge, stop, refrain from ■ *n* **assistance**, aid, benefit, support, service *Opposite*: hindrance

helper *n* **assistant**, aid, aide, collaborator, coworker. *See* COMPARE AND CONTRAST *at* assistant.

helpful *adj* **1 useful**, beneficial, advantageous, of use, effective *Opposite*: useless **2 obliging**, accommodating, supportive, caring, cooperative *Opposite*: unhelpful

helpfulness *n* **1 usefulness**, effectiveness, utility, benefit, advantageousness *Opposite*: uselessness **2 kindness** neighborliness, goodwill, concern, care *Opposite*: unhelpfulness

helping *n* **serving**, plateful, portion, ration, selection

helping hand *n* **help**, assistance, support, aid, boost

helpless *adj* **powerless**, weak, feeble, dependent, vulnerable *Opposite*: self-reliant

helplessness *n* **powerlessness**, weakness, feebleness, vulnerability, dependence *Opposite*: confidence

helpmate *n* **assistant**, associate, spouse, teammate, partner

help out *v* **help**, lend a hand, abet, aid, assist

help yourself *v* **use**, make use of, appropriate, take, have

helter-skelter *adv* **hurriedly**, in confusion, carelessly, haphazardly, pell-mell *Opposite*: calmly ■ *adj* **chaotic**, disorganized, confused, haphazard *Opposite*: ordered

hem *v* **edge**, turn up, shorten, lengthen, sew up *Opposite*: let down

hem in *v* **enclose**, close in, encircle, confine, restrict *Opposite*: release

hemorrhage *n* **loss**, outflow, outpouring, seeping away, depletion ■ *v* **lose**, flow away, seep away, pour out, drain away

hence *(fml)* *adv* **1 therefore**, for this reason, consequently, that's why, and so **2 from now on**, from this time, henceforth, later, in future

henceforth *adv* **from now on**, from this time, in future, hereafter *(fml)*, henceforward *(fml)*

henhouse *n* **coop**, pen, barn, shelter, shed

herald *n* **1 messenger**, crier, announcer, proclaimer, courier **2** *(literary)* **sign**, harbinger, indication, omen, portent ■ *v* **1 signal**, prefigure, foreshadow, presage, indicate **2 proclaim**, announce, give out, publish, tout

herculean *adj* **superhuman**, colossal, enormous, phenomenal, extraordinary *Opposite*: small

herd *n* **1 people**, masses, mob, crowd, sheep **2 group**, set, cluster ■ *v* **1 round up**, steer, gather together, collect, drove **2 shepherd**, usher, direct, guide, funnel

---

WORD BANK

❏ **types of herds** bale (of turtles), band (of gorillas), bevy (of roe deer), colony (of ants/sea lions), drove (of sheep), flock (of sheep), gam (of whales), gang (of elk), kennel (of dogs), leash (of foxes), litter (of cubs/kittens), mob (of kangaroos), pack (of wolves), pod (of porpoises/seals/walrus/whales), pride (of lions), rookery (of seals), school (of porpoises/whales), skulk (of foxes), troop (of kangaroos/monkeys)

---

here *adv* **at this time**, at this point, now, at this juncture

hereabout *adj* **nearby**, near, around here, close

hereafter *(fml)* *adv* **after this**, in future, henceforth, from now on, from this time

hereditary *adj* **1 genetic**, transmissible, inborn, inbred, innate **2 inherited**, heritable, traditional, family

heresy *n* **dissent**, deviation, unorthodoxy, sacrilege, profanation *(fml)*

heretical *adj* **unorthodox**, sacrilegious, dissenting, unconventional, deviating

herewith adv **with this**, together with this, enclosed, with, attached

heritable adj **inheritable**, transferable, transmissible, hereditary

heritage n **inheritance**, legacy, tradition, birthright, custom

hermaphrodite adj **androgynous**, epicene, intersexual

hermetic adj **airtight**, enclosed, closed

hermit n **recluse**, loner, solitary

hero n **1 superman**, champion, conqueror, idol Opposite: loser **2 male lead**, leading actor, leading man, star, protagonist

heroic adj **daring**, stout, valiant, brave, epic

heroics n **recklessness**, rashness, irresponsibility, going over the top, overdoing it Opposite: timidity

heroine n **1 superwoman**, champion, conqueror, idol **2 female lead**, leading actress, leading lady, star, protagonist

heroism n **valor**, bravery, courage, fearlessness, boldness

hero worship n **adulation**, idolization, idealization, admiration, glorification

hesitancy n **indecision**, caution, uncertainty, tentativeness, timidity Opposite: decisiveness

hesitant adj **cautious**, tentative, timid, shy, undecided Opposite: decisive. See COMPARE AND CONTRAST at **unwilling**.

hesitate v **1 be uncertain**, be indecisive, vacillate, waver, falter **2 be unwilling**, think twice, scruple, have qualms, be reluctant

---

COMPARE AND CONTRAST CORE MEANING: show uncertainty or indecision

hesitate be slow in doing something, or take a short break in an activity, as a result of uncertainty or reluctance; **pause** stop doing something briefly before continuing, or wait intentionally for a short period before doing something; **falter** show a loss of confidence when speaking, for example, because of nervousness, fear, awkwardness, or incompetence; **stumble** speak or act hesitatingly, confusedly, or incompetently; **waver** become unsure or begin to change from a previous opinion; **vacillate** be indecisive or irresolute, changing between one opinion and another.

---

hesitation n **1 uncertainty**, indecision, vacillation, wavering, faltering Opposite: decisiveness **2 unwillingness**, qualms, reluctance, disinclination, hesitancy Opposite: willingness

heterogeneous adj **varied**, mixed, assorted, diverse, various Opposite: homogeneous

het up adj **on edge**, agitated, jittery, jumpy, excited

heuristic adj **experiential**, empirical, experimental, investigative, exploratory

hew v **1 cut**, chop, fell, cleave, ax **2 carve**, fashion, sculpt, shape, model

hex n **curse**, spell, jinx, voodoo

heyday n **prime**, zenith, glory days, peak, halcyon days (literary)

hiatus n **pause**, break, interruption, space, lull

hibernate v **lie dormant**, take cover, overwinter, hide, hide away

hiccup (infml) n **hitch**, glitch, interruption, delay, setback

hidden adj **1 concealed**, out of sight, unseen, secreted, veiled **2 unknown**, secret, mysterious, clandestine, covert

hidden agenda n **ulterior motive**, secret plan, motivation, driving force, impetus

hide v **1 conceal**, put out of sight, hide from view, secrete, veil Opposite: flaunt **2 go underground**, take cover, disappear, keep cover, hole up (slang) **3 keep secret**, withhold, hold back, keep back, suppress Opposite: disclose

hideaway n **hiding place**, refuge, sanctuary, asylum, retreat

hidebound adj **narrow-minded**, prejudiced, conservative, conventional, parochial Opposite: broad-minded

hideous adj **1 ugly**, unattractive, grotesque, repellent, unsightly Opposite: attractive **2 revolting**, repugnant, repulsive, gruesome, shocking Opposite: pleasant. See COMPARE AND CONTRAST at **unattractive**.

hideousness n **ugliness**, repulsiveness, unsightliness, gruesomeness, dreadfulness

hideout n **safe house**, refuge, sanctuary, retreat, den

hidey-hole (infml) n **hiding place**, hideaway, safe house, safe place, shelter

hiding (infml) n **beating**, whacking, thumping, smacking, spanking

hiding place n **hideaway**, hole, place of escape, den, safe house

hierarchical adj **ranked**, graded, tiered, ordered, classified

hierarchy n **chain of command**, ladder, pecking order, grading, order

hieroglyph n **symbol**, pictograph, picture, ideogram, cipher

hifalutin (infml) see **highfalutin**

hi-fi (dated) n **sound system**, stereo system, stereo, CD player, cassette recorder

higgledy-piggledy adj **untidy**, topsy-turvy, in a mess, jumbled, confused Opposite: ordered

high adj **1 tall**, lofty, elevated, towering, soaring Opposite: low **2 in height**, from top to bottom, from head to foot, from top to toe, tall **3 above average**, great, extraordinary, elevated, extreme Opposite: normal **4 high-pitched**, shrill, piercing, penetrating, sharp Opposite: low-pitched

5 important, eminent, prominent, high-ranking, superior *Opposite*: low ■ *n* **1 high point**, peak, climax, summit *Opposite*: low point **2** (*infml*) **thrill**, boost, lift, excitement, pleasure

high achiever *n* **high flier**, success, star, winner, success story

high and dry *adj* **helpless**, in the lurch, washed up, stranded, abandoned

high and low *adv* **everywhere**, all over, here, there, and everywhere, in every nook and cranny, all over the place (*infml*)

high and mighty *adj* **arrogant**, disdainful, overbearing, conceited, proud

highbrow *adj* **intellectual**, cultured, academic, scholarly, exclusive *Opposite*: lowbrow ■ *n* **intellectual**, academic, scholar, philosopher, sage (*literary*)

high-class *adj* **high-quality**, fancy, formal, elegant, superior *Opposite*: cheap

high court *n* **court**, supreme court, principal court

highest *adj* **top**, topmost, utmost, ultimate, premier

highfalutin (*infml*) *adj* **pretentious**, pompous, affected, grandiose, snobbish *Opposite*: down-to-earth

high-flier *n* **high achiever**, success, winner, success story, star *Opposite*: plodder

high-flown *adj* **affected**, pretentious, grandiose, high-sounding, grandiloquent *Opposite*: down-to-earth

high-flyer *see* **high-flier**

high-grade *adj* **high-quality**, quality, finest, superior, prime *Opposite*: low-grade

high ground *n* **1 upland**, highland, plateau, hillside, hilltop *Opposite*: lowland **2 refuge**, shelter, cover, protection, sanctuary **3 principled stance**, moral stand, high road

high-handed *adj* **bossy**, autocratic, dominant, undemocratic, domineering

high-handedness *n* **bossiness**, arrogance, imperiousness, inconsiderateness, overbearingness

high jinks (*infml*) *n* **mischief**, mischievousness, trouble, no good, nonsense

highland *n* **upland**, plateau, high ground, hilltop *Opposite*: lowland

high-level *adj* **sophisticated**, elevated, advanced, complex, top *Opposite*: unsophisticated

high life *n* **good life**, life of Riley, life of ease, lap of luxury, easy street

highlight *n* **high point**, climax, best part, icing on the cake, acme ■ *v* **emphasize**, draw attention to, underline, stress, focus on *Opposite*: downplay

highly *adv* **1 extremely**, very, exceedingly, very much, greatly *Opposite*: modestly **2 favorably**, approvingly, kindly, warmly, graciously *Opposite*: unfavorably

high-minded *adj* **principled**, worthy, moral, noble, upright *Opposite*: base

high-pitched *adj* **shrill**, high, piercing, penetrating, sharp

high point *n* **best moment**, climax, icing on the cake, acme, highlight *Opposite*: low point

high-powered *adj* **successful**, dynamic, driven, ambitious, energetic

high-pressure *adj* **stressful**, difficult, relentless, pressured, intense *Opposite*: easy

high profile *n* **prominence**, conspicuousness, eminence, celebrity, notoriety *Opposite*: anonymity

high-profile *adj* **prominent**, prestigious, conspicuous, famous, eminent *Opposite*: discreet

high-rise *adj* **multistory**, high, tall, big, lofty *Opposite*: low-rise ■ *n* **skyscraper**, apartment building, apartment house, office tower, office block

high society *n* **upper classes**, elite, polite society, beautiful people, Four Hundred

high-sounding *adj* **imposing**, high-flown, grandiloquent, grandiose, lofty

high-spirited *adj* **lively**, exuberant, merry, cheerful, vivacious *Opposite*: lethargic

high spirits *n* **liveliness**, exuberance, merriness, cheerfulness, vivacity *Opposite*: depression

high-strung *adj* **excitable**, nervous, edgy, tense, jittery *Opposite*: laid-back (*infml*)

high-tech *adj* **advanced**, technological, computerized, digital, modern

hijack *v* **1 take over**, seize, commandeer, capture, skyjack **2** (*infml*) **steal**, appropriate, take over, commandeer, borrow ■ *n* **takeover**, skyjacking, capture, seizure

hijinks (*infml*) *see* **high jinks**

hike *v* **ramble**, trek, walk, climb

hiker *n* **walker**, rambler, backpacker, trekker

hilarious *adj* **funny**, sidesplitting, comic, comical, humorous

hilariousness *n* **humorousness**, uproariousness, comicalness, mirthfulness, funniness

hilarity *n* **amusement**, laughter, merriment, mirth, glee *Opposite*: sadness

hill *n* **1 mountain**, peak, mount, knoll, mound *Opposite*: valley **2 gradient**, slope, incline, rise *Opposite*: drop

hillock *n* **mound**, hump, hill, knoll

hilltop *n* **top**, summit, peak, pinnacle, brow *Opposite*: base

hilly *adj* **mountainous**, undulating, bumpy, alpine, craggy *Opposite*: flat

hind *adj* **back**, rear, rearmost, posterior (*fml*), hindmost (*literary*) *Opposite*: fore (*literary*)

hinder *v* **hold back**, obstruct, impede, block, hamper *Opposite*: facilitate

COMPARE AND CONTRAST CORE MEANING: put difficulties in the way of progress hinder delay or restrict the development or progress of something, either accidentally or by deliberate interference; **block** prevent movement through, into, or out of something, or prevent something from taking place; **hamper** restrict the free movement or action of somebody or something; **hold back** keep something from happening or restrain somebody from doing something; **impede** interfere with the movement, progress, or development of somebody or something; **obstruct** cause a serious delay in action or progress, or cause a major physical blockage in a road or passageway.

hindmost (literary) adj **last**, rear, final, back, rearmost Opposite: foremost

hindquarters n **back**, rear, rear legs, hind legs Opposite: front

hindrance n 1 **obstruction**, impediment, barrier, obstacle, encumbrance 2 **interference**, interruption, limitation, prevention, sabotage Opposite: assistance

hindsight n **reflection**, retrospection, perception, observation, remembrance Opposite: foresight

hinge n **pivot**, axis, fulcrum, joint, crux

hinge on v **depend on**, hang on, turn on, be dependent on, rest on

hint v **suggest**, intimate, insinuate, imply, mention ■ n 1 **suggestion**, clue, intimation, mention, indication 2 **tip**, advice, pointer, suggestion, clue 3 **trace**, tinge, suggestion, dash, taste

hinterland n **vicinity**, environs, surroundings, neighborhood Opposite: heartland

hire v **employ**, appoint, take on, contract, sign up Opposite: fire

hirsute adj **hairy**, bearded, bushy, furry, long-haired Opposite: bald

hiss v 1 **jeer**, boo, hoot, mock, ridicule Opposite: cheer 2 **whisper**, murmur, rustle, whistle, susurrate

historic adj 1 **significant**, momentous, notable, famous, remarkable Opposite: insignificant 2 **past**, old, ancient, antique, historical Opposite: modern

historical adj **past**, old, ancient, antique, historic Opposite: modern

historically adv 1 **in history**, over all, factually, archaeologically 2 **traditionally**, generally, usually, as a rule, in the main

history n 1 **past**, times gone by, times past, olden times, antiquity Opposite: present 2 **account**, record, chronicle, narration, memoir

histrionic adj **theatrical**, dramatic, exaggerated, melodramatic, unrestrained Opposite: restrained

histrionics n **dramatics**, tantrums, hysterics, scene, melodrama

hit v 1 **strike**, punch, thump, slap, beat 2 **crash into**, strike, bang into, bump into, collide with 3 **affect**, afflict, damage, hurt,

disadvantage ■ n 1 **blow**, knock, smack, slap, bump 2 **success**, winner, triumph, sensation, market leader Opposite: flop (infml)

hit back v **retaliate**, get even, strike back, react, even the score

hitch n **snag**, catch, drawback, glitch, delay ■ v 1 **fasten**, hook, harness, join, tether Opposite: undo 2 **hitchhike**, get a ride, be given a ride, put your thumb out, get a lift

hitchhike v **hitch**, get a lift, be given a lift, thumb a lift, put your thumb out

hitherto adv **up till now**, up till then, until now, until then, till now

hit it off (infml) v **get along well**, connect, get along, make friends, take to each other Opposite: clash

hit on v **think of**, chance upon, discover, realize, arrive at

hit-or-miss adj **haphazard**, random, unplanned, unpredictable, careless Opposite: planned

hit out v 1 **strike out**, lash out, lunge, go for, attack 2 **criticize**, attack, assail, condemn, lambaste

hit the hay (infml) v **go to bed**, say goodnight, get to sleep, get some rest, retire

hit the roof v **lose your temper**, be angry, fly into a rage, go berserk, see red (infml) Opposite: calm down

hit the sack (infml) see **hit the hay**

hit upon v **stumble on**, chance upon, discover, realize, arrive at

hive v **store**, put away, save, put aside, hoard Opposite: discard

hive off v **cream off**, skim off, transfer, separate, split off Opposite: merge

hoard v **save**, store, amass, stockpile, accumulate Opposite: throw away ■ n **store**, pile, mass, reserve, supply. See COMPARE AND CONTRAST at **collect**.

hoarder n **collector**, saver, accumulator, miser, squirrel (infml)

hoar frost n **frost**, ice, rime

hoarse adj **croaky**, gruff, gravelly, husky, rough Opposite: smooth

hoarseness n **croakiness**, gruffness, huskiness, roughness, harshness Opposite: smoothness

hoary adj 1 **overused**, old, ancient, age-old, stale Opposite: fresh 2 **white**, snow-white, whitened, snowy, silvery

hoax n **trick**, deception, practical joke, joke, swindle ■ v **deceive**, trick, con, swindle, mislead

hoaxer n **trickster**, practical joker, joker, swindler, deceiver

hobble v **limp**, hop, shuffle, shamble, totter ■ n **limp**, shuffle, stagger, shamble, stumble

hobby n **pastime**, leisure pursuit, diversion, relaxation, sideline Opposite: job

hobbyhorse n **favorite subject**, pet topic, bee

in your bonnet, obsession, idée fixe

hobgoblin *n* goblin, imp, elf, pixie, sprite

hobnob *v* socialize, mix, fraternize, associate, go around *Opposite*: shun

hobo *n* traveler, itinerant, vagrant, tramp, drifter

hodgepodge *n* jumble, medley, mass, assortment, mishmash

hoe *v* turn over, weed, dig, dig out, loosen

hog (*infml*) *v* monopolize, take over, help yourself, take the lion's share of, hang onto

hogwash (*infml*) *n* nonsense, gibberish, humbug, garbage, rubbish

hoi polloi *n* common herd, general public, masses, ordinary people, proletariat *Opposite*: aristocracy

hoist *v* lift, raise, pull, heave, erect ■ *n* winch, crane, elevator, pulley

hoity-toity (*infml*) *adj* haughty, arrogant, snobbish, proud, disdainful *Opposite*: down-to-earth

hokum (*infml*) *n* nonsense, humbug, garbage, claptrap (*infml*), hooey (*infml*)

hold *v* 1 grasp, clutch, grip, clasp, seize *Opposite*: release 2 fix, secure, fasten, bind, attach 3 embrace, hug, cuddle, enfold, squeeze 4 contain, accommodate, stow, carry, take in 5 detain, restrain, confine, shut in, imprison *Opposite*: let go 6 arrange, convene, call, conduct, have 7 possess, have, keep, retain, own 8 believe, think, maintain, presume, consider 9 sustain, maintain, continue, keep up, carry on 10 wait, hold on, hang on, stay on the line *Opposite*: hang up ■ *n* 1 grip, grasp, clasp, clutch, embrace 2 control, power, influence, claim, sway 3 storage space, storeroom, cargo bay, compartment, storage

hold back *v* 1 restrain, inhibit, suppress, repress, hamper *Opposite*: let go 2 keep back, retain, keep, reserve, keep hold of *Opposite*: release. *See* COMPARE AND CONTRAST *at* hinder.

hold close *v* hug, embrace, hold tight, cuddle, enfold *Opposite*: release

hold down (*infml*) *v* keep, retain, maintain, manage, hang onto *Opposite*: lose

holder *n* 1 container, pouch, receptacle, vessel, box 2 owner, possessor, proprietor, controller, bearer

hold forth *v* speak out, harangue, preach, lecture, discourse *Opposite*: bottle up

hold in *v* 1 keep in check, restrain, keep back, hold back, control *Opposite*: release 2 restrain, keep the lid on, control, bridle, suppress *Opposite*: let out

holding *n* 1 land, field, property, farm, croft 2 stock, investment, share, property, interest

hold in high regard *v* revere, respect, venerate, idolize, esteem *Opposite*: despise

hold off *v* 1 refrain, desist, leave off, abstain, avoid *Opposite*: speed up 2 resist, fend off, keep away, keep off, repel *Opposite*: yield

hold on *v* 1 wait, hang on, be patient, wait a minute, hold your horses (*infml*) 2 persist, persevere, keep on, stand your ground, stand firm *Opposite*: give up 3 grasp, grip, keep hold of, hold fast, stick to *Opposite*: let go

hold onto *v* 1 retain, keep, hang onto, save, hoard *Opposite*: give up 2 grasp, clasp, clutch, grip, stick *Opposite*: release

hold out *v* 1 extend, give, present, offer, proffer *Opposite*: withdraw 2 endure, stand your ground, persist, stand firm, withstand *Opposite*: give in

hold out on *v* not tell, keep something from, hide something from, withhold something from *Opposite*: tell

hold over *v* defer, delay, postpone, put off, suspend *Opposite*: bring forward

hold sway *v* have authority, have influence, have power, be in power, be in control

hold the fort *v* look after things, take care of things, take over, take charge, mind things

hold up *v* 1 delay, slow down, slow up, impede, hinder *Opposite*: speed up 2 rob, raid, mug, stick up (*infml*), do (*slang*) 3 survive, bear up, keep up, endure, keep going *Opposite*: give up 4 support, shore up, keep up, prop, sustain *Opposite*: bring down

holdup *n* 1 theft, raid, robbery, assault, mugging 2 delay, hitch, glitch, snag, stoppage

hold with *v* approve of, endorse, support, subscribe to, agree with *Opposite*: disapprove

hold your own *v* 1 bear up, persevere, be stable, be comfortable, persist *Opposite*: succumb 2 match up, stand your ground, stand firm, look after yourself, take care of yourself

hole *n* 1 cavity, hollow, void, chasm, gulf 2 aperture, gap, opening, crack, break 3 burrow, lair, retreat, run, sett 4 flaw, weakness, fault, error, defect *Opposite*: strength 5 (*infml*) hovel, slum, shack, pigpen, dump (*infml*)

hole-in-the-wall (*infml*) *n* restaurant, bar, bistro, café, dive (*infml*)

holey *adj* leaky, porous, perforated, worn, torn

holiday *n* 1 day off, day's leave, personal day 2 leave, time off, break, sabbatical, vacation *Opposite*: work 3 legal holiday, federal holiday, anniversary, feast, saint's day

holier-than-thou (*infml*) *adj* self-righteous, pious, smug, superior, sanctimonious *Opposite*: self-effacing

holiness *n* sanctity, sacredness, piety, godliness, religiousness

holistic *adj* **all-inclusive**, rounded, full, complete, general

holler *(infml)* *v* **shout**, yell, scream, shriek, howl *Opposite*: whisper

hollow *adj* **1 empty**, void, unfilled, vacant, unoccupied *Opposite*: solid **2 concave**, depressed, sunken, indented, cavernous *Opposite*: convex **3 resonating**, echoing, deep, low, dull *Opposite*: high-pitched **4 insincere**, empty, worthless, futile, vain *Opposite*: sincere ■ *n* **1 cavity**, recess, indentation, cup, nook *Opposite*: bulge **2 valley**, crater, dip, depression, basin *Opposite*: hill ■ *v* **excavate**, scoop, dig out, gouge, tunnel *Opposite*: fill. *See* COMPARE AND CONTRAST *at* vain.

hollowness *n* **1 void**, empty space, cavity, emptiness, concavity *Opposite*: solidity **2 insincerity**, emptiness, worthlessness, futility, vainness *Opposite*: sincerity

holy *adj* **1 sacred**, consecrated, hallowed, sanctified, blessed **2 saintly**, righteous, devout, religious, godly *Opposite*: irreligious

homage *n* **deference**, reverence, respect, service, duty *Opposite*: disrespect

home *n* **1 residence**, house, habitat, quarters, address **2 family**, household, family circle, family unit, background **3 birthplace**, place of birth, homeland, home town, native land **4 institution**, residence, residential home, children's home, assisted living ■ *adj* **1 internal**, domestic, inland, interior, local *Opposite*: foreign **2 home-based**, household, homegrown, family, domestic *Opposite*: industrial ■ *adv* **homeward**, back home, in, home sweet home, back at the ranch *(infml)*

homecoming *n* **return**, arrival, repatriation, visit, revisiting *Opposite*: emigration

home in *v* **focus**, zoom in, move in, aim, take aim *Opposite*: draw back

homeland *n* **native country**, mother country, native land, fatherland, motherland

homeless *adj* **on the streets**, living rough, dispossessed, destitute, vagrant *Opposite*: housed

homely *adj* **1 unattractive**, plain, unappealing, ugly, mousy *Opposite*: attractive **2 simple**, plain, ordinary, unpretentious, cozy *Opposite*: fancy. *See* COMPARE AND CONTRAST *at* unattractive.

home rule *n* **self-government**, autonomy, self-rule, independence, separatism

homesick *adj* **nostalgic**, sad, melancholy, pining, unsettled *Opposite*: content

homespun *adj* **plain**, simple, ordinary, unsophisticated, down-to-earth *Opposite*: sophisticated

homestead *n* **farm**, farmstead, ranch, croft, estate

home town *n* **birthplace**, home, home base, back yard, home ground

home truth *n* **fact**, truth, bitter pill, criticism *Opposite*: lie

homework *n* **1 schoolwork**, exercise, lesson, study, assignment **2** *(infml)* **preparation**, reading up, research, groundwork

homicidal *adj* **murderous**, destructive, killer, killing, bloodthirsty *Opposite*: harmless

homicide *n* **killing**, murder, slaughter, manslaughter, assassination

homily *n* **lecture**, sermon, talk, speech, discourse

hominid *n* **primate**, hominoid, anthropoid

hominoid *see* **hominid**

homogeneity *n* **1 sameness**, similarity, equality, consistency, regularity *Opposite*: dissimilarity **2 uniformity**, constancy, consistency, stability, regularity *Opposite*: variability

homogeneous *adj* **1 same**, similar, standardized, consistent, equal *Opposite*: heterogeneous **2 uniform**, consistent, constant, stable, regular *Opposite*: variable

homogeneousness *see* **homogeneity**

homogenize *v* **1 standardize**, normalize, even out, regulate, make the same *Opposite*: distinguish **2 smooth**, emulsify, mix, beat, whip *Opposite*: separate out

hone *v* **1 improve**, refine, enhance, polish, perfect *Opposite*: impair **2 sharpen**, whet, file, grind, polish *Opposite*: blunt

honest *adj* **1 upright**, trustworthy, moral, good, decent *Opposite*: immoral **2 truthful**, authentic, true, sincere, frank *Opposite*: untruthful

honestly *adv* **1 fairly**, justly, in all conscience, decently, reliably *Opposite*: immorally **2 really**, truly, truthfully, candidly, openly *Opposite*: untruthfully

honesty *n* **1 uprightness**, morality, trustworthiness, goodness, scrupulousness *Opposite*: immorality **2 sincerity**, truthfulness, integrity, frankness, candor *Opposite*: dishonesty

honey *(infml)* *n* **darling**, dear, dearest, sweetheart, sugar *(infml)*

honeyed *adj* **1 ingratiating**, sugarcoated, cloying, flattering, fawning *Opposite*: sharp **2 melodious**, soft, dulcet, sweet, pleasing *Opposite*: harsh

honk *v* **beep**, hoot, toot, blare, blast

honor *n* **1 integrity**, decency, righteousness, principle, uprightness *Opposite*: baseness **2 respect**, admiration, esteem, regard, reverence *Opposite*: scorn **3 dignity**, distinction, nobility, pride, decorum **4 reputation**, image, good name, name, renown *Opposite*: disgrace **5 award**, distinction, tribute, credit, accolade *Opposite*: blot **6 privilege**, occasion, opportunity, milestone, high-water mark *Opposite*: disgrace ■ *v* **1 esteem**, respect, admire, revere, reverence *Opposite*: disparage **2 keep**, stick to, carry out, fulfill *Opposite*: break

honorable adj 1 moral, decent, worthy, proper, upright Opposite: immoral 2 respectable, decent, admirable, praiseworthy, worthy Opposite: shameful

honorarium n payment, fee, grant, scholarship, stipend. See COMPARE AND CONTRAST at **wage**.

honorary adj 1 nominal, token, symbolic, titular 2 unpaid, voluntary, unsalaried, amateur, volunteer Opposite: salaried

honored adj privileged, pleased, flattered, grateful, thrilled Opposite: insulted

hoodlum n gangster, criminal, lawbreaker, thug, vandal

hoodwink v trick, deceive, dupe, delude, take in

hooey (infml) n nonsense, humbug, gibberish, garbage, rubbish Opposite: fact

hook n peg, hanger, nail, knob, catch ■ v fasten, attach, secure, join, tie Opposite: unhook

hook and eye n fastener, fastening, clasp, catch, clip

hooked adj bent, curved, bowed, curving, angular Opposite: straight

hook up v 1 connect, link up, plug in, wire up, electrify Opposite: disconnect 2 (infml) get together, take up with, meet up, meet, pair off Opposite: part

hooligan (infml) n criminal, gangster, lawbreaker, thug, hoodlum

hoop n ring, loop, band, circle, round

hoot v 1 toot, beep, honk, blare, blow 2 shout, howl, whoop, roar, cry out

hop v 1 jump, skip, leap, spring n 1 leap, jump, skip, bound, step 2 (infml) flight, journey, trip, stage, leg 3 (dated infml) dance, party, disco, hoedown, barn dance

hope v want, expect, trust, anticipate, wish Opposite: despair ■ n 1 confidence, expectation, optimism, anticipation, faith Opposite: despair 2 likelihood, prospect, possibility, promise, potential Opposite: impossibility 3 desire, aspiration, dream, expectation, plan

hopeful adj 1 confident, expectant, optimistic, positive, encouraged Opposite: pessimistic 2 promising, encouraging, positive, rosy, propitious Opposite: discouraging 3 aspiring, prospective, would-be, potential, budding ■ n aspirant, candidate, applicant, contender, seeker

hopefully adv 1 with any luck, with a bit of luck, all being well 2 confidently, expectantly, optimistically, positively, buoyantly Opposite: despairingly

hopefulness n 1 confidence, hope, optimism, expectation, anticipation Opposite: despair 2 promise, encouragement, positiveness, positivity, rosiness

hopeless adj 1 impossible, desperate, unpromising, fruitless, bleak Opposite: promising 2 despairing, desperate, in despair, despondent, disheartened Opposite: positive 3 useless, bad, pathetic, inept, incompetent Opposite: excellent

hopelessly adv 1 terribly, desperately, badly, completely, totally Opposite: slightly 2 despairingly, in despair, desperately, despondently, downheartedly Opposite: positively

hopelessness n 1 despair, desperation, despondency, bleakness, depression Opposite: hope 2 impossibility, desperateness, fruitlessness, bleakness, futility Opposite: promise 3 uselessness, ineptness, ineptitude, incompetence, inability Opposite: excellence

horde n throng, crowd, mass, gang, group

horizon n skyline, distance, vanishing point, vista, prospect

horizontal adj level, flat, straight, plane Opposite: vertical

horn n 1 siren, hooter, alarm, buzzer, bleeper 2 antler, spine, barb, projection, tusk

horn of plenty n cornucopia, abundance, treasure chest, ready supply, never-ending supply Opposite: famine

horrendous adj 1 dreadful, awful, terrible, dire, unbearable Opposite: wonderful 2 (infml) outrageous, exorbitant, sky-high, shocking, dreadful

horrible adj unpleasant, bad, awful, vile, nasty Opposite: pleasant

horribly adv 1 unpleasantly, dreadfully, badly, terribly, unbearably Opposite: pleasantly 2 extremely, greatly, very, totally, utterly

horrid adj 1 disgusting, awful, dreadful, nasty, vile Opposite: pleasant 2 dreadful, shocking, appalling, horrific, frightful

horridness n 1 nastiness, beastliness, unpleasantness, hatefulness, meanness Opposite: pleasantness 2 disgustingness, loathsomeness, vileness, dreadfulness, unpleasantness Opposite: attractiveness 3 dreadfulness, frightfulness, terribleness, awfulness, horror

horrific adj appalling, dreadful, awful, horrendous, horrifying Opposite: wonderful

horrified adj 1 appalled, shocked, aghast, sickened, disgusted Opposite: delighted 2 dismayed, depressed, shocked, perplexed, disturbed

horrify v 1 appall, disgust, revolt, shock, sicken Opposite: delight 2 dismay, depress, shock, perplex, disturb

horrifying adj 1 horrific, horrible, horrendous, terrible, sickening Opposite: delightful 2 shocking, upsetting, disturbing, perplexing, perturbing

horror n fear, shock, revulsion, dismay, disgust Opposite: delight

horror-stricken see **horror-struck**

horror-struck adj petrified, scared stiff, terrified, horrified, stunned

hors d'oeuvre n **appetizer**, starter, entrée, crudités, first course

horse n **mount**, pony, charger, steed (literary)

WORD BANK
❑ **types of horses** Arabian horse, bronco, broodmare, carthorse, charger, cob, hack, hunter, mustang, pacer, packhorse, pony, racehorse, saddle horse, Shetland pony, shire horse, thoroughbred, trotter, warhorse, workhorse
❑ **parts of a horse** croup, fetlock, flank, foreleg, forelock, hindquarters, hock, hoof, mane, pastern, shank, withers

horse around v **fool around**, play around, clown, act the fool, cavort

horseman n **rider**, jockey, equestrian, huntsman, knight

horseplay n **rough-and-tumble**, boisterousness, play, fun, horsing around

horse sense (infml) n **common sense**, good sense, sense, wit, judgment

horseshoe n **1 lucky charm**, talisman, mascot, amulet, token **2 crescent**, curve, arc, loop, bend

horsewoman n **rider**, jockey, equestrian, huntswoman

horticultural adj **gardening**, garden, agricultural, nursery

horticulture n **gardening**, cultivation, propagation, agriculture, truck farming

hose n **tube**, pipe, line, hosepipe, garden hose ■ v **rinse**, water, spray, sluice, wash

hose down v **wash**, clean, sluice, rinse, hose Opposite: dry

hosepipe n **tube**, pipe, line, hose, garden hose

hospice n **nursing home**, hospital, rest home, sanatorium, clinic

hospitable adj **welcoming**, friendly, warm, open, generous Opposite: unfriendly

hospital n **infirmary**, sanatorium, rest home, hospice, sickbay

hospitality n **welcome**, friendliness, warmth, kindness, generosity Opposite: unfriendliness

host n **1 entertainer**, master of ceremonies, MC, emcee (infml) **2 crowd**, swarm, cloud, congregation, mass ■ v **accommodate**, lay on, hold, present, introduce

hostage n **captive**, prisoner, detainee, victim

hostel n **1 shelter**, refuge, boarding house, single room occupancy, flophouse (infml) **2 inn**, hotel, bed and breakfast, guesthouse, motel

hostess n **entertainer**, MC, emcee (infml)

hostile adj **1 unfriendly**, aggressive, intimidating, antagonistic, unreceptive Opposite: friendly **2 adverse**, harsh, unfavorable, unwelcoming, unpleasant Opposite: pleasant

hostilities n **fighting**, warfare, conflict, battle, aggression

hostility n **aggression**, anger, unfriendliness, resentment, antagonism Opposite: friendliness

hot adj **1 warm**, burning, boiling, searing, fiery Opposite: cold **2 sweltering**, stifling, muggy, sultry, boiling Opposite: chilly **3 spicy**, peppery, piquant, pungent, fiery Opposite: bland **4 passionate**, fierce, angry, emotional, strong Opposite: dispassionate

hot air (infml) n **nonsense**, drivel, lies, bravado, bragging

hot and bothered adj **worried**, anxious, edgy, flustered, in a panic Opposite: composed

hotbed n **breeding ground**, source, focus, hothouse, center

hot-blooded adj **passionate**, volatile, hot-tempered, ardent, fierce Opposite: coldblooded

hotelier n **innkeeper**, landlord, landlady, proprietor, manager

hotfoot adv **immediately**, at once, without delay, instantly, urgently Opposite: slowly

hothead n **firebrand**, tearaway, madcap, loose cannon (slang)

hotheaded adj **impetuous**, volatile, rash, irascible, on a short fuse Opposite: prudent

hothouse n **greenhouse**, orangery, conservatory, winter garden

hotly adv **passionately**, fiercely, ardently, fervently, vehemently Opposite: dispassionately

hotness n **1 heat**, high temperature, temperature, warmness, warmth Opposite: coldness **2 overheating**, sweatiness, stickiness, warmness, warmth **3 spiciness**, heat, fieriness, piquancy, pepperiness Opposite: mildness

hot potato n **difficulty**, controversy, tricky problem, thorny problem, knotty problem

hotshot (infml) n **high-flier**, achiever, star, expert, top gun (infml)

hot-tempered adj **excitable**, fiery, hot-blooded, volatile, quick-tempered Opposite: relaxed

hot water (infml) n **trouble**, bother, difficulty, controversy, conflict

hound n **dog**, wolfhound, deerhound, basset hound, foxhound ■ v **pursue**, chase, harass, pester, persecute

hour n **1 60 minutes**, time, period, o'clock **2 time**, period, era, age, day

house n **1 residence**, home, address, building, crib (slang) **2 household**, family, dynasty, community, line **3 company**, firm, organization, business, establishment ■ v **1 accommodate**, lodge, shelter, give shelter to, take in **2 contain**, keep, store, hold, retain

WORD BANK
❑ **types of apartments** apartment, bed-sitter, condominium, dockominium, duplex, efficiency apartment, garden apartment, loft, penthouse, split-level, studio

❑ **types of houses** brownstone, bungalow, cabana, cabin, cape, Cape Cod, chalet, chateau, colonial, contemporary, cottage, country house, detached house, Dutch colonial, farmhouse, hacienda, homestead, igloo, lodge, manor, manor house, mansion, mobile home, palace, pied-à-terre, raised ranch, ranch, ranch house, row house, semidetached, shack, starter home, timeshare, town house, villa, walk-up

housecoat *n* robe, wrap, bathrobe, kimono, gown

house guest *n* visitor, guest, lodger, boarder

household *n* family, home, family circle, family unit, house ■ *adj* domestic, home, family, everyday, domiciliary *Opposite*: industrial

household name *n* celebrity, star, superstar, megastar, luminary *Opposite*: unknown

housekeeping *n* 1 organization, maintenance, upkeep, management, running 2 housework, chores, cleaning, housecleaning, tidying

house of worship *n* house of God, church, cathedral, synagogue, mosque

houseplant *n* plant, indoor plant, potted plant, foliage plant

WORD BANK
❑ **types of houseplants** aspidistra, coleus, fern, moss, poinsettia, rubber plant, sansevieria, spider plant, yucca

housing *n* 1 lodging, shelter, board, accommodations, home 2 cover, covering, case, casing, frame

housing estate *n* estate, development, urban development, residential area, housing development

hovel *n* slum, shack, squat, dump *(infml)*, hole *(infml)*

hover *v* 1 float, hang, drift, soar, fly *Opposite*: descend 2 linger, stay close, hang around, wait, remain *Opposite*: leave

how *adv* in what way, by what means, by what method, in what manner, just how

however *adv* though, but, on the other hand, yet, still *Opposite*: also

howl *v* yowl, bay, cry, wail, scream *Opposite*: murmur

howl down *v* drown out, shout down, boo, jeer, mock *Opposite*: cheer

howling *adj* violent, whistling, gale-force, hurricane-force, breathtaking *Opposite*: gentle

hub *n* 1 center, core, heart, focus, focal point *Opposite*: periphery 2 center, middle, boss, pivot *Opposite*: spoke

hubbub *n* noise, racket, hullabaloo, din, uproar *Opposite*: silence

huddle *n* group, cluster, knot, crowd, clump *Opposite*: scattering ■ *v* 1 gather together, crowd together, throng together, cluster, come together *Opposite*: scatter 2 crouch, bend, cower, nestle, hunch

hue *n* 1 color, tint, tinge, tone, shade 2 type, kind, sort, description, manner

hue and cry *n* uproar, furor, commotion, protest, public outcry *Opposite*: acceptance

huff *n* sulk, mood, bad mood, fit of pique, temper ■ *v* 1 puff, pant, wheeze, gasp, blow 2 bluster, grumble, complain, rant, gripe *(infml)* *Opposite*: calm down

huffy *adj* touchy, sensitive, moody, grumpy, sulky *Opposite*: good-natured

hug *v* embrace, hold close, enfold, cuddle, clasp ■ *n* cuddle, clinch, clasp, bear hug, embrace

huge *adj* 1 enormous, vast, gigantic, massive, giant *Opposite*: tiny 2 *(infml)* incredible, awesome, phenomenal, amazing, mind-blowing *(infml)*

hugely *adv* enormously, immensely, overwhelmingly, vastly, tremendously *Opposite*: slightly

hulk *n* 1 giant, goliath, colossus, titan, ogre 2 shell, skeleton, frame, carcass, wreck

hulking *adj* bulky, vast, massive, colossal, enormous *Opposite*: dainty

hull *n* body, exterior, underside, keel, casing *Opposite*: interior

hullaballoo *see* hullabaloo

hullabaloo *n* noise, racket, hubbub, din, uproar *Opposite*: silence

hum *v* drone, whine, purr, buzz, whir ■ *n* whine, drone, purr, buzz, vibration

human *n* person, being, human being, individual, creature ■ *adj* humanoid, hominid, hominoid, anthropological, anthropoid *Opposite*: animal

human being *n* person, human, being, individual, creature

humane *adj* compassionate, caring, kind, gentle, humanitarian *Opposite*: cruel

humanitarian *adj* caring, charitable, benevolent, philanthropic, public-spirited *Opposite*: uncaring

humanity *n* 1 humankind, people, human race, mortality, homo sapiens 2 kindness, charity, compassion, sympathy, mercy *Opposite*: cruelty

humanize *v* 1 civilize, cultivate, improve, soften, refine *Opposite*: brutalize 2 anthropomorphize, personify personalize

humanizing *adj* civilizing, improving, progressive, refining, softening *Opposite*: brutalizing

humankind *n* human race, humanity, people, mortality, homo sapiens

humanly *adv* at all, feasibly, physically, realistically, in any way

human race *n* humankind, humanity, people, mortality, homo sapiens

human rights *n* basic rights, civil liberties, civil rights, citizens' rights, inalienable rights

humble adj 1 modest, unassuming, retiring, meek, self-effacing Opposite: arrogant 2 lowly, poor, modest, simple, underprivileged Opposite: privileged 3 respectful, subservient, servile, deferential, obliging Opposite: aloof ■ v 1 humiliate, chasten, shame, bring down a peg, force to eat humble pie Opposite: glorify 2 degrade, debase, demean, lower, reduce Opposite: exalt (fml)

humbled adj shamed, chastened, crestfallen, mortified, sheepish Opposite: proud

humbleness n humility, modesty, meekness, self-effacement, shyness Opposite: arrogance

humbling adj 1 chastening, awe-inspiring, awesome, overwhelming Opposite: uplifting (fml) 2 mortifying, embarrassing, shaming, sobering, crushing Opposite: heartening

humbug n 1 nonsense, gibberish, garbage, rubbish, claptrap (infml) Opposite: fact 2 deception, hypocrisy, lies, deceit, propaganda Opposite: sincerity

humdrum adj dull, boring, routine, unexciting, everyday Opposite: exciting

humid adj moist, damp, steamy, tropical, sticky Opposite: arid

humidify v moisten, dampen, saturate, impregnate Opposite: dry out

humidity n moisture, moistness, dampness, clamminess, stickiness Opposite: aridity

humiliate v chasten, embarrass, demean, degrade, disgrace Opposite: dignify

humiliated adj chastened, humbled, shamed, mortified, disgraced Opposite: proud

humiliating adj chastening, humbling, embarrassing, mortifying, shameful Opposite: gratifying

humiliation n disgrace, shame, mortification, embarrassment, dishonor Opposite: dignity

humility n self-effacement, unpretentiousness, humbleness, modesty, meekness Opposite: arrogance

humming adj droning, whining, purring, buzzing, whirring Opposite: silent

hummock n hillock, mound, knoll, hill, rise Opposite: dip

humongous (infml) adj enormous, gigantic, colossal, massive, vast Opposite: tiny

humor n 1 funniness, wit, comedy, comicality, comicalness Opposite: seriousness 2 wit, wittiness, sense of humor, sparkle, drollness Opposite: dourness 3 comedy, satire, black humor, spoof, slapstick ■ v go along with, indulge, accommodate, please, pacify Opposite: oppose

humorist n 1 comedian, comic, standup comedian, impressionist, entertainer 2 joker, wit, satirist, punster, clown

humorless adj 1 sullen, serious, sour, dour, dull Opposite: merry 2 unfunny, unamusing, dull, serious, straight Opposite: funny

humorous adj funny, amusing, entertaining, hilarious, comical Opposite: serious

hump n bulge, bump, lump, swelling, protuberance Opposite: dip

humungous see humongous

hunch n feeling, gut feeling, sixth sense, premonition, intuition ■ v bend, huddle, stoop, crouch, lean forward Opposite: straighten

hunger n 1 starvation, food shortage, lack of food, malnutrition, famine Opposite: surfeit 2 appetite, emptiness, craving, hungriness, ravenousness 3 craving, desire, need, wish, yearning ■ v crave, yearn, long, desire, hanker Opposite: spurn

hungrily adv 1 eagerly, impatiently, keenly, enthusiastically, excitedly Opposite: nonchalantly 2 ravenously, greedily, voraciously, raveningly

hungry adj 1 famished, ravenous, empty, ravening, voracious Opposite: full 2 (infml) ambitious, driven, thrusting, powerhungry, aggressive Opposite: content 3 avid, eager, keen, greedy, thirsty Opposite: nonchalant

hunk n chunk, piece, lump, slab, wedge

hunker v squat, squat down, hunker down, crouch, crouch down Opposite: stand

hunky (infml) adj muscular, well-built, masculine, stocky, solid Opposite: puny

hunt v 1 chase, pursue, stalk, follow, track Opposite: flee 2 seek out, hunt down, track down, chase, pursue Opposite: evade 3 search, seek, rummage, look, ferret around Opposite: find ■ n search, quest, chase, pursuit, expedition

hunt down v find, catch, track down, capture, get hold of Opposite: flee

hunted adj panic-stricken, alarmed, startled, frightened, unsettled Opposite: relaxed

hunter n 1 seeker, searcher, quester, forager, scout Opposite: prey 2 stalker, predator, tracker, pursuer, chaser Opposite: prey

hunting n blood sport, fox hunting, deer stalking, hare coursing, shooting

hurdle n obstacle, difficulty, problem, stumbling block, snag Opposite: aid ■ v jump, leap, jump over, leap over, clear

hurl v throw, fling, launch, toss, heave. See COMPARE AND CONTRAST at throw.

hurly-burly n commotion, chaos, turmoil, confusion, bustle Opposite: peace

hurricane n storm, gale, tempest, tropical storm, tornado

hurried adj 1 quick, rushed, speedy, swift, sudden Opposite: leisurely 2 rushed, pressurized, under pressure, harried, hassled (infml) Opposite: relaxed

hurry v 1 rush, speed, hasten, run, dash Opposite: delay 2 speed up, accelerate, quicken, hasten, hustle Opposite: slow down ■ n **1 haste**, rush, dash, flurry, frenzy **2 urgency**, time pressure, panic, rush, haste

hurry up v **speed up**, accelerate, quicken, hasten, hustle Opposite: slow down

hurt v **1 injure**, harm, wound, damage, mar Opposite: benefit **2 impair**, damage, mar, spoil, ruin Opposite: improve **3 ache**, be sore, be painful, throb, trouble Opposite: soothe **4 offend**, upset, insult, injure, wound Opposite: comfort ■ n **1 injury**, damage, harm, pain, soreness Opposite: benefit **2 upset**, pain, distress, sadness, injury Opposite: gratification ■ adj **upset**, offended, wounded, unhappy, indignant Opposite: gratified. See COMPARE AND CONTRAST at **harm**.

hurtful adj **upsetting**, unkind, cruel, spiteful, cutting Opposite: kind

hurting adj **sad**, aching, heartbroken, brokenhearted, down Opposite: happy

hurtle v **dash**, career, tear, race, plunge Opposite: plod

husband n **spouse**, partner, other half, significant other, mate Opposite: wife

hushed adj **quiet**, silent, muted, soft, whispered Opposite: loud

hush-hush (infml) adj **secret**, confidential, top-secret, cloak-and-dagger, clandestine Opposite: public

hush money (infml) n **bribe**, pacifier, incentive, payoff (infml), sweetener (infml)

hush up (infml) v **cover up**, suppress, conceal, keep quiet, keep secret Opposite: reveal

husk n **shell**, casing, pod, covering, skin Opposite: kernel

huskiness n **throatiness**, hoarseness, dryness, roughness, gruffness Opposite: clearness

husky adj **1 burly**, strong, solid, broad, hulking **2 throaty**, hoarse, dry, rough, gruff Opposite: clear

hustle v **1 propel**, jostle, manhandle, push, shove **2** (infml) **hurry**, hurry up, get going, get cracking, get a move on (infml) Opposite: slow down

hustle and bustle n **commotion**, chaos, turmoil, confusion, hurly-burly Opposite: calm

hut n **shed**, lean-to, cabin, shelter, shack

hutzpah see **chutzpah**

hybrid n **cross**, crossbreed, mix, amalgam, mixture

hydroplane v **skid**, slide, swerve, slew, veer

hygiene n **cleanliness**, sanitation, sanitariness, cleanness, sterility

hygienic adj **clean**, sterile, disinfected, sanitary, germ-free Opposite: unhygienic

hymn n **song**, chant, carol, chorus, anthem ■

v **praise**, celebrate, eulogize, extol, laud Opposite: criticize

hype n **publicity**, propaganda, buildup, excitement, puff ■ v **publicize**, advertise, build up, tout, push

hyper (infml) adj **1 hyperactive**, restless, frenzied, agitated, overactive Opposite: placid **2 excitable**, hotheaded, on the edge, volatile, high-strung Opposite: calm

hyperactive adj **restless**, agitated, frenzied, overactive, manic (infml) Opposite: placid

hyperbole n **exaggeration**, overstatement, overemphasis, magnification, inflation Opposite: understatement

hypercritical adj **overcritical**, censorious, nitpicking, finicky, pedantic Opposite: lenient

hypersensitive adj **touchy**, oversensitive, thin-skinned, easily offended, easily hurt Opposite: thick-skinned

hypnotic (infml) adj **fascinating**, mesmerizing, entrancing, spellbinding, compelling Opposite: uninteresting

hypnotize v **fascinate**, mesmerize, spellbind, entrance, entrall Opposite: bore

hypocrisy n **insincerity**, double standard, pretense, duplicity, two-facedness Opposite: sincerity

hypocrite n **charlatan**, fraud, phony, double-dealer, pretender

hypocritical adj **insincere**, two-faced, duplicitous, deceitful, phony Opposite: genuine

hypothesis n **theory**, premise, suggestion, supposition, proposition

hypothesize v **imagine**, conjecture, put forward, assume, theorize

hypothetical adj **theoretical**, imaginary, supposed, conjectural, proposed Opposite: real

hysteria n **panic**, hysterics, frenzy, madness, emotion Opposite: calm

hysterical adj **1 panic-stricken**, out of control, agitated, overexcited, feverish Opposite: composed **2 uncontrollable**, frenzied, intense, violent, unrestrained Opposite: controlled **3** (infml) **hilarious**, uproarious, highly amusing, sidesplitting, comical Opposite: sad

hysterically adv **1 frantically**, feverishly, frenziedly, frenetically, agitatedly Opposite: calmly **2 uncontrollably**, violently, wildly, frenziedly, unrestrainedly Opposite: quietly **3** (infml) **uproariously**, hilariously, sidesplittingly, riotously, screamingly Opposite: mildly

hysterics n **1 hysteria**, panic, frenzy, agitation, distraction Opposite: calmness **2** (infml) **fits**, fits of laughter, stitches, laughter

I

ice *n* frost, snow, hoar frost, rime, black ice ■ *v* 1 freeze up, freeze, freeze solid, freeze over, ice over *Opposite*: thaw 2 decorate, finish off, frost, embellish, adorn 3 chill, cool, cool down *Opposite*: heat

icebox *n* refrigerator, fridge, freezer

icebreaker *n* opener, starter, opening, introduction

ice-cold *adj* freezing, frozen, icy, subzero, chilled *Opposite*: boiling

ice cream *n* ice, cone, ice-cream cone, sherbet, sorbet

iced *adj* chilled, cool, refrigerated, frozen, cold *Opposite*: hot

ice over *v* freeze, freeze over, freeze up, harden, solidify *Opposite*: thaw

ice pack *n* compress, cold compress, wrapping, poultice

ice up *v* freeze, freeze over, freeze up, ice over, frost up *Opposite*: thaw

iciness *n* coldness, coolness, frostiness, unfriendliness, hostility *Opposite*: warmth

icing *n* 1 frosting, decoration, glaze, glazing, ganache 2 freezing, freezing over, freezing up

icky (*infml*) *adj* 1 sticky, gooey, tacky, messy, disgusting 2 nasty, unpleasant, horrid, uncomfortable, horrible 3 sentimental, too much, saccharine, over-the-top (*infml*), sloppy (*infml*)

icon *n* 1 image, likeness, representation, sign, picture 2 idol, star, model, symbol, embodiment

iconoclast *n* revolutionary, radical, free thinker, subversive, individualist *Opposite*: conservative

iconoclastic *adj* radical, revolutionary, subversive, individualistic, free-thinking *Opposite*: conservative

icy *adj* 1 freezing, frozen, frosty, ice-cold, subzero 2 unfriendly, frosty, hostile, distant, aloof *Opposite*: warm

ID *n* identification, identity card, passport, papers, documents

idea *n* 1 opinion, belief, view, viewpoint, outlook 2 suggestion, design, plan, scheme, proposal 3 concept, impression, notion, understanding, perception 4 plan, inspiration, solution, brainchild, notion 5 aim, objective, plan, object, goal 6 gist, précis, outline, sketch, overview

ideal *n* 1 principle, standard, belief, value 2 epitome, model, archetype, essence, stereotype ■ *adj* best, model, ultimate, idyllic, supreme

idealism *n* 1 naiveté, romanticism, impracticality, optimism *Opposite*: realism 2 perfectionism, fundamentalism, commitment, principle, morality

idealist *n* 1 romantic, optimist, dreamer *Opposite*: realist 2 perfectionist, fundamentalist, crusader, zealot, fanatic

idealistic *adj* 1 naive, unrealistic, romantic, impractical, optimistic *Opposite*: realistic 2 uncompromising, principled, committed, unswerving, unwavering

idealize *v* romanticize, put on a pedestal, view through rose-tinted glasses, venerate, overemphasize

idealized *adj* perfect, flawless, faultless, ideal, unrealistic

ideally *adv* 1 in an ideal world, preferably, if possible, if at all possible 2 perfectly, supremely, superlatively, well

idée fixe *n* obsession, pet topic, hobbyhorse, fixation, bee in your bonnet

idem *adv* the same, the same thing, the same as before

identical *adj* same, indistinguishable, equal, matching, alike *Opposite*: different

identifiable *adj* recognizable, distinguishable, perceptible, discernible, detectable

identification *n* 1 recognition, classification, naming, detection, discovery 2 ID, documentation, proof of identity, papers, credentials 3 empathy, sympathy, affinity, rapport, bonding

identify *v* 1 recognize, classify, name, find, categorize 2 equate, connect, relate, link, associate

identify with *v* empathize with, sympathize with, relate to, feel for, have sympathy for

identity *n* individuality, uniqueness, distinctiveness, self, character

identity card *n* pass, card, passport, ID card (*infml*)

ideological *adj* conceptual, philosophical, moral, political, ethical

ideology *n* philosophy, belief, creed, dogma, line

idiolect *n* speech pattern, turn of phrase, style, dialect, idiom

idiom *n* 1 expression, phrase, set phrase, turn of phrase, saying 2 language, dialect, speech, style, vernacular

idiomatic *adj* natural, fluent, colloquial, vernacular, native *Opposite*: stilted

idiosyncrasy *n* quirk, peculiarity, eccentricity, foible, habit

idiosyncratic adj **characteristic**, personal, individual, distinctive, eccentric

idle adj **1 inactive**, inoperative, unoccupied, at rest, still Opposite: working **2 lazy**, indolent, shiftless, slothful, sluggish Opposite: diligent **3 frivolous**, futile, pointless, worthless, vain **4 unfounded**, baseless, groundless, frivolous, meaningless **5 empty**, hollow, ineffectual, impotent, meaningless ■ v **1 laze**, laze around, hang around, sit around, loaf around **2 turn over**, run, tick over (infml) **3 dismiss**, fire, lay off (infml), can (slang). See COMPARE AND CONTRAST at **vain**.

idle away v while away, fritter away, waste, pass, spend

idleness n laziness, sloth, inertia, indolence, apathy Opposite: activity

idler n **loafer**, malingerer, timewaster, shirker, slacker Opposite: workaholic

idly adv **1 lazily**, indolently, shiftlessly, slothfully (fml) Opposite: diligently **2 frivolously**, futilely, pointlessly, worthlessly, uselessly Opposite: seriously

idol n **1 hero**, star, pinup, obsession, ideal **2 icon**, graven image, statue, carving, sculpture

idolater n **fan**, admirer, fanatic, devotee, aficionado

idolatry n worship, hero worship, adoration, admiration, veneration Opposite: denigration

idolization see idolatry

idolize v worship, hero-worship, adore, look up to, admire Opposite: denigrate

idyll n nirvana, honeymoon, honeymoon period, heaven, paradise Opposite: nightmare

idyllic adj **1 peaceful**, calm, tranquil, restful, relaxing Opposite: nightmarish **2 picturesque**, scenic, unspoiled, beautiful, charming

i.e. adv that is to say, that is, namely, viz., to be precise

if n **1 doubt**, uncertainty, question mark, unknown, unknown quantity **2 stipulation**, condition, rider, proviso, qualification

iffy (infml) adj **1 risky**, chancy, shaky, suspicious, dubious Opposite: reliable **2 unsure**, undecided, doubtful, hesitant, up in the air Opposite: certain

ignite v **1 catch fire**, catch light, go up in flames, burst into flames, flare up Opposite: go out **2 set fire to**, light, put a match to, set alight, kindle Opposite: put out **3 stir up**, stir, inflame, fan the flames of, kindle Opposite: dampen

ignition n explosion, detonation, eruption, burst, blastoff

ignoble adj **dishonorable**, shameful, despicable, immoral, dastardly Opposite: honorable

ignominious adj **humiliating**, embarrassing, shameful, disgraceful, reprehensible Opposite: honorable

ignominy n **humiliation**, embarrassment, shame, disgrace dishonor Opposite: honor

ignorance n **unawareness**, unfamiliarity, obliviousness, inexperience, witlessness Opposite: knowledge

ignorant adj **unaware**, uninformed, illinformed, unfamiliar, oblivious Opposite: aware

ignore v pay no attention to, take no notice of, close your eyes to, pay no heed to, disregard Opposite: notice

ignored adj **overlooked**, unnoticed, disregarded, discounted, unheeded Opposite: noted

ilk n **type**, like, sort, kind, class

ill adj **1 unwell**, sick, under the weather, laid up, in poor health Opposite: well **2 unkind**, unfriendly, hostile, harsh, mean Opposite: good **3 harmful**, adverse, detrimental, unfavorable, unpropitious Opposite: good **4 wicked**, evil, immoral, bad, iniquitous Opposite: good ■ adv **1 unkindly**, hostilely, harshly, cruelly, unpleasantly Opposite: well **2 unfavorably**, adversely, unpropitiously, inauspiciously, ominously Opposite: well **3 hardly**, barely, scarcely Opposite: well ■ n **harm**, evil, misfortune, trouble mischief Opposite: good

ill-advised adj **foolish**, foolhardy, misguided, rash, reckless Opposite: well-advised

ill-bred adj **rude**, impolite, boorish, bad-mannered, ill-mannered Opposite: well-bred

ill-conceived adj **doomed**, impractical, vague, ill-judged, half-baked (infml)

ill-considered adj **careless**, reckless, irresponsible, rash, hasty Opposite: prudent

ill-defined adj **imprecise**, vague, hazy, unclear, nebulous Opposite: clear

ill-disguised adj **obvious**, blatant, clear, apparent, plain Opposite: concealed

ill-disposed adj **hostile**, unfriendly, cold, cool, antagonistic Opposite: well-disposed

illegal adj against the law, unlawful, illicit, illegitimate, prohibited Opposite: legal. See COMPARE AND CONTRAST at **unlawful**.

illegality n **1 unlawfulness**, illicitness, illegitimacy, impropriety, wrongfulness Opposite: legality **2 crime**, misdemeanor, felony, infraction, offense

illegible adj **unreadable**, indecipherable, scrawled, scribbled, spidery Opposite: legible

illegitimate adj **unlawful**, illegal, illicit, prohibited, banned Opposite: legitimate

ill-fated adj **doomed**, ill-starred, unlucky, unfortunate, hapless Opposite: lucky

ill-favored adj **unattractive**, ugly, repulsive, horrible, repellent Opposite: good-looking

ill feeling n animosity, hostility, ill will, antagonism, enmity Opposite: friendliness

ill-founded adj illogical, false, inaccurate, trumped-up, unreliable Opposite: reliable

ill-gotten adj illegal, illicit, fraudulent, contraband, unlawful

ill health n infirmity, illness, sickness, disease, frailty Opposite: good health

ill humor n grouchiness, bad mood, mood, bad temper, foul mood

illiberal adj 1 intolerant, bigoted, narrow-minded, reactionary, parochial Opposite: liberal 2 (fml) mean, parsimonious, stingy, miserly, niggardly Opposite: generous

illicit adj illegal, unlawful, illegitimate, dishonest, criminal Opposite: legal. See COMPARE AND CONTRAST at unlawful.

illiterate adj uneducated, untaught, unschooled, untrained, uninformed Opposite: literate

ill-judged adj misguided, injudicious, inappropriate, unwise, imprudent Opposite: prudent

ill-mannered adj rude, bad-mannered, impolite, discourteous, disrespectful Opposite: well-mannered

ill-natured adj unpleasant, disagreeable, ill-tempered, bad-tempered, ill-humored Opposite: good-natured

illness n 1 disease, sickness, complaint, ailment, infection 2 ill health, sickness, disease, infirmity, disability Opposite: good health

illogical adj 1 irrational, unreasoned, unscientific, specious, unsound Opposite: logical 2 unreasonable, senseless, absurd, ludicrous, nonsensical Opposite: logical

illogicality n 1 irrationality, speciousness, unsoundness, inconsistency, contradiction 2 unreasonableness, senselessness, absurdity, ludicrousness, nonsensicality

ill-omened adj inauspicious, unlucky, unfortunate, ominous, fateful Opposite: blessed

ill-sorted adj incompatible, mismatched, unsuited, incongruous, antagonistic Opposite: compatible

ill-starred adj unlucky, doomed, ill-fated, unfortunate, hapless Opposite: lucky

ill-tempered adj bad-tempered, ill-humored, short-tempered, irascible, irritable Opposite: good-tempered

ill-timed adj inopportune, mistimed, untimely, inconvenient, intrusive Opposite: opportune

ill-treat v abuse, harm, mistreat, misuse, ill-use Opposite: take care of. See COMPARE AND CONTRAST at misuse.

ill-treated adj abused, harmed, mistreated, maltreated, ill-used Opposite: cherished

ill-treatment n abuse, harm, maltreatment, mistreatment, cruelty Opposite: care

illuminate v 1 light up, light, brighten, lighten, irradiate Opposite: darken 2 clarify, elucidate, explain, clear up, illustrate Opposite: confuse

illuminating adj enlightening, revealing, informative, instructive, educational Opposite: confusing

illumination n 1 light, lighting, lights, brightness, brilliance 2 enlightenment, clarification, explanation, insight, knowledge Opposite: confusion

illuminations n lights, Christmas lights, colored lights, decorations

ill-use v abuse, harm, mistreat, maltreat, treat badly Opposite: take care of

ill-used adj mistreated, maltreated, badly treated, abused, hurt Opposite: cherished

illusion n 1 delusion, misapprehension, deception, misconception, magic 2 impression, semblance, appearance, feeling, sensation 3 fantasy, daydream, figment of your imagination, chimera, mirage Opposite: reality

illusive see illusory

illusory adj deceptive, false, imagined, misleading, unreal Opposite: real

illustrate v exemplify, demonstrate, show, point up, prove

illustration n 1 picture, drawing, figure, diagram, photograph 2 example, demonstration, instance, case in point, exemplification

illustrative adj descriptive, explanatory, graphic, expressive, demonstrative

illustrious adj distinguished, celebrated, renowned, famous, eminent Opposite: obscure

ill will n animosity, hostility, ill feeling, antagonism, enmity Opposite: goodwill

image n 1 picture, representation, drawing, icon, figure 2 impression, picture, idea, concept, notion 3 copy, twin, double, duplicate, carbon copy 4 appearance, look, persona, aura, air

imagery n images, pictures, descriptions, metaphors, similes

imaginable adj conceivable, possible, thinkable, supposable, presumable Opposite: unimaginable

imaginary adj fantasy, make-believe, made-up, unreal, invented Opposite: real

imagination n 1 mind's eye, mind, head, thoughts, dreams 2 resourcefulness, ingenuity, creativity, inventiveness, vision

imaginative adj creative, inventive, original, ingenious, artistic Opposite: unimaginative

imaginativeness n creativeness, inventiveness, originality, ingeniousness, resourcefulness

imagine v 1 picture, envisage, visualize, see, conjure up 2 make up, dream, dream up, invent, make believe 3 suppose, think, expect, assume, presume

imagined *adj* **fictional**, imaginary, abstract, unreal, illusory *Opposite*: real

imbalance *n* **inequity**, disparity, unevenness, disproportion, inequality *Opposite*: balance

imbibe *(fml)* *v* **drink**, down, swallow, take in, absorb

imbroglio *n* **mess**, embarrassment, entanglement, complication, enmeshment

imbue *v* **instill**, fill, permeate, infuse, saturate

imitate *v* **1 mimic**, copy, ape, emulate, take off *(infml)* **2 reproduce**, copy, duplicate, replicate, rip off *(infml)*

COMPARE AND CONTRAST CORE MEANING: adopt the behavior of another person
imitate copy another's behavior, voice, or manner, sometimes in order to make fun of him or her; **copy** do exactly what somebody else does; **emulate** try to equal or surpass somebody else who is successful or admired; **mimic** imitate somebody in a deliberate and exaggerated way, especially to amuse people; **take off** *(infml)* imitate somebody to amuse people; **ape** imitate somebody in an absurd or grotesque way.

imitation *n* **1 simulation**, reproduction, replication, copy, facsimile **2 impersonation**, impression, skit, parody, sendup *(infml)* **■** *adj* **mock**, fake, simulated, artificial, pretend *Opposite*: real

imitative *adj* **unoriginal**, derivative, plagiarized, copied, secondhand *Opposite*: original

imitator *n* **1 impersonator**, impressionist, mimic, double, actor **2 follower**, sheep, copier, clone, imitation *Opposite*: original

immaculate *adj* **1 spotless**, perfect, neat and tidy, clean, spick-and-span *Opposite*: messy **2 perfect**, flawless, faultless, pristine, pure *Opposite*: flawed

immanent *(fml)* *adj* **inherent**, intrinsic, innate, ingrained, internal

immaterial *adj* **irrelevant**, unimportant, of no importance, of no consequence, inconsequential *Opposite*: relevant

immature *adj* **1 young**, undeveloped, small, unformed, juvenile *Opposite*: mature **2 childish**, babyish, infantile, juvenile, adolescent *Opposite*: mature

immaturity *n* **1 adolescence**, infancy, reproductive immaturity, youth, babyhood *Opposite*: maturity **2 childishness**, irresponsibility, naiveté, ingenuousness, silliness *Opposite*: maturity **3 inexperience**, greenness, naiveté, rawness, awkwardness *Opposite*: maturity

immeasurable *adj* **vast**, beyond measure, endless, infinite, incalculable *Opposite*: slight

immeasurably *adv* **extremely**, infinitely, vastly, incalculably, inestimably *Opposite*: slightly

immediate *adj* **1 instant**, direct, instantaneous, abrupt, fast **2 direct**, close, near, proximate *Opposite*: distant **3 urgent**, current, pressing, high priority, burning

immediately *adv* **1 right away**, at once, without delay, instantly, directly *Opposite*: later **2 directly**, closely, nearly, proximately *Opposite*: distantly **■** *conj* **as soon as**, the moment, the instant, the minute, the second

immemorial *adj* **ancient**, age-old, old, centuries old, timeworn

immense *adj* **huge**, vast, enormous, massive, gigantic *Opposite*: tiny

immensely *adv* **hugely**, vastly, enormously, immeasurably, greatly

immensity *n* **hugeness**, vastness, enormity, sheer size, extent

immerse *v* **1 submerge**, dip, plunge, duck, dunk **2 engross**, throw yourself into, absorb yourself in, engage, occupy

immersed *adj* **engrossed**, wrapped up, absorbed, deep, occupied *Opposite*: distracted

immersion *n* **1 involvement**, engagement, absorption, entanglement, preoccupation **2 dipping**, soaking, wetting, dunking, steeping

immigrant *n* **settler**, émigré, migrant, refugee, colonist *Opposite*: emigrant

immigrate *v* **settle**, arrive, colonize, discover, found *Opposite*: emigrate

immigration *n* **migration**, settlement, arrival, entry, colonization

imminent *adj* **impending**, forthcoming, pending, looming, about to happen *Opposite*: distant

immobile *adj* **1 motionless**, stationary, still, stock-still, inert *Opposite*: mobile **2 fixed**, immovable, secure, steady, permanent *Opposite*: mobile

immobility *n* **stillness**, motionlessness, immovability, fixity, stasis *Opposite*: mobility

immobilize *v* **stop**, halt, restrain, arrest, bring to a halt *Opposite*: mobilize

immoderate *adj* **excessive**, extreme, intemperate, extravagant, unrestrained *Opposite*: moderate

immoderateness *(fml)* *see* **immoderation**

immoderation *(fml)* *n* **excess**, intemperance, extravagance, prodigality, abandon *Opposite*: moderation

immodest *adj* **boastful**, arrogant, conceited, ostentatious, bombastic *Opposite*: modest

immodesty *n* **arrogance**, conceit, boastfulness, pretentiousness, ostentatiousness *Opposite*: modesty

immolate *(literary)* *v* **sacrifice**, offer up, slaughter, make an offering of, kill

immoral *adj* **wicked**, depraved, corrupt, dissolute, dishonest *Opposite*: moral

immorality *n* **wickedness**, sin, depravity, corruption, dissoluteness *Opposite*: morality

immortal *adj* 1 **eternal**, everlasting, undying, perpetual, enduring *Opposite*: mortal 2 **memorable**, well-known, famous, illustrious, unforgettable *Opposite*: forgotten

immortalize *v* **commemorate**, celebrate, preserve, make immortal, memorialize

immovable *adj* 1 **fixed**, immobile, secure, steady, permanent *Opposite*: movable 2 **resolute**, unbending, rigid, stubborn, obstinate *Opposite*: irresolute

immune *adj* 1 **resistant**, protected, invulnerable, safe, insusceptible *(fml)* *Opposite*: susceptible 2 **exempt**, excepted, absolved, excused, not liable *Opposite*: liable 3 **impervious**, invulnerable, untouchable, untouched, unaffected *Opposite*: vulnerable

immune system *n* **body's defenses**, natural defenses, immune response, white blood cells, natural resistance

immunity *n* 1 **resistance**, protection, invulnerability, imperviousness, insusceptibility *(fml)* *Opposite*: susceptibility 2 **exemption**, exception, liberty, freedom, protection *Opposite*: liability

immunization *n* **vaccination**, inoculation, injection, shot *(infml)*

immunize *v* **vaccinate**, inoculate, inject, protect

immure *(literary)* *v* **imprison**, confine, shut away, shut up, hold captive *Opposite*: free

immutable *adj* **unchanging**, irreversible, fixed, absolute, unchangeable *Opposite*: mercurial

imp *n* 1 **elf**, goblin, pixie, sprite, fairy 2 **mischief**, urchin, rascal, scamp *(infml)*, scalawag *(dated infml)*

impact *n* 1 **crash**, collision, shock, bang, blow 2 **influence**, impression, effect, bearing, power

impacted *adj* **wedged**, stuck, jammed, squeezed, obstructed

impair *v* **damage**, harm, spoil, weaken, worsen *Opposite*: enhance

impaired *adj* **reduced**, lessened, decreased, weakened, diminished *Opposite*: unimpaired

impairment *n* **damage**, injury, hurt, loss, weakening *Opposite*: enhancement

impale *v* **spear**, pierce, stab, bayonet, spike

impalpable *(fml)* *adj* **intangible**, shadowy, vague, unclear, indefinable *Opposite*: palpable

impart *v* **communicate**, inform, tell, convey, divulge

impartial *adj* **neutral**, fair, unbiased, independent, objective *Opposite*: biased

impartiality *n* **neutrality**, fairness, independence, objectivity, detachment *Opposite*: bias

impassable *adj* **blocked**, impenetrable, closed, obstructed, inaccessible *Opposite*: open

impasse *n* **stalemate**, standoff, deadlock, gridlock, bottleneck

impassioned *adj* **emotional**, ardent, fervent, passionate, heated *Opposite*: impassive

impassive *adj* 1 **expressionless**, blank, inexpressive, poker-faced, deadpan *Opposite*: expressive 2 **unemotional**, unmoved, stolid, stoic, phlegmatic *Opposite*: impassioned

COMPARE AND CONTRAST CORE MEANING: showing no emotional response or interest **impassive** showing no outward sign of emotion, especially on the face; **apathetic** not taking any interest in anything, or not bothering to do anything; **phlegmatic** generally unemotional and difficult to arouse; **stolid** solemn, unemotional, and not easily excited or upset; **stoic** showing admirable patience and endurance in the face of adversity without complaining or getting upset; **unmoved** showing no emotion, surprise, or excitement when this would normally have been expected.

impatience *n* 1 **annoyance**, irritation, edginess, intolerance, displeasure *Opposite*: patience 2 **eagerness**, anxiety, hurry, haste, impulsiveness *Opposite*: patience

impatient *adj* 1 **annoyed**, irritated, edgy, intolerant, exasperated *Opposite*: patient 2 **eager**, raring, anxious, in a hurry, hurried *Opposite*: patient

impeach *v* **indict**, accuse, arraign, charge, inculpate *(fml)*

impeccable *adj* **perfect**, flawless, faultless, unimpeachable, above reproach *Opposite*: flawed

impecunious *adj* **poor**, impoverished, penniless, poverty-stricken, destitute *Opposite*: wealthy

impede *v* **obstruct**, hinder, hamper, slow down, delay *Opposite*: facilitate. *See* COMPARE AND CONTRAST *at* hinder.

impediment *n* 1 **impairment**, disablement, weakness, disorder, inhibition 2 **obstacle**, obstruction, barrier, hurdle, hindrance

impel *v* 1 **compel**, urge, force, drive, coerce *Opposite*: hold back 2 *(fml)* **propel**, force, drive, throw, push

impend *v* 1 *(fml)* **loom**, approach, be on the horizon, be imminent, be in the offing *Opposite*: recede 2 *(literary)* **menace**, loom, threaten, hover, hang

impending *adj* **imminent**, looming, in the near future, approaching, coming *Opposite*: far-off

impenetrability *n* 1 **impassability**, impermeability, density, denseness, thickness 2 **incomprehensibility**, complexity, opacity, intricacy, obscurity *Opposite*: lucidity

impenetrable *adj* 1 **impassable**, dense, tightly packed, thick, solid 2 **incomprehensible**, unfathomable, indecipherable, inscrutable, unsolvable Opposite: understandable

impenitent adj unrepentant, unremorseful, unapologetic, defiant, shameless Opposite: remorseful

imperative adj 1 **necessary**, vital, crucial, essential, urgent Opposite: unimportant 2 (fml) **commanding**, domineering, bossy, imperious, overbearing Opposite: subservient ▪ n priority, essential, requirement, necessity, obligation Opposite: option

imperceptible adj **slight**, gradual, subtle, invisible, undetectable Opposite: obvious

imperceptibly adv **slightly**, gradually, invisibly, subtly, little by little Opposite: obviously

imperfect adj **faulty**, defective, deficient, damaged, flawed Opposite: perfect

imperfection n 1 **fault**, defect, deficiency, blemish, flaw 2 **faultiness**, inadequacy, limitation, deficiency, failure Opposite: perfection. See COMPARE AND CONTRAST at flaw.

imperial adj **grand**, majestic, imposing, regal, stately

imperialism n **expansionism**, colonialism, empire-building, colonization, interventionism

imperil (fml) v **endanger**, put in danger, risk, put at risk, jeopardize Opposite: protect

imperious adj **domineering**, authoritative, commanding, arrogant, superior Opposite: humble

imperiousness n **haughtiness**, overbearingness, arrogance, superiority, bossiness Opposite: humility

imperishability n 1 **durability**, resilience, stability, endurance, hardiness 2 (literary) **permanence**, immortality, everlastingness, enduringness Opposite: transience

imperishable adj 1 **permanent**, durable, indestructible, resilient, stable 2 (literary) **enduring**, eternal, everlasting, permanent, immortal Opposite: transient

impermanence n **transience**, transitoriness, evanescence, ephemerality, temporariness Opposite: permanence

impermanent adj **temporary**, transitory, passing, transient, evanescent Opposite: permanent

impermeability n **watertightness**, airtightness, waterproofness, protection, impenetrability Opposite: permeability

impermeable adj **resistant**, impervious, waterproof, water-resistant, rainproof Opposite: permeable

impersonal adj 1 **objective**, cool, detached, measured, careful Opposite: personal 2 **anonymous**, faceless, soulless, featureless, depersonalized 3 **unfriendly**, cool, cold, aloof, frosty Opposite: friendly

impersonate v 1 **mimic**, imitate, ape, copy, satirize 2 **pretend to be**, pose as, masquerade as, personate, pass off

impersonation n 1 **impression**, parody, caricature, takeoff (infml), sendup (infml) 2 **imitation**, pretense, masquerade, personation, imposture (fml)

impertinence n **impudence**, insolence, disrespect, impoliteness, brazenness Opposite: respect

impertinent adj **impudent**, insolent, disrespectful, impolite, brazen Opposite: respectful

imperturbable adj **calm**, cool, unflappable, collected, composed Opposite: excitable

impervious adj 1 **unreceptive**, unbending, unyielding, unwavering, rigid Opposite: responsive 2 **impermeable**, solid, resistant, waterproof, water-resistant Opposite: permeable

imperviousness n 1 **obduracy**, unyieldingness, rigidity, inflexibility Opposite: responsiveness 2 **impermeability**, resistance, invulnerability, watertightness, solidity Opposite: permeability

impetuosity n **impulsiveness**, rashness, hastiness, hotheadedness, recklessness Opposite: consideration

impetuous adj **impulsive**, rash, hasty, hotheaded, unthinking Opposite: considered

impetuousness see **impetuosity**

impetus n 1 **force**, momentum, impulsion, thrust, forward motion Opposite: inertia 2 **push** motivation, incentive, energy, stimulus

impiety n **irreverence**, sin, wickedness, transgression, immorality Opposite: piety

impinge (fml) v **impose**, intrude, interrupt, encroach, impact

impious adj **sinful**, irreverent, wicked, immoral, irreligious Opposite: pious

impish adj **mischievous**, naughty, wicked, playful, puckish

impishness n **mischievousness**, naughtiness, wickedness, playfulness, puckishness

implacability n **pitilessness**, mercilessness, relentlessness, ruthlessness, cruelty Opposite: kindness

implacable adj **pitiless**, merciless, relentless, ruthless, cruel Opposite: kind

implant v **establish**, embed, plant, insert, instill

implantation n **embedding**, establishment, grafting, attaching, joining

implausibility n **improbability** unlikelihood, inconceivability, doubtfulness, questionability Opposite: plausibility

implausible adj **unlikely**, improbable, unbelievable, incredible, fantastic Opposite: plausible

implement n **tool**, device, gadget, instrument, contrivance ▪ v **carry out**, put into practice, apply, realize, execute

implementation n **carrying out**, application, putting into practice, operation, execution Opposite: proposal

implicate v 1 **connect**, involve, associate, link, incriminate *Opposite*: clear 2 *(fml)* **imply**, suggest, assume, hint at, point to

implication n 1 **insinuation**, inference, suggestion, innuendo, hint 2 **involvement**, association, connection, link, part 3 **consequence**, repercussion, outcome, result

implicit adj 1 **understood**, implied, unspoken, tacit, hidden *Opposite*: explicit 2 **unreserved**, absolute, total, complete, utter *Opposite*: qualified

implicitly adv 1 **indirectly**, covertly, tacitly, obliquely, subtly 2 **unreservedly**, absolutely, totally, completely, wholly

implied adj **indirect**, understood, implicit, unspoken, tacit

implode v **collapse**, fail, cave in, fall in, subside *Opposite*: explode

implore *(fml)* v **beg**, plead, pray, appeal, entreat

imploring *(fml)* adj **pleading**, desperate, longing, heartfelt, suppliant *(fml)*

implosion n **collapse**, falling-in, subsidence, cave-in, disintegration *Opposite*: explosion

imply v 1 **suggest**, hint at, point to, indicate, insinuate 2 **involve**, entail, mean, denote

impolite adj **rude**, ill-mannered, bad-mannered, boorish, disrespectful *Opposite*: polite

impoliteness n **rudeness**, bad manners, loutishness, boorishness, disrespect *Opposite*: politeness

impolitic adj **unwise**, inappropriate, misguided, ill-advised, ill-judged *Opposite*: wise

imponderable adj **unknown**, unquantifiable, incalculable, indeterminable, inestimable ■ n **unknown**, mystery, enigma, paradox, uncertainty

import v **bring in**, introduce, trade in, smuggle *Opposite*: export ■ n 1 **introduction**, importation, ingress *(fml)* *Opposite*: export 2 **significance**, importance, meaning, consequence *(fml)*

importance n 1 **significance**, meaning, weight, magnitude, import *Opposite*: triviality 2 **rank**, position, standing, status, reputation

important adj 1 **significant**, vital, imperative, central, chief *Opposite*: trivial 2 **high-ranking**, eminent, worthy, notable, prominent *Opposite*: insignificant

importantly adv **significantly**, notably, crucially, critically, vitally

importation n **import**, introduction, ingress *(fml)* *Opposite*: export

importer n **trader**, shipper, carrier, hauler, distributor

importunate *(fml)* adj **persistent**, demanding, unrelenting, annoying, overeager

importune *(fml)* v **bother**, pester, badger, harass, plague

importunity *(fml)* n 1 **persistence**, insistence, obstinacy, doggedness, stubbornness 2 **demand**, request, entreaty, appeal, petition

impose v 1 **enforce**, levy, exact, execute, carry out 2 **inflict**, force, foist, dump, insist 3 **intrude**, be in the way, be a nuisance, disturb, trespass

imposing adj **impressive**, striking, grand, magnificent, stately *Opposite*: unimpressive

imposition n **burden**, nuisance, annoyance, obligation, bother

impossibility n **unfeasibility**, impracticality, hopelessness, ridiculousness, unlikelihood *Opposite*: possibility

impossible adj 1 **irresolvable**, irresoluble, unfeasible, impracticable, unattainable *Opposite*: possible 2 **unbearable**, terrible, dreadful, intolerable, insufferable *Opposite*: manageable

impossibly adv **dreadfully**, terribly, hopelessly, unbearably, ridiculously *Opposite*: reasonably

impostor n **deceiver**, imitator, impersonator, pretender, fake *Opposite*: the real McCoy *(infml)*

imposture *(fml)* n **deception**, impersonation, masquerade, imitation, pretense

impotence n **ineffectiveness**, incapability, ineffectualness, feebleness, powerlessness *Opposite*: strength

impotent adj **powerless**, weak, helpless, unable, incapable *Opposite*: powerful

impound v **confiscate**, seize, lock up, take away, hold *Opposite*: release

impoverish v **deprive**, ruin, bankrupt, diminish, weaken *Opposite*: enrich

impoverished adj **needy**, poor, penniless, disadvantaged, underprivileged *Opposite*: rich

impoverishment n 1 **destitution**, failure, disadvantage, poverty, insolvency *Opposite*: prosperity 2 **diminishment**, ruination, decline, depletion, degeneration *Opposite*: enrichment

impracticability n **unworkability**, impossibility, impracticality, impracticableness, unworkableness *Opposite*: feasibility

impracticable adj **unviable**, useless, unrealistic, unfeasible, unpractical *Opposite*: viable

impractical adj 1 **unpractical**, unreasonable, unviable, unfeasible, unworkable *Opposite*: practical 2 **unrealistic**, idealistic, starry-eyed, not down to earth, clueless *(infml)* *Opposite*: realistic

impracticality n **unviability**, unfeasibility, impracticability, inconvenience, hopelessness *Opposite*: practicality

imprecate *(fml)* v **curse**, revile, call down, execrate *(literary or fml)*, maledict *(literary)*

imprecation *(fml)* n 1 **oath**, insult,

swearword, expletive, curse **2 swearing**, cursing, blasphemy, profanity, cussing (infml)

imprecise adj **sketchy**, vague, inexact, rough, inaccurate Opposite: precise

imprecision n **fuzziness**, roughness, sketchiness, inaccuracy, inexactitude Opposite: accuracy

impregnable adj **unassailable**, invincible, secure, unconquerable impenetrable Opposite: vulnerable

impregnate v **saturate**, soak, steep, infuse, permeate Opposite: dry out

impresario n **manager** producer, promoter, agent, entrepreneur

impress v **1 excite**, move, amaze, influence, affect Opposite: disappoint **2 emphasize**, stress, drive home, drum into, din into Opposite: gloss over

impression n **1 feeling**, idea, notion, thought, sense Opposite: certainty **2 imprint**, dent, mark, print, hollow **3 mark**, impact, effect, influence, cause **4 impersonation**, imitation, parody, takeoff (infml), sendup (infml)

impressionable adj **susceptible**, suggestible, vulnerable, receptive, sensitive Opposite: unreceptive

impressionist n **impersonator**, mimic, imitator, comic, entertainer

impressionistic adj **ill-defined**, rough, loose, unfocused, imprecise Opposite: detailed

impressive adj **imposing**, inspiring, striking, remarkable, notable Opposite: unimpressive

impressiveness n **grandeur**, magnificence, brilliance, eminence, powerfulness

imprint n **1 impression**, print, mark, indentation, hollow **2 stamp**, inscription, name, print, printer's mark **3 hallmark**, emblem, stamp, seal, sign **4 indication**, mark, impression, effect, sign ■ v **impress**, fix, establish, drive home, drum into

imprison v **confine**, detain, intern, lock up, lock away

imprisoned adj **confined**, jailed, captive, restrained, trapped Opposite: free

imprisonment n **custody**, captivity, detention, term, internment

improbability n **unlikelihood**, implausibility, dubiousness, doubtfulness, questionability Opposite: probability

improbable adj **unlikely**, doubtful, implausible, questionable, dubious Opposite: likely

impromptu adj **unprepared**, unrehearsed, unplanned, spontaneous, spur-of-the-moment Opposite: prepared

improper adj **1** (fml) **indecorous**, inappropriate, unsuitable, out of place, unfitting Opposite: fitting **2 rude**, shocking, indecent, inappropriate, unacceptable Opposite: proper **3 dishonest**, irregular, shady,

illegal, criminal Opposite: honest

impropriety n **rudeness**, indecency, unseemliness, immodesty, bad behavior Opposite: propriety

improve v **1 look up**, perk up, get better, rally, mend Opposite: worsen **2 better**, enhance, ameliorate, enrich, upgrade Opposite: deteriorate **3 correct**, adjust, touch up, titivate, amend

improved adj **better**, enhanced, amended, upgraded, developed Opposite: deteriorated

improvement n **1 amendment**, correction, development, upgrade, enhancement Opposite: deterioration **2 recovery**, recuperation, rally, progress, advance Opposite: decline

improve on v **better**, go one better, top, beat, exceed

improvident adj **imprudent**, careless, reckless, negligent irresponsible Opposite: prudent

improvisation n **1 inventiveness**, invention, creativeness, lateral thinking **2 extemporization**, ad-libbing, standup

improvise v **1 ad-lib**, extemporize, create, make up, invent Opposite: orchestrate **2 contrive**, concoct, invent, create, devise

improvised adj **unpremeditated**, ad hoc, unplanned, makeshift, spontaneous Opposite: prepared

imprudence n **profligacy**, carelessness, indiscretion, rashness, injudiciousness Opposite: prudence

imprudent adj **foolish**, impulsive, indiscreet, irresponsible, rash Opposite: prudent

impudence n **impertinence**, boldness, insolence, nerve, effrontery Opposite: respect

impudent adj **bold**, brazen, insolent, rude, disrespectful Opposite: respectful

impugn (fml) v **question**, dispute, call into question, doubt, query

impulse n **1 instinct**, desire, urge, whim, compulsion Opposite: aversion (fml) **2 propulsion**, motive power, drive, stimulus, pressure **3 tick**, pulse, nerve, pulsation, beat

impulsion n **1 push**, propulsion, thrust, momentum, impetus **2 desire**, yen, compulsion, instinct, whim Opposite: aversion (fml)

impulsive adj **unwary**, thoughtless, impetuous, imprudent, precipitate Opposite: cautious

impulsively adv **unwarily**, thoughtlessly, on impulse, impetuously, spontaneously Opposite: deliberately

impulsiveness n **precipitateness**, suddenness, thoughtlessness, impetuosity, spontaneity Opposite: deliberation (fml)

impunity n **license**, exemption, freedom, liberty, latitude

impure adj **contaminated**, adulterated, mixed, tainted, polluted Opposite: pure

impurity n **contamination**, pollution, adulteration, uncleanness, infection *Opposite*: purity

imputation n **accusation**, assertion, attribution, reproach, complaint

impute v **1 credit**, chalk up, attribute, accredit, assign **2 complain**, accuse, implicate, allege, assert

in prep **inside**, within, around *Opposite*: outside ■ adv **around**, inside, accessible, available, at home *Opposite*: out ■ adj **cutting-edge**, fashionable, popular, now, in vogue *Opposite*: out

inability n **incapability**, incapacity, powerlessness, helplessness, failure *Opposite*: ability

inaccessibility n **1 unreachability**, remoteness, distance, isolation, unapproachability *Opposite*: approachability **2 unattainability**, unavailability, unaffordability, impossibility, confidentiality *Opposite*: accessibility **3 difficulty**, obscurity, obscureness, obliqueness, impenetrability *Opposite*: lucidity

inaccessible adj **1 unreachable**, out-of-the-way, unapproachable, hard to find, remote *Opposite*: approachable **2 difficult**, obscure, esoteric, abstruse, oblique *Opposite*: simple

inaccuracy n **1 imprecision**, inexactness, mistakenness, wrongness, erroneousness *Opposite*: precision **2 error**, mistake, slip, flaw, blunder. *See* COMPARE AND CONTRAST *at* **mistake**.

inaccurate adj **imprecise**, inexact, mistaken, erroneous, wrong *Opposite*: precise

inaction n **1 failure to act**, indecision, procrastination, fumbling, delay *Opposite*: decisiveness **2 inactivity**, laziness, idleness, inertia, apathy *Opposite*: energy

inactivate v **deactivate**, put out of action, incapacitate, disable, turn off *Opposite*: set in motion

inactive adj **1 motionless**, stationary, unmoving, immobile, stopped *Opposite*: moving **2 idle**, dormant, out of action, unused, inoperative *Opposite*: working **3 sedentary**, lazy, slothful, indolent, sluggish *Opposite*: energetic

inactivity n **1 motionlessness**, immobility, stillness *Opposite*: motion **2 idleness**, dormancy, inoperativeness *Opposite*: activity **3 sedentariness**, laziness, sloth, indolence, sluggishness *Opposite*: energy

in addition to prep **as well as**, along with, on top of, besides, over and above

inadequacy n **1 insufficiency**, meagerness, scantiness, lack, shortage *Opposite*: sufficiency **2 fault**, failure, failing, incompetence, defectiveness *Opposite*: asset

inadequate adj **1 insufficient**, scarce, derisory, laughable, poor *Opposite*: sufficient **2 incompetent**, lacking, deficient, ineffective, inefficient *Opposite*: capable

inadmissible adj **unacceptable**, prohibited, excluded, barred, disallowed *Opposite*: acceptable

inadvertence n **1 carelessness**, inattention, negligence, thoughtlessness, laxity **2 oversight**, omission, error, mistake, blunder

inadvertency *see* **inadvertence**

inadvertent adj **unintentional**, careless, unintended, involuntary, unplanned *Opposite*: intentional

inadvisable adj **ill-advised**, imprudent, unwise, foolish, injudicious *Opposite*: wise

inalienable (fml) adj **unchallengeable**, absolute, immutable, unassailable, incontrovertible *Opposite*: disputable

in all adv **ultimately**, altogether, all in all, as a whole, all told

inane adj **silly**, unintelligent, absurd, ridiculous, stupid *Opposite*: sensible

inanimate adj **1 lifeless**, dead, nonliving, inorganic, inert *Opposite*: alive **2 inactive**, dull, unresponsive, apathetic, listless *Opposite*: spirited

inanity n **1 meaninglessness**, senselessness, stupidity, ridiculousness, absurdity *Opposite*: logic **2 silliness**, foolishness, frivolousness, stupidity, ridiculousness *Opposite*: sensibleness

inapplicability n **unsuitability**, inappropriateness, irrelevance, inaptness, wrongness *Opposite*: suitability

inapplicable adj **unsuitable**, irrelevant, inappropriate, inapposite, inapt *Opposite*: suitable

inapposite adj **unsuitable**, out of place, inappropriate, inapt, unfitting *Opposite*: suitable

inappositeness n **unsuitability**, inappropriateness, inaptness, wrongness, irrelevance *Opposite*: suitability

inappreciable adj **insignificant**, imperceptible, negligible, unimportant, immaterial *Opposite*: significant

inappreciably adv **insignificantly**, imperceptibly, negligibly, immaterially, microscopically *Opposite*: significantly

inappropriate adj **unsuitable**, unfitting, untimely, inapt, wrong *Opposite*: fitting

inappropriateness n **unsuitability**, impropriety, wrongness, incorrectness, unseemliness *Opposite*: appropriateness

inarticulacy n **1 incoherence**, hesitation, lack of fluency, stumbling, stuttering *Opposite*: eloquence **2 unintelligibility**, incomprehensibility, inaudibility, indistinctness, unclearness *Opposite*: clarity

inarticulate adj **1 tongue-tied**, incoherent, mumbling, hesitant, faltering *Opposite*: eloquent **2 garbled**, muttered, incoherent, unintelligible, incomprehensible *Opposite*: clear

inasmuch as conj **because**, insofar as, considering that, since, as

inattention n inattentiveness, daydreaming, woolgathering, distraction, abstraction Opposite: concentration

inattentive adj careless, distracted, abstracted, daydreaming, woolgathering Opposite: careful

inattentiveness n carelessness, inattention, daydreaming, distraction, abstraction Opposite: attention

inaudibility n quietness, faintness, imperceptibility, noiselessness, silence Opposite: audibility

inaudible adj quiet, low, faint, soft, silent Opposite: perceptible

inaugural adj opening, initial, first, introductory, foundational

inaugurate v 1 swear in, install, induct, instate, initiate Opposite: dismiss 2 open, launch, dedicate, initiate, unveil Opposite: close 3 initiate, establish, put in place, set up, start up Opposite: terminate (fml)

inauguration n 1 induction, investiture, installation, swearing in, inaugural ceremony Opposite: dismissal 2 opening, launch, opening ceremony, initiation ceremony, start Opposite: closure 3 initiation, creation, introduction, setting up, conception Opposite: closedown

inauspicious adj unpromising, discouraging, ill-starred, ill-fated, unfavorable Opposite: promising

inauthentic adj false, imitation, fake, forged, counterfeit Opposite: genuine

in between prep between, next to, sandwiched by, in the middle of, amid

in-between adj intermediate, separating, isolating, halfway, indeterminate ■ adv meanwhile, in the interval, in the intervening time, between times, at the same time

inborn adj innate, natural, instinctive, intuitive, inherited Opposite: acquired

inbound adj incoming, arriving, inward bound, coming in, heading toward

in-box n tray, pigeonhole, mailbox

inbred adj congenital, inherited, hereditary, ingrained, deep-seated Opposite: acquired

in brief adv briefly, in a few words, in short, to sum up, in a word

in-built adj innate, natural, inborn, inherent, instinctive Opposite: learned

incalculable adj 1 countless, without number, innumerable, infinite, multitudinous Opposite: finite 2 unpredictable, unforeseeable, indeterminable, uncertain, haphazard Opposite: predictable

incalculably adv greatly, infinitely, immeasurably, inestimably, immensely

incandesce v glow, radiate, shine, luminesce, fluoresce

incandescence n glow, luminosity, light, luminescence, fluorescence

incandescent adj glowing, radiant, luminous, shining, bright

incantation n chant, invocation, prayer, spell, charm

incapable adj 1 unable, powerless, inept, inexpert, unqualified Opposite: able 2 helpless, weak, vulnerable, feeble, frail Opposite: strong

incapacitate v debilitate, injure, harm, disable, lay up Opposite: enable

incapacitated adj debilitated, injured, harmed, disabled, laid up Opposite: fit

incapacity n 1 inability, ineffectiveness, incapability, powerlessness, weakness Opposite: ability 2 disability, infirmity, frailty, ill health

incarcerate (fml) v imprison, jail, lock up, hold prisoner, intern Opposite: free

incarceration (fml) n imprisonment, confinement, custody, captivity, internment Opposite: freedom

incarnate adj personified, in person, in the flesh, alive, embodied

incarnation n personification, embodiment, manifestation, avatar, living form

in case conj just in case, in the event, lest, if, whether or no

incautious adj careless, rash, reckless, impetuous, impulsive Opposite: careful

incendiary adj 1 inflammable, combustible, flammable 2 inflammatory, provocative, rabble-rousing, aggressive, stirring Opposite: conciliatory ■ n 1 (fml) troublemaker, agitator, demagogue, activist, firebrand 2 arsonist, pyromaniac, burner, firebomber, torcher (slang)

incense v enrage, anger, exasperate, infuriate, annoy Opposite: calm

incensed adj enraged, angry, exasperated, infuriated, irate Opposite: calm

incentive n inducement, motive, motivation, encouragement Opposite: disincentive. See COMPARE AND CONTRAST at motive.

inception (fml) n beginning, start, inauguration, initiation, foundation Opposite: culmination

incessant adj nonstop, never-ending, ceaseless, continuous, continual Opposite: sporadic

inch v creep, crawl, shuffle, edge

in charge adj in command, in control, at the helm, responsible, giving the orders

inchoate (fml) adj undeveloped, incipient, immature, beginning, budding Opposite: mature

incidence n occurrence, frequency, rate, commonness, prevalence

incident n 1 event, occurrence, occasion, happening, episode 2 confrontation, clash, skirmish, fight, episode

incidental adj related, accompanying, secondary, subsidiary, supplementary Opposite: essential

incidentally *adv* by the way, by the by, while we're on the subject, before I forget, parenthetically

incinerate *v* burn, burn up, set fire to, cremate, reduce to ashes

incinerator *n* furnace, brazier, kiln, oven, burner

incipient *adj* emerging, initial, embryonic, budding, early *Opposite*: final

incise *v* cut, slit, notch, score, carve

incision *n* cut, slit, opening, notch, scratch

incisive *adj* keen, perceptive, insightful, sharp, penetrating *Opposite*: dull

incite *v* provoke, inflame, rouse, goad, spur *Opposite*: quell

incitement *n* provocation, stimulation, agitation, encouragement, goad *Opposite*: deterrent

incivility *n* rudeness, impoliteness, discourteousness, discourtesy, lack of respect *Opposite*: politeness

inclement *adj* intemperate, extreme, severe, bad, foul *Opposite*: pleasant

inclination *n* 1 feeling, predisposition, disposition, leaning, proclivity *Opposite*: antipathy 2 slope, slant, incline, gradient, pitch

incline *v* 1 slant, slope, tilt, rise, fall 2 dispose, persuade, prejudice, bias, bring around *Opposite*: deter ■ *n* slope, slant, gradient, rise, ascent

inclined *adj* 1 motivated, persuaded, tending, disposed, apt *Opposite*: averse (*fml*) 2 leaning, sloping, slanting, tilting, orientated

include *v* 1 contain, comprise, take in, consist of, take account of *Opposite*: omit 2 bring in, incorporate, add in, enter, involve *Opposite*: reject

included *adj* contained within, counted in, comprised, encompassed, involved *Opposite*: omitted

including *prep* counting, as well as, with, together with, plus *Opposite*: excluding

inclusion *n* presence, addition, enclosure, insertion, annexation *Opposite*: absence

inclusive *adj* comprehensive, wide-ranging, all-encompassing, complete, broad *Opposite*: restricted

incognito *adv* in disguise, disguised, undercover, anonymously, secretly *Opposite*: openly

incoherence *n* unintelligibility, inarticulateness, disjointedness, illogicality, confusedness *Opposite*: coherence

incoherent *adj* 1 disjointed, confused, jumbled, illogical, all over the place (*infml*) *Opposite*: clear 2 inarticulate, unintelligible, incomprehensible, garbled, mumbled *Opposite*: articulate

incombustible *adj* fireproof, flameproof, fire-resistant, flame-resistant, fire-retardant *Opposite*: flammable

income *n* profits, proceeds, returns, revenue, earnings *Opposite*: expenditure

income tax *n* tax, toll, duty, excise, tariff

incoming *adj* 1 inbound, inward bound, homeward bound, arriving, entering *Opposite*: outgoing 2 new, next, succeeding, newly appointed, newly elected *Opposite*: outgoing

incommensurate *adj* disproportionate, unequal, inadequate, insufficient, lacking parity *Opposite*: proportionate

incommode (*fml*) *v* inconvenience, trouble, disturb, bother, put out

incommodious (*fml*) *adj* 1 cramped, restricted, confined, tiny, small *Opposite*: roomy 2 inconvenient, troublesome, awkward, annoying, bothersome

incommunicado *adj* not in contact, out of touch, not in communication, not able to communicate, unwilling to communicate

incomparable *adj* unequaled, unrivaled, unparalleled, unsurpassed, unmatched *Opposite*: ordinary

incompatibility *n* 1 mismatch, unsuitability, discordancy, inharmoniousness, irreconcilability 2 inconsistency, illogicality, irreconcilability, incongruity, mismatch *Opposite*: consistency

incompatible *adj* mismatched, unsuited, discordant, dissenting, irreconcilable *Opposite*: like-minded

incompetence *n* ineptitude, unskillfulness, inability, ineffectiveness, stupidity *Opposite*: ability

incompetent *adj* inept, useless, unskilled, ineffectual, hopeless *Opposite*: able

incomplete *adj* 1 imperfect, partial, unfinished, inadequate, half-finished *Opposite*: entire 2 unfinished, undeveloped, curtailed, shortened, deficient *Opposite*: finished

incomprehensible *adj* unintelligible, unfathomable, impenetrable, inexplicable, inconceivable *Opposite*: understandable

incomprehension *n* disbelief, incredulity, incredulousness, perplexity, blankness *Opposite*: understanding

inconceivable *adj* unimaginable, unthinkable, beyond belief, unbelievable, incredible *Opposite*: imaginable

inconclusive *adj* indecisive, questionable, unconvincing, unsatisfying, unsettled *Opposite*: decisive

in confidence *adv* in secret, confidentially, between ourselves, in private, privately *Opposite*: openly

incongruity *n* oddness, strangeness, absurdity, inappropriateness, inaptness *Opposite*: consistency

incongruous *adj* odd, strange, out of place, incompatible, inappropriate *Opposite*: consistent

in conjunction with *prep* together with, com-

bined with, along with, with, in addition
to Opposite: apart from

in consequence (fml) adv **accordingly**, as a
result, consequently, therefore, so

inconsequence n **unimportance**, irrelevance,
insignificance, triviality, inconsequentiality Opposite: importance

inconsequential adj **unimportant**, trivial,
petty, negligible, minor Opposite: important

inconsequentiality n **unimportance**, insignificance, triviality, frivolity, inconsequence Opposite: importance

inconsiderable adj **small**, minor, tiny,
paltry, negligible Opposite: sizable

inconsiderate adj **selfish**, thoughtless,
insensitive, uncharitable, unkind Opposite: caring

inconsistency n 1 **discrepancy**, contradiction, variation, variance, irregularity
2 **changeability**, unpredictability, unreliability, fickleness, capriciousness Opposite: consistency

inconsistent adj 1 **conflicting**, contradictory,
incompatible, incongruous, paradoxical
Opposite: consistent 2 **unpredictable**, variable, unreliable, erratic, changeable Opposite: constant

inconsolable adj **grief-stricken**, brokenhearted, devastated, desolate, despairing
Opposite: ecstatic

inconspicuous adj **unobtrusive**, discreet,
unremarkable, ordinary, modest Opposite:
obvious

inconstant adj 1 (literary) **unfaithful**, disloyal,
fickle, deceitful, false Opposite: faithful
2 **changeable**, variable, irregular, unpredictable, fluctuating Opposite: unchanging

incontestable adj **indisputable**, incontrovertible, irrefutable, unquestionable,
indubitable Opposite: arguable

incontrovertible adj **undeniable**, unquestionable, irrefutable, incontestable, indisputable Opposite: questionable

inconvenience n 1 **troublesomeness**, tire-
someness, inopportuneness, untimeliness,
awkwardness Opposite: benefit 2 **problem**,
trouble, bother, difficulty, nuisance ■
v **disrupt**, put out, trouble, bother, disturb
Opposite: help

inconvenient adj **troublesome**, tiresome,
inopportune, problematic, untimely Opposite: beneficial

in cooperation with prep **together with**, in
association with, in collaboration with,
alongside, in conjunction with

incorporate v 1 **include**, integrate, assimilate, fit in, add in Opposite: exclude
2 **merge**, combine, feature, contain, include Opposite: divide

incorporated adj **combined**, united, unified,
merged, fused Opposite: separate

incorporation n **combination**, amalgamation,
integration, assimilation, merger Opposite: separation

incorporeal (fml) adj **intangible**, ethereal,
spiritual, unreal, disembodied Opposite:
tangible

incorrect adj 1 **erroneous**, wrong, mistaken,
untrue, inaccurate Opposite: right 2 **improper**, unfitting, inappropriate, unseemly,
unbecoming Opposite: proper

incorrectness n 1 **erroneousness**, error,
fallacy, wrongness, mistakenness Opposite: correctness 2 **impropriety**, inappropriateness, unsuitability, unseemliness,
indecorousness Opposite: propriety

incorrigible adj **irredeemable**, habitual,
inveterate, dyed-in-the-wool, persistent
Opposite: tractable

incorruptible adj 1 **moral**, principled, just,
straight, honorable Opposite: venal
2 **imperishable**, everlasting, immortal,
indestructible, unchanging Opposite: perishable

increase v **enlarge**, extend, expand, amplify,
swell Opposite: decrease ■ n **upsurge**,
surge, rise, growth, intensification Opposite: decrease

COMPARE AND CONTRAST CORE MEANING: make
larger or greater
increase become or cause to become larger
in number, quantity, degree, or scope; **expand**
become or cause to become larger or more
extensive; **enlarge** become or cause to become
larger generally, or broaden in scope and detail;
extend make larger in terms of length, area,
period of time, or other existing limits; **augment**
(fml) add to something in order to make it larger
or more substantial; **intensify** become or cause
to become greater in strength or degree; **amplify**
become or cause to become louder, or greater
in intensity or scope.

incredible adj 1 **unbelievable**, implausible,
improbable, far-fetched, absurd Opposite:
believable 2 **amazing**, astonishing, extraordinary, staggering, unbelievable Opposite: unremarkable 3 (infml) **excellent**,
superb, tremendous, prodigious, phenomenal Opposite: mediocre

incredibly adv 1 **unbelievably**, implausibly,
inconceivably, absurdly, improbably
Opposite: believably 2 (infml) **very**, extremely, unbelievably, amazingly, really

incredulity n **disbelief**, amazement, astonishment, doubt, skepticism Opposite:
belief

incredulous adj **disbelieving**, skeptical,
unbelieving, doubtful, doubting Opposite:
believing

increment n **increase**, addition, raise, rise,
growth Opposite: cut

incriminate v **implicate**, impeach, give away,
lay the blame on, convict Opposite: exonerate

in-crowd *(infml)* n **inner circle**, beau monde, high society, clique, elite

incrustation n **coating**, crust, layer, covering, accumulation

incubate v **hatch**, gestate, raise, rear, nurture

incubation n **development**, gestation, cultivation, nurture, growth *Opposite*: destruction

inculcate v **impress upon**, teach, drum into, instruct, drill into

incumbency *(fml)* n **1 tenure**, period of office, term of office, term, time **2 post**, position, office, appointment **3 duty**, obligation, responsibility, office, task

incumbent *adj (fml)* **obligatory**, mandatory, compulsory, binding, unavoidable *Opposite*: optional ■ n **official**, office holder, occupant, appointee, officer

incur v **1 experience**, suffer, sustain, bring upon yourself, lay yourself open to *Opposite*: avoid **2 sustain**, meet with, encounter, experience, suffer

incurable *adj* **1 terminal**, fatal, deadly, inoperable, untreatable *Opposite*: curable **2 irredeemable**, inveterate, incorrigible, hopeless, undying *Opposite*: redeemable

incurious *adj* **uninterested**, indifferent, unmoved, unconcerned, detached *Opposite*: inquisitive

incursion n **1 raid**, night raid, attack, sortie, invasion *Opposite*: retreat **2** *(fml)* **intrusion**, invasion, spread, infiltration, arrival

in custody *adj* **under arrest**, in prison, in detention, detained, remanded

indebted *adj* **obligated**, obliged, grateful, thankful, in somebody's debt *Opposite*: ungrateful

indebtedness n **obligation**, gratitude, appreciation, thankfulness, gratefulness *Opposite*: ingratitude

indecency n **1 offensiveness**, coarseness, crudeness, lewdness, obscenity *Opposite*: decency **2 impropriety**, unsuitability, unseemliness, indecorousness, indelicacy *Opposite*: propriety

indecent *adj* **1 offensive**, coarse, rude, crude, obscene *Opposite*: decorous **2 improper**, unsuitable, unseemly, indecorous, unbecoming *Opposite*: proper

indecipherable *adj* **1 illegible**, incomprehensible, unintelligible, unreadable, indistinct *Opposite*: legible **2 impenetrable**, inscrutable, obscure, unfathomable, enigmatic *Opposite*: clear

indecision n **irresolution**, hesitancy, indecisiveness, uncertainty, vacillation *Opposite*: decisiveness

indecisive *adj* **1 irresolute**, vacillating, wavering, hesitant, unsure *Opposite*: decisive **2 inconclusive**, indefinite, indeterminate, tentative, unclear *Opposite*: conclusive

indecisiveness n **1 irresolution**, hesitancy, hesitation, vacillation, uncertainty *Opposite*: decisiveness **2 indefiniteness**, inconclusiveness, woolliness, vagueness, indeterminacy *Opposite*: certainty

indecorous *adj* **impolite**, rude, shocking, inappropriate, unseemly *Opposite*: polite

indecorum n **impoliteness**, bad behavior, rudeness, offensiveness, impropriety *Opposite*: politeness

indeed *adv* **1 certainly**, really, to be sure, undeniably, definitely **2 in reality**, in fact, actually, in truth, as a matter of fact

indefatigable *adj* **untiring**, unflagging, unrelenting, remorseless, unfaltering *Opposite*: half-hearted

indefensible *adj* **1 inexcusable**, unpardonable, unforgivable, unjustifiable, unwarrantable *Opposite*: excusable **2 unprotected**, exposed, vulnerable, undefended, defenseless *Opposite*: impregnable **3 invalid**, untenable, unsustainable, shaky, weak *Opposite*: valid

indefinable *adj* **indescribable**, inexpressible, vague, indefinite, obscure

indefinite *adj* **1 unlimited**, unfixed, unspecified, unknown, indeterminate *Opposite*: specified **2 unclear**, imprecise, vague, hazy, woolly *Opposite*: precise **3 vague**, uncertain, undecided, unclear, noncommittal *Opposite*: certain

indefinitely *adv* **until further notice**, for the foreseeable future, for life, forever, ad infinitum

indelible *adj* **1 permanent**, fixed, ineradicable, fast, stubborn *Opposite*: temporary **2 unforgettable**, deep-seated, deep-rooted, lasting, enduring *Opposite*: temporary

indelibly *adv* **permanently**, ineradicably, lastingly, forever, for good *Opposite*: temporarily

indelicacy n **tactlessness**, offensiveness, tastelessness, crudeness, unseemliness *Opposite*: politeness

indelicate *adj* **tactless**, offensive, improper, unseemly, impolite *Opposite*: polite

indemnify v **1 insure**, underwrite, cover, assure, protect **2 reimburse**, compensate, repay, pay, refund

indemnity n **1 insurance**, protection, cover, life insurance, security **2 compensation**, reimbursement, remuneration, reparation, payment

indent v **1 hollow out**, dent, depress, stave in, scoop **2 notch**, serrate, nick, pink, incise

indentation n **1 notch**, groove, serration, nick, incision **2 hollow**, dent, depression, scoop, gouge

indenture n **contract**, arrangement, pact, deal, agreement

independence n **1 self-sufficiency**, self-reliance, self-determination, freedom, autonomy *Opposite*: helplessness **2 self-government**, sovereignty, autonomy, self-rule, self-determination *Opposite*: subjection **3 individuality**, freedom, liberation, unconventionality *Opposite*: conventionality **4 impartiality**, objectivity, disinterest, neutrality, disinterestedness *Opposite*: partiality

independent *adj* **1 self-governing**, sovereign, autonomous, self-determining, self-regulating *Opposite*: dependent **2 self-sufficient**, self-reliant, autonomous, self-supporting, self-contained *Opposite*: dependent **3 free**, liberated, individual, individualistic, unconventional *Opposite*: conventional **4 impartial**, detached, objective, dispassionate, neutral *Opposite*: partial

in depth *adv* **at length**, painstakingly, in detail, thoroughly, exhaustively *Opposite*: superficially

in-depth *adj* **painstaking**, detailed, exhaustive, thorough, comprehensive *Opposite*: superficial

indescribable *adj* **1 indefinable**, inexpressible, unutterable, incommunicable, unspeakable **2 extreme**, great, tremendous, intense, dramatic

indestructible *adj* **1 abiding**, durable, everlasting, imperishable, eternal *Opposite*: perishable **2 unbreakable**, nonbreaking, resistant, shatterproof, rock-solid *Opposite*: fragile

indeterminable *adj* **1 unknowable**, indefinable, indescribable, impalpable *(fml) Opposite*: knowable **2 unresolvable**, unanswerable, uncountable *Opposite*: answerable

indeterminate *adj* **1 unknown**, unpredictable, undefined, unspecified, unstipulated *Opposite*: known **2 vague**, imprecise, uncertain, unclear, inexact *Opposite*: definite

index *n* **1 catalog**, directory, guide, file, key **2 indication**, indicator, symbol, pointer, sign

indicate *v* **1 point to**, point at, point out, show, point toward **2 denote**, signify, be a sign of, imply, suggest **3 make known**, demonstrate, show, display, express

indication *n* **sign**, suggestion, signal, hint, warning

indicative *adj* **revealing**, symptomatic, telling, telltale, suggestive

indicator *n* **pointer**, needle, gauge, dial, display

indict *v* **accuse**, impeach, summons, prosecute, arraign *Opposite*: exonerate

indictable *adj* **criminal**, unlawful, illegal, chargeable, felonious

indictment *n* **1 accusation**, impeachment, summons, prosecution, arraignment *Opposite*: exoneration **2 condemnation**, denunciation, criticism, comment, censure *Opposite*: praise

indifference *n* **1 apathy**, coldness, coolness, unconcern, disinterest *Opposite*: concern **2 unimportance**, insignificance, inconsequence, meaninglessness, irrelevance *Opposite*: importance

indifferent *adj* **1 uncaring**, uninterested, unresponsive, apathetic, unsympathetic *Opposite*: concerned **2 average**, mediocre, moderate, undistinguished, middling *Opposite*: exceptional

indigence *(fml) n* **poverty**, need, penury, deprivation, destitution *Opposite*: wealth

indigenous *adj* **native**, original, aboriginal, homegrown, local *Opposite*: immigrant. *See* COMPARE AND CONTRAST *at* **native**.

indigent *(fml) adj* **poor**, needy, impoverished, poverty-stricken, penniless *Opposite*: wealthy

indigestible *adj* **1 heavy**, rich, tough, inedible, stodgy *(infml) Opposite*: edible **2 incomprehensible**, impenetrable, unreadable, complex, obscure *Opposite*: readable

indigestion *n* **heartburn**, stomachache, upset stomach, colic, gastritis

indignant *adj* **angry**, furious, vexed, irate, outraged *Opposite*: mollified

indignation *n* **anger**, resentment, outrage, annoyance, exasperation *Opposite*: delight. *See* COMPARE AND CONTRAST *at* **anger**.

indignity *n* **humiliation**, shame, disgrace, mortification, embarrassment *Opposite*: glory

indirect *adj* **1 circuitous**, roundabout, rambling, circumlocutory, tortuous *Opposite*: straight **2 unintended**, unplanned, secondary, ancillary, subsidiary *Opposite*: intended **3 devious**, oblique, implicit, tacit, implied *Opposite*: overt

indiscernible *adj* **imperceptible**, invisible, inaudible, unnoticeable, undetectable *Opposite*: perceptible

indiscipline *n* **disorderliness**, rowdiness, unruliness, insubordination, disruptiveness *Opposite*: control

indiscreet *adj* **1 careless**, injudicious, imprudent, incautious, unthinking *Opposite*: careful **2 tactless**, undiplomatic, unsubtle, garrulous, indelicate *Opposite*: tactful

indiscretion *n* **1 carelessness**, injudiciousness, imprudence, lack of caution, recklessness *Opposite*: carefulness **2 tactlessness**, garrulousness, indelicateness, nosiness *(infml)* **3 transgression**, impropriety, peccadillo, misdemeanor, misdeed

indiscriminate *adj* **1 unselective**, undiscriminating, undiscerning, uncritical, broad *Opposite*: selective **2 haphazard**, random, arbitrary, wholesale, blanket *Opposite*: planned

indispensable *adj* **necessary**, essential, crucial, vital, required *Opposite*: unnecessary. *See* COMPARE AND CONTRAST *at* **necessary**.

indisposed *(fml)* adj **1 sick**, unwell, ill, laid up, under the weather *Opposite*: well **2 unwilling**, disinclined, reluctant, loath, loth *Opposite*: willing

indisposition n **1 illness**, complaint, condition, problem, debility *Opposite*: health **2 reluctance**, unwillingness, disinclination, refusal, resistance *Opposite*: willingness

indisputable *(fml)* adj **indubitable**, unquestionable, undeniable, incontrovertible, irrefutable *Opposite*: debatable

indissoluble adj **binding**, unbreakable, enduring, everlasting, eternal *Opposite*: temporary

indistinct adj **1 unclear**, hazy, dim, misty, blurred *Opposite*: clear **2 inaudible**, imperceptible, faint, soft, low *Opposite*: audible **3 vague**, imprecise, inexact, indefinite, indeterminate *Opposite*: definite

indistinctive adj **ordinary**, dull, everyday, unexceptional, unmemorable *Opposite*: unique

indistinctness n **1 blurriness**, haziness, fuzziness, mistiness, dimness *Opposite*: clarity **2 unclearness**, inarticulacy, faintness, softness *Opposite*: audibility

indistinguishable adj **1 undifferentiated**, homogeneous, identical, the same, interchangeable *Opposite*: separable **2 vague**, blurry, hazy, fuzzy, misty *Opposite*: clear **3 inaudible**, inarticulate, unintelligible, faint, soft *Opposite*: clear

individual n **person**, human being, entity, character, personality ■ adj **1 separable**, singular, separate, discrete, distinct **2 particularized**, special, private, exclusive, particular *Opposite*: collective **3 unusual**, distinctive, original, idiosyncratic, individualistic *Opposite*: ordinary

individualism n **uniqueness**, egoism, individuality, independence, selfishness *Opposite*: conformity

individualist n **free spirit**, nonconformist, eccentric, rebel, maverick *Opposite*: conformist

individuality n **independence**, uniqueness, eccentricity, personality, distinctiveness *Opposite*: conformity

individualize v **adapt**, modify, customize, personalize, convert

individually adv **separately**, independently, alone, on your own, by yourself *Opposite*: together

indivisible adj **inseparable**, united, amalgamated, blended, conjoined *(fml)* *Opposite*: separable

indoctrinate v **instruct**, program, train, teach, coach

indoctrination n **instruction**, programming, propaganda, brainwashing, training

indolence n **laziness**, idleness, lethargy, sloth, inactivity *Opposite*: energy

indolent adj **lazy**, lethargic, idle, sluggish, slothful *Opposite*: energetic

indomitable adj **unconquerable**, strong, resolute, determined, stubborn *Opposite*: submissive

indoor adj **inside**, interior, covered, enclosed, internal *Opposite*: outdoor

indoors adv **inside**, in, within, at home, in the house *Opposite*: outside

indubitable adj **unquestionable**, definite, certain, positive, undoubted *Opposite*: questionable

induce v **1 persuade**, encourage, tempt, make, bring *Opposite*: dissuade **2 bring on**, bring about, provoke, stimulate, produce *Opposite*: deter

inducement n **stimulus**, incentive, encouragement, carrot, enticement *Opposite*: disincentive. *See* COMPARE AND CONTRAST *at* **motive**.

induct v **1 inaugurate**, swear in, initiate, welcome, receive **2 introduce**, initiate, train, instruct, educate

induction n **1 introduction**, initiation, training, instruction, orientation **2 inauguration**, investiture, reception, installment, swearing in **3 bringing on**, stimulation, generation, production, provocation

in due course adv **afterward**, eventually, in good time, ultimately, in the end

indulge v **treat**, spoil, pamper, pander, cosset *Opposite*: deny

indulgence n **1 treat**, luxury, extravagance, pleasure *Opposite*: necessity **2 tolerance**, lenience, understanding, clemency, sympathy *Opposite*: strictness

indulgent adj **permissive**, kind, lenient, tolerant, generous *Opposite*: strict

industrial adj **1 manufacturing**, engineering, trade, business, work **2 developed**, built-up, industrialized, mechanized, manufacturing

industrial espionage n **espionage**, spying, intelligence gathering, surveillance, bugging

industrialist n **manufacturer**, entrepreneur, magnate, mogul, captain of industry

industrialization n **industrial development**, economic development, development, economic growth, progress

industrialize v **change**, mechanize, develop, mass-produce, automate

industrialized adj **industrial**, developed, technologically advanced, manufacturing, commercial *Opposite*: agrarian

industrial park n **industrial zone**, enterprise zone, business park, industrial development, science park

industrious adj **diligent**, hard-working, busy, productive, conscientious *Opposite*: indolent

industriousness n **diligence**, hard work, application, conscientiousness, productiveness *Opposite*: indolence

industry n 1 **manufacturing**, business, commerce, trade, engineering 2 *(fml or literary)* **hard work**, diligence, productivity, conscientiousness, activity *Opposite*: indolence

inebriated adj **drunk**, intoxicated, liquored up *(infml)*, plastered *(infml)*, smashed *(infml)* *Opposite*: sober

inedible adj **uneatable**, indigestible, unpalatable, revolting, bad *Opposite*: edible

ineffable *(fml)* adj **indescribable**, inexpressible, unutterable, beyond words, overwhelming

ineffective adj **unsuccessful**, unproductive, useless, vain, futile *Opposite*: successful

ineffectiveness n **unsuccessfulness**, unproductiveness, uselessness, futility, hopelessness *Opposite*: success

ineffectual adj **incompetent**, indecisive, weak, feeble, useless *Opposite*: competent

ineffectuality n **incompetence**, indecisiveness, inadequacy, uselessness, feebleness *Opposite*: competence

inefficiency n 1 **unproductiveness**, wastefulness, laxness *Opposite*: efficiency 2 **disorganization**, incompetence, inadequacy, ineptitude, ineffectiveness *Opposite*: competence

inefficient adj 1 **unproductive**, wasteful, uneconomical, lax, timewasting *Opposite*: efficient 2 **incompetent**, inept, disorganized, ineffectual, inadequate *Opposite*: competent

inelastic adj **inflexible**, rigid, unbendable, stiff, unyielding *Opposite*: stretchy

inelegance n 1 **unsophistication**, lack of style, tastelessness, bad taste, vulgarity *Opposite*: stylishness 2 **clumsiness**, awkwardness, gracelessness, coarseness, roughness *Opposite*: grace

inelegant adj 1 **unstylish**, unsophisticated, tasteless, vulgar, unpolished *Opposite*: stylish 2 **clumsy**, awkward, ungainly, maladroit, graceless *Opposite*: graceful

ineligible adj **unqualified**, disqualified, barred, disallowed, banned *Opposite*: entitled

ineluctable *(literary)* adj **unavoidable**, inescapable, inevitable, certain, sure *Opposite*: avoidable

inept adj **incompetent**, inexpert, clumsy, useless, hopeless *Opposite*: competent

ineptitude n **incompetence**, clumsiness, uselessness, ineffectiveness, lack of ability *Opposite*: competence

ineptness see **ineptitude**

inequality n **disparity**, dissimilarity, variation, difference, discrimination *Opposite*: parity

inequitable adj **unfair**, unjust, unbalanced, undemocratic, unequal *Opposite*: fair

inequity *(fml)* n **unfairness**, injustice, discrimination, inequality, bias *Opposite*: fairness

ineradicable adj **indelible**, enduring, lasting, ingrained, stubborn *Opposite*: fleeting

inert adj 1 **motionless**, still, lifeless, immobile, unmoving *Opposite*: moving 2 **sluggish**, slow, inactive, passive, torpid *Opposite*: active

inertia n **apathy**, inactivity, torpor, lethargy, inaction *Opposite*: activity

inescapable adj **inevitable**, unavoidable, bound to happen, certain, patent *Opposite*: avoidable

in essence adv **fundamentally**, intrinsically, basically, essentially, at heart

inessential adj **unnecessary**, unneeded, superfluous, redundant, dispensable *Opposite*: necessary

inestimable adj **incalculable**, immeasurable, great, fathomless, enormous *Opposite*: measurable

inevitability n **unavoidability**, predictability, certainty, inescapability, irrevocability

inevitable adj **unavoidable**, predictable, expected, foreseeable to be expected *Opposite*: avoidable

inevitably adv **unavoidably**, inescapably, without doubt, certainly, predictably

inexact adj **imprecise**, inaccurate, vague, rough, approximate *Opposite*: precise

inexactness n **imprecision**, vagueness, uncertainty, roughness approximation *Opposite*: precision

in excess of prep **more than**, beyond, above, over and above, exceeding *Opposite*: below

inexcusable adj **unpardonable**, unforgivable, uncalled-for, intolerable, indefensible *Opposite*: excusable

inexhaustible adj **everlasting**, infinite, unlimited, never-ending, bottomless *Opposite*: limited

inexorability *(fml)* n **inevitability**, unavoidability, inescapability, relentlessness, certainty

inexorable adj 1 *(fml)* **unstoppable**, inevitable, unavoidable, inescapable, unchangeable 2 **adamant**, obstinate, obdurate, unyielding, unbending

inexorableness *(fml)* see **inexorability**

inexpedient adj 1 **inconvenient**, impractical, inopportune, untimely, ill-timed *Opposite*: convenient 2 *(fml)* **inadvisable**, inappropriate, unwise, unsuitable, injudicious *Opposite*: advisable

inexpensive adj **cheap**, low-cost, low-priced, economical, budget *Opposite*: costly

inexperience n **greenness**, rawness, innocence, immaturity, naiveté *Opposite*: experience

inexperienced adj **green**, inexpert, raw, new, innocent *Opposite*: seasoned

inexpert adj **unskilled**, clumsy, inept, inexperienced, untrained *Opposite*: skilled

inexplicable *adj* **unaccountable**, mysterious, incomprehensible, unfathomable, bizarre *Opposite*: explicable

inexplicit *adj* **imprecise**, vague, ambiguous, hazy, sketchy *Opposite*: precise

inexpressible *adj* **indescribable**, beyond words, overwhelming, deep, indefinable

inexpressive *adj* **emotionless**, impassive, soulless, deadpan, unemotional *Opposite*: animated

inextricable *adj* **complicated**, complex, tricky, involved, knotty *Opposite*: simple

inextricably *adv* **indissolubly**, inseparably, indistinguishably, intimately, indivisibly

in fact *adv* **actually**, in actual fact, in effect, in reality, really *Opposite*: in theory

infallibility *n* **1 dependability**, soundness, reliability, trustworthiness, steadiness *Opposite*: fallibility **2 perfection**, rightness, flawlessness, correctness, exactitude *Opposite*: inaccuracy

infallible *adj* **1 dependable**, unfailing, foolproof, reliable, sound *Opposite*: unreliable **2 perfect**, right, correct, exact, accurate *Opposite*: imperfect

infallibly *adv* **dependably**, unfailingly, without fail, reliably, always *Opposite*: unreliably

infamous *adj* **1 notorious**, disreputable, ill-famed, ill-reputed, dishonorable *Opposite*: reputable **2 abominable**, villainous, wicked, iniquitous, loathsome *Opposite*: illustrious

infamy *n* **1 notoriety**, ill repute, ill fame, shame, disrepute *Opposite*: esteem **2 disgrace**, scandal, outrage, abomination, atrocity *Opposite*: good deed

infancy *n* **1 babyhood**, childhood, early years, youth, immaturity *Opposite*: adulthood **2 beginning**, early stages, embryonic stage, initial stages, first phase *Opposite*: conclusion

infant *n* **baby**, child, newborn, babe in arms, toddler *Opposite*: adult

infantile *adj* **1 childish**, babyish, immature, puerile, juvenile *Opposite*: mature **2 childhood**, juvenile, infant, baby, youthful *Opposite*: adult

infatuated *adj* **in love**, lovesick, obsessed, besotted, captivated *Opposite*: disenchanted

infatuation *n* **passion**, obsession, craze, love, fascination *Opposite*: disenchantment. *See* COMPARE AND CONTRAST *at* **love**.

in favor of *prep* **for**, all for, supporting, on the side of, supportive of *Opposite*: against

infect *v* **1 contaminate**, pollute, taint, poison, blight *Opposite*: cleanse **2 pervert**, corrupt, deprave, debase, defile *(fml) Opposite*: redeem **3 influence**, affect, afflict, touch, inspire

infected *adj* **1 contaminated**, polluted,

tainted, poisoned, impure *Opposite*: pure **2 ill**, diseased, sick, infested, disease-ridden *Opposite*: healthy **3 septic**, festering, weeping, pus-filled, purulent *Opposite*: healthy **4 affected**, influenced, touched, inspired, moved *Opposite*: untouched

infection *n* **1 contagion**, contamination, pollution, taint, poison **2 disease**, illness, virus, blight, bug *(infm)* **3 corruption**, perversion, depravity, debasement, debauchery *(fml)*

infectious *adj* **1 communicable**, catching, transferable, transmittable, transmissible **2 irresistible**, compelling, captivating, alluring, contagious

infective *adj* **infectious**, communicable, catching, transferable, transmittable

infer *v* **1 conclude**, deduce, suppose, gather, understand **2 imply**, suggest, insinuate, hint

inference *n* **1 implication**, extrapolation, corollary, interpretation, reading **2 conclusion**, deduction, supposition, conjecture, presumption

inferior *adj* **1 mediocre**, lesser, lower, substandard, poorer *Opposite*: superior **2 lower**, junior, secondary, subordinate, subsidiary *Opposite*: superior ■ *n* junior, subordinate, underling, vassal, menial *(fml) Opposite*: superior

inferiority *n* **1 mediocrity**, weakness, inadequacy, shoddiness, meanness *Opposite*: superiority **2 lowliness**, humbleness, subordination, subservience, subsidiarity *Opposite*: superiority

inferiority complex *n* **inadequacy**, anxiety, phobia, depression, obsession

inferno *n* **1 conflagration**, blaze, fire, firestorm, flames **2 hellhole**, hell, underworld, perdition, fire and brimstone *Opposite*: heaven

infertile *adj* **sterile**, unproductive, barren, unfruitful, childless *Opposite*: fertile

infertility *n* **sterility**, barrenness, childlessness, aridity, unproductiveness *Opposite*: fertility

infest *v* **overrun**, fill, invade, infiltrate, pervade

infestation *n* **plague**, invasion, swarm, influx, infiltration

infidelity *n* **unfaithfulness**, faithlessness, disloyalty, betrayal, adultery *Opposite*: faithfulness

infighting *n* **rivalry**, internal strife, competitiveness, backbiting, squabbling

infiltrate *v* **penetrate**, permeate, gain access to, break into, creep into

infiltration *n* **penetration**, permeation, access, intrusion, insinuation

infiltrator *n* **mole**, spy, secret agent, double agent, subversive

infinite *adj* **1 immeasurable**, never-ending,

endless, countless, unbounded *Opposite*: limited **2 extreme**, stupendous, great, immense, large *Opposite*: slight

infinitely *adv* **markedly**, a great deal, substantially, enormously, interminably *Opposite*: slightly

infinitesimal *adj* **tiny**, minute, minuscule, microscopic, insignificant *Opposite*: huge

infinity *n* **eternity**, immensity, endlessness, infinitude, boundlessness

infirm *adj* **unwell**, sick, ill, frail, in poor health *Opposite*: healthy. *See* COMPARE AND CONTRAST *at* **weak**.

infirmary *n* **hospital**, sanatorium, sickbay, hospice, medical center

infirmity *n* **ill health**, illness, frailty, disability, weakness *Opposite*: health

inflame *v* **1 arouse**, anger, fan, provoke, stir up *Opposite*: calm **2 exacerbate**, aggravate, fuel, intensify, increase *Opposite*: diminish

inflamed *adj* **reddened**, swollen, irritated, tender, sore

inflammable *adj* **flammable**, combustible, ignitable, incendiary *Opposite*: nonflammable

inflammation *n* **irritation**, swelling, soreness, tenderness, redness

inflammatory *adj* **provocative**, seditious, rabble-rousing, fiery, stirring *Opposite*: placatory

inflatable *adj* **blow-up**, pump-up, expandable

inflate *v* **1 blow up**, pump up, fill with air, expand, fill *Opposite*: deflate **2 exaggerate**, amplify, embellish, magnify, overestimate *Opposite*: understate **3 increase**, go up, drive up, escalate, boost *Opposite*: deflate

inflated *adj* **exaggerated**, overstated, overblown, puffed up, magnified *Opposite*: understated

inflation *n* **price rises**, rise, increase, price increases *Opposite*: deflation

inflationary *adj* **price-raising**, price-increasing, spiraling

inflect *v* **change**, modulate, vary, adjust, modify

inflection *n* **modulation**, nuance, variation, variety, accent

inflexibility *n* **1 stubbornness**, obstinacy, intransigence, rigor, dogmatism *Opposite*: tractability **2 rigidity**, stiffness, hardness, firmness, tautness *Opposite*: flexibility

inflexible *adj* **1 unbending**, stubborn, obstinate, uncompromising, strict *Opposite*: tractable **2 rigid**, stiff, hard, unbendable, firm *Opposite*: bendable

inflict *v* **impose**, exact, mete out, wreak, perpetrate *Opposite*: remove

in-flight *adj* **onboard**, mid-flight, airborne, midair

inflow *n* **influx**, arrival, invasion, incursion, introduction *Opposite*: outflow

influence *n* **1 effect**, inspiration, impact, stimulus, encouragement **2 power**, sway, authority, weight, control ■ *v* **1 sway**, manipulate, persuade, induce, win over **2 affect**, motivate, inspire, shape, have an effect on

influential *adj* **powerful**, important, significant, persuasive, dominant *Opposite*: ineffectual

influenza *n* **flu**, cold, virus, infection, respiratory tract infection

influx *n* **arrival**, invasion, incursion, flood, entry *Opposite*: outflow

info *(infml)* *n* **1 information**, data, statistics, facts, figures **2 news**, report, tidings, word, communication

infomercial *n* **commercial**, advertisement, promotional film, ad *(infml)*, promo *(infml)*

inform *v* **1 tell**, notify, let know, update, bring up-to-date *Opposite*: keep in the dark **2 blow the whistle on**, betray, denounce, tell on, tattle *Opposite*: keep mum *(infml)*

informal *adj* **1 relaxed**, casual, familiar, easy, comfortable *Opposite*: ceremonious **2 unofficial**, off-the-record, unauthorized, unsanctioned, confidential *Opposite*: official **3 colloquial**, idiomatic, vernacular, everyday, familiar *Opposite*: formal

informality *n* **casualness**, familiarity, ease, unpretentiousness, lack of formality *Opposite*: formality

informally *adv* **1 casually**, nonchalantly, easily, unceremoniously, offhandedly *Opposite*: ceremoniously **2 unofficially**, off the record, confidentially *Opposite*: officially

informant *n* **1 source**, guide, interpreter, adviser, tipster **2 informer**, spy, mole, tattletale, stool pigeon *(slang)*

information *n* **1 data**, statistics, facts, figures, material **2 news**, report, tidings, word, communication

information processing *n* **data processing**, data handling, data manipulation, data analysis, data transmission

information retrieval *n* **data storage and retrieval**, data storage, data retrieval, data processing, computer processing

information sheet *n* **newsletter**, brochure, leaflet, bulletin, communiqué

information superhighway *n* **Internet**, World Wide Web, infobahn, the Net *(infml)*, the Web *(infml)*

information technology *n* **IT**, computing, telecommunications, computer technology, electronic technology

informative *adj* **educational**, revealing, edifying, enlightening, useful *Opposite*: uncommunicative

informed *adj* **knowledgeable**, well-versed, conversant, up-to-date, educated *Opposite*: ignorant

informer n **informant**, spy, mole, tattletale, stool pigeon (slang)

infraction n **breach**, violation, infringement, contravention, transgression

infrastructure n **1 substructure**, organization, structure, setup, arrangement **2 public services**, communications, public transport, power supplies, water supplies

infrequency n **rarity**, irregularity, uncommonness, paucity, scarcity Opposite: frequency

infrequent adj **rare**, uncommon, occasional, intermittent, sporadic Opposite: frequent

infringe v **1 encroach on**, intrude on, interfere with, trespass, invade Opposite: respect **2 disobey**, disregard, breach, break, violate Opposite: obey

infringement n **1 breach**, violation, contravention, transgression, flouting Opposite: compliance **2 encroachment**, intrusion, invasion, interference, trespass

in front of prep **1 before**, ahead of, facing, opposite Opposite: behind **2 in the presence of**, with, in the company of, before, watched by

in full adv **completely**, fully, totally, in total, wholly Opposite: in part

infuriate v **enrage**, madden, incense, make your blood boil, annoy Opposite: calm

infuriated adj **enraged**, exasperated, furious, angry, incensed Opposite: calm

infuriating adj **maddening**, annoying, irritating, exasperating, galling Opposite: calming

infuse v **1 pervade**, fill, permeate, suffuse, imbue **2 instill**, impart, introduce, inculcate, imbue **3 steep**, soak, brew, immerse, saturate Opposite: drain

infusion n **brew**, tea, distillation, fermentation, drink

in general adv **1 as a whole**, generally, altogether, overall Opposite: in particular **2 in most cases**, generally, mainly, normally, usually Opposite: occasionally

ingenious adj **1 inventive**, clever, imaginative, resourceful, original Opposite: unimaginative **2 effective**, cunning, inspired, nifty (infml)

ingenuity n **inventiveness**, cleverness, resourcefulness, imagination, originality

ingenuous adj **1 innocent**, unworldly, artless, unsophisticated, naive Opposite: artful **2 honest**, direct, frank, open, straightforward Opposite: dishonest

ingenuousness n **1 openness**, straightforwardness, directness, honesty, candor Opposite: dishonesty **2 innocence**, unpretentiousness, unworldliness, gullibility, simplicity Opposite: artfulness

ingest v **absorb**, swallow, take in, consume, eat Opposite: vomit

inglenook n **hearthside**, fireside, nook, corner, recess

inglorious adj **shameful**, dishonorable, disgraceful, humiliating, unsuccessful Opposite: glorious

ingoing adj **incoming**, new, inward Opposite: outgoing

ingot n **slab**, nugget, lump, brick, block

ingrain v **impress**, etch, drill in, fix, root

ingrained adj **deep-seated**, in-built, entrenched, fixed, deep-rooted Opposite: superficial

ingratiate v **curry favor**, insinuate yourself, toady, get in with, grovel Opposite: alienate

ingratiating adj **sycophantic**, insinuative, obsequious, smarmy, deferential Opposite: proud

ingratitude n **rudeness**, unmannerliness, lack of appreciation, ungratefulness, thanklessness Opposite: gratitude

ingredient n **element**, component, part, constituent, factor

ingress (fml) n **entry**, entrance, opening, door, admission

in-group n **clique**, gang, faction, circle, elite

ingrowing adj **ingrown**, impacted, malformed, deformed

inhabit v **live**, reside, populate, occupy, squat

inhabitable adj **habitable**, civilized, usable, hospitable, livable Opposite: uninhabitable

inhabitant n **occupant**, resident, citizen, native, denizen

inhabited adj **populated**, populous, tenanted Opposite: uninhabited

inhalation n **breath**, gulp, gasp, pant, mouthful

inhale v **breathe in**, gasp, gulp, huff, pant Opposite: exhale

inhaler n **bronchodilator**, nebulizer, spray

in hand adj **1 under control**, receiving attention, under consideration, under deliberation, being dealt with Opposite: pending **2 unused**, remaining, spare, superfluous, available

inharmonious adj **1 discordant**, clashing, harsh, jarring, unmusical Opposite: harmonious **2 argumentative**, clashing, incompatible, disagreeable, antagonistic Opposite: cordial

inherent adj **characteristic**, essential, innate, natural, intrinsic Opposite: acquired

inherit v **receive**, accede to, come into, succeed to, take over Opposite: bequeath

inheritance n **heirloom**, tradition, legacy, bequest, birthright

inhibit v **1 slow**, stop, hold back, restrain, hinder **2 constrain**, hinder, prevent, impede, obstruct

inhibited adj **self-conscious**, reserved, introverted, repressed, subdued Opposite: uninhibited

inhibition n **reserve**, shyness, embarrassment, self-consciousness, reticence *Opposite*: spontaneity

inhospitable adj **1 unwelcoming**, unfriendly, unreceptive, uncongenial, uninviting *Opposite*: hospitable **2 harsh**, forbidding, bleak, desolate, barren *Opposite*: inviting

inhuman adj **1 cruel**, vicious, cold-blooded, inhumane, brutal *Opposite*: kind **2 cold-hearted**, unfeeling, insensitive, merciless, callous *Opposite*: sensitive **3 otherworldly**, weird, strange, unearthly, eerie *Opposite*: earthly

inhumane adj **cold-hearted**, cold-blooded, cruel, callous, brutal *Opposite*: humane

inhumanity n **cruelty**, cold-heartedness, mercilessness, viciousness, ruthlessness *Opposite*: humanity

inimical adj **1 unfavorable**, contrary, opposed, adverse, detrimental *Opposite*: favorable **2 hostile**, unfriendly, unwelcoming, cold, ill-disposed *Opposite*: friendly

inimitable adj **unique**, matchless, unmatched, incomparable, peerless *Opposite*: common

iniquitous adj **wicked**, heinous, sinful, bad, evil *Opposite*: good

iniquity n **wickedness**, evil, sin, vice, immorality *Opposite*: goodness

initial adj **first**, early, original, preliminary, opening *Opposite*: final

initialize v **reset**, prime, prepare, set, make ready *Opposite*: disable

initiate v **1 start**, introduce, originate, begin, open *Opposite*: finish **2 instruct**, induct, admit, introduce, teach *Opposite*: expel

initiation n **1 beginning**, start, opening, instigation, launch *Opposite*: end **2 introduction**, admission, induction, admittance, instruction *Opposite*: expulsion

initiative n **1 inventiveness**, creativity, wits, enterprise, resourcefulness **2 plan**, proposal, scheme, program, idea **3 pole position**, upper hand, advantage, edge, lead

initiator n **motivator**, inventor, originator, author, creator

inject v **1 vaccinate**, inoculate, give a shot *(infml)* **2 bring**, add, introduce, insert, instill *Opposite*: remove

injection n **1 inoculation**, dose, vaccination, booster, shot *(infml)* **2 addition**, instillation, insertion, introduction, infusion *Opposite*: removal

in-joke n **private joke**, inside joke, running joke, witticism

injudicious adj **ill-advised**, unwise, foolish, imprudent, careless *Opposite*: judicious

injudiciousness n **indiscretion**, imprudence, foolishness, rashness, impulsiveness *Opposite*: prudence

injunction n **ban**, sanction, embargo, restriction, order

injure v **damage**, harm, hurt, wound, cut *Opposite*: heal. *See* COMPARE AND CONTRAST *at* harm.

injured adj **hurt**, incapacitated, wounded, battered, bruised *Opposite*: unscathed

injurious adj **harmful**, distressing, damaging, adverse, detrimental *Opposite*: beneficial

injury n **wound**, damage, grievance, wrong, hurt

injustice n **discrimination**, unfairness, inequality, bias, prejudice *Opposite*: justice

in keeping with prep **consistent with**, suitable for, in accordance with, in line with, according to

inkling n **suspicion**, hint, clue, hunch, feeling *Opposite*: certainty

inkwell n **jar**, inkstand, pot, container, well

inlaid adj **decorated**, veneered, enameled, ornamented, mosaic

inland adj **interior**, internal, upcountry, inward, central *Opposite*: coastal ■ adv **within**, inshore, upcountry, inside, inward

inlay n **1 enamel**, tile, piece, ornament, inset **2 pattern**, enameling, decoration, ornament, mosaic

inlet n **bay**, cove, fjord, creek, tidal creek

in line with prep **in agreement with**, according to, in keeping with, corresponding to, consistent with

inmate n **prisoner**, internee, patient, convict, jailbird *(slang)*

in memoriam prep **in memory of**, in remembrance of, as a memorial to, in commemoration of, for

inmost *see* innermost

innards *(infml)* n **entrails**, guts, intestines, bowels, viscera

innate adj **essential**, inborn, native, distinctive, natural

inner adj **1 innermost** inward, internal, inside, central *Opposite*: outer **2 private**, secret, intimate, deep, hidden *Opposite*: public

inner city n **downtown**, city center, center, town center

inner-city adj **city**, metropolitan, town, downtown, central *Opposite*: suburban

innermost adj **deepest**, private, secret, intimate, inmost *Opposite*: outermost

innings n **runs**, turn, batting, score, round

innocence n **1 blamelessness**, goodness, guiltlessness, incorruptibility, virtue *Opposite*: guilt **2 inexperience**, unworldliness, naiveté, unsophistication, gullibility *Opposite*: experience

innocent adj **1 blameless**, acquitted, guiltless, cleared, not guilty *Opposite*: guilty **2 harmless**, unknowing, unintended, unintentional, inoffensive *Opposite*: malicious **3 virtuous**, untouched, unsullied, chaste, immaculate *Opposite*: tainted **4 unsophis-**

ticated, unworldly, artless, harmless, naive *Opposite*: worldly

innocuous *adj* **inoffensive**, harmless, innocent, safe, mild *Opposite*: offensive

innovate *v* **invent**, modernize, originate, revolutionize, transform *Opposite*: stagnate

innovation *n* **novelty**, invention, revolution, modernization, origination *Opposite*: stagnation

innovative *adj* **groundbreaking**, advanced, state-of-the-art, pioneering, inventive *Opposite*: outdated

innuendo *n* **insinuation**, ambiguity, double entendre, inference, intimation

innumerable *adj* **countless**, uncountable, numerous, incalculable, immeasurable

inoculate *v* **immunize**, vaccinate, inject, protect, give a shot *(infml) Opposite*: infect

inoculation *n* **vaccination**, injection, booster, immunization, shot *(infml)*

inoffensive *adj* **innocuous**, harmless, bland, dull, safe *Opposite*: offensive

inoperable *adj* **1 incurable**, untreatable, terminal, grave, fatal *Opposite*: operable **2 impracticable**, unworkable, unfeasible, impossible, unachievable *Opposite*: doable

inoperative *adj* **out of action**, out of order, out of use, broken, broken down *Opposite*: operative

inopportune *adj* **ill-timed**, unfortunate, inconvenient, mistimed, untimely *Opposite*: opportune

in order to *conj* **so as to**, to, with the intention of, with the purpose of, with the aim of

inordinate *adj* **excessive**, undue, unwarranted, immoderate, unreasonable *Opposite*: moderate

inorganic *adj* **mineral**, inanimate, inert, lifeless *Opposite*: organic

in particular *adv* **specifically**, especially, specially, particularly, above all *Opposite*: generally

in person *adv* **personally**, yourself, in the flesh, physically, individually

input *n* **contribution**, effort, say, participation, involvement ■ *v* **enter**, key, key in, record, store

inquest *n* **investigation**, inquiry, examination, postmortem, autopsy

inquire *v* **ask**, query, request, question, find out

inquire into *v* **investigate**, go into, delve into, look into, probe into

inquiring *adj* **1 inquisitive**, interested, curious, questioning, analytical *Opposite*: incurious **2 searching**, questioning, penetrating, probing, prying

inquiry *n* **1 review**, postmortem, autopsy, investigation, examination **2 request**, question, query, interrogation, quiz

inquisition *n* **inquiry**, inquest, investigation, examination, interrogation

inquisitive *adj* **1 curious**, inquiring, interested, questioning, probing *Opposite*: indifferent **2 prying**, intrusive, prurient, meddlesome, officious *Opposite*: incurious

inquisitiveness *n* **1 curiosity**, interest, keenness, desire for knowledge, thirst for knowledge *Opposite*: indifference **2 prurience**, meddlesomeness, prying, questioning, officiousness *Opposite*: indifference

inquisitor *n* **cross-examiner**, examiner, investigator, interrogator, questioner

inquisitorial *adj* **interrogational**, cross-examining, investigative, interviewing, questioning

in reality *adv* **in actual fact**, really, actually, in fact, in effect

in retrospect *adv* **with hindsight**, looking back, retrospectively, on second thought, on reflection

insalubrious *(fml) adj* **unhealthy**, unsavory, unwholesome, harmful, unhygienic *Opposite*: healthy

ins and outs *n* **details**, fine points, particulars, facts, minutiae

insane *adj* **1 of unsound mind**, mentally disordered, mentally ill, deranged *Opposite*: sane **2 foolish**, silly, stupid, irrational, impractical *Opposite*: sensible

insanitary *adj* **unhygienic**, dirty, unclean, contaminated, unhealthy *Opposite*: hygienic

insanity *n* **foolishness**, stupidity, irrationality, folly, senselessness *Opposite*: common sense

insatiability *n* **voraciousness**, greed, greediness, gluttony, ravenousness

insatiable *adj* **voracious**, greedy, avid, ravenous, unquenchable

inscribe *v* **1 engrave**, carve, etch, cut, scratch *Opposite*: erase **2 list**, enter, record, register, enroll *Opposite*: delete **3 dedicate**, autograph, address, sign, assign

inscription *n* **1 writing**, caption, label, engraving, legend **2 dedication**, autograph, signature, personal note, initials

inscrutability *n* **mystique**, mystery, mysteriousness, enigma, incomprehensibility *Opposite*: clarity

inscrutable *adj* **enigmatic**, sphinx-like, unfathomable, mysterious, impenetrable *Opposite*: transparent

in secret *adv* **secretly**, privately, in private, confidentially, clandestinely *Opposite*: openly

insect *n* **bug**, fly, pest, creature, creepy-crawly *(infml)*

WORD BANK
❑ **parts of an insect** abdomen, antenna, feeler, proboscis, thorax, wing

❏ **types of stages of insect development** caterpillar, chrysalis, glowworm, grub, imago, larva, maggot, nit, pupa, silkworm, woodworm

insecure adj 1 **unconfident**, anxious, self-doubting, uncertain, timid Opposite: confident 2 **vulnerable**, unprotected, unguarded, undefended, at risk Opposite: secure 3 **shaky**, rickety, unstable, unsteady, loose Opposite: steady

insecurity n **lack of confidence**, anxiety, uncertainty, timidity, self-doubt Opposite: confidence

insensate adj 1 **unconscious**, comatose, inert, numbed, numb Opposite: animate 2 (literary) **heartless**, callous, cold, insensitive, unsympathetic Opposite: sympathetic 3 (literary) **thoughtless**, inconsiderate, inattentive, heedless, unthinking Opposite: considerate

insensible adj 1 **unaware**, unresponsive, insensitive, oblivious, numb Opposite: sensitive 2 **unconscious**, comatose, inert, insentient, numb Opposite: conscious 3 **imperceptible**, indiscernible, unnoticeable, indistinguishable, inappreciable Opposite: obvious

insensitive adj 1 **unresponsive**, oblivious, unmoved, inured to, indifferent Opposite: responsive 2 **tactless**, thoughtless, inconsiderate, uncaring, unsympathetic Opposite: sensitive 3 **numb**, unfeeling, insensate, insensible, dead Opposite: sensitive

insensitivity n **selfishness**, thoughtlessness, inconsiderateness, tactlessness, inattentiveness Opposite: sensitivity

insentient adj **lifeless**, inert, inanimate, insensate, unconscious Opposite: sentient

inseparable adj 1 **close**, devoted, intimate, joined at the hip, in each other's pocket Opposite: distant 2 **indivisible**, indissoluble, inextricable, united, conjoined (fml) Opposite: independent

insert v 1 **introduce**, implant, inject, put in, place in Opposite: take out 2 **add**, include, enclose, append, incorporate Opposite: extract ■ n **supplement**, pullout, addition, enclosure, inset

insertion n 1 **supplement**, pullout, addition, inset, insert 2 **addition**, inclusion, incorporation, enclosure, attachment Opposite: extraction

in-service adj **work-related**, occupational, professional, vocational, job-related

inset v **insert**, put in, add, include, incorporate Opposite: extract ■ n **supplement**, insert, pullout, insertion, inclusion

inshore adv **landward**, coastward, ashore, shoreward

in short adv **in brief**, briefly, in a word, in summary, in a nutshell Opposite: at length

inside adv **indoors**, in, within, in the interior, at home Opposite: outside ■ adj 1 **confidential**, privileged, secret, private, exclu-

sive 2 **inner**, innermost, inmost, inward Opposite: outer 3 **indoor**, interior, internal Opposite: outside 4 (infml) **locked up**, imprisoned, put away (infml), doing time (slang) ■ n **interior**, inner recesses, inner parts, contents Opposite: outside ■ prep **in**, within, surrounded by, contained by Opposite: outside

insides (infml) n **internal organs**, guts, entrails, bowels, viscera

insidious adj **sinister**, treacherous, crafty, sneaky, deceptive Opposite: harmless

insight n **vision**, understanding, awareness, intuition, perception

insightful adj **perceptive**, astute, shrewd, understanding, discerning Opposite: unperceptive

insightfulness n **perspicacity**, perceptiveness, astuteness, discernment, sensitivity

insignia n **emblem**, crest, badge, sign, symbol

insignificance n **unimportance**, irrelevance, inconsequentiality, triviality, paltriness Opposite: significance

insignificant adj **unimportant**, irrelevant, immaterial, inconsequential, trivial Opposite: significant

insincere adj **dishonest**, two-faced, hypocritical, disingenuous, deceitful Opposite: sincere

insincerity n **dishonesty**, disingenuousness, hypocrisy, deceit, mendacity Opposite: sincerity

insinuate v 1 **imply**, suggest, hint, intimate, indicate Opposite: declare 2 **ingratiate yourself**, worm your way in, wheedle, cozy up, curry favor Opposite: insult

insinuation n **suggestion**, implication, hint, intimation, allusion Opposite: statement

insipid adj 1 **dull**, bland, characterless, colorless, trite Opposite: exciting 2 **bland**, tasteless, unappetizing, flavorless, watery Opposite: tasty

insipidness n 1 **dullness**, blandness, feebleness, characterlessness, colorlessness 2 **tastelessness**, blandness, wateriness, weakness, lack of flavor Opposite: tastiness

insist v 1 **maintain**, claim, assert, contend, swear Opposite: deny 2 **require**, demand, press for, stipulate, enforce

insistence n **persistence**, resolve, firmness, perseverance, doggedness

insistent adj 1 **adamant**, firm, persistent, unrelenting, resolute Opposite: half-hearted 2 **incessant**, repeated, persistent, relentless, unrelenting Opposite: occasional

insofar as conj **inasmuch as**, insomuch as, to the extent that, to the degree that, because

insolence n **impudence**, impertinence, rudeness, audacity, disrespect Opposite: respect

insolent *adj* **impudent**, rude, disrespectful, brazen, impertinent *(fml)* *Opposite*: respectful

insolubility *n* **mysteriousness**, indecipherability, intricacy, difficulty, impenetrability *Opposite*: solubility

insoluble *adj* **inexplicable**, mysterious, insolvable, unfathomable, indecipherable *Opposite*: solvable

insolvency *n* **bankruptcy**, liquidation, indebtedness, ruin, collapse *Opposite*: solvency

insolvent *adj* **bankrupt**, ruined, in debt, in receivership, broke *(infml)* *Opposite*: solvent

insomnia *n* **sleeplessness**, wakefulness, restlessness

insomuch as *conj* **insofar as**, inasmuch as, to the extent that, to the degree that, because

insouciance *n* **carefreeness**, nonchalance, indifference, happiness, unconcern *Opposite*: worry

inspect *v* **look at**, review, examine, scrutinize, look over *Opposite*: ignore

inspection *n* **review**, examination, scrutiny, assessment, check

inspector *n* **examiner**, superintendent, overseer, assessor, supervisor

inspiration *n* **1 stimulus**, spur, motivation, stimulation, encouragement *Opposite*: disincentive **2 creativeness**, inventiveness, brilliance, vision, creativity **3 insight**, flash, idea, revelation, brainstorm *(infml)*

inspirational *adj* **stimulating**, inspiring, stirring, rousing, moving *Opposite*: boring

inspire *v* **stimulate**, motivate, stir, move, encourage *Opposite*: bore

inspired *adj* **1 brilliant**, outstanding, superb, exceptional, dazzling *Opposite*: uninspired **2 stimulated**, stirred, moved, encouraged, motivated *Opposite*: uninspired

inspiring *adj* **inspirational**, stirring, rousing, moving, exciting *Opposite*: uninspiring

in spite of *prep* **despite**, regardless of, in the face of, notwithstanding *(fml)*

instability *n* **unpredictability**, variability, uncertainty, unsteadiness, volatility *Opposite*: stability

install *v* **1 connect**, fit, put in, set up, fix *Opposite*: remove **2 ordain**, establish, inaugurate, instate, induct *Opposite*: oust **3 settle in**, settle, settle down, ensconce, position

installation *n* **1 connection**, fitting, setting up, fixing, putting in *Opposite*: removal **2 system**, mechanism, machinery, equipment, apparatus **3 appointment**, ordination, inauguration, investiture, instatement *Opposite*: removal

installment *n* **1 payment**, portion, part, section, segment **2 part**, episode, chapter

instance *n* **example**, case, case in point, occurrence, illustration

instant *adj* **1 prompt**, immediate, sudden, swift, instantaneous *Opposite*: gradual **2 prepared**, precooked, premixed, powdered, microwavable **3 urgent**, pressing, immediate ■ *n* **moment**, second, split second, the twinkling of an eye, minute

instantaneous *adj* **prompt**, rapid, sudden, immediate, instant *Opposite*: gradual

instantly *adv* **promptly**, right away, instantaneously, immediately, directly *Opposite*: gradually

instate *v* **appoint**, ordain, inaugurate, establish, install *Opposite*: oust

instead *adv* **in its place**, as an alternative, as a substitute, as a replacement

instead of *prep* **in place of**, rather than, as opposed to, in preference to

in step *adv* **1 in line**, in accordance, in harmony, in concordance, in agreement **2 keeping pace**, in time, in synchronization, keeping up, in harmony

instigate *v* **bring about**, prompt, initiate, start, activate *Opposite*: stifle

instigation *n* **1 start**, beginning, initiation, establishment, commencement *(fml)* *Opposite*: end **2 initiation**, prompting, urging, encouragement, provocation *Opposite*: discouragement

instigator *n* **initiator**, prime mover, mastermind, troublemaker, ringleader

instill *v* **1 impart**, implant, inculcate, introduce, drum into **2 drip**, pour, infuse, inject, introduce

instinct *n* **1 nature**, character, makeup, predisposition, disposition **2 drive**, reflex, feeling, impulse, urge *Opposite*: reason **3 feeling**, intuition, gut feeling, sixth sense, sense **4 talent**, knack, gift, flair, ability

instinctive *adj* **1 involuntary**, automatic, reflex, natural, unconscious *Opposite*: conscious **2 natural**, intuitive, innate, inherent, inborn *Opposite*: learned

instinctively *adv* **impulsively**, mechanically, on impulse, automatically, unconsciously

institute *v* **introduce**, establish, set up, bring about, found ■ *n* **organization**, institution, establishment, foundation, association

institution *n* **1 establishment**, organization, body, association, society **2 tradition**, custom, convention, ritual **3 introduction**, establishment, setting up, foundation, creation

institutional *adj* **1 official**, recognized, formal, established, organized *Opposite*: unofficial **2 utilitarian**, uniform, dull, ugly, ordinary *Opposite*: unique

institutionalized *adj* **established**, existing, long-standing, traditional, entrenched *Opposite*: innovative

in store *adv* **to come**, coming up, in the making, for the future, waiting

instruct *v* **1 teach**, train, coach, tutor, educate **2 command**, order, tell, give orders to, charge. See COMPARE AND CONTRAST at teach.

instruction n 1 **teaching**, training, lessons, tuition, education 2 **order**, command, direction, directive

instructive adj **informative**, educational, useful, helpful, enlightening

instructor n **teacher**, coach, tutor, trainer, mentor

instrument n 1 **tool**, gadget, device, utensil, apparatus 2 **means**, channel, vehicle, method, medium

instrumental adj **contributory**, active, involved, helpful, influential Opposite: tangential

instrumentalist n **musician**, player, performer

instrumentation n 1 **arrangement**, composition, musical arrangement, music, score 2 **instrument panel**, equipment, instruments, controls, console

insubordinate adj **disobedient**, defiant, rebellious, mutinous, unruly Opposite: obedient

insubordination n **disobedience**, defiance, rebelliousness, mutiny, unruliness Opposite: obedience

insubstantial adj **flimsy**, light, slight, weak, frail Opposite: weighty

insubstantiality n **weakness**, fragility, thinness, flimsiness, lightness Opposite: robustness

insufferable adj **excruciating**, unbearable, intolerable, insupportable, unendurable

insufficiency n 1 **lack**, deficiency, dearth, absence, shortage 2 **inadequacy**, deficiency, unfitness, failure, inefficiency Opposite: adequacy

insufficient adj **inadequate**, deficient, lacking, in short supply, scarce Opposite: surplus

insular adj **inward-looking**, blinkered, narrow-minded, narrow, limited Opposite: open-minded

insularity n **narrow-mindedness**, narrowness, parochialism, intolerance, small-mindedness Opposite: openness

insulate v 1 **lag**, wad, line, fill, pad 2 **cloister**, protect, shield, cut off, isolate Opposite: expose

insulation n 1 **lining**, lagging, wadding, padding, filling 2 **protection**, isolation, separation, segregation, sequestration Opposite: exposure

insulator n **insulation**, padding, soundproofing, lagging

insult v **offend**, affront, abuse, slur, slight Opposite: praise ■ n **affront**, slight, slur, offense, rudeness Opposite: compliment

insulting adj **abusive**, offensive, rude, insolent, wounding Opposite: polite

insuperable adj **insurmountable**, impossible, unbeatable, challenging, overwhelming Opposite: easy

insupportable adj **unbearable**, intolerable, unendurable, insufferable, unspeakable Opposite: bearable

insurance n **cover**, indemnity, assurance, protection, coverage

insurance policy n 1 **document**, contract, cover, agreement, guarantee 2 **safety net**, safeguard, precaution, protection, provision

insure v **protect**, cover, assure, indemnify, underwrite

insurer n **underwriter**, broker, guarantor

insurgence see insurgency

insurgency n **uprising**, rebellion, revolt, insurrection, revolution

insurgent n **rebel**, insurrectionary, revolutionary, guerrilla, mutineer ■ adj **mutinous**, rebellious, rebel, insurrectionary

insurmountable adj **unbeatable**, insuperable, unassailable, invincible, impossible Opposite: easy

insurrection n **uprising**, rebellion, revolt, insurgency, revolution

intact adj **complete**, whole, unbroken, in one piece, integral Opposite: broken

intake n 1 **consumption**, eating, drinking, ingestion 2 **opening**, pipe, tube, aperture, inlet Opposite: out let 3 **entry**, entrants, students

intangibility n 1 **imperceptibility**, immateriality, immaterialness, untouchability, insubstantiality Opposite: tangibility 2 **indescribability**, elusiveness, vagueness, subtlety, abstractness

intangible adj 1 **imperceptible**, immaterial, insubstantial, incorporeal (fml), impalpable (fml) Opposite: concrete 2 **unquantifiable**, elusive, vague, ethereal, subtle

integer n **whole number**, number, numeral, digit, figure Opposite: fraction

integral adj 1 **essential**, vital, important, basic, fundamental 2 **connected**, internal, central, at the heart of Opposite: unimportant 3 **complete**, whole, intact, undivided, unbroken

integrate v 1 **mix**, fit in, join in, assimilate, take part 2 **put together**, mix, incorporate, add, join together Opposite: separate 3 **open up**, desegregate, combine, mix, assimilate

integrated adj 1 **combined**, united, joined, unified, cohesive Opposite: separated 2 **open**, desegregated, multiethnic, multicultural, multilingual Opposite: segregated

integration n **addition**, mixing, incorporation, combination, amalgamation

integrity n **honesty**, truth, truthfulness, honor, veracity Opposite: dishonesty

intellect n **intelligence**, brainpower, brain, brains, mind Opposite: emotion

intellectual adj **knowledgeable**, intelligent, highbrow, academic, cerebral ■ n philo-

sopher, thinker, academic, scholar, highbrow

intelligence n **1 brain**, cleverness, aptitude, intellect, brains Opposite: stupidity **2 information**, news, reports, communication, word

intelligence quotient n **IQ**, mental ability, aptitude

intelligent adj **1 clever**, bright, smart, quick, able Opposite: stupid **2 sensible**, rational, wise, logical, perceptive Opposite: irrational

---

COMPARE AND CONTRAST CORE MEANING: having the ability to learn and understand easily **intelligent** quick to learn and understand; **bright** showing an ability to think, learn, or respond quickly, especially used of younger people; **quick** alert, perceptive, and able to respond quickly; **smart** showing intelligence and mental alertness; **clever** having sharp mental abilities, sometimes suggesting showy or superficial cleverness; **able** capable or talented, also used in educational circles of children who are intelligent; **gifted** talented, especially artistically or creatively, also used in educational circles of children who are exceptionally intelligent.

---

intelligentsia n **intellectuals**, academics, highbrows, cognoscenti, literati (fml)

intelligible adj **comprehensible**, understandable, clear, plain, lucid Opposite: unintelligible

intemperance n **self-indulgence**, overindulgence, excess, hedonism, gluttony Opposite: moderation

intemperate adj **self-indulgent**, uncontrolled, unrestrained, inordinate, immoderate Opposite: moderate

intend v **mean**, aim, propose, plan, have in mind

intended adj **1 envisioned**, future, planned, proposed, projected **2 planned**, intentional, deliberate, on purpose, premeditated Opposite: accidental ■ n (dated) **fiancé**, fiancée, husband-to-be, wife-to-be, girlfriend

intense adj **penetrating**, strong, powerful, forceful, concentrated Opposite: moderate

intensely adv **forcefully**, powerfully, strongly, deeply, extremely Opposite: mildly

intensification n **strengthening**, increase, rise, spiraling, escalation Opposite: reduction

intensify v **strengthen**, deepen, step up, exaggerate, increase Opposite: weaken. See COMPARE AND CONTRAST at **increase**.

intensity n **strength**, concentration, power, force, passion Opposite: moderation

intensive adj **concentrated**, rigorous, exhaustive, severe, thorough Opposite: easy

intensive care n **monitoring**, nursing, 24-hour care, one-to-one care

intent n (fml) **intention**, aim, goal, target, objective ■ adj **1 concentrated**, absorbed, focused, directed, fixed **2 intending to**, bent on, determined, resolved, set on

intention n **aim**, purpose, goal, target, objective

intentional adj **deliberate**, planned, intended, premeditated, calculated Opposite: accidental

intently adv **closely**, fixedly, carefully, keenly, attentively Opposite: abstractedly

intentness n **attentiveness**, concentration, focus, attention, close attention Opposite: abstraction

inter v **bury**, entomb, lay to rest

interact v **interrelate**, act together, cooperate, relate, intermingle

interaction n **communication**, contact, interface, dealings, relations

interactive adj **communicating**, collaborating, cooperating, collaborative, cooperative

interbreed v **breed**, reproduce, multiply, mate, produce

intercalate v **insert**, introduce, interpolate, add, interpose Opposite: extrapolate

intercede v **intervene**, mediate, plead, negotiate, arbitrate

intercept v **cut off**, catch, interrupt, stop, seize

interception n **capture**, seizure, interruption, interference, intervention

intercession n **intervention**, mediation, arbitration, negotiation

interchange v **switch**, trade, exchange, substitute, trade off ■ n **1 trading**, exchange, transaction, substitution, swapping **2 crossroads**, junction, intersection

interchangeable adj **substitutable**, identical, the same, compatible, transposable Opposite: incompatible

intercommunicate v **talk**, communicate, converse, discuss, contact

interconnect v **join**, intersect, connect, interrelate, interlock

intercontinental adj **international**, transnational, global, worldwide, large-scale Opposite: national

intercourse n **dealings**, contact, communication, interaction, association

intercut v **interpose**, insert, alternate, interweave, interject

interdependent adj **symbiotic**, dependent, reliant, codependent

interdict n **order**, court order, ban, prohibition, veto ■ v **ban**, prohibit, forbid, veto, embargo Opposite: permit

interest n **1 attention**, notice, curiosity, concentration, awareness Opposite: indifference **2 concern**, importance, significance, relevance, note **3 hobby**, activity, pursuit, pastime, leisure activity

4 good, advantage, benefit, gain, profit ■ *v* **attract**, draw, appeal, fascinate, be of interest *Opposite*: bore

interested *adj* **absorbed**, attentive, involved, concerned, attracted *Opposite*: indifferent

interest group *n* **1 alliance**, association, cartel, trade union, pressure group **2 club**, association, group, society

interesting *adj* **stimulating**, thought-provoking, motivating, exciting, fascinating *Opposite*: boring

interface *n* **border**, boundary, line, crossing point, edge

interfere *v* **1 delay**, inhibit, restrict, affect, get in the way **2 pry**, intrude, meddle, disturb, intervene

interference *n* **1 meddling**, intrusion, prying, interfering, intervention **2 restriction**, obstruction, hindrance, obstacle, delay

interfering *adj* **intrusive**, meddlesome, prying, inquisitive, meddling

intergalactic *adj* **interstellar**, interplanetary, space

intergovernmental *adj* **interstate**, international, diplomatic, foreign, high-level

interim *adj* **temporary**, provisional, short-term, intervening, acting *Opposite*: permanent ■ *n* **interlude**, pause, break, interval, pause in the action

interior *n* **inside**, core, center, heart *Opposite*: outside ■ *adj* **internal**, inner, central, inland, inside *Opposite*: peripheral

interior decoration *n* **decoration**, furnishings, decorating scheme, interior design, decor

interject *v* **butt in**, exclaim, interrupt, interpose, cut in

interjection *n* **1 exclamation**, outburst, cry, utterance, shout **2 interruption**, interpolation, introduction, addition, insertion

interlace *v* **interweave**, intertwine, interlock, entwine, knit

interlard *v* **interpose**, insert, introduce, intersperse, interweave

interleave *v* **slot in**, put in, enclose, interweave, add

interlink *v* **interweave**, intertwine, interlace, interconnect, knit

interlock *v* **mesh**, dovetail, link, join, interconnect

interlocutor *n* **speaker**, talker, discusser, panelist, converser

interloper *n* **1 intruder**, trespasser, gatecrasher, persona non grata, impostor **2 meddler**, busybody *(infml)*, snoop *(infml)*

interlude *n* **interval**, break, rest, pause, interim

intermediary *n* **intercessor**, arbitrator, negotiator, go-between, mediator ■ *adj* **intermediate**, middle, midway, in-between, transitional

intermediate *adj* **middle**, midway, in-between, transitional, halfway *Opposite*: extreme

interment *n* **burial**, entombment, committal, funeral, funeral rites *Opposite*: disinterment

intermesh *v* **join**, interlink, knit, mesh, interconnect

interminable *adj* **endless**, ceaseless, everlasting, perpetual, never-ending *Opposite*: finite

intermingle *v* **intermix**, mingle, interact, combine, fuse

intermission *n* **intermezzo**, interval, break, interlude, pause

intermittent *adj* **spasmodic**, periodic, sporadic, occasional, irregular *Opposite*: constant. *See* COMPARE AND CONTRAST *at* **periodic**.

intermix *v* **meld**, intermingle, mix, mingle, blend *Opposite*: separate

intern *v* **imprison**, detain, confine, hold, jail *Opposite*: release ■ *n* **medical student**, doctor, student doctor, med student, medic *(infml)*

internal *adj* **1 interior**, inner, inside *Opposite*: external **2 domestic**, in-house, home, intramural *Opposite*: external

internalize *v* **1 adopt**, affect, take on, assume, co-opt **2 stew**, mull over, bottle up, suppress *Opposite*: externalize

international *adj* **global**, worldwide, intercontinental, universal, transnational *Opposite*: domestic

internecine *adj* **1 internal**, inner, civil, domestic **2 destructive**, devastating, decimating, deadly, injurious

internee *n* **prisoner**, captive, detainee, hostage, inmate

Internet *n* **World Wide Web**, information superhighway, cyberspace, the Net *(infml)*, the Web *(infml)*

WORD BANK

❑ **types of Internet facilities and activities** bot, browser, bulletin board, chat room, cookie, home page, instant messaging, ISP, newsgroup, portal, robot, router, search engine, service provider, URL, Web site, Webcast, Web-conferencing, Web page, Webzine

internment *n* **imprisonment**, captivity, confinement, custody, detention *Opposite*: release

internship *n* **residency**, medical training, practicum, medical school, training period

interpersonal *adj* **relational**, social, personal, interactive *Opposite*: solitary

interplanetary *adj* **space**, planetary, interstellar, intergalactic, astronomical

interplay *n* **chemistry**, interaction, relationship, interchange, back-and-forth

interpolate *v* **1 insert**, interpose, intercalate, incorporate, include **2 interrupt**, interject, interpose, throw in, cut in

interpose v 1 **interrupt**, cut in, throw in, interpolate, interject 2 **intervene**, interfere, intercede, meddle, butt in

interpret v 1 **explain**, clarify, account for, elucidate, make clear 2 **take to mean**, understand, read, construe, infer *Opposite*: misread 3 **translate**, decode, decipher, unravel, figure out

interpretation n **clarification**, understanding, reading, explanation, analysis

interpretative adj **explanatory**, revelatory, informational, informative, revealing

interpreter n 1 **translator**, linguist, transcriber, polyglot, explainer 2 **performer**, portrayer, exponent, promoter, medium

interpretive *see* **interpretative**

interracial adj **mixed**, of mixed race, multicultural, multiethnic, integrated *Opposite*: segregated

interregnum n **interval**, pause, lag, lapse, wait

interrelate v **interconnect**, relate, connect, link up, correlate

interrogate v **question**, cross-examine, quiz, interview, debrief. *See* COMPARE AND CONTRAST at **question**.

interrogation n **questioning**, examination, cross-examination, grilling, interview

interrogative adj **questioning**, curious, inquisitive, inquiring, probing

interrogator n **questioner**, interviewer, investigator, examiner

interrupt v 1 **butt in**, barge in, interject, disturb, intrude 2 **break off**, cut short, disrupt, break up, stop

interruption n **break**, pause, disruption, stoppage, disturbance *Opposite*: continuity

intersect v **cross**, interconnect, meet, traverse, overlap

intersection n 1 **connection**, meeting, node, joint, joining 2 **junction**, crossroads, fork, interchange, cloverleaf

intersperse v **mix together**, combine, intermingle, sprinkle, scatter

interstate adj **regional**, national, federal, political, administrative

interstellar adj **interplanetary**, space, star, intergalactic, stellar

interstice n **space**, gap, crack, opening, aperture

intertwine v **interweave**, entwine, interlace, link, interleave *Opposite*: divide

interval n **gap**, space, distance, hiatus, separation

intervene v 1 **intercede**, arbitrate, mediate, interfere, get involved *Opposite*: hold back 2 **happen**, occur, take place, ensue, succeed

intervention n **interference**, involvement, intrusion, intercession, interposition

interview n **meeting**, talk, consultation, conference, discussion ∎ v **question**, interrogate, talk to, converse with, put questions to

interviewee n **applicant**, candidate, hopeful, aspirant, contender *Opposite*: interviewer

interviewer n 1 **examiner**, assessor, questioner, interrogator, evaluator *Opposite*: interviewee 2 **questioner**, correspondent, personality, journalist

interweave v **intertwine**, interlace, mingle, intermingle, entwine

intestate adj **without a will**, unrepresented, unaccounted for, voiceless, unheard

intestinal adj **duodenal**, colonic, abdominal, stomach, bowel

in that conj **because**, as, since, given that

in the air adj **imminent**, about to happen, in the pipeline, forthcoming, coming

in the altogether (infml) adj **naked**, nude, unclothed, stark-naked, in the buff (infml) *Opposite*: clothed

in the clear adj **innocent**, let off, free of blame, cleared, guiltless *Opposite*: guilty

in the end adv **finally**, eventually, after some time, at long last, after a while *Opposite*: initially

in the event adv **as it turned out**, as it was, unexpectedly, surprisingly, when it came to it

in the face of prep **despite**, in spite of, regardless of, notwithstanding (fml)

in the flesh adv **in person**, personally, in real life, physically, face to face

in the know adj **informed**, in the picture, well-informed, aware, enlightened *Opposite*: ignorant

in the light of prep **taking into consideration**, in view of, considering, taking into account, with regard to

in the main adv **largely**, in general, on the whole, generally, generally speaking *Opposite*: in part

in the making adj **future**, potential, budding, prospective, to be *Opposite*: established

in the midst of prep **in the middle of**, at the heart of, amid, among, between

in the money adj **rich**, in clover, well-off, affluent, prosperous *Opposite*: poor

in the name of prep **on behalf of**, for, for the benefit of, for the sake of, on the authority of

in the offing adj **imminent**, coming up, on the agenda, on the horizon, forthcoming

in the open adj **unconcealed**, revealed, on show, public, public knowledge *Opposite*: concealed ∎ adv **openly**, publicly, in full view, for everyone to see, in public *Opposite*: furtively

in the right adj **correct**, right, justified, blameless, not to blame *Opposite*: wrong

in the running adj **in contention**, in competition, up there, in with a shout (infml)

in the throes of prep **in the process of**, in the

middle of, in the midst of, in the thick of, involved in

in the wrong adj 1 **to blame**, at fault, culpable, responsible, blameworthy Opposite: in the right 2 **mistaken**, incorrect, wide of the mark, off beam, wrong Opposite: in the right

intimacy n 1 **familiarity**, closeness, understanding, confidence, caring Opposite: distance 2 **quietness**, seclusion, privacy, informality, friendliness Opposite: formality

intimate adj 1 **close**, dear, near, warm, friendly Opposite: distant 2 **quiet**, cozy, informal, friendly, warm Opposite: formal 3 **personal**, confidential, private, secret, innermost Opposite: public 4 **thorough**, detailed, in-depth, profound, firsthand Opposite: superficial ■ v **suggest**, hint, insinuate, imply, indicate

intimately adv 1 **closely**, warmly, familiarly, confidentially, personally Opposite: distantly 2 **quietly**, informally, cozily, warmly, comfortably Opposite: formally 3 **thoroughly**, very well, fully, in detail, closely Opposite: superficially

intimation n **hint**, allusion, insinuation, suggestion, warning

intimidate v **threaten**, frighten, bully, coerce, terrorize

intimidated adj **daunted**, scared, frightened, overwhelmed, unsettled Opposite: relaxed

intimidating adj **threatening**, unapproachable, frightening, daunting, menacing Opposite: approachable

intimidation n **coercion**, pressure, bullying, threats, terrorization

into (infml) adj **addicted to**, interested in, obsessed by, mad about, crazy about (infml)

intolerable adj **unbearable**, insufferable, impossible, unendurable, insupportable Opposite: bearable

intolerance n **bigotry**, prejudice, narrow-mindedness, fanaticism, narrowness Opposite: tolerance

intolerant adj **bigoted**, prejudiced, narrow-minded, fanatical, blinkered Opposite: tolerant

intonation n 1 **pitch**, inflection, lilt, cadence, timbre 2 **chanting**, chant, incantation, invocation, intoning

intone v 1 **say**, utter, speak, articulate, pronounce 2 (fml) **chant**, sing, croon, drone, hum

intoxicating adj 1 **exciting**, invigorating, stimulating, exhilarating, fascinating Opposite: dull 2 (fml) **alcoholic**, strong, powerful, heady, mind-altering Opposite: soft

intoxication n **alcoholism**, drunkenness, inebriation, intemperance, heavy drinking

intractability n 1 **difficulty**, knottiness, complexity, awkwardness, unwieldiness Opposite: simplicity 2 (fml) **unmanageability**, uncontrollability, obstinacy, stubbornness, pigheadedness Opposite: tractability

intractable adj 1 **difficult**, problematic, troublesome, awkward, thorny Opposite: easy 2 (fml) **stubborn**, obstinate, obdurate, willful, headstrong Opposite: easygoing. See COMPARE AND CONTRAST at **unruly**.

intramural adj **internal**, inner, in-house, college, school Opposite: extramural

intransigence n **inflexibility**, stubbornness, narrow-mindedness, obstinacy, unyieldingness Opposite: flexibility

intransigent adj **inflexible**, stubborn, obdurate obstinate, uncompromising Opposite: flexible ■ n (fml) **conservative**, dinosaur, diehard, reactionary, extremist Opposite: progressive

intravenous adj **venous**, vein, arterial, blood, circulatory

intrepid adj **fearless**, bold, courageous, valiant, heroic Opposite: cowardly

intricacies n **details**, ins and outs, workings, particulars, minutiae

intricacy n **complexity**, difficulty, obscurity, sophistication convolutedness

intricate adj **complicated**, complex, involved, difficult, elaborate Opposite: simple

intrigue n 1 **plotting**, conspiracy, trickery, scheming, maneuvering 2 **conspiracy**, plot, deception, scheme, stratagem ■ v **interest**, fascinate, charm, attract, captivate

intriguing adj **interesting**, fascinating, exciting, stimulating, absorbing Opposite: uninteresting

intrinsic adj **basic**, essential, inherent, fundamental, central Opposite: acquired

introduce v 1 **present**, make known to, acquaint with, familiarize, announce 2 **host**, present, preside over, lead, head 3 **bring in**, set up, initiate, usher in, pioneer Opposite: conclude 4 **make somebody aware of**, bring to somebody's attention, acquaint somebody with, turn somebody on to, get somebody into

introduction n 1 **foreword**, opening, preface, prologue, preamble Opposite: conclusion 2 **outline**, overview, primer, summary, starter 3 **institution**, presentation, insertion, ushering in

introductory adj 1 **preliminary**, initial, opening, starting, early Opposite: final 2 **basic**, entry-level, preliminary, first, simple

introspection n **self-examination**, contemplation, brooding, meditation, self-analysis

introspective adj **self-examining**, self-absorbed, inward-looking, contemplative, brooding

introversion n **introspection**, self-absorption, contemplation, navel-gazing, shyness *Opposite*: extroversion

introvert n **recluse**, hermit, loner, homebody (*infml*), shrinking violet (*infml*) *Opposite*: extrovert ■ *adj* **introverted**, shy, withdrawn, reclusive, reserved *Opposite*: extrovert

introverted *adj* **shy**, withdrawn, reclusive, reserved, reticent *Opposite*: extrovert

intrude v **encroach**, break in, interrupt, interfere, impose

intruder n **interloper**, burglar, trespasser, prowler, stalker

intrusion n **disturbance**, interruption, imposition, interference, invasion

intrusive *adj* **invasive**, indiscreet, interfering, insensitive, upsetting *Opposite*: discreet

intuit v **sense**, perceive, discern, feel, understand

intuition n **1 instinct**, perception, insight, sixth sense, awareness **2 hunch**, feeling, inkling, suspicion, sense

intuitive *adj* **1 instinctive**, spontaneous, innate, in-built, instinctual *Opposite*: cerebral **2 perceptive**, sensitive, shrewd, discerning, insightful

intuitively *adv* **instinctively**, automatically, by instinct, spontaneously, naturally

intuitiveness n **instinct**, perceptiveness, perception, insightfulness, insight

inundate v **1 flood**, deluge, drown, immerse, submerge *Opposite*: drain **2 overwhelm**, snow under, swamp, overburden, besiege

inundation n **1 deluge**, flood, sea, stream, shower *Opposite*: trickle **2 flood**, blizzard, sea, wave, barrage

inure v **harden**, toughen, accustom, season, acclimatize

inurement n **hardening**, toughening, acclimatization, seasoning, desensitization

invade v **1 attack**, occupy, enter, conquer, annex **2 overrun**, infect, infest, plague, colonize

invader n **attacker**, aggressor, raider, intruder, assailant

in vain *adv* **without success**, unsuccessfully, uselessly, hopelessly, fruitlessly *Opposite*: successfully

invalid *adj* **1 null and void**, unacceptable, unenforceable, illegal, worthless *Opposite*: valid **2 unsound**, untrue, unfounded, illogical, untenable *Opposite*: valid **3 infirm**, enfeebled, debilitated, disabled, sick *Opposite*: well ■ n **convalescent**, patient, sick person

invalidate v **overturn**, cancel, annul, nullify, undo *Opposite*: validate. *See* COMPARE AND CONTRAST *at* **nullify**.

invalidation n **annulment**, undoing, overthrow, nullification, cancellation *Opposite*: validation

invalidity n **1 unsoundness**, inaccuracy, base-lessness, irrationality, falsehood *Opposite*: validity **2 illegality**, inoperativeness, ineffectiveness, unsoundness, voidness *Opposite*: legality

invaluable *adj* **priceless**, irreplaceable, vital, instrumental, precious *Opposite*: worthless

invaluableness n **pricelessness**, irreplaceability, helpfulness, importance, value *Opposite*: worthlessness

invariable *adj* **constant**, set, unchanging, inflexible, consistent *Opposite*: erratic

invasion n **attack**, assault, incursion, raid, foray *Opposite*: withdrawal

invasive *adj* **1 aggressive**, offensive, hostile, warlike, bellicose **2 intrusive**, disturbing, interfering, insensitive, imposing *Opposite*: discreet

invective (*fml*) n **diatribe**, tirade, attack, broadside, counterblast *Opposite*: eulogy

inveigh v **protest**, complain, fulminate, criticize, rail

inveigle v **persuade**, entice, charm, cajole, trick

invent v **1 create**, devise, formulate, originate, conceive **2 make up**, think up, concoct, fabricate, contrive

invented *adj* **false**, made-up, fictitious, imaginary, pretend *Opposite*: real

invention n **1 creation**, discovery, development, brainchild, origination **2 device**, innovation, contraption, gadget, design **3 creativity**, imagination, ingenuity, inventiveness, resourcefulness **4 fabrication**, forgery, falsehood, deceit, lies *Opposite*: truth

inventive *adj* **creative**, imaginative, ingenious, resourceful, original *Opposite*: unimaginative

inventiveness n **ingenuity**, resourcefulness, originality, creativity, imagination

inventor n **discoverer**, originator, creator, architect, author

inventory n **1 list**, record, account, register, catalog **2 supply**, range, array, stock, accounting

inverse *adj* **opposite**, converse, reverse, contrary, counter *Opposite*: same ■ n **reverse**, opposite, other, contrary, converse

inversion n **1 reversal**, overturn, downturn, upturn **2 reverse**, transposition, antithesis, contrary, converse

invert v **turn over**, upset, capsize, overturn, reverse *Opposite*: right

invest v **1 capitalize**, put in, devote, advance, finance **2 endow**, provide, supply, empower, authorize **3** (*fml*) **appoint**, ordain, instate, inaugurate, establish

investigate v **examine**, look into, explore, inspect, study

investigation n **study**, examination, analysis, research, survey

investigative *adj* **analytical**, exploratory, undercover, fact-finding, research

investigator *n* **detective**, private detective, private investigator, agent, plainclothesman

investiture *n* **installation**, inauguration, swearing-in, instatement, admission

investment *n* 1 **savings**, speculation, venture, asset, share 2 *(fml)* **investiture**, swearing-in, instatement, installation, enthronement

investor *n* 1 **saver**, shareholder, depositor, stakeholder, financier 2 **backer**, sponsor, patron, guarantor, security

inveterate *adj* **chronic**, confirmed, hardened, ingrained, incurable *Opposite*: occasional

invidious *adj* **unpleasant**, discriminatory, unenviable, unfair, undesirable *Opposite*: pleasant

in view of *prep* **considering**, bearing in mind, taking into consideration, taking into account, in consideration of *(fml)* *Opposite*: notwithstanding *(fml)*

invigilate *v* **supervise**, monitor, inspect, observe, check

invigilator *n* **supervisor**, inspector, monitor, overseer, scrutineer

invigorate *v* **energize**, revitalize, refresh, stimulate, enliven *Opposite*: exhaust

invigorated *adj* **strengthened**, fortified, energized, refreshed, restored *Opposite*: weakened

invigorating *adj* **bracing**, brisk, stimulating, refreshing, revitalizing *Opposite*: enervating

invincibility *n* **strength**, insuperability, invulnerability, impregnability, indomitability *Opposite*: vulnerability

invincible *adj* **unbeatable**, invulnerable, unconquerable, indomitable, impregnable *Opposite*: vulnerable

inviolable *adj* **unbreakable**, sacred, sacrosanct, firm, unchallengeable

inviolate *adj* 1 **unaltered**, unchanged, unbroken, intact, entire *Opposite*: altered 2 **pure**, unsullied, untouched, whole, intact *Opposite*: contaminated

invisibility *n* **hiddenness**, inconspicuousness, indiscernibility, faintness, indistinctness *Opposite*: visibility

invisible *adj* 1 **imperceptible**, unseen, indistinguishable, indiscernible, undetectable *Opposite*: visible 2 **hidden**, concealed, disguised, unnoticed, obscured *Opposite*: obvious 3 **imaginary**, nonexistent, intangible, shadowy, insubstantial *Opposite*: palpable

invitation *n* 1 **offer**, request, call, summons, bidding 2 **encouragement**, inducement, provocation, incitement, enticement *Opposite*: discouragement

invite *n* *(infml)* **invitation**, request, call,

summons, offer ■ *v* 1 **ask**, request, call, summon, bid *(archaic)* *Opposite*: blackball 2 **provoke**, incite, induce, attract, encourage *Opposite*: forbid

inviting *adj* **attractive**, appealing, alluring, tempting, welcoming *Opposite*: unappealing

invocation *n* **prayer**, call, request, entreaty, petition

invoice *n* **bill**, account, statement, demand, proof of purchase *Opposite*: receipt ■ *v* **bill**, debit, charge

invoke *v* 1 **appeal**, call upon, call up, beg, summon 2 **cite**, quote, use, refer, mention 3 **evoke**, call to mind, conjure up, incite, arouse

involuntarily *adv* **unwillingly**, reluctantly, unhappily, against your will, compulsorily *Opposite*: willingly

involuntary *adj* 1 **compulsory**, obligatory, forced, unwilling, reluctant *Opposite*: willing 2 **instinctive**, spontaneous, reflex, unintentional, automatic *Opposite*: intentional

involve *v* 1 **contain**, include, take in, comprise, consist of 2 **concern**, have to do with, affect, interest, encompass 3 **implicate**, draw in, mix up, get into, embroil 4 **engage**, engross, absorb, grip, occupy *Opposite*: bore 5 **imply**, mean, entail, necessitate, require

involved *adj* 1 **complicated**, complex, intricate, elaborate, knotty *Opposite*: simple 2 **concerned**, caught up, mixed up, occupied, implicated *Opposite*: uninvolved

involvement *n* 1 **participation**, association, connection, contribution, engrossment 2 **attachment**, interest, concern, enthusiasm, commitment *Opposite*: detachment

invulnerable *adj* **untouchable**, invincible, unassailable, safe, impenetrable *Opposite*: vulnerable

inward *adj* 1 **inner**, innermost, inmost, private, deep *Opposite*: external 2 **internal**, interior, inner, inner-directed, innermost *Opposite*: outer 3 **incoming**, ingoing, entering, inward bound, inflowing *Opposite*: outward ■ *adv* **within**, inwardly, inside, in *Opposite*: outward

inwardly *adv* **secretly**, privately, to yourself, silently, deeply *Opposite*: openly

iota *n* **jot**, bit, scrap, speck, grain *Opposite*: lot

I.Q. *n* **intelligence quotient**, level of intelligence, degree of intelligence, intelligence

irascible *adj* **quick-tempered**, irritable, petulant, hot-tempered, short-tempered *Opposite*: easygoing

irate *adj* **angry**, incensed, furious, mad, irritated *Opposite*: calm

ire *(literary)* *n* **fury**, rage, anger, wrath, annoyance *Opposite*: calmness. *See* COMPARE AND CONTRAST *at* **anger**.

iridescent *adj* **lustrous**, rainbowlike, shimmering, shimmery, opalescent *Opposite*: monochrome

irk *v* **annoy**, vex, displease, trouble, bother *Opposite*: please. *See* COMPARE AND CONTRAST *at* bother.

irksome *adj* **annoying**, irritating, exasperating, tiresome, tedious *Opposite*: pleasant

iron *v* **press**, smooth out, iron out, smooth, flatten *Opposite*: crumple ▪ *adj* **firm**, hard, strong, determined, tough *Opposite*: soft

iron-clad *adj* **definite**, firm, sure, watertight, unimpeachable

iron curtain *n* **obstacle**, impediment, hurdle, line, border

ironic *adj* **1 caustic**, dry, biting, sarcastic, satirical **2 incongruous**, paradoxical, poignant, peculiar, odd. *See* COMPARE AND CONTRAST *at* sarcastic.

ironical *see* **ironic**

iron out *v* **sort out**, resolve, smooth over, clear up, settle

ironwork *n* **wrought iron**, metalwork, ironware, iron object, hardware

irony *n* **1 satire**, dryness, causticness, sardonicism, sarcasm *Opposite*: sincerity **2 paradox**, incongruity, fatefulness, dramatic irony, contrariety

irradiate *v* **1 light up**, light, illuminate, brighten, cast light on *Opposite*: darken **2 enlighten**, clarify, inform, instruct, inspire *Opposite*: obfuscate

irradiation *n* **1 radioactivity**, radiation, contamination, X-ray, treatment **2 preservation**, treatment, sterilization, purification

irrational *adj* **illogical**, unreasonable, foolish, ridiculous, absurd *Opposite*: rational

irrationality *n* **illogicality**, unreasonableness, foolishness, ludicrousness, absurdity *Opposite*: sense

irreconcilable *adj* **incompatible**, irresoluble, conflicting, opposing, opposed *Opposite*: compatible

irrecoverable *adj* **1 irretrievable**, gone, lost, given up, written off *(infml)* **2 irreparable**, beyond repair, irreversible, irredeemable, irremediable

irredeemable *adj* **hopeless**, unalterable, absolute, complete, incorrigible *Opposite*: redeemable

irreducible *adj* **complex**, complicated, involved, intricate, difficult

irrefutable *adj* **indisputable**, certain, unquestionable, overwhelming, unassailable *Opposite*: disputable

irregular *adj* **1 uneven**, unequal, asymmetrical, unbalanced, rough *Opposite*: even **2 erratic**, variable, random, haphazard, intermittent *Opposite*: regular **3 improper**, unacceptable, abnormal,

wrong, unsuitable *Opposite*: proper

irregularity *n* **1 indiscretion**, abnormality, wrongdoing, misdeed, anomaly **2 unevenness**, inequality, variability, randomness, haphazardness *Opposite*: regularity

irrelevance *n* **1 insignificance**, unimportance, inappropriateness, worthlessness, triviality *Opposite*: relevance **2 inconsequence**, side issue, detail, technicality, red herring

irrelevant *adj* **immaterial**, neither here nor there, unrelated, inappropriate, extraneous *Opposite*: relevant

irreligious *adj* **ungodly**, unspiritual, nonreligious, blasphemous, sacrilegious *Opposite*: devout

irremediable *adj* **irreparable**, irreversible, irredeemable, beyond repair, irrevocable

irreparable *adj* **beyond repair**, irreversible, irretrievable, severe, lasting

irreplaceable *adj* **unique**, inimitable, matchless, exceptional, rare *Opposite*: common

irrepressible *adj* **uncontrollable**, out of control, wild, unruly, disorderly *Opposite*: contained

irreproachable *adj* **blameless**, faultless, flawless, perfect, impeccable *Opposite*: blameworthy

irresistible *adj* **1 overwhelming**, overpowering, uncontrollable, compelling, strong *Opposite*: weak **2 desirable**, tempting, appealing, enticing, alluring *Opposite*: unappealing

irresolute *adj* **indecisive**, vacillating, unsure, weak, undetermined *Opposite*: determined

irresolution *n* **indecision**, indecisiveness, vacillation, weakness, hesitancy *Opposite*: determination

irrespective *adv* **regardless**, nevertheless, nonetheless, heedlessly, notwithstanding *(fml)*

irrespective of *prep* **regardless of**, despite, no matter, in spite of, heedless of *Opposite*: considering

irresponsibility *n* **recklessness**, carelessness, inattention, negligence, rashness *Opposite*: responsibility

irresponsible *adj* **reckless**, careless, negligent, rash, foolish *Opposite*: responsible

irretrievable *adj* **irreparable**, irreversible, irrevocable, severe, irrecoverable

irreverence *n* **disrespect**, mockery, derision, impertinence, impudence *Opposite*: respect

irreverent *adj* **disrespectful**, mocking, derisive, rude, impudent *Opposite*: respectful

irreversible *adj* **irreparable**, irretrievable, irrevocable, unalterable, irremediable *Opposite*: temporary

irrevocable *adj* **binding**, irreversible, final, unalterable, unchangeable *Opposite*: flexible

irrevocably *adv* irreversibly, forever, permanently, once and for all, for all time

irrigate *v* water, flood, wet, moisten, hose down *Opposite*: dry out

irritability *n* touchiness, bad temper, petulance, cantankerousness, tetchiness *(infml)* *Opposite*: equanimity *(fml)*

irritable *adj* bad-tempered, short-tempered, ill-tempered, petulant, cantankerous *Opposite*: easygoing

irritant *n* nuisance, annoyance, aggravation, irritation, bane *Opposite*: balm

irritate *v* 1 annoy, infuriate, bother, exasperate, aggravate *(infml)* *Opposite*: soothe 2 inflame, rub, chafe, sting, hurt *Opposite*: soothe. *See* COMPARE AND CONTRAST *at* annoy.

irritated *adj* annoyed, bothered, angry, exasperated, wound up *(infml)* *Opposite*: unperturbed

irritating *adj* annoying, exasperating, irksome, infuriating, frustrating *Opposite*: soothing

irritation *n* 1 annoyance, frustration, impatience, exasperation, aggravation *(infml)* *Opposite*: calmness 2 nuisance, bother, irritant, bane, pain *(infml)* 3 inflammation, soreness, tenderness, itchiness, rash. *See* COMPARE AND CONTRAST *at* anger.

island *n* isle, islet, atoll, desert island, key *Opposite*: mainland

islander *n* inhabitant, local, resident, occupant, native

island-hop *v* travel around, tour, sail around, sail, cruise

isle *n* island, islet, atoll, desert island, key

islet *see* isle

ism *(infml)* *n* doctrine, ideology, belief, belief system, creed

isolate *v* cut off, separate, segregate, detach, set apart *Opposite*: include

isolated *adj* 1 remote, cut off, inaccessible, lonely, secluded *Opposite*: nearby 2 exceptional, unique, solitary, unrepeated, special *Opposite*: common 3 lonely, alone, solitary, insular, friendless

isolation *n* separation, segregation, remoteness, loneliness, seclusion *Opposite*: inclusion

isolationism *n* separateness, remoteness, seclusion, independence, standoffishness

isometrics *n* exercise, workout, bodybuilding

isotope *n* element, form, variant, version

issue *n* 1 subject, matter, question, topic, problem 2 copy, number, edition, installment, back number 3 production, release, distribution, circulation, publication 4 progeny, offspring, children, young, descendants ■ *v* 1 supply, give out, hand out, deliver, distribute 2 announce, broadcast, send out, make, declare 3 publish, release, broadcast, disseminate, distribute *Opposite*: withdraw 4 originate, stem, spring, arise, rise 5 emanate, emerge, issue forth, gush, flow

isthmus *n* strip, neck, bridge, peninsula, spit

IT *n* information technology, computer science, data processing, information processing, data retrieval

italic *adj* sloping, slanted, oblique *Opposite*: roman

itch *v* 1 irritate, prickle, scratch, tickle, crawl *Opposite*: soothe 2 long, desire, wish, hanker, yearn ■ *n* 1 itchiness, tickle, irritation, prickling, tingling 2 desire, longing, wish, eagerness, hankering

itchiness *n* irritation, tickle, inflammation, tingling, prickliness

itching *adj* eager, longing, dying, keen, burning *Opposite*: reluctant

itchy *adj* prickly, tickly, scratchy, uncomfortable, irritated

item *n* 1 thing, article, piece, entry, point 2 *(infml)* couple, pair, twosome, match, duo

itemize *v* list, detail, enumerate, record, document

iterate *v* repeat, restate, reiterate, go over, retell

iteration *n* repetition, restatement, reiteration, rehearsal, duplication

itinerant *adj* peripatetic, roving, wandering, nomadic, roaming *Opposite*: settled

itinerary *n* route, schedule, journey, circuit, tour

itsy-bitsy *(infml)* *adj* tiny, little, small, minute, minuscule *Opposite*: huge

ivory tower *n* seclusion, isolation, retreat, remoteness, academic world *Opposite*: real world

J

jab v stab, prod, thrust, dig, poke ■ n prod, stab, thrust, dig, poke

jabber v chatter, babble, prattle, gabble, ramble

jacket n cover, covering, casing, sheathing, sheath

jackknife v turn, skid, swerve, veer, swivel

jackpot n prize, bonanza, winnings, windfall, pool

jack up v 1 lift, lift up, raise, raise up, put up Opposite: lower 2 increase, raise, put up, hike up, boost Opposite: slash

jaded adj 1 bored, world-weary, jaundiced, cynical, fed up (infml) Opposite: enthusiastic 2 tired, weary, exhausted, worn-out, burned-out Opposite: fresh

jagged adj 1 sharp, pointed, pointy, rough, serrated Opposite: smooth 2 uneven, rough, ragged, crude, irregular Opposite: even

jaggedness n 1 sharpness, pointedness, pointiness, roughness, serration Opposite: smoothness 2 unevenness, raggedness, roughness, irregularity, bumpiness Opposite: evenness

jail n prison, penitentiary, lockup, detention home, open prison ■ v imprison, lock up, lock away, put behind bars, confine Opposite: free

jailbreak n breakout, escape, getaway, exodus, flight

jailer n prison officer, guard, warden, governor, keeper Opposite: liberator

jalopy (dated infml) n wreck, tin lizzie (infml), rattletrap (infml), beater (infml), heap (slang)

jam v 1 push, squash, cram, stuff, pack 2 fill, fill up, throng, pack, block 3 stop, seize, seize up, grind to a halt, stick ■ n 1 traffic jam, gridlock, bottleneck, logjam, roadblock 2 (infml) predicament, mess, quandary, pickle (infml), fix (infml)

jamb n upright, post, support, column, doorpost

jamboree n celebration, party, fete, carnival, garden party

jammed adj 1 stuck, wedged, stuck fast, lodged, caught Opposite: free 2 blocked, congested, thronged, packed, crammed Opposite: deserted

jam-packed (infml) adj crowded, full, full up, packed, filled to capacity Opposite: empty

jangle v rattle, jingle, clank, clink, clatter

jape (literary) n prank, trick, practical joke, joke, lark ■ v joke, fool around, make mischief, trick, play with

jar n pot, container, vessel, crock, urn ■ v 1 shake, jolt, jerk, bump, hit 2 irritate, grate, annoy, irk, get on somebody's nerves Opposite: harmonize

jargon n 1 terminology, slang, argot, parlance, language 2 nonsense, verbiage, cant, gobbledygook (infml), mumbo jumbo (infml)

jarring adj 1 irritating, grating, annoying, unpleasant, unbearable Opposite: calming 2 disturbing, unsettling, shocking, destabilizing, uncomfortable Opposite: reassuring 3 clashing, incongruous, uncharacteristic, discordant, inharmonious Opposite: harmonious

jaundiced adj cynical, pessimistic, skeptical, unenthusiastic, jaded

jaunt n outing, trip, excursion, break, day out

jauntiness n cheerfulness, jolliness, gaiety, dash, spryness

jaunty adj carefree, cheerful, cheery, jolly, spry

javelin n spear, projectile, missile, lance, harpoon

jaw n chin, jawbone, jawline, jowl, mouth

jawbone n jaw, chin, maxilla, mandible

jaywalk v cross, cross over, walk across, stroll across, go across

jaywalker n pedestrian, walker, crosser, traverser, stroller

jazz up (infml) v enhance, spice, spice up, liven up, enliven

jealous adj 1 envious, covetous, resentful, green with envy, green 2 protective, suspicious, wary, watchful, mistrustful Opposite: trusting

jealousy n 1 envy, covetousness, resentment, resentfulness, desirousness (fml) 2 protectiveness, suspicion, suspiciousness, wariness, watchfulness

jeer v boo, hiss, heckle, catcall, taunt Opposite: applaud ■ n hiss, boo, taunt, catcall, hoot

jeer at v insult, taunt, sneer, mock, deride Opposite: cheer

jeering n derision, mockery, name-calling, mocking, taunting Opposite: applause ■ adj derisive, scornful, mocking, sardonic, contemptuous

jejune adj 1 boring, undemanding, uninteresting, lightweight, insubstantial Opposite: interesting 2 childish, immature, adolescent, unsophisticated, crude Opposite: mature

jell v **1 solidify**, set, congeal, firm, harden Opposite: liquefy **2 take shape**, shape up, crystallize, come together, firm up Opposite: disintegrate **3 bond**, be compatible, be on the same wavelength, get along, click (infml) Opposite: clash

jellied adj **gelatinous**, set, solid, congealed

jellify v **set**, gelatinize, congeal, jell, gel Opposite: liquefy

jelly n **1 gelatin**, aspic, gel **2 petroleum jelly**, lubricant, ointment ■ v **set**, thicken, jellify, gelatinize, congeal Opposite: liquefy

jeopardize v **put at risk**, risk, put in danger, endanger, expose

jeopardy n **danger**, risk, threat, peril, hazard

jerk v **1 yank**, tug, pull, wrench, haul **2 lurch**, jolt, shudder, judder, bump **3 twitch**, shudder, tremble, shake ■ n **1 pull**, tug, yank, wrench, haul **2 jolt**, bump, shudder, judder, lurch **3 spasm**, twitch, shudder, tremble, shake

jerkin n **jacket**, body warmer, tunic, vest

jerkiness n **bumpiness**, jumpiness, bounciness, lurching, shuddering Opposite: smoothness

jerky adj **irregular**, spasmodic, erratic, fitful, bumpy Opposite: smooth

jerrybuild v **throw up**, fling up, throw together (infml), knock together (infml)

jerrybuilt adj **badly built**, poor, poor quality, shoddy, flimsy

jerry can n **can**, container, canister

jest (literary) n **joke**, prank, hoax, quip, spoof ■ v **banter**, joke, kid, tease, quip

jester n **fool**, clown, comedian, entertainer, comic

jesting (literary) adj **jokey**, lighthearted, flippant, funny, humorous Opposite: serious ■ n **joking**, clowning, kidding, slapstick, fun

jet n **spurt**, spout, fountain, squirt, stream

jetsam n **odds and ends**, flotsam, debris, detritus, trash

jet set (infml) n **glitterati**, high society, rich and famous, beautiful people, idle rich Opposite: hoi polloi

jettison v **throw away**, throw out, get rid of, abandon, discard Opposite: keep

jetty n **dock**, breakwater, quay, landing stage, pier

jewel n **1 gemstone**, gem, precious stone, semiprecious stone, crystal **2 ornament**, trinket, accessory

jibe see gibe

jiffy (infml) n **moment**, second, minute, flash, instant

jig v **jerk**, skip, hop, caper, leap

jiggle v **wiggle**, waggle, shake, joggle, rattle

jigsaw n **puzzle**, jigsaw puzzle, picture puzzle, Chinese puzzle, tangram

jigsaw puzzle see jigsaw

jilt v **reject**, turn down, break up, split up, walk out Opposite: stick by

jimmy v **lever**, open, force, pry, prize

jingle n **tune**, song, refrain, chorus, ditty ■ v **tinkle**, rattle, ring, clink, clank

jingoism n **chauvinism**, patriotism, nationalism, xenophobia, hostility

jingoistic adj **chauvinistic**, patriotic, nationalistic, xenophobic, hostile

jinx n **curse**, plague, evil eye, spell, bad luck

jinxed adj **unlucky**, luckless, hapless, unfortunate, star-crossed Opposite: lucky

jitters (infml) n **nervousness**, agitation, uneasiness, anxiety, apprehension Opposite: calmness

jittery adj **nervous**, jumpy, on edge, edgy, fidgety Opposite: calm

job n **1 occupation**, work, line, line of work, trade **2 position**, post, appointment, vacancy, role **3 task**, duty, responsibility, chore, assignment

jobbing adj **casual**, occasional, freelance, part-time, temporary Opposite: regular

jobless adj **unemployed**, out of work, on welfare, laid off Opposite: employed

job-sharing n **part-time work**, work-sharing, sharing

jockey n **rider**, equestrian, steeplechaser, showjumper, competitor ■ v **1 ride**, race, steeplechase, show jump, compete **2 compete**, contend, fight, struggle, juggle **3 manipulate**, cajole, trick, deceive, talk into

jocular adj **funny**, joking, jokey, jovial, playful Opposite: solemn

jocularity n **wittiness**, comicality, playfulness, jokiness, humorousness Opposite: solemnity

jocund (literary) adj **cheerful**, good-humored, cheery, merry, ebullient

jog v **1 trot**, run, train, exercise, sprint **2 nudge**, prod, bump, push, bang

jogger n **runner**, sprinter, cross-country runner, athlete

joggle v **shake**, wiggle, waggle, jiggle, jerk

John Hancock (infml) n **signature**, autograph, name, mark

joie de vivre n **vitality**, enthusiasm, liveliness, exuberance, high-spiritedness Opposite: lethargy

join v **1 fasten**, connect, link, unite, stick Opposite: separate **2 connect**, link up, merge, bring together, unite Opposite: disengage **3 sign up**, enroll, enlist, join up, go in with Opposite: leave ■ n **joint**, seam, connection, intersection, link

joined adj **1 bonded**, fixed together, hinged, hitched, linked Opposite: detached **2 associated**, allied, affiliated, twinned, connected Opposite: independent

joinery n **woodworking**, cabinetmaking, furniture making, carving, carpentry

join forces v **team up**, collaborate, get together, come together, rally *Opposite*: split

join in v **participate**, become involved, take part, enter into, take a turn *Opposite*: leave

joint *adj* **combined**, dual, shared, multiparty, united *Opposite*: individual ■ *n* **join**, linkage, link, junction, intersection

join together v **merge**, amalgamate, integrate, dovetail, associate *Opposite*: split

join up v **enroll**, enroll, sign up, join, subscribe *Opposite*: quit

joist *n* **beam**, spar, truss, support

joke *n* **1 witticism**, tall story, pun, anecdote, tale **2 prank**, trick, practical joke, stunt, hoax **3 butt**, laughingstock, object of ridicule, fool, buffoon ■ v **kid**, pretend, clown, play the fool, pull somebody's leg (*infml*)

joker *n* **clown**, fool, buffoon, comedian, comic

jokey *adj* **amusing**, lighthearted, flippant, funny, witty *Opposite*: serious

joking *adj* **jokey**, playful, flippant, lighthearted, facetious *Opposite*: serious ■ *n* **clowning**, teasing, raillery, fooling around, horseplay

jollification *n* **festivity**, revelry, celebration, merrymaking, party

jolliness *see* **jollity**

jollity *n* **cheerfulness**, fun, hilarity, joviality, jolliness *Opposite*: seriousness

jolly *adj* **cheerful**, happy, fun, jovial, bright *Opposite*: sad

jolt v **shake**, jerk, bump, joggle, nudge ■ *n* **1 shock**, surprise, bolt from the blue, blow, reminder **2 bump**, shake, jerk, joggle, bounce

josh (*infml*) v **tease**, make fun of, chaff, ridicule, mock

jostle v **push**, knock, bump, elbow, shove

jot *n* **iota**, atom, bit, speck, tittle

jot down v **write down**, make a note of, scribble down, put on paper, put down

journal *n* **1 periodical**, magazine, paper, weekly, monthly **2 diary**, log, chronicle, record, register

journalism *n* **reporting**, reportage, broadcasting, commentary, fourth estate

journalist *n* **correspondent**, reporter, broadcaster, columnist, newscaster

journalistic *adj* **reporting**, editorial, newspaper, current affairs

journey *n* **trip**, voyage, expedition, ride, flight ■ v **travel**, tour, go, trek, voyage

joust v **fight**, tilt, compete, battle, engage *Opposite*: agree

jovial *adj* **cheerful**, jolly, fun-loving, breezy, happy *Opposite*: glum

joviality *n* **cheerfulness**, jollity, jolliness, cheeriness, bonhomie *Opposite*: glumness

jovialness *see* **joviality**

jowl *n* **jaw**, chin, jawbone, jawline, muzzle

joy *n* **1 happiness**, delight, enjoyment, bliss, ecstasy *Opposite*: sadness **2 delight**, jewel, treasure, pearl, angel

joyful *adj* **1 happy**, elated, ecstatic, thrilled, pleased *Opposite*: sad **2 wonderful**, blissful, pleasurable, fantastic, enjoyable *Opposite*: unpleasant

joyfulness *n* **happiness**, enjoyment, bliss, ecstasy, merriment *Opposite*: sadness

joyless *adj* **miserable**, cheerless, depressing, bleak, desolate *Opposite*: happy

joylessness *n* **cheerlessness**, misery, gloom, unhappiness, bleakness *Opposite*: happiness

joyous *adj* **happy**, merry, blissful, festive, cheerful *Opposite*: glum

joyousness *n* **happiness**, pleasure, bliss, joyfulness, jubilation *Opposite*: glumness

joyrider *n* **carjacker**, car thief, speeder, hot-rodder (*slang*)

joyriding *n* **carjacking**, car theft, speeding, hot-rodding (*slang*)

JP *n* **Justice of the Peace**, magistrate, justice, judge, arbitrator

jubilant *adj* **triumphant**, proud, thrilled, ecstatic, delighted *Opposite*: disappointed

jubilation *n* **elation**, triumph, joyousness, euphoria, delight *Opposite*: disappointment

jubilee *n* **anniversary**, celebration, commemoration, festival, festivity

judder v **shake**, vibrate, shudder, quiver, tremble ■ *n* **shudder**, vibration, quiver, tremor, jerk

judge *n* **1 magistrate**, justice, justice of the peace, judge advocate **2 arbitrator**, adjudicator, moderator, umpire, referee **3 evaluator**, critic, reviewer, arbiter, expert ■ v **1 arbitrate**, adjudicate, mediate, referee, umpire **2 estimate**, guess, consider, say, assess **3 condemn**, criticize, sneer at, belittle, pass judgment on **4 assess**, evaluate, weigh, look at, appraise **5 consider**, reckon, think, believe, maintain

judgment *n* **1 verdict**, ruling, decision, finding, sentence **2 discernment**, good sense, shrewdness, wisdom, common sense **3 opinion**, view, considered opinion, feeling, thoughts

judgmental *adj* **critical**, hypercritical, condemnatory, negative, disapproving *Opposite*: complimentary

judicial *adj* **legal**, court, justice, official

judiciary *n* **judges**, bench, courts, magistrates

judicious *adj* **sensible**, wise, careful, shrewd, astute *Opposite*: foolish

judiciousness *n* **wisdom**, prudence, shrewdness, sense, care *Opposite*: foolishness

jug *n* **pitcher**, ewer, carafe, crock

juggle v **1 fit in**, manage, cope with, run,

deal with **2 manipulate,** falsify, alter, misrepresent, tamper with

juice n extract, sap, liquid, fluid, liquor

juiciness n **succulence,** ripeness, lusciousness, moistness Opposite: dryness

juicy adj **1 succulent,** luscious, thirst-quenching, moist, ripe Opposite: dry **2** (infml) titillating, scandalous, salacious, exciting, sensational Opposite: dull

jumble v **mix up,** muddle, clutter, disarrange, shuffle Opposite: tidy ■ n **muddle,** heap, clutter, hodgepodge, mishmash

jumbled adj **untidy,** topsy-turvy, muddled, chaotic, disorderly Opposite: orderly

jumbo adj **oversize,** outsize, huge, enormous, giant-sized Opposite: tiny

jump v **1 bound,** leap, hop, skip, soar **2 be startled,** be surprised, start, get a fright, be frightened **3** (infml) **obey,** do as you are told, conform, toe the line, play the game ■ n **1 leap,** bound, hop, skip, spring **2 obstacle,** hurdle, fence, wall, hedge **3 start,** jolt, jerk, lurch, jar

jump back v **rebound,** recoil, bounce back, ricochet

jumper n **athlete,** high jumper, long jumper, hurdler, steeplechaser

jump in v **make a start,** take the plunge, get going, leap in, take the bull by the horns

jumpiness n **1 jitteriness,** anxiety, nervousness, agitation, edginess Opposite: calmness **2 jerkiness,** erraticism, unsteadiness, suddenness, abruptness Opposite: smoothness

jump-start v **1 kick-start,** start up, get going, set in motion, goose (infml) **2 stimulate,** trigger, set off, start up, kick-start ■ n **1 kick-start,** startup, start **2 stimulus,** momentum, spur, drive, impetus

jumpy adj **1 jittery,** anxious, nervous, worried, tense Opposite: calm **2 jerky,** erratic, unsteady, sudden, abrupt Opposite: smooth

junction n **connection,** intersection, seam, link, joint

juncture n **1 point in time,** stage, moment, occasion, interval **2** (fml) **join,** connection, joint, link, seam

jungle n **1 tropical forest,** rain forest, forest, wilderness, bush **2 tangle,** muddle, maze, jumble, mess

junior adj **low-ranking,** subordinate, inferior, lower, low-grade Opposite: senior ■ n **subordinate,** underling, beginner, trainee, novice Opposite: old hand

junk (infml) n **1 secondhand goods,** unwanted items, castoffs, odds and ends **2 rubbish,** trash, scrap, debris, litter ■ v **discard,** throw away, throw out, get rid of, scrap Opposite: keep

junket n **trip,** excursion, visit, outing, spree

junk food n **snack food,** convenience food, fast food, TV dinner

junk mail n **fliers,** leaflets, brochures, direct mail

junta n **1 military government,** military rule, regime, martial law, government **2 cabal,** faction, clique, gang, band **3 council,** committee, legislative body, assembly, forum

jurisdiction n **1 authority,** dominion, influence, power, control **2 area,** state, extent of power, territory, province

juror n **jury member,** assessor, estimator, judge, adjudicator

jury n **adjudicators,** judges, bench, panel, board

just adv **1 a minute ago,** a moment ago, a second ago, only this minute, in the past few minutes **2 at this moment,** now, immediately, presently, in a minute **3 only,** merely, simply, solely, purely **4 barely,** hardly, scarcely, slightly **5 simply,** really, truly, definitely, emphatically **6 exactly,** precisely, absolutely, emphatically, completely ■ adj **1 fair,** impartial, objective, unbiased, unprejudiced Opposite: unfair **2 correct,** moral, ethical, good, appropriate Opposite: unjust **3 reasonable,** valid, sensible, sound, balanced

just deserts n **what you deserve,** what was coming to you, just reward, comeuppance (infml)

just-folks (infml) adj **unaffected,** unsophisticated, folksy, simple, friendly Opposite: pretentious

justice n **1 fairness,** reasonableness, impartiality, evenhandedness, righteousness Opposite: unfairness **2 validity,** legitimacy, rightfulness, acceptability, reasonableness **3 judge,** magistrate, justice of the peace, judge advocate

justifiable adj **defensible,** admissible, justified, reasonable, correct Opposite: indefensible

justification n **defense,** reason, reasoning, explanation, validation

justified adj **warranted,** defensible, vindicated, correct, right Opposite: unwarranted

justify v **1 defend,** validate, explain, rationalize, excuse **2 align,** adjust, straighten up, line up

justly adv **1 fairly,** impartially, rightly, reasonably, honorably Opposite: unfairly **2 correctly,** morally, deservedly, reasonably, justifiably Opposite: unjustly

just reward see **just deserts**

jut v **stick out,** protrude, overhang, poke out, project

juvenile adj **1 youthful,** young, immature, adolescent, baby-faced Opposite: mature **2 childish,** infantile, babyish, puerile, immature Opposite: grown-up ■ n **youngster,** adolescent, young person, teenager, youth Opposite: adult

juxtapose v put side by side, put together, put next to, put beside, put adjacent to

juxtaposition n collocation, association, apposition, comparison, contrast

K

kaleidoscope n 1 **complex pattern**, phantasmagoria, display, mixture, medley 2 **series**, web, set, chain reaction, domino effect

kaleidoscopic adj **colorful**, variegated, multicolored, many-colored, motley Opposite: monochromatic

kaolin n **clay**, kaolinite, argil, potter's clay, potter's earth

kaput (infml) adj **broken**, ruined, wrecked, finished, ended Opposite: working

karaoke n **sing-along**, singing, karaoke night, music, entertainment

karma n 1 **destiny**, fate, kismet, fortune, providence 2 (infml) **atmosphere**, aura, feeling, ambiance, vibrations (infml)

keel v **capsize**, turn upside down, upset, overturn, turn over Opposite: right

keel over (infml) v 1 **collapse**, fall over, faint, pass out, lose consciousness Opposite: come to 2 **capsize**, keel, turn upside down, upset, overturn Opposite: right

keen adj 1 **intense**, strong, acute, deep, powerful Opposite: mild 2 **sensitive**, responsive, finely honed, finely tuned, well-developed Opposite: insensitive 3 (literary) **sharp**, sharpened, whetted, bright, steely Opposite: blunt 4 **eager**, enthusiastic, willing, fanatical, dedicated Opposite: indifferent 5 **icy**, bitter, cold, chilly, wintry Opposite: mild 6 **acute**, quick, clever, perceptive, alert Opposite: dull ■ v **cry out**, wail, howl, weep, sob

keenness n 1 **enthusiasm**, eagerness, zeal, passion, willingness Opposite: reluctance 2 **intensity**, intenseness, strength, acuteness, depth Opposite: mildness 3 (literary) **sharpness**, razor-sharpness, brightness, steeliness Opposite: bluntness 4 **iciness**, bitterness, coldness, chill, wintriness Opposite: mildness 5 **acuteness**, perception, quickness, cleverness, perceptiveness Opposite: dullness

keen-sighted adj **sharp-sighted**, sharp-eyed, eagle-eyed, hawk-eyed

keep v 1 **hold onto**, hang onto, save, retain, have Opposite: let go 2 **maintain**, hold, sustain, preserve, conserve Opposite: abandon 3 **hide**, conceal, repress, withhold, hold back Opposite: let out 4 **store**, hold, stash, stack, shelve Opposite: get rid of 5 **continue**, go on, keep on, persist in, persevere with Opposite: stop 6 **detain**, delay, hold up, hold back, keep back Oppo-

site: release 7 **take care of**, care for, tend, look after, watch over 8 **honor**, fulfill, carry out, comply with, obey Opposite: break 9 **stay**, remain, be, keep yourself Opposite: become 10 **own**, look after, care for, farm, rear

keep abreast v **stay current**, keep up, keep up to date, be well-informed, stay in touch

keep an eye on v 1 **watch closely**, keep a close watch on, observe, spy on, watch 2 **look after**, watch over, keep in check, mind, take care of

keep a secret v **not tell a soul**, be discreet, keep quiet, be the soul of discretion, keep mum (infml) Opposite: spill the beans (infml)

keep a straight face v **show no emotion**, have a poker face, look blank, dissemble

keep at v **persevere**, persist, soldier on, plow through, keep your nose to the grindstone Opposite: give up

keep at bay v **hold off**, keep away, ward off, stave off, fend off Opposite: encourage

keep away v **hold off**, ward off, keep at bay, stave off, fend off Opposite: encourage

keep back v 1 **restrain**, curb, control, restrict, limit 2 **withhold**, keep secret, suppress, omit, hide Opposite: reveal 3 **reserve**, conserve, hold on to, save, withhold Opposite: use up

keep count v **record**, note, keep a record of, note down, keep a note of Opposite: lose track of

keep down v 1 **oppress**, suppress, repress, subjugate, subdue Opposite: liberate 2 **limit**, curb, restrain, control, check

keeper n **custodian**, guard, guardian, caretaker, attendant

keep from v 1 **prevent**, restrain, stop, deter, prohibit Opposite: allow 2 **protect**, shield, shelter, save, cushion Opposite: expose 3 **withhold**, omit, hide, conceal, keep back Opposite: reveal

keep going v **persevere**, carry on, persist, hold up, last Opposite: stop

keep in v **hold in**, repress, withhold, hold back, retain Opposite: let out

keep in check v **control**, restrict, restrain, curb, limit

keeping n **charge**, custody, possession, care, trust

keep in mind v **bear in mind**, remember, recall, retain Opposite: forget

keep in the dark v keep in ignorance, withhold information from, keep something back from, hold something back from, conceal something from *Opposite*: inform

keep mum (infml) v keep quiet, not tell a soul, be discreet, keep secret, keep under wraps *Opposite*: spill the beans (infml)

keep off v 1 abstain, do without, go without, avoid, not touch *Opposite*: indulge 2 **hold off**, hold back, separate, shut out, ward off *Opposite*: encourage

keep on v continue, persist, persevere, carry on, go on *Opposite*: give up

keep out v exclude, shut out, bar, ban, deny entry *Opposite*: admit

keepsake n memento, reminder, souvenir, gift, token

keep secret v withhold, suppress, sit on, keep from, keep under wraps *Opposite*: let slip

keep the ball rolling v continue, keep things moving, keep things going, keep up the momentum, maintain momentum *Opposite*: stop

keep the lid on v keep under control, contain, control, suppress, restrain

keep to v obey, comply with, abide by, stick to, adhere to

keep track of v follow, keep an eye on, keep up with, monitor, keep up to date with *Opposite*: lose track of

keep under control v keep in check, restrain, contain, keep the lid on, suppress

keep under wraps v keep secret, keep to yourself, keep back, keep quiet, hide *Opposite*: reveal

keep up v 1 continue, sustain, maintain, carry on, persevere *Opposite*: stop 2 **stay beside**, keep abreast, keep pace, stay even, match *Opposite*: fall behind 3 **stay in touch**, keep in touch, keep in contact, keep abreast, keep up to date *Opposite*: lose touch

keep your chin up v make the best of things, take the bad with the good, look on the bright side, not let things get the better of you *Opposite*: go under

keep your cool (infml) v stay calm, keep your head, calm down, simmer down, cool off

keep your word v be as good as your word, keep your promise, deliver on a promise, be true to your word, keep your side of the bargain *Opposite*: go back on

keg n barrel, cask, tub, firkin, drum

ken n knowledge, acquaintance, understanding, awareness, comprehension

kennel n house, hut, shelter

kernel n 1 pip, pit, stone *Opposite*: husk 2 core, nub, root, heart, essence

kerosene n fuel, oil, fuel oil, lamp oil

kerosine see **kerosene**

kettle n pot, pan, caldron, steamer, fish kettle

kettle of fish n mess, predicament, difficulty, problem, quagmire

key n 1 skeleton key, master key, passepartout, passkey, latchkey 2 **pitch**, register, tone, scale, note 3 **button**, knob, control 4 **solution**, answer, explanation, means, secret ■ adj important, main, crucial, significant, vital *Opposite*: unimportant ■ v input, keyboard, enter, key in, type

keyboard n control panel, console, controls ■ v type, key, key in, input, enter

keyboarder n keyboard operator, typist, data entry clerk, typesetter

keyhole n hole, aperture, spyhole, peephole, opening

key in v key, type, input, enter, typeset

keynote n theme, essence, idea, gist, core ■ adj important, crucial, major, essential, defining

key player n leading light, principal, kingpin (infml), big cheese (infml), honcho (slang)

keystone n foundation, basis, bedrock, underpinning, grounding

kibbutz n collective, commune, cooperative, community, settlement

kick v 1 boot, strike, hack 2 **dribble**, punt, place-kick, kick off 3 **jolt**, jerk, recoil, flex, reflex 4 (infml) **give up**, quit, end, cease, stop *Opposite*: take up ■ n 1 **recoil**, rebound, return, reaction, reflex 2 (infml) **thrill**, boost, pleasure, excitement, frisson

kick back (infml) v relax, take it easy, lounge, loaf, veg out (infml)

kickback n bribe, softener, payment, reward, inducement

kick in v 1 (infml) **take effect**, come on-line, get going, get underway, start *Opposite*: run out 2 **break down**, smash, demolish, flatten, destroy

kick in the teeth n setback, blow, shock, betrayal, letdown *Opposite*: boost

kick off (infml) v start, begin, start the ball rolling, get underway, commence *Opposite*: end

kickoff (infml) n start, beginning, opening, initiation, commencement (fml) *Opposite*: end

kick out (infml) v throw out, sling out, eject, force out, show the door *Opposite*: appoint

kick-start v 1 start up, start, get going, turn over, crank up *Opposite*: stop 2 **restart**, start, revive, resuscitate, jump-start *Opposite*: kill off ■ n (infml) fillip, shot in the arm, spur, stimulus, boost

kick up a fuss v protest, rampage, make a scene, make a fuss, complain *Opposite*: smooth over

kid n (infml) child, teenager, adolescent, youngster, toddler *Opposite*: adult ■ v 1 tease, joke, poke fun at, make fun of, mock 2 (infml) fool, trick, delude, hoodwink, con. See COMPARE AND CONTRAST at youth.

kidder n **joker**, tease, trickster, clown, prankster

kidnap v **abduct**, take hostage, capture, take prisoner, hijack Opposite: release

kid's stuff n **child's play**, piece of cake, pushover

kill v 1 **murder**, assassinate, execute, put to death, slaughter Opposite: revive 2 (infml) **turn off**, shut down, deactivate, disconnect, cut Opposite: start up

---

COMPARE AND CONTRAST CORE MEANING: deprive of life

kill cause the death of a person or animal; **murder** take the life of another person deliberately and not in self-defense in a serious criminal act; **assassinate** murder a public figure by a sudden violent attack; **execute** take somebody's life as part of a judicial or extrajudicial process; **put to death** deliberately take somebody's life, especially in accordance with a legal death sentence; **slaughter** kill farm animals for food, or to kill a person or large numbers of people brutally; **slay** (fml or literary) to kill a person or animal; **put down** or **put to sleep** kill a sick or injured animal, especially when done by a vet.

---

killer n 1 **murderer**, assassin, slaughterer, executioner, exterminator 2 **disease**, destroyer, natural disaster, predator

killing n **murder**, assassination, butchery, slaughter, carnage

killjoy n **spoilsport**, party pooper (infml), sourpuss (infml), wet blanket (infml) Opposite: merrymaker

kill off v **put an end to**, stop, halt, destroy, end Opposite: set up

kill time v **pass the time**, waste time, wait, loiter, twiddle your thumbs

kill yourself v **commit suicide**, end it all, take your own life

kill yourself laughing v **laugh your head off**, double over, have hysterics (infml), split your sides (infml)

kiln n **oven**, furnace, forge

kimono n **dressing gown**, peignoir, bathrobe, robe, negligee

kin n **family**, relatives, relations, nearest and dearest, kith and kin

kind adj **caring**, nice, generous, gentle, compassionate Opposite: inhumane ■ n **type**, sort, class, variety, category. See COMPARE AND CONTRAST at **type**, **generous**.

kindergarten n **nursery school**, playschool, playgroup, nursery, day nursery

kindhearted adj **kind**, friendly, generous, sympathetic, caring Opposite: cruel

kindheartedness n **kindness**, sympathy, compassion, benevolence, thoughtfulness Opposite: cruelty

kindle v 1 **encourage**, stimulate, stir up, fire up, promote Opposite: quench 2 **spark**, light, set alight, burn, ignite Opposite: douse

kindliness n **kindness**, compassion, sympathy, amiability, gentleness Opposite: cruelty

kindly adj **friendly**, sympathetic, generous, kindhearted, caring ■ adv **gently**, compassionately, sympathetically, benevolently, kindheartedly Opposite: cruelly

kindness n **compassion**, gentleness, sympathy, kindheartedness, benevolence Opposite: cruelty

kindred adj **associated**, close, like, alike, allied Opposite: dissimilar ■ n 1 **kinship**, family, kin, blood, ties 2 **family**, relations, relatives, kinfolk, nearest and dearest

kinfolk n **family**, relatives, relations, kindred, kith and kin

king n 1 **monarch**, sovereign, ruler, rajah, tsar Opposite: subject 2 **ruler**, chief, head, leader, dictator 3 **leader**, star, superstar, luminary, leading light

kingdom n **realm**, empire, monarchy, territory, domain

kingly adj **magnificent**, stately, grand, majestic, regal

kingpin (infml) n **key player**, leading light, principal, superstar, linchpin

kingship n **monarchy**, sovereignty, crown, power, authority

king-size adj **extra-large**, outsize, enormous, huge, giant Opposite: miniature

kink n **bend**, twist, crook, hook, bow

kinky adj 1 **crinkled**, crinkly, twisty, knotted, twisted Opposite: straight 2 (infml) **unusual**, strange, idiosyncratic, quirky, unnatural Opposite: conventional

kinship n 1 **relationship**, connection, tie, link, bond 2 **relatedness**, understanding, empathy, affiliation, affinity

kinsman (fml) n **relative**, relation, family member

kinswoman (fml) n **relative**, relation, family member

kiosk n **booth**, stall, stand, hut

kismet n **fate**, fortune, luck, destiny, doom

kiss v 1 **peck**, make out (infml), smooch (infml), canoodle (infml), neck (infml) 2 **touch**, brush, glance, graze, caress ■ n 1 **caress**, light touch, contact, graze, pat 2 **peck**, embrace, smacker (infml), smooch (infml), canoodle (infml)

kiss-and-tell (infml) adj **revealing**, exposing, divulging, sensational, scandalous

kit n 1 **tackle**, tools, equipment, implements, supplies 2 **set of clothes**, dress, apparel, costume, clothing 3 **belongings**, things, stuff, baggage, luggage

kit bag n **canvas bag**, duffel bag, backpack, knapsack, rucksack

kitchen n **kitchenette**, galley, scullery

kith and kin n **relatives**, family, relations, folks, kinfolk

kitsch n 1 **vulgarity**, tastelessness, sentimentality, ostentation, showiness *Opposite*: tastefulness **2 trash**, frippery, junk (*infml*), tack (*infml*) ■ *adj* **tasteless**, in poor taste, vulgar, common, loud *Opposite*: tasteful

kittenish *adj* **1 playful**, frisky, lively, coltish, frolicsome *Opposite*: staid **2 flirtatious**, coy, frisky, cute, coquettish (*literary*)

kitty *n* **1** (*infml*) **cat**, kitten, puss (*infml*), pussy (*infml*), pussycat (*infml*) **2 fund**, pool, stake, ante, pot (*infml*)

kitty-cornered *adv* **cater-cornered**, crosswise, crossways, sideways, catty-cornered

Klaxon *n* **horn**, siren, alarm, signal, buzzer

knack *n* **ability**, skill, talent, flair, aptitude. *See* COMPARE AND CONTRAST *at* **talent**.

knapsack *n* **bag**, shoulder bag, rucksack, backpack, daypack

knead *v* **massage**, rub, work, manipulate, press

knee-deep *adj* **involved**, occupied, engrossed, absorbed, immersed *Opposite*: uninvolved

knee-jerk (*infml*) *adj* **1 unthinking**, automatic, reflex, habitual, immediate *Opposite*: considered **2 predictable**, prejudging, prejudiced, biased, dyed-in-the-wool *Opposite*: unpredictable

kneel *v* **go down on your knees**, genuflect, kneel down, kowtow *Opposite*: rise

knell *n* **toll**, ring, peal, sound, ringing

knickknack *n* **trinket**, curio, souvenir, object, decoration

knife *v* **stab**, spear, stick, wound, lacerate

WORD BANK

❏ **types of knives** bread knife, butcher knife, carving knife, clasp knife, cleaver, jackknife, paperknife, paring knife, penknife, pocketknife, steak knife, switchblade, table knife

knife-edge *n* **critical point**, decisive point, turning point, watershed, crisis

knight *n* **cavalier**, caballero, knight-errant, adventurer

knit *v* **1 unite**, join, interweave, weave, interlace **2 heal**, mend, set, join, meld

knob *n* **1 handle**, doorknob, dial, button, handhold **2 lump**, bump, bulge, protuberance, protrusion

knobby *adj* **lumpy**, bumpy, ridged, bony, protuberant

knock *v* **hit**, bump, collide, bang, thump ■ *n* **1** (*infml*) **blow**, setback, upset, misfortune, kick in the teeth **2 blow**, collision, hit, bump, bang

knockabout *adj* **1 physical**, slapstick, boisterous, rowdy, rough *Opposite*: decorous **2 sturdy**, stout, strong, solid, substantial *Opposite*: flimsy ■ *n* **slapstick**, physical comedy, visual comedy, clowning, buffoonery

knock around (*infml*) *v* **1 hit**, beat, mistreat,

abuse, batter **2 hang around**, spend time, relax, hang out (*infml*), kick around (*infml*)

knock back (*infml*) *v* **down**, gulp, swallow, drink, put back

knock down *v* **1 floor**, fell, knock over, hit, strike **2 destroy**, demolish, dismantle, bulldoze, pull down *Opposite*: build **3 reduce the price of**, discount, mark down, lower, reduce *Opposite*: put up

knockdown *adj* **cheap**, reduced, low, rock-bottom, bargain *Opposite*: inflated

knocker *n* **door fixture**, knob, handle, bell, doorbell

knock off (*infml*) *v* **1 stop work**, finish, call it a day, leave, head off *Opposite*: start **2 deduct**, take off, discount, subtract, reduce *Opposite*: add **3 mass-produce**, churn out, knock out, turn out, rattle off

knockoff (*infml*) *n* **copy**, fake, forgery, reproduction, counterfeit *Opposite*: original

knock out *v* **1 make unconscious**, hit, floor, fell, knock down **2 eliminate**, put out, defeat, overcome, beat **3 surprise**, amaze, astound, impress, overwhelm

knockout (*infml*) *n* **big success**, hit, sensation, triumph, winner *Opposite*: flop (*infml*)

knock over *v* **1 upset**, topple, overturn, tip over, spill **2** (*infml*) **surprise**, amaze, astound, impress, overwhelm

knock together *v* **assemble**, improvise, make up, concoct, cobble together

knoll *n* **hill**, hillock, hummock, mound, mount

knot *n* **1 tie**, loop, reef knot, square knot, granny knot **2 lump**, bump, bulge, protuberance, nub **3 cluster**, huddle, clutch, band, collection ■ *v* **join**, tie, bind, tether, secure *Opposite*: untie

knotted *adj* **tied**, tense, secured, taut, tangled *Opposite*: relaxed

knotty *adj* **tricky**, awkward, complicated, complex, thorny *Opposite*: simple

know *v* **1 understand**, be aware of, be knowledgeable about, comprehend, appreciate **2 experience**, go through, undergo **3 be acquainted with**, be familiar with, distinguish, see, have knowledge of

knowable *adj* **intelligible**, comprehensible, understandable, coherent, identifiable *Opposite*: unknowable

know backward and forward *v* **know well**, know inside out, know like the back of your hand

know-how (*infml*) *n* **knowledge**, experience, expertise, savoir-faire, proficiency

knowing *adj* **1 meaningful**, significant, expressive, eloquent, perceptive *Opposite*: innocent **2 deliberate**, intentional, intended, conscious, calculating *Opposite*: unconscious

know-it-all (*infml*) *n* **smart aleck** (*infml*), smarty pants (*infml*), wise guy (*infml*), wiseacre (*infml*),

knowledge n 1 **acquaintance**, familiarity, awareness, understanding, comprehension Opposite: ignorance 2 **information**, facts, data 3 **wisdom**, learning, education, scholarship, erudition

knowledgeable adj **well-informed**, au fait, conversant, familiar, informed Opposite: ignorant

known adj **recognized**, identified, acknowledged, accepted, branded Opposite: unknown

knuckle n **protuberance**, projection, lump, prominence, bulge

knuckle down (infml) v **work hard**, apply yourself, get down to it, buckle down (infml)

knuckle under v **give in**, give up, admit defeat, concede defeat, concede Opposite: continue

kohl n **eyeliner**, eye pencil, mascara

kosher (infml) adj 1 **lawful**, acceptable, legitimate, aboveboard, proper Opposite: unlawful 2 **genuine**, authentic, true, real, bona fide Opposite: fake

kowtow v 1 **kneel**, bow, genuflect, prostrate oneself, salaam Opposite: stand up 2 **grovel**, be servile, be obsequious, show deference, bow and scrape Opposite: lord it over ■ n **bow**, genuflection, prostration, salaam, homage

kudos n **glory**, praise, credit, fame, admiration Opposite: discredit

kvetch (infml) v **complain**, whine, grumble, moan (infml)

L

laager n **camp**, encampment, settlement, defensive position, shelter

lab (infml) n **workroom**, workshop, test center, test bed, laboratory

label n 1 **tag**, ticket, sticker, marker, sticky tag 2 **make**, brand name, trade name, trademark, mark 3 **description**, categorization, classification, characterization ■ v 1 **put a label on**, mark, identify, stamp 2 **consider**, regard, describe, categorize, class

labor n 1 **work**, toil, hard work, manual labor, efforts 2 **workers**, work force, employees, labor force, hands Opposite: management 3 **task**, job, chore, effort, exertion 4 **childbirth**, delivery, giving birth, confinement (dated) ■ v 1 **strive**, strain, grind away, keep at it, burn the candle at both ends Opposite: idle 2 **struggle**, exert, grapple, wrestle, agonize 3 **malfunction**, struggle, complain, seize up, falter 4 **drag yourself**, stagger, struggle, plod, trudge Opposite: skip 5 **overemphasize**, go on, dwell on, exaggerate, drive home Opposite: pass over

laboratory n **workroom**, workshop, test bed, test center, research laboratory

labored adj **tortured**, tortuous, difficult, strenuous, arduous Opposite: effortless

laborer n **manual worker**, blue-collar worker, hand, workhand, drudge

laborious adj **arduous**, backbreaking, strenuous, hard, tough Opposite: easy. See COMPARE AND CONTRAST at hard.

laboriousness n **difficulty**, arduousness, hardness, toughness, tedium Opposite: ease

labor under v **suffer from**, struggle with, be disadvantaged by, be burdened with, be swayed by

labor union n **workers' association**, organized labor, staff association, syndicate, union

labyrinth n **maze**, warren, web, tangle, jumble

labyrinthine adj **complex**, convoluted, intricate, complicated, tortuous Opposite: straightforward

lace n **tie**, shoelace, bootlace, cord ■ v 1 **do up**, tie up, lace up, fasten Opposite: undo 2 **spike**, mix, fortify

lacerate v **slash**, tear, cut, score, scratch

laceration n **cut**, slash, graze, scratch, tear

lachrymose (literary) adj 1 **tearful**, crying, easily moved, in tears, in floods of tears Opposite: dry-eyed 2 **sad**, tragic, unhappy, moving, dismal Opposite: cheerful

lack n **shortage**, absence, want, dearth, deficiency Opposite: surplus ■ v **be short of**, not have, be deficient in, want for, need Opposite: have

COMPARE AND CONTRAST CORE MEANING: an insufficiency or absence of something
lack a complete absence of a particular thing; **shortage** a lack of something that is needed or required; **deficiency** a shortfall in the amount of something necessary, e.g., a particular nutrient in the human body, or an inadequacy in the supply or performance of something; **deficit** the amount by which something falls short of a target amount or level; **want** or **dearth** a scarcity or absence of something.

lackadaisical adj **apathetic**, careless, lazy, relaxed, half-hearted Opposite: energetic

lackey n **minion**, lapdog, sycophant, toady, creature

lacking *adj* **missing**, not there, wanting, absent *Opposite*: present

lacking in *adj* **short of**, without, not having, bereft of, devoid of *Opposite*: full of

lackluster *adj* **dull**, lifeless, dreary, unexciting, uninspiring *Opposite*: brilliant

laconic *adj* **terse**, brief, short, concise, economical *Opposite*: long-winded

lacquer *n* **polish**, varnish, gloss

lacuna *(literary)* *n* **space**, empty space, void, hole, omission

lacy *adj* **delicate**, lacelike, net, filigree, fine

lad *n* **1 boy**, young man, youngster, youth, teenager *Opposite*: lass **2** *(infml)* **man**, fellow, guy *(infml)*, fella *(infml)* *Opposite*: lass

ladder *n* **1 ranking**, tree, table, pecking order, hierarchy **2 stepladder**, folding ladder, loft ladder, roof ladder, rope ladder

laddie *(infml)* *see* **lad**

laden *adj* **weighed down**, burdened, overloaded, loaded *Opposite*: empty

la-di-da *(infml)* *adj* **affected**, pretentious, snobbish, put-on, full of airs and graces *Opposite*: common

lady *n* **woman**, female, matron

lady friend *(infml)* *n* **female companion**, girlfriend, partner

lag *v* **1 drop back**, drop behind, fall back, fall behind, trail *Opposite*: lead **2 insulate**, wrap, wad, protect, pad ■ *n* **interval**, wait, delay, intermission, pause

laggard *n* **straggler**, dawdler, shirker, slacker, idler *Opposite*: leader

lagging *n* **insulation**, wadding, padding, sleeve, skin

lagoon *n* **1 inlet**, cove, bay, creek **2 lake**, pond, pool, mere *(literary)*

lah-di-dah *(infml)* *see* **la-di-da**

laid-back *(infml)* *adj* **relaxed**, easygoing, easy, phlegmatic, cool *Opposite*: tense

lair *(infml)* *n* **hideout**, den, haunt, retreat, hideaway

laissez-faire *n* **noninterventionism**, nonintervention, noninvolvement, laxity *Opposite*: intervention ■ *adj* **noninterventionist**, unrestrictive, permissive, freewheeling, lax *Opposite*: proactive

laity *n* **1 laypeople**, flock, congregation, worshipers *Opposite*: clergy **2 nonprofessionals**, outsiders, amateurs, uninitiated

lake *n* **pond**, lagoon, tarn, water, sea

lakeside *n* **shore**, waterside, water's edge, bank, land

lama *n* **monk**, priest, brother, father, clergyman

lambaste *v* **attack**, upbraid, reprimand, criticize, reprove *Opposite*: praise

lambent *adj* **1** *(literary)* **gleaming**, glowing, radiant, luminous, shining *Opposite*: dull **2 brilliant**, scintillating, witty, sharp, rapier-like *Opposite*: leaden

lament *v* **mourn**, grieve, cry for, weep, bemoan *Opposite*: celebrate ■ *n* **lamentation**, cry, dirge, crying, weeping *Opposite*: celebration

lamentable *adj* **1 regrettable**, deplorable, inexcusable, appalling, dreadful *Opposite*: laudable **2** *(literary)* **woeful**, sad, mournful, pitiful

lamentation *n* **lament**, dirge, cry, weeping, crying *Opposite*: celebration

laminate *v* **cover**, seal, coat, protect, enclose

laminated *adj* **plastic-coated**, coated, covered, bonded, composite

lampoon *v* **ridicule**, satirize, make fun of, parody, caricature ■ *n* **satire**, parody, skit, sketch, caricature

lamppost *n* **streetlight**, streetlamp, light

lance *n* **spear**, weapon, bayonet, javelin ■ *v* **cut**, pierce, prick, slice into, slice open

land *n* **1 earth**, ground, terrain, countryside **2 homeland**, nation, country, territory **3 property**, plot, parcel, lot, acreage ■ *v* **1 arrive**, set down, alight, come down, touch down *Opposite*: take off **2 acquire**, get, annex, gain, obtain *Opposite*: lose

landed *adj* **property-owning**, landowning, wealthy, propertied, rich *Opposite*: landless

landfall *n* **1 arrival**, landing, touchdown, docking, mooring **2 land**, dry land, mainland, terra firma, shore

land forces *n* **army**, ground forces, troops, infantry, soldiers

landholder *n* **landowner**, landlord, property owner, proprietor, owner

landing *n* **1 arrival**, alighting, touchdown, docking, mooring **2 mooring**, pier, jetty, quay, landing stage **3 mezzanine**, half floor, top of the stairs

landing field *see* **landing strip**

landing stage *n* **jetty**, quay, mooring, landing

landing strip *n* **runway**, airstrip, airfield, airdrome, landing field

landlady *n* **1 property owner**, landowner, landholder, proprietor, owner *Opposite*: tenant **2 licensee**, proprietor, manager, hotelier, innkeeper

landless *adj* **dispossessed**, evicted, ousted, powerless *Opposite*: landed

landline *n* **cable**, line, phone line, wire, link

landlocked *adj* **closed in**, blocked-in, noncoastal, interior *Opposite*: coastal

landlord *n* **1 property-owner**, landowner, landholder, proprietor, owner *Opposite*: tenant **2 licensee**, proprietor, manager, hotelier, innkeeper

landmark *n* **1 marker**, sight, attraction, sign, signpost **2 breakthrough**, milestone, revolution, innovation, benchmark ■ *adj* **milestone**, breakthrough, momentous, revolutionary, innovative *Opposite*: run-of-the-mill

landmass n **continent**, land, landform, island, mainland

land on your feet v **come out on top**, succeed, get lucky, come through unscathed, find yourself Opposite: fail

landowner n **property owner**, landlord, owner, proprietor, landlady Opposite: tenant

landscape n **1 scenery**, countryside, land, site, scene **2 painting**, picture, watercolor, oil painting, drawing **3 background**, backdrop, circumstances, situation, setting ■ v **design**, model, form, shape, plan out

landslide n **1 avalanche**, landslip, rock fall, mudslide **2 victory**, rout, win, success, triumph

landslip n **landslide**, avalanche, rock fall, mudslide

landward adj **inland**, inward, inward-looking, inner, innermost ■ adv **ashore**, inland, inward, in

lane n **traffic lane**, fast lane, inside lane, passing lane, left-hand lane

language n **1 communication**, speech, talking **2 tongue**, idiom, dialect, parlance, lingo (infml) **3 words**, vocabulary, writing, prose, poetry

COMPARE AND CONTRAST CORE MEANING: communication by words

language the human use of spoken or written words as a communication system, or the particular system of communication prevailing in a specific country, nation, or community; **vocabulary** the body of words that make up a particular language; **tongue** a particular language used by a specific country, nation, or community; **dialect** a form of a language spoken in a particular region or by members of a particular social class or profession; **slang** words and expressions used instead of standard terms in casual speech or writing, or by a particular group of people; **jargon** terms associated with a particular specialized activity, profession, or culture, especially terms that are not generally understood by outsiders; **parlance** the style of speech or writing used by people in a particular context or profession; **lingo** (infml) the way of speaking associated with a particular, usually specialized, group of people; **-speak** a suffix added to nouns to describe the language used by a particular group of people or in a particular context, suggesting that this way of speaking or writing is obscure or difficult to follow; **-ese** a suffix added to nouns to describe the language associated with a group of people, especially when it resembles jargon.

languid adj **unhurried**, relaxed, languorous, lazy, indolent Opposite: vigorous

languish v **1 suffer**, weaken, fail, flag, deteriorate Opposite: thrive **2 pine**, pine away, long for, grieve **3 decline**, fail, sink, teeter, fade away Opposite: thrive

languor n **tiredness**, listlessness, lethargy, sluggishness, dreaminess Opposite: vigor

languorous adj **tired**, listless, lethargic, languid, sluggish Opposite: vigorous

laniard see lanyard

lank adj **limp**, lifeless, dull, thin, floppy

lanky adj **gangling**, gangly, long-legged, leggy, angular Opposite: rotund

lanyard n **rope**, cord, line, cable, halyard

lap n **1 circuit**, tour, round, circle **2 stage**, leg, part, segment, section ■ v **lick up**, slurp, lap up, drink

lapdog n **minion**, toady, sycophant, lackey, creature

lap of luxury n **bed of roses**, the life of Riley, life of ease, Easy Street

lapse n **1 error**, slip, failure, mistake, blunder **2 interval**, space, break, delay, pause ■ v **1 decline**, tumble, descend, drop, fail Opposite: rise **2 come to an end**, end, fail, give up, stop Opposite: renew **3 slip**, tail off, trail off, drift, falter Opposite: start up

lapsed adj **failed**, onetime, former, erstwhile, recent Opposite: current

lapse into v **1 slide into**, slip into, fall into, drift into, resort to Opposite: choose **2 revert**, regress, backslide, relapse, fall back Opposite: progress

lap up v **1 lick up**, slurp up, lap **2 enjoy**, soak up, bask in, love, glory in Opposite: hate **3 swallow**, fall for, believe, be fooled by, take in Opposite: disbelieve

larceny n **theft**, robbery, burglary, stealing, thieving

larder n **pantry**, storeroom, room, cupboard, store

large adj **1 big**, huge, sizable, immense, colossal Opposite: tiny **2 well-built**, outsized, hefty, bulky, ample Opposite: small **3 sizable**, considerable, not inconsiderable, significant, substantial Opposite: insignificant

large-hearted adj **generous**, giving, kind, kindly, kindhearted Opposite: meanspirited

largely adv **mainly**, in the main, mostly, for the most part, principally Opposite: particularly

largeness n **size**, bulk, expansiveness, mass, extent Opposite: smallness

larger-than-life adj **flamboyant**, confident, impressive, exaggerated, overstated Opposite: understated

large-scale adj **major**, important, significant, extensive, sweeping Opposite: small-scale

largesse n **1 generosity**, charity, liberality, munificence, benevolence Opposite: miserliness **2 gifts**, handouts, aid, assistance, donations

lariat n **noose**, loop, rope, tether, lasso

lark n **game**, joke, prank, caper, shines

lash n **1 hit**, whip, blow, stroke, whiplash

2 cat-o'-nine-tails, cat, whip, belt, switch ■ *v* **1** smash, pound, beat, impact, bump **2** criticize, lambaste, upbraid, condemn, lay into *(infml)* **3** whip, flog, flay, thrash, strike **4** shake, jerk, thrash, twitch, thump **5** tie, bind, fasten, knot, secure *Opposite*: loosen

lash out *v* **1** attack, strike out, hit out, let fly, flail around **2** criticize, lambaste, berate, hit out, tear into *Opposite*: praise

lass *n* girl, miss, young woman, daughter, adolescent *Opposite*: lad

lassitude *n* weariness, listlessness, apathy, lethargy, fatigue *Opposite*: liveliness

lasso *see* lariat

last *adj* **1** previous, latter, past, preceding, latest *Opposite*: next **2** final, end, ultimate, closing, concluding *Opposite*: first **3** remaining, surviving, extant, final, sole remaining *Opposite*: original ■ *v* keep, stay fresh, keep going, carry on, go on *Opposite*: die out

last-ditch *adj* eleventh-hour, desperate, emergency, frantic, frenzied

lasting *adj* permanent, long-lasting, longterm, lifelong, eternal *Opposite*: temporary

lastly *adv* finally, last of all, to finish, to conclude, to end *Opposite*: firstly

last minute *n* eleventh hour, final moment, last ditch, last gasp

last-minute *adj* late, tardy, delayed, overdue, belated *Opposite*: prompt

last name *n* surname, family name, name, patronymic, matronymic *Opposite*: given name

last out *v* survive, live, go on, continue, persist *Opposite*: fail

last resort *n* last chance, only hope, lastditch effort, fallback

last straw *n* final straw, limit, end, breaking point, deciding factor

latch *n* fastener, handle, bolt, key, bar

latch onto *(infml)* *v* **1** fall in with, befriend, take to, get in good with, take up with *Opposite*: abandon **2** take up, discover, get into, pursue, go in for *Opposite*: give up

late *adj* **1** delayed, tardy, overdue, belated, unpunctual *Opposite*: early **2** later, delayed, deferred, postponed *Opposite*: early **3** late-night, nighttime, evening, twilight *Opposite*: early **4** dead, much lamented, late lamented, deceased *(fml)*, dear departed *(fml or literary)* *Opposite*: living **5** last-minute, eleventh-hour, lastditch, final *Opposite*: early ■ *adv* **1** recently, until recently, lately, of late, latterly **2** belatedly, unpunctually, tardily, behind schedule, behind time *Opposite*: early **3** at the last minute, too late, finally, at the end, in the nick of time *Opposite*: early **4** at night, in the small hours, in the dead of night, in the evening, after dark *Opposite*:

early. *See* COMPARE AND CONTRAST *at* dead.

latecomer *n* straggler, dawdler, laggard

lately *adv* recently, of late, these days, latterly, currently

latency *n* dormancy, inactivity, potential, expectancy, underdevelopment *Opposite*: expression

lateness *n* tardiness, unpunctuality, delay, belatedness, deferment *Opposite*: promptness

latent *adj* **1** hidden, covert, buried, concealed, invisible *Opposite*: manifest **2** dormant, inactive, lurking, embryonic, underlying

later *adv* afterward, later on, in a while, shortly, soon *Opposite*: earlier

lateral *adj* side, on the side, adjacent, crossways, horizontal

latest *adj* newest, up-to-the-minute, hottest, state-of-the-art, modern *Opposite*: outdated

latex *n* sap, fluid, liquid

lather *n* **1** foam, suds, froth, bubbles, soapsuds **2** *(infml)* agitation, anxiety, panic, dither, pother *Opposite*: calmness ■ *v* soap, lather up, soap up

latitude *n* **1** parallel, position, location, coordinate *Opposite*: longitude **2** leeway, freedom, autonomy, liberty, room *Opposite*: restriction

latter *adj* last, final, concluding, second, end *Opposite*: former

latter-day *adj* modern, modern-day, contemporary, current *Opposite*: former

latterly *adv* **1** recently, lately, up till now, currently, of late *Opposite*: formerly **2** at the end, in the last part, toward the end, finally *Opposite*: initially

lattice *n* frame, mesh, framework, web, matrix

laud *v* praise, applaud, extol, acclaim, glorify *Opposite*: criticize

laudable *adj* admirable, praiseworthy, creditable, worthy, commendable *Opposite*: despicable

laudatory *adj* admiring, congratulatory, praising, complimentary, approving *Opposite*: damning

laugh *v* chuckle, chortle, guffaw, giggle, hoot *Opposite*: cry ■ *n* **1** chuckle, chortle, guffaw, giggle, hoot **2** *(infml)* fun, joke, teasing, giggle, prank

laughable *adj* pathetic, pitiful, derisory, inadequate, ridiculous *Opposite*: impressive

laugh at *v* sneer, jeer, mock, make fun of, ridicule *Opposite*: respect

laughingstock *n* figure of fun, joke, fool, buffoon, butt

laugh off *v* downplay, trivialize, shrug off, joke about, dismiss *Opposite*: face up to

laugh out of court *v* ridicule, mock, make fun of, scoff at, pour scorn on

laughter n **happiness**, amusement, hilarity, mirth, merriment *Opposite*: sadness

launch v **1 dispatch**, send off, send, shoot, fire **2 open**, start, begin, commence, initiate **3 introduce**, present, inaugurate, unveil, reveal **4 hurl**, throw, toss, fling, propel ■ n **presentation**, introduction, promotion, unveiling, inauguration

launching pad n **takeoff point**, springboard, start, base, foundation

launch into v **embark on**, get going on, break into, begin, commence

launder v **1 wash**, clean, dry-clean, valet **2 legalize**, filter, clean, decontaminate

laundry n **washing**, wash, clean wash, dirty wash

laurels n **success**, glory, honor, achievements

lavish adj **1 abundant**, plentiful, sumptuous, copious, prolific *Opposite*: scanty **2 extravagant**, profligate, wasteful, unrestrained, excessive *Opposite*: frugal ■ v **heap**, pour, smother, cover, load *Opposite*: deprive

law n **1 rule**, regulation, decree, act, edict **2 principle**, theory, formula, rule

law-abiding adj **honest**, straight, upright, upstanding, peaceable *Opposite*: crooked *(infml)*

law and order n **1 law enforcement**, keeping the peace, order, orderliness, policing *Opposite*: crime **2 stability**, harmony, peace, peace and quiet, peacefulness *Opposite*: unrest

lawbreaker n **criminal**, felon, wrongdoer, convict, offender

lawful adj **legal**, legalized, legitimate, official, endorsed *Opposite*: unlawful. *See* COMPARE AND CONTRAST *at* legal.

lawless adj **unruly**, anarchic, uncontrolled, unregulated, ungovernable *Opposite*: law-abiding

lawlessness n **anarchy**, chaos, disorder, unruliness, mayhem *(infml)* *Opposite*: order

lawmaker n **legislator**, policymaker, lawgiver

lawsuit n **court case**, proceedings, litigation, process

lawyer n **legal representative**, attorney, notary, trial lawyer, public prosecutor

lax adj **1 lenient**, soft, tolerant, permissive, accepting **2 negligent**, slack, careless, slipshod, sloppy *Opposite*: strict **3 limp**, loose, flaccid, relaxed, floppy *Opposite*: tense

laxity n **1 leniency**, tolerance, permissiveness, softness, forbearance *(fml)* *Opposite*: severity **2 carelessness**, negligence, sloppiness, slackness, indifference *Opposite*: vigilance

laxness *see* laxity

lay v **put down**, place, rest, put, arrange *Opposite*: pick up ■ adj **untrained**, amateur, non-

professional, uninitiated, unqualified *Opposite*: professional

layabout n **slacker**, shirker, timewaster, idler, lounger *Opposite*: go-getter *(infml)*

lay bare v **reveal**, explain, show, expose, display *Opposite*: cover up

lay before v **set before**, present, put before, submit, set out *Opposite*: withdraw

lay bets v **bet**, gamble, wager, stake money on

lay claim to v **appropriate**, claim, stake a claim to, demand, insist on *Opposite*: renounce

lay down v **1 put down**, lay aside, put aside, give up, surrender *Opposite*: take up **2 decree**, set down, put down, formulate, rule

lay down the law v **order**, boss, order around, boss around, dictate to

layer n **1 coating**, coat, sheet, film, deposit **2 level**, tier, seam, gradation, stratum *(fml)*

layette n **baby clothes**, babywear, baby linen, nursery equipment

lay in v **store**, acquire, hoard, save, stock up *Opposite*: use up

lay into v **1** *(infml)* **criticize**, attack, lambaste, get at, round on *Opposite*: praise **2 hit**, attack, beat, thump, thrash *Opposite*: protect

lay it on v **exaggerate**, embroider, embellish, overdo, overstate *Opposite*: understate

lay it on the line *(infml)* v **be honest**, be direct, be blunt, be straight, be clear *Opposite*: lie

lay off v **1 dismiss**, suspend, sack, let go, discharge *(fml)* *Opposite*: hire **2** *(infml)* **stop**, cease, desist, discontinue, cut out *Opposite*: continue

layoff n **1 dismissal**, downsizing, streamlining, sacking *(infml)*, discharge *(fml)* **2 unemployment**, career break, inactivity, rest, joblessness *Opposite*: employment

lay of the land *(infml)* n **general state**, general situation, prospect, state of affairs, picture

lay on v **provide**, supply, make available, organize, cater

lay out v **1 explain**, present, describe, outline, set out **2 design**, plan, arrange, organize, prepare

layout n **plan**, design, arrangement, outline, draft

layover n **stopover**, stop, halt, break, stay

lay to rest v **bury**, entomb, inter *(fml)*

laze v **idle**, lounge, loaf, bask, relax *Opposite*: toil

laze around *see* laze

laziness n **idleness**, lethargy, indolence, languor, sluggishness *Opposite*: energy

lazy adj **indolent**, idle, lethargic, languid, sluggish *Opposite*: energetic

lazybones *(infml)* n **layabout**, slacker, shirker, loafer, idler *Opposite*: worker

leach v **leak**, filter, percolate, trickle, seep

lead v 1 **guide**, indicate, direct, escort, pilot *Opposite*: follow 2 **be in charge of**, run, control, command, direct 3 **be in the lead**, take the lead, be the forerunner, be in front, have an advantage *Opposite*: trail ■ n 1 **leader**, spearhead, leading light, trailblazer, groundbreaker 2 **advantage**, advance start, head start, flying start 3 **precedent**, example, style, pattern, model 4 **clue**, tip, indication, information, hint 5 **leash**, chain, tether, restraint, rope ■ adj **principal**, chief, main, central, prime

lead astray v **mislead**, misinform, lead on, hoodwink, delude

leaden adj 1 **gray**, steely, ashen, dull, grim *Opposite*: bright 2 **heavy**, ponderous, weighty, sluggish, stodgy (infml) *Opposite*: light 3 **labored**, slow, sluggish, dragging, crawling *Opposite*: quick 4 **lifeless**, dull, dreary, flat, monotonous *Opposite*: lively

leader n 1 **guide**, director, organizer, mentor, guru *Opposite*: disciple 2 **spearhead**, leading light, trailblazer, groundbreaker, lead 3 **head**, chief, manager, superior, principal *Opposite*: underling

leadership n **management**, control, guidance, headship, direction

lead-in n **introduction**, preamble, preface, prelude, preliminary *Opposite*: conclusion

leading adj **prominent**, foremost, important, principal, chief *Opposite*: secondary

leading edge n **forefront**, cutting edge, sharp end, vanguard, avant-garde

leading light n **big name**, top name, star, superstar, celebrity *Opposite*: unknown

lead off v **begin**, start, start off, commence, open *Opposite*: end

lead on v **entice**, lure, tempt, seduce, attract

lead the way v **blaze a trail**, set a trend, originate, break new ground, break through

lead time n **notice**, advance notice, warning, notification, foreknowledge

lead to v **cause**, bring about, make possible, initiate, set in motion

lead up to v 1 **prepare for**, prepare the way, prepare the ground, sow the seeds, gear up 2 **approach**, get around to, come to, get to

leaf n 1 **foliage**, greenery, sprig, spray, frond 2 **page**, sheet, folio, side 3 **sheet**, foil, plate, lamina, film 4 **flap**, foldout, projection, section, piece

leaflet n **booklet**, brochure, pamphlet, flier, handbill

leaf through v **look through**, flick through, skim, browse, flip

leafy adj **green**, verdant, lush, luxuriant, rank *Opposite*: bare

league n **association**, group, union, confederation, club

leak n 1 **escape**, seepage, leakage, outflow, drip 2 **disclosure**, betrayal, giveaway,

revelation, release ■ v 1 **seep**, escape, pour out, trickle, drip 2 **disclose**, reveal, give away, betray, uncover *Opposite*: keep under wraps (infml)

leakage n **leak**, escape, seepage, outflow, drip

leak out v **emerge**, get out, slip out, come out, come to light

leakproof adj **watertight**, waterproof, sealed, hermetic, rainproof *Opposite*: leaky

leaky adj 1 **leaking**, holey, sieve-like, dripping, drippy *Opposite*: watertight 2 (infml) **unsecured**, unsafe, indiscreet, loose, lax *Opposite*: secure

lean v 1 **bend**, bend over, bend forward, incline, tilt 2 **rest**, prop, support, place, put 3 **tend**, incline, be disposed, favor, prefer ■ adj **thin**, slender, slim, wiry, sinewy *Opposite*: stout. *See* COMPARE AND CONTRAST *at* thin.

leaning n **inclination**, tendency, bent, affinity, preference *Opposite*: aversion (fml)

lean on v 1 **depend on**, rely on, trust, count on 2 (infml) **intimidate**, pressurize, put pressure on, oblige, coerce

leap v 1 **jump**, bound, dive, soar, fly 2 **increase**, rise, shoot up, go up, jump *Opposite*: drop ■ n 1 **bound**, jump, dive, spring, hop 2 **rise**, increase, jump, hike, climb *Opposite*: drop

leap at v **jump at**, seize, grab, clutch, accept *Opposite*: balk

leapfrog v 1 **jump**, vault, leap, bound, spring 2 **advance**, shoot ahead, get ahead, pull ahead, catapult 3 **overtake**, pass, leave behind, outstrip, leave standing 4 **circumvent** evade, avoid, sidestep, bypass

leap out at v **stand out**, stick out, jump out, hit somebody in the face, impact

learn v 1 **study**, absorb, pick up, acquire, hit the books (infml) *Opposite*: teach 2 **find out**, hear, discover, realize, gather

learned adj **erudite**, educated, scholarly, academic, cultured *Opposite*: uneducated

learner n **beginner**, apprentice, student, pupil, novice *Opposite*: expert

learning n **knowledge**, education, erudition, scholarship, culture *Opposite*: ignorance

lease v **rent**, rent out, let, charter, lease out

lease out *see* lease

leash n **lead**, chain, tether, string, rope

least adj **smallest**, slightest, tiniest, minimum *Opposite*: most

leastways *see* leastwise

leastwise (infml) adv **in any case**, anyway, at least, at any rate, in spite of

leave v 1 **go away**, depart, go, run off, abscond *Opposite*: stay 2 **put down**, set down, put, put away, place *Opposite*: remove 3 **set aside**, allow, give, permit, assign 4 **result in**, cause, bring about, effect (fml) 5 **bequeath**, pass on, hand down, donate, entrust *Opposite*: withhold

6 abandon, desert, renounce, forsake, ditch *(infml)* *Opposite*: stand by **7 delay**, defer, put off, avoid, hold off *Opposite*: bring forward ■ *n* **1 sabbatical**, time off, leave of absence, time out, vacation **2** *(fml)* **permission**, consent, authority, authorization, dispensation

leave alone *v* **let alone**, let be, leave well enough alone, pay no attention, ignore *Opposite*: harass

leave be *see* **leave alone**

leave behind *v* **1 overtake**, outstrip, outpace, leave in the dust, surpass *Opposite*: fall behind **2 put behind you**, escape, evade, get away from, put to one side *Opposite*: suffer **3 abandon**, get rid of, cast off, leave, forget *Opposite*: retain

leave cold *v* **bore**, do nothing for, bore rigid, bore stiff, bore to tears *Opposite*: inspire

leave in peace *see* **leave alone**

leave much to be desired *v* **be unsatisfactory**, disappoint, let down, not make the grade, fall short *Opposite*: pass muster

leave no stone unturned *v* **do all you can**, do your utmost, pull out all the stops, spare no effort, try everything

leave of absence *n* **sabbatical**, time off, time out, leave

leave off *v* **stop**, desist, cease, refrain, discontinue *Opposite*: carry on

leave out *v* **omit**, exclude, count out, ignore, overlook *Opposite*: include

leave-taking *(literary)* *n* **farewell**, goodbye, sendoff, departure, separation *Opposite*: greeting

leavings *n* **leftovers**, scraps, remnants, remains, castoffs

lecherous *adj* **lewd**, lustful, lascivious, libidinous, lusty

lectern *n* **bookstand**, reading stand, reading desk, stand, booktrest

lecture *n* **1 talk**, address, sermon, speech, homily **2 reprimand**, dressing-down, scolding, tongue-lashing, telling-off *(infml)* ■ *v* **1 teach**, address, instruct, talk, hold forth **2 harangue**, criticize, scold, reprove, censure

lecturer *n* **1 speaker**, public speaker, speechmaker, orator, spokesperson **2 teacher**, professor, instructor, academic

ledge *n* **1 shelf**, sill, niche, ridge, rack **2 outcrop**, ridge, sill, shelf, foothold

ledger *n* **book**, account book, record book, record, register

lee *n* **shelter**, cover, protection, shadow, shade

leer *v* **smirk**, ogle, eye, sneer, stare ■ *n* **sneer**, grimace, smirk, evil eye, stare

leery *adj* **suspicious**, wary, doubting, doubtful, circumspect

lees *n* **dregs**, remains, leftovers, remnants

leeward *adj* **protected**, sheltered, shielded *Opposite*: upwind

leeway *n* **scope**, flexibility, margin, freedom, latitude

left-hand *adj* **left**, leftward, port *Opposite*: right-hand

left-handed *adj* **counterclockwise**, right to left, circular, round, helical *Opposite*: right-handed

leftover *n* **relic**, hangover, vestige, remnant, remainder

leftovers *n* **scraps**, remains, what's left, table scraps, leavings

left-wing *adj* **progressive**, reformist, leftist, socialist, communist *Opposite*: right-wing

left-winger *n* **progressive**, reformist, leftist, socialist, communist *Opposite*: right-winger

leg *n* **1 limb**, foreleg, member, extremity, hind leg **2 pole**, foot, support, stand, base **3 stage**, phase, lap, step, part

WORD BANK

❑ **parts of a leg or foot** ankle, big toe, calf, haunch, heel, instep, knee, lap, little toe, shin, sole, thigh, toe, toenail

legacy *n* **1 bequest**, inheritance, heirloom, heritage, birthright **2 relic**, hangover, vestige, remnant, remainder ■ *adj* **superseded**, obsolete, discontinued, outdated, antiquated *Opposite*: up-to-date

legal *adj* **lawful**, permissible, permitted, allowed, authorized *Opposite*: illegal

COMPARE AND CONTRAST CORE MEANING: describes something that is permitted, recognized, or required by law
legal permitted, recognized, or required by law; **lawful** a less common word meaning legal; **decriminalized** no longer categorized as a criminal offense; **legalized** previously categorized as illegal and now declared legal; **legitimate** complying with the law, or under the law; **licit** *(fml)* a rarely used word meaning legal.

legalese *n* **jargon**, cant, mumbo jumbo *(infml)*, gobbledygook *(infml)*

legality *n* **validity**, lawfulness, rightfulness, legitimacy *Opposite*: illegality

legalization *n* **ratification**, authorization, certification, validation, endorsement *Opposite*: criminalization

legalize *v* **decriminalize**, authorize, sanction, allow, permit *Opposite*: prohibit

legate *n* **representative**, envoy, ambassador, emissary, diplomat

legend *n* **1 fable**, myth, tale, lore, folklore **2 star**, celebrity, big name, icon, personality *Opposite*: unknown

legendary *adj* **1 fabled**, mythical, mythological, imaginary, fabulous *Opposite*: real-life **2 famous**, renowned, well-known, celebrated, great *Opposite*: unknown

legible *adj* **clear**, readable, intelligible, decipherable, understandable *Opposite*: illegible

legion *n* **multitude**, host, team, crowd, throng

legislate *v* **enact**, pass, establish, lay down the law, decree

legislation *n* **1 lawmaking**, lawgiving, legislature, regulation **2 laws**, legal code, body of law, bill, rule

legislative *adj* **lawmaking**, parliamentary, governmental, judicial, jurisdictive

legislature *n* **government**, parliament, administration, senate, assembly

legit *(slang) see* legitimate

legitimacy *n* **1 legality**, lawfulness, validity, rightfulness, justice **2 acceptability**, rightfulness, correctness **3 sincerity**, genuineness, realness, authenticity, validity

legitimate *adj* **1 lawful**, rightful, valid, legal, legit *(slang) Opposite*: unlawful **2 reasonable**, acceptable, justifiable, logical, valid *Opposite*: unreasonable **3 genuine**, sincere, real, valid, authentic *Opposite*: spurious

legroom *n* **room**, space, freedom, elbowroom *(infml)*

legume *n* **leguminous plant**, pulse, pea, bean

legwarmer *n* **sock**, stocking, legging, gaiter, puttee

legwork *(infml) n* **research**, preparation, homework, groundwork, spadework

lei *n* **garland**, wreath, chaplet, coronet, circlet

leisure *n* **free time**, spare time, time off, leisure time, R & R *Opposite*: work

leisured *adj* **rich**, wealthy, affluent, moneyed, propertied *Opposite*: poor

leisurely *adj* **unhurried**, easy, relaxed, restful, relaxing *Opposite*: frantic

leisurewear *n* **sportswear**, casualwear, casual clothes, mufti

leitmotif *n* **motif**, theme, strand, element, topic

lemming *n* **conformist**, sheep, imitator, follower, copycat *(infml) Opposite*: nonconformist

lemon *(infml) n* **failure**, dud *(infml)*, nonstarter *(infml)*, washout *(infml)*, flop *(infml) Opposite*: winner

lemony *adj* **lemon-flavored**, lemon, citrus *Opposite*: sweet

lend *v* **1 loan**, advance, give, offer *Opposite*: borrow **2 provide**, offer, give, impart, add *Opposite*: take away

lend a hand *v* **help**, help out, give somebody a hand, do your bit, assist *Opposite*: hinder

lend an ear *v* **listen**, pay attention, hang on the words of, listen up *(slang)*

lender *n* **giver**, moneylender, financier, creditor, investor

length *n* **1 distance**, span, measurement, extent, dimension **2 duration**, time, timespan, extent **3 piece**, strip, segment, section, bit

lengthen *v* **grow**, increase, extend, elongate, stretch *Opposite*: shorten

lengthwise *adv* **lengthways**, along, end to end, sideways, laterally *Opposite*: endwise

lengthy *adj* **long**, long-lasting, extensive, prolonged, protracted *Opposite*: brief

lenience *see* leniency

leniency *n* **clemency**, mercy, compassion, humanity, tolerance *Opposite*: severity

lenient *adj* **compassionate**, merciful, humane, tolerant, indulgent *Opposite*: severe

leonine *adj* **impressive**, imposing, majestic, proud, dignified

leper *n* **outcast**, untouchable, pariah, outsider, exile

leprechaun *n* **sprite**, elf, imp, pixie, dwarf

lèse majesté *see* lese majesty

lese majesty *n* **1 disrespect**, disregard, dishonor, contempt, disdain *Opposite*: respect **2 treason**, high treason, sedition, betrayal, treachery *Opposite*: loyalty

lesion *n* **wound**, injury, cut, graze, scratch

less *adj* **a smaller amount of**, not as much of, a lesser amount of, a reduced amount of *Opposite*: more ■ *prep* **minus**, take away, with a reduction of, excluding *Opposite*: plus

lessen *v* **diminish**, decrease, decline, tail off, ease off *Opposite*: increase

lesser *adj* **smaller**, slighter, minor, reduced *Opposite*: greater

lesson *n* **1 class**, lecture, session, tutorial, seminar **2 example**, message, moral, warning, object lesson

lest *(fml) conj* **in case**, for fear that, so as not to

let *v* **1 allow**, give permission, permit, agree to, consent to *Opposite*: forbid **2 rent**, rent out, lease, lease out, hire ■ *n (fml)* **problem**, difficulty, hindrance, impediment, complication

let alone *see* let be

let be *v* **leave alone**, leave in peace, leave be, leave off, leave well enough alone *Opposite*: pester

let down *v* **1 disappoint**, fail, abandon, betray, disillusion **2 lower**, drop, sink, let fall, move down *Opposite*: raise **3 lengthen**, extend, let out, expand, enlarge *Opposite*: take up

letdown *n* **disappointment**, anticlimax, failure, disillusionment, discouragement *Opposite*: success

let drop *v* **disclose**, reveal, divulge, let slip, let out

let fly *v* **1 throw**, fling, toss, hurl, pitch **2 lose your temper**, explode, rage, hit the roof *(infml)*, see red *(infml) Opposite*: keep your cool *(infml)*

let go *v* **release**, liberate, set free, free, set loose *Opposite*: retain

lethal *adj* **deadly**, fatal, mortal, poisonous,

toxic. *See* COMPARE AND CONTRAST *at* **deadly**.

lethargic *adj* **sluggish**, tired, weary, lackluster, exhausted *Opposite*: energetic

lethargy *n* **sluggishness**, tiredness, weariness, exhaustion, fatigue *Opposite*: energy

let in *v* **admit**, allow in, open the door to, show in, receive *Opposite*: keep out

let in for *(infml)* *v* **involve in**, entangle in, ensnare in, mix up in, entrap in *Opposite*: get out of

let in on *v* **make aware of**, tell, acquaint with, reveal to, disclose to *Opposite*: keep from

let into *v* **1 admit to**, welcome into, usher into, take into, show into **2 accept into**, receive into, allow into, enlist into, enroll into

let know *v* **tell**, inform, advise, alert, warn *Opposite*: keep in the dark

let loose *v* **let out**, let go, set free, set loose, release *Opposite*: confine

let off *v* **excuse**, pardon, release, free, acquit *Opposite*: punish

let on *v* **1 admit**, disclose, divulge, reveal, declare *Opposite*: conceal **2 pretend**, make out, claim, profess, act *Opposite*: come clean *(infml)*

let out *v* **1 emit**, give, utter, release, produce *Opposite*: suppress **2 free**, let go, release, set free, let loose *Opposite*: keep in **3 enlarge**, expand, extend, widen, broaden *Opposite*: take in **4 let slip**, reveal, divulge, disclose, blurt out *Opposite*: conceal

let pass *v* **1 ignore**, let go, overlook, let ride, pay no attention to *Opposite*: pick up on *(infml)* **2 let through**, let by, let past, stand aside for, make way for *Opposite*: bar

let ride *v* **ignore**, close your eyes to, turn a blind eye to, let go, let pass *Opposite*: stop

let slip *v* **1 reveal**, disclose, divulge, give away, let out *Opposite*: hold back **2 let go**, lose, lose track of, lose sight of, take your eyes off *Opposite*: keep an eye on

letter *n* **1 communication**, note, message, memo, dispatch **2 character**, symbol, sign, capital, capital letter

lettered *adj* **educated**, knowledgeable, cultured, cultivated, literary *Opposite*: uneducated

lettering *n* **writing**, print, calligraphy, letters, inscription

letter-perfect *adj* **exact**, precise, perfect, faultless, flawless *Opposite*: unprepared

letters *n* **literature**, culture, cultivation, knowledge, education

let the cat out of the bag *v* **talk**, let on, tell a secret, tell, spill the beans *(infml)* *Opposite*: keep mum *(infml)*

let through *v* **make way for**, stand aside for, clear the way for, let pass, let past *Opposite*: block

let up *v* **ease off**, ease, ease up, lessen, slacken *Opposite*: intensify

letup *(infml)* *n* **respite**, break, rest, relief, interval *Opposite*: intensification

let up on *v* **ease up on**, ease off on, slack off on, soften up on, spare

let your hair down *(infml)* *v* **relax**, have a good time, enjoy yourself, let yourself go, have fun

let yourself go *v* **1 unwind**, relax, mellow, let your hair down, throw caution to the winds **2 give up**, lose heart, go downhill, lose your self-respect, go to the dogs *(infml)*

levee *n* **1 embankment**, earthwork, bank, wall, rampart **2 reception**, royal reception, royal function, court reception, court function

level *adj* **1 flat**, smooth, flat as a pancake, even, dead flat *Opposite*: bumpy **2 horizontal**, parallel with the ground, even, flat *Opposite*: slanted **3 equal**, neck and neck, side by side, close, near ■ *n* **1 height**, altitude, stage, point, plane **2 intensity**, quantity, concentration, amount, degree ■ *v* **1 flatten**, smooth, steamroll, press flat, even out **2 aim**, direct, point, turn **3 demolish**, knock down, raze, blow up, raze to the ground *Opposite*: rebuild

level-headed *adj* **sensible**, calm, sound, even-tempered, reliable *Opposite*: rash

level-headedness *n* **composure**, calmness, good sense, reliability, balance *Opposite*: rashness

levelly *adv* **1 calmly**, steadily, sensibly, evenly, equably *Opposite*: excitedly **2 smoothly**, flatly, evenly *Opposite*: unevenly

level off *v* **stabilize**, even out, settle, settle down, smooth out

level out *v* **settle down**, stabilize, settle, even out, even up

lever *n* **handle**, control, regulator, knob

leverage *n* **influence**, power, force, control, weight

leviathan *n* **giant**, colossus, behemoth, monster

levitate *v* **float**, rise up, ascend, drift up, soar *Opposite*: sink

levitation *n* **defiance of gravity**, rising, raising, hovering, floating

levity *n* **lightheartedness**, cheerfulness, humor, lightness, flippancy *Opposite*: gravity

levy *v* **impose**, tax, collect, put, charge ■ *n* **tax**, rates, toll, duty, tariff

lewd *adj* **salacious**, obscene, crude, vulgar, indecent

lexical *adj* **verbal**, word, vocabulary, philological, etymological

lexicon *n* **1 vocabulary**, vocabulary list, word list, glossary, dictionary **2 language**, lexis, idiolect

liability *n* **1 legal responsibility**, obligation, accountability, responsibility, charge **2 disadvantage**, problem, burden, millstone, jinx

liable *adj* **1 legally responsible**, accountable, answerable, responsible *Opposite*: unaccountable **2 likely**, apt, predisposed, prone *Opposite*: unlikely

liaise *v* **act as a go-between**, communicate, link, bridge, mediate

liaison *n* **link**, connection, contact, cooperation, relationship

liar *n* **deceiver**, fast talker, perjurer, fibber *(infml)*, storyteller *(infml)*

libation *n* **1 drink**, alcoholic drink, potion, brew *(infml)*, beverage *(fml)* **2 offering**, oblation, offertory, sacrifice, tribute

libel *n* **defamation**, vilification, slander, smear, denigration *Opposite*: praise ■ *v* **defame**, vilify, sully, tarnish, malign *Opposite*: praise. *See* COMPARE AND CONTRAST *at* **malign**.

libelous *adj* **defamatory**, vilifying, slanderous, unfounded *Opposite*: admiring

liberal *adj* **1 open-minded**, broad-minded, moderate, noninterventionist, free-thinking *Opposite*: narrow-minded **2 generous**, copious, abundant, profuse, substantial *Opposite*: meager. *See* COMPARE AND CONTRAST *at* **generous**.

liberalism *n* **tolerance**, broad-mindedness, open-mindedness, moderation, free-thinking *Opposite*: narrow-mindedness

liberalize *v* **relax**, slacken, loosen, ease up, open *Opposite*: tighten

liberate *v* **release**, free, set free, unshackle, unfetter *Opposite*: imprison

liberated *adj* **unconventional**, open-minded, freethinking, modern, enlightened *Opposite*: unenlightened

liberation *n* **freedom**, liberty, release, discharge, emancipation *Opposite*: captivity

liberator *n* **deliverer**, savior, emancipator, releaser *Opposite*: captor

liberty *n* **1 freedom**, independence, autonomy, emancipation, liberation *Opposite*: captivity **2 right**, freedom, authorization, authority, permission *Opposite*: suppression

libidinous *adj* **lustful**, lecherous, lusty, lascivious, salacious

library *n* **collection**, archive, books, papers, records

librettist *n* **libretto writer**, lyricist, songwriter, writer, author

license *v* **certify**, permit, allow, authorize, accredit ■ *n* **1 certificate**, authorization, pass, card, permit **2 excess**, abandon, lawlessness, unrestraint, intemperance **3 freedom**, liberty, carte blanche, dispensation, authority

licensed *adj* **approved**, qualified, certified, accredited, registered

licentiate *n* **license holder**, licensee, certified professional, qualified practitioner

licentious *adj* **immoral**, degenerate, decadent, dissipated, depraved

licit *adj* **lawful**, legitimate, legal, valid, right *Opposite*: illegal. *See* COMPARE AND CONTRAST *at* **legal**.

lick *(infml)* *v* **defeat**, conquer, get the better of, overcome, thrash

lickety-split *(infml)* *adv* **quickly**, fast, at high speed, swiftly, rapidly *Opposite*: sluggishly

licking *(infml)* *n* **trouncing**, thrashing, drubbing, hammering *(infml)*, pasting *(infml)*

lick your lips *v* **relish**, salivate, drool, anticipate, await

lid *n* **top**, cover, cap, closure

lie *v* **1 recline**, stretch out, lounge, lie down, slouch **2 be positioned**, be arranged, be placed, be situated, sit **3 remain**, rest, stay, be, stop **4 tell lies**, tell untruths, perjure yourself, tell stories, be economical with the truth *Opposite*: tell the truth ■ *n* **untruth**, falsehood, fabrication, white lie, fib *(infml)* *Opposite*: truth

COMPARE AND CONTRAST CORE MEANING: something that is not true

lie a false statement made deliberately; **untruth** something that is presented as being true but is actually false; **falsehood** a lie or an untruth; **fabrication** an invented statement, story, or account devised with intent to deceive; **fib** *(infml)* an insignificant harmless lie; **white lie** a minor harmless lie, usually told to avoid hurting somebody's feelings.

lie around *(infml)* *v* **1 laze**, lounge around, sit around, laze around, loaf **2 be scattered about**, be all over the place, clutter up the place, be distributed, litter

lie back *v* **recline**, stretch out, lounge, sprawl, relax

lie down *v* **recline**, rest, stretch out, relax, lounge *Opposite*: stand up

lie in wait *v* **lurk**, hide, conceal yourself, ambush, prowl

life *n* **1 existence**, being, living *Opposite*: death **2 lifetime**, life span, life cycle, life expectancy, natural life **3 verve**, vivacity, animation, energy, excitement

life-and-death *adj* **critical**, crucial, vital, pivotal, paramount *Opposite*: unimportant

lifeblood *n* **1** *(literary)* **blood**, sap, essence, life force, élan vital **2 essential**, essence, quintessence, sine qua non, necessity

life cycle *n* **life span**, development, maturation, growth

life expectancy *n* **life span**, lifetime, allotted span, natural life

lifeguard *n* **rescuer**, beach attendant, swimming pool attendant, pool attendant, lifesaver *(infml)*

lifeless *adj* **1 dead**, unconscious, unresponsive, unmoving, inert *Opposite*: alive **2 unexciting**, dull, uninteresting, tedious, listless *Opposite*: animated. *See* COMPARE AND CONTRAST *at* **dead**.

lifelike *adj* **realistic**, natural, believable, convincing, credible *Opposite*: unrealistic

lifeline *n* **salvation**, link, help, support, helping hand

lifelong *adj* **enduring**, all-time, permanent, ultimate, lasting *Opposite*: temporary

life-or-death *see* **life-and-death**

life-size *adj* **full-scale**, full-size, actual size *Opposite*: miniature

life span *n* **natural life**, lifetime, life cycle, life expectancy, life

lifestyle *n* **way of life**, standard of living, existence, routine, life

life-threatening *adj* **dangerous**, serious, severe, grave, incurable

lifetime *n* **1 life**, time, life span, natural life, life cycle **2 era**, generation, time, period, epoch **3** (*infml*) **days**, eternity (*infml*), forever (*infml*), ages (*infml*)

lifework *n* **product of working life**, result of working life, achievement, accomplishment, success

lift *v* **1 winch up**, haul up, elevate, boost, raise **2 revoke**, cancel, take back, relax, rescind *Opposite*: impose **3 lighten**, buoy up, brighten, elate, uplift **4** (*infml*) **steal**, walk off with, help yourself, pocket, take ■ *n* **boost**, revitalization, tonic, encouragement, kick (*infml*)

ligature *n* **1 cord**, string, rope, tie, line **2** (*fml*) **bond**, connection, link, linkage, union

light *n* **glow**, beam, brightness, luminosity, daylight *Opposite*: darkness ■ *adj* **1 bright**, sunny, sunlit, well-lit *Opposite*: dark **2 pastel**, subtle, neutral, fair, pale *Opposite*: deep **3 weightless**, buoyant, fluffy, insubstantial, frothy *Opposite*: heavy **4 gentle**, delicate, soft, noiseless, featherlike *Opposite*: heavy **5 nimble**, graceful, dainty, elegant, agile *Opposite*: awkward **6 carefree**, happy, cheerful, untroubled, joyful *Opposite*: oppressive **7 easy**, manageable, undemanding, simple, effortless *Opposite*: demanding **8 entertaining**, lightweight, fun, frivolous, amusing *Opposite*: somber ■ *v* **set alight**, set on fire, ignite, strike, set fire to *Opposite*: extinguish

WORD BANK
❑ **types of lights** arc lamp, chandelier, flashlight, floodlight, floorlamp, fluorescent lamp, footlights, headlight, hurricane lamp, lamp, lamppost, lantern, LED, light bulb, neon light, nightlight, penlight, searchlight, spotlight, streetlamp, streetlight, sunlamp, traffic light

light-colored *adj* **pale**, light, pastel, subtle, fair

lighten *v* **1 ease**, lessen, alleviate, reduce, lift *Opposite*: overload **2 cheer up**, improve, lift, refresh, buoy up *Opposite*: depress

lighten up (*infml*) *v* **relax**, take it easy, loosen up, unwind, cool it (*slang*)

lightface *adj* **faint**, light *Opposite*: boldface

light-fingered *adj* **thieving**, kleptomaniacal, larcenous, dishonest

light-footed *adj* **nimble**, graceful, dainty, elegant, agile *Opposite*: clumsy

lightheaded *adj* **dizzy**, faint, giddy, woozy, unsteady

lighthearted *adj* **1 carefree**, happy-go-lucky, happy, cheerful, cheery *Opposite*: troubled **2 enjoyable**, entertaining, amusing, diverting, fun *Opposite*: serious **3 cheerful**, jokey, cheery, funny, bright *Opposite*: gloomy

lighting *n* **illumination**, light, lights

light into (*infml*) *v* **attack**, tear into, set upon, lay into, let have it *Opposite*: defend

lightly *adv* **1 gently**, softly, delicately, imperceptibly, quietly *Opposite*: heavily **2 flippantly**, frivolously, jokily, informally, casually *Opposite*: seriously **3 nimbly**, gracefully, trippingly, adeptly, dexterously *Opposite*: awkwardly

light-minded *adj* **frivolous**, silly, foolish, vacuous, inane *Opposite*: serious-minded

lightness *n* **1 weightlessness**, buoyancy, fluffiness, frothiness, flimsiness *Opposite*: heaviness **2 nimbleness**, precision, grace, agility, dexterity *Opposite*: clumsiness

lightning *n* **flash of lightning**, sheet lightning, heat lightning, lightning bolt, lightning strike ■ *adj* **fast**, quick, speedy, whirlwind, sudden *Opposite*: slow

light out (*infml*) *v* **run away**, run off, leave in a hurry, cut and run, run for it

lights out *n* **1 bedtime**, time for bed, sleep time, bye-bye (*infml*) **2 signal**, taps, bugle call, curfew *Opposite*: reveille

light up *v* **1 illuminate**, light, cast light on, shed light on, shine a light on *Opposite*: darken **2 cheer up**, brighten up, perk up, liven up, brighten **3 shine**, glow, gleam, beam, burn *Opposite*: darken

lightweight *adj* **frivolous**, trivial, insubstantial, inconsequential, unimportant *Opposite*: serious ■ *n* (*infml*) **person of little consequence**, small fry, little man, little guy, pawn *Opposite*: heavyweight

likable *adj* **pleasant**, nice, affable, agreeable, amiable *Opposite*: abominable

like *prep* **similar to**, akin to, approximating to, in the vein of, reminiscent of *Opposite*: unlike ■ *adj* **similar**, comparable, alike, corresponding, identical *Opposite*: dissimilar ■ *v* **be fond of**, love, enjoy, be partial to, adore *Opposite*: dislike

likelihood *n* **probability**, possibility, prospect, chance, chances

likely *adj* **1 probable**, possible, expected, prospective, to be expected *Opposite*: unlikely **2 liable**, apt, prone, tending, having a tendency to

like-minded *adj* **in agreement**, concurring, compatible, in accord, of one mind *Opposite*: incompatible

liken *v* compare, equate, relate, associate *Opposite*: contrast

likeness *n* 1 similarity, resemblance, correspondence 2 portrait, image, reproduction, picture, rendering

likewise *adv* similarly, the same, equally, also, as well

liking *n* taste, fondness, partiality, love, penchant *Opposite*: dislike. *See* COMPARE AND CONTRAST at love.

lilt *n* intonation, inflection, rise and fall, cadence, stress

lily-livered *(dated) adj* cowardly, faint-hearted, spineless, weak, chicken *(infml) Opposite*: courageous

limb *n* 1 extremity, appendage, member 2 branch, bough, spur

limber *adj* lithe, supple, agile, nimble, lissome *Opposite*: stiff

limber up *v* warm up, loosen up, exercise, practice, prepare

limelight *n* attention, public interest, public eye, fame, renown

limit *n* 1 boundary, bounds, border, edge, perimeter 2 threshold, cutoff point, check, cap, constraint ▪ *v* control, regulate, restrain, curb, constrain *Opposite*: deregulate

limitation *n* drawback, inadequacy, imperfection, weakness, weak point

limited *adj* incomplete, imperfect, partial, inadequate, restricted *Opposite*: boundless

limited company *n* public limited company, joint-stock company, company, corporation, firm

limited edition *n* special edition, limited printing, limited issue, limited print run, deluxe edition

limiter *n* regulator, controller, control, restraint, check

limitless *adj* boundless, unbounded, immeasurable, infinite, vast *Opposite*: limited

limits *n* bounds, restrictions, confines, parameters, boundaries

limp *v* hobble, shuffle, shamble, stagger, wobble ▪ *adj* floppy, wilted, flaccid, lifeless, drooping *Opposite*: stiff

limpid *adj* 1 transparent, clear, translucent, diaphanous, see-through *Opposite*: opaque 2 lucid, clear, crystal clear, clear as day, understandable *Opposite*: obscure

limpness *n* floppiness, flaccidity, droopiness, lifelessness, sagginess *Opposite*: stiffness

limy *adj* lime-flavored, lime, citrus

linchpin *n* keystone, cornerstone, hub, essential, kingpin *(infml) Opposite*: accessory

line *n* 1 streak, stripe, contour, mark, stroke 2 edge, profile, contour, outline, silhouette 3 boundary, limit, border, edge, frontier 4 link, route, track, connection, course 5 string, cable, rope, thread, twine 6 ancestry, family, lineage, descent, race 7 policy, attitude, method, approach, ideology 8 area, occupation, field, interest, specialty 9 row, column, procession, lineup ▪ *v* coat, cover, face, reinforce, pad

lineage *n* ancestry, family, line, heredity, extraction

lineament *(literary) n* facial feature, feature, contour

linear *adj* 1 in lines, lined, line 2 straight, rectilinear, direct, undeviating, right

lined *adj* 1 wrinkled, creased, wizened, furrowed, crinkled *Opposite*: smooth 2 ruled, feint *Opposite*: plain

line manager *n* manager, production manager, sales manager, boss, superior

line of attack *n* stratagem, tactic, technique, method, modus operandi

line officer *n* combat officer, frontline officer, fighting officer, field officer, officer

line of sight *n* sightline, line of vision, view

line of work *n* profession, career, job, occupation

liner *n* lining, pool liner, facing, insert

line up *v* 1 arrange, collect, order, organize, place *Opposite*: disarrange 2 form ranks, fall in to line, marshal, order, align 3 assemble, queue, gather together, collect, align 4 plan, organize, arrange, prepare, set up

lineup *n* 1 team list, roster, team, listing, side 2 schedule, listing, program 3 group, team, alliance, association, league

linger *v* remain, stay behind, hang on, loiter, stay *Opposite*: leave

lingerie *n* underwear, underclothes, underclothing, undergarments, undies *(infml)*

lingering *adj* 1 lasting, remaining, persistent, enduring, haunting 2 drawn-out, slow, protracted, long-drawn-out, prolonged *Opposite*: quick

lingo *(infml) n* language, speech, idiom, vernacular, jargon

linguistic *adj* language, verbal, philological, dialectal, etymological

liniment *n* ointment, cream, unguent, rub, salve

lining *n* coating, liner, insert, facing

link *n* connection, relation, association, relationship, linkage ▪ *v* connect, relate, associate, bring together, link up *Opposite*: separate

linkage *n* connection, relation, association, relationship, link

linked *adj* related, connected, accompanying, allied, associated *Opposite*: unrelated

linkup *n* connection, association, link, linkage, bond *Opposite*: separation

lionhearted *adj* brave, courageous, stouthearted, bold, audacious *Opposite*: cowardly

lionize v **glorify**, idolize, praise, fete, celebrate Opposite: censure

lion's share n **largest part**, bulk, most, majority, mass

lip n **edge**, rim, brim, brink

lip-smacking adj **delicious**, delectable, tasty, flavorful, flavorsome

liquefy v **dissolve**, soften, melt, run, thaw Opposite: solidify

liquescent adj **melting**, runny, gooey, liquefying Opposite: solid

liquid n **fluid**, water, juice, solution, liquor ∎ adj **runny**, fluid, gooey, watery, melted Opposite: solid

liquidate v 1 **settle**, clear up, pay, pay off, satisfy 2 **shut down**, sell out, sell off, bankrupt, wind up 3 **kill**, murder, execute, eliminate, assassinate

liquidation n **insolvency**, bankruptcy, closing, winding up, selling out

liquidator n **receiver**, official receiver, administrative receiver, overseer

liquidity n 1 **liquidness**, fluidity, fluidness, wateriness Opposite: solidity 2 **assets**, liquid assets, convertible assets, resources, financial resources

liquidize v **purée**, blend, pulverize, mash, pulp

liquor n 1 **alcohol**, spirits, strong drink 2 **liquid**, fluid, solution, juice

lissom see lissome

lissome adj 1 **lithe**, supple, flexible, willowy, svelte Opposite: stiff 2 **agile**, nimble, lively, quick, light Opposite: awkward

list n 1 **catalog**, register, record, roll, listing 2 **tilt**, slant, slope, gradient, lean ∎ v 1 **record**, catalog, register, itemize, enumerate 2 **slant**, tilt, incline, lean, bank

listed adj **registered**, recorded, itemized, enumerated Opposite: unlisted

listen v **lend an ear**, pay attention, take note, attend, give heed Opposite: ignore

listener n **hearer**, radio listener, audience member, audiophile, eavesdropper

listen in v **eavesdrop**, monitor, wiretap, bug, snoop (infml)

listening post n **observation post**, lookout post, surveillance post, sentry post

listing n 1 **list**, catalog, register, record, roll 2 **citation**, item, entry

listings n **schedule**, program, guide

listless adj **languid**, lethargic, indolent, enervated, limp Opposite: energetic

litany n 1 **prayers**, liturgical prayers, petitions, invocations, responses 2 **list**, listing, catalog, series, recital

lite adj **low-fat**, slimming, light, diet, low-calorie Opposite: fattening

literacy n 1 **reading ability**, the three Rs, literateness 2 **knowledge**, learning, mastery, savvy (infml)

literal adj 1 **factual**, truthful, honest, exact, accurate Opposite: figurative 2 **word for word**, verbatim, accurate, exact, correct Opposite: inaccurate

literary adj 1 **fictional**, mythical, legendary, storybook, fictitious Opposite: historical 2 **bookish**, erudite, scholarly, well-read, literate

literate adj **well-educated**, well-read, knowledgeable, cultured, erudite Opposite: illiterate

literati (fml) n 1 **intellectuals**, intellects, highbrows, intelligentsia, academics 2 **authors**, writers, poets, playwrights, editors

literature n 1 **writings**, works, collected works, texts, books 2 **information**, sources, reading matter, brochures, pamphlets

lithe adj **supple**, flexible, lissome, agile, nimble Opposite: stiff

litigable adj **responsible**, liable, accountable, answerable, actionable

litigate v **take proceedings**, sue, contest, file, petition

litigation n **court case**, proceedings, lawsuit, legal action, legal process

litmus test n **acid test**, proof, confirmation, test, measure

litter n 1 **waste**, trash, garbage, debris, refuse 2 **disorder**, confusion, jumble, clutter, untidiness 3 **offspring**, young, progeny, brood, family ∎ v **drop litter**, scatter, spoil, strew, clutter Opposite: clean up

little adj 1 **small**, slight, petite, diminutive, tiny Opposite: large 2 **unimportant**, trivial, slight, petty, trifling Opposite: major ∎ pron **bit**, touch, spot, some, pittance Opposite: lot ∎ adv **not very**, not much, not sufficiently, insufficiently, inadequately Opposite: well

little folk see little people

little green man n **alien**, Martian, extraterrestrial

little people n **supernatural beings**, imaginary beings, fairies, elves, pixies

littoral adj **coastal**, shoreline, seaside Opposite: inland ∎ n **shore**, coast, seaside, shoreline, beach

liturgy n **church service**, mass, ritual, religious ceremony, rite

livable adj 1 **habitable**, functional, civilized, comfortable, agreeable Opposite: uninhabitable 2 **bearable**, endurable, acceptable, tolerable, worthwhile Opposite: intolerable

live v 1 **exist**, be alive, be in this world, survive, subsist Opposite: die 2 **reside**, stay, have your home, inhabit, settle ∎ adj **living**, animate, conscious, breathing, aware Opposite: dead

liveable see livable

lived-in adj 1 **comfortable**, relaxed, disheveled, untidy, homey 2 **careworn**, haggard, worn, lined, tired

live down v get over, recover, from, shake off, forget

livelihood n 1 **employment**, occupation, trade, business, work **2 living**, income, source of revenue, means of support, maintenance

liveliness n **energy**, sparkle, joie de vivre, vivacity, dynamism Opposite: lethargy

lively adj **energetic**, vigorous, sparkling, active, vivacious Opposite: lethargic

liven v **perk up**, cheer up, boost, quicken, energize Opposite: depress

liven up v **enliven**, stimulate, revive, cheer up, perk up

live off v **rely on**, depend on, impose on, sponge (infml), mooch (infml)

live on v 1 **survive on**, get by on, exist on, subsist on, eke out a living **2 remain**, continue, survive, persist, prevail Opposite: die away

liveried adj **uniformed**, costumed, dressed up, caparisoned

liverish adj **irritable**, bad-tempered, moody, irascible, volatile

livery n 1 **uniform**, dress, costume, vestments, regalia **2** (literary) **insignia**, colors, corporate colors, racing colors

livestock n animals, cattle, stock

live through v **survive**, come through, get through, experience, undergo Opposite: succumb

live up to v **match**, achieve, reach, come up to, meet

live wire (infml) n **doer**, activist, high-flier, extrovert, go-getter (infml)

live with v **tolerate**, put up with, bear, endure, manage

livid adj 1 **furious**, enraged, up in arms, beside yourself, incensed Opposite: pleased **2 bruised**, purple, discolored, black-and-blue, contused

living adj **alive**, breathing, existing, live, active Opposite: dead ■ n **livelihood**, income, living wage, source of revenue, subsistence

COMPARE AND CONTRAST CORE MEANING: having life or existence

living not dead, or, of inanimate things, still in existence; **alive** not dead; **animate** used especially to distinguish living animals and plants from inanimate objects such as rocks, water, or buildings; **extant** still in existence.

living thing n **creature**, being, living being, life form, organism

load n **weight**, cargo, freight, consignment, shipment ■ v 1 **fill**, pack, stack, load up, pile Opposite: unload **2 put in**, insert, slot in, pop in (infml) Opposite: eject **3 burden**, encumber, weigh down, overload, oppress Opposite: alleviate

loaded adj 1 **laden**, weighed down, encumbered, burdened, overloaded Opposite: empty **2 biased**, leading, deceptive, trick, manipulative Opposite: innocent

loads (infml) n **many**, much, lots, tons (infml), heaps (infml) Opposite: handful

load up v **fill up**, stack, pack, pile, fill Opposite: unload

loaf v be **idle**, be unoccupied, laze, loiter, loll

loafer n **idler**, slacker, shirker, sloth, loiterer

loan n **advance**, credit, finance, mortgage ■ v **lend**, advance, give a loan, give an advance, allow Opposite: borrow

loath adj **wary**, unwilling, reluctant, chary, against Opposite: eager. See COMPARE AND CONTRAST at **unwilling**.

loathe v **hate**, dislike, detest, despise, scorn Opposite: adore

loathing n **hate**, hatred, antipathy, repugnance, dislike Opposite: love. See COMPARE AND CONTRAST at **dislike**.

loathsome adj **hateful**, despicable, disgusting, repugnant, detestable Opposite: delightful

lob v 1 **throw**, toss, fling, pitch, hurl **2 hit**, knock, strike, bat, whack ■ n **toss**, throw, pitch, hit, ball

lobby n 1 **entrance hall**, foyer, reception area, vestibule, atrium **2 pressure group**, interest group, campaign group, special interest group, faction ■ v **petition**, press your case, try to influence, apply pressure, sway opinion

lobe n **part**, section, portion, hemisphere

local adj 1 **home**, neighboring, neighborhood, community, district Opposite: national **2 native**, indigenous, resident, homegrown Opposite: foreign **3 restricted**, limited, confined, narrow, insular Opposite: universal ■ n **resident**, inhabitant, citizen, native Opposite: stranger

locale n **location**, place, setting, site, spot

locality n 1 **area**, district, neighborhood, region, zone **2 position**, place, site, spot, setting

localize v 1 **restrict**, confine, limit, focus, contain **2 pinpoint**, locate, identify, find exactly, narrow down

localized adj **contained**, limited, restricted, confined, local Opposite: generalized

locally adv **nearby**, close by, in the vicinity, in the neighborhood

locate v 1 **find**, trace, discover, track down, detect Opposite: lose **2 place**, put, position, situate, set

location n **site**, place, position, spot, setting

lock n 1 **security device**, padlock, combination lock, latch, bolt **2 curl**, strand, tuft, wisp, ringlet ■ v 1 **fasten**, bolt, secure, lock up, padlock Opposite: unlock **2 fix in place**, lodge, wedge, secure, confine Opposite: free **3 brace**, clench, stiffen, tighten Opposite: flex **4 link**, clasp, intertwine, join, unite

lock away v 1 **imprison**, lock up, jail, send to prison, sentence to prison *Opposite*: release 2 **shut away**, keep safe, secure, seal up, hide away *Opposite*: bring out

lock horns v **argue**, disagree, fight, contest, dispute

lock on v **home in on**, track, follow, shadow

lock, stock, and barrel adv **completely**, entirely, totally

lock up v **imprison**, put in jail, put in prison, put behind bars, confine *Opposite*: release

lockup n **jail**, prison, reformatory, penitentiary, detention center

locomotion n **movement**, motion, propulsion, kinetic energy, kinesis *Opposite*: immobility

locomotive n **train**, engine, steam engine, tank engine

lodge n 1 **small house**, cabin, cottage, chalet, hunting lodge 2 **hotel**, inn, resort, motel ■ v 1 **stay**, live, board, be a lodger, take lodgings 2 **accommodate**, board, billet, put up, quarter 3 **fix in place**, embed, implant, stick, catch

lodger n **tenant**, boarder, paying guest, cotenant, lessee

lodging n **accommodations**, room, space, place to stay, housing

lodgings (dated) n **rooms**, quarters, accommodations

loftiness n 1 **haughtiness**, superior manner, disdain, arrogance, condescension *Opposite*: humility 2 **grandeur**, nobility, dignity *Opposite*: baseness 3 **height**, elevation, altitude

lofty adj 1 **supercilious**, superior, disdainful, lordly, arrogant *Opposite*: humble 2 **grand**, elevated, noble, admirable, distinguished *Opposite*: base 3 **tall**, high, towering, soaring, high-ceilinged *Opposite*: low

log n **record**, journal, notes, minutes, logbook ■ v **make a note of**, chart, record, note down, note

logbook n **record**, record book, log, journal, report

loge n **box**, enclosure, box seat, skybox

logic n **reason**, judgment, sense, common sense, lucidity

logical adj 1 **rational**, reasonable, sound, commonsense, commonsensical *Opposite*: illogical 2 **plausible**, reasonable, obvious, sensible, understandable *Opposite*: implausible

log in v **gain access**, open up, start, switch on, sign in

logjam n 1 **deadlock**, standstill, standoff, stalemate, impasse 2 **traffic jam**, holdup, buildup, snarl

logo n **symbol**, sign, emblem, badge, insignia

log off v **leave**, quit, exit, log out, close down *Opposite*: log on

log on v **gain access**, open up, start, switch on, sign in *Opposite*: log off

log out *see* **log off**

logy adj **tired**, run-down, enervated, sleepy, washed out

loiter v 1 **amble**, stroll, wander, drift, dally 2 **wait**, linger, lurk, skulk, hang around

loll v 1 **lie**, lounge, lie back, sprawl, slouch 2 **droop**, hang down, dangle, sag, flop

lollop v **bound**, bounce, bumble, stride, lope

lollygagger (dated) n **loafer**, dawdler, idler, lazybones (infml)

lone adj 1 **solitary**, single, single-handed, solo *Opposite*: accompanied 2 **only**, sole, unique, singular 3 **isolated**, lonely, separate, distinct, discrete

loneliness n **aloneness**, solitude, isolation, lonesomeness, seclusion *Opposite*: companionship

lonely adj 1 **forlorn**, lost, alone, friendless, without a friend in the world 2 **isolated**, solitary, secluded, cut off, deserted

loner n **recluse**, hermit, lone wolf, outsider

lonesome adj 1 **lonely**, forlorn, lost, alone, friendless 2 **solitary**, isolated, secluded, lonely, cut off

long adj 1 **extended**, extensive, elongated, lengthy, stretched *Opposite*: short 2 **time-consuming**, protracted, lengthy, slow, prolonged *Opposite*: brief ■ v **long for**, want, yearn, crave, desire. *See* COMPARE AND CONTRAST *at* **want**.

long-ago adj **past**, old, historic, early, prehistoric *Opposite*: modern

long-drawn-out adj **protracted**, prolonged, lengthy, drawn-out, dragged-out *Opposite*: brief

long-established adj **age-old**, time-honored, timeworn, ancient, old *Opposite*: new

longevity n **long life**, permanence, durability, endurance

long haul (infml) n 1 **ordeal**, marathon, trial, struggle, endurance test 2 **trek**, hike, distance, way, schlep (infml)

longing n **desire**, wish, yearning, hunger, craving

longitude n **position**, meridian, coordinate, location *Opposite*: latitude

long-lasting adj **long-term**, continuing, enduring, long-standing, long-running *Opposite*: short-lived

long-lived adj **long-lasting**, long-standing, prolonged, abiding, long-term *Opposite*: short-lived

long-lost adj **lost**, gone, forgotten, missing

long-range adj **long-term**, future, distant, far-off

long shot n **slim chance**, long odds, poor prospect, remote possibility, outside chance

long-standing adj **established**, age-old, ancient, enduring, ongoing

long-suffering adj **forgiving**, resigned, tolerant, accommodating, patient *Opposite*: intolerant

long-term *adj* **lasting**, long-standing, enduring, continuing, durable *Opposite*: short-term

long-winded *adj* **long-drawn-out**, rambling, interminable, wordy, prolix *Opposite*: concise. *See* COMPARE AND CONTRAST *at* **wordy**.

loofa *n* **sponge**, scrubber, exfoliator

look *v* **1 seem**, appear, come across, seem to be **2 observe**, watch, see, view, regard **3 examine**, inspect, scrutinize, pore over, study **4 focus on**, gaze, stare, glare, glance **5 explore**, investigate, examine, consider, discuss ■ *n* **appearance**, expression, air, aspect, guise

look after *v* **care for**, take care of, see to, watch over, guard *Opposite*: neglect

look ahead *v* **look forward**, project, plan, anticipate, think about *Opposite*: look back

look-alike (*infml*) *n* **double**, twin, doppelgänger, mirror image, duplicate

look back *v* **1 remember**, reminisce, recall, recollect, relive *Opposite*: look ahead **2 review**, check, return, revisit

look daggers *v* **glare**, glower, scowl, give somebody a dirty look

look down on *v* **scorn**, disdain, despise, frown on, abhor *Opposite*: look up to

looked-for *adj* **anticipated**, expected, awaited, foreseen, hoped-for *Opposite*: unexpected

looker *n* **observer**, watcher, spectator, viewer, onlooker

look for *v* **search for**, seek, hunt for, rummage

look forward to *v* **anticipate**, hope for, expect, await, wait for *Opposite*: dread

looking glass *n* **mirror**, glass, hand mirror, shaving mirror

look into *v* **investigate**, go into, check out, research, study

look like *v* **resemble**, be like, be similar to, mimic, seem like

look on the bright side *v* **be positive**, be optimistic, make the best of something, make the best of things, hope for the best *Opposite*: despair

look out *v* **1 watch out**, beware, take care, pay attention, be alert **2 look over**, look on to, look out on, overlook, face

lookout *n* **1 guard**, sentry, sentinel, watch **2 viewpoint**, vantage point, lookout tower, crow's nest, belvedere

look over *v* **inspect**, examine, check, peruse, scan

lookover (*infml*) *n* **inspection**, examination, scan, check, scrutiny

look-see (*infml*) *n* **look**, glance, glimpse, peep, peek

look through *v* **ignore**, take no notice of, give the cold shoulder, snub, cut *Opposite*: acknowledge

look up *v* **1 search**, hunt, research, find, consult **2 get better**, improve, take a turn for the better, mend, recuperate *Opposite*: worsen **3 visit**, call on, contact, get in touch, locate

look up to *v* **admire**, respect, esteem, worship, adore *Opposite*: look down on

loom *v* **1 appear**, emerge, come out, materialize, show *Opposite*: recede **2 hang over**, approach, come up, threaten, menace *Opposite*: recede

looming *adj* **impending**, pending, forthcoming, coming up, approaching

loop *n* **ring**, coil, twist, circlet, hoop ■ *v* **wind**, twist, coil, entwine, encircle

loophole *n* **dodge**, gap, ambiguity, excuse, escape

loose *adj* **1 movable**, slack, wobbly, unfastened, free *Opposite*: fixed **2 floppy**, relaxed, supple, slack, droopy *Opposite*: tight **3 loose-fitting**, baggy, unrestricting, flowing, roomy *Opposite*: tight **4 free**, freed, at liberty, unchained, untied *Opposite*: secure **5 assorted**, diverse, free, miscellaneous, eclectic **6** (*dated*) **irresponsible**, lax, slack, relaxed, free *Opposite*: strict

loose-fitting *adj* **loose**, baggy, voluminous, roomy, ample *Opposite*: tight

loose-limbed *adj* **supple**, lissome, agile, lithe, elastic *Opposite*: stiff

loosen *v* **come loose**, work loose, untie, undo, release *Opposite*: tighten

looseness *n* **1 bagginess**, shapelessness, roominess, ampleness *Opposite*: tightness **2** (*dated*) **irresponsibility**, laxity, slackness, freeness, carelessness *Opposite*: strictness

loosen up *v* **1 warm up**, limber up, stretch, exercise, prepare **2 relax**, take it easy, kick back (*infml*), let your hair down (*infml*), chill out (*infml*)

loot *n* **1 booty**, spoils, plunder, swag (*slang*) **2** (*infml*) **money**, cash, wealth, assets, dough (*slang*) ■ *v* **burgle**, plunder, ransack, pillage, rob

looter *n* **robber**, raider, plunderer, burglar, thief

lop *v* **1 cut**, chop, hack, sever, crop *Opposite*: graft **2 cut off**, chop off, slice off, remove, amputate *Opposite*: attach **3 deduct**, take off, subtract, discount, reduce *Opposite*: add

lope *n* **pace**, stride, step, gait, tread ■ *v* **stride**, move, walk, lollop

lopsided *adj* **uneven**, askew, crooked, cockeyed, disproportionate *Opposite*: even

lopsidedness *n* **unevenness**, crookedness, skewedness, imbalance, disproportionateness *Opposite*: evenness

loquacious *adj* **talkative**, garrulous, chatty, voluble, verbose *Opposite*: silent. *See* COMPARE AND CONTRAST *at* **talkative**.

lore *n* **wisdom**, tradition, teachings, knowledge, experience

lose *v* **1 misplace**, be unable to find, mislay, drop, miss *Opposite*: find **2 be defeated**, be beaten, go under, fail, suffer defeat *Opposite*: win **3 shake off**, evade, give somebody the slip, leave behind, get away from **4 waste**, squander, exhaust, use up, consume *Opposite*: save

lose consciousness *v* **faint**, blackout, pass out, swoon, collapse *Opposite*: come to

lose control *v* **lose your temper**, get carried away, go berserk, hit the roof *(infml)*, lose it *(infml) Opposite*: keep your cool *(infml)*

lose heart *v* **become despondent**, become demoralized, give up, give in, lose motivation *Opposite*: take heart

lose it *(infml) see* **lose control**

lose out *(infml) v* **miss out**, get the worst of it, come off second best, fail to benefit, miss the boat *Opposite*: gain

loser *n* **failure**, also-ran, underdog, dud *(infml)*, has-been *(infml) Opposite*: achiever

lose the thread *v* **get off the point**, lose the point, digress, go off on a tangent, deviate *Opposite*: follow

lose touch *v* **lose contact**, drift apart, lose track of, be out of the loop *(infml) Opposite*: keep up

lose track of *v* **misplace**, lose sight of, lose, be unable to follow, mislay *Opposite*: keep track of

lose weight *v* **diet**, go on a diet, slim down, watch your weight, count the calories

lose your bearings *v* **get lost**, lose your way, stray, become disoriented, take a wrong turn

lose your cool *(infml) v* **lose control**, go off the deep end, go berserk, lose your head, lose your rag *(infml) Opposite*: keep your cool *(infml)*

lose your footing *v* **stumble**, trip, trip up, fall over, slip

lose your nerve *v* **go to pieces**, break down, get flustered, give up, fall apart *Opposite*: keep your cool *(infml)*

lose your patience *v* **flare up**, snap, hit the roof *(infml)*, lose your cool *(infml)*, lose it *(infml) Opposite*: keep your cool *(infml)*

lose your rag *(infml) see* **lose your temper**

lose your temper *v* **fly into a rage**, explode, hit the roof *(infml)*, fly off the handle *(infml)*, blow your top *(infml) Opposite*: keep your cool *(infml)*

lose your way *v* **lose your bearings**, get lost, become disoriented, stray, take a wrong turn

losing *adj* **behind**, trailing, bringing up the rear, down *Opposite*: winning

loss *n* **1 deprivation**, removal, withdrawal, forfeiture, depletion **2 bereavement**, passing, passing away, death, demise *(fml)* **3 deficit**, debit, deficiency, shortfall *Opposite*: profit **4 damage**, harm, injury, cost, hurt **5 defeat**, beating, thrashing, trouncing, hammering *(infml) Opposite*: victory

loss of consciousness *n* **blackout**, faint, fainting fit, swoon, collapse

lost *adj* **1 misplaced**, mislaid, missing, gone, nowhere to be found *Opposite*: found **2 disoriented**, adrift, astray **3 deep in thought**, spellbound, entranced, rapt, engrossed **4 confused**, bewildered, bemused, at sea, stumped **5 forlorn**, vulnerable, abandoned, alone, aimless

lost in thought *adj* **faraway**, dreamy, engrossed, absorbed, deep in thought

lot *n* **1 batch**, set, assortment, grouping, bundle **2 ration**, share, slice, proportion, percentage **3 fate**, destiny, luck, kismet, fortune

loth *see* **loath**

lotion *n* **oil**, ointment, liniment, unguent, rub

lots *n* **plenty**, many, tons *(infml)*, heaps *(infml)*, loads *(infml) Opposite*: a few

lottery *n* **1 draw**, sweepstakes, raffle, lotto, bingo **2 risk**, gamble, chance, fortune, luck *Opposite*: certainty

lotus-eater *n* **lazy person**, hedonist, dreamer, daydreamer, idler

louche *adj* **disreputable**, shady, dubious, immoral, suspect *Opposite*: respectable

loud *adj* **1 noisy**, deafening, piercing, strident, thunderous *Opposite*: quiet **2 vociferous**, rowdy, boisterous, raucous, noisy *Opposite*: gentle **3 lurid**, flamboyant, brash, flashy, gaudy *Opposite*: muted

loudmouthed *(infml) adj* **blustering**, loud, noisy, vociferous, voluble *Opposite*: quiet

loudness *n* **volume**, noise, decibels, level, intensity *Opposite*: quietness

lounge *n* **living room**, drawing room, sitting room, family room, salon ■ *v* **sprawl**, recline, laze, loaf, loll

lounger *n* **reclining seat**, recliner, tanning bed, folding chair, deck chair

lousy *(infml) adj* **1 useless**, worthless, stupid, second-rate, mean *Opposite*: great **2 awful**, rotten, miserable, dreadful, abysmal *Opposite*: great

lout *n* **hulk**, oaf, ox *(infml)*, lug *(infml)*, lummox *(infml)*

loutish *adj* **coarse**, impolite, rough, uncouth, rude *Opposite*: genteel

loutishness *n* **uncouthness**, rudeness, incivility, vulgarity, bad behavior *Opposite*: politeness

lovable *adj* **endearing**, adorable, enchanting, attractive, delightful

love *n* **1 affection**, fondness, passion, liking, tenderness *Opposite*: hatred **2 darling**, dear, dearest, sweetheart, honey *(infml)* ■ *v* **1 feel affection for**, adore, worship, be in love with, be devoted to *Opposite*: hate **2 like**, enjoy, appreciate, be partial to, have a weakness for *Opposite*: dislike

---

COMPARE AND CONTRAST CORE MEANING: a strong positive feeling toward somebody or something

love an intense feeling of tender affection and compassion, especially strong romantic or sexual feelings between people; **liking** a feeling of enjoying something or finding it pleasant, or personal taste or choice; **affection** fond or tender feelings toward somebody or something; **fondness** a feeling of affection or preference; **passion** intense or overpowering emotion, either love for somebody, usually of a strong sexual nature, or strong liking or enthusiasm for something; **infatuation** an intense but short-lived, often unrealistic love for somebody, usually of a romantic or sexual nature; **crush** (*infml*) a temporary romantic *infatuation*, especially in teenagers and young people.

loved *adj* **precious**, treasured, respected, important, adored *Opposite*: detested

loved ones *n* **family**, nearest and dearest, relations, relatives, kin

loveless *adj* **harsh**, hard, unhappy, unkind, cruel *Opposite*: loving

loveliness *n* **beauty**, attractiveness, good looks, exquisiteness, charm *Opposite*: ugliness

lovely *adj* **1 beautiful**, attractive, pretty, good-looking, gorgeous *Opposite*: ugly **2 pleasant**, agreeable, delightful, perfect, wonderful *Opposite*: unpleasant. *See* COMPARE AND CONTRAST *at* good-looking.

lovesick *adj* **infatuated**, sentimental, overly affectionate, obsessed, pining

loving *adj* **affectionate**, tender, fond, devoted, caring *Opposite*: cold

low *adj* **1 near to the ground**, close to the ground, low down, short, small *Opposite*: high **2 depleted**, at a low level, down, short, in short supply *Opposite*: high **3 soft**, muted, soothing, muffled, subdued *Opposite*: loud **4 sad**, miserable, unhappy, down, depressed *Opposite*: cheerful ■ *n* **low point**, slump, depression, depths, nadir *Opposite*: peak

lowbrow *adj* **popular**, mass-market, philistine, undemanding, middle-of-the-road *Opposite*: highbrow

lowdown (*infml*) *n* **facts**, fundamentals, basics, ins and outs, particulars

lower *adj* **inferior**, subordinate, lesser, junior, poorer *Opposite*: superior ■ *v* **1 let down**, drop, let fall, hand down, sink *Opposite*: raise **2 lessen**, drop, cut, bring down, decrease *Opposite*: raise

lower class *n* **working class**, masses, hoi polloi, lower classes, proletariat *Opposite*: upper class

lower-class *adj* **working-class**, blue-collar, plebeian, popular *Opposite*: aristocratic

lowermost *adj* **lowest**, bottommost, deepest, bottom, last

lower yourself *v* **deign**, condescend, cheapen yourself, stoop, humiliate yourself

low-grade *adj* **low-quality**, inferior, cheap, substandard, second-rate *Opposite*: premium

low-key *adj* **simple**, unglamorous, unspectacular, understated, subdued *Opposite*: elaborate

lowland *n* **plain**, fen, flat, valley, swamp *Opposite*: high ground

lowliness *n* **humbleness**, meekness, submissiveness, inferiority, commonness *Opposite*: eminence

lowly *adj* **humble**, poor, deprived, ordinary, modest *Opposite*: exalted (*fml*)

low-lying *adj* **low**, lowland, sea-level, below sea level, coastal *Opposite*: high

low-minded *adj* **coarse**, common, vulgar, base, uncouth *Opposite*: refined

low-pitched *adj* **low**, deep, throaty, gruff *Opposite*: high-pitched

low point *n* **low**, all-time low, nadir, rock bottom *Opposite*: high point

low-rise *adj* **single-story**, two-story, small, three-story, low *Opposite*: high-rise

loyal *adj* **faithful**, trustworthy, devoted, reliable, dependable *Opposite*: disloyal

loyalist *n* **stalwart**, partisan, supporter, devotee, advocate *Opposite*: rebel

loyalty *n* **faithfulness**, allegiance, constancy, fidelity, devotion *Opposite*: disloyalty

lozenge *n* **pastille**, tablet, pill

lubricate *v* **oil**, grease, loosen

lucid *adj* **1 articulate**, clear, well-spoken, silver-tongued, smooth-tongued *Opposite*: incoherent **2 rational**, sane, sober, clear-headed, compos mentis *Opposite*: delirious **3 luminous**, shining, luminescent, limpid, translucent *Opposite*: dull

lucidity *n* **1 intelligibility**, perspicuity, fluency, eloquence, lucidness *Opposite*: ambiguousness **2 rationality**, lucidness, clarity, reason, sanity *Opposite*: confusion **3 luminousness**, luminescence, limpidness, lucidness, translucence *Opposite*: dullness

lucidness *see* lucidity

luck *n* **1 good fortune**, good luck, stroke of luck, windfall, blessing *Opposite*: misfortune **2 chance**, fate, fortune, destiny, providence

luckless *adj* **hapless**, unlucky, unfortunate, jinxed, ill-fated *Opposite*: lucky

lucky *adj* **fortunate**, blessed, auspicious, propitious, providential *Opposite*: unlucky

---

COMPARE AND CONTRAST CORE MEANING: relating to advantage or good fortune
lucky bringing or experiencing success or advantage, especially when this seems to happen by chance; **fortunate** bringing or experiencing unexpectedly great success or advantage; **happy** resulting in something pleasant or welcome; **providential** happening at a favorable time; **serendipitous** favorable and happening entirely by chance.

---

lucky break *n* **opportunity**, opening, chance, blessing, boon

lucky charm *n* **amulet**, mascot, good luck charm, juju, talisman

lucrative *adj* **profitable**, well-paid, rewarding, worthwhile, beneficial *Opposite*: unprofitable

ludicrous *adj* **absurd**, ridiculous, preposterous, nonsensical, comical *Opposite*: sensible

ludicrousness *n* **absurdity**, ridiculousness, unreasonableness, foolishness, nonsicalness *Opposite*: sensibleness

lug *v* **drag**, heave, cart, carry, haul

luggage *n* **baggage**, bags, cases, suitcases, stuff

luggage compartment *n* **hold**, trunk, locker

lugubrious *adj* **sad**, mournful, gloomy, depressing, doleful *Opposite*: cheerful

lugubriousness *n* **moroseness**, gloominess, melancholy, depression, sadness *Opposite*: cheerfulness

lukewarm *adj* **1 tepid**, warm, cool **2 unenthusiastic**, half-hearted, cool, unexcited, indifferent *Opposite*: enthusiastic

lull *v* **soothe**, calm, reassure, quiet, settle down *Opposite*: rouse ▪ *n* **quiet**, calm, stillness, silence, pause *Opposite*: storm

lullaby *n* **cradlesong**, song, ditty, child's bedtime song, serenade

lumbago *n* **backache**, back pain, bad back

lumber *n* **wood**, boards, planks, logs ▪ *v* **trudge**, shamble, hobble, plod, clump

lumbering *adj* **awkward**, clumsy, unwieldy, hulking, graceless *Opposite*: dainty

luminary *n* **celebrity**, star, achiever, personality, personage *Opposite*: nobody

luminosity *n* **glow**, light, brilliance, radiance, shine

luminous *adj* **glowing**, shining, brilliant, bright, radiant *Opposite*: dull

lump *n* **1 piece**, chunk, morsel, block, section **2 bump**, swelling, protuberance, knob, inflammation *Opposite*: dent ▪ *v* **1 group**, collect, combine, join, amalgamate *Opposite*: split **2** (*infml*) **put up with**, deal with, take, endure, bear

lumpy *adj* **1 clumpy**, uneven, bumpy, knobbly **2 cumbersome**, awkward, lumbering, unwieldy, graceless *Opposite*: graceful

lunge *n* **swipe**, grab, swing, thrust, stab ▪ *v* **1 attack**, dive, spring, leap, charge **2 grab**, swipe, swing, thrust, stab

lurch *v* **1 pitch**, stagger, rock, tilt, list **2 totter**, stagger, stumble, sway, reel

lure *v* **entice**, tempt, attract, decoy, draw in ▪ *n* **bait**, trap, decoy, enticement, temptation

lurid *adj* **1 shocking**, explicit, sensational, vivid, juicy (*infml*) *Opposite*: bland **2 loud**, garish, gaudy, bright, vivid *Opposite*: dull

luridness *n* **1 explicitness**, sensationalism, vividness, juiciness (*infml*) **2 garishness**, brightness, vividness, gaudiness, colorfulness

lurk *v* **lie in wait for**, loiter, prowl, skulk, wait

luscious *adj* **juicy**, moist, delicious, succulent, sweet *Opposite*: dry

lusciousness *n* **juiciness**, succulence, moistness, palatability, sweetness *Opposite*: dryness

lush *adj* **1 verdant**, abundant, green, flourishing, thriving *Opposite*: arid **2 luxurious**, lavish, opulent, sumptuous, deluxe *Opposite*: downscale

lushness *n* **1 greenness**, abundance, fertility, leafiness, luxuriance *Opposite*: aridity **2 luxury**, lavishness, sumptuousness, opulence, richness

lust *n* **desire**, envy, covetousness, longing, yearning ▪ *v* **yearn**, desire, long, hanker, hunger

luster *n* **sheen**, shine, gleam, patina, glint *Opposite*: lusterless

lusterless *adj* **dull**, matte, drab, faded, unpolished *Opposite*: shiny

lustful *adj* **lecherous**, libidinous, lascivious, passionate, amorous

lustrous *adj* **shiny**, glossy, radiant, gleaming, shimmering *Opposite*: dull

lusty *adj* **hearty**, healthy, vigorous, forceful, robust *Opposite*: feeble

luxuriance *n* **lavishness**, luxury, extravagance, abundance, richness

luxuriant *adj* **1 lush**, flourishing, thriving, exuberant, rank *Opposite*: sparse **2 abundant**, lavish, plentiful, copious, ample *Opposite*: meager

luxuriate *v* **enjoy**, wallow, indulge, bask, relish

luxurious *adj* **1 deluxe**, sumptuous, opulent, expensive, lavish *Opposite*: simple **2 extravagant**, indulgent, decadent, prodigal, epicurean *Opposite*: simple

luxuriousness *n* **expensiveness**, luxury, sumptuousness, magnificence, fulsomeness

luxury *n* **1 treat**, extra, extravagance, indulgence, bonus *Opposite*: necessity **2 lavishness**, comfort, sumptuousness, opulence, magnificence

lying *adj* **deceitful**, dishonest, two-faced, insincere, untruthful *Opposite*: truthful ▪ *n* **dishonesty**, deceit, duplicity, falseness, untruthfulness *Opposite*: truthfulness

lynch *v* **hang**, string up, murder, mob, assassinate

lynchpin *see* **linchpin**

lyric *adj* **1 poetic**, romantic, emotional, expressive, inspired **2 musical**, melodic, harmonious, tuneful, lilting

lyrical *adj* **poetic**, romantic, emotional, expressive, inspired

lyricism *n* **poeticality**, expressiveness, eloquence, floweriness

lyrics *n* **words**, lines, libretto

M

ma (infml) n **mother**, mom (infml), mommy (infml), mama (infml), mammy (infml)

macabre adj **ghoulish**, ghastly, grisly, chilling, gruesome

macadam n **asphalt**, tar, paving, blacktop, pavement

macerate v 1 **soften**, soak, steep, marinate, marinade 2 **break up**, separate, soak, mash, pulp 3 **waste away**, starve, fast, slim down, lose weight

Machiavellian adj **cunning**, unscrupulous, tricky, amoral, devious Opposite: honest

machinate v **plot**, scheme, conspire, intrigue, hatch

machination n **intrigue**, plotting, maneuvering, scheming, planning

machine n 1 **mechanism**, engine, appliance, apparatus, contraption 2 **system**, machinery, structure, procedure, mechanism 3 **automaton**, robot, cyborg, android

machine-gun v **shoot**, kill, fire at, blaze, strafe ■ adj **staccato**, rapid, abrupt, fast, quick Opposite: slow

machinery n 1 **machines**, apparatus, tackle, gear, technology 2 **mechanism**, moving parts, workings, works, cogs 3 **organization**, system, procedure, machine, structure

machinist n **machine operator**, operator, factory worker, operative, technician

machismo n **manliness**, masculinity, masculineness, maleness, virility

macho adj **manly**, masculine, virile, laddish

macro n **instruction**, command, key code, function, shortcut

macrobiotic adj **wholefood**, vegan, vegetarian, organic, natural

macrocosm n **system**, structure, formation, composition, whole Opposite: microcosm

mad adj 1 **angry**, furious, livid, irate, infuriated Opposite: calm 2 **uncontrolled**, frenzied, frenetic, panic-stricken, frantic Opposite: calm 3 **passionate**, wild about, infatuated with, enthusiastic, crazy about (infml) Opposite: indifferent

madcap adj **silly**, zany, chaotic, wild, crazy (infml) Opposite: sensible

madden v **infuriate**, enrage, annoy, anger, irritate Opposite: pacify

maddened adj **infuriated**, incensed, annoyed, angered, enraged Opposite: calm

maddening adj **infuriating**, annoying, irritating, exasperating, frustrating Opposite: pleasing

made-to-measure adj **tailor-made**, custom-made, made-to-order, customized, custom-built Opposite: off-the-rack

made-to-order adj **custom-made**, custom-built, made-to-measure, tailor-made Opposite: mass-produced

made-up adj **pretend**, invented, concocted, fictional, fictitious Opposite: real

madly adv 1 **intensely**, extremely, strongly, deeply, very 2 **wildly**, frantically, frenetically, rashly, riotously Opposite: calmly

madness n **folly**, foolishness, stupidity, foolhardiness

maelstrom n **tumult**, turbulence, flurry, whirl, turmoil

maestro n **genius**, talent, virtuoso, marvel, expert Opposite: amateur

mafia n **clique**, gang, coterie, faction, set

magazine n 1 **periodical**, publication, slick, journal, weekly 2 **arsenal**, depot, repository, ordnance, stockpile

magic n 1 **enchantment**, sorcery, witchcraft, voodoo, augury 2 **conjuring**, tricks, trickery, illusion, sleight of hand 3 **mystery**, charm, appeal, allure, attraction ■ adj 1 **enchanted**, magical, fairylike, charmed, dreamlike 2 **supernatural**, magical, paranormal, mysterious, miraculous Opposite: normal 3 **thrilling**, magical, enchanting, delightful, wonderful Opposite: mundane 4 **powerful**, special, key, all-important, famous

magical adj 1 **enchanted**, magic, fairylike, charmed, dreamlike 2 **supernatural**, magic, paranormal, mysterious, miraculous Opposite: normal 3 **thrilling**, magic, enchanting, delightful, wonderful Opposite: mundane

magician n 1 **conjurer**, illusionist, entertainer, escape artist, performer 2 **sorcerer**, wizard, warlock, enchanter, necromancer (literary) 3 **genius**, virtuoso, expert, wizard, marvel

magisterial adj 1 **overbearing**, arrogant, superior, domineering, imperious Opposite: diffident 2 **commanding**, authoritative, majestic, stately, dignified Opposite: lightweight 3 **authoritative**, expert, able, knowledgeable scholarly

magistrate n **law officer**, justice of the peace, judge, JP, justice

magma n **molten rock**, lava, tuff, igneous rock, pumice

magnanimity n **nobility**, high-mindedness, fairness, generousness, generosity *Opposite*: pettiness

magnanimous adj **generous**, benevolent, big-hearted, openhanded, altruistic *Opposite*: petty. *See* COMPARE AND CONTRAST *at* **generous**.

magnate n **tycoon**, mogul, entrepreneur, industrialist, baron

magnet n **1 magnetic body**, lodestone, horseshoe magnet, electromagnet, bar magnet **2 lure**, draw, attraction, inducement, center of attention

magnetic adj **attractive**, charming, compelling, alluring, captivating *Opposite*: repellent

magnetism n **1 magnetic field**, attraction, pull **2 charisma**, appeal, allure, charm, magic

magnetize v **attract**, charm, influence, draw, fascinate *Opposite*: repel

magnification n **exaggeration**, intensification, enlargement, increase, amplification *Opposite*: reduction

magnificence n **splendor**, glory, brilliance, radiance, majesty

magnificent adj **superb**, wonderful, splendid, glorious, brilliant *Opposite*: unimpressive

magnify v **1 enlarge**, blow up, expand, amplify, increase *Opposite*: shrink **2** *(fml)* **worship**, praise, extol, laud, glorify

magnitude n **1 greatness**, size, extent, degree, amount **2 importance**, significance, enormity, weight, consequence *(fml)* *Opposite*: triviality

magnum n **bottle**, jeroboam, demijohn

magpie *(infml)* n **1 collector**, hoarder, saver, accumulator, pack rat *(infml)* **2 chatterer**, babbler, prattler, talker, gossip

maharishi n **religious teacher**, guru, mahatma, prophet, evangelist *Opposite*: follower

maiden n **girl**, lass, young woman, young lady, damsel *(literary)* ■ adj **first**, earliest, initial, original

mail n **letters**, correspondence, packages, parcels, junk mail ■ v **send**, dispatch, transmit, email

mailbag n **1 mail sack**, sack, bag, satchel, shoulder bag **2 correspondence**, feedback, mail, letters, communications

mailbox n **maildrop**, post office box, mail slot, box, in-box

mailer n **1 envelope**, padded envelope, carton, mailing tube, container **2 advertisement**, circular, flier, leaflet, brochure

mailing list n **distribution list**, register, circulation list, newsgroup, address book

mail order n **home shopping**, electronic shopping, cybershopping, online shopping, teleshopping

maim v **wound**, injure, hurt, mutilate, damage

main adj **major**, chief, key, foremost, core *Opposite*: minor

mainland n **landmass**, continent, land *Opposite*: island

main line n **rail route**, principal route, trunk route, major route, line

mainly adv **mostly**, largely, chiefly, for the most part, primarily

mainspring n **driving force**, motive force, motivating force, chief reason, chief motive

mainstay n **cornerstone**, linchpin, keystone, foundation, basis

mainstream adj **normal**, typical, conventional, ordinary, middle-of-the-road *Opposite*: unconventional

maintain v **1 uphold**, keep, keep up, continue, sustain *Opposite*: destroy **2 look after**, care for, take care of, keep up, keep in good condition *Opposite*: neglect **3 argue**, claim, insist, assert, hold *Opposite*: deny

maintenance n **1 repairs**, upkeep, looking after, care, keep *Opposite*: neglect **2 preservation**, upholding, protection, continuation, continuance *Opposite*: destruction **3 alimony**, allowance, child support, child maintenance, grant

majestic adj **1 impressive**, superb, grand, wonderful, splendid *Opposite*: modest **2 regal**, royal, grand, stately, imposing *Opposite*: humble

majesty n **magnificence**, splendor, dignity, grandeur, illustriousness

major adj **1 main**, chief, key, foremost, leading *Opposite*: minor **2 significant**, important, weighty, substantial, crucial *Opposite*: trivial **3 serious**, grave, life-threatening *Opposite*: minor

majority n **1 bulk**, preponderance, mass, greater part, lion's share **2 margin**, difference, gap, advantage, lead **3 adulthood**, maturity, manhood, womanhood, adult years *Opposite*: childhood ■ adj **mainstream**, popular, common, widely held, middle-of-the-road *Opposite*: minority

make v **1 create**, fashion, compose, craft, build *Opposite*: destroy **2 put together**, assemble, make up, put up, cobble together **3 manufacture**, produce, fabricate, churn out, yield *Opposite*: consume **4 cook**, prepare, concoct, produce, create **5 cause**, bring about, create, give rise to, occasion **6 earn**, bring in, get, take home, get paid *Opposite*: spend **7 force**, compel, pressure, command, cause *Opposite*: ask **8 become**, turn into, change into, be **9 appoint**, elect, designate, nominate, name **10 manage**, accomplish, find time for, fit in, finish **11 achieve**, get into, get on to, succeed, progress to *Opposite*: miss **12 form**, make up, constitute, comprise, be **13 reach**, get to, make it to, get as far as, arrive at ■ n **sort**, type, kind, style, variety

make a beeline for v **make straight for**, go directly to, head for, target

make a big thing of v make a mountain out of a molehill, make a point of, make a show of, make a big deal out of (infml) Opposite: play down

make a clean breast of things v admit, confess, own up, tell all, tell the truth

make a difference v have an effect, matter, be important, change things

make a fool of v con, deceive, dupe, fool, mislead

make a fool of yourself v appear foolish, embarrass yourself, expose yourself to ridicule, humiliate yourself, make an exhibition of yourself

make a fuss v complain, fuss, make a scene, kick up a fuss, make a mountain out of a molehill

make a fuss of v make much of, indulge, spoil, cosset, coddle Opposite: ignore

make a hash of (infml) v muddle, confuse, jumble, spoil, mix up

make allowances v take into account, bear in mind, consider, take into consideration, cut somebody some slack (slang)

make amends v compensate, make reparations, make up for, pay back, recompense

make a mess of v do badly, manage badly, mishandle, mismanage, ruin

make a mountain out of a molehill v exaggerate, make a big thing of, make a fuss, make too much of, overstate

make a name for yourself v succeed, rise to fame, make it to the top, become known, gain respect

make an effort v attempt, put yourself out, try, work hard, endeavor (fml)

make an exhibition of yourself v make a fool of yourself, expose yourself to ridicule, embarrass yourself, behave foolishly, show off

make a note of v 1 mark, memorize, notice, observe, remark upon 2 write down, jot down, take down, keep a record of

make a point of v 1 make sure to, not forget to, take care to, remember to, make an effort to 2 let people know about, make a big thing of, make a fuss, make a show of, make a song and dance about (infml)

make a scene v be angry, carry on, make an exhibition of yourself, make a fuss, throw a tantrum

make a splash v make an impression, impress, get noticed, make an impact, turn heads

make a stab at (infml) v attempt, try, strive, have a go at (infml), take a stab at (infml)

make a start v begin, get going, jump in, start, get cracking (infml) Opposite: procrastinate

make a statement v say something, send a message, catch the eye, turn heads, make an impact

make available v free up, find, set aside, release, provide Opposite: refuse

make believe v pretend, imagine, fantasize, daydream, muse

make-believe n fantasy, pretense, role-playing, play-acting, story Opposite: reality ■ adj pretend, imaginary, fantasy, made-up, invented Opposite: real

make better v cure, heal, treat, alleviate, relieve

make certain v check, double-check, ensure, make sure, be in no doubt

make clear v clarify, elucidate, spell out, explain, give details Opposite: obscure

make contact v speak to, approach, communicate, touch base, get in touch Opposite: drop

make contacts v meet people, exchange cards, introduce yourself, make friends, network

make do v manage, put up with, cope, accept, tolerate

make ends meet v cope, manage, pay your bills, break even, get by

make enquiries see make inquiries

make for v 1 head for, head toward, go toward, proceed toward, aim for 2 produce, create, bring about, give rise to, generate

make friends v befriend, take up with, get in with, get to know, become acquainted Opposite: repel

make fun of v mock, poke fun at, laugh at, tease, ridicule Opposite: respect

make good v succeed, arrive, be somebody, do well, become successful Opposite: fail

make happen v cause, bring about, realize, make real, produce

make headway v make progress, progress, get somewhere, get on, make ground

make inquiries v research, investigate, explore, look into, inspect

make inroads v 1 produce a result, have an effect on, get somewhere, make something happen, make headway 2 encroach, creep up on, dent, overstep, infringe

make it (infml) v succeed, achieve, accomplish, attain, manage Opposite: give up

make known v publicize, announce, communicate, proclaim, broadcast

make light of v play down, make little of, minimize, underestimate, understate Opposite: overstate

make mincemeat of v defeat heavily, thrash, rout, overwhelm, overpower

make much of v make a fuss of, mollycoddle, baby, pet, pat

make off v run away, run off, decamp, make a break for it, make a run for it Opposite: come back

make off with v appropriate, run away with, steal, remove, pilfer Opposite: return

make out v 1 **distinguish**, see, hear, perceive, pick out 2 **understand**, work out, decipher, decode, figure out 3 **fill in**, write out, make, compose, draw up 4 **imply**, suggest, give the impression, make somebody believe, insinuate 5 **get by**, get on, manage, fare, do 6 (infml) **kiss**, make love, embrace, smooch (infml), canoodle (infml)

makeover n 1 **transformation**, change, restyling, cosmetic treatment, beautification 2 **remodeling**, renovation, restoration, transformation, alteration

make points with v **get on the good side of**, get in good with, pander to, ingratiate yourself with, flatter

make progress v 1 **make headway**, progress, advance, get somewhere, forge ahead Opposite: stall 2 **recover**, get well, get better, improve, be on the mend Opposite: deteriorate

make public v **publicize**, publish, release, put out, reveal

maker n **creator**, manufacturer, fabricator, producer, architect Opposite: destroyer

make sense v **add up**, fit, seem sensible, seem right

make sense of v **understand**, decode, decipher, follow, grasp Opposite: misunderstand

makeshift adj **rough-and-ready**, crude, temporary, improvised, provisional Opposite: permanent

make short work of v **make short shrift of**, do quickly, dash through, rush through, dash off (infml)

make somebody's acquaintance v **meet for the first time**, meet, get to know, become acquainted, bump into

make somebody's blood boil v **anger**, annoy, exasperate, irritate, enrage Opposite: delight

make somebody's hackles rise v **anger**, antagonize, get up somebody's nose, annoy, get somebody's back up Opposite: placate

make sure v **validate**, confirm, certify, take care, ensure Opposite: assume

make the best of things v **take the bad with the good**, look on the bright side, keep your chin up, keep smiling, grin and bear it (infml) Opposite: complain

make the grade v **meet the standards**, be good enough, measure up, hit the mark, satisfy Opposite: fail

make the most of v **capitalize on**, take advantage of, maximize, profit from, make hay while the sun shines (infml) Opposite: squander

make tracks (infml) v **leave**, depart, go away, make a move, vamoose (slang) Opposite: stay

make up v 1 **prepare**, make ready, get ready, set up, put together 2 **contribute**, add,

supply, come up with, provide Opposite: deduct 3 **form**, comprise, constitute, add up to, make 4 **invent**, concoct, forge, fabricate, think up 5 **top up**, subsidize, complete, supplement, round up 6 **be reconciled**, make peace, forgive and forget, kiss and make up, bury the hatchet Opposite: fall out 7 **compensate**, make amends, make good, recompense, redeem

makeup n 1 **cosmetics**, face paint, greasepaint, powder and paint, maquillage 2 **composition**, constitution, structure, formation, construction 3 **temperament**, character, personality, nature, disposition

make up your mind v **decide**, come to a decision, resolve, determine

make use of v **utilize**, use, draw on, take advantage of, avail yourself of. See COMPARE AND CONTRAST at use.

make waves v **kick up a fuss**, create a stir, rock the boat, dissent, revolt

makeweight n 1 **counterpoise**, weight, counterbalance, ballast, counterweight 2 **extra**, complement, supplement, compensation, reinforcement

make your mark v **succeed**, arrive, make an impact, make an impression, make your presence felt

make yourself known v **introduce yourself**, say who you are, identify yourself, give your name, come forward

make yourself useful v **help out**, be of service, lend a hand, assist, rally round Opposite: hinder

make your way v **go**, move, head, wend your way, pick your way

making n **creation**, manufacture, production, construction, assembly

makings n 1 **ingredients**, requirements, components, elements, materials 2 **qualities**, potential, wherewithal, what it takes, assets

maladjusted adj **disturbed**, neurotic, unstable, confused, alienated Opposite: well-adjusted

maladjustment n **instability**, disturbance, confusion, alienation, estrangement Opposite: stability

maladroit adj **awkward**, clumsy, inept, gauche, ungainly Opposite: dexterous

maladroitness n **clumsiness**, insensitivity, awkwardness, ineptitude, gaucheness Opposite: gracefulness

malady n **sickness**, illness, disease, disorder, condition

malaise n 1 **sickness**, illness, disease, disorder, condition 2 **dissatisfaction**, discontent, unease, disquiet, anxiety

malcontent n **complainer**, mischief-maker, protester, rebel, whiner ■ adj **discontented**, disgruntled, dissatisfied, unhappy, complaining Opposite: content

male *adj* **masculine,** mannish, manlike, manly, virile *Opposite*: feminine ■ *n* **man,** fellow, boy, guy *(infml)*, fella *(infml) Opposite*: female

malediction *(fml) n* **curse,** spell, blight, charm, hex *Opposite*: blessing

malefactor *(fml) n* **lawbreaker,** wrongdoer, criminal, outlaw, offender

malevolence *n* **wickedness,** malice, ill will, evil, spite *Opposite*: benevolence

malevolent *adj* **malicious,** spiteful, wicked, nasty, mean *Opposite*: benevolent

malformation *n* **deformity,** defect, fault, abnormality, distortion

malformed *adj* **misshapen,** deformed, abnormal, crooked, distorted *Opposite*: perfect

malfunction *v* **act up,** break down, crash, fail, go wrong *Opposite*: function ■ *n* **fault,** breakdown, failure, error, blip

malice *n* **hatred,** spite, malevolence, meanness, nastiness *Opposite*: kindness

malicious *adj* **hateful,** spiteful, malevolent, mean, nasty *Opposite*: kind

malign *v* **criticize,** defame, vilify, denigrate, disparage *Opposite*: praise ■ *adj* **harmful,** hurtful, damaging, destructive, negative *Opposite*: benign

---

COMPARE AND CONTRAST CORE MEANING: say or write something damaging about somebody **malign** criticize somebody in a spiteful and false or misleading way; **defame** make an attack on somebody's good name or reputation with a view to damaging or destroying it; **slander** in legal terms, make spoken false accusations about somebody that are damaging to the person's reputation; **libel** in legal terms, make false damaging accusations about somebody in writing, signs, or pictures; **vilify** make viciously defamatory statements about somebody.

---

malignancy *n* **1 spite,** malevolence, menace, evil, malice *Opposite*: kindness **2 melanoma,** tumor, disease, growth, cancer

malignant *adj* **1 evil,** malevolent, hateful, spiteful, malicious *Opposite*: kind **2 cancerous,** spreading, harmful, fatal, life-threatening *Opposite*: benign

malinger *v* **shirk,** be AWOL, duck, sidestep, shun

malleability *n* **1 ductility,** flexibility, plasticity, pliability, softness *Opposite*: rigidity **2 impressionability,** pliability, manipulability, compliance, acquiescence *Opposite*: inflexibility

malleable *adj* **1 soft,** supple, flexible, pliable, ductile *Opposite*: rigid **2 impressionable,** compliant, acquiescent, manipulable, biddable. *See* COMPARE AND CONTRAST *at* pliable.

malnourished *adj* **underfed,** undernourished, underweight, starving, famished *Opposite*: well-fed

malnutrition *n* **undernourishment,** malnourishment, underfeeding, starvation, famine

malodorous *adj* **foul-smelling,** fetid, reeking, smelly, stinking *Opposite*: fragrant

malpractice *n* **misconduct,** negligence, abuse, dereliction, mismanagement

maltreat *v* **hurt,** injure, harm, damage, misuse. *See* COMPARE AND CONTRAST *at* misuse.

maltreatment *n* **mistreatment,** abuse, ill-treatment, harm, damage

mama *(infml) n* **mother,** mom *(infml)*, momma *(infml)*, mommy *(infml)*, mammy *(infml)*

mamma *(infml) see* mama

mammal *n* **animal,** marsupial, placental mammal, marine mammal

---

WORD BANK

❑ **types of large mammals** alpaca, bactrian camel, bear, bison, boar, buffalo, camel, dromedary, elephant, giraffe, hippopotamus, llama, panda, polar bear, rhinoceros, wart hog

❑ **types of marine mammals** dolphin, dugong, grampus, manatee, narwhal, porpoise, sea lion, seal, walrus, whale

❑ **types of small mammals** anteater, armadillo, badger, ferret, hare, hedgehog, hyrax, marten, mink, mongoose, otter, pine marten, polecat, porcupine, rabbit, raccoon, skunk, sloth, stoat, weasel, wolverine

---

mammon *n* **ambition,** greed, loot, money, riches

mammoth *adj* **enormous,** huge, massive, immense, epic *Opposite*: tiny

man *n* **gentleman,** male, fellow, fella *(infml)*, guy *(infml) Opposite*: woman ■ *v* **operate,** staff, crew, work, manage

manacle *n* **handcuff,** chain, shackle, bond, fetter ■ *v* **bind,** chain, chain up, fetter, handcuff *Opposite*: release

manage *v* **1 achieve,** accomplish, succeed, be able to, bring about *Opposite*: fail **2 cope,** fare, get on, do, get by *Opposite*: give up **3 run,** direct, administer, supervise, be in charge **4 handle,** deal with, control, cope with **5 control,** discipline, master, dominate, boss

manageable *adj* **1 feasible,** doable, practicable, viable, possible *Opposite*: unmanageable **2 controllable,** handy, user-friendly, adaptable, easy to use *Opposite*: unwieldy

management *n* **1 organization,** running, administration, supervision, managing **2 directors,** managers, executives, employers, board

manager *n* **boss,** director, executive, administrator, supervisor

managerial *adj* **executive,** management, supervisory, directorial, decision-making

mandarin *n* **bureaucrat,** official, public servant, civil servant, manager

mandate *n* **1** order, command, directive, decree, dictate **2** authority, authorization, consent, permission, support **3** term of office, reign, tenure, stay ■ *v* assign, authorize, command, delegate, instruct

mandatory *adj* obligatory, compulsory, required, fixed, binding *Opposite*: optional

mandible *n* jaw, jawbone, maxilla, mouth, mouthpart

mane *(literary or infml)* *n* tresses, curls, shock, head of hair, locks *(literary)*

man-eating *adj* carnivorous, ferocious, fierce, wild, aggressive

maneuver *n* **1** move, movement, operation, exercise **2** ploy, trick, plot, scheme, device ■ *v* manipulate, plot, scheme, contrive, plan

man friend *(infml)* *n* male companion, boyfriend, partner

manful *adj* brave, strong, resolute, bold, determined *Opposite*: cowardly

manger *n* trough, feeding-box, container, crib

mangle *v* crush, mash, smash, contort, twist

mangy *(infml)* *adj* unpleasant, dirty, shabby, disgusting, filthy *Opposite*: pristine

manhandle *v* push, shove, jostle, hustle, move

manhood *n* **1** maturity, independence, adulthood **2** men, menfolk, males **3** strength, courage, determination, virility, boldness *Opposite*: unmanliness

mania *n* obsession, desire, love, craze, passion

maniac *n* enthusiast, fanatic, zealot, fiend, freak *(infml)*

manic *(infml)* *adj* overexcited, agitated, hectic, frenzied, busy *Opposite*: calm

manicure *v* trim, file, shape, cut, clip

manifest *adj* apparent, unmistakable, clear, plain, obvious *Opposite*: unclear ■ *v* make plain, establish, demonstrate, display, reveal

manifestation *n* sign, indication, index, indicator, appearance

manifesto *n* declaration, statement, policy, guidelines, proposal

manifold *adj* various, diverse, many, multiple, assorted *Opposite*: uniform

manipulate *v* **1** operate, work, use, deploy, employ **2** influence, control, bias, direct, sway **3** maneuver, direct, control, stagemanage, engineer

manipulation *n* **1** operation, handling, management, use, guidance **2** running, control, maneuvering, exploitation, persuasion **3** falsification, forgery, alteration, misuse, tampering **4** osteopathy, massage, movement, flexing, rubbing

manipulative *adj* scheming, calculating, controlling, devious, unscrupulous

manipulator *n* Machiavelli, exploiter, schemer, Svengali, wheeler-dealer *(infml)*

mankind *n* **1** *(dated)* men, menfolk, manhood, males **2** human race, humankind, humanity, human beings, people

manliness *n* masculinity, machismo, manhood *Opposite*: unmanliness

manly *adj* virile, mannish, male, masculine, macho *Opposite*: womanly

man-made *adj* artificial, synthetic, manufactured, substitute, imitation *Opposite*: natural

manna *n* **1** food, sustenance, victuals, fodder, provisions **2** godsend, blessing, boon, gift, help

mannequin *n* dummy, model, figure, tailor's dummy, dressmaker's dummy

manner *n* **1** way, means, method, style, custom **2** type, kind, sort, class, category **3** behavior, conduct, demeanor, bearing, comportment *(fml)*

mannered *adj* affected, artificial, put-on, false, simpering *Opposite*: natural

mannerism *n* **1** gesture, trait, characteristic, gesticulation, habit **2** affectation, show, act, display, pretense

mannerly *adj* well-behaved, polite, refined, well-mannered, respectful *Opposite*: rude

manners *n* **1** etiquette, protocol, good manners **2** behavior, conduct, demeanor, deportment, manner

manqué *adj* failed, near, would-be, unfulfilled, unsuccessful *Opposite*: successful

mansard *n* attic, loft, roof, eaves, rafters

manse *n* vicarage, rectory, parsonage, residence, church house

manslaughter *n* murder, homicide, killing, assassination, slaying

mantle *n* **1** *(literary)* layer, blanket, covering, shroud, veil **2** *(fml)* responsibility, function, role, position, duty

mantra *n* chant, intonation, repetition, refrain, hymn

manual *adj* physical, labor-intensive, bluecollar *Opposite*: mental ■ *n* instruction booklet, guide, handbook, guidebook, instruction manual

manufacture *v* build, assemble, construct, produce, create ■ *n* production, making, creation, building, assembly

manufactured *adj* factory-made, mass-produced, industrial, man-made, synthetic

manufacturer *n* builder, producer, constructor, creator, industrialist

manufacturing *n* production, manufacture, making, assembly, construction

manure *n* dung, compost, guano, muck, fertilizer

manuscript *n* document, copy, text, script

many *adj* a lot of, lots of, numerous, countless, several *Opposite*: a few

many-sided *adj* multifaceted, complex, complicated, deep, multidimensional *Opposite*: one-dimensional

map n **plan**, chart, atlas, record, drawing ■ v **chart**, plot, plan, record, draw

map out v **work out**, plan, devise, outline, arrange

map reading n **route-planning**, routing, direction-finding, orienteering, navigation

mar v **deface**, ruin, mutilate, damage, disfigure Opposite: repair

marathon adj **lengthy**, epic, long-drawn-out, grueling, difficult

maraud v **raid**, plunder, ransack, loot, pillage

marauder n **raider**, robber, bandit, pillager, plunderer

marble n **glass ball**, agate, cat's eye

marbled adj **veined**, streaked, mottled, lined, shot through

march v 1 **parade**, file, step, troop, process 2 **stride**, stomp, storm, sweep, flounce ■ n 1 **hike**, trek, walk, tramp, trudge 2 **protest**, picket, mass lobby, rally. demonstration

marcher n **demonstrator**, protester, walker, campaigner, supporter

march-past n **parade**, review, muster, procession

margin n 1 **boundary**, border, brim, sideline, edge 2 **surplus**, room, leeway, allowance, scope

marginal adj 1 **negligible**, minimal, low, minor, slight Opposite: major 2 **irrelevant**, insignificant, unimportant, borderline, fringe Opposite: central

marginalization n **relegation**, sidelining, demotion, downgrading, disregarding

marginalize v **relegate**, sideline, demote, downgrade, disregard Opposite: include

marginally adv **slightly**, a little, a touch, a bit (infml), a tad (infml)

marina n **harbor**, port, dock, quay, yacht haven

marinade n 1 **dressing**, sauce, flavoring, juices, infusion 2 see **marinate**

marinate v **steep**, soak, infuse, immerse, douse

marine adj 1 **saltwater**, seawater, sea, aquatic 2 **nautical**, oceangoing, naval, seafaring, seagoing

mariner n **sailor**, seafarer, seadog, old salt, tar (archaic infml)

marital adj **conjugal**, nuptial, wedded, spousal, matrimonial

maritime adj 1 **nautical**, naval, oceanic, seafaring, seagoing 2 **seaside**, coastal, shoreline, littoral

mark n 1 **spot**, scratch, dent, stain, smear 2 **sign**, indication, feature, characteristic, symbol 3 **score**, point, assessment, evaluation, grade ■ v 1 **stain**, scratch, smudge, smear, blot 2 **correct**, assess, grade, evaluate, score 3 **indicate**, denote, show, demonstrate, evidence 4 **celebrate**, commemorate, keep, observe, solemnize

markdown n **discount**, price cutting, reduction Opposite: markup

marked adj **clear**, apparent, evident, noticeable, conspicuous

marker n **indicator**, sign, indication, symbol, pointer

market n **marketplace**, souk, bazaar, arcade, fair ■ v **sell**, promote, advertise, peddle, trade

marketable adj **in demand**, sought-after, wanted, vendible, merchantable

marketing n **advertising**, selling, presentation, publicizing, promotion

marketplace n 1 **bazaar**, market, souk, flea market, open market 2 **trading floor**, sphere, arena, market

marking n **pattern**, coloration, design

mark out v 1 **outline**, demarcate, sketch, delimit, delineate 2 **distinguish**, differentiate, single out, identify, characterize

markup n **price increase**, rise, hike, profit, profit margin Opposite: markdown

maroon v **abandon**, leave high and dry, leave, cast aside, cast adrift

marooned adj **stranded**, deserted, abandoned, isolated, stuck

marque n **make**, label, trademark, brand

marquee n **tent**, pavilion, canvas, shelter, erection (fmi)

marquetry n **inlay**, pattern, design, veneer

marred adj **blemished**, flawed, stained, disfigured, tarnished Opposite: unblemished

marriage n 1 **wedding**, matrimony, wedding ceremony, marriage ceremony, nuptials (fml) Opposite: divorce 2 **union**, fusion, combination, coming together, alliance Opposite: separation

marriageability n **eligibility**, suitability, availability, fitness

marriageable adj **eligible**, suitable, available, adult, grown-up

married adj **wedded**, matrimonial, nuptial, conjugal, marital

marrow (literary) n **core**, heart, soul, spirit, essence

marry v **get married**, join in matrimony, walk down the aisle, tie the knot (infml), get hitched (infml)

marsh n **bog**, swamp, quagmire, swampland, marshland

marshal n **officer**, sheriff, deputy, law officer ■ v 1 **assemble**, position, gather together, collect, shepherd Opposite: disperse 2 **arrange**, order, sort out, put in order, organize Opposite: muddle

marshland n **bog**, swamp, swampland, marsh, wetland

marshy adj **boggy**, swampy, soggy, muddy, peaty Opposite: dry

mart n **auction**, sale, market, store, trading place

martial *adj* **1 military**, soldierly, warlike, battle-hardened, fighting *Opposite*: civilian **2 warlike**, fierce, aggressive, belligerent, hostile *Opposite*: peaceful

martial law *n* **state of emergency**, militarism, junta, dictatorship, emergency powers

Martian *n* **alien**, extraterrestrial, ET, spaceman, invader *Opposite*: terrestrial

martinet *n* **disciplinarian**, stickler, despot, hardliner, perfectionist *Opposite*: softy (*infml*)

martyr *n* **1 sacrifice**, sacrificial victim, victim, scapegoat, ransom (*literary*) **2 idealist**, witness, believer, supporter **3 sufferer**, invalid, patient

martyrdom *n* **1 death**, killing, slaughter, torture, ritual murder **2 suffering**, misery, pain, sacrifice, torment

marvel *n* **1 wonder**, miracle, spectacle, sight, curiosity **2 genius**, prodigy, phenomenon, wunderkind, whiz (*infml*) ■ *v* **be amazed**, be surprised, be impressed, admire, wonder *Opposite*: deride

marvellous *see* **marvelous**

marvelous *adj* **1 amazing**, impressive, remarkable, magnificent, superb *Opposite*: ordinary **2 great**, brilliant, wonderful, fantastic, fabulous

mascot *n* **symbol**, charm, talisman, amulet, periapt *Opposite*: hex

masculine *adj* **male**, manly, mannish, macho, virile *Opposite*: feminine

masculinity *n* **maleness**, manliness, mannishness, manhood, boyhood *Opposite*: femininity

mash *n* **purée**, pulp, mush ■ *v* **pulp**, squash, pound, crush, smash

mask *n* **cover**, disguise, guise, façade, front ■ *v* **hide**, conceal, disguise, cover, camouflage *Opposite*: expose

masked *adj* **1 disguised**, incognito, camouflaged, concealed, screened *Opposite*: exposed **2 undetectable**, imperceptible, latent, hidden, invisible *Opposite*: detectable

masonry *n* **stonework**, brickwork, building materials, granite, sandstone

masque *n* **1 performance**, allegory, theatricals, play, opera **2 masquerade**, dance, ball, masked ball

masquerade *n* **1 pretense**, deception, cover-up, subterfuge, ruse **2 masked ball**, masque, ball, dance ■ *v* **pretend to be**, impersonate, pose, disguise yourself, make-believe

mass *n* **1 form**, figure, frame, physique, build **2 quantity**, corpus, amount, area, reservoir **3 bulk**, main part, essence, majority, better part ■ *v* **gather**, assemble, group, congregate, collect *Opposite*: disperse ■ *adj* **general**, widespread, common, universal, wholesale

massacre *n* **extermination**, annihilation, carnage, butchery, mass slaughter ■ *v* **slaughter**, murder, exterminate, butcher, mow down

massage *n* **manipulation**, pressure, kneading, rubbing, reflexology ■ *v* **1 knead**, manipulate, rub, rub down **2 falsify**, manipulate, alter, amend, misrepresent

masses *n* **common people**, crowd, multitude, commonality, hoi polloi *Opposite*: elite

massif *n* **mountain range**, chain, sierra, ridge, line

massive *adj* **1 bulky**, heavy, solid, weighty, hulking *Opposite*: slight **2 huge**, enormous, gigantic, immense, colossal *Opposite*: tiny

massively (*infml*) *adv* **enormously**, immensely, hugely, tremendously, vastly *Opposite*: slightly

mass-produce *v* **churn out**, turn out, manufacture, process, knock out

mass-produced *adj* **ready-to-wear**, off-the-shelf, off-the-rack, ready-made, machine-made *Opposite*: personalized

master *n* **1 controller**, ruler, leader, chief, boss *Opposite*: underling **2 teacher**, guru, tutor, instructor, guide *Opposite*: pupil **3 expert**, virtuoso, maestro, genius, prodigy *Opposite*: novice ■ *adj* **chief**, principal, main, major, leading *Opposite*: secondary ■ *v* **1 become skilled at**, become proficient at, grasp, learn, understand *Opposite*: fail **2 conquer**, gain control of, overcome, subdue, get the better of

masterful *adj* **1 expert**, skilled, proficient, skillful, accomplished *Opposite*: incompetent **2 authoritative**, commanding, imposing, assured, forceful *Opposite*: weak

masterly *adj* **skilled**, skillful, proficient, talented, gifted *Opposite*: incompetent

mastermind *n* **brains**, architect, organizer, instigator, brain (*infml*) ■ *v* **plan**, engineer, oversee, organize, devise *Opposite*: carry out

masterpiece *n* **work of art**, magnum opus, tour de force, stroke of genius, masterwork

masterwork *see* **masterpiece**

mastery *n* **1 expertise**, skill, knowledge, proficiency, command **2 control**, power, supremacy, authority, command

masthead *n* **title**, banner, strip, logo, header

masticate *v* **chew**, munch, crunch, champ, grind

mastication *n* **chewing**, munching, eating, grinding, champing

mat *n* **1 rug**, carpet, doormat, bathmat, floorcovering **2 table mat**, place mat, doily, coaster, pad ■ *v* **tangle**, entwine, entangle, intertwine, knot *Opposite*: disentangle ■ *adj* **dull**, lusterless, nonglossy, muted *Opposite*: glossy

match n 1 competition, bout, contest, game, tie 2 equal, counterpart, equivalent, pair, partner ■ v 1 go with, complement, harmonize, accord, coordinate Opposite: clash 2 be alike, correspond, be identical, tally, fit Opposite: differ

matching adj 1 corresponding, identical, similar, alike, same Opposite: different 2 toning, harmonizing, complementary, coordinative, coordinating Opposite: clashing

matchless adj peerless, outstanding, unparalleled, incomparable, unrivaled Opposite: ordinary

matchmaker n marriage broker, go-between, fixer, intermediary, cupid

mate n helper, assistant, colleague, partner, coworker ■ v breed, reproduce, couple (fml), copulate (fml)

material n 1 substance, matter, raw material, stuff 2 data, information, ideas, facts, notes 3 fabric, textile, stuff, cloth, yard goods ■ adj 1 physical, substantial, solid, factual, quantifiable Opposite: insubstantial 2 significant, relevant, pertinent, important, central Opposite: immaterial

materialism n acquisitiveness, avariciousness, avarice, covetousness, avidity Opposite: detachment

materialistic adj money-oriented, grasping, acquisitive, avaricious, covetous Opposite: spiritual

materialization n appearance, arrival, advent, embodiment, manifestation Opposite: disappearance

materialize v 1 appear, turn up, show up, arrive, reveal yourself Opposite: disappear 2 come into existence, happen, occur, exist, take shape Opposite: evaporate

materially adv significantly, considerably, substantially, importantly, essentially Opposite: slightly

materials n resources, supplies, ingredients, constituents, equipment

maternal adj 1 motherly, parental, nurturing, protective, guiding 2 caring, devoted, kind, tender, gentle Opposite: uncaring

maternity n motherhood, childbearing, parenthood

mathematical adj 1 arithmetical, numerical, arithmetic, geometric, algebraic 2 exact, precise, scientific, accurate, measured Opposite: random

mathematics n calculation, reckoning, math, algebra, arithmetic

matinée n afternoon showing, show, performance, presentation

matriarch n mother, matron, grandmother, older woman, materfamilias (fml) Opposite: patriarch

matriculate v 1 admit, register, enlist, enroll, inscribe Opposite: strike off 2 enroll, be admitted, sign up, join, be enrolled Opposite: drop out

matriculation n enrollment, admission, registration, admittance, enlistment Opposite: expulsion

matrimonial adj marital, wedded, married, nuptial, conjugal

matrimony n marriage, wedlock, wedding, ceremony, service Opposite: divorce

matrix n 1 substance, medium, carrier, solution, base 2 situation, environment, milieu, conditions, background 3 template, mold, format, pattern, mint

matron n older woman, mature woman, middle-aged woman, matriarch, doyenne

matronly adj full-figured, plump, portly, stout, well-rounded

matted adj tangled, entwined, entangled, disheveled, intertwined

matter n 1 substance, stuff, stock, staple, material 2 trouble, problem, difficulty, worry, concern 3 subject, topic, theme, issue, affair ■ v be of importance, be important, count, signify, be significant. See COMPARE AND CONTRAST at subject.

matter-of-fact adj 1 down-to-earth, straightforward, rational, unemotional, realistic 2 factual, unvarnished, down-to-earth, literal, unembroidered Opposite: fictional

matting n floorcovering, tatami, mats, coconut matting, rush matting

mattress n futon, air mattress, pallet, pad, paillasse

maturation n maturing, ripening, mellowing, development, growth

mature adj 1 established, developed, advanced, settled, matured Opposite: undeveloped 2 experienced, responsible, prudent, wise, sensible Opposite: naive 3 grown-up, adult, full-grown, middle-aged, older Opposite: immature 4 ripe, mellow, ready, strong, sweet Opposite: young ■ v grow up, develop, ripen, mellow, age

matured adj mature, ripe, ripened, mellowed, aged Opposite: young

maturely adv wisely, sensibly, responsibly, prudently Opposite: immaturely

maturity n 1 adulthood, prime of life, middle age, old age Opposite: youth 2 ripeness, mellowness, development, age Opposite: youth 3 wisdom, experience, responsibility, reliability, sensibleness Opposite: inexperience

maudlin adj oversentimental, mawkish, slushy, mushy, syrupy Opposite: unemotional

maul v 1 claw, attack, ill-treat, paw, mangle 2 criticize, attack, savage, slam (infml), pan (infml)

mauling n criticism, disparagement, censure, barrage, blast

mausoleum n tomb, vault, crypt, resting place, grave

maven n expert, doyen, doyenne, enthusiast, pundit

maverick *n* **nonconformist**, eccentric, individualist, rebel, odd one out *Opposite*: conformist

mawkish *adj* **oversentimental**, slushy, mushy, syrupy, overemotional *Opposite*: unemotional

mawkishness *n* **sentimentality**, tearfulness, mushiness, slushiness, weepiness *(infml)*

max *v* **win**, succeed, come first, come out on top, triumph

maxi *adj* **large**, mega, big, jumbo, king-size *Opposite*: mini

maxim *n* **1 saying**, adage, proverb, saw, aphorism **2 rule**, tenet, guideline, truth, principle

maximal *adj* **best**, greatest, most, utmost, highest *Opposite*: minimal

maximization *n* **expansion**, growth, enlargement, extension, intensification

maximize *v* **1 make the most of**, make best use of, exploit, take full advantage of, capitalize on *Opposite*: minimize **2 increase**, expand, amplify, make bigger, boost *Opposite*: minimize

maximum *n* **1 limit**, ceiling, greatest extent, top figure, upper limit *Opposite*: minimum **2 most**, greatest, highest, utmost *Opposite*: minimum

maybe *adv* **perhaps**, possibly, it could be, perchance *(literary)*, mayhap *(archaic)* *Opposite*: definitely

mayday *n* **SOS**, distress signal, emergency call, distress call, alert

mayhem *(infml)* *n* **chaos**, disorder, confusion, turmoil, havoc *Opposite*: order

maypole *n* **column**, post, pole, support

maze *n* **1 labyrinth**, warren, web, network **2 confusion**, muddle, jumble, mess, intricacy *Opposite*: order

MC *n* **master of ceremonies**, host, toastmaster, moderator, emcee *(infml)*

meadow *n* **field**, pasture, paddock, grazing land, lea *(literary)*

meager *adj* **small**, slight, insufficient, inadequate, sparse *Opposite*: plentiful

meagerness *n* **insufficiency**, inadequacy, scantness, stinginess, sparseness *Opposite*: abundance

meal *n* **food**, bite, snack, something to eat

WORD BANK

❏ **types of meals** banquet, barbecue, breakfast, brunch, buffet, clambake, continental breakfast, cookout, dinner, English breakfast, lunch, luncheon, picnic, ready-made meal, snack, supper, takeout, tea, tidbit, TV dinner

❏ **parts of a meal** antipasto, aperitif, appetizer, canapé, delicacy, dessert, entrée, hors d'oeuvre, main course, meze, side dish, starter, tapas

mealtime *n* **breakfast time**, lunchtime, dinnertime, suppertime

mealy-mouthed *adj* **hypocritical**, insincere, euphemistic, indirect, devious *Opposite*: frank

mean *v* **1 denote**, signify, indicate, stand for, represent **2 intend**, propose, aim, plan, want **3 entail**, involve, require, lead to, necessitate ▪ *adj* **1 nasty**, unkind, cruel, callous, vile *Opposite*: kind **2 poor**, shabby, squalid, humble, lowly *Opposite*: comfortable **3** *(archaic)* **humble**, lowly, poor, simple, underprivileged **4 paltry**, derisory, meager, miserable, scanty *Opposite*: plentiful **5 middle**, mid, average, normal, standard *Opposite*: extreme ▪ *n* **average**, norm, median, middle, midpoint *Opposite*: extremity

COMPARE AND CONTRAST CORE MEANING: referring to somebody or something below normal standards of decency

mean unkind or malicious; **nasty** showing spitefulness, malice, or ill-nature; **vile** despicable or shameful; **low** without principles or morals; **base** lacking proper social values or moral principles; **ignoble** dishonorable and contrary to the high standards of conduct expected.

mean business *v* **be serious**, mean what you say, mean it, be determined, be deadly serious

meander *v* **1 wind**, zigzag, twist and turn, twist, snake **2 wander**, roam, amble, ramble, stroll *Opposite*: rush

meandering *adj* **twisting**, winding, twisty, tortuous, snaking *Opposite*: straight

meaning *n* **1 sense**, connotation, denotation, import, gist **2 significance**, importance, implication, worth, value *Opposite*: insignificance

meaningful *adj* **1 expressive**, evocative, telling, eloquent, speaking **2 significant**, important, consequential, momentous, deep *Opposite*: meaningless

meaningfulness *n* **meaning**, importance, significance, seriousness, relevance *Opposite*: meaninglessness

meaningless *adj* **1 empty**, worthless, throwaway, hollow, pointless *Opposite*: meaningful **2 unimportant**, trivial, inconsequential, irrelevant, insignificant *Opposite*: significant

meaninglessness *n* **emptiness**, insignificance, futility, purposelessness, worthlessness *Opposite*: importance

mean it *v* **be in earnest**, not be joking, be deadly serious, mean business, mean what you say

meanness *n* **nastiness**, unkindness, cruelty, callousness, spitefulness *Opposite*: kindness

means *n* **1 way**, method, process, measures, channel **2 income**, earnings, resources, revenue, funds

mean-spirited *adj* **ungenerous**, uncharitable, harsh, mean, unkind *Opposite*: generous

meant *adj* **1 intended**, designed, planned, aimed, targeted *Opposite*: unexpected **2 inevitable**, preordained, fated, predestined *Opposite*: accidental

meantime *n* **interim**, intervening time, period in-between, the time being

mean well *v* **have good intentions**, have your heart in the right place, try to do the right thing, try hard, have the best intentions

meanwhile *adv* **in the meantime**, for the meantime, in the interim, in the intervening time, for now

measly (*infml*) *adj* **stingy**, ungenerous, meager, mean, derisory *Opposite*: ample

measurable *adj* **1 quantifiable**, assessable, gaugeable, computable, calculable *Opposite*: indeterminate **2 considerable**, appreciable, noticeable, detectable, perceptible *Opposite*: imperceptible

measurably *adv* **noticeably**, evidently, significantly, demonstrably, obviously *Opposite*: insignificantly

measure *n* **1 amount**, degree, quantity, portion, ration **2 measuring device**, gauge, meter, counter ▪ *v* **gauge**, calculate, compute, determine, assess

measured *adj* **1 slow**, unhurried, unrushed, restrained, stately *Opposite*: hurried **2 deliberate**, calculated, precise, exact, careful *Opposite*: unthinking

measureless *adj* **incalculable**, immeasurable, immense, vast, without limit *Opposite*: negligible

measurement *n* **dimension**, size, extent, quantity, amount

WORD BANK

❑ **types of metric units** centigram, centiliter, centimeter, decagram, decaliter, decameter, decigram, deciliter, decimeter, gram, hectare, hectogram, hectoliter, hectometer, kilogram, kiloliter, kilometer, liter, meter, microgram, micrometer, milligram, milliliter, millimeter, tonne

❑ **types of nonmetric units** acre, barrel, bushel, degree Fahrenheit, dram, fluid dram, fluid ounce, foot, gallon, gill, inch, mile, ounce, peck, pint, pound, quart, rod, ton, yard

❑ **types of SI units** becquerel (radioactivity), coulomb (electric charge), degree Celsius (temperature), farad (capacitance), gray (radiation dose), henry (inductance), hertz (frequency), joule (energy), lumen (luminous flux), lux (illuminance), newton (force), ohm (electric resistance), pascal (pressure), siemens (electric conductance), sievert (radiation effects), tesla (magnetic flux density), volt (electric potential), watt (power), weber (magnetic flux)

measure up *v* **hit the mark**, satisfy, deliver, do, meet the required standards *Opposite*: fall short

measuring device *n* **gauge**, measure, meter, counter

WORD BANK

❑ **types of measuring devices** altimeter, anemometer, aneroid barometer, balance, barograph, barometer, calipers, clock, compass, dipstick, dividers, cropper, Geiger counter, level, measuring tape, micrometer, odometer, pipette, protractor, quadrant, rule, scale, speedometer, statoscope, tachometer, tape, tape measure, theodolite, thermometer, weather vane, weighing machine, weighing scale, wind gauge, windsock

meat *n* **1 flesh**, food, carrion **2 substance**, heart, gist, pith, kernel

WORD BANK

❑ **types of cuts** breast, brisket, chop, chuck, cutlet, drumstick, flank, foreshank, hock, joint, leg, loin, neck, rasher, rib, round, scrag end, shoulder, side, sparerib, steak, top round, wing

❑ **types of meats** beef, chicken, duck, gammon, goat, goose, grouse, hare, lamb, mutton, partridge, pheasant, pork, rabbit, turkey, veal, venison, wild boar

❑ **types of processed meats** bacon, beefburger, bologna, bratwurst, bresaola, burger, chorizo, foie gras, frankfurter, ground beef, ground meat, ham, hamburger, jerky, liverwurst, meat loaf, meatball, merguez, mincemeat, mortadella, pancetta, parma ham, pastrami, pâté, patty, pepperoni, rissole, salami, sausage, wiener, wienerwurst

❑ **types of steaks** Chateaubriand, fillet, fillet mignon, porterhouse steak, rump, sirloin, T-bone steak, tenderloin

meat-and-potatoes *adj* **basic**, fundamental, essential, primary, central

meaty *adj* **1 substantial**, profound, deep, weighty, solid *Opposite*: lightweight **2 brawny**, burly, muscular, fleshy, husky *Opposite*: weedy

mecca *n* **center**, focus, focal point, magnet, hub

mechanical *adj* **1 motorized**, powered, power-driven, machine-driven, automated *Opposite*: manual **2 automatic**, perfunctory, unconscious, unthinking, reflex

mechanics *n* **workings**, technicalities, procedure, mechanism, process

mechanism *n* **1 device**, instrument, apparatus, machine, machinery **2 means**, method, system, procedure, process

mechanistic *adj* **automatic**, mechanical, machine-like, automatous, robotic

mechanization *n* **automation**, computerization, streamlining, modernization, systematization

mechanize *v* **automate**, power, systematize, industrialize, program

mechanized *adj* **automated**, mechanical, industrialized, automatic, computerized

medal *n* **award**, decoration, honor, distinction, laurel

medalist n winner, champion, victor, runner-up

medallion n medal, decoration, pendant, ornament

meddle v interfere, butt in, stick your nose in, intrude, pry

meddler n troublemaker, nuisance, gossip, interferer, busybody (infml)

meddlesome adj interfering, intrusive, meddling, officious, prying Opposite: detached

meddling n interference, inquisitiveness, intrusion, prying, intrusiveness ■ adj interfering, meddlesome, inquisitive, intrusive, prying Opposite: uninterested

media n mass media, television, radio, newspapers, magazines

median n mean, midpoint, middle, norm, standard

mediate v arbitrate, intercede, facilitate, intermediate, referee Opposite: provoke

mediation n arbitration, intercession, conciliation, intervention, negotiation Opposite: provocation

mediator n go-between, intermediary, third party, arbitrator, negotiator

medic (infml) n doctor, medical student, physician, surgeon, general practitioner

medical adj medicinal, remedial, health, homeopathic, curative ■ n checkup, physical, physical exam, health check, examination

WORD BANK

❑ **types of complementary therapies** acupressure, acupuncture, Alexander technique, Ayurvedic medicine, Bach flower remedy, chiropractic, color therapy, cranial osteopathy, flotation, herbal medicine, homeopathy, hydrotherapy, hypnotherapy, iridology, kinesiology, massage, music therapy, naturopathy, neurolinguistic programming, osteopathy, Pilates, reflexology, reiki, shiatsu, tai chi, yoga

❑ **types of medical procedures** amniocentesis, amputation, anesthesia, angioplasty, appendectomy, biopsy, booster, bypass, CAT scan, Cesarean section, checkup, chemotherapy, diagnosis, dialysis, endoscopy, facelift, graft, hysterectomy, immunization, keyhole surgery, laparoscopy, manipulation, mastectomy, operation, physical therapy, plastic surgery, radiotherapy, resuscitation, sedation, tracheotomy, transfusion, ultrasound scan, vaccination, vasectomy, X-ray

❑ **types of medical specialties** anesthesiology, cardiology, dermatology, endocrinology, family medicine, geriatrics, hematology, internal medicine, neurology, ob-gyn, oncology, ophthalmology, pediatrics, psychiatry, radiology, rheumatology, surgery

medicament n medicine, remedy, treatment, pharmaceutical, curative

medicated adj medicinal, antiseptic, antibacterial, antiviral, analgesic

medication n drug, pharmaceutical, pill, tablet, capsule

medicinal adj medicated, remedial, healing, therapeutic, curative

medicine n drug, remedy, medication, treatment, prescription

medieval adj old-fashioned, out-of-date, primitive, feudal, unenlightened Opposite: modern

mediocre adj middling, average, unexceptional, ordinary, middle-of-the-road Opposite: excellent

mediocrity n patchiness, unevenness, poorness, weakness, averageness Opposite: excellence

meditate v contemplate, ponder, think, consider, deliberate

meditation n thought, consideration, contemplation, reflection, rumination

meditative adj thoughtful, reflective, contemplative, pensive, introspective Opposite: active

medium adj average, intermediate, middle, middling, standard Opposite: extraordinary ■ n means, vehicle, channel, mode, method

medley n mixture, combination, assortment, mix, jumble

meek adj 1 mild, quiet, humble, gentle, docile Opposite: overbearing 2 timid, compliant, weak, cowed, fearful Opposite: assertive

meekness n 1 humbleness, quietness, docility, humility, gentleness 2 timidity, submissiveness, fearfulness, compliance, weakness Opposite: assertiveness

meet v 1 come across, encounter, bump into, run into, chance on Opposite: avoid 2 gather, get together, come together, convene, assemble Opposite: disperse 3 be introduced to, make somebody's acquaintance, get to know, greet, become acquainted with 4 touch, contact, connect, join, converge Opposite: separate 5 experience, encounter, come across, endure, go through

meeting n 1 business meeting, conference, assembly, summit, seminar 2 encounter, introduction, reunion, appointment, engagement

meetinghouse n assembly hall, church, building

megalith n prehistoric monument, standing stone, menhir, dolmen, sarsen

megalomania n power lust, overbearingness, tyranny, totalitarianism, autocracy

megalomaniac n tyrant, dictator, autocrat, despot ■ adj power-hungry, power-crazy, self-important, tyrannical, dictatorial

melancholic adj dejected, sad, unhappy, miserable, forlorn Opposite: cheerful

melancholy adj sad, downhearted, miserable, down, low Opposite: cheerful ■

n **sadness**, unhappiness, dejection, sorrow, the blues *Opposite*: cheerfulness

melange *(literary or fml)* *n* **mixture**, mix, jumble, potpourri, mishmash

meld *v* **mix**, merge, blend, fuse, combine *Opposite*: separate ■ *n* **combination**, mix, mixture, blend, amalgamation

melee *n* 1 **fight**, commotion, brawl, fracas, uproar 2 **muddle**, jumble, mix, confusion, mixture

mellifluous *adj* **pleasant**, soothing, sweet, melodious, honeyed *Opposite*: jarring

mellow *adj* 1 **smooth**, rich, full, warm, soft *Opposite*: harsh 2 **mature**, full-flavored, ripe, aged, strong *Opposite*: young 3 **easygoing**, tolerant, approachable, genial, equable *Opposite*: uptight *(infml)* ■ *v* 1 **calm down**, ease up, settle down, relax, soften 2 **mature**, soften, develop, ripen, improve *Opposite*: deteriorate

mellowness *n* 1 **smoothness**, richness, warmth, fullness, mellifluousness *Opposite*: harshness 2 **ripeness**, sweetness, fullness, matureness, maturity *Opposite*: rawness 3 **geniality**, amiability, warmth, affability, expansiveness

melodic *see* **melodious**

melodious *adj* **tuneful**, harmonious, musical, easy on the ear, mellow *Opposite*: discordant

melodiousness *n* **tunefulness**, musicalness, pleasantness, euphoniousness, euphony *Opposite*: cacophony

melodrama *n* 1 **play**, drama, tragedy, farce, stage show 2 **fuss**, drama, scene, exaggeration, histrionics

melodramatic *adj* **histrionic**, overdramatic, overemotional, exaggerated, sensational *Opposite*: low-key

melody *n* **tune**, song, air, phrase, strain

melt *v* 1 **thaw**, thaw out, dissolve, soften, liquefy *Opposite*: freeze 2 **disappear**, dissolve, fade, vanish, evaporate *Opposite*: materialize

meltdown *(infml)* *n* **collapse**, breakdown, failure, disaster, disintegration *Opposite*: success

melting *adj* **tender**, sweet, loving, sentimental, soft *Opposite*: harsh

melting pot *n* **mixture**, mix, mishmash, blend, hodgepodge

member *n* 1 **associate**, affiliate, fellow, adherent, participant 2 **limb**, appendage, organ, extremity, leg 3 **part**, constituent, component, element, portion

membership *n* 1 **association**, affiliation, involvement, connection, relationship *Opposite*: exclusion 2 **members**, associates, affiliates, fellows, adherents

membrane *n* **skin**, film, sheath, casing, tissue

memento *n* **souvenir**, reminder, vestige, keepsake, token

memo *n* **memorandum**, note, minute, letter, message

memoir *n* 1 **account**, biography, history, chronicle, description 2 **essay**, article, report, paper, thesis

memoirs *n* **autobiography**, journal, life story, life history, diary

memorabilia *n* **collectibles**, collector's items, souvenirs, mementos, ephemera

memorability *n* **importance**, note, momentousness, uncommonness, impressiveness *Opposite*: inconsequence

memorable *adj* **unforgettable**, notable, remarkable, outstanding, impressive *Opposite*: forgettable

memorandum *n* **memo**, note, minute, letter, message

memorial *n* **monument**, cenotaph, statue, bust, plaque

memorize *v* **learn by heart**, learn by rote, learn, commit to memory, remember *Opposite*: forget

memory *n* 1 **reminiscence**, recollection, recall, remembrance, retention 2 **commemoration**, remembrance, celebration, memorial

menace *n* 1 **threat**, danger, hazard, peril, jeopardy *Opposite*: reassurance 2 *(infml)* **thorn in the flesh**, nuisance, troublemaker, annoyance, bother ■ *v* 1 **endanger**, threaten, jeopardize, hang over, loom over 2 **threaten**, intimidate, terrorize, frighten, alarm *Opposite*: reassure

menacing *adj* **threatening**, ominous, frightening, alarming, intimidating *Opposite*: reassuring

menagerie *n* **zoo**, zoological gardens, petting zoo, farm park

mend *v* 1 **repair**, fix, put right, put back together, restore *Opposite*: break 2 **stitch**, sew, sew up, patch, patch up *Opposite*: rip 3 **improve**, amend, rectify, reform, transform 4 **recover**, get better, get well, recuperate, heal *Opposite*: deteriorate ■ *n* **patch**, darn, repair

mendacious *adj* 1 **untruthful**, dishonest, deceitful, unreliable, lying *Opposite*: truthful 2 **untrue**, misleading, false, spurious, untruthful *Opposite*: true

mendaciously *adv* **untruthfully**, dishonestly, deceitfully, falsely, unreliably *Opposite*: truthfully

mendacity *n* **lies**, deception, deceit, falsehood, fabrication *Opposite*: truthfulness

mendicant *adj* **homeless**, vagrant, vagabond, begging, penniless ■ *n* *(fml)* **beggar**, vagrant, panhandler, tramp, down-and-out

mending *n* **sewing**, darning, stitching, fixing, patching

menfolk *n* **kinsmen**, men, boys, husbands, sons

menial *adj* **unskilled**, boring, tedious, basic, lowly *Opposite*: skilled

menswear *n* **men's clothing**, sportswear, outerwear, haberdashery

mental *adj* **psychological**, cerebral, rational, intellectual, spiritual *Opposite*: physical

mentality *n* **attitude**, approach, outlook, mindset, state of mind

mention *v* **talk about**, state, say, cite, bring up *Opposite*: conceal ■ *n* **reference**, indication, discussion, remark, comment

mentor *n* **adviser**, counselor, guide, tutor, teacher *Opposite*: pupil

menu *n* **bill of fare**, carte du jour, tariff, blackboard, set menu

meow *v* **cry**, purr, mew, whimper, caterwaul

mercantile *adj* **merchant**, commercial, trade, trading, business

mercenary *n* **soldier of fortune**, soldier, legionnaire, freedom fighter, guerrilla ■ *adj* **acquisitive**, grasping, greedy, avaricious, covetous *Opposite*: altruistic

merchandise *n* **goods**, products, produce, commodities, stock ■ *v* **sell**, retail, trade in, deal in, handle

merchant *n* **1 wholesaler**, dealer, trader, supplier, broker **2 retailer**, seller, vendor, storekeeper

merciful *adj* **1 compassionate**, kind, kindhearted, lenient, humane *Opposite*: hardhearted **2 thankful**, fortunate, welcome, lucky, happy *Opposite*: unfortunate

merciless *adj* **cruel**, hardhearted, pitiless, harsh, heartless *Opposite*: kind

mercilessness *n* **cruelty**, hardheartedness, pitilessness, harshness, heartlessness *Opposite*: kindness

mercurial *adj* **changeable**, unpredictable, lively, active, impulsive *Opposite*: consistent

mercy *n* **1 compassion**, pity, clemency, kindness, leniency *Opposite*: cruelty **2 blessing**, relief, kindness, stroke of luck, piece of luck *Opposite*: blow

mere *adj* **1 ordinary**, simple, sheer, plain, unadorned **2 scant**, paltry, mean, miserable, meager ■ *n* (*literary*) **lake**, lagoon, tarn

merely *adv* **just**, only, simply, purely

meretricious *adj* **1** (*fml*) **superficial**, flashy, vulgar, tawdry, showy **2 specious**, plausible, deceptive, insincere, glib *Opposite*: genuine

merge *v* **1 combine**, unite, come together, join, amalgamate *Opposite*: separate **2 blend**, meld, blur, fuse, unify *Opposite*: separate

merger *n* **1 amalgamation**, union, combination, joining, fusion *Opposite*: separation **2 blend**, meld, blur, fusion, union *Opposite*: separation

meridian (*literary*) *n* **zenith**, height, high point, peak, apogee *Opposite*: nadir

merit *n* **1 value**, worth, quality, excellence, distinction *Opposite*: ineptitude **2 ability**, accomplishment, capability, aptitude, skill *Opposite*: worthlessness **3 advantage**, good point, pro, asset, virtue *Opposite*: disadvantage ■ *v* **deserve**, warrant, earn, call for, be worthy of

meritorious *adj* **commendable**, praiseworthy, estimable, admirable, laudable *Opposite*: despicable

merriment *n* **cheerfulness**, happiness, fun, high spirits, jollity *Opposite*: misery

merry *adj* **cheerful**, happy, cheery, jolly, joyful *Opposite*: miserable

merry-go-round *n* **whirl**, round, series, succession, string

merrymaker *n* **reveler**, partygoer, party guest, life and soul of the party, social butterfly *Opposite*: killjoy

merrymaking *n* **celebration**, revels, partying, jollification, jollity *Opposite*: misery

mesa *n* **butte**, hill, mound, tor, peak

mesh *n* **net**, web, network, netting, webbing ■ *v* **interlock**, interconnect, engage, fit together, enmesh *Opposite*: separate

mesmeric *adj* **fascinating**, absorbing, compelling, compulsive, mesmerizing *Opposite*: boring

mesmerize *v* **hypnotize**, fascinate, enthrall, absorb, entrance *Opposite*: bore

mesmerizing *see* **mesmeric**

mess *n* **1 untidiness**, muddle, chaos, confusion, clutter *Opposite*: order **2 tight spot**, disaster, predicament, plight, bind **3 canteen**, refectory, dining room, dining hall, restaurant

message *n* **1 communication**, memo, memorandum, note, letter **2 meaning**, significance, point, lesson, moral

mess around (*infml*) *v* **1 waste time**, fool around, play, mooch (*slang*) *Opposite*: behave **2 relax**, laze around, lounge around, loll around, rest up **3 tamper**, fiddle, meddle, interfere, mess **4 hang around**, associate, go around, go out, spend time **5 joke**, fool around, play the fool, act the fool, tease **6 mistreat**, treat badly, treat unfairly, fool with, toy with **7 putter**, tinker, dabble, fiddle, play around

messenger *n* **courier**, envoy, go-between, emissary, herald

messiah *n* **champion**, liberator, leader, defender, savior

messiness *n* **1 untidiness**, disorderliness, scruffiness, dirtiness, scrappiness *Opposite*: neatness **2 unpleasantness**, acrimony, bitterness, awkwardness, nastiness

mess up (*infml*) *v* **1 spoil**, ruin, wreck, scupper, blunder **2 make untidy**, muddle up, mix up, make a mess, clutter *Opposite*: tidy up **3 upset**, confuse, put out, put somebody off their stride, throw (*infml*) *Opposite*: sort out

mess-up *(infml)* n **muddle**, mix-up, mess, confusion, blunder

messy adj 1 **untidy**, muddled, chaotic, cluttered, in disarray *Opposite*: neat 2 **unpleasant**, acrimonious, bitter, awkward, complicated *Opposite*: amicable

metabolism n **breakdown**, absorption, digestion, uptake, use

metabolize v **break down**, absorb, digest, take up, make use of

metallic adj 1 **metal**, iron, steel, copper, brass 2 **shiny**, reflective, glossy, glittering, polished *Opposite*: dull 3 **tinny**, brassy, ringing, clanging, sharp *Opposite*: soft

metamorphose v **change**, transform, transmute, mutate, alter

metamorphosis n **transformation**, change, mutation, conversion, alteration

metaphor n **symbol**, image, figure of speech, allegory, comparison

metaphorical adj **figurative**, symbolic, allegorical, emblematic, representational *Opposite*: literal

metaphysical adj **abstract**, theoretical, philosophical, hypothetical, conjectural

meteoric adj **dramatic**, sudden, swift, spectacular, impressive *Opposite*: gradual

meteorological adj **climatological**, climatic, atmospheric, weather, weather-related

meteorology n **weather forecasting**, climatology, weather prediction, weather-casting

mete out v **give out**, deal out, allocate, impose, exact

meter n 1 **rhythm**, beat, tempo, pulse, pattern 2 **measuring device**, gauge, counter

method n 1 **means**, way, process, system, procedure 2 **orderliness**, organization, order, form, structure

methodical adj **systematic**, logical, disciplined, precise, orderly *Opposite*: haphazard

methodological adj **procedural**, organizational, working, running, operational

methodology n **organizing system**, practice, procedure, organization, policy

meticulous adj **careful**, scrupulous, thorough, particular, painstaking *Opposite*: careless. *See* COMPARE AND CONTRAST *at* careful.

meticulously adv **exactly**, accurately, precisely, squarely, methodically *Opposite*: carelessly

meticulousness n **care**, thoroughness, strictness, diligence, perfectionism *Opposite*: carelessness

métier n **vocation**, occupation, profession, calling, sphere

metropolis n **city**, conurbation, capital, metropolitan area, megalopolis. *See* COMPARE AND CONTRAST *at* city.

metropolitan adj **city**, urban, municipal, civic

mettle n **courage**, bravery, determination, spirit, grit. *See* COMPARE AND CONTRAST *at* courage.

mettlesome adj **lively**, spirited, high-spirited, courageous, plucky *Opposite*: lethargic

mew v **cry**, meow, sob, whimper, yowl

mezzanine n **mezzanine floor**, entresol, story, level

miasma n **mist**, fog, haze, cloud, murk

microbe n **microorganism**, germ, bug *(infml)*

microbiological adj **biological**, bacteriological, fungal, viral, microparasitic

microcosm n **small-scale version**, version in miniature, miniature copy, miniature *Opposite*: macrocosm

micromanage v **interfere**, intervene, nitpick, breathe down somebody's neck, control

microorganism n **microbe**, germ, bug *(infml)*

microscopic adj **tiny**, minute, infinitesimal, minuscule, atomic *Opposite*: gigantic

microscopically adv **meticulously**, minutely, closely, carefully, painstakingly

microwave v **heat**, heat up, warm, warm up, cook

mid adj **middle**, median, medium, midway, central *Opposite*: extreme

midair adj 1 **in the air**, up in the air, in the sky, overhead, above the ground 2 **air**, airborne, in-flight, mid-flight, midcourse

midday n **noon**, noontime, twelve noon, lunchtime, the middle of the day

middle adj 1 **central**, mid, internal, intermediate, inside 2 **median**, average, intermediate, medium, middling ■ n 1 **midpoint**, halfway point, median, mean, norm 2 **center**, heart, focus, core, hub *Opposite*: circumference

middlebrow *(infml)* adj **unintellectual**, conventional, unchallenging, middle-of-the-road, mediocre

middleman n 1 **trader**, distributor, wholesaler, retailer, broker 2 **intermediary**, agent, go-between, mediator, negotiator

middle-of-the-road adj **normal**, mainstream, majority, standard, typical

middling adj 1 **usual**, typical, ordinary, average, run-of-the-mill *Opposite*: unusual 2 **adequate**, all right, tolerable, fair, passable *Opposite*: exceptional

midnight n **twelve o'clock**, twelve midnight, middle of the night, night, nighttime *Opposite*: noon

midpoint n **center**, middle, nucleus, median, mean

midriff n **waist**, stomach, belly, middle, abdomen

midst n **middle**, center, heart, focus, core

midstream adv **halfway through**, midway, in the middle, in full flow

midsummer n **middle of the summer**, summertime, summer solstice, dog days, the height of summer *Opposite*: midwinter

midway *adj* **central**, middle, mid, halfway ■ *adv* **halfway**, in the middle, midstream, in full flow, halfway through

midwinter *n* **middle of winter**, wintertime, winter solstice, the winter months, the depths of winter *Opposite*: midsummer

mien *(fml) n* **appearance**, bearing, expression, manner, look

miff *(infml) v* **irritate**, upset, annoy, vex, peeve *(infml)*

miffed *(infml) adj* **annoyed**, displeased, put out, chagrined, bothered

might *n* **strength**, power, force, capacity, valor

mightily *adv* **tremendously**, greatly, extremely, awfully, decidedly *Opposite*: slightly

mighty *adj* **1 powerful**, strong, forceful, potent, great *Opposite*: weak **2 huge**, enormous, vast, expansive, massive *Opposite*: insignificant

migrant *n* **1 refugee**, immigrant, emigrant, asylum seeker **2 wanderer**, traveler, nomad, itinerant, wayfarer *(literary) Opposite*: resident ■ *adj* **migratory**, traveling, wandering, drifting, itinerant *Opposite*: resident

migrate *v* **travel**, journey, wander, drift, roam

migration *n* **relocation**, immigration, emigration, exodus, movement

migratory *adj* **traveling**, wandering, drifting, migrant, itinerant

mild *adj* **1 slight**, unimportant, insignificant, trifling, trivial *Opposite*: serious **2 gentle**, kind, soft, easygoing, meek *Opposite*: harsh **3 warm**, balmy, pleasant, clement, temperate *Opposite*: harsh **4 weak**, bland, tasteless, insipid, flat *Opposite*: strong

mildly *adv* **1 slightly**, a little, somewhat, a touch, insignificantly *Opposite*: considerably **2 gently**, kindly, meekly, placidly, calmly *Opposite*: harshly

mild-mannered *adj* **gentle**, kind, polite, good-natured, placid *Opposite*: fierce

mildness *n* **gentleness**, kindness, leniency, tenderness, warmth *Opposite*: harshness

mileage *n* **1 distance**, traveling distance, range, extent, way **2** *(infml)* **benefit**, profit, advantage, usefulness, assistance

milepost *n* **marker**, sign, mark, indicator, signpost

miles *(infml) n* **a long way**, a great distance, miles and miles, miles away, a long way away

milestone *n* **1 sign**, signpost, indicator, mark, marker **2 landmark**, highlight, high point, achievement, record

milieu *n* **setting**, environment, scene, background, surroundings

militancy *n* **aggressiveness**, combativeness, belligerence, forcefulness, violence

militant *adj* **confrontational**, aggressive, radical, revolutionary, combative *Opposite*: peaceable ■ *n* **activist**, revolutionary, radical, fighter, supporter

militarism *n* **belligerence**, aggression, aggressiveness, pugnaciousness, bellicosity

militarist *adj* **bellicose**, aggressive, warmongering, martial, military *Opposite*: pacific

militaristic *see* **militarist**

militarized *adj* **mobilized**, armed, battle-ready, prepared, organized

military *adj* **armed**, martial, soldierly, fighting *Opposite*: civilian ■ *n* **services**, forces, armed forces, military establishment, army

militate *v* **influence**, inspire, affect, work, act on

militia *n* **reservists**, local militia, paramilitaries, mercenaries, soldiers

milk *(infml) v* **exploit**, drain, tap, take advantage of, cash in on

milky *adj* **cloudy**, chalky, creamy, pale, translucent *Opposite*: clear

millennial *adj* **utopian**, idealistic, visionary, romantic, optimistic

millennium *n* **epoch**, era, age, period, time

millionaire *n* **tycoon**, mogul, magnate, billionaire, baron *Opposite*: pauper

millions *n* **many**, masses, lots, loads *(infml)*, heaps *(infml)*

millstone *n* **burden**, weight, dead weight, albatross, shackle

mime *v* **1 act out**, represent, simulate, express, symbolize **2 mimic**, satirize, caricature, parody, ape

mimetic *adj* **imitative**, derivative, copied, representational, simulated *Opposite*: original

mimic *v* **1 imitate**, impersonate, represent, mirror, simulate **2 caricature**, ape, satirize, parody, mock ■ *n* **impersonator**, impressionist, imitator, caricaturist, parodist. *See* COMPARE AND CONTRAST *at* imitate.

mimicry *n* **imitation**, impersonation, impression, parody, caricature

minaret *n* **turret**, tower, spire

mince *v* **shred**, cut up, chop up, crumble, hash

mincing *adj* **dainty**, prim, fussy, precious, affected

mind *n* **1 brain**, intellect, wits, brains, brainpower **2 attention**, concentration, thoughts, awareness, observance **3 thinker**, intellect, intellectual, brain *(infml)*, egghead *(infml)* **4 point of view**, mentality, opinion, thinking, view ■ *v* **1 pay attention**, take care, beware, heed, be careful **2 object**, care, demur, take offense, resent *Opposite*: approve **3 take care of**, look after, tend, care for, attend to

mind-bending *see* **mind-boggling**

mind-blowing *(infml)* *adj* **astonishing**, amazing, incredible, inconceivable, astounding *Opposite*: unexceptional

mind-boggling *(infml)* *adj* **overwhelming**, complex, difficult, complicated, puzzling *Opposite*: simple

minded *(fml)* *adj* **inclined**, of a mind to, set, intent, prepared *Opposite*: disinclined

mindful *adj* **watchful**, aware, wary, heedful, alert *Opposite*: unwary. *See* COMPARE AND CONTRAST *at* **aware**.

mindless *adj* **1 tedious**, dull, boring, monotonous, mechanical *Opposite*: enthralling **2 senseless**, gratuitous, unnecessary, pointless, needless

mindlessly *adv* **1 automatically**, mechanically, unconsciously, unthinkingly, robotically *Opposite*: deliberately **2 senselessly**, stupidly, thoughtlessly, carelessly, foolishly *Opposite*: thoughtfully

mind-numbing *adj* **boring**, dull, tedious, tiresome, wearisome *Opposite*: interesting

mindset *n* **attitude**, outlook, mind, mentality, way of thinking

mind your own business *v* **keep it to yourself**, keep your nose out of it, keep off, keep out of it, mind your own beeswax *(infml)* *Opposite*: snoop

mine *n* **1 pit**, excavation, colliery, coalfield, coalmine **2 source**, repository, fund, gold mine, store *Opposite*: dearth ■ *v* **extract**, excavate, quarry, dig, dig out

minefield *n* **problem**, trial, test, ordeal, hazard

miner *n* **sapper**, coalminer, collier, tunneler, driller

mingle *v* **1 mix**, blend, fuse, join, unite *Opposite*: separate **2 circulate**, associate, intermingle, socialize, mix

mini *(infml)* *adj* **small**, miniature, baby, diminutive, tiny *Opposite*: maxi

miniature *adj* **small-scale**, small, tiny, minute, little *Opposite*: enormous

miniaturization *n* **reduction**, shrinking, contraction, diminishment *Opposite*: enlargement

miniaturize *v* **reduce**, scale down, shrink, contract, diminish *Opposite*: enlarge

minibar *n* **bar**, fridge, cupboard, cooler, cocktail cabinet

minimal *adj* **1 negligible**, trifling, slight, nominal, token *Opposite*: significant **2 least**, smallest, minimum, tiniest, minutest *Opposite*: maximum

minimalism *n* **simplicity**, plainness, cleanness, austereness, starkness *Opposite*: elaboration

minimalist *adj* **simple**, uncluttered, understated, discreet, plain *Opposite*: baroque

minimize *v* **1 minimalize**, diminish, curtail, lessen, reduce *Opposite*: maximize **2 play down**, make light of, reduce, dismiss, shrug off *Opposite*: exaggerate

minimum *n* **least**, bare minimum, smallest amount, iota, jot *Opposite*: maximum ■ *adj* **smallest**, least, lowest, tiniest, minutest *Opposite*: maximum

minion *n* **follower**, assistant, hanger-on, crony, underling *Opposite*: superior

miniseries *n* **series**, serial, soap, drama, serialization

minister *n* **priest**, vicar, rector, parson, reverend ■ *v* *(fml)* **attend**, look after, care for, tend, nurse *Opposite*: neglect

ministerial *adj* **governmental**, parliamentary, cabinet, official, legislative

ministration *(fml)* *n* **care**, support, attention, nurture, aid *Opposite*: neglect

ministry *n* **office**, bureau, department, agency, organization

minnow *n* **small fry**, little man, little guy, nobody, sprat

minor *adj* **1 slight**, small, negligible, inconsequential, trivial *Opposite*: major **2 lesser**, inferior, junior, secondary, minor-league *Opposite*: major ■ *n* **juvenile**, youth, adolescent, child, teenager *Opposite*: adult

minority *n* **section**, faction, interest group, pressure group, subgroup ■ *adj* **alternative**, underground, marginal, sectional, smaller *Opposite*: majority

minstrel *n* **musician**, troubadour, wandering minstrel, player, entertainer

mint *n* *(infml)* **fortune**, millions, billions, pile *(infml)*, bundle *(slang)* *Opposite*: pittance ■ *v* **cast**, issue, imprint, make, strike

minus *prep* **1 less**, take away, excluding, reduced by, with the subtraction of *Opposite*: plus **2 without**, lacking, excluding, exclusive of, with the exception of *Opposite*: including ■ *n* **1 disadvantage**, detriment, handicap, hindrance, drawback *Opposite*: plus **2 deficiency**, loss, drop, fall, decrease *Opposite*: addition

minuscule *adj* **tiny**, minute, microscopic, infinitesimal, little *Opposite*: gigantic

minute *n* **moment**, instant, second, flash, sec *(infml)* *Opposite*: ages *(infml)* ■ *v* **record**, summarize, write down, précis, transcribe ■ *adj* **1 miniature**, tiny, minuscule, microscopic, infinitesimal *Opposite*: enormous **2 close**, detailed, thorough, exhaustive, painstaking *Opposite*: cursory

minuteness *n* **smallness**, tininess, shortness, compactness

minutes *n* **notes**, record, proceedings, transcript, transcription

minutiae *n* **details**, niceties, intricacies, particulars, ins and outs *Opposite*: gist

miracle *n* **wonder**, phenomenon, marvel, sensation, vision

miraculous *adj* **amazing**, astounding, astonishing, incredible, unbelievable *Opposite*: mundane

mirage n **hallucination**, optical illusion, illusion, vision, delusion *Opposite*: reality

mire n **swamp**, marsh, mud, sludge, slush

mirror n **glass**, hand mirror, shaving mirror, looking glass *(dated)* ■ v **1 reflect**, echo, copy, parallel, emulate **2 represent**, symbolize, illustrate, typify, signify

mirror image n **double**, twin, copy, replica, likeness

mirth n **laughter**, hilarity, humor, jollity, fun *Opposite*: sadness

mirthful adj **joyful**, merry, gleeful, jovial, cheery *Opposite*: mirthless

mirthless adj **cheerless**, dour, gloomy, grim, dismal *Opposite*: cheerful

misadventure n **accident**, mishap, misfortune, disaster, calamity

misaligned adj **askew**, skewed, awry, cockeyed, crooked *Opposite*: straight

misalliance n **mismatch**, inequality, bad match, disparity, mésalliance

misanthropic adj **cynical**, pessimistic, distrustful, disdainful, sardonic *Opposite*: philanthropic

misanthropy n **cynicism**, pessimism, distrust, disdain, sardonicism *Opposite*: philanthropy

misapplication n **misuse**, abuse, misemployment, mishandling, exploitation

misapply v **misuse**, abuse, misemploy, mishandle, mismanage

misapprehend v **mistake**, misunderstand, misinterpret, misconstrue, misjudge

misapprehension n **misunderstanding**, misinterpretation, wrong idea, false impression, misconception *Opposite*: comprehension

misappropriate v **steal**, embezzle, pocket, take, help yourself *Opposite*: reimburse. *See* COMPARE AND CONTRAST *at steal*.

misappropriation n **embezzlement**, misuse, stealing, dishonesty, fraud

misbegotten adj **ill-conceived**, bad, inappropriate, foolish, deplorable

misbehave v **be naughty**, be bad, act up, behave badly, disobey *Opposite*: behave

misbehavior n **naughtiness**, misconduct, mischief, disobedience, waywardness

miscalculate v **misjudge**, underestimate, overestimate, get it wrong, overvalue

miscalculation n **error**, mistake, inaccuracy, blunder, slip

miscarriage *(fml)* n **failure**, lapse, breakdown, insufficiency, mistake

miscarriage of justice n **wrongful conviction**, unfair ruling, injustice, judicial error, mistake

miscarry *(fml)* v **fail**, founder, backfire, go wrong, go amiss

miscellaneous adj **various**, varied, assorted, mixed, diverse *Opposite*: homogeneous

miscellany n **assortment**, collection, selection, grouping, medley

mischance n **misfortune**, ill fortune, bad luck, ill luck, misadventure

mischief n **1 misbehavior**, naughtiness, trouble, disobedience, waywardness **2 harm**, damage, trouble, disruption, injury **3 troublemaker**, nuisance, rascal, scamp *(infml)*, monkey *(infml)*

mischief-maker n **meddler**, troublemaker, gossip, ringleader, instigator

mischievous adj **1 naughty**, playful, impish, roguish, badly behaved *Opposite*: well-behaved **2** *(fml)* **harmful**, damaging, malicious, wicked, negative *Opposite*: harmless. *See* COMPARE AND CONTRAST *at bad*.

mischievousness n **1 naughtiness**, bad behavior, impishness, playfulness, disobedience **2** *(fml)* **malice**, hatred, harm, animosity, spite

misconceive v **misunderstand**, misapprehend, misinterpret, get the wrong impression, get the wrong idea *Opposite*: understand

misconceived adj **ill-conceived**, ill-thought-out, flawed, misguided, inappropriate

misconception n **fallacy**, delusion, misapprehension, misconstruction, mistaken belief *Opposite*: fact

misconduct n **bad behavior**, misbehavior, delinquency, transgression, wrongdoing

misconstruction n **misinterpretation**, misunderstanding, misreading, false impression, misjudgment *Opposite*: understanding

misconstrue v **misinterpret**, misunderstand, misread, get the wrong idea about, get the wrong impression about *Opposite*: understand

miscount v **lose count**, miscalculate, make a mistake, underestimate, overestimate

miscreant *(literary)* n **troublemaker**, scoundrel, mischief-maker, wrongdoer, criminal

misdeed n **crime**, offense, wrong, transgression, misdemeanor

misdemeanor n **1 petty larceny**, crime, offense, transgression, infringement **2 misdeed**, wrongdoing, indiscretion, lapse, transgression

misdirect v **1 point in the wrong direction**, lead astray, send off course, send on a wild goose chase *Opposite*: direct **2 misallocate**, misuse, misapply, waste, misemploy

miser n **1 hoarder**, accumulator, saver, collector, squirrel *(infml)* **2 skinflint**, pinchpenny, penny pincher *(infml)*, cheapskate *(infml)*, tightwad *(infml)* *Opposite*: spendthrift

miserable adj **1 unhappy**, sad, depressed, down, despondent *Opposite*: happy **2 depressing**, cheerless, wretched, desolate, gloomy *Opposite*: cheery **3 inadequate**, paltry, derisory, miserly, mean *Opposite*: generous **4 gloomy**, dull, gray, overcast, dreary *Opposite*: bright

miserliness *n* parsimoniousness, greed, greediness, tightfistedness, avariciousness *Opposite*: generosity

miserly *adj* **1 mean**, stingy, tightfisted, parsimonious, tight *Opposite*: generous **2 paltry**, derisory, meager, mean, stingy *Opposite*: generous

misery *n* **1 unhappiness**, sadness, depression, desolation, gloom *Opposite*: happiness **2 deprivation**, destitution, distress, poverty, privation

misfire *v* **go wrong**, backfire, fail, fall through, not come off *Opposite*: succeed

misfit *n* **oddity**, eccentric, loner, odd one out, nonconformist *Opposite*: conformist

misfortune *n* **disaster**, calamity, trial, tribulation, misadventure *Opposite*: opportunity

misgiving *n* **scruple**, qualm, doubt, suspicion, hesitation

misguided *adj* **mistaken**, foolish, ill-advised, unwise, erroneous *Opposite*: wise

mishandle *v* **1 mismanage**, make a mess of, misapply, misuse, botch (*infml*) **2 abuse**, mistreat, exploit, ill-treat, rough up (*infml*)

mishap *n* **accident**, calamity, misfortune, disaster, catastrophe

mishear *v* **hear wrong**, get wrong, pick up wrong, not get, be mistaken

mishit *v* **miss**, nick, clip, hit a foul, foul ■ *n* **error**, slice, hook, miss, nick

mishmash *n* **hodgepodge**, jumble, muddle, miscellany, mixture

misinform *v* **mislead**, deceive, lie to, lead on, lead astray

misinformation *n* **propaganda**, dishonesty, distortion, fabrication, bending of the truth *Opposite*: fact

misinterpret *v* **misconstrue**, misunderstand, misread, get the wrong idea about, get the wrong impression about *Opposite*: understand

misinterpretation *n* **misunderstanding**, misconception, misapprehension, misreading, confusion *Opposite*: understanding

misjudge *v* **miscalculate**, underestimate, overestimate, be wrong about, get the wrong idea

misjudgment *n* **1 poor judgment**, error of judgment, error, miscalculation, slip **2 wrong impression**, misinterpretation, misconstruction, false reading, prejudice *Opposite*: understanding

mislaid *adj* **lost**, missing, nowhere to be found, gone astray, misplaced

mislay *v* **lose**, misplace, be unable to find, miss, put in the wrong place *Opposite*: find

mislead *v* **give the wrong impression**, misinform, deceive, lie, delude

misleading *adj* **deceptive**, ambiguous, confusing, false, disingenuous *Opposite*: truthful

mismanage *v* **mishandle**, make a mess of, misuse, manage badly, botch (*infml*)

mismanagement *n* **mishandling**, misconduct, negligence, malpractice, maladministration *Opposite*: efficiency

mismatch *n* **incongruity**, discrepancy, gap, disparity, misalliance *Opposite*: harmony

mismatched *adj* **incompatible**, unequal, uneven, unjust, one-sided

misnomer *n* **misleading term**, inaccurate term, poor description, loose term, contradiction

misplace *v* **lose**, mislay, be unable to put your hands on, drop, leave behind *Opposite*: find

misplaced *adj* **1 mislaid**, nowhere to be found, missing, lost, gone astray **2 inappropriate**, erroneous, misdirected, out-of-place, inapt *Opposite*: appropriate

misprint *n* **typographical error**, error, mistake, blunder, oversight

mispronounce *v* **say wrong**, distort, mangle, make a mess of, stumble through *Opposite*: articulate

mispronunciation *n* **distortion**, error, misstatement, slip, blunder

misquote *v* **put words in somebody's mouth**, misreport, misrepresent, misattribute, quote out of context

misread *v* **misjudge**, misinterpret, misunderstand, misconstrue, get the wrong idea *Opposite*: interpret

misrepresent *v* **parody**, pervert, twist, distort, pass off

misrepresentation *n* **parody**, caricature, distortion, falsification, twisting

misrule *n* **1 misgovernment**, mishandling, corruption, maladministration, mismanagement **2 lawlessness**, anarchy, unruliness, chaos, turmoil *Opposite*: order

miss *v* **1 overlook**, fail to spot, let pass, fail to notice, fail to see *Opposite*: see **2 skip**, fail to attend, escape, avoid, forget *Opposite*: attend **3 forego**, lose, pass up, let pass, let go *Opposite*: take up **4 pine for**, long for, yearn for, wish for, grieve for ■ *n* **1 failure**, false step, error, slip, miscue **2 omission**, oversight, delinquency, neglect, mistake

missal *n* **service book**, prayer book, liturgical book, breviary, Psalter

misshapen *adj* **distorted**, twisted, deformed, malformed, warped *Opposite*: shapely

missing *adj* **lost**, absent, gone astray, misplaced, mislaid *Opposite*: present

mission *n* **1 assignment**, task, job, work, undertaking **2 delegation**, deputation, task force, legation, embassy **3 calling**, vocation, purpose, goal, aim

missionary *n* **1 evangelist**, proselytizer, preacher, minister, priest **2 campaigner**, champion, crusader, proselytizer, propagandist

missive *n* **letter**, communiqué, note, communication, memo

miss out *v* **fail to benefit**, forgo, miss the boat, miss an opportunity, miss a chance *Opposite*: benefit

misspelling *n* **spelling mistake**, wrong spelling, slip, error, orthographical error

misspend *v* **squander**, fritter away, waste, throw away, misuse *Opposite*: save

misspent *adj* **wasted**, squandered, frittered away, misused, thrown away *Opposite*: profitable

misstep *n* **mistake**, slip, gaffe, blunder, error

miss the boat *v* **miss an opportunity**, miss a chance, miss out, fail to benefit, forego

miss the point *v* **misunderstand**, misinterpret, misconstrue, fail to understand, misread *Opposite*: understand

mist *n* **haze**, fog, smog, vapor, spray

mistake *n* **1 blunder**, gaffe, slip, lapse, miscalculation **2 error**, fault, inaccuracy, oversight, misspelling ■ *v* **1 misunderstand**, misjudge, misinterpret, misconstrue, confuse *Opposite*: understand **2 confuse with**, take for, mix up with, confound, mix *Opposite*: recognize

---

COMPARE AND CONTRAST CORE MEANING: something incorrect or improper
mistake an unwise decision or an error resulting from a lack of care; **error** something that unintentionally deviates from a recognized standard or guide; **inaccuracy** something that is incorrect because it has been measured, calculated, copied, or conveyed incorrectly; **slip** a minor mistake or oversight, especially one caused by carelessness; **blunder** a serious or embarrassing mistake, usually the result of carelessness or ignorance; **faux pas** (*literary*) an embarrassing mistake that breaks a social convention.

---

mistaken *adj* **wrong**, incorrect, false, erroneous, faulty *Opposite*: correct

mistime *v* **misjudge**, miss the boat, anticipate, jump the gun, preempt *Opposite*: coordinate

mistiness *n* **1 haziness**, murkiness, duskiness, cloudiness, fogginess *Opposite*: clearness **2 vagueness**, indistinctness, obscurity, opacity, lack of clarity *Opposite*: clarity

mist over *v* **mist**, mist up, fog over, become hazy, become clouded *Opposite*: clear

mistreat *v* **abuse**, misuse, ill-treat, harm, mishandle *Opposite*: pamper. *See* COMPARE AND CONTRAST *at* misuse.

mistreated *adj* **abused**, neglected, wronged, injured, victimized *Opposite*: pampered

mistreatment *n* **maltreatment**, exploitation, abuse, ill-treatment, neglect *Opposite*: pampering

mistress *n* **1 lover**, concubine, courtesan, kept woman, lady friend (*infml*) *Opposite*: wife **2 manager**, employer, controller, proprietor, owner *Opposite*: servant **3 expert**, specialist, queen, doyenne, leading exponent *Opposite*: novice **4 owner**, trainer, keeper, rider

mistrial *n* **invalid trial**, unfair trial, miscarriage of justice, travesty, injustice

mistrust *n* **suspicion**, distrust, doubt, wariness, uncertainty *Opposite*: trust ■ *v* **distrust**, doubt, suspect, be wary of, be suspicious of *Opposite*: trust

mistrustful *adj* **distrustful**, wary, suspicious, doubtful, skeptical *Opposite*: trusting

misty *adj* **1 hazy**, foggy, murky, cloudy, steamy *Opposite*: clear **2 indistinct**, vague, obscure, dim, opaque *Opposite*: clear

misty-eyed *adj* **1 tearful**, emotional, teary, teary-eyed, close to tears *Opposite*: dry-eyed **2 sentimental**, nostalgic, romantic, weepy (*infml*), soppy (*infml*) *Opposite*: unsentimental

misunderstand *v* **get the wrong idea**, misinterpret, misread, misconstrue, get the wrong impression *Opposite*: understand

misunderstanding *n* **1 mistake**, mix-up, confusion, misinterpretation, misconstruction **2 quarrel**, row, argument, difference of opinion, disagreement *Opposite*: agreement

misunderstood *adj* **unacknowledged**, unrecognized, unappreciated, undervalued, misjudged *Opposite*: valued

misuse *n* **misappropriation**, misapplication, waste, ill use, mismanagement ■ *v* **1 abuse**, exploit, mistreat, maltreat, ill-treat *Opposite*: cherish **2 waste**, misappropriate, squander, misapply, mishandle

---

COMPARE AND CONTRAST CORE MEANING: treat somebody or something wrongly or badly
misuse put something to an inappropriate use or purpose, or treat a person or animal badly or harshly; **abuse** use in a wrong or inappropriate way something that should be used responsibly, for example, a power, privilege, or a substance such as alcohol or a drug. It is also used to refer to cruel or violent treatment of a person or animal, especially on a regular or habitual basis; **ill-treat** or **maltreat** behave cruelly toward a person or animal, or treat something roughly and carelessly; **mistreat** treat a person badly, inconsiderately, or unfairly, not necessarily in a way involving physical cruelty, or treat something roughly and carelessly.

---

mite (*dated*) *n* **jot**, bit, scrap, speck, grain

mitigate *v* **alleviate**, lessen, ease, allay, moderate *Opposite*: aggravate

mitigating *adj* **justifying**, extenuating, modifying, qualifying, vindicating *Opposite*: aggravating

mitigation *n* **1 extenuation**, vindication, justification, qualification, moderation **2 alleviation**, easing, improvement, lessening, relief *Opposite*: intensification

mix v 1 **mix up**, mingle, intermingle, blend, intersperse *Opposite*: separate 2 **combine**, blend, unite, merge, join *Opposite*: separate out 3 **fraternize**, mingle, associate, get together, socialize 4 **go together**, accord, agree, fit, harmonize *Opposite*: clash ∎ n **combination**, mixture, blend, assortment, fusion

mixed adj 1 **varied**, diverse, assorted, sundry, miscellaneous *Opposite*: uniform 2 **cosmopolitan**, integrated, international, interracial, multiracial *Opposite*: segregated

mixed bag n **ragbag**, assortment, combination, jumble, variety

mixed-up (infml) adj 1 **confused**, muddled, bewildered, puzzled, perplexed *Opposite*: clear 2 **disturbed**, maladjusted, confused, troubled, rebellious *Opposite*: well-adjusted

mixture n **combination**, mix, blend, amalgam, concoction

COMPARE AND CONTRAST CORE MEANING: something formed by mixing materials
mixture a number of elements or ingredients brought together; **blend** something formed by putting together two or more different kinds of things, especially in a skilled way, to form a new whole in which the original elements lose their distinctness; **combination** something formed by the association of two or more things that retain their distinctness; **compound** a technical word for a chemical formed from two or more elements, also used generally to describe anything composed of two or more separate parts; **alloy** a technical word for a metal such as steel that is formed by combining two or more different metallic elements; **amalgam** a technical word for an alloy formed by combining mercury with another metal, also used generally to describe something that is a mixture of two or more elements or characteristics.

---

mix up v 1 **confuse**, misunderstand, muddle, confound, mistake *Opposite*: straighten out 2 **mix**, combine, merge, blend, fuse *Opposite*: separate

mix-up n **mistake**, muddle, misunderstanding, confusion, error

mnemonic n **memory aid**, reminder, prompt, cue, aide-mémoire (fml)

moan v 1 **groan**, sigh, whine, whimper, wail 2 (infml) **complain**, grumble, whine, gripe (infml), grouse (infml) ∎ n (infml) **complaint**, grumble, gripe (infml), grouse (infml) *Opposite*: compliment

moaner (infml) n **grumbler**, complainer, whiner, wailer, objector

moat n **ditch**, trench, fosse, channel, dike *Opposite*: bank

mob n 1 **crowd**, horde, mass, multitude, throng 2 (infml) **populace**, plebs, hoi polloi, rabble, the masses *Opposite*: elite ∎ v 1 **besiege**, descend on, crowd around, surround, swarm around *Opposite*: avoid 2 **attack**, jostle, pester, set upon, set about *Opposite*: defend

mobile adj 1 **movable**, portable, transportable, itinerant, peripatetic *Opposite*: fixed 2 **active**, flexible, limber, supple, agile *Opposite*: immobile 3 **expressive**, changing, changeable, lively, communicative *Opposite*: inexpressive 4 **upwardly mobile**, successful, ambitious, aspiring, rising *Opposite*: unambitious

mobility n 1 **flexibility**, freedom of movement, agility, suppleness, movement *Opposite*: stasis 2 **progress**, social mobility, upward mobility, success, promotion

mobilization n **enlistment**, deployment, armament, organization, utilization *Opposite*: demobilization

mobilize v **rally**, assemble, muster, drum up, gather together *Opposite*: demobilize

mobster (infml) n **gangster**, hoodlum, thug, tough, racketeer

mock v 1 **ridicule**, tease, make fun of, laugh at, poke fun at *Opposite*: praise 2 **mimic**, imitate, parody, ape, simulate ∎ adj **fake**, pretend, simulated, imitation, artificial *Opposite*: genuine. See COMPARE AND CONTRAST at ridicule.

mocker n **ridiculer**, derider, scorner, scoffer, caricaturist

mockery n 1 **ridicule**, scorn, derision, contempt, disdain *Opposite*: respect 2 **travesty**, charade, farce, sham, caricature *Opposite*: exemplar (literary)

mocking adj **scornful**, derisive, contemptuous, disdainful, sardonic *Opposite*: respectful

mock-up n **replica**, copy, model, sample, dummy

mode n **form**, style, manner, method, means

model n 1 **replica**, mock-up, representation, copy, reproduction 2 **type**, sort, style, kind, version 3 **example**, paradigm, pattern, standard, prototype ∎ v 1 **demonstrate**, show, exhibit, display, show off 2 **sculpt**, mold, form, shape, fashion ∎ adj **perfect**, classical, prototypical, typical, archetypal *Opposite*: atypical

moderate adj 1 **reasonable**, modest, sensible, restrained, judicious *Opposite*: excessive 2 **average**, medium, normal, balanced, middling *Opposite*: extraordinary ∎ v 1 **curb**, control, tone down, play down, diminish *Opposite*: intensify 2 **arbitrate**, mediate, referee, facilitate, umpire

moderately adv **reasonably**, rather, somewhat, fairly, comparatively *Opposite*: excessively

moderation n **restraint**, control, self-control, temperance, fairness *Opposite*: excess

moderator n **mediator**, go-between, arbiter, arbitrator, referee

modern adj 1 **contemporary**, current, up-to-date, up-to-the-minute, recent Opposite: old-fashioned 2 **state-of-the-art**, latest, cutting-edge, leading-edge, novel Opposite: outdated 3 **progressive**, enlightened, forward-looking, avant-garde, advanced Opposite: traditional. See COMPARE AND CONTRAST at new.

modern-day adj **contemporary**, modern, current, recent, present-day Opposite: past

modernism n **innovation**, innovativeness, novelty, originality, modernization Opposite: traditionalism

modernistic adj **ultramodern**, modern, radical, futuristic, avant-garde Opposite: traditional

modernity n **modernism**, innovation, innovativeness, freshness, newness Opposite: traditionalism

modernization n **transformation**, upgrading, innovation, reconstruction, renewal

modernize v **update**, renovate, streamline, revolutionize, reform

modernizer n **innovator**, pacesetter, trendsetter, new broom, visionary

modest adj 1 **self-effacing**, humble, reserved, discreet, unpretentious Opposite: arrogant 2 **shy**, meek, diffident, quiet, reserved Opposite: overbearing 3 **unexceptional**, ordinary, humble, unpretentious, plain Opposite: showy 4 **moderate**, reasonable, acceptable, small, low Opposite: excessive

modesty n **humility**, reserve, reticence, diffidence, shyness Opposite: arrogance

modicum n **little**, bit, degree, scrap, ounce

modification n **change**, alteration, adjustment, amendment, reform

modified adj **adapted**, altered, changed, improved, revised Opposite: unmodified

modify v 1 **alter**, change, adapt, adjust, amend Opposite: maintain 2 **lessen**, reduce, restrain, moderate, curb Opposite: intensify. See COMPARE AND CONTRAST at change.

modish adj **fashionable**, stylish, in, chic, up-to-the-minute Opposite: unfashionable

modular adj **linked**, flexible, integrated, prefabricated, segmental

modulate v 1 **adjust**, alter, amend, vary, modify 2 **moderate**, curb, control, tone down, play down Opposite: intensify

modulation n 1 **inflection**, intonation, accent, lilt, cadence Opposite: flatness 2 **adjustment**, change, alteration, swing, variation

module n **unit**, component, part, element, section

modus operandi n **method**, formula, technique, way, protocol

modus vivendi n 1 **compromise**, arrangement, settlement, deal, bargain 2 **practice**, way of life, lifestyle, standard of living, habit

mogul n **tycoon**, entrepreneur, magnate, industrialist, dynast

moist adj **damp**, wet, humid, soggy, clammy Opposite: dry

moisten v **dampen**, wet, moisturize, humidify, sprinkle Opposite: dry

moistness n **dampness**, humidity, wetness, clamminess, sogginess Opposite: aridity

moisture n **damp**, dampness, wetness, humidity, moistness Opposite: dryness

moisturize v 1 **cream**, nourish, soothe, oil, condition Opposite: dry 2 **moisten**, dampen, wet, humidify, spray

moisturizer n **cold cream**, cream, lotion, conditioner, night cream

mold n 1 **container**, cast, form, die, shape 2 **impression**, cast, plaster cast, molding, prototype 3 **frame**, pattern, template, stencil, outline 4 **character**, type, variety, kind, shape 5 **mildew**, fungus, growth, decay, rot ▪ v 1 **shape**, make, fashion, cast, style 2 **influence**, affect, change, shape, fashion 3 **cling**, hug, follow, fit, press

molder v **rot**, gather dust, disintegrate, crumble, decay

moldiness n **decay**, mustiness, mildew, rottenness, disintegration

molding n **decoration**, detail, cornice, dado, beading

moldy adj 1 **fungal**, decaying, decayed, rotting, rotten Opposite: fresh 2 **stale**, neglected, dingy, seedy, shabby Opposite: fresh

mole n **spy**, infiltrator, secret agent, undercover agent, plant

molecule n **particle**, bit, iota, speck, shred

molest v 1 **assault**, mistreat, abuse, attack, feel up (infml) 2 **bother**, pester, annoy, torment, harass

mollify v **pacify**, calm, placate, appease, calm down Opposite: enrage

mollycoddle v **pamper**, fuss over, spoil, overprotect, cosset

molt v **shed**, cast, peel, skin, slough Opposite: grow

molten adj **melted**, liquefied, liquid, fluid, heated Opposite: solid

moment n 1 **instant**, second, minute, split second, flash Opposite: age 2 (fml) **importance**, significance, weight, import, substance

momentarily adv 1 **for a moment**, briefly, temporarily, fleetingly, transitorily 2 **soon**, right away, in a moment, before long, any time now

momentary adj **brief**, fleeting, passing, temporary, transitory Opposite: interminable

momentous adj **important**, significant, historic, earthshattering, crucial Opposite: insignificant

momentum n **impetus**, thrust, energy, force, drive Opposite: brake

monarch n **ruler**, sovereign, crowned head, emperor, king Opposite: subject

monarchism n royalism, imperialism, elitism, tsarism, traditionalism Opposite: republicanism

monarchist n royalist, loyalist, counter-revolutionary, traditionalist, imperialist Opposite: revolutionary

monarchy n realm, kingdom, dominion, domain, empire Opposite: republic

monastery n religious foundation, religious community, cloister, friary, abbey

monastic adj austere, reclusive, simple, spartan, frugal

monetary adj financial, fiscal, economic, monetarist, pecuniary

money n 1 cash, currency, ready money, ready cash, coinage 2 capital, funds, riches, means, wherewithal

moneybags (infml) n millionaire, multimillionaire, billionaire, tycoon, mogul

money box n piggy bank, cash box, collecting box, safe

moneyed adj wealthy, rich, affluent, prosperous, comfortable

moneylender n lender, financier, banker, pawnbroker, loan shark

moneymaker n 1 tycoon, speculator, magnate, investor, mogul 2 hit, success, gold mine, profit center, cash cow (slang)

moneymaking adj profitable, commercial, economic, fruitful, lucrative

mongrel n dog, cur, hound, crossbreed, pye-dog Opposite: pedigree

monitor n 1 screen, display, video display terminal, television set, closed-circuit television 2 observer, supervisor, overseer, inspector, invigilator ■ v observe, keep an eye on, supervise, scrutinize, examine

monk n holy man, religious, monastic, friar, abbot

monkey (infml) n 1 mischief, rogue, rascal, scamp (infml), scalawag (dated infml) 2 fool, dupe, laughingstock, butt, buffoon

monkey around v fool around, joke, play the fool, clown around, lark

monkey business (infml) n tricks, mischief, trouble, pranks, monkeyshines (infml)

monkey with v tamper, meddle, interfere, fiddle, tinker

monkish adj reclusive, austere, withdrawn, cloistered, simple Opposite: worldly

monochromatic adj 1 one-color, homochromous, unicolor, homochromatic, shaded 2 dull, indistinct, neutral, uniform, toneless Opposite: colorful

monochrome adj 1 unicolor, self-colored, homochromous, homochromatic, monochromatic 2 neutral, colorless, dull, indeterminate, toneless

monocle n eyeglass, glass, lens

monogamous adj faithful, exclusive, committed, married, steady Opposite: bigamous

monogamy n exclusivity, fidelity, commitment, marriage, coupledom Opposite: bigamy

monogram n initials, signet, logo, seal, stamp ■ v mark, initial, sign, seal, identify

monograph n book, article, paper, essay, thesis

monolith n standing stone, menhir, megalith, sarsen, stone

monolithic adj colossal, monumental, massive, uniform, immovable

monologue n 1 soliloquy, speech, prologue, epilogue, aside Opposite: dialogue 2 harangue, rant, speech, running commentary, lecture Opposite: conversation

monopolistic adj anticompetitive, unchallenged, controlling, autocratic, exploitative Opposite: competitive

monopolization n control, domination, appropriation, takeover, expropriation Opposite: cooperation

monopolize v control, dominate, take over, corner, exploit Opposite: share

monopoly n control, domination, cartel, trust, corner

monosyllabic adj uncommunicative, curt, gruff, brief, short Opposite: verbose

monosyllable n word, syllable, grunt, squeak Opposite: polysyllable

monotheism n theism, deism Opposite: polytheism

monotone n drone, whine, chant, intonation, mutter

monotonous adj dull, repetitious, uninteresting, repetitive, boring Opposite: varied

monotony n 1 tedium, dullness, boredom, flatness, dreariness Opposite: excitement 2 uniformity, repetitiousness, sameness, repetitiveness, predictability Opposite: variety

monsoon n rainy season, wet season, rains

monster n 1 fiend, ogre, beast, brute 2 giant, behemoth, leviathan, whopper (infml), biggie (infml) ■ adj huge, enormous, giant, monstrous, gigantic Opposite: small

monstrosity n eyesore, blot on the landscape, atrocity, sight, horror

monstrous adj 1 atrocious, outrageous, horrific, immoral, evil 2 huge, enormous, giant, monster, gigantic Opposite: small 3 hideous, grotesque, gruesome, ugly, horrible Opposite: lovely

monstrously adv preposterously, shockingly, offensively, unbelievably, prodigiously Opposite: unexceptionally

montage n mosaic, tableau, medley, mixture, pastiche

monthly adj 1 regular, periodic, frequent, once-a-month, scheduled Opposite: occasional 2 month-long, 30-day, period, season, medium-term ■ adv regularly, once a month, periodically, frequently, at monthly intervals *Opposite*: irregularly ■ *n* **magazine**, publication, periodical, journal, bulletin

monument *n* 1 **memorial**, testimonial, testament, tribute 2 **headstone**, marker, tombstone, gravestone

monumental *adj* 1 **colossal**, epic, immense, massive, enormous *Opposite*: small 2 **historic**, classic, significant, important, epic *Opposite*: minor

mooch *(infml)* v **wheedle**, beg, sponge *(infml)*, cadge *(infml)*, scrounge *(infml)*

moocher *(infml)* n **scrounger**, taker, cadger *(infml)*, freeloader *(infml)*, sponger *(infml)*

mood *n* 1 **frame of mind**, disposition, temper, attitude, temperament 2 **atmosphere**, feel, ambiance, air, feeling 3 **temper**, bad temper, sulk, the doldrums, anger

moodiness *n* **sulkiness**, changeableness, sullenness, grumpiness, glumness *Opposite*: cheeriness

moody *adj* **temperamental**, morose, sulky, sullen, glum *Opposite*: predictable

moon v 1 **wander**, drift, meander, amble, dawdle 2 *(literary)* **fantasize**, dream, daydream, languish, pine

moonbeam *n* **ray**, moonlight, shaft of light, moonshine, glint *Opposite*: sunbeam

moonlight *(infml)* v **do work on the side**, do two jobs, supplement your income, have a second job, have a night job

moonscape *n* **wasteland**, desert, wilderness, barren land, waste

moonshine *n* 1 *(infml)* **poteen**, bootleg alcohol, homebrew, white lightning, mountain dew *(infml)* 2 **nonsense**, fantasy, silliness, fiction, gibberish

moonshot *n* **rocket launch**, launch, lunar expedition, lunar exploration, mission

moonstruck *(infml)* adj **dazed**, confused, irrational, distracted, in a daze *Opposite*: alert

moor *n* **heath**, moorland, common, upland, hill ■ v **tie**, fix, secure, chain, attach *Opposite*: untie

mooring *n* **anchorage**, berth, tie-up, bay, reserved space

moot *adj* **debatable**, arguable, doubtful, controversial, unresolved *Opposite*: established ■ v **propose**, put forward, suggest, bring up, introduce

mop v **wipe**, clean, swab, dust, mop up

mope v **brood**, languish, pine, sulk, pout

moppet *(infml)* n **child**, toddler, little one, tot *(infml)*, kid *(infml)*

mop up v 1 **wipe up**, clear up, mop, wipe, swab 2 *(infml)* **finish off**, dispose of, see to, deal with, polish off

moraine *n* **glacial deposit**, debris, rubble, residue

moral *adj* **ethical**, good, right, honest, decent *Opposite*: immoral ■ n **message**, meaning, significance, rule, maxim

morale *n* **confidence**, self-esteem, spirits, self-confidence, assurance *Opposite*: aimlessness

moralist *n* 1 **moralizer**, censor, preacher, critic, philosopher 2 **virtuous person**, upright person, puritan, saint, prude

moralistic *adj* **moralizing**, didactic, straitlaced, serious, upright

morality *n* 1 **ethics**, morals, principles, standards, scruples 2 **goodness**, decency, probity, honesty, integrity *Opposite*: wickedness

moralize v **preach**, lecture, sermonize, criticize, nag

moralizing *n* **lecturing**, sermonizing, instruction, remonstration, admonishment ■ *adj* **lecturing**, critical, preaching, exhorting, hectoring *Opposite*: unprincipled

morals *n* **ethics**, morality, standards, scruples, principles

morass *n* 1 **bog**, marsh, mire, swamp, wetland 2 **mess**, chaos, muddle, quagmire, mire

moratorium *n* **suspension**, freeze, halt, pause, cessation

morbid *adj* 1 **morose**, gloomy, dark, moody, melancholic *Opposite*: cheerful 2 **gruesome**, dark, sinister, macabre, perverse

morbidity *n* **illness**, injury, disease, ill health, indisposition *Opposite*: health

mordant *adj* **caustic**, astringent, acerbic, penetrating, sarcastic *Opposite*: gentle

more *adj* **additional**, extra, supplementary, added, further *Opposite*: less

moreover *adv* **furthermore**, what is more, in addition, besides, also

mores *n* **customs**, values, habits, traditions, patterns

morgue *n* **mortuary**, funeral parlor, funeral home, chapel of rest

moribund *adj* 1 **dying**, failing, expiring, on your last legs, at death's door *Opposite*: well 2 **declining**, on the way out, waning, on its last legs, dilapidated *Opposite*: thriving

morning *n* **dawn**, daybreak, sunrise, break of day, first light *Opposite*: evening

morose *adj* **miserable**, glum, depressed, down, low *Opposite*: cheery

morph v **transform**, alter, switch, convert, adapt

morphology *n* **shape**, form, contours, formation

morsel *n* **scrap**, crumb, bit, piece, fragment *Opposite*: chunk

mortal *adj* 1 **earthly**, worldly, human, corporeal, finite *Opposite*: immortal 2 **deadly**, fatal, lethal, life-threatening, terminal 3 **extreme**, great, grave, severe, serious *Opposite*: mild ■ *n* **human being**, human, person, individual, soul. *See* COMPARE AND CONTRAST *at* **deadly**.

mortality n **humanity**, death, transience, impermanence

mortally adv **1 fatally**, lethally, incurably, terminally **2 extremely**, severely, seriously, greatly, very Opposite: mildly

mortgage n **loan**, bank loan, advance, secured loan, debt ■ v **pledge**, forfeit, offer as security, use as a guarantee, pawn

mortification n **shame**, degradation, indignity, embarrassment, chagrin

mortified adj **ashamed**, embarrassed, humiliated, horrified, offended Opposite: proud

mortify v **degrade**, humiliate, take down, embarrass, crush

mortifying adj **humiliating**, shameful, embarrassing, degrading, chastening Opposite: uplifting

mortuary n **morgue**, funeral parlor, funeral home, chapel of rest

mosaic n **medley**, assortment, mixture, variety, montage

mosey (infml) v **saunter**, wander, amble, stroll, dawdle Opposite: rush

mossy adj **moss-covered**, moss-grown, moss-topped, overgrown, green

most pron **the majority**, nearly everyone, nearly all, a good number, a large amount Opposite: few ■ adv **very**, highly, extremely, really, truly Opposite: fairly

mostly adv **1 for the most part**, above all, mainly, generally, on the whole **2 usually**, more often than not, normally, typically, commonly Opposite: rarely

mote n **speck**, particle, jot, iota, bit Opposite: mass

mothball v **1 postpone**, delay, put on the back burner, put aside, put on ice **2 shut up**, pack away, decommission, put into storage, put out of commission Opposite: open up

moth-eaten adj **tattered**, threadbare, tatty, dog-eared, worn Opposite: brand-new

mother v **look after**, care for, protect, nurse, tend Opposite: neglect

motherhood n **maternity**, parenthood, kinship Opposite: fatherhood

motherland n **mother country**, native country, birthplace, homeland, fatherland

motherly adj **maternal**, protective, caring, loving, kind Opposite: uncaring

motif n **1 design**, pattern, image, decoration, shape **2 theme**, idea, subject, topic, keynote

motion n **1 gesture**, wave, signal, sign, gesticulation **2 movement**, action, activity, change, mobility Opposite: stillness **3 proposal**, suggestion, proposition, submission, recommendation ■ v **signal**, indicate, wave, gesture, beckon

motionless adj **stationary**, immobile, still, stock-still, static Opposite: moving

motionlessness n **stillness**, calm, immobility, paralysis, rigidity Opposite: mobility

motion picture n **film**, movie, picture, feature film, video

motivate v **1 inspire**, stimulate, encourage, egg on, persuade Opposite: discourage **2 cause**, prompt, provoke, induce, spur Opposite: deter

motivated adj **interested**, driven, inspired, moved, stirred Opposite: unmotivated

motivating adj **stimulating**, interesting, inspiring, galvanizing, encouraging Opposite: uninspiring

motivation n **1 incentive**, inspiration, enthusiasm, impetus, stimulus Opposite: disincentive **2 reason**, cause, motive, purpose, rationale

motivator n **instigator**, persuader, promoter, cheerleader, stimulus

motive n **reason**, motivation, spur, incentive, inducement Opposite: deterrent

COMPARE AND CONTRAST CORE MEANING: something that prompts action

motive the reason for doing something or behaving in a particular way; **incentive** something external, often some kind of reward, that inspires extra enthusiasm or effort; **inducement** something external that persuades or attracts somebody to a particular course of action, especially something that is offered as a reward; **spur** something such as the hope of a reward or the fear of punishment that encourages action or effort or energy; **goad** a stimulus that motivates somebody or stirs somebody into action, often against his or her will.

motiveless adj **unprovoked**, gratuitous, wanton, senseless, unwarranted Opposite: justified

motley adj **assorted**, miscellaneous, diverse, varied, mixed Opposite: uniform

motocross n **scramble**, cross-country race, motorcycle race, trail biking, motorcycle racing

motor n **engine**, diesel engine, gasoline engine, internal combustion engine, electric motor ■ adj **motorized**, motor-powered, gas-powered, diesel-powered, electrically powered ■ v (fml) **drive**, travel, proceed, journey, ride

motorcade n **convoy**, procession, parade, file, escort

motorist n **driver**, car driver, car user, car owner, chauffeur Opposite: passenger

motorized adj **motor**, motor-powered, gas-powered, diesel-powered, electrically powered

mottled adj **dappled**, spotted, blotchy, speckled, stippled Opposite: plain

motto n **slogan**, saying, maxim, aphorism, adage

mound n **1 pile**, stack, mass, bundle, mountain **2 knoll**, hillock, embankment, bank, hill Opposite: valley

mount v **1 rise**, mount up, increase, accumulate, grow *Opposite*: decrease **2 climb**, ascend, go up, climb up, clamber up *Opposite*: descend **3 prepare**, set up, produce, launch, arrange **4 get on**, climb on, jump on, board, go on *Opposite*: dismount **5 frame**, box, encase, inset, affix ■ *n* **1 base**, stand, support, pedestal, plinth **2 horse**, mule, ass, donkey, pony

mountain *n* **1 peak**, mount, crag, massif, hill *Opposite*: valley **2 pile**, mass, stack, bundle, mound

mountaineer *n* **climber**, alpinist, rock climber

mountainous *adj* **1 hilly**, high, steep, precipitous, rocky *Opposite*: flat **2 huge**, enormous, immense, monumental, gigantic *Opposite*: tiny

mountainside *n* **slope**, shoulder, gradient, incline, hillside

mountaintop *n* **peak**, summit, crest, hilltop, pinnacle *Opposite*: bottom

mountebank *(literary) n* **fraud**, deceiver, trickster, cheat, charlatan

mounted *adj* **1 on horseback**, equestrian, astride, straddling, riding *Opposite*: on foot **2 attached**, fixed, affixed, screwed on, displayed *Opposite*: loose

mounting *adj* **rising**, increasing, growing, swelling, escalating *Opposite*: decreasing

mourn *v* **grieve**, lament, grieve for, grieve over, weep for *Opposite*: rejoice *(literary)*

mourner *n* **bereaved person**, funeral-goer, griever, widow, widower

mournful *adj* **sad**, sorrowful, somber, woeful, doleful *Opposite*: cheerful

mournfulness *n* **sadness**, somberness, melancholy, gloominess, despondency *Opposite*: cheerfulness

mourning *n* **grief**, bereavement, sorrow, sadness, lamentation *Opposite*: rejoicing

mouth *n* **1 entrance**, opening, door, doorway, aperture **2 estuary**, outlet, bay, inlet **3** *(infml)* **insolence**, impertinence, rudeness, back talk, cheek *(infml)* ■ *v* **say**, mime, state, utter, reply

WORD BANK
❑ **parts of a mouth** adenoids, denture, gum, lip, palate, roof, soft palate, taste bud, tongue, tonsils, tooth, uvula

mouthful *n* **1 bite**, taste, piece, spoonful, forkful **2 harangue**, sermon, lecture, tirade, earful *(infml)*

mouthpiece *n* **spokesperson**, representative, agent, ambassador, delegate

mouth-to-mouth *n* **artificial respiration**, kiss of life, resuscitation, cardiopulmonary resuscitation, CPR

mouthwash *n* **gargle**, rinse, breath freshener, mouth spray

mouthwatering *adj* **delicious**, delectable, lip-smacking, luscious, tasty *Opposite*: revolting

movable *adj* **1 portable**, transportable, transferable, mobile, detachable *Opposite*: fixed **2 changeable**, variable, mutable, impermanent, adjustable *Opposite*: fixed

move *v* **1 reposition**, shift, budge, shove, stir **2 go**, progress, transport, walk, step **3 relocate**, transfer, redeploy, change, shift *Opposite*: stay put **4 cause**, provoke, persuade, encourage, prod **5 affect**, touch, stir the emotions, impress, upset ■ *n* **1 movement**, action, motion, gesture, transfer **2 attempt**, effort, step, action, activity **3 shift**, realignment, rearrangement, repositioning, relocation

move ahead *v* **progress**, move on, press forward, go on, move forward *Opposite*: retreat

move along *v* **1 proceed**, hasten, go on, advance, press on **2 move aside**, move over, make way, make room, shift *Opposite*: stay put

move away *v* **retreat**, back off, diverge, distance, deviate

move back *v* **recoil**, recede, shrink back, retreat, regress *Opposite*: advance

move fast *v* **streak**, zoom, speed, tear, whiz

move forward *v* **advance**, progress, push on, go ahead, proceed *Opposite*: fall back

move heaven and earth *v* **do your utmost**, pull out all the stops, make every effort, move mountains, leave no stone unturned

move in on *v* **approach**, surround, converge, come closer, draw near *Opposite*: retreat

move into *v* **enter**, start, enter on, begin, set the ball rolling *Opposite*: back out

movement *n* **1 motion**, mobility, locomotion, circulation *Opposite*: stillness **2 move**, action, motion, gesture, lift **3 drive**, crusade, program, undertaking, measure **4 pressure group**, association, society, lobby, faction **5 progress**, advance, development, improvement, headway *Opposite*: stagnation

movements *n* **actions**, activities, travels, schedule, arrangements

move on *v* **1 leave**, depart, go, make off, set off *Opposite*: stay put **2 progress**, get going, go on, take the next step, uproot *Opposite*: backtrack

move out *v* **leave**, depart, go, relocate, move on *Opposite*: stay put

move over *v* **move aside**, make way, make room, shift, step aside *Opposite*: stay put

mover *n* **1 motivator**, driving force, agent, doer, goer **2 initiator**, proposer, introducer, advocate, sponsor *Opposite*: seconder

move toward *v* **draw near**, move in on, approach, converge, creep up on *Opposite*: move away

move up *v* **go up**, rise, increase, progress, advance *Opposite*: drop

movie *n* **moving picture**, show, picture, picture show, film

movies n cinema, big screen, silver screen, films, pictures (dated infml)

moving adj touching, poignant, affecting, pathetic, heartrending

COMPARE AND CONTRAST CORE MEANING: arousing emotion

moving causing deep feelings, especially of sadness or compassion; **pathetic** arousing feelings of compassion and pity, often centered on somebody who is vulnerable, helpless, or unfortunate; **pitiful** arousing compassion and pity, or arousing contempt or derision; **poignant** causing strong, often bittersweet feelings of sadness, pity, or regret; **touching** causing feelings of warmth, sympathy, and tenderness; **heartwarming** inspiring warm or kindly feelings, usually by showing life and human nature in a positive and reassuring light; **heartrending** causing intense sadness or distress, especially in sympathy with somebody else's unhappiness or hardship because it involves suffering or tragic events.

moving parts n mechanism, machinery, workings, components, gears

mow v cut, scythe, cut down, shear, trim

mow down v 1 shoot, kill, slaughter, massacre, butcher 2 knock down, run over, knock over, floor, topple

much adv 1 significantly, noticeably, considerably, greatly, substantially 2 often, frequently, over and over again, time and again, repeatedly ▪ adj a good deal of, a great deal of, lots of, abundant, ample

much-loved adj adored, favorite, preferred, chosen, desired

muck n 1 manure, sewage, waste, sludge, dung 2 (infml) dirt, mess, grime, mud, filth

muck around (infml) v fool around, waste time, be silly, mess around (infml)

muckiness (infml) n filthiness, muddiness, dirtiness, grubbiness, griminess

muckraker n scandalmonger, gossipmonger, troublemaker, mudslinger, slanderer

muckraking n scandalmongering, dishing the dirt, mudslinging, slander, libel

muck up (infml) v spoil, ruin, damage, make a mess of, muddy up

mucky (infml) adj dirty, muddy, messy, grubby, smeared Opposite: clean

mucous adj self-lubricating, slimy, slippery, lubricated

mucus n slime, secretion, saliva, lubricant, phlegm

mud n mire, sludge, dirt, muck (infml)

muddiness n 1 dirtiness, grubbiness, filthiness, griminess, muckiness (infml) Opposite: cleanness 2 cloudiness, murkiness, dullness, opacity, thickness Opposite: clarity

muddle v 1 mix up, jumble, disorder, disorganize, disarrange Opposite: disentangle 2 confuse, bewilder, baffle,

puzzle, perplex Opposite: clarify ▪ n disorder, jumble, confusion, mix-up, chaos Opposite: order

muddled adj 1 jumbled, scrambled, mixed up, topsy-turvy, upside down Opposite: ordered 2 confused, befuddled, bewildered, bemused, perplexed Opposite: clear

muddleheaded adj 1 baffled, mixed up, confused, befuddled, bewildered Opposite: clear-headed 2 inept, illogical, impractical, random, ineffective Opposite: logical

muddle up v mix up, jumble, disorder, disorganize, disarrange

muddy adj 1 mud-spattered, dirty, grubby, grimy, filthy Opposite: clean 2 cloudy, murky, unclear, opaque, thick Opposite: clear

mud flap n mudguard, splashguard, flap, shield, guard

mudpack n face mask, facial, face pack, treatment, beauty treatment

mudslinger n slanderer, defamer, denigrator, character assassin, attacker

mudslinging n defamation, backbiting, slander, denigration, character assassination Opposite: praise

muff v 1 miss, drop, fumble, mishit, mishandle 2 get wrong, mishandle, botch (infml), bungle (infml), mess up (infml)

muffle v deaden, dampen, quiet, silence, mute Opposite: amplify

muffled adj stifled, muted, inaudible, soft, lowered Opposite: loud

mufti n civilian clothes, ordinary clothes, street clothes, casual wear, civvies (infml) Opposite: uniform

mug v attack, assault, rob, ambush, hold up

mugger n robber, assailant, thug, attacker, assaulter

mugginess n humidity, closeness, clamminess, oppressiveness, warmth Opposite: freshness

mugging n attack, assault, robbery, ambush, theft

muggy adj humid, close, sultry, clammy, oppressive Opposite: fresh

mug shot n photo, photograph, close-up, police photo, passport photo

mulch n covering, protection, insulation, organic matter, leaves ▪ v cover, protect, insulate, dress, top dress

mulish adj stubborn, obstinate, defiant, headstrong, obdurate Opposite: amenable

mulishness n stubbornness, obstinacy, defiance, obduracy, determination Opposite: amenability

mulled adj spiced, warmed, sweetened, warm, heated

mull over v ponder, consider, contemplate, think over, think about

multicolor adj colorful, rainbow, rainbow-colored, many-hued, variegated

multicultural *adj* **diverse**, multiethnic, multi-racial, inclusive, all-inclusive

multifaceted *adj* **multilayered**, complex, complicated, many-sided, polygonal *Opposite*: simple

multifarious *adj* **diverse**, varied, assorted, mixed, miscellaneous *Opposite*: homogeneous

multilateral *adj* **1 many-sided**, polygonal, multifaceted, multidimensional **2 mutual**, all-party, multiparty, joint, bilateral *Opposite*: unilateral

multilingual *adj* **polyglot**, trilingual, bilingual

multimedia *n* **1 hypermedia**, software, interactive program, program **2 collage**, combination, montage, assemblage, construction

multimillionaire *n* **millionaire**, magnate, billionaire, tycoon, mogul

multinational *adj* **international**, cosmopolitan, transnational, global, worldwide *Opposite*: national ■ *n* **conglomerate**, corporation, transnational, international business, international company

multipartite *adj* **multiple**, multifarious, multifaceted, composite, compound

multiple *adj* **manifold**, numerous, many, several, various *Opposite*: few

multiplication *n* **increase**, growth, development, reproduction, duplication *Opposite*: decrease

multiplicity *n* **array**, diversity, variety, large quantity, range *Opposite*: dearth

multiply *v* **increase**, grow, reproduce, swell, proliferate *Opposite*: decrease

multipurpose *adj* **versatile**, flexible, adaptable, multiuse *Opposite*: dedicated

multiracial *adj* **interracial**, multicultural, multiethnic, inclusive, all-inclusive *Opposite*: exclusive

multistory *adj* **high-rise**, multistoried, tall, high, towering *Opposite*: low-rise

multitude *n* **1 crowd**, horde, host, mass, throng *Opposite*: handful **2 variety**, assortment, array, collection, wealth *Opposite*: few

mum *(infml) adj* **silent**, tight-lipped, mute, quiet, dumb *Opposite*: communicative

mumble *v* **mutter**, murmur, drone, intone, gabble *Opposite*: enunciate

mumbled *adj* **muttered**, murmured, muffled, inaudible, slurred *Opposite*: enunciated

mumbo jumbo *(infml) n* **jargon**, gibberish, doublespeak, cant, technobabble *Opposite*: sense

mummify *v* **1 embalm**, preserve, wrap up, prepare, dress **2 shrivel**, dry out, dry up, wrinkle, wither *Opposite*: flourish

mummy *n* **mummified body**, body, cadaver, corpse

munch *v* **chew**, masticate, crunch, grind, eat

mundane *adj* **ordinary**, dull, routine, everyday, commonplace *Opposite*: exotic

mundaneness *n* **ordinariness**, routine, tedium, flatness, unimaginativeness *Opposite*: excitement

municipal *adj* **civic**, public, community, urban, metropolitan *Opposite*: private

municipality *n* **city**, metropolis, town, borough, burg. See COMPARE AND CONTRAST *at* city.

munificence *n* **generosity**, largesse, benevolence, kindness, philanthropy *Opposite*: miserliness

munificent *adj* **generous**, liberal, magnanimous, unstinting, unsparing *Opposite*: miserly. See COMPARE AND CONTRAST *at* generous.

munitions *n* **weaponry**, ammunition, arms, guns, armaments

mural *n* **wall painting**, fresco, frieze, painting

murder *n* **homicide**, manslaughter, assassination, killing, slaying ■ *v* **kill**, assassinate, execute, put to death, slaughter. See COMPARE AND CONTRAST *at* kill.

murderer *n* **killer**, assassin, butcher, slaughterer, executioner

murderous *adj* **1 fatal**, lethal, mortal, deadly, homicidal **2** *(infml)* **difficult**, testing, arduous, rigorous, exhausting *Opposite*: easy

murk *n* **gloom**, darkness, shadows, dark, dimness *Opposite*: light

murkiness *n* **darkness**, fogginess, mistiness, cloudiness, gloom *Opposite*: brightness

murky *adj* **dark**, gloomy, foggy, misty, cloudy *Opposite*: clear

murmur *v* **1 whisper**, mutter, mumble, purr, croon *Opposite*: bray **2 complain**, grumble, grouch, mutter, grouse *(infml) Opposite*: praise

muscle *n* **1 sinew**, brawn, musculature, thew *(archaic)* **2 influence**, power, authority, force, control **3** *(infml)* **strength**, vigor, power, force, elbow grease *(infml)*

WORD BANK
❑ **types of muscles or tendons** abdominals, Achilles tendon, biceps, diaphragm, hamstring, pectoral, quadriceps, sinew, smooth muscle, sphincter, striated muscle, tendon, triceps

muscle in *(infml) v* **intrude**, intervene, barge in, butt in, interfere

muscular *adj* **brawny**, beefy, well-built, burly, well-developed *Opposite*: puny

muse *v* **think**, ponder, consider, mull over, deliberate

museum *n* **gallery**, exhibition hall, arts center, academy, institution

mush *n* **1 pap**, purée, mash, paste, slop **2 sentimentality**, sentimentalism, slush, sugariness, slop *(infml)*

mushroom *v* **grow**, increase, expand, flourish, swell *Opposite*: decline

mushy adj **1 soggy**, soft, squashy, squishy, spongy Opposite: firm **2 oversentimental**, mawkish, maudlin, syrupy, romantic

music n **melody**, tune, harmony, composition, song

WORD BANK

❏ **types of musical forms** anthem, aria, bagatelle, ballad, cantata, canticle, capriccio, chorale, coloratura, concerto, étude, fantasia, fugue, hymn, intermezzo, madrigal, mass, nocturne, oratorio, overture, prelude, requiem, rondo, scherzo, sinfonia, sonata, song, suite, symphony, tone poem, waltz

❏ **types of musical registers** alto, baritone, bass, countertenor, falsetto, mezzo-soprano, soprano, tenor

❏ **types of musical terms** a cappella, adagio, allegro, andante, appassionato, arpeggio, capriccioso, con brio, con moto, crescendo, decrescendo, diminuendo, forte, fortissimo, grave, larghetto, largo, legato, lentissimo, lento, moderato, pianissimo, piano, pizzicato, rubato, sotto voce, staccato

❏ **types of classical music** Baroque, chamber music, comic opera, early music, opera, operetta, Romantic, twelve-tone

❏ **types of dance music** acid house, acid jazz, big beat, boogie, broken beat, disco, drum 'n' bass, funk, garage, hard core, hip hop, house, jungle, ragga, ragamuffin, rap, rave, reggae, rock steady, ska, speed garage, techno, trance, two step

❏ **types of electronic music** ambient, breakbeat, breaks and beats, chillout, downbeat, dub, electro, electronica, new age, trip hop

❏ **types of jazz music** bebop, boogie-woogie, cool jazz, Dixieland, honky-tonk, jazz, jazz funk, jazz fusion, jazz rock, jive, modal jazz, New Orleans jazz, ragtime, swing

❏ **types of pop and vocal music** bluegrass, blues, country and western, doowop, easy listening, folk, gangsta rap, gospel, lounge, Motown, new wave, pop, R&B, rap metal, rare soul, rockabilly, soul, spiritual, urban

❏ **types of rock music** grunge, heavy metal, indie, metal, punk, rock, rock 'n' roll, thrash metal

❏ **types of world music** afrobeat, bhangra, calypso, flamenco, Latin, mento, raga, rai, roots, salsa, yodel

musical adj **melodic**, harmonious, melodious, tuneful, easy on the ear Opposite: discordant

musician n **performer**, instrumentalist, player, artiste, composer

musing n **thinking**, reflection, reverie, daydream, consideration ■ adj **thoughtful**, reflective, pensive, contemplative, absorbed

musk n **perfume**, scent, smell, fragrance, aroma

musky adj **pungent**, perfumed, scented, odorous, aromatic

must v **have to**, have got to, be obliged to, ought to, should ■ n **necessity**, obligation, duty, essential, requirement Opposite: option

mustache n **whiskers**, walrus mustache, pencil mustache handlebar mustache, mustachio (archaic)

muster v **gather**, gather together, congregate, collect, get together Opposite: disperse ■ n **gathering**, assembly, meeting, congregation, congress

mustiness n **dankness**, staleness, moldiness, stuffiness, fustiness Opposite: freshness

musty adj **mildewed**, moldy, stale, fusty, stuffy Opposite: fresh

mutable adj **changeable**, alterable, changing, variable, fluctuating Opposite: fixed

mutant adj **distorted**, misshapen, malformed, transformed, altered

mutate v **change**, alter, transform, transmute, metamorphose

mutation n **change**, alteration, transformation, transmutation, metamorphosis

mute adj **silent**, speechless, voiceless, unspeaking, quiet Opposite: vocal

muted adj **subdued**, hushed, soft, quiet, gentle Opposite: loud

mutilate v **maim**, injure, hurt, disfigure, harm

mutilation n **disfigurement**, defacement, damage, injury, maiming

mutineer n **rebel**, insurgent, rioter, radical, insurrectionist

mutinous adj **rebellious**, revolutionary, seditious, subversive, disobedient Opposite: obedient

mutiny n **rebellion**, revolt, sedition, uprising, insubordination

mutter v **1 mumble**, murmur, drone, burble, slur Opposite: speak up **2 complain**, grouch, grumble, murmur, grouse (infml) Opposite: praise

mutual adj **joint**, shared, common, communal, reciprocated

muzzle v **silence**, gag, hush, quiet, stifle

muzzy adj **1 fuzzy**, woozy, groggy, bleary, shaky Opposite: clear-headed **2 vague**, fuzzy, out of focus, blurred, bleary Opposite: clear

myopia n **1 nearsightedness**, poor sight, short-sightedness **2 bigotry**, prejudice, bias, intolerance, narrow-mindedness

myopic adj **1 short-sighted**, owlish, nearsighted **2 narrow-minded**, bigoted, parochial, prejudiced, intolerant Opposite: broad-minded

myriad adj **countless**, innumerable, numberless, numerous, many Opposite: few ■ n **multitude**, mass, host, army, crowd Opposite: few

mysterious adj **1 strange**, unexplained, inexplicable, unsolved, odd **2 secretive**, enigmatic, shadowy, furtive, cryptic *Opposite*: open

mysteriousness *n* **strangeness**, oddness, weirdness, curiousness, inexplicableness *Opposite*: normality

mystery *n* **1 problem**, puzzle, conundrum, enigma, riddle **2 secrecy**, obscurity, ambiguity, inscrutability, vagueness **3 whodunit**, detective novel, thriller, crime novel ■ *adj* **unknown**, anonymous, unidentified, secret, clandestine

mystic *n* **spiritualist**, medium, shaman, sorcerer, wizard ■ *adj* **mystical**, spiritual, supernatural, magical, cabalistic

mystical *adj* **spiritual**, mystic, magical, supernatural, magic

mystification *n* **bewilderment**, confusion, perplexity, bafflement, puzzlement

mystified *adj* **puzzled**, confused, bewildered, baffled, perplexed *Opposite*: enlightened

mystify *v* **puzzle**, confuse, bewilder, confound, baffle

mystifying *adj* **mysterious**, baffling, inexplicable, puzzling, confusing

mystique *n* **air of mystery**, air of secrecy, aura, charisma, magic

myth *n* **1 legend**, fable, saga, fairy tale, allegory **2 falsehood**, fiction, illusion, invention, fabrication *Opposite*: fact

---

WORD BANK

❑ **types of mythical beings** Abominable Snowman, Bigfoot, bogey, bogeyman, bugaboo, daemon, demon, dryad, giant, gnome, goblin, gremlin *(infml)*, hobgoblin, leprechaun, naiad, nymph, ogre, sasquatch, sylph, troll, wood nymph, yeti

---

mythic *see* **mythical**

mythical *adj* **1 legendary**, mythological, fabled, fabulous, storybook *Opposite*: factual **2 imaginary**, untrue, fictitious, fictional, made-up *Opposite*: real

mythological *adj* **mythical**, mythic, fabulous, fairy-tale, fabled *Opposite*: factual

mythology *n* **myths**, legends, folklore, tradition, mythos

N

nab *v* **1** *(infml)* **arrest**, seize, capture, detain, catch **2 steal**, walk off with, rip off *(infml)*, swipe *(infml)*, lift *(infml)*

nadir *n* **lowest point**, all-time low, depths of despair, depths, base *Opposite*: zenith

nag *v* **1 badger**, pester, plague, harass, harry **2 criticize**, find fault, carp, grumble, complain **3 irritate**, annoy, worry, trouble, torment. *See* COMPARE AND CONTRAST *at* **complain**.

nagging *adj* **irritating**, niggling, troublesome, distressing, irksome

nail *n* **pin**, spike, tack, peg ■ *v* **tack**, pin, fix, fasten, attach

nail-biting *adj* **nerve-racking**, tense, exciting, stressful, anxious *Opposite*: relaxing

nail down *v* **pin down**, get an agreement on, get a decision on, settle, confirm

naive *adj* **1 simple**, trusting, innocent, childlike, inexperienced *Opposite*: suspicious **2 unsophisticated**, gullible, wet behind the ears, green, foolish *Opposite*: shrewd

naiveté *n* **innocence**, ingenuousness, candor, artlessness, naturalness *Opposite*: sophistication

naked *adj* **1 bare**, nude, undressed, unclothed, with nothing on *Opposite*: clothed **2 uncovered**, unprotected, exposed, unsheathed, unwrapped *Opposite*: covered **3 open**, undisguised, unadorned, unadulterated, unvarnished *Opposite*: hidden

---

COMPARE AND CONTRAST CORE MEANING: devoid of clothes or covering

naked not covered or concealed, especially not covered by clothing on any part of the body; **bare** without the usual furnishings or decorations, or not covered by clothing; **nude** not wearing any clothes at all, especially in artistic contexts; **undressed** not wearing any or many clothes, used especially when clothes have just been removed or are about to be put on.

---

nakedly *adv* **openly**, blatantly, starkly, obviously, overtly *Opposite*: covertly

nakedness *n* **1 nudity**, bareness, state of undress **2 defenselessness**, helplessness, exposure, vulnerability **3 blatancy**, obviousness, openness, overtness, starkness *Opposite*: covertness

namby-pamby *(infml insult)* *adj* **feeble**, soft, spineless, ineffectual, pathetic *(infml)* *Opposite*: tough

name *n* **1 first name**, Christian name, forename, surname, family name **2 designation**, term, tag, title, label **3 reputation**, renown, character, respectability, honor *Opposite*: notoriety **4 celebrity**, star, big name, public figure, VIP *Opposite*: nobody ■ *v* **1 call**, christen, baptize, nickname, label **2 identify**, specify, refer to, mention, cite *Opposite*: conceal **3 nominate**, appoint, assign, choose, suggest *Opposite*: reject

name-calling *n* **abuse**, insults, foul language, swearing, invective *(fml)*

named *adj* **called**, baptized, christened, entitled, titled *Opposite*: nameless

name-drop *v* **boast**, brag, show off, vaunt

name-dropper *n* **boaster**, bragger, braggart, show-off *(infml)*, blower *(infml)*

nameless *adj* **1 anonymous**, unknown, unidentified, unnamed, unspecified *Opposite*: named **2 indescribable**, awful, dreadful, horrible, ghastly

namely *adv* **that is**, that is to say, viz., specifically, explicitly

nameplate *n* **plate**, sign, plaque, notice, panel

naming *n* **identification**, designation, nomenclature, christening, baptism

nanny *n* **1 caretaker**, au pair, caregiver **2** *(infml)* **grandmother**, nana *(infml)*, nan *(infml)*, granny *(infml)*, gran *(infml)*

nanosecond *n* **moment**, split second, second, instant, trice

nap *n* **1 doze**, catnap, siesta, sleep, rest **2 pile**, surface, finish, weave, texture ■ *v* **sleep**, catnap, have a siesta, doze, drowse

napkin *n* **bib**, paper towel, table linen, napery *(archaic)*

narcissism *n* **self-love**, self-absorption, egotism, conceit, self-importance *Opposite*: selflessness

narcissistic *adj* **vain**, self-absorbed, egotistic, egotistical, selfish *Opposite*: selfless

narrate *v* **relate**, recount, tell, describe, recite

narration *n* **1 telling**, recitation, relating, unfolding, recounting **2 tale**, account, description, chronicle, history

narrative *n* **1 tale**, account, description, chronicle, history **2 plot**, story line, sequence of events

narrator *n* **storyteller**, speaker, raconteur, teller of tales, relator *Opposite*: listener

narrow *adj* **thin**, fine, slim, slender, slight *Opposite*: wide ■ *v* **1 get thinner**, get smaller, taper, contract, tighten *Opposite*: widen **2 restrict**, limit, narrow down, confine, focus *Opposite*: broaden

narrow down *v* **focus**, restrict, limit, confine, concentrate *Opposite*: broaden

narrow escape *n* **close call**, near miss, close shave, lucky escape, narrow squeak

narrowing *n* **tapering**, contraction, thinning, reduction, tightening

narrowly *adv* **1 only just**, barely, hardly, scarcely, by a hair's breadth **2 closely**, intently, carefully, attentively, assiduously

narrow-minded *adj* **bigoted**, insular, intolerant, prejudiced, biased *Opposite*: broadminded

narrow-mindedness *n* **bigotry**, insularity, prejudice, bias, intolerance *Opposite*: broad-mindedness

narrowness *n* **thinness**, fineness, slimness, slightness, constriction *Opposite*: width

narrow squeak *see* **narrow escape**

nascent *adj* **budding**, promising, embryonic, emerging, blossoming *Opposite*: moribund

nastiness *n* **spite**, meanness, malice, viciousness, cruelty *Opposite*: kindness

nasty *adj* **1 spiteful**, mean, malicious, vicious, cruel *Opposite*: kind **2 foul**, horrid, horrible, revolting, offensive *Opposite*: pleasant **3 severe**, painful, horrible, serious, grave *Opposite*: slight **4** *(infml)* **obscene**, offensive, indecent, vulgar, crude **5** *(infml)* **difficult**, tricky, hard, complicated, knotty. *See* COMPARE AND CONTRAST *at* **mean**.

nation *n* **1 state**, country, land, realm, homeland **2 people**, population, inhabitants, residents, populace

national *adj* **1 nationwide**, countrywide, state, general, coast-to-coast *Opposite*: local **2 state**, public, nationalized, state-run state-owned *Opposite*: private ■ *n* **resident**, citizen, inhabitant, subject, native *Opposite*: visitor

nationalism *n* **1 independence**, autonomy, home rule, self-rule, self-government **2 patriotism**, chauvinism, jingoism, xenophobia

nationalist *n* **separatist**, autonomist, separationist

nationalistic *adj* **patriotic**, jingoistic, chauvinistic, xenophobic

nationality *n* **people**, population, race, ethnic group

nationalize *v* **make public**, take over, municipalize *Opposite*: privatize

nationalized *adj* **state-owned**, publicly owned, public sector, state, national *Opposite*: private

nationally *adv* **countrywide**, all over the country, on a national scale, nationwide, generally *Opposite*: locally

nation-state *n* **state**, country, land, nation, sovereign state

nationwide *adj* **countrywide**, general, national, state, coast-to-coast *Opposite*: local ■ *adv* **nationally**, countrywide, all over the country, on a national scale, generally *Opposite*: locally

native *adj* **1 innate**, natural, inborn, instinctive, inherent *Opposite*: acquired **2 indigenous**, local, aboriginal, resident, autochthonous *Opposite*: foreign ■ *n* **inhabitant**, resident, local, citizen, subject *Opposite*: foreigner

---

COMPARE AND CONTRAST CORE MEANING: originating in a particular place

native born or originating in a particular place; **aboriginal** existing in a region from the earliest known times; **indigenous** originating in and typical of a region or country; **autochthonous** originating where currently found, especially used of rocks and minerals that were formed in their present position, or flora, fauna, or inhabitants descended from those present in a region from earliest times.

native land *n* **land of origin**, land of birth, birthplace, native country, motherland

nativity *n* **origin**, birth, genesis, conception, dawn *Opposite*: demise *(fml)*

natter *(infml)* *v* **have a chat**, chat, chatter, gossip, talk

natty *adj* **smart**, fashionable, trim, dapper, chic *Opposite*: unfashionable

natural *adj* **1 usual**, normal, ordinary, accepted, expected *Opposite*: unusual **2 physical**, biological, environmental, ecological, geographic *Opposite*: technological **3 innate**, native, inborn, instinctive, effortless *Opposite*: learned **4 unaffected**, unpretentious, spontaneous, genuine, artless *Opposite*: affected **5 untreated**, unprocessed, pure, raw, crude *Opposite*: artificial **6 biological**, physical, birth, true, actual *Opposite*: adoptive

naturalistic *adj* **realistic**, real, true-to-life, natural, lifelike

naturalize *v* **1 accept**, adopt, enfranchise **2 adapt**, become established, grow wild, grow naturally, acclimatize

naturally *adv* **1 of course**, obviously, logically, as expected, unsurprisingly *Opposite*: surprisingly **2 innately**, inherently, instinctively, intuitively, effortlessly **3 unaffectedly**, unpretentiously, spontaneously, genuinely, artlessly *Opposite*: pretentiously **4 in nature**, physically, biologically, geographically, geologically *Opposite*: artificially

naturalness *n* **unaffectedness**, spontaneity, genuineness, artlessness, sincerity *Opposite*: affectedness

natural resource *n* **raw material**, mineral, mineral deposit, reserve, resource

natural world *n* **environment**, nature, biosphere, ecosphere

nature *n* **1 Mother Nature**, countryside, natural surroundings, wildlife, flora **2 class**, kind, sort, type, description **3 character**, personality, temperament, disposition, spirit

naught *n* **zero**, nil, nothing, zilch *(infml)*

naughtiness *n* **disobedience**, bad behavior, wickedness, ill-discipline, waywardness *Opposite*: obedience

naughty *adj* **disobedient**, bad, badly behaved, wicked, ill-disciplined *Opposite*: good. *See* COMPARE AND CONTRAST *at* bad.

nausea *n* **1 biliousness**, queasiness, sickness, vomiting, unsettled stomach **2** *(literary)* **revulsion**, repugnance, repulsion, abhorrence, disgust

nauseate *v* **1 sicken**, turn your stomach, make you feel sick *Opposite*: please **2** *(literary)* **disgust**, repel, revolt, upset, put off *Opposite*: attract

nauseating *(literary) adj* **disgusting**, sickening, repellent, revolting, repulsive *Opposite*: pleasant

nauseous *adj* **1 sick**, bilious, queasy, unwell, nauseated *Opposite*: well **2 disgusting**, sickening, repellent, revolting, repulsive *Opposite*: pleasant

nautical *adj* **maritime**, seafaring, sailing, marine, naval

naval *see* **nautical**

navel-gazing *n* **self-analysis**, reflection, rumination, brooding, self-absorption

navigable *adj* **1 passable**, negotiable, crossable, traversable *Opposite*: impassable **2 maneuverable**, controllable, seaworthy, sturdy, steerable

navigate *v* **1 find the way**, plot a course, plot a route, map read, follow the map **2 sail across**, circumnavigate, steer, pilot, take the helm

navigation *n* **direction finding**, steering, course plotting, map reading, celestial navigation

navigational *adj* **directional**, direction-finding, course-plotting, route-finding

navigator *n* **guide**, autopilot, skipper, pilot, direction finder

navvy *(dated) n* **manual worker**, laborer, manual laborer, worker, hand

navy *n* **fleet**, armada, flotilla, merchant marine

nay *(literary) adv* **or rather**, and also, more correctly, indeed, even

near *prep* **1 close to**, by, next to, in close proximity to, in the vicinity of *Opposite*: far from **2 like**, close to, similar to, resembling, approaching **3 on the verge of**, approaching, nearing, close to, bordering on ■ *adv* **1 nearby**, close, close by, close at hand, in close proximity **2 almost**, nearly, virtually, practically, just about ■ *adj* **close**, nearby, neighboring, adjacent, adjoining *Opposite*: far ■ *v* **approach**, reach, draw up to, draw near to, go up to *Opposite*: leave

nearby *adj* **close**, near, neighboring, adjacent, adjoining *Opposite*: distant ■ *adv* **near**, close, close by, close at hand, in close proximity

nearly *adv* **closely**, approximately, almost, near, virtually

near miss *n* **lucky escape**, close thing, close call, close shave, narrow escape

nearness *n* **immediacy**, imminence, proximity, closeness, juxtaposition *Opposite*: distance

nearsighted *adj* **short-sighted**, myopic, owlish *Opposite*: farsighted

neat *adj* **1 well-ordered**, in order, straight, arranged, tidy *Opposite*: untidy **2 well-organized**, organized, methodical, systematic, careful *Opposite*: disorganized **3 straight**, undiluted, unmixed, full-strength, pure *Opposite*: diluted **4 simple**, ingenious, elegant, convenient, effective **5 graceful**, effortless, practiced, precise, deft *Opposite*: clumsy **6 natty**, trim,

compact, well-designed, elegant *Opposite*:
cumbersome

neaten *v* order, arrange, sort out, put in
order, tidy *Opposite*: mess up *(infml)*

neatness *n* **1** orderliness, immaculateness,
carefulness, trimness, tidiness *Opposite*:
messiness **2** ingeniousness, elegance,
cleverness, effectiveness, handiness *Opposite*: ineffectiveness **3** gracefulness, effortlessness, preciseness, deftness, skillfulness
Opposite: clumsiness **4** simplicity, elegance, nattiness, trimness, compactness

nebulous *adj* unclear, vague, imprecise,
hazy, unformulated *Opposite*: precise

necessary *adj* essential, indispensable,
needed, vital, requisite *(fml) Opposite*:
optional

COMPARE AND CONTRAST CORE MEANING:
describes something that is required
necessary important in order to achieve a
desired result, or required by authority or convention; **essential** of the highest importance for
achieving something; **vital** extremely important
to the survival or continuing effectiveness of
something; **indispensable** absolutely essential,
or extremely desirable or useful; **requisite** *(fml)*
necessary for a particular purpose; **needed**
required or desired.

---

necessitate *v* require, demand, need, call
for, dictate

necessitude *n* need, necessity, demand,
requirement, want

necessity *n* **1** essential, requirement, prerequisite, basic, necessary *Opposite*:
luxury **2** need, requirement, inevitability,
obligation, stipulation

neck *n* narrow part, stem, shank, shaft ■
v (infml) kiss, cuddle, hug, embrace,
smooch *(infml)*

neckerchief *n* bandanna, cravat, scarf, tie,
band

necklace *n* chain, string, choker, band, rope

necktie *n* tie, scarf, bandanna, cravat

necropolis *n* cemetery, burial ground, graveyard, resting place, churchyard

nectar *n* liquid, juice, sap, fluid, syrup

née *adj* formerly, previously, originally

need *v* **1** demand, require, call for, want,
necessitate **2** have to, must, should, ought ■
n **1** essential, necessity, requirement, want,
prerequisite *Opposite*: option **2** privation,
poverty, want, hardship, neediness *Opposite*: luxury. *See* COMPARE AND CONTRAST *at*
necessary.

needed *adj* necessary, desired, required,
wanted. *See* COMPARE AND CONTRAST *at* **necessary**.

needful *adj* **1** *(fml or archaic)* necessary,
obligatory, compulsory, mandatory,
essential **2** *(fml)* requiring, necessitating,
demanding, calling for, needing

neediness *n* need, poverty, want, penury,
destitution

needle *n* **1** pointer, indicator, hand **2** spine,
spike, prickle, barb, pine needle ■ *v (infml)*
irritate, provoke, annoy, pester, niggle

needless *adj* unnecessary, pointless,
uncalled-for, useless, unneeded *Opposite*:
necessary

needlessness *n* uselessness, unhelpfulness,
fruitlessness, impracticality, pointlessness
Opposite: usefulness

needy *adj* poor, in need, deprived, disadvantaged, destitute

ne'er-do-well *n* layabout, waster, idler,
slacker, shirker

nefarious *adj* wicked, evil, despicable,
immoral, reprehensible *Opposite*: reputable

negate *(fml) v* **1** refute, contradict, disprove,
deny, repudiate *Opposite*: affirm **2** invalidate, cancel, reverse, render null and void,
nullify *Opposite*: validate. *See* COMPARE AND
CONTRAST *at* **nullify**.

negation *n* **1** denial, annulment, nullification, repudiation, cancellation *Opposite*: affirmation **2** opposite, contrary,
absence, lack, antithesis *Opposite*: confirmation

negative *adj* **1** unenthusiastic, unconstructive, unhelpful, pessimistic, disapproving *Opposite*: encouraging **2** bad,
undesirable, adverse, harmful, damaging
Opposite: positive ■ *n* rejection, rebuff,
veto, no, refusal *Opposite*: approval

negatively *adv* **1** in the negative, with a no,
with a refusal, with a denial *Opposite*:
affirmatively **2** damagingly, harmfully,
destructively, undesirably, adversely
Opposite: positively **3** offputtingly, dis-
couragingly, unenthusiastically, uncon-
structively, unhelpfully *Opposite*:
encouragingly

negativity *n* unconstructiveness, unhelpfulness, pessimism, disapproval *Opposite*:
enthusiasm

neglect *v* **1** abandon, desert, forget, forsake,
ignore *Opposite*: look after **2** omit, forget,
overlook, ignore, disregard ■ *n* negligence,
abandonment, desertion, disregard,
inattention *Opposite*: care

COMPARE AND CONTRAST CORE MEANING: fail
to do something
neglect fail to give the proper or required care
and attention to somebody or something, or fail
to do something, especially because of carelessness, forgetfulness, or indifference; **forget**
fail, or fail to remember, to give due attention
to somebody or something; **omit** fail to do something, either deliberately or accidentally; **overlook** fail to notice or check something as a result
of inattention, preoccupation, or haste.

---

neglected *adj* deserted, abandoned,
unkempt, uncared for, mistreated *Opposite*: looked after

neglectful *adj* negligent, careless, slipshod, remiss, lax *Opposite*: attentive

negligee *n* nightgown, nightdress, dressing gown, peignoir, nightie *(infml)*

negligence *n* neglect, inattention, disregard, laxity, slackness *Opposite*: attention

negligent *adj* 1 neglectful, careless, inattentive, slipshod, remiss *Opposite*: careful 2 *(literary)* nonchalant, relaxed, casual, informal, easy *Opposite*: formal

negligible *adj* insignificant, tiny, small, slight, unimportant *Opposite*: significant

negligibly *adv* not noticeably, just, insignificantly, trivially, marginally *Opposite*: significantly

negotiable *adj* 1 open to discussion, unfixed, flexible, open-ended, up for grabs *(infml)* *Opposite*: nonnegotiable 2 transferable, exchangeable, convertible, assignable, movable 3 passable, navigable, crossable, traversable, accessible *Opposite*: impassable

negotiate *v* 1 talk, discuss, confer, consult, bargain 2 sell, transfer, exchange, convert, convey 3 get past, pass, navigate, go around, cross

negotiation *n* arbitration, mediation, discussion, cooperation, diplomacy

negotiations *n* talks, discussions, conference, consultation, dialogue

negotiator *n* speaker, representative, envoy, delegate, mediator

neighborhood *n* area, district, barrio, region, locality

neighboring *adj* adjacent, adjoining, bordering, next door, near *Opposite*: distant

neighborliness *n* friendliness, kindness, helpfulness, consideration, sociability *Opposite*: unfriendliness

nemesis *(literary)* *n* 1 punishment, vengeance, retribution, fate, doom 2 opponent, archenemy, archrival, adversary, competitor 3 avenger, retaliator, revenger, vindicator

neologism *n* new word, coinage, buzzword *(infml)*

neonatal *adj* newborn, new, brand-new

neophyte *n* novice, beginner, recruit, learner, trainee

nepotism *n* favoritism, preferential treatment, partiality, bias, preference

nerve *n* 1 courage, bravery, spirit, audacity, bravado *Opposite*: cowardice 2 boldness, impudence, insolence, effrontery, bravado. *See* COMPARE AND CONTRAST *at* courage.

nerve center *n* hub, control room, headquarters, H.Q., nexus

nerve-racking *adj* worrying, anxious, tense, stressful, scary *(infml)*

nerves *(infml)* *n* anxiety, worry, tension, stress, mental strain

nerve-wracking *see* **nerve-racking**

nerviness *n* edginess, anxiety, jumpiness, tenseness, uneasiness *Opposite*: calmness

nervous *adj* anxious, worried, edgy, jumpy, panicky *Opposite*: calm

nervousness *n* anxiety, edginess, jumpiness, tenseness, uneasiness *Opposite*: calmness

nervy *(infml)* *adj* fearless, brave, daring, bold, gutsy *(infml)*

nest egg *n* savings, reserve, capital, fund, store

nestle *v* 1 cuddle up, cozy up, huddle, nuzzle, settle 2 cushion, place, lie, soften, shelter

net *n* mesh, web, netting, lattice, grid ■ *v* 1 *(infml)* get, catch, achieve, obtain, procure 2 earn, make, gain, make a profit of, profit ■ *adj* remaining, disposable, clear, after deductions, left *Opposite*: gross

nether *(fml)* *adj* rear, hind, hinder, back, after

netherworld *(fml)* *n* hell, inferno, purgatory, underworld, perdition

netting *n* mesh, net, web, fabric, meshwork

nettle *(infml)* *v* irritate, annoy, infuriate, bother, exasperate

network *n* net, system, grid, web, link

neurological *adj* nervous, nerve, neural

neurosis *n* quirk, complex, obsession, inhibition, idiosyncrasy

neurotic *adj* anxious, fearful, phobic, fixated, disturbed *Opposite*: rational

neuter *v* spay, sterilize, castrate, fix

neutral *adj* 1 unbiased, impartial, disinterested, dispassionate, middle-of-the-road *Opposite*: biased 2 drab, light-colored, indistinct, indeterminate, pale *Opposite*: colorful

neutrality *n* impartiality, detachment, objectivity, noninvolvement, disinterest *Opposite*: bias

neutralization *n* canceling out, nullification, off-setting, frustration, counteraction *Opposite*: activation

neutralize *v* counteract, counterbalance, defuse, deactivate, nullify

never *adv* 1 not ever, not once, on no occasion, at no time *Opposite*: always 2 certainly not, under no circumstances, by no means, in no way, not at all

never-ending *adj* endless, everlasting, continual, continuous, nonstop

nevertheless *adv* yet, but, however, nonetheless, on the other hand

new *adj* 1 novel, newfangled, original, innovative, fresh *Opposite*: old 2 recent, latest, up-to-the-minute, contemporary, up-to-date *Opposite*: outmoded 3 another, additional, extra, further, different 4 brand-new, pristine, newborn, in mint condition, newfound *Opposite*: used 5 inexperienced, new to the job, just starting out, wet behind the ears, green *Opposite*: experienced

COMPARE AND CONTRAST CORE MEANING: never experienced before or having recently come into being
new recently invented, discovered, made, bought, experienced, or not previously known or encountered; **fresh** excitingly or refreshingly different from what has been done or experienced previously; **modern** of the latest kind, or characterized by up-to-date ideas, techniques, design, or equipment; **newfangled** puzzlingly or worryingly new or different, especially because it seems gimmicky or overcomplicated; **novel** new and different, often in an interesting, unusual, or inventive way; **original** unique and not copied or derived from anything else.

newborn *adj* **1 new**, brand-new, neonatal **2 newfound**, new, brand-new, fresh, recent *Opposite*: established ■ *n* **baby**, infant, child, neonate, babe (*literary*)

newcomer *n* **1 new arrival**, stranger, Johnny-come-lately (*infml*) **2 novice**, recruit, beginner, neophyte, trainee *Opposite*: old hand

newfangled *adj* **novel**, new, innovative, up-to-date, up-to-the-minute *Opposite*: old-fashioned. *See* COMPARE AND CONTRAST *at* **new**.

newly *adv* **1 recently**, lately, freshly, just now, just this minute **2 afresh**, anew, again, once more

newlyweds *n* **just marrieds**, wedding couple, happy couple, bride and groom

newness *n* **novelty**, innovation, originality, freshness, inventiveness

news *n* **1 information**, reports, intelligence, gossip, rumor **2 news bulletin**, news broadcast, newscast, news summary, news flash

newscast *n* **news**, news bulletin, news broadcast, news summary, news flash

newscaster *n* **broadcaster**, telecaster, anchor, announcer

newshawk (*infml*) *n* **reporter**, journalist, investigative reporter, correspondent, newsgatherer

newshound *see* **newshawk**

newsletter *n* **information sheet**, bulletin, circular

newspaper *n* **1 paper**, broadsheet, daily, weekly, broadside **2 newsprint**, printing paper, coarse paper

newsprint *n* **newspaper**, printing paper, coarse paper

newsreel *n* **news film**, documentary, news movie, news report, news bulletin

newsroom *n* **news studio**, broadcasting studio, TV studio

newsstand *n* **kiosk**, stand, stall, booth

newsworthy *adj* **interesting**, exciting, remarkable, out of the ordinary, extraordinary *Opposite*: unremarkable

newsy *adj* **chatty**, gossipy, friendly, interesting, informative

next *adv* **after that**, then, afterward, after, thereafter *Opposite*: first

next-door *adj* **adjacent**, adjoining, neighboring, flanking, next

next of kin *n* **close relative**, blood relation, blood relative, spouse, partner

nexus *n* **connection**, link, tie, relationship, node

nib *n* **tip**, point, end

nibble *v* **chew**, nip, peck, gnaw, bite *Opposite*: chomp (*infml*) ■ *n* **bite**, morsel, tidbit, crumb, speck

nice *adj* **1 enjoyable**, agreeable, pleasant, good, lovely *Opposite*: unpleasant **2 polite**, considerate, friendly, courteous, charming *Opposite*: nasty **3 respectable**, proper, refined, virtuous, genteel *Opposite*: improper **4 attractive**, lovely, pleasant, delightful, appealing *Opposite*: unattractive **5 precise**, exact, fine-drawn, meticulous, narrow *Opposite*: broad **6 discriminating**, painstaking, particular, scrupulous, precise

nice-looking *adj* **good-looking**, pretty, attractive, handsome, appealing *Opposite*: unattractive

nicely *adv* **1 agreeably**, kindly, well, politely, courteously *Opposite*: unpleasantly **2 suitably**, effectively, satisfactorily, accurately, carefully *Opposite*: unsatisfactorily **3 carefully**, meticulously, finely, subtly, narrowly *Opposite*: broadly

nicety *n* **1 distinction**, precision, detail, small point, refinement **2 delicacy**, tactfulness, particularity, finesse, polish

niche *n* **1 place**, position, slot, function, role **2 alcove**, bay, nook, cubbyhole, recess

nick *n* **incision**, groove, mark, notch, cut ■ *v* **score**, incise, mark, cut, scratch

nicknack *see* **knickknack**

nickname *n* **name**, pet name, epithet, sobriquet, diminutive ■ *v* **label**, call, name, designate, dub

nifty *adj* **1 smart**, attractive, well-designed, neat, natty *Opposite*: unattractive **2 good**, quick, clever, neat, slick *Opposite*: clumsy **3 useful**, handy, convenient, effective, ingenious *Opposite*: useless

niggardly *adj* **1 ungenerous**, stingy, mean, miserly, tight *Opposite*: generous **2 miserable**, meager, wretched, insufficient, paltry

niggle *v* **1 criticize**, cavil, carp, nag, nitpick **2 trouble**, bother, nag, annoy, irritate ■ *n* **1 complaint**, grumble, objection, grievance, criticism **2 doubt**, anxiety, twinge, misgiving, concern

niggling *adj* **1 trivial**, petty, unimportant, inconsequential, insignificant *Opposite*: important **2 irritating**, awkward, finicky, troublesome, difficult

nigh *adj* **imminent**, close, near, at hand, approaching *Opposite*: remote

night *n* **1 nighttime**, hours of darkness, dark, darkness, nightfall *Opposite*: day **2 early**

hours, small hours, middle of the night

nightcap n **1 drink**, bedtime drink, hot drink, hot toddy **2 sleeping cap**, hat, cap

nightclothes n **pajamas**, sleepwear, nightwear

nightdress see **nightgown**

nightfall n **dusk**, twilight, evening, sunset, end of the day Opposite: daybreak

nightgown n **negligee**, nightshirt, nightie (infml)

nightlife n **nightspots**, social life, entertainment, club scene, discos

nightly adj **night**, evening, nocturnal ■ adv **every night**, night by night, once a night, through the night

nightmare n **dream**, bad dream, hallucination, vision, incubus ■ adj **traumatic**, frightening, dreadful, terrible, horrendous Opposite: wonderful

nightmarish adj **nightmare**, frightening, terrifying, horrendous, terrible Opposite: lovely

nightspot n **bar**, nightclub, disco, club

nighttime n **night**, evening, dark, hours of darkness, middle of the night Opposite: daytime

nightwear n **sleepwear**, nightclothes, pajamas

nihilism n **negativism**, pessimism, nothingness, emptiness, anarchism

nihilist n **pessimist**, existentialist, anarchist, revolutionary, radical

nihilistic adj **negativistic**, pessimistic, existentialist, destructive, anarchic

nil n **nothing**, zero, none, naught, null

nimble adj **sprightly**, lithe, deft, agile, quick Opposite: awkward

nimbleness n **sprightliness**, litheness, agility, quickness, dexterity Opposite: awkwardness

nimbus n **circle of light**, halo, corona, aura, radiance

nip v **1 squeeze**, compress, grasp, grab, grip **2 peck**, nibble, snap, gnaw, bite **3 steal**, snatch, pilfer, make off with, make away with ■ n **1 pinch**, tweak, grasp, grab, squeeze **2 peck**, bite, nibble, snippet, clipping **3 sip**, drink, swallow, tot, swig (infml)

nip in the bud (infml) v **stop**, prevent, hinder, block, thwart Opposite: encourage

nipper n **pincer**, claw, gripper, appendage

nippy adj **cold**, chilly, freezing, biting, icy Opposite: warm

nirvana n **1 enlightenment**, spiritual enlightenment, state of grace **2 bliss**, heaven, joy, paradise, pleasure Opposite: hell

nitpick v **cavil**, complain, quibble, find fault, criticize. See COMPARE AND CONTRAST at **criticize**.

nitpicker n **faultfinder**, critic, carper, nagger, pedant

nitpicking n **criticism**, faultfinding, carping, hairsplitting, quibbling ■ adj **critical**, faultfinding, carping, finicky, fussy

nitty-gritty (infml) n **essentials**, brass tacks, fundamentals, basics, crux of the matter

no adv **on no account**, not at all, certainly not, definitely not, by no means ■ n **rejection**, negative, denial, rebuff, refusal ■ adj **not any**, not one, not at all

nobility n **1 aristocracy**, upper class, landed gentry, upper crust (infml) Opposite: hoi polloi **2 dignity**, graciousness, decency, goodness, nobleness Opposite: baseness

noble adj **1 honorable**, principled, moral, decent, upright Opposite: unprincipled **2 magnificent**, impressive, imposing, fine, splendid Opposite: unimpressive **3 aristocratic**, patrician, blue-blooded, titled, upper-class ■ n **aristocrat**, nobleman, noblewoman, peer, patrician Opposite: commoner

nobleness n **honorableness**, honor, morality, magnanimity, dignity

nobody pron **not one person**, not a single person, no one, not a soul Opposite: everybody ■ n **nonentity**, mediocrity, unknown, upstart, nothing Opposite: somebody

nocturnal adj **nighttime**, night, nightly Opposite: diurnal

nod v **move**, bow, bob, jiggle, dip ■ n **permission**, affirmation, signal, sign, gesture

noddle (dated infml) n **head**, nut (infml), noggin (dated infml), noodle (slang)

node n **1 bulge**, protuberance, lump, swelling, bump **2 meeting point**, join, connection, intersection, point

nod off v **doze off**, fall asleep, drift off, doze, catnap Opposite: wake up

no doubt adv **undoubtedly**, surely, certainly, without a doubt, for sure (infml)

nod to v **acknowledge**, greet, signal to, salute

nodule n **lump**, knot, knob, lump, bump

no end (infml) pron **a lot**, a great deal, very much, enormously, greatly

no-frills (infml) adj **basic**, utilitarian, unadorned, economy, generic Opposite: luxury

noggin (dated infml) n **head**, nut (infml), noddle (dated infml), noodle (slang)

noise n **sound**, din, racket, clamor, clatter Opposite: silence

noiseless adj **soundless**, silent, muted, hushed, quiet Opposite: noisy

noisome adj **foul**, offensive, disgusting, repulsive, repellent Opposite: pleasant

noisy adj **loud**, deafening, earsplitting, piercing, raucous Opposite: quiet

nomad n **wanderer**, traveler, itinerant, migrant, drifter

nomadic adj **itinerant**, traveling, roaming, wandering, roving

no matter what adv **come what may**, anyhow, regardless, by hook or by crook, anyway

nom de plume n **pen name**, pseudonym,

alias, assumed name, nom de guerre

nomenclature n 1 **classification**, taxonomy, codification, categorization, organization 2 **terminology**, vocabulary, language, terms, jargon

nominal adj 1 **supposed**, ostensible, so-called, in name only, titular Opposite: actual 2 **small**, trifling, token, minimal, insignificant Opposite: great

nominate v 1 **propose**, put forward, suggest, name, submit Opposite: reject 2 **appoint**, elect, designate, choose, select Opposite: reject

nomination n 1 **proposal**, suggestion, recommendation, submission 2 **choice**, selection, appointment, nominee, candidate

nominee n **candidate**, entrant, applicant, nomination, contender

nonaggression n **pacifism**, peaceful coexistence, nonviolence, inaction Opposite: aggression

nonalcoholic adj **soft**, lite, low-alcohol, virgin Opposite: alcoholic

nonaligned adj **neutral**, independent, unallied, unconnected, unrelated Opposite: aligned

nonalignment n **neutrality**, independence, autonomy, self-determination, impartiality Opposite: alignment

nonattendance n 1 **truancy**, skipping class, playing truant, playing hooky, cutting class Opposite: attendance 2 **absence**, default, absenteeism, nonappearance Opposite: presence

nonbeliever n **disbeliever**, unbeliever, doubter, skeptic, agnostic Opposite: believer

nonchalance n **indifference**, detachment, disinterest, calmness, dispassion Opposite: interest

nonchalant adj **casual**, offhand, cool, calm, relaxed Opposite: concerned

noncombatant n **civilian**, citizen, conscientious objector Opposite: soldier

noncommittal adj **guarded**, evasive, vague, wary, tactful Opposite: definite

noncompliance n **nonfulfillment**, nonconformity, refusal, failure, denial Opposite: compliance

noncompliant adj **disobedient**, recalcitrant, rebellious, uncooperative, dissenting Opposite: cooperative

nonconformist adj **unconventional**, eccentric, alternative, rebellious, radical Opposite: conformist ■ n **rebel**, dissenter, maverick, radical, eccentric Opposite: conformist

nonconformity n 1 **unconventionality**, originality, eccentricity, idiosyncrasy, individuality Opposite: conformity 2 **noncooperation**, noncompliance, divergence, variation, difference Opposite: conformity

noncooperation n **defiance**, disobedience, insubordination, rebellion, rebelliousness Opposite: cooperation

nondescript adj **unremarkable**, ordinary, unexceptional, dull, uninteresting Opposite: special

nondiscriminatory adj **fair**, equal, unbiased, evenhanded, just Opposite: discriminatory

none pron 1 **no one**, nobody, not a soul, not a single person Opposite: everyone 2 **not any**, nothing, not a bit, not an iota, not a hint Opposite: some

nonentity n **nobody**, unknown, mediocrity, nothing Opposite: somebody

nonessential adj **luxury**, extra, supplementary, additional, dispensable Opposite: essential ■ n **extra**, luxury, perk Opposite: essential

nonetheless adv **however**, nevertheless, even so, on the other hand

nonevent n **failure**, anticlimax, disappointment, letdown, flop Opposite: success

nonexistence n 1 **absence**, lack, want, dearth, deficiency 2 **nothingness**, unreality, fictionality Opposite: existence

nonexistent adj **missing**, unreal, fictional, imaginary, absent Opposite: existent (fml)

nonfiction adj **factual**, true-life, reference, fact-based Opposite: fiction

nonflammable adj **noninflammable**, fireproof, flameproof, fire-retardant, fire-resistant Opposite: inflammable

nonintervention n **inaction**, noninvolvement, noninterventionism, laissez-faire, abstention Opposite: intervention

noninterventionist adj **laissez-faire**, noninterfering, nonaligned, nonpartisan, neutral

nonjudgmental adj **indulgent**, lax, easygoing, relaxed, lenient Opposite: judgmental

nonmember n **outsider**, visitor, guest Opposite: member

nonnegotiable adj 1 **firm**, immutable, unchanging, inflexible, fixed Opposite: negotiable 2 **nontransferable**, unmarketable, nonsalable, nonexchangeable, nonconvertible

no-no (infml) n **taboo**, forbidden thing, breaking of convention, social restriction

no-nonsense adj **straightforward**, plain, practical, down-to-earth, plain-speaking

nonpareil adj **unparalleled**, peerless, best, unequalled, unique Opposite: common

nonpartisan adj **unbiased**, impartial, unprejudiced, independent, neutral Opposite: partisan

nonpayment n **defaulting**, evasion, default, avoidance Opposite: payment

nonperformance n **delinquency**, default, arrears

nonplus v unnerve, befuddle, stump, bewilder, mystify

nonplussed adj **confused**, baffled, bewildered, puzzled, stumped

nonprofessional adj **amateur**, blue-collar, manual, lay Opposite: professional

nonprofit adj **not-for-profit**, public, state, charitable Opposite: profitmaking

nonproliferation n **limitation**, reduction, control, prevention Opposite: proliferation

nonresident adj **transient**, visiting, commuting, vacationing Opposite: resident ■ n **visitor**, transient, guest, vacationer, tourist Opposite: resident

nonsense n **rubbish**, drivel, gibberish, noise, babble Opposite: sense

nonsensical adj **ridiculous**, stupid, senseless, absurd, illogical Opposite: sensible

nonspecific adj **generic**, general, broad, broad-based, broad-spectrum Opposite: specific

nonstandard adj **unusual**, out of the ordinary, atypical, special, modified Opposite: standard

nonstarter (infml) n **hopeless case**, loser, failure, dud (infml) Opposite: winner

nonstick adj **coated**, protected, surfaced, covered

nonstop adj **continuous**, never-ending, uninterrupted, around-the-clock, constant Opposite: intermittent

nontoxic adj **harmless**, safe, nonhazardous, innocuous, risk-free Opposite: toxic

nonviolence n **pacifism**, passivity, nonaggression, civil disobedience Opposite: aggression

nonviolent adj **peaceful**, nonaggressive, pacific, peaceable, passive Opposite: violent

nook n **corner**, alcove, cranny, niche, recess

noon n **midday**, twelve noon, noontime, noonday (literary)

noonday (literary) see **noon**

no one pron **not one person**, not a single person, nobody, not a soul Opposite: everyone

noose n 1 **loop**, lasso, lariat, halter, rope 2 **snare**, trap, booby trap, trick, con

norm n **standard**, average, custom, rule, model Opposite: exception

normal adj **usual**, standard, ordinary, typical, customary Opposite: abnormal

normalcy see **normality**

normality n **routine**, regularity, status quo, normalcy

normalization n **regularization**, standardization, stabilization, regulation, control Opposite: deviation

normalize v **regularize**, standardize, regulate, put on a normal footing, control Opposite: destabilize

normally adv 1 **usually**, in general, as a rule, on the whole, by and large Opposite: rarely 2 **as normal**, as usual, naturally, unexceptionally, conventionally Opposite: abnormally

nose n **snout**, muzzle, beak, proboscis, hooter (slang) ■ v (infml) **poke around**, watch, sneak, pry, snoop (infml)

nosebleed n **bloody nose**, blood, hemorrhage, blood loss

nosedive n 1 **drop**, fall, dive, plunge, tumble Opposite: ascent 2 **decrease**, fall, deterioration, drop, crash Opposite: increase

nose-dive v 1 **plummet**, drop, plunge, dive, tumble Opposite: ascend 2 **decrease**, deteriorate, plummet, drop, slump Opposite: rocket

nosegay n **posy**, spray, bouquet, bunch, sprig

nosh (infml) n **snack**, food, rations, goodies, grub (infml) ■ v **eat**, munch, champ, eat up, consume

no-show n **absentee**, nonattender, dropout

nostalgia n **homesickness**, reminiscence, wistfulness, longing, melancholy

nostalgic adj **sentimental**, wistful, misty, longing, yearning Opposite: expectant

nostrum n **remedy**, plan, scheme, big idea, solution

nosy (infml) adj **inquisitive**, curious, interfering, prying, meddlesome

notability n 1 **famous person**, celebrity, dignitary, VIP, notable Opposite: nobody 2 **significance**, importance, relevance, import, weight

notable adj **noteworthy**, distinguished, outstanding, prominent, extraordinary Opposite: insignificant ■ n **celebrity**, dignity, VIP, personality, somebody Opposite: nobody

notarize v **authenticate**, certify, endorse, validate, rubber stamp

notary n **lawyer**, attorney, legal official, legal clerk

notation n 1 **representation**, symbolization, system, code, cipher 2 **note**, footnote, jotting, memo, annotation

not bad adj **reasonable**, average, fair, acceptable, passable Opposite: unacceptable

notch n 1 **nick**, indentation, cut, mark, slash 2 **level**, degree, step, stage, rung

not counting prep **apart from**, excluding, aside from, besides, except

note n 1 **letter**, memo, memorandum, message, communication 2 **footnote**, annotation, gloss, comment, addendum 3 **tone**, edge, tinge, shade, hint ■ v 1 **notice**, take note of, take notice of, take in, observe Opposite: disregard 2 **mention**, observe, state, say, remark 3 **make a note of**, note down, write down, record, jot down

noted adj **renowned**, well-known, famous, distinguished, celebrated

notepad *n* **writing pad**, pad of paper, memo pad, scratchpad, pad

notepaper *n* **writing paper**, writing pad, stationery, headed paper, letterhead

noteworthy *adj* **of note**, notable, striking, remarkable, important *Opposite*: insignificant

nothing *pron* **naught**, nil, zero, zilch *(infml)* ■ *n* **nonentity**, nobody, unknown

nothingness *n* **oblivion**, nothing, emptiness, void, vacuum

notice *n* **1 sign**, poster, announcement, advertisement, bill **2 warning**, notification, announcement, communication ■ *v* **become aware of**, see, take in, observe, perceive *Opposite*: close your eyes to

noticeable *adj* **obvious**, clear, visible, perceptible, conspicuous *Opposite*: inconspicuous

notification *n* **announcement**, notice, warning, statement, report

notify *v* **inform**, alert, advise, warn, report

notion *n* **1 idea**, view, concept, belief, conception **2 impulse**, urge, whim, fancy, instinct

notional *adj* **1 theoretical**, estimated, speculative, academic, hypothetical **2 imaginary**, unreal, fancied, fanciful, whimsical *Opposite*: real

not mince words *v* **be direct**, speak plainly, call a spade a spade, be blunt, speak your mind *Opposite*: prevaricate

notoriety *n* **disrepute**, infamy, dishonor, bad reputation, bad name

notorious *adj* **1 infamous**, disreputable, dishonorable, tarnished *Opposite*: reputable **2** *(archaic)* **famous**, renowned, eminent, familiar, recognized *Opposite*: unknown

notoriously *adv* **particularly**, especially, extremely, very

not quite *adv* **almost**, virtually, as good as, roughly, nearly

notwithstanding *(fml) prep* **despite**, in spite of, aside from, excluding, setting aside ■ *adv* **nevertheless**, all the same, nonetheless, anyhow

nourish *v* **1 nurture**, give food to, sustain, suckle, feed **2 encourage**, promote, cultivate, support, foster

nourishing *adj* **nutritious**, wholesome, beneficial, healthful *Opposite*: unhealthy

nourishment *n* **food**, sustenance, diet, nutrition

nous *n* **intellect**, ability, intelligence, rationality, reason

novel *n* **book**, narrative, work of fiction, tale, story ■ *adj* **original**, new, fresh, different, innovative *Opposite*: well-worn. *See* COMPARE AND CONTRAST *at new*.

novelette *see* **novella**

novelist *n* **writer**, author, story writer

novella *n* **short story**, short novel, novelette, tale, fable

novelty *n* **innovation**, originality, newness, freshness, uniqueness

novice *n* **beginner**, learner, trainee, apprentice, greenhorn *Opposite*: old hand. *See* COMPARE AND CONTRAST *at beginner*.

now *adv* **1 at the present**, at the moment, at this time, currently, presently *Opposite*: then **2 immediately**, right away, straightaway, at once, instantly *Opposite*: later

nowadays *adv* **these days**, today, now, at the present time, at the moment *Opposite*: formerly

now and then *adv* **from time to time**, sometimes, at times, now and again, occasionally *Opposite*: regularly

noxious *adj* **1 harmful**, toxic, poisonous, deadly, lethal *Opposite*: harmless **2 nasty**, unpleasant, offensive, foul, horrible *Opposite*: pleasant

nozzle *n* **spout**, jet, control valve, spigot, outlet

nuance *n* **tone**, gradation, distinction, tinge, hint

nub *n* **crux**, crucial point, essence, core, heart

nuclear *adj* **atomic**, nuclear-powered, fissile, fissionable

nucleus *n* **center**, basis, core, heart, nub

nude *adj* **unclothed**, in the nude, undressed, in a state of undress, stripped *Opposite*: clothed. *See* COMPARE AND CONTRAST *at naked*.

nudge *v* **push**, bump, elbow, shove, jolt ■ *n* **prod**, push, shove, bump, jolt

nudity *n* **bareness**, nakedness, undress, dishabille

nugatory *adj* **trifling**, petty, insignificant, trivial, unimportant *Opposite*: significant

nugget *n* **piece**, bit, chunk, lump, hunk

nuisance *n* **irritation**, annoyance, bother, trouble, irritant *Opposite*: boon

null *adj* **1 invalid**, null and void, void, unacceptable, unsound *Opposite*: valid **2 worthless**, valueless, unimportant, insignificant, useless *Opposite*: useful

null and void *adj* **invalid**, void, null, unacceptable, flawed *Opposite*: valid

nullify *v* **invalidate**, annul, cancel out, abolish, negate *(fml) Opposite*: validate

---

COMPARE AND CONTRAST CORE MEANING: put an end to the effective existence of something **nullify** make something legally invalid or ineffective, or cancel something out; **abrogate** *(fml)* end an agreement or contract formally and publicly; **annul** declare something officially or legally invalid or ineffective; **repeal** end a law officially **invalidate** deprive something of its legal force or value, e.g., by failing to comply with certain terms and conditions; **negate** *(fml)* render something ineffective, e.g., by doing something that counterbalances its force or effectiveness.

---

numb *adj* **1 frozen**, anesthetized, dead, deadened, unfeeling **2 emotionless**, shocked, dazed, traumatized, disoriented *Opposite*: animated ■ *v* **deaden**, freeze, anesthetize, stun, dull

number *n* 1 **figure**, numeral, digit, integer 2 **amount**, quantity, sum ■ *v* **come to**, add up to, total, amount to, run to

numberless *adj* **countless**, innumerable, numerous, endless, myriad *Opposite*: few

number one *adj* 1 **first**, top, leading, best, most important 2 *(infml)* **excellent**, high quality, first-rate, top, top quality ■ *n* 1 *(infml)* **important person**, key player, linchpin, leader, prime candidate 2 *(infml)* **chief executive officer**, chief executive, boss, chief, head honcho

numbing *adj* 1 **deadening**, freezing, anesthetizing 2 **shocking**, distressing, dazing, upsetting, disorienting

numbness *n* 1 **deadness**, unresponsiveness, lack of sensation *Opposite*: sensation 2 **emotionlessness**, impassiveness, coldness, detachment, shock

numeracy *n* **mathematical ability**, numerical competence, skill, proficiency, expertise

numeral *n* **number**, figure, digit, cipher

numerate *adj* **mathematically competent**, good with numbers, proficient, accomplished, competent

numerical *adj* **mathematical**, arithmetic, arithmetical, statistical

numerous *adj* **many**, frequent, plentiful, abundant, several *Opposite*: few

numinous *(fml) adj* **mystic**, magical, magic, supernatural, transcendent

nunnery *n* **convent**, monastery, abbey, religious foundation, religious community

nuptial *adj* **marriage**, wedding, bridal, matrimonial, marital

nuptials *(fml) n* **wedding**, marriage, happy day

nurse *v* 1 **care for**, look after, tend, foster, nurture *Opposite*: neglect 2 **harbor**, cherish, nurture, have, foster

nursery *n* 1 **nursery school**, day nursery, playgroup, kindergarten 2 **plant sales outlet**, garden center, plant market

nurture *v* 1 **care for**, take care of, raise, rear, foster 2 **cultivate**, cherish, develop, support, encourage

nut *(infml) n* 1 **skull**, cranium, dome, crown, bean *(slang)* 2 **enthusiast**, fan, aficionado, aficionada, buff

WORD BANK
❏ **types of nuts** acorn, almond, brazil nut, cashew, chestnut, cob, cobnut, coconut, cola nut, hazelnut, hickory nut, horse chestnut, macadamia nut, peanut, pecan, pine nut, pistachio, walnut

nutrition *n* **nourishment**, diet, food, sustenance

nutritional *adj* **nutritious**, nourishing, nutritive, dietary, alimentary

nutritious *adj* **nourishing**, healthy, wholesome, healthful, beneficial *Opposite*: unhealthy

nutritive *adj* 1 **nutritional**, dietary, dietetic, alimentary, food 2 **nutritious**, nourishing, healthy, wholesome, healthful *Opposite*: unhealthy

nuts and bolts *(infml) n* **basics**, brass tacks, practicalities, fundamentals, details

nutshell *n* **husk**, casing, shell

nuzzle *v* **nestle**, cuddle, burrow, snuggle, push

nymph *n* **fairy**, sprite, spirit, dryad, elf

O

oaf *n* **buffoon**, bumbler, lummox *(infml)*, klutz *(slang)*

oar *n* **paddle**, scull, sweep, blade

oasis *n* **retreat**, refuge, haven, sanctuary, escape

oath *n* 1 **promise**, pledge, vow, word, assurance 2 **curse**, swearword, expletive, four-letter word, cussword *(infml)*

obduracy *n* **obstinacy**, stubbornness, inflexibility, mulishness, pigheadedness *Opposite*: compliance

obdurate *adj* 1 **obstinate**, stubborn, inflexible, unyielding, unbending *Opposite*: compliant 2 **hardhearted**, callous, unfeeling, heartless, pitiless *Opposite*: warmhearted

obedience *n* **compliance**, agreement, submission, respect, duty *Opposite*: disobedience

obedient *adj* **compliant**, dutiful, submissive, respectful, biddable *Opposite*: disobedient

obeisance *n* 1 *(fml)* **bow**, curtsy, bob, nod, genuflection 2 **homage**, respect, deference, duty, loyalty

obelisk *n* **pillar**, column, pylon, needle, tower

obese *adj* **fat**, overweight, heavy, stout, plump *Opposite*: underweight

obesity *n* **plumpness**, fatness, stoutness, portliness, corpulence *Opposite*: thinness

obey *v* **do as you are told**, submit, follow, comply with, act upon *Opposite*: disobey

obfuscate v obscure, complicate, confuse, muddy, cloud Opposite: clarify

obfuscation n **complication**, mystification, confusion, muddying, clouding Opposite: clarification

obituary n **tribute**, article, announcement, eulogy, epitaph ∎ adj **funerary**, funereal, memorial, epitaphic, death

object n 1 **thing**, article, item, entity, body 2 **purpose**, objective, aim, point, idea ∎ v **oppose**, protest, challenge, expostulate, demur Opposite: approve

COMPARE AND CONTRAST CORE MEANING: indicate opposition to something

object be opposed or averse to something, or express opposition to it; **protest** express strong disapproval of or disagreement with something, or refuse to obey or accept something, often by making a formal statement or taking action in public; **demur** raise objections in a hesitant or tentative way; **remonstrate** reason or argue forcefully with somebody about something; **expostulate** express disagreement or disapproval vehemently, or attempt to dissuade somebody from doing something.

objectify v 1 **actualize**, realize, represent, portray, reify 2 **diminish**, reduce, simplify, trivialize

objection n 1 **opposition**, protest, protestation, hostility, demurral Opposite: approval 2 **doubt**, concern, problem, worry, difficulty Opposite: confidence

objectionable adj **offensive**, obnoxious, horrible, unpleasant, intolerable Opposite: inoffensive

objective adj 1 **impartial**, detached, neutral, unbiased, unprejudiced Opposite: subjective 2 **factual**, actual, tangible, factbased, demonstrable Opposite: subjective ∎ n **object**, purpose, aim, point, idea

objectivity n **impartiality**, detachment, independence, neutrality, fairness Opposite: subjectivity

objet d'art n **work of art**, masterpiece, creation, piece, ornament

obligate v **compel**, oblige, force, make, require Opposite: request

obligation n 1 **duty**, responsibility, requirement, compulsion, commitment Opposite: option 2 **debt**, contract, commitment, promise, agreement

obligatory adj 1 **compulsory**, required, necessary, essential, de rigueur (fml) Opposite: optional 2 **required**, statutory, mandatory, binding, the law Opposite: discretionary

oblige v 1 **compel**, obligate, force, make, require Opposite: request 2 **gratify**, please, indulge, accommodate, help Opposite: disappoint

obliged adj **grateful**, thankful, appreciative, gratified, indebted

obliging adj **helpful**, kind, considerate,

willing, agreeable Opposite: unhelpful

oblique adj 1 **slanting**, slanted, tilted, sloping, leaning Opposite: upright 2 **indirect**, implicit, implied, roundabout, circuitous Opposite: direct

obliqueness n 1 **tilt**, inclination, slant, steepness, lean 2 **indirectness**, circuitousness, circumlocution, obscureness, opaqueness Opposite: directness

obliterate v **destroy**, demolish, eliminate, eradicate, annihilate Opposite: create

obliteration n **destruction**, annihilation, eradication, elimination, abolition Opposite: creation

oblivion n 1 **forgetfulness**, unconsciousness, stupor, insensibility, obliviousness Opposite: awareness 2 **obscurity**, extinction, the past, the annals of history, nothingness Opposite: existence

oblivious adj **unaware**, unconscious, unmindful, ignorant, insensible Opposite: conscious

obloquy (fml or literary) n 1 **censure**, criticism, defamation, blame, opprobrium Opposite: praise 2 **disgrace**, shame, infamy, ignominy, disfavor

obnoxious adj **loathsome**, hateful, horrible, insufferable, intolerable Opposite: delightful

obscene adj 1 **indecent**, lewd, explicit, offensive, crude Opposite: decent 2 **disgusting**, nauseating, sickening, offensive, rude Opposite: decent 3 **tasteless**, foulmouthed, crude, loutish, boorish

obscenity n 1 **offensiveness**, atrocity, tastelessness, vulgarity, rudeness Opposite: tastefulness 2 **indecency**, lewdness, offensiveness, explicitness, crudeness Opposite: decency 3 **curse**, swearword, four-letter word, expletive, cuss word (infml)

obscurantism n **conservatism**, traditionalism, dogmatism, reaction, illiberalism Opposite: liberalism

obscurantist adj **reactionary**, conservative, backward-looking, traditionalist, old-fashioned Opposite: liberal ∎ n **conservative**, reactionary, traditionalist, diehard, dogmatist Opposite: liberal

obscure adj 1 **incomprehensible**, unclear, vague, ambiguous, abstruse Opposite: clear 2 **indistinct**, faint, shadowy, murky, blurry Opposite: clear 3 **unknown**, little-known, minor, unseen, unheard of Opposite: famous ∎ v 1 **confuse**, disguise, conceal, complicate, obfuscate Opposite: clarify 2 **darken**, cloak, mask, hide, shroud Opposite: disclose

COMPARE AND CONTRAST CORE MEANING: difficult to understand

obscure difficult to understand because it is expressed in a complicated way or because it involves areas of knowledge or study that are not known to most people; **abstruse** not easy to understand, often because it involves specialist knowledge or is expressed in specialist language; **recondite** requiring a high degree of scholarship or specialist knowledge to be understood; **arcane** requiring information that is secret or known only to a few people in order to be understood; **cryptic** deliberately mysterious or ambiguous and seeming to have a hidden meaning; **enigmatic** having a quality of mystery and ambiguity that makes it difficult to understand or interpret.

obscurity *n* 1 **anonymity**, insignificance, unimportance, inconspicuousness, oblivion *Opposite*: fame 2 **incomprehensibility**, vagueness, ambiguousness, doubt, opacity *Opposite*: clarity

obsequious *adj* **servile**, sycophantic, flattering, toadying, submissive *Opposite*: assertive

obsequiousness *n* **sycophancy**, servility, flattery, submissiveness, compliance *Opposite*: assertiveness

observable *adj* **noticeable**, visible, apparent, evident, obvious *Opposite*: imperceptible

observance *n* 1 **adherence**, compliance, execution, performance, observation *Opposite*: violation 2 **ritual**, ceremony, ceremonial, rite, celebration

observant *adj* **sharp-eyed**, alert, attentive, watchful, vigilant *Opposite*: unobservant

observation *n* 1 **surveillance**, scrutiny, watching, inspection, examination *Opposite*: neglect 2 **remark**, comment, opinion, thought, reflection

observatory *n* **building**, station, laboratory, telescope, observe

observe *v* 1 **detect**, perceive, witness, see, spot *Opposite*: miss 2 **watch**, view, scrutinize, monitor, study *Opposite*: ignore 3 **remark**, comment, say, declare, state 4 **abide by**, respect, follow, comply with, heed *Opposite*: violate 5 **celebrate**, keep, remember, take part in, perform *Opposite*: break

observer *n* **spectator**, witness, viewer, onlooker, bystander *Opposite*: participant

obsess *v* **preoccupy**, grip, consume, fixate, possess *Opposite*: bore

obsessed *adj* **fanatical**, gripped, preoccupied, infatuated, fixated *Opposite*: indifferent

obsession *n* **mania**, fascination, fixation, passion, preoccupation *Opposite*: indifference

obsessive *adj* **compulsive**, fanatical, fixated, infatuated, neurotic *Opposite*: easygoing

obsolescence *n* **unfashionableness**, oldness, undesirability, uselessness *Opposite*: modernity

obsolescent *see* **obsolete**

obsolete *adj* **archaic**, outmoded, antiquated, passé, unfashionable *Opposite*: up-to-date

obstacle *n* 1 **problem**, difficulty, hindrance, impediment, complication *Opposite*: help 2 **obstruction**, barrier, blockage, blockade, impediment *Opposite*: passage

obstinacy *n* **stubbornness**, determination, pigheadedness, inflexibility, unreasonableness *Opposite*: compliance

obstinate *adj* **stubborn**, determined, pigheaded, fixed, inflexible *Opposite*: compliant

obstreperous *adj* **disruptive**, rowdy, disorderly, loud, noisy *Opposite*: demure. *See* COMPARE AND CONTRAST *at* **unruly**.

obstruct *v* 1 **block**, barricade, impede, hold up, stop *Opposite*: clear 2 **hinder**, thwart, frustrate, hamper, complicate *Opposite*: assist. *See* COMPARE AND CONTRAST *at* **hinder**.

obstruction *n* **obstacle**, barrier, block, blockade, barricade *Opposite*: help

obstructionism *n* **timewasting**, stalling, filibustering, sabotage, hindrance *Opposite*: helpfulness

obstructionist *adj* **stalling**, timewasting, filibustering, delaying, delay ■ *n* **staller**, timewaster, filibusterer, wrecker, saboteur

obstructive *adj* **disruptive**, uncooperative, unhelpful, obstreperous, awkward *Opposite*: helpful

obtain *v* **get**, get hold of, acquire, procure, attain *Opposite*: lose. *See* COMPARE AND CONTRAST *at* **get**.

obtainable *adj* **available**, accessible, reachable, attainable, at hand *Opposite*: unavailable

obtrude *v* 1 **interfere**, impose, meddle, pry, interrupt 2 **extend**, thrust, stick out, push out

obtrusive *adj* 1 **conspicuous**, unmistakable, blatant, prominent, garish *Opposite*: inconspicuous 2 **interfering**, intruding, meddlesome, forward, presumptuous

obtuse *adj* **insensitive**, dull-witted, simpleminded, imperceptive, stupid *Opposite*: astute

obverse *n* 1 **front**, head, heads, side, face 2 **counterpart**, complement, opposite, equivalent, opposite number ■ *adj* 1 **front**, forward-facing, opposite, visible, anterior *Opposite*: reverse 2 **equivalent**, complementary, opposite, other, opposing

obviate *v* **do away with**, avoid, remove, forestall, prevent

obvious *adj* **clear**, understandable, palpable, noticeable, apparent *Opposite*: obscure

obviousness *n* **clearness**, certainty, overtness, unmistakability, conspicuousness *Opposite*: obscurity

occasion *n* 1 **time**, juncture, case, instance, event 2 **possibility**, opportunity, opening, season, contingency 3 **reason**, cause, motive, justification, rationale ■ *v* **cause**, motivate, give rise to, bring about, induce

occasional *adj* **infrequent**, irregular, chance,

sporadic, rare *Opposite*: regular. *See* COMPARE AND CONTRAST *at* **periodic**.

occlude *v* 1 block, stop up, close off, seal, shut off *Opposite*: free 2 **cut off**, cut out, close, block off, shut *Opposite*: open

occlusion *n* 1 blocking, obstruction, closing off, sealing, shutting off 2 **cutting off**, cutting out, closure, blocking, sealing

occupancy *n* tenancy, tenure, habitation, possession, residence *Opposite*: vacancy

occupant *n* inhabitant, tenant, lodger, resident, occupier

occupation *n* 1 job, profession, work, career, livelihood 2 **activity**, pursuit, enterprise, task

occupational *adj* work-related, job-related, professional, industrial, working

occupied *adj* 1 busy, engaged, employed, unavailable, working *Opposite*: free 2 **in use**, full, engaged, tied down, taken *Opposite*: empty 3 **conquered**, subjugated, subject, dominated, ruled *Opposite*: liberated

occupier *n* inhabitant, resident, tenant, occupant, lodger

occupy *v* 1 live in, inhabit, reside in, dwell in *(literary)*, lodge *(dated)* *Opposite*: vacate 2 **interest**, engage, divert, take up, entertain 3 **conquer**, subjugate, dominate, rule, seize *Opposite*: liberate

occur *v* 1 happen, take place, arise, come about, transpire 2 **hit**, strike, cross your mind, appear, come to mind

occurrence *n* 1 incidence, rate, amount, existence, manifestation 2 **happening**, event, incident, episode, occasion

ocean *n* sea, deep, water ■ *adj* marine, sea, deep-sea, oceanic

oceangoing *adj* seagoing, sea, seaworthy, maritime, seafaring

oceanic *adj* sea, deep-sea, ocean, saltwater, marine

ocular *adj* visual, optical, ophthalmic

odd *adj* strange, peculiar, unusual, abnormal, anomalous *Opposite*: ordinary

oddity *n* 1 peculiarity, quirk, foible, idiosyncrasy, twist 2 **strangeness**, peculiarity, quirkiness, oddness, bizarreness *Opposite*: normality 3 **eccentric**, character, original, exception, misfit 4 **curiosity**, rarity, phenomenon, freak

oddments *n* 1 odds and ends, leftovers, offcuts, bits, fragments 2 **knickknacks**, notions, sundries, curios, gewgaws

oddness *n* strangeness, peculiarity, mysteriousness, incongruity, weirdness *Opposite*: normality

odds *n* chances, probability, likelihood, balance

odds and ends *n* remnants, leftovers, loose ends, offcuts, fragments

odds-on *(infml)* *adv* probably, most likely,

likely, dependably, reliably *Opposite*: unlikely

ode *n* poem, elegy, verse, sonnet, song *(literary)*

odious *adj* hateful, horrible, loathsome, revolting, detestable *Opposite*: delightful

odium *n* abhorrence, hatred, disgust, revulsion, hate *Opposite*: approval

odor *n* 1 scent, perfume, smell, redolence, fragrance 2 **air**, aura, atmosphere, flavor, spirit. *See* COMPARE AND CONTRAST *at* **smell**.

odorless *adj* unscented, fragrance-free, neutral *Opposite*: scented

odorous *(literary)* *adj* scented, aromatic, redolent, fragrant, perfumed

odyssey *n* journey, trek, crusade, pilgrimage, wanderings

oeuvre *(fml)* *n* work, piece, composition, opus, works

of course *adv* 1 obviously, unquestionably, undeniably, certainly, indubitably *(fml)* 2 **yes**, certainly, naturally, evidently, no problem *(infml)* 3 **naturally**, not surprisingly, sure enough, needless to say *Opposite*: surprisingly

off *adj* rotten, rancid, bad, moldy, tainted *Opposite*: fresh

off and on *adv* intermittently, infrequently, by fits and starts, discontinuously *Opposite*: regularly

offbeat *adj* unusual, unconventional, eccentric, quirky, off-center *Opposite*: typical

off-center *adj* 1 asymmetrical, skewed, uneven, unbalanced, eccentric 2 **quirky**, eccentric, unconventional, odd, out in left field *(infml)*

off chance *n* likelihood, probability, possibility, chance, prospect

off-color *(infml)* *adj* risqué, indecorous, improper, indiscreet, racy

off course *adj* disoriented, lost, out, astray, adrift

offend *v* 1 hurt somebody's feelings, upset, insult, affront, be rude to 2 **commit an offense**, commit a crime, commit a felony, transgress, break the law

offended *adj* affronted, insulted, hurt, upset, slighted

offender *n* criminal, wrongdoer, reprobate, delinquent, lawbreaker

offense *n* 1 crime, wrongdoing, felony, fault, transgression 2 **insult**, affront, outrage, slight, slur 3 **umbrage**, resentment, pique, indignation 4 **attack**, offensive, assault, onslaught, bombardment *Opposite*: defense

offensive *adj* 1 unpleasant, distasteful, disgusting, odious, hateful *Opposite*: agreeable 2 **insulting**, rude, impolite, provoking, provocative *Opposite*: courteous 3 **aggressive**, attacking, violent, invasive, belligerent *Opposite*: peaceful

offensiveness *n* **rudeness**, impoliteness, indecency, vulgarity, abusiveness *Opposite*: politeness

offer *v* **1 proffer**, tender, present, bid **2 propose**, suggest, pose, recommend, put forward *Opposite*: withdraw ■ *n* **proposal**, suggestion, bid, proposition, bargain

offering *n* **contribution**, gift, donation, present, submission

off-guard *adj* **unready**, unawares, napping, unprepared *Opposite*: ready

offhand *adj* **1 impromptu**, extemporaneous, improvised, unrehearsed, spontaneous *Opposite*: premeditated **2 informal**, casual, nonchalant, easygoing, indifferent *Opposite*: serious

office *n* **bureau**, workplace, administrative center, headquarters, agency

office holder *n* **official**, officer, politician, public servant, elected official

officer *n* **1 police officer**, patrolman, policeman, policewoman, cop *(slang)* **2 official**, bureaucrat, representative, administrator, office holder

official *n* **bureaucrat**, administrator, representative, spokesperson, officer ■ *adj* **authorized**, certified, endorsed, sanctioned, allowed *Opposite*: informal

officialdom *(infml)* *n* **the powers that be**, bureaucracy, administrative system, red tape *(infml)*

officiate *v* **preside**, manage, perform official duties, carry out official duties, solemnize

officious *adj* **meddlesome**, bossy, bureaucratic, self-important, overbearing

off-key *adj* **out of key**, tuneless, out of tune, discordant, screeching *Opposite*: melodious ■ *adv* **tunelessly**, out of tune, discordantly, unmusically *Opposite*: melodiously

off-limits *adj* **forbidden**, prohibited, proscribed, outlawed, verboten *Opposite*: permitted

off-line *adj* **off**, disconnected, down *Opposite*: online

offload *v* **1 discharge**, unload, deposit, dump, leave *Opposite*: load **2 pass on**, get rid of, dump, deposit, devolve *Opposite*: keep **3** *(infml)* **relieve of**, divest, rid, free from, unburden

off-putting *adj* **1 repellent**, repulsive, disgusting, distasteful, offensive *Opposite*: attractive **2 forbidding**, disconcerting, upsetting, disturbing, daunting *Opposite*: comforting

offset *n* **counterbalance**, balance, counterpoise, equalizer, counterweight ■ *v* **counterweigh**, counterbalance, make up for, counteract, compensate

offshoot *n* **1 sideshoot**, sprout, sucker, branch, twig **2 derivative**, subsidiary, consequence, result, outcome

offspring *n* **descendants**, progeny, children, issue, young

---

WORD BANK
❏ **types of offspring** only child, quadruplet, quintuplet, singleton, triplet, twin

---

off-the-cuff *adj* **impromptu**, spontaneous, improvised, unprepared, unrehearsed

off-the-rack *adj* **ready-made**, ready-to-wear, mass-produced, prêt-à-porter *Opposite*: made-to-measure

off the record *adj* **private**, confidential, secret, unofficial, privy *(archaic)* *Opposite*: official

off-the-shelf *adj* **standard**, regular, mass-produced, ordinary, run-of-the-mill *Opposite*: tailor-made

off-the-wall *(infml)* *adj* **bizarre**, strange, eccentric, unusual, unconventional

of its own accord *adv* **by itself**, on its own, unaided, voluntarily

of no account *adj* **unimportant**, of no consequence, inconsequential, insignificant, minor *Opposite*: important

of note *adj* **important**, well-known, worth mentioning, notable, acclaimed *Opposite*: unknown

often *adv* **frequently**, over and over again, time and again, repeatedly, habitually *Opposite*: seldom

of your own accord *adv* **voluntarily**, willingly, spontaneously, independently, by choice

ogle *v* **look at**, eye, leer, stare, gaze *Opposite*: ignore. See COMPARE AND CONTRAST at **gaze**.

ogre *n* **giant**, troll, tyrant, monster, fiend

oil *n* **1 lubricant**, emollient, grease **2 grease**, fat, lard ■ *v* **apply oil**, lubricate, smear with oil, grease, loosen

---

WORD BANK
❏ **types of cooking fats and oils** butter, canola oil, corn oil, drippings, ghee, lard, margarine, olive oil, peanut oil, rape oil, sesame oil, shortening, suet, sunflower oil, vegetable oil

---

oily *adj* **greasy**, fatty, slick, slippery, oleaginous

ointment *n* **gel**, liniment, lotion, balm, salve

old *adj* **1 aged**, elderly, senior, mature, getting on *Opposite*: young **2 from the past**, ancient, from way back, long-standing, long forgotten *Opposite*: recent **3 previous**, last, other, former, erstwhile *Opposite*: current

olden *(literary)* *adj* **past**, ancient, historic, bygone, aged *Opposite*: modern

old-fashioned *adj* **1 antiquated**, outdated, unfashionable, behind the times, archaic *Opposite*: up-to-date **2 fogyish**, traditional, conservative, conventional, old-school *Opposite*: modern

---

COMPARE AND CONTRAST CORE MEANING: no longer in current use or no longer considered fashionable

old-fashioned no longer considered fashionable or suitable because of changes in taste or technology, or nostalgically favoring or maintaining the style of a former time; **outdated** no longer relevant to modern life because it has been superseded by something better, more fashionable, or more technologically advanced; **antiquated** regarded as in need of updating or replacing, though still functioning or in use; **archaic** belonging to a much earlier period of time, often suggesting a lack of relevance to modern life; **obsolete** superseded by something new, and in some cases therefore no longer in use; **passé** dismissed as no longer current or fashionable; **antediluvian** (*infml*) extremely old-fashioned and outdated

old hand *n* veteran, expert, professional, connoisseur, authority *Opposite*: novice

old-style *adj* traditional, outdated, outmoded, out-of-date, old *Opposite*: modern

old-time *adj* old-fashioned, outdated, outmoded, traditional, old-style *Opposite*: modern

old-world *adj* outdated, outmoded, quaint, traditional, old-style *Opposite*: modern

olive branch *n* peace offering, compromise, concession, gesture, apology

omen *n* sign, portent, warning, forecast, premonition

ominous *adj* threatening, warning, worrying, gloomy, portentous *Opposite*: promising

omission *n* 1 oversight, lapse, slip, error, blunder 2 exclusion, exception, absence, leaving out, hiatus *Opposite*: inclusion

omit *v* 1 leave out, miss out, pass over, skip, skip over *Opposite*: include 2 neglect, forget, not take the trouble, not bother, overlook *Opposite*: remember. *See* COMPARE AND CONTRAST *at* neglect.

omnibus *n* compilation, collection, anthology, edition, album

omnipotence *n* authority, power, all-powerfulness, supremacy, influence *Opposite*: powerlessness

omnipotent *adj* almighty, all-powerful, invincible, unstoppable, supreme *Opposite*: powerless

omnipresent *adj* ubiquitous, all-pervading, universal, ever-present, pervasive *Opposite*: absent

omniscience *n* knowledge, awareness, insight, wisdom, sapience *Opposite*: ignorance

omniscient *adj* all-knowing, all-seeing, wise, well-informed, sagacious

on *prep* 1 sitting on, on top of, resting on, lying on, upon *Opposite*: under 2 at, next to, by the side of, by ▪ *adv* 1 happening, taking place, scheduled, arranged, proceeding *Opposite*: off 2 without stopping, continuously, without a break, constantly, unceasingly

on account of *prep* owing to, because of, due to, through, as a result of

once *adv* 1 some time ago, formerly, previously, a long time ago, once upon a time *Opposite*: now 2 as soon as, when, after, the minute

once in a while *adv* every so often, every now and then, now and again, from time to time, occasionally *Opposite*: frequently

once-over (*infml*) *n* examination, inspection, check, review, survey

oncoming *adj* approaching, looming, nearing, advancing, onrushing

one *adj* unique, single, solitary, lone, individual

one and all *pron* everyone, everybody, all, all and sundry, ladies and gentlemen *Opposite*: nobody

one and only *adj* unique, inimitable, incomparable, amazing, incredible *Opposite*: common

one and the same *adj* identical, the same, the very same *Opposite*: different

one by one *adv* one after another, one after the other, one at a time, sequentially, separately *Opposite*: all together

one-dimensional *adj* superficial, lacking in depth, simplistic, simple-minded, basic

one-liner *n* joke, witticism, quip, bon mot, epigram

oneness *n* 1 singleness, cohesion, coherence *Opposite*: diversity 2 agreement, unanimity, unity, togetherness, solidarity *Opposite*: divergence

one of a kind *adj* unique, exceptional, irreplaceable, special, inimitable *Opposite*: commonplace

one-on-one *adj* individual, private, personal, intimate, personalized ▪ *adv* individually, privately, personally, alone

one or two *adj* a few, a couple, a handful, some, not many *Opposite*: lots

onerous *adj* difficult, burdensome, arduous, heavy, tiring *Opposite*: easy

one-sided *adj* biased, unfair, prejudiced, weighted, unrepresentative *Opposite*: balanced

one-sidedness *n* bias, partiality, unfairness, prejudice, unrepresentativeness

onetime *adj* former, previous, ex, past, old *Opposite*: current

one-way *adj* single, outward *Opposite*: round-trip

ongoing *adj* continuing, rolling, in progress, current, open-ended

online *adj* connected, on, operational, working, available *Opposite*: off-line

onlooker *n* bystander, spectator, viewer, observer, witness

only *adv* merely, simply, just, barely, no more than ▪ *adj* single, lone, solitary, individual

onrush *n* surge, rush, wave, tide, deluge

onrushing *adj* oncoming, surging, rushing, approaching, nearing

on-screen *adj* **televised**, television, live, on-air, televisual

onset *n* **start**, beginning, arrival, inception *(fml)*, commencement *(fml) Opposite*: conclusion

onside *adj* **legal**, safe, clear, in the clear ■ *adv* **legally**, safely, legitimately

onslaught *n* **attack**, assault, offensive, ambush, blitz

on the strength of *prep* **because of**, on the basis of, on account of, by reason of, by virtue of *Opposite*: notwithstanding *(fml)*

on the subject of *prep* **concerning**, with reference to, regarding, as regards, re

on the threshold of *prep* **on the brink of**, on the point of, at the start of, verging on, bordering on

on the way *adj* **imminent**, near, close, about to happen, under discussion

on the whole *adv* **in general**, overall, generally, generally speaking, usually

on top *adv* **ahead**, leading, with the upper hand, in the lead, in front

on top of *prep* **over**, lying on, resting on, on, above *Opposite*: beneath ■ *adj* **ahead of**, in control of, dealing with, abreast of, aware of

onus *n* **responsibility**, burden, obligation, duty

onward *adj* **forward**, headlong *Opposite*: backward ■ *adv* **on**, forward, ahead, headlong, straight on *Opposite*: backward

onwards *see* **onward**

oodles *(infml) n* **plenty**, lots, piles *(infml)*, tons *(infml)*, loads *(infml)*

oomph *n* **energy**, enthusiasm, life, dynamism, vivacity

ooze *v* 1 **seep**, leach, leak, trickle, dribble 2 **exude**, be full of, reek of, radiate, overflow with

opacity *n* 1 **opaqueness**, imperviousness, impenetrability, denseness, cloudiness *Opposite*: transparency 2 **obscurity**, obtuseness, impenetrability, complexity, vagueness *Opposite*: transparency

opaque *adj* 1 **impervious**, cloudy, muddy, milky, misty *Opposite*: transparent 2 **obscure**, unclear, incomprehensible, impenetrable, difficult *Opposite*: clear

open *adj* 1 **unlocked**, ajar, wide open, gaping *Opposite*: closed 2 **exposed**, uncluttered, sweeping, undeveloped, unspoiled *Opposite*: built-up 3 **approachable**, friendly, amenable, receptive, amicable *Opposite*: standoffish 4 **honest**, unguarded, direct, straight, frank *Opposite*: guarded 5 **vulnerable**, exposed, undefended, unprotected, unguarded *Opposite*: safe 6 **accessible**, public, unrestricted, free *Opposite*: restricted ■ *v* 1 **unlock**, unbolt, undo, unfasten, release *Opposite*: close 2 **begin**, start, commence, initiate, launch *Opposite*: conclude

open-air *adj* **outside**, outdoor, alfresco, uncovered *Opposite*: indoor

open-and-shut *adj* **simple**, clear, straightforward, clear-cut, obvious *Opposite*: ambiguous

open-ended *adj* **open**, flexible, undecided, unrestricted, fluid *Opposite*: fixed

opener *n* 1 **bottle opener**, can opener, corkscrew 2 *(infml)* **starter**, introduction, icebreaker, preamble

openhanded *adj* **generous**, unstinting, lavish, unselfish, philanthropic *Opposite*: miserly

openhandedness *n* **generosity**, lavishness, unselfishness, philanthropy, bounty *(literary) Opposite*: miserliness

openhearted *adj* **sincere**, genuine, honest, open, kind

openheartedness *n* **sincerity**, genuineness, honesty, kindness, love

opening *n* 1 **gap**, breach, aperture, hole, fissure 2 **start**, beginning, introduction, lead-in, prologue *Opposite*: end 3 **opportunity**, chance, lucky break, break *(infml)*

openly *adv* **candidly**, explicitly, frankly, honestly, plainly *Opposite*: secretly

open-minded *adj* **unbiased**, unprejudiced, tolerant, liberal, progressive *Opposite*: narrow-minded

open-mindedness *n* **broad-mindedness**, impartiality, tolerance, liberalism, progressiveness *Opposite*: narrow-mindedness

open-mouthed *adj* **astonished**, amazed, astounded, horrified, aghast

openness *n* **honesty**, directness, frankness, sincerity, candidness *Opposite*: reticence

open out *v* 1 **unfold**, spread out, open, open up, stretch out *Opposite*: fold up 2 **spread out**, radiate, separate, divide 3 **expand**, flower, spread, spread wide, get bigger

open up *v* 1 **unfold**, expand, spread out, open out, stretch 2 **excavate**, cut through, open, dig out, expose 3 **unwrap**, open, uncover, expose 4 **speak freely**, bare your soul, unwind, speak your mind, speak openly *Opposite*: clam up *(infml)* 5 **open fire**, start firing, start shooting 6 **begin trading**, open, unlock *Opposite*: close 7 *(infml)* **accelerate**, open the throttle, speed up, step on it, get going *Opposite*: slow down

operable *adj* 1 **treatable**, curable, nonfatal *Opposite*: inoperable 2 **practicable**, doable, possible, feasible, workable *Opposite*: impracticable

operate *v* 1 **function**, work, run, go, activate 2 **trade**, work, manage, run, carry on

operation *n* 1 **control**, management, use, controlling, maneuvering 2 **process**, action, act, procedure, maneuver 3 **campaign**, procedure, raid, attack, strategy 4 **business**, company, venture, undertaking, outfit *(infml)*

operational *adj* in use, in operation, in order, working, active

operative *adj* in effect, functioning, working, effective, operational *Opposite*: inoperative ■ *n* worker, operator, machinist, hand, technician

operator *n* worker, operative, machinist, hand

operose *(fml) adj* arduous, taxing, difficult, strenuous, hard *Opposite*: easy

opine *(fml) v* pronounce, hold forth, discourse, lecture, preach

opinion *n* view, estimation, belief, judgment, attitude

opinionated *adj* voluble, bigoted, narrow-minded, partisan, prejudiced *Opposite*: open-minded

opinion poll *n* survey, poll, questionnaire, investigation

opponent *n* adversary, enemy, rival, challenger, antagonist *Opposite*: ally

opportune *adj* fitting, favorable, appropriate, apt, right *Opposite*: inopportune

opportunism *n* resourcefulness, unscrupulousness, cunning, deviousness, speculation

opportunist *n* speculator, freebooter, fortune hunter, buccaneer, swashbuckler

opportunistic *adj* unscrupulous, resourceful, unprincipled, devious, cunning *Opposite*: principled

opportunity *n* occasion, opening, prospect, chance, break *(infml) Opposite*: misfortune

oppose *v* 1 be against, resist, fight, contest, combat *Opposite*: support 2 compete with, face, compete against, do battle with, clash with

opposed *adj* opposite, different, contrasting, divergent, conflicting *Opposite*: similar

opposed to *adj* against, hostile to, antagonistic to, resistant to, anti *(infml) Opposite*: in favor of

opposing *adj* 1 opposite, contrasting, differing, disparate, conflicting *Opposite*: similar 2 rival, opposite, hostile, competing, antagonistic *Opposite*: allied

opposite *adj* 1 conflicting, contradictory, differing, reverse, contrary *Opposite*: matching 2 far, other, furthest, facing, opposing *Opposite*: adjacent ■ *n* contrary, reverse, converse, inverse, opposite number *Opposite*: same ■ *prep* facing, across from, in front of, overlooking *Opposite*: beside

opposite number *n* counterpart, equivalent, parallel, equal, match

opposition *n* 1 resistance, antagonism, hostility, disapproval, disagreement *Opposite*: friendliness 2 opponent, challenger, competitor, enemy, rival

oppress *v* 1 keep down, coerce, tyrannize, dominate, repress *Opposite*: liberate 2 afflict, worry, torment, depress, distress *Opposite*: relieve

oppression *n* domination, coercion, cruelty, tyranny, repression

oppressive *adj* 1 cruel, harsh, domineering, tyrannical, repressive *Opposite*: fair 2 humid, hot, close, muggy, stifling *Opposite*: fresh 3 overwhelming, crushing, depressing, distressing, stressful *Opposite*: relaxing

oppressor *n* autocrat, despot, persecutor, bully, tyrant *Opposite*: liberator

opprobrious *adj* 1 scornful, contemptuous, damning, dismissive, reproachful *Opposite*: approving 2 shameful, humiliating, ignominious, embarrassing, belittling *Opposite*: glorious

opprobriousness *n* 1 scorn, contempt, censoriousness, dismissiveness, reproachfulness *Opposite*: approval 2 shamefulness, shame, humiliation, ignominy, embarrassment *Opposite*: glory

opprobrium *n* 1 scorn, contempt, condemnation, criticism, reproach *Opposite*: approval 2 shame, disgrace, ignominy, humiliation, embarrassment *Opposite*: glory

opt *v* choose, elect, decide, determine, plump for

optical *adj* visual, ocular, ophthalmic, photosensitive

optical illusion *n* 1 illusion, impression, effect, visual effect, mirage 2 trick, illusion, trick of the light, special effect, visual effect

optima *adj* best, ideal, optimum, top, finest *Opposite*: worst

optimism *n* 1 hopefulness, sanguinity, confidence, positiveness, assurance *Opposite*: pessimism 2 cheerfulness, enthusiasm, buoyancy, sunniness, brightness *Opposite*: pessimism

optimist *n* idealist, romantic, utopian, visionary, hoper *Opposite*: pessimist

optimistic *adj* hopeful, positive, bright, cheerful, expectant *Opposite*: pessimistic

optimize *v* enhance, improve, adjust, heighten, elevate

optimum *n* ideal situation, best-case scenario, goal, ideal, best ■ *adj* best, ideal, optimal, top, finest *Opposite*: worst

option *n* choice, alternative, possibility, route, opportunity *Opposite*: imperative

optional *adj* elective, voluntary, discretionary, possible, free *Opposite*: compulsory

opt out *(infml) v* bow out, bail out, withdraw, get out, leave

opulence *n* 1 lavishness, luxury, richness, magnificence, sumptuousness *Opposite*: simplicity 2 wealth, affluence, riches, prosperity, fortune *Opposite*: poverty

opulent *adj* 1 wealthy, lavish, luxurious, rich, magnificent *Opposite*: poor 2 abundant, ample, lavish, profuse, rich *Opposite*: sparse

opus *n* composition, work, piece, production, brainchild

oracle *n* 1 prophesy, vision, revelation, foreshadowing, prediction 2 prophet, augur, soothsayer, seer, visionary

oral *adj* spoken, verbal, uttered, said, verbalized *Opposite:* written. *See* COMPARE AND CONTRAST *at* verbal.

orangery *n* greenhouse, hothouse, conservatory, winter garden

orate *v* 1 speak, lecture, make a speech, take the floor, discourse 2 *(fml)* hold forth, preach, lecture, speak, declaim

oration *n* speech, discourse, address, lecture, sermon

orator *n* speaker, debater, lecturer, raconteur, storyteller

oratorical *adj* rhetorical, debating, declamatory, speechmaking, eloquent *Opposite:* halting

oratory *n* 1 debating, discussion, rhetoric, declamation, speechifying *(infml)* 2 eloquence, persuasiveness, cogency, skill, style 3 pomposity, prolixity, grandiloquence, verbosity, speechifying *(infml)*

orb *n* globe, sphere, planet, ball, round

orbit *n* 1 path, track, trajectory, flight path, course 2 scope, range, compass, influence, ambit ■ *v* circle, circumnavigate, loop, encircle, revolve

orchard *n* plantation, wood, copse, grove, coppice

orchestral *adj* instrumental, classical, symphonic, musical

orchestrate *v* 1 score, arrange, compose, write, rewrite 2 plan out, work out, arrange, coordinate, organize *Opposite:* improvise

orchestration *n* 1 instrumentation, transposition, arrangement, scoring, composition 2 planning, organization, stage-management, arrangement, preplanning *Opposite:* improvisation

ordain *(fml)* *v* order, decree, proclaim, enact, command *Opposite:* suggest

ordeal *n* trial, torment, suffering, tribulation, test

order *n* 1 instruction, command, directive, direction, demand *Opposite:* suggestion 2 stability, calm, harmony, peace, peacefulness *Opposite:* upheaval 3 orderliness, neatness, tidiness, method, regulation *Opposite:* disorder 4 sequence, succession, rank, classification, arrangement *Opposite:* chaos 5 contract, purchase, sale, request, requisition 6 sect, organization, group, class, lodge ■ *v* 1 arrange, organize, regulate, classify, categorize *Opposite:* confuse 2 command, instruct, tell, require, charge *Opposite:* request 3 requisition, request, ask for, send for, send off for *Opposite:* supply

order around *v* boss around, bully, lord it over, push around *(infml)*

ordered *adj* 1 well-ordered, neat, tidy, methodical, well-organized *Opposite:* disorganized 2 controlled, regimented, consistent, steady, efficient *Opposite:* irregular

orderliness *n* neatness, order, tidiness, method, organization *Opposite:* disorderliness

orderly *adj* 1 arranged, tidy, methodical, neat, logical *Opposite:* disorderly 2 obedient, disciplined, well-behaved, decorous, compliant *Opposite:* disorderly

ordinance *n* decree, order, rule, regulation, law

ordinarily *adv* normally, usually, generally, customarily, in general *Opposite:* unusually

ordinariness *n* 1 normality, commonplaceness, usualness, commonness, familiarity 2 dullness, triteness, drabness, dreariness, predictability

ordinary *adj* 1 normal, commonplace, usual, regular, common *Opposite:* unusual 2 dull, trite, drab, dreary, predictable *Opposite:* extraordinary

ordination *n* investiture, consecration, ceremony, conferment, installation

ordnance *n* weapons, artillery, arms, guns, weaponry

ordure *(fml)* *n* excrement, filth, dung, manure, feces

ore *n* mineral, rock, metal, element, aggregate

organ *n* 1 body part, tissue, structure 2 *(fml)* publication, mouthpiece, newspaper, magazine, periodical 3 *(fml)* agency, organization, body, representative, voice

organic *adj* 1 carbon-based, biological, living, animate, animal *Opposite:* inorganic 2 natural, unprocessed, unrefined, untreated, raw *Opposite:* synthetic 3 gradual, natural, spontaneous, slow, unforced *Opposite:* artificial

organism *n* living thing, creature, animal, plant, virus

organization *n* 1 group, body, society, association, party 2 orderliness, order, method, regulation, neatness *Opposite:* chaos 3 arrangement, configuration, design, format, composition

organizational *adj* structural, administrative, legislative, executive, logistic

organize *v* 1 establish, form, shape, unify, unite 2 systematize, arrange, sort out, classify, categorize *Opposite:* disarrange 3 coordinate, manage, control, run, set up

organized *adj* 1 prearranged, structured, ordered, systematized, well thought-out *Opposite:* spontaneous 2 methodical, logical, orderly, reasonable, sensible *Opposite:* disorganized

organizer *n* 1 manager, director, coordinator, planner, controller 2 calendar, appointment book, PDA, personal digital assistant, daybook

orient *see* **orientate**

orientate *v* **1** familiarize, adjust, learn about, orient, adapt **2 position**, turn, angle, face, place

orientation *n* **1 location**, alignment, direction, positioning, angle **2 emphasis**, focus, character, slant, thrust **3 leaning**, tendency, proclivity, preference, inclination **4 adjustment**, acclimatization, assimilation, acclimation, settling in **5 initiation**, briefing, induction, training, introduction

oriented *adj* concerned with, focused on, preoccupied with, slanted toward, adapted to

orifice *(literary) n* **opening**, hole, vent, cavity, outlet

origin *n* **source**, derivation, provenance, cause, root

COMPARE AND CONTRAST CORE MEANING: the beginning of something

origin the beginning of something in terms of the time, place, situation, or idea from which it arose, or somebody's ancestry, social background, or country; **source** the place, person, or thing through which something has come into being or from which it has been obtained; **derivation** the origin or source of something, especially a word, phrase, or name; **provenance** the place of origin of something, or the source and ownership history of a work of art or archaeological artifact; **root** the fundamental cause, basis, or origin of something, especially a feeling or a problem.

---

original *adj* **1 unique**, innovative, novel, inventive, creative *Opposite*: unoriginal **2 first**, initial, previous, fundamental, primary *Opposite*: last ■ *n* **prototype**, genuine article, pattern, archetype, template *Opposite*: copy. See COMPARE AND CONTRAST at **new**.

originality *n* **innovation**, novelty, uniqueness, inventiveness, creativity *Opposite*: unoriginality

originally *adv* **first**, initially, in the beginning, formerly, at first *Opposite*: eventually

originate *v* **1 create**, invent, initiate, instigate, inaugurate **2 begin**, derive, stem from, start, commence *Opposite*: finish

originator *n* **inventor**, creator, instigator, designer, maker

ornament *n* **1 embellishment**, adornment, enhancement, enrichment, trimming **2 knickknack**, figurine, objet d'art, bauble, decoration ■ *v* **adorn**, decorate, beautify, embellish, paint

ornamental *adj* **decorative**, attractive, for show, ornate, patterned *Opposite*: functional

ornamentation *n* **decoration**, adornment, embellishment, enhancement, garnishing

ornate *adj* **1 decorative**, overelaborate,

baroque, elaborate, ornamental *Opposite*: unadorned **2 high-flown**, flowery, wordy, verbose, elaborate *Opposite*: plain

ornery *(infml) adj* **irritable**, crabby, cantankerous, bad-tempered, awkward *Opposite*: good-tempered

orotund *(fml) adj* **1 loud**, clear, strong, ringing, stentorian *Opposite*: soft **2 wordy**, verbose, grandiloquent, pompous, bombastic *Opposite*: humble

orphan *n* **child**, baby, boy, girl, waif ■ *v* **bereave**, leave alone, leave all alone, make an orphan

orphanage *n* **home**, residential home, hostel, poorhouse, workhouse

orthodox *adj* **conventional**, accepted, traditional, mainstream, conformist *Opposite*: unorthodox

orthodoxy *n* **accepted view**, convention, accepted belief, prevailing attitude, tenet

oscillate *v* **1 swing**, move back and forth, move to and fro, move backward and forward, fluctuate **2 waver**, hesitate, vacillate, blow hot and cold, dither

oscillation *n* **swaying**, fluctuation, vacillation, alternation, swinging

osculate *(fml) v* **kiss**, give a kiss, give a smacker *(infml)*, canoodle with *(infml)*, smooch *(infml)*

ossify *v* **petrify**, fossilize, harden, become inflexible, become fixed

ossuary *(fml) n* **vault**, grave, tomb, crypt, charnel house

ostensible *adj* **ostensive**, apparent, professed, supposed, perceived *Opposite*: real

ostentation *n* **flashiness**, showiness, display, flamboyance, pretension *Opposite*: modesty

ostentatious *adj* **flashy**, showy, flamboyant, affected, pretentious *Opposite*: modest

ostracism *n* **shunning**, snubbing, exclusion, barring, keeping out *Opposite*: inclusion

ostracize *v* **coldshoulder**, exclude, banish, shun, ignore *Opposite*: include

other *adj* **additional**, new, more, fresh, extra

otherness *n* **strangeness**, difference, uniqueness, distinctiveness, oddness *Opposite*: normality

otherwise *adv* **or else**, if not, else, alternatively

otiose *adj* **futile**, ineffectual, useless, impractical, ineffective *Opposite*: effective

ottoman *n* **divan**, couch, day bed, chaise lounge, settee

oubliette *n* **prison cell**, dungeon, prison, cell

ounce *n* **grain**, jot, scrap, small amount, modicum

oust *v* **expel**, throw out, get rid of, drive out, exile *Opposite*: appoint

ouster *n* **removal**, ejection, dismissal, expulsion, coup

out *adv* **outdoors**, out-of-doors, in the open,

in the open air, alfresco *Opposite*: indoors ■ *adj* **1 elsewhere**, not in, not at home, away, away from home *Opposite*: in **2 available**, on view, obtainable, ready, on show *Opposite*: unavailable **3 banned**, prohibited, disallowed, barred, prevented *Opposite*: legitimate **4 unacceptable**, impossible, improbable, not worth it, unthinkable *Opposite*: acceptable **5 unconscious**, out cold, asleep, comatose, dazed *Opposite*: conscious **6 old-fashioned**, unfashionable, outdated, dated, passé *Opposite*: fashionable **7 exposed**, revealed, given away, made known, shown *Opposite*: hidden

out-and-out *adj* **complete**, blatant, obvious, outright, utter

outback *n* **wilderness**, scrubland, wilds, desert, badlands

outbid *v* **offer more than**, outspend, outdo, leave standing, overpay

outboard *adj* **external**, on the outside, outside, outward, exterior

outbrave (*archaic*) *v* **defy**, confront, brave, stand up to, face up to

outbreak *n* **eruption**, outburst, epidemic, occurrence, rash

outbuilding *n* **shed**, outhouse, lean-to, barn, shack

WORD BANK
❏ **types of outbuildings** barn, booth, carport, conservatory, cowshed, garage, garden shed, gatehouse, gazebo, greenhouse, guardhouse, hothouse, hut, kiosk, lean-to, lodge, orangery, outhouse, pavilion, privy (*infml*), sentry box, shed, stall, stand, summerhouse

outburst *n* **outpouring**, upsurge, surge, eruption, explosion

outcast *n* **untouchable**, exile, pariah, recluse, outsider

outclass *v* **surpass**, outshine, excel, do better than, better

outcome *n* **consequence**, result, ending, product, conclusion

outcrop *n* **rocky outcrop**, crag, ridge, bluff, boulder

outcry *n* **1 protest**, disagreement, objection, chorus of disapproval, quarrel *Opposite*: acceptance **2 uproar**, hullabaloo, hue and cry, turmoil, clamor

outdated *adj* **antiquated**, passé, outmoded, obsolete, dated *Opposite*: up-to-date. *See* COMPARE AND CONTRAST *at* **old-fashioned**.

outdistance *v* **outdo**, beat, do better than, outrun, outstrip

outdo *v* **exceed**, surpass, top, outdistance, outshine

outdoor *adj* **outside**, open-air, out-of-doors, alfresco *Opposite*: indoor

outdoors *adv* **out-of-doors**, outside, in the open, in the open air, alfresco *Opposite*: indoors

outer *adj* **outside**, external, on the outside, surface, superficial *Opposite*: inner

outermost *adj* **furthest**, farthest, remotest, outmost *Opposite*: innermost

outer space *n* **space**, the heavens, the universe, the solar system, the cosmos

outface *v* **1 stare down**, outstare *Opposite*: give in **2 brave**, stand up to, face up to, defy, confront *Opposite*: capitulate

outfall *n* **vent**, mouth, duct, channel, culvert

outfit *n* **1 suit**, clothes, clothing, ensemble, dress **2** (*infml*) **company**, team, business, group, unit ■ *v* **supply**, equip, fit out, arm, furnish (*fml*)

outflank *v* **1 go around**, attack from behind, attack from the rear, outmaneuver **2 outwit**, outmaneuver, outdo, bypass, outclass

outflow *n* **1 discharge**, drainage, seepage, leakage, depletion *Opposite*: influx **2 expenditure**, debit, expenses, spending, outlay *Opposite*: income

outfox *v* **defeat**, outwit, get the better of, outflank, take in

outgo *n* **expense**, expenditure, cost, overhead, outlay *Opposite*: income

outgoing *adj* **1 outward-bound**, outbound, outward, departing, leaving *Opposite*: incoming **2 retiring**, leaving, departing, withdrawing, resigning *Opposite*: incoming **3 sociable**, friendly, gregarious, extrovert, genial *Opposite*: introvert

outgrow *v* **1 get too large for**, grow too big for, get too big for, enlarge, grow up **2 move beyond**, be too grown-up for, be too old for, mature, develop **3 grow bigger than**, grow larger than, grow faster than, grow quicker than, outnumber

outgrowth *n* **extension**, result, development, product, consequence

outhouse *n* **outdoor toilet**, latrine, toilet, privy (*infml*)

outing *n* **visit**, excursion, trip, day trip, jaunt

outjockey *v* **outfox**, outdo, outwit, outmaneuver, outflank

outlandish *adj* **unusual**, bizarre, peculiar, strange, eccentric *Opposite*: usual

outlast *v* **outlive**, survive, live longer than, last longer than, endure

outlaw *n* **runaway**, criminal, fugitive, bandit, desperado ■ *v* **forbid**, ban, prohibit, proscribe, veto *Opposite*: allow

outlay *n* **expenditure**, expense, cost, spending, sum *Opposite*: return ■ *v* **expend**, spend, lay out, pay out, disburse

outlet *n* **1 opening**, passage, vent, exit, channel **2 means**, channel, conduit, vent, instrument **3 department store**, shop, retailer, market, store

outline *n* **1 shape**, form, figure, contour, silhouette **2 plan**, rough draft, summary, sketch, rough idea ■ *v* **1 draw round**, sketch, draw, delineate, chart *Opposite*: fill in **2 summarize**, sketch out, delineate, run through, give a rough idea *Opposite:* expand

outlive *v* live longer than, outlast, survive, last longer than, endure

outlook *n* 1 viewpoint, view, attitude, position, point of view 2 future, prospect, time to come, time ahead 3 view, panorama, vista

out loud *adv* loudly, audibly, distinctly, aloud, vocally *Opposite:* inaudibly

outlying *adj* remote, out-of-the-way, distant, faraway, far-off *Opposite:* neighboring

outmaneuver *v* outsmart, outfox, outwit, outflank, beat

outmoded *adj* 1 unfashionable, dated, passé, old-fashioned, out-of-date *Opposite:* fashionable 2 obsolete, out of use, out of commission, archaic, antiquated

outmost *adj* outermost, remotest, furthest, most remote, extreme

outnumber *v* be more than, be more numerous than, outstrip

out of bounds *adj* off-limits, forbidden, prohibited, banned, barred *Opposite:* open

out of breath *adj* breathless, panting, gasping, puffing, winded

out-of-date *adj* outdated, obsolete, outmoded, old-fashioned, dated *Opposite:* up-to-date

out-of-doors *adv* outdoors, outside, in the open, in the open air, alfresco *Opposite:* indoors

out of order *adj* not working, unusable, broken, out of commission, out of use *Opposite:* functional

out of the blue *adv* unexpectedly, without warning, all of a sudden, suddenly, surprisingly

out of the ordinary *adj* unusual, exceptional, atypical, extraordinary, uncommon *Opposite:* ordinary

out of the question *adj* impossible, unthinkable, unacceptable, highly unlikely, improbable *Opposite:* possible

out-of-the-way *adj* 1 distant, off the beaten path, off the beaten track, remote, isolated *Opposite:* accessible 2 uncommon, unconventional, different, out of the ordinary, special *Opposite:* common

out of this world (*infml*) *adj* exceptional, superb, wonderful, fabulous, amazing *Opposite:* unexceptional

outpace *v* outstrip, outperform, overtake, outdo, beat

outperform *v* outdo, outstrip, outpace, outclass, beat *Opposite:* underperform

outpost *n* garrison, base, station, settlement, colony

outpouring *n* expression, outburst, torrent, spate, flood

output *n* production, productivity, amount produced, yield, harvest

outrage *n* 1 crime, barbarity, disgrace, scandal, horror 2 indignation, anger, rage, fury, annoyance ■ *v* infuriate, offend, insult, anger, enrage *Opposite:* placate

outraged *adj* angry, incensed, livid, infuriated, furious *Opposite:* calm

outrageous *adj* disgraceful, shameful, shocking, offensive, contemptible *Opposite:* commendable

outré *adj* shocking, eccentric, unconventional, excessive, too much

outride *v* 1 outpace, outstrip, outclass, beat, overtake 2 survive, last out, endure, ride out, make it through

outrider *n* patrol, guard, bodyguard, attendant, escort

outright *adv* 1 completely, entirely, totally, fully, absolutely *Opposite:* partially 2 immediately, straightaway, right away, without hesitation, at once *Opposite:* hesitantly 3 openly, unreservedly, frankly, forthrightly, unequivocally *Opposite:* equivocally ■ *adj* 1 absolute, complete, total, utter, downright *Opposite:* partial 2 out-and-out, clear, transparent, obvious, direct

outrun *v* 1 outpace, outstrip, outclass, beat, overtake 2 leave behind, flee, run faster than, elude, get away from 3 go beyond, overrun, exceed, excel, surpass

outsell *v* beat, overtake, outpace, outstrip, sell more than *Opposite:* underperform

outset *n* beginning, start, onset, kickoff (*infml*), inception (*fml*)

outshine *v* surpass, outdo, outstrip, outperform, do better than

outside *adv* 1 outdoors, in the open air, alfresco, out of doors, in the fresh air 2 beyond, out there, elsewhere, yonder ■ *adj* 1 outdoor, external, separate, open-air, exterior 2 external, unknown, unfamiliar, independent, freelance 3 slight, faint, remote, scarce, slim *Opposite:* strong ■ *prep* beyond, out of, further than, farther than, past *Opposite:* within ■ *n* exterior, outer surface, surface, external surface *Opposite:* inside

outsider *n* stranger, foreigner, unknown, interloper, outcast

outsize *adj* enormous, massive, huge, immense, gigantic

outsized *see* outsize

outskirts *n* border, fringes, periphery, bounds, outer reaches *Opposite:* center

outsmart *v* outwit, outfox, outmaneuver, get the better of, overcome

outspoken *adj* frank, opinionated, honest, candid, open *Opposite:* tactful

outspokenness *n* frankness, honesty, candor, openness, bluntness *Opposite:* tact

outspread *adj* extended, spread-out, stretched, widely spread, open *Opposite:* folded ■ *v* extend, expand, stretch, spread, spread out *Opposite:* close in

outstanding *adj* **1 exceptional**, wonderful, stupendous, dazzling, marvelous *Opposite*: abysmal **2 unresolved**, unsettled, unpaid, remaining, owing *Opposite*: settled

outstandingly *adv* **exceptionally**, terrifically, wonderfully, stupendously, marvelously *Opposite*: abysmally

outstay *v* **outlast**, outlive, survive, stay longer than

outstretched *adj* **outspread**, extended, stretched out, spread-out, stretched *Opposite*: folded

outstrip *v* **outdo**, outshine, surpass, exceed, do better than *Opposite*: fall behind

outward *adj* **visible**, external, apparent, obvious, noticeable *Opposite*: inward ■ *adv* **out**, away, centrifugally *Opposite*: inward

outweigh *v* **overshadow**, be more important than, prevail over, be greater than, dwarf

outwit *v* **outsmart**, outfox, outmaneuver, get the better of, take in

outworn *adj* **obsolete**, outmoded, out-of-date, antiquated, archaic *Opposite*: current

ovate *adj* **oval**, egg-shaped, ellipsoid

ovation *n* **standing ovation**, cheer, vote of confidence, endorsement, thumbs up *(infml)*

over *prep* **1 in excess of**, more than, greater than, larger than, above *Opposite*: under **2 throughout**, around, the length and breadth of, round, across **3 on top of**, above, on, upon *Opposite*: beneath ■ *adj* **ended**, finished, done, completed, concluded

overabundance *n* **excess**, surplus, glut, superfluity, flood *Opposite*: shortage

overact *v* **ham it up**, ham, overdo it, exaggerate, overplay

overactive *adj* **feverish**, overexcited, overcharged, intense, fervid

overall *adj* **general**, complete, total, global, inclusive ■ *adv* **on the whole**, in general, generally, taken as a whole, largely *Opposite*: in particular

over and above *prep* **in addition to**, besides, as well as, added to, on top of

overarching *adj* **all-embracing**, main, all-encompassing, predominant, principal

overawe *v* **intimidate**, scare, impress, subdue

overbearing *adj* **arrogant**, domineering, bossy, imperious, pompous *Opposite*: meek

overblown *adj* **1 overdone**, excessive, exaggerated, unrestrained, immoderate *Opposite*: understated **2 pretentious**, pompous, puffed-up, extravagant *Opposite*: unassuming

overburden *v* **overload**, overtax, overstrain, burden, load

overcast *adj* **cloudy**, gray, gloomy, dark, dull *Opposite*: bright

overcharge *v* **charge too much**, take advantage of, cheat, swindle, rip off *(infml)*

overcome *v* **1 overwhelm**, overpower, incapacitate, disable, knock out **2 carry away**, affect, move to tears, reduce to tears, grip **3 surmount**, prevail over, rise above, triumph over, conquer *Opposite*: yield. *See* COMPARE AND CONTRAST *at* defeat.

overcompensate *v* **overreact**, overcorrect, overplay, give too much weight to, try too hard

overconfidence *n* **arrogance**, overoptimism, boldness, pride, nerve *Opposite*: caution

overconfident *adj* **arrogant**, full of yourself, brash, overoptimistic, bullish *(infml)* *Opposite*: modest

overcook *v* **overdo**, stew, burn, char, spoil

overcooked *adj* **overdone**, burnt, well done, chewy, hard *Opposite*: underdone

overcritical *adj* **harsh**, hypercritical, censorious, severe, critical

overcrowded *adj* **filled to capacity**, congested, overloaded, teeming, swarming *Opposite*: deserted

overcrowding *n* **congestion**, overloading, overpopulation, excess, excess numbers

overdo *v* **1 overcook**, burn, stew, char, spoil **2 exaggerate**, overstate, overplay, overemphasize, take to extremes *Opposite*: play down

overdone *adj* **1 overcooked**, stewed, charred, spoiled, burned *Opposite*: underdone **2 exaggerated**, overstated, overplayed, overemphasized, extreme *Opposite*: restrained

overdo things *v* **strain yourself**, burn the candle at both ends, overtax yourself, overexert yourself, overdo it *Opposite*: relax

overdrawn *adj* **in debt**, in the red, overspent, insolvent, over your limit *Opposite*: in credit

overdue *adj* **late**, tardy, unpaid, unsettled, belated *Opposite*: early

overeat *v* **overindulge**, eat too much, gorge, stuff yourself, binge

overemotional *adj* **emotional**, sentimental, melodramatic, maudlin, histrionic *Opposite*: unemotional

overemphasize *v* **exaggerate**, overstate, overstress, stress, go over the top about

overenthusiasm *n* **fanaticism**, mania, obsessiveness, obsession, fever

overenthusiastic *adj* **overzealous**, carried away, fanatical, obsessive, obsessional

overestimate *v* **1 misjudge**, overrate, miscalculate, overvalue, allow too much for *Opposite*: underestimate **2 overrate**, expect too much of, misjudge, miscalculate, overemphasize *Opposite*: underestimate

overexcite *v* **work up**, excite, get in a state, get carried away, wind up *(infml)* *Opposite*: calm down

overexcited adj carried away, high, frenzied, in a frenzy, feverish Opposite: calm

overexcitement n frenzy, mania, feverishness, anxiety, emotion

overextend v overstretch, overreach, go too far, bite off more than you can chew, exceed your limit

overflow v run over, flood, spill over, brim over, pour out ■ n excess, runoff, extra, surfeit, surplus Opposite: lack

overflowing adj spilling over, teeming, swarming, brimming, abundant Opposite: empty

overflow with v be full of, brim with, abound with, bubble with, be bursting at the seams with Opposite: lack

overgrown adj dense, thick, overrun, lush, untidy Opposite: tidy

overhang v project, extend, jut out, hang over, extend beyond ■ n projection, extension, outcrop, ledge, outcropping

overhaul v 1 repair, renovate, fix, refit, refurbish 2 overtake, surpass, leave behind, outdo, pass Opposite: fall behind ■ n service, refit, refurbishment

overhead adv above, in the air, upstairs, directly above, above your head Opposite: below ■ n cost, expense, payment, business cost, bill

overhear v eavesdrop, listen in, hear, eavesdrop on, listen to

overheated adj excited, impassioned, agitated, inflamed, hot and bothered Opposite: calm

overindulge v overeat, eat too much, stuff yourself, gorge, gorge yourself

overindulgence n excess, greed, intemperance, hedonism, gluttony

overindulgent adj excessive, greedy, immoderate, intemperate, hedonistic

overjoyed adj delighted, joyful, elated, ecstatic, jubilant Opposite: disappointed

overkill n excess, too much, overstatement, too much of a good thing, heavy-handedness Opposite: restraint

overladen adj overloaded, overfilled, crammed, overburdened, weighed down

overlap v 1 partly cover, overlie, meet, touch, cover 2 coincide, correspond, intersect, meet, come together ■ n 1 overlay, intersection, edge, join, connection 2 correspondence, connection, similarity, common ground, commonality

overlay v cover, coat, put over, overlap, drape

overload v overburden, overwork, tax, weigh down, overexert ■ n excess, surplus, overwork, burden, overkill Opposite: lack

overloaded adj weighed down, weighted down, loaded, laden, full

overlook v 1 ignore, miss, forget, skip, neglect Opposite: notice 2 excuse,

condone, spare, let pass, pardon Opposite: punish 3 give onto, be opposite, face, back onto 4 supervise, oversee, superintend, boss, observe 5 inspect, survey, examine, peruse, scan. See COMPARE AND CONTRAST at neglect.

overly adv excessively, too, desperately, exaggeratedly, exceedingly Opposite: slightly

overmuch adv excessively, too much, very much, unnecessarily overly ■ adj excessive, extreme, too much, immoderate, extravagant ■ n excess, superfluity, surplus, overage

overnight adv suddenly, at once, quickly, instantly, abruptly Opposite: gradually ■ adj instant, immediate, abrupt, instantaneous, sudden Opposite: gradual

overpitch v exaggerate, overdo, overcompensate, overplay, overemphasize

overplay v overemphasize, exaggerate, overdo, overstress, overstate Opposite: underplay

overpower v 1 subdue, override, suppress, subjugate, conquer Opposite: yield 2 overwhelm, overshadow, floor, overcome, dumbfound

overpowering adj overwhelming, intense, overriding, uncontrollable, consuming Opposite: weak

overpoweringly adv irresistibly, overwhelmingly, devastatingly, strongly, intensely

overprice v overrate, overvalue, hike up, write up, mark up Opposite: underprice

overpriced adj high-priced, costly, extortionate, expensive, exorbitant Opposite: cheap

overprotect v fuss over, cocoon, indulge, protect, mollycoddle Opposite: neglect

overrate v overprize, overestimate, exaggerate, overvalue Opposite: underrate

overrated adj overvalued, overestimated, hyped, puffed up, glorified Opposite: underrated

overreach v 1 overdo, bite off more than you can chew, overstretch, overextend, go too far 2 overstrain overextend, overdo, overstress 3 outwit, outsmart, outfox, outplay, deceive

overreact v exaggerate, make a big deal, make something out of nothing, make a mountain out of a molehill, make a drama out of a crisis

override v 1 disregard, overrule, defy, flout, countermand Opposite: follow 2 supersede, dominate, prevail, predominate, overrule

overriding adj overruling, superseding, intervening, dominant, prevailing Opposite: insignificant

overrule v 1 override, cancel, rule against, refuse, make null and void 2 master, exercise authority, domineer, pull rank

overrun v invade, attack, assail, assault, besiege ■ adj **swarming**, infested, teeming, flooded, swamped

overseas adj **foreign**, external, ultramarine *(literary)* ■ adv **abroad**, out of the country, in foreign parts

oversee v **supervise**, manage, superintend, run, direct

overseer n **supervisor**, manager, administrator, chief, boss

oversell v **exaggerate**, overvalue, overrate, hype, overstate *Opposite*: undersell

oversensitive adj **emotional**, thin-skinned, hypersensitive, vulnerable, touchy *Opposite*: thick-skinned

oversentimental adj **mawkish**, syrupy, maudlin, sad, mushy *Opposite*: callous

overshadow v **outshine**, outdo, dominate, surpass, eclipse

overshoot v **pass**, exceed, overreach, overpass, overrun *Opposite*: hit

oversight n 1 **mistake**, failure to notice, slip, omission, misunderstanding 2 **supervision**, control, overseeing, management, administration

oversimplify v **generalize**, overgeneralize, simplify, distort *Opposite*: complicate

oversize adj **extra large**, large, huge, king-size, oversized

oversized *see* **oversize**

overspill n **flood**, overflow, runoff, excess, surplus ■ v **spill over**, overflow, brim over, pour out, flood

overstate v **exaggerate**, make too much of, overdo, overstress, overemphasize *Opposite*: understate

overstated adj **exaggerated**, extravagant, excessive, inflated, overelaborate *Opposite*: understated

overstatement n **exaggeration**, hyperbole, overemphasis *Opposite*: understatement

overstay v **prolong**, protract, extend

overstep v 1 **exceed**, go beyond, pass, surpass, step over 2 **transgress**, violate, disregard, disobey, contravene *Opposite*: obey

overstrain v **overstretch**, overstress, overreach, overtax, overload

overstress v 1 **overstretch**, overstrain, overreach, overtax, overload 2 **overemphasize**, exaggerate, overplay, overpitch, overstate ■ n **overstating**, overplaying, overdoing, dwelling on, going on about

overstretch v 1 **overstrain**, overstress, overreach, overdo 2 **overburden**, overtax, overload, overdo, overreach

overstrung adj **nervous**, tense, oversensitive, high-strung, temperamental *Opposite*: placid

overstuffed adj **brimming**, overfilled, brimful, overflowing, bursting at the seams *Opposite*: empty

oversupply n **overflow**, excess, surplus, glut, superfluity ■ v **glut**, overwhelm, flood, inundate, swamp

overt adj **obvious**, unconcealed, explicit, evident, open *Opposite*: covert

overtake v 1 **pass**, go beyond, go past, overhaul, leave behind *Opposite*: fall behind 2 **hit**, sweep over, engulf, assail, strike

overtax v **strain**, overload, overdo it, overstretch, overstrain

over-the-hill adj **old**, past your prime, ancient, decrepit *(archaic) Opposite*: up-and-coming

over-the-top *(infml)* adj **exaggerated**, excessive, overdone, extravagant, overblown *Opposite*: understated

overthrow v **conquer**, defeat, dethrone, bring down, depose *Opposite*: uphold

overtime n **extra pay**, extra hours, time and a half, additional hours, double time ■ adv **energetically**, tirelessly, actively, strenuously, intensely

overtone n **implication**, association, hint, undertone, connotation

overturn v 1 **turn over**, knock over, tip over, upend, capsize *Opposite*: right 2 **nullify**, abolish, invalidate, annul, reverse

overuse n **misuse**, abuse, overconsumption ■ v **overdo**, go to extremes, overplay, do to death, misuse

overused adj **overworked**, clichéd, hackneyed, commonplace, trite

overvalue v **overrate**, overprize, overestimate *Opposite*: undervalue

overview n **indication**, summary, outline, gestalt, synopsis

overweening adj **arrogant**, conceited, pompous, presumptuous, haughty *Opposite*: unassuming

overweight adj **heavy**, big, large, weighty, cumbersome *Opposite*: underweight

overwhelm v **overpower**, overcome, engulf, devastate, crush

overwhelmed adj 1 **overcome**, overawed, speechless, dazed, stunned *Opposite*: unimpressed 2 **overpowered physically**, overcome, beaten, conquered, crushed 3 **inundated**, snowed under, swamped, flooded, exhausted

overwhelming adj **irresistible**, overpowering, devastating, crushing, awe-inspiring *Opposite*: insignificant

overwinter v **hibernate**, lie dormant, stagnate, vegetate, lie fallow

overwork v **burn the midnight oil**, overdo it, work your fingers to the bone, overburden, overtax

overwrought adj **tense**, stressed, distraught, emotional, strained *Opposite*: calm

owe v **be beholden**, be obligated *Opposite*: repay

owed adj **owing**, unpaid, outstanding, due, payable *Opposite*: paid

owing *adj* **in arrears**, owed, due, in the red *Opposite*: paid

owing to *prep* **because of**, due to, on account of, thanks to, as a result of

owlish *adj* **owl-like**, serious, wise, solemn, bespectacled

own *adj* **individual**, private, particular, peculiar, specific ■ *v* **1 possess**, have, have possession of, keep, retain **2** (*fml*) **confess**, admit, own up, acknowledge, profess *Opposite*: deny

owner *n* **proprietor**, landlord, possessor, holder, titleholder

ownership *n* **possession**, rights, tenure, title, proprietorship

own up *v* **confess**, admit, profess, express, utter

ox *n* **bull**, bullock, steer

oxidization *n* **reaction**, rust, tarnishing, corrosion, verdigris

oxidize *v* **react**, rust, tarnish, corrode, dissolve

P

PA *n* **public-address system**, loudspeaker, speaker, amplifier, amp

pace *n* **1 speed**, rapidity, swiftness, velocity, rate of knots **2 rate**, speed, tempo, time, regularity **3 step**, stride, leap, bound, hop ■ *v* **1 walk**, stride, march, walk back and forth, walk up and down **2 govern**, regulate, restrict, manage, limit

pacemaker *n* **leader**, pacesetter, pacer, innovator, trendsetter

pacific *adj* **1 soothing**, appeasing, conciliatory, comforting, placatory *Opposite*: antagonistic **2 tranquil**, peaceful, calm, untroubled, gentle *Opposite*: violent

pacifist *n* **peace lover**, conscientious objector, dove, peacemaker, peacekeeper ■ *adj* **pacific**, appeasing, conciliatory, placatory, comforting *Opposite*: antagonistic

pacify *v* **calm**, soothe, mollify, placate, calm down *Opposite*: antagonize

pack *v* **1 store**, arrange, put, place, sort **2 package**, wrap, wrap up, box, bundle *Opposite*: unpack **3 fill**, cram, stuff, jam, load **4 compact**, press, compress, squash, flatten ■ *n* **1 carton**, packet, box, parcel, container **2 folder**, packet, wallet, dossier, file **3 set**, bunch, group, quantity, collection **4 bag**, backpack, rucksack, haversack, daypack **5 crowd**, horde, mob, gang, bunch

package *n* **1 parcel**, packet, box, envelope **2 set**, bundle, suite, raft, compendium ■ *v* **1 pack**, wrap, wrap up, parcel, box *Opposite*: unwrap **2 promote**, present, market, advertise, put across

packaging *n* **wrapping**, packing, wrapper, packet, box

packed *adj* **crowded**, crammed, full, full to capacity, filled *Opposite*: empty

packet *n* **pack**, package, sachet, container, carton

pack in *v* **1 attract**, interest, excite, fill the seats, be a box office success *Opposite*: flop (*infml*) **2** (*infml*) **stop**, give up, quit,

abandon, drop *Opposite*: take up

packing *n* **stuffing**, filling, filler, wadding, padding

pack up *v* **stop**, give up, quit, abandon, drop *Opposite*: start

pact *n* **deal**, agreement, treaty, contract, accord

pad *n* **1 cushion**, cloth, wad, swab, pack **2 notepad**, sketchpad, notebook, sketchbook, scratchpad **3 mat**, place mat, coaster, doily ■ *v* **1 creep**, tiptoe, steal, walk, sneak **2 line**, cover, fill, stuff, wad **3 fill out**, flesh out, amplify, lengthen, expand

padding *n* **1 stuffing**, filling, wadding, lining, packing **2 verbiage**, circumlocution, periphrasis, garbage, rubbish

paddle *n* **oar**, scull, sweep, blade ■ *v* **row**, scull, propel

page *n* **1 sheet**, piece of paper, sheet of paper, leaf, folio **2 call**, beep, summons, message ■ *v* **call**, contact, beep, summon

pageant *n* **procession**, parade, cavalcade, display, carnival

pageantry *n* **spectacle**, display, pomp, ceremony, ritual

paid *adj* **salaried**, professional, funded *Opposite*: unpaid

pain *n* **1 discomfort**, agony, aching, hurt, ache *Opposite*: pleasure **2 grief**, sorrow, anguish, ache, torture *Opposite*: joy **3** (*infml*) **nuisance**, bother, menace, bind, drag (*infml*) *Opposite*: pleasure ■ *v* **sadden**, distress, upset, disturb, grieve *Opposite*: hearten

pained *adj* **hurt**, aggrieved, indignant, wounded, injured

painful *adj* **1 tender**, aching, raw, throbbing, excruciating *Opposite*: painless **2 sorrowful**, distressing, anguished, heartbreaking, upsetting *Opposite*: pleasant **3 laborious**, troublesome, awkward, labored, tedious *Opposite*: easy **4 awful**, excruciating, dire, dreadful, agonizing *Opposite*: wonderful

painkiller *n* **analgesic**, sedative, anesthetic, drug

painkilling *adj* **analgesic**, calming, sedative, deadening, numbing

painless *adj* **effortless**, easy, trouble-free, simple, unproblematic *Opposite*: problematic

pains *n* **care**, effort, trouble, lengths

painstaking *adj* **thorough**, careful, meticulous, conscientious, scrupulous *Opposite*: careless. *See* COMPARE AND CONTRAST *at* **careful**.

paint *v* **1 coat**, decorate, smear, daub, splatter **2 portray**, capture, catch, show, render (*fml*)

painter *n* **artist**, watercolorist, portraitist, miniaturist

painting *n* **1 picture**, work of art, image, canvas, oil painting **2 art**, fine art, portraiture, landscape, oils

paint the town red (*infml*) *v* **celebrate**, have a good time, have fun, revel, go out

pair *n* **couple**, duo, twosome, brace, set ■ *v* **pair off**, team up, join up, match up, put together *Opposite*: separate

pal (*infml*) *n* **friend**, comrade, crony, chum (*infml*), buddy (*infml*)

palatable *adj* **1 edible**, pleasant, tasty, appetizing, toothsome *Opposite*: inedible **2 acceptable**, agreeable, satisfactory, pleasant, passable *Opposite*: disagreeable

palatial *adj* **luxurious**, lavish, grand, impressive, splendid *Opposite*: miserable

palaver *n* **chatter**, chat, gossip, talk, chitchat (*infml*)

pale *adj* **1 light**, pastel, soft, whitish, insipid *Opposite*: dark **2 pallid**, colorless, fair, ashen, white *Opposite*: deep **3 faint**, dim, feeble, weak, watery *Opposite*: bright ■ *v* **1 diminish**, reduce, recede, lessen *Opposite*: intensify **2 lose color**, fade, become washed out, soften, lighten *Opposite*: deepen **3 go white**, whiten, go pale, blanch, bleach *Opposite*: color

pall *v* **lose its attraction**, fade, diminish, wither, go sour ■ *n* **1 cloud**, blanket, shroud, sheet, wall **2 gloom**, despair, sadness, depression, melancholy

palliative *adj* **1 soothing**, calming, relaxing, comforting, mollifying **2 analgesic**, painkilling, anesthetic, sedative

pallid *adj* **pale**, white, ashen, pasty, colorless *Opposite*: dark

pallor *n* **paleness**, whiteness, pastiness, wanness, sallowness *Opposite*: bloom

palpable *adj* **1 intense**, tangible, physical, real, deep *Opposite*: intangible **2 obvious**, clear, demonstrable, unmistakable, evident *Opposite*: hidden

palpitate *v* **flutter**, pound, race, tremble, quiver

paltry *adj* **1 worthless**, trivial, trifling, miserable, insignificant *Opposite*: substantial **2 despicable**, wretched, mean, miserable, contemptible

pamper *v* **spoil**, indulge, coddle, mollycoddle, cosset *Opposite*: mistreat

pamphlet *n* **leaflet**, brochure, booklet, guide, tract

pan *n* **pot**, saucepan, casserole, wok, frying pan ■ *v* (*infml*) **criticize**, berate, disparage, deride, slam (*infml*) *Opposite*: praise

panacea *n* **cure-all**, cure, solution, answer, remedy

panache *n* **flair**, flamboyance, style, spirit, confidence *Opposite*: awkwardness

pandemic *n* **epidemic**, plague, contagion, sickness, disease

pandemonium *n* **chaos**, bedlam, uproar, hubbub, racket

pander to *v* **indulge**, satisfy, gratify, bow to, go along with *Opposite*: resist

pane *n* **windowpane**, glass, window, sheet, panel

panel *n* **1 piece**, board, pane, sheet, plate **2 board**, team, jury, group, council

pang *n* **twinge**, spasm, paroxysm, shooting pain, cramp

panic *n* **fear**, anxiety, fright, terror, dread *Opposite*: calm ■ *v* **1 be frightened**, be terrified, lose your nerve, go to pieces, get flustered *Opposite*: calm down **2 terrify**, unnerve, scare, frighten, fluster

panicky *adj* **frightened**, scared, alarmed, fearful, anxious *Opposite*: calm

panic-stricken *adj* **terrified**, unnerved, frightened, fearful, scared out of your wits *Opposite*: calm

panoply *n* **display**, array, show, parade, exhibition

panorama *n* **view**, scene, vista, outlook, landscape

pan out (*infml*) *v* **turn out**, work out, develop, end up, resolve itself

pant *v* **gasp**, puff, wheeze, blow, gasp for air

pap *n* **drivel**, nonsense, rubbish, trash, garbage

paper *n* **1 newspaper**, daily, weekly, broadsheet, broadside **2 document**, manuscript, thesis, term paper, dissertation

paperback *n* **book**, softback, softcover, novel

paper over *v* **1 wallpaper**, cover, cover up, obscure, disguise *Opposite*: strip **2 conceal**, sweep under the carpet, hide, cover up, make light of *Opposite*: highlight

paperwork *n* **form-filling**, accounts, bookkeeping, correspondence, administration

papery *adj* **flimsy**, frail, thin, paper-thin, delicate

par *n* **average**, standard, norm, the usual

parable *n* **allegory**, fable, moral tale, folktale, tale

parade *n* **procession**, pageant, cavalcade, display, carnival ■ *v* **1 process**, march, file, strut, turn out **2 show off**, exhibit, display, trumpet, flaunt *Opposite*: hide **3 walk**, stalk, march, strut, stroll *Opposite*: skulk

paradigm n 1 epitome, archetype, model, example, exemplar (literary) Opposite: antithesis 2 model, template, prototype, standard, pattern

paradise n 1 heaven, seventh heaven, nirvana, happy hunting ground Opposite: hell 2 (infml) dream world, wonderland, cloud nine, utopia, bliss

paradox n inconsistency, absurdity, irony, contradiction, contradiction in terms

paradoxical adj inconsistent, absurd, ironic, contradictory, illogical Opposite: logical

paradoxically adv 1 illogically, absurdly, inconsistently, puzzlingly, unexpectedly Opposite: logically 2 strangely enough, oddly enough, funnily enough, surprisingly, ironically

paragon n model, shining example, epitome, archetype, quintessence Opposite: rake

paragraph n 1 section, subsection, passage, part, clause 2 article, piece, item, story, editorial

parallel adj similar, equivalent, corresponding, analogous, matching Opposite: dissimilar ■ n 1 counterpart, match, equal, equivalent, peer Opposite: opposite 2 similarity, correspondence, equivalence, resemblance, analogy Opposite: dissimilarity

paramedic n first aider, first responder, emergency worker, rescue worker

parameter n limit, boundary, limitation, restriction, constraint

paramilitary adj guerrilla, rebel, revolutionary, terrorist ■ n rebel, revolutionary, terrorist, guerrilla, fighter

paramount adj supreme, utmost, dominant, chief, principal Opposite: minimal

paranoia n fear, suspicion, mistrust, distrust, obsession Opposite: confidence

paranoid adj suspicious, fearful, mistrustful, distrustful, obsessed Opposite: trusting

paraphernalia n things, stuff, equipment, trappings, odds and ends

paraphrase v rephrase, summarize, reword, interpret, translate ■ n summary, rewording, précis, translation, interpretation

parasite n 1 pest, bug, bloodsucker, insect, flea Opposite: host 2 leech, scrounger (infml), sponger (infml), freeloader (infml)

WORD BANK

❏ **types of parasitic insects** bedbug, botfly, chigger, chigoe, crab louse, deer tick, flea, gadfly, harvest mite, head louse, louse, mite, sand flea, sandfly, tapeworm, tick

parasitic adj 1 biting, bloodsucking, dependent, opportunistic Opposite: host 2 dependent, lazy, scrounging (infml), sponging (infml), freeloading (infml)

parasol n sunshade, umbrella, shade

parcel n 1 package, packet, bundle, carton, box 2 tract, plot, piece, section, portion

■ / **pack**, package, wrap, wrap up, box Opposite: unwrap

parcel out v distribute, divide, give out, hand out, apportion

parch v dry, dry out, scorch, dehydrate, desiccate

parched adj 1 dry, arid, dried up, dried out, scorched Opposite: waterlogged 2 (infml) thirsty, gasping, dehydrated, dry, panting Opposite: refreshed. See COMPARE AND CONTRAST at dry.

pardon v 1 forgive, absolve, exonerate, let off, acquit Opposite: condemn 2 excuse, forgive, overlook, let pass, take no notice of Opposite: resent ■ n forgiveness, absolution, exoneration, amnesty, mercy

pare v 1 peel, skin, strip, trim, shave 2 cut, trim, clip, cut back, tidy up Opposite: grow

pare down v cut back, cut down, reduce, scale down, pare Opposite: increase

parentage n 1 parents, paternity, maternity 2 ancestry, background, pedigree, origin, derivation

parental adj parent, maternal, paternal Opposite: filial

parenthesis n digression, afterthought, addition, aside, comment

parenthood n parentage, fatherhood, motherhood, parenting, paternity

parenting n childcare, child-rearing, babycare, nurturing, child raising

parish n community, district, village, locality, area

parity n equivalence, equality, uniformity, similarity, correspondence Opposite: disparity

park n gardens, botanical gardens, common, green, grounds

parking n parking lot, parking garage, parking space, parking bay, parking place

parkland n grassland, land, fields, meadows, estate

parlance n idiom, turn of phrase, phraseology, phrasing, jargon

parley v confer, negotiate, talk, discuss, deliberate ■ n conference, meeting, discussion, negotiations, consultation

parliament n government, legislative body, legislature, assembly

parliamentarian n member of parliament, politician, legislator, minister, backbencher

parliamentary adj governmental, legislative, lawmaking, congressional, senatorial

parlor n business premises, salon, store, business establishment, studio

parlous (archaic) adj dangerous, perilous, risky, unsafe, uncertain Opposite: comfortable

parochial adj narrow, narrow-minded, closed-minded, provincial, insular Opposite: broad-minded

parochialism n narrow-mindedness, provincialism, insularity, closed-mindedness, narrowness *Opposite*: broad-mindedness

parodist *n* satirist, humorist, imitator, lampooner, burlesquer

parody *n* 1 **caricature**, imitation, lampoon, satire, burlesque 2 **distortion**, travesty, misrepresentation, perversion, pale imitation *Opposite*: model ■ *v* 1 **distort**, pervert, misrepresent, twist 2 **lampoon**, imitate, caricature, satirize, burlesque

parole *n* **conditional release**, early release, bail, liberation ■ *v* **release on parole**, release conditionally, liberate, bail, give terms

paroxysm *n* 1 **convulsion**, spasm, fit, seizure, attack 2 **outburst**, fit, frenzy, outpouring, explosion

paroxysmal *adj* **convulsive**, violent, spasmodic, uncontrollable, involuntary

parquet *n* **flooring**, parquetry, floor, floorboards, inlay

parrot *n* **imitator**, mimic, impersonator, impressionist, copier ■ *v* **mimic**, imitate, copy, impersonate, echo

parry *v* 1 **deflect**, block, fend off, shield yourself from, dodge *Opposite*: take 2 **evade**, avoid, dodge, elude, sidestep *Opposite*: answer

parse *v* **analyze**, describe, break down, explain, construe

parsimonious *adj* **stingy**, thrifty, frugal, ungenerous, miserly *Opposite*: extravagant

parsimoniousness *see* parsimony

parsimony *n* **stinginess**, thrift, thriftiness, meanness, frugality *Opposite*: extravagance

parson *n* **cleric**, priest, minister, pastor, parish priest

parsonage *n* **church house**, rectory, vicarage, manse, residence

part *n* 1 **portion**, division, section, fraction, piece *Opposite*: whole 2 **feature**, ingredient, element, component, bit 3 **share**, portion, fragment, slice, chunk *Opposite*: whole 4 **function**, role, duty, job, position ■ *v* **divide**, separate, open, split, segregate *Opposite*: join

partake *v* 1 **consume**, dine, eat, drink, taste *Opposite*: abstain 2 **participate**, share, contribute, take part, play a part *Opposite*: refrain

partial *adj* 1 **incomplete**, fractional, limited, restricted, unfinished *Opposite*: complete 2 **biased**, prejudiced, subjective, one-sided, inequitable *Opposite*: impartial

partiality *n* 1 **fondness**, liking, penchant, inclination, affection *Opposite*: dislike 2 **bias**, prejudice, preference, leaning, favoritism *Opposite*: impartiality

partially *adv* **partly**, in part, incompletely, to some extent, somewhat *Opposite*: completely

partial to *adj* **fond of**, keen on, into *(infml)*

participant *n* **member**, contributor, contestant, applicant, partaker *Opposite*: observer

participate *v* **contribute**, partake, take part, join, join in *Opposite*: observe

participation *n* **contribution**, input, sharing, partaking, involvement *Opposite*: observation

participatory *adj* **taking part**, participating, sharing, partaking, hands-on

particle *n* 1 **bit**, speck, spot, crumb, grain 2 **iota**, bit, jot, scrap, shred

parti-colored *adj* **variegated**, multicolored, pied, piebald, rainbow *Opposite*: monochrome

particular *adj* 1 **specific**, precise, certain, exact, actual *Opposite*: vague 2 **individual**, distinct, noteworthy, special, unique *Opposite*: general 3 **exacting**, meticulous, scrupulous, fastidious, fussy *Opposite*: relaxed

particularity *n* 1 **fastidiousness**, meticulousness, fussiness, carefulness, discrimination *Opposite*: carelessness 2 **peculiarity**, characteristic, trait, idiosyncrasy, quirk 3 **individuality**, distinctiveness, idiosyncrasy, singularity, originality *Opposite*: similarity

particularize *v* **detail**, itemize, specify, enumerate, stipulate

particularly *adv* 1 **chiefly**, mainly, above all, predominantly, mostly 2 **exceptionally**, intensely, acutely, especially, specifically *Opposite*: unexceptionally

particulars *n* **details**, facts, information, essentials, basics

parting *n* **leaving**, departure, separation, going, goodbye *Opposite*: reunion

parting shot *n* **Parthian shot**, last word, final remark, retort, hostile remark

partisan *n* **supporter**, follower, adherent, fan, member *Opposite*: opponent ■ *adj* **biased**, prejudiced, opinionated, one-sided, bigoted *Opposite*: impartial

partisanship *n* 1 **support**, devotion, membership, sponsorship, adherence 2 **bias**, prejudice, bigotry, narrow-mindedness, one-sidedness *Opposite*: impartiality

partition *n* 1 **divider**, panel, dividing wall, screen, sliding doors 2 **separation**, division, rift, split, dividing up ■ *v* **divide**, separate, wall off, fence off, split

partly *adv* **partially**, in part, somewhat, partway, moderately *Opposite*: wholly

partner *n* 1 **spouse**, wife, husband, other half, lover 2 **associate**, colleague, collaborator, equal, coworker *Opposite*: superior ■ *v* **team up**, unite, join, link up, accompany

partner in crime *n* **accessory**, accomplice, crony, associate, sidekick *(infml)*

partnership *n* 1 **company**, business, firm, corporation, enterprise **2 affiliation**, association, collaboration, companionship, alliance *Opposite*: opposition

part-time *adj* **job-sharing**, evening, weekend, freelance, casual *Opposite*: full-time

part-timer *n* **part-time worker**, job-sharer, freelance, freelancer, casual *Opposite*: full-timer

partway *adv* **partly**, partially, halfway, in part, somewhat *Opposite*: completely

party *n* **1 social gathering**, gathering, festivity, revelry, event **2 faction**, political party, interest group, society, splinter group **3 participant**, accomplice, accessory, partaker, contributor **4 company**, band, gang, crew, contingent **5** *(fml)* **individual**, person, one, person concerned, someone ■ *v (infml)* **celebrate**, have fun, revel, whoop it up *(infml)*, paint the town red *(infml)*

party crasher *n* **interloper**, trespasser, invader, persona non grata *Opposite*: guest

partygoer *n* **celebrator**, socializer, guest, sociable person, attendee

party line *n* **official policy**, official position, party policy, official line, dogma

party pooper *(infml)* *n* **spoilsport**, killjoy, bore, wet blanket *(infml)*

parvenu *n* **upstart**, nouveau riche, social climber, arriviste, pretender

pass *v* **1 go by**, overtake, exceed, outdo, surpass *Opposite*: stop **2 elapse**, go by, pass by, lapse, go **3 hand over**, give, deliver, hand, forward *Opposite*: withhold **4 happen**, occur, arise, take place, come about **5 approve**, ratify, adopt, permit, accept **6 succeed**, qualify, make the grade, excel, exceed *Opposite*: fail **7 throw**, kick, hit, toss, lob ■ *n* **1 permit**, license, authorization, card, documentation *Opposite*: ban **2 passage**, gorge, route, corridor, valley **3 toss**, kick, hit, throw, lob **4 state of affairs**, state, plight, predicament, circumstances

passable *adj* **1 traversable**, crossable, drivable, safe, penetrable *Opposite*: impassable **2 acceptable**, adequate, good enough, all right, respectable *Opposite*: unacceptable

passage *n* **1 way through**, way, road, channel, course **2 section**, part, chapter, paragraph, segment **3 corridor**, pathway, walkway, hall, hallway **4 approval**, enactment, passing, ratification, acceptance **5 journey**, voyage, transfer, run, crossing **6 migration**, movement, exodus, flood, transit

passageway *n* **passage**, corridor, pathway, hallway, hall

pass away *v* **1 die**, succumb, pass on, kick the bucket *(slang)*, depart *(fml)* **2 come to an end**, finish, end, cease, terminate

pass by *v* **1 disregard**, overlook, pass over, ignore, look the other way **2 overtake**, go by, pass, surpass, leave behind **3 reject**, turn down, decline, refuse, ignore

passé *adj* **out-of-date**, old, faded, aged, worn-out *Opposite*: fashionable

passenger *n* **traveler**, customer, fare, commuter, rail user

passer-by *n* **onlooker**, bystander, spectator, witness, pedestrian

pass for *v* **impersonate**, pass as, look like, go as, do as

passim *(fml)* *adv* **here and there**, throughout, frequently, in various places, in several places

passing *adj* **1 transitory**, short-lived, ephemeral, fleeting, fly-by-night *Opposite*: permanent **2 cursory**, quick, casual, superficial, surface *Opposite*: thorough ■ *n* **1 departure**, departing, leaving, disappearance, desertion **2 death**, dying, passing away, end, departure. *See* COMPARE AND CONTRAST *at* **temporary**.

passion *n* **1 fervor**, ardor, obsession, infatuation, love **2 desire**, hunger, thirst, appetite, craving **3 rage**, fury, outburst, fever, anger. *See* COMPARE AND CONTRAST *at* **love**.

passionate *adj* **1 fervent**, ardent, zealous, avid, obsessive *Opposite*: indifferent **2 fiery**, quick-tempered, incensed, inflamed, enraged *Opposite*: easygoing

passionately *adv* **fervently**, ardently, avidly, single-mindedly, overpoweringly *Opposite*: indifferently

passionless *adj* **loveless**, detached, unromantic, emotionless, frigid *Opposite*: passionate

passive *adj* **inert**, inactive, unreceptive, reflexive, flaccid *Opposite*: active

passiveness *see* **passivity**

passivity *n* **inactivity**, inaction, nonparticipation, indifference, apathy *Opposite*: activeness

pass judgment *v* **give an opinion**, judge, criticize, condemn, deliver judgment

pass muster *v* **measure up**, be all right, check out, qualify, do

pass off *v* **masquerade**, pretend, misrepresent, palm off, falsify

pass on *v* **convey**, send, forward, impart, communicate

pass out *v* **1 faint**, black out, lose consciousness, have a fainting fit, swoon *Opposite*: come to **2 distribute**, hand out, give out, assign, deal out

pass over *v* **ignore**, neglect, discount, disregard, let go *Opposite*: consider

passport *n* **1 official document**, travel document, ID, papers, permit **2 access**, gateway, entry, opening, door

pass the buck *(infml)* *v* **shift the blame**, evade responsibility, lay something at somebody's door

pass through *v* **cross**, go through, lead through, traverse, move across

password *n* **code word**, open sesame, secret word, PIN, key

past *adj* **1 previous**, historical, earlier, former, bygone *Opposite*: future **2 elapsed**, completed, accomplished, over and done, done *Opposite*: ongoing ■ *n* **history**, earlier period, ancient times, times of yore, antiquity *Opposite*: future

paste *n* **1 adhesive**, glue, gum, fixative, wallpaper paste **2 slime**, gunk *(infml)*, goo *(infml)*, glop *(infml)*, goop *(infml)* **3 pastry**, dough, pie crust ■ *v* **glue**, stick, gum, fix, bond

pastel *adj* **pale**, light, soft, muted, neutral *Opposite*: vivid ■ *n* **crayon**, colored chalk, chalk, oil pastel

pasteurization *n* **sterilization**, heat treatment, purification, decontamination, disinfection

pasteurize *v* **sterilize**, heat, purify, decontaminate, disinfect

pasteurized *adj* **sterilized**, treated, purified, decontaminated, disinfected

pastiche *n* **imitation**, spoof, satire, lampoon, parody

pastime *n* **hobby**, interest, activity, pursuit, amusement

pasting *(infml)* *n* **beating**, defeat, thrashing, drubbing, pounding

past love *n* **first love**, ex *(infml)*, old flame *(infml)*, blast from the past *(infml)*

pastor *n* **minister**, priest, vicar, clergyman, cleric

pastoral *adj* **rural**, rustic, countryside, countrified, idyllic *Opposite*: urban

pastry *n* **1 dough**, paste, pie crust, puff pastry, flaky pastry **2 pie**, tart, tartlet, flan, Danish pastry

pasture *n* **meadow**, meadowland, fallow, grassland, prairie

pasty *adj* **pale**, unhealthy-looking, ashen, pallid, wan

pasty-faced *adj* **pasty**, pale, unhealthy-looking, ashen, pallid

pat *v* **1 tap**, touch, stroke, caress, massage **2 shape**, smooth, work, knead, mold ■ *n* **touch**, tap, stroke ■ *adv* **perfectly**, faultlessly, fluently, impeccably, by heart

patch *n* **1 cover**, reinforcement, covering, square **2 area**, spot, blotch, bit, smear **3 badge**, award, stripe, tag, square ■ *v* **repair**, cover, mend, strengthen, reinforce

patchiness *n* **1 unevenness**, intermittence, sparseness *Opposite*: evenness **2 variability**, inconsistency, unreliability, irregularity, unevenness *Opposite*: consistency

patchouli *n* **aromatic oil**, oil, perfume, scent, essential oil

patch up *v* **mend**, repair, fix, strengthen, reinforce

patchwork *n* **mixture**, mix, collage, assortment, potpourri ■ *adj* **pieced together**, jury-rigged, makeshift, jerrybuilt, piecemeal

patchy *adj* **1 occasional**, irregular, sporadic, intermittent, sparse **2 variable**, inconsistent, unreliable, erratic, unpredictable

pate *(archaic)* *n* **head**, crown, cranium, skull, noggin *(dated infml)*

patent *n* **copyright**, charter, right ■ *adj* **clear**, obvious, blatant, bald-faced, flagrant *Opposite*: unclear

paterfamilias *n* **father**, head of household, head, headman, paternalist

paternal *adj* **fatherly**, parental, nurturing, protective, guiding

paternalism *n* **authoritarianism**, interventionism, protectiveness, overprotectiveness, control

paternalistic *adj* **authoritarian**, patriarchal, protective, overprotective

paternity *n* **fatherhood**, parenthood, role, status, responsibility

path *n* **1 track**, trail, pathway, footpath, route **2 course**, route, way, orbit, direction

pathetic *adj* **1 pitiful**, sad, moving, tragic, doleful **2** *(infml)* **contemptible**, useless, risible, derisory, laughable. *See* COMPARE AND CONTRAST *at* moving.

pathfinder *n* **leader**, trailblazer, scout, pioneer, guide

pathological *adj* **1 extreme**, compulsive, uncontrolled, unreasonable, unreasoning **2 medical**, clinical, scientific, diagnostic, immunological **3 morbid**, systemic, allergic, viral, bacteriological

pathos *n* **sadness**, tragedy, bleakness, despair, anguish

pathway *n* **trail**, path, way, lane, alleyway

patience *n* **1 endurance**, staying power, stamina, persistence, perseverance *Opposite*: impatience **2 tolerance**, fortitude, serenity, imperturbability, unflappability *Opposite*: impatience

patient *adj* **1 enduring**, persistent, persevering, easygoing **2 tolerant**, long-suffering, serene, fortitudinous, imperturbable

patina *n* **1 discoloration**, tarnishing, staining, coating, verdigris **2 sheen**, shine, gloss, luster **3 layer**, veneer, covering, coating, coat

patois *n* **1 dialect**, vernacular, idiom, language, speech **2 jargon**, slang, cant, patter, argot

pat on the back *(infml)* *n* **handshake**, round of applause, endorsement, seal of approval

patriarch *n* **1 head of family**, paterfamilias, father, head, headman *Opposite*: matriarch **2 bishop**, archbishop, prelate, leader

patriarchal *adj* **male-controlled**, male, masculine, macho

patrician *adj* **aristocratic**, refined, upper-class, noble, blue-blooded ■ *n* **aristocrat**, noble, peer, squire

patricide n 1 **murder**, killing, parricide, slaughter, manslaughter 2 **murderer**, killer, parricide, slaughterer, homicide

patriot n **nationalist**, loyalist, flag-waver

patriotic adj **nationalist**, loyal, jingoistic, xenophobic, chauvinistic

patriotism n **loyalty**, partisanship, nationalism, jingoism, xenophobia

patrol n 1 **tour**, round, beat, circuit, perambulation 2 **unit**, detachment, squad, troop, group ■ v **guard**, watch, tour, make the rounds, walk the beat

patron n 1 **sponsor**, benefactor, supporter, investor, backer 2 **customer**, client, user, shopper, diner. See COMPARE AND CONTRAST at **backer**.

patronage n **investment**, backing, aid, sponsorship, benefaction

patronize v 1 **be condescending to**, demean, denigrate, belittle, talk down to 2 *(fml)* **frequent**, shop at, use, utilize, visit

patronizing adj **condescending**, superior, denigrating, belittling, full of yourself

patter n 1 **tapping**, drumming, beating, pitter-patter, rhythm 2 **speech**, script, talk, spiel *(infml)* 3 **jargon**, slang, cant, patois, argot ■ v 1 **tap**, drum, beat, pitter-patter, knock 2 **jabber**, prattle, rattle on, rant, go on and on

pattern n 1 **prototype**, outline, model, example, blueprint 2 **design**, decoration, shape, outline, form

patterned adj **decorated**, spotted, lined, squared, dotted

patty n 1 **pie**, pastry, meat pie 2 **cake**, burger, rissole

paucity n **dearth**, scarcity, rareness, scantiness, lack

paunch n **stomach**, belly, gut, potbelly, pot *(infml)*

paunchy adj **potbellied**, portly, corpulent, fleshy, plump

pauper n **poor person**, down-and-out, bankrupt, indigent *(fml)* Opposite: millionaire

pause v 1 **stop**, wait, break off, rest, stop what you're doing Opposite: continue 2 **hesitate**, falter, waver, wait, hold back 3 **linger**, stop, rest, tarry, halt Opposite: move on ■ n 1 **silence**, awkward moment, hiatus, gap 2 **break**, recess, suspension, intermission, hiatus Opposite: continuation. See COMPARE AND CONTRAST at **hesitate**.

pave v **cover**, surface, floor, tile, flag

paved adj **cemented**, flagged, surfaced, covered, tiled

pavement n **road surface**, roadway, asphalt, street, tarmac

paving n **flagging**, pavement, tiling, flooring, concrete

paw n *(infml)* **hand**, fist, mitt *(slang)* ■ v **maul**, molest, fondle, stroke, touch

pawn v **trade in**, wager, put up, place as collateral, pledge Opposite: redeem

pay v **disburse**, reimburse, compensate, forfeit, recompense Opposite: receive ■ n **wage**, salary, recompense, reimbursement, earnings. See COMPARE AND CONTRAST at **wage**.

payable adj **owed**, billed, due, allocated, to be paid

pay back v 1 **repay**, reimburse, pay off, settle up, restore Opposite: keep 2 **retaliate**, get even, take revenge, give tit for tat, settle scores

payback n 1 **return**, reimbursement, profit, remuneration, repayment 2 *(infml)* **revenge**, retaliation, retribution, vengeance, reprisal

paycheck n **wages**, salary, pay, payment, earnings

payee n **recipient**, beneficiary, receiver, collector, acceptor Opposite: payer

pay envelope n **wages**, salary, paycheck, earnings, income

payer n **spender**, financier, customer, client, paymaster Opposite: payee

pay in v **deposit**, bank, put away, put in, save Opposite: withdraw

payload n **cargo**, load, freight, shipment, consignment

payment n **sum**, expense, compensation, recompense, disbursement

pay off v 1 **settle**, square, repay, pay back, reimburse 2 **succeed**, bear fruit, work, be effective, prosper

payoff *(infml)* n 1 **payment**, settlement, reckoning, payout, remuneration 2 **bribe**, graft take, inducement, bribery

payola *(infml)* n **payment**, bribe, bribery, inducement, graft

payout n 1 **disbursement**, expenditure, expenses, outgoing, charge Opposite: income 2 **payment**, pay, wages, money, cash

payroll n **employees**, personnel, staff, workforce, workers

paystub n **statement**, stub, record, note, pay

pdq *(infml)* adv **immediately**, at once, quickly, fast, right away Opposite: later

peace n 1 **concord**, peacetime, harmony, armistice, reconciliation Opposite: war 2 **harmony**, calm, quiet, tranquility, stillness Opposite: uproar

peaceable adj 1 **peace-loving**, amiable, agreeable, easygoing, willing to please Opposite: aggressive 2 **tranquil**, peaceful, serene, harmonious, calm Opposite: chaotic

peace agreement n **treaty**, truce, ceasefire, armistice, agreement

peaceful adj 1 **quiet**, serene, calm, still, peaceable Opposite: disordered 2 **nonviolent**, passive, diplomatic, peaceable, pacific Opposite: violent

peacekeeper *n* **intermediary**, mediator, go-between, diplomat, pacifist

peacekeeping *n* **mediation**, intermediation, diplomacy, pacification, negotiation

peacemaker *n* **negotiator**, arbitrator, diplomat, mediator, intermediary *Opposite*: fighter

peacemaking *n* **reconciliation**, conciliation, mediation, arbitration, appeasement

peace offering *n* **olive branch**, apology, overture, approach, gesture

peacetime *n* **peace**, harmony, armistice, truce, ceasefire

peach *(infml)* *n* **beauty**, pearl, wow *(infml)*, honey *(infml)*, jim-dandy *(infml)* *Opposite*: dud *(infml)*

peachy *adj* **1** **peachlike**, downy, fuzzy, velvety, soft **2** *(infml)* **excellent**, wonderful, nice, splendid, great *Opposite*: terrible

peacock *n* **egoist**, exhibitionist, fop, show-off *(infml)*, dandy *(dated)*

peak *n* **1** **mountain**, mountaintop, summit, crest, point *Opposite*: valley **2** **tip**, pinnacle, zenith, top, summit *Opposite*: base ■ *v* **climax**, crest, max out, top *Opposite*: dip ■ *adj* **top**, highest, crowning, topmost, ultimate *Opposite*: bottom

peaked *adj* **1** **pointed**, sharp, pointy, spiky, tipped *Opposite*: rounded **2** **sickly-looking**, pale, thin, wan, emaciated

peal *n* **clangor**, ringing, tolling, din, clang

peanuts *(infml)* *n* **a small sum**, a trifling amount, a trifle, a trifling sum, a paltry sum *Opposite*: fortune

pearl *n* **treasure**, precious thing, nugget, prize, gem *(infml)* *Opposite*: dud *(infml)*

pearly *adj* **iridescent**, lustrous, gleaming, shining, translucent *Opposite*: dull

pear-shaped *adj* **bottom-heavy**, broadening, widening, bulging, rotund *Opposite*: top-heavy

peasant *n* **1** **farmer**, laborer, farm hand, farmworker, crofter **2** **country-dweller**, rustic, provincial

peat *n* **mulch**, moss, compost, fertilizer, turf

pebble *n* **stone**, nugget, grit, shingle

peccadillo *n* **sin**, offense, failing, indulgence, crime *Opposite*: virtue

peck *v* **1** **strike**, bite, jab, poke, dig **2** **nibble**, pick at, eat, play with, toy with *Opposite*: gobble **3** *(infml)* **kiss**, brush, caress, osculate *(fml)*, buss *(dated)* ■ *n* **1** **bite**, blow, stroke, jab, dig **2** *(infml)* **kiss**, brush, caress, smack, osculation *(fml)*

pecking order *n* **hierarchy**, class structure, social order, social structure, ladder

peculiar *adj* **1** **unusual**, odd, strange, weird, irregular *Opposite*: normal **2** **unique**, idiosyncratic, local, individual, special *Opposite*: universal

peculiarity *n* **1** **individuality**, idiosyncrasy, distinctiveness, particularity, uniqueness **2** **oddness**, strangeness, weirdness, eccentricity, abnormality *Opposite*: normality

peculiarly *adv* **1** **uniquely**, abnormally, unusually, curiously, strangely *Opposite*: typically **2** **particularly**, especially, extremely, very, extraordinarily *Opposite*: slightly

pecuniary *adj* **monetary**, financial, fiscal, economic, commercial

pedagogic *see* pedagogical

pedagogical *adj* **educational**, academic, instructive, tutorial, didactic

pedagogue *n* **teacher**, educator, schoolteacher, instructor, tutor

pedagogy *n* **teaching**, education, instruction, training, tutoring

pedal *n* **lever**, device, control, treadle ■ *v* **1** **cycle**, ride, drive, steer, travel **2** **ride**, operate, propel, control, guide

pedant *n* **doctrinaire**, obfuscator, nitpicker, sophist, hairsplitter *Opposite*: dilettante

pedantic *adj* **finicky**, plodding, obscure, arcane, dull *Opposite*: dilettante

pedantry *n* **literalism**, laboriousness, sophistry, meticulousness, thoroughness *Opposite*: creativity

peddle *v* **1** **sell**, tout, hawk, vend, retail **2** **promote**, market, hype, espouse, advocate

peddler *n* **seller**, dealer, trader, vendor, hawker

pedestal *n* **base**, plinth, stand, dais, platform

pedestrian *n* **walker**, rambler, ambler, hiker, strider ■ *adj* **dull**, ordinary, unimaginative, uninspired, prosaic *Opposite*: exciting

pedestrianized *adj* **traffic-free**, pedestrian, closed off

pedicure *n* **beauty treatment**, foot massage, cosmetic treatment, cosmetic session, chiropody treatment

pedigree *n* **lineage**, family background, ancestry, derivation, history ■ *adj* **pure-bred**, full-blooded, thoroughbred, noble, aristocratic

peek *v* **peep**, glance, peer, steal a look, have a look-see *Opposite*: stare ■ *n* **look**, glance, peep, glimpse, once-over *(infml)* *Opposite*: gaze

peel *v* **1** **skin**, strip, pare, hull, bark **2** **flake**, come off in layers, shed, desquamate **3** **unwrap**, remove, strip off, take off ■ *n* **skin**, rind, peelings, covering, shell

peeler *n* **potato peeler**, carrot peeler, paring knife, scraper

peeling *adj* **flaking**, shedding, cracking, coming off, coming loose *Opposite*: smooth

peelings *n* **parings**, skin, peel, rind, shavings

peep *v* **1** **peek**, peer, steal a look, glance, sneak a look *Opposite*: gaze **2** **chirp**, twitter, chirrup, squeak, beep ■ *n* **1** **look**, peek, glance, glimpse, gander *(infml)* **2 sound**, utterance, noise, word

peephole *n* **1 opening**, crack, hole, aperture, knothole **2 spyhole**, eyehole, keyhole

peer *n* **1 equal**, colleague, contemporary, friend, match **2 noble**, aristocrat, lord, patrician, member of the aristocracy ■ *v* **look**, scrutinize, gaze, stare, examine *Opposite*: glance

peer group *n* **cohort**, coequals, generation, age group, classmates

peerless *adj* **incomparable**, unequaled, matchless, unrivaled, without equal *Opposite*: commonplace

peeve *(infml)* *v* **vex**, annoy, irritate, irk, upset *Opposite*: please ■ *n* **gripe** *(infml)*, bugbear, irritation, vexation, nuisance *Opposite*: pleasure

peeved *(infml)* *adj* **annoyed**, irritated, irked, piqued, upset *Opposite*: pleased

peevish *adj* **irritable**, crabby, bad-tempered, cross, grumpy *Opposite*: good-tempered

peevishness *n* **irritability**, crabbiness, spitefulness, crossness, grumpiness

peewee *(infml)* *adj* **toy**, miniature, undersized, tiny, small *Opposite*: jumbo

peg *n* **pin**, fastener, dowel, hook, bolt ■ *v* **1 fasten**, secure, attach, fix, hang *Opposite*: detach **2 mark**, keep score, track, gauge, measure **3 freeze**, fix, set, control, limit *Opposite*: free

pejorative *(fml)* *adj* **disapproving**, judgmental, harsh, scornful, derogatory *Opposite*: positive

pell-mell *adv* **1 helter-skelter**, hurriedly, headlong, recklessly, tumultuously *Opposite*: carefully **2 untidily**, higgledy-piggledy, haphazardly, chaotically, topsyturvily *Opposite*: neatly

pelt *n* **hide**, fur, skin, hair, coat ■ *v* **1 bombard**, assail, assault, strafe, attack **2 pour**, cascade, come down in sheets *(infml)*, rain cats and dogs *(infml)* *Opposite*: drizzle

pen *n* **enclosure**, run, cage, coop ■ *v* **1 scribble**, jot, compose, scrawl, write **2 confine**, shut in, hold in, trap, capture *Opposite*: release

---

WORD BANK

❏ **types of pens** ballpoint, felt-tipped pen, fountain pen, highlighter, marker, quill, rollerball

---

penal *adj* **punitive**, punishing, disciplinary, corrective

penalization *n* **punishment**, disciplining, fining, discipline, correction *Opposite*: rewarding

penalize *v* **punish**, discipline, fine, reprimand, correct *Opposite*: let off

penalty *n* **1 punishment**, fine, sentence, penalization **2 consequence**, disadvantage, drawback, forfeit, price *Opposite*: advantage

penance *n* **self-punishment**, reparation, forfeit, atonement, amends

penchant *n* **liking**, fondness, partiality, taste, proclivity *Opposite*: antipathy

pencil *v* **write**, draw, mark, color, sketch

pendent *adj* **1 hanging**, suspended, dangling, sagging, perdulous *(fml or literary)* **pending** incomplete, unresolved, awaiting, undecided

pending *adj* **1 undecided**, incomplete, awaiting, unresolved, pendent *(fml or literary)* *Opposite*: in hand **2 imminent**, impending, expected, around the corner, approaching ■ *prep* **1 awaiting**, until, till **2 during**, throughout, in the course of

pendulous *adj* **1 hanging**, swinging, overhanging, drooping, loose **2 undecided**, wavering, vacillating, uncommitted, uncertain *Opposite*: decided

pendulum *n* **weight**, bob, plumb, swing

penetrate *v* **1 enter**, pass through, go through, go in, break in **2 diffuse**, seep in, soak in, infiltrate, imbue **3 grasp**, see into, perceive, figure out, comprehend **4 work out**, solve, decipher, figure out, understand

penetrating *adj* **1 all-pervading**, powerful, pungent, sharp, piercing **2 probing**, piercing, searching, questioning, inquiring **3 sharp**, intelligent, astute, perceptive, insightful *Opposite*: obtuse **4 piercing**, shrill, high-pitched, earsplitting, sharp

penetration *n* **1 diffusion**, infiltration, saturation, dispersion, dissemination **2 perception**, astuteness, understanding, discernment, comprehension **3 incursion**, access, breach entrance, infringement

penetrative *adj* **1 penetrating**, piercing, penetrant, permeating, pervasive **2 keen**, perceptive, insightful, acute, sharp *Opposite*: unperceptive

peninsula *n* **neck of land**, finger of land, cape, point, headland

penitence *n* **shame**, repentance, contrition, atonement, remorse *Opposite*: shamelessness

penitent *adj* **repentant**, repenting, contrite, remorseful, regretful *Opposite*: unrepentant

penitential *see* **penitent**

penitentiary *n* **prison**, penal colony, labor camp, house of correction, reformatory

pen name *n* **pseudonym**, nom de plume, alias, nom de guerre

pennant *n* **banner**, flag, ensign, emblem, streamer

penniless *adj* **poor**, impoverished, impecunious, destitute, bankrupt *Opposite*: rich

pennon *n* **flag**, pennant, banner, standard, emblem

penny pincher *(infml)* *n* **skinflint**, miser, pinchpenny, cheapskate *(infml)*, scrooge *(infml)* *Opposite*: spendthrift

penny-pinching *(infml)* *adj* **frugal**, thrifty,

stingy, tightfisted, parsimonious *Opposite*: generous

pension *n* **retirement pension**, retirement fund, annuity, income, retirement income

pensioner *n* **retiree**, retired person, senior citizen, senior

pensive *adj* **thoughtful**, meditative, contemplative, thinking, brooding

pensiveness *n* **thoughtfulness**, dreaminess, wistfulness, meditativeness, reflectiveness

pent-up *adj* **repressed**, stifled, unexpressed, contained, constrained *Opposite*: voiced

penultimate *adj* **second to last**, one before the last, next to last

penumbra *n* **1 shadow**, shade, darkness **2 obscurity**, uncertainty, cloudiness, indistinctness

pen up *v* **cage**, round up, shut within, corral, enclose *Opposite*: free

penurious *(literary) adj* **1 poor**, impoverished, destitute, needy, penniless *Opposite*: well-off **2 miserly**, grudging, cheap, niggardly, frugal *Opposite*: generous

penury *n* **poverty**, pennilessness, destitution, neediness, impoverishment *Opposite*: luxury

people *n* **1 nation**, community, nationality, populace, population **2 persons**, folks, individuals, public, general public **3** *(infml)* **relatives**, relations, family, folks, ancestors ■ *v* **populate**, fill, inhabit, immigrate, colonize

pep *(infml) n* **energy**, liveliness, vigor, perkiness, zest

pepper *v* **1 sprinkle**, shower, spray, scatter, speckle **2 intersperse**, sprinkle, interleave, infuse, scatter

peppery *adj* **spicy**, piquant, hot, fiery, pungent *Opposite*: mild

peppy *(infml) adj* **lively**, vigorous, sprightly, perky, frisky *Opposite*: lethargic

pep talk *(infml) n* **team talk**, speech, support, encouragement, inspiration

pep up *(infml) v* **spice up**, add zest, liven up, make something swing, give a bit of zing *(infml)*

per *prep* **for each**, apiece, for every, each, per capita

perceive *v* **1 notice**, observe, see, take in, remark *Opposite*: ignore **2 understand**, comprehend, sense, feel, become aware of

percent *adv* **out of a hundred**, out of each hundred, in each hundred, in a hundred, per hundred ■ *n* **percentage**, part, proportion, ratio, percentile

percentage *n* **1 fraction**, proportion, ratio, part, section **2** *(infml)* **commission**, proportion, fraction, take, profit

perceptible *adj* **noticeable**, traceable, observable, appreciable, visible *Opposite*: imperceptible

perception *n* **1 reading**, view, opinion, picture, take **2 insight**, acuity, awareness, discernment, observation

perceptive *adj* **discerning**, sensitive, insightful, keen, observant *Opposite*: insensitive

perceptiveness *n* **insight**, insightfulness, understanding, intuition, discernment

perch *v* **rest**, sit, settle, balance, alight

perchance *(literary) adv* **perhaps**, maybe, possibly, by chance, conceivably *Opposite*: definitely

percipience *n* **insight**, insightfulness, perceptiveness, discernment, understanding *Opposite*: insensitivity

percipient *adj* **insightful**, perceptive, observant, discerning, understanding *Opposite*: insensitive

percolate *v* **1 drip**, filter, trickle, ooze, leach **2 seep into**, infiltrate, permeate, penetrate, get into

percolator *n* **coffeepot**, coffee maker, coffee machine

percussion *(fml) n* **drumming**, beating, striking, hitting, bass beat

perdition *n* **hell**, purgatory, punishment, damnation, abyss

peregrination *(literary) n* **journey**, voyage, passage, traversing, crossing

peremptory *adj* **1 dictatorial**, authoritative, unconditional, absolute, dogmatic *Opposite*: polite **2 decisive**, no-nonsense, quick, hasty, direct *Opposite*: roundabout

perennial *adj* **recurrent**, returning, perpetual, constant, persistent *Opposite*: occasional

perestroika *n* **restructuring**, reform, reconstruction, reorganization, modernization

perfect *adj* **1 faultless**, flawless, textbook, picture-perfect, seamless *Opposite*: flawed **2 complete**, absolute, unqualified, whole, finished *Opposite*: incomplete **3 ideal**, just right, just the thing, wonderful, just what the doctor ordered *Opposite*: wrong **4 precise**, exact, accurate, on target, just right ■ *v* **1 achieve**, finish, complete, finalize, reach the summit of **2 improve**, refine, hone, tighten up, work on *Opposite*: spoil

perfection *n* **1 excellence**, rightness, faultlessness, exactness, precision **2 accomplishment**, fulfillment, completion, realization, achievement *Opposite*: abandonment

perfectionism *n* **fastidiousness**, fussiness, nitpicking, hairsplitting, pedantry *Opposite*: carelessness

perfectionist *n* **stickler**, purist, pedant, obsessive, quibbler

perfectly *adv* **1 flawlessly**, faultlessly, impeccably, effortlessly, seamlessly *Opposite*: badly **2 entirely**, wholly, absolutely, utterly *Opposite*: partially

perfidious *(fml) adj* **disloyal**, treacherous, deceitful, dishonest, lying *Opposite*: honest

perfidy *(fml)* n **treachery**, disloyalty, deceit, duplicity, betrayal *Opposite*: honesty

perforate v **puncture**, prick, pierce, hole, go through

perforation n **hole**, puncture, tear, rip, slash

perforce *(literary)* adv **unavoidably**, inevitably, of necessity, necessarily, inescapably

perform v 1 **do**, carry out, fulfill, accomplish, execute 2 **present**, act, play, put on, stage 3 **function**, work, behave, act, go

COMPARE AND CONTRAST CORE MEANING: complete a task

perform complete an action or accomplish a task, especially when this requires skill or care or when it forms part of a set procedure; **do** complete an action or accomplish a task of any kind; **carry out** complete any action or task; **fulfill** do what is necessary to achieve the successful accomplishment or realization of something planned, promised, or anticipated; **discharge** *(fml)* complete duties or responsibilities successfully; **execute** put an instruction or plan into effect, or complete an action or procedure that requires skill and expertise.

performance n 1 **presentation**, recital, act, routine, concert 2 **functioning**, implementation, execution, performing, carrying out 3 **feat**, deed, act, accomplishment, occurrence

performer n 1 **doer**, perpetrator, executor, architect, operator 2 **player**, actor, musician, recitalist, actress *Opposite*: spectator

perfume n 1 **fragrance**, scent, cologne, body spray, toilet water 2 **smell**, aroma, scent, odor, fragrance *Opposite*: stench ∎ v **scent**, fragrance, imbue, freshen, lace. *See* COMPARE AND CONTRAST *at* smell.

perfumed adj **scented**, sweet-smelling, sweet-scented, aromatic, fragrant

perfunctory adj 1 **unthinking**, automatic, mechanical, dutiful, obligatory *Opposite*: thoughtful 2 **hasty**, superficial, quick, fleeting, hurried *Opposite*: thorough

pergola n **arch**, trellis, framework, arbor, structure

perhaps adv **maybe**, possibly, conceivably, feasibly, imaginably *Opposite*: definitely

peril n **danger**, threat, risk, hazard, jeopardy *Opposite*: safety

perilous adj **dangerous**, unsafe, hazardous, risky, death-defying *Opposite*: safe

perimeter n **boundary**, border, edge, limit, outskirts

period n 1 **era**, age, epoch, stage, phase 2 **interval**, episode, interlude, phase, cycle

periodic adj 1 **episodic**, intermittent, interrupted, sporadic, occasional *Opposite*: constant 2 **cyclic**, recurring, recurrent, serial, regular *Opposite*: irregular

COMPARE AND CONTRAST CORE MEANING: recurring over a period of time

periodic recurring or reappearing from time to time with a degree of regularity; **intermittent** occurring at irregular intervals; **occasional** occurring infrequently at irregular intervals; **sporadic** occurring irregularly and unpredictably.

periodical n **journal**, bulletin, magazine, review, publication

peripatetic adj **itinerant**, traveling, nomadic, wandering, roving *Opposite*: settled

peripheral adj 1 **outlying**, marginal, fringe, bordering, exterior *Opposite*: major 2 **minor**, incidental, tangential, marginal, unimportant *Opposite*: central

periphery n **boundary**, margin, edge, sideline, border *Opposite*: center

perish *(literary)* v **die**, pass away, take your last breath, succumb, depart this life *(fml)* *Opposite*: live

perishable adj **unpreserved**, fresh, untreated *Opposite*: preserved

perishing adj **cold**, freezing, bitter, raw, chilly *Opposite*: boiling

periwig n **wig**, hairpiece, toupee, rug *(infml)*, peruke *(archaic)*

perjure v **lie**, bear false witness, commit perjury, fabricate, stretch the truth *Opposite*: tell the truth

perjury n **lying**, untruthfulness, lie, falsehood, untruth *Opposite*: honesty

perk n **bonus**, benefit, incentive, perquisite, extra *Opposite*: disadvantage

perk up v 1 **liven up**, cheer up, brighten up, wake up, awaken 2 **stick up**, stand up, prick up, pop up, straighten up *Opposite*: droop

perky adj 1 **lively**, cheerful, energetic, jaunty, pert *Opposite*: despondent 2 **overconfident**, confident, self-confident, self-important, self-assured *Opposite*: timid

perm v **curl**, wave, kink, crimp, frizz *Opposite*: straighten

permanence n **perpetuity**, durability, durableness, longevity, solidity *Opposite*: transience

permanency *see* permanence

permanent adj **perpetual**, enduring, lasting, eternal, everlasting *Opposite*: temporary

permeability n **porousness**, penetrability, perviousness, absorbency, sponginess *Opposite*: impermeability

permeable adj **porous**, penetrable, pervious, absorbent, absorptive *Opposite*: impermeable

permeate v 1 **infuse**, flood, fill, infiltrate, invade 2 **filter**, seep, leak, pervade, penetrate

permeation n 1 **infusion**, pervasion, flood, infiltration, invasion 2 **filtration**, seepage, leakage, penetration, percolation

permissible adj **allowable**, allowed, permitted, acceptable, accepted *Opposite*: unacceptable

permission *n* **consent**, authorization, approval, agreement, acquiescence *Opposite*: embargo

permissive *adj* **tolerant**, lenient, liberal, accommodating, lax *Opposite*: strict

permit *v* **authorize**, allow, let, approve, consent to *Opposite*: forbid ■ *n* **license**, document, certification, certificate, authorization

permitted *adj* **allowed**, allowable, permissible, acceptable, accepted *Opposite*: forbidden

permutation *n* **variation**, transformation, version, arrangement, rearrangement

pernicious *adj* **1 malicious**, wicked, evil, malevolent, malign *Opposite*: benign **2 destructive**, harmful, deadly, fatal, insidious *Opposite*: harmless

perniciousness *n* **1 maliciousness**, malice, wickedness, evil, malevolence *Opposite*: benignity **2 destructiveness**, harmfulness, deadliness, insidiousness, ruinousness *Opposite*: harmlessness

peroration *(fml) n* **speech**, oration, discourse, address, talk

peroxide *n* **hydrogen peroxide**, bleaching agent, bleach, tint ■ *v* **bleach**, tint, lighten, dye, discolor

perpendicular *adj* **vertical**, at right angles, upright, bolt upright, erect *Opposite*: parallel

perpetrate *v* **commit**, carry out, do, be responsible for, be behind

perpetration *n* **commission**, enactment, transaction, action, responsibility

perpetrator *n* **culprit**, criminal, wrongdoer, guilty party, offender

perpetual *adj* **continuous**, everlasting, uninterrupted, lasting, unending *Opposite*: temporary

perpetuate *v* **continue**, preserve, prolong, carry on, spread *Opposite*: stop

perpetuation *n* **continuation**, continuance, preservation, prolongation, spread *Opposite*: ending

perpetuity *n* **eternity**, time without end, all time, infinity, permanence

perplex *v* **puzzle**, baffle, confuse, stun, mystify *Opposite*: enlighten

perplexed *adj* **puzzled**, baffled, confused, at a loss, stunned *Opposite*: comprehending

perplexing *adj* **puzzling**, baffling, confusing, mystifying, confounding *Opposite*: simple

perplexity *n* **puzzlement**, bafflement, confusion, bewilderment, mystification *Opposite*: comprehension

perquisite *(fml) n* **privilege**, gratuity, perk, bonus, benefit *Opposite*: disadvantage

persecute *v* **1 oppress**, hound, harass, maltreat, pursue *Opposite*: protect **2 pester**, harass, torment, bother, bait *Opposite*: leave alone

persecution *n* **1 oppression**, harassment, maltreatment, pursuit, discrimination *Opposite*: protection **2 harassment**, torment, annoyance, irritation, suffering

persecutor *n* **1 oppressor**, harasser, pursuer, bully, torturer *Opposite*: protector **2 pesterer**, harasser, tormentor, nuisance, baiter

perseverance *n* **persistence**, determination, resolve, resolution, doggedness

persevere *v* **persist**, continue, keep at, keep it up, keep on *Opposite*: give up

persevering *adj* **persistent**, determined, resolute, resolved, dogged *Opposite*: irresolute

persist *v* **1 persevere**, continue, keep at, keep it up, keep on *Opposite*: give up **2 continue**, endure, live on, stay, go on *Opposite*: fade away

persistence *n* **1 perseverance**, determination, tenacity, resolve, resolution **2 continuance**, continuation, endurance, permanence, preservation *Opposite*: transience

persistent *adj* **1 tenacious**, determined, obstinate, insistent, dogged *Opposite*: irresolute **2 continuing**, continual, continued, unrelenting, incessant *Opposite*: fleeting

persnickety *(infml) adj* **1 painstaking**, meticulous, demanding, exacting, finicky *Opposite*: slapdash **2 exacting**, detailed, precise, painstaking, finicky *Opposite*: straightforward

person *n* **1 being**, human being, individual, creature, soul **2 body**, form, frame, figure **3** *(fml)* **appearance**, persona, personality, character, ego

persona *n* **1 character**, figure, person, role, part **2 identity**, role, guise, personality, character

personable *adj* **amiable**, friendly, pleasant, affable, agreeable *Opposite*: disagreeable

personage *(fml) n* **VIP**, celebrity, star, public figure, dignitary *Opposite*: nobody

personal *adj* **1 individual**, private, own, special, particular *Opposite*: public **2 offensive**, rude, derogatory, familiar, intrusive *Opposite*: complimentary ■ *n* **advertisement**, announcement, public notice, ad *(infml)*

personal assistant *n* **secretary**, assistant, administrative assistant, administrator, right arm

personal computer *n* **PC**, computer, terminal, laptop, notebook

personal effects *n* **belongings**, possessions, personal property, things, stuff

personality *n* **1 character**, nature, disposition, behavior, temperament **2 celebrity**, star, public figure, somebody, VIP *Opposite*: nobody

personalize *v* **1 initial**, monogram, mark, engrave, identify **2 customize**, individualize, differentiate, distinguish, specify *Opposite*: generalize

personally *adv* 1 **for myself**, in my opinion, in my view, for my part, myself *Opposite*: generally 2 **in person**, face to face, individually, myself, directly *Opposite*: indirectly

personal organizer *n* 1 **planner**, appointment book, address book, engagement book, datebook 2 **hand-held computer**, electronic planner, palmtop

personification *n* **epitome**, image, embodiment, incarnation, representation

personify *v* 1 **epitomize**, embody, incarnate, exemplify, characterize 2 **anthropomorphize**, humanize, personalize, give a human face, bring alive

personnel *n* **workers**, staff, employees, work force, human resources

perspective *n* 1 **viewpoint**, standpoint, outlook, view, perception 2 **proportion**, scale, ratio, size, depth 3 **vista**, view, prospect, scene, lookout

perspicacious *adj* **discerning**, perceptive, astute, insightful, wise *Opposite*: obtuse

perspicacity *n* **discernment**, perceptiveness, astuteness, shrewdness, clear-sightedness

perspiration *n* **sweat**, fluid, exudate, secretion, moisture

perspire *v* **sweat**, exude, ooze, swelter, drip

persuade *v* 1 **encourage**, coax, influence, induce, motivate *Opposite*: dissuade 2 **convince**, win over, sway, convert, bring around

persuasion *n* 1 **persuading**, encouragement, coaxing, influence, urging 2 **affiliation**, belief, order, denomination, faith

persuasive *adj* **convincing**, influential, winning, swaying, believable *Opposite*: unconvincing

persuasiveness *n* **persuasion**, influence, cogency, smoothness, eloquence

pert *adj* **lively**, flippant, impudent, perky, breezy

pertain to *v* **relate**, refer to, apply to, belong to, affect

pertinacious *adj* **resolute**, stubborn, obstinate, persistent, headstrong *Opposite*: malleable

pertinence *n* **relevance**, relatedness, appositeness, appropriateness, suitability *Opposite*: irrelevance

pertinent *adj* **relevant**, related, apposite, appropriate, germane *Opposite*: irrelevant

pertness *n* **cheekiness**, liveliness, flippancy, perkiness, breeziness

perturb *v* **trouble**, bother, disturb, worry, agitate

perturbation *n* **alarm**, worry, agitation, disquiet, trepidation *Opposite*: composure

perturbed *adj* **troubled**, disturbed, worried, anxious, disconcerted *Opposite*: composed

perusal *n* **examination**, scrutiny, inspection, checking, read-through

peruse *v* **read**, examine, scan, pore over, scrutinize *Opposite*: skim

pervade *v* **permeate**, pass through, saturate, spread through, infuse

pervasive *adj* **extensive**, universal, general, inescapable, prevalent *Opposite*: localized

pervasiveness *n* **extensiveness**, universality, generality, ubiquity, ubiquitousness

perverse *adj* 1 **obstinate**, willful, stubborn, headstrong, pertinacious *Opposite*: malleable 2 **aberrant**, irrational, deviant, abnormal, unreasonable *Opposite*: obliging

perverseness *n* 1 **aberrance**, irrationality, deviance, disobedience, unreasonableness 2 **willfulness**, stubbornness, contrariness, recalcitrance *Opposite*: malleability

perversion *n* **distortion**, misinterpretation, twisting, corruption, misapplication

perversity *n* **obstinacy**, willfulness, stubbornness, unreasonableness, contrariness *Opposite*: malleability

pervert *v* 1 **deprave**, corrupt, lead astray, spoil, warp 2 **distort**, misinterpret, twist, misrepresent, alter

perverted *adj* 1 **distorted**, misinterpreted, twisted, garbled, changed *Opposite*: undistorted 2 **depraved**, corrupt, debauched, warped, degenerate

pervious *adj* 1 **porous**, penetrable, absorbent, permeable *Opposite*: impervious 2 **receptive**, amenable, responsive, flexible, open *Opposite*: impervious

pesky *(infml)* *adj* **irritating**, troublesome, annoying, harassing, bothersome

pessimism *n* **negativity**, cynicism, doubt, distrust, gloom *Opposite*: optimism

pessimist *n* **cynic**, doubter, worrier, nihilist, defeatist *Opposite*: optimist

pessimistic *adj* **negative**, cynical, doubtful, distrustful, gloomy *Opposite*: optimistic

pest *n* 1 **vermin**, bug, insect, fly, mosquito 2 *(infml)* **bother**, nuisance, annoyance, vexation, irritant

pester *v* **annoy**, harass, worry, beleaguer, disturb *Opposite*: delight

pestilence *(archaic)* *n* **plague**, epidemic, virus, disease, bubonic plague

pestilent *adj* 1 **deadly**, lethal, fatal, virulent, killer *Opposite*: mild 2 **infected**, plague-ridden, contaminated, polluted, plague-ridden *Opposite*: healthy 3 *(literary)* **annoying**, irksome, irritating, bothersome, troublesome *Opposite*: pleasing

pet *n* 1 **animal**, domestic animal, domesticated animal, tame animal, companion 2 **favorite**, darling, treasure, jewel, idol 3 **sulk**, huff, pique, temper, tantrum ■ *adj* **favorite**, special, cherished, indulged, preferred ■ *v* 1 **stroke**, pat, fondle, caress, nuzzle 2 **indulge**, pamper, cosset, mollycoddle, spoil

peter out v disappear, dwindle, fade, recede, decrease Opposite: grow

petite adj small, diminutive, short, little, tiny Opposite: big

petition n request, appeal, entreaty, requisition, application ■ v appeal, lobby, request, beg, plead

petitioner n lobbyist, activist, campaigner, requester, asker

pet name n name, nickname, sobriquet, diminutive, epithet

petrified adj 1 frightened, terrified, scared, alarmed, scared stiff Opposite: reassured 2 fossilized, hardened, solidified, fixed, calcified

petrify v 1 frighten, terrify, scare, alarm, fill with fear Opposite: reassure 2 fossilize, harden, solidify, ossify, fix

petrifying adj frightening, terrifying, horrifying, shocking, spine-chilling Opposite: reassuring

pettifogging adj trivial, petty, unimportant, minor, insignificant Opposite: important

pettiness n 1 triviality, unimportance, inconsequence, paltriness, irrelevance Opposite: importance 2 petty-mindedness, mean-mindedness, triviality, pettifoggery, narrow-mindedness 3 spitefulness, grudgingness, resentfulness, maliciousness, vindictiveness

pettish adj peevish, irritable, sulky, bad-tempered, petulant Opposite: even-tempered

petty adj 1 trivial, unimportant, inconsequential, insignificant, paltry Opposite: important 2 petty-minded, mean-minded, niggling, narrow-minded, trivial 3 spiteful, grudging, resentful, malicious, vindictive Opposite: generous

petty cash n cash fund, office fund, coffee fund

petulance n sulkiness, crabbiness, peevishness, sullenness, moodiness Opposite: affability

petulant adj sulky, crabby, peevish, grumpy, sullen Opposite: affable

pew n bench, form, seat, bleacher

phalanx n group, body, mass, unit, formation

phantasm n ghost, spirit, apparition, specter, phantom

phantasmagoria n image, dream, hallucination, optical illusion, mirage

phantasmagoric adj dreamlike, bizarre, surreal, psychedelic, fantastical

phantasmagory see phantasmagoria

phantom n ghost, apparition, spirit, specter, phantasm

Pharaoh n ruler, king, sovereign, monarch, emperor

pharmaceutical adj medicinal, medical, pharmacological, therapeutic, curative ■ n drug, medicine, medication, treatment, narcotic

pharmacist n druggist, pharmacologist, posologist, apothecary (archaic)

pharmacy n drugstore, dispensary, druggist's, apothecary (archaic)

phase n stage, point, chapter, time, segment

phenomenal adj 1 remarkable, extraordinary, impressive, prodigious, outstanding Opposite: unremarkable 2 (infml) fantastic, marvelous, wonderful, amazing, brilliant Opposite: moderate

phenomenon n 1 occurrence, fact, experience, happening, incident 2 marvel, wonder, singularity, miracle, spectacle 3 prodigy, genius, bright star, enfant terrible, whiz kid (infml)

phial n vial, bottle, vessel, flask, flagon

philanderer n flirt, Casanova, adulterer, lady-killer, ladies' man

philanthropic adj charitable, benevolent, humanitarian, generous, big-hearted Opposite: misanthropic

philanthropist n patron, humanitarian, donor, sponsor, promoter Opposite: misanthropist

philanthropy n charity, compassion, humanity, patronage, generosity Opposite: misanthropy

philippic n diatribe, tirade, discourse, denunciation, insult

philistine n barbarian, boor, vulgarian Opposite: aesthete ■ adj uncultured, unsophisticated, uninformed, untutored, boorish Opposite: cultured

philistinism n barbarism, unsophistication, boorishness, ignorance

philosopher n theorist, thinker, logician, truth-seeker, academic Opposite: realist

philosophic see philosophical

philosophical adj 1 logical, ethical, metaphysical, moral, theoretical 2 deep-thinking, learned, thoughtful, studious, enlightened Opposite: shallow 3 calm, resigned, restrained, stoical, patient Opposite: emotional

philosophize v moralize, speculate, theorize, pronounce, meditate

philosophy n beliefs, viewpoint, thinking, values, attitude

philter (literary) n potion, charm, drug, aphrodisiac, magic potion

phlegm n 1 mucus, catarrh, rheum 2 calmness, composure, unflappability, self-possession, imperturbability Opposite: nervousness

phlegmatic adj calm, unemotional, composed, impassive, placid Opposite: nervous. See COMPARE AND CONTRAST at impassive.

phobia n fear, terror, dread, horror, fright

WORD BANK

❏ types of phobias acrophobia (fear of high places), agoraphobia (fear of public or open spaces), ailurophobia (fear of cats), arachnophobia (fear of spiders), claustrophobia (fear of confined or enclosed spaces), hydrophobia (fear of water), necrophobia (fear of death or dead bodies), nyctophobia (fear of night or darkness), photophobia (fear of light or lighted spaces), pyrophobia (fear of fire), technophobia (fear of new technology or computerization), zoophobia (fear of animals)

phobic adj **1 fearful**, scared, terrified, nervous, anxious **2 irrational**, neurotic, obsessed, disturbed, fixated

phone n **telephone**, mobile phone, mobile, cellphone, cellular phone ■ v **call**, ring, ring up, telephone, make a call

phoney see **phony**

phony adj **1 false**, fake, counterfeit, bogus, artificial Opposite: genuine **2 affected**, pretentious, deceiving, insincere, deceptive Opposite: sincere ■ n **fake**, counterfeit, impostor, hypocrite, forgery

photo see **photograph**

photocopy n **copy**, duplicate, reproduction, print ■ v **copy**, reproduce, make a copy of, run off, duplicate

photo finish n **close contest**, close thing, tie, neck-and-neck finish (infml)

photogenic adj **camera-friendly**, attractive, picturesque, appealing, good-looking

photograph n **picture**, snap, shot, snapshot, print ■ v **photo**, snap, shoot, get on film

photographer n **professional photographer**, press photographer, paparazzo, amateur photographer, photojournalist

photographic adj **1 pictorial**, graphic, picturesque, photogenic, camera-friendly **2 vivid**, clear, accurate, exact, detailed

photography n **cinematography**, filmmaking, picture making, shooting, camerawork

WORD BANK

❑ **parts of a camera** autofocus, diaphragm, exposure meter, film, filter, fisheye lens, flash, lens, lens cap, rangefinder, shutter, telephoto lens, viewfinder, zoom lens

❑ **types of photographic equipment** box camera, camera, developer, disc camera, enlarger, headcam, microfiche, microfilm, movie camera, pinhole camera, printer, projector, reflex camera, single-lens reflex, speed camera, tripod, twin-lens reflex

photojournalism n **photography**, news photography, reportage, camerawork, filmmaking

photo opportunity n **media event**, photo shoot, photo op, public-relations exercise, publicity event

photosensitive adj **light sensitive**, sensitive, reactive, light reactive, hypersensitive

phrasal adj **linguistic**, verbal, expressive, semantic, phraseological

phrase n **expression**, saying, idiom, axiom,

slogan ■ v **express**, couch, put, say, put into words

phrase book n **glossary**, bilingual dictionary, foreign-language dictionary, dictionary, lexicon

phraseology n **phrasing**, wording, choice of words, word choice, terminology

phrasing n **wording**, turn of phrase, style, word choice, diction

physical adj **1 bodily**, corporeal, animal, corporal, fleshly Opposite: mental **2 substantial**, material, objective, natural, real Opposite: ethereal **3 brute**, instinctive, visceral, instinctual, basic Opposite: refined

physical education n **sports**, gymnastics, athletics, exercise, aerobics

physically adv **bodily**, actually, in the flesh, really, materially Opposite: mentally

physical therapy n **treatment**, remedial exercise, rehabilitation, exercise

physician n **doctor**, medical doctor, doctor of medicine, general practitioner, GP

physics n **dynamics**, forces, physical processes, interactions, properties

physiognomy n **appearance**, face, features, characteristics, physical appearance

physiological adj **physical**, bodily, biological, functional

physique n **build**, body type, physical type, figure, form

piazza n **square**, forum, gathering place, village square, town square

picaresque adj **roguish**, mischievous, rascally, impish, villainous

pick v **1 harvest**, gather, cut, collect, pluck **2 select**, single out, choose, pick and choose, make a choice ■ n **best choice**, top choice, choice, cream of the crop, pick of the litter

picked adj **chosen**, selected, select, elect, handpicked

picket n **1 stake**, post, fence post, peg, rod **2 lookout**, sentinel, watch, sentry, guard **3 striker**, protester, boycotter, blockader ■ v **1 enclose**, fence, restrain, hedge in, pen in **2 protest**, strike, demonstrate, strike against, demonstrate at

pick holes in v **find fault with**, fault, criticize, attack, tear to shreds Opposite: praise

pickings n **earnings**, profits, takings, proceeds, spoils

pickle n (infml) **difficulty**, bind, predicament, plight, quandary ■ v **preserve**, marinate, cure, keep, conserve

pickled adj **preserved**, marinated, soused

pick-me-up (infml) n **refreshment**, stimulant, tonic, boost, lift

pick on v **tease**, make fun of, bully, harass, criticize

pick out v **1 choose**, make a choice, select, pick, pull out **2 identify**, distinguish, isolate, recognize, single out **3 highlight**, outline, emphasize

pickpocket *n* **thief**, sneak thief, robber, bag-snatcher, purse snatcher

pick up *v* **1 lift**, raise, hoist, raise up, elevate *Opposite*: put down **2** *(infml)* **improve**, recover, bounce back, buck up, change for the better *Opposite*: deteriorate **3 give a ride to**, give a lift to, come and get, call for, stop for *Opposite*: drop off *(infml)* **4 learn**, understand, grasp, get the hang of, remember **5 speed up**, accelerate, go faster, get better, improve *Opposite*: slow down **6 restart**, take up again, continue, carry on, jump back in *Opposite*: drop

pick up on *(infml)* *v* **notice**, point out, focus on, single out, call attention to *Opposite*: miss

picky *adj* **fastidious**, fussy, hard to please, finicky, particular *Opposite*: easygoing

picnic *n* *(infml)* **nothing**, walkover *(infml)*, cinch *(infml)*, piece of cake *(infml)*, breeze *(infml)* ■ *v* **have a picnic**, eat al fresco, eat outside

pictograph *n* **symbol**, hieroglyph, primitive writing, character, drawing

pictographic *adj* **graphic**, symbolic, pictorial, illustrative, visual

pictorial *adj* **graphic**, symbolic, illustrative, pictographic, clear

picture *n* **1 image**, depiction, portrait, representation, photograph **2 movie**, film, feature, motion picture, flick *(infml)* **3 embodiment**, epitome, perfect example, essence, personification ■ *v* **1 imagine**, create in your mind, visualize, see, conceive of **2 describe**, depict, illustrate, draw, show

picture book *n* **illustrated book**, children's book, story book, annual, coffee-table book

picture-postcard *adj* **picturesque**, attractive, pretty, chocolate-box, scenic *Opposite*: unattractive

picturesque *adj* **1 attractive**, pretty, scenic, charming, chocolate-box *Opposite*: unattractive **2 pictorial**, graphic, symbolic, pictographic, vivid

piddling *(infml)* *adj* **small**, petty, puny, paltry, trifling *Opposite*: enormous

pidgin *n* **lingua franca**, creole, patois, dialect, lingo *(infml)*

piebald *adj* **parti-colored**, pied, skewbald, spotted, mottled *Opposite*: plain

piece *n* **1 part**, fragment, bit, member, part of a set *Opposite*: whole **2 bit**, portion, hunk, wedge, slice *Opposite*: whole **3 example**, case, sample, instance, occurrence ■ *v* **patch**, mend, repair, restore, fix

piecemeal *adv* **1 gradually**, by degrees, little by little, a little at a time, a bit at a time *Opposite*: together **2 piece by piece**, bit by bit, one by one, separately, one at a time ■ *adj* **fragmentary**, disjointed, disconnected, disorganized, haphazard *Opposite*: cohesive

piece of cake *(infml)* *n* **snap**, child's play, nothing, breeze *(infml)*, cinch *(infml)*

piece of music *n* **composition**, creation, tune, melody, work

piece of writing *n* **article**, essay, composition, report, discourse

piece out *v* **piece together**, work out, reconstruct, restore, make sense of

piece together *v* **1 work out**, piece out, restore, reconstruct, make sense of **2 assemble**, join, fix, repair, mend *Opposite*: take apart

piecework *n* **freelance work**, part-time work, casual work, commission

piechart *n* **graph**, chart, diagram, illustration, figure

pied *adj* **multicolored**, variegated, mottled, piebald, flecked *Opposite*: plain

pied-à-terre *n* **second home**, vacation home, apartment, city apartment, studio

pier *n* **dock**, wharf, berth, jetty, landing-stage

pierce *v* **1 bore into**, stab, impale, cut, penetrate **2 hurt**, sting, pain, wound, affront *Opposite*: heal

piercing *adj* **1 penetrating**, intense, sharp, loud, earsplitting *Opposite*: soothing **2 perceptive**, searching, shrewd, acute, keen *Opposite*: gentle **3 cold**, bitter, freezing, wintry, raw *Opposite*: mild

piety *n* **1 piousness**, devoutness, devotion, religiousness, virtue *Opposite*: impiety **2 sanctimoniousness**, moralizing, hypocrisy, smugness, self-righteousness

piffle *(infml)* *n* **nonsense**, garbage, rubbish, twaddle *(infml)*, bunkum *(infml)* *Opposite*: sense

piffling *(infml)* *adj* **trifling**, unimportant, trivial, insignificant, petty *Opposite*: important

pig *(infml)* *n* **1 glutton**, gourmand, greedy pig *(infml)*, guzzler *(infml)* **2 brute**, beast, monster, rat *(slang)*

pigeon *(infml)* *n* **easy target**, dupe, sitting duck *(infml)*, sucker *(infml)*, chump *(infml)*

pigeon-breasted *adj* **barrel-chested**, top-heavy, stout

pigeonhole *n* **1 cubbyhole**, compartment, box, shelf, slot **2 category**, class, slot, classification, compartment ■ *v* **categorize**, class, classify, label, compartmentalize

piggish *adj* **1 greedy**, gluttonous, hoggish, self-indulgent *Opposite*: abstemious **2 stubborn**, uncooperative, obstructive, selfish, self-centered *Opposite*: considerate

piggy *adj* **greedy**, gluttonous, hoggish, self-indulgent, piggish *Opposite*: abstemious

piggyback *adj* **allied**, attached, associated, linked, added

piggy bank *n* **money box**, cash box, collecting box, savings box

pigheaded *adj* **stubborn**, obstinate, mulish,

dogged, single-minded *Opposite*: flexible

pigheadedness *n* **stubbornness**, obstinacy, mulishness, single-mindedness, intransigence *Opposite*: flexibility

pigment *n* **color**, dye, stain, tint, coloring

pigmentation *n* **coloring**, coloration, skincolor, pigment, color

pig out (*infml*) *v* **gobble**, gorge, devour, eat, scarf (*infml*)

pigpen *n* **filthy surroundings**, mess, dump (*infml*), hole (*infml*)

pile *n* **1 mound**, mountain, quantity, mass, heap **2** (*infml*) **big money**, fortune, mint (*infml*), wad (*infml*), megabucks (*slang*) **3 stake**, post, support, pillar, column **4 soft surface**, fiber, down, nap, fur ▪ *v* **heap**, load, stack, pile up, amass *Opposite*: scatter

pile up *v* **stack**, heap up, amass, mound, collect *Opposite*: scatter

pileup (*infml*) *n* **crash**, car crash, collision, car accident, road accident

pilfer *v* **steal**, rob, thieve, poach, take. *See* COMPARE AND CONTRAST *at* **steal**.

pilferer *n* **thief**, petty thief, sneak thief, robber, shoplifter

pilgrim *n* **traveler**, hajji, tourist, visitor, wayfarer (*literary*)

pilgrimage *n* **journey**, trip, visit, hajj, tour

pill *n* **tablet**, capsule, medication

pillage *v* **plunder**, sack, rob, loot, steal ▪ *n* **loot**, spoils, plunder, booty, prize

pillager *n* **plunderer**, robber, looter, raider, thief

pillar *n* **1 support**, column, post, prop, mast **2 rock**, mainstay, tower of strength, stalwart

pillbox *n* **1 box**, tin, container, étui **2 lookout post**, shelter, gun emplacement, gun shelter

pillory *v* **ridicule**, denounce, scorn, deride, humiliate *Opposite*: praise

pillow *n* **cushion**, support, pad, throw pillow, bolster ▪ *v* **protect**, support, prop up, hold up

pillowcase *n* **pillowslip**, pillow sham, sham, slipcover, slipcase

pilot *v* **guide**, conduct, control, navigate, lead ▪ *adj* **experimental**, trial, model, test, preliminary

pimple *n* **spot**, blemish, blackhead, boil, pustule

pimply *adj* **spotty**, blemished, acned *Opposite*: clear

pin *n* **1 brooch**, badge, stick pin **2** (*dated infml*) **iota**, tittle, pinch, bit, dash ▪ *v* **1 fasten**, attach, fix, secure **2 hold**, pin down, hold down, restrain, stick

pinch *v* **1 squeeze**, nip, tweak, grasp, press **2** (*infml*) **steal**, take, pilfer, thieve ▪ *n* **touch**, dash, soupçon, bit, taste. *See* COMPARE AND CONTRAST *at* **steal**.

pinched *adj* **haggard**, gaunt, drawn, pale, thin

pinchpenny *adj* **stingy**, ungenerous, miserly, tightfisted, mean *Opposite*: generous ▪ *n* **miser**, skinflint, penny pincher (*infml*), scrooge (*infml*), cheapskate (*infml*)

pin down *v* **1 identify**, determine, locate, pinpoint, isolate **2 hold down**, restrain, trap, pinion, pin

pine *v* **1 long**, yearn, ache, want, wish **2 waste away**, fade, fade away, suffer, go downhill *Opposite*: thrive

pine cone *n* **cone**, fir cone, seed case

ping *v* **sound**, ring, ding, beep, tinkle

pinion *v* **hold down**, trap, restrain, pin down, immobilize

pink *adj* **1 flushed**, red, rosy, glowing, blushing **2 undercooked**, rare, underdone, raw

WORD BANK
❑ **types of pink** cerise, coral, fuchsia, raspberry, rose, salmon pink, shell pink, shocking pink

pin money *n* **pocket money**, spending money, allowance, change, small change

pinnacle *n* **1 summit**, peak, height, top, apex *Opposite*: base **2 high point**, peak, acme, zenith, apex *Opposite*: nadir

pinpoint *v* **locate**, identify, pin down, isolate, find

pinprick *n* **hole**, puncture, pinhole, perforation, prick

pins and needles *n* **tingling**, prickling, numbness

pint-size (*infml*) *adj* **miniature**, pocket-sized, pocket-size, little, minuscule

pioneer *n* **innovator**, inventor, forerunner, developer, creator ▪ *v* **lead the way**, open up, forge, found, initiate

pioneering *adj* **groundbreaking**, revolutionary, cutting-edge, inventive, innovative

pious *adj* **1 devout**, religious, virtuous, moral, spiritual *Opposite*: impious **2 self-righteous**, sanctimonious, moralizing, hypocritical, smug

piousness *n* **1 piety**, devoutness, devotion, religiousness, virtue *Opposite*: impiety **2 self-righteousness**, sanctimoniousness, moralizing, hypocrisy, smugness

pip *n* **1 seed**, pit, fruit seed, stone, nut **2 spot**, speck, blemish, dot, mark

pipe *n* **tube**, cylinder, channel, conduit, pipeline ▪ *v* **1 supply**, channel, convey, transmit, bring in **2 whistle**, twitter, tweet, cheep, peep

pipe down (*infml*) *v* **quiet down**, keep it down, be quiet, hush, shut up (*infml*)

pipe dream *n* **fantasy**, aspiration, ambition, castle in the air, castle in Spain

pipeline *n* **conduit**, pipe, duct, channel, tube

pipe up *v* **speak up**, speak, make yourself heard, have your say, chip in (*infml*)

piping n **1** pipes, tubing, plumbing **2** edging, trimming, fringing ■ adj **high-pitched**, shrill, piercing, penetrating, high

piquancy n spiciness, tastiness, sharpness, tang, kick Opposite: blandness

piquant adj **1** spicy, tasty, sharp, hot, tangy Opposite: bland **2** stimulating, provocative, interesting, exciting **3** critical, biting, severe, sharp, harsh

pique n temper, resentment, annoyance, anger, ill will ■ v **1** irritate, annoy, upset, offend, bother **2** interest, intrigue, attract, stimulate, arouse Opposite: bore

piqued adj resentful, irritated, annoyed, upset, in high dudgeon

piratic adj freebooting, marauding, attacking, robbing, lawless

pirouette n spin, twirl, whirl, turn, revolution ■ v twirl, rotate, spin, turn, whirl

pit n **1** hole, ditch, well, crater, trench **2** dent, pock, indentation, hollow, depression **3** coal mine, mine, quarry, colliery **4** nadir, bottom, depths ■ v set as rivals, set against, fight, oppose

pitch v **1** throw, hurl, lob, toss, fling Opposite: catch **2** erect, set up, fix, plant, put up **3** sway, move, teeter, tilt, stumble **4** slope, slant, fall away, descend, dip **5** roll, lurch, plunge, rock, buck **6** propose, sell, throw, offer, deliver ■ n tone, highness, lowness, note

pitch-black adj black, inky, jet-black, black as night, dark Opposite: pale

pitch-dark adj unlit, pitch-black, dark, black, jet-black Opposite: light

pitched battle n argument, disagreement, fight, head-to-head, battle

pitcher n jug, decanter, carafe

pitchfork v **1** turn, lift, fork, toss **2** thrust, push, force, propel, drive

pitching adj rolling, lurching, plunging, rocking, bucking

piteous adj pathetic, pitiful, wretched, sad, pitiable Opposite: enviable

pitfall n drawback, snare, snag, danger, downside Opposite: advantage

pith n essence, crux, heart, nub, core

pithead n colliery, pit, coalmine, mineshaft, mine

pithiness n concision, terseness, brevity, succinctness, briefness Opposite: verbosity

pithy adj concise, terse, to the point, brief, succinct Opposite: long-winded

pitiable adj **1** contemptible, wretched, deplorable, disgraceful, miserable Opposite: admirable **2** pitiful, pathetic, unfortunate, sad, piteous Opposite: heartening

pitiful adj **1** disgraceful, deplorable, contemptible, abject, despicable Opposite: admirable **2** piteous, pathetic, pitiable, unfortunate, sad Opposite: heartening **3** meager, inadequate, derisory, small, paltry Opposite: magnanimous

pitiless adj merciless, heartless, callous, hard, unfeeling Opposite: compassionate

pitilessness n mercilessness, heartlessness, callousness, ruthlessness, harshness Opposite: compassion

pit stop n refueling stop, stop, rest stop, break, servicing stop

pittance n subsistence wage, small change, trifle, nothing, mite Opposite: fortune

pitted adj potholed, rutted, eroded, rough, bumpy Opposite: smooth

pity n **1** shame, disappointment, bad luck, tough luck, letdown Opposite: luck **2** sympathy, compassion, mercy, mercifulness, kindliness Opposite: pitilessness ■ v sympathize, commiserate, empathize, be there for somebody, show concern Opposite: blame

pitying adj sympathetic, understanding, compassionate, concerned, solicitous Opposite: unsympathetic

pivot n hinge, axle, axis, swivel, spindle ■ v spin, revolve, twist, rotate, whirl

pivotal adj essential, key, crucial, fundamental, critical Opposite: unimportant

pixie n fairy, elf, sprite, hobgoblin, Puck

pizzazz (infml) n vitality, spark, zest, style, glamour Opposite: dullness

placard n poster, sign, board, advertisement, notice

placate v appease, pacify, mollify, propitiate, conciliate Opposite: enrage

placation n appeasement, pacification, mollification, conciliation, satisfaction

placatory adj appeasing, mollifying, conciliatory, calming, soothing Opposite: inflammatory

place n **1** space, spot, position, point, area **2** location, spot, area, position, locality **3** home, house, residence, room, habitation **4** status, rank, position, station, circumstance ■ v **1** assign, hire, employ, engage, retain Opposite: fire **2** position, put, set, lay, leave Opposite: jettison **3** consign, identify, file, locate, arrange

placebo n dummy, palliative, control, sample, try-on (infml) Opposite: treatment

place mat n table mat, mat, cover, cloth, coaster

placement n **1** location, settlement, assignment, situation, employment **2** siting, positioning, location, arrangement, situation

place setting n setting, cover, place, tableware, flatware

placid adj calm, equable, even-tempered, imperturbable, easygoing Opposite: excitable

placidity n calmness, equability, serenity, imperturbability, even-temperedness Opposite: excitability

plagiarism n copy, piracy, theft, bootlegging, fraud

plagiarist n copyist, pirate, bootlegger, imitator, cheat Opposite: originator

plagiarize v copy, pirate, bootleg, steal, pass off as your own Opposite: originate

plague n 1 epidemic, disease, infection, pandemic, wave 2 curse, affliction, scourge, blight, visitation Opposite: blessing ■ v 1 afflict, trouble, pursue, hound, harass Opposite: bless 2 pester, badger, bother, harass, trouble Opposite: leave alone

plaid adj checkered, checked, tartan Opposite: plain

plain adj 1 simple, basic, unadorned, natural, pure Opposite: elaborate 2 clear, evident, obvious, apparent, manifest Opposite: obscure 3 blunt, straightforward, direct, frank, open Opposite: evasive 4 plain-featured, ordinary, unattractive, unappealing, homely Opposite: pretty ■ n prairie, savanna, steppe, pampas. See COMPARE AND CONTRAST at unattractive.

plain-clothes adj undercover, secret, disguised, out of uniform

plainly adv 1 simply, normally, basically, naturally, purely Opposite: elaborately 2 clearly, evidently, obviously, apparently, palpably Opposite: obscurely 3 bluntly, straightforwardly, directly, frankly, openly Opposite: evasively

plainness n 1 simplicity, ordinariness, naturalness, purity, bareness 2 clarity, clearness, palpability, tangibility, transparency Opposite: obscurity 3 bluntness, straightforwardness, directness, frankness, openness Opposite: evasiveness

plain-spoken adj direct, frank, blunt, forthright, bald Opposite: mealy-mouthed

plaint n plea, charge, accusation, complaint, action Opposite: defense

plaintiff n accuser, applicant, complainant, petitioner, litigant Opposite: defendant

plaintive adj mournful, lamenting, nostalgic, sorrowful, wistful Opposite: cheerful

plait v braid, interweave, weave, intertwine, crisscross Opposite: unravel

plan n 1 strategy, scheme, project, plan of action, tactic 2 idea, proposal, plot, scheme, aspiration 3 design, diagram, layout, blueprint, outline ■ v 1 work out, arrange, scheme, plot, organize Opposite: improvise 2 intend, propose, mean, line up, schedule

plane n aircraft, airplane, crate (dated infml), bird (slang)

planet n Earth, world, globe

WORD BANK
❏ types of planets Earth, Jupiter, Mars, Mercury, Neptune, Pluto, Saturn, Uranus, Venus

planned adj deliberate, intentional, prearranged, strategic, premeditated Opposite: unplanned

planner n 1 town planner, organizer, developer, city planner, designer 2 diary, calendar, appointment book, wall chart, planning aid

planning n preparation, setting up, development, arrangement, scheduling

plant n 1 shrub, bush, flower, herb, potted plant 2 factory works, installation, industrial unit, manufacturing plant 3 (infml) spy, informant, infiltrator, secret agent, mole ■ v 1 introduce, lodge, establish, implant, fix Opposite: erase 2 place, fix, stand transplant, deposit 3 sow, seed, scatter, root, transplant 4 (infml) conceal, hide, bury

plantation n estate, farm, homestead, farmstead, manor

planter n pot, flower pot, container, window box, urn

plaque n sign, panel, commemoration, inscription, plate

plaster v surface, coat, cover, face, plaster over

plasterwork n plaster, molding, stuccowork, stucco, pargeting

plastic adj 1 malleable, soft, pliable, elastic, flexible Opposite: hard 2 artificial, fake, synthetic, false, forced Opposite: genuine

WORD BANK
❏ types of plastic acetate, celluloid, epoxide, latex, melamine, neoprene, PET, polyethylene, polystyrene, polyurethane, PVC, vinyl

plasticity n malleability, softness, pliability, elasticity, flexibility Opposite: hardness

plate n dish, platter, salver, serving dish, bowl ■ v cover, coat, overlay, protect, shield

plateau n 1 upland, highland, hill, mesa, tableland 2 level, stage, period, phase

plated adj coated, overlaid, gold-plated, covered, finished Opposite: solid

platform n 1 stage, display place, raised area, podium, stand 2 policy, proposal, manifesto, program

plating n 1 electroplating, silver-plating, gilding, coating, luster 2 armor, armor plate, cladding, metal casing, outer casing Opposite: core

platitude n 1 cliché, inanity, tired expression, commonplace, banality 2 dullness, boredom, insipidity, triteness, plainness

platitudinous adj clichéd, trite, banal, corny, hackneyed Opposite: original

platonic adj spiritual companionable, friendly, nonsexual, nonphysical

platoon n squad, legion, team, detachment, subdivision

platter n plate, serving dish, salver, dish, tray

plaudit n applause, approval, praise, positive feedback, appreciation Opposite: criticism

plausibility n believability, credibility, reasonableness, probability, conceivability *Opposite*: implausibility

plausible *adj* believable, credible, reasonable, probable, conceivable *Opposite*: implausible

play *v* **1 enjoy yourself**, occupy yourself, amuse yourself, have fun, frolic **2 joke**, tease, fool around, mess around *(infml)*, kid *(infml)* **3 participate**, take part, join in, compete, engage in **4 perform**, act, play-act, portray, star as ∎ *n* **1 recreation**, amusement, fun, diversion, games *Opposite*: work **2 production**, drama, show, piece, performance

play-act *(infml)* *v* pretend, ham it up, put it on, put on an act, play to the gallery

playback *n* replay, rerun, reshowing, repetition, reproduction *Opposite*: recording

play down *v* minimize, make light of, underplay, underestimate, make little of *Opposite*: accentuate

player *n* **1 participant**, team member, competitor, contestant **2 actor**, thespian, performer, entertainer, play-actor

playfellow *(archaic)* *n* friend, playmate, chum *(infml)*, pal *(infml)*, buddy *(infml)* *Opposite*: enemy

playful *adj* **1 lively**, bouncy, full of fun, full of life, frisky *Opposite*: subdued **2 good-humored**, lighthearted, good-natured, teasing, jokey *Opposite*: serious

playfulness *n* **1 liveliness**, bounce, bounciness, friskiness, spirit **2 lightheartedness**, good humor, teasing, mischief, impishness *Opposite*: seriousness

play games with *v* deceive, trick, confuse, mistreat, abuse

playgoer *n* theatergoer, theater buff, spectator

playground *n* park, play area, community playground, adventure playground, outdoor play area

play hooky *(infml)* *v* play truant, truant, skip classes, miss school, absent yourself *Opposite*: attend

playhouse *n* theater, auditorium, studio, venue

playing field *n* sports grounds, sports field, park, ground, field

playmate *n* friend, pal *(infml)*, chum *(infml)*, buddy *(infml)*, playfellow *(archaic)* *Opposite*: enemy

play off *v* oppose, set against, pit against, go against, challenge

playoff *n* final, final round, semifinal, quarterfinal, tiebreaker

play safe *v* take no risks, hedge your bets, take care, be cautious, be careful *Opposite*: gamble

playschool *n* playgroup, nursery school, preschool, nursery, kindergarten

play the game *v* toe the line, follow the rules, conform, comply, obey *Opposite*: act up

plaything *n* toy, doll, bauble, curio, game

playtime *n* break, recess, interval, free time, leisure time

play to the gallery *v* show off, play up, posture, perform, play to the crowd

play up *v* exaggerate, emphasize, embellish, highlight, draw attention to *Opposite*: play down

play up to *v* flatter, toady, ingratiate yourself with, win the favor of, butter up *(infml)*

playwright *n* dramatist, writer, author, tragedian, dramaturge

play your cards close to your vest *v* be secretive, be a dark horse, keep secret, keep under wraps, keep mum *(infml)*

plaza *n* **1 square**, piazza, mall, marketplace, court **2 shopping center**, arcade, mall

plea *n* **1 appeal**, entreaty, prayer, request, petition *Opposite*: demand **2 statement**, claim, defense, declaration, assertion *Opposite*: denial **3 excuse**, pretext, reason, explanation, alibi

plea-bargain *v* plead guilty, do a deal, negotiate, come to an agreement, contract

plead *v* **1 beg**, appeal, pray, entreat, request *Opposite*: demand **2 declare**, assert, claim, state, put forward **3 support**, defend, argue, contend, vindicate

pleading *adj* begging, piteous, persuasive, suppliant *(fml)*, imploring *(fml)*

pleasant *adj* **1 enjoyable**, agreeable, pleasing, lovely, nice *Opposite*: unpleasant **2 amiable**, friendly, congenial, likable, genial *Opposite*: nasty

pleasantness *n* **1 appeal**, loveliness, niceness, pleasurableness, satisfaction *Opposite*: unpleasantness **2 amiability**, friendliness, congeniality, likability, likableness *Opposite*: nastiness

pleasantries *n* small talk, chat, gossip, banter, conversation

pleasantry *n* remark, civility, banality, politeness, observation *Opposite*: insult

please *v* **1 satisfy**, gratify, make happy, delight, thrill *Opposite*: displease **2 like**, prefer, choose, desire, wish *Opposite*: dislike

pleased *adj* satisfied, happy, content, delighted, contented *Opposite*: displeased

pleasing *adj* agreeable, pleasant, enjoyable, lovely, nice *Opposite*: disagreeable

pleasurable *adj* agreeable, enjoyable, pleasing, pleasant, gratifying *Opposite*: disagreeable

pleasure *n* **1 enjoyment**, happiness, delight, bliss, contentment *Opposite*: displeasure **2 gratification**, indulgence, hedonism, decadence, sensuality **3 amusement**, recreation, fun, leisure, diversion *Opposite*: work **4** *(fml or literary)* **desire**, preference, wish, choice, liking *Opposite*: displeasure

pleat n **crease**, fold, tuck, gather, crimp ■ v **fold**, crease, tuck, gather, crimp

plebiscite n **referendum**, poll, vote, ballot, opinion poll

pledge n 1 **vow**, oath, promise, assurance, guarantee 2 **initiate**, new member, recruit, freshman, inductee 3 **security**, deposit, guarantee, warranty, collateral ■ v **promise**, vow, swear, guarantee, give your word

plenary adj (fml) **full**, complete, entire, whole, unlimited ■ n **meeting** session, general assembly, plenary meeting, plenary session

plenipotentiary adj **presiding**, all-powerful, in charge, officiating, supreme Opposite: powerless ■ n **minister**, minister plenipotentiary, ambassador, special envoy, envoy Opposite: pawn

plenteous (literary) adj 1 **plentiful**, abundant, copious, overflowing, ample Opposite: sparse

plentiful adj **abundant**, copious, overflowing, ample, lavish Opposite: scarce

plenty n **prosperity**, abundance, copiousness, profusion, plethora Opposite: insufficiency ■ adj (infml) **ample**, a lot, lots, a load, sufficient Opposite: inadequate ■ adv (infml) **sufficiently**, adequately, amply, abundantly, profusely Opposite: insufficiently

plenum n **general assembly**, meeting, session, plenary meeting, plenary session

plethora n **overabundance**, excess, surfeit, glut, surplus Opposite: shortage

pliability n 1 **flexibility**, bendability, pliancy, softness Opposite: rigidity 2 **compliance**, pliancy, adaptability, flexibility, obedience Opposite: inflexibility

pliable adj 1 **flexible**, bendable, workable, pliant, plastic Opposite: rigid 2 **compliant**, pliant, docile, flexible, yielding Opposite: inflexible

---

COMPARE AND CONTRAST CORE MEANING: able to be bent or molded

pliable flexible and easily bent or molded; **ductile** describes metals that can be easily drawn out into a long continuous wire or hammered into thin sheets; **malleable** describes metals that can be hammered or pressed into various shapes without breaking or cracking; **elastic** describes substances or materials that can be stretched without breaking and then return to their original shape; **pliant** supple and springy and therefore easily bent.

---

pliancy n 1 **pliability**, flexibility, suppleness, elasticity, plasticity Opposite: stiffness 2 **compliance**, pliability, adaptability, flexibility, obedience Opposite: obstinacy

pliant adj 1 **supple**, springy, pliable, flexible, elastic Opposite: stiff 2 **compliant**, pliable, adaptable, flexible, accommodating Opposite: inflexible. See COMPARE AND CONTRAST at pliable.

plight n **dilemma**, trouble, predicament, difficulty, quandary

plinth n **pedestal**, platform, base, stand, support

plod v **trudge**, slog, tread, lumber, tramp Opposite: race

plodder n **snail**, toiler, slogger, idler, slowpoke (infml) Opposite: high-flier

plodding adj **slow**, dull, slow but sure, ponderous, tedious Opposite: rapid

plonk see **plunk**

plop v **place**, put, put down, set down, dump

plop down v **flop down**, sit down heavily, collapse, subside, plunk down

plot n 1 **conspiracy**, plan, scheme, subversion, strategy 2 **story line**, action, scenario, outline, narrative 3 **area**, section, parcel, piece, lot ■ v 1 **plan**, scheme, strategize, conspire, design 2 **chart**, map, draw, mark, map out

plotter n **schemer**, conspirator, conniver, contriver, strategist

plow v **cultivate**, till, turn over, work

plow into v **crash into**, bang into, drive into, run into, career into

plow on v **keep at it**, struggle on, persevere, persist, keep your nose to the grindstone

plow through v **keep at**, struggle on, plow on, persevere, persist

plow under v **overwhelm**, inundate, snow under, overburden, deluge

ploy n **trick**, maneuver, strategy, plan, ruse

pluck v 1 **pull**, tug, pick at, grasp, take 2 **pull out**, remove, yank, tweak, uproot 3 **pick**, collect, gather, harvest 4 **strum**, play, twang, plunk, pick ■ n **courage**, determination, bravery, fortitude, nerve Opposite: cowardice. See COMPARE AND CONTRAST at courage.

pluckiness n **bravery**, courage, pluck, fearlessness, boldness Opposite: cowardice

pluck up courage v **dare**, take the plunge, brace yourself, take a deep breath, steel yourself Opposite: lose your nerve

plucky adj **brave**, courageous, fearless, bold, audacious Opposite: cowardly

plug n 1 **stopper**, cork, cap, bung, top 2 **wad**, mass, lump, wadding, padding 3 **sample**, core, piece, wedge, extract 4 (infml) **socket**, outlet, wall outlet 5 (infml) **advertisement**, recommendation, mention, puff, ad (infml) ■ v 1 **stop**, cap, bung, cork, seal Opposite: unplug 2 (infml) **work**, carry on, keep at it, keep going, persevere 3 (infml) **puff**, hype, sell, push, spin Opposite: run down

plug in v **connect**, link up, hook up (infml) Opposite: unplug

plum (infml) n **reward**, award, bonus, windfall, trophy ■ adj **desirable**, choice, covetable, prestigious, profitable

plumage n **feathers**, down, fluff, fuzz

plumb adv 1 (infml) **exactly**, precisely, right,

bang, slap *(infml)* **2** *(infml)* **completely**, truly, totally, absolutely, utterly ■ *adj* **perpendicular**, upright, vertical, true, aligned *Opposite*: horizontal ■ *v* **1 comprehend**, understand, fathom, grasp, know **2 experience**, undergo, face, suffer, go through

plumbing *n* **drains**, sanitation, drainage system, water system, heating system

plume *n* **trail**, cloud, spiral, column, curl

plummet *v* **plunge**, drop, dive, tumble, crash *Opposite*: climb

plummy *adj* **resonant**, mellow, rich, sonorous *Opposite*: reedy

plump *adj* **fat**, overweight, chubby, stout, fleshy *Opposite*: slender ■ *v* **flop down**, drop, plop down, flop, fall *Opposite*: stand up

plump for *v* **support**, root for, cheer on, pull for, encourage

plumpness *n* **fatness**, chubbiness, fleshiness, curviness, obesity *Opposite*: slenderness

plump up *v* **fatten**, shake up, plump, fluff up

plunder *v* **steal**, rob, loot, pillage, raid ■ *n* **stolen goods**, loot, booty, spoils, ill-gotten gains

plunge *v* **1 thrust**, force, throw, push, pitch **2 rush**, jump, leap, lurch, throw yourself *Opposite*: hesitate **3 drop**, dive, plummet, sink, nose-dive *Opposite*: soar ■ *n* **dive**, drop, plummet, fall, nosedive *Opposite*: climb

plunging *adj* **1 plummeting**, dipping, dropping, tumbling, reducing *Opposite*: rising **2 low**, low-cut, revealing, décolleté *Opposite*: high

plunk *v* **1 twang**, strum, plonk, play, pick **2 drop**, dump, fall, push, throw

plunk down *v* **plump down**, flop down, plop down, drop down, collapse *Opposite*: stand up

pluralism *n* **variety**, diversity, multiplicity, heterogeneity *Opposite*: homogeneity

pluralistic *adj* **varied**, mixed, diverse, multicultural, multiethnic *Opposite*: homogeneous

plurality *n* **1 number**, range, variety, multiplicity, multitude *Opposite*: single **2 majority**, landslide, margin

plus *prep* **in addition to**, added to, as well as, along with, together with *Opposite*: minus ■ *adj* **1 and above**, and over, and more **2 desirable**, positive, advantageous, favorable, good *Opposite*: minus ■ *n* *(infml)* **advantage**, bonus, benefit, boon, pro *Opposite*: minus

plush *(infml) adj* **lush**, luxurious, expensive, rich, lavish

plutocrat *n* **tycoon**, magnate, mogul, big shot *(infml)*

ply *v* **1 work**, practice, pursue, carry out, wage **2 use**, work with, apply, utilize, employ **3 supply**, pile, load, provide, furnish *(fml)* **4 badger**, hound, harass,

overwhelm, bombard ■ *n* **layer**, thickness, strand, tier

p.m. *adj* **afternoon**, after lunch, evening, night *Opposite*: a.m.

pneumatic *adj* **air-filled**, inflated, inflatable, air *Opposite*: solid

poach *v* **1 steal**, thieve, rustle, pilfer, plunder **2 simmer**, boil, steam, braise

poacher *n* **thief**, rustler, robber, pilferer

pocked *adj* **pitted**, pockmarked, dented, cratered, scarred *Opposite*: unblemished

pocket *n* **pouch**, compartment, receptacle, sack, bag ■ *v* **help yourself to**, steal, appropriate, take, pinch *(infml)* ■ *adj* **concise**, abridged, reduced, short, small

pocketbook *n* **1 shoulder bag**, handbag, purse **2 notecase** *(dated)*, wallet, purse, case, organizer

pocket money *n* **spending money**, pin money, expenses, extra cash, personal money

pocket-size *see* **pocket-sized**

pocket-sized *adj* **little**, small, handy, compact, portable *Opposite*: bulky

pockmark *n* **blemish**, scar, indentation, hollow, blotch

pockmarked *adj* **pitted**, pocked, dented, cratered, scarred *Opposite*: unblemished

pod *n* **shell**, husk, peapod, case, hull

podium *n* **1 dais**, platform, stage, plinth **2 lectern**, pedestal, stand, support

poem *n* **verse**, rhyme, ode, sonnet, elegy *Opposite*: prose

poet *n* **writer**, lyricist, rhymester, versifier, composer

poetic *adj* **1 lyrical**, elegiac, graceful, rhythmical, flowing *Opposite*: prosaic **2 sensitive**, full of feeling, profound, deep, moving *Opposite*: insensitive

poeticality *n* **lyricism**, expressivity, eloquence

poetry *n* **verse**, rhyme, poems, rhymes, lyrics *Opposite*: prose

pogrom *n* **persecution**, extermination, massacre, devastation, slaughter

poignance *see* **poignancy**

poignancy *n* **pathos**, sadness, tragedy, nostalgia, tenderness

poignant *adj* **moving**, emotional, touching, distressing, sad *Opposite*: unemotional. *See* COMPARE AND CONTRAST *at* **moving**.

point *n* **1 opinion**, fact, idea, argument, theme **2 instant**, time, stage, moment, juncture *(fml)* **3 aim**, meaning, central theme, intention, heart **4 purpose**, advantage, use, sense, object **5 argument**, statement, line of reasoning, thrust, viewpoint **6 detail**, item, feature, aspect, thing **7 position**, spot, place, situation, site **8 tip**, end, top, summit, peak **9 headland**, cape, promontory, spit, peninsula ■ *v* **direct**, aim, face, indicate, draw attention to

point-blank *adv* **1 at close range**, straight

on, dead on, close up, close to 2 **frankly**, bluntly, outright, straightforwardly, directly *Opposite*: indirectly

pointed *adj* 1 **sharp**, piercing, keen, pointy, jagged *Opposite*: blunt 2 **barbed**, critical, meaningful, incisive, sharp *Opposite*: mild

pointedly *adv* **deliberately**, purposely, intentionally, meaningfully, openly *Opposite*: subtly

pointer *n* 1 **cane**, baton, stick, pole 2 **needle**, indicator, hand, cursor 3 **tip**, advice, hint, suggestion, warning

pointless *adj* **useless**, futile, senseless, meaningless, worthless *Opposite*: useful

pointlessness *n* **uselessness**, futility, senselessness, meaninglessness, worthlessness *Opposite*: usefulness

point of view *n* **opinion**, attitude, standpoint, viewpoint, position

point out *v* 1 **indicate**, show, reveal, point at, identify 2 **call attention to**, draw attention to, highlight, indicate, mention *Opposite*: hide

point-to-point *n* **steeplechase**, horserace, equestrian event, cross-country racing

point up *v* **emphasize**, draw attention to, underline, make clear, show

poise *n* 1 **composure**, dignity, self-assurance, self-confidence, self-control *Opposite*: insecurity 2 **grace**, bearing, deportment, good posture, composure *Opposite*: clumsiness ■ *v* **hover**, balance, float, perch, hang

poised *adj* 1 **ready**, prepared, primed, in position, in place *Opposite*: unprepared 2 **balanced**, suspended, hovering, on the edge, on the brink 3 **composed**, dignified, self-assured, self-confident, controlled *Opposite*: insecure

poison *n* **venom**, toxin, contagion, toxic substance *Opposite*: antidote ■ *v* 1 **kill**, murder, exterminate, destroy, harm 2 **pollute**, taint, corrupt, contaminate, adulterate

poisoner *n* **murderer**, killer, exterminator, assassin, slaughterer

poisonous *adj* 1 **toxic**, venomous, noxious, fatal, lethal *Opposite*: harmless 2 **malicious**, evil, wicked, nasty, spiteful *Opposite*: kindly

poke *v* 1 **jab**, stab, push, prod, thrust 2 **protrude**, stick out, project, jut, extend 3 **search through**, look through, root, browse, rummage ■ *n* **stab**, jab, push, prod, thrust

poke fun at *v* **make fun of**, ridicule, tease, mock, laugh at

poker-faced *adj* **expressionless**, blank, impassive, emotionless, deadpan *Opposite*: expressive

poky (*infml*) *adj* 1 **slow**, plodding, sluggish, leaden, dilatory *Opposite*: quick 2 **frumpy**, dowdy, shabby, drab, plain 3 **small**, tiny, cramped, restricted, tight *Opposite*: spacious

polar *adj* **glacial**, Arctic, Antarctic *Opposite*: tropical

polarity *n* **division**, split, schism, divergence, polarization *Opposite*: convergence

polarization *n* **divergence**, separation, division, opposition, schism *Opposite*: union

polarize *v* **diverge**, split, drive apart, separate, create a rift in *Opposite*: unite

pole *n* 1 **opposite** extreme, extremity, limit, end 2 **rod**, shaft, stick, post, dowel ■ *v* **push**, propel, raft, punt, shove

poleax *v* **astonish**, amaze, stupefy, stun, shock

polemic *n* **argument**, plea, diatribe, speech, discourse ■ *adj* **controversial**, outspoken, impassioned, uncompromising, bold *Opposite*: dispassionate

polemicist *n* **debater**, orator, speaker, essayist, lecturer

pole position *n* **prime position**, lead, front, advantage, catbird seat (*infml*) *Opposite*: rear

pole-vault *v* **jump**, vault, leap, bound

police *n* **police department**, law enforcement agency, police force, force, constabulary ■ *v* **regulate**, control, keep watch over, monitor, patrol

policeman *see* **police officer**

police officer *n* **officer**, sheriff, law enforcement officer, peace officer, cop (*slang*)

policewoman *see* **police officer**

policy *n* 1 **course of action**, rule, strategy, plan, guiding principle 2 **contract**, document, certificate, statement, papers

polish *v* 1 **shine**, buff, buff up, rub, clean *Opposite*: tarnish 2 **improve**, enhance, refine, perfect, hone ■ *n* 1 **shine**, luster, gleam, sheen, brilliance *Opposite*: dullness 2 **refinement**, skill, control, sophistication, grace

polished *adj* 1 **smooth**, shiny, gleaming, glossy, slippery *Opposite*: dull 2 **practiced**, skillful, accomplished, professional, impeccable *Opposite*: amateur 3 **refined**, elegant, cultured, sophisticated, graceful *Opposite*: coarse

polish off *v* **finish**, finish off, dispose of, complete, eliminate *Opposite*: leave

polish up *v* 1 **shine**, buff, rub, clean, dust *Opposite*: tarnish 2 **refine**, improve, practice, brush up, work on *Opposite*: let go

polite *adj* 1 **well-mannered**, good-mannered, civil, well-bred, gracious *Opposite*: rude 2 **refined**, cultured, sophisticated, polished, elegant *Opposite*: coarse

politeness *n* **good manners**, graciousness, manners, civility, breeding *Opposite*: rudeness

politic *adj* **tactful**, diplomatic, prudent, wise, expedient *Opposite*: foolish

political *adj* 1 **governmental**, administrative, electoral, civil, diplomatic 2 **politically**

aware, radical, partisan, dogmatic, party-political

political correctness *n* **appropriateness**, sensitivity, awareness, tactfulness, inclusiveness *Opposite*: insensitivity

politically correct *adj* **inclusive**, sensitive, tactful, inoffensive, appropriate *Opposite*: politically incorrect

politically incorrect *adj* **exclusive**, insensitive, inappropriate, unaware, tactless *Opposite*: politically correct

politician *n* **political figure**, representative, candidate, official, legislator

politicization *n* **awareness raising**, consciousness raising, lobbying

politicize *v* **raise awareness of**, put on the agenda, debate, discuss, air *Opposite*: depoliticize

politicking *n* **campaigning**, speechmaking, lobbying, politics, scheming

politics *n* **1. government**, political affairs, affairs of state, policy, policymaking **2 beliefs**, principles, opinions, views, theory

polity *n* **political entity**, organization, institution, state, society

poll *n* **election**, census, survey, opinion poll, sample ■ *v* **sample**, survey, question, ask, interview

pollinate *v* **fertilize**, cross-fertilize, self-fertilize, cross-pollinate, self-pollinate

pollination *n* **fertilization**, cross-fertilization, self-fertilization, cross-pollination, self-pollination

polling *n* **voting**, casting your vote, balloting, going to the polls

polling booth *n* **cubicle**, voting booth, booth, stall, box

pollutant *n* **contaminant**, impurity, toxin, poison, waste product

pollute *v* **1 contaminate**, poison, adulterate, infest, infect *Opposite*: clean **2 corrupt**, pervert, demoralize, violate, damage *Opposite*: purify

polluted *adj* **contaminated**, dirty, poisoned, adulterated, unclean *Opposite*: clean

polluter *n* **contaminator**, dumper, poisoner, emitter, discharger *Opposite*: environmentalist

pollution *n* **1 contamination**, infection, adulteration, corruption **2 contaminant**, toxic waste, effluence, greenhouse gasses, smog

poltergeist *n* **ghost**, spirit, manifestation, apparition, specter

polyglot *n* **linguist**, multilingual person, bilingual person

polygonal *adj* **many-sided**, multilateral, triangular, quadrilateral, pentagonal

polygraph *n* **detector**, lie detector, recorder, tester

polymath *n* **fount of knowledge**, Renaissance man, Renaissance woman, walking encyclopedia, mine of information *Opposite*: specialist

polyp *n* **growth**, tumor, cyst, nodule, swelling

polysyllabic *adj* **long**, compound, complex, multisyllabic *Opposite*: monosyllabic

polysyllable *n* **long word**, compound, complex word *Opposite*: monosyllable

polytechnic *n* **college**, technical college, university, tech (*infml*)

polytheism *n* **dualism**, animism, pantheism *Opposite*: monotheism

pomp *n* **splendor**, spectacle, display, ceremony, show *Opposite*: understatement

pom-pom *n* **tassel**, decoration, detail, ball

pomposity *n* **self-importance**, arrogance, pretentiousness, pretension, snobbishness *Opposite*: modesty

pompous *adj* **1 self-important**, arrogant, pretentious, snobbish, affected *Opposite*: modest **2 showy**, flaunting, spectacular, magnificent, grand *Opposite*: modest

pompousness *see* pomposity

poncho *n* **cloak**, cape, wrap

pond *n* **pool**, tarn, fishpond, millpond, mere (*literary*)

ponder *v* **consider**, think about, contemplate, deliberate, wonder about

ponderable *adj* **appreciable**, significant, considerable, substantial, weighty *Opposite*: insignificant

ponderous *adj* **1 heavy**, laborious, lumbering, weighty, unwieldy *Opposite*: light **2 tedious**, boring, laborious, tiresome, dull *Opposite*: lively

pontiff *n* **pope**, bishop of Rome, Holy Father

pontifical *adj* **1 episcopal**, papal, prelatic **2 pompous**, self-important, pontificating, grandiose, portentous *Opposite*: humble

pontificate *v* **hold forth**, preach, go on, sound off

pontoon *n* **platform**, float, buoy, support, base

pooch (*infml*) *n* **dog**, lapdog, canine companion, canine, hound

pooh-pooh *v* **reject**, dismiss, spurn, scorn, scoff at *Opposite*: praise

pool *n* **1 pond**, puddle, lake, swimming pool, tarn **2 team**, band, collection, consortium, collective **3 kitty**, fund, pot (*infml*) ■ *v* **share**, combine, bring together, put together, assemble *Opposite*: ration out

pooped (*infml*) *adj* **exhausted**, tired out, worn out, drained, ready to drop *Opposite*: invigorated

poor *adj* **1 destitute**, needy, poverty-stricken, impoverished, penniless *Opposite*: rich **2 deprived**, unfortunate, underprivileged, meager, reduced *Opposite*: privileged **3 weak**, inadequate, feeble, meager, bad *Opposite*: superior **4 humble**, lowly, modest, insignificant *Opposite*: noble

poorly *adv* **badly**, inadequately, weakly, feebly, scantily *Opposite*: well

poorness *n* **1 poverty**, impoverishment, destitution, pennilessness, neediness *Opposite*: wealth **2 weakness**, inadequacy, feebleness, inferiority, poor quality *Opposite*: superiority

poor quality *n* **cheapness**, tawdriness, mediocrity, inferiority, weakness *Opposite*: quality

poor-quality *adj* **cheap**, shoddy, trashy, jerrybuilt, junky *Opposite*: first-rate

pop *n* **explosion**, bang, crack, report, snap ▪ *v* **1 explode**, burst, go off, crack **2** (*infml*) **dash**, dart, go, call, nip (*infml*) **3** (*infml*) **put**, place, insert, drop, shove ▪ *adj* (*infml*) **popular**, modern, current, accessible, easy

pope *n* **pontiff**, bishop of Rome, Holy Father

popeyed *adj* **goggle-eyed**, swollen-eyed, wide-eyed, bug-eyed (*infml*)

pop in (*infml*) *v* **visit**, go, stop at, look in, drop in

poppycock (*dated infml*) *n* **nonsense**, absurdity, untruth, rubbish, twaddle (*infml*)

populace *n* **public**, population, general public, common people, lay people

popular *adj* **1 well-liked**, accepted, admired, in style, all the rage *Opposite*: unpopular **2 common**, general, prevalent, widely held, current *Opposite*: rare

popularity *n* **admiration**, approval, acceptance, fame, status *Opposite*: infamy

popularization *n* **1 promotion**, spread, commercialization, propagation, universalization **2 simplification**, vulgarization, interpretation, explanation, universalization

popularize *v* **1 make popular**, promote, spread, propagate, commercialize **2 simplify**, interpret, vulgarize, put in layperson's terms, explain

popularly *adv* **generally**, commonly, prevalently, readily, widely

populate *v* **inhabit**, people, settle, colonize, fill *Opposite*: desert

population *n* **inhabitants**, populace, people, residents

populist *adj* **mainstream**, majority, democratic, general, accessible *Opposite*: elitist

populous *adj* **crowded**, overcrowded, populated, full of people, packed *Opposite*: desolate

pop-up *adj* **spring-operated**, automatic, self-opening, folding, foldaway

porcine *adj* **piggy**, piggish, swinish, hoglike

pore *n* **hole**, opening, aperture, stoma

pore over *v* **examine**, scour, read, study, go over

porous *adj* **absorbent**, permeable, leaky, spongy *Opposite*: impermeable

port *n* **seaport**, anchorage, dock, harbor, haven (*literary*)

portability *n* **movability**, transportability, transferability, lightness, compactness *Opposite*: bulkiness

portable *adj* **movable**, transportable, transferable, handy, convenient *Opposite*: fixed

portal (*literary*) *n* **gateway**, doorway, porch, entrance, entry

portcullis *n* **gate**, door, grating, drawbridge, entry

portend *v* **foreshadow**, foretell, signify, mean, warn of

portent *n* **1 omen**, sign, presage, warning, indication **2** (*fml*) **marvel**, phenomenon, prodigy, wonder, miracle

portentous *adj* **1 significant**, important, crucial, ominous, fateful *Opposite*: trivial **2 pompous**, pretentious, self-important, haughty, arrogant *Opposite*: modest

porter *n* **gatekeeper**, doorkeeper, concierge, janitor, receptionist

portfolio *n* **1 case**, folder, file, wallet **2** (*fml*) **range**, collection, selection, group, set

portico *n* **porch**, entrance, doorway, entry, entryway

portion *n* **1 helping**, share, slice, serving, percentage **2 fraction**, piece, bit, part, segment *Opposite*: whole **3** (*literary*) **fate**, destiny, lot, karma, kismet ▪ *v* **divide**, distribute, allocate, assign, share out

portliness *n* **stoutness**, stockiness, roundness, heaviness, heftiness *Opposite*: slimness

portly *adj* **overweight**, stout, stocky, round, heavy *Opposite*: slim

portmanteau *n* **suitcase**, case, bag, valise, holdall

portrait *n* **picture**, representation, portrayal, likeness, photograph

portraiture *n* **portrait making**, portrait painting, photography, painting, drawing

portray *v* **depict**, represent, describe, show, interpret

portrayal *n* **representation**, interpretation, depiction, picture, description

pose *v* **1 model**, stand, sit, sit for, posture **2 impersonate**, pretend, play the part of, masquerade, profess **3 present**, cause, create, set, establish **4 ask**, put, put forward, present, propound ▪ *n* **1 posture**, stance, position, attitude, carriage (*fml*) **2 pretense**, sham, fake, front, façade

poser *n* **1** (*infml*) **poseur**, show-off, exhibitionist, posturer, narcissist **2 problem**, question, puzzle, conundrum, challenge

poseur *n* **exhibitionist**, posturer, narcissist, swaggerer, peacock

posh (*infml*) *adj* **upmarket**, elegant, fashionable, expensive, luxurious *Opposite*: downmarket

posit (*fml*) *v* **put forward**, postulate, suggest, theorize, speculate

position *n* **1 location**, place, site, spot, point **2 posture**, stance, pose, arrangement, attitude **3 rank**, status, standing, station **4 view**, opinion, policy, stance, perception ▪ *v* **put**, place, locate, stand, sit

positive *adj* **1 sure**, certain, clear, convinced, assured *Opposite*: uncertain **2 irrefutable**, definite, explicit, clear-cut, conclusive *Opposite*: dubious **3 optimistic**, confident, constructive, helpful, encouraging *Opposite*: negative

positively *adv* **1 definitely**, absolutely, completely, really, certainly **2 encouragingly**, confidently, optimistically, supportively, constructively *Opposite*: negatively

posse *(infml) n* **gang**, band, party, group, company

possess *v* **1 own**, have, hold, enjoy, keep *Opposite*: lack **2 take control**, influence, take, occupy, seize

possessed *adj* **controlled**, influenced, obsessed, crazed, overcome

possession *n* **ownership**, control, tenure, custody, proprietorship

possessions *n* **property**, belongings, wealth, goods, assets

possessive *adj* **1 domineering**, jealous, controlling, overprotective, covetous *Opposite*: trusting **2 selfish**, greedy, grasping, tightfisted, mean *Opposite*: generous

possessiveness *n* **1 selfishness**, greed, tightfistedness, meanness, greediness *Opposite*: generosity **2 jealousy**, jealousness, suspiciousness, overprotectiveness, insecurity

possessor *n* **owner**, holder, bearer, keeper, proprietor

possibility *n* **likelihood**, prospect, risk, chance, probability

possible *adj* **1 likely**, conceivable, imaginable, thinkable, probable *Opposite*: unlikely **2 achievable**, doable, feasible, viable, workable *Opposite*: impossible

possibly *adv* **perhaps**, maybe, probably, conceivably, feasibly *Opposite*: certainly

post *n* **1 pole**, column, stake, upright, marker **2 position**, placement, job, station, place ■ *v* **display**, announce, advertise, put up, publish

postage *n* **stamp price**, postage fee, postage charge, postage cost

postcard *n* **card**, picture postcard, message, note, letter

poster *n* **1 picture**, print, reproduction, artwork, photograph **2 advertisement**, placard, notice, bill, announcement

posterior *adj* **1 rear**, hind, back, hindmost *Opposite*: front **2** *(fml)* **latter**, subsequent, following, next, later *Opposite*: former

posterity *n* **future generations**, later generations, generations to come, successors, future

postgraduate *n* **student**, postgraduate student, graduate student, Ph.D. student, graduate

posthaste *adv* **fast**, immediately, right away, quickly, straight away *Opposite*: slowly

posthumous *adj* **subsequent**, retrospective, delayed, following, postmortem

posting *n* **placement**, relocation, position, post, military posting

postmark *n* **date stamp**, frank, stamp, mark, rubber stamp ■ *v* **frank**, stamp, date, mark, rubber-stamp

postmortem *n* **1 autopsy**, postmortem examination, medical examination, examination, inquest **2 investigation**, analysis, examination, inquest, review

postnatal *adj* **postpartum**, post-delivery, perinatal

post office *n* **1 P.O.**, mail depot, mailroom **2 mail system**, mail service, postal service, postal communications, mail

postpone *v* **delay**, put off, put back, shelve, put on the back burner *Opposite*: bring forward

postponement *n* **delay**, rescheduling, rearrangement, deferment, adjournment

postscript *n* **afterthought**, addition, supplement, afterword, epilogue *Opposite*: preface

postulate *v* **assume**, guess, hypothesize, suggest, claim

posture *n* **bearing**, stance, attitude, position, pose

posturing *n* **self-importance**, pomposity, swagger, bravado, bluster

posy *n* **1 bouquet**, bunch of flowers, spray, nosegay, arrangement **2 blossom**, flower, bloom *(literary)*

pot *n* **1 container**, pan, vessel, jar, tub **2** *(infml)* **potbelly**, paunch, beer belly *(slang)* ■ *v* **1 shoot**, bag, catch, get, hit **2 preserve**, seal, pickle, can

potable *adj* **drinkable**, clean, filtered, fit to drink, drinking

potato *n* **tuber**, new potato, seed potato, spud *(infml)*, tater *(infml)*

WORD BANK
❑ **types of processed potatoes** croquette, French fries, fries, hash browns, home fries, knish, latke, potato cake, potato chips, potato pancake, rösti

poteen *n* **bootleg alcohol**, spirit, bootleg whiskey, whiskey, white lightning

potency *n* **strength**, force, power, might, vigor *Opposite*: weakness

potent *adj* **1 strong**, effective, powerful, forceful, mighty *Opposite*: weak **2 persuasive**, convincing, influential, forceful

potentate *n* **monarch**, ruler, leader, emperor, sovereign

potential *n* **ability**, capacity, possibility, makings, what it takes ■ *adj* **possible**, hypothetical, conceivable, likely, probable *Opposite*: unlikely

pothole *n* **1 rut**, hole, dip, depression, fault **2 cave**, cavern, catacomb, pit, hole

potholed adj rutted, pitted, holed, eroded, uneven Opposite: smooth

potholer n speleologist, caver, spelunker

potion n liquid, medicine, concoction, mixture, brew

potluck n luck of the draw, whatever is going, whatever is on offer, chance, whatever is available

potpourri n miscellany, mixture, assortment, hodgepodge, collection

pots (infml) n bags, heaps (infml), piles (infml), tons (infml), loads (infml)

potshot n shot, pot, go, aim, try

potted adj preserved, sealed, conserved, pickled, canned Opposite: fresh

pottery n ceramic objects, earthenware, stoneware, ceramics

WORD BANK

❑ **types of pottery** bone china, ceramic, china, delft, earthenware, enamel, faience, Limoges, Meissen, porcelain, Sèvres, stoneware, terra cotta

---

pouch n bag, pocket, money bag, purse, sack

poultice n dressing, compress, bandage

pounce v 1 attack, seize upon, seize, tackle, ambush 2 spring, swoop, leap, jump, dive Opposite: recoil ■ n leap, jump, spring, bound, swoop

pound v 1 hit, strike, batter, beat, hammer 2 throb, thump, beat, pulsate, pulse 3 grind, crush, pulverize, bruise, mash

pounding n 1 beating, thrashing, drubbing, defeat, pasting (infml) 2 throbbing, thumping, pulsation, pulse, hammering

pour v 1 decant, drizzle, dispense, discharge, transfer 2 spill out, gush, stream, flow, rush Opposite: trickle 3 swarm, crowd, teem, stream, rush Opposite: trickle 4 rain, drench, lash, rain cats and dogs (infml) Opposite: drizzle

pouring adj torrential, heavy, hammering, driving Opposite: light

pour out v reveal, blurt out, disclose, give away, tell

pour scorn on v disparage, ridicule, deride, sneer at, mock

pour with rain v pour down, teem, come down in torrents, rain cats and dogs (infml)

pout v 1 purse your lips, pucker, frown, scowl, glower Opposite: smile 2 sulk, mope, glower, scowl, grouch (infml) Opposite: smile

poverty n 1 lack, deficiency, scarcity, shortage, dearth Opposite: surplus 2 neediness, destitution, hardship, deprivation, privation Opposite: affluence

poverty-stricken adj destitute, in need, poor, penniless, impoverished Opposite: rich

powder n fine particles, dust, residue, precipitate, ash ■ v crush, grind, pound, pulverize, mill

powdered adj ground, crushed, pulverized, milled, processed Opposite: whole

powder keg n tinderbox, minefield, time bomb, recipe for disaster, explosive combination

powdery adj fine, crumbly, chalky, dusty, dry

power n 1 control, influence, authority, supremacy, rule Opposite: powerlessness 2 ability, capacity, faculty, potential, capability Opposite: inability 3 authority, right, prerogative, license, privilege Opposite: powerlessness 4 nation, country, state, player, superpower 5 strength, force, might, energy, brawn Opposite: weakness

power base n stronghold, seat of power, headquarters, home base, base

powerful adj 1 influential, commanding, authoritative, controlling, prevailing Opposite: powerless 2 strong, mighty, brawny, muscular, sturdy Opposite: weak 3 effective, potent, strong, pungent, overwhelming Opposite: impotent 4 persuasive, compelling, forceful, effective, convincing Opposite: unimpressive

powerhouse (infml) n driving force, heart, center, dynamo, live wire (infml)

powerless adj helpless, incapable, unable, weak, feeble Opposite: powerful

powerlessness n helplessness, hopelessness, weakness, feebleness, ineffectiveness

power line n electricity cable, overhead cable, cable, wire, overhead wire

practicability n feasibility, viability, workability, attainability, operability Opposite: impossibility

practicable adj feasible, realistic, possible, workable, attainable Opposite: impossible

practical adj 1 applied, real-world, hands-on, everyday, real Opposite: theoretical 2 realistic, down-to-earth, level-headed, sensible, pragmatic Opposite: unrealistic 3 useful, sensible, feasible, sound, workable 4 everyday, workaday, serviceable, functional, plain Opposite: decorative 5 handy, step-by-step, helpful, user-friendly, useful

practicality n 1 realism, common sense, level-headedness, pragmatism, sensibleness Opposite: impracticality 2 usefulness, sensibleness, feasibility, soundness, workability Opposite: uselessness

practical joke n trick, prank, joke, lark, hoax

practically adv 1 almost, nearly, virtually, just about, well-nigh 2 realistically, sensibly, rationally, reasonably, level-headedly Opposite: unrealistically

practice n 1 repetition, rehearsal, exercise, preparation, training 2 habit, custom, tradition, way, system ■ v 1 rehearse, prepare, exercise, repeat, try 2 live out, carry out, perform, apply, follow *Opposite*: reject. *See* COMPARE AND CONTRAST *at* **habit**.

practiced *adj* **skillful**, experienced, trained, expert, adept *Opposite*: untrained

practitioner *n* **physician**, medical practitioner, general practitioner, GP, doctor

pragmatic *adj* **practical**, realistic, logical, rational, reasonable *Opposite*: idealistic

pragmatism *n* **practicality**, realism, logicality, rationality, reasonableness *Opposite*: idealism

pragmatist *n* **practical person**, down-to-earth person, realist, doer, rationalist *Opposite*: idealist

prairie *n* **plain**, savanna, steppe, pampas

praise *n* **1 admiration**, commendation, approval, acclaim, tribute *Opposite*: criticism **2 worship**, honor, adoration, devotion, thanks *Opposite*: vilification ■ *v* **1 admire**, commend, extol, honor, compliment *Opposite*: criticize **2 glorify**, honor, laud, worship, adore *Opposite*: vilify

praiseworthy *adj* **admirable**, commendable, laudable, worthy, exemplary *Opposite*: blameworthy

prance *v* **1 cavort**, dance, frolic, gambol, caper **2 swagger**, strut, parade, flounce, sashay

prank *n* **trick**, practical joke, hoax, joke, lark

prankster *n* **trickster**, joker, practical joker, mischief-maker, imp

prate *v* **chatter**, gibber, prattle, babble, jabber

prattle *v* **prate**, gibber, chatter, jabber, babble ■ *n* **chatter**, gibber, drivel, nonsense, jabber

pray *v* **1 request**, plead, beg, crave, ask **2 hope**, wish, cross your fingers, hope against hope, yearn **3 meditate**, contemplate, say your prayers, call upon, invoke

prayer *n* **1 entreaty**, appeal, plea, request, desire **2 invocation**, meditation, contemplation, devotions, chant

preach *v* **1 give a sermon**, speak, discourse, talk, deliver an address **2 advise**, lecture, sermonize, moralize, advocate

preacher *n* **minister**, pastor, missionary, lay preacher, vicar

preamble *n* **introduction**, preface, foreword, prelude, overture *Opposite*: postscript

prearrange *v* **organize**, set up, arrange, plan, settle upon

prearranged *adj* **planned**, arranged, agreed, preset, specified *Opposite*: chance

precarious *adj* **shaky**, unstable, insecure, wobbly, unsteady *Opposite*: stable

precaution *n* **protection**, safety measure, preventive measure, insurance, safeguard

precautionary *adj* **protective**, defensive, safety, cautionary, preventive *Opposite*: remedial

precede *v* **lead**, come first, go before, pave the way, herald *Opposite*: follow

precedence *n* **superiority**, priority, preference, primacy, antecedence

precedent *n* **example**, model, guide, pattern, standard

preceding *adj* **previous**, earlier, prior, former, past *Opposite*: following

precept *(fml) n* **principle**, teaching, rule, guideline, instruction

precinct *n* **district**, zone, area, sector, quarter

precious *adj* **1 valuable**, costly, expensive, dear, treasurable *Opposite*: worthless **2 valued**, loved, beloved, important, dear *Opposite*: despised **3 fastidious**, affected, overrefined, fussy, self-conscious *Opposite*: natural

preciousness *n* **1 valuableness**, value, costliness, expensiveness, dearness *Opposite*: worthlessness **2 fastidiousness**, affectation, fussiness, self-consciousness, daintiness *Opposite*: naturalness

precious stone *n* **gemstone**, jewel, stone, gem, sparkler *(infml)*

precipice *n* **rock face**, cliff, crag, sheer drop, abyss

precipitate *adj* **1 rash**, impulsive, impetuous, careless, reckless *Opposite*: considered **2 abrupt**, sudden, unexpected, surprising, unforeseen *Opposite*: expected **3 hurried**, hasty, swift, quick, rapid *Opposite*: slow ■ *v* **hasten**, bring on, cause, lead to, occasion *Opposite*: retard

precipitation *n* **rain**, rainfall, snow, sleet, hail

precipitous *adj* **1 rash**, quick, hurried, swift, impulsive *Opposite*: careful **2 steep**, sheer, abrupt, high, vertical *Opposite*: gentle

précis *n* **summary**, synopsis, résumé, abstract, sketch ■ *v* **summarize**, sum up, condense, outline, abridge *Opposite*: expand

precise *adj* **1 exact**, detailed, accurate, specific, particular *Opposite*: vague **2 meticulous**, scrupulous, particular, careful, fastidious *Opposite*: careless

precision *n* **exactness**, accuracy, exactitude, care, meticulousness *Opposite*: vagueness

preclude *(fml) v* **prevent**, impede, stop, rule out, exclude *Opposite*: permit

preclusion *(fml) n* **prevention**, exclusion, disqualification, prohibition, deterrence *Opposite*: permission

precocious *adj* **advanced**, developed, intelligent, bright, gifted *Opposite*: immature

precociousness *see* **precocity**

precocity *n* **talent**, cleverness, brightness, intelligence, precociousness *Opposite*: immaturity

precognition *n* **clairvoyance**, foreknowledge, premonition, foresight, second sight

preconceived *adj* **fixed**, set, defined, rigid, inflexible *Opposite*: unprejudiced

preconception n prejudice, bias, fixed idea, presumption, notion

precondition n condition, requirement, prerequisite, qualification, must

precook v parboil, soften, blanch

precursor n forerunner, ancestor, predecessor, antecedent, pioneer Opposite: successor

predate v precede, go before, antedate, exist before, preexist

predator n marauder, killer, hunter, pillager, raider

predatory adj greedy, destructive, rapacious, grasping, voracious

predecessor n precursor, forerunner, ancestor, antecedent, prototype Opposite: successor

predestination n destiny, fate, doom, kismet, lot Opposite: free will

predestine v destine, fate, preordain, doom, predetermine

predestined adj fated, destined, bound, preordained, appointed

predetermination n 1 prearrangement, arrangement, intention, decision, resolution 2 predestination, preordination, preordainment, lot, destiny Opposite: free will

predetermine v 1 set, program, encode, determine, decide 2 predestine, destine, fate, preordain, doom

predetermined adj 1 prearranged, programmed, encoded, fixed, determined 2 predestined, destined, fated, bound, preordained

predicament n difficulty, quandary, dilemma, tight spot, tight corner

predicate (fml) v base, establish, found, ground, build

predict v forecast, foresee, envisage, expect, guess

predictability n 1 likelihood, probability, sureness, certainty, liability Opposite: unpredictability 2 unoriginality, banality, triteness, obviousness, staleness Opposite: originality

predictable adj 1 foreseeable, expectable, expected, likely, probable Opposite: unlikely 2 unsurprising, unoriginal, banal, trite, obvious Opposite: original

predictableness see predictability

predicted adj foretold, forecast, foreseen, prophesied, projected Opposite: unforeseen

prediction n forecast, guess, calculation, estimate, prophecy

predictive adj prognostic, extrapolative, prophetic, projecting, foretelling

predilection (fml) n liking, preference, fondness, partiality, penchant Opposite: dislike

predispose (fml) v incline, dispose, prompt, influence, prejudice

predisposed (fml) adj inclined, disposed, subject, liable, susceptible Opposite: unwilling

predisposition n tendency, disposition, inclination, penchant, bias

predominance n 1 superiority, power, dominance, control, supremacy 2 majority, prevalence, preponderance, numerousness Opposite: minority

predominant adj main, major, chief, principal, prime Opposite: minor

predominantly adv mainly, mostly, largely, chiefly, principally Opposite: partially

predominate v prevail, dominate, outweigh, preponderate, be in the majority

preeminence n superiority, authority, excellence, eminence, renown Opposite: obscurity

preeminent adj distinguished, outstanding, famous, well-known, foremost Opposite: obscure

preempt v forestall, anticipate, obstruct, block, prevent Opposite: react

preemption n preemptive action, preventive action, preventive measures, prevention, anticipation Opposite: reaction

preemptive adj preventive, preventative, proactive, anticipatory, blocking Opposite: reactive

preen v groom, smarten, clean, tidy, smooth

preexist v predate, precede, antecede, go before, prelude

preexisting adj previous, prior, earlier, former, established Opposite: new

prefabricate v manufacture, make up, assemble, produce, mass-produce

preface n foreword, preamble, introduction, prologue, prelude Opposite: postscript ■ v prefix, precede, introduce, start, begin

prefect n senior pupil, monitor, captain

prefer v favor, have a preference, like better, wish, desire

preferable adj better, desirable, nicer, superior choice Opposite: inferior

preference n favorite, first choice, partiality, penchant, fondness Opposite: dislike

preferential adj special, favored, privileged, superior, better Opposite: disadvantageous

preferment (fml) n promotion, upgrading, appointment, advancement, elevation Opposite: demotion

preferred adj favored, favorite, chosen, number one, in

prefigure v anticipate, herald, foreshadow, portend, presage

prefix v preface, precede, begin, start, start off

pregnancy n 1 gestation, prenatal period, perinatal period, gravidity, gravidness 2 significance, importance, import, meaning

pregnant adj 1 **expectant**, antenatal, prenatal, gravid, expecting (infml) 2 **charged**, significant, weighty, meaningful, pointed

preheat v **heat**, heat up, warm, warm up, turn on Opposite: cool

prehistoric adj 1 **primeval**, primitive, antediluvian, early, ancient 2 **old-fashioned**, out-of-date, ancient, outmoded, antiquated Opposite: modern

prehistory n **early history**, olden days, times gone by, dawn of time, Stone Age

prejudge v **jump to conclusions**, presume, presuppose, anticipate, assume

prejudice n 1 **bias**, preconception, prejudgment, predisposition, partiality Opposite: impartiality 2 **bigotry**, chauvinism, narrow-mindedness, discrimination, intolerance Opposite: tolerance ■ v **influence**, bias, sway, slant, distort

prejudiced adj **biased**, intolerant, bigoted, narrow-minded, discriminatory Opposite: tolerant

prejudicial adj **harmful**, detrimental, hurtful, damaging, injurious Opposite: helpful

prelate n **archbishop**, cardinal, bishop, abbot

preliminary adj **initial**, first, opening, pilot, introductory Opposite: closing ■ n **beginning**, first round, introduction, opening, groundwork Opposite: finale

prelude n **introduction**, overture, prologue, preface, foreword Opposite: finale

premature adj **early**, untimely, hasty, rash, precipitate Opposite: overdue

premeditated adj **planned**, deliberate, intentional, calculated, thought-out Opposite: spontaneous

premeditation n 1 **planning**, calculation, cold-bloodedness, coldness, contemplation Opposite: impulsiveness 2 **reflection**, contemplation, thought, consideration, cogitation (fml) Opposite: spontaneity

premier adj **best**, first, leading, foremost, highest Opposite: worst ■ n **president**, head of state, head of government, prime minister, PM

premiere n **opening**, first night, first performance, first showing, debut

premiership n **presidency**, prime ministership, leadership, term of office, tenure

premise n 1 **evidence**, principle, idea, foundation, ground 2 **proposition**, supposition, hypothesis, assertion, thesis

premises n **building**, grounds, location, site, property

premium n **payment**, percentage, bonus, reward, perk ■ adj **best**, top, finest, quality, first-class Opposite: low-grade

premonition n 1 **intuition**, presentiment, feeling, hunch, fear 2 **warning**, omen, sign, portent, indication

premonitory adj 1 **intuitive**, predictive, clairvoyant, prophetic, precognitive 2 **warning**, prognostic, precautionary, cautionary, sobering

preoccupation n **worry**, obsession, anxiety, concern, fixation

preoccupied adj **worried**, anxious, lost in thought, elsewhere, inattentive Opposite: carefree

preoccupy v **worry**, concern, disturb, trouble, consume

preordained adj **inevitable**, fated, predetermined, destined, doomed

preparation n 1 **groundwork**, training, grounding, homework, research 2 **planning**, provision, arrangement, formulation, organization

preparatory adj **introductory**, foundation, preliminary, elementary, opening Opposite: final

prepare v 1 **get ready**, arrange, organize, plan, set up 2 **train**, groom, coach, prime, make ready 3 **make**, cook, get ready, concoct, formulate

prepared adj **ready**, set, equipped, geared up, organized

preparedness n **readiness**, preparation, alertness, attentiveness, awareness

prepare yourself v **steel yourself**, brace yourself, nerve yourself, compose yourself, get ready

prepayment n **advance payment**, down payment, payment, advance, deposit Opposite: debt

preponderance (fml) n 1 **majority**, mass, great number, multitude, many Opposite: minority 2 **dominance**, superiority, prevalence, predominance, weight

preponderant adj **greater**, more numerous, more powerful, more important, more significant Opposite: lesser

preponderantly adv **generally**, largely, in the main, by and large, for the most part

prepossessing (fml) adj **attractive**, pleasant, alluring, good-looking, eye-catching Opposite: unattractive

preposterous adj **outrageous**, absurd, ridiculous, ludicrous, unbelievable Opposite: sensible

preposterousness n **outrageousness**, absurdity, ridiculousness, ludicrousness, silliness Opposite: sensibleness

preppy (infml) adj **yuppie**, conservative, classic, traditional, tailored

preproduction n **planning**, groundwork, organization, scheduling, planning stage

prepubescent adj **preadolescent**, preteen, preteenager, young, childish Opposite: adult ■ n **youngster**, preadolescent, preteenager, preteen, subteen Opposite: adult

prequel n **prelude**, prologue, spinoff Opposite: sequel

prerecord v **record**, tape, film, copy

prerequisite n **precondition**, requirement, condition, qualification, criterion

prerogative n **right**, privilege, due, entitlement, birthright

presage n **portent**, omen, sign, warning, signal ■ v **foretell**, foreshadow, portend, bode, augur

preschool adj **young**, toddler, infant, kindergarten, nursery

preschooler n **young child**, preschool child, toddler, infant, baby

prescience n **foresight**, precognition, clairvoyance, prophecy, prediction Opposite: hindsight

prescient adj **prophetic**, psychic, clairvoyant, discerning, perceptive

prescribe v 1 **recommend**, suggest, advise, propose, advocate 2 **lay down**, stipulate, impose, order, set down

prescribed adj **set**, agreed, arranged, prearranged, given

prescript (fml) n **rule**, regulation, law, convention, canon

prescription n **medicine**, treatment, drug preparation, remedy

prescriptive adj **narrow**, rigid, strict unbending, inflexible Opposite: lax

prescriptiveness n **narrowness**, rigidity strictness, inflexibility, dogmatism Opposite: laxity

presence n 1 **attendance**, company, occurrence, incidence, existence Opposite: absence 2 **dignity**, charisma, aura, authority, poise 3 **ghost**, apparition, spirit, ghoul, manifestation

presence of mind n **nerve**, composure, levelheadedness, common sense, sense

present v 1 **give**, hand over, award, donate, offer Opposite: deny 2 **show**, display, exhibit, put on view, reveal 3 **cause**, represent, pose, raise, produce 4 **portray**, represent, depict, cast, show 5 **appear**, report, arrive, turn up, visit 6 **put forward**, bring forward, introduce, announce, offer for consideration 7 **exhibit**, mount, stage, put on view, organize ■ n 1 **gift**, offering, grant, dowry, largesse 2 **now**, here and now, present day, today, nowadays Opposite: past ■ adj 1 **current**, contemporary, present-day, existing, extant Opposite: past 2 **there**, here, in attendance, at hand, near Opposite: absent. See COMPARE AND CONTRAST at give.

presentable adj 1 **respectable**, personable, fit to be seen, smart, well-dressed Opposite: scruffy 2 **reasonable**, acceptable, satisfactory, good enough, passable Opposite: unsatisfactory

presentation n 1 **performance**, exhibition, demonstration, appearance, arrangement 2 **award**, donation, giving, offer, bestowal 3 **talk**, lecture, seminar, speech, address

present day n **now**, here and now, present, today, nowadays Opposite: past

present-day adj **contemporary**, current, existing, present, modern Opposite: past

presentiment n **feeling**, intuition, foreboding, fear, sense

presently adv **currently**, at the moment, at present, right now, now

preservation n 1 **protection**, conservation, safeguarding, defense, conservancy Opposite: destruction 2 **maintenance**, continuation, perpetuation, keeping, upholding Opposite: abolition

preservative adj **preserving**, conserving, protective, antibacterial, antifungal Opposite: destructive ■ n **additive**, preserver, stabilizer

preserve n **game reserve**, reservation, sanctuary, game preserve

preserved adj 1 **conserved**, well-looked-after, well-maintained, well-preserved, well-kept-up Opposite: dilapidated 2 **treated**, pickled, frozen, dried, salted Opposite: fresh

preserver n **protector**, guard, guardian, savior, conserver Opposite: destroyer

preset adj **set**, predetermined, fixed, stipulated, specific

preside v **take the chair**, chair, control, supervise, head

presidency n **premiership**, leadership, term of office, tenure .

president n **leader**, premier, head, head of state, chair

presidential adj 1 **political**, constitutional, high-level, governmental, top-level 2 **dignified**, authoritative, monarchic, judicious, regal

presidium n **executive committee**, committee, council, group, body

press v 1 **push**, depress, force down, bear down on, compress Opposite: pull 2 **iron**, smooth, steam, flatten, hot-press 3 **pursue**, lobby, beg, entreat, enjoin 4 **force**, urge, push, compel, oblige 5 (literary) **surge**, crowd, swarm, mill, cluster ■ n 1 **journalists**, media, reporters, newspapers, correspondents 2 **crowd**, horde, throng, mob, multitude

press conference n **news conference**, question and answer session, interview, conference, photo opportunity

pressed adj **busy**, pushed, hard-pressed, constrained, compelled

press for v **demand**, seek, urge, push for, campaign for

press-gang v **force**, coerce, bully, pressure, make

pressing adj 1 **urgent**, important, serious, crucial, vital Opposite: unimportant 2 **persistent**, insistent, unrelenting, unyielding, demanding Opposite: half-hearted

press officer n **spokesperson**, media spokesperson, press liaison officer, press agent

press on v **continue**, push on, forge ahead, keep going, press ahead Opposite: give up

press release n **statement**, document, announcement, bulletin

press together v squeeze together, force together, clamp, join together, close *Opposite*: pull apart

pressure n 1 force, weight, heaviness, burden, compression 2 stress, anxiety, weight, strain, tension ■ v coerce, force, bully, insist, compel

pressured adj worried, stressed, under pressure, overstretched, edgy *Opposite*: relaxed

prestige n status, standing, stature, kudos, esteem *Opposite*: notoriety

prestigious adj admired, respected, significant, important, impressive *Opposite*: insignificant

presumably adv most probably, I assume, I imagine, in all probability, most likely

presume v 1 believe, assume, guess, deduce, imagine *Opposite*: know 2 venture, dare, be so bold, take the liberty, make free

presumption n 1 belief, assumption, conjecture, supposition, presupposition 2 impertinence, audacity, nerve, gall, impudence

presumptive (fml) adj probable, likely, plausible, convincing, reasonable *Opposite*: implausible

presumptuous adj overfamiliar, rude, presuming, audacious, insolent *Opposite*: modest

presumptuousness n rudeness, arrogance, impropriety, disrespect, inappropriateness *Opposite*: modesty

presuppose v assume, take for granted, take as read, take as fact, presume

presupposition n assumption, supposition, conjecture, belief, guess

prêt-à-porter adj off-the-rack, ready-made, ready-to-wear, mass-produced *Opposite*: made-to-measure

pretend v 1 make believe, imagine, fantasize, make up, play 2 feign, put on, affect, profess, simulate ■ adj imaginary, make-believe, made-up, invented, false *Opposite*: real

pretender n aspirant, aspiring leader, candidate, opponent, claimant

pretend to be v impersonate, masquerade as, pose as, imitate, pass for

pretense n 1 trick, con, sham, hoax, fabrication 2 make-believe, fantasy, fancy, imagination, castles in the air *Opposite*: reality 3 claim, suggestion, allegation, hint, supposition

pretension n affectation, airs, posing, posturing, pretentiousness *Opposite*: humility

pretentious adj affected, ostentatious, showy, exaggerated, pompous *Opposite*: down-to-earth

pretentiousness see pretension

preternatural (literary) adj supernatural, paranormal, uncanny, unnatural, otherworldly *Opposite*: natural

pretext n excuse, cause, con, ploy, ruse

prettify v smarten up, do up, beautify, improve, adorn *Opposite*: mess up (infml)

prettiness n good looks, handsomeness, attractiveness, beauty, cuteness *Opposite*: ugliness

pretty adj attractive, beautiful, handsome, cute, good-looking *Opposite*: unattractive ■ adv rather, fairly, reasonably, quite, moderately. *See* COMPARE AND CONTRAST *at* good-looking.

prevail v 1 triumph, succeed, be victorious, overcome, win out *Opposite*: fail 2 (fml) exist, reign, be happening, occur, predominate

prevailing adj 1 usual, main, dominant, predominant, principal *Opposite*: underlying 2 current, existing, customary, established, popular

prevail on v persuade, convince, cajole, sway, coax into

prevalence n occurrence, commonness, pervasiveness, incidence, frequency

prevalent adj common, dominant, predominant, widespread, rampant *Opposite*: rare. *See* COMPARE AND CONTRAST *at* widespread.

prevaricate v hedge, evade, beat around the bush, lie, quibble *Opposite*: call a spade a spade

prevarication n evasiveness, evasion, equivocation, avoidance, hedging *Opposite*: forthrightness

prevent v stop, avert, avoid, foil, thwart *Opposite*: encourage

preventable adj avoidable, needless, unnecessary, avertible, escapable *Opposite*: inevitable

prevention n 1 avoidance, deterrence, stoppage, inhibition, hindrance *Opposite*: promotion 2 obstacle, hindrance, impediment, inhibition, restraint

preventive adj anticipatory, preemptive, defensive, prophylactic, deterrent ■ n protection, anticipatory measure, preemptive measure, deterrent, disincentive

preview n 1 showing, performance, broadcast, screening, opening 2 trailer, clip, foretaste, extract, coming attraction ■ v 1 show, perform, broadcast, screen, promote 2 review, describe, introduce, advertise, trail

previous adj preceding, earlier, prior, former, past *Opposite*: subsequent

prey n quarry, victim, target, kill, game *Opposite*: hunter

prey on v 1 live on, live off, feed on, hunt, kill 2 worry, preoccupy, bother, haunt, oppress 3 take advantage of, exploit, victimize, intimidate, bully

price n 1 cost, worth, fee, face value, amount 2 penalty, cost, punishment, consequences, fine ■ v set a price, assess, estimate, rate, evaluate

priceless adj 1 **invaluable**, inestimable, beyond price, incalculable, costly Opposite: worthless 2 (infml) **hilarious**, funny, comic, amusing, entertaining

pricey (infml) adj **costly**, expensive, dear, high-priced, exorbitant Opposite: cheap

prick v **pierce**, stab, puncture, perforate, jab ■ n **hole**, puncture, perforation, pinhole

prickle n 1 **spike**, spine, barb, thorn, quill 2 **itch**, tickle, sting, irritation, tingling ■ v **sting**, itch, tickle, prick, irritate

prickling n **scratchiness**, pricking, itchiness, itching, prickle

prickly adj 1 **spiny**, thorny, barbed, bristly, spiky Opposite: smooth 2 **itchy**, tickly, scratchy, stinging, tingling 3 (infml) **sensitive**, snappy, irritable, grumpy, snappish Opposite: impervious

pride n 1 **arrogance**, conceit smugness, superiority, self-importance Opposite: humility 2 **self-respect**, dignity, self-esteem, honor 3 **satisfaction**, delight, gratification, enjoyment, joy

pride and joy n **most prized possession**, the apple of your eye, poster child, treasure, pride

pride yourself on v **be proud of**, take satisfaction in, revel in, take pride in, glory in

priest n **minister**, pastor, vicar, rector, presbyter

priesthood n **clergy**, ministry, cloth Opposite: laity

prim adj 1 **prudish**, prissy, strait-laced, puritanical, moralistic Opposite: broadminded 2 **formal**, proper, dignified, starchy, stiff Opposite: informal 3 **tidy**, orderly, precise, meticulous, fussy Opposite: messy

primacy n **preeminence**, importance, predominance, dominance, prevalence

primal adj **primitive**, primeval aboriginal, primordial, prehistoric Opposite: new

primarily adv **first and foremost**, above all, chiefly, mainly, principally

primary adj 1 **first**, initial, top, leading, foremost Opposite: last 2 **main**, chief, most important, key, prime Opposite: secondary 3 **basic**, core, central, fundamental, essential Opposite: minor

primate n 1 **ape**, monkey, hominid, human 2 **archbishop**, bishop, prelate, cardinal

---

WORD BANK

❑ types of primates aye-aye, baboon, Barbary ape, bonnet monkey, capuchin, chimp, chimpanzee, colobus, gibbon, gorilla, lemur, macaque, mandrill, marmoset, orangutan, proboscis monkey, rhesus monkey, spider monkey

---

prime adj 1 **top**, superior, superlative, best, premier Opposite: inferior 2 **major**, main, key, chief, leading ■ n **peak**, zenith, heyday, summit, high point Opposite:

nadir ■ v 1 **prepare**, ready, get ready, make ready 2 **brief**, fill in, instruct, give somebody the lowdown (infml)

primed adj 1 **aware** well-informed, geared up, informed, in the picture Opposite: unprepared 2 **prepared**, ready, set, in position, poised

prime minister n **premier**, chief minister, head of cabinet, PM, head of government

primer n **textbook**, reader, grammar, introduction, how-to (infml)

primeval adj 1 **prehistoric**, original, ancient, archaic Opposite: modern 2 **primitive**, primordial primal, basic, instinctive Opposite: considered

primitive adj 1 **embryonic**, primeval, original, aboriginal, nascent Opposite: developed 2 **simple**, basic, uncomplicated, unsophisticated, crude Opposite: sophisticated 3 **prehistoric**, ancient, primordial, primal, archaic Opposite: modern

primitiveness n 1 **antiquity**, ancientness, primitive stage, early stage, primeval stage 2 **crudeness**, simplicity, roughness, coarseness, unsophisticatedness Opposite: sophistication

primness n 1 **prudishness**, narrowness, shockability, oversensitivity, strait-lacedness Opposite: broad-mindedness 2 **formality**, properness, starchiness, propriety, stiffness Opposite: informality 3 **neatness**, tidiness, orderliness, fastidiousness, meticulousness Opposite: messiness

primordial adj 1 **primeval**, prehistoric, primal, ancient, primitive 2 **embryonic**, developing, early, nascent

primp v **fuss**, fuss over, groom, preen, adorn

prince n 1 **leader**, leading figure, leading light, doyen, big shot (infml) 2 (infml) **gentleman**, mensch (infml), trump (infml)

princely adj **generous**, handsome, large, significant, huge Opposite: measly (infml)

principal adj **main**, major, chief, most important, primary ■ n 1 **leader**, chief, doyenne, doyen, head Opposite: follower 2 **head of school**, headmaster, headmistress, dean, provost

principality n **princedom**, territory, country, domain

principally adv **mainly**, chiefly, above all, first and foremost, primarily

principle n 1 **rule**, theory, notion, concept, tenet 2 **code**, standard, belief, attitude, value 3 **source**, wellspring, origin, cause, basis

principled adj **honorable**, righteous, upright, ethical, just Opposite: unethical

print n 1 **pattern**, design motif 2 **reproduction**, copy, lithograph, photograph, photocopy ■ v 1 **turn out**, produce, make, issue, run off 2 **publish**, carry, make known, advertise, broadcast 3 **stamp**, imprint, engrave, emboss

printed *adj* **in print**, in black and white, on paper, published, reproduced

printing *n* **1 production**, reproduction, lithography, offset lithography, letterpress **2 text**, lettering, words, writing, wording **3 lettering**, capitals, upper case, lower case, block lettering *Opposite*: script **4 edition**, print run, run, impression

prior *adj* **previous**, preceding, past, erstwhile, former *Opposite*: subsequent

prioritization *n* **ordering**, ranking, arranging, arrangement, listing

prioritize *v* **1 order**, rank, arrange, list, line up **2 concentrate on**, give precedence to, select, highlight, rank first

priority *n* **importance**, precedence, urgency, import, significance

prior to *prep* **before**, previous to, earlier than, preceding, in advance of *Opposite*: after

priory *n* **monastery**, convent, religious community, abbey, ashram

prison *n* **1 jail**, penitentiary, penal complex, detention center, house of correction **2 imprisonment**, confinement, solitary confinement, detention, custody

prisoner *n* **1 detainee**, inmate, convict, political prisoner, prisoner of war **2 captive**, hostage, kidnap victim

prissiness *n* **primness**, prudishness, properness, starchiness, stiffness *Opposite*: informality

prissy *adj* **prim**, prudish, proper, starchy, stiff *Opposite*: informal

pristine *adj* **1 immaculate**, perfect, faultless, spotless, pure *Opposite*: soiled **2 unspoiled**, untouched, primeval, original, virgin *Opposite*: developed

privacy *n* **1 solitude**, time alone, space, seclusion, isolation *Opposite*: company **2 confidentiality**, discretion, secrecy, concealment *Opposite*: disclosure

private *adj* **1 confidential**, secret, concealed, undisclosed, classified *Opposite*: public **2 secluded**, set apart, isolated, remote, cloistered **3 privileged**, restricted, reserved, exclusive, not in the public domain *Opposite*: public **4 secretive**, reserved, reticent, tight-lipped, self-contained *Opposite*: forthcoming

private detective *n* **private investigator**, PI, sleuth, private eye *(infml)*, gumshoe *(dated infml)*

private eye *(infml) see* **private detective**

private investigator *see* **private detective**

privately *adv* **confidentially**, in confidence, in private, secretly, in secret *Opposite*: publicly

privation *n* **hardship**, deprivation, adversity, poverty, need

privatization *n* **sale**, transfer, denationalization

privatize *v* **sell**, transfer, denationalize, go public *Opposite*: nationalize

privilege *n* **1 freedom**, license, opportunity, dispensation, advantage **2 honor**, source of pride, treat, pleasure, joy ■ *v* **favor**, show partiality toward, benefit *Opposite*: persecute

privileged *adj* **1 advantaged**, lucky, fortunate, honored *Opposite*: disadvantaged **2 confidential**, private, restricted, controlled, limited *Opposite*: public

privy *adj* **in the know**, sharing in, aware of, party to, partaking of ■ *n* *(infml)* **outside toilet**, outhouse, outside lavatory, latrine, toilet

prize *n* **award**, reward, trophy, medal, accolade ■ *v* **1 lever**, open, work loose, work free, force **2 extract**, drag out, pry out of, wheedle, coax **3 treasure**, cherish, value, respect, esteem

prized *adj* **award-winning**, high-quality, valued, respected, esteemed

prizewinning *adj* **award-winning**, victorious, successful, triumphant, winning *Opposite*: unsuccessful

pro *prep* **for**, in favor of, all for, in support of *Opposite*: against ■ *n* **professional**, authority, maven, expert, specialist *Opposite*: amateur

proactive *adj* **practical**, taking the initiative, hands-on, active, down to business *Opposite*: passive

probability *n* **likelihood**, prospect, odds, possibility, chance *Opposite*: improbability

probable *adj* **likely**, credible, possible, feasible, plausible *Opposite*: unlikely

probate *n* **certification**, validation, confirmation, validity

probation *n* **trial**, test, audition, experimentation, tryout

probationary *adj* **provisional**, trial, test, experimental, sample *Opposite*: permanent

probe *n* **investigation**, inquiry, review, examination, analysis ■ *v* **investigate**, research, delve, inquire, look into

probing *adj* **searching**, penetrating, analytical, inquisitive, curious *Opposite*: cursory

probity *n* **correctness**, scrupulousness, rectitude, righteousness, integrity *Opposite*: immorality

problem *n* **1 difficulty**, setback, hitch, drawback, glitch *Opposite*: boost **2 puzzle**, poser, riddle, conundrum, challenge *Opposite*: solution ■ *adj* **problematic**, tricky, unruly, badly-behaved, delinquent *Opposite*: easy

COMPARE AND CONTRAST CORE MEANING: something difficult to solve or understand **problem** a difficult situation, matter, or person; **mystery** an event or situation that has never been fully explained or understood, or a person who is puzzling or mysterious; **puzzle** a problem whose solution requires ingenuity, or a situation that it is difficult to resolve, or somebody whose behavior or motives are difficult to understand; **riddle** a perplexing or confusing issue; **conundrum** something puzzling, confusing, or mysterious; **enigma** somebody or something that is mysterious and hard to understand.

problematic *adj* tricky, challenging, sticky, awkward, knotty *Opposite*: easy

problematical *see* **problematic**

proboscis *n* nose, snout, feeler, trunk, antenna

procedural *adj* technical, practical, bureaucratic, routine, ritual

procedure *n* process, modus operandi, way, technique, method

proceed *v* go on, carry on, continue, ensue, advance *Opposite*: recede

proceedings *n* 1 events, actions, measures, trial, procedures 2 minutes, record, account, report, chronicle

proceeds *n* profits, income, earnings, gate, box office

process *n* procedure, course, activity, development, progression ■ *v* deal with, handle, treat, sort out, administer

procession *n* 1 march, parade, pageant, march-past, motorcade 2 sequence, succession, string, series, line

processional *adj* ceremonial, ritual, commemorative, celebratory, sacred

proclaim *v* state publicly, announce, declare, state, make known

proclamation *n* public statement, announcement, declaration, decree, assertion

proclivity *n* liking, appetite, taste, penchant, inclination

procrastinate *v* put off, delay, postpone, adjourn, dally *Opposite*: make a start

procrastination *n* deferment, putting off, postponement, stalling, delay *Opposite*: action

procure *v* obtain, acquire, secure, get hold of, get. *See* COMPARE AND CONTRAST *at* get.

procurement *n* 1 gaining, obtaining, finding, locating, tracking down *Opposite*: giving up 2 buying, purchasing, ordering, obtaining *Opposite*: selling

procurer *n* buyer, purchaser, customer, client, consumer

prod *v* 1 elbow, nudge, dig, jab, push 2 urge, stimulate, stir, prompt, provoke ■ *n* nudge, elbow, dig, jab, push

prodigal *adj* wasteful, reckless, dissolute, profligate, uncontrolled *Opposite*: cautious

prodigious *adj* 1 huge, vast, copious, giant, gigantic *Opposite*: small 2 abnormal, extraordinary, phenomenal, unusual, exceptional *Opposite*: average

prodigy *n* genius, sensation, phenomenon, wonder, star

produce *v* 1 create, make, manufacture, construct, fabricate 2 give, give off, yield, churn out, be the source of ■ *n* crop, foodstuffs, harvest, products, goods

producer *n* creator, manufacturer, maker, fabricator

product *n* 1 manufactured article, commodity, artifact 2 output, merchandise, goods, wares 3 result, outcome, upshot, consequence, effect *Opposite*: cause 4 creation, invention, achievement, work

production *n* manufacture, making, construction, creation, invention

productive *adj* 1 creative, prolific, fecund, industrious, fruitful *Opposite*: destructive 2 useful, helpful, constructive, beneficial, valuable *Opposite*: negative

productiveness *n* usefulness, constructiveness, use, utility, fruitfulness

productivity *n* output, efficiency, yield, production, throughput

profane *(fml)* *adj* irreverent, blasphemous, irreligious, disrespectful, wicked *Opposite*: sacred

profanity *n* blasphemy, oath, vulgarity, curse, swearword

profess *v* 1 declare, announce, state, affirm, proclaim 2 claim, maintain, make out, feign 3 admit, own up, confess, acknowledge, agree

professed *adj* 1 declared, acknowledged, open, stated, blatant *Opposite*: unspoken 2 supposed, alleged, so-called, ostensible, seeming *Opposite*: proven

profession *n* job, work, occupation, line of work, career

professional *adj* specialized, qualified, proficient, skilled, trained *Opposite*: amateur ■ *n* specialist, expert, authority, pro, maven *Opposite*: amateur

professionalism *n* skill, competence, expertise, proficiency, efficiency *Opposite*: incompetence

professor *n* university teacher, lecturer, tutor, instructor, dean

professorial *adj* academic, pedagogical, intellectual, educational, senior

proffer *v* offer, hold out, extend, tender, volunteer *Opposite*: withdraw

proficiency *n* skill, ability, talent, expertise, aptitude *Opposite*: incompetence

proficient *adj* capable, talented, expert, gifted, adroit *Opposite*: incompetent

profile *n* 1 outline, side view, shape, silhouette, contour 2 summary, sketch, outline, report, précis ■ *v* summarize, sum up, sketch, outline, report

profit *n* 1 income, earnings, revenue, proceeds, turnover *Opposite*: loss 2 advantage, gain, benefit, use, reward *Opposite*: loss ■ *v* 1 earn, bring in, make, make money on, turn a profit *Opposite*: lose 2 benefit, gain, be of advantage to, help, aid

profitability n 1 **success**, effectiveness, productivity, viability, cost-effectiveness 2 **usefulness**, worth, fruitfulness, use, value *Opposite*: uselessness

profitable adj 1 **lucrative**, moneymaking, gainful, commercial, cost-effective *Opposite*: unprofitable 2 **advantageous**, beneficial, rewarding, useful, valuable *Opposite*: unhelpful

profiteer v **exploit**, take advantage of, make use of, racketeer, abuse ▪ n **swindler**, racketeer, embezzler, crook *(infml)*, con man *(slang)*

profitmaking adj **profitable**, viable, moneymaking, economic, cost-effective *Opposite*: draining

profligacy n **wastefulness**, recklessness, dissolution, decadence, extravagance *Opposite*: parsimony

profligate adj 1 **wasteful**, reckless, spendthrift, squandering, decadent *Opposite*: parsimonious 2 **dissolute**, licentious, immoral, wicked, shameless

profound adj 1 **deep**, thoughtful, reflective, philosophical, weighty *Opposite*: superficial 2 **intense**, great, overpowering, overwhelming, extreme *Opposite*: shallow

profoundly adv **intensely**, greatly, extremely, strongly, very much

profoundness *see* profundity

profundity n 1 **understanding**, perceptiveness, wisdom, acuity, perspicacity *Opposite*: superficiality 2 **complexity**, abstruseness, difficulty, depth, intricacy *Opposite*: simplicity 3 **intensity**, greatness, strength, seriousness, enormity *Opposite*: mildness 4 **depth**, immensity, fathomlessness, extent, reach

profuse adj **plentiful**, copious, abundant, teeming, generous *Opposite*: scanty

profusion n **abundance**, large amount, excess, cornucopia, plethora *Opposite*: dearth

progenitor n 1 **ancestor**, forebear *Opposite*: descendant 2 **antecedent**, originator, forerunner, prototype, predecessor *Opposite*: copy

progeny n **offspring**, children, young, descendants, issue

prognosis n **forecast**, prediction, projection, scenario, diagnosis

prognosticate v 1 **predict**, divine, foresee, foretell, forecast *Opposite*: recall 2 **indicate**, suggest, point to, augur, signify *Opposite*: prove

prognostication n 1 **prediction**, prognosis, projection, divination, foreseeing *Opposite*: recollection 2 **indication**, suggestion, pointer, token, portent *Opposite*: proof

prognosticator n **predictor**, diviner, prophet, seer, clairvoyant

program n 1 **plan**, agenda, schedule, timetable, list 2 **broadcast**, presentation, production, performance, show 3 **brochure**, booklet, pamphlet, listing, synopsis 4 **system**, procedure, course, series, setup 5 **setting**, option, cycle, mode, instruction ▪ v 1 **schedule**, arrange, book, plan, line up 2 **train**, condition, compel, brainwash, hypnotize 3 **write instructions**, load instructions, write software, load software, set

programmed adj **automatic**, involuntary, planned, automated, set *Opposite*: spontaneous

programmer n **computer operator**, computer programmer, computer scientist, program writer, systems analyst

programming n **software design**, program design, program writing, user interface design, software development

progress n **development**, improvement, advancement, evolution, growth *Opposite*: regression ▪ v 1 **improve**, develop, advance, evolve, increase *Opposite*: regress 2 **move forward**, advance, proceed, continue, make progress *Opposite*: retreat

progression n 1 **development**, evolution, movement, advance, advancement *Opposite*: regression 2 **series**, sequence, succession, string, chain

progressive adj 1 **liberal**, reformist, openminded, broad-minded, radical *Opposite*: reactionary 2 **gradual**, ongoing, increasing, continuing, developing *Opposite*: sudden

progressively adv **increasingly**, more and more, with time, gradually, little by little *Opposite*: suddenly

progressiveness n **liberalism**, reformism, progressivism, modernism, tolerance

progressivism n **liberalism**, reformism, modernism, radicalism, leftism

prohibit v **forbid**, ban, proscribe, disallow, veto *Opposite*: permit

prohibited adj **forbidden**, banned, verboten, illegal, proscribed *Opposite*: permitted

prohibition n **ban**, exclusion, embargo, prevention, veto *Opposite*: permission

prohibitive adj **high-priced**, excessive, exorbitant, extortionate, unaffordable *Opposite*: affordable

project n **assignment**, task, undertaking, job, plan ▪ v 1 **forecast**, predict, estimate, foresee, foretell 2 **stick out**, jut out, protrude, bulge, distend 3 **throw**, launch, shoot, propel, cast 4 **plan**, envisage, propose, intend, anticipate

projected adj **estimated**, planned, proposed, outlined, expected *Opposite*: actual

projection n 1 **forecast**, prediction, plan, prognosis, estimate *Opposite*: outcome 2 **outcrop**, protuberance, bulge, protrusion, ledge

proletarian adj **popular**, grassroots, people's, working-class, blue-collar *Opposite*: aristocratic

proletariat n **hoi polloi**, rank and file, grassroots, working class, workers *Opposite*: gentry

proliferate *v* **1** multiply, thrive, flourish, boom, increase *Opposite*: dwindle **2** reproduce, propagate, multiply, breed, procreate *Opposite*: die out

proliferation *n* propagation, explosion, spread, multiplying, production

prolific *adj* **1** productive, creative, fertile, inexhaustible, high-volume *Opposite*: unproductive **2** abundant, abounding, plentiful, copious, profuse *Opposite*: scarce

prolix *adj* wordy, verbose, long-winded, flowery, protracted *Opposite*: concise. *See* COMPARE AND CONTRAST *at* wordy.

prologue *n* introduction, preface, foreword, preamble, opening *Opposite*: epilogue

prolong *v* extend, lengthen, protract, draw out, spin out *Opposite*: curtail

prolongation *n* continuation, perpetuation, drawing out, protraction, extension *Opposite*: curtailment

prolonged *adj* lengthy, protracted, long, continued, extended *Opposite*: curtailed

prom *n* dance, college dance, high-school dance, formal dance, ball

promenade *n* **1** walkway, path, boardwalk, esplanade **2** *(fml)* stroll, walk, saunter, amble, constitutional ■ *v* *(fml)* walk, stroll, amble, saunter, wander

prominence *n* **1** fame, importance, distinction, celebrity, eminence *Opposite*: obscurity **2** bump, lump, bulge, swelling, protrusion *Opposite*: crater

prominent *adj* **1** protuberant, protruding, projecting, bulbous, bulging *Opposite*: flat **2** noticeable, conspicuous, obvious, blatant, flagrant *Opposite*: subtle **3** famous, well-known, important, high-flying, top *Opposite*: obscure

promiscuous *adj* immoral, loose, licentious, wanton, uninhibited

promise *v* **1** assure, swear, vow, undertake, guarantee **2** suggest, augur, bode, look like, show all the signs ■ *n* **1** assurance, undertaking, guarantee, contract, word *Opposite*: threat **2** potential, possibilities, aptitude, ability, capacity

promising *adj* **1** talented, gifted, capable, able **2** auspicious, hopeful, likely, encouraging, favorable *Opposite*: disappointing

promisingly *adv* favorably, auspiciously, hopefully, well, nicely *Opposite*: disappointingly

promo *(infml)* *n* promotion, advertisement, publicity stunt, publicity, profile-raiser

promontory *n* cape, headland, peninsula, outcrop, point

promote *v* **1** advance, upgrade, further, elevate, put forward *Opposite*: demote **2** endorse, encourage, help, support, stimulate *Opposite*: suppress **3** advertise,

publicize, make known, market, tout *Opposite*: defame **4** further, progress, move forward, develop, encourage *Opposite*: hinder **5** stage, put on, organize, arrange

promoter *n* organizer, agent, sponsor, advocate, supporter

promot on *n* **1** upgrade, raise, advancement, elevation, preferment *(fml)* *Opposite*: demotion **2** advertising, marketing, publicity, publicity campaign, public relations **3** endorsement, encouragement, help, support, stimulation **4** offer, special promotion, deal, loss leader

promotional *adj* publicity, advertising, public relations, P.R. positive

prompt *adj* **1** punctual, on time, at the appointed time, without delay, timely *Opposite*: late **2** quick, rapid, swift, without delay, speedy *Opposite*: slow ■ *v* **1** stimulate, encourage, provoke, incite, urge *Opposite*: prevent **2** bring about, induce, occasion, set off, trigger *Opposite*: prevent ■ *n* stimulus, prod, goad, reminder, heads-up

prompting *n* encouragement, warning, pressure, motivation, instigation

promptness *n* **1** speed, rapidity, swiftness, alacrity, velocity *Opposite*: slowness **2** punctuality, timeliness, timekeeping *Opposite*: tardiness

promulgate *(fml)* *v* **1** publicize, spread, disseminate, circulate, transmit *Opposite*: suppress **2** declare, proclaim, decree, announce, pronounce *Opposite*: withdraw

promulgation *(fml)* *n* **1** declaration, proclamation, decree, announcement, pronouncement *Opposite*: withdrawal **2** publicizing, spreading, dissemination, circulation, broadcasting *Opposite*: suppression

prone *adj* **1** disposed, predisposed, liable, inclined, likely **2** flat, horizontal, flat out, face down, motionless *Opposite*: upright

prong *n* point, spike, spine, tine

pronounce *v* **1** say, speak, utter, articulate, voice **2** state, assert, declare, announce, decree

pronounced *adj* marked, noticeable, distinct, definite, obvious *Opposite*: subtle

pronouncement *n* statement, assertion, declaration, announcement, decree

pronto *(infml)* *adv* straightaway, right away, quick, on the double, quickly *Opposite*: sluggishly

pronunciation *n* articulation, accent, elocution, intonation, enunciation

proof *n* evidence, testimony, verification, confirmation, attestation ■ *adj* resistant, resilient, impervious, immune *Opposite*: vulnerable

proofread *v* check, correct, check through, check over, look through

proofreader *n* checker, reader, editor, copy editor, corrector

prop *n* support, leg, crutch, buttress, pile ∎ *v* hold up, support, prop up, sustain, buttress *Opposite*: destabilize

propaganda *n* 1 publicity, advertising, marketing, literature, information 2 misinformation, disinformation, party line, half truths, cant

propagandist *n* 1 publicist, polemicist, essayist, writer, speaker 2 partisan, apologist, mouthpiece, sophist, spin doctor *(slang)* ∎ *adj* slanted, distorted, one-sided, polemical, partisan

propagate *v* 1 breed, grow, raise, reproduce, proliferate 2 spread, broadcast, proliferate, circulate, disseminate

propagation *n* 1 breeding, reproduction, proliferation, procreation 2 spread, circulation, dissemination, transmission, proliferation

propagator *n* 1 spreader, broadcaster, transmitter, communicator, diffuser 2 tray, box, seed tray, cloche, cold frame

propel *v* push, drive, force, boost, thrust

propensity *n* tendency, inclination, partiality, bent, proclivity

proper *adj* 1 good, correct, appropriate, suitable, right *Opposite*: wrong 2 polite, modest, decorous, prim, genteel *Opposite*: improper 3 own, personal, characteristic, identifiable, individual

properly *adv* correctly, right, appropriately, as it should be, by the book *Opposite*: incorrectly

propertied *adj* property-owning, land-owning, landed, affluent, moneyed *Opposite*: dispossessed

property *n* 1 possessions, belongings, goods, assets, material goods 2 land, home, house, estate, acreage

property owner *n* proprietor, owner, landowner, homeowner, property holder *Opposite*: tenant

prophecy *n* prediction, forecast, divination, foretelling, insight

prophesy *v* predict, forecast, divine, foretell, see the future

prophet *n* clairvoyant, forecaster, fortune teller, seer, prescient

prophetic *adj* visionary, farsighted, predictive, foretelling, forewarning

propinquity *(fml)* *n* nearness, closeness, proximity, convenience, relationship *Opposite*: remoteness

propitiate *v* appease, placate, mollify, pacify, soothe *Opposite*: provoke *(infml)*

propitiation *(fml)* *n* placation, appeasement, mollification, pacification, soothing *Opposite*: provocation

propitiatory *adj* placatory, conciliatory, soothing, mollifying, calming *Opposite*: provocative

proponent *n* advocate, supporter, exponent, protagonist, follower *Opposite*: opponent

proportion *n* 1 amount, quantity, part, share, percentage 2 ratio, comparison, relative amount, relationship

proportional *adj* relative, comparative, relational, related, proportionate

proportionate *adj* balanced, proportional, comparable, equal, equivalent

proposal *n* suggestion, offer, application, tender, bid

propose *v* 1 suggest, offer, recommend, proposition, advise 2 intend, plan, have in mind, aim, mean

proposer *n* nominator, supporter, sponsor, advocate, advocator

proposition *n* proposal, plan, scheme, intention, suggestion

propound *v* put forward, advocate, submit, set out, offer

proprietary *adj* 1 branded, exclusive, patented, registered, trademarked *Opposite*: generic 2 private, privately owned, privately run, privately operated, commercial 3 protective, jealous, territorial, possessive, suspicious

proprietor *n* owner, manager, administrator, landowner, property owner

proprietorial *adj* possessive, protective, jealous, suspicious, territorial

propriety *n* 1 politeness, decorum, modesty, good manners, respectability *Opposite*: impropriety 2 correctness, aptness, appropriateness, decency, suitability *Opposite*: impropriety

propulsion *n* force, forward motion, thrust, impulsion, momentum

prop up *v* hold up, support, prop, sustain, buttress *Opposite*: destabilize

prosaic *adj* 1 straightforward, matter-of-fact, simple, plain, ordinary 2 banal, mundane, everyday, dull, humdrum *Opposite*: extraordinary

proscribe *v* ban, bar, forbid, exclude, veto *Opposite*: permit

proscribed *adj* prohibited, banned, forbidden, verboten, inadmissible *Opposite*: permissible

proscription *(fml)* *n* prohibition, banning, exclusion, forbidding, interdiction

prose *n* writing style, style, text *Opposite*: poetry

prosecute *v* put on trial, impeach, arraign, indict, take legal action

prosecution *n* trial, action, suit, case, examination

prosecutor *n* prosecuting attorney, public prosecutor, DA, district attorney

proselytization *n* preaching, evangelization, agitation, propagandizing, campaigning

proselytize *v* 1 preach, evangelize, spread the word, make somebody see the light, convert 2 persuade, cajole, lecture, bend somebody's ear, talk into

proselytizer n preacher, evangelist, missionary, zealot, agitator

prospect n 1 view, scene, vision, outlook, panorama 2 hope, possibility, expectation, outlook, likelihood ■ v search, mine, dig, seek, pan

prospective adj potential, future, forthcoming, likely, probable

prospectus n brochure, list, document, catalog, booklet

prosper v 1 flourish, thrive, do well, get on, grow Opposite: decline 2 succeed, make money, show a profit, be in the black

prosperity n wealth, affluence, opulence, riches, success Opposite: poverty

prosperous adj 1 wealthy, affluent, rich, well-off, well-to-do Opposite: poor 2 flourishing, thriving, successful, booming Opposite: failing

prostrate adj 1 flat, face down, horizontal, level, prone Opposite: upright 2 drained, exhausted, desperate, powerless, at a low ebb

prostrate yourself v bow, genuflect, bend low, humble yourself, grovel

prostration n 1 bowing, kneeling, falling down, worship, adoration 2 incapacitation, breakdown, exhaustion, helplessness, weakness Opposite: robustness

protagonist n character, hero, central character, leading role, good guy (infml)

protean adj variable, changeable, mutable, adjustable, fluctuating Opposite: constant

protect v defend, guard, keep, safeguard, care for Opposite: neglect. See COMPARE AND CONTRAST at **safeguard**.

protected adj 1 endangered, threatened, nearing extinction, dwindling Opposite: thriving 2 sheltered, safe, secure, safeguarded, shielded Opposite: exposed 3 locked, tamperproof, inaccessible, sealed, impenetrable Opposite: open

protection n 1 safeguard, defense, guard, fortification, shield 2 security, safety, defense, asylum, sanctuary Opposite: exposure

protectionism n isolationism, protection, tariff barriers, trade barriers

protectionist n isolationist, nationalist, patriot, xenophobe ■ adj protective, isolationist, nationalist, preferential, xenophobic

protective adj defensive, caring, shielding, protecting, defending

protective covering n shell, armor, cladding, shield

protectiveness n 1 safety, security, secureness, strength, robustness 2 solicitousness, jealousness, jealousy, possessiveness, suspicion 3 protectionism, isolationism, protection, tariff barriers, trade barriers

protector n 1 shield, armor, mask, apron 2 guard, guardian, defender, handler, bodyguard

protectorate n dominion, colony, dependency, region, territory

protégé n ward, pupil, apprentice, dependent, student Opposite: protector

protest v 1 complain, object, remonstrate, dissent, dispute 2 declare, affirm, assert, insist, claim ■ n 1 complaint, objection, remonstration, dissent, dispute 2 demonstration, march, rally, campaign, dispute. See COMPARE AND CONTRAST at **complain**, object.

protestation n assertion, declaration, affirmation, pronouncement, disclosure

protester n activist, campaigner, demonstrator, marcher, picketer Opposite: supporter

protest march n demonstration, march, rally, protest, protest rally

protest rally see **protest march**

protocol n procedure, etiquette, code of behavior, conventions, rules

prototype n example, sample, model, original, archetype Opposite: copy

protract v draw out, prolong, extend, spin out, drag out Opposite: shorten

protracted adj long-drawn-out, prolonged, extended, lingering, expanded Opposite: brief

protraction n 1 extension, lengthening, drawing out, continuation Opposite: shortening 2 scale drawing, plan, elevation, blueprint, diagram

protrude v stick out, jut, project, overhang, obtrude

protrusion n lump, lip, flange, overhang, outcrop

protrusive adj 1 prominent, bulging, swelling, jutting, extending Opposite: sunken 2 brash, forward, presumptuous, rude, fresh (infml) Opposite: retiring

protuberance n swelling, bulge, bump, lump, knob

protuberant adj sticking out, prominent, bulging, swelling, popping Opposite: concave

proud adj 1 pleased, satisfied, gratified, honored, delighted Opposite: ashamed 2 independent, self-sufficient, honorable, dignified, scrupulous 3 rewarding, satisfying, pleasurable, pleasing, uplifting 4 arrogant, conceited, smug, superior, self-important Opposite: humble 5 impressive, stately, majestic, noble, magnificent

---

COMPARE AND CONTRAST CORE MEANING: describing somebody who is pleased with himself or herself

proud justifiably pleased and satisfied about a situation, or self-satisfied and having an exaggerated opinion of self-worth; **arrogant** feeling or showing self-importance and contempt for others; **conceited** showing excessive satisfaction with one's personal qualities or abilities; **egot-**

istic having an inflated sense of self-importance, especially when this is shown through constantly talking or thinking about oneself; **vain** excessively self-satisfied, especially suggesting that somebody is overly concerned with and admires his or her own personal appearance.

proudly *adv* **1 delightedly**, happily, triumphantly, joyfully *Opposite*: ashamedly **2 arrogantly**, conceitedly, smugly, self-importantly, pompously *Opposite*: humbly

provable *adj* **demonstrable**, verifiable, watertight, incontestable, unarguable

prove *v* **1 show**, establish, confirm, demonstrate, verify *Opposite*: disprove **2 turn out**, develop, offer, arrange for, run

proven *adj* **established**, confirmed, demonstrated, verified, recognized *Opposite*: unproven

provenance *n* **origin**, derivation, attribution, source, birthplace. *See* COMPARE AND CONTRAST *at* origin.

provender *n* **1** *(archaic)* **fodder**, feed, hay, forage, silage **2** *(literary)* **food**, fare, provisions, victuals, grub *(infml)*

proverb *n* **maxim**, axiom, adage, saying, aphorism

proverbial *adj* **1 well-known**, axiomatic, familiar, legendary, famous **2 archetypal**, clichéd, typical, regular, common *Opposite*: novel

provide *v* **1 give**, supply, present, endow, grant *Opposite*: withhold **2 make available**, deliver, offer, arrange for, run *Opposite*: withdraw **3 stipulate**, postulate, specify, require **4 take care of**, support, look after, care for, keep *Opposite*: neglect

provided *see* provided that

provided that *conj* **on condition that**, if, only if, as long as, so long as

providence *n* **1 fate**, luck, destiny, fortune, divine intervention **2 wisdom**, foresight, prudence, sense, frugality

provident *adj* **1 prudent**, foresighted, well-prepared, wise, careful *Opposite*: improvident **2 frugal**, thrifty, cautious, careful, sparing *Opposite*: spendthrift

providential *adj* **1 fortunate**, lucky, beneficial, advantageous, convenient *Opposite*: unfortunate **2 preordained**, destined, fated, God-given, divine *Opposite*: arbitrary. *See* COMPARE AND CONTRAST *at* lucky.

provider *n* **1 breadwinner**, wage-earner, earner, worker, benefactor *Opposite*: dependent **2 supplier**, source, contributor, donor, bringer *Opposite*: beneficiary

providing *conj* **on condition that**, if, only if, as long as, so long as

province *n* **1 region**, area, state, county, prefecture **2 area**, sphere, field, jurisdiction, domain

provinces *n* **outlying areas**, countryside, backwaters, hinterland, sticks *(infml)* *Opposite*: capital

provincial *adj* **1 local**, regional, county, district, small-town *Opposite*: central **2 unsophisticated**, unfashionable, simple, outmoded, parochial *Opposite*: worldly

provincialism *n* **lack of sophistication**, lack of refinement, parochialism, narrow-mindedness, insularity *Opposite*: worldliness

provision *n* **1 delivery**, facility, running, setting up, establishment **2 anticipation**, prearrangement, forethought, wherewithal, readiness **3 stipulation**, rider, condition, proviso, if

provisional *adj* **temporary**, interim, conditional, makeshift, short-term *Opposite*: permanent

provisions *n* **supplies**, necessities, requirements, food, rations

proviso *n* **stipulation**, rider, condition, provision, if

provisory *adj* **conditional**, subject to, dependent upon, provisional, contingent *Opposite*: unconditional

provocation *n* **1 incitement**, needling, goading, baiting, niggling *Opposite*: appeasement **2 vexation**, frustration, irritation, annoyance, affront

provocative *adj* **1 challenging**, provoking, stimulating, inflammatory, incendiary *Opposite*: conciliatory **2 suggestive**, enticing, seductive, alluring, encouraging *Opposite*: forbidding

provoke *v* **1 incite**, needle, goad, bait, irritate *Opposite*: soothe **2 cause**, elicit, produce, trigger, bring about *Opposite*: prevent

provoked *adj* **irritated**, annoyed, angered, goaded, frustrated *Opposite*: unaffected

provoking *adj* **infuriating**, irritating, annoying, frustrating, maddening *Opposite*: soothing

provost *n* **principal**, director, head, chancellor, leader

prowess *n* **1 ability**, skill, expertise, competence, dexterity *Opposite*: incompetence **2 bravery**, valor, heroism, gallantry, courage *Opposite*: cowardice

prowl *v* **stalk**, lurk, skulk, lie in wait, hang around

prowler *n* **stalker**, pursuer, intruder, tormentor, Peeping Tom

proximity *n* **nearness**, closeness, juxtaposition, vicinity, immediacy *Opposite*: remoteness

proxy *n* **1 substitute**, alternate, stand-in, deputy, delegate **2 indirect means**, substitution, deputation, commission, delegation

prudence *n* **practicality**, carefulness, caution, discretion, forethought *Opposite*: imprudence

prudent adj **practical**, careful, cautious, sensible, discreet Opposite: imprudent. See COMPARE AND CONTRAST at **cautious**.

prudential adj **sensible**, wise, sagacious, provident, practical Opposite: foolish

prudery n **primness**, stuffiness, reserve, puritanism, prudishness Opposite: broadmindedness

prudish adj **prim**, stuffy, strait-laced, starchy, formal Opposite: relaxed

prudishness see **prudery**

prune v 1 **clip**, trim, snip, cut back, cut 2 **shorten**, cut, abridge, condense, tighten up Opposite: expand

prurient adj **unwholesome**, unhealthy, immodest, indecent, salacious Opposite: healthy

pry v 1 **interfere**, poke your nose in, meddle, inquire, peer Opposite: leave alone 2 **lever open**, force, force open, wrench, wrest

prying adj **interfering**, inquisitive, curious, meddling, peeping Opposite: incurious

P.S. n **postscript**, addendum, afterthought, addition, coda

psalm n **sacred song**, hymn, poem, canticle, prayer

Psalter n **book of psalms**, prayer book, breviary, hymnal, missal

pseudonym n **alias**, false name, assumed name, fictitious name, stage name

psych v 1 **panic**, frighten, scare, worry, trouble 2 **nerve**, steel, brace, motivate, gear up

psyche n 1 **soul**, spirit, inner self, essence, being 2 **mind**, consciousness, awareness, ego, intellect

psychedelic adj 1 **hallucinogenic**, mind-altering, mind-expanding, mood-altering, mind-blowing (infml) 2 **colored**, patterned, vibrant, vivid, loud Opposite: dull

psychic adj 1 **mental**, cerebral, intellectual, cognitive, psychosomatic 2 **supernatural**, extrasensory, mysterious, unexplained, paranormal Opposite: physical 3 **telepathic**, clairvoyant, intuitive, second-sighted, stargazing ■ n **clairvoyant**, spiritualist, soothsayer, sensitive, diviner

psychical adj **supernatural**, paranormal, spiritual, extrasensory, subliminal Opposite: physical

psychological adj **mental**, emotional, inner, spiritual, psychosomatic Opposite: physical

psychology n **mind**, thinking, mindset, makeup, sensibility

psychosomatic adj **self-induced**, mental, psychological, inner, all in the mind

puberty n **sexual maturity**, adolescence, youth, teens

pubescent adj **pubertal**, teenage, adolescent, teen (infml)

public adj 1 **community**, civic, communal, municipal, free Opposite: private 2 **freely available**, shared, known, open, in the public domain Opposite: secret ■ n **everyone**, people, populace, community, society

publication n **book**, magazine, newspaper, journal, periodical

public disgrace n **dishonor**, disgrace, ignominy, humiliation, exposure

public figure n **celebrity**, name, personality, personage, household name

public image n **façade**, front, public face, persona, identity

publicity n **advertising**, promotion, exposure, hype, media hype

publicize v **make public**, make known, broadcast, advertise, announce Opposite: suppress

publicly adv **openly**, in public, overtly, widely, freely Opposite: secretly

public relations n **image management**, publicity, media, relations, P.R.

public-spirited adj **philanthropic**, charitable, altruistic, humanitarian, benevolent Opposite: selfish

publish v 1 **issue**, put out, bring out, print, distribute 2 **make public**, make known, announce, broadcast, advertise Opposite: keep secret

publisher n **producer**, originator, commissioner, editor, issuer

publishing n **publication**, printing, issuing, reproducing, dissemination

pucker v **wrinkle**, crease, gather, pull together, ruck up Opposite: smooth ■ n **gather**, wrinkle, crease, ruck, pull

puckish adj **mischievous**, playful, naughty, impish, elfin

puddle n **pool**, slick, wet patch ■ v **splash**, dabble, paddle, wade

pudgy (infml) adj **fat**, chubby, stubby, heavy, round

puerile adj **childish**, immature, infantile, foolish, silly Opposite: mature

puerility n **immaturity**, childishness, silliness, foolishness, inanity

puff n 1 **gust**, breath, draft, current, flurry 2 **cloud**, wisp, waft, billow 3 **praise**, recommendation, advertisement, publicity, blurb (slang) ■ v 1 **blow**, exhale, breathe out, breathe Opposite: inhale 2 **pant**, breathe heavily, wheeze, gasp, gasp for breath

puffed-up adj **pompous**, self-important, arrogant, conceited, boastful Opposite: humble

puffiness n 1 **swelling**, enlargement, inflammation, edema, distension 2 **pomposity**, pompousness, arrogance, haughtiness, pride Opposite: humility

puffing n **wheezing**, wheeziness, breathlessness, heavy breathing, breathing ■ adj **breathless**, out of breath, panting, gasping, winded

puff out see **puff up**

puff up v enlarge, swell, inflate, expand, bulge Opposite: deflate

puffy adj swollen, distended, inflated, bloated, bulbous

pugilism n boxing, fighting, prizefighting

pugilist n boxer, fighter, prizefighter, pug (infml)

pugnacious adj aggressive, confrontational, belligerent, truculent, argumentative Opposite: peaceable

pugnaciousness see **pugnacity**

pugnacity n aggression, fierceness, forcefulness, hostility, confrontational attitude

pukka adj fine, well-made, excellent, high-quality, first-class

pull v 1 drag, draw, heave, haul, tow Opposite: push 2 tug, jerk, yank, wrench, pluck 3 attract, draw, bring in, pull in, lure Opposite: put off 4 strain, sprain, damage, injure, tear 5 remove, extract, withdraw, draw out, pluck out Opposite: put in ■ n 1 (infml) attraction, appeal, power, influence, draw 2 jerk, tug, yank, twitch, tweak

---

COMPARE AND CONTRAST CORE MEANING: move something toward you or in the same direction as you

pull move something toward you or in the same direction as you; **drag** move something large or heavy with effort across a surface; **draw** pull something with a smooth movement; **haul** pull something with a steady strong movement, often involving strenuous effort; **tow** pull something along behind by means of a rope or chain; **tug** pull at something with a sharp forceful movement, without necessarily moving the object; **yank** pull something suddenly and sharply with a single strong movement.

---

pull apart v disintegrate, tear apart, dismantle, pull to pieces, demolish Opposite: assemble

pull back v recoil, shrink, shrink away, back off, retract

pull down v demolish, tear down, destroy, fell, flatten Opposite: build up

pulley n winch, hoist, block and tackle

pull in v attract, draw, bring in, pull, entice Opposite: put off

pull off (infml) v achieve, succeed, be successful, accomplish, carry out Opposite: fail. See COMPARE AND CONTRAST at **accomplish**.

pull out v 1 remove, extract, withdraw, draw out, pluck out Opposite: insert 2 leave, depart, abandon, drop out, go away Opposite: remain

pullout n 1 insert, flier, supplement, enclosure, addendum 2 retreat, withdrawal, departure

pull out all the stops v do your utmost, go all-out, move heaven and earth, make a supreme effort, do all you can

pull somebody's leg (infml) v tease some-body, joke, have a joke on somebody, have a laugh, tell stories

pull the plug v end, discontinue, close down, cut off, wind up

pull the wool over somebody's eyes v deceive, delude, hoodwink, swindle, con

pull through v recover, get better, pick up, survive, get through

pull together v 1 unite, join forces, rally, cooperate, team up 2 organize, arrange, assemble, draw together, bring together

pull to pieces v 1 dismantle, pull to bits, pull apart, take to pieces, rip to pieces 2 criticize, vilify, make short work of, make mincemeat of, shoot down

pull up v stop, halt, draw to a halt, brake, pull in

pull yourself together (infml) v compose yourself, regain your composure, think straight, calm down, regain your self-control

pulmonary adj pulmonic, lung, respiratory

pulp n 1 soft tissue, fleshy tissue, tissue, flesh 2 paste, mush, mash, blend, soft mass ■ v mash, crush, squash, pound, grind

pulpit n 1 podium, dais, stand, lectern, reading desk 2 clergy, church, church authorities

pulsate v throb, beat, pulse, thump, thud

pulsation n throb, beat, pulse, rhythm, pounding

pulse n 1 throb, pulsation, rhythm, pounding, thump 2 legume, leguminous plant, bean, pea ■ v throb, beat, pulsate, pound, palpitate

---

WORD BANK

❑ types of pulses bean, black bean, black-eyed pea, broad bean, butter bean, chickpea, fava bean, French bean, garbanzo, haricot, kidney bean, lentil, lima bean, mung bean, navy bean, pea, petits pois, pinto bean, runner bean, snow pea, soybean, string bean

---

pulverization n 1 maceration, liquidization, crushing, reduction, grinding 2 (infml) defeat, humiliation, thrashing, beating, whipping

pulverize v 1 grind, crush, macerate, pulp, mash 2 (infml) thrash, crush, annihilate, destroy, defeat

pummel v beat, thump, thrash, pound, punch

pump v 1 force, drive, impel, propel, thrust 2 question, interrogate, quiz, probe, debrief

pump out v produce, give off, generate, churn out, emit

pump up v inflate, blow up, puff up, puff out, expand Opposite: deflate

pun n witticism, joke, double entendre, quip, bon mot ■ v play with words, joke, quip, make a joke, banter

punch v 1 stamp, press, perforate, cut, pierce 2 hit, beat, strike, pummel, thump ■ n 1 blow, hit, thump, clout, knock 2 vigor, drive, energy, power, verve

punch-drunk (infml) adj dazed, confused, bewildered, stupefied, stunned Opposite: alert

punchiness n vigor, energy, verve, liveliness, drive Opposite: lethargy

punchy (infml) adj 1 pithy, hard-hitting, forceful, terse, effective Opposite: bland 2 dazed, confused, bewildered, stupefied, stunned Opposite: alert

punctilious adj 1 fastidious, scrupulous, painstaking, assiduous, meticulous Opposite: sloppy (infml) 2 correct, seemly, courteous, polite, civil Opposite: boorish. See COMPARE AND CONTRAST at careful.

punctiliousness n 1 fastidiousness, precision, correctness, exactitude, efficiency Opposite: carelessness 2 propriety, courteousness, correctness, politeness, decorum Opposite: boorishness

punctual adj on time, in good time, prompt, on the dot Opposite: late

punctuality n promptness, timekeeping, reliability, regularity Opposite: lateness

punctuate v 1 interrupt, intersperse, scatter, interpose, pepper 2 mark, edit, correct, mark up, proofread

puncture n hole, perforation, wound, lesion, pinhole ■ v 1 pierce, stab, perforate, prick, stick in 2 undermine, deflate, erode, ruin, destroy Opposite: inflate

pundit n expert, specialist, authority, commentator, guru

pungency n 1 spiciness, strong flavor, bitterness, sharpness, acidity Opposite: blandness 2 pithiness, pointedness, wit, force, bite Opposite: mildness

pungent adj 1 strong, powerful, spicy, hot, overpowering Opposite: bland 2 caustic, pithy, pointed, witty, forceful Opposite: mild

punish v chastise, discipline, penalize, reprove, rebuke Opposite: commend

punishable adj serious, indictable, bookable, hanging, capital

punishing adj grueling, exhausting, demanding, tiring, arduous Opposite: undemanding

punishment n 1 sentence, penalty, reprimand, retribution, penance Opposite: reward 2 rough treatment, abuse, mistreatment, heavy use, ill-use

punitive adj disciplinary, penal, corrective, retaliatory, retributive

punk (infml) adj inferior, second rate, cheap, nasty, poor

punt v kick, hit, strike, boot, shoot

puny adj 1 small, weak, tiny, feeble, frail Opposite: robust 2 inadequate, trifling, paltry, minor, feeble Opposite: considerable

pup n upstart, brat, puppy, smart aleck (infml), know-it-all (infml) ■ v whelp, litter, bear, deliver, give birth

pupil n acolyte, understudy, follower, apprentice, student Opposite: teacher

puppet n 1 marionette, dummy, doll, hand puppet, finger-puppet 2 pawn, lackey, instrument, tool, lapdog

puppy n upstart, brat, pup, smart aleck (infml), know-it-all (infml)

purchase v 1 buy, pay for, acquire, obtain, procure Opposite: sell 2 obtain, win, gain, secure, acquire ■ n 1 acquisition, buying, obtaining, procurement, securing Opposite: sale 2 buy, acquisition, goods, merchandise, item 3 grip, grasp, hold, leverage, foothold

purchaser n buyer, procurer, customer, client, consumer Opposite: seller

purdah n 1 seclusion, withdrawal, separation, retirement, isolation 2 screen, curtain, barrier, divider, shield

pure adj 1 unmixed, one hundred percent, genuine, real, authentic 2 uncontaminated, unadulterated, unpolluted, clean, untainted Opposite: tainted 3 sheer, complete, utter, absolute, downright 4 (literary) chaste, unsullied, uncorrupted, innocent, sinless Opposite: corrupt 5 clear, vivid, strong, vibrant, rich Opposite: weak 6 theoretical, abstract, fundamental, basic, higher Opposite: applied

purebred adj thoroughbred, pedigree, pure

purée n pulp, paste, mush, pap, sauce ■ v mash, blend, process, liquidize, pound

purely adv 1 entirely, wholly, totally, thoroughly, completely Opposite: partly 2 merely, only, simply, just, solely 3 chastely, virtuously, decently, morally, innocently Opposite: indecently

pureness n 1 cleanliness, wholesomeness, spotlessness, clarity, transparency Opposite: dirtiness 2 clarity, vividness, strength, vibrancy, richness

purgative (fml) n enema, emetic, suppository, laxative, purge ■ adj cleansing, emetic, laxative, emptying, purging

purgatory n agony, limbo, hell, anguish, despair

purge v 1 get rid of, eliminate, remove, eradicate, do away with 2 wash out, cleanse, clean, flush out, sluice 3 (fml) pardon, exonerate, absolve, forgive, excuse Opposite: castigate (fml) ■ n 1 laxative, cathartic, emetic, purgative (fml) 2 elimination, removal, eradication, expulsion, ridding

purification n cleansing, sanitization, decontamination, distillation, sterilization

purifier n cleanser, filter, sterilizer, disinfectant, antiseptic

purify v cleanse, disinfect, sanitize, decontaminate, clean Opposite: contaminate

purist n traditionalist, perfectionist, stickler, pedant, conformist

purity n **1 cleanliness**, spotlessness, clarity, transparency, limpidness *Opposite*: dirtiness **2 innocence**, wholesomeness, virtue, virtuousness, chasteness

purl n **1 thread**, gold thread, silver thread, wire, filigree **2 border**, edge, frill, trim, fringe ■ v (*literary*) **flow**, ripple, babble, murmur, gurgle

purlieu n **suburb**, exurb, outskirts, suburbia, vicinity

purloin (*fml*) v **steal**, appropriate, walk off with, pocket, help yourself to. *See* COMPARE AND CONTRAST *at* steal.

purple adj **elaborate**, exaggerated, florid, overwritten, ornate

---

WORD BANK
❏ **types of purple** amethyst, aubergine, heliotrope, lavender, lilac, mauve, orchid, plum, violet

---

purport v **1 claim**, assert, allege, profess, contend **2** (*fml*) **intend**, aim, mean, plan ■ n **1** (*fml*) **sense**, significance, importance, meaning, implication **2** (*fml*) **purpose**, intention, aim, design, plan

purported adj **supposed**, claimed, alleged, ostensible, unsupported

purpose n **1 intention**, aim, object, objective, goal **2 determination**, resolution, resolve, persistence, perseverance *Opposite*: indifference

purposeful adj **focused**, determined, decisive, resolute, firm *Opposite*: indecisive

purposefulness n **determination**, resolution, single-mindedness, commitment, tenacity *Opposite*: aimlessness

purposeless adj **1 pointless**, irrational, useless, illogical, unreasonable **2 empty**, aimless, meaningless, pointless, senseless *Opposite*: meaningful

purposely adv **deliberately**, intentionally, on purpose, knowingly, wittingly *Opposite*: accidentally

purr v **vibrate**, hum, rumble, whir, buzz

purse n **1 handbag**, bag, pocketbook **2 change purse**, wallet, pouch, money bag **3 reward**, winnings, takings, prize ■ v **pucker**, tighten, squeeze, press, compress *Opposite*: relax

pursuance (*fml*) n **enactment**, undertaking, fulfillment, achievement, acquirement

pursue v **1 follow**, chase, hunt, trail, track **2 practice**, engage in, work at, go in for, take up. *See* COMPARE AND CONTRAST *at* follow.

pursuer n **follower**, chaser, hunter, trailer, tracker

pursuit n **1 chase**, hunt, search, quest, detection **2 hobby**, recreation, activity, pastime, interest

purulent adj **infected**, pus-filled, pussy, weeping, oozing

purvey v **1** (*fml*) **sell**, provide, supply, deal

in, furnish (*fml*) *Opposite*: buy **2 gossip**, tattle, whisper, spread, tell

purveyor (*fml*) n **1 supplier**, seller, vendor, outlet, source **2 spreader**, gossipmonger, teller, tattler, source

pus n **discharge**, secretion, excretion, fluid, infection

push v **1 shove**, thrust, ram, press, set in motion *Opposite*: pull **2 impel**, urge, goad, force, make *Opposite*: restrain **3 advocate**, promote, advance, endorse, boost *Opposite*: oppose ■ n **ambition**, energy, force, vigor, impetus *Opposite*: apathy

push-button adj **automatic**, high-tech, remote-control, electronic *Opposite*: manual

pushcart n **cart**, handcart, trolley, wagon

pushed (*infml*) adj **1 lacking**, short, short of cash, strapped (*infml*), hard up (*infml*) **2 hard-pressed**, pressed, busy, struggling, hard at it

push in v **cut in**, barge in, shove in, squeeze in, cut in line

pushiness n **forcefulness**, nerve, aggressiveness, assertiveness, brashness *Opposite*: reluctance

pushing adj **1 assertive**, forceful, aggressive, strident, brash *Opposite*: retiring **2 approaching**, nearly, almost, just about, roughly

push off v **1 cast off**, shove off, embark, depart, set sail **2 go away**, leave, depart, get going, set out *Opposite*: remain

pushover (*infml*) n **dupe**, soft touch, gull, target, softy (*infml*)

push through v **put into force**, enforce, enact, introduce, force through

pushy (*infml*) adj **assertive**, forceful, aggressive, strident, brash *Opposite*: retiring

pusillanimity n **timidity**, fear, cowardice, nervousness, hesitation *Opposite*: confidence

pusillanimous adj **timid**, cowardly, fainthearted, weak, spineless *Opposite*: brave. *See* COMPARE AND CONTRAST *at* cowardly.

pussy n (*infml*) **cat**, kitten, puss (*infml*), pussycat (*infml*), kitty (*infml*) ■ adj **infected**, purulent, pus-filled, weeping, oozing

pussycat n **1 cat**, kitten, pussy (*infml*), puss (*infml*), kitty (*infml*) **2 dear**, soft touch, pushover, softy (*infml*), sweetie (*infml*)

pussyfoot (*infml*) v **1 hesitate**, waver, wander, prevaricate, procrastinate **2 tiptoe**, creep, steal, pick your way, ghost

pustule n **boil**, abscess, eruption, pimple, carbuncle

put v **place**, set, lay, position, situate *Opposite*: remove

put about v **spread**, circulate, tell, inform, give out *Opposite*: keep secret

put across v **get across**, express, transmit, articulate, explain

put a damper on v **deflate**, spoil, mar, subdue, depress *Opposite*: enliven

put a match to v **set alight**, set fire to, set on fire, light, ignite *Opposite*: put out

put an end to v **stop**, discontinue, halt, suspend, call a halt to *Opposite*: continue

put a premium on v **value**, appreciate, prize, favor, rate highly

put aside v 1 **save**, earmark, allocate, put by, set aside 2 **disregard**, ignore, close your eyes to, forget, waive 3 **set down**, set aside, deposit, lay down, put down

put a stop to v **put an end to**, stop, bring to an end, pull the plug on, call a halt *Opposite*: continue

putative adj 1 **accepted**, acknowledged, recognized, known, believed 2 **supposed**, reputed, alleged, assumed, presumed

put at risk v **endanger**, jeopardize, gamble with, risk, imperil *(fml)*

put away v 1 **tidy up**, pack away, clear up, store, pack up *Opposite*: scatter 2 **save**, put aside, keep, stash away, put by 3 *(infml)* **consume**, eat, drink, swallow, devour 4 *(infml)* **imprison**, jail, commit, confine

put a wrench in the works v **foil**, thwart, cause havoc, frustrate, wreak havoc *Opposite*: help

put back v 1 **put away**, replace, pack away, return, clear away 2 **pay back**, repay, reimburse, compensate, recompense 3 **postpone**, defer, suspend, put on hold, put off 4 **drink**, throw back, put away, gulp down, swallow down

put back together v **mend**, repair, reassemble, rebuild, reconstruct *Opposite*: take apart

put behind you v **forget**, get over, recover from, put down to experience, get out of your system *Opposite*: brood

put by v **save**, put aside, stash away, earmark, put away

put down v 1 **set down**, lay down, down, deposit, leave *Opposite*: pick up 2 **enter**, write down, put in writing, record, log 3 **quell**, crush, suppress, quash, repress 4 *(infml)* **ridicule**, mock, criticize, deride, disparage *Opposite*: praise 5 **attribute**, ascribe, lay at the door of, impute, blame on 6 **kill**, put to death, dispatch, destroy

putdown *(infml)* n **insult**, attack, gibe, criticism, dig *Opposite*: compliment

put forth *(fml)* v 1 **state**, make known, publish, present, give 2 **leave**, set out, depart, head off, start out

put forward v 1 **state**, make known, publish, present, give 2 **suggest**, propose, present, submit, offer

put in v 1 **donate**, contribute, dedicate, allocate, give *Opposite*: take out 2 **present**, submit, offer, make, claim *Opposite*: withdraw 3 **interrupt**, break in, interpose, interject, butt in

put in an appearance v **attend**, drop in, appear, turn up, be present

put in danger v **endanger**, jeopardize, hazard, risk, compromise

put in the shade v **outshine**, be head and shoulders above, eclipse, be way ahead of, humiliate

put into action v **implement**, put into practice, apply, realize, carry out

put into effect v **enforce**, put into practice, exercise, apply, carry out

put into operation v **implement**, put into action, put into practice, apply, set up

put into practice v **carry out**, practice, do, realize, implement

put into words v **phrase**, articulate, formulate, express, convey

put in writing v **put down on paper**, put down in black and white, put down, confirm in writing, write down

put off v 1 **postpone**, delay, defer, shelve, suspend *Opposite*: bring forward 2 **hinder**, discourage, delay, obstruct, prevent 3 **disgust**, repel, offend, sicken, revolt *Opposite*: attract

put on v 1 **dress in**, wear, change into, get into, don *Opposite*: take off 2 **stage**, present, produce, mount, direct 3 **gain**, add, increase, accumulate, acquire *Opposite*: lose 4 **pretend**, feign, simulate, fake, play-act

put-on adj **pretend**, false, fake, sham, feigned *Opposite*: genuine ■ n *(infml)* **deception**, simulation, trick, hoax, con

put on a brave front v **put a brave face on it**, keep up appearances, be brave, keep your chin up

put on an act v **pretend**, put it on, put on a pretense, sham, feign

put on a pedestal v **elevate**, idolize, worship, admire, regard highly

put on hold v **put off**, delay, postpone, adjourn, defer

put on ice *see* put on hold

put on the back burner *see* put on hold

put on the market v **offer for sale**, put up for sale, market, advertise

put out v 1 **extinguish**, douse, snuff out, stifle, snuff *Opposite*: light 2 **annoy**, irritate, slight, offend, exasperate *Opposite*: please 3 **make public**, make known, publicize, circulate, spread *Opposite*: keep secret

putrefaction n **decay**, decomposition, rot, breakdown, corruption

putrefy v **rot**, decay, decompose, go moldy, go bad

putrid adj **rotten**, rotting, decayed, decaying, decomposed *Opposite*: fresh

put right v **repair**, fix, mend, rectify, restore

putsch n **coup**, insurrection, uprising, revolution, revolt

put somebody's back up *(infml)* v **annoy**,

irritate, get on somebody's nerves, get on the wrong side of somebody, alienate *Opposite*: soothe

putt v hit, tap, stroke, knock, push ■ n tap, stroke, hit, knock, push

putter v dawdle, idle, do nothing much, fiddle, fool around

put to death v kill, execute, murder, assassinate, liquidate. *See* COMPARE AND CONTRAST *at* kill.

put together v 1 assemble, piece together, construct, build, fabricate 2 draw up, formulate, devise, develop, prepare

put to good use v use, apply, exploit, exercise, make use of *Opposite*: discard

put to sleep v knock out, anesthetize, sedate, put under, put out *Opposite*: bring around

put under v sedate, put to sleep, put out, knock out, anesthetize *Opposite*: bring around

put up v 1 erect, raise, build, construct, create *Opposite*: tear down 2 accommodate, house, lodge, take in *Opposite*: evict 3 offer, provide, proffer, extend, advance

put-upon adj overburdened, exploited, used, overworked, abused

put up to v induce, persuade, encourage, make, cause *Opposite*: dissuade

put up with v tolerate, endure, bear, stand, submit

put your back into v try hard, give your all, work hard, give it your best shot, give it all you've got

put your faith in v trust, rely on, count on, have confidence in, bank on

put your feet up v relax, rest, nap, lounge around, lie down

put your foot down v demand, stand firm, stand fast, be resolute, be determined

put your foot in it (*infml*) v blunder, err, goof, speak out of turn, be indiscreet

put your foot in your mouth (*infml*) see **put your foot in it**

puzzle v 1 mystify, bewilder, perplex, baffle, confuse 2 wonder, mull, brood, ponder ■ n mystery, enigma, conundrum, problem, dilemma *Opposite*: explanation. *See* COMPARE AND CONTRAST *at* problem.

puzzled adj mystified, bewildered, perplexed, baffled, confused *Opposite*: enlightened

puzzlement n bafflement, perplexity, uncertainty, disorientation, bemusement *Opposite*: understanding

puzzle out v work out, solve, figure out, resolve, decipher

puzzler n conundrum, puzzle, mystery, riddle, brainteaser

puzzling adj mystifying, bewildering, perplexing, baffling, confusing *Opposite*: enlightening

pygmy adj miniature, small, tiny, dwarf, little

pylon n tower, mast, post, pillar

pyre n fire, bonfire, furnace

pyromaniac n fire setter, arsonist, torcher

Q

quack n imposter, charlatan, fraud, fake, pretender

quackery n deception, trickery, dishonesty, fraud, deceit *Opposite*: honesty

quad (*infml*) n quadrangle, courtyard, yard, square, patio

quadrangle n 1 courtyard, yard, square, patio, piazza 2 four-sided figure, rectangle, oblong, quadrilateral, parallelogram

quadrilateral n rectangle, oblong, square, parallelogram, rhombus ■ adj four-sided, rectangular, square, quadrangular, quadrate

quadruped n animal, four-footed animal, tetrapod

quadruple v increase fourfold, multiply, times, magnify, augment *Opposite*: decrease

quaff (*literary*) v drink, gulp down, put away, throw back, swallow down

quagmire n 1 swamp, marsh, bog, mire, quicksand 2 predicament, dilemma, quandary, sticky situation, muddle

quail v flinch, recoil, cringe, balk. *See* COMPARE AND CONTRAST *at* recoil.

quaint adj 1 old-world, old-fashioned, picturesque, antiquated, charming *Opposite*: modern 2 strange, peculiar, odd, curious, bizarre *Opposite*: ordinary

quake v 1 quail, tremble, shudder, quaver, cower 2 shake, tremble, quiver, shudder, shiver ■ n (*infml*) earthquake, tremor, temblor, seismic wave, seismic activity

qualification n 1 skill, quality, attribute, ability, aptitude *Opposite*: failing 2 credential, diploma, certificate, license 3 requirement, condition, prerequisite, criterion, sine qua non 4 restriction, reservation, modification, limitation, tempering

question

qualified *adj* **1 trained**, licensed, registered, certified, recognized *Opposite*: unqualified **2 suitable**, eligible, capable, competent, skilled *Opposite*: unsuitable **3 limited**, contingent, modified *Opposite*: unconditional

qualify *v* **1 be suitable**, be in the running, meet the requirements, be eligible, make the grade *Opposite*: fail **2 train**, certify, license, empower, entitle **3 restrict**, limit, modify, temper, moderate

quality *n* **1 characteristic**, feature, attribute, property, trait **2 standard**, grade, level, caliber, class **3 excellence**, superiority, distinction, merit, eminence *Opposite*: inferiority

qualm *n* **1 misgiving**, doubt, pang, fear, apprehensiveness **2 scruple**, pang of conscience, remorse, contrition, compunction

quandary *n* **dilemma**, predicament, difficulty, Catch-22, fix *(infml)*

quantifiable *adj* **calculable**, computable, measurable, assessable, determinable *Opposite*: unquantifiable

quantify *v* **calculate**, count, enumerate, measure, compute

quantitative *adj* **1 measurable**, quantifiable, calculable, numerical, computable *Opposite*: unquantifiable **2 numerical**, enumerative, arithmetical, mathematical, variable

quantity *n* **amount**, number, measure, extent, size

quantum *adj* **major**, dramatic, significant, important, considerable *Opposite*: minor

quarantine *n* **isolation**, seclusion, confinement, solitary confinement, cordon sanitaire *Opposite*: integration ■ *v* **1 isolate**, seclude, set apart, confine, separate *Opposite*: integrate **2 detain**, imprison, hold, lock up, intern *Opposite*: release

quarrel *n* **1 argument**, dispute, disagreement, row, squabble *Opposite*: reconciliation **2 complaint**, grievance, grumble, problem *(infml)*, bone to pick *(infml)* ■ *v* **argue**, row, fall out, clash, fight *Opposite*: make up

quarrelsome *adj* **argumentative**, cantankerous, irritable, petulant, confrontational *Opposite*: agreeable

quarry *n* **1 excavation**, mine, pit, diggings **2 prey**, victim, target, kill, game *Opposite*: hunter ■ *v* **mine**, dig out, extract, excavate, dig up

quarter *n* **1 fourth**, division, part, section, quadrant **2 district**, neighborhood, sector, zone, precinct ■ *v* **1 divide**, subdivide, cut up, section, split up **2 lodge**, house, billet, accommodate, put up *Opposite*: evict

quarterfinal *n* **round**, heat, leg, match, game

quarterly *adj* **three-monthly**, trimestral, four times a year ■ *n* **magazine**, periodical, journal, publication, slick

quarters *n* **rooms**, accommodations, billet, housing, lodgings *(dated)*

quash *v* **1 put down**, suppress, quell, subdue, crush *Opposite*: allow **2 nullify**, cancel, repeal, overturn, annul *Opposite*: validate

quasi *adj* **virtual**, to all intents and purposes, pseudo, would-be, self-styled *Opposite*: through and through

quatrain *n* **verse**, stanza, rhyme

quaver *v* **1 tremble**, shudder, shake, quiver, quake **2 trill**, warble, wobble, vibrate, quiver

quay *n* **dockside**, wharf, dock, pier, seafront

quayside *see* **quay**

queasily *adv* **nauseously**, biliously, dizzily, groggily, woozily

queasiness *n* **nausea**, sickness, biliousness, vomiting, upset stomach

queasy *adj* **1 nauseous**, sick, ill, indisposed, seasick *Opposite*: well **2 uneasy**, uncomfortable, doubtful, dubious, troubling *Opposite*: reassuring

queen *n* **1 monarch**, sovereign, ruler, crowned head, empress **2 icon**, star, prima donna, doyenne **3 epitome**, model, essence, ideal, crème de la crème

queenly *adj* **majestic**, royal, regal, dignified, stately

queen-size *adj* **large**, largish, medium-large

queer *(dated) adj* **1 unusual**, unexpected, strange, surprising, funny *Opposite*: commonplace **2 eccentric**, unconventional, idiosyncratic, curious, bizarre *Opposite*: normal **3 eccentric**, unconventional, idiosyncratic, curious, bizarre *Opposite*: normal **4 unwell**, sick, nauseous, queasy, faint *Opposite*: well

quell *v* **1 suppress**, put down, subdue, crush, quash *Opposite*: incite **2 allay**, assuage, alleviate, mollify, mitigate *Opposite*: aggravate

quench *v* **1 slake**, satisfy, satiate, reduce, sate *Opposite*: stimulate **2 extinguish**, put out, douse, smother, stifle *Opposite*: ignite

querulous *adj* **1 complaining**, carping, critical, difficult, hard to please *Opposite*: equable **2 whining**, cantankerous, grumbling, complaining, moaning *(infml)* *Opposite*: good-natured

querulousness *n* **peevishness**, negativity, cantankerousness, criticalness, argumentativeness

query *n* **1 inquiry**, question, request, interrogation, demand *Opposite*: answer **2 doubt**, uncertainty, reservation, question, question mark *Opposite*: certainty ■ *v* **1 question**, cast doubt on, doubt, suspect, challenge *Opposite*: trust **2 inquire**, ask, interrogate, quiz, demand *Opposite*: answer

quest *n* **mission**, expedition, pursuit, search, hunt ■ *v* **search**, hunt, seek, chase, pursue *Opposite*: find

question *n* **1 inquiry**, query, request, interrogation, demand *Opposite*: answer

2 issue, subject, matter, point at issue, problem *Opposite*: resolution **3 uncertainty**, doubt, reservation, query, question mark *Opposite*: certainty ■ *v* **1 interrogate**, quiz, probe, grill (*infml*) give somebody the third degree (*infml*) *Opposite*: reply **2 query**, cast doubt on, doubt, suspect, challenge *Opposite*: trust

COMPARE AND CONTRAST CORE MEANING: ask for information
question ask for information on a particular topic, especially formally or officially; **quiz** subject somebody to persistent questions; **interrogate** question somebody systematically and intensively in a formal or official context, such as in a police investigation or court case; **grill** (*infml*) question somebody intensively; **give the third degree** (*infml*) question somebody intensively, especially in an aggressive way.

questionable *adj* **dubious**, doubtful, open to discussion, open to doubt, moot *Opposite*: indisputable

questioner *n* **interviewer**, interrogator, cross-examiner, asker, inquirer *Opposite*: interviewee

questioning *adj* **interrogative**, inquisitorial, searching, quizzical, inquiring *Opposite*: responsive

question mark *n* **doubt**, uncertainty, reservation, query, question *Opposite*: certainty

questionnaire *n* **survey**, opinion poll, inquiry form, form, feedback form

queue *v* **line up**, get in line, wait your turn, stand in line, wait in line

quibble *v* **equivocate**, hedge, split hairs, nitpick, cavil *Opposite*: agree ■ *n* **objection**, cavil, equivocation, quiddity (*fml*)

quiche *n* **tart**, egg pie, pastry, flan, tartlet

quick *adj* **1 rapid**, fast, speedy, swift, hasty *Opposite*: slow **2 sudden**, immediate, instant, prompt, abrupt *Opposite*: delayed **3 brief**, short, cursory, fleeting, momentary *Opposite*: lasting **4 intelligent**, clever, bright, quick-thinking, quick-witted **5 nimble**, lively, sprightly, spry, agile *Opposite*: sluggish. *See* COMPARE AND CONTRAST *at* **intelligent**.

quicken *v* **speed up**, accelerate, hasten, pick up speed, go faster *Opposite*: slow down

quick-fire *adj* **rapid**, swift, successive, automatic, fast *Opposite*: measured

quickly *adv* **1 rapidly**, fast, speedily, swiftly, hurriedly *Opposite*: slowly **2 suddenly**, immediately, promptly, without delay, at once *Opposite*: slowly **3 briefly**, cursorily, fleetingly, momentarily, passingly *Opposite*: lastingly

quickness *n* **1 rapidity**, speed, speediness, swiftness, promptness *Opposite*: sluggishness **2 alertness**, cleverness, quick-wittedness, adroitness, sharpness

quicksand *n* **swamp**, marsh, quagmire, bog, mire

quicksilver *adj* **volatile**, mercurial, changeable, inconstant, unpredictable *Opposite*: constant

quick-tempered *adj* **fiery**, temperamental, excitable, volatile, passionate *Opposite*: calm

quick-witted *adj* **smart**, intelligent, clever, bright, sharp

quick-wittedness *n* **adroitness**, inventiveness, sharpness, intelligence, cleverness

quid pro quo *n* **deal**, trade, agreement, exchange, tradeoff

quiescence *n* **dormancy**, latency, rest, inertness, calm *Opposite*: action

quiescent *adj* **calm**, inactive, dormant, gentle, sluggish *Opposite*: active

quiet *adj* **1 silent**, noiseless, inaudible, low, soft *Opposite*: noisy **2 peaceful**, still, tranquil, uninterrupted, undisturbed *Opposite*: noisy **3 private**, discreet, unofficial, off-the-record, confidential *Opposite*: public **4 trouble-free**, straightforward, uncomplicated, simple, easy **5 relaxing**, restful, leisurely, peaceful, pleasant *Opposite*: busy **6 discreet**, modest, subtle, subdued, muted *Opposite*: showy ■ *n* **silence**, hush, peace, stillness, tranquillity *Opposite*: noise ■ *v* **1 fall silent**, calm down, settle down, calm, hush *Opposite*: animate **2 alleviate**, allay, soothe, assuage, quell *Opposite*: aggravate. *See* COMPARE AND CONTRAST *at* **silent**.

quiet down *v* **stop talking**, fall silent, keep it down, shut up (*infml*), shush (*infml*)

quietly *adv* **1 silently**, gently, inaudibly, softly, in silence *Opposite*: loudly **2 calmly**, peacefully, tranquilly, serenely, uninterrupted *Opposite*: noisily **3 peacefully**, tranquilly, pleasantly, agreeably, restfully

quietness *n* **1 silence**, softness, quiet, noiselessness, inaudibility *Opposite*: noise **2 peace**, stillness, serenity, calm, quiet

quill *n* **feather**, plume, barb, spine, spike

quilt *n* **comforter**, patchwork quilt, bedspread, eiderdown, coverlet

quintessence *n* **essence**, embodiment, epitome, personification, soul

quintessential *adj* **typical**, essential, archetypal, prototypical, model *Opposite*: atypical

quip *n* **witticism**, joke, sally, one-liner, clever remark ■ *v* **joke**, gibe, remark, banter, retort

quirk *n* **1 twist of fate**, coincidence, accident, chance, oddity **2 idiosyncrasy**, peculiarity, foible, oddity, habit

quirky *adj* **idiosyncratic**, individual, unusual, peculiar, odd *Opposite*: normal

quit *v* **1 resign**, leave, walk out, abandon, vacate *Opposite*: stay **2 give up**, stop, relinquish, refrain from, renounce *Opposite*: take up

quite *adv* **1 very**, entirely, completely, totally, utterly *Opposite*: slightly **2 fairly**, rather, moderately, relatively, reasonably *Opposite*: extremely

quits *(infml)* *adj* **even**, square, settled, level, even-steven *(infml)*

quitter *(infml)* *n* **defeatist**, deserter, loser, pessimist, coward *Opposite*: go-getter *(infml)*

quiver *v* **tremble**, shake, shudder, shiver, quake ■ *n* **shudder**, shiver, tremble, palpitation, tremor

quivering *adj* **trembling**, quaking, quavering, unsteady, shaky *Opposite*: steady ■ *n* **pulsation**, vibration, spasm, palpitation, tremor

quixotic *adj* **romantic**, unrealistic, idealistic, impractical, dreamy *Opposite*: down-to-earth

quiz *n* **test**, puzzle, game, contest, competition ■ *v* **question**, interrogate, cross-examine, interview, examine. *See* COMPARE AND CONTRAST *at* **question**.

quiz master *r* **host**, emcee, interviewer, questioner, chair *Opposite*: contestant

quizzical *adj* **questioning**, curious, puzzled, surprised, perplexed

quorum *n* **minimum**, minimum number, least, required number, lower limit

quota *n* **share**, allocation, allowance, part, ration

quotation *n* **1 quote**, citation, line, passage, extract **2 estimate**, price, figure, costing, quote

quote *v* **1 cite**, recite, repeat, refer to, mention **2 give an estimate**, estimate, bid, give a price, give a figure ■ *n* **1 quotation**, citation, line, passage, extract **2 estimate**, price, figure, bid, quotation

quotient *n* **proportion**, measure, amount, share, percentage

R

rabbi *n* **religious leader**, scholar, teacher, official, leader

rabbit *n* **bunny**, coney, cottontail

rabble *n* **mob**, crowd, swarm, throng, horde

rabble-rouser *n* **troublemaker**, agitator, demagogue, activist, firebrand

rabble-rousing *n* **troublemaking**, sedition, provocation, agitation, activism ■ *adj* **provocative**, inflammatory, seditious, incendiary, troublemaking

rabid *adj* **1 foaming at the mouth**, diseased, sick, ill, infected *Opposite*: well **2 fanatical**, extreme, radical, uncompromising, militant *Opposite*: lukewarm **3 intense**, fervent, ardent, violent, zealous *Opposite*: moderate

rabidly *adv* **fervently**, ardently, intensely, single-mindedly, zealously *Opposite*: moderately

race *n* **1 contest**, competition, heat, sprint, marathon **2 ethnic group**, nation, tribe, line, people *(infml)* **3 struggle**, fight, rivalry, battle, competition ■ *v* **1 compete**, take part, run, sprint, contest *Opposite*: withdraw **2 speed**, go fast, run, sprint, hurry *Opposite*: crawl

racecourse *n* **track**, stadium, running track, circuit, speedway

racer *n* **competitor**, contender, entrant, sprinter, runner

racetrack *n* **track**, turf, course, hippodrome

raceway *n* **1 channel**, race, conduit, canal, course **2 track**, circuit, course, stadium, racecourse

racial *adj* **ethnic**, cultural, tribal, national

racism *n* **racial discrimination**, discrimination, prejudice, bigotry, intolerance

racist *adj* **chauvinistic**, bigoted, xenophobic, prejudiced, discriminatory *Opposite*: tolerant

rack *n* **stand**, frame, framework, holder, shelf ■ *v* **1 afflict**, torment, plague, torture, beset *Opposite*: comfort **2 shake**, rock, devastate, play havoc with, wreck *Opposite*: restore **3 store**, shelve, stack, stow, put away *Opposite*: unpack

racket *n* **1 noise**, din, rumpus, commotion, hullabaloo **2 swindle**, con, fraud, scheme, scam *(slang)*

racketeer *n* **criminal**, swindler, hoodlum, shark *(infml)*, con artist *(slang)*

rack up *(infml)* *v* **accumulate**, chalk up, score, make, achieve

rack your brains *v* **try to remember**, think hard, concentrate, make an effort, focus

raconteur *n* **narrator**, storyteller, conversationalist, after-dinner speaker, wit

racy *adj* **indecent**, risqué, indelicate, improper, sexy *Opposite*: clean

radar *n* **detector**, locater, sensor, locating system, position finder

raddled *adj* **haggard**, debauched, worn-out, unkempt, disheveled *Opposite*: fresh

radial *adj* **circular**, outward, centrifugal, radiated, outspread

radiance *n* **1 happiness**, sparkle, joy, vivacity, joie de vivre *Opposite*: dullness

2 light, brightness, glow, luminosity, brilliance

radiant *adj* **1 happy**, healthy, glowing, beaming, sunny *Opposite*: unhappy **2 shining**, luminous, brilliant, bright, dazzling *Opposite*: dull

radiate *v* **1 give out**, give off, emit, discharge, issue **2 exude**, emanate, glow with, bristle with, brim with **3 spread out**, branch out, diverge, spread, circulate

radiation *n* **particle emission**, energy, radioactivity, fallout, contamination

radiator *n* **heater**, room heater, storage heater, space heater

radical *adj* **1 basic**, fundamental, essential, profound, deep-seated **2 sweeping**, pervasive, thorough, far-reaching, wide-ranging *Opposite*: minor **3 revolutionary**, extreme, extremist, uncompromising, militant *Opposite*: conservative ■ *n* **extremist**, activist, militant, revolutionary, fanatic *Opposite*: conservative

radicalism *n* **extremism**, militancy, fanaticism, zealotry, radicalness

radio *n* **radio set**, transistor, receiver, boom box *(infml)*, wireless *(dated)*

radioactive *adj* **emitting radiation**, dangerous, harmful, hot, active

radioactivity *n* **radiation**, particle emission, energy, fallout

radio-controlled *adj* **remote-controlled**, automatic, remote

radius *n* **1 area**, range, circle, ambit, extent **2 line**, distance, length **3 scope**, area of influence, umbrella, reach, range

raffia *n* **straw**, fiber, grass, natural fiber

raffish *adj* **1 unconventional**, dashing, rakish, disreputable, louche *Opposite*: conventional **2 showy**, ostentatious, gaudy, loud, garish *Opposite*: discreet

raffle *n* **lottery**, draw, sweepstakes, drawing ■ *v* **offer**, give away, award, present, donate

raft *(infml)* *n* **bundle**, number, tranche, portfolio, range

rafter *n* **beam**, roof beam, support, joist, strut

rag *n* **1 scrap**, shred, wisp, tatter, thread **2** *(infml)* **newspaper**, paper, daily, tabloid ■ *v* *(dated)* **tease**, taunt, make fun of, call names, poke fun at

ragamuffin *(dated)* *n* **urchin**, waif, child

ragbag *(infml)* *n* **mixture**, mixed bag, miscellany, hodgepodge, jumble

rage *n* **fury**, anger, wrath, temper, frenzy *Opposite*: calmness ■ *v* **fume**, rant and rave, storm, seethe, thunder. *See* COMPARE AND CONTRAST *at* anger.

ragged *adj* **1 tattered**, torn, worn-out, raggedy, in tatters *Opposite*: pristine **2 jagged**, serrated, uneven, irregular, rough *Opposite*: even **3 unkempt**, untidy, shabby, raggedy, in rags *Opposite*: neat

raggedness *n* **1 untidiness**, shabbiness, scruffiness, sloppiness, messiness *Opposite*: neatness **2 unevenness**, jaggedness, roughness, irregularity, sharpness *Opposite*: smoothness

raggedy *see* **ragged**

raging *adj* **powerful**, intense, furious, strong, rampant *Opposite*: mild

ragtag *adj* **1 motley**, disparate, assorted, miscellaneous, multifarious **2 untidy**, shabby, unkempt, scruffy, ragged *Opposite*: neat

raid *n* **attack**, search, forced entry, break-in, incursion ■ *v* **1 storm**, attack, invade, search, break into **2 rob**, loot, plunder, hold up, burgle

raider *n* **attacker**, thief, robber, marauder, invader

rail *n* **railing**, handrail, banister, bar, support ■ *v* **protest**, complain, object, criticize, condemn *Opposite*: accept

railhead *n* **terminus**, starting point, end of the line

railing *n* **fence**, paling, barrier, balustrade, boundary line

raillery *n* **teasing**, joking, banter, repartee, kidding *Opposite*: bullying

railroad *n* **1 track**, line, train track, route, rail **2 rail network**, network, train system, train network, rail transportation system ■ *v* *(infml)* **push**, force, steamroller, bulldoze, shove

---

WORD BANK

❏ **types of railroads** cable railroad, light rail, metro, monorail, streetcar line, subway, underground

❏ **types of rail vehicles** cable car, funicular, locomotive, steam engine, streetcar, TGV, train

❏ **parts of a train** box car, cabin, caboose, car, coach, compartment, dining car, freight car, locomotive, luggage compartment, observation car, Pullman, sleeper, sleeping car, smoker, smoking car, smoking compartment, steam engine, tank engine, wagon

---

raiment *(literary)* *n* **clothing**, apparel, clothes, wear, dress

rain *n* **1 rainfall**, drizzle, shower, torrent, precipitation **2 volley**, hail, stream, torrent, flood ■ *v* **1 pour**, drizzle, pelt down, shower, sprinkle **2 lavish**, shower, pour, deluge, overwhelm

rainbow *n* **arc**, arch, bow ■ *adj* **multicolored**, colorful, variegated, spectral, polychromatic *Opposite*: monochrome

rain cats and dogs *(infml)* *v* **pour rain**, pour down rain, come down in torrents, come down in buckets, come down in sheets *(infml)*

rainfall *n* **rain**, shower, drizzle, torrent, precipitation *Opposite*: sunshine

rainmaker *(infml)* *n* **achiever**, triumph, success, star, celebrity *Opposite*: failure

rain out *v* **postpone**, put back, call off, move

on, move forward *Opposite*: bring forward

rainproof *adj* **impermeable**, water-resistant, waterproof, showerproof, impervious *Opposite*: permeable

rainstorm *n* **cloudburst**, downpour, deluge, thunderstorm, shower

rainwater *n* **rain**, precipitation, rainfall, raindrops

rainy *adj* **wet**, raining, drizzling, showery, drizzly *Opposite*: dry

raise *v* **1 hoist**, lift up, uplift, elevate, move up *Opposite*: let down **2 look after**, bring up, foster, grow, breed *Opposite*: neglect **3 increase**, put up, inflate, boost, jack up *Opposite*: lower **4 build**, erect, set up, construct, put up **5 mention**, bring up, present, put forward, moot *Opposite*: withdraw **6 solicit**, canvass, obtain, bring in, procure **7 lift**, end, terminate, conclude *Opposite*: impose **8 improve**, better, enhance, uplift, advance *Opposite*: deteriorate **9 cause**, elicit, stimulate, induce, excite *Opposite*: quell ■ *n* **increase**, promotion, advance, elevation

raise objections *v* **object**, protest about, demur, remonstrate, contest *Opposite*: agree

raise your spirits *v* **cheer up**, lift your spirits, gladden, hearten, buoy up *Opposite*: depress

raison d'être *n* **meaning**, purpose, rationale, motivation, inspiration

rajah *n* **king**, prince, maharajah, chief, ruler *Opposite*: subject

rake *v* **1 gather**, clear up, scrape, collect, scrape up *Opposite*: scatter **2 enfilade**, pepper, spray, shoot **3 search through**, go through, sift, rummage, comb *Opposite*: find ■ *n* **reprobate**, degenerate, prodigal, profligate, squanderer *Opposite*: paragon

rake-off *(infml)* *n* **bribe**, kickback, favor, sweetener *(infml)*, cut *(infml)* *Opposite*: cost

rake up *(infml)* *v* **mention**, drag up, dredge up, bring up, dig up *Opposite*: keep mum *(infml)*

rakish *adj* **1 dashing**, stylish, natty, sporty, jaunty *Opposite*: bland **2 dissolute**, profligate, degenerate, louche, dubious *Opposite*: upright

rally *n* **1 resurgence**, revival, comeback, recovery, revitalization **2 gathering**, meeting, assembly, convention, demonstration ■ *v* **1 come together**, gather, call together, bring together, unite *Opposite*: disperse **2 revive**, improve, recover, pull through, get better *Opposite*: decline

ram *v* **1 strike**, hit, bump, slam, collide with **2 force**, stuff, jam, cram, compress

ramble *v* **1 go on**, digress, go off on a tangent, ramble on, blather *(infml)* *Opposite*: focus **2 walk**, hike, wander, roam, go for a walk ■ *n* **hike**, walk, roam, stroll, wander

ramble on *v* **go on**, ramble, digress, go off on a tangent, blather *(infml)* *Opposite*: focus

rambler *n* **walker**, hiker, backpacker, roamer, wanderer

rambling *adj* **1 long-winded**, wordy, discursive, digressive, incoherent *Opposite*: concise **2 spread out**, sprawling, trailing, straggling, irregular *Opposite*: compact. *See* COMPARE AND CONTRAST *at* wordy.

rambunctious *adj* **rowdy**, high-spirited, lively, disorderly, riotous *Opposite*: mellow

ramekin *n* **dish**, pot, container, vessel, baking dish

ramequin *see* ramekin

ram home *v* **emphasize**, stress, accentuate, drive home, underline *Opposite*: pass over

ramification *n* **complication**, difficulty, consequence, result, implication

ramify *v* **1 branch**, divide, subdivide, fork, split *Opposite*: unite **2 complicate**, confuse, confound, compound, intensify *Opposite*: simplify

ramp *n* **slope**, incline, rise, upgrade, gradient

rampage *n* **riot**, uproar, tumult, furor, turmoil ■ *v* **run riot**, riot, rage, run amok, tear

rampant *adj* **1 unchecked**, unrestrained, threatening, out of control, uncontrolled *Opposite*: contained **2 wild**, widespread, extensive, lush, rambling *Opposite*: tamed

rampart *n* **fortification**, embankment, bastion, wall, earthwork

ramshackle *adj* **rickety**, tumbledown, dilapidated, broken down, falling to pieces *Opposite*: sturdy

ranch *n* **farm**, farmstead, estate, rancho, hacienda

rancher *n* **farmer**, livestock farmer, landowner, squire, planter

rancid *adj* **reeking**, fetid, sour, bad, rotten *Opposite*: fresh

rancidness *n* **sourness**, rankness, fetidness, rottenness, smelliness *Opposite*: freshness

rancor *n* **acrimony**, bitterness, malice, resentment, vindictiveness

rancorous *adj* **acrimonious**, bitter, malicious, resentful, vindictive *Opposite*: amicable

rancorousness *see* rancor

random *adj* **haphazard**, arbitrary, accidental, casual, hit and miss *Opposite*: deliberate

randomness *n* **haphazardness**, arbitrariness, casualness, chanciness, unpredictability *Opposite*: predictability

range *n* **1 variety**, choice, series, assortment, array **2 scope**, span, breadth, reach, extent ■ *v* **vary between**, fluctuate, vacillate, oscillate, alternate

ranger *n* **1 warden**, park ranger, steward, overseer, guardian **2 wanderer**, roamer, rambler, walker, hiker

rangy *adj* **long-legged**, tall, lanky, gangling, gangly *Opposite*: thickset

rani *n* queen, princess, maharani, consort

rank *n* status, title, category, position, level ■ *v* rate, position, place, categorize, class ■ *adj* 1 sheer, utter, complete, blatant, absolute *Opposite*: minimal 2 vigorous, rampant, exuberant, abundant, flourishing *Opposite*: sparse 3 *(literary)* pungent, fetid, stinking, smelly, bad *Opposite*: fresh

ranking *n* position, status, place, standing, rank

rankle *v* irritate, fester, gnaw, eat up, irk *Opposite*: soothe

ransack *v* 1 rob, despoil, vandalize, strip, loot 2 search, go through, rummage, turn upside down, turn out *Opposite*: find

ransom *n* payment, money, sum, deal, exchange ■ *v* redeem, buy back, set free, strike a deal, pay up

rant *v* rage, go on, bluster, fume, seethe *Opposite*: sweet-talk *(infml)* ■ *n* outburst, tirade, histrionics, bombast, bluster

rant and rave *v* rage, go on, keep on, bluster, shout *Opposite*: calm down

rap *v* hit, thwack, strike, tap, crack ■ *n* 1 blow, tap, knock, smack, crack *Opposite*: caress 2 rebuke, criticism, reprimand, reproach, tongue-lashing

rapacious *adj* 1 grasping, greedy, avid, voracious, avaricious *Opposite*: temperate 2 destructive, vicious, harmful, aggressive, dangerous *Opposite*: harmless

rapaciousness *n* 1 voraciousness, greediness, unscrupulousness, greed, avarice 2 destructiveness, violence, viciousness, harmfulness, aggressiveness *Opposite*: gentleness

rapid *adj* swift, quick, fast, speedy, hasty *Opposite*: slow

rapidity *n* swiftness, quickness, speed, speediness, haste *Opposite*: slowness

rapids *n* fast-moving water, white water, torrents, waterfall, fall

rap on/over the knuckles *(infml)* *v* reprimand, scold, rebuke, censure, upbraid *Opposite*: praise

rap out *v* bark, shout, snap, bawl, yell *Opposite*: whisper

rapper *n* singer, vocalist, rhymer, performer

rapport *n* relationship, bond, understanding, link, affinity *Opposite*: friction

rapprochement *n* reconciliation, reunion, understanding, settlement, compromise *Opposite*: hostility

rapt *adj* 1 engrossed, fascinated, absorbed, captivated, gripped *Opposite*: bored 2 happy, blissful, delighted, content, joyful *Opposite*: sullen

rapture *n* bliss, ecstasy, euphoria, delight, joy *Opposite*: depression

rapturous *adj* delighted, enthusiastic, thrilled, overjoyed, elated *Opposite*: unenthusiastic

rare *adj* 1 valuable, unique, singular, scarce, exceptional *Opposite*: common 2 infrequent, occasional, sporadic, intermittent, erratic *Opposite*: frequent 3 underdone, bloody, juicy, red, pink *Opposite*: overcooked

rarefied *adj* esoteric, abstruse, exclusive, obscure, complex *Opposite*: simple

rarely *adv* seldom, infrequently, on the odd occasion, hardly ever, not often *Opposite*: often

rareness *n* 1 scarcity, paucity, dearth, lack, scarceness *Opposite*: abundance 2 uniqueness, matchlessness, exclusivity, exceptionality, individuality *Opposite*: commonness

rarified *see* rarefied

raring *adj* enthusiastic, eager, keen, ready, impatient *Opposite*: reluctant

rarity *n* 1 infrequency, shortage, scarcity, uncommonness, fewness 2 find, unusual object, curiosity, oddity, singularity

rascal *n* 1 rogue, mischief, mischief-maker, scoundrel, scamp *(infml)* 2 tease, joker, prankster, trickster, jester

rascally *adj* 1 mischievous, impish, naughty, puckish, playful *Opposite*: well-behaved 2 dishonest, wicked, bad, mean, untrustworthy *Opposite*: good

rash *adj* impetuous, thoughtless, hasty, impulsive, reckless *Opposite*: sensible ■ *n* 1 eruption, spots, reaction, itchiness, inflammation 2 outbreak, flush, spate, string, eruption *Opposite*: incident

rashness *n* impetuousness, thoughtlessness, haste, recklessness, foolishness *Opposite*: prudence

rasp *n* file, scraper, tool ■ *v* 1 scrape, rub, grate, chafe, grind *Opposite*: smooth 2 grate, bark, snarl, growl *Opposite*: murmur

rasping *adj* harsh, rough, grating, hoarse, jarring *Opposite*: smooth

ratchet *n* notch, tooth, cog, wheel, pawl ■ *v* intensify, inflame, step up, stir up, increase *Opposite*: lessen

rate *n* 1 speed, tempo, pace, velocity 2 amount, frequency, level, degree, proportion 3 charge, fee, price, tariff, toll ■ *v* value, regard, rank, esteem, appraise

rather *adv* 1 somewhat, to a certain extent, slightly, pretty, fairly 2 very, considerably, significantly, noticeably, extremely *Opposite*: hardly 3 sooner, preferably, instead, by preference

ratification *n* approval, sanction, endorsement, confirmation, authorization *Opposite*: rejection

ratify *v* approve, sanction, endorse, confirm, authorize *Opposite*: reject

rating *n* assessment, score, evaluation, grade, ranking

ratio *n* proportion, relative amount, relation, percentage, share

ration n **share**, portion, allowance, quota, allotment ■ v **restrict**, control, limit, put a ceiling on, regulate Opposite: lavish

rational adj **1 reasonable**, sensible, logical, realistic, sound Opposite: illogical **2 lucid**, balanced, sane, normal, cogent Opposite: irrational

rationale n **reasoning**, basis, foundation, justification, motivation

rationality n **logic**, reason, shrewdness, judgment, lucidity Opposite: irrationality

rationalization n **1 justification**, explanation, reasoning, validation, excuse **2 streamlining**, restructuring, reorganization, rearrangement, reshuffling

rationalize v **1 justify**, give good reason for, vindicate, excuse, explain **2 make more efficient**, reduce, downsize, streamline, slim down Opposite: increase **3 adjust**, tune, level, straighten out, unravel

ration out v **distribute**, share out, apportion, divide up, allot Opposite: pool

rations n **provisions**, supplies, food, consignment, distribution

rat on (infml) v **betray**, tell on, inform on, set up, spill the beans on (infml)

rattily (infml) adv **messily**, shabbily, tattily, raggedly, scruffily Opposite: tidily

rattle v **1 shake**, clatter, bang, crash, jangle **2 unnerve**, fluster, faze, shock, disconcert Opposite: calm

rattle off v **say quickly**, reel off, run through, list, recite Opposite: stammer

rattle on v **chatter**, go on and on, drone on, talk nineteen to the dozen, jabber Opposite: clam up (infml)

rattletrap (infml) n **wreck**, beater (infml), clunker (infml), rust bucket (infml), heap (slang)

rattling adj **fast**, brisk, lively, speedy, fast-moving Opposite: plodding

ratty (infml) adj **1 messy**, unkempt, shabby, seedy, tatty Opposite: tidy **2 shabby**, dilapidated, worn, seedy, decrepit Opposite: pristine

raucous adj **loud**, harsh, rough, hoarse, disorderly Opposite: subdued

raucousness n **boisterousness**, wildness, disorderliness, unruliness, riotousness Opposite: quietness

ravage v **1 wreck**, devastate, destroy, ruin, damage Opposite: create **2 despoil**, pillage, plunder, sack, lay waste Opposite: restore

ravages n **effects**, consequences, results, aftereffects

rave v **1 rant**, rage, fume, fulminate, hold forth Opposite: reason **2 enthuse**, praise, go on about, laud, extol Opposite: criticize ■ n **party**, bash, event, revelry, festivity

ravel v **tangle**, knot, twist, snag, catch Opposite: untangle

raven (literary) v **wolf**, wolf down, gobble, gobble up, bolt

ravening adj **voracious**, greedy, hungry, predatory, vicious Opposite: sated

ravenous adj **1 hungry**, famished, starving (infml), starved (infml) Opposite: sated **2 greedy**, voracious, rapacious, ravening, predatory Opposite: generous

ravenousness n **greediness**, insatiability, hunger, greed, gluttony

raver (infml) n **partygoer**, hedonist, clubber, party animal (infml), sybarite (literary)

ravine n **valley**, gorge, gap, gully, canyon

raving adj **frenzied**, gibbering, crazed, raging, delirious Opposite: controlled

ravish v **overwhelm**, overcome, transport, overpower, delight

ravishing adj **beautiful**, stunning, gorgeous, striking, eye-catching Opposite: plain

raw adj **1 uncooked**, fresh, rare, red, underdone Opposite: cooked **2 unprocessed**, unrefined, untreated, crude, basic Opposite: processed **3 painful**, sore, sensitive, tender, bleeding Opposite: healed **4 inexperienced**, green, untrained, wet behind the ears, untried Opposite: experienced **5 bitter**, chilly, bleak, freezing, inclement Opposite: mild **6 visceral**, brutal, crude, rude, primal Opposite: bland

rawness n **1 inflammation**, painfulness, soreness, pain, redness **2 inexperience**, naiveté, ingenuousness, innocence, immaturity Opposite: poise **3 cold**, chill, bitterness, iciness, chilliness Opposite: mildness **4 brutality**, crudeness, rudeness, primitiveness, atavism Opposite: polish

ray n **beam**, shaft, gleam, glimmer, flicker

raze v **destroy**, demolish, annihilate, level, flatten Opposite: build

razor v **shave**, cut, trim, style, clip

razz (infml) v **tease**, taunt, make fun of, poke fun at, ridicule

razzmatazz n **showiness**, flashiness, hype, razzle-dazzle, glitziness Opposite: dullness

re prep **on the subject of**, with regard to, with reference to, concerning, regarding

reach v **1 stretch**, touch, get hold of, grasp, extend **2 go**, move, feel, fumble, lunge **3 arrive at**, get to, attain, make, achieve **4 influence**, touch, affect, impact on, get to **5 contact**, get in touch with, access, get through to, get hold of ■ n **scope**, spread, range, orbit, grasp

reachable adj **within reach**, on hand, nearby, easy to get to, accessible Opposite: remote

react v **1 respond**, counter, retort, answer, reply Opposite: ignore **2 change**, alter, oxidize, reduce, bond

reaction n **response**, repercussion, comeback, feedback, blowback (infml)

reactionary adj **backward-looking**, conservative, right-wing, illiberal, unreceptive Opposite: progressive ■ n **conservative**, right-winger, dinosaur, diehard, extremist *Opposite*: progressive

reactivate *v* **restart**, reboot, galvanize, resuscitate, revitalize *Opposite*: deactivate

reactive *adj* **responsive**, sensitive, oversensitive, volatile, mercurial *Opposite*: phlegmatic

read *v* **1 understand**, comprehend, make sense of, follow **2 read out**, recite, deliver, speak, declaim **3 peruse**, scan, glance at, look at, study **4 interpret**, decipher, figure out, translate, convert **5 study**, take, research, take a degree in

readable *adj* **clear**, legible, decipherable, understandable, comprehensible *Opposite*: illegible

reader *n* **booklover**, bibliophile, bookworm (*infml*)

readership *n* **circulation**, audience, distribution, market share, niche

readily *adv* **1 willingly**, gamely, eagerly, voluntarily, gladly *Opposite*: grudgingly **2 promptly**, unhesitatingly, quickly, at once, without delay *Opposite*: belatedly **3 without difficulty**, easily, effortlessly, with no trouble, smoothly *Opposite*: painfully

readiness *n* **1 willingness**, gameness, eagerness, keenness, enthusiasm *Opposite*: unwillingness **2 promptness**, speediness, quickness, alacrity, skill *Opposite*: delay

reading *n* **1 understanding**, comprehension, construing, interpretation, analysis **2 recitation**, recital, rendition, performance, presentation

readjust *v* **1 get used to**, settle, settle in, accommodate, come to terms with **2 rearrange**, realign, modify, calibrate, rectify *Opposite*: leave alone

readjustment *n* **rearrangement**, change, modification, alteration, reformation

read out *v* **announce**, recite, deliver, declaim, reel off

readout *n* **1 data**, information, figures, statistics, details **2 display**, retrieval, record, screen, monitor

read up *v* **study**, find out about, look into, investigate, research

ready *adj* **1 prepared**, set, all set, complete, standing by *Opposite*: unprepared **2 likely to**, about to, on the verge of, on the point of, liable to *Opposite*: unlikely **3 willing**, eager, prepared, disposed, keen *Opposite*: unwilling **4 quick**, prompt, apt, timely, swift *Opposite*: slow **5 perceptive**, discerning, attentive, wide-awake, astute *Opposite*: dull ■ *v* **prepare**, set, arrange, prime, make plans for

ready-made *adj* **off-the-rack**, prêt-à-porter, retail, convenient, handy *Opposite*: personalized

ready-to-wear *see* ready-made

reaffirm *v* **repeat**, reassert, confirm, reiterate, endorse *Opposite*: contradict

reaffirmation *n* **restatement**, repetition, reiteration, endorsement, confirmation *Opposite*: contradiction

reagent *n* **substance**, component, element, chemical, mixture

real *adj* **1 actual**, factual, material, tangible, physical *Opposite*: nonexistent **2 genuine**, original, authentic, bona fide, valid *Opposite*: false **3 sincere**, unfeigned, genuine, frank, heartfelt *Opposite*: artificial ■ *adv* (*infml*) **very**, truly, extremely, honestly, really *Opposite*: hardly

real estate *n* **land**, property, realty, commercial property, houses

realign *v* **readjust**, straighten, manipulate, rearrange, restore *Opposite*: disarrange

realignment *n* **readjustment**, rearrangement, shift, repositioning, relocation

realism *n* **practicality**, pragmatism, levelheadedness, common sense, sanity *Opposite*: impracticality

realist *n* **pragmatist**, doer, experimenter, radical, stoic *Opposite*: idealist

realistic *adj* **1 practical**, sensible, pragmatic, down-to-earth, level-headed *Opposite*: impractical **2 convincing**, lifelike, representative, truthful, accurate *Opposite*: unnatural

reality *n* **1 realism**, authenticity, truth, certainty, veracity *Opposite*: idealism **2 actuality**, the everyday, experience, existence, life *Opposite*: make-believe

realizable *adj* **achievable**, attainable, realistic, viable, possible *Opposite*: unattainable

realization *n* **1 understanding**, comprehension, consciousness, awareness, recognition *Opposite*: ignorance **2 achievement**, accomplishment, carrying out, attainment, completion *Opposite*: failure

realize *v* **1 understand**, comprehend, become conscious, appreciate, grasp *Opposite*: misunderstand **2 fulfill**, achieve, accomplish, carry out, bring to fruition *Opposite*: fail. *See* COMPARE AND CONTRAST *at* accomplish.

real-life *adj* **actual**, true, factual, real, realistic *Opposite*: imaginary

reallocate *v* **redistribute**, reshuffle, reorganize, transfer, rationalize

really *adv* **1 actually**, in fact, in truth, in reality, truly **2 very**, thoroughly, truly, genuinely, sincerely *Opposite*: hardly

realm *n* **1 kingdom**, monarchy, dominion, empire, land **2 scope**, area, range, domain, sphere

realness *n* **reality**, actuality, authenticity, genuineness, sincerity

realty *n* **real estate**, real property, land, property, estate

real world *n* **reality**, life, everyday, the world, actuality *Opposite*: ivory tower

real-world *adj* **practical**, actual, everyday, real, real-life *Opposite*: imaginary

ream n quantity, amount, pack, pile

reanimate v revive, restore, reawaken, awaken, resuscitate Opposite: deaden

reap v 1 gather, harvest, garner, collect, pick Opposite: sow 2 obtain, acquire, gain, earn, secure Opposite: lose

reaper n gatherer, harvester, cutter, gleaner, mower

reappear v come back, recur, resurface, return, come again Opposite: disappear

reappearance n recurrence, repetition, reemergence, return, comeback Opposite: disappearance

reappraisal n reassessment, review, reconsideration, check, second look

reappraise v reassess, check, reevaluate, reconsider, reexamine

rear v raise, bring up, care for, nurture, take care of Opposite: neglect ■ n back, stern, tail, tail end, back end Opposite: front

rear-end v crash into, bang into, bump into, collide, hit

rearguard n tail end, rear, back end, tail, back Opposite: vanguard

rear its head v appear, loom, turn up, materialize, rise up Opposite: disappear

rearm v 1 arm, equip, provide, supply, sell 2 build up, upgrade, reinforce, fortify, secure Opposite: disarm

rearmament n 1 equipment, armament, provision, supply, sale 2 buildup, upgrade, fortification, reinforcement, securement Opposite: disarmament

rearmost adj backmost, last, final, ultimate, terminal Opposite: foremost

rearrange v 1 reorder, reorganize, reposition, move, move around Opposite: leave 2 reschedule, change the date, postpone, delay, adjourn

rearrangement n 1 reorganization, reordering, movement, change, relocation 2 rescheduling, postponement, change of date, delay, adjournment

rearward adv backward, toward the rear, behind, back, to the rear Opposite: forward ■ adj backward, to the rear, toward the rear, back, behind Opposite: forward

reason n 1 justification, explanation, basis, grounds, cause 2 motive, cause, aim, end, goal 3 thought, judgment, logic, sense, mind 4 sanity, right mind, mind, wits, senses Opposite: insanity ■ v 1 think, rationalize, deduce, analyze, work out 2 argue, debate, discuss, influence, persuade. See COMPARE AND CONTRAST at deduce.

reasonable adj 1 sensible, rational, acceptable, practical, realistic Opposite: unreasonable 2 not bad, quite good, passable, tolerable, all right Opposite: appalling 3 inexpensive, affordable, cheap, moderate, economical Opposite: expensive. See COMPARE AND CONTRAST at valid.

reasonableness n sensibleness, rationality,

fairness, common sense, level-headedness Opposite: irrationality

reasonably adv 1 sensibly, rationally, judiciously, level-headedly, soundly Opposite: irrationally 2 quite, fairly, moderately, rather, relatively Opposite: extremely

reasoned adj rational, coherent, logical, lucid, analytic Opposite: illogical

reasoning n analysis, logic, calculation, reckoning, interpretation

reassemble v 1 put back together, reconstruct, rebuild, repair, mend Opposite: take apart 2 meet again, reconvene, reunite, get back together, congregate Opposite: disperse

reassert v restate, reaffirm, repeat, reiterate, confirm Opposite: abandon

reassertion n reaffirmation, restatement, repetition, reiteration, confirmation Opposite: abandonment

reassess v reconsider, review, have another look at, think again, check

reassessment n reconsideration, review, reexamination, check, revision

reassurance n comfort, assurance, support, encouragement, hope Opposite: discouragement

reassure v assure, comfort, support, encourage, set your mind at rest Opposite: discourage

reassuring adj encouraging, comforting, supportive, cheering, heartening Opposite: discouraging

reawaken v stir up, revive, bring back, rekindle, resuscitate Opposite: obliterate

rebadge v rebrand, rename, retitle, change the name of, give another name

rebarbative (fml) adj unpleasant, unattractive, objectionable, annoying, forbidding Opposite: pleasant

rebate n refund, repayment, return, discount, reimbursement Opposite: supplement

rebel n protester, objector, campaigner, agitator, radical Opposite: loyalist ■ v 1 revolt, rise up, mutiny, resist, mount the barricades Opposite: comply with 2 protest, campaign, agitate, defy, dissent Opposite: obey

rebellion n revolt, uprising, insurgence, upheaval, mutiny Opposite: compliance

rebellious adj 1 disobedient, unruly, insubordinate, recalcitrant, defiant Opposite: obedient 2 revolutionary, militant, armed, treacherous, mutinous Opposite: law-abiding

rebelliousness n 1 disobedience, unruliness, recalcitrance, insubordination, defiance Opposite: obedience 2 revolution, insurrection, sedition, mutiny, treachery Opposite: compliance

rebirth n 1 revival, renaissance, reawakening, renascence, return Opposite: disappearance **2 regeneration**, renewal, restoration, revitalization, rejuvenation *Opposite*: degeneration

reboot v **restart**, start up again, open again, boot up

reborn adj **born again**, recreated, regenerated, renewed, revitalized

rebound v **1 spring back**, recoil, ricochet, jump back, return **2 recover**, bounce back, rally, pick up, return to normal

rebuff v **reject**, snub, refuse, repulse, slight *Opposite*: accept ■ n **rejection**, refusal, snub, slight, denial *Opposite*: acceptance

rebuild v **1 reconstruct**, build, restructure, reerect, remake *Opposite*: destroy **2 restore**, renovate, recreate, reconstitute, do up *Opposite*: neglect

rebuke v **reprimand**, reprove, censure, reproach, take to task *Opposite*: praise ■ n **reproach**, reproof, censure, reprimand, scolding *Opposite*: compliment

rebut v **refute**, disprove, deny, invalidate, contradict *Opposite*: accept

rebuttal n **refutation**, disproof, denial, negation, contradiction *Opposite*: endorsement

recalcitrance n **resistance**, noncooperation, stubbornness, obstinacy, obduracy *Opposite*: cooperation

recalcitrant adj **unruly**, refractory, disobedient, wayward, headstrong *Opposite*: cooperative. *See* COMPARE AND CONTRAST *at* **unruly**.

recall v **1 remember**, bring to mind, evoke, call to mind, recollect *Opposite*: forget **2 call back**, call in, take back, withdraw, take out ■ n **memory**, recollection, remembrance, reminiscence *Opposite*: amnesia

recant v **take back**, renounce, repudiate, disavow, retract *Opposite*: avow (fml)

recantation n **denial**, withdrawal, repudiation, retraction, revocation *Opposite*: affirmation

recap v **sum up**, summarize, go over, run through, review ■ n **summary**, outline, summing up, review, restatement

recapitulate (fml) v **sum up**, recap, summarize, run through, review

recapitulation (fml) n **recap**, summary, restatement, review, outline

recapture v **1 regain**, retake, take back, reclaim, repossess **2 summon up**, recall, evoke, bring back, recollect

recast v **1 reorganize**, re-present, re-form, modify, alter **2 reassign**, reallocate, reselect, redistribute

recede v **1 move away**, retreat, go back, withdraw, draw back *Opposite*: advance **2 diminish**, lessen, decline, wane, fade *Opposite*: increase

receding adj **retreating**, withdrawing, disappearing, ebbing, declining *Opposite*: growing

receipt n **1 acknowledgment**, proof of purchase, slip, voucher, chit (dated) *Opposite*: invoice **2 receiving**, reception, delivery, unloading, acceptance *Opposite*: dispatch

receive v **1 get**, obtain, accept, take, have *Opposite*: dispatch **2 hear**, catch, sense, gather, grasp **3 entertain**, greet, welcome, meet

receivership n **bankruptcy**, insolvency, liquidation, failure, ruin

recent adj **new**, of late, fresh, current, topical *Opposite*: old

recently adv **lately**, in recent times, a moment ago, a short time ago, newly

receptacle n **container**, vessel, holder, repository, magazine

reception n **1 party**, function, cocktail party, gathering, get-together (infml) **2 welcome**, greeting, reaction, response, treatment **3 signal**, clarity, picture, sound **4 receipt**, receiving, delivery, unloading, acceptance *Opposite*: dispatch

receptionist n **receiver**, welcomer, greeter, telephonist, switchboard operator

receptive adj **1 open**, amenable, accessible, interested, approachable *Opposite*: hostile **2 alert**, sensitive, responsive, sharp, bright *Opposite*: slow

receptiveness n **1 approachability**, friendliness, openness, accessibility, interest *Opposite*: hostility **2 alertness**, sensitivity, responsiveness, acuteness, brightness *Opposite*: slowness

receptivity *see* **receptiveness**

recess n **1 break**, vacation, time off, rest, retreat **2 alcove**, nook, indentation, niche, bay

recession n **depression**, slump, downturn, collapse, decline *Opposite*: boom

recessionary adj **falling**, declining, failing, in slump, in depression *Opposite*: booming

recessive adj **1 receding**, falling, retreating, ebbing, declining *Opposite*: growing **2 latent**, suppressed, dormant, hidden, masked *Opposite*: dominant

recharge v **renew**, refresh, boost, revive, revitalize *Opposite*: drain

recherché adj **rare**, exotic, obscure, exquisite, unusual *Opposite*: ordinary

recidivism n **reoffending**, backsliding, reoffense, lapse, regression

recidivist n **reoffender**, hardened criminal, repeat offender, backslider, lawbreaker

recipe n **formula**, guidelines, instructions, method, steps

recipient n **receiver**, beneficiary, heir, addressee, inheritor *Opposite*: donor

reciprocal adj **mutual**, joint, shared, equal, common *Opposite*: one-sided

reciprocate v **give in return**, respond, return, give back, counter

reciprocation n **giving in return**, correspondence, exchange, trade, interchange

reciprocity n **mutual benefit**, mutuality, exchange, trade, tradeoff Opposite: isolation

recital n **performance**, concert, presentation, reading, recitation

recitation n **recital**, reading, performance, narration, presentation

recitative n **declamation**, narrative, oratorio, opera, singing

recite v **1 declaim**, narrate, perform, rehearse, speak publicly **2 list**, enumerate, reel off, regurgitate, itemize

reckless adj **irresponsible**, wild, thoughtless, uncontrolled, out of control Opposite: cautious

reckon v **1 regard**, consider, judge, rate, deem (fml) **2 think**, believe, suppose, imagine, feel Opposite: know

reckonable adj **calculable**, countable, quantifiable, finite, measurable Opposite: incalculable

reckoning n **1 calculation**, estimate, weighing up, computation, arithmetic **2 opinion**, judgment, view, estimation

reckon on (infml) v **depend**, rely, count on, bank on, be prepared for

reckon with v **allow for**, bargain for, be prepared for, expect, anticipate

reclaim v **get back**, regain, retrieve, recover, repossess

reclamation n **recovery**, retrieval, repossession, recuperation, renovation

recline v **lie down**, lie back, stretch out, loll, lounge Opposite: stand

recluse n **hermit**, loner, outsider, lone wolf, solitary

reclusive adj **isolated**, cloistered, solitary, withdrawn, secluded Opposite: sociable

recognition n **1 identification**, detection, distinguishing, perception, differentiation **2 credit**, gratitude, acknowledgment, thanks, appreciation Opposite: blame **3 acceptance**, admission, concession, acknowledgement Opposite: denial

recognizable adj **familiar**, identifiable, decipherable, detectable, distinguishable Opposite: unfamiliar

recognize v **1 know**, identify, distinguish, make out, be familiar with **2 accept**, acknowledge, appreciate, understand, admit Opposite: deny **3 acknowledge**, credit, cherish, value, have appreciation for

recognized adj **1 documented**, familiar, known, standard, predictable Opposite: unknown **2 established**, acclaimed, professional, accepted, important

recoil v **shrink**, withdraw, quail, wince, flinch Opposite: confront ■ n **shrinking**, wince, withdrawal, start, retreat

COMPARE AND CONTRAST CORE MEANING: draw back in fear or distaste

recoil draw back suddenly or react mentally in fear, horror, disgust, or distaste; **flinch** draw back physically because of fear or pain, or avoid confronting something unpleasant; **quail** tremble or cower with fear or apprehension; **shrink** move away physically from something because of fear or disgust, or feel reluctance to do something because of fear or apprehension; **wince** make an involuntary movement away from something in response to a stimulus such as pain or embarrassment.

recollect v **remember**, recall, call to mind, summon up, think of Opposite: forget

recollection n **memory**, recall, remembrance, reminiscence, calling to mind

recommence v **begin again**, restart, resume, take up again, continue

recommend v **1 suggest**, advocate, propose, advise, urge Opposite: oppose **2 endorse**, commend, vouch for, mention, put in a good word for Opposite: criticize

COMPARE AND CONTRAST CORE MEANING: put forward ideas to somebody deciding on a course of action

recommend put forward a course of action as being worthy of acceptance in the circumstances; **advise** give advice in a relatively open and objective way; **advocate** support or speak in favor of something; **counsel** (fml or literary) advise somebody on a particular course of action; **suggest** propose something in a tentative way as a possible course of action for somebody else to consider.

recommendation n **1 advice**, proposal, suggestion, counsel (fml or literary) **2 reference**, endorsement, commendation, blessing, approval Opposite: disparagement

recompense v **reward**, compensate, repay, pay, remunerate Opposite: charge ■ n **payment**, reward, remuneration, repayment, return Opposite: cost

reconcile v **settle**, bring together, square, reunite, resolve Opposite: fall out

reconciliation n **settlement**, understanding, squaring off, resolution, compromise Opposite: conflict

recondite adj **obscure**, abstruse, complex, out-of-the-way, little known Opposite: mainstream. See COMPARE AND CONTRAST at **obscure**.

recondition v **overhaul**, service, tune, clean, repair. See COMPARE AND CONTRAST at **renew**.

reconnaissance n **investigation**, scouting, inspection, exploration, survey

reconnect v **connect up**, rewire, rejoin, join up, put together again Opposite: sever

reconnection n **connecting again**, connecting up, rejoining, rewiring, recombination Opposite: severance

reconnoiter v **explore**, look out, patrol, watch, search ■ n **exploration**, reconnaissance, look, lookout, watch

reconsider v **reassess**, review, think again, go back over, reexamine

reconsideration n **reassessment**, reevaluation, review, reexamination

reconstitute v **1 reconstruct**, rebuild, reform, put back together, build again Opposite: take apart **2 alter**, change, reorganize, modify, revise Opposite: maintain

reconstitution n **1 reconstruction**, rebuilding, re-formation, putting back together, building again Opposite: breakup **2 alteration**, modification, reorganization, revision, change

reconstruct v **rebuild**, renovate, recreate, redo, restructure Opposite: take apart

reconstructed adj **rebuilt**, recreated, reassembled, restored, renovated Opposite: original

reconstruction n **rebuilding**, renovation, reform, modernization, renewal

reconvene v **resume**, come together again, call together again, gather again, call again

record n **1 account**, report, archive, chronicle, document **2 past performance**, track record, reputation, background, history **3 personal best**, top score, high, world record, best ■ v **1 note down**, make a note, keep a note, take notes, keep details **2 make a recording**, tape, video, film, pick up

recording n **footage**, video recording, copy, soundtrack, tape

recount v **tell**, narrate, relate, report, describe

re-count n **verification**, second opinion, check ■ v **count again**, verify, tally up, check

recoup v **get back**, earn, make back, recover, regain Opposite: lose

recourse n **option**, alternative, remedy, way out, choice

recover v **1 get back**, claim, regain, recuperate, recoup Opposite: lose **2 get well**, get better, pull through, recuperate, make progress Opposite: deteriorate

recovery n **1 revival**, upturn, recuperation, mending, healing Opposite: deterioration **2 retrieval**, salvage, recapture, repossession, regaining Opposite: loss

re-create v **reproduce**, copy, redesign, reinvent, reconstruct. See COMPARE AND CONTRAST at **copy**.

recreation n **1 leisure**, hobby, pastime, exercise, play Opposite: work **2 regeneration**, rebirth, reformation, restoration, restitution Opposite: exhaustion

recreational adj **leisure**, spare time, fun, frivolous, entertaining

recreation room n **playroom**, game room, rec room, den

recrimination n **accusation**, blame, reproach, allegation, retort Opposite: appeasement

recriminatory adj **counter-accusatory**, accusing, retaliatory, counterattacking Opposite: placatory

recrudescence n **reactivation**, recurrence, breaking out again, repetition, happening again

recruit v **employ**, take on, enlist, engage, draft Opposite: fire (infml) ■ n **employee**, trainee, beginner, novice, newcomer Opposite: old hand

recruitment n **staffing**, employment, enrollment, conscription, enlistment Opposite: dismissal

rectangular adj **four-sided**, quadrilateral, quadrangular, oblong

rectification n **correction**, improvement, adjustment, minor adjustment, modification

rectify v **put right**, set right, correct, remedy, cure Opposite: damage

rectilinear adj **straight-lined**, with straight lines, direct, unbending, uncurving Opposite: serpentine

rectitude n **1 righteousness**, morality, goodness, correctness, decency Opposite: immorality **2** (fml) **correctness**, rightness, precision, accuracy, exactness

rector n **1 minister**, cleric, parson, priest, vicar **2 principal**, director, chancellor, dean, president

rectory n **vicarage**, manse, church house, residence

recumbent (literary) adj **lying down**, leaning, lying back, reclining, resting Opposite: upright

recuperate v **1 convalesce**, build up your strength, recover, get better, get well Opposite: deteriorate **2 get back**, retrieve, reclaim, recover, recapture Opposite: lose

recuperation n **1 convalescence**, healing, recovery, getting better, restoration Opposite: deterioration **2 retrieval**, recovery, repossession, salvage, reclamation Opposite: loss

recuperative adj **curative**, restorative, invigorating, convalescent, healing

recur v **happen again**, persist, return, come back, reappear Opposite: cease

recurrence n **reappearance**, return, repetition, relapse Opposite: cessation

recurrent adj **repeated**, persistent, frequent, periodic, intermittent Opposite: finished

recurring see **recurrent**

recurvate adj **curved**, bowed, arched, rounded, bent Opposite: straight

recycle v **reprocess**, salvage, reuse, recover, reutilize Opposite: throw away

red-blooded adj **vigorous**, strong, robust, hearty, lusty Opposite: weak

red-carpet adj **preferential**, VIP, no-expense-spared, special, favored

redden v **flush**, blush, color, glow Opposite: redden

redecorate v **revamp**, spruce up, refurbish, restore, repaint

redeem v 1 **compensate for**, make up for, make amends for, restore, redress 2 **cash in**, cash, trade in, exchange, convert Opposite: keep 3 **release**, liberate, free, emancipate, deliver Opposite: arrest

redeemable adj **exchangeable**, valid, good, convertible, equivalent Opposite: irredeemable

redeeming adj **saving**, good, positive, abiding, compensating

redemption n 1 **improvement**, recovery, renovation, reclamation, refurbishment Opposite: deterioration 2 **salvation**, rescue, release, liberation, emancipation Opposite: downfall 3 **exchange**, use, conversion, trade-in, buying back

redemptive adj **liberating**, redeeming, saving, rescuing, delivering

redeploy v **redistribute**, divert, post, send, dispatch

redeployment n **redistribution**, posting, reorganization, relocation, rearrangement

redevelop v **improve**, revitalize, renovate, revamp, restore Opposite: neglect

redevelopment n **improvement**, renovation, revitalization, revamping, restoration Opposite: neglect

red-faced adj 1 **blushing**, flushed, embarrassed, hot and bothered, sweating 2 **ruddy**, weather-beaten, rosy, florid, rubicund (literary)

redheaded adj **auburn**, chestnut-haired, auburn-haired, strawberry blond, sandy

red herring n **decoy**, trick, ploy, lure, diversion

red-hot adj **burning**, boiling, scalding, fiery, scorching (infml) Opposite: cold

redirect v **forward**, send, readdress, transmit, convey

redirection n **sending on**, resending, rerouting, transferal, forwarding

rediscover v **find again**, revive, experience again, remember, relive

rediscovery n **finding again**, discovering again, reawakening, seeing afresh, rekindling

redistribute v **reallocate**, reorder, sort out, restructure, rearrange

redistribution n **redeployment**, rearrangement, relocation, reorganization, restructuring

red-letter day n **special day**, day to remember, occasion, event, turning point

red light n 1 **traffic light**, stop light, warning signal, warning light, stop sign Opposite: green light 2 (infml) **rejection**, disapproval, refusal, no, prohibition Opposite: approval

redness n 1 **blush**, flush, rosiness, glow, pinkness Opposite: pallor 2 **soreness**, rawness, tenderness, inflammation, painfulness

redo v **rebuild**, do from scratch, do again, recreate, start again

redolence n 1 **suggestion**, hint, trace, evocation, reminiscence 2 (literary) **fragrance**, scent, aroma, odor, smell

redolent adj 1 **suggestive**, reminiscent, evocative, indicative, recalling 2 **scented**, aromatic, fragrant, sweet-smelling, perfumed

redouble v **intensify**, renew, increase, multiply, amplify Opposite: reduce

redoubt (literary) n **stronghold**, castle, fortification, fort, fortress

redoubtable adj **formidable**, impressive, terrible, mighty, fearsome Opposite: unimpressive

redraft n **rewrite**, reworking, alteration, modification, change ■ v **rewrite**, reword, rework, revise, rephrase

redress n **compensation**, reparation, damages, recompense, reimbursement ■ v 1 **reimburse**, repay, pay damages, pay reparations, remunerate 2 **restore**, level out, equalize, right, rectify

red tape (infml) n **formalities**, bureaucracy, paperwork, official procedure, rules and regulations

reduce v 1 **decrease**, lessen, diminish, cut, trim down Opposite: increase 2 **downgrade**, cut down, demote, degrade, slash Opposite: upgrade 3 **lose weight**, slim, slim down, go on a diet, diet

reduced adj **cheap**, bargain, low-price, cut-rate, on sale

reduction n **discount**, decrease, lessening, drop, saving Opposite: increase

redundant adj **superfluous**, outmoded, disused, surplus, unneeded Opposite: needed

reduplicate v **repeat**, double, copy, redo, recast

reduplication n **repetition**, copying, imitation, doubling, duplication

reed n **cane**, stalk, stem

reediness n **squeakiness**, shrillness, stridency, screechiness, squawkiness Opposite: sonority

reeducate v **retrain**, reskill, retool, requalify, reinstruct

reeducation n **retraining**, reskilling, retooling, reequipping, requalification

reedy adj 1 **high-pitched**, thin, shrill, high, feeble Opposite: full-bodied 2 **thin**, narrow, slim, skinny, long Opposite: squat

reef n **ridge**, bar, bank, mound, range

reek v **show signs**, smack, smell, suggest, be

redolent of ■ *n* **stench**, stink, smell, odor, whiff. *See* COMPARE AND CONTRAST *at* **smell**.

reel *n* roll, spool, cylinder, bobbin, roller ■ *v* **1 lurch**, stagger, totter, stumble, wobble **2 wind**, whirl, spin, go round and round, revolve

reelect *v* **appoint again**, vote in again, reappoint, reconfirm, endorse

reelection *n* **reappointment**, endorsement, confirmation *Opposite*: defeat

reel off *v* **recite**, rattle off, list, repeat, go through

reenter *v* **return**, go back into, withdraw into, retire into, turn back into *Opposite*: leave

reentry *n* **return**, going back into, going into again, going in again

reestablish *v* **establish again**, create again, regenerate, reinvent, rebuild

reexamination *n* **reappraisal**, reconsideration, reassessment, reevaluation, verification

reexamine *v* **reconsider**, go back over, review, reassess, go over

ref *(infml)* *n* **referee**, umpire, arbitrator, adjudicator, mediator

refectory *n* **cafeteria**, dining hall, mess hall, lunchroom

refer *v* **1 mention**, denote, talk about, bring up, speak of **2 signify**, mean, indicate, suggest, insinuate **3 apply to**, relate to, concern, belong, be relevant to **4 consult**, check, turn to, look up, examine **5 send to**, direct to, pass on to, consign to, turn over to

referee *n* umpire, arbitrator, judge, arbiter, adjudicator *Opposite*: partisan ■ *v* **arbitrate**, adjudicate, umpire, mediate, judge

reference *n* **1 allusion**, mention, suggestion, indication, citation **2 recommendation**, testimonial, character reference, endorsement, commendation **3 orientation**, position, situation, location, locus

referendum *n* **vote**, poll, plebiscite, survey, ballot

referral *n* **transfer**, recommendation, appointment, medical appointment

refill *v* **replenish**, top up, fill up, restock, stock up *Opposite*: empty

refine *v* **1 purify**, process, treat, filter, distill *Opposite*: contaminate **2 improve**, polish, perfect, hone, enhance *Opposite*: coarsen

refined *adj* **1 sophisticated**, advanced, superior, polished, distinguished *Opposite*: coarse **2 purified**, processed, treated, filtered, distilled

refinement *n* **1 sophistication**, finesse, class, maturity, delicacy *Opposite*: vulgarity **2 modification**, alteration, minor change, improvement, enhancement

refining *n* **1 purifying**, sanitizing, decontaminating, cleansing, filtering *Opposite*: adulterating **2 improving**, cultivating, educating, taming, enlightening *Opposite*:

coarsening ■ *adj* **improving**, educating, cultivating, civilizing, enlightening *Opposite*: coarsening

refit *v* **overhaul**, renovate, service, reequip, repair ■ *n* **overhaul**, reequipping, repair, refurbishment, service

reflate *v* **expand**, increase, stimulate, spur on, build up *Opposite*: deflate

reflation *n* **expansion**, increase, stimulation, boost, advance *Opposite*: deflation

reflect *v* **1 reproduce**, mirror, imitate, replicate, redirect **2 be a sign of**, reveal, expose, suggest, signal **3 think**, consider, ponder, mull over, contemplate

reflection *n* **1 mirror image**, likeness, echo, image, replication **2 consideration**, thinking, thought, contemplation, meditation *Opposite*: impulse **3 indication**, sign, manifestation, suggestion, expression

reflective *adj* **thoughtful**, pensive, wistful, meditative, contemplative *Opposite*: impulsive

reflex *n* **reaction**, impulse, instinct, spontaneous effect, response

reflexive *adj* **automatic**, impulsive, spontaneous, involuntary, instinctive *Opposite*: premeditated

reform *v* **improve**, restructure, revolutionize, remodel, modernize ■ *n* **improvement**, reorganization, restructuring, modification, transformation

re-form *v* **recreate**, reconstruct, refashion, rebuild, remake

reformation *n* **improvement**, renovation, reorganization, restructuring, overhaul

reformatory *n* **institution**, reform school, detention center, jail, penitentiary

reformed *adj* **rehabilitated**, transformed, changed, converted, renewed

reformer *n* **improver**, campaigner, activist, crusader, agitator *Opposite*: conservative

refract *v* **bend**, divert, change course, detour, deflect

refraction *n* **bending**, change of direction, change of course, diversion, detour

refractory *adj* **headstrong**, stubborn, rebellious, obstinate, wayward *Opposite*: placid

refrain *v* **desist**, abstain, hold back, leave off, cease *Opposite*: persist ■ *n* **chorus**, strain, theme

refresh *v* **revive**, cool down, enliven, invigorate, rejuvenate *Opposite*: wear out

refresher *n* **reminder**, revision, update, review

refreshing *adj* **stimulating**, uplifting, inspirational, invigorating, energizing *Opposite*: draining

refreshment *n* **drink**, food, nourishment, sustenance, nutriment

refreshments n food and drink, snacks, drinks, nibbles, hors d'oeuvres

refrigerate v keep cold, store at a low temperature, cool, ice, chill Opposite: heat

refrigeration n cooling, chilling, preservation, freezing, conserving

refuel v refill, replenish, top up, restock, resupply Opposite: run down

refuge n haven, sanctuary, harbor, shelter, protection

refugee n person in exile, immigrant, migrant, expatriate, exile

refulgence (literary) n brilliance, splendor, shine, brightness, glitter Opposite: dullness

refulgent (literary) adj brilliant, shining, bright, sparkling, glittering Opposite: dull

refund v repay, reimburse, give back, pay back, compensate Opposite: keep ■ n repayment, reimbursement, money back, compensation, recompense Opposite: payment

refurbish v renovate, restore, refit, fix up, spruce up

refurbishment n restoration, renovation, overhaul, renewal, repair

refusal n negative response, snub, denial, rejection, negation Opposite: acceptance

refuse v say no, decline, reject, snub, rebuff Opposite: accept ■ n waste, garbage, rubbish, trash, litter

refutation n repudiation, disproof, negation, rejection, contradiction Opposite: confirmation

refute v disprove, contest, rebut, counter, repudiate Opposite: prove

regain v recover, get back, recuperate, recoup, reclaim Opposite: lose

regal adj royal, majestic, noble, imperial, stately

regale v entertain, amuse, delight, divert

regalia n symbols of office, ceremonial objects, ceremonial dress, insignia

regard v 1 consider, hold, think, see, view 2 look upon, stare, observe, gaze at, view 3 relate to, concern, touch on, connect with, have to do with ■ n 1 respect, esteem, favor, admiration, honor Opposite: disregard 2 (fml) look, stare, gaze, glance

---

COMPARE AND CONTRAST CORE MEANING: appreciation of the worth of somebody or something

regard a mixture of liking and appreciation of somebody or something; **admiration** warm approval and appreciation of somebody or something, often suggesting a desire to copy or resemble somebody; **esteem** a high opinion and appreciation of somebody or something; **favor** a liking and preference for somebody or something; **respect** a strong acknowledgment and appreciation of somebody's abilities and achievements; **reverence** a feeling of deep respect and devotion combined with a slight sense of awe; **veneration** a profound feeling of respect and awe.

---

regarding prep concerning, about, on the subject of, on the topic of, as regards

regardless adv anyway, anyhow, no matter what, whatever happens, nevertheless

regardless of prep in spite of, despite, apart from, not considering, not withstanding

regatta n boat race, race, gala, competition, contest

regenerate v renew, restore, revive, redevelop, reinforce Opposite: degenerate

regeneration n renewal, rebirth, revival, renaissance, rejuvenation

regenerative adj growing back, reformative, recreating, re-forming, recovering Opposite: degenerative

regent n substitute, proxy, replacement, protector

regime n 1 government, command, rule, administration, management 2 routine, system, regimen, treatment, course of therapy

regimen n routine, schedule, treatment, regime, course of therapy

regiment n military unit, troop, squadron, battalion, brigade ■ v 1 control strictly, regulate, oppress, suppress, order Opposite: liberate 2 organize systematically, arrange, order, file, organize

regimental adj strict, rigid, disciplined, harsh, ordered Opposite: lax

regimentation n control, regulation, oppression, suppression, organization

regimented adj 1 controlled, disciplined, restricted, strict, rigid Opposite: undisciplined 2 well-ordered, neatly arranged, organized, systematic, structured Opposite: disordered

region n area, district, county, section, province

regional adj local, area, district, provincial, county Opposite: national

regionalism n 1 regional loyalty, regional prejudice, decentralization, home loyalty, area loyalty 2 linguistic feature, local expression, dialect word

register n list, record, catalog, roll, index ■ v 1 enter, list, record, catalog, keep details 2 enroll, join, sign up, matriculate, enlist 3 reveal, disclose, show, convey, score Opposite: hide 4 reach, touch, record, measure, indicate

registrar n 1 administrative officer, school administrator, university official, administrator, bursar 2 public official, recorder, public administrator, record-keeper, clerk

registration n 1 registering, recording, record-keeping, cataloguing, listing 2 enrollment, enlisting, course enrollment, signing up, class enrollment

registry *n* records office, registrar's office, archive, administrative office, office

regress *v* 1 relapse, revert, lapse, backslide, retrogress *Opposite*: progress 2 go back, lose headway, lose ground, retreat, move back *Opposite*: advance

regression *n* 1 reversion, deterioration, relapse, worsening, getting worse *Opposite*: progression 2 going backward, recession, retreat, retrogression, return *Opposite*: advance

regressive *adj* reverting, returning, going back, degenerating, deteriorating *Opposite*: progressive

regret *v* 1 be sorry, be apologetic, apologize for, be repentant, feel sorry 2 *(fml)* be disappointed, be unhappy, lament, be remorseful, express grief ■ *n* 1 remorse, guilt, repentance, compunction, pang of conscience *Opposite*: shamelessness 2 disappointment, sorrow, unhappiness, grief, distress *Opposite*: contentment

regretful *adj* 1 apologetic, remorseful, repentant, sorry, penitent *Opposite*: unapologetic 2 disappointed, unhappy, sorrowful, sad *Opposite*: content

regrettable *adj* unfortunate, deplorable, lamentable, undesirable, unwelcome *Opposite*: fortunate

regroup *v* re-form, recover, rearrange, recuperate, reorder *Opposite*: scatter

regular *adj* 1 usual, normal, standard, ordinary, customary *Opposite*: unusual 2 even, steady, unvarying, consistent, systematic *Opposite*: irregular 3 recurring, recurrent, frequent, repeated, fixed *Opposite*: intermittent 4 ordered, methodical, even, consistent, reliable *Opposite*: inconsistent ■ *n* soldier, combatant, legionnaire, GI

regularity *n* orderliness, symmetry, uniformity, consistency, constancy *Opposite*: inconsistency

regularize *v* standardize, normalize, make conform, legalize, regulate

regulate *v* 1 control, order, adjust, set, synchronize *Opposite*: deregulate 2 *(fml)* direct, control, guide, manage, handle

regulation *n* 1 rule, directive, guideline, parameter, instruction 2 control, adjustment, adaptation, alteration, management

regulator *n* 1 watchdog, controller, supervisory body, manager, supervisor 2 device, valve, mechanism, controller, rheostat

regulatory *adj* controlling, supervisory, governing, monitoring, directing

regurgitate *v* 1 bring up, vomit, spew up, spit up, throw up *(infml)* *Opposite*: ingest 2 repeat, rehearse, go over, do again, reiterate

regurgitation *n* 1 bringing up, vomiting, spitting out, spewing, spewing out 2 repetition, rehearsal, restating, churning out, recitation

rehabilitate *v* 1 restore, recover, mend, repair, revitalize 2 assimilate, acclimatize, reeducate, naturalize, reorient

rehabilitation *n* reintegration, restoration, therapy, recuperation, convalescence

rehash *v* rework, reuse, do again, go over, repeat

rehearsal *n* practice, preparation, trial, run-through, tryout *Opposite*: performance

rehearse *v* practice, go over, run through, prepare, train

rehearsed *adj* practiced, prepared, learned, studied, planned out *Opposite*: ad-lib

reheat *v* heat up, warm up, warm, heat

rehouse *v* move, transfer, relocate, resettle

reign *n* rule, sovereignty, control, supremacy, sway ■ *v* rule, hold sway, govern, control, lead

reimburse *v* repay, pay back, give money back, compensate, refund

reimbursement *n* repayment, compensation, recompense, settlement, damages

rein *n* bridle, restraint, harness, leash, lead

reincarnate *v* revive, bring back, revitalize, rejuvenate, reawaken

reincarnation *n* re-embodiment, rebirth, recreation, reawakening, restoration

reinforce *v* 1 strengthen, support, underpin, buttress, bolster *Opposite*: underplay 2 emphasize, underline, highlight, add force to, boost *Opposite*: weaken

reinforcement *n* 1 strengthening, support, underpinning, fortification, buttressing *Opposite*: weakening 2 emphasis, underlining, underscoring, corroboration, backup *Opposite*: underplaying

rein in *v* hold back, cut back, restrain, reduce, decrease *Opposite*: unleash

reinstate *v* restore, return, give back, put back, replace

reinstatement *n* restoration, return, recall, replacement, reestablishment

reinsurance *n* provision, protection, additional coverage

reintroduce *v* introduce again, bring into effect again, reinstate, restore, reestablish

reintroduction *n* reinstatement, restoration, reestablishment

reinvigorated *adj* revitalized, refreshed, restored, recharged, fresh *Opposite*: exhausted

reissue *v* rerelease, redistribute, recirculate, republish, send out again ■ *n* new issue, reprint, rerelease, new edition, new copy

reiterate *v* repeat, go over, restate, stress, reinforce

reiteration *n* repetition, replication, restatement, echo, recap

reject *v* refuse, rebuff, decline, snub, throw out *Opposite*: accept

rejection *n* refusal, denial, rebuff, denunciation, refutation *Opposite*: acceptance

rejigger (infml) v **rearrange**, alter, readjust, reorganize, change

rejoice (literary) v **celebrate**, be pleased about, cheer, exult, be glad Opposite: lament

rejoin (fml) v **reply**, answer, respond, retort, return

rejoinder (fml) n **response**, answer, reply, comeback, retort. See COMPARE AND CONTRAST at **answer**.

rejuvenate v **revitalize**, invigorate, revive, make younger, revivify

rejuvenation n **revitalization**, reinvigoration, regeneration, renewal, renovation

rekindle v **renew**, reawaken, revive, regenerate, relight Opposite: kill

relapse v **go back to**, revert, deteriorate, degenerate, fall back Opposite: improve ■ n **deterioration**, decline, degeneration, reversion, waning Opposite: improvement

relate v 1 **tell**, narrate, speak about, recount, relay 2 **connect**, link, associate, correlate, link up 3 **interact**, form a relationship, connect, cooperate, get along

related adj **connected**, linked, associated, correlated, interrelated Opposite: unconnected

relating to prep **about**, regarding, re, apropos of, in relation to

relation n **family member**, relative, next of kin

relations n 1 **kith and kin**, kin, family members, relatives, family 2 **relationships**, dealings, associations, affairs, contact

relationship n **association**, connection, affiliation, rapport, liaison

relative adj **comparative**, qualified, virtual Opposite: absolute ■ n **family member**, relation, next of kin

relative to prep **in relation to**, compared with, proportionate to, corresponding to

relativism n **contingency**, belief, doctrine Opposite: absolutism

relativist n **equivocator**, fence sitter, trimmer, agnostic, waverer

relativity n **relativeness**, dependence, contingency

relax v 1 **unwind**, calm down, slow down, let go, loosen up 2 **rest**, put your feet up, take it easy, have a break, lie down 3 **loosen**, slacken, ease, let up on, let out Opposite: tense 4 **lessen**, decrease, diminish, lower, ease Opposite: increase

relaxation n 1 **recreation**, leisure, entertainment, rest, repose 2 **reduction**, lessening, easing, slackening, moderation Opposite: increase

relaxed adj 1 **tranquil**, calm, comfortable, stress-free, unperturbed Opposite: tense 2 **lenient**, easygoing, untroubled, casual, laid-back (infml) Opposite: strict

relaxing adj **calming**, soothing, comforting, peaceful, tranquil Opposite: harrowing

relay v **communicate**, pass on, transmit, spread, convey

release v 1 **let go**, free discharge, liberate, let loose Opposite: hold 2 **make public**, make available, announce, publish, circulate Opposite: withhold ■ n 1 **relief**, discharge, freedom, liberation, emancipation Opposite: arrest 2 **announcement**, issue, statement, publication, proclamation

relegate v **demote**, downgrade, transfer, consign, refer Opposite: promote

relegation n **demotion**, sending down, transfer down, lowering of rank, downgrade Opposite: promotion

relent v **give in**, cave in, change your mind, concede, yield Opposite: stand firm

relentless adj 1 **ceaseless**, unremitting, persistent, endless, steady 2 **remorseless**, merciless, pitiless, ruthless, heartless

relentlessness n 1 **ceaselessness**, unremittingness, persistence, intensity, steadiness 2 **remorselessness**, mercilessness, pitilessness, ruthlessness, harshness

relevance n **significance**, bearing, application, importance, weight Opposite: irrelevance

relevancy see **relevance**

relevant adj **pertinent**, applicable, germane, related, appropriate Opposite: unrelated

reliability n **dependability**, consistency, steadfastness, trustworthiness Opposite: untrustworthiness

reliable adj **dependable**, consistent, steadfast, unswerving, unfailing Opposite: unreliable

reliance n **dependence**, confidence, trust, belief, faith Opposite: independence

reliant adj **dependent**, needful, conditional, subject to, contingent Opposite: independent

relic n **historical object**, artifact, remnant, remains, vestige

relief n 1 **respite**, release, reprieve, break, liberation 2 **assistance**, aid, help, reinforcement, support

relieve v 1 **ease**, release, alleviate, reduce, mitigate Opposite: exacerbate 2 **take the place of**, take over for, substitute for, stand in for, replace 3 **dismiss**, release, let go, discharge, get rid of Opposite: appoint

relieved adj **reassured**, thankful, calmed, pleased, comforted Opposite: worried

religion n **faith**, belief, creed, conviction, denomination

religious adj 1 **theological**, sacred, holy, consecrated, church Opposite: secular 2 **spiritual**, devout, pious, holy, observant Opposite: irreligious 3 **thorough**, conscientious, dutiful, faithful, reliable Opposite: unreliable

religiousness n **devoutness**, piousness, spirituality, sense of God, faithfulness

relinquish v **give up**, surrender, hand over, abandon, renounce *Opposite*: retain

reliquary n **repository**, casket, container, shrine

relish v **enjoy**, delight in, savor, take pleasure in, like *Opposite*: dislike ■ n **enjoyment**, delight, pleasure, elation, appreciation *Opposite*: displeasure

---

WORD BANK
☐ **types of relishes** caponata, chow-chow, chutney, piccalilli, salsa, sweet pickle

---

relive v **experience again**, go through again, live through again, remember, recall *Opposite*: forget

reload v **refill**, fill, load again, replenish, recharge *Opposite*: unload

relocate v **move**, change place, reposition, transfer, displace *Opposite*: remain

relocation n **transfer**, moving, rearrangement, repositioning, replacement

reluctance n **unwillingness**, lack of enthusiasm, disinclination, hesitancy, foot-dragging *(infml)* *Opposite*: enthusiasm

reluctant adj **unwilling**, unenthusiastic, disinclined, loath, hesitant *Opposite*: enthusiastic. *See* COMPARE AND CONTRAST *at* **unwilling**.

rely v **depend on**, bank on, count on, trust, be sure of *Opposite*: distrust

remain v **1 stay**, stay put, stay behind, stay on, linger *Opposite*: leave **2 continue**, keep on, endure, persist, go on *Opposite*: stop

remainder n **rest**, residue, remnants, remains, leftovers

remaining adj **residual**, outstanding, left over, excess, lingering

remains n **1 leftovers**, remnants, relics, remainder, ruins **2 dead body**, corpse, cadaver, ashes, cremains

remake n **new version**, cover version, cover, new edition, re-creation ■ v **produce again**, re-create, re-form, change the format, reshape

remand v **return to custody**, return to prison, commit to custody, imprison, jail ■ n **return to custody**, return to prison, committal to custody, custody, prison

remark n **comment**, statement, observation, aside, mention ■ v **say**, comment, state, observe, pronounce

remarkable adj **extraordinary**, amazing, notable, outstanding, noteworthy *Opposite*: ordinary

remarry v **get married again**, marry again, get wed again, re-wed, wed again *(fml or literary)*

remedial adj **corrective**, counteractive, helpful, educative, curative *Opposite*: precautionary

remedy n **1 medicine**, medication, preparation, mixture, therapy **2 solution**, cure, answer, antidote, resolution ■ v **1 cure**, relieve, improve, alleviate, ease **2 resolve**,

deal with, correct, improve, make better *Opposite*: exacerbate

remember v **1 recall**, think of, recollect, dredge up, hark back to *Opposite*: forget **2 keep in mind**, bear in mind, retain, memorize, learn *Opposite*: forget

remembrance n **commemoration**, memory, tribute, recollection, reminiscence

remind v **1 be reminiscent**, strike a chord, take you back, jog your memory, ring a bell *(infml)* **2 repeat**, retell, prompt, recap, run by again

reminder n **1 cue**, notice, prompt, recap, aide-mémoire *(fml)* **2 souvenir**, token, memento, knickknack, keepsake

reminisce v **recall**, talk about, hark back to, muse over, evoke

reminiscence n **1 nostalgia**, recollection, looking back, musing, rumination **2 memory**, recollection, reminder

reminiscent adj **suggestive**, evocative, resonant, redolent, similar

remiss adj **careless**, negligent, lax, slipshod, slapdash *Opposite*: diligent

remission n **reduction**, decrease, lessening, diminution, cutback

remissive adj **pardoning**, forgiving, absolving, exonerating

remit v **1 send**, forward, dispatch, pay, settle **2 submit**, refer, pass on *Opposite*: handle **3 slacken**, decrease, lessen, diminish, cancel *Opposite*: increase

remittance n **1 payment**, transfer of funds, transmittal, fee, transfer **2 release**, dispatch, discharge *(fml)*

remix v **produce a new version of**, rehash, reproduce, alter, change ■ n **new recording**, different version, new version, latest version, revised version

remnant n **remainder**, remains, relic, residue, trace

remodel v **alter**, modify, modernize, adapt, adjust

remonstrance n **1 argument**, evidence, backup, proof, case **2 protest**, complaint, objection, petition, dispute

remonstrate v **argue**, protest, object, oppose, complain *Opposite*: agree. *See* COMPARE AND CONTRAST *at* **object**.

remorse n **regret**, sorrow, repentance, penitence, guilt

remorseful adj **regretful**, repentant, penitent, contrite, apologetic *Opposite*: unrepentant

remorseless adj **1 pitiless**, ruthless, merciless, callous, cruel *Opposite*: merciful **2 inexorable**, implacable, indefatigable, unbending, unyielding

remote adj **1 distant**, isolated, inaccessible, far-flung, far-off *Opposite*: nearby **2 slight**, outside, slim, unlikely, improbable *Opposite*: likely **3 aloof**, detached, withdrawn, reserved, cool *Opposite*: approachable

remotely *adv* 1 **slightly**, tenuously, marginally, minimally, a little *Opposite*: closely 2 **at all**, in the least, the least bit, the slightest bit *Opposite*: greatly

remoteness *n* 1 **isolation**, seclusion, distance, solitude, inaccessibility *Opposite*: closeness 2 **aloofness**, detachment, reserve, inaccessibility, coolness *Opposite*: approachability 3 **slightness**, improbability, faintness, slimness *Opposite*: likelihood

remount *v* **get on again**, get back on, mount again, ride again, get back in the saddle

removable *adj* **detachable**, not fixed, can be removed, changeable, transferable *Opposite*: attached

removal *n* **taking away**, elimination, exclusion, subtraction, deletion *Opposite*: addition

remove *v* 1 **take away**, get rid of, eliminate, do away with, eradicate *Opposite*: add 2 **take off**, detach, cut off, amputate, disconnect

remunerate *v* **pay**, reward, compensate, recompense, repay

remuneration *n* **payment**, fee, salary, wage, compensation. *See* COMPARE AND CONTRAST *at* **wage**.

renaissance *n* **rebirth**, new start, new beginning, resurgence, revitalization *Opposite*: decline

rename *v* **give a new name**, retitle, rechristen, nickname, change the name of

renascent *adj* **becoming active**, budding, burgeoning, appearing, becoming popular

rend *v* **tear**, tear apart, rip, come apart, split *Opposite*: mend. *See* COMPARE AND CONTRAST *at* **tear**.

render *v* 1 *(fml)* **provide**, give, deliver, submit, make available 2 *(fml)* **portray**, depict, represent, execute, translate 3 *(fml)* **decide**, decree, judge, adjudicate, declare 4 **make**, cause, cause to become 5 **melt down**, reduce, condense, concentrate, boil down *Opposite*: solidify

rendering *n* 1 **portrayal**, depiction, picture, image, portrait 2 **version**, translation, interpretation, interpreting, execution 3 **plaster coating**, plaster, coating, cladding, siding

rendezvous *n* 1 **engagement**, meeting, appointment, tryst, assignation 2 **meeting place**, meeting point, assembly point, location, site ■ *v* **meet**, come together, make contact, get together, assemble

rendition *n* **version**, interpretation, performance, rendering, execution

renegade *n* **apostate**, traitor, rebel, turncoat, betrayer *Opposite*: loyalist

renege *v* **go back on**, break your word, break a promise, back out, default

renew *v* 1 **return to**, reintroduce, repeat, restart, begin again 2 **recondition**, renovate, refurbish, revamp, restore 3 **rekindle**, revit-

alize, rejuvenate, refresh, revive

renewal *n* **regeneration**, restitution, rekindling, revitalization, rejuvenation

renounce *v* 1 **relinquish**, surrender, hand over, give up, abdicate *Opposite*: accept 2 **disavow**, repudiate, reject, abandon, forsake *Opposite*: embrace

renovate *v* **renew**, recondition, modernize, refurbish, repair *Opposite*: wear out. *See* COMPARE AND CONTRAST *at* **renew**.

renovation *n* **facelift**, revamp, makeover, restoration, redecoration

renown *n* **fame**, celebrity, notoriety, prominence, popularity *Opposite*: obscurity

renowned *adj* **famous**, well-known, celebrated, prominent, popular *Opposite*: unknown

rent *n* 1 **rental**, rent payment, hire charge, fee, payment 2 **hole**, tear, rip, split, slash ■ *v* **et**, hire out, lend out, rent out, charter

rental *n* **rent payment**, fee, payment, hire charge, charge

renunciation *n* 1 **repudiation**, abandonment, denial, renouncement, rejection *Opposite*: acceptance 2 **surrender**, disowning, abdication, relinquishment

reorder *v* **rearrange**, reorganize, regroup, restructure, move around

reorganization *n* **reform**, restructuring, reshuffle, redeployment, reformation

reorganize *v* **regroup**, move around, reorder, rearrange, restructure

rep *(infml)* *n* **representative**, agent, courier, delegate, deputy

repaint *v* **redecorate**, renovate, touch up, patch up, freshen up

repair *v* **mend**, fix, patch up, restore, darn *Opposite*: damage ■ *n* **overhaul**, reparation, restoration, patch-up, mending

reparation *n* **amends**, compensation, damages, recompense, reimbursement

repartee *n* **banter**, wit, wordplay, badinage, raillery

repast *(literary)* *n* **meal**, banquet, feast, buffet, collation

repatriate *v* **send home**, deport, send back, banish, exile

repatriation *n* **sending home**, going home, deportation, return, exile

repay v pay, pay back, reimburse, refund, pay off

repayment n **payment**, refund, reimbursement, settlement, compensation

repeal v cancel, revoke, rescind, annul, nullify Opposite: enact

repeat v 1 reiterate, recap, go over, echo, retell 2 do again, replicate, duplicate, show again, copy ■ n recurrence, replication, reiteration, duplication, reappearance

repeated adj recurrent, frequent, recurring, repetitive, constant Opposite: rare

repel v 1 disgust, revolt, nauseate, repulse, make you feel sick 2 keep away, fend off, drive back, keep at bay, deter Opposite: attract

repellent adj 1 disgusting, revolting, nauseating, repulsive, repugnant Opposite: attractive 2 impervious, impermeable, resistant, proof, tight

repent v regret, be sorry, apologize, ask forgiveness, feel sorrow

repentance n regret, sorrow, remorse, penitence, atonement Opposite: shamelessness

repentant adj regretful, remorseful, apologetic, penitent, rueful Opposite: unrepentant

repercussion n consequence, effect, upshot, impact, aftermath

repertoire n repertory, collection, selection, series, stock

repertory n 1 theater, company, theater company, theater group, repertory company 2 repertoire, selection, series, stock, range

repetition n recurrence, replication, duplication, reiteration, reappearance

repetitious adj boring, monotonous, tedious, dull, repetitive Opposite: innovative

repetitive see repetitious

repetitively adv repeatedly, continually, over and over again, cyclically, frequently Opposite: infrequently

rephrase v restate, retell, say differently, express in other words, put another way

replace v 1 substitute, trade, use instead, exchange, switch 2 replenish, put back, restore, return, reinstate

replacement n substitute, stand-in, substitution, proxy, surrogate Opposite: original

replay v play again, rerun, repeat, retell, reiterate ■ n rerun, repetition, reiteration, echo, repeat

replenish v replace, refill, fill, stock up, top up Opposite: deplete

replenishment n replacement, refill, renewal

replete adj 1 full, complete, supplied, abounding, brimming Opposite: lacking 2 sated, satisfied, satiated, full, full up Opposite: hungry

repletion n fullness, surfeit, glut, satiety

replica n copy, reproduction, imitation, model, facsimile Opposite: original

replicate v duplicate, repeat, copy, imitate, reproduce. See COMPARE AND CONTRAST at copy.

replication n repetition, duplication, imitation, copying, reproduction

reply v respond, answer, retort, answer back, react Opposite: ask ■ n response, account, answer, retort, riposte Opposite: question. See COMPARE AND CONTRAST at answer.

report v 1 give an account, tell, state, describe, give details 2 register, check in, present yourself, turn up, show up ■ n 1 tale, statement, description, testimony, story 2 loud noise, bang, boom, crash, explosion

reportage n news coverage, reporting, coverage, mention, analysis

reportedly adv allegedly, supposedly, apparently, seemingly, they say Opposite: actually

reporter n foreign correspondent, special correspondent, journalist, correspondent, writer

repose n 1 inactivity, sleep, rest, relaxation, restfulness Opposite: activity 2 calmness, peace, stillness, tranquillity, calm Opposite: agitation ■ v (fml) relax, rest, take it easy, recline, put your feet up

reposition v shift, transpose, move, relocate

repositioning n transposition, relocation, moving, move

repository n 1 store, container, storage area, storage place, receptacle 2 source, fountain, mine, storehouse, origin

repossess v recoup, take back, reclaim, recover, recuperate

repossession n recovery, reclamation, retrieval, taking back, seizure

repot v transplant, transfer, replant, pot

reprehensible adj wrong, bad, disgraceful, shameful, inexcusable Opposite: praiseworthy

reprehension n criticism, censure, condemnation, telling off, admonition Opposite: praise

reprehensive adj condemnatory, reproachful, accusing, reproving, critical Opposite: praiseworthy

represent v 1 act for, speak for, stand for, stand in for 2 stand for, symbolize, correspond to, signify, exemplify Opposite: misrepresent

representation n 1 picture, image, symbol, depiction, illustration 2 statement, complaint, submission, argument 3 account, version, portrayal, description, interpretation

representational adj realistic, representative, figurative, depictive, mimetic Opposite: abstract

representative n 1 envoy, delegate, agent, spokesperson, diplomat 2 agent, courier, delegate, deputy, rep *(infml)* ▪ *adj* **1 illustrative**, typical, characteristic, demonstrative, archetypal **2 symbolic**, descriptive, illustrative, evocative, expressive

repress *v* **1 curb**, block, suppress, contain, keep inside *Opposite*: express **2 dominate**, subdue, overpower, subjugate, quell

repressed *adj* **1 stifled**, bottled-up, suppressed, blocked, curbed *Opposite*: expressed **2 intimidated**, crushed, suppressed, subjugated, overpowered *Opposite*: liberated

repression *n* **suppression**, subjugation, domination, authoritarianism, tyranny

repressive *adj* **oppressive**, suppressive, tyrannical, authoritarian, brutal *Opposite*: liberal

reprieve *v* **let off**, pardon, grant a stay of execution, acquit, stay *Opposite*: punish ▪ *n* **official pardon**, stay of execution, amnesty, pardon, acquittal

reprimand *v* **chastise**, reproach, lecture, scold, admonish *Opposite*: praise ▪ *n* **rebuke**, admonishment, warning, dressing-down, reproof

reprint *v* **reissue**, print again, publish again, produce again, republish ▪ *n* **reissue**, copy, edition

reprisal *n* **retaliation**, revenge, act of vengeance, punishment, payback *(infml)*

reprise *n* **reappearance**, echo, recap, repeat, repetition ▪ *v* **repeat**, reinterpret, reenact, re-present

reproach *v* **admonish**, accuse, reprove, criticize, scold *Opposite*: praise ▪ *n* **criticism**, censure, reprimand, blame, accusation *Opposite*: praise

reproachful *adj* **censorious**, accusing, disapproving, reproving, critical *Opposite*: approving

reprobate *n* **degenerate**, rascal, troublemaker, ne'er-do-well, sinner

reprocess *v* **process again**, reuse, recycle, recover, reclaim

reproduce *v* **1 copy**, replicate, duplicate, repeat, imitate **2 have children**, produce offspring, produce young, breed, give birth. *See* COMPARE AND CONTRAST *at* COPY.

reproduction *n* **1 copy**, imitation, replica, duplicate, facsimile *Opposite*: original **2 breeding**, procreation, propagation, generation, multiplication ▪ *adj* **imitation**, replica, fake, faux *Opposite*: genuine

reproductive *adj* **generative**, multiplicative, procreative, procreant, propagative

reproof *n* **criticism**, blame, accusation, rebuke, scolding *Opposite*: compliment

reprove *v* **criticize**, take to task, accuse, rebuke, scold *Opposite*: praise

reproving *adj* **disapproving**, condemnatory, reproachful, admonitory, censorious *Opposite*: approving

reptilian *adj* **cold-blooded**, unfriendly, emotionless, inhuman, stony *Opposite*: warm

republic *n* **state**, nation, democracy *Opposite*: monarchy

republican *n* **antiroyalist**, antimonarchist *Opposite*: monarchist ▪ *adj* **pro-republic**, antiroyalist, antimonarchist *Opposite*: monarchist

republicanism *n* **antimonarchism**, antiroyalism, political belief *Opposite*: monarchism

repudiate *v* **1 reject**, renounce, retract, disavow, turn your back on *Opposite*: acknowledge **2 deny**, refute, contradict, gainsay, disclaim *Opposite*: accept

repudiation *n* **1 retraction**, renunciation, rejection, abandonment, disavowal *(fml)* *Opposite*: acknowledgment **2 denial**, refutation, negation, disclaimer, contradiction *Opposite*: acceptance

repugnance *n* **disgust**, revulsion, hatred, hate, abhorrence *Opposite*: attraction. *See* COMPARE AND CONTRAST *at* dislike.

repugnant *adj* **1 disgusting**, revolting, nauseating, repulsive, hideous *Opposite*: attractive **2 offensive**, objectionable, distasteful, unacceptable, obnoxious *Opposite*: agreeable

repulse *v* **1 repel**, drive away, force away, hold back, hold off *Opposite*: yield **2 disgust**, revolt, sicken, nauseate, repel **3 reject**, rebuff, resist, spurn, snub *Opposite*: welcome

repulsed *adj* **disgusted**, nauseated, revolted, repelled, sickened *Opposite*: attracted

repulsion *n* **disgust**, revulsion, nausea, loathing, repugnance *Opposite*: attraction

repulsive *adj* **disgusting**, revolting, nauseating, hideous, vile *Opposite*: attractive

repulsiveness *n* **hideousness**, repugnance, foulness, abhorrence, vileness *Opposite*: attractiveness

reputable *adj* **highly regarded**, trustworthy, well-thought-of, sound, upright *Opposite*: disreputable

reputation *n* **standing**, status, name, character, repute *(fml)*

repute *(fml) see* reputation

reputed *adj* **supposed**, alleged, presumed, apparent, believed *Opposite*: actual

request *v* **ask for**, apply for, call for, entreat, invite *Opposite*: demand ▪ *n* **appeal**, call, application, entreaty, invitation *Opposite*: demand

requiem *n* **1 service**, Mass, funeral, funeral Mass, service for the dead **2 funeral music**, lament, dirge, funeral hymn, funeral song

require *v* **1 need**, necessitate, want, have need of, entail **2 oblige**, compel, demand, expect, force

required *adj* **necessary**, obligatory, compulsory, mandatory, essential *Opposite*: optional

requirement n obligation, condition, prerequisite, must, necessity *Opposite*: option

requisite *(fml) adj* necessary, mandatory, vital, essential, indispensable *Opposite*: optional. *See* COMPARE AND CONTRAST *at* necessary.

requisition n demand, request, application, summons ■ v 1 take over, commandeer, seize, take possession of, appropriate *Opposite*: relinquish 2 demand, apply for, call for, request, put in for

reread v revisit, look back over, check through, go through, read again

rerun v replay, repeat, play again, air again, show again ■ n repeat, repeat showing, replay

reschedule v postpone, rearrange, defer, reorganize, suspend *Opposite*: bring forward

rescheduling n postponement, deferment, putting off, rearrangement, rearranging

rescind v withdraw, annul, cancel, repeal, overturn *Opposite*: authorize

rescue v save, free, set free, liberate, release *Opposite*: abandon ■ n release, liberation, saving, salvage *Opposite*: capture

rescuer n savior, champion, liberator, salvation, redeemer *Opposite*: captor

research n investigation, study, exploration, examination, inquiries ■ v investigate, study, explore, do research, delve into

researcher n investigator, academic, scholar, scientist, student

resemblance n similarity, likeness, semblance, sameness, alikeness *Opposite*: difference

resemble v look like, bear a resemblance to, be similar to, be like, look a lot like *Opposite*: differ

resembling adj like, similar to, not unlike, close to, reminiscent of

resent v 1 dislike, not like, hate, be offended by, show antipathy towards *Opposite*: like 2 begrudge, bear a grudge, feel bitter about, have hard feelings about, feel aggrieved *Opposite*: accept

resentful adj angry, bitter, indignant, offended, aggrieved

resentment n anger, bitterness, dislike, hatred, antipathy. *See* COMPARE AND CONTRAST *at* anger.

reservation n 1 advance booking, booking, registration, reserved seat, arrangement 2 condition, proviso, rider, corollary, stipulation 3 unwillingness, reluctance, hesitation, distance, aloofness *Opposite*: enthusiasm 4 protected area, sanctuary, refuge, game park, preserve

reservations n misgivings, doubts, hesitation, questions, uncertainties

reserve v 1 set aside, keep, keep back, hold back, put to one side *Opposite*: use 2 book, retain, put your name down for, make a

reservation *Opposite*: cancel ■ n 1 store, cache, hoard, stock, emergency supply 2 reservation, park, game park, protected area, game reserve 3 substitute, stand-in, alternate, fallback, replacement

reserved adj 1 booked, retained, taken, engaged *Opposite*: free 2 earmarked, kept, set aside, held in reserve, kept back *Opposite*: used 3 aloof, reticent, standoffish, snobbish, distant *Opposite*: outgoing

reserves n 1 assets, funds, contingency fund, financial resources, capital 2 stocks, supplies, hoard, resources, stores

reservist n soldier, reserve, reserve member, part-time soldier

reservoir n tank, pool, basin, lake, artificial lake

reset v rearrange, reorganize, retune, change, right

resettle v relocate, transfer, transplant, emigrate, immigrate

resettlement n relocation, immigration, emigration, migration, transfer

reshape v redesign, reform, rewrite, restructure, reformat

reshuffle n reorganization, rearrangement, rationalization, reallocation, reordering ■ v reorganize, rearrange, rationalize, reallocate, reorder

reside v 1 exist in, be inherent in, be located in, be a feature of, be present in 2 live, live in, inhabit, have your home, be a resident of

residence n house, home, seat, habitation, dwelling *(fml)*

residency n placement, position, job, post, internship

resident n occupant, inhabitant, denizen, tenant, occupier

residential adj domestic, suburban, housing, domiciliary *Opposite*: business

residual adj left over, remaining, lingering, left behind, outstanding

residue n remains, remainder, rest, deposit, scum

resign v leave, leave your job, quit, walk out, give notice *Opposite*: sign on

resignation n 1 notice, notification, letter of resignation 2 acceptance, acquiescence, acknowledgment, submission, forbearance *(fml) Opposite*: defiance

resigned adj reconciled, accepting, acquiescent, submissive, stoic *Opposite*: resistant

resign yourself v accept, acknowledge, give in to, yield to, reconcile yourself *Opposite*: resist

resilience n 1 buoyancy, spirit, hardiness, toughness, resistance *Opposite*: defeatism 2 pliability, flexibility, elasticity, suppleness, bounciness *Opposite*: rigidity

resilient adj 1 hardy, strong, tough, robust,

buoyant *Opposite*: defeatist **2 elastic**, pliable, flexible, supple, resistant *Opposite*: rigid

resin *n* **mastic**, gum, balm, kauri gum, gamboge

resinous *adj* **sticky**, viscous, tacky, gummy

resist *v* **1 fight**, battle, struggle, fight back, attack *Opposite*: surrender **2 oppose**, defy, stand firm, contest, challenge *Opposite*: accept **3 withstand**, survive, endure, weather, be proof against *Opposite*: succumb **4 keep from**, avoid, refuse, refrain, withstand *Opposite*: give in

resistance *n* **1 confrontation**, fight, battle, fighting, struggle *Opposite*: surrender **2 opposition**, defiance, challenge, endurance *Opposite*: acceptance

resistant *adj* **1 opposed**, dead set against, unwilling, defiant, challenging *Opposite*: accepting **2 resilient**, hardy, unaffected, impervious, tough *Opposite*: weak

resistor *n* **regulator**, rheostat, controller

resolute *adj* **firm**, staunch, unyielding, stubborn, unbendable *Opposite*: irresolute

resoluteness *n* **firmness**, determination, steadfastness, staunchness, single-mindedness *Opposite*: indecisiveness

resolution *n* **1 decree**, declaration, decision, motion, ruling **2 promise**, pledge, oath, vow **3 resolve**, determination, steadfastness, tenacity, firmness *Opposite*: indecision **4 solution**, answer, end, upshot, outcome

resolve *v* **1 make up your mind**, decide, determine, make a decision, undertake **2 solve**, get to the bottom of, sort out, put an end to, settle ■ *n* **resolution**, determination, steadfastness, tenacity, doggedness *Opposite*: indecision

resolved *adj* **determined**, set, resolute, fixed, committed *Opposite*: undecided

resonance *n* **1 timbre**, character, quality, tone, reverberation **2 significance**, meaning, importance, suggestion, echo

resonant *adj* **1 booming**, ringing, echoing, reverberating, resounding *Opposite*: tinny **2 significant**, meaningful, important, evocative, indicative *Opposite*: insignificant

resonate *v* **reverberate**, vibrate, resound, ring, echo

resort *n* **option**, recourse, alternative, course of action, possibility

resort to *v* **turn to**, give in to, have recourse to, fall back on, avail yourself of

resound *v* **echo**, resonate, boom, ring, reverberate

resounding *adj* **1 unqualified**, categorical, unambiguous, definite, unquestionable *Opposite*: qualified **2 loud**, booming, echoing, ringing, resonant *Opposite*: weak

resource *n* **reserve**, supply, source, means, store

resourceful *adj* **ingenious**, imaginative, inventive, practical, quick-witted *Opposite*: unimaginative

resourcefulness *n* **ingenuity**, imagination, inventiveness, wits, originality

resources *n* **capital**, income, possessions, wealth, property

respect *n* **1 admiration**, high opinion, regard, esteem reverence *Opposite*: disrespect **2 detail**, regard, matter, particular, point ■ *v* **1 value**, revere, think a lot of, esteem, defer to *Opposite*: disrespect **2 show consideration for**, appreciate, regard, have a high regard for, recognize *Opposite*: disregard **3 follow**, abide by, comply with, obey, acknowledge *Opposite*: deny. *See* COMPARE AND CONTRAST *at* regard.

respectability *n* **decency**, propriety, uprightness decorum, morality *Opposite*: indecency

respectable *adj* **1 reputable**, highly regarded, well-thought-of, decent, good *Opposite*: disreputable **2 adequate**, decent, reasonable, acceptable, satisfactory *Opposite*: inadequate

respected *adj* **reliable**, authoritative, distinguished, venerable, esteemed

respectful *adj* **deferential**, reverential, reverent, humble, dutiful *Opposite*: disrespectful

respectfulness *n* **deference**, respect, consideration, regard, honor *Opposite*: contemptuousness

respecting *prep* **with regard to**, regarding, with respect to, in respect of, relating to

respective *adj* **own**, individual, particular, separate, corresponding

respects *n* **compliments**, good wishes, greetings, salutations (*fml*)

respiration *n* **breathing**, inhalation, exhalation

respirator *n* **breathing apparatus**, ventilator, gas mask, oxygen mask

respiratory *adj* **breathing**, lung, respirational

WORD BANK
❏ **parts of a respiratory system** air sac, airway, alveolus, bronchial tube, bronchiole, bronchus, larynx, lung, pharynx, throat, trachea, vocal cords, voice box, windpipe

respire *v* **breathe**, take breaths, inhale, exhale

respite *n* **1 interval**, break, breathing space, lull, relief **2 reprieve**, delay, adjournment, hiatus, break

resplendent *adj* **splendid**, dazzling, magnificent, glorious, brilliant *Opposite*: unimpressive

respond *v* **1 reply**, answer, retort, answer back, rejoin (*fml*) **2 react**, act in response, take action, counter, act *Opposite*: ignore

respondent *n* **defendant**, accused, plaintiff

response *n* **reply**, answer, retort, comeback, reaction. *See* COMPARE AND CONTRAST *at* answer.

responsibility n 1 **accountability**, duty, charge, concern, obligation *Opposite*: irresponsibility 2 **blame**, liability, guilt, answerability, fault 3 **task**, brief, assignment, concern, job

responsible adj 1 **accountable**, in charge, in control, in authority, answerable 2 **dependable**, conscientious, trustworthy, reliable, sensible *Opposite*: irresponsible 3 **to blame**, liable, guilty, at fault, blamable

responsive adj **receptive**, open, approachable, reactive, quick to respond *Opposite*: sluggish

responsively adv **sensitively**, quick-wittedly, instinctively, positively, favorably

responsiveness n **receptiveness**, openness, reaction, sensitivity, awareness *Opposite*: sluggishness

rest n 1 **break**, respite, time out, relaxation, recreation 2 **remainder**, residue, leftovers, remnants, surplus 3 **stand**, support, holder, rack, frame ■ v 1 **relax**, take it easy, have a rest, take a break, have a break 2 **lie**, lean, lay, place, put

restart v 1 **resume**, take up, start again, pick up, start over *Opposite*: halt 2 **revive**, resurrect, save, renew, reopen *Opposite*: wind down

restate v **repeat**, reaffirm, reiterate, say again, regurgitate

rested adj **refreshed**, relaxed, restored, reinvigorated, revitalized *Opposite*: exhausted

restful adj **soothing**, relaxing, soporific, calming, peaceful *Opposite*: stimulating

restitution n 1 **compensation**, recompense, reimbursement, amends, repayment 2 **restoration**, return, reinstatement

restive see **restless**

restiveness n **restlessness**, impatience, agitation, edginess, nervousness *Opposite*: calmness

restless adj **fidgety**, agitated, edgy, impatient, on edge *Opposite*: relaxed

restlessness n **agitation**, impatience, restiveness, edginess *Opposite*: calmness

restock v **refill**, replenish, top off, top up, fill up

rest on v **hinge on**, turn on, depend on, rely, hang on

restoration n 1 **reinstatement**, reestablishment, return, restitution, reinstallation *Opposite*: abolition 2 **refurbishment**, renovation, repair, renewal, rebuilding

restorative adj **healing**, uplifting, invigorating, soothing, recuperative *Opposite*: draining

restore v 1 **reinstate**, reestablish, bring back, return, give back 2 **refurbish**, renovate, repair, renew, recondition. *See* COMPARE AND CONTRAST *at* renew.

restrain v 1 **hold back**, prevent, stop, keep, deter 2 **control**, bring under control, keep under control, keep in check, check 3 **confine**, detain, jail, lock up, imprison *Opposite*: free

restrained adj **reserved**, controlled, in control of yourself, self-possessed, calm *Opposite*: demonstrative

restraining order n **injunction**, court order, gag order, stay

restraint n 1 **self-control**, control, command, self-possession, self-discipline *Opposite*: self-indulgence 2 **limit**, limitation, curb, ceiling, restriction 3 **captivity**, arrest, imprisonment, confinement, detention *Opposite*: freedom 4 **belt**, chain, shackle, fetter, bond

restrict v **limit**, confine, put a ceiling on, curb, control *Opposite*: loosen

restricted adj 1 **limited**, controlled, constrained, regulated, delimited *Opposite*: open 2 **classified**, top-secret, secret, confidential, privileged *Opposite*: public

restriction n **limit**, constraint, restraint, control, ceiling

restrictive adj **preventive**, obstructive, limiting, deterring, restraining *Opposite*: free

restructure v **rearrange**, reorganize, reform, reshuffle, redistribute

restructuring n **rearrangement**, reorganization, shake-up, reform, reshuffle

result n 1 **consequence**, outcome, upshot, effect, product 2 **mark**, grade, score, outcome 3 **calculation**, solution, answer, findings, conclusion ■ v 1 **cause**, bring about, give rise to, occasion, lead to 2 **ensue**, be caused by, stem, rise, be brought about by

resultant adj **subsequent**, ensuing, resulting, consequential, follow-on

resulting adj **subsequent**, resultant, ensuing, consequential, follow-on

resume v 1 **recommence**, start again, continue, begin again, pick up where you left off *Opposite*: stop 2 **return**, go back, reoccupy, take up again

resumé see **résumé**

résumé n **précis**, review, outline, rundown, summary

resumption n **recommencement**, continuation, carrying on, renewal, reopening

resurface v 1 **float up**, come up, break the surface, rise *Opposite*: sink 2 **reappear**, come back, rematerialize, reemerge, return 3 **coat**, cover, skim, overlay, surface

resurgence n **revival**, renaissance, rebirth, resurrection, recovery *Opposite*: disappearance

resurgent adj **burgeoning**, growing, rising, increasing, reviving

resurrect v 1 **resuscitate**, bring back to life, raise from the dead, restore to life, revive *Opposite*: kill 2 **save**, breathe new life into, revive, revivify, restart

resurrection n **revival**, renaissance, rebirth, revivification, reappearance

resuscitate v **1 give artificial respiration to**, bring around, save, give the kiss of life to *Opposite*: asphyxiate **2 breathe new life into**, revive, revivify, resurrect, boost

resuscitation n **1 artificial respiration**, cardiac massage, revival, recovery **2 restoration**, resurgence, renewal, revival, revitalization

retail n **trade**, selling, marketing, merchandising, wholesale ■ v **sell**, trade, put on the market, put up for sale, vend

retailer n **1 shop**, store, retail outlet **2 seller**, vendor, merchant, trader, dealer

retain v **1 keep**, keep hold of, hold on to, hold, hang on to *Opposite*: let go **2 recall**, recollect, keep in mind, remember, hold *Opposite*: forget

retainer n **deposit**, down payment, fee, payment

retake v **take back**, recapture, regain, reconquer, win back ■ n **exam**, examination, repeat

retaliate v **hit back**, strike back, get even, even the score, react *Opposite*: forgive

retaliation n **reprisal**, revenge, vengeance, retribution *Opposite*: forgiveness

retaliatory adj **tit-for-tat**, reciprocal, reactive, punitive, revengeful *Opposite*: forgiving

retard v **delay**, slow down, hold up, hold back, hinder *Opposite*: speed up

retardation n **delay**, check, obstruction, hindrance, obstacle *Opposite*: acceleration

retarded adj **underdeveloped**, slow, stunted, arrested, lagging *Opposite*: accelerated

retch v **vomit**, gag, be sick, heave (*infml*), throw up (*infml*)

retell v **repeat**, restate, go over, reiterate, recite

retention n **1 holding**, retaining, preservation, withholding, maintenance *Opposite*: release **2 remembering**, memorizing, recalling, memory, recollection *Opposite*: forgetting

retentive adj **retaining**, absorbent, spongy

rethink v **reconsider**, change your mind, change direction, change tack, change course ■ n **reconsideration**, change of mind, change of heart, second thoughts, volteface

reticence n **1 reserve**, silence, uncommunicativeness, discretion, restraint *Opposite*: openness **2 shyness**, bashfulness, reserve, quietness, modesty *Opposite*: boldness

reticent adj **reserved**, discreet, restrained, unforthcoming, uncommunicative *Opposite*: talkative. *See* COMPARE AND CONTRAST *at* silent.

retinue n **entourage**, followers, attendants, servants, aides

retire v **1 give up work**, stop working, step down, be pensioned off, be superannuated **2 leave**, take your leave, withdraw, go away, go off **3 go to bed**, call it a day, turn in (*infml*), hit the sack (*infml*), hit the hay (*infml*)

retired adj **superannuated**, pensioned off, discharged, emeritus, emerita *Opposite*: working

retirement n **1 superannuation**, departure, leaving, giving up work, stepping down **2 withdrawal**, retreat, sequestration, seclusion

retiring adj **reticent**, self-effacing, unassuming, shy, reserved

retort v **reply**, answer, respond, counter, rejoin (*fml*) ■ n **reply**, response, riposte, answer, squelch (*slang*). *See* COMPARE AND CONTRAST *at* answer.

retouch v **touch up**, correct, restore, renovate, improve

retrace v **review**, redo, go back over, repeat

retract v **1 draw in**, draw back, pull in, pull back, withdraw *Opposite*: extend **2 deny**, take back, withdraw, apologize, recant *Opposite*: stand by

retractable adj **telescopic**, folding, collapsible

retraction n **withdrawal**, refutation, disclaimer, denial, negation *Opposite*: confirmation

retreat n **1 departure**, withdrawal, flight, evacuation *Opposite*: advance **2 haven**, hideaway, sanctuary, refuge, shelter ■ v **move away**, move back, draw back, back away, run away *Opposite*: advance

retrench v **cut back**, economize, save, save money, tighten your belt

retrenchment n **cutback**, economizing, cuts, cost-cutting, belt-tightening

retribution n **vengeance**, revenge, reprisal, reckoning, justice

retributive adj **punitive**, retaliatory, vengeful, punishing, revengeful

retrieval n **recovery**, repossession, rescue, reclamation, salvage *Opposite*: loss

retrieve v **save**, get back, recover, regain, repossess *Opposite*: lose

retro adj **period**, old-fashioned, dated, historical, passé

retrograde adj **1 backward**, reversing, rearward *Opposite*: forward **2 regressive**, declining, worsening, getting worse, deteriorating *Opposite*: improving

retrogress v **1 regress**, decline, revert, degenerate, worsen *Opposite*: progress **2 move backward**, reverse, go back, retreat, draw back *Opposite*: move forward

retrogression n **decline**, regression, return, relapse, deterioration *Opposite*: progression

retrogressive adj **1 regressive**, reverting, degenerating, worsening, getting worse

Opposite: progressive **2 reversing**, retreating, withdrawing, moving back, drawing back

retrospect *n* **recollection**, remembrance, review, reconsideration, survey *Opposite*: prospect

retrospective *adj* **1 backward-looking**, nostalgic, retrograde, traditional, conservative *Opposite*: forward-thinking **2 reviewing**, reflective, surveying, reconsidering **3 retroactive**, backdated, ex post facto ■ *n* **exhibition**, show, presentation, showcase, display

retrospectively *adv* **on reflection**, in retrospect, with hindsight, with the benefit of hindsight, on second thought

return *v* **1 revisit**, come back, go again, come again, go back *Opposite*: depart **2 repay**, pay back, refund, reimburse, give back *Opposite*: keep **3 resume**, go back, revert, revisit, begin again *Opposite*: stop **4 send back**, take back, replace, restore *Opposite*: retain ■ *n* **1 coming back**, reappearance, reoccurrence, arrival, homecoming *Opposite*: departure **2 profit**, earnings, yield, revenue, proceeds

returns *n* **revenue**, earnings, yield, proceeds, takings *Opposite*: outlay

reunification *n* **reunion**, reconsolidation, amalgamation, recombination, reintegration

reunify *v* **reunite**, come together, rejoin, bring together, reintegrate

reunion *n* **1 gathering**, meeting, event, get-together (*infml*) **2 reunification**, reintegration, recombination, reconsolidation

reunite *v* **reunify**, unite, bring together, unify, come together *Opposite*: split

reusable *adj* **refillable**, returnable, recyclable, green, ecofriendly *Opposite*: disposable

reuse *v* **recycle**, reclaim, reprocess, salvage *Opposite*: discard

rev *n* **revolution**, cycle, rotation, turn, revolution per minute ■ *v* **race**, roar, scream, increase power, accelerate

revaluation *n* **revision**, reappraisal, reassessment, readjustment, redefinition

revalue *v* **1 raise**, increase, up, enhance, augment (*fml*) *Opposite*: devalue **2 reappraise**, reevaluate, adjust, reset, change

revamp *v* **restore**, make over, renew, refurbish, give a facelift ■ *n* **facelift**, refurbishment, restoration, renovation, overhaul. *See* COMPARE AND CONTRAST *at* **renew**.

reveal *v* **1 make known**, disclose, divulge, expose, make public *Opposite*: conceal **2 expose**, uncover, show, bare, bring to light *Opposite*: cover up

revealing *adj* **1 skimpy**, see-through, figure-hugging, close-fitting, tight-fitting **2 enlightening**, illuminating, telling, telltale, informative *Opposite*: obscure

revealingly *adv* **tellingly**, significantly, interestingly, importantly, conspicuously

reveille *n* **1 wake-up call**, early-morning call, bugle call *Opposite*: lights out **2 early morning**, daybreak, dawn, sunup, the crack of dawn *Opposite*: dusk

revel *v* **1 make merry**, celebrate, have fun, socialize, let your hair down (*infml*) **2 delight**, enjoy, take pleasure in, luxuriate, bask ■ *n* **celebration**, party, festivities, carnival, merrymaking

revelation *n* **1 exposé**, exposure, disclosure, leak, admission **2 surprise**, shock, eye opener

reveler *n* **partygoer**, roisterer, merrymaker, pleasure-seeker, celebrator

revelry *n* **festivities**, revels, celebrations, partying, merriment

revenge *n* **retaliation**, vengeance, retribution, settling of scores, reprisal ■ *v* **requite**, avenge, even the score, get back, retaliate

revenue *n* **income**, proceeds, profits, returns, takings *Opposite*: expenses

reverberate *v* **echo**, resound, ring, vibrate, resonate

reverberating *adj* **resounding**, echoing, resonant, rich, rumbling

reverberation *n* **echo**, sound, noise, boom

reverberations *n* **aftershock**, aftereffects, impact, shock

revere *v* **admire**, respect, look up to, hold in the highest regard, be in awe of *Opposite*: despise

revered *adj* **1 respected**, valued, illustrious, distinguished, esteemed *Opposite*: vilified **2 holy**, sacred, blessed, venerated, hallowed *Opposite*: vilified

reverence *n* **respect**, admiration, worship, veneration, regard *Opposite*: contempt. *See* COMPARE AND CONTRAST *at* **regard**.

reverent *see* **reverential**

reverential *adj* **respectful**, deferential, worshipful, humble, awed *Opposite*: disrespectful

reverie *n* **daydream**, dream, trance, musing, contemplation

reversal *n* **1 turnaround**, U-turn, about-face, volte-face **2 setback**, hitch, problem, reverse, blow

reverse *v* **1 overturn**, turn around, undo, annul, invalidate *Opposite*: carry out **2 move backward**, back up, drive backward, go backward, retreat *Opposite*: advance **3 transpose**, switch, invert, reorder, rearrange ■ *n* **1 contrary**, opposite, antithesis, converse **2 back**, rear, underneath, other side, opposite side *Opposite*: front

3 setback, reversal, hitch, problem, misfortune ■ adj **opposite**, contrary, converse, inverse Opposite: same

reversible adj 1 **rescindable**, revocable, alterable, adjustable, changeable Opposite: irreversible **2 two-sided**, dual-purpose, multipurpose, double-sided, two-in-one

reversion n 1 **return**, decline, deterioration, degeneration, retreat **2 reversal**, turnaround, about-face, U-turn, change of direction

revert v 1 **return**, go back, take a step back, relapse, regress **2 go back**, revisit, go over again, take another look at, return **3 regress**, change back, return, mutate, degenerate **4 lapse**, backslide, go back to your old ways, slip back, reoffend **5 be returned**, pass, pass back, return, go back

review v 1 **study**, go over, go through, look over, reread **2 appraise**, evaluate, assess, look at, examine **3 reconsider**, reassess, go over, check, make another study of ■ n 1 **appraisal**, evaluation, assessment, examination, analysis **2 publication**, magazine, journal, periodical **3 reconsideration**, reassessment, check, reexamination, revision

reviewer n **critic**, commentator, assessor, referee

revile v **insult**, abuse, scorn, condemn, censure Opposite: praise

revise v **amend**, modify, adjust, alter, change

revision n **amendment**, reconsideration, modification, adjustment, alteration

revisionism n **reassessment**, reconsideration, reinterpretation, pragmatism, alteration

revisionist adj **pragmatic**, heretical, progressive, modernizing, controversial ■ n **pragmatist**, modernizer, heretic, liberal

revisit v 1 **return to**, go back to, come back to, retreat to, reenter Opposite: abandon **2 reconsider**, reexamine, reassess, reevaluate, rethink

revitalization n **renewal**, renaissance, revival, new life, recovery Opposite: decline

revitalize v **refresh**, invigorate, revive, rejuvenate, regenerate Opposite: wear out

revitalizing adj **energizing**, vitalizing, stimulating, uplifting, invigorating

revival n 1 **revitalization**, renewal, restoration, stimulation, reinforcement Opposite: disappearance **2 resuscitation**, recovery, waking, coming to, bringing around Opposite: relapse

revive v 1 **revitalize**, renew, breathe life into, restore, refresh Opposite: kill **2 recover**, pick up, perk up, resume, develop Opposite: die down **3 resuscitate**, come around, recover, come to, bring around Opposite: lose consciousness **4 put on**, stage, restage, perform, redo

revivify v **rejuvenate**, breathe new life into, refresh, resurrect, resuscitate Opposite: exhaust

revocation n **cancellation**, withdrawal, reversal, overturning, annulment Opposite: enactment

revoke v **cancel**, annul, rescind, withdraw, retract

revolt v 1 **rebel**, rise up, mutiny, riot **2 repel**, repulse, sicken, nauseate, turn your stomach Opposite: attract ■ n **rebellion**, revolution, uprising, upheaval, insurgency

revolted adj **nauseated**, appalled, horrorstruck, horror-stricken, dismayed Opposite: charmed

revolting adj **disgusting**, repellent, repulsive, sickening, nauseating Opposite: appealing

revolution n 1 **rebellion**, revolt, uprising, upheaval, insurgency **2 transformation**, conversion, alteration, upheaval, development **3 rotation**, turn, spin, cycle, circle

revolutionary adj 1 **rebellious**, radical, insurgent, mutinous, anarchist **2 radical**, groundbreaking, world-shattering, innovative, innovatory Opposite: conventional ■ n **rebel**, radical, insurgent, rioter, mutineer

revolutionize v **transform**, transfigure, reform, alter, change Opposite: maintain

revolve v **rotate**, turn, spin, circle, orbit

revolving adj **rotating**, turning, spinning, circling, gyrating

revue n **variety show**, show, skit, sketch show, satire

revulsion n **disgust**, repulsion, repugnance, distaste, dislike Opposite: attraction

reward n **recompense**, payment, repayment, return, remuneration Opposite: penalty ■ v **recompense**, pay, repay, remunerate, compensate Opposite: penalize

rewarding adj **satisfying**, worthwhile, gratifying, pleasing, fulfilling Opposite: disappointing

rewind v **wind back**, spool back, reverse

rewire v **redo**, renovate, renew, refurbish, revamp

reword v **rephrase**, redraft, rewrite, rework, revise

rework v **revise**, amend, redo, alter, modify

rewrite v **redraft**, rephrase, reword, rework, revise ■ n **revision**, amendment, alteration, modification

rhapsodic adj **ecstatic**, enthusiastic, lyrical, rapturous, fervent Opposite: unenthusiastic

rhapsodize v **enthuse**, be ecstatic, eulogize, go over the top (infml), wax lyrical (literary)

rhapsody n **ecstasy**, rapture, bliss, enthusiasm, eagerness Opposite: gloom

rheostat n **control**, regulator, resistor, controller

rhetoric *n* **1 oratory**, public speaking, speechmaking, speechifying *(infml)* **2 bombast**, pomposity, grandiloquence, fustian, loftiness **3 language**, expression, style, idiom, words

rhetorical *adj* **1 oratorical**, verbal, linguistic, stylistic **2 bombastic**, pompous, pretentious, periphrastic, voluble

rhetorician *n* **orator**, speaker, public speaker, debater, advocate

rheumatic *adj* **stiff**, aching, sore, inflexible, rigid *Opposite*: flexible

rhinestone *n* **paste**, strass, diamanté

rhizome *n* **stem**, shoot, root, tuber, corm

rhomboid *see* **rhombus**

rhombus *n* **diamond**, lozenge, parallelogram, rhomboid

rhubarb *n* **argument**, quarrel, fight, disagreement, dispute

rhyme *n* **1 poem**, verse, nursery rhyme, jingle, limerick **2 assonance**, consonance, rhyming

rhyme or reason *n* **sense**, logic, meaning, pattern

rhythm *n* **1 beat**, pace, tempo, time, measure **2 regularity**, pattern, progression, sequence

rhythmic *adj* **1 musical**, cadenced, metrical **2 recurring**, regular, periodic, recurrent

rib *n* **beam**, strut, spoke, spine, spar ■ *v (infml)* **tease**, make fun of, laugh at, mock, kid

ribald *adj* **coarse**, vulgar, bawdy, rude, lewd *Opposite*: refined

ribaldry *n* **coarseness**, vulgarity, bawdiness, rudeness, lewdness *Opposite*: refinement

ribbed *adj* **grooved**, corrugated, ridged, bumpy, uneven

ribbon *n* **1 band**, tie, trimming, decoration, tape **2 decoration**, award, honor, badge of honor, medal **3 strip**, stretch, band, length

rich *adj* **1 wealthy**, well-off, affluent, prosperous, moneyed *Opposite*: poor **2 opulent**, gorgeous, lush, luxuriant, splendid *Opposite*: shabby **3 full**, abounding, plentiful, stuffed, heavy *Opposite*: lacking **4 productive**, fertile, abundant, plentiful, fruitful *Opposite*: infertile **5 heavy**, indigestible, calorific, cloying, unhealthy *Opposite*: light **6 intense**, deep, strong, full, powerful *Opposite*: weak **7** *(infml)* **ironic**, amusing, irritating, annoying, ridiculous

riches *n* **resources**, treasures, reserves, materials, raw materials

richly *adv* **1 opulently**, luxuriantly, luxuriously, splendidly, ornately *Opposite*: shabbily **2 thoroughly**, fully, completely, totally, deeply *Opposite*: barely

richness *n* **1 prosperity**, fortune, affluence, wealth *Opposite*: poverty **2 opulence**, luxury, sumptuousness, splendor, luxuriousness *Opposite*: shabbiness **3 fertility**, fruitfulness, productivity, lushness, fullness *Opposite*: infertility **4 intensity**, depth,

strength, fullness, power *Opposite*: weakness

rickety *adj* **shaky**, unsteady, unstable, rocky, unbalanced *Opposite*: firm

ricochet *v* **recoil**, rebound, glance off, bounce off, reflect ■ *n* **rebound**, recoil, reverberation, reflection, echo

rictus *n* **grimace**, grin, fixed expression, contortion

rid *v* **1** *(archaic)* **free**, clear, purge, liberate, cleanse **2 get rid of**, dispense with, do away with, divest, drop

riddle *n* **puzzle**, conundrum, question, brainteaser, problem ■ *v* **1 pierce**, perforate, puncture, pepper, damage **2 sift**, screen, sieve, separate. *See* COMPARE AND CONTRAST *at* **problem**.

ride *v* **1 gallop**, canter, trot, jockey **2 travel**, journey, go, be carried, be conveyed *Opposite*: walk **3** *(infml)* **tease**, torment, criticize, mock, provoke **4 depend on**, rest on, center on, rely on, be contingent on ■ *n* **trip**, outing, jaunt, journey, drive

ride out *v* **endure**, brave, stick out, survive, live through *Opposite*: succumb

rider *n* **proviso**, qualification, provision, condition, stipulation

ride up *v* **roll up**, slide up, wriggle up, move up, wrinkle *Opposite*: fall down

ridge *n* **crest**, point, edge, rim, elevation ■ *v* **fold**, crumple, crinkle, crease, wrinkle

ridicule *v* **belittle**, mock, deride, scorn, scoff at ■ *n* **mockery**, scorn, derision, laughter, mimicry

---

COMPARE AND CONTRAST CORE MEANING: belittle by making fun of somebody or something **ridicule** make fun of somebody or something in a cruel contemptuous way; **deride** trivialize somebody or something; **laugh at** make scornful fun of somebody or their behavior; **mock** treat somebody or something with scorn, often by cruel mimicking; **send up** *(infml)* parody or mimic somebody or something.

---

ridiculous *adj* **ludicrous**, preposterous, absurd, silly, outlandish *Opposite*: sensible

ridiculousness *n* **ludicrousness**, preposterousness, absurdity, irrationality, outlandishness *Opposite*: sense

riding *n* **show jumping**, racing, hunting, dressage, cross-country

rife *adj* **1 widespread**, common, endemic, extensive, prevalent *Opposite*: rare **2 full**, abounding, bursting, laden, loaded *Opposite*: lacking. *See* COMPARE AND CONTRAST *at* **widespread**.

riff *n* **phrase**, refrain, melody, tune, groove ■ *v* **play**, jam, improvise, strum, perform

riffle *v* **1 flick through**, turn the pages of, peruse, glance at, scan **2 shuffle**, mix, mix up, randomize, jumble up **3 ripple**, roughen, undulate, get choppy, ruffle ■

n **flick**, quick look, glance, perusal, skim

rifle *v* **ransack**, search, search through, rummage, go through

rift *n* 1 **crack**, hole, fissure, split, crevice 2 **disagreement**, difference, conflict, falling-out, quarrel

rig *v* 1 **fix**, engineer, arrange, prepare, fit 2 **improvise**, fix up, invent, set up, assemble *Opposite*: plan 3 **manipulate**, falsify, mock up, fix, set up ■ *n* 1 **oil rig**, platform, derrick 2 *(infml)* **dress**, clothes, clothing, outfit, getup *(infml)*

rigamarole *see* rigmarole

rigging *n* **ropes**, chains, wires, supports, pulleys

right *adj* 1 **correct**, accurate, true, exact, precise *Opposite*: wrong 2 **just**, proper, fair, moral, honorable *Opposite*: immoral 3 **appropriate**, respectable, fitting, proper, desirable *Opposite*: inappropriate 4 **well**, healthy, in shape, fit, very well *Opposite*: ill ■ *adv* 1 **appropriately**, as it should be, acceptably, suitably, properly *Opposite*: unsuitably 2 **correctly**, exactly, accurately, precisely, directly *Opposite*: inexactly 3 *(infml)* **utterly**, entirely, completely, absolutely, totally ■ *n* 1 **truth**, honesty, goodness, morality, fairness *Opposite*: wrong 2 **entitlement**, privilege, due, birthright, justification ■ *v* **redress**, rectify, amend, remedy, correct

right-angled *adj* **angled**, square, perpendicular, ninety-degree, right-angle

right away *adv* **immediately**, at once, instantaneously, right now, just now

righteous *adj* **virtuous**, moral, good, just, blameless *Opposite*: sinful

righteousness *n* **virtue**, morality, justice, decency, uprightness *Opposite*: wickedness

rightful *adj* **fair**, correct, legal, due, just *Opposite*: unlawful

rightfulness *n* **truth**, fairness, correctness, legality, lawfulness

right hand *n* **assistant**, aide, deputy, lieutenant, helper

right-hand *adj* 1 **right**, rightward, starboard *Opposite*: left-hand 2 **trusted**, important, reliable, principal, main

right-handed *adj* **clockwise**, left to right, circular, round, helical *Opposite*: left-handed

rightist *adj* **right-wing**, conservative, traditionalist

rightly *adv* 1 **correctly**, truly, exactly, accurately, precisely *Opposite*: wrongly 2 **justly**, fittingly, justifiably, suitably, rightfully *Opposite*: unreasonably 3 *(infml)* **for certain**, without a shadow of a doubt, for sure, certainly, positively

right-minded *adj* **reasonable**, sensible, fair-minded, decent, rational

rightness *n* 1 **rectitude**, correctness, faultlessness, truth, precision 2 **aptness**, suit-

ability, appropriateness, timeliness, properness *Opposite*: inappropriateness

right-wing *adj* **conservative**, rightist, traditionalist *Opposite*: left-wing

right-winger *n* **conservative**, rightist, traditionalist *Opposite*: liberal

rigid *adj* 1 **unbending**, inflexible, stiff, firm, set *Opposite*: floppy 2 **severe**, strict, harsh, stern, inflexible *Opposite*: lax

rigidity *n* 1 **stiffness**, inflexibility, hardness, firmness, rigor *Opposite*: floppiness 2 **inflexibility**, firmness, severity, strictness, stringency *Opposite*: laxity

rigmarole *n* 1 **fuss**, bother, ritual, business, hassle *(infml)* 2 **explanation**, account, excuse, palaver, verbiage

rigor *n* 1 **severity**, strictness, harshness, intransigence, dogmatism *Opposite*: flexibility 2 **thoroughness**, consistency, attention to detail, precision, accuracy *Opposite*: negligence 3 **hardship**, difficulty, hard time, difficult time, demand *Opposite*: mildness 4 **stiffness**, rigidity, unresponsiveness, stiffening, rigor mortis *Opposite*: flexibility

rigorous *adj* 1 **hard**, severe, harsh, demanding, laborious *Opposite*: mild 2 **exact**, thorough, precise, meticulous, painstaking *Opposite*: slapdash

rigorousness *n* 1 **strictness**, discipline, severity, harshness, difficulty *Opposite*: leniency 2 **exactness**, thoroughness, discipline, meticulousness, scrupulousness *Opposite*: negligence

rig out *(infml)* *v* 1 **equip**, provide, prepare, arrange, fit out 2 **dress up**, clothe, get up *(infml)*, attire *(fml)*

rig up *v* **improvise**, cobble together, set up, assemble, fix up *Opposite*: plan

rile *(infml)* *v* **anger**, enrage, annoy, irritate, irk *Opposite*: placate

rim *n* **edge**, border, lip, perimeter, circumference *Opposite*: center

rime *n* **frost**, hoar frost, ice

rind *n* **peel**, skin, husk, crust, coat *Opposite*: flesh

ring *n* 1 **circle**, loop, hoop, band, halo 2 **group**, band, gang, organization, team 3 **impression**, semblance, appearance, feel, air 4 **call**, phone call, telephone call, buzz *(infml)* ■ *v* 1 **encircle**, enclose, circle, surround 2 **peal**, tinkle, chime, toll, ding-dong 3 **resonate**, resound, ring out, reverberate, echo

ring a bell *(infml)* *v* **strike a chord**, jog somebody's memory, sound familiar, be reminiscent, remind

ringleader *n* **gang leader**, leader of the pack, agitator, instigator, inciter

ringlet *n* **curl**, lock, twist, coil, spiral

ringmaster *n* **master of ceremonies**, MC, host, chair, chairperson

ring out v be heard, sound, rise, pierce the silence, blast out

ringside adj front row, grandstand, unimpeded, unobstructed, clear

rink n arena, floor, space, area

rinse n 1 wash, clean, bathe, sluice, dip 2 solution, dye, tint, bleach, stain

riot n 1 uprising, insurrection, disturbance, unrest, demonstration 2 (infml) laugh (infml), scream (infml), hoot (slang), gas (slang) ■ v mutiny, demonstrate, run riot, rebel, protest

rioter n demonstrator, rebel, revolutionary, insurgent, protester

riotous adj 1 violent, disorderly, unruly, uncontrolled, uproarious Opposite: peaceful 2 wild, debauched, uncontrolled, out of control, hedonistic Opposite: subdued

riotously adv 1 hilariously, madly, side-splittingly, screamingly, wildly 2 raucously, rowdily, wildly, rambunctiously, noisily Opposite: quietly

rip v 1 tear, split, cleave, shred, scratch Opposite: mend 2 snatch, tear, seize, grab, pluck Opposite: give 3 speed, tear, dash, rush, fly Opposite: amble ■ n tear, split, scratch, cleft, slash. See COMPARE AND CONTRAST at tear.

ripcord n cord, line, string, cable, rope

ripe adj 1 (infml) pungent, strong, sour, strong-smelling, off Opposite: sweet 2 mature, ready, grown, fully grown, matured Opposite: unripe 3 ready, suitable, prepared, crying out, disposed

ripen v mature, season, grow, develop, evolve

ripeness n maturity, readiness, mellowness, age

rip off (infml) v overcharge, cheat, swindle, dupe, deceive

rip-off (infml) n swindle, con, cheat, diddle (slang)

riposte n reply, retort, comeback, response, answer ■ v retort, reply, come back, return, counter. See COMPARE AND CONTRAST at answer.

ripple v undulate, swell, flow, move, rise and fall ■ n wave, undulation, swell, current, wrinkle Opposite: stillness

rip-roaring (infml) adj exciting, uproarious, boisterous, rollicking, energetic Opposite: boring

rip up v tear up, shred, pull apart, chew up, pull to pieces Opposite: piece together

rise v 1 stand up, get up, get to your feet, arise (literary) Opposite: sit down 2 go up, increase, climb, mount, get higher Opposite: drop 3 rebel, revolt, mutiny, rise up, riot Opposite: conform 4 originate, begin, start, come out of, be set in motion Opposite: end 5 emerge, come up, appear, arise, be apparent Opposite: disappear 6 wake up, get up, get out of bed, arise, awaken Opposite: retire ■ n 1 increase, growth,

upsurge, intensification, escalation Opposite: decrease 2 growth, spread, development, expansion, advance Opposite: decline 3 hill, slope, incline, acclivity, elevation Opposite: hollow 4 climb, ascent, elevation Opposite: fall

rise above v surmount, overcome, conquer, triumph over, surpass

rise and fall n swell, undulation, ripple, movement, rolling Opposite: stability

rise to (infml) v respond, meet, shine, succeed, perform

rise to the bait v respond, react, get angry, be provoked, answer Opposite: ignore

rise up v 1 rebel, revolt, riot, rise, mutiny 2 emerge, stand up, float up, soar, arise (literary) Opposite: sink

risibility n 1 (fml) humorousness, sense of humor, happiness, wit, humor Opposite: soberness 2 ridiculousness, ludicrousness, absurdity, laughableness, stupidity Opposite: seriousness

risible adj 1 laughable, ludicrous, absurd, ridiculous, stupid Opposite: serious 2 (fml) humorous, good-humored, happy, cheerful, cheery Opposite: somber

rising adj increasing, growing, going up, mounting, getting higher Opposite: falling ■ n uprising, rebellion, revolt, mutiny, riot

risk n 1 danger, jeopardy, peril, hazard, menace Opposite: safety 2 possibility, chance, danger, hazard, gamble ■ v 1 endanger, jeopardize, lay bare, expose, imperil (fml) Opposite: protect 2 chance, hazard, attempt, gamble, venture Opposite: play safe

riskiness n hazardousness, perilousness, precariousness, dangerousness, audaciousness Opposite: safety

risky adj dangerous, hazardous, chancy, precarious, perilous Opposite: safe

risqué adj racy, rude, lewd, salacious, naughty Opposite: decorous

rite n 1 ritual, ceremony, formal procedure, service, sacrament 2 custom, habit, practice, routine, procedure

ritual n 1 rite, ceremony, service, formal procedure, sacrament 2 custom, habit, practice, routine, procedure ■ adj 1 ceremonial, procedural, ceremonious, sacramental, formal 2 customary, habitual, usual, normal, expected

ritualistic adj ceremonial, formalized, formulaic, ritualized, sacred

rival n 1 competitor, opponent, adversary, contender, challenger Opposite: ally 2 equal, match, counterpart, peer, equivalent ■ v 1 match, equal, be the equal of, be similar to, compare with 2 oppose, compete with, challenge, go up against, be against 3 outdo, surpass, exceed, beat, top ■ adj competing, opposing, challenging, contending, enemy

rivalry n **competition**, opposition, contention, competitiveness, enmity Opposite: cooperation

riven (literary) adj **split**, torn apart, divided, fragmented, torn asunder (fml) Opposite: united

river n **stream**, waterway, tributary, canal, watercourse

riverside n **waterside**, water's edge, bank, shore

rivet n **pin**, nail, fastener, bolt, screw ■ v 1 (infml) **fascinate**, enthrall, entrance, interest, mesmerize Opposite: bore 2 **fasten**, hold, pin, bolt, nail

riveting (infml) adj **fascinating**, enthralling, exciting, spellbinding, entrancing Opposite: boring

rivulet n **stream**, creek, gully, brook (literary)

RNA n **nucleic acid**, ribonucleic acid, genetic material

road n **street**, thoroughfare, lane, way

WORD BANK

❑ **types of highways** artery, avenue, beltway, boulevard, bypass, divided highway, expressway, freeway, highway, interstate, limited-access highway, main road, overpass, parkway, speedway, superhighway, thruway, toll road, trunk route, turnpike

❑ **types of secondary roads** access road, access strip, alley, alleyway, backstreet, blind alley, byroad, byway, corniche, cul-de-sac, dead end, dirt track, driveway, esplanade, lane, parade, path, service road, side street, street, track

roadblock n **barricade**, barrier, sentry post, obstruction, blockade

roadhouse n **hotel**, motel, inn, tavern, bar

road show n 1 **radio show**, live broadcast, open-air broadcast, broadcast, tour 2 **campaign**, publicity campaign, advertising campaign, dog-and-pony show, media circus (infml)

road sign n **sign**, signpost, notice, stop sign, yield sign

road-test v **try out**, test, test drive, trial, run

roadway n **road**, street, thoroughfare, highway

roadworthiness n **safety**, soundness, reliability, working order

roadworthy adj **safe**, fit, legal, driveable, suitable

roam v **wander**, rove, travel, journey, stray Opposite: settle

roamer n **wanderer**, traveler, rover, itinerant, nomad

roaming adj **wandering**, roving, itinerant, nomadic, peripatetic Opposite: stationary

roaring adj 1 **noisy**, loud, deafening, boisterous, thunderous Opposite: quiet 2 **busy** thriving, prosperous, active Opposite: slack

roast v **bake**, cook, heat

roasting (infml) adj **boiling**, hot, red-hot, sweltering, burning up Opposite: cool

rob v 1 **steal from**, take from, hold up, raid, mug 2 **deprive**, cheat, strip, drain, fleece (infml)

robber n **thief**, burglar, pickpocket, shoplifter, mugger

robbery n **theft**, burglary, break-in, mugging, stealing

robe n **dressing gown**, negligee, housecoat, bathrobe, gown

robot n **automaton**, android, machine, computer, mechanical device

robotic adj 1 **mechanical**, mechanized, automated, automatic, cybernetic 2 **machine-like**, mechanical, unresponsive, unfeeling, humorless Opposite: warm

robotics n **cybernetics**, automation, engineering, manufacturing, science

robust adj **healthy**, vigorous, hearty, strong, tough Opposite: weak

robustness n **heftiness**, sturdiness, strength, toughness, forcefulness Opposite: weakness

rock n 1 **stone**, boulder, pebble 2 **pillar**, mainstay, tower of strength, stalwart ■ v 1 **sway**, swing, shake, move up and down, pitch 2 (infml) **astound**, shock, shake, stun, disturb

rock bottom n **the lowest**, the bottom, the depths, all-time low, nadir

rocker (infml) n 1 **rock star**, rock musician, rock singer, rock and roller, pop star 2 **rock fan**, groupie (infml), headbanger (slang)

rockery n **garden**, rock garden, alpine garden, terrace

rocket v 1 **speed**, whiz, hurtle, fly, zoom 2 (infml) **shoot up**, soar, increase rapidly, go through the roof (infml), go sky-high (infml) Opposite: plummet

rock face n **cliff face**, face, precipice, crag, cliff

rock garden n **garden**, rockery, alpine garden, terrace

rock-hard adj **solid**, firm, cast-iron, hard as nails, like granite Opposite: soft

rockiness n **shakiness**, unsteadiness, uncertainty, insecurity, instability Opposite: steadiness

rock-solid adj 1 **firm**, unshakable, solid, rigid, unyielding Opposite: shaky 2 **durable**, unbreakable, strong, firm, enduring Opposite: breakable

rock-strewn adj **stony**, rocky, gravelly, pebbly, rough Opposite: smooth

rock the boat (infml) v **cause an argument**, cause an upset, cause trouble

rocky adj 1 **stony**, rock-strewn, pebbly, gravelly 2 **shaky**, unsteady, wobbly, unsound, insecure Opposite: stable 3 **difficult**, troubled, uncertain, not easy, hard Opposite: easy

rod *n* bar, pole, stick, shaft, dowel

rodeo *n* competition, display, festival, meet, fair

rogue *n* scoundrel, rascal, reprobate, ne'er-do-well, cad *(dated)*

roguery *n* 1 dishonesty, deceit, unscrupulousness, double-dealing, sharp practice *Opposite*: honesty 2 mischief, mischievousness, playfulness, naughtiness, tricks

roguish *adj* 1 mischievous, naughty, impish, wicked, malicious 2 dishonest, deceitful, unscrupulous, double-dealing, criminal *Opposite*: honest

roguishness *n* 1 unscrupulousness, dishonesty, deceit, double-dealing, sharp practice *Opposite*: honesty 2 mischievousness, mischief, playfulness, naughtiness, tricks

roister *v* 1 revel, make merry, celebrate, drink, party *(infml)* 2 brag, boast, show off, swagger, gloat

roisterer *n* 1 reveler, partygoer, merrymaker, pleasure-seeker, celebrator 2 braggart, boaster, show-off *(infml)*, loudmouth *(infml)*, bigmouth *(infml)*

role *n* 1 position, function, responsibility, job, task 2 part, character, person, title role, starring role

role model *n* example, model, paradigm, exemplar *(literary)*

role-play *v* act, act out, enact, play, imagine

role-playing *n* acting, acting out, game-playing, imagination, play-acting

roil *v* 1 bowl, trundle, troll, set rolling, roll along 2 revolve, turn, turn over, turn around, spin ■ *n* reel, cylinder, spool, tube, bolt

roll call *n* attendance check, register check, checkup, check, monitoring

roller *n* breaker, wave, whitecap

roller-skate *v* skate, blade, Rollerblade

rollicking *adj* boisterous, rowdy, loud, carefree, swashbuckling

roll·in *v* arrive, enter, land, roll up, appear *Opposite*: leave

rolling *adj* 1 undulating, rising and falling, gently sloping *Opposite*: steep 2 progressing, continuing, ongoing, continuous, constant

rolling in it *(infml) adj* rich, wealthy, in the money *(infml)*, loaded *(slang)* *Opposite*: broke *(infml)*

roll out *v* introduce, launch, inaugurate, issue, bring out

roll out the red carpet *v* treat like royalty, give a hero's welcome, lionize, make a fuss of, welcome

roll up *v* 1 appear, turn up, ride up, show up, roll in *Opposite*: leave 2 turn up, push back, furl *Opposite*: unroll

roman *adj* 1 upright, straight, plain *Opposite*: italic 2 in classical style, classical, ancient

romance *n* 1 love, passion, amorousness, sex, eroticism 2 relationship, love affair, affair, involvement, fling *(infml)* 3 allure, excitement, adventure, nostalgia, feeling 4 fascination, enthusiasm, passion, love, love affair 5 love story, romantic story, romantic tale, weepie *(infml)*, tearjerker *(infml)* *Opposite*: tragedy 6 adventure story, adventure, tale, story, narrative 7 fantasy, story, tall tale, fiction, daydream ■ *v* 1 tell stories, fantasize, romanticize 2 be romantic, act romantically, swoon, daydream, be in love 3 court *(dated)*, woo *(literary)*, pay court to *(dated)* 4 have an affair with, have a love affair with, have a relationship with, date, have a fling with

romantic *adj* 1 idealistic, dreamy, quixotic, impractical, starry-eyed *Opposite*: prosaic 2 loving, passionate, tender, amorous, adoring *Opposite*: platonic

romanticism *n* idealization, fantasy, nostalgia, soft focus, rose-tinted glasses

romanticize *v* 1 idealize, glamorize, sentimentalize, put on a pedestal, look at through rose-colored glasses 2 daydream, swoon, gush, dream, rhapsodize

Romeo *n* Don Juan, Casanova, seducer, wolf, womanizer

romp *v* 1 cavort, frolic, horse around, caper, prance 2 sail, steam, coast, cruise, whiz *Opposite*: struggle 3 *(infml)* win, coast, excel yourself, surpass yourself *Opposite*: lose ■ *n* 1 frolic, frisk, gambol, run, scramble 2 *(infml)* page-turner, thriller, chiller, potboiler *Opposite*: bore 3 *(infml)* foregone conclusion, one-horse race, piece of cake *(infml)*, cinch *(infml)*, walkover *(infml)*

roofed *adj* covered, enclosed, vaulted, topped *Opposite*: open

roofing *n* tiling, slating, tiles, slates, shingles

rooftop *n* roof, top, tiles, slates, gable

rookie *(infml) n* beginner, novice, recruit, trainee, learner *Opposite*: old hand

room *n* 1 space, extent, span, capacity, volume 2 compartment, apartment *(fml)*, chamber *(literary)* 3 scope, opportunity, possibility, occasion, chance

WORD BANK

❑ **types of rooms in public buildings** antechamber, anteroom, ballroom, banquet hall, boardroom, bunkhouse, cell, classroom, dining hall, dormitory, dressing room, entrance hall, foyer, gallery, games room, hall, lavatory, library, lobby, lounge, meeting room, men's room, office, operating room, powder room, reception room, refectory, restroom, schoolroom, stateroom, vault, waiting room, ward, washroom

❑ **types of rooms in the home** atelier, attic, bathroom, bedchamber *(literary)*, bedroom, boudoir, closet, day room, den, dining room, drawing room, family room, garret, great room, guestroom, kitchen, kitchenette, laundry room, living room, loft, parlor, playroom, rec room, recreation room, salon, scullery, sitting room, sleeping quarters, spare room, study, sunroom, toilet, utility room

roomer *n* **lodger**, tenant, boarder, renter, resident *Opposite*: landlord

roomie *(infml) see* **roommate**

roominess *n* **spaciousness**, largeness, capaciousness, generousness, sizableness *Opposite*: smallness

roommate *n* **cotenant**, housemate, lodger, buddy *(infml)*, roomie *(infml)*

rooms *n* **housing**, accommodations, quarters, place, lodgings *(dated)*

roomy *adj* **spacious**, large, generous, sizable, capacious *Opposite*: cramped

roost *v* **settle**, rest, stay, perch, sleep

root *n* **1** stem, rhizome, tuber, radicle, radix **2** origin, cause, source, basis, starting place ■ *v* **1** dig, grub, forage, delve. burrow **2** search, delve, rifle, burrow, rummage **3** cheer, shout, applaud, yell, clap *Opposite*: jeer. *See* COMPARE AND CONTRAST *at* **origin**.

rooted *adj* **entrenched**, ingrained, fixed, deep-rooted, deep-seated

rootless *adj* **drifting**, freewheeling, roving, nomadic, itinerant *Opposite*: rooted

root out *v* **1** eradicate, remove, get rid of, do away with, eliminate **2** find, discover, locate, turn up, unearth *Opposite*: hide

roots *n* **origins**, ancestry, background, heritage, pedigree

rope *n* **cord**, line, cable, lead, twine ■ *v* tie, fasten, lash, secure, attach *Opposite*: untie

rose *n* **1** design, rosette, ornament, representation, emblem **2** sprinkler, jet, nozzle, spray, attachment **3** ceiling rose, fitting, boss, connector, socket

roseate *adj* **reddish**, rose, fuchsia, magenta, rose-colored

rosebud *n* **bud**, bloom, rose, flower, blossom

rose-colored *adj* **idealistic**, optimistic, hopeful, romantic, sentimental *Opposite*: pessimistic

rosette *n* **1** badge, decoration, prize **2** ornament, design, rose, shape, representation

rosiness *n* **blush**, flush, pinkness, redness, glow

roster *n* **list**, schedule, roll, register

rostrum *n* **platform**, podium, stage, dais, stand

rosy *adj* **1** pink, rose-colored, reddish, pinkish, rose **2** blushing, flushed, glowing, healthy, ruddy *Opposite*: pale **3** promising, auspicious, successful, happy, favorable *Opposite*: unpromising **4** optimistic, idealistic, unrealistic, hopeful, encouraging *Opposite*: pessimistic

rot *v* **decompose**, decay, putrefy, disintegrate, break down ■ *n* **1** *(infml)* nonsense, balderdash, rubbish, garbage, twaddle *(infml)*

Opposite: sense **2** decay, deterioration, putrefaction, decomposition, corrosion

rotary *adj* **rotating**, turning, revolving, rotational, gyratory

rotate *v* **1** turn, revolve, go, spin, swivel **2** alternate, take turns, interchange, switch, swap *(infml)* **3** replace, switch, alternate, exchange, swap *(infml)*

rotation *n* **1** revolution, turning, spin, gyration **2** switching, replacement, cycle, sequence **3** alternation, variation, interchange

rote *n* **repetition**, memorization, routine, habit, rotation

rotisserie *n* **spit**, skewer, brochette, grill, barbecue

rotor *n* **blade**, propeller, airfoil

rotten *adj* **1** decayed, putrid, bad, decomposed moldy *Opposite*: fresh **2** *(infml)* awful, bad, nasty, terrible, unpleasant *Opposite*: pleasant **3** *(infml)* inferior, poor, bad, dreadful, incompetent *Opposite*: good **4** *(infml)* unhappy, uncomfortable, guilty, embarrassed, bad *Opposite*: happy **5** *(infml)* unwell, ill, sick, seedy *(infml)* *Opposite*: healthy *(infml.* **6** unfair, unethical, immoral, unprincipled, dishonest *Opposite*: just ■ *adv* *(infml)* terribly, unduly, excessively, overly, outrageously *Opposite*: slightly

rottenness *n* **1** decay, moldiness, dry rot, wet rot, badness *Opposite*: freshness **2** *(infml)* unpleasantness, awfulness, dreadfulness, hideousness, ghastliness *Opposite*: pleasantness **3** *(infml)* beastliness, nastiness, cruelness, cruelty, horridness *Opposite*: goodness

rotter *(dated infml)* *n* **scoundrel**, liar, swindler, cheat, cad *(dated)* *Opposite*: angel

rotting *adj* **decomposing**, decaying, putrid, bad, contaminated *Opposite*: fresh

rotund *adj* **overweight**, stout, fat, plump, corpulent *Opposite*: slender

rotunda *n* **pavilion**, tower, dome, cupola

rotundity *n* **roundness**, sphericalness, rotundness, overweight, stoutness *Opposite*: slenderness

rouge *(dated)* *n* **lipstick**, blush, makeup, face paint, coloring ■ *v* make up, redden, color, highlight paint

rough *adj* **1** uneven, bumpy, irregular, jagged, lumpy *Opposite*: even **2** coarse, shaggy, hairy, bristly, bushy *Opposite*: smooth **3** turbulent, stormy, tempestuous, squally, wild *Opposite*: calm **4** rugged, wild, uncultivated, rocky, hilly *Opposite*: cultivated **5** violent, forceful, tough, physical, forcible *Opposite*: gentle **6** boorish, unrefined, rough-and-ready, coarse, crude *Opposite*: refined **7** harsh, grating, jarring, discordant, rasping *Opposite*: melodious **8** approximate, sketchy, vague, estimated, imprecise *Opposite*: exact **9** difficult, trying, challenging, unpleasant, uncomfortable

Opposite: easy **10 rowdy**, boisterous, noisy, violent, tough *Opposite:* quiet ■ *n* **outline**, sketch, summary, draft, mock-up

roughage *n* **fiber**, bulk, cellulose, bran

rough-and-ready *adj* **1 crude**, simple, basic, primitive, serviceable *Opposite:* sophisticated **2 down-to-earth**, unpretentious, honest, rough-hewn, decent *Opposite:* refined

rough-and-tumble *n* **hurly-burly**, cut and thrust, infighting, sparring, fracas

roughcast *n* **coating**, cladding, facing, plasterwork, rendering

rough copy *n* **outline**, sketch, summary, draft, rough

roughen *v* **coarsen**, toughen, scratch, abrade, rough *Opposite:* soften

rough-hewn *adj* **1 rough**, unfinished, undressed, incomplete **2 crude**, basic, primitive, simple, rough *Opposite:* polished **3 rugged**, rough, unrefined, coarse, crude

roughhouse *(infml)* *n* **rowdiness**, boisterousness, rough-and-tumble, horseplay, roughness

roughneck *(infml)* *n* **thug**, hoodlum, rowdy, hooligan *(infml)*, ruffian *(dated)*

roughness *n* **1 unevenness**, coarseness, bumpiness, irregularity, jaggedness *Opposite:* smoothness **2 coarseness**, shagginess, hairiness, bristliness, bushiness *Opposite:* smoothness **3 turbulence**, storminess, tempestuousness, wildness *Opposite:* calmness **4 ruggedness**, wildness, rockiness, hilliness, cragginess *Opposite:* gentleness **5 violence**, force, toughness, power, brutality *Opposite:* gentleness **6 brusqueness**, rudeness, gruffness, harshness, coarseness *Opposite:* refinement **7 harshness**, discordance, astringency, gruffness, raucousness *Opposite:* smoothness **8 vagueness**, sketchiness, ambiguity, inexactness, haziness *Opposite:* exactness **9 rowdiness**, boisterousness, noisiness, violence, toughness *Opposite:* quietness

rough out *v* **draft**, outline, prepare, sketch, block out *Opposite:* finalize

rough up *(infml)* *v* **maltreat**, mistreat, abuse, batter, manhandle *Opposite:* take care of

round *n* **circle**, disk, slice, ring, band ■ *v* **turn**, circumnavigate, negotiate, skirt, pass ■ *prep* **surrounding**, around, about, encircling, encompassing ■ *adv* **around**, about, near, on all sides

round about *prep* **around**, about, circa, say, in the neighborhood of

roundabout *n* **merry-go-round**, carousel, ride, attraction ■ *adj* **indirect**, oblique, circuitous, winding, meandering *Opposite:* direct

rounded *adj* **curved**, smoothed, smooth-edged, round, curvy *Opposite:* pointed

round-eyed *adj* **open-mouthed**, amazed, gaping, staring, fascinated

roundly *adv* **severely**, forcefully, completely, utterly, bluntly

roundness *n* **roundedness**, plumpness, chubbiness *Opposite:* slenderness

round-shouldered *adj* **stooping**, hunched, slouching, bent, bent over *Opposite:* erect

roundtable *n* **discussion**, negotiation, debate, forum, meeting

round-the-clock *adj* **24-hour**, day-and-night, 24/7, continuous, constant

round trip *n* **both ways**, circuit, tour

round up *v* **capture**, gather together, collect, arrest, amass *Opposite:* disperse

roundup *n* **1 assembly**, capture, hunt, herding, rodeo *Opposite:* release **2 summary**, rundown, review, summing up, recap

rouse *v* **1 stir**, wake up, revive, awaken, disturb *Opposite:* lull **2 stir up**, provoke, incite, move, galvanize *Opposite:* lull

rousing *adj* **stirring**, inspiring, moving, exciting, stimulating *Opposite:* soothing

rout *n* **1 retreat**, flight, stampede, surrender, collapse *Opposite:* advance **2 defeat**, massacre, landslide, thrashing, beating *Opposite:* victory **3 tumult**, disorder, riot, disturbance, hubbub ■ *v* **beat back**, overpower, overwhelm, beat, defeat *Opposite:* retreat

route *n* **1 road**, path, way, track, itinerary **2 course**, means, method, way, direction ■ *v* **direct**, send, transmit, move, channel

routine *n* **1 procedure**, practice, habit, custom, sequence **2 tedium**, monotony, mundaneness, dullness, dreariness *Opposite:* variety ■ *adj* **1 usual**, standard, everyday, normal, customary *Opposite:* unusual **2 monotonous**, dull, tedious, repetitive, humdrum *Opposite:* exciting. *See* COMPARE AND CONTRAST *at* habit.

rove *v* **wander**, roam, range, meander, travel

rover *n* **wanderer**, traveler, rolling stone, nomad, drifter

roving *adj* **1 roaming**, traveling, wandering, rambling, nomadic *Opposite:* stationary **2 erratic**, wandering, fickle, capricious, inconsistent *Opposite:* steady

row *n* **1 line**, chain, string, file, rank **2 disagreement**, dispute, quarrel, controversy, argument *Opposite:* agreement **3 noise**, racket, ruckus, rumpus, din *Opposite:* lull ■ *v* **1 paddle**, scull, punt take the oars, propel **2 fight**, quarrel, have a row, disagree, argue *Opposite:* agree

rowdiness *n* **disorderliness**, unruliness, noisiness, loudness, raucousness *Opposite:* restraint

rowdy *adj* **disorderly**, unruly, noisy, loud, raucous *Opposite:* restrained

rower *n* **oarsperson**, sculler, coxswain, cox

row house *n* **row home**, terrace, town house

royal *adj* **1 regal**, imperial, majestic, stately, noble **2 magnificent**, splendid, noble, excellent, grand *Opposite:* ordinary

royalist *n* **monarchist**, traditionalist, constitutionalist, conservative, loyal subject *Opposite*: republican

royals *n* **royalty**, crowned heads, monarchs, sovereigns, royal family

royalty *n* **1 royals**, crowned heads, monarchs, sovereigns, royal family **2 fee**, payment, percentage, credit, token

R.P. *n* **Received Pronunciation**, BBC English, the Queen's English, Standard English

RSI *n* **repetitive strain injury**, tenosynovitis, carpal tunnel syndrome, industrial injury, work-related injury

R.S.V.P. *n* **reply**, acknowledgment, answer, response ■ *v* **answer**, reply, acknowledge, respond

rub *v* **1 massage**, stroke, caress, knead, pat **2 polish**, wipe, buff, shine, clean **3 chafe**, hurt, gall, irritate, scrape *Opposite*: soothe

rubber *n* **foam rubber**, neoprene, gum, elastic, latex

rubberneck *(infml)* *v* **stare**, gaze, gape, goggle, ogle. *See* COMPARE AND CONTRAST *at* **gaze**.

rubbernecking *(infml)* *n* **staring**, gazing, gaping, ogling, gawking *(infml)*

rubber stamp *n* **stamping device**, stamp, seal, stamper, signet

rubber-stamp *v* **approve**, authorize, sanction, pass, let through *Opposite*: veto

rubbery *adj* **tough**, elastic, chewy, hard, overcooked *Opposite*: tender

rubbing *n* **1 impression**, brass rubbing, copy, reproduction, relief **2 friction**, scraping, abrasion, resistance, chafing **3 soreness**, chafing, irritation, blistering, saddle sores

rubbish *n* **1 refuse**, debris, litter, waste, garbage **2 nonsense**, drivel, garbage, claptrap *(infml)*, hogwash *(infml)*

rubbishy *adj* **inferior**, poor quality, poor, bad *Opposite*: quality

rubble *n* **debris**, ruins, wreckage, remains, bricks

rub down *v* **1 dry**, rub, dry off, towel dry, towel **2 massage**, rub, go over, oil, stroke **3 finish**, wipe down, sand, scour, prepare

rubicund *(literary)* *adj* **red**, rosy, ruddy, redfaced, flushed *Opposite*: pale

rub out *v* **erase**, delete, wipe, expunge, efface

rubric *n* **1 title**, heading, header, head, introduction **2 rules**, instructions, guidelines, directions, rulebook **3 custom**, tradition, practice, system, convention **4 class**, category, classification, division, type

rub the wrong way *v* **irritate**, annoy, make somebody's hackles rise, get on the wrong side of somebody, offend

ruched *adj* **pleated**, gathered, frilled, frilly, edged *Opposite*: plain

ruck *n* **1 mass**, pile, heap, accumulation, conglomeration **2 crease**, wrinkle, fold, crumple, rumple ■ *v* **wrinkle**, crease, fold,

crumple, gather *Opposite*: smooth

rucksack *n* **backpack**, haversack, knapsack, frame rucksack, daypack

ruckus *n* **commotion**, disturbance, rumpus, riot, uproar

ruction *n* **quarrel**, fight, dispute, disturbance, row

ructions *n* **rumpus**, fuss, uproar, dispute, controversy

ruddiness *n* **redness**, rosiness, glow, blush, flush *Opposite*: pallor

ruddy *adj* **reddish**, rosy, flushed, glowing, healthy-looking *Opposite*: pale

rude *adj* **1 impolite**, discourteous, insolent, bad-mannered, ill-mannered *Opposite*: polite **2 foul**, crude, offensive, vulgar, foul-mouthed *Opposite*: polite

rudeness *n* **impoliteness**, insolence, discourtesy, offensiveness, vulgarity *Opposite*: politeness

rudimentary *adj* **basic**, elementary, simple, fundamental, primary *Opposite*: advanced

rudiments *n* **basics**, essentials, fundamentals, principles, beginnings

rue *v* **regret**, lament, repent, deplore, feel sorry about

rueful *adj* **regretful**, remorseful, apologetic, repentant, contrite *Opposite*: cheerful

ruffian *(dated)* *n* **thug**, tough guy, gangster, hooligan *(infml)*, hood *(slang)*

ruffle *v* **1 disturb**, tousle, rumple, upset, dishevel *Opposite*: smooth **2 perturb**, upset, annoy, disrupt, distress *Opposite*: calm

rug *n* **1 carpet**, mat, hearth rug, sheepskin, runner **2** *(infml)* **wig**, toupee, hairpiece, periwig **3 blanket**, car rug, throw, cover, bedspread

rugged *adj* **1 rocky**, rough, craggy, uneven, jagged *Opposite*: rolling **2 strong-featured**, craggy, weathered, furrowed, rough **3 strong**, hardy, tough, robust, resilient *Opposite*: weak **4 testing**, demanding, difficult, harsh, tough *Opposite*: easy **5 well-built**, sturdy, tough, robust, strong *Opposite*: flimsy

ruggedness *n* **1 roughness**, rockiness, harshness, jaggedness, cragginess *Opposite*: smoothness **2 strong features**, cragginess, handsomeness, manliness, masculinity *Opposite*: roundness **3 toughness**, resilience, stamina, endurance, strength *Opposite*: weakness **4 unforgiving nature**, difficulty, harshness, toughness, severity *Opposite*: gentleness **5 resilience**, sturdiness, toughness, robustness, strength *Opposite*: flimsiness

rug rat *(infml)* *n* **child**, infant, toddler

ruin *n* **1 remains**, wreck, debris, wreckage, shell **2 devastation**, shambles, decay, destruction, collapse *Opposite*: regeneration **3 decline**, downfall, defeat, fall, disaster *Opposite*: improvement ■

v **damage**, wreck, spoil, destroy, devastate *Opposite*: mend

ruination *n* 1 **undoing**, downfall, ruin, curse, destruction *Opposite*: making 2 **destruction**, loss, ruin, calamity, devastation *Opposite*: salvation

ruined *adj* 1 **bankrupt**, insolvent, out of business, broke *(infml)*, cleaned out *(infml) Opposite*: solvent 2 **tumbledown**, crumbling, derelict, abandoned, uninhabited *Opposite*: renovated

ruinous *adj* **disastrous**, damaging, harmful, devastating, catastrophic *Opposite*: advantageous

rule *n* 1 **instruction**, law, regulation, decree, statute 2 **regime**, power, control, leadership, reign ■ *v* **govern**, reign, run, administrate, have power over *Opposite*: follow

rulebook *n* **manual**, rules, instructions, directory, rubric

rule out *v* 1 **exclude**, dismiss, reject, discount, discard *Opposite*: consider 2 **prevent**, exclude, ban, prohibit, forbid *Opposite*: facilitate

ruler *n* **monarch**, sovereign, leader, head of state, potentate *Opposite*: subject

---

WORD BANK

❏ **types of rulers** chief, chieftain, emir, emperor, empress, governor, head of state, king, maharajah, maharani, Pharoah, president, queen, rajah, rani, regent, sultan, tsar, tsarina, tsaritsa

---

rule the roost *v* **be in control**, be in charge, reign supreme, hold sway, be in the driver's seat

ruling *n* **decision**, verdict, edict, judgment, declaration ■ *adj* **presiding**, reigning, governing, dominant, sovereign *Opposite*: subordinate

ruling body *n* **council**, administration, government, assembly, legislative body

rumble *v* **grumble**, thunder, crash, growl, roll

rumbling *(infml)* *n* **indication**, early sign, beginning, warning sign, rumor

rumbustious *adj* **boisterous**, exuberant, swashbuckling, swaggering, rambunctious *Opposite*: reticent

ruminate *v* 1 **ponder**, think over, reflect, chew over, meditate 2 **chew**, graze, browse, crop, pasture

rumination *n* 1 **reflection**, pondering, contemplation, musing, thought 2 **chewing**, grazing, browsing, chewing the cud

ruminative *adj* **thoughtful**, pensive, reflective, contemplative, speculative *Opposite*: blithe

rummage *v* **search**, look through, grope, fumble, poke around

rummage sale *n* **sale**, yard sale, garage sale, tag sale

rumor *n* 1 **claim**, report, unconfirmed report, belief, allegation *Opposite*: fact 2 **specu-**

lation, opinion, gossip, talk, tittle-tattle ■ *v* **say**, believe, allege, claim, speculate *Opposite*: confirm

rumored *adj* **supposed**, thought, whispered, alleged, held *Opposite*: true

rumor mill *n* **grapevine**, network, newsmongers, gossips, tattlers

rumormonger *n* **gossip**, tattletale, scandalmonger, gossipmonger, telltale

rump *n* **hindquarters**, back end, rear, buttocks, rear end

rumple *v* **wrinkle**, crumple, crease, crinkle, pucker *Opposite*: tidy

rumpled *adj* **crumpled**, creased, untidy, messy, bedraggled *Opposite*: tidy

rumpus *n* **disturbance**, commotion, furor, brouhaha, fuss

run *v* 1 **sprint**, jog, lope, scuttle, scamper 2 **flow**, stream, trickle, course, pour out 3 **proceed**, happen, go, progress, move along 4 **manage**, administer, govern, administrate, lead 5 **operate**, function, process 6 **move**, pass, cast, throw 7 **continue**, extend, reach, stretch, go 8 **compete**, enter, participate, take part, contend ■ *n* 1 **course**, track, route, lane, path 2 **sequence**, series, chain, string, list 3 **enclosure**, pen, cage, coop, paddock 4 **outing**, trip, ride, excursion, visit 5 **sprint**, race, lope, dart, dash

runabout *n* **wanderer**, rover, rolling stone, nomad, traveler

run after *v* **pursue**, chase, go after, follow, hound

run along *v* **go away**, go, leave, depart, take leave *Opposite*: stay

run amok *v* **go berserk**, be in a frenzy, run riot, go on the rampage, rampage

run a risk *v* **take a risk**, play a dangerous game, sail close to the wind, court disaster, play Russian roulette

run around *v* **associate**, spend time, keep company, hang out *(infml)*, hang *(slang)*

run away *v* **escape**, flee, run off, abscond, elope

runaway *n* **escapee**, absentee, absconder, fugitive ■ *adj* *(infml)* **bestselling**, blockbusting, hit, roaring, huge

runaway success *n* **big hit**, smash, smash hit, blockbuster *(infml)*, barnburner *(infml)*

run by *v* **explain**, describe, tell, impart, acquaint

run down *v* 1 **belittle**, criticize, knock, disparage, put down *Opposite*: praise 2 **bring to an end**, close down, wind up, shut down, peter out *Opposite*: start

rundown *n* **background**, details, information, lowdown *(infml)*, info *(infml)*

run-down *adj* 1 **dilapidated**, ramshackle, shabby, neglected, derelict *Opposite*: well-kept 2 **exhausted**, tired, weak, wearied, worn-out *Opposite*: energetic 3 **under the weather**, worn out, tired, weary, washed out *Opposite*: well

rune n **character**, letter, symbol, sign, hieroglyph

rung n **step**, stair, tread, stage

run-in (infml) n **argument**, confrontation, quarrel, clash, disagreement

run into v 1 **come across**, bump into, meet by chance, encounter 2 **hit**, bump into, crash into, collide with, run over Opposite: miss

runner n 1 **sprinter**, jogger, racer, contender, competitor 2 **messenger**, courier, gofer (infml) 3 **candidate**, contender, entrant, participant, competitor

runner-up n **second place**, person in second place, silver medalist, second to finish, next best person

running n **management**, administration, organization, operation, controlling ■ adv **in a row**, consecutively, successively, in succession, seriatim

runny adj **liquid**, fluid, gooey, soft, thin Opposite: set

run off v **flee**, escape, run away, decamp

run-of-the-mill adj **mediocre**, ordinary, middling, average, undistinguished Opposite: extraordinary

run on v **go on**, carry on, continue, keep going Opposite: stop

run out v **end**, expire, come to an end, finish

run over v 1 **crush**, hit, squash, flatten, collide with 2 **explain**, summarize, go over, run through, cover

run rings around v **outshine**, beat, outdo, outstrip, outperform

run riot v **run amok**, go on the rampage, riot, go berserk, rampage

runt n **smallest**, weakest, littlest

run the gauntlet v **undergo**, experience, face, suffer, endure

run through v 1 **use up**, exhaust, eat through, go through, deplete Opposite: conserve 2 **review**, go over, examine, consider, look over 3 **pervade**, spread through, underlie, permeate 4 **rehearse**, practice, try out, go through 5 **infect**, contaminate, pollute 6 (literary) **spear**, impale, stab, jab

run-through n 1 **rehearsal**, practice, dry run, test run, test 2 **review**, survey, summary, overview, résumé

run up v 1 **accumulate**, amass, collect, incur, build up Opposite: discharge 2 **sew**, create, make, put together

run-up n **approach**, advance, run

runway n **landing strip**, airstrip, landing field, taxiway, flight strip

rupture n 1 **break**, crack, tear, split, fissure 2 **disagreement**, falling-out, split, breakup, separation ■ v **break**, crack, burst, come apart, rip apart

rural adj **country**, rustic, pastoral, bucolic, countryside Opposite: urban

ruse n **trick**, dodge, subterfuge, wile, con

rush v 1 **run**, hurry, dash, sprint, flash Opposite: dawdle 2 **hurry**, precipitate, hasten, dash, bolt ■ n 1 **haste**, hurry, urgency, flash 2 **blast**, current, gale, gust, blow

rushed adj **hurried**, quick, swift, hasty Opposite: leisurely

rushes n **unedited prints**, dailies, first prints, raw footage, footage

rust n **corrosion**, oxidation, erosion, corruption, decomposition ■ v **corrode**, oxidize, tarnish, erode, decompose

rustic adj **rural**, country, pastoral, bucolic, countryside Opposite: urban

rustle v **crunch**, crackle, whisper, swish

rustler n **thief**, poacher, robber, horse thief, cattle thief

rustle up (infml) v **prepare**, concoct, put together, make, produce

rustproof adj **nonrusting**, rust-free, rustproofed, stainless-steel, corrosion-proof ■ v **seal**, make rustproof, waterproof, coat, paint

rusty adj 1 **corroded**, oxidized, tarnished, eroded 2 **out of practice**, unpracticed, unaccustomed, off form, out of shape

rut n **furrow**, groove, channel, runnel, pothole

ruthless adj **cruel**, callous, brutal, pitiless, merciless Opposite: merciful

ruthlessness n **callousness**, cruelty, mercilessness, brutality, heartlessness Opposite: mercy

rutted adj **uneven**, furrowed, potholed, bumpy Opposite: smooth

RV n **recreational vehicle**, camper, motor home, mobile home, trailer

S

sabbatical n **study leave**, leave, time off, retreat, time out

saber rattling n **display of force**, bravado, empty threats, bluffing, aggression

sabotage n **disruption**, damage, vandalism, interference, interruption ■ v **disrupt**, damage, vandalize, interfere with, interrupt

saboteur n **vandal**, terrorist, ecowarrior, computer hacker, hunt saboteur

sac n **bag**, sack, pouch, case, pod

saccharine adj 1 **sugary**, sickly, sweet, syrupy, treacly Opposite: sour 2 **sentimental**, slushy, gushy, mawkish, cloying Opposite: unsentimental

sacerdotal *adj* **priestly**, clerical, ecclesiastic, religious, spiritual

sachet *n* **envelope**, packet, pouch

sack *n* **1 bag**, brown bag, gunnysack, carryall, pouch **2** *(infml)* **dismissal**, termination, layoff, pink slip, discharge ■ *v* **1** *(infml)* **dismiss**, give somebody notice, throw out, terminate, lay off *Opposite*: employ **2 ransack**, plunder, destroy, pillage, tear apart

sacking *(infml)* *n* **dismissal**, discharge, job loss, notice, layoff

sacrament *n* **rite**, ceremony, ritual, service, mass

sacred *adj* **holy**, blessed, consecrated, hallowed, revered *Opposite*: secular

sacrifice *n* **price**, toll, cost, loss, expense ■ *v* **give up**, forgo, forfeit, let go, surrender

sacrilege *n* **blasphemy**, desecration, profanity, irreverence, violation *Opposite*: reverence

sacrilegious *adj* **blasphemous**, irreverent, heretical, impious, disrespectful *Opposite*: pious

sacrosanct *adj* **1 sacred**, revered, holy, sanctified **2 inviolable**, untouchable, off limits, protected

sad *adj* **1 unhappy**, miserable, depressed, gloomy, low *Opposite*: happy **2 depressing**, gloomy, miserable, cheerless, distressing *Opposite*: cheerful

sadden *v* **depress**, distress, upset, dismay, pain *Opposite*: cheer

saddlebag *n* **basket**, bag, pannier, carrier

saddle with *v* **burden**, encumber, weigh down, land, load

sadistic *adj* **cruel**, nasty, callous, heartless, vicious *Opposite*: kind

sadly *adv* **1 unhappily**, miserably, gloomily, wretchedly, dejectedly *Opposite*: happily **2 unfortunately**, unluckily, regrettably, alas *Opposite*: luckily

sadness *n* **unhappiness**, misery, depression, dejection, despondency *Opposite*: happiness

safari *n* **trek**, expedition, trip, search, quest

safe *adj* **1 harmless**, benign, innocuous, innocent, nonviolent *Opposite*: dangerous **2 secure**, protected, sheltered, in safe hands, out of harm's way *Opposite*: unsafe **3 unharmed**, undamaged, uninjured, unhurt, unscathed **4 reliable**, dependable, trustworthy, careful, cautious *Opposite*: unsafe ■ *n* **strongbox**, lockbox, safe-deposit box, vault

safeguard *n* **protection**, precaution, defense, safety measure, safety device *Opposite*: hazard ■ *v* **defend**, protect, preserve, guard, shield *Opposite*: endanger

COMPARE AND CONTRAST CORE MEANING: keep safe from actual or potential damage or attack **safeguard** take steps to prevent somebody or

something from being harmed or damaged; **protect** keep somebody or something from any kind of harm or damage; **defend** deter an actual or threatened attack; **guard** work to prevent damage, loss, or attack by being vigilant and taking defensive measures; **shield** prevent harm, damage, or attack by using a physical barrier or by intervening in a protective way.

safeguarding *n* **protection**, preservation, conservation, maintenance, upkeep *Opposite*: destruction

safe haven *n* **refuge**, asylum, haven, sanctuary

safe house *n* **hideout**, hideaway, retreat, refuge, hidey-hole *(infml)*

safekeeping *n* **protection**, care, security, custody, charge

safe place *n* **refuge**, safe haven, hideaway, haven, sanctuary

safety *n* **care**, security, protection, shelter, well-being *Opposite*: danger

safety belt *n* **seat belt**, strap, restraint, harness, safety harness

safety net *n* **safety device**, safeguard, fail-safe, guard, shield

safety valve *n* **1 fail-safe**, valve, safety device, safety precaution, overflow **2 release**, channel, outlet

sag *v* **droop**, wilt, slump, flag, drop ■ *n* **drop**, slump, dip, fall, depression

saga *n* **epic**, account, chronicle, tale, legend

sagacious *adj* **wise**, knowledgeable, learned, erudite, perceptive *Opposite*: foolish

sagaciousness *(fml)* *see* **sagacity**

sagacity *n* **wisdom**, knowledge, erudition, perceptiveness, intelligence *Opposite*: stupidity

sage *(literary)* *n* **adviser**, mentor, elder, savant, statesman ■ *adj* **learned**, erudite, perceptive, intelligent, astute

sagging *adj* **drooping**, wilting, flaccid, floppy, slumped

saggy *see* **sagging**

said *adj* **1 alleged**, supposed, assumed **2 previously mentioned**, above, aforesaid *(fml)*, aforementioned *(fml)*

sail *v* **1 set sail**, navigate, cruise, voyage, put out to sea **2 glide**, float, flow, drift, fly

sailing *n* **boating**, cruising, yachting, navigation

sailor *n* **seafarer**, mariner, navigator, deckhand, salt *(infml)*

sail through *v* **do well**, do with ease, pass with flying colors, breeze through, ace *(slang)* *Opposite*: fail

saintliness *n* **virtue**, goodness, piety, holiness, devoutness *Opposite*: evil

saintly *adj* **virtuous**, good, holy, pious, devout *Opposite*: evil

salaam *n* **greeting**, salutation, bow, nod, acknowledgment ■ v **greet**, bow, salute, nod, acknowledge

salacious adj **risqué**, indecent, crude, improper, obscene

salad days (dated) n **youth**, prime, heyday

salaried adj **remunerated**, on the payroll, on the books, paid, compensated

salary n **income**, pay, wage payment, remuneration. See COMPARE AND CONTRAST at **wage**.

sale n 1 **transaction**, deal, selling, retailing, vending Opposite: purchase 2 **auction**, clearance sale, rummage sale, garage sale, tag sale

sales assistant n **salesperson**, cashier, floorwalker, salesclerk

salesclerk see **sales assistant**

salesperson n 1 **rep**, seller, trader, marketer, peddler 2 **sales assistant**, salesclerk, cashier, floorwalker

sales representative n **salesperson**, rep, seller, trader, marketer

salient adj **noticeable**, striking, prominent, outstanding, relevant Opposite: minor

saline adj **salty**, salt, brackish, briny, salted

saliva n **spittle**, spit, drool, dribble, slobber

salivate v **drool**, dribble, slobber, slaver

sallow adj **yellow**, sickly, wan, washed-out, ashen

sally n 1 **attack**, sortie, breakout, breakthrough, raid 2 **rush**, charge, dash, push ■ v 1 **attack**, charge, raid, strike 2 **go forth**, go out, venture forth, venture out, set out Opposite: retreat

salon n 1 **soiree**, gathering, rendezvous, meeting, group 2 **beauty parlor**, beauty salon, hair salon, hairdresser's, barbershop

salt-and-pepper adj **flecked**, streaked, grizzled, graying, patchy

salt away v **hoard**, save, squirrel away, put by, set aside Opposite: fritter away

salt water n **brine**, sea water, saline

salty adj **salt**, saline, brackish, salted, briny Opposite: sweet

salubrious (fml) adj **healthy**, wholesome, respectable, decent, hygienic Opposite: insalubrious (fml)

salutary adj **beneficial**, helpful, useful, valuable, constructive

salutation n **greeting**, acknowledgment, welcome, gesture, salute

salute v **acknowledge**, greet, welcome, gesture, wave ■ n **sign of respect**, salutation, greeting, acknowledgment, signal

salvage v **save**, recover, rescue, retrieve, reclaim

salvation n **redemption**, rescue, recovery, escape, deliverance (fml) Opposite: ruination

salve n **lotion**, ointment, balm, balsam, liniment Opposite: irritant ■ v **appease**, soothe, comfort, mollify, calm Opposite: irritate

salver n **tray**, platter, plate, serving dish, dish

salvo n **barrage**, bombardment, round, torrent, hail

same adj 1 **identical**, alike, matching, similar, equal Opposite: different 2 **unchanged**, constant, consistent, uniform, even Opposite: changed

sameness n 1 **similarity**, likeness, resemblance, uniformity, equivalence Opposite: difference 2 **monotony**, repetitiveness, uniformity, consistency, evenness Opposite: variety

samovar n **tea urn**, urn, teapot, jug, kettle

sample n **example**, model, trial, illustration, mock-up ■ v **test**, try, appraise, try out, check out

sampler n 1 **technician**, tester, analyst, quality control analyst, laboratory technician 2 **selection**, sample, cross section, sampling, representative selection 3 **sample**, tryout, example, taste, illustration 4 **embroidery**, sewing, needlework, handwork

sampling n **sample**, specimen, cross section, selection, test group

sanatorium n **clinic**, hospital, infirmary, hospice, spa

sanctified adj **sacred**, holy, blessed, consecrated, hallowed Opposite: desecrated

sanctify v **bless**, consecrate, hallow, dedicate, purify Opposite: desecrate

sanctimonious adj **self-righteous**, smug, pious, pompous, self-satisfied Opposite: humble

sanctimoniousness n **self-righteousness**, smugness, pomposity, superiority

sanction n 1 **authorization**, permission, approval, agreement, consent Opposite: prohibition 2 **support**, approval, encouragement, agreement, affirmation 3 **restriction**, penalty, ban, punishment, injunction ■ v **authorize**, permit, approve, allow, pass Opposite: veto

sanctity n **holiness**, blessedness, sacredness, inviolability, purity Opposite: profanity

sanctuary n 1 **refuge**, asylum, shelter, safe haven, haven 2 **reserve**, reservation, national park, nature reserve, preserve 3 **safety**, protection, refuge, asylum, shelter

sanctum n 1 **holy of holies**, sanctum sanctorum, temple, altar, shrine 2 **retreat**, den, refuge, study, hideaway

sand n 1 **shingle**, grit, gravel, powder, silt 2 **beach**, strand, dune, shore, shoreline ■ v **rub down**, smooth, sandpaper, polish, rub

sandbank n **sandbar**, dune, mound, bank, hummock

sandbar n **sandbank**, ridge, shallows, shoal

sandpaper v **rub down**, smooth, sand, polish, rub

sandwich v **squeeze in**, squash in, pack in, cram, slot in

WORD BANK

❏ **types of sandwich** club sandwich, double-decker, hero, hoagie, open sandwich, panini, Reuben, sub *(infml)*, submarine, torpedo, wrap

sane *adj* **1 well-balanced**, compos mentis, rational, stable, healthy *Opposite*: insane **2 sensible**, reasonable, rational, sound, wise *Opposite*: irrational

saneness *see* sanity

sang-froid *n* **self-possession**, calmness, poise, aplomb, self-assurance *Opposite*: anxiety

sanguinary *(fml) adj* **1 bloody**, gory, brutal, grim, gruesome **2 bloodthirsty**, murderous, ruthless, savage, cruel

sanguine *adj* **confident**, optimistic, cheerful, hopeful, positive *Opposite*: pessimistic

sanitarium *n* **clinic**, rest home, convalescent home, hospital, infirmary

sanitary *adj* **hygienic**, clean, healthy, wholesome, sterile *Opposite*: insanitary

sanitation *n* **hygiene**, cleanliness, cleanness, public health, health

sanitize *v* **1 purify**, fumigate, disinfect, clean, cleanse *Opposite*: contaminate **2 censor**, clean up, bowdlerize, water down

sanity *n* **1 rationality**, lucidity, reason, stability, saneness *Opposite*: insanity **2 reasonableness**, sense, rationality, soundness, wisdom *Opposite*: unreasonableness

sans *(literary) prep* **without**, lacking, missing, wanting, less

sap *n* **1 juice**, fluid, liquid, latex **2 energy**, vitality, health, strength, life ■ *v* **1 dig down**, burrow, bore, tunnel, mine **2 weaken**, drain, undermine, deplete, eat away *Opposite*: boost

sapient *adj* **wise**, learned, educated, intelligent, knowing *Opposite*: ignorant

sapling *n* **1 tree**, seedling, plantlet, sprout, scion **2** *(literary)* **youth**, adolescent, youngster, juvenile, teenager

sarcasm *n* **irony**, mockery, cynicism, derision, acerbity

sarcastic *adj* **ironic**, mocking, sardonic, cynical, caustic

---

COMPARE AND CONTRAST CORE MEANING: describes remarks that are designed to hurt or mock

sarcastic contemptuous, scornful, or mocking and intended to hurt or belittle; **ironic** deliberately stating the opposite of the truth, usually with the intention of being amusing; **sardonic** mocking and cynical or disdainful, though not deliberately hurtful; **satirical** using ridicule, especially in a work of art, to criticize somebody's or something's faults, especially in the arts or politics; **caustic** harsh and bitter and intended to mock, offend, or belittle.

---

sarcophagus *n* **coffin**, tomb, casket

sardonic *adj* **mocking**, scornful, ironic, sarcastic, derisive. *See* COMPARE AND CONTRAST *at* sarcastic.

sarsen *n* **rock**, boulder, stone, cairn, block

sartorial *adj* **dress**, fashion, clothing

sash *n* **band**, ribbon, belt, cummerbund, tie

sashay *v* **flounce**, sway, strut, prance, swagger

sass *(infml) n* **impertinence**, impudence, rudeness, attitude, cheek

sassiness *n* **1 impudence**, impertinence, brazenness, insolence, impishness *Opposite*: respectfulness **2 liveliness**, high spirits, jauntiness, vivacity, vivaciousness *Opposite*: quietness

sassy *adj* **1 impudent**, brazen, insolent, impish, mischievous *Opposite*: respectful **2 lively**, high-spirited, spirited, jaunty, vivacious *Opposite*: subdued

satchel *n* **bag**, shoulder bag, haversack, school bag, backpack

sate *v* **fill up**, fill, satiate, stuff, gorge

sated *adj* **full**, satiated, gorged, bursting, satisfied *Opposite*: hungry

satellite *n* **1 dependency**, protectorate, colony, overseas territory, subject population **2 satellite television**, satellite TV, satellite broadcasting, digital television, digital TV

satiate *v* **1 gratify**, satisfy, quench, sate, slake **2 glut**, fill, satisfy, sate, fill up

satiated *adj* **1 gratified**, satisfied, quenched, sated, slaked **2 full**, satisfied, replete, sated, full up *Opposite*: unsatisfied

satiety *n* **fullness**, surfeit, glut, repletion

satiny *adj* **lustrous**, luminous, shiny, radiant, glossy *Opposite*: dull

satire *n* **1 mockery**, irony, sarcasm, ridicule, wit **2 parody**, lampoon, burlesque, caricature, travesty

satirical *adj* **mocking**, ironic, sardonic, humorous, sarcastic. *See* COMPARE AND CONTRAST *at* sarcastic.

satirist *n* **humorist**, wit, joker, satirizer, comic

satirize *v* **mock**, ridicule, parody, lampoon, deride

satisfaction *n* **1 contentment**, pleasure, happiness, joy, enjoyment *Opposite*: dissatisfaction **2 gratification**, consummation, fulfillment **3 approval**, liking, taste, contentment, agreement *Opposite*: dissatisfaction **4 redress**, reparation, compensation, settlement, repayment

satisfactory *adj* **acceptable**, reasonable, pleasing, fitting, agreeable *Opposite*: unsatisfactory

satisfied *adj* **content**, pleased, happy, gratified, fulfilled *Opposite*: dissatisfied

satisfy *v* **1 content**, please, gratify, mollify, placate *Opposite*: dissatisfy **2 gratify**, satiate, quench, sate, slake **3 convince**, assure, persuade, reassure, win over

4 fulfill, comply with, meet, suit, fill

satisfying adj **1 pleasing**, gratifying, fulfilling, rewarding, enjoyable Opposite: dissatisfying **2 filling**, sustaining, nourishing, substantial, satiating Opposite: insufficient

saturate v **1 soak**, drench, wet through, douse, steep Opposite: dry out **2 oversupply**, overwhelm, overload, flood, inundate

saturated adj **1 soaked**, soaking, drenched, wet through, wet Opposite: dry **2 packed**, full, brimming, brimful, overfull Opposite: empty

saturation n **1 wetness**, soaking, drenching, wetting, moistening Opposite: dryness **2 fullness**, capacity, overload, satiety, permeation

saturnalia n **orgy**, celebration, bacchanalia, revel, party

saturnine adj **melancholy**, morose, gloomy, sad, sullen Opposite: cheerful

sauce (infml) n **impudence**, impertinence, rudeness, insolence, nerve

WORD BANK

❑ **types of seasonings, sauces, and dips** aioli, applesauce, barbecue sauce, béarnaise, béchamel, catsup, chili sauce, coulis, dressing, French dressing, gravy, guacamole, hollandaise, horseradish, hummus, ketchup, marinade, mayonnaise, mint sauce, raita, ranch dressing, Russian dressing, salsa, satay, soy sauce, tabasco, tahini, taramasalata, tartar sauce, teriyaki, Thousand Island dressing, vinegar, vinaigrette, wasabi, Worcestershire sauce

saucepan n **pan**, pot, cooking pot

saucer n **plate**, bowl, dish

saucy adj **impudent**, smart, rude, sassy, cheeky (infml)

saunter v **stroll**, walk, amble, meander, ramble Opposite: hurry ■ n **walk**, stroll, amble, ramble, meander

sauté v **fry**, stir-fry, pan-fry, brown

savage adj **1 violent**, unrestrained, vicious, fierce, ferocious Opposite: gentle **2 severe**, harsh, drastic, stringent, ruthless Opposite: mild **3 undomesticated**, wild, ferocious, fierce, feral Opposite: tame ■ v **1 attack**, brutalize, mug, maul, mangle **2 criticize**, tear apart, maul, destroy, attack Opposite: praise

savagery n **cruelty**, violence, barbarity, viciousness, barbarism Opposite: gentleness

savanna n **grassland**, pampas, plains, prairie

savant n **guru**, philosopher, thinker, pundit, expert

save v **1 rescue**, recover, salvage, bail out, revive Opposite: abandon **2 accumulate**, bank, salt away, collect Opposite: spend **3 keep back**, set aside, put aside, put away, hold back Opposite: use up **4 avoid**, prevent, stop, avert, bar ■ prep **but**, except, apart from, with the exception of, excluding Opposite: including

save for prep **but**, except, apart from, with the exception of, excluding

saver n **investor**, collector, hoarder, gatherer, squirrel (infml)

saving n **economy**, reduction, cutback, discount, cut Opposite: increase

saving grace n **merit**, advantage, strong point, strong suit, virtue Opposite: failing

savings n **investments**, reserves, nest egg, funds, hoard Opposite: expenditure

savior r **redeemer**, rescuer, knight in shining armor, liberator, deliverer

savoir-faire n **confidence**, style, flair, poise, sense

savor n **taste**, smell, flavor, aroma, tang ■ v **enjoy**, relish, appreciate, delight in, cherish

savorless adj **tasteless**, insipid, bland, flavorless Opposite: flavorful

savorlessness n **tastelessness**, insipidness, blandness, flavorlessness Opposite: tastiness

savory adj **1 appetizing**, tasty, flavorful, palatable, delicious Opposite: insipid **2 salty**, salt, spicy, piquant, pungent Opposite: sweet **3 respectable**, pleasant, acceptable, nice, wholesome Opposite: unsavory

savvy (infml) n **shrewdness**, practicality, knowledge, perception, understanding Opposite: ignorance

saw n **saying**, proverb, adage, maxim, motto ■ v **cut**, slice, sever, divide, chop

say v **1 speak**, utter, articulate, declare, pronounce **2 convey**, indicate, reveal, give away, tell ■ n **input**, voice, opinion, view, two cents' worth ■ adv **approximately**, roughly, about, around, give or take Opposite: exactly

saying n **proverb**, adage, maxim, axiom, motto

say-so (infml) n **authorization**, authority, permission, approval, agreement Opposite: veto

say yes v **agree**, accept, consent, acquiesce, assent Opposite: refuse

say you're sorry v **apologize**, excuse yourself, crawl, grovel, beg forgiveness

say your piece v **speak out**, speak up, protest, take a stand, make a stand Opposite: hold back

scab n **crust**, layer, skin, shell, covering

scabbard n **sheath**, case, covering, cover, casing

scabby adj **mangy**, scaly, diseased, shabby, dirty Opposite: unblemished

scabrous adj **rough**, flaky, scaly, mangy, leprous Opposite: smooth

scads (infml) n **lots**, scores, tons (infml), heaps (infml), buckets (infml) Opposite: none

scaffold *n* **1 support**, framework, frame, platform, shell **2 gallows**, gibbet, halter, noose

scaffolding *n* **support**, framework, frame, platform, shell

scalawag *(dated infml)* *n* **mischief-maker**, imp, monkey *(infml)*, scamp *(infml)*, rascal *Opposite*: angel

scald *v* **burn**, blister, singe, sear, injure **2 sterilize**, boil, steam, autoclave, heat *Opposite*: contaminate **3 bring to the boil**, boil, heat, warm, simmer *Opposite*: chill

scalding *adj* **1 boiling**, piping hot, baking, burning, blistering *Opposite*: icy **2 scathing**, blistering, critical, fierce, scornful *Opposite*: complimentary

scale *n* **1 weighing machine**, balance, scales, measure **2 gradation**, tier, band, ratio, progression **3 range**, extent, size, gamut, degree **4 deposit**, crust, fur, covering, plaque **5 plate**, flake, skin, scab, scurf ■ *v* **1 ascend**, climb, mount, go up, clamber up **2 peel**, pare, skin, exfoliate, flake

scale down *v* **reduce**, decrease, lower, cut back, cut down *Opposite*: scale up

scale up *v* **increase**, expand, extend, raise, step up *Opposite*: scale down

scallop *n* **pinking**, edging, scalloping, piping, border

scallywag *see* **scalawag**

scaly *adj* **flaking**, peeling, crusty, encrusted, scabby *Opposite*: smooth

scamp *(infml)* *n* **rogue**, imp, urchin, rascal, monkey *(infml)* *Opposite*: angel

scamper *v* **scurry**, scuttle, run, hurry, dash *Opposite*: dawdle

scan *v* **1 scrutinize**, examine, look into, pore over, inspect **2 skim**, skim through, glance at, glance over, browse *Opposite*: study **3 examine**, photograph, visualize, image, X-ray ■ *n* **1 image**, X-ray, CT scan, MRI scan, PET scan **2 perusal**, skim, examination, inspection, look

scandal *n* **1 disgrace**, shame, dishonor, humiliation, outrage **2 gossip**, tittle-tattle, rumor, talk, rumormongering

scandalize *v* **horrify**, outrage, shock, disgust, dismay *Opposite*: impress

scandalmonger *n* **gossip**, rumormonger, gossipmonger, newsmonger, snoop *(infml)*

scandalous *adj* **shocking**, outrageous, disgraceful, immoral, shameful *Opposite*: admirable

scant *adj* **slight**, limited, negligible, little, scarce *Opposite*: extensive

scanty *adj* **1 revealing**, flimsy, light, low-cut, tight **2 insufficient**, inadequate, meager, little, scarce *Opposite*: abundant

scapegoat *n* **stooge**, victim, accused, culprit, fall guy *(slang)* ■ *v* **blame**, incriminate, condemn, accuse, reproach *Opposite*: exonerate

scar *n* **1 mark**, blemish, mutilation, scratch, wound **2 effect**, wound, trauma, hurt,

aftereffect ■ *v* **1 damage**, mark, blemish, mutilate, disfigure **2 traumatize**, hurt, affect, damage, mark

scarce *adj* **1 in short supply**, limited, insufficient, inadequate, scant *Opposite*: abundant **2 rare**, uncommon, unusual, infrequent, threatened *Opposite*: common

scarcely *adv* **barely**, hardly, not quite, only just, just *Opposite*: fully

scarceness *see* **scarcity**

scarcity *n* **1 shortage**, lack, dearth, insufficiency, scarceness *Opposite*: abundance **2 rarity**, uncommonness, infrequency, lack, want *Opposite*: commonness

scare *v* **frighten**, terrify, startle, alarm, panic *Opposite*: reassure ■ *n* **fright**, shock, start, jolt, alarm *Opposite*: reassurance

scarecrow *n* **figure**, effigy, mannequin

scared *adj* **frightened**, afraid, fearful, terrified, nervous *Opposite*: fearless

scaremonger *n* **alarmist**, doomsayer, troublemaker, rumormonger, newsmonger *Opposite*: optimist

scare off *v* **frighten away**, drive away, chase off, scare away, frighten *Opposite*: welcome

scare up *(infml)* *v* **1 get**, get hold of, lay hands on, rustle up, search out **2 prepare**, concoct, put together, whip up, rustle up *(infml)*

scarf *n* **muffler**, headscarf, bandana, cravat, shawl ■ *v* *(infml)* **gobble**, wolf, bolt, devour, scarf down *(infml)* *Opposite*: refuse

scarf down *(infml)* *v* **gobble**, wolf, bolt, devour, scarf *(infml)* *Opposite*: refuse

scarify *v* **1** *(infml)* **scare**, frighten, alarm, worry, startle *Opposite*: reassure **2 lacerate**, scratch, score, cut, incise

scariness *n* **menace**, creepiness *(infml)*, spookiness *(infml)* *Opposite*: reassurance

scarp *n* **escarpment**, ridge, cliff, bluff, crag

scarred *adj* **1 mutilated**, disfigured, marked, injured, wounded **2 damaged**, defaced, blemished, marked, scratched

scary *(infml)* *adj* **frightening**, chilling, terrifying, petrifying, daunting *Opposite*: reassuring

scat *(infml)* *v* **run away**, run off, escape, flee, abscond

scathing *adj* **scornful**, mocking, derisive, sarcastic, contemptuous *Opposite*: complimentary

scatter *v* **1 throw**, strew, fling, sprinkle, distribute *Opposite*: collect **2 disperse**, spread out, spread, flee, take flight *Opposite*: gather

---

COMPARE AND CONTRAST CORE MEANING: spread around

scatter spread things around physically, especially in a random widespread manner; **broadcast** spread or transmit information, especially by means of radio or television, or scatter seeds over the ground; **distribute** allocate, share, or give out something in a structured or organized way, or spread something over a particular surface or area; **disseminate** spread ideas, information, or attitudes such as goodwill.

scatterbrained *adj* **absent-minded**, vague, forgetful, woolly-headed, careless *Opposite*: focused

scattered *adj* **1 dispersed**, distributed, strewn, sprinkled, disseminated *Opposite*: concentrated **2 infrequent**, isolated, discrete, separate, occasional *Opposite*: frequent

scattering *n* **handful**, sprinkling, trickle, bit, smattering

scattershot *adj* **disorganized**, indiscriminate, random, chaotic, slapdash *Opposite*: focused

scavenge *v* **hunt**, forage, search, rummage, sift

scenario *n* **situation**, state of affairs, state, setup, circumstances

scene *n* **1 act**, division, part, section, passage **2 setting**, site, place, background, backdrop **3 sight**, prospect, picture, panorama, view **4 fuss**, commotion, exhibition, incident, spectacle

scenery *n* **1 set**, backdrop, backcloth, background, decor **2 landscape**, panorama, vista, outlook, view

scenic *adj* **picturesque**, beautiful, attractive, lovely, charming *Opposite*: unsightly

scent *n* **1 smell**, odor, aroma, perfume, bouquet **2 trail**, trace, track, spoor **3 perfume**, fragrance, cologne, toilet water, eau de cologne **4 hint**, trace, air, whiff, suggestion ■ *v* **1 sniff**, smell, detect, sense, pick up **2 predict**, foresee, foretell, sense, feel **3 imbue**, perfume, fill, infuse, suffuse *See* COMPARE AND CONTRAST *at* smell.

scented *adj* **perfumed**, fragrant, aromatic, sweet-smelling, fragranced *Opposite*: odorless

scepter *n* **staff**, staff of office, mace, rod, insignia

schedule *n* **agenda**, timetable, calendar, list, plan ■ *v* **arrange**, plan, program, book, organize *Opposite*: cancel

scheduled *adj* **arranged**, planned, programmed, listed, booked *Opposite*: unplanned

schema *n* **plan**, diagram, scheme, schematic, representation

schematize *v* **systematize**, arrange, structure, organize, draft *Opposite*: disarrange

scheme *n* **1 plot**, plan, conspiracy, ploy, ruse **2 plan**, method, stratagem, program, idea **3 arrangement**, system, structure, outline, organization *Opposite*: chaos **4 diagram**, plan, schematic, graphic, representation ■ *v* **plot**, conspire, intrigue, connive, plan

schemer *n* **plotter**, conspirator, conniver, traitor, intriguer

scheming *adj* **devious**, calculating, conniving, conspiratorial, treacherous *Opposite*: honest

schism *n* **split**, break, division, rupture, rift *Opposite*: union

schismatic *adj* **factional**, divisive, clashing, conflicting, controversial *Opposite*: unifying

schlep *(nfml)* *v* **lug**, haul, heave, drag, cart ■ *n* **trek**, trudge, hike, bore, bind

schmaltz *(infml)* *n* **sentimentality**, slush, mush, corniness, mawkishness

schmaltzy *(infml)* *adj* **sentimental**, cloying, sugary, saccharine, slushy

scholar *n* **academic**, researcher, professor, doctor, intellectual

scholarly *adj* **learned**, academic, erudite, intellectual, educated *Opposite*: lowbrow

scholarship *n* **1 grant**, bursary, studentship, subsidy, allowance **2 learning**, erudition, study, knowledge, research *Opposite*: ignorance

scholastic *adj* **educational**, academic, pedagogic, school, college

school *n* **1 university**, college, seminary, conservatory, graduate school **2 group**, set, coterie, brotherhood, sisterhood *Opposite*: individual ■ *v* **train**, instruct, educate, discipline, teach

---

WORD BANK

❏ **types of schools** academy, boarding school, elementary school, grade school, grammar school, high school, junior high, kindergarten, middle school, military academy, nursery school, prep school, preschool, primary school, private school, public school, trade school, vocational school

---

schoolchild *n* **pupil**, student, scholar, schoolboy, schoolgirl

schooling *n* **education**, teaching, training, instruction, tuition

school of thought *n* **philosophy**, doctrine, ideology, outlook, attitude

science *n* **discipline**, knowledge, skill, learning, scholarship

scientific *adj* **technical**, methodical, systematic, logical, precise *Opposite*: unscientific

scintilla *n* **jot**, iota, scrap, shred, speck

scintillate *v* **1 sparkle**, glitter, gleam, flash, glint **2 fascinate**, dazzle, charm, shine, sparkle *Opposite*: bore

scintillating *adj* **sparkling**, dazzling, brilliant, bright, glittering *Opposite*: dull

scintillation *n* **sparkling**, glittering, gleaming, flashing, glinting *Opposite*: dullness

scion *n* **1 cutting**, graft, shoot, implant, implantation **2 offspring**, child, heir, descendant, son *Opposite*: parent

scoff *v* **1 jeer**, sneer, mock, ridicule, make fun of *Opposite*: praise **2** *(infml)* **eat**, gobble, stuff your face, bolt, wolf *Opposite*: nibble

scoffing *adj* **mocking**, jeering, sneering, dismissive, contemptuous

scold *v* **rebuke**, admonish, reprimand, reproach, discipline *Opposite*: praise

scolding *n* **admonishment**, reprimand, reproach, rebuke, caution *Opposite*: praise

sconce *n* **light fixture**, bracket, wall lamp, candleholder

scoop *n* **1 ladle**, dipper, serving spoon, server, soup ladle **2** (*infml*) **news story**, story, exclusive, revelation, exposé ■ *v* **1 dig**, hollow, scrape, shovel, excavate *Opposite*: fill **2 lift**, gather up, pick up, raise, take *Opposite*: drop

scoot (*infml*) *v* **1 move quickly**, rush, hurry, scurry, dash *Opposite*: dawdle **2 go away**, leave, scat (*infml*), make yourself scarce (*infml*), skedaddle (*slang*) *Opposite*: arrive

scope *n* **1 possibility**, choice, room, opportunity, space *Opposite*: constraint **2 range**, extent, capacity, span, reach

scorch *v* **burn**, singe, sear, char, blacken

scorched *adj* **1 burned**, singed, seared, charred, blackened **2 dried**, dry as a bone, dry, parched, baked *Opposite*: drenched

scorching (*infml*) *adj* **boiling**, baking, sweltering, sizzling (*infml*), blazing *Opposite*: freezing

score *n* **1 total**, tally, mark, result, count **2 notch**, cut, slash, groove, nick ■ *v* **1 achieve**, chalk up, attain, make, gain **2 keep count**, keep a tally, keep score, count, tot up **3 cut into**, slash, notch, nick, slice **4 scratch**, etch, carve, mark, scrape

scoreboard *n* **display**, board, panel, bulletin board

scorecard *n* **tally**, scoresheet, record, card

scores *n* **lots**, tons (*infml*), heaps (*infml*), buckets (*infml*), piles (*infml*) *Opposite*: none

scoresheet *n* **sheet**, scorecard, tally, record

scorn *n* **contempt**, disdain, disrespect, derision, scornfulness *Opposite*: admiration ■ *v* **1 show contempt for**, despise, disdain, belittle, deride *Opposite*: admire **2 reject**, spurn, rebuff, turn down, refuse *Opposite*: choose

scorned *adj* **1 despised**, disdained, belittled, derided, disparaged *Opposite*: admired **2 rejected**, spurned, rebuffed, turned down, refused *Opposite*: chosen

scornful *adj* **contemptuous**, disdainful, disrespectful, mocking, derisive *Opposite*: admiring

scornfulness *n* **contempt**, disdain, disrespect, mockery, derision

scotch *v* **stop**, spoil, foil, scuttle, scupper *Opposite*: initiate

scot-free *adv* **unpunished**, without punishment, with impunity, lightly, easily

scoundrel *n* **rogue**, rascal, villain, cheat, crook (*infml*) *Opposite*: hero

scour *v* **1 scrub**, rub, clean, wash, polish *Opposite*: dirty **2 search**, comb, hunt, go over with a fine-tooth comb, rake through

scourge *n* **bane**, blight, plague, curse, menace *Opposite*: blessing ■ *v* **plague**, curse, afflict, terrorize, torment *Opposite*: bless

scout *n* **lookout**, spy, watch, undercover agent, detective ■ *v* **1 search**, hunt, scout around, look around, cast around *Opposite*: find **2 check out**, survey, investigate, spy out, explore

scout around *v* **search**, hunt, scout, look around, scout out

scowl *n* **glare**, frown, glower, grimace, stare *Opposite*: smile ■ *v* **look daggers**, glare, frown, glower, grimace *Opposite*: smile

scrabble *v* **1 scratch**, dig, scrape, claw, pick **2 grope**, fumble, clutch, rummage, scrape around

scragginess *n* **scrawniness**, boniness, gauntness, skinniness, thinness *Opposite*: plumpness

scraggly *adj* **messy**, disheveled, untidy, unkempt, tangled *Opposite*: tidy

scraggy *adj* **scrawny**, skinny, bony, gaunt, thin *Opposite*: plump. *See* COMPARE AND CONTRAST *at* thin.

scram (*infml*) *v* **run off**, run away, get out, get away, bolt

scramble *v* **1 climb**, clamber, crawl, scrabble, struggle *Opposite*: descend **2 move quickly**, rush, run, scuttle, jostle *Opposite*: plod **3 mix up**, jumble, mix, muddle, confuse *Opposite*: unscramble ■ *n* **1 ascent**, climb, clamber, hike *Opposite*: descent **2 rush**, run, stampede, commotion, dash *Opposite*: calm

scrap *n* **1 piece**, bit, fragment, slip, wisp **2** (*infml*) **fight**, scuffle, tussle, row, clash ■ *v* **1 cancel**, abandon, get rid of, do away with, give up *Opposite*: adopt **2 scuffle**, fight, tussle, spar, brawl

scrape *v* **1 rub**, scratch, scuff, abrade, scour **2 graze**, scratch, scuff, mark, abrade ■ *n* **1 scratch**, scuff, graze, mark, abrasion **2** (*infml*) **predicament**, plight, problem, fix (*infml*), pickle (*infml*) **3** (*infml*) **fight**, brawl, clash, fracas, scuffle

scrape by *v* **make do**, survive, make ends meet, get by, scratch a living *Opposite*: prosper

scrape out *v* **hollow out**, scoop out, gouge out, carve out, gouge *Opposite*: fill

scrape together *v* **collect**, amass, put by, put aside, scrape up *Opposite*: disperse

scrapheap *n* **garbage dump**, junkyard, landfill

scrappy *adj* **1 fragmentary**, fragmented, patchy, piecemeal, incomplete *Opposite*: complete **2 disjointed**, inconsistent, disconnected, incoherent, patchy *Opposite*: uniform **3** (*infml*) **plucky**, courageous, determined, spirited, spunky (infml) Opposite: timid **4** (infml) **argumentative**, contrary, confrontational, hotheaded, quarrelsome Opposite: docile

scraps n leftovers, scrapings, slops, crumbs, leavings

scratch v **1 scrape**, graze, grate, rub, cut **2 itch**, rub, scrape, worry at **3 cancel**, abandon, forget, scrap, leave out Opposite: keep **4 pull out**, drop out, bow out, withdraw, abandon Opposite: continue ■ n **cut**, scrape, graze, score, nick

scratched adj **scuffed**, scored, scraped, marked, damaged

scratch together v **collect**, amass, put by, put aside, scratch up Opposite: disperse

scratchy adj **itchy**, prickly, tickly, irritating, uncomfortable Opposite: soft

scrawl v **scribble**, doodle, pencil, write, draw ■ n **illegible writing**, scribble, doodle, graffiti, squiggle

scrawled adj **indecipherable**, illegible, incomprehensible, scribbled, untidy Opposite: neat

scrawniness n **gauntness**, skinniness, boniness, scragginess, thinness Opposite: plumpness

scrawny adj **scraggy**, skinny, bony, gaunt, thin Opposite: plump. See COMPARE AND CONTRAST at **thin**.

screak v **1 screech**, howl, yowl, yell, scream Opposite: murmur **2 creak**, groan, grate, squeak, squeal

scream n **1 shriek**, yell, cry, yelp, shout Opposite: murmur **2** (infml) **laugh**, riot (infml), card (dated infml), gas (slang), hoot (slang) ■ v **shout**, shriek, yell, cry, screech Opposite: whisper

scree n **rock debris**, talus, rubble, gravel, stones

screech n **scream**, shriek, squeal, cry, yelp Opposite: whisper ■ v **shriek**, scream, squeal, cry, yelp Opposite: whisper

screen n **1 partition**, divider, panel, shield, guard **2 shade**, awning, canopy, shelter, curtain **3 monitor**, VDT, display, computer screen, television ■ v **1 hide**, conceal, cover, protect, shelter Opposite: reveal **2 partition**, separate, divide, mark off, curtain Opposite: open out **3 broadcast**, put on, show, transmit, project **4 test**, inspect, examine, diagnose, check **5 vet**, select, assess, investigate, test

screening n **1 show**, showing, viewing, program, projection **2 broadcast**, showing, transmission, run, airing **3 inspection**, testing, examination, diagnosis, checking **4 selection**, vetting, assessment, investigation, inspection

screenplay n **script**, dialogue, scenario, text, writing

screenwriter n **scriptwriter**, writer, dramatist, author, playwright

screw v **1 attach**, bolt, fasten, fix, secure **2 twist**, rotate, coil, turn, wind Opposite: unscrew **3 crumple**, twist, distort, contort, crinkle Opposite: smooth

screw up v **muster**, gather, summon, call up, pluck up Opposite: lose

scribble v **1 scrawl**, jot, write, dash off (infml) **2 draw**, doodle, scrawl, squiggle ■ n **1 doodle**, scrawl, jotting, squiggle, design **2 writing**, handwriting, scrawl, lettering

scribbled adj **scrawled**, jotted, untidy, illegible, indecipherable Opposite: neat

scribe n **transcriber**, copyist, clerk, illuminator, transcriptionist

scrimmage n **1 practice**, drill, practice play, exercise **2 struggle**, tussle, fray, ruckus, free-for-all (infml)

scrimp v **economize**, save, skimp, tighten your belt, pull in your horns Opposite: squander

script n **1 screenplay**, text, dialogue, words, libretto **2 writing**, calligraphy, handwriting, hand, cursive

scriptwriter n **writer**, author, playwright, screenwriter, dramatist

scroll n **roll**, parchment, document, certificate, manuscript

scrooge (infml) n **miser**, skinflint, niggard, pinchpenny, cheapskate (infml)

scrounge (infml) v **1 beg**, borrow, solicit, sponge (infml), cadge (infml) Opposite: give **2 scavenge**, rummage, forage, go through, search

scrounger (infml) n **beggar**, borrower, cadger (infml), sponger (infml), freeloader (infml) Opposite: donor

scrub v **1 clean**, rub, scour, polish, brush Opposite: dirty **2** (infml) **cancel**, delete, erase, forget about, scratch Opposite: schedule ■ n **1 undergrowth**, brush, bush, brushwood, vegetation **2 rub**, clean, scour, polish, brush

scruffy adj **untidy**, shabby, tatty, unkempt, disheveled Opposite: tidy

scrummy (infml) see **scrumptious**

scrumptious (infml) adj **delicious**, delectable, mouthwatering, tasty, delightful Opposite: revolting

scrunch v **crumple**, crush, crunch, crease, wrinkle Opposite: smooth

scruple n **misgiving**, doubt, qualm, compunction, hesitation

scrupulous adj **1 honorable**, trustworthy, reliable, dependable, trusty **2 conscientious**, meticulous, thorough, careful, rigorous Opposite: sloppy. See COMPARE AND CONTRAST at **careful**.

scrupulousness n **1 honesty**, reliability, dependability, trustworthiness, decency **2 conscientiousness**, meticulousness, thoroughness, carefulness, rigor

scrutinize v **examine**, inspect, study, pore over, analyze Opposite: skim

scrutiny *n* **examination**, inspection, study, analysis, search

scud *v* **speed**, sweep, fly, sail, rush *Opposite*: crawl

scuff *v* **scrape**, wear away, rub, graze, scratch ■ *n* **scratch**, scrape, graze, abrasion

scuffle *n* **fight**, brawl, fracas, fray, scrap (*infml*) ■ *v* **wrestle**, fight, come to blows, exchange blows, scrap

scull *n* **oar**, paddle, blade, sweep ■ *v* **row**, paddle, propel, canoe

sculpt *v* **carve**, shape, mold, form, fashion

sculpture *n* **statue**, statuette, figure, figurine, carving

scum *n* **froth**, foam, impurities, filth, crust

scurf *n* **1 dandruff**, dander, dead skin, flakes **2 encrustation**, scale, crust, deposit, coat

scurrilous *adj* **scandalous**, slanderous, defamatory, outrageous, abusive *Opposite*: complimentary

scurry *v* **dash**, scuttle, scamper, dart, rush *Opposite*: saunter

scuttle *v* **1 destroy**, stymie, thwart, spoil, ruin **2 scurry**, scamper, dart, dash, rush *Opposite*: saunter

scythe *v* **cut**, cut down, hack, slice, sweep

sea *n* **ocean**, deep, depths *Opposite*: dry land ■ *adj* **maritime**, aquatic, oceanic, marine, nautical *Opposite*: land

seaboard *n* **coast**, coastline, shore, seashore, shoreline *Opposite*: interior

sea change *n* **transformation**, metamorphosis, shift, turnaround, U-turn

seacoast *see* **seaboard**

seafaring *adj* **maritime**, nautical, oceangoing, seagoing, marine

seafront *n* **waterfront**, esplanade, boardwalk, beach, seashore

seagoing *see* **seafaring**

seal *n* **1 closure**, cover, stopper, lid, cap **2 stamp**, hallmark, impression, signet, sigil ■ *v* **1 close**, fasten, stick, close up, shut *Opposite*: open **2 guarantee**, settle, finalize, wrap up, confirm

sea lane *n* **seaway**, shipping lane, sea route, channel, corridor

sealed *adj* **1 closed**, stuck down, wrapped, taped up *Opposite*: unsealed **2 impenetrable**, hermetically sealed, vacuum-packed, airtight, watertight *Opposite*: unsealed

seal off *v* **close off**, cordon off, fence off, isolate, quarantine *Opposite*: open

seam *n* **1 join**, joint, closure, ridge **2 layer**, stratum, vein, lode

seaman *n* **sailor**, mariner, seafarer, navigator, deckhand

seamless *adj* **1 unified**, all-in-one, one-piece, whole, continuous *Opposite*: joined **2 smooth**, perfect, faultless, uniform, unified

seamy *adj* **unpleasant**, degenerate, sordid,

unsavory, squalid *Opposite*: wholesome

seaport *n* **harbor**, port, coastal town, anchorage, dock

sear *v* **burn**, scorch, solder, singe, char

search *v* **examine**, rifle, comb, look for, seek ■ *n* **examination**, hunt, quest, pursuit, exploration

searching *adj* **thorough**, penetrating, incisive, probing, pointed *Opposite*: superficial

searchlight *n* **light**, spotlight, beam, lamp, flashlight

search out *v* **discover**, uncover, find out, find, research

search party *n* **searchers**, rescue party, rescuers, rescue patrol, emergency workers

search through *v* **sift through**, sort through, rummage, hunt through, ransack

searing *adj* **1 blistering**, sweltering, scorching (*infml*), sizzling (*infml*), roasting (*infml*) *Opposite*: freezing **2 intense**, shooting, stabbing, agonizing, excruciating *Opposite*: mild

seashore *n* **coastline**, shore, shoreline, coast, seacoast

seasick *adj* **sick**, nauseous, queasy, travelsick, ill

seaside *n* **beach**, seafront, seashore, coast, shore

season *n* **period**, term, spell, time, time of year ■ *v* **flavor**, spice, spike, pepper, salt

seasonable *adj* **appropriate**, fitting, timely, opportune, suitable *Opposite*: unseasonable

seasonal *adj* **1 cyclical**, periodic, cyclic, recurrent, spring *Opposite*: year-round **2 limited**, sporadic, intermittent, temporary, casual *Opposite*: permanent

seasoned *adj* **experienced**, veteran, hardened, tested, weathered *Opposite*: inexperienced

seasoning *n* **zest**, flavoring, flavor, zing (*infml*)

seat *n* **1 chair**, bench, couch, pew, stool **2 base**, HQ, headquarters, center, station ■ *v* **1 place**, sit, sit down, set, install **2 accommodate**, hold, sit, contain, take

seating *n* **seats**, chairs, spaces, places, places to sit

WORD BANK

❏ **types of seating** Adirondack chair, armchair, beach chair, bench, bleachers, Boston rocker, bucket seat, chair, chaise longue, chesterfield, couch, davenport, deck chair, easy chair, highchair, ladder-back, lounger, love seat, pew, recliner, rocking chair, settee, sofa, stall, stool, swivel chair, Windsor chair, wing chair

sea wall *n* **dike**, jetty, breakwater, groyne, embankment

seaway *n* **channel**, sea lane, shipping lane, sea route, canal

secede v **withdraw**, break away, break from, disaffiliate, pull out Opposite: affiliate

secession n **withdrawal**, departure, separation, retreat, retirement

seclude v **isolate**, separate, keep away, keep apart, remove

secluded adj **private**, sheltered, quiet, isolated, out-of-the-way Opposite: public

seclusion n **privacy**, shelter, isolation, quiet, solitude

second adj **additional**, another, next, subsequent, following ■ n **moment**, minute, instant, trice, flash Opposite: age ■ v **support**, agree with, endorse, subscribe, uphold Opposite: oppose

secondary adj **1 subordinate**, minor, inferior, lesser, tributary Opposite: primary **2 derived**, derivative, resulting, resultant, consequent Opposite: original

second best adj **second-rate**, second class, second choice, next best, inferior Opposite: best

second-class adj **second-rate**, mediocre, indifferent, middling, second best Opposite: first-class

seconder n **supporter**, endorser, backer, advocate, assenter

second-guess v **predict**, guess, foretell, anticipate

secondhand adj **used**, nearly new, hand-me-down, preowned, previously owned Opposite: new ■ adv **indirectly**, circuitously, through the grapevine, in a roundabout way, on the rumor mill Opposite: firsthand

secondly adv **then**, furthermore, in addition, what is more, also Opposite: firstly

second-rate adj **inadequate**, mediocre, unsatisfactory, poor, below standard Opposite: first-rate

second sight n **clairvoyance**, foresight, foreknowledge, precognition, intuition

second thoughts n **reconsideration**, pangs, doubts, qualms, misgivings

secrecy n **concealment**, confidentiality, privacy, mystery, silence Opposite: openness

secret adj **1 clandestine**, covert, stealthy, surreptitious, furtive Opposite: open **2 confidential**, private, classified, top-secret, restricted Opposite: public ■ n **confidence**, skeleton in the closet, mystery, riddle, enigma

---

COMPARE AND CONTRAST CORE MEANING: conveying a desire or need for concealment
secret intentionally withheld from general knowledge; **clandestine** describes an activity that needs to be concealed, usually because it is illegal or unauthorized; **covert** not intended to be known, seen, or found out, suggesting a lack of honesty or openness; **furtive** cautious and careful in order to escape notice; **stealthy** quiet, slow, and cautious in order to escape notice;

---

surreptitious done in a concealed or underhand way to escape notice.

secret agent n **spy**, undercover agent, double agent, mole, infiltrator

secretary n **clerical worker**, administrative assistant, personal assistant, office assistant, typist

secretary-general n **chief executive officer**, C.E.O., head, chief, chair

secrete v **1 hide**, hide away, conceal, stow, squirrel away Opposite: display **2 exude**, ooze, emit, produce, squirt Opposite: absorb

secretion n **discharge**, excretion, exudation, emission, ooze

secretive adj **private**, mysterious, enigmatic, guarded, reticent Opposite: open

secretly adv **clandestinely**, covertly, in secret, surreptitiously, furtively Opposite: openly

sect n **1 group**, clique, faction, camp, party **2 religious group**, religious persuasion, denomination, cult, movement

sectarian adj **1 religious**, denominational, sectional, factional **2 dogmatic**, intolerant, bigoted, biased, partisan Opposite: tolerant

section n **part**, unit, piece, segment, slice Opposite: whole ■ v **divide**, divide up, partition, split, segment Opposite: combine

sector n **1 part**, division, subdivision, segment, portion Opposite: whole **2 area**, zone, region, quarter, district

secular adj **earthly**, worldly, nonspiritual, profane, lay Opposite: spiritual

secure adj **1 confident**, assured, self-confident, sure of yourself, self-assured Opposite: insecure **2 fixed firmly**, closed, fastened, locked Opposite: unfastened **3 dependable**, reliable, safe, stable, steady Opposite: unreliable **4 safe**, protected, safe and sound, sheltered Opposite: vulnerable ■ v **1 fix**, fasten, make fast, position, attach Opposite: loosen **2 make safe**, safeguard, fortify, lock, lock up **3 obtain**, acquire, get, get hold of, capture Opposite: lose **4 guarantee**, ensure, give security, indemnify, assure. See COMPARE AND CONTRAST at get.

securely adv **firmly**, steadily, tightly, strongly, safely

security n **1 safety**, refuge, sanctuary, haven, safekeeping Opposite: danger **2 confidence**, well-being, self-assurance, reassurance, self-confidence Opposite: insecurity **3 precautions**, safety measures, defense, protection **4 guarantee**, collateral, surety, insurance, indemnity

sedate adj **1 dignified**, calm, cool, demure, serene Opposite: boisterous **2 staid**, unexciting, dull, slow-moving, slow Opposite: exciting ■ v **anesthetize**, tranquilize, drug, put under sedation, knock out Opposite: revive

sedateness n 1 dignity, calmness, coolness, demureness, composedness 2 **staidness**, dullness, slowness

sedation n calm, restfulness, drowsiness, torpor, tranquility *Opposite*: excitement

sedative n tranquilizer, narcotic, barbiturate, downer *(slang)* *Opposite*: stimulant ■ adj **tranquilizing**, calming, soothing, relaxing, soporific *Opposite*: stimulating

sedentary adj sitting, inactive, deskbound, desk *Opposite*: active

sediment n residue, deposit, dregs, remains, grounds

sedition n 1 incitement to rebellion, agitation, treason, subversion, rabble-rousing 2 **rebellion**, mutiny, defiance, unrest, civil disobedience

seditious adj rebellious, subversive, treasonable, disloyal, mutinous *Opposite*: loyal

seduce v 1 entice, lead astray, lure, allure, tempt 2 **persuade**, wheedle, inveigle, talk into, coax

sedulous *(literary)* adj zealous, assiduous, diligent, hard-working, keen *Opposite*: lazy

see v 1 perceive, observe, distinguish, notice, witness 2 **understand**, realize, perceive, grasp, appreciate *Opposite*: misunderstand 3 **meet**, visit, pay a visit to, go to see, call on 4 **find out**, establish, investigate, look into, check 5 **imagine**, picture, envisage, predict, foresee 6 **make sure**, see to it, ensure, make certain, guarantee 7 **consider it**, think about it, weigh it up, give it some thought, think it over 8 **date**, escort, accompany, go with, go out with 9 **look at**, refer to, consult, view, regard

see about v take care of, look into, investigate, find out about, attend to *Opposite*: leave alone

seed n 1 kernel, pip, spore, germ, stone 2 **source**, beginning, start, starting point, nucleus ■ v **sow**, plant, broadcast, scatter *Opposite*: harvest

seediness n 1 dinginess, grubbiness, shabbiness, squalor, tattiness 2 *(infml)* **sickliness**, paleness, roughness *(infml)*

seedling n sprout, sapling, plantlet, slip, twig

seed money n startup funds, venture capital, initial investment, working capital

seedy adj 1 dingy, sordid, shabby, squalid, sleazy *Opposite*: respectable 2 *(infml)* **unwell**, ill, sick, pale, wan *Opposite*: healthy

see eye to eye v agree, see things the same way, have the same opinion, be of the same mind *Opposite*: disagree

seeing conj considering, bearing in mind, as, since, in view of

see into v discern, understand, penetrate, comprehend, figure out

see in your mind's eye v imagine, picture, visualize, envision, see

seek v 1 search for, try to find, hunt for, pursue, seek out *Opposite*: find 2 **strive for**, try for, go after, work toward, pursue *Opposite*: achieve 3 **ask for**, request, inquire about *Opposite*: obtain

seek out v look for, seek, search for, try to find, hunt for *Opposite*: find

seek to v try to, aspire to, aim to, attempt to, strive to *Opposite*: succeed

seem v appear, give the impression, seem like, look, look as if

seeming adj apparent, outward, ostensible, surface, superficial *Opposite*: real

seemingly adv 1 by all accounts, on the face of it, to all appearances, rumor has it, or so it seems *Opposite*: actually 2 **apparently**, outwardly, ostensibly, superficially, externally *Opposite*: really

seemly adj appropriate, decorous, fitting, fit, decent *Opposite*: unseemly

see off v say goodbye to, bid farewell to, send off, take to the station, take to the airport *Opposite*: welcome

see out v 1 show to the door, show out, say goodbye to, accompany, go with *Opposite*: usher in 2 **stay**, last, last out, live out, survive

seep v leak, ooze, trickle, dribble, soak

seepage n leakage, leak, outflow, waste, escape

seer n prophet, soothsayer, clairvoyant, oracle, fortune-teller

see red *(infml)* v lose your temper, go berserk, be enraged, fly into a rage, rage *Opposite*: calm down

seesaw v alternate, go up and down, oscillate, fluctuate, swing *Opposite*: stabilize

seethe v 1 boil, bubble, froth, foam, churn 2 **fume**, rage, be furious, be livid, boil with rage *Opposite*: calm down 3 **teem**, swarm, be alive with, be crawling with

seething adj 1 fuming, furious, livid, beside yourself, enraged *Opposite*: calm 2 **boiling**, bubbling, foaming, simmering *Opposite*: still 3 **bustling**, busy, frantic, teeming, packed *Opposite*: quiet

see through v 1 understand, get to the bottom of, be wise to, know inside out, read like a book 2 **persevere with**, persist at, stick at, stay with, carry out *Opposite*: quit

see-through adj transparent, translucent, sheer, diaphanous, gauzy *Opposite*: opaque

see to v deal with, sort out, handle, take care of, manage

see to it v make sure, see, ensure, make certain, guarantee

segment n section, part, piece, slice, sector *Opposite*: whole ■ v divide, split, subdivide, section, portion

segmentation n division, subdivision, separation, splitting up, dissection *Opposite*: integration

segregate v separate, separate out, isolate, keep apart, set apart *Opposite*: integrate

segregation n separation, isolation, exclusion, setting apart, apartheid *Opposite*: integration

seize v 1 take hold of, grab, grab hold of, get hold of, snatch *Opposite*: relinquish 2 **appropriate**, confiscate, take away, sequester, remove *Opposite*: return 3 **take control of**, capture, take, take over, annex *Opposite*: lose 4 **arrest**, capture, take into custody, apprehend, take hostage *Opposite*: release 5 **take advantage of**, grab, jump at, take

seize up v 1 grind to a halt, jam, fail, stop working, stall 2 **stiffen**, stiffen up, freeze up, stick, cramp

seizure n 1 attack, fit, spasm, convulsion 2 **capture**, arrest, abduction, apprehension *Opposite*: release 3 **appropriation**, confiscation, commandeering, annexation, capture *Opposite*: return

seldom adv not often, hardly ever, rarely, infrequently, occasionally *Opposite*: often

select v choose, pick, pick out, decide on, opt for *Opposite*: deselect ■ adj 1 **choice**, top quality, first-class, excellent, first-rate *Opposite*: inferior 2 **exclusive**, elite, privileged, cliquey, restricted

selected adj carefully chosen, designated, nominated, particular, certain *Opposite*: all

selection n range, assortment, collection, choice, variety

selective adj discerning, discriminating, discriminatory, careful, choosy *(infml)* *Opposite*: indiscriminate

selectivity n discrimination, discernment, choosiness *(infml)*

selector n chooser, picker, committee member, jury member, panel member

self n personality, nature, character, psyche, identity

self-abasement n humbling, humiliation, mortification, prostration, eating humble pie *Opposite*: self-aggrandizement

self-absorbed adj full of yourself, self-regarding, self-centered, narcissistic, egocentric *Opposite*: considerate

self-absorption n self-preoccupation, egotism, egoism, egocentricity, self-centeredness *Opposite*: generosity

self-acting adj self-operating, automatic, automated, mechanized, mechanical

self-aggrandizement n ambition, self-promotion, braggadocio, self-importance, self-glorification

self-assertive adj confident, self-confident, forceful, assured, aggressive *Opposite*: timid

self-assurance n confidence, self-confidence, self-possession, poise, assurance *Opposite*: timidity

self-assured adj confident, self-confident, poised, assured, self-possessed *Opposite*: timid

self-centered adj selfish, self-interested, egocentric, egoistic, egotistic *Opposite*: altruistic

self-centeredness n selfishness, self-interest, egocentricity, egoism, egotism *Opposite*: altruism

self-colored adj uniform, plain, single-color, unpatterned, monochrome *Opposite*: patterned

self-conceit n smugness, arrogance, boastfulness, conceit, superiority *Opposite*: modesty

self-confessed adj admitted, by your own admission, self-proclaimed, acknowledged, known *Opposite*: closet

self-confidence n confidence, self-assurance, self-possession, poise, assurance *Opposite*: insecurity

self-confident adj confident, self-assured, self-possessed poised, assured *Opposite*: insecure

self-congratulation n self-satisfaction, smugness, self-praise, self-glorification, self-flattery *Opposite*: self-hatred

self-conscious adj ill at ease, awkward, uncomfortable, embarrassed, insecure *Opposite*: self-confident

self-contained adj independent, self-sufficient, self-reliant, autonomous *Opposite*: dependent

self-contradictory adj inconsistent, self-contradicting, contradictory, illogical, unreasonable *Opposite*: consistent

self-control n self-discipline, discipline, willpower, restraint, strength of mind *Opposite*: self-indulgence

self-critical adj self-deprecatory, self-deprecating, self-effacing, reticent, humble

self-defense n self-protection, self-preservation, defense, resistance

self-denial n abstinence, abstemiousness, frugality, asceticism, self-discipline *Opposite*: self-indulgence

self-deprecating adj self-critical, self-deprecatory, self-effacing, modest, humble *Opposite*: boastful

self-deprecation n self-criticism, self-depreciation, self-effacement, modesty, humility *Opposite*: boasting

self-determination n autonomy, self-rule, self-government, freedom, independence

self-discipline n self-control, discipline, willpower, restraint, strength of mind *Opposite*: self-indulgence

self-doubt n uncertainty, lack of confidence, insecurity, self-loathing, self-hatred *Opposite*: self-confidence

self-effacing adj modest, quiet, meek, diffident, unassuming Opposite: brash

self-employed adj freelance, your own boss, working for yourself, independent, freelancing Opposite: employed

self-esteem n confidence, self-confidence, self-worth, sense of worth, self-respect Opposite: insecurity

self-evident adj obvious, clear, plain, manifest, undeniable Opposite: unclear

self-explanatory adj clear, easy to understand, easy to follow, transparent, understandable Opposite: unclear

self-expression n creativity, making a statement, assertiveness, individualism, expressing yourself

self-fertilization n self-fertilizing, self-pollination, self-pollinating, autogamy, hermaphroditism Opposite: cross-fertilization

self-flattery n self-congratulation, self-satisfaction, self-praise, self-glorification, self-aggrandizement Opposite: self-abasement

self-glorification n self-promotion, self-congratulation, self-satisfaction, self-praise, self-flattery Opposite: self-deprecation

self-governing adj autonomous, independent, sovereign, self-determining, self-sufficient Opposite: dependent

self-government n autonomy, independence, self-governance, sovereignty, self-rule Opposite: dependence

self-gratification n self-indulgence, hedonism, pleasure-seeking, high living, selfishness Opposite: self-sacrifice

self-hatred n self-contempt, self-loathing, self-disgust, self-denigration, self-dislike Opposite: self-love

self-help n support, mutual support, group support, help, counseling

self-image n opinion of yourself, self-perception, self-esteem, self-regard, self-respect

self-immolation n suicide, self-sacrifice, hara-kiri, suttee, martyrdom

self-importance n arrogance, pride, egotism, haughtiness, pomposity Opposite: humility

self-important adj arrogant, pompous, conceited, egotistic, bumptious Opposite: humble

self-imposed adj chosen, voluntary, self-inflicted, self-induced, of your own free will Opposite: enforced

self-incrimination n self-accusation, self-implication, confession, admission of guilt, self-blame

self-indulgence n 1 decadence, indulgence, hedonism, pleasure, luxury Opposite: restraint 2 self-pity, childishness, selfishness, self-centeredness, self-absorption Opposite: restraint

self-indulgent adj 1 decadent, indulgent, hedonistic, epicurean, luxurious Opposite: restrained 2 self-pitying, wallowing, childish, selfish, self-centered Opposite: restrained

self-interest n selfishness, self-centeredness, egotism, self-regard, egocentricity Opposite: altruism

self-interested adj selfish, self-centered, self-seeking, egocentric, egoistic Opposite: altruistic

selfish adj self-centered, self-seeking, self-interested, egotistic, egoistic Opposite: selfless

selfishness n self-centeredness, self-interest, egotism, egoism, egocentricity Opposite: selflessness

selfless adj unselfish, self-sacrificing, altruistic, generous, noble Opposite: selfish

selflessness n unselfishness, self-sacrifice, altruism, generosity, gallantry Opposite: selfishness

self-love n egotism, selfishness, egocentricity, narcissism, egoism Opposite: modesty

self-motivated adj energetic, dynamic, keen, enthusiastic, driven Opposite: unmotivated

self-obsessed adj self-centered, egocentric, egomaniacal, egotistical, narcissistic

self-opinionated adj 1 overconfident, sure of yourself, cocksure, self-confident, opinionated Opposite: diffident 2 conceited, vain, full of yourself, self-satisfied, big-headed (infml) Opposite: self-deprecating

self-opinioned see self-opinionated

self-pity n self-indulgence, misery, unhappiness, defeatism, self-absorption Opposite: cheerfulness

self-pitying adj self-absorbed, wallowing, defeatist, sorry for yourself, miserable Opposite: happy-go-lucky

self-possessed adj confident, self-assured, self-confident, assured, poised Opposite: insecure

self-possession n confidence, self-assurance, self-confidence, assurance, poise Opposite: insecurity

self-preservation n self-protection, self-defense, survival, preservation instinct, survival instinct

self-promotion n self-aggrandizement, self-importance, self-glorification, self-glory, self-praise Opposite: self-deprecation

self-regard n 1 self-interest, self-centeredness, selfishness, egotism, egocentricity Opposite: altruism 2 self-respect, self-esteem, self-worth, dignity, pride Opposite: self-hatred

self-regarding adj selfish, self-centered, egocentric, egotistic, self-absorbed Opposite: selfless

self-reliance n independence, self-sufficiency, autonomy, self-confidence, self-assurance *Opposite*: dependence

self-reliant *adj* **independent**, self-sufficient, autonomous, self-confident, self-assured *Opposite*: dependent

self-reproach *n* **self-criticism**, remorse, contrition, shame, guilt *Opposite*: self-congratulation

self-respect *n* **self-esteem**, self-confidence, confidence, dignity, pride *Opposite*: self-hatred

self-restraint *n* **self-control**, self-discipline, discipline, willpower, moderation *Opposite*: abandon

self-righteous *adj* **sanctimonious**, smug, self-satisfied, complacent, pious *Opposite*: humble

self-righteousness *n* **sanctimoniousness**, smugness, complacency, piety, superciliousness *Opposite*: humility

self-rule *n* **self-government**, independence, self-determination, autonomy, self-governance *Opposite*: dependence

self-sacrifice *n* **altruism**, unselfishness, selflessness, self-denial, martyrdom *Opposite*: abandon

self-sacrificing *adj* **altruistic**, unselfish, selfless, noble, self-denying *Opposite*: selfish

selfsame *adj* **very same**, identical, very, exact, same *Opposite*: different

self-satisfaction *n* **smugness**, complacency, self-righteousness, conceit, arrogance *Opposite*: self-doubt

self-satisfied *adj* **smug**, pleased with yourself, self-righteous, conceited, arrogant

self-seeking *adj* **selfish**, self-centered, self-regarding, egocentric, egoistic *Opposite*: selfless

self-serving *adj* **selfish**, egotistic, self-centered, narcissistic, egocentric *Opposite*: altruistic

self-styled *adj* **self-appointed**, self-proclaimed, so-called, professed, would-be *Opposite*: certified

self-sufficiency *n* **independence**, autonomy, self-reliance, self-support *Opposite*: dependence

self-sufficient *adj* **independent**, autonomous, self-reliant, self-supporting, self-financing *Opposite*: dependent

self-supporting *adj* **self-sufficient**, self-financing, profitable, healthy, successful *Opposite*: struggling

self-will *n* **determination**, obstinacy, stubbornness, willfulness, pigheadedness *Opposite*: weakness

self-willed *adj* **headstrong**, obstinate, determined, stubborn, pigheaded *Opposite*: weak-willed

self-worth *n* **self-esteem**, self-respect, self-confidence, pride, dignity

sell *v* 1 **vend**, wholesale, trade, retail *Opposite*: buy 2 **put up for sale**, market, offer, deal in, auction *Opposite*: buy 3 **be bought**, go, sell like hotcakes, be snapped up, be popular 4 **persuade people to buy**, market, promote, advertise, traffic in

seller *n* **vendor**, retailer, wholesaler, supplier, merchant *Opposite*: buyer

selling *n* **vending**, sales, marketing, trade, retailing *Opposite*: buying

sell out *v* 1 **run out**, be out of stock, be snapped up, go, be unavailable *Opposite*: stock up 2 **give in**, give up, sell your soul, betray your principles, be co-opted

sellout *n* 1 **box-office hit**, hit, smash hit, smash, bestseller *Opposite*: flop *(infml)* 2 *(infml)* **betrayal**, treachery, disloyalty, apostasy, co-optation *Opposite*: loyalty 3 *(infml)* **traitor**, opportunist, turncoat, renegade, apostate *Opposite*: loyalist

semblance *n* 1 **appearance**, impression, air, resemblance, façade 2 **trace**, shred, fragment, measure, modicum

semiconscious *adj* **half-conscious**, half-awake, half-asleep, surfacing, dazed

semidarkness *n* **twilight**, half-light, dusk, dimness, gloom

semifinal *n* **round**, heat, leg, game, match

seminal *adj* **influential**, important, formative, pivotal, inspirational *Opposite*: insignificant

seminar *n* 1 **meeting**, session, roundtable, discussion, conference 2 **discussion group**, tutorial, class, evening class, talk

seminary *n* **theological college**, divinity school, college, academy, institute

senate *n* **governing body**, legislature, congress, parliament, diet

senator *n* **senate member**, politician, representative, legislator, congresswoman

send *v* 1 **mail**, transmit, dispatch, forward, convey *Opposite*: receive 2 **direct**, refer, guide, show, lead 3 **propel**, hurl, fling, throw, fire *Opposite*: bring 4 **transmit**, project, broadcast, disseminate, give off

send for *v* **request**, summon, call for, order, assemble *Opposite*: dismiss

send forth *(literary)* *v* **produce**, give out, emit, spout, put out *Opposite*: retract

send off *v* **dispatch**, send, send away, transmit, forward *Opposite*: receive

sendoff *n* **goodbye**, farewell, leaving party, valediction *(fml)*, leave-taking *(literary)* *Opposite*: welcome

send over the edge *v* **derange**, unhinge, unsettle, stress out *(infml)*

send packing *(infml)* *v* **dismiss**, expel, evict, turn out, throw out *Opposite*: welcome

send up *v* 1 **raise**, elevate, heighten, boost, bump up *(infml)* *Opposite*: lower 2 *(infml)* **lampoon**, satirize, mock, parody, ridicule

sendup *(infml) n* **parody**, lampoon, takeoff, impersonation, caricature

senile *adj* **confused**, disoriented, forgetful, failing, absent-minded

senior *adj* **1 older**, elder, oldest, eldest, first-born *Opposite:* junior **2 high-ranking**, high-grade, superior, higher, leading *Opposite:* junior ■ *n* **1 elder**, first-born, elder sibling, big brother, big sister *Opposite:* junior **2 senior citizen**, pensioner, golden ager, retiree, retired person **3 boss**, superior, chief, manager, leader *Opposite:* junior

senior citizen *n* **pensioner**, retired person, retiree, senior, golden ager

seniority *n* **superiority**, supremacy, precedence, priority, position

sensation *n* **1 feeling**, sense, impression, awareness, consciousness *Opposite:* numbness **2 commotion**, stir, fuss, uproar, rumpus *Opposite:* lull **3 phenomenon**, miracle, wonder, marvel, spectacle

sensational *adj* **1 outstanding**, excellent, dramatic, amazing, extraordinary *Opposite:* predictable **2 startling**, shocking, scandalous, melodramatic, lurid *Opposite:* understated **3** *(infml)* **amazing**, astounding, marvelous, exciting, thrilling *Opposite:* boring

sensationalism *n* **exaggeration**, overstatement, luridness, scandal, melodrama *Opposite:* understatement

sensationalist *adj* **startling**, shocking, scandalous, melodramatic, lurid *Opposite:* understated

sense *n* **1 feeling**, sensation, awareness, perception **2 appreciation**, impression, consciousness, awareness, feeling **3 intelligence**, brains, intellect, wisdom, sagacity *Opposite:* folly **4 purpose**, point, reason, function, end **5 opinion**, view, viewpoint, consensus, mood **6 gist**, substance, drift, nub, idea **7 meaning**, denotation, significance, signification, implication ■ *v* **1 detect**, identify, distinguish, recognize, know **2 perceive**, feel, have a feeling, get the impression, discern *Opposite:* observe **3 intuit**, guess, suspect, pick up, feel

senseless *adj* **1 pointless**, ridiculous, absurd, meaningless, futile *Opposite:* worthwhile **2 stupid**, silly, foolish, mindless, idiotic *Opposite:* sensible **3 unconscious**, comatose, numb, deadened, knocked out *Opposite:* conscious

senselessness *n* **1 pointlessness**, ridiculousness, absurdity, irrationality, meaninglessness **2 stupidity**, silliness, foolishness, madness, idiocy *Opposite:* sense

sensibility *n* **responsiveness**, deep feeling, emotional response, receptivity, susceptibility *Opposite:* insensitivity

sensible *adj* **1 level-headed**, sane, rational, reasonable, shrewd *Opposite:* foolish **2 practical**, serviceable, workable, functional, utilitarian *Opposite:* impractical **3** *(fml)* **aware**, conscious, mindful, cognizant *(fml)*. *See* COMPARE AND CONTRAST *at* **aware**.

sensibleness *n* **rationality**, level-headedness, reasonableness, shrewdness, wisdom *Opposite:* foolishness

sensitive *adj* **1 responsive**, receptive, susceptible, aware, perceptive *Opposite:* indifferent **2 delicate**, irritable, susceptible, allergic, difficult *Opposite:* robust **3 subtle**, delicate, complex, searching, penetrating *Opposite:* superficial **4 thoughtful**, sympathetic, understanding, perceptive, considerate *Opposite:* unsympathetic **5 thin-skinned**, easily upset, easily hurt, hypersensitive, vulnerable *Opposite:* impervious **6 secret**, confidential, classified, top secret, restricted *Opposite:* public **7 awkward**, tricky, difficult, sticky, delicate *Opposite:* straightforward **8 precise**, exact, delicate, finely tuned, responsive *Opposite:* imprecise

sensitivity *n* **compassion**, sympathy, understanding, kindliness, warmth *Opposite:* indifference

sensitize *v* **1 alert**, make aware, inform, explain, brief *Opposite:* desensitize **2 expose**, make sensitive, irritate, trigger, induce *Opposite:* desensitize

sensor *n* **device**, measuring device, instrument, radar, beam

sensual *adj* **1 sensory**, carnal, bodily, physical, corporeal *Opposite:* intellectual **2 sexual**, erotic, voluptuous, fleshly, carnal *Opposite:* ascetic

sensuous *adj* **sumptuous**, opulent, rich, deep, intense *Opposite:* ascetic

sentence *n* **judgment**, verdict, ruling, decree, condemnation ■ *v* **pass judgment on**, condemn, punish, send to prison, pronounce judgment on *Opposite:* acquit

sententious *adj* **moralizing**, moralistic, judgmental, critical, censorious *Opposite:* approving

sentient *adj* **1 conscious**, animate, flesh-and-blood, alive, living *Opposite:* inanimate **2 emotional**, responsive, sensitive, perceptive, feeling *Opposite:* intellectual

sentiment *n* **1 feeling**, emotion, response, reaction, attitude **2 sentimentality**, mawkishness, gush, romanticism, corn *(infml)*

sentimental *adj* **mawkish**, romantic, slushy, mushy, maudlin *Opposite:* cynical

sentimentality *n* **mawkishness**, corniness, slushiness, mushiness, romanticism *Opposite:* cynicism

sentimentalize *v* **gush**, emotionalize, romanticize, wax lyrical *(literary)*

sentinel *see* **sentry**

sentry *n* **guard**, patrol, lookout, watch, sentinel

separable *adj* **divisible**, distinguishable, detachable, removable, discrete *Opposite*: inseparable

separate *adj* **1 unconnected**, disconnected, individual, independent, unattached *Opposite*: connected **2 distinct**, discrete, detached, loose, dispersed *Opposite*: attached ■ *v* **1 divide**, part, disconnect, undo, split *Opposite*: unite **2 break away**, secede, branch out, break free, break *Opposite*: join **3 split up**, split, divorce, part, part company

separately *adv* **1 distinctly**, unconnectedly, disjointedly, discretely, severally *Opposite*: together **2 independently**, alone, individually, one at a time, singly *Opposite*: together

separateness *n* **distinctness**, disconnectedness, separation, distinctiveness, difference

separate off *v* **divide**, divide off, split off, detach, sever

separate out *v* **strain**, filter, pass through a filter, sieve, extract *Opposite*: cohere *(fml)*

separation *n* **1 division**, severance, taking apart, partition, disjunction *Opposite*: unification **2 parting**, departure, goodbye, farewell, leave-taking *(literary) Opposite*: meeting **3 split-up**, split, divorce, estrangement, rift

separatist *n* **dissenter**, secessionist, protester, rebel, freedom fighter

separator *n* **1 divider**, barrier, partition, dividing wall, screen **2 sieve**, strainer, filter, extractor, centrifuge *Opposite*: blender

septic *adj* **poisoned**, infected, festering, gangrenous, diseased *Opposite*: healthy

sepulcher *n* **vault**, tomb, grave, crypt, burial chamber

sepulchral *adj* **funereal**, sad, dismal, somber, melancholy *Opposite*: cheery

sequel *n* **1 follow-on**, continuation, conclusion, follow-up *Opposite*: prequel **2 consequence**, development, result, outcome, upshot *Opposite*: prelude

sequence *n* **1 series**, succession, run, progression, chain **2 order**, arrangement, classification, categorization, system *Opposite*: disarray

sequential *adj* **1 in sequence**, consecutive, in order, successive, chronological *Opposite*: jumbled **2 consequent**, resulting, resultant, ensuing, following *Opposite*: previous

sequentially *adv* **in sequence**, in succession, successively, in order, consecutively *Opposite*: out of order

sequester *v* **1 confiscate**, requisition, appropriate, impound, seize *Opposite*: restore **2** *(fml)* **isolate**, separate, segregate, cut off, set apart

sequestration *n* **confiscation**, appropriation, impounding, seizure, requisitioning *Opposite*: restoration

sequin *n* **spangle**, bead, bauble, star, decoration

serenade *v* **sing**, croon, court, entertain, divert

serendipitous *adj* **fortunate**, lucky, happy, fortuitous, providential. *See* COMPARE AND CONTRAST *at* lucky.

serendipity *n* **fate**, destiny, karma, providence, luck *Opposite*: design

serene *adj* **1 calm**, composed, unruffled, cool, unflustered *Opposite*: agitated **2 tranquil**, calm, peaceful, still, quiet *Opposite*: bustling

serenity *n* **1 composure**, coolness, peace of mind, poise, contentment *Opposite*: panic **2 tranquility**, calmness, peacefulness, quietude, quietness *Opposite*: bustle

serial *adj* **sequential**, successive, consecutive, ongoing, in order *Opposite*: random

series *n* **sequence**, succession, run, chain, string

serious *adj* **1 dangerous**, acute, life-threatening, critical, grave *Opposite*: minor **2 important**, momentous, significant, crucial, vital *Opposite*: trivial **3 thoughtful**, grave, solemn, somber, stern *Opposite*: lighthearted **4 thought-provoking**, meaningful, intense, deep, profound *Opposite*: lightweight **5 earnest**, sincere, genuine, honest, resolute *Opposite*: flippant

seriously *adv* **1 badly**, dangerously, critically, fatally, acutely *Opposite*: slightly **2 earnestly**, truly, sincerely, genuinely, honestly *Opposite*: jokingly **3** *(infml)* **extremely**, very, really, totally, utterly

serious-minded *adj* **earnest**, sensible, sedate, steady, determined *Opposite*: frivolous

seriousness *n* **1 importance**, significance, gravity, weightiness, momentousness *Opposite*: triviality **2 earnestness**, sincerity, genuineness, honesty, resoluteness *Opposite*: flippancy

sermon *n* **1 talk**, address, homily, discourse, oration *Opposite*: conversation **2 lecture**, harangue, homily, talking-to *(infml)*, ticking-off *(infml) Opposite*: praise

sermonize *v* **preach**, pontificate, moralize, hold forth, lecture *Opposite*: flatter

serpent *n* **1** *(literary)* **snake**, sea serpent, sea snake, viper, reptile **2 traitor**, liar, cheat, troublemaker, snake in the grass *Opposite*: friend

serpentine *adj* **winding**, meandering, twisting, sinuous, bending *Opposite*: straight

serrated *adj* **jagged**, toothed, notched, ragged, saw-toothed *Opposite*: smooth

servant *n* **domestic**, retainer, help *Opposite*: employer

---

WORD BANK

❏ **types of servants** butler, chambermaid, cleaner, cook, factotum, flunky, footman, lackey, maid, maidservant, major-domo, valet

serve v 1 **work for**, help, aid, attend, assist 2 **function**, work, operate, act, perform 3 **supply**, dish up, serve up, hand out, give out 4 **wait on**, wait, attend, tend, minister to

service n 1 **help**, assistance, aid, use, benefit *Opposite*: disservice 2 **facility**, provision, package, deal, amenity 3 **overhaul**, examination, check, tune-up, maintenance 4 **ceremony**, ritual, rite, sacrament, mass 5 **armed forces**, military, service, defense force, army ■ v **repair**, overhaul, examine, tune, check

serviceable adj 1 **durable**, strong, stout, tough, sturdy *Opposite*: flimsy 2 **working**, operative, functional, in working order, usable *Opposite*: broken 3 **effective**, helpful, practical, useful, practicable *Opposite*: impractical

servile adj **submissive**, abject, fawning, subservient, sycophantic *Opposite*: proud

serving n **portion**, helping, plateful, ration, quota

serving dish n **platter**, salver, plate, tray, dish

servitude n 1 **slavery**, bondage, serfdom, enslavement, vassalage *Opposite*: freedom 2 **subjection**, subjugation, subordination, dependence, dependency *Opposite*: liberty

session n 1 **meeting**, sitting, assembly, conference, gathering 2 **term**, period, semester, trimester, quarter 3 **shift**, stint, go, spell, turn

set v 1 **put**, place, locate, position, situate *Opposite*: pick up 2 **become hard**, harden, solidify, congeal, coagulate *Opposite*: liquefy 3 **establish**, fix, agree on, appoint, decide *Opposite*: change 4 **adjust**, regulate, synchronize, align, program ■ n 1 **scenery**, stage set, movie set, setting, location 2 **collection**, group, arrangement, array, series *Opposite*: individual 3 **circle**, group, clique, gang, crowd ■ adj 1 **established**, usual, customary, traditional, conventional *Opposite*: changing 2 **inflexible**, obstinate, determined, resolute, resolved *Opposite*: flexible 3 **ready**, prepared, fit, primed, organized *Opposite*: unprepared 4 **firm**, congealed, solid, hard, fixed *Opposite*: liquid 5 *see* **sett**

set about v **begin**, tackle, start, launch into, get down to

set against v 1 **compare**, contrast, consider, set side by side, oppose 2 **pit against**, turn against, set as rivals, set in opposition, alienate *Opposite*: bring together

set alight v **kindle**, light, ignite, set fire to, set on fire *Opposite*: put out

set apart v 1 **reserve**, put aside, keep on one side, set aside, separate 2 **distinguish**, differentiate, single out, make something stand out, mark out

set aside v 1 **reserve**, save, keep back, put to one side, lay by *Opposite*: use up 2 **reject**, discard, annul, break free from, shake off

set back v **delay**, hinder, hold up, impede, slow down *Opposite*: facilitate

setback n **hindrance**, holdup, delay, impediment, stumbling block *Opposite*: boost

set down v 1 **put down**, lay down, place, deposit, put 2 **write down**, report, record, chronicle, write out

set eyes on v **catch sight of**, observe, notice, sight, spot

set fire to v **kindle**, light, ignite, set alight, set on fire *Opposite*: put out

set foot in v **enter**, go in, come into, show your face, turn up

set forth v 1 (*fml*) **state**, describe, express, lay down, present 2 (*literary*) **leave**, depart, set out, set off, start out *Opposite*: arrive

set free v 1 **liberate**, free, release, discharge, let go *Opposite*: imprison 2 **untie**, unloose, unshackle, unleash, let loose *Opposite*: tie up

set in v **come to stay**, be here to stay, take root, become established, become entrenched *Opposite*: pass

set in motion v **start**, initiate, begin, kick-start, set off *Opposite*: stop

set off v 1 **start out**, set out, go, depart, leave *Opposite*: arrive 2 **detonate**, explode, light, ignite, trigger *Opposite*: defuse 3 **start**, begin, commence, start off, burst out *Opposite*: finish 4 **initiate**, instigate, launch, inaugurate, begin 5 **draw attention to**, display, bring out, highlight, enhance

set on v **attack**, set upon, assault, lay into, terrorize

set on fire v **kindle**, light, ignite, set alight, set fire to *Opposite*: put out

set out v 1 **leave**, set off, depart, go, move off *Opposite*: arrive 2 **embark on**, start, begin, commence, set off *Opposite*: finish 3 **plan**, aim, intend, determine, design 4 **display**, lay out, arrange, present, show 5 **explain**, specify, define, describe, detail

set phrase n **expression**, phrase, idiom, turn of phrase, saying

set right v **correct**, rectify, right, put right, put to rights

set store by v **deem important**, value, esteem, prize, regard highly

sett n **paving stone**, paving slab, paver, stone, slab

settee n **sofa**, couch, loveseat, chaise lounge, divan

setting n **location**, surroundings, scenery, situation, background

settle v 1 **resolve**, reconcile, clear up, straighten out, mend 2 **stay**, inhabit, put down roots, set up house, establish yourself 3 **sink**, drop, descend, fall, go to the bottom *Opposite*: rise 4 **pay**, defray, discharge, clear, foot *Opposite*: owe 5 **land**, perch, alight, roost, come to rest *Opposite*: take off **6 become peaceful**, become calm, settle down, calm down, relax *Opposite*: fluster

settled *adj* **established**, stable, solid, firm, steady *Opposite*: unsettled

settle down *v* **1 become less restless**, quiet down, relax, calm down, snuggle down *Opposite*: agitate **2 sink**, drop, descend, fall, stabilize *Opposite*: rise

settle for *v* **agree to**, accept, make do with, take, be happy with *Opposite*: refuse

settle in *v* **1 adapt**, acclimatize, adjust, get used to it, find your feet **2 get comfortable**, snuggle down, ensconce yourself, bed down, get comfy

settlement *n* **1 resolution**, conclusion, completion, decision, agreement **2 payment**, defrayal, clearance, clearing, reimbursement *Opposite*: receipt **3 community**, village, town, township, colony

settle on *v* **choose**, pick, select, decide on, agree on *Opposite*: reject

settler *n* **colonizer**, colonist, pioneer, pilgrim, immigrant

settle up *v* **pay the bill**, pay, pay up, settle the debt, settle your account *Opposite*: quibble

set to *v* **1 get on with it**, put your shoulder to the wheel, make a start, get started, start work **2 come to blows**, start fighting, lay into, grapple, tussle

set-to *(infml)* *n* **confrontation**, quarrel, altercation, disagreement, row *Opposite*: reconciliation

set up *v* **1 erect**, raise, build, construct, put up **2 establish**, inaugurate, found, institute, launch **3** *(infml)* **frame**, trap, entrap, trick, con

setup *n* **1 system**, arrangement, format, situation, structure **2** *(infml)* **frame**, trap, trick, deception, con

set upon *v* **attack**, assault, lay into, assail, pounce on *Opposite*: defend

seventh heaven *n* **bliss**, ecstasy, heaven, nirvana, cloud nine *Opposite*: despair

sever *v* **1 cut**, split, separate, undo, disunite *Opposite*: unite **2 cut off**, chop off, lop off, shear off, slice off *Opposite*: attach

several *adj* **some**, quite a lot of, a number of, numerous, many

severally *adv* **separately**, individually, singly, one at a time, one by one *Opposite*: together

severance *n* **1 separation**, detachment, disconnection, division, taking apart *Opposite*: joining **2 compensation**, severance pay, golden handshake *(infml)*, golden parachute *(infml)*

severe *adj* **1 harsh**, stern, strict, cruel, brutal *Opposite*: gentle **2 acute**, grave, critical, mortal, serious *Opposite*: slight **3 plain**, simple, spartan, unadorned, unembellished *Opposite*: ornate

severity *n* **1 harshness**, sternness, strictness, cruelty, brutality *Opposite*: gentleness **2 gravity**, seriousness, acuteness, dangerousness, awfulness *Opposite*: insignificance **3 plainness**, simplicity, starkness, bareness, austerity *Opposite*: opulence

sew *v* **stitch**, seam, baste, tack, hem *Opposite*: unpick

sewer *n* **drain**, septic tank, cesspit, cesspool, open drain

sewing *n* **stitching**, embroidery, tapestry, needlework, needlepoint

sew up *v* **1 settle**, clinch, tie up, finalize, finish **2 stitch up**, sew, stitch, darn, repair *Opposite*: unpick

sex *n* **gender**, sexual category, masculinity, femininity

sexy *adj* **1 erotic**, sensual, sexual, suggestive, pleasurable **2 voluptuous**, curvaceous, sensuous, alluring, attractive

shabbiness *n* **1 scruffiness**, untidiness, dilapidation, seediness, raggedness *Opposite*: elegance **2 inconsiderateness**, unfairness, meanness, disrespect, negligence *Opposite*: decency

shabby *adj* **1 scruffy**, untidy, ragged, tattered, worn out *Opposite*: elegant **2 inconsiderate**, unjust, mean, dishonorable, contemptible *Opposite*: decent

shack *n* **hut**, shanty, hovel, lean-to, shed

shackle *v* **1 fetter**, manacle, handcuff, chain, put in irons *Opposite*: free **2 constrain**, restrict, impede, hamper, hinder *Opposite*: facilitate

shackles *n* **fetters**, manacles, chains, restraints, irons

shade *n* **1 shadow**, dark, darkness, gloom, gloominess *Opposite*: light **2 blind**, screen, awning, canopy, cover **3 hue**, tint, tinge, color, tone **4 hint**, trace, suggestion, touch, dash ■ *v* **1 cover**, shield, protect, screen, veil *Opposite*: expose **2 darken**, eclipse, blot out, shadow, block out *Opposite*: brighten **3 fill in**, hatch, color, color in, block in

shades *(infml)* *n* **sunglasses**, dark glasses, tinted lenses

shadiness *n* **1 dishonesty**, crookedness, underhandedness, shiftiness, suspiciousness *Opposite*: honesty **2 dimness**, dark, darkness, shadowiness, obscurity *Opposite*: brightness

shadow *n* **1 silhouette**, outline, shape, figure, form **2 shade**, dark, darkness, gloom, gloominess *Opposite*: light **3 hint**, trace, suggestion, touch, shade **4 constant companion**, alter ego, sidekick, other self, double **5 private investigator**, private detective, private eye *(infml)*, sleuth *(infml)*, gumshoe *(dated infml)* **6 follower**, stalker, pursuer, tracker, tail *(infml)* **7 ghost**, specter, spirit, wraith, apparition ■ *v* **1 follow**, trail, track, stalk, observe **2 darken**, eclipse, blot out, shade *Opposite*:

brighten. *See* COMPARE AND CONTRAST *at* **follow**.

shadows n **shade**, dark, darkness, obscurity, dimness *Opposite*: light

shadowy adj **1 indistinct**, obscure, vague, indistinguishable, unclear *Opposite*: distinct **2 dim**, dark, murky, gloomy, poorly lit *Opposite*: bright **3 ghostly**, spectral, ethereal, sinister, mysterious *Opposite*: material

shady adj **1 out of the sun**, in the shade, shaded, under the trees, cool *Opposite*: sunny **2 dishonest**, underhand, shifty, suspicious, devious *Opposite*: aboveboard

shagginess n **hairiness**, dishevelment, untidiness, bushiness, scruffiness *Opposite*: neatness

shaggy adj **hairy**, unkempt, disheveled, bushy, unshaven *Opposite*: tidy

shake v **1 wobble**, jolt, jerk, bounce, sway **2 tremble**, quiver, quake, shudder, shiver **3 agitate**, stir, blend, mix **4 unsettle**, unnerve, disturb, distress, upset *Opposite*: reassure **5 brandish**, flourish, flaunt, wave, wield ■ n **1 tremor**, vibration, wobble, lurch, sway **2 shudder**, quiver, quake, tremble, shiver **3 waggle**, wave, flourish, twirl

shake off v **1 get rid of**, get away from, lose, elude, leave behind **2 recover from**, recuperate from, get over, get rid of *Opposite*: succumb

shakeout n **transformation**, radical change, overhaul, reorganization, reform

shake up v **1 transform**, overhaul, change drastically, revamp, rethink *Opposite*: leave alone **2 upset**, disturb, distress, shock, alarm *Opposite*: calm down **3 mix**, blend, combine, agitate, shake

shake-up n **transformation**, radical change, upheaval, overhaul, reorganization

shakiness n **1 tremor**, shaking, trembling, shake, jerkiness *Opposite*: control **2 wobbliness**, instability, flimsiness, fragility, insubstantiality *Opposite*: sturdiness **3 uncertainty**, precariousness, instability, unreliability, weakness *Opposite*: reliability

shaking n **vibration**, jolting, rocking, rattling, shuddering

shaky adj **1 trembling**, shaking, quivering, quaking, shuddering *Opposite*: composed **2 wobbly**, unstable, unsteady, insecure, rickety *Opposite*: steady **3 unsupported**, unsound, questionable, dubious, doubtful *Opposite*: dependable

shallow adj **1 low**, thin, light, narrow, surface *Opposite*: deep **2 superficial**, trivial, slight, insubstantial, petty *Opposite*: profound

sham n **1 pretense**, deception, charade, con, fraud **2 impostor**, charlatan, con, fake, fraud ■ adj **fake**, mock, bogus, imitation, pretended *Opposite*: bona fide ■ v **pretend**, fake, put it on, act, play *Opposite*: real

shamble v **shuffle**, amble, waddle, drag your feet, walk *Opposite*: stride

shambles n **1 fiasco**, disaster, failure, mess, botch (infml) *Opposite*: success **2 chaos**, muddle, tip, clutter, dump

shambling adj **awkward**, ungainly, clumsy, uncoordinated, lumbering *Opposite*: graceful

shame n **disgrace**, embarrassment, dishonor, humiliation, mortification *Opposite*: pride ■ v **embarrass**, discredit, disgrace, humiliate, mortify *Opposite*: honor

shamefaced adj **ashamed**, embarrassed, abashed, sheepish, hangdog *Opposite*: proud

shameful adj **disgraceful**, reprehensible, dishonorable, discreditable, shocking *Opposite*: honorable

shameless adj **brazen**, barefaced, unabashed, blatant, unashamed *Opposite*: ashamed

shamelessness n **lack of remorse**, brazenness, hardheartedness, boldness, impudence *Opposite*: repentance

shank n **stem**, shaft, trunk, rod, bar

shape n **1 form**, figure, outline, silhouette, profile **2 character**, nature, form, identity, structure ■ v **1 model**, mold, whittle, manipulate, smooth **2 sway**, determine, cause, influence, affect

WORD BANK

❏ **types of angular shapes** box, cross, cube, diamond, dodecahedron, dogleg, lozenge, oblong, parallelogram, pentagon, polygon, pyramid, quadrangle, quadrilateral, rectangle, rhomboid, rhombus, square, star, tetragon, tetrahedron, trapezium, trapezoid, triangle

❏ **types of rounded shapes** arc, arch, ball, bend, bow, bulb, circle, circlet, coil, cone, crescent, curl, curve, cylinder, dome, figure eight, globe, heart, helix, hemisphere, hoop, horseshoe, kidney, loop, orb, oval, ring, round, semicircle, sphere, spheroid, spiral, teardrop

shapeless adj **baggy**, loose-fitting, formless, ill-defined, amorphous *Opposite*: defined

shapelessness n **amorphousness**, formlessness, bagginess, fluidity *Opposite*: definition

shapely adj **well-formed**, attractive, well-rounded, well-proportioned, pleasing

shape up v **1 develop**, progress, improve, come along, come together **2 improve**, pull yourself together, get it together, reform, mend your ways

shard n **sliver**, splinter, spike, shaving, chip

share v **1 split**, go halves, divide, divide up, divvy (infml) **2 distribute**, allocate, assign, apportion, allot **3 communicate**, let somebody in on, impart, reveal, disclose ■ n **part**, portion, segment, cut, stake *Opposite*: whole

shared adj **common**, communal, joint, mutual, collective

share out v **divide up**, give out, parcel out, distribute, allot

sharp adj 1 **pointed**, razor-sharp, tapered, pointy, jagged Opposite: blunt 2 **quick**, intelligent, razor-sharp, incisive, astute Opposite: dull 3 **abrupt**, sudden, quick, brusque, urgent Opposite: gentle 4 **shrill**, piercing, loud, high-pitched, strident Opposite: soft 5 **harsh**, severe, snappy, sarcastic, snappish Opposite: gentle 6 **severe**, acute, strong, hard, intense Opposite: mild 7 **sour**, tangy, acid, acrid, pungent Opposite: sweet 8 **clear**, well-defined, definite, clear-cut, distinct Opposite: imprecise ■ adv **exactly**, precisely, on the dot, promptly, punctually

sharpen v 1 **hone**, whet, grind, file, strop Opposite: blunt 2 **improve**, hone, perfect, brush up, refine Opposite: worsen

sharp-eyed adj 1 **observant**, watchful, alert, vigilant, attentive Opposite: unobservant 2 **eagle-eyed**, with good eyesight, with good vision, with eyes like a hawk, hawk-eyed Opposite: nearsighted

sharply adv 1 **abruptly**, suddenly, all at once, hard, tight Opposite: gradually 2 **harshly**, severely, cuttingly, unkindly, snappishly Opposite: gently 3 **alarmingly**, steeply, greatly, dramatically, suddenly Opposite: gradually 4 **briskly**, abruptly, suddenly, smartly, swiftly Opposite: slowly 5 **extremely**, clearly, acutely, distinctly, deeply Opposite: subtly 6 **clearly**, distinctly, strikingly, obviously, eye-catchingly Opposite: hazily

sharpness n 1 **acuity**, perceptiveness, intelligence, quickness, keenness Opposite: slowness 2 **harshness**, severity, unkindness, snappishness, terseness Opposite: gentleness 3 **clarity**, definition, distinctness, contrast, intensity Opposite: haziness 4 **acidity**, sourness, bitterness, bite, pungency Opposite: sweetness

sharp-sighted adj 1 **eagle-eyed**, with good eyesight, with good vision, with eyes like a hawk, hawk-eyed 2 **observant**, watchful, alert, vigilant, attentive Opposite: unobservant

sharp-tongued adj **sarcastic**, caustic, harsh, mean, brusque Opposite: gentle

sharp-witted adj **quick**, sharp, quick-witted, acute, bright

shatter v 1 **smash**, break, smash to smithereens, splinter, fragment 2 **destroy**, wreck, crush, blast, demolish Opposite: build up

shattered adj **devastated**, crushed, traumatized, horrified, suffering

shattering adj **devastating**, crushing, shocking, earthshattering, cataclysmic Opposite: wonderful

shatterproof adj **indestructible**, unbreakable, nonbreaking, resistant, strengthened

shave v **cut off**, shear, cut, trim, clip

shaving n **chip**, splinter, flake, shred, sliver Opposite: chunk

shawl n **wrap**, stole, scarf, rebozo, cloak

sheaf n **bundle**, cluster, clump, wad, stack

shear v **cut off**, shave, clip, trim, crop

sheath n **cover**, case, casing, covering, scabbard

sheathe v 1 **put away**, replace, retract, stash (infml) Opposite: take out 2 **envelop**, swathe, cloak, wrap, drape

sheathing n **casing**, covering, outer layer, jacket, shield

shed v 1 **radiate**, emit, disperse, cast, project 2 **cast off**, slough off, get rid of, molt, lose

shed light on v **clarify**, explain, illuminate, elucidate, clear up

sheen n **shine**, polish, luster, gloss, gleam

sheep n 1 **ewe**, ram, lamb 2 **conformist**, follower, traditionalist, lemming, yes man Opposite: individualist

sheepish adj **ashamed**, shamefaced, embarrassed, hangdog, guilty Opposite: unashamed

sheepishness n **shame**, embarrassment, guilt, awkwardness, self-consciousness

sheer adj 1 **pure**, complete, absolute, utter, unalloyed 2 **steep**, vertical, perpendicular, precipitous, abrupt Opposite: gentle 3 **fine**, transparent, translucent, thin, diaphanous Opposite: thick ■ adv **vertically**, straight up, plumb, precipitously, steeply

sheerness n **fineness**, thinness, translucence, transparency, gauziness Opposite: thickness

sheet n 1 **piece**, page, leaf, folio, slip 2 **expanse**, mass, area, layer

sheik n **leader**, ruler, chief, chieftain, head

shelf n 1 **ledge**, sill, projection, bookshelf, mantelpiece 2 **layer**, ridge, step, ledge, rock shelf

shell n 1 **case**, casing, covering, shield, crust 2 **husk**, skeleton, carcass, remains 3 **bomb**, explosive, missile, mortar, projectile ■ v **bombard**, shoot at, fire at, open fire on, shoot down

shellfish n **crustacean**, mollusk, seafood

WORD BANK

❏ **types of shellfish** abalone, clam, crab, crayfish, langoustine, lobster, mussel, oyster, prawn, quahog, scallop, shrimp

---

shell out (infml) v **pay out**, pay up, pay, spend, give

shelter n 1 **protection**, cover, refuge, retreat, haven 2 **housing**, accommodations, living quarters, lodging, somewhere to stay ■ v 1 **protect**, shield, cover, defend, harbor 2 **take shelter**, take refuge, take cover, hide

sheltered adj 1 **protected**, privileged, comfortable, shielded, cozy Opposite: harsh 2 **secluded**, protected, shielded, isolated, insulated Opposite: exposed

shelve v **put on hold**, put on ice, defer, abandon, cancel

shenanigans *(infml)* n **1 trickery**, mischief, trouble, monkeyshines, to-do *(infml)* **2 playfulness**, joking around, pranks, tricks, tomfoolery *(infml)*

shepherd v marshal, drive, guide, steer, pilot

sherd see shard

shield n **protection**, armor, defense, safeguard, buffer ■ v **protect**, guard, defend, shelter, safeguard *Opposite*: expose. *See* COMPARE AND CONTRAST *at* **safeguard**.

shielded *adj* **protected**, safeguarded, isolated, defended, sheltered *Opposite*: exposed

shift v **move**, budge, vary, transfer, change ■ n **1 move**, swing, modification, alteration, change **2 stint**, spell, scheduled time, period, turn. *See* COMPARE AND CONTRAST *at* **change**.

shifting *adj* **unstable**, ever-changing, fluctuating, fluid, flowing *Opposite*: fixed

shiftless *adj* **lazy**, idle, good-for-nothing, indolent, slothful *Opposite*: industrious

shifty *adj* **suspicious**, suspect, dubious, dishonest, untrustworthy *Opposite*: trustworthy

shilly-shally v **1 waver**, dilly-dally, dither, hesitate, vacillate *Opposite*: decide **2 waste time**, hang around, dawdle, delay, dally *Opposite*: forge ahead

shimmer v **sparkle**, glisten, shine, glitter, gleam

shimmering *adj* **iridescent**, sparkling, shining, gleaming, glistening

shindig *(infml)* n **party**, bash, jamboree, get-together *(infml)*

shine v **1 glow**, gleam, glimmer, sparkle, glitter **2 excel**, be good at, stand out, have a gift for, be skilled at *Opposite*: bomb *(infml)* **3 polish**, burnish, wax, buff, buff up ■ n **sheen**, polish, luster, gloss, gleam

shining *adj* **outstanding**, excellent, admirable, brilliant, superb *Opposite*: poor

shiny *adj* **glossy**, gleaming, glittery, polished, shimmering *Opposite*: dull

ship n **vessel**, craft, boat ■ v **send**, transport, distribute, dispatch, convey

WORD BANK

❏ **types of historical vessels** clipper, flagship, galleon, galley, Indiaman, longboat, longship, man-of-war, tall ship, windjammer

❏ **types of military vessels** aircraft carrier, battle cruiser, battleship, cruiser, cutter, destroyer, frigate, gunboat, minesweeper, PT boat, submarine, warship

❏ **types of motor vessels** barge, cabin cruiser, canal boat, coaster, container ship, cutter, dredger, factory ship, ferry, ferryboat, freighter, houseboat, hovercraft, hydrofoil, icebreaker, launch, lifeboat, lighter, lightship, motorboat, powerboat, speedboat, steamboat, steamer, tanker, trawler, tug, tugboat

❏ **types of sailing vessels** bark, brig, brigantine, catamaran, catboat, dhow, felucca, junk, ketch, sailboat, schooner, sloop, smack, trimaran, yacht

❏ **types of small vessels** canoe, dinghy, dory, dugout, gondola, kayak, life raft, pirogue, punt, raft, rowboat, sampan, scull, skiff

❏ **parts of a sailing vessel** boom, bowsprit, fore-and-aft sail, gaff, jib, mainsail, mainstay, mast, mizzen, pennant, sheet, shroud, spanker, spinnaker, topsail

❏ **parts of a ship or boat** bilge, bow, bridge, cabin, capstan, crow's nest, deck, engine room, forecastle, galley, gunwale, helm, hold, hull, keel, oarlock, outboard motor, outrigger, poop, prow, rudder, stateroom, stern, superstructure, tiller

shipment n **consignment**, delivery, batch, load, cargo

shipping n **delivery**, transportation, distribution, carriage, freight

shipshape *adj* **in order**, neat, tidy, organized, spick-and-span *Opposite*: untidy

shirk v **evade**, avoid, dodge, duck, get out of *Opposite*: accept

shirker n **lazy person**, slacker, idler, loafer, malingerer *Opposite*: worker

shiver v **shake**, tremble, quiver, quake, shudder ■ n **quiver**, shudder, tremor, tremble, quake

shoal n **sandbar**, sandbank, ridge, shallows

shock n **1 distress**, numbness, devastation, disbelief, astonishment **2 surprise**, jolt, blow, bombshell, kick in the teeth ■ v **1 stun**, alarm, surprise, frighten, astonish *Opposite*: calm **2 scandalize**, outrage, appall, offend, horrify **3 traumatize**, upset, devastate, shake up, alarm *Opposite*: reassure

shocked *adj* **1 surprised**, stunned, dazed, upset, shaken *Opposite*: indifferent **2 scandalized**, outraged, appalled, offended *Opposite*: indifferent

shocking *adj* **1 outrageous**, scandalous, offensive, disgraceful, reprehensible *Opposite*: acceptable **2 distressing**, startling, upsetting, disturbing, worrying *Opposite*: comforting **3** *(infml)* **dreadful**, awful, bad, appalling, lamentable *Opposite*: pleasant

shockingly *adv* **1 outrageously**, scandalously, disgracefully, reprehensibly, unpardonably *Opposite*: acceptably **2 startlingly**, distressingly, upsettingly, disturbingly, worryingly *Opposite*: comfortingly **3 dreadfully**, awfully, appallingly, lamentably, horribly

shock wave n **1 repercussion**, reaction, shock, effect **2 tremor**, shudder, shock, trembling, agitation

shoddy *adj* **1 careless**, slapdash, inferior, cheap, substandard *Opposite*: fine **2 inconsiderate**, mean, unkind, dishonest, rotten *Opposite*: considerate

shoelace n **cord**, lace, bootlace, tie, fastener

shoo away v chase off, drive away, frighten away, scare off Opposite: invite

shoot v 1 fire, open fire, fire off, fire at, bombard 2 kill, slaughter, shoot down, bring down, gun down (infml) 3 spurt, squirt, burst, jet, gush 4 film, photograph, take, snap, capture 5 aim, point, direct, cast, score 6 start to grow, produce buds, develop, appear, sprout 7 (infml) dart, dash, run, race, speed ■ n new growth, branch, leaf bud, outgrowth, stem

shoot down v 1 kill, slaughter, destroy, murder, bring down 2 attack, tear to shreds, pick holes in, pillory, criticize

shooting n 1 gunfire, shelling, bombardment, fire, firing 2 killing, murder, assassination, execution, slaying

shoot up v appear, soar, rocket, spring up, mushroom Opposite: plummet

shop n 1 store, outlet, emporium, showroom 2 spree, shopping spree, shopping expedition, binge, retail therapy 3 workshop, plant, factory, garage, yard ■ v go shopping, buy groceries, go window-shopping, go on a spree, do the marketing

shoplift v steal, rob, pilfer, thieve, pocket

shoplifting n stealing, theft, thieving, pilfering, larceny

shopper n customer, consumer, buyer, purchaser, bargain hunter

shopping n errands, spending, clothes shopping, grocery shopping, supermarket run

shopping mall n shopping center, arcade, mall, strip mall, shopping plaza

shore n coast, beach, seashore, coastline, seaboard

shoreline n beach, shore, seashore, water's edge, coastline

shore up v prop up, support, hold up, buttress, bolster

shorn of adj deprived of, stripped of, minus, less, lacking

short adj 1 small, little, petite, tiny, diminutive Opposite: tall 2 brief, quick, rapid, fleeting, passing Opposite: lengthy 3 concise, succinct, condensed, brief, to the point Opposite: long 4 curt, brusque, snappy, abrupt, unfriendly Opposite: friendly ■ adv midstream, abruptly, suddenly, sharply Opposite: gradually

shortage n lack, scarcity, deficiency, dearth, famine Opposite: excess. See COMPARE AND CONTRAST at lack.

short break n break, rest, weekend away, midweek break, a few days away

shortcoming n inadequacy, failing, fault, deficiency, limitation Opposite: virtue

short course n crash course, intensive course, introductory course, refresher course

shorten v cut down, cut, cut back, curtail, abbreviate Opposite: lengthen

shortening n fat, lard, margarine, butter, suet

shortfall n deficit, loss, underperformance, gap, lack Opposite: excess

short form n abbreviation, shortening, contraction, acronym, ellipsis

short-handed adj short-staffed, understaffed, short

short-list v select, choose, pick out, cream off, narrow down

short-lived adj brief, fleeting, transitory, passing, short Opposite: long-lasting. See COMPARE AND CONTRAST at temporary.

shortly adv 1 soon, before long, in a while, in a minute, in a moment Opposite: later 2 curtly, brusquely, abruptly, briskly, tersely Opposite: pleasantly

shortness n 1 smallness, tininess, squatness, dumpiness Opposite: tallness 2 quickness, rapidity, speed, transience Opposite: length 3 briefness, brevity, terseness, conciseness, concision Opposite: length 4 curtness, brusqueness, abruptness, briskness, terseness Opposite: pleasantness

short of prep apart from, other than, without, bar Opposite: including

short-sighted adj ill-considered, thoughtless, unthinking, imprudent, ill-advised Opposite: farsighted

short-sightedness n thoughtlessness, imprudence, rashness, hastiness Opposite: farsightedness

short-staffed adj short-handed, understaffed, understrength

short story n novella, tale, story, fable, parable Opposite: epic

short-tempered adj quick-tempered, irritable, impatient, irascible, touchy

short-term adj temporary, immediate, instant, short-range, interim Opposite: long-term

shot n 1 gunshot, potshot, round, volley, report 2 bullet, cannonball, slug, gunshot, buckshot 3 picture, photo, photograph, snapshot, snap 4 try, go, attempt, turn, crack (infml) 5 (infml) injection, inoculation, vaccination 6 (infml) measure, drink, glass, tot, slug (infml)

shot in the arm n boost, fillip, spur, kickstart, stimulus

shot in the dark n guess, conjecture, speculation, potshot, attempt

should v ought to, had better, have a duty to, be duty-bound to, must

shoulder v bear, take on, accept, assume, carry Opposite: refuse

shout v yell, cry, scream, bellow, screech Opposite: whisper ■ n cry, yell, scream, bellow, screech Opposite: whisper

shout at v yell at, scold, reprimand, haul over the coals, berate Opposite: praise

shove v 1 push, thrust, heave, propel, jostle

Opposite: pull **2 put**, throw, toss, slap, sling ■ *n* thrust, push, heave, jolt

shovel *n* **spade**, scoop, trowel, tool ■ *v* **scoop**, move, dig, spoon, heap

show *v* **1 present**, display, exhibit, expose, disclose *Opposite*: hide **2 stand out**, stick out, show up, appear, surface **3 accompany**, take, guide, direct, point **4 prove**, illustrate, demonstrate, confirm, indicate *Opposite*: disprove **5 demonstrate**, illustrate, explain, teach, point out ■ *n* **1 demonstration**, display, expression, illustration, appearance **2 performance**, musical, cabaret, play, film **3 fair**, exhibition, trade show, agricultural show, fashion show

show business *n* **the stage**, theater, the boards, films, movies

showcase *n* **1 glass case**, cabinet, display case, display cabinet, vitrine **2 platform**, vehicle, setting, stage

showdown *n* **confrontation**, head-to-head, face-off, fight, argument

shower *n* **1 wash**, dip, rinse, spray **2 cascade**, burst, deluge, hail, spray **3 cloudburst**, downpour, storm, rainstorm, flurry ■ *v* **1 wash**, clean up, freshen up, rinse **2 rain**, rain down, pour, pour down, sprinkle **3 overwhelm**, inundate, flood, deluge, bombard

showery *adj* **rainy**, wet, changeable, damp, spitting *Opposite*: dry

showground *n* **arena**, ring, enclosure, field, ground

showing *n* **presentation**, performance, viewing, screening, display

showing off *n* **bravado**, boastfulness, boasting, bragging, posturing

show off *v* **1 boast**, brag, shoot your mouth off, sing your own praises, pose **2 display**, flaunt, parade, flourish, flash *(infml)* *Opposite*: hide

show-off *(infml)* *n* **boaster**, braggart, bragger, exhibitionist, know-it-all *(infml)*

showpiece *n* **centerpiece**, pride and joy, focus, attraction, pièce de résistance

showroom *n* **shop**, outlet, store

show up *v* **1** *(infml)* **come**, turn up, arrive, put in an appearance, appear **2 highlight**, emphasize, point up, bring to light, reveal *Opposite*: hide **3 stand out**, stick out, show, catch your eye, come to light **4 embarrass**, humiliate, put somebody to shame, mortify, shame

showy *adj* **1 impressive**, attractive, eye-catching, splendid, magnificent *Opposite*: modest **2 ostentatious**, flashy, gaudy, garish, tasteless *Opposite*: restrained

show your face *v* **turn up**, appear, put in an appearance, come, arrive *Opposite*: hide

shred *n* **scrap**, strip, bit, piece, sliver *Opposite*: whole ■ *v* **slice**, cut up, tear up, rip up, grate

shrewd *adj* **astute**, sharp, smart, perceptive, discerning *Opposite*: naive

shrewdness *n* **astuteness**, sharpness, smartness, perceptiveness, discernment *Opposite*: naiveté

shriek *n* **screech**, scream, yell, cry, yelp *Opposite*: whisper

shrill *adj* **piercing**, high-pitched, strident, penetrating, harsh *Opposite*: low

shrine *n* **memorial**, monument, tomb, grave, sanctuary

shrink *v* **1 contract**, shrivel, wither, telescope, shorten *Opposite*: grow **2 fall**, drop, decrease, decline, diminish *Opposite*: rise **3 cower**, cringe, flinch, recoil, draw back *Opposite*: stand your ground. *See* COMPARE AND CONTRAST *at* recoil.

shrinkage *n* **reduction**, decrease, decline, contraction, fall *Opposite*: growth

shrink back *v* **recoil**, cringe, shrink away, shy away, flinch *Opposite*: advance

shrink from *v* **recoil from**, balk at, avoid, shirk, shun *Opposite*: welcome

shrivel *v* **shrink**, wither, dry up, contract, curl up *Opposite*: expand

shroud *n* **covering**, cover, blanket, layer, cloak

shrub *n* **bush**, plant, tree, flowering shrub

WORD BANK
❏ **types of shrubs or bushs** azalea, bramble, brier, broom, camellia, elder, forsythia, gardenia, gorse, hawthorn, heather, hydrangea, laurel, lavender, lilac, magnolia, privet, pussy willow, rhododendron, rose, sagebrush, witch hazel

---

shrubbery *n* **bushes**, undergrowth, border, herbaceous border, hedging

shrug off *v* **dismiss**, pooh-pooh, ignore, treat lightly, make light of

shrunken *adj* **wasted**, emaciated, dried up, withered, shriveled *Opposite*: bloated

shudder *v* **shake**, tremble, shiver, wince, quake ■ *n* **tremble**, shake, shiver, tremor, jolt

shuffle *v* **1 scuffle**, hobble, shamble, lumber, slouch **2 mix up**, jumble up, muddle up, rearrange, reorder

shun *v* **avoid**, turn away from, spurn, reject, eschew *Opposite*: court

shunt *v* **push**, shove, move, shift, propel ■ *n* **shove**, thrust, jolt, push

shush *(infml)* *v* **silence**, hush, quiet, quiet down, shut up *(infml)*

shut *v* **1 close**, close up, fasten, secure, bolt *Opposite*: open **2 close down**, close, close up shop, shut down, go out of business *Opposite*: start up

shutdown *n* **closure**, cessation, stoppage, halt, end

shut off *v* **1 switch off**, turn off, close off, close down, shut down *Opposite*: turn on

2 isolate, cut off, separate, seclude, set apart

shut out v **lock out**, keep out, exclude, keep off, debar Opposite: let in

shuttle v **go back and forth**, travel between, ply between, commute, ferry

shut up v **1** (infml) **be quiet**, fall silent, quiet down, clam up (infml), pipe down (infml) **2 confine**, imprison, cage, shut in, lock in Opposite: let loose **3** (infml) **silence**, hush, gag, muzzle, cut off

shy adj **1 introverted**, retiring, withdrawn, timid, bashful Opposite: outgoing **2 cautious**, wary, nervous, afraid, fearful Opposite: confident

shy away v **retreat**, shrink, recoil, flinch, back off

shyness n **introversion**, timidity, bashfulness, inhibition, reticence Opposite: boldness

sick adj **1 ill**, unwell, bad, under the weather, out of sorts Opposite: well **2 nauseous**, queasy, bilious, dizzy, green around the gills (infml) **3 bored**, up to here, sick to death, sick and tired (infml), fed up (infml) **4** (infml) **tasteless**, in bad taste, gruesome, bizarre, sickening

sickbay n **infirmary**, sanatorium, sickroom, hospital

sicken v **nauseate**, turn your stomach, repel, disgust, appall

sickening adj **disgusting**, nauseating, stomach-turning, shocking, appalling Opposite: appealing

sickly adj **1 unhealthy**, weak, ill, unwell, pale Opposite: healthy **2 cloying**, overpowering, disgusting, suffocating, nauseating Opposite: appealing **3 saccharine**, sentimental, cloying, sickly-sweet, mawkish Opposite: tough

sickly-sweet adj **saccharine**, cloying, mawkish, sentimental, nauseating

sickness n **1 illness**, disease, virus, condition, bad health Opposite: health **2 nausea**, vomiting, queasiness, biliousness, throwing up (infml)

side n **1 surface**, face, elevation, wall, plane **2 part**, area, region, section, segment **3 edge**, boundary, flank, bank, periphery **4 aspect**, facet, feature, quality, characteristic **5 team**, squad, line-up, group, gang

side effect n **unexpected result**, secondary effect, byproduct, consequence, result

sidekick (infml) n **assistant**, helper, associate, subordinate, partner Opposite: boss

sideline n **hobby**, pastime, offshoot, secondary activity, second job Opposite: career ■ v **1 put aside**, shelve, put off, put on the back burner, suspend Opposite: promote **2 relegate**, demote, exclude, downgrade, lay off Opposite: promote

sidelong adj **sideways**, oblique, slanting, indirect, askew Opposite: direct

sidesplitting adj **hilarious**, riotous, uproarious, rollicking, funny Opposite: dull

sidestep v **avoid**, evade, dodge, duck, bypass

side street n **alley**, back street, lane, side road

sidetrack v **distract**, deflect, divert, change the subject, get off the point

side view n **cross section**, profile, section, side, aspect

sidewalk n **path**, footway, walkway, footpath

sideways adj **oblique**, slanting, indirect, sidelong, slanted Opposite: straight ■ adv **to one side**, to the left, to the right, askew, askance Opposite: straight

side with v **back**, support, take somebody's side, be in somebody's camp, take somebody's part Opposite: oppose

sidle v **edge**, creep, slither, snake, inch

siege n **blockade**, cordon, barrier, barricade, obstruction

siesta n **rest**, nap, sleep, catnap, snooze (infml)

sift v **1 sieve**, filter, separate, put through a sieve, strain **2 sort through**, go through, go through with a fine-tooth comb, examine, select

sigh v **1 exhale**, heave a sigh, moan, groan, breathe Opposite: inhale **2 yearn**, long, hanker, pine, want Opposite: dislike ■ n **exhalation**, moan, groan, complaint, lament

sight n **1 view**, spectacle, prospect, picture, scene **2 vision**, eyesight, ability to see ■ v **notice**, catch sight of, spot, see, glimpse Opposite: miss

sighted adj **seeing**, keen-sighted, partially sighted, nearsighted, farsighted Opposite: blind

sights n **tourist attractions**, places of interest, highlights, wonders, marvels

sightseeing n **tourism**, visiting the attractions, going to places of interest, seeing the sights, exploration

sightseer n **tourist**, visitor, day tripper, vacationer Opposite: resident

sign n **1 symbol**, mark, emblem, insignia, logo **2 signal**, indication, symptom, warning, clue **3 notice**, poster, road sign, placard, billboard **4 trace**, track, trail, footprint, mark **5 omen**, warning, portent, premonition, indication ■ v **1 autograph**, sign your name, initial, authorize, endorse **2 make signs**, signal, gesture, motion, indicate **3 employ**, contract, hire, engage, take on Opposite: dismiss

signal n **sign**, indication, gesture, indicator, motion ■ v **1 communicate**, indicate, suggest, intimate, hint **2 gesture**, gesticulate, motion, sign, beckon **3 indicate**, mark, herald, portend, announce

signally adv **completely**, notably, totally,

absolutely, one hundred percent

signatory n **party**, participant, guarantor, the undersigned, cosignatory

signature n **name**, autograph, cross, mark, initials

significance n **1 meaning**, implication, import, worth, connotation **2 importance**, impact, substance, weight, magnitude Opposite: meaninglessness

significant adj **1 important**, major, noteworthy, momentous, substantial Opposite: insignificant **2 meaningful**, knowing, meaning, suggestive, expressive Opposite: blank **3 considerable**, large, major, big, sizable Opposite: paltry

significantly adv **1 considerably**, appreciably, drastically, notably, radically **2 meaningfully**, knowingly, suggestively, pointedly, expressively Opposite: innocently

significant other n **partner**, lover, spouse, other half, better half

signification n **meaning**, sense, gist, significance, denotation

signify v **mean**, indicate, show, imply, suggest

signing n **ratification**, validation, adoption, passing, authorization Opposite: rejection

sign on v **enlist**, sign up, enroll, put your name down, register

signpost n **1 signboard**, sign, notice, marker, road sign **2 indication**, suggestion, pointer, marker, sign ■ v **flag**, mark, indicate, label, designate Opposite: conceal

sign up v **1 recruit**, employ, sign, take somebody on, contract Opposite: fire **2 enlist**, join, enroll, become a member, put your name down Opposite: quit

silage n **fodder**, feed, grass, forage

silence n **1 quietness**, quiet, hush, stillness, peace Opposite: noise **2 muteness**, taciturnity, reticence, reserve, uncommunicativeness Opposite: chatter ■ v **1 make quiet**, hush, muzzle, quiet, shut up (infml) **2 stop**, put an end to, gag, stifle, suppress Opposite: encourage

silent adj **1 still**, hushed, soundless, noiseless, quiet Opposite: noisy **2 unspoken**, unvoiced, voiceless, tacit, wordless Opposite: spoken **3 mute**, tongue-tied, uncommunicative, taciturn, reticent Opposite: talkative

---

COMPARE AND CONTRAST CORE MEANING: not speaking or not saying much

silent not speaking or communicating at any particular time, especially through choice, or not inclined to speak much; **quiet** not inclined to speak much, often because of shyness; **reticent** unwilling to communicate very much, talk freely, or reveal all the facts; **taciturn** habitually reserved in speech and manner; **uncommunicative** not willing to say much, especially not to reveal information, or tending not to say much.

---

silhouette n **outline**, shape, shadow, profile, line

silken adj **smooth**, soft, silky, silky-smooth, glossy Opposite: coarse

silky adj **1 glossy**, smooth, soft, silken, silky-smooth Opposite: rough **2 smooth**, honeyed, mellifluous, sweet, unctuous Opposite: harsh

sill n **ledge**, shelf, ridge, projection, windowsill

silliness n **1 stupidity**, ridiculousness, childishness, madness, idiocy Opposite: sense **2 triviality**, meaninglessness, mindlessness, puerility, inanity Opposite: importance

silly adj **1 stupid**, ridiculous, impractical, childish, asinine Opposite: sensible **2 trivial**, meaningless, mindless, puerile, senseless Opposite: important

silt n **deposit**, mud, sediment, sludge, residue

silver-tongued adj **eloquent**, smooth-talking, grandiloquent, fluent, flattering Opposite: tongue-tied

silvery adj **silver**, gray, hoary, shiny

similar adj **alike**, like, comparable, parallel, analogous Opposite: dissimilar

similarity n **resemblance**, comparison, likeness, parallel, correspondence Opposite: difference

similarly adv **1 likewise**, also, in the same way, correspondingly, equally Opposite: on the contrary **2 alike**, in the same way, comparably, analogously, relatedly Opposite: differently

similitude (fml) n **similarity**, resemblance, likeness, sameness, semblance Opposite: difference

simmer v **1 boil**, bubble, cook **2 seethe**, rumble, bubble, boil, fester

simmer down v **cool down**, calm down, settle down, regain your self-control, compose yourself Opposite: blow your top (infml)

simper v **smirk**, grimace, sneer, look smug, look coy Opposite: frown ■ n **grimace**, smirk, sneer, smug look, coy look Opposite: frown

simple adj **1 easy**, straightforward, uncomplicated, trouble-free, effortless Opposite: difficult **2 plain**, minimal, unadorned, unfussy, down-to-earth Opposite: fancy **3 humble**, modest, unassuming, unpretentious, meek Opposite: pretentious **4 guileless**, ingenuous, naive, unsophisticated, green Opposite: sophisticated

simple-minded adj **1 naive**, childlike, unsophisticated, artless, guileless Opposite: sophisticated **2 simplistic**, crude, basic, one-dimensional, unsophisticated Opposite: subtle

simplicity n **1 ease**, straightforwardness, effortlessness, easiness, lack of complication Opposite: difficulty **2 plainness**, minimalism, cleanness, lack of adornment, austerity 3 **humility**, modesty, unpretentiousness, meekness, unassumingness *Opposite*: pride 4 **guilelessness**, naiveté, ingenuousness, lack of sophistication, artlessness *Opposite*: sophistication

simplified *adj* **cut down**, basic, easy, abridged, shortened *Opposite*: complex

simplify *v* **make simpler**, make easier, make straightforward, abridge, shorten *Opposite*: complicate

simplistic *adj* **naive**, unsophisticated, crude, basic, one-dimensional *Opposite*: sophisticated

simply *adv* 1 **just**, only, merely, purely, basically 2 **plainly**, minimally, cleanly, austerely, unpretentiously *Opposite*: elaborately 3 **modestly**, humbly, unassumingly, meekly, unpretentiously *Opposite*: proudly 4 **easily**, straightforwardly, in basic terms, in simple terms, in words of one syllable *Opposite*: elaborately 5 **naively**, guilelessly, ingenuously, candidly, innocently *Opposite*: knowingly 6 **frankly**, absolutely, obviously, undeniably, unquestionably

simulate *v* 1 **replicate**, reproduce, imitate, suggest, copy 2 **fake**, pretend, feign, put on, sham 3 **mimic**, ape, copy, imitate, parrot

simulated *adj* 1 **virtual**, cyber-, computer-generated 2 **fake**, imitation, pretend, counterfeit, sham *Opposite*: genuine

simulation *n* imitation, reproduction, replication, recreation, mock-up

simulator *n* simulant, emulator, trainer

simultaneous *adj* concurrent, immediate, instantaneous, real-time, synchronized *Opposite*: separate

sin *n* 1 **crime**, misdemeanor, transgression, misdeed, wrongdoing *Opposite*: good deed 2 **wickedness**, iniquity, depravity, immorality, debauchery *Opposite*: goodness ■ *v* **transgress**, do wrong, commit a crime, err, lapse

since *conj* **as**, because, given that, seeing as, in view of the fact that ■ *adv* **meanwhile**, in the meantime, subsequently, later, then

sincere *adj* 1 **honest**, open, frank, natural, straight *Opposite*: disingenuous 2 **heartfelt**, genuine, real, true, truthful *Opposite*: insincere

sincerity *n* **genuineness**, honesty, earnestness, naturalness, unaffectedness *Opposite*: insincerity

sinecure *n* **easy ride**, plum job, soft option, cushy job (*infml*), plum (*infml*)

sine qua non *n* **prerequisite**, essential condition, precondition, requirement, necessity

sinew (*literary*) *n* **strength**, vigor, muscularity, brawn, power *Opposite*: frailty

sinewy *adj* **wiry**, lean, strong, muscly, brawny *Opposite*: frail

sinful *adj* **wicked**, bad, evil, corrupt, errant *Opposite*: virtuous

sing *v* 1 **croon**, chant, hum, warble, carol 2 **resonate**, buzz, hum, purr, vibrate

singe *v* **scorch**, burn, char, sear

singer *n* **vocalist**, songster, lead singer, soloist, chorister

singing *n* **vocals**, songs, vocal music, chanting, warbling ■ *adj* **vocal**, choral, melodic, whistling, humming *Opposite*: instrumental

single *adj* 1 **solitary**, on its own, lone, sole, solo 2 **particular**, distinct, separate, specific, definite *Opposite*: general 3 **unmarried**, unattached, lone, free *Opposite*: attached ■ *n* **record**, song, track, release

single-handed *adj* **unassisted**, unaided, lone, solo, unaccompanied *Opposite*: assisted ■ *adv* **by yourself**, on your own, alone, without help, without assistance

single-minded *adj* **focused**, dedicated, resolute, dogged, driven *Opposite*: unfocused

single-mindedness *n* **sense of purpose**, concentration, application, attention, focus *Opposite*: aimlessness

single out *v* **pick out**, choose, select, identify, pull out

singly *adv* **individually**, alone, one by one, one at a time, piecemeal *Opposite*: together

sing out *v* **call out**, pipe up, speak up, speak out, shout

sing the praises of *v* **eulogize**, acclaim, praise, lionize, extol *Opposite*: criticize

singular *adj* **remarkable**, extraordinary, particular, outstanding, curious

singularity *n* **distinctiveness**, individuality, originality, uniqueness, peculiarity

sing your own praises *v* **boast**, swagger, swank, try to make an impression, brag

sinister *adj* **menacing**, ominous, threatening, evil, disturbing

sink *v* 1 **go under**, go down, go under the surface, be submerged, go downwards *Opposite*: float 2 **fall**, descend, drop, decline, go down *Opposite*: rise 3 **dig**, drill, mine, bore ■ *n* **basin**, bowl, hand basin, washbasin

sink in *v* **go in**, enter, penetrate, diffuse, permeate

sinuous *adj* **lithe**, supple, twisting, winding, graceful

sip *v* **taste**, drink, swallow, sup *Opposite*: gulp ■ *n* **drink**, swallow, taste, drop, mouthful

siphon *v* **draw off**, tap, drain off

siren *n* **alarm**, alert, warning, alarm bell, danger signal

sister *n* 1 **nun**, holy sister, religious, vestal (*literary*) 2 **friend**, supporter, ally, associate ■ *adj* **fellow**, parallel, associated, corresponding, equivalent

sit *v* 1 **be seated**, sit down, take a seat, take

the weight off your feet, park yourself *Opposite*: stand **2 assemble**, meet, convene, be in session *Opposite*: disperse **3 be placed**, be positioned, lie, rest, be on top of

sit around *v* **kill time**, do nothing, lounge around, hang around, hang out *(infml)*

sit down *v* **be seated**, take a seat, take the weight off your feet, park yourself *Opposite*: stand up

sit-down *(infml)* *n* **rest**, break, respite, breather *(infml)*

site *n* **place**, location, spot, position ■ *v* **put**, position, place, situate, locate

sit-in *n* **protest**, demonstration, rally, vigil, demo *(infml)*

sitting *n* **session**, meeting, hearing

situate *v* **place**, set, put, locate, position

situated *(fml)* *adj* **located**, positioned, set, placed, sited

situation *n* **1 state of affairs**, circumstances, state, condition, status quo **2 location**, position, site, place, setting

sixth sense *n* **intuition**, feeling, hunch, ESP

sizable *adj* **substantial**, generous, good-sized, ample, large *Opposite*: small

size *n* **dimension**, mass, bulk, amount, extent

sizeable *see* **sizable**

size up *v* **assess**, look somebody up and down, take stock of, evaluate, appraise

sizzle *v* **crackle**, hiss, sputter, spit

sizzling *(infml)* *adj* **boiling**, red-hot, baking, blistering, sweltering *Opposite*: freezing

skein *n* **hank**, ball, bundle, length, coil

skeletal *adj* **thin**, emaciated, skinny, gaunt, wasted *Opposite*: obese

skeleton *n* **1 frame**, bones, carcass **2 plan**, outline, framework, sketch, bare bones *(infml)* ■ *adj* **minimum**, basic, essential, minimal *Opposite*: full

skeptic *n* **cynic**, disbeliever, doubter, doubting Thomas, questioner *Opposite*: believer

skeptical *adj* **cynical**, disbelieving, doubtful, doubting, unconvinced *Opposite*: convinced

skepticism *n* **cynicism**, disbelief, doubt, incredulity, uncertainty *Opposite*: conviction

sketch *n* **draft**, plan, drawing, rough copy, rough ■ *v* **draw**, outline, draft, delineate, block in

sketchy *adj* **vague**, unclear, hazy, imprecise, woolly *Opposite*: detailed

skew *v* **1 tilt**, slant, twist, angle, slope *Opposite*: straighten **2 distort**, bias, slant, twist, spin

skewed *adj* **1 tilted**, slanted, twisted, crooked, askew *Opposite*: straight **2 distorted**, biased, slanted, prejudiced, partial *Opposite*: objective

skewer *n* **spit**, brochette, spike, spear, needle

■ *v* **impale**, spear, spike, pierce, stab

skid *v* **slip**, slide, slew, slither, spin out

skill *n* **ability**, talent, cleverness, dexterity, expertise. *See* COMPARE AND CONTRAST *at* **ability**.

skilled *adj* **accomplished**, expert, capable, able, trained *Opposite*: untrained

skillful *adj* **clever**, adroit, dexterous, skilled, expert *Opposite*: incompetent

skim *v* **1 glide**, fly, float, soar **2 scan**, speed-read, browse, glance at, flick through *Opposite*: peruse

skim off *v* **cull**, cream off, hive off, handpick, choose

skimp *v* **stint**, withhold, hold back on, be sparing with, pinch *Opposite*: lavish

skimpy *adj* **meager**, insufficient, scanty, inadequate, sparse *Opposite*: generous

skin *n* **1 hide**, pelt, fur, coat **2 casing**, covering, membrane, crust, coating ■ *v* **1 peel**, pare, excoriate, desquamate **2 graze**, scrape, flay, scuff

skin-deep *adj* **superficial**, on the surface, on the outside, shallow, artificial

skinflint *n* **miser**, pinchpenny, cheapskate *(infml)*, penny pincher *(infml)*, tightwad *(infml)*

skinniness *n* **gauntness**, scrawniness, thinness, boniness, leanness *Opposite*: plumpness

skinny *adj* **thin**, lean, undernourished, emaciated, scrawny *Opposite*: fat. *See* COMPARE AND CONTRAST *at* **thin**.

skin tone *n* **skin color**, complexion, skin, facial appearance, natural coloring

skip *v* **1 hop**, bounce, prance, gambol, caper **2 omit**, leave out, miss, pass over **3** *(infml)* **avoid**, miss, cut *(infml)* *Opposite*: attend

skipper *(infml)* *n* **captain**, boss, chief, head, person in charge

skirmish *n* **battle**, fight, engagement, scuffle, clash ■ *v* **clash**, fight, scuffle, tussle, scrap. *See* COMPARE AND CONTRAST *at* **fight**.

skirt *v* **1 border**, edge, adjoin, abut, neighbor **2 go around**, avoid, evade, bypass, edge past **3 skim over**, pass over, avoid, evade, bypass *Opposite*: tackle

WORD BANK

❑ **types of skirts** dirndl, hobble skirt, kilt, maxi skirt, miniskirt, pencil skirt, sarong, tutu, wrap-around

skit *n* **parody**, satire, spoof, sketch, burlesque

skittish *adj* **1 wary**, jumpy, edgy, nervous, uneasy **2 playful**, lively, frisky, excited, restless

skulduggery *n* **trickery**, tricks, dishonesty, cheating, mischief *Opposite*: honesty

skulk *v* **lurk**, loiter, creep, prowl, lie in wait

skull *(infml)* *n* **mind**, brain, head, noggin, pate *(archaic)*

sky *n* **heaven**, blue, atmosphere, firmament *(literary)*

sky-high *adj* **excessive**, very high, elevated, exorbitant, over-the-top

skyjack *v* **hijack**, seize, take over, take control of, capture

skyline *n* **horizon**, distance, prospect, vista

skyrocket *(infml)* *v* **rise steeply**, go through the ceiling, climb sharply, shoot up, hit the roof *(infml)* Opposite: plummet

skyscraper *n* **multistory building**, tower, high-rise, high-rise building

skyward *adv* **heavenward**, upward, up, above, aloft ■ *adj* **upward**, heavenward, aloft

slab *n* **lump**, chunk, block, hunk, piece

slack *adj* **1 loose**, limp, relaxed, baggy, floppy Opposite: taut **2 careless**, inattentive, idle, inefficient, unprofessional Opposite: diligent **3 slow-moving**, slow, dull, quiet, sluggish Opposite: brisk

slacken *v* **loosen**, relax, release, slacken off Opposite: tighten

slacker *n* **idler**, loafer, shirker, lazybones *(infml)*, freeloader *(infml)*

slackness *n* **1 looseness**, limpness, bagginess, floppiness, droopiness Opposite: tautness **2 carelessness**, negligence, laxity, inattention, laziness Opposite: meticulousness

slake *v* **quench**, satisfy, satiate, sate, extinguish Opposite: exacerbate

slam *(infml)* *v* **criticize**, berate, disparage, deride, pan *(infml)* Opposite: praise

slander *n* **1 defamation**, character assassination, disparagement, vilification, calumny *(fml)* **2 slur**, smear, slight, insult, calumny *(fml)* ■ *v* **insult**, malign, slur, smear, disparage Opposite: compliment. See COMPARE AND CONTRAST at **malign**.

slanderous *adj* **libelous**, defamatory, insulting, malicious, disparaging

slang *n* **jargon**, vernacular, colloquial speech, dialect, argot

slant *v* **incline**, lean, skew, slope, tilt ■ *n* **1 angle**, incline, diagonal, pitch, gradient **2 viewpoint**, angle, attitude, point of view, perspective

slanted *adj* **biased**, prejudiced, one-sided, partial, unfair Opposite: balanced

slanting *adj* **angled**, at an angle, sloping, on a slope, oblique Opposite: level

slantways see **slantwise**

slantwise *adv* **diagonally**, crosswise, crossways, at an angle, obliquely Opposite: straight

slap *n* **smack**, blow, spank, cuff, clout ■ *v* **hit**, smack, spank, cuff, swipe

slapdash *adj* **careless**, messy, clumsy, hasty, hurried Opposite: meticulous

slaphappy *adj* **slapdash**, careless, haphazard, hit-or-miss, irresponsible Opposite: meticulous

slapstick *n* **farce**, clowning, burlesque, comedy, humor

slash *v* **1 cut**, hack, slice, gash, slit **2 reduce**, cut, lower, drop, decrease Opposite: increase ■ *n* **laceration**, gash, slit, tear, rip

slat *n* **plank**, board, lath

slaughter *v* **kill**, murder, massacre, butcher, slay *(fml or literary)* ■ *n* **killing**, murder, massacre, carnage, butchery. See COMPARE AND CONTRAST at **kill**.

slaver *v* **drool**, slobber, dribble, salivate

slay *(fml or literary)* *v* **kill**, murder, assassinate, massacre, eliminate

slayer *(fml or literary)* *n* **killer**, butcher, homicide, murderer, executioner

sleaze *n* **corruption**, dishonesty, malpractice, scandal, foul play Opposite: probity

sleazy *adj* **1 seedy**, sordid, squalid, grubby **2 corrupt**, immoral, dishonest, shady, slimy Opposite: honest

sleek *adj* **smooth**, shiny, glossy, silky, lustrous

sleep *n* **slumber**, nap, doze, siesta, catnap ■ *v* **be asleep**, slumber, be dead to the world, nap doze

sleepily *adv* **drowsily**, dozily, woozily, wearily, blearily Opposite: alertly

sleep in *v* **oversleep**, sleep late, stay in bed, snooze on, ignore the alarm

sleepiness *n* **drowsiness**, tiredness, lethargy, somnolence, lassitude Opposite: alertness

sleepless *adj* **1 wakeful**, restless, disturbed, unsleeping, awake **2 alert**, active, vigilant, attentive, ready

sleeplessness *n* **1 insomnia**, wakefulness, restlessness **2 alertness**, vigilance, readiness, liveliness

sleepy *adj* **1 drowsy**, tired, lethargic, heavy-eyed, sluggish Opposite: alert **2 quiet**, dull, slow, inactive, peaceful Opposite: lively

sleet *n* **slush**, snow, frozen rain

sleeve *n* **cover**, jacket, protective cover, envelope, dust jacket

sleight of hand *n* **dexterity**, skill, adroitness, cunning, trickery

slender *adj* **1 slim**, slight, lean, trim, thin Opposite: fat **2 small**, slim, meager, slight, little Opposite: considerable. See COMPARE AND CONTRAST at **thin**.

slenderness *n* **thinness**, slimness, skinniness, fineness, narrowness Opposite: stoutness

sleuth *v* **1 investigate**, look for clues, spy, look into things, check things out **2 track**, tail, follow, pursue, stalk ■ *n* *(infml)* **detective**, Sherlock Holmes, investigator, private eye *(infml)*, gumshoe *(dated infml)*

slew see **slue**

slice *n* **1 piece**, sliver, wedge, portion, segment **2 share**, cut, portion, part, percentage ■ *v* **cut**, share, carve, divide, cut up

slick *adj* **1 slippery**, smooth, glossy, shiny, glassy **2 glib**, superficial, untrustworthy, shallow, facile **3 polished**, professional, efficient, glossy, smooth *Opposite*: shoddy

slide v **1 glide**, slither, slip, skim, skate **2 go down**, fall, decrease, diminish, drop *Opposite*: rise

slight *adj* **1 small**, minor, unimportant, trivial, insignificant *Opposite*: considerable **2 slim**, delicate, thin, feeble, slender *Opposite*: stocky ■ *n* **snub**, insult, slur, smear, rebuff ■ *v* **insult**, offend, snub, scorn, affront

slightly *adv* **somewhat**, to some extent, a little, a touch, marginally *Opposite*: considerably

slim *adj* **1 thin**, trim, slender, slight, lean *Opposite*: fat **2 faint**, slender, remote, poor, slight *Opposite*: considerable. *See* COMPARE AND CONTRAST *at* thin.

slim down v **reduce**, streamline, rationalize, cut, scale back *Opposite*: expand

slime *n* **paste**, mucus, glop (*infml*), goop (*infml*), goo (*infml*)

slimming *adj* **1 flattering**, becoming, thinning *Opposite*: unflattering **2 low-fat**, lite, light, diet, low-calorie *Opposite*: fattening

slimness *n* **1 narrowness**, fineness, slightness, thinness, flatness *Opposite*: bulkiness **2 slenderness**, leanness, svelteness, trimness, thinness *Opposite*: plumpness

slimy *adj* **1 greasy**, oily, slippery, slick **2 smarmy**, oily, groveling, sycophantic, unctuous

sling v **1 throw**, toss, lob, fling, hurl **2 hang**, suspend, dangle, drape, hook up

slink v **creep**, sneak, tiptoe, steal, skulk

slip v **1 trip**, fall, lose your balance, lose your footing, tumble **2 slide**, glide, slither, skid, skate **3 sneak**, steal, creep, flit, slink ■ *n* **blunder**, mistake, error, omission, gaffe. *See* COMPARE AND CONTRAST *at* mistake.

slip back v **revert**, relapse, lapse, slide back, return

slippery *adj* **1 greasy**, oily, slick, icy, slimy *Opposite*: dry **2 sneaky**, shifty, crafty, devious, dishonest *Opposite*: trustworthy

slipshod *adj* **careless**, shoddy, slapdash, slack, sloppy (*infml*) *Opposite*: thorough

slip up (*infml*) v **make a mistake**, go wrong, get it wrong, blunder, trip up

slip-up (*infml*) *n* **blunder**, slip, mistake, error, omission

slit v **cut**, slash, gash, nick, tear ■ *n* **opening**, cut, slash, gash, slot. *See* COMPARE AND CONTRAST *at* tear.

slither v **slide**, glide, slink, slip, skid

sliver *n* **slice**, shaving, splinter, flake, shard

slobber v **drool**, dribble, salivate, slaver

slog v **1 plod**, trudge, tramp, trek, hike **2 work**, labor, toil, grind, struggle ■ *n* **1 trek**, hike, tramp, trail, marathon **2 drag**, effort, strain, grind, struggle

slogan *n* **motto**, saying, jingle, catch phrase, watchword

slop v **spill**, slosh, splatter, splash, swill

slope *n* **gradient**, grade, incline, hill, rise ■ *v* **incline**, slant, tilt, lean, rise

sloppy *adj* **1 messy**, untidy, disordered, chaotic, slovenly *Opposite*: tidy **2** (*infml*) **slack**, shoddy, careless, poor, slipshod *Opposite*: meticulous **3** (*infml*) **slushy**, sentimental, romantic, corny, gushing

slosh v **spill**, slop, splatter, splash, swill

slot *n* **1 slit**, hole, opening, niche, space **2 time**, window, opening, space, period ■ *v* **position**, locate, fit, insert, slip

sloth *n* **laziness**, idleness, indolence, apathy, sluggishness *Opposite*: liveliness

slothful *adj* **lazy**, idle, sluggish, inactive, indolent *Opposite*: energetic

slothfulness *see* **sloth**

slot in v **fit in**, squeeze in, accommodate, accept, see

slouch v **slump**, droop, stoop, sprawl, lounge ■ *n* (*infml*) **idler**, loafer, slacker, shirker, freeloader (*infml*)

slovenly *adj* **careless**, disheveled, untidy, messy, unkempt

slow *adj* **1 sluggish**, unhurried, measured, deliberate, dawdling *Opposite*: fast **2 time-consuming**, drawn-out, protracted, lengthy, lingering *Opposite*: quick ■ *v* **slow down**, decelerate, brake, reduce, slacken

slow down v **1 decelerate**, slow up, slow, brake, reduce speed *Opposite*: speed up **2 hold up**, hold back, delay, slow, retard *Opposite*: speed up

slowly *adv* **gradually**, unhurriedly, bit by bit, little by little, at a snail's pace *Opposite*: quickly

slowness *n* **leisureliness**, sluggishness, deliberateness, gradualness *Opposite*: fastness

slow up v **1 hold up**, hold back, delay, slow, retard *Opposite*: speed up **2 decelerate**, slow down, slow, brake, reduce speed

sludge *n* **mud**, slush, mire, muck, slop

slue v **veer**, swing, slide, skid, swerve

slug *n* **1 bullet**, shot, shell, cartridge, pellet **2** (*infml*) **shot**, gulp, swallow, mouthful, glassful *Opposite*: sip **3 blow**, hit, thump, punch, whack ■ *v* **1** (*infml*) **swallow**, gulp, down, drink, swill *Opposite*: sip **2 hit**, thump, strike, punch, whack

sluggish *adj* **inactive**, lethargic, slow, listless, slothful *Opposite*: energetic

sluggishness *n* **lethargy**, slowness, listlessness, sloth, laziness *Opposite*: alertness

sluice *n* **channel**, conduit, race, drain, gutter ■ *v* **clean**, flush, rinse, hose, wash

slum *n* **shanty town**, ghetto, project, favela, colonia

slumber v **sleep**, drowse, doze, be dead to the world, catnap ■ *n* **1 sleep**, doze, nap, catnap, siesta **2 rest**, inactivity, inertia, torpor, laziness

slump v 1 **collapse**, fall, sink, tumble, lurch 2 **slouch**, bend, hunch, droop, sprawl 3 **decrease**, decline, collapse, crash, plummet Opposite: rise ∎ n **recession**, crash, collapse, decline, plummet Opposite: rise

slur v 1 **speak**, run together, blend, overlap, overrun 2 **demean**, smear, insult, slight, besmirch ∎ n **smear**, disgrace, insult, slight, stain

slurp v **gulp**, suck, drink, swallow, down ∎ n **mouthful**, swallow, drink, sip, gulp

slurred adj **indistinct**, inaudible, unclear, garbled, incoherent Opposite: distinct

slush n **sludge**, mud, mire, muck, slurry

slushy adj 1 **snowy**, icy, wet, mushy, sloppy Opposite: dry 2 **sentimental**, mushy, corny, syrupy, mawkish Opposite: unsentimental

sly adj 1 **crafty**, cunning, clever, knowing, artful 2 **evasive**, wily, devious, furtive, underhand Opposite: honest

slyness n 1 **craftiness**, cunning, skill, artfulness, cleverness Opposite: clumsiness 2 **sneakiness**, evasiveness, furtiveness, dishonesty, underhandedness Opposite: openness

smack v 1 **hit**, clout, slap, cuff, spank 2 **suggest**, imply, hint at, look like, sound like ∎ n 1 **slap**, blow, clout, cuff, spank 2 **taste**, tang, bite, flavor, savor

small adj 1 **little**, minute, tiny, diminutive, miniature Opposite: big 2 **unimportant**, trivial, slight, lesser, minor Opposite: major

small arms n **weapons**, guns, firearms, side arms, pistols

smallness n **tininess**, littleness, minuteness, compactness Opposite: largeness

small-scale adj 1 **limited**, modest, moderate, minor, unimportant Opposite: large-scale 2 **little**, small, miniature, minuscule, tiny Opposite: large-scale

small screen (infml) n **television**, tube (infml), TV (infml), boob tube (infml)

small talk n **chat**, conversation, pleasantries, gossip, chatter

small-time (infml) adj **petty**, unimportant, local, minor, insignificant Opposite: major

smarmy adj **sycophantic**, oily, groveling, slimy, unctuous

smart adj 1 **intelligent**, bright, sharp, quick, clever Opposite: stupid 2 **insolent**, rude, facetious, disrespectful, sarcastic 3 **elegant**, tidy, stylish, chic, well-dressed Opposite: shabby 4 **fashionable**, chic, glamorous, stylish, voguish 5 **lively**, brisk, vigorous, energetic, quick ∎ v **sting**, burn, hurt, chafe, tingle. See COMPARE AND CONTRAST at **intelligent**.

smart aleck (infml) n **wise guy** (infml), know-it-all (infml), smarty pants (infml), wag (infml), wiseacre (infml)

smarten v **spruce up**, clean up, revamp, do up, redecorate Opposite: let go

smarten up v 1 **spruce up**, clean up, revamp, do up, redecorate Opposite: let go 2 **brighten up**, liven up, cheer up, enliven, energize Opposite: stagnate

smartly adv 1 **intelligently**, cleverly, ably, knowledgeably Opposite: stupidly 2 **vigorously**, briskly, energetically, quickly, rapidly 3 **stylishly**, nattily, neatly, tidily, elegantly Opposite: untidily

smartness n **neatness**, tidiness, elegance, stylishness, chicness Opposite: untidiness

smarty pants (infml) n **know-it-all** (infml), smart aleck (infml), wise guy (infml), wiseacre (infml), wag (infml)

smash v **shatter**, break, demolish, destroy, crush Opposite: repair ∎ n 1 **crash**, bang, crunch 2 **blow**, chop, punch, kick, volley 3 **accident**, crash, collision, wreck, fender-bender (infml)

smash up v **wreck**, damage, ruin, trash (infml), total (slang)

smashup n **crash**, collision, accident, wreck, pileup (infml)

smattering n **bit**, modicum, dash, iota, little Opposite: lot

smear v 1 **spread**, coat, daub, cover, wipe 2 **sully**, discredit, disgrace, besmirch, tarnish Opposite: praise ∎ n 1 **mark**, smudge, blotch, stain, splotch 2 **slur**, insult, slight, affront, slander

smear campaign n **mudslinging**, whispering campaign, muckraking, defamation, slander

smell v **sniff**, sense, get a whiff of, suspect, taste ∎ n **odor**, aroma, scent, perfume, fragrance

---

COMPARE AND CONTRAST CORE MEANING: the way something smells

smell a neutral, pleasant, or unpleasant quality detected by the nerves of the nose; **odor** a neutral or unpleasant smell; **aroma** a distinctive pleasant smell, especially one related to cooking or food; **bouquet** a characteristic pleasant smell, usually associated with fine wines; **scent** a pleasant, sweet smell, for example, the smell of flowers, or the characteristic smell given off by a particular animal; **perfume** a sweet, pleasant, and heady smell, especially the smell of flowers or plants; **fragrance** a sweet pleasant smell, especially a delicate or subtle one; **stink** a strong unpleasant smell; **stench** a strong unpleasant smell, especially one associated with burning or decay; **reek** a strong unpleasant smell.

---

smelly adj **stinking**, reeking, foul, malodorous, putrid Opposite: fragrant

smelt v 1 **melt**, melt down, liquefy, flux 2 **found**, cast, produce, manufacture

smidge (infml) see **smidgen**

smidgen (infml) n **dash**, drop, bit, splash, morsel

smile v **grin**, beam, smirk, leer, sneer Oppo-

site: frown ■ *n* beam, grin, smirk, leer *Opposite*: frown

smiley *adj* smiling, happy, cheery, sunny, cheerful *Opposite*: miserable ■ *n* emoticon, smiley face, symbol, sign-off

smirk *n* grin, leer, sneer, simper ■ *v* sneer, leer, grin, simper

smite *(literary)* *v* hit, strike, beat, punch, thrash

smithereens *(infml)* *n* pieces, bits, fragments, shards

smitten *(literary)* *adj* in love, besotted, enamored, head over heels in love, infatuated *Opposite*: indifferent

smog *n* pollution, smoke, fog, haze

smoke *n* fumes, smog, poisonous gas, firedamp, chokedamp ■ *v* burn, be on fire, smolder

smoke detector *n* smoke alarm, fire alarm, sensor

smoke out *v* 1 drive out, force out, turn out, eject, expel *Opposite*: bring in 2 bring to light, reveal, expose, unearth, discover *Opposite*: conceal

smoker *n* cigarette smoker, pipe smoker, cigar smoker, chain-smoker, heavy smoker

smoke screen *n* 1 cover-up, cover, camouflage, screen, mask 2 cloud of smoke, wall of smoke, smoke

smoky *adj* misty, murky, cloudy, foggy, hazy *Opposite*: clear

smolder *v* 1 burn, smoke, glow 2 fume, seethe, glower, burn, boil 3 lurk, fester, rumble, linger, persist

smooch *(infml)* *v* kiss, cuddle, hug, hold each other close, caress ■ *n* cuddle, kiss, hug, caress, embrace

smooth *adj* 1 flat, even, level, horizontal, plane. *Opposite*: uneven 2 easy, flowing, effortless, efficient 3 charming, suave, persuasive, glib, silver-tongued *Opposite*: gauche 4 soft, silky, downy, velvety, shiny *Opposite*: rough ■ *v* flatten, smooth out, level, iron, press *Opposite*: crumple

smooth down *v* flatten, iron out, paste down, smooth out, even out *Opposite*: scrunch

smoothie *n* 1 *(infml)* charmer, smooth talker, smooth character, fast talker, poser *(infml)* 2 drink, fruit juice, milk shake, yogurt drink

smoothly *adv* easily, effortlessly, efficiently, well, slickly *Opposite*: awkwardly

smoothness *n* 1 flatness, evenness, levelness *Opposite*: unevenness 2 softness, silkiness, velveteness, sleekness *Opposite*: roughness 3 ease, effortlessness, efficiency *Opposite*: awkwardness 4 charm, suaveness, persuasiveness, glibness, slickness

smooth out *v* 1 flatten, iron out, paste down, smooth down, even out *Opposite*: crease 2 ease, calm, defuse, soothe, smooth over *Opposite*: stir up

smooth over *v* ease, calm, defuse, soothe, smooth out *Opposite*: stir up

smooth talk *n* flattery, nonsense, rubbish, garbage, sweet talk *(infml)* *Opposite*: sincerity

smooth-tongued *adj* smooth-talking, silver-tongued, eloquent, persuasive, convincing

smoothy *see* smoothie

smother *v* 1 suffocate, stifle, choke, asphyxiate 2 overwhelm, overpower, oppress, suffocate, stifle 3 suppress, repress, stifle, hold back, restrain *Opposite*: express

smudge *n* blotch, smear, stain, mark, blemish ■ *v* smear, blur, distort, blot, smirch

smug *adj* self-satisfied, superior, self-righteous, arrogant, conceited *Opposite*: humble

smuggle *v* handle contraband, traffic, run, sneak in, bring in

smugness *n* complacency, arrogance, self-satisfaction, conceit, self-righteousness *Opposite*: humility

smut *n* 1 soot, smudge, ash, grime, dirt 2 obscenity, dirt, filth, pornography, erotica

smutty *adj* 1 sooty, smudged, grimy, dirty, grubby *Opposite*: pristine 2 obscene, dirty, pornographic, filthy, explicit 3 crude, foul-mouthed, indelicate, tasteless, loutish

snag *n* problem, hitch, difficulty, obstacle, hurdle *Opposite*: solution ■ *v* catch, rip, tear

snail mail *(infml)* *n* postal service, surface mail, airmail, mail

snake *n* sea snake, water snake, serpent *(literary)* ■ *v* wind, bend, twist, meander, turn

---

WORD BANK

❑ **types of nonpoisonous snakes** anaconda, blacksnake, boa, boa constrictor, garter snake, grass snake, king snake, python, rat snake, water snake, whip snake

❑ **types of poisonous snakes** adder, asp, cobra, copperhead, coral snake, diamondback, fer-de-lance, horned viper, mamba, pit viper, puff adder, rattler, rattlesnake, ringhals, sea snake, sidewinder, taipan, viper, water moccasin

---

snaky *adj* winding, twisting, meandering, zigzagged, coiling *Opposite*: straight

snap *v* 1 break, crack, shatter, give way, come apart 2 retort, bark, shout, yell, speak sharply 3 bite, nip, bite at ■ *n* 1 child's play, nothing, piece of cake *(infml)*, breeze *(infml)*, walk in the park *(infml)* 2 fastening, fastener, stud ■ *adj* sudden, spur-of-the-moment, impulsive, spontaneous, instant *Opposite*: considered

snappish *adj* irritable, snappy, bad-tempered, short-tempered, sharp *Opposite*: good-natured

snappy adj 1 (infml) **stylish**, chic, fashionable, smart, elegant Opposite: dowdy 2 (infml) **lively**, brisk, interesting, stimulating, to the point Opposite: dull 3 **irritable**, bad-tempered, short-tempered, sharp, ill-humored Opposite: good-natured 4 **hasty**, quick, fast, speedy, rapid Opposite: slow

snapshot n 1 **photo**, photograph, picture, snap, portrait 2 **view**, glimpse, outline, idea, thumbnail sketch

snap up v **grab**, seize, pounce on, take up

snare n **trap**, noose, gin, lasso ■ v **catch**, trap, capture, ensnare, entrap

snarl v 1 **growl**, roar, bellow 2 **speak angrily**, bark, growl, snap, rasp

snatch v 1 **grab**, grasp, seize, take 2 **steal**, run off with, filch (infml), pinch (infml) 3 (infml) **kidnap**, abduct, seize, shanghai, capture Opposite: release

snazzy (infml) adj **flashy**, bright, colorful, loud, ostentatious Opposite: drab

sneak v **slip**, steal, creep, slink, tiptoe

sneakiness n **slyness**, furtiveness, stealth, deviousness, cunning Opposite: openness

sneaking adj **niggling**, uneasy, nagging, uncomfortable, worrying

sneak preview n **advance showing**, premiere, preview, screening, advance screening

sneak thief n **pickpocket**, shoplifter, burglar, thief, robber

sneak up on v 1 **creep up on**, steal up on, come up on, come up behind, surprise 2 **catch napping**, catch unawares, take by surprise, surprise, creep up on

sneaky adj **sly**, devious, shifty, underhand, mean Opposite: honest

sneer v **scorn**, scoff, turn your nose up at, mock, deride

sneering adj **scornful**, contemptuous, disdainful, sarcastic, arrogant Opposite: admiring

sneeze n **sniff**, sniffle, snuffle, splutter, snort ■ v **sniffle**, sniff, snuffle, splutter, snort

snicker v **laugh**, smirk, mock, deride, sneer ■ n **laugh**, sneer, jeer, snort, snigger

snide adj **sarcastic**, mean, unpleasant, malicious, spiteful Opposite: pleasant

sniff v 1 **snuffle**, breathe, inhale Opposite: exhale 2 **smell**, scent, get a whiff of, catch the scent of ■ n **breath**, snort, snuffle, lungful, inhalation

sniff at v **turn your nose up at**, sneer at, hold in contempt, look down on, scorn Opposite: accept

sniffle v 1 **sniff**, snuffle, snivel, snort, splutter 2 **whimper**, snivel, cry, weep, sob

sniff out (infml) v **discover**, find, unearth, track down, detect

sniffy (infml) adj **contemptuous**, haughty, disdainful, scornful, superior Opposite: humble

snifter (infml) n **drink**, nightcap, tot, splash, nip

snigger v **snicker**, laugh, smirk, mock, deride ■ n **snicker**, laugh, sneer, snort

snip v **cut**, shear, slice, nick, trim

sniper n **gunman**, marksman, assassin, rifleman, shooter

snippet n **extract**, piece, bit, scrap

snippy (infml) adj **irritable**, snappy, grumpy, crabby, sharp Opposite: good-tempered

snivel v **sob**, sniff, cry, weep, whimper

snob n **social climber**, name-dropper, elitist

snobbery n **arrogance**, superciliousness, condescension, pretentiousness, conceit Opposite: humility

snobbish adj **high and mighty**, superior, arrogant, condescending, supercilious Opposite: humble

snobbishness see snobbery

snobby see snobbish

snooker (infml) v **thwart**, stymie, obstruct, hinder, stop Opposite: assist

snoop (infml) v **spy**, poke around, watch, sneak, pry Opposite: mind your own business ■ n **spy**, sneak, meddler, intruder, eavesdropper

snooty (infml) adj 1 **high and mighty**, condescending, hoity-toity, supercilious, snobbish Opposite: humble 2 **exclusive**, select, posh (infml)

snooze (infml) v **doze**, sleep, doze off, nap, nod off Opposite: wake up ■ n **sleep**, doze, nap, catnap, siesta

snore v **snort**, breathe heavily, snuffle, wheeze

snorkel v **swim**, dive, scuba dive

snort v **grunt**, exhale, breathe out, inhale, draw in

snout n **nose**, muzzle, proboscis, schnozzle (slang)

snow n **sleet**, snowflake, slush, hail, ice

snowball v **increase**, mount, balloon, swell, grow quickly Opposite: decrease

snowbound adj **snowed in**, cut off, isolated, shut in, blockaded

snowfall n **snowstorm**, blizzard, whiteout, flurry

snowstorm n **blizzard**, whiteout, snowfall, flurry

snow under v 1 **defeat**, beat, overcome, crush, rout 2 **inundate**, swamp, bury, overwhelm, overload

snowy adj **snow-white**, hoary, white

snub v **ignore**, coldshoulder, slight, look right through, cut Opposite: acknowledge ■ n **rebuff**, slight, rejection, rebuke, insult

snub-nosed adj **button-nosed**, pug-nosed, retroussé

snuff v 1 **extinguish**, put out, douse, snuff out, blow out Opposite: light 2 (infml) **destroy**, kill, eliminate, abolish, eradicate Opposite: save

snuffle v **sniff**, sniffle, snort, snivel, splutter

■ *n* **snort**, sniff, sniffle, snivel, splutter

snug *adj* **1 cozy**, warm, comfortable, homely, inviting *Opposite*: uncomfortable **2 close**, well-fitting, neat, close-fitting, tight *Opposite*: loose

snuggle *v* **nestle**, nuzzle, cuddle, burrow, huddle

so *adv* **consequently**, as a result, therefore, subsequently, accordingly

soak *v* **1 immerse**, steep, marinate, infuse, saturate **2 drench**, douse, saturate, wet, drown *Opposite*: dry out

soaked *adj* **wet through**, saturated, sodden, waterlogged, drenched *Opposite*: dry

soaking *adj* **drenched**, soaked, soaking wet, sopping wet, sopping *Opposite*: dry

so-and-so (*infml*) *n* **whatchamacallit** (*infml*), thingamajig (*infml*), thingummy (*infml*), thingamabob (*infml*), whatshisname (*infml*)

soap *n* **1 cleanser**, detergent, shampoo, soap powder, lather **2** (*infml*) **serial**, soap opera, series, program ■ *v* **cleanse**, lather, wash, wash down, shampoo

soap opera *n* **serial**, series, soap (*infml*)

soap powder *n* **detergent**, soap, soapsuds, cleanser, suds

soapsuds *n* **foam**, lather, suds, froth, bubbles

soar *v* **1 fly**, ascend, climb, wheel, circle *Opposite*: plummet **2 rise**, rocket, climb, mount, go through the roof *Opposite*: plummet

soaring *adj* **rising**, mounting, climbing, spiraling, increasing *Opposite*: plummeting

sob *v* **moan**, cry, weep, snivel, sniffle

sobbing *n* **crying**, weeping, howling, tears, sniveling

sober *adj* **1 abstemious**, clear-headed, temperate, teetotal, moderate **2 serious**, somber, solemn, thoughtful, calm *Opposite*: frivolous **3 dull**, somber, drab, dreary, staid *Opposite*: bright **4 rational**, judicious, level-headed, clear-headed, sensible *Opposite*: speculative

soberness *n* **1 seriousness**, solemnity, somberness, gravity, glumness *Opposite*: frivolity **2 dullness**, drabness, somberness, plainness, simplicity *Opposite*: brightness **3 rationality**, judiciousness, level-headedness, clear-headedness, lucidity

sobriety *n* **1 abstemiousness**, abstinence, temperance, moderation, soberness **2 seriousness**, somberness, solemnity, thoughtfulness, calm *Opposite*: flippancy

sobriquet *n* **nickname**, pet name, term of endearment, alias, assumed name

sob story (*infml*) *n* **tale of woe**, hard-luck story, sorry tale, sad story

so-called *adj* **supposed**, alleged, ostensible, purported, self-styled

sociability *n* **1 gregariousness**, companionability, conviviality, hospitability

2 friendliness, pleasantness, amiability, affability, geniality

sociable *adj* **1 gregarious**, companionable, convivial, good company, hospitable *Opposite*: retiring **2 friendly**, outgoing, amiable, warm, affable *Opposite*: unsociable

social *adj* **communal**, community, common, societal, public ■ *n* **party**, gathering, get-together (*infml*)

social climber *n* **hanger-on**, sycophant, toady, snob, socialite

socialism *n* **collectivism**, social democracy, public ownership, communism, communalism

socialist *n* **collectivist**, social democrat, communist, communalist

socialite *n* **trendsetter**, social climber, one of the beautiful people, one of the glitterati, member of café society

socialize *v* **meet people**, go out, get out, mix, mingle

socially *adv* **1 communally**, publicly, within society, generally, collectively **2 in public**, in a social context, with other people, in a crowd **3 as a friend**, outside of work, informally, on a social basis

societal *adj* **social**, group, shared, general, common

society *n* **1 civilization**, culture, humanity, the social order, the world **2 people**, the public, the general public, the populace, the population **3 association**, union, group, guild, league **4 high society**, the upper classes, polite society, the upper crust (*infml*)

sock (*infml*) *n* **hit**, punch, thump, whack, thwack ■ *v* **hit**, punch, thump, whack, thwack

socket *n* **hole**, opening, hollow

sod *n* **turf**, clod, grass, earth

sodden *adj* **saturated**, soaking, soaked, soaking wet, sopping *Opposite*: dry

sofa *n* **settee**, couch, chaise longue, day bed, futon

so far *adv* **up to now**, thus far, hitherto, until now, to date

soft *adj* **1 yielding**, squashy, spongy, pliable, elastic *Opposite*: hard **2 smooth**, silky, supple, velvety *Opposite*: rough **3 low**, mellifluous, melodious, faint, muted *Opposite*: loud **4 gentle**, flowing, delicate, subtle, understated *Opposite*: harsh **5 dim**, diffused, mellow, subtle, gentle *Opposite*: bright **6 lenient**, lax, easy, forgiving, over-indulgent *Opposite*: strict **7 tender**, sensitive, gentle, kind, sympathetic *Opposite*: hardhearted **8 wet**, spineless, weak, soppy (*infml*), pathetic (*infml*)

soft-boiled *adj* **soft-hearted**, soft, sympathetic, sentimental, indulgent *Opposite*: hard-boiled (*infml*)

soften *v* **1 make softer**, relax, make pliable

Opposite: harden **2 alleviate**, lessen, reduce, diminish, mitigate *Opposite*: exacerbate **3 moderate**, relax, temper, tone down, assuage

soft furnishings *n* upholstery, curtains, rugs, drapes, cushions

soft-hearted *adj* sympathetic, kind, caring, warm, good-natured *Opposite*: hard-hearted

softie *see* **softy**

softly *adv* **1 tenderly**, delicately, gently, kindly, sympathetically *Opposite*: severely **2 quietly**, gently, mellifluously, melodiously, faintly *Opposite*: harshly **3 dimly**, gently, subtly, lightly, faintly *Opposite*: brightly

softness *n* **1 gentleness**, smoothness, quietness, faintness *Opposite*: harshness **2 pliability**, suppleness, flexibility, elasticity, malleability

soft-pedal (*infml*) *v* play down, downplay, make light of, underplay, minimize *Opposite*: emphasize

soft sell (*infml*) *n* persuasion, persuasiveness, subtlety, sweet-talking (*infml*), soft-soaping (*infml*)

soft-soap (*infml*) *v* flatter, play up to, lay it on thick, sweet-talk (*infml*), butter up (*infml*)

soft-spoken *adj* quiet, gentle, calm, tranquil, serene *Opposite*: loud

soft spot *n* weakness, partiality, affection, weak spot, liking

soft touch *n* easy prey, easy target, easy mark, pushover (*infml*), sucker (*infml*)

softy (*infml*) *n* soft touch, easy prey, easy target, sucker (*infml*)

soggy *adj* damp, wet, moist, mushy, squelchy *Opposite*: dry

soi-disant (*literary*) *adj* self-styled, so-called, self-proclaimed, self-confessed, self-appointed

soigné *adj* well-groomed, neat, elegant, chic, stylish *Opposite*: dowdy

soil *n* **1 earth**, dirt, topsoil, mud, dust **2 territory**, land, country, ground ■ *v* dirty, get dirty, foul, muddy, stain *Opposite*: cleanse

soiled *adj* dirty, grubby, muddy, stained, filthy *Opposite*: clean. *See* COMPARE AND CONTRAST *at* dirty.

soiree *n* party, celebration, dinner party, evening, gathering

soirée *see* **soiree**

sojourn (*literary*) *n* visit, stay, stop, stopover ■ *v* stay, stop, remain, dwell (*literary*), abide (*archaic*)

solace *n* comfort, consolation, support, relief, help *Opposite*: aggravation

solarium *n* conservatory, sun parlor, suntrap, greenhouse

solder *v* join, fuse, weld, bond, connect

soldier *n* **1 fighter**, combatant, warrior, regular, legionnaire *Opposite*: non-combatant **2 sapper**, gunner, corporal, sergeant **3 worker**, supporter, campaigner, crusader, workhorse

soldier of fortune *n* mercenary, adventurer, hired gun (*slang*) *Opposite*: regular

soldier on *v* persevere, continue, carry on, keep on, keep going *Opposite*: give up

sole *adj* **1 only**, solitary, single, individual, singular **2 exclusive**, private, unique, special, individual

solecism *n* error, mistake, blunder, slip, gaffe

solely *adv* exclusively, only, merely, just, uniquely

solemn *adj* **1 somber**, grave, serious, sober, sad *Opposite*: cheerful **2 earnest**, sincere, serious, firm, grave *Opposite*: flippant **3 formal**, official, ceremonial, ritual, sacred

solemnity *n* somberness, gravity, seriousness, soberness, sadness

solemnize *v* celebrate, honor, make official, formalize, sanctify

solicit *v* **1 ask for**, beg, seek, petition for, plead for *Opposite*: grant **2 ask**, petition, lobby, plead with, implore (*fml*)

solicitous *adj* considerate, caring, attentive, concerned, kind *Opposite*: uncaring

solicitousness *n* concern, attentiveness, consideration, care, kindness

solicitude *n* **1 concern**, attentiveness, consideration, care, kindness *Opposite*: negligence **2 anxiety**, concern, worry, unease, apprehension *Opposite*: serenity

solid *adj* **1 hard**, rock-hard, rock-solid, concrete, firm *Opposite*: soft **2 dense**, unbroken, continuous, closed, blocked *Opposite*: hollow **3 pure**, genuine, unadulterated, one hundred percent, unmixed **4 sturdy**, strong, secure, firm, stable *Opposite*: weak **5 reliable**, dependable, sound, trustworthy, level-headed *Opposite*: unreliable **6 unanimous**, universal, widespread, popular, general *Opposite*: patchy ■ *n* **1 object**, thing, artifact, item, entity **2 figure**, pyramid, tetrahedron, sphere, icosahedron

solidarity *n* unity, harmony, cohesion, commonality, camaraderie *Opposite*: discord

solidify *v* harden, coagulate, congeal, set, get hard *Opposite*: dissolve

solidity *n* hardness, firmness, sturdiness, strength, toughness *Opposite*: softness

solidness *see* **solidity**

soliloquy *n* monologue, speech, declamation, oration, dramatic monologue

solitaire *n* single stone, gemstone, jewel, diamond, precious stone

solitary *adj* **1 private**, unsociable, unsocial, self-contained, self-sufficient *Opposite*: sociable **2 lone**, single, sole, individual, solo *Opposite*: accompanied **3 isolated**, desolate, out-of-the-way, secluded, unfrequented

solitary confinement n **isolation**, imprisonment, confinement, detention, custody

solitude n **loneliness**, privacy, isolation, seclusion, separateness

solo adj **single**, unaccompanied, lone Opposite: joint ■ adv **alone**, on your own, singly, by yourself Opposite: together

soloist n **artist**, artiste, musician, singer, vocalist Opposite: accompanist

solon (literary) n **statesman**, adviser, mentor, elder statesman, sage (literary)

solubility n **dissolvability**, deliquescence Opposite: insolubility

soluble adj **1 solvable**, answerable, fathomable, resolvable, decipherable Opposite: insoluble **2 dissolvable**, deliquescent Opposite: insoluble

solution n **1 answer**, key, explanation, resolution, way out Opposite: problem **2 mix**, mixture, liquid, blend, cocktail

solvable adj **soluble**, resolvable, fathomable, answerable, decipherable Opposite: insoluble

solve v **resolve**, crack, answer, explain, get to the bottom of

solvency n **creditworthiness**, affluence, wealth, soundness, comfort Opposite: insolvency

solvent adj **in the black**, in credit, in the chips, in the money, in clover Opposite: insolvent

somber adj **1 dark**, dull, gloomy, drab, dingy Opposite: bright **2 muted**, subdued, drab, dull, dark Opposite: light **3 melancholy**, lugubrious, sad, depressed, dismal Opposite: cheerful

some adv **approximately**, about, around, roughly, more or less Opposite: exactly ■ adj **1 a number of**, a little, a few, several, various Opposite: all **2 certain**, particular, selected, specific

somebody pron **some person**, someone Opposite: nobody ■ n **celebrity**, someone, name, superstar, bigwig (infml) Opposite: nobody

someday adv **one day**, sooner or later, sometime, soon, in the future Opposite: never

somehow adv **one way or another**, someway, by hook or by crook, come what may, come hell or high water

someone see **somebody**

someplace (infml) adv **somewhere**, wherever, anywhere, anyplace (infml)

somersault n **tumble**, forward roll, flip-flop, cartwheel, flip ■ v **turn over**, tumble, flip over, cartwheel, flip

something adv **a little**, somewhat, to some degree, rather, slightly Opposite: completely

sometime adv **at some point**, someday, at some time, in the future, one day Opposite: never ■ adj (fml) **former**, onetime, previous, earlier, ex (infml) Opposite: current

sometimes adv **occasionally**, now and then, every now and then, every so often, now and again Opposite: always

someway adv **somehow**, one way or another, in some way, by some means, by hook or by crook

somewhat adv **rather**, fairly, slightly, to some extent, to a certain extent

somewhere adv **wherever**, anywhere, anyplace (infml), someplace (infml)

somnolent adj **sleepy**, drowsy, dozy, half asleep, half awake

son n **child**, lad, boy, kid (infml)

son et lumière n **entertainment**, spectacle, light show, tableau, spectacular

song n **1 tune**, melody, air, refrain, jingle **2 birdsong**, call, warble, warbling, cry

songbook n **anthology**, collection, hymnbook, book, hymnal

songster n **singer**, vocalist, lead singer, soloist, chanteuse

songwriter n **composer**, lyricist, songsmith, librettist

sonic adj **auditory**, aural, audible, sound

sonic boom n **boom**, shock wave, noise, rumble, roar

sonnet n **poem**, verse, rhyme

sonny (infml) n **lad**, young man, my boy, my lad, sonny boy (infml)

sonny boy (infml) see **sonny**

sonority n **resonance**, fullness, roundness, richness, reverberation

sonorous adj **loud**, deep, resonant, echoing, booming Opposite: thin

soon adv **almost immediately**, quickly, rapidly, shortly, before long Opposite: eventually

sooner adv **1 earlier**, faster, more quickly, more rapidly, nearer Opposite: later **2 rather**, more readily, more willingly, preferably, as soon Opposite: reluctantly

sooner or later adv **eventually**, one day, someday, in time, in due course Opposite: never

soot n **dust**, powder, grime, ashes, dirt

soothe v **1 calm**, pacify, quiet, appease, mollify Opposite: excite **2 ease**, relieve, alleviate, reduce, palliate Opposite: aggravate

soothing adj **calming**, comforting, restful, gentle, peaceful Opposite: irritating

soothsayer n **fortune-teller**, oracle, seer, astrologer, clairvoyant

sooty adj **dirty**, grimy, black, filthy, dusty Opposite: clean

sop n **concession**, offering, bribe, pacifier, gesture

sophisticate v **educate**, school, mold, acculturate, tutor ■ n **socialite**, trendsetter, connoisseur, aesthete, cognoscente Opposite: hoi polloi

sophisticated adj 1 urbane, cultured, chic, erudite, refined Opposite: gauche 2 **clever**, advanced, high-level, complex, erudite Opposite: crude

sophistication n 1 **complexity**, erudition, difficulty, intricacy Opposite: crudeness 2 **refinement**, style, chic, urbanity, elegance Opposite: naiveté

sophistry n casuistry, fallaciousness, illogicality, sophism, dishonesty Opposite: logic

soporific adj 1 **sleep-inducing**, calming, tranquilizing, narcotic, hypnotic (infml) Opposite: energizing 2 **tedious**, boring, interminable, turgid, endless Opposite: stimulating

sopping adj **drenched**, soaked, dripping, sodden, saturated Opposite: dry

soppy adj **soaked**, wet, sopping wet, sopping, dripping Opposite: dry

soprano n singer, vocalist, soloist, chanteuse, diva ■ adj **high**, high-pitched, shrill, piercing, soaring Opposite: bass

sop up v soak up, mop up, sponge, absorb, wipe

sorbet n fruit ice, ice, sherbet

sorcerer n wizard, magician, enchanter, magus, witch

sorceress n witch, enchantress, sibyl, magician, necromancer (literary)

sorcery n witchcraft, wizardry, magic, black magic, enchantment

sordid adj 1 **base**, disreputable, sleazy, repugnant, disgusting Opposite: uplifting 2 **squalid**, distasteful, disgusting, low, dirty Opposite: pleasant

sordidness n 1 **baseness**, sleaze, unpleasantness, repugnance, wretchedness Opposite: pleasantness 2 **squalor**, grime, filth, squalidness, grubbiness Opposite: cleanliness

sore adj 1 **painful**, tender, uncomfortable, stinging, aching Opposite: comfortable 2 **annoying**, sensitive, embarrassing, controversial, difficult Opposite: uncontroversial 3 (infml) **angry**, cross, mad, annoyed, upset Opposite: pleased ■ n **wound**, abscess, lesion, eruption, blister

sorely (fml) adv **deeply**, truly, greatly, very much, really Opposite: not at all

soreness n **tenderness**, pain, discomfort, distress, agony

sorrow n **grief**, mourning, sadness, distress, sorrowfulness Opposite: joy ■ v (literary) **grieve**, mourn, wail, lament, weep Opposite: rejoice (literary)

sorrowful adj 1 **distressed**, sad, mournful, grief-stricken, unhappy Opposite: joyful 2 **distressing**, tragic, sad, solemn, unhappy Opposite: happy

sorrowing adj **sad**, mournful, grief-stricken, distressed, unhappy Opposite: joyful

sorry adj 1 **apologetic**, regretful, remorseful, repentant, sad Opposite: glad 2 **pitiful**, miserable, wretched, forlorn, pathetic Opposite: fine

sort n 1 **category**, kind, class, type, genus 2 (infml) **personality type**, person, character, type, individual ■ v **arrange**, classify, rank, place, sort out Opposite: mix up. See COMPARE AND CONTRAST at **type**.

sortie n 1 **attack**, maneuver, foray, incursion, inroad Opposite: retreat 2 **excursion**, trip, outing, journey, jaunt

sort out v 1 **resolve**, deal with, solve, iron out, fix 2 **put in order**, arrange, file, disentangle, tidy up Opposite: mix up 3 **separate**, distinguish, segregate, sort, divide

SOS n **distress signal**, cry for help, call for help, alarm, flare

so-so (infml) adj **average**, fair, mediocre, unremarkable, indifferent Opposite: exceptional

sought-after adj **desirable**, coveted, in demand, exclusive, fashionable Opposite: unpopular

souk n **bazaar**, market, marketplace, flea market, emporium

soul n 1 **spirit**, consciousness, psyche, will, essence 2 **depth**, personality, atmosphere, emotion, passion 3 **individual**, person, anyone, someone, example 4 **soul music**, gospel, R & B, rhythm and blues, blues

soul-destroying adj **demoralizing**, depressing, disheartening, unfulfilling, boring Opposite: uplifting

soulful adj **expressive**, affecting, sad, moving, poignant Opposite: emotionless

soulfulness n **expressiveness**, sadness, poignancy, emotion, mournfulness

soulless adj **bleak**, utilitarian, characterless, inexpressive, insensitive Opposite: soulful

soul mate n **friend**, mate, boon companion, confidant, confidante

soul-searching n **thought**, consideration, contemplation, introspection, assessment

sound n 1 **noise**, resonance, hum, echo, thud Opposite: silence 2 **strait**, channel, inlet, fjord ■ v 1 **seem**, appear, look 2 **announce**, ring out, declare, signal, express 3 **go off**, ring out, explode, ring, wail ■ adj 1 **complete**, comprehensive, wide-ranging, all-encompassing, thorough Opposite: superficial 2 **sensible**, good, firm, unassailable, reliable Opposite: unsound 3 **whole**, healthy, unblemished, perfect, normal Opposite: infirm 4 **firm**, rigorous, good, hard, severe Opposite: half-hearted

---

WORD BANK

❏ **types of animal sounds** baa, bark, bay, bleat, bray, caterwaul, croak, growl, grunt, howl, meow, mew, moo, neigh, oink, purr, roar, snarl, squeak, squeal, whinny, woof, yap, yelp

❏ **types of bird sounds** caw, cheep, chirp, chirrup, cluck, cock-a-doodle-doo, coo, hoot, peep, quack, screak, screech, squawk, trill, tweet, twitter, warble

❑ **types of human sounds** babble, bawl, bellow, boo, catcall, chatter, chortle, chuckle, cry, gasp, giggle, groan, grunt, holler (infml), howl, hum, moan, murmur, mutter, peep, screak, scream, screech, shout, shriek, sigh, slurp, snicker, sniffle, splutter, squeal, titter, wail, wheeze, whimper, whine, whisper, whistle, whoop, yell

❑ **types of continuous sounds** beep, bleep, boom, burble, buzz, chug, crackle, creak, drone, gurgle, hiss, honk, hoot, hum, purl (literary), purr, rasp, rattle, roar, rumble, rustle, sizzle, sonic boom, swish, swoosh, throb, thunder, whir, whiz, whoosh

❑ **types of impact sounds** bang, beat, bong, bonk (infml), bump, clang, clank, clap, clash, clatter, click, clip-clop, clop, clunk, crack, crash, patter, pitter-patter, plop, plunk, pop, rat-a-tat-tat, rattle, slam, smash, splash, splat, squelch, squish, tap, thud, thump, thwack, tick, tick-tock, wham

❑ **types of ringing sounds** chime, chink, clink, ding, ding-a-ling, ding-dong, honk, hoot, jangle, jingle, knell, peal, ping, ring, ting, tinkle, toll, tootle (infml)

sound bite n comment, announcement, statement, declaration, response

sound effect n sound, recording, effect, special effect

sounding board n confidant, confidante, close friend, best friend, intimate

soundings n investigations, inquiries, research, surveys, market research

soundless adj silent, noiseless, still, quiet, mute Opposite: noisy

soundly adv 1 thoroughly, roundly, severely, firmly, decisively 2 deeply, well, like a log, peacefully, fast Opposite: fitfully

soundness n 1 reliability, unassailability, security, accuracy, dependability Opposite: unreliability 2 completeness, comprehensiveness, thoroughness, depth, range Opposite: superficiality 3 wholeness, completeness, health, healthiness, fitness Opposite: infirmity 4 thoroughness, firmness, severity, rigorousness Opposite: halfheartedness

sound off (infml) v hold forth, go on, have your say, speak up, speak out

sound out v investigate, test, explore, survey, look into

soundproof adj impenetrable, insulated, lined, padded, sealed ■ v insulate, line, seal, pad, protect

sound system n hi-fi, stereo, stereo system, audio system, CD player

soundtrack n 1 recording, music, dialogue, sound, sound effects 2 music, album, LP, tape, CD

soupçon n hint, touch, speck, morsel, modicum Opposite: surfeit

soup up (infml) v boost, enhance, tune up, modify, upgrade

sour adj 1 acid, tart, bitter, acerbic, vinegary Opposite: sweet 2 bad, rancid, off, curdled, fetid Opposite: fresh 3 bitter, disagreeable, unpleasant, bad-tempered, resentful Opposite: agreeable ■ v 1 curdle, go sour, ferment, turn, go bad 2 taint, ruin, harm, spoil, embitter Opposite: improve

source n 1 basis, foundation, origin, cause, font 2 informant, spokesperson, informer, supplier, stool pigeon (slang) 3 resource, supply, fund, mine, well 4 natural spring, upwelling, fount, fountain Opposite: estuary ■ v obtain, find, track down, trace, track. See COMPARE AND CONTRAST at origin.

sour grapes n resentment, jealousy, bitterness, ill feeling, envy

sourly adv 1 tartly, bitterly, drily, acridly, acidly Opposite: sweetly 2 disagreeably, unpleasantly, bitterly, resentfully, spitefully Opposite: agreeably

sourness n 1 acidity, tartness, bitterness, tang, acridness Opposite: sweetness 2 bitterness, resentment, acrimony, unpleasantness, hostility Opposite: pleasantness

sourpuss (infml) n complainer, grumbler, whiner, grouch (infml), moaner (infml)

souse v 1 pickle, marinade, soak, steep, preserve 2 soak, steep, douse, saturate, immerse

souvenir n memento, reminder, keepsake, knickknack, remembrance

sovereign n monarch, ruler, potentate, king, queen Opposite: subject ■ adj 1 independent, autonomous, self-governing, free, self-determining 2 supreme, dominant, ascendant, predominant, absolute 3 outstanding, superior, supreme, excellent, matchless

sovereignty n 1 dominion, control, rule, power, authority 2 independence, autonomy, self-government, freedom, self-determination

sow v spread, propagate, disseminate, scatter, strew Opposite: reap

spa n 1 health resort, sanatorium, health spa, thalassotherapy center, fat farm (infml) 2 plunge pool, Turkish bath, sauna, hot tub

space n 1 solar system, galaxy, outer space, deep space, universe 2 interval, time, period, pause, window 3 area, place, seat, bay, plot 4 (infml) leeway, freedom, autonomy, liberty, latitude ■ v spread out, move apart, space out, set apart

space-age adj hi-tech, automated, up-to-the-minute, state-of-the-art, new

space capsule n spacecraft, spaceship, rocket, capsule, vehicle

spacecraft n spaceship, space rocket, rocket, rocket ship

WORD BANK
❑ **types of spacecraft** biosatellite, lander, launch vehicle, lunar module, multistage rocket, orbital space station, orbiter, rocket, rocket ship, rover, satellite, space capsule, spacelab,

space probe, space rocket, space shuttle, space station

❑ **parts of a spacecraft** booster rocket, bus cabin, command module, drogue parachute, footpad, grain, life-support system, nose cone, plasma engine, pod, retropack, rocket engine, shroud, solar cell, stage, thruster

spaceflight *n* **flight**, rocket flight, shuttle flight, space travel, orbiting

space platform *see* **space station**

space probe *n* **rover**, lander, spacecraft, satellite, probe

spacer *n* **insertion**, insert, piece, part, bar

spaceship *n* **1 space capsule**, space shuttle, lunar module, ship, capsule **2 flying saucer**, alien craft, UFO, unidentified flying object

space station *n* **space platform**, orbital space station, spacelab, extraterrestrial base

spacewalk *n* **extravehicular activity**, EVA, moonwalk

spacing *n* **1 space**, arrangement, layout, spaces, gaps **2 arranging**, positioning, placing, ordering, spacing out

spacious *adj* **roomy**, airy, large, open, expansive *Opposite*: cramped

spade *n* **garden spade**, shovel, scoop, snow shovel ■ *v* **dig**, shovel, scoop, excavate, fill in

spadework *n* **groundwork**, research, drudgery, preliminaries, preparatory work

spam *n* **junk mail**, unsolicited mail, garbage, mail, direct mail ■ *v* **e-mail**, post, block, send, distribute

span *n* **1 distance**, width, length, extent, area **2 time**, duration, period, limit ■ *v* **cross**, cover, reach over, extend over, bridge

spangle *n* **sequin**, bead, bauble, star ■ *v* **1 sprinkle**, stud, pepper, dot, spot **2 sparkle**, glitter, shine, glisten, twinkle

spank *v* **whack**, smack, slap, hit, strike

spanking *n* **smacking**, smack, slap, thrashing, beating ■ *adj* **1 remarkable**, excellent, outstanding, wonderful, marvelous *Opposite*: ordinary **2 vigorous**, brisk, rapid, fast, lively *Opposite*: weak

spar *n* **pole**, arm, boom, mast, rod ■ *v* **1 scuffle**, fight, box, exchange blows, scrap **2 argue**, fence, dispute, squabble, bicker *Opposite*: agree

spare *v* **1 afford**, do without, get by without, manage without, give up *Opposite*: need **2 show mercy to**, free, release, save, pardon *Opposite*: condemn ■ *adj* **1 replacement**, extra, auxiliary, standby, additional *Opposite*: main **2 sparse**, thin, mean, insubstantial, frugal *Opposite*: abundant

spare part *n* **reserve**, extra, standby, part, replacement

spare time *n* **free time**, leisure time, time off, downtime

sparing *adj* **1 frugal**, parsimonious, economical, careful, thrifty *Opposite*: gen-

erous **2 sparse**, limited, meager, restricted, insufficient *Opposite*: plentiful

spark *n* **1 flash**, flicker, sparkle, arc, glint **2 stimulus**, catalyst, incentive, spur, trigger ■ *v* **1 sparkle**, flicker, glimmer, glint, glow **2 generate**, produce, inspire, initiate, set off

sparkle *v* **1 fizzle**, bubble, fizz, ferment, effervesce **2 shine**, glitter, glisten, flash, flicker **3 excel**, scintillate, shine, come into your own, come to life ■ *n* **1 life**, vivacity, energy, enthusiasm, gusto *Opposite*: apathy **2 effervescence**, carbonation, bubbles, aeration, gassiness

sparkler *(infml)* *n* **gem**, diamond, gemstone, jewel, precious stone

sparkling *adj* **1 glittering**, glistening, twinkling, iridescent, spangled *Opposite*: dull **2 vivacious**, witty, brilliant, scintillating, vibrant *Opposite*: dull **3 fizzy**, effervescent, carbonated, bubbly, aerated *Opposite*: still

sparkly *see* **sparkling**

spark off *v* **generate**, produce, inspire, initiate, set off

sparky *adj* **lively**, spirited, enthusiastic, bubbly, feisty *(infml)* *Opposite*: lifeless

sparring partner *n* **opponent**, adversary, sworn enemy, counterpart, opposite number

sparse *adj* **thin**, spare, scant, light, scarce *Opposite*: dense

sparseness *n* **thinness**, scarceness, scarcity, meagerness, bareness

spartan *adj* **frugal**, simple, basic, meager, bare *Opposite*: luxurious

spasm *n* **shudder**, contraction, seizure, ripple, paroxysm

spasmodic *adj* **fitful**, irregular, intermittent, occasional, sporadic *Opposite*: continuous

spat *n* **quarrel**, fight, row, argument, tiff

spate *n* **flood**, rash, epidemic, wave, sequence

spatial *adj* **three-dimensional**, 3-D, longitudinal, latitudinal, altitudinal

spatter *v* **1 shower**, spray, sprinkle, scatter, splash **2 spray**, splatter, shower, mark, splash

spawn *n* **1 roe**, fish eggs, eggs, seed **2 brood**, issue, offspring, progeny, young ■ *v* **1 lay**, deposit, produce **2 reproduce**, give birth, procreate, breed, hatch **3 create**, generate, produce, initiate, set off

spay *v* **neuter**, sterilize, castrate, operate on, geld

speak *v* **1 chatter**, talk, verbalize, articulate, chat *Opposite*: shut up *(infml)* **2 say**, tell, express, state, voice **3 be fluent in**, converse in, speak a language **4 address**, lecture, preach, give a talk, give a lecture

speaker *n* **1 utterer**, chatterer, reciter, talker **2 orator**, lecturer, narrator, spokesman, spokeswoman

speak for v **speak on behalf of**, represent, act on behalf of, stand for, argue for

speaking n **speech**, language, communication, discourse, talking

speak out v **1 talk loudly**, raise your voice, exclaim, shout, speak up *Opposite*: mutter **2 be frank**, speak your mind, say your piece, have your say, speak up *Opposite*: equivocate

speak to v **1 get in touch with**, contact, approach, talk to, address **2 reprimand**, discipline, reprove, talk to, have a word with **3** (*fml*) **discuss**, consider, go into, deal with, address

speak up v **1 be frank**, speak your mind, say your piece, have your say, protest *Opposite*: equivocate **2 speak out**, exclaim, talk loudly, raise your voice, shout *Opposite*: mutter

speak up for v **support**, back, argue for, defend, approve *Opposite*: attack

speak your mind v **be frank**, not beat around the bush, speak up, speak out, make yourself heard *Opposite*: equivocate

spear n **lance**, spike, javelin, assegai, harpoon ■ v **impale**, spike, stab, pierce, gouge

spearhead n **driving force**, forefront, head, lead, leader ■ v **lead**, front, head, organize, direct

special adj **1 superior**, distinct, different, exceptional, distinctive *Opposite*: ordinary **2 individual**, specific, particular, distinct, one *Opposite*: general

special consideration n **dispensation**, concession, allowance, indulgence, preference

special delivery n **express**, courier, premium rate, overnight delivery, registered mail

special education n **special needs education**, remedial education, compensatory education

special effects n **effects**, FX, computer graphics, lighting, morphing

specialism n **1 specialization**, narrowing down, concentration, focusing in, gaining expertise **2 specialty**, area of expertise, subject, sphere, forte

specialist n **authority**, expert, maven, consultant, doyen

specialization n **1 narrowing down**, concentration, focusing in, gaining expertise, gaining in-depth knowledge *Opposite*: diversification **2 adaptation**, change, mutation, selection, evolution

specialize v **concentrate**, focus, dedicate yourself to, major in *Opposite*: diversify

specialized adj **particular**, dedicated, focused, specific, expert *Opposite*: generalized

specially adv **1 particularly**, in particular, especially, specifically, expressly *Opposite*: generally **2 personally**, individually, to order

specialty n **area of expertise**, subject, sphere, forte, area

species n **class**, type, kind, sort, genus. *See* COMPARE AND CONTRAST *at* **type**.

specific adj **1 exact**, precise, detailed, explicit, definite *Opposite*: vague **2 particular**, peculiar, exclusive, special, restricted *Opposite*: general **3 distinctive**, particular, express, identifiable, certain *Opposite*: indefinite ■ n **detail**, particular, aspect, feature, fact *Opposite*: generality

specification n **requirement**, condition, plan, order, arrangement

specified adj **1 stated**, quantified, definite, spelled out, detailed *Opposite*: unstated **2 stipulated**, required, postulated, restricted, insisted on *Opposite*: optional

specify v **1 state**, identify, spell out, detail, give *Opposite*: suggest **2 stipulate**, agree, lay down, postulate, require

specious adj **false**, hollow, erroneous, baseless, inaccurate *Opposite*: valid

speciousness n **falsity**, hollowness, inaccuracy, falseness, deceptiveness *Opposite*: validity

speck n **1 dot**, fleck, spot, dab, blob **2 particle**, fragment, crumb, iota, scrap ■ v **dot**, fleck, spot, speckle, stipple

speckle n **fleck**, mark, speck, spot, dot ■ v **mark**, fleck, dust, stipple, dot

speckled adj **spotted**, freckled, dotted, stippled, dappled

specs (*infml*) *see* **spectacles**

spectacle n **1 sight**, scene, vision, marvel, phenomenon **2 display**, show, demonstration, exhibition, event

spectacles n **glasses**, goggles, specs (*infml*)

spectacular adj **1 stunning**, impressive, amazing, fantastic, fabulous *Opposite*: humdrum **2 remarkable**, huge, great, enormous, mighty *Opposite*: unimpressive ■ n **show**, display, performance, extravaganza, special

spectacularly adv **extremely**, enormously, hugely, monumentally, prodigiously *Opposite*: mildly

spectate v **watch**, look on, observe, take in, look *Opposite*: participate

spectator n **viewer**, watcher, observer, onlooker, bystander *Opposite*: participant

specter n **1 ghost**, apparition, phantom, spirit, spook **2 threat**, menace, shadow, danger, possibility

spectral adj **ghostly**, phantom, ethereal, supernatural, ghostlike *Opposite*: real

spectrum n **range**, band, field, gamut, variety

speculate v **1 wonder**, guess, conjecture, hypothesize, reason *Opposite*: know **2 consider**, contemplate, reflect on, ponder, deliberate *Opposite*: decide **3 gamble**, take risks, hazard, risk, venture

speculation n conjecture, rumor, opinion, gossip, assumption Opposite: fact

speculative adj 1 tentative, approximate, rough, exploratory, provisional Opposite: definite 2 hypothetical, notional, theoretical, academic, abstract Opposite: proven 3 dangerous, risky, unpredictable, uncertain, dicey (infml) Opposite: safe

speculator n risk-taker, investor, entrepreneur, opportunist, adventurer

speech n 1 language, talking, verbal communication, dialogue, words 2 tongue, idiom, dialect, vernacular, native tongue 3 lecture, oration, sermon, talk, homily

speechify (infml) v pontificate, lecture, pronounce, preach, hold forth

speechless adj astonished, astounded, amazed, dumbstruck, wordless

speechmaker n speaker, orator, raconteur, preacher, lecturer

speed n 1 pace, rate, velocity, momentum, tempo 2 haste, hurry, swiftness, speediness, hustle Opposite: slowness ■ v race, fly, zoom, break the speed limit, drive too fast Opposite: crawl

speedily adv quickly, promptly, soon, hastily, hurriedly Opposite: slowly

speediness n 1 quickness, promptness, hastiness, rapidity, speed Opposite: slowness 2 fastness, swiftness, nimbleness, rapidness, fleetness (literary) Opposite: sluggishness

speeding adj fast-moving, hurtling, flying, moving, fast Opposite: slow

speed limit n maximum speed, top speed, permitted speed, limit, restriction

speedometer n clock, gauge, recorder

speed-read v skim, scan, read

speed trap n radar trap, police trap, traffic control

speed up v accelerate, get faster, get moving, get going, hurry up Opposite: slow down

speedway n track, course, circuit, racecourse

speedy adj 1 quick, immediate, prompt, early, fast Opposite: slow 2 fast-moving, speeding, fast, swift, nimble Opposite: slow

spell v signify, mean, bring, predict, imply ■ n 1 incantation, curse, enchantment, hex, evil eye 2 influence, fascination, thrall, glamour, enchantment 3 (infml) bout, interlude, stretch, session, time period

spellbinding adj mesmerizing, enthralling, entrancing, fascinating, captivating Opposite: boring

spellbound adj enthralled, fascinated, awestruck, rapt, captivated Opposite: distracted

spell-check v check, check over, check through, correct, proofread

spell out v make obvious, explain in simple terms, make clear, explain, interpret Opposite: obfuscate

spend v 1 pay, expend, pay out, splurge, lay out 2 devote, apply, employ, fill, occupy 3 use, use up, waste, fritter, squander Opposite: save

spending n expenditure, expenses, costs, payments, outlay Opposite: earnings

spending money n cash, money, ready cash, pin money, pocket money Opposite: savings

spendthrift n wastrel, squanderer, waster, prodigal, profligate Opposite: miser ■ adj wasteful, extravagant, improvident, prodigal, reckless Opposite: miserly

spent adj 1 consumed, used up, expended, paid, paid out Opposite: saved 2 exhausted, tired, washed-out, worn-out, shattered Opposite: fresh 3 finished, over, done, completed, over and done with Opposite: new

sperm n 1 semen, seed, ejaculate 2 cell, gamete, spermatozoon

spermatozoon n sperm, cell, gamete

spew v 1 disgorge, discharge, vomit, send out, churn out 2 pour out, pour forth, gush, flow, stream Opposite: dribble

sphere n 1 ball, globe, orb, bubble 2 area, specialty, subject, field, area of interest 3 sphere of influence compass, scope, range, domain

spherical adj sphere-shaped, globular, rotund, circular, round

sphinxlike adj enigmatic, mysterious, cryptic, bemusing, baffling Opposite: transparent

spice n 1 seasoning, flavoring, additive 2 interest, excitement, a little something, zest, flavor Opposite: blandness ■ v 1 season, flavor, enhance, lace 2 enliven, liven up, lace, add zest to, add a little something to Opposite: tone down

---

WORD BANK

❑ types of spices allspice, aniseed, black pepper, caraway seed, cardamom, cayenne pepper, chili, cinnamon, clove, coriander, cumin, fenugreek, ginger, ginseng, mace, mustard, nutmeg, paprika, pepper, peppercorn, saffron, turmeric, white pepper

---

spick-and-span adj 1 tidy, clean, neat, immaculate, spotless Opposite: untidy 2 in perfect condition, immaculate, as new, in tiptop condition, in mint condition Opposite: used

spicy adj hot, spiced, curried, piquant, peppery Opposite: mild

spidery adj 1 thin, spindly, angular, squiggly, jerky Opposite: bold 2 gangling, spirdly, lanky, skinny, thin Opposite: plump

spiel (infml) n patter, speech, lecture, talk, waffle (infml) ■ v prattle, pitch, go on, hold forth, jabber

spigot n 1 faucet, tap, spout, standpipe, valve 2 stopper, plug, bung, cork, peg

spike n point, barb, spear, thorn, spine ■ v 1 **spear**, impale, pierce, skewer, run through (literary) 2 (infml) **thwart**, confound, frustrate, dash, quash Opposite: foster

spiked adj **spiky**, sharp, pointed, hobnailed, jagged Opposite: smooth

spiky adj **prickly**, thorny, sharp, bristly, spiny Opposite: smooth

spill v **slop**, drip, leak, trickle, dribble Opposite: absorb ■ n 1 **leak**, spillage, escape, discharge, overflow 2 (infml) **tumble**, fall, roll, trip, stumble

spillage n 1 **spilling**, spill, discharge, emission, leak 2 **wastage**, waste, loss, spill, slick

spill over v 1 **overflow**, brim over, leak out, run over, spill out 2 **spread**, extend, overflow, advance, creep

spill the beans (infml) v **let the cat out of the bag**, give the game away, tell, confess, let on Opposite: keep secret

spin v **turn**, rotate, revolve, gyrate, whirl ■ n 1 **gyration**, rotation, turn, whirl, swirl 2 **drive**, outing, run, trip, jaunt

spinal adj **back**, backbone, vertebral

spinal column n **spine**, back, backbone, vertebrae, vertebral column

spindle n 1 **rod**, bar, shaft, axle, pole 2 **leg**, baluster, support, vertical, upright

spindly adj **skinny**, gangly, lanky, thin, frail Opposite: sturdy

spindrift n **spray**, sea spray, foam, mist, vapor

spine n **spinal column**, vertebral column, backbone, back, vertebrae

spine-chilling adj **bloodcurdling**, chilling, terrifying, petrifying, frightening Opposite: comforting

spineless adj **gutless**, cowardly, weak, timid, spiritless Opposite: courageous. See COMPARE AND CONTRAST at **cowardly**.

spinelessness n **weakness**, gutlessness, cowardice, feebleness, faint-heartedness Opposite: courage

spine-tingling adj **hair-raising**, thrilling, frightening, gripping, exciting Opposite: soothing

spinner n **rotator**, whirler, whirligig, turner, gyrator

spinoff v **derive**, result, develop, grow, follow on ■ n **byproduct**, derivative, offshoot, extra, bonus

spin out v **drag out**, prolong, keep going, draw out, eke out Opposite: cut

spiny adj **barbed**, prickly, spiky, bristly, thorny Opposite: smooth

spiral v 1 **escalate**, increase, get worse, run away, rise Opposite: plummet 2 **fly**, rise, ascend, descend, soar

spire n **tip**, spike, pinnacle, point, top Opposite: base

spirit n 1 **will**, strength, courage, character, strength of mind 2 **soul**, inner self, life force, chi, essence Opposite: body 3 **disposition**, temperament, attitude, nature, temper 4 **feeling**, attitude, mood, tendency, atmosphere 5 **ghost**, soul, ghoul, phantom, apparition ■ v **remove**, take away, whisk off, steal, abduct

spirited adj **forceful**, determined, strong-willed, vigorous, energetic Opposite: lackluster

spiritless adj **spineless**, gutless, cowardly, sad, dejected Opposite: energetic

spirits n **emotional state**, frame of mind, state of mind, mental state, feelings

spiritual adj 1 **religious**, holy, sacred, divine, heavenly Opposite: secular 2 **mental**, emotional, psychological, temperamental, internal Opposite: physical

spiritualist n **medium**, clairvoyant, seer, psychic, mystic

spirituality n **holiness**, sanctity, religiousness, otherworldliness, unworldliness

spit v 1 **expectorate**, splutter, hawk, expel Opposite: swallow 2 **sputter**, sizzle, pop, spatter, spurt 3 **utter**, splutter, hiss, mutter, say 4 **rain**, shower, drizzle, sprinkle, mizzle 5 **impale**, skewer, spear, spike, run through (literary) ■ n 1 **saliva**, spittle, sputum, dribble 2 **skewer**, rotisserie, brochette, rod, broach

spit and polish (infml) n **meticulousness**, tidiness, cleanliness, orderliness, neatness

spite n **malice**, ill will, ill feeling, vindictiveness, meanness Opposite: goodwill

spiteful adj **malicious**, vindictive, mean, nasty, vicious Opposite: kind

spitefulness see **spite**

spitting image (infml) n **double**, twin, clone, image, spit Opposite: opposite

spittle n **saliva**, spit, sputum, dribble

splash v 1 **wallow**, wade, plop, flap, flop Opposite: glide 2 **splatter**, get water on, wet, dash, spray Opposite: dab 3 **plop**, slop, spatter, spray, slap

splashy adj 1 **gaudy**, garish, bright, bold, colorful Opposite: drab 2 (infml) **showy**, ostentatious, flamboyant, flashy, bold Opposite: restrained

splat n **smack**, splash, plop, slop, slap

splatter v **splash**, spatter, bespatter, dash, spray

splay v 1 **spread**, spread out, spread wide, open, open out Opposite: close up 2 **turn out**, turn outward, twist, bend, distort ■ adj **outspread**, splayed, splayed-out, spread, spread-out ■ n **slope**, bevel, slant, angle, incline

spleen n **ill temper**, anger, irritation, annoyance, grumpiness Opposite: contentment

splendid adj 1 **magnificent**, grand, superb, impressive, fine Opposite: unimpressive 2 **excellent**, wonderful, fabulous, marvelous, great

splendiferous *adj* magnificent, splendid, superlative, wonderful, superb *Opposite*: abysmal

splendor *n* 1 magnificence, glory, grandeur, brilliance, finery *Opposite*: drabness 2 wonder, marvel, miracle, glory, triumph

splenetic *adj* bad-tempered, spiteful, irritable, peevish, waspish *Opposite*: good-tempered

splice *v* join, intertwine, interweave, merge, fix together *Opposite*: split ■ *n* seam, join, connection, link, joint

spline *n* 1 key, tooth, blade, fin, projection 2 connecting strip, connector, connection, joining strip, link

splint *v* immobilize, strap, bind, bandage, secure

splinter *n* fragment, particle, piece, shard, sliver ■ *v* fall apart, crack, disintegrate, come apart, break up *Opposite*: mend

splinter group *n* faction, sect, offshoot, subset, minority

split *v* 1 divide, rip, tear, crack, come apart *Opposite*: join 2 cause a rift in, breach, divide, partition ■ *n* 1 tear, hole, rip, crack, fissure 2 difference, breach, breakup, divergence, rift *Opposite*: reconciliation 3 splitting, ripping, tearing, cracking, rupture 4 crack, division, rift, rent, break. *See* COMPARE AND CONTRAST *at* tear.

split hairs *v* quibble, equivocate, be pedantic, argue, mince matters

split-level *adj* two-tier, twin-tier, twin-level, two-level

split second *n* instant, moment, flash, the twinkling of an eye, second

split-second *adj* instant, instantaneous, immediate, prompt, high-speed *Opposite*: tardy

splitting *adj* excruciating, unbearable, piercing, intense, severe *Opposite*: slight

split up *v* part, break up, split, go your separate ways, end things *Opposite*: unite

split-up *n* breakup, separation, dissolution, ending, divorce *Opposite*: marriage

splurge *v* 1 spend, fritter, waste, squander, run through *Opposite*: save 2 *(infml)* indulge, binge, wallow, spoil, treat ■ *n* 1 *(infml)* bout, spree, binge, orgy, session 2 *(infml)* display, exhibition, show, parade, demonstration

splutter *v* choke, gasp, cough, spit, stutter

spoil *v* 1 ruin, blemish, blot, blight, impair *Opposite*: improve 2 indulge, pander to, be soft on, pamper, cosset *Opposite*: neglect 3 decay, go rotten, rot, go bad, putrefy

spoilage *n* 1 decay, rot, decomposition, degeneration, putrefaction 2 waste, wastage, loss, leakage, spillage

spoiled *adj* 1 ruined, damaged, decayed, rotted, rotten *Opposite*: fresh 2 over-indulged, ruined, willful, brattish, self-centered *Opposite*: neglected

spoils *n* 1 plunder, loot, booty, haul, pickings 2 reward, prize, gain, profit, earnings

spoilsport *n* killjoy, stuffed shirt, dog in the manger, curmudgeon, wet blanket *(infml)*

spoke *n* 1 rod, bar, rib, strut, shaft 2 rung, step, foothold, strut, bar

spoken *adj* verbal, vocal, oral, articulated, vocalized *Opposite*: written. *See* COMPARE AND CONTRAST *at* verbal.

spoken for *adj* reserved, kept back, taken, booked, earmarked *Opposite*: available

spokesperson *n* representative, speaker, voice, spokesman, spokeswoman

sponge *n (infml)* parasite, hanger-on, idler, user, sponger *(infml)* ■ *v* clean, wipe, wash, rub, mop

sponger *(infml) n* parasite, hanger-on, idler, user, scrounger *(infml) Opposite*: donor

spongy *adj* 1 soft, springy, malleable, elastic, flexible *Opposite*: firm 2 absorbent, porous, osmotic, permeable, penetrable *Opposite*: impermeable 3 soggy, squishy, moist, sodden, waterlogged *Opposite*: dry

sponsor *n* backer, guarantor, patron, promoter, champion ■ *v* back, support, pay for, subsidize, fund. *See* COMPARE AND CONTRAST *at* backer.

sponsorship *n* backing, support, protection, patronage, funding

spontaneity *n* impulsiveness, naturalness, artlessness, extemporaneity, freedom *Opposite*: constraint

spontaneous *adj* impulsive, unprompted, spur-of-the-moment, natural, artless *Opposite*: planned

spoof *n* 1 parody, satire, skit, burlesque, caricature 2 hoax, prank, deception, trick, bluff ■ *v* 1 deceive, fool, trick, bluff, hoax 2 satirize, burlesque, parody, caricature, take off *(infml)*

spook *n* 1 spy, mole, double agent, sleuth *(infml)*, snoop *(infml)* 2 *(infml)* ghost, wraith, phantom, specter, apparition ■ *v* startle, surprise, shock, alarm, agitate *Opposite*: soothe

spooky *adj* 1 strange, amazing, odd, unnerving, extraordinary *Opposite*: normal 2 *(infml)* frightening, ghostly, unnerving, mysterious, eerie *Opposite*: reassuring

spool *n* reel, coil, pin, bobbin ■ *v* wind, reel, coil, roll

spoon *v* serve, ladle, spoon over, spoon out, serve up

spoonerism *n* slip of the tongue, mistake, error, Freudian slip, tongue twister

spoon-feed *v* 1 feed, nourish, take care of, look after, care for *Opposite*: neglect 2 coddle, overindulge, wait on hand and foot, do everything for, run around after *Opposite*: neglect

spoonful *n* spoon, portion, serving, teaspoonful, dessertspoonful

spoor n **trail**, track, paw prints, hoof marks, footmarks ■ v **track**, stalk, follow, trail, hunt

sporadic adj **irregular**, intermittent, infrequent, periodic, erratic Opposite: regular. See COMPARE AND CONTRAST at **periodic**.

spore n **reproductive structure**, dormant bacterium, bacterium, microorganism

sporran n **pouch**, purse, bag

sport n **1 diversion**, game, amusement, hobby, pastime Opposite: work **2** (fml) **joking**, clowning, teasing, fooling around, fooling about ■ v (infml) **wear**, don, display, exhibit, show off

---

WORD BANK

❑ **types of ball games** Australian Rules, baseball, basketball, cricket, field hockey, football, hurling, lacrosse, netball, polo, rounders, rugby, Rugby League, Rugby Union, shinty, soccer, softball, water polo

❑ **types of combat sports** aikido, boxing, fencing, judo, karate, kendo, kickboxing, kung fu, sumo, tae kwon do, wrestling

❑ **types of court games** badminton, jai alai, pelota, rackets, squash, table tennis, tennis, volleyball

❑ **types of extreme sports** barefoot waterskiing, basejumping, bungee jumping, in-line skating, mountain biking, mountain boarding, skateboarding, skysurfing, sport climbing, street luge, stunt bicycling, wakeboarding

❑ **types of sports equipment** ball, bat, bowl, club, cue, discus, football, glove, helmet, hockey stick, javelin, lacrosse stick, mallet, mitt, pad, pigskin, puck, racket, shot, shuttlecock, spikes, tee, wicket

❑ **types of target ball games** billiards, boules, bowling, croquet, golf, lawn bowling, pool, snooker

❑ **types of track and field** cross-country, decathlon, discus, hammer throw, heptathlon, high jump, javelin, long jump, marathon, modern pentathlon, pole vault, relay race, shot put, sprint, steeplechase, triathlon, triple jump

❑ **types of winter sports** alpine skiing, biathlon, bobsled, cross-country skiing, curling, downhill, figure skating, hockey, ice dancing, langlauf, Nordic skiing, skiing, ski jump, slalom, snowboarding, speed skating, toboggan, XC skiing

---

sporting adj **fair**, honorable, generous, decent, honest Opposite: dishonest

sporting chance n **fair chance**, good chance, decent chance, fair shot, reasonable chance

sports adj **1 sporting**, games, athletic **2 casual**, informal, leisure, outdoor, leisurewear

sportscast n **sports broadcast**, sports update, sports program, televised sports event, televised match

sportscaster n **sports broadcaster**, sports presenter, sports commentator, sports reporter, sports correspondent

sports grounds n **stadium**, arena, bowl, field, ground

sportsperson n **competitor**, player, contestant, athlete

sporty adj **1 athletic**, active, good at sport, fit, muscular Opposite: lazy **2 flashy**, stylish, jaunty, natty, snazzy (infml) Opposite: formal

spot n **1 mark**, blemish, stain, smudge, speck **2 bit**, touch, dash, soupçon, tad (infml) **3 place**, location, site, setting, corner **4 advertisement**, commercial, promotion, ad (infml), plug (infml) **5** (infml) **predicament**, mess, difficulty, awkward situation, quandary ■ v **1 notice**, spy, recognize, catch a glimpse of, catch sight of Opposite: miss **2 stain**, dirty, blemish, smudge, speck Opposite: clean

spot check n **inspection**, check, search, examination, visit

spot-check v **inspect**, check, search, examine, double-check

spotless adj **1 immaculate**, spick-and-span, clean, clean as a whistle, pristine Opposite: dirty **2 unblemished**, flawless, perfect, faultless, impeccable Opposite: flawed

spotlessly adv **immaculately**, extremely, perfectly, absolutely, very

spotlessness n **1 cleanliness**, cleanness, pristineness, immaculateness, neatness Opposite: dirtiness **2 flawlessness**, wholesomeness, innocence, stainlessness, irreproachability Opposite: imperfection

spotlight n **attention**, limelight, fuss, focus, interest Opposite: anonymity ■ v **highlight**, point up, draw attention to, underline, focus on Opposite: obscure

spotted adj **dotted**, marked, speckled, dappled, mottled Opposite: plain

spotty adj **mottled**, patterned, blotchy, spotted, dotted

spousal equivalent n **cohabitee**, partner, domestic partner, significant other

spouse n **other half**, wife, husband, next of kin, partner

spout v **1 spew out**, shoot out, discharge, spurt, emit Opposite: retain **2 talk**, utter, pontificate, ramble on, sermonize ■ n **1 jet**, fountain, stream, column, spurt **2 tube**, pipe, nozzle, outlet, spray

sprain v **twist**, pull, injure, strain, crick

sprawl v **1 slump**, collapse, lounge, loll, slouch Opposite: curl up **2 spread out**, cover, extend over, stretch over, trail Opposite: shrink ■ n **stretch**, mass, extension, spread, straggle

sprawling adj **extensive**, rambling, expansive, straggling, straggly Opposite: contained

spray n **1 gush**, squirt, mist, jet, fountain **2 atomizer**, aerosol, spray can, pump dispenser, sprayer **3 sprig**, bouquet, stem, posy, bunch ■ v **1 scatter**, squirt, send out, spew, spurt **2 cover**, drench, squirt, mist, dose

spray can *n* aerosol, atomizer, spray, pump dispenser, sprayer

spray gun *n* spray, atomizer, airbrush, sprayer, diffuser

spread *v* **1 increase**, extend, multiply, reach, stretch *Opposite*: shrink **2 open out**, unfold, place, lay out, put out *Opposite*: furl **3 apply**, put on, smear, daub, butter *Opposite*: remove **4 disperse**, distribute, share out, allot, divide *Opposite*: collect **5 broadcast**, disseminate, circulate, publish, propagate **6 last**, continue, go on, carry on, persist ■ *n* **1 range**, extent, increase, coverage, span **2 variety**, range, selection, array, assortment **3 ranch**, estate, farm, plantation, station **4** (*infml*) **feast**, banquet, binge, meal, supper

spread-eagled *adj* **sprawled**, sprawling, prone, prostrate, face down *Opposite*: erect

spread out *v* **1 move apart**, divide up, split up *Opposite*: amass **2 extend**, cover, spread, go as far as, stretch **3 share out**, share, divide up, split up

spreadsheet *n* worksheet, database, table

spree *n* **1 binge**, extravaganza, fling, orgy, splurge (*infml*) **2 jaunt**, outing, trip, excursion, break

sprig *n* spray, twig, stem, branch, shoot

sprightly *adj* energetic, active, spry, lively, agile *Opposite*: lethargic

spring *v* jump, leap, bounce, pounce, launch yourself ■ *n* **1 coil**, spiral, helix, mainspring, hairspring **2 springtime**, season, seedtime, springtide (*literary*) **3 elasticity**, springiness, bounce, give, flexibility *Opposite*: rigidity **4 leap**, bound, jump, bounce, vault **5 source**, upwelling, fount, fountain, water source

spring back *v* ricochet, recoil, shrink

springboard *n* catalyst, facilitator, spur, trigger, launch pad *Opposite*: brake

spring-clean *v* scour, scrub, wash down, dust down, clean out *Opposite*: dirty

springtime *n* season, spring, seedtime, springtide (*literary*)

spring up *v* appear, emerge, pop up, come into existence, mushroom *Opposite*: disappear

springy *adj* bouncy, elastic, supple, pliable, soft *Opposite*: unyielding

sprinkle *v* **1 shake over**, dust, scatter, cover **2 intersperse**, pepper, strew, scatter, litter **3 rain**, drizzle, shower ■ *n* **sprinkling**, shake, dusting, scattering, scatter

sprinkler *n* **1 sprayer**, irrigator, waterer, spray, hose **2 nozzle**, rose, showerhead, spray, diffuser

sprinkling *n* **scattering**, dash, shake, pinch, bit *Opposite*: heap

sprint *n* dash, burst, race, run, cycle race

Opposite: marathon ■ *v* hurry, run, dash, race, gallop *Opposite*: dawdle

sprinter *n* runner, racer, competitor

sprite *n* fairy, nymph, elf, dryad, leprechaun

sprocket *n* tooth, cog, notch, projection, sprocket wheel

sprout *v* **1 grow**, shoot, develop, bud, spring *Opposite*: wither **2 spring up**, spring, emerge, appear, pop up ■ *n* **shoot**, bud, leaf, young branch, new growth

spruce *adj* smart, neat, dapper, trim, elegant *Opposite*: scruffy

spruce up *v* smarten, smarten up, tidy, neaten, improve *Opposite*: mess up (*infml*)

spry *adj* **sprightly**, lively, active, agile, energetic *Opposite*: slow

spume (*literary*) *n* foam, surf, spray, froth, bubbles

spunk (*infml*) *n* pluck, spirit, toughness, determination, nerve *Opposite*: cowardice

spunky (*infml*) *adj* plucky, spirited, tough, determined, energetic *Opposite*: cowardly

spur *n* **1 incentive**, stimulus, incitement, provocation, motive *Opposite*: disincentive **2 branch**, limb, shoot, offshoot, outgrowth **3 spike**, point, barb, spine **4 ridge**, mountainside, projection, edge, saddle ■ *v* **1 urge**, encourage, incite, prompt, stimulate *Opposite*: discourage **2** (*literary*) **hurry up**, hasten, speed up, speed, rush *Opposite*: delay. *See* COMPARE AND CONTRAST at **motive**

spurious *adj* false, bogus, fake, forged, counterfeit *Opposite*: genuine

spurn *v* reject, snub, slight, rebuff, repulse *Opposite*: accept

spur-of-the-moment *adj* **spontaneous**, impulsive, unplanned, impromptu, unpremeditated *Opposite*: planned

spurt *n* **1 jet**, spray, squirt, gush, spout *Opposite*: trickle **2 increase**, burst, surge, rush, swell ■ *v* gush, spray, burst, jet, erupt *Opposite*: trickle

splutter *v* **1 pop**, splutter, spit, sizzle, crackle **2 splutter**, gasp, spit, stammer, snort

sputum *n* mucus, phlegm, saliva, spit, spittle

spy *n* secret agent, undercover agent, double agent, mole, infiltrator ■ *v* **1 work undercover**, pry, reconnoiter, snoop (*infml*), nose around (*infml*) **2 watch**, eavesdrop, listen in, observe, scrutinize **3 spot**, glimpse, notice, observe, see **4 discover**, search out, detect, find out, observe *Opposite*: overlook **5 investigate**, poke around, explore, search, research

spyhole *n* peephole, slot, chink, opening, window

spying *n* undercover work, intelligence work, espionage, eavesdropping, infiltration

spy out *v* discover, uncover, seek out, sniff out, nose out *Opposite*: overlook

squabble *n* quarrel, row, tiff, dispute, argument *Opposite*: reconciliation ■ *v* argue, bicker, quarrel, disagree, have words *Opposite*: make up

squad *n* group, team, crew, company, gang

squad car *n* police car, patrol car, prowl car, cruiser

squadron *n* regiment, troop, team, squad, company

squalid *adj* 1 filthy, dirty, foul, nasty, fetid *Opposite*: clean 2 seedy, repulsive, sordid, sleazy, low *Opposite*: charming. *See* COMPARE AND CONTRAST *at* dirty.

squall *n* storm, gust of wind, windstorm, gust, shower

squally *adj* stormy, gusty, blustery, wild, inclement *Opposite*: fine

squalor *n* 1 filth, dirt, dirtiness, foulness, grime *Opposite*: cleanliness 2 nastiness, sordidness, unpleasantness, degradation, immorality *Opposite*: charm

squander *v* waste, spend, throw away, fritter away, dissipate *Opposite*: save

square *n* 1 four-sided figure, quadrangle, tetragon, rectangle, parallelogram 2 plaza, open area, marketplace, place, parade ■ *adj* 1 four-sided, right-angled, rectangular, quadrangular, tetragonal 2 fair, honest, genuine, just, straight *Opposite*: dishonest ■ *v* 1 shape, form, file down, sharpen, even up 2 adjust, align, realign, set straight, straighten *Opposite*: unbalance 3 pay off, settle, clear, pay, balance 4 agree, harmonize, accord, tally *Opposite*: conflict ■ *adv* 1 at right angles, directly, straight 2 *(infml)* fairly, honestly, openly, straightforwardly, straight

squarely *adv* directly, exactly, evenly, head-on, straight *Opposite*: indirectly

square meal *n* nourishment, hot meal, proper meal, food, sustenance *Opposite*: nibble

square up *v* 1 settle up, even up, settle your debts, settle the bill, pay up 2 work out, turn out fine, sort itself out, be arranged, be organized *Opposite*: go wrong 3 face up to, confront, look something in the eye, tackle, take on *Opposite*: evade 4 put up your fists, make a stand, put up a fight, stand your ground, take up the gauntlet *Opposite*: run away

squash *v* 1 crush, flatten, compress, pulp, mash *Opposite*: reshape 2 cram, squeeze, wedge, force, jam *Opposite*: coax 3 overcome, stop, conquer, suppress, quash *Opposite*: encourage ■ *n* squeeze, crush, congestion, crowd, jam

squashy *adj* soft, yielding, spongy, springy, mushy *Opposite*: firm

squat *v* crouch, sit on your heels, hunker down, bend *Opposite*: stand ■ *adj* short, thickset, thick, stubby, stocky *Opposite*: tall

squatter *n* unlawful tenant, unlawful resident, resident, trespasser

squawk *v* 1 screech, call, cry, squeal, shriek 2 *(infml)* complain, protest, whine, wail, grumble ■ *n* *(infml)* protest, complaint, whine, wail, grumble.

squeak *v* squeal, whine, yelp, shrill, pipe

squeak through *(infml)* *v* scrape through, scrape by, manage, achieve, do

squeaky *adj* high-pitched, shrill, whiny, noisy, creaky

squeaky-clean *adj* 1 virtuous, righteous, pure, honorable, unimpeachable *Opposite*: corrupt 2 clean, clean as a whistle, spotless, dirt-free, pristine

squeal *n* screech, yelp, shriek, yell, cry ■ *v* yell, cry, shriek, yelp, howl

squeamish *adj* 1 nauseous, queasy, sick, woozy 2 prudish, delicate, easily upset, easily offended, puritanical *Opposite*: strong 3 fastidious, particular, scrupulous, fussy, uncompromising *Opposite*: easygoing

squeamishness *n* 1 queasiness, nauseousness, sickness, qualmishness, seediness *(infml)* 2 delicacy, prudishness, prudery, shockability, puritanism *Opposite*: toughness

squeeze *v* 1 press, squash, compress, constrict, pinch 2 grip, hold on, grasp, hug, clutch *Opposite*: release 3 hug, embrace, cuddle, enfold, clasp *Opposite*: release 4 crush, squash, cram, crowd, jam *Opposite*: coax 5 find time for, make time for, make room for, fit in, slot in 6 extract, wring, expel, drive out, mangle 7 put pressure on, harass, oppress, lean on *(infml)*, hassle *(infml)*

squeeze out *v* exclude, express, force out, freeze out, ostracize

squelch *v* 1 squish, splash, splish-splash, suck, gurgle 2 crush, squash, flatten, trample, squish

squelchy *adj* soggy, squishy, wet, watery, damp *Opposite*: dry

squiggle *n* scribble, wavy line, doodle, ornamentation, flourish

squiggly *adj* wavy, curvy, wobbly, bumpy, scribbly *Opposite*: straight

squint *v* narrow your eyes, peer, peek, look, glance ■ *n* peep, peer, quick look, glance, glimpse ■ *adj* *(infml)* crooked, lopsided, cross-eyed, off balance, uneven *Opposite*: straight ■ *adv* *(infml)* lopsidedly, askew, crookedly, unevenly *Opposite*: straight

squire *n* 1 landowner, lord, landlord, owner, proprietor *Opposite*: tenant 2 attendant, retainer, steward, man, servant

squirm *v* 1 wriggle, writhe, twist, turn, fidget 2 feel shame, feel embarrassment, feel remorse, feel guilty, feel awkward

squirrel *v* hoard, collect, accumulate, store, put aside *Opposite*: throw out

squirt *v* spurt, shoot, jet, gush, spray ■ *n* spurt, jet, fountain, stream, spray

squish v 1 squeeze, crush, squash, squelch, pinch 2 splash, squelch, splish-splash, suck, gurgle

squishy adj squelchy, soggy, soft, mushy, spongy Opposite: firm

stab v knife, wound, pierce, cut, spear ■ n 1 pang, twinge, ache, pain, prick 2 (infml) attempt, go, try, shot, guess

stabbing n knife attack, assault, wounding, attack ■ adj sharp, acute, piercing, shooting, intense

stability n constancy, steadiness, firmness, solidity, permanence Opposite: instability

stabilization n steadying, steadiness, maintenance, balance, equilibrium Opposite: change

stabilize v become stable, even out, become constant, calm, calm down Opposite: change

stab in the back (infml) v betray, let down, be disloyal to, sell out, wound ■ n betrayal, wound, attack, act of disloyalty, act of treachery

stable adj 1 steady, unchanging, even, constant, firm Opposite: changeable 2 secure, fixed, firm, permanent, rigid Opposite: unstable 3 calm, steady, even, settled, level-headed Opposite: erratic ■ n 1 stall, shed, stabling 2 team, gang, string, group, lineup

staccato adj clipped, disjointed, disconnected, faltering, monosyllabic

stack n 1 pile, heap, mass, mound, mountain 2 chimney, smokestack, flue ■ v pile, load, heap, mound, amass

stacked adj loaded, weighted, set, slanted, fixed

stacks (infml) n lots, masses, piles (infml), tons (infml), loads (infml) Opposite: a few

stack up v 1 measure up, stand up, compare, line up, stand comparison 2 add up, come to, accumulate, make, total

stadium n sports grounds, arena, ground, field, ring

staff n 1 employees, personnel, workers, work force, team 2 rod, cane, pole, wand, stick ■ v operate, run, work, control, supervise

stage n 1 phase, period, step, point, leg 2 platform, rostrum, stand, scaffold, podium 3 theater, arena, playhouse, the boards ■ v put on, perform, present, show, play

stagecoach n carriage, horse-drawn carriage, cart

stage door n back door, side door, entrance, way in, exit

stage fright n first-night nerves, fear, panic, nerves (infml)

stage-manage v engineer, contrive, manipulate, devise, set up

stage name n pseudonym, alias, assumed name, professional name

stage whisper n aside, mutter, murmur Opposite: shout

stagey see stagy

stagflation n slump, recession, downturn, stagnation, inflation Opposite: growth

stagger v 1 reel, lurch, sway, totter, wobble 2 astound, amaze, shock, stun, surprise 3 alternate, vary, zigzag, rotate, space out Opposite: overlap

staggered adj 1 stunned, shocked, amazed, astounded, taken aback Opposite: unaffected 2 alternated, spread out, spaced out, zigzagged

staggering adj astounding, amazing, confounding, overwhelming, stunning

staging n performance, dramatization, production, enactment, presentation

stagnant adj 1 still, motionless, stationary, standing, immobile Opposite: moving 2 sluggish, inactive, inert, torpid, dull Opposite: active

stagnate v 1 stand still, come to a halt, grind to a halt, be idle, languish Opposite: progress 2 fester, rot, deteriorate, decay, go rancid 3 vegetate, be inactive, idle, be idle, sit around

stagnation n inactivity, inaction, inertia, torpor, sluggishness Opposite: movement

stagy adj theatrical, dramatic, histrionic, exaggerated, artificial Opposite: unaffected

staid adj sedate, serious, grave, sober, dull Opposite: exciting

stain n 1 mark, blemish, spot, blot, imperfection 2 tint, dye, color, tinge, pigment 3 stigma, slur, disgrace, dishonor, blemish ■ v 1 blemish, tarnish, soil, discolor, mark 2 disgrace, sully, taint, debase, dishonor Opposite: honor

stained adj discolored, marked, blemished, tainted, tarnished

stair n 1 step, tread, rung 2 staircase, stairway, flight of steps, set of steps, flight of stairs

stairs n staircase, stair, stairway, flight of steps, set of steps

stairwell n hall, entrance hall, vestibule, shaft

stake n 1 bet, wager, ante, risk, venture 2 post, pale, pole, palisade, picket 3 investment, claim, share, involvement, concern 4 prize, winnings, purse, stakes ■ v risk, gamble, bet, venture, hazard

stakeholder n investor, shareholder, backer, sponsor, participant

stake out v 1 mark out, demarcate, delimit, measure out, fence off 2 establish, clarify, define, limit, restrict 3 (infml) spy on, watch, keep under surveillance, keep watch on, keep an eye on

stakeout (infml) n close watch, watch, observation, investigation, examination

stakes n 1 risk, risk factor, danger, element

of danger **2 reward**, prize, recompense, incentive, winnings

stale adj **1 decayed**, sour, old, musty, hard Opposite: fresh **2 hackneyed**, worn-out, tired, overused, boring Opposite: original

stalemate n **impasse**, deadlock, standoff, logjam, standstill

staleness n **1 mustiness**, moldiness, decay, flatness, sourness Opposite: freshness **2 unoriginality**, overuse, insipidness

stalk n **stem**, shoot, twig, branch, trunk ■ v **follow**, trail, track, pursue, shadow

stalker n **prowler**, pursuer, shadow, tracker, follower

stall n **1 booth**, stand, arcade, shop, kiosk **2 compartment**, pen, coop, shed, cubicle ■ v **1 stop**, cut out, freeze, pause, halt Opposite: keep going **2 delay**, put off, defer, postpone, suspend Opposite: advance **3 play for time**, prevaricate, equivocate, hedge, hesitate

stalwart adj **1 resolute**, vigorous, determined, committed, unfaltering Opposite: uncommitted **2 strong**, muscular, athletic, brawny, sturdy Opposite: feeble **3 brave**, courageous, daring, fearless, bold Opposite: cowardly

stamina n **staying power**, endurance, energy, resilience, resistance Opposite: frailty

stammer v **stumble**, stutter, falter, hesitate, pause ■ n **stutter**, hesitant speech, speech impediment

stamp n **1 mark**, imprint, mold, cast, hallmark **2 character**, kind, make, sort, type ■ v **1 imprint**, engrave, inscribe, fix, impress **2 trample**, stomp, crush, squash, plod Opposite: tiptoe

stampede n **rush**, mad dash, flight, rout, pandemonium ■ v **rush**, hurry, run, dash, sprint

stamping ground (infml) n **patch**, haunt, place, home, territory

stamp out v **eradicate**, banish, destroy, remove, eliminate Opposite: cultivate

stance n **1 attitude**, position, stand, standpoint, view **2 posture**, deportment, bearing, attitude, carriage (fml)

stanch see **staunch**

stand v **1 erect**, mount, hoist, put up, stick up **2 rise**, get up, stand up, get to your feet, be on your feet Opposite: sit **3 place**, situate, position, set, put **4 tolerate**, endure, put up with, abide, bear **5 remain**, halt, stop, continue, exist ■ n **1 stop**, standstill, stay, rest, halt **2 attitude**, opinion, stance, position, viewpoint **3 rack**, frame, support, holder, shelf **4 platform**, rostrum, stage, place, post **5 stall**, counter, booth, kiosk, tent

standard n **1 criterion**, benchmark, touchstone, paradigm, yardstick **2 norm**, average, mean, par, level **3 flag**, banner, ensign, pennant, colors ■ adj **normal**,

typical, average, usual, ordinary Opposite: unusual

standard-bearer n **leader**, ringleader, prime mover, spearhead, director

standardize v **regulate**, homogenize, normalize, even out, regiment Opposite: vary

standard of living n **level of comfort**, means, level of affluence, wealth, lifestyle

standards n **principles**, values, morals, ethics, ideals

stand by v **support**, stick by, back, stick up for, side with Opposite: abandon

standby n **1 fallback**, reserve, replacement, resource, stand-in **2 backup**, substitute, replacement, spare, reserve ■ adj **1 reserve**, fallback, replacement, stand-in, deputy Opposite: main **2 unreserved**, last-minute, late, for immediate use Opposite: reserved

stand down v **resign**, step down, quit, bow out, give up

stand firm v **persevere**, stand your ground, hold on, hold out, dig in your heels Opposite: yield

stand for v **1 mean**, signify, represent, denote, symbolize **2 advocate**, promote, support, champion, endorse **3 put up with**, tolerate, abide, withstand, stand

stand in v **fill in**, substitute, deputize, take somebody's place, do somebody's work

stand-in n **replacement**, understudy, deputy, substitute, reserve

stand in for v **take the place of**, deputize for, substitute for, cover for, do the work of

standing n **1 rank**, status, position, reputation, station **2 duration**, existence, continuance, age, tenure ■ adj **1 established**, settled, fixed, immovable, durable Opposite: temporary **2 standup**, vertical, upright, upended, perpendicular Opposite: horizontal

standing order n **rule**, order, instruction, protocol, procedure

standing stone n **obelisk**, menhir, dolmen, megalith, column

standoff n **1 stalemate**, impasse, deadlock, logjam, standstill **2 tie**, draw, dead heat, photo finish

standoffish adj **distant**, aloof, superior, unapproachable, cold Opposite: affable

stand out v **1 be obvious**, be prominent, show up, be conspicuous, stick out **2 project**, jut, protrude, jut out, stick out

standpipe n **water pipe**, faucet, emergency pipe, water supply, hydrant

standpoint n **point of view**, position, stance, angle, viewpoint

standstill n **halt**, stop, stoppage, cessation, end

stand up v **1 rise**, stand, get to your feet, get up, arise (literary) Opposite: sit down **2 endure**, last, survive, continue, hold out

standup adj **solo**, improvised, spontaneous,

off-the-cuff, improv *(infml) Opposite*: rehearsed

stand up to *v* face, brave, take on, meet head-on, confront *Opposite*: avoid

stand your ground *v* stand firm, persist, persevere, reserve, hold out *Opposite*: give in

stanza *n* verse, section, stave, couplet, triplet

staple *n* clip, fastener, nail, tack, pin ■ *v* fasten, affix, clip, attach, secure ■ *adj* main, chief, principal, essential, primary *Opposite*: minor

star *n* celebrity, superstar, personality, icon ■ *v* 1 feature, showcase, head the cast, top the bill, play the lead 2 do well, excel, shine, succeed, stand out

---

WORD BANK

❏ **types of stars or star systems** binary star, black hole, brown dwarf, dark star, dwarf star, galaxy, giant star, nebula, nova, pulsar, quasar, red giant, sun, supernova, white dwarf

---

star billing *n* top billing, star status, top of the bill, main attraction, big name

starboard *adj* right-hand, right, right-side *Opposite*: port

starchy *adj* stiff, solemn, prudish, prim, austere *Opposite*: relaxed

star-crossed *adj* ill-fated, unlucky, ill-starred, doomed, unfortunate *Opposite*: lucky

stardom *n* fame, celebrity, prominence, renown, glory *Opposite*: anonymity

stardust *n* romance, dreaminess, sentiment, emotion, feeling

stare *v* gaze, gape, look intently, ogle, glare *Opposite*: ignore ■ *n* intent look, gaze, gape, glare, glower. *See* COMPARE AND CONTRAST *at* gaze.

star in *v* play the lead in, feature in, act in, play in, head the cast

stark *adj* 1 bleak, bare, barren, desolate, austere *Opposite*: opulent 2 plain, unambiguous, simple, blunt, unadulterated *Opposite*: ambiguous 3 complete, utter, absolute, sheer, downright *Opposite*: partial ■ *adv* completely, utterly, entirely, wholly, fully *Opposite*: partially

starkness *n* 1 austerity, bleakness, harshness, severity, sparseness *Opposite*: opulence 2 frankness, unambiguity, blatancy, harshness, bluntness *Opposite*: ambiguity

starlet *n* actor, rising young star, new talent, star of tomorrow, star in the making

starlight *n* glow, gleam, sheen, twinkle, sparkle

starlit *adj* starry, bright, glowing, gleaming, twinkling *Opposite*: dark

starry *adj* glittery, shiny, bright, sparkly, brilliant *Opposite*: dull

starry-eyed *adj* dreamy, optimistic, idealistic, head-in-the-clouds, happy *Opposite*: cynical

starship *n* spaceship, space shuttle, space station, flying saucer

star sign *n* sign of the zodiac, birth sign, sun sign, sign, astrological sign

star-studded *adj* star-spangled, all-star, celebrity, big-name, glittering *Opposite*: unknown

star system *n* constellation, galaxy, Milky Way, solar system

start *v* 1 create, found, begin, establish, set up *Opposite*: close 2 begin, commence, start off, get going, set off *Opposite*: finish 3 set out, leave, set off, depart, get going *Opposite*: arrive 4 jump, recoil, flinch, shrink, twitch ■ *n* 1 beginning, birth, foundation, onset, dawn *Opposite*: end 2 twitch, jump, jerk, flinch, jolt 3 shock, fright, surprise, turn 4 lead, advantage, edge, boon, gain

starter *n* hors d'oeuvre, first course, entrée, appetizer, meze

starting point *n* 1 basis, base, foundation, point of departure, beginning 2 starting line, starting block, starting grid, starting post, starting gate *Opposite*: finishing line

startle *v* surprise, disconcert, shock, alarm, frighten

startled *adj* surprised, disconcerted, alarmed, astonished, amazed

startling *adj* surprising, astonishing, amazing, astounding, staggering *Opposite*: comforting

start off *v* 1 begin, commence, get going, start out, start *Opposite*: finish 2 set off, start out, be off, get going, start *Opposite*: arrive

start on *v* 1 begin, tackle, deal with, embark on, get going on *Opposite*: finish 2 *(infml)* scold, harass, pester, nag, annoy

start out *v* 1 start off, start, begin, set off, get going *Opposite*: arrive 2 intend, mean, plan, propose, expect

start up *v* 1 switch on, turn on, fire up, power up, ignite *Opposite*: turn off 2 set up, open, begin, launch, create *Opposite*: close down 3 pipe up, resound, be heard, begin, start *Opposite*: quiet down 4 leap up, jump up, stand up, get up, rise *Opposite*: sit down

starvation *n* hunger, malnourishment, undernourishment, famishment, famine

starve *v* have nothing to eat, go hungry, famish, be malnourished, go short of food *Opposite*: eat

starved *adj* 1 deprived, bereft, devoid, lacking, without 2 *(infml)* ravenous, hungry, famished, starving *(infml) Opposite*: replete

starving *(infml) adj* ravenous, hungry, famished, starved *(infml) Opposite*: replete

stash *n* supply, hideaway, hoard, mass, pile ■ *v* *(infml)* hide, hoard, put away, put by, stockpile

stasis *n* stability, motionlessness, status quo,

continuity, inertia *Opposite*: change

state n 1 **condition**, situation, position, status, circumstances 2 **federation**, kingdom, nation, land, territory 3 **grandeur**, ceremony, pomp, splendor, glory 4 *(infml)* **confusion**, turmoil, disarray, disorder, chaos ■ *adj* 1 **public**, government, municipal, state-run, state-owned 2 **formal**, official, stately, imperial, royal ■ *v* **utter**, affirm, declare, assert, express

statecraft n **government**, management, governance, administration, direction

stateless *adj* **homeless**, nationless, displaced, refugee, outlawed

state line n **border**, border line, frontier, boundary

stateliness n **grandeur**, pomp, glory, dignity, majesty

stately *adj* **grand**, splendid, dignified, imperial, majestic *Opposite*: modest

statement n 1 **declaration**, announcement, report, account, speech 2 **record**, account, receipt, invoice

state of affairs n **situation**, set of circumstances, condition, setup, position

state of mind n **mood**, temper, attitude, feelings, spirits

state-of-the-art *adj* **advanced**, high-tech, cutting-edge, up-to-the-minute, up-to-date *Opposite*: antiquated

state-owned *adj* **public**, public-sector, state, state-run, nationalized *Opposite*: private

stateroom n **first-class compartment**, first-class cabin, sleeping compartment, berth, sleeper

state school *(infml)* n **state university**, state college, public university, community college, public school

state secret n **confidential matter**, affair of state, top-secret matter, confidential information, classified material

static *adj* 1 **still**, motionless, stationary, inert, standing *Opposite*: moving 2 **unchanging**, constant, invariable, unvarying *Opposite*: dynamic

station n 1 **rank**, class, status, position, level 2 **position**, place, post, location, situation ■ *v* **post**, base, position, place, situate

stationary *adj* **motionless**, still, immobile, inactive, fixed *Opposite*: moving

stationery n **writing materials**, writing implements, pen and paper, writing paper, notepaper

statistic n **number**, figure, digit, piece of data, measurement

statistics n **figures**, data, numbers, information

statuary n **sculptures**, statues, figures, monuments, busts

statue n **figurine**, figure, sculpture, effigy, statuette

statuesque *adj* **stately**, elegant, graceful, majestic, dignified *Opposite*: ungainly

statuette *see* **statue**

stature n 1 **build**, height, physique, figure, tallness 2 **standing**, importance, prominence, status, rank

status n 1 **rank**, position, standing, grade, station 2 **eminence**, prestige, prominence, importance, significance 3 **category**, condition, class, type, stage

status quo n **current situation**, existing state of affairs, present circumstances, how things stand

status symbol n **asset**, must-have, prize possession

statute n **decree**, act, ruling, edict, order

statute book n **body of law**, record, legislation, legal code, law book

statute law n **written law**, law, constitution, legislation, acts of Congress

statutory *adj* **constitutional**, legislative, legal

staunch *v* **stop**, stem, halt, hold back, curb ■ *adj* **loyal**, faithful, steadfast, reliable, dependable *Opposite*: wavering

stave n 1 **plank**, slat, board, lath, band 2 **bar**, rung, tread, step, crosspiece 3 **stanza**, verse, section, couplet, triplet

stave off *v* **fend off**, keep at bay, hold off, delay, deflect

stay *v* 1 **remain**, wait, continue, keep on, hang around *Opposite*: go 2 **reside**, live, inhabit, settle, dwell *(literary)* 3 **stop**, halt, delay, defer, put off ■ *n* 1 **visit**, break, stopover, vacation, sojourn *(literary)* 2 **halt**, stop, delay, deferment, adjournment

staying power n **stamina**, endurance, determination, doggedness, vigor *Opposite*: frailty

stay on *v* **remain**, stay, stay put, stay behind, stay out *Opposite*: leave

stay out *v* **be out**, not come home, not come back

stay put *v* **remain**, stay, stay still, tarry, hang on *Opposite*: move

stay up *v* **burn the candle at both ends**, stay up till all hours, burn the midnight oil, make a night of it, pull an all-nighter *(infml)*

steadfast *adj* 1 **unwavering**, unfaltering, resolute, committed, dedicated *Opposite*: wavering 2 **loyal**, trusty, dependable, faithful, trustworthy *Opposite*: inconstant *(literary)*

steadfastness n 1 **resoluteness**, commitment, dedication, persistence, determination *Opposite*: wavering 2 **loyalty**, faithfulness, trustworthiness, devotion, dependability *Opposite*: disloyalty

steadily *adv* **progressively**, gradually, increasingly, little by little, bit by bit *Opposite*: suddenly

steadiness n 1 **control**, stability, firmness, balance, equilibrium *Opposite*: unsteadiness 2 **calmness**, composure, serenity, reliability, dependability *Opposite*: excitability **3 regularity**, uniformity, constancy

steady *adj* **1 stable**, firm, fixed, solid, sturdy *Opposite*: rickety **2 continual**, constant, perpetual, never-ending, ceaseless *Opposite*: intermittent **3 even**, regular, uniform, unchanging, unvarying *Opposite*: irregular **4 calm**, cool, collected, composed, unruffled *Opposite*: excitable ■ *v* **stabilize**, secure, fix, support, strengthen *Opposite*: undermine

steal *v* **1 pilfer**, misappropriate, embezzle, take, pocket **2 creep**, sneak, slip, slink, tiptoe ■ *n* (*infml*) **bargain**, good deal, good buy, giveaway (*infml*) *Opposite*: rip-off (*infml*)

COMPARE AND CONTRAST CORE MEANING: the taking of property unlawfully

steal take something that belongs to somebody else, illegally or without the owner's permission; **pinch** (*infml*) steal something; **nick** (*slang*) steal something; **filch** (*infml*) steal something furtively and opportunistically, usually a small item or something of little value; **purloin** (*fml*) steal something, sometimes used humorously or euphemistically; **pilfer** steal small items of little value, especially habitually; **embezzle** take for personal use money or property that has been given on trust by others, without their knowledge; **misappropriate** take something, especially money, dishonestly or in order to use it for an improper or illegal purpose.

stealing *n* **theft**, robbery, burglary, larceny, thieving

stealth *n* **furtiveness**, surreptitiousness, sneakiness, slyness, craftiness *Opposite*: openness

stealthy *adj* **furtive**, surreptitious, sly, silent, cautious *Opposite*: blatant. *See* COMPARE AND CONTRAST *at* **secret**.

steam *n* **vapor**, condensation, haze, mist, fog

steamroller *v* **1 compress**, bulldoze, flatten, crush, squash **2 crush**, squash, demolish, destroy, overwhelm **3 force**, compel, coerce, bludgeon, bully

steam up *v* **mist up**, fog up, cloud, cloud over, mist over

steamy *adj* **1 humid**, muggy, damp, sticky, hot and sticky **2 misted up**, misty, fogged up, foggy, steamed up *Opposite*: clear

steed (*literary*) *n* **horse**, pony, mount, charger

steel *v* **strengthen**, toughen, harden, fortify, brace

steely *adj* **1 hard**, strong, tough, sturdy, rugged *Opposite*: soft **2 determined**, resolute, unyielding, unbending, rigid *Opposite*: irresolute

steel yourself *v* **brace yourself**, harden your heart, pluck up your courage, prepare yourself, compose yourself

steep *adj* **1 sheer**, vertical, sharp, precipitous, abrupt *Opposite*: gentle **2** (*infml*) **unreasonable**, extreme, excessive, expensive, dear *Opposite*: reasonable ■ *v* **1 soak**, immerse, drench, submerge, suffuse **2 imbue**, permeate, infuse

steeple *n* **tower**, spire, turret, bell tower, belfry

steeply *adv* **sharply**, precipitously, abruptly, suddenly *Opposite*: gently

steepness *n* **sharpness**, abruptness, gradient, sheerness *Opposite*: gentleness

steer *v* **1 control**, drive, pilot, navigate, maneuver **2 direct**, guide, point, conduct, lead. *See* COMPARE AND CONTRAST *at* **guide**.

steerage *n* **third class**, bottom deck, tourist class, lower deck

steering committee *n* **steering group**, board, panel, team, commission

stellar *adj* **1 astral**, astronomical, astrophysical, solar, planetary *Opposite*: earthly **2 all-star**, star-studded, star-spangled, starry, celebrity *Opposite*: unknown

stem *n* **stalk**, shoot, trunk, twig, branch ■ *v* **stop**, staunch, halt, curtail, restrict *Opposite*: accelerate

stem from *v* **arise from**, originate from, come from, derive from, develop from

stench *n* **stink**, reek, unpleasant smell, disgusting odor, foul smell *Opposite*: fragrance. *See* COMPARE AND CONTRAST *at* **smell**.

stencil *n* **1 template**, cutout, guide, plate, shape **2 design**, pattern, lettering, motif, border ■ *v* **1 apply**, paint, work, draw, trace **2 decorate**, adorn, paint, ornament

stentorian *adj* **loud**, powerful, booming, thunderous, deafening *Opposite*: quiet

step *n* **1 pace**, footstep, stride **2 stair**, rung, tread **3 move**, movement, action, measure **4 stage**, phase, period ■ *v* **walk**, tread, march, pace, move

step down *v* **1 stand down**, resign, retire, bow out, withdraw *Opposite*: stay on **2 decrease**, reduce, lower, lessen, restrict *Opposite*: step up

step in *v* **intervene**, intercede, interpose, interrupt, get involved

stepladder *n* **ladder**, portable ladder, folding ladder, stairs

step out *v* **1 go out**, step outside, leave, absent yourself, pop out (*infml*) *Opposite*: stay put **2 march**, tear along, rush, stride, dash *Opposite*: crawl

steppe *n* **prairie**, grassland, plain, savanna, pampas

stepping stone *n* **1 stone**, boulder, rock, foothold, bridge **2 stage**, step, means of access, stage of progress, stage of advancement

step up *v* **increase**, intensify, improve, maximize, accelerate *Opposite*: lower

stereophonic *adj* **stereo**, audio, binaural, hi-fi, high-fidelity

stereotype *v* typecast, label, pigeonhole, categorize, cast

stereotypical *adj* **conventional**, orthodox, formulaic, banal, hackneyed *Opposite*: original

sterile *adj* **1** germ-free, disinfected, antiseptic, sterilized, spotlessly clean *Opposite*: dirty **2** infertile, unproductive, barren *Opposite*: fertile **3** bare, fruitless, unfruitful, unproductive, desolate *Opposite*: verdant **4** dull, unimaginative, banal, unstimulating *Opposite*: creative

sterility *n* **1** barrenness, unfruitfulness, unproductiveness, desolation, bareness *Opposite*: fruitfulness **2** infertility, barrenness, childlessness, unproductiveness, impotence *Opposite*: fertility **3** cleanness, antisepsis, disinfection, decontamination, purity *Opposite*: contamination **4** dullness, unimaginativeness, lack of imagination, lack of creativity, banality *Opposite*: creativity

sterilization *n* **1** purification, cleansing, disinfection, fumigation, decontamination **2** neutering, castration, gelding, spaying

sterilize *v* **1** disinfect, bleach, make germ-free, fumigate, sanitize **2** neuter, spay, geld, castrate

sterilizer *n* disinfectant, germicide, antiseptic, bactericide, sanitizer

sterling *adj* **1** genuine, authentic, true, pure, real *Opposite*: spurious **2** excellent, exceptional, matchless, incomparable, worthy *Opposite*: mediocre

stern *adj* **1** strict, harsh, severe, austere, unsympathetic *Opposite*: easygoing **2** grim, forbidding, formidable, dour, serious *Opposite*: cheerful

sternness *n* **1** severity, strictness, harshness, firmness, austerity *Opposite*: leniency **2** grimness, seriousness, somberness, gravity, humorlessness *Opposite*: cheerfulness

stet *v* let it stand, restore, retain, undo, ignore *Opposite*: delete

stew *n* (*infml*) difficult situation, state (*infml*), flap (*infml*), tizzy (*infml*), lather (*infml*) ■ *v* **1** simmer, boil slowly, braise, casserole, parboil **2** be upset, be troubled, be agitated, worry, trouble

stick *n* twig, cane, baton, rod, staff ■ *v* **1** spear, stab, penetrate, pierce, spike **2** attach, glue, fix, fasten, join *Opposite*: detach **3** (*infml*) put, lay, place, set, deposit **4** (*infml*) push, put, thrust, shove, poke *Opposite*: withdraw

stick around (*infml*) *v* linger, wait, stay, remain, hang around (*infml*) *Opposite*: leave

stick at *v* persist at, continue with, persist, persevere with, see through *Opposite*: give up

stick by *v* remain loyal to, stay loyal to, remain faithful to, support, adhere to *Opposite*: let down

sticker *n* label, sign, marker, decal, bumper sticker

stickiness *n* tackiness, gluiness, gumminess, adhesiveness, pastiness

sticking point *n* stumbling block, bone of contention, impasse, obstacle, deadlock

stick-in-the-mud (*infml*) *n* reactionary, diehard, fogy, fuddy-duddy (*infml*), stuffed shirt (*infml*) *Opposite*: daredevil

stickler *n* pedant, nitpicker, perfectionist, martinet, hard taskmaster

stick out *v* **1** extend, poke out, jut out, push out, thrust out **2** put up with, endure, bear, weather, see through *Opposite*: give up

stick to *v* **1** adhere, cling, follow, cling to, hold **2** follow, obey, abide by, stand by, remain faithful to *Opposite*: abandon

stick together *v* stay close, remain unified, remain loyal, remain friendly, concur *Opposite*: split up

stick up *v* **1** protrude, point up, point upward, stand up, bristle *Opposite*: hang down **2** point up, cock, prick up, make vertical, raise up **3** (*infml*) rob, hold up, mug, steal from, pull a gun on

stickup (*infml*) *n* armed robbery, robbery, mugging, attack, assault

stick up for *v* support, defend, stand up for, stand by, argue for

stick with *v* **1** persist with, continue with, persevere with, see through, stay with *Opposite*: give up **2** stay loyal to, remain loyal to, remain faithful to, stay close to, stay with *Opposite*: abandon

sticky *adj* **1** tacky, gluey, gummy, adhesive, pasty **2** (*infml*) difficult, tricky, delicate, awkward, sensitive **3** muggy, humid, close, clammy, sultry *Opposite*: dry

sticky wicket (*infml*) *n* tricky situation, awkward situation, difficult situation, difficult problem, embarrassing problem

stiff *adj* **1** rigid, firm, inflexible, unbending, unbendable *Opposite*: limp **2** aching, painful, arthritic, tender, sore **3** severe, harsh, drastic, stringent, excessive *Opposite*: lenient **4** demanding, exacting, arduous, testing, tough *Opposite*: easy **5** strong, vigorous, powerful, robust, intense *Opposite*: weak **6** formal, stuffy, standoffish, aloof, pompous *Opposite*: relaxed

stiffen *v* **1** harden, thicken, solidify, congeal, become rigid *Opposite*: soften **2** strengthen, make stronger, reinforce, toughen, brace *Opposite*: weaken

stiffly *adv* rigidly, firmly, inflexibly, unbendingly, tautly

stiff-necked *adj* obstinate, arrogant, stubborn, proud, haughty *Opposite*: yielding

stiffness *n* **1** rigidity, firmness, inflexibility, tautness, hardness *Opposite*: limpness

2 difficulty, arduousness, laboriousness, rigorousness, toughness *Opposite*: ease **3 severity**, harshness, stringency, excessiveness, extremity *Opposite*: leniency **4 strength**, vigor, power, robustness, intensity *Opposite*: weakness **5 formality**, stuffiness, standoffishness, aloofness, pomposity *Opposite*: informality

stifle *v* **1 smother**, asphyxiate, throttle, suffocate, choke **2 suppress**, repress, restrain, curb, hold back *Opposite*: let out

stifling *adj* **1 hot**, boiling, airless, muggy, close *Opposite*: cool **2 oppressive**, repressive, overpowering, restrictive, inhibiting *Opposite*: liberating

stigma *n* shame, disgrace, dishonor, humiliation

stigmatize *v* brand, slur, defame, mark out, pillory

still *adj* **1 motionless**, immobile, unmoving, at rest, at a standstill *Opposite*: moving **2 flat**, nonsparkling, uncarbonated. ■ *v* **calm**, allay, dispel, banish, quiet *Opposite*: stir up ■ *adv* **even now**, in spite of everything, even so, nevertheless, nonetheless

stillborn *adj* **1 born dead**, dead at birth, miscarried, aborted, dead **2 ineffectual**, useless, ineffective, unsuccessful, abortive *Opposite*: successful

stillness *n* **motionlessness**, immobility, silence, quietness, tranquillity *Opposite*: movement

stilt *n* post, column, support, pillar, pole

stilted *adj* **affected**, stiff, wooden, mannered, unnatural *Opposite*: natural

stimulant *n* **stimulating substance**, tonic, pick-me-up *(infml)*, upper *(slang)*, pep pill *(dated) Opposite*: sedative ■ *adj* **stimulating**, tonic, restorative, intoxicant, energizing *Opposite*: sedative

stimulate *v* **1 rouse**, arouse, kindle, excite, inspire *Opposite*: dampen **2 quicken**, accelerate, increase, invigorate, promote *Opposite*: slow down

stimulating *adj* **1 inspiring**, encouraging, motivating, interesting, thought-provoking *Opposite*: boring **2 invigorating**, refreshing, energizing, rousing *Opposite*: relaxing

stimulation *n* **inspiration**, motivation, encouragement, stimulus, incentive

stimulus *n* **incentive**, spur, inducement, impetus, provocation

sting *v* smart, prick, tingle, throb, hurt

stinging *adj* hurtful, cutting, harsh, hard, cruel

stingy *adj* **ungenerous**, miserly, parsimonious, sparing, grudging *Opposite*: generous

stink *v* **smell horrible**, reek, smell ■ *n* **1 stench**, smell, horrible smell, unpleasant odor, reek *Opposite*: perfume **2** *(infml)* **fuss**,

scandal, uproar, rumpus, commotion. *See* COMPARE AND CONTRAST *at* smell.

stinker *n* **problem**, nightmare, shocker *(infml)*, horror *(infml) Opposite*: delight

stinking *adj* **foul-smelling**, reeking, smelly, stinky, rotten

stink up *v* **make smelly**, permeate, pervade, overpower, fill with a smell *Opposite*: deodorize

stinky *adj* **1 smelly**, stinking, foul-smelling, putrid, rotten *Opposite*: fragrant **2 nasty**, unfair, dishonest, devious, mean-spirited *Opposite*: pleasant

stint *n* **spell**, stretch, time, shift, period

stint on *v* **be sparing with**, be mean with, be parsimonious with, be frugal with, ration

stipend *n* **allowance**, salary, payment, pay, wage. *See* COMPARE AND CONTRAST *at* wage.

stipendiary *adj* **paid**, salaried, remunerated ■ *n* **earner**, wage earner, breadwinner, payee, employee

stipple *v* **dab**, paint, dot, speckle, fleck

stippled *adj* **mottled**, dappled, speckled, spotted, flecked

stipulate *v* **specify**, lay down, instruct, order, require

stipulation *n* **condition**, requirement, proviso, demand, specification

stir *v* **1 mix**, blend, swirl, fold, whip **2 awaken**, arouse, revive, call to mind, bring back **3 rouse**, wake up, move, budge, shift **4 agitate**, cause feeling, disturb, trouble, upset **5 motivate**, incite, provoke, excite, inspire ■ *n* **commotion**, disturbance, fuss, uproar, hue and cry

stir-crazy *(infml) adj* **mentally unsettled**, restless, frantic, distraught, agitated

stir-fry *v* **fry**, pan-fry, sauté

stirring *adj* **rousing**, inspiring, moving, emotive, exciting *Opposite*: uninspiring

stirrup *n* **foot support**, strap, loop, ring

stir up *v* **awaken**, reawaken, bring back, kindle, inflame *Opposite*: calm

stitch *v* **1 sew**, sew up, stitch up, darn, baste **2 suture**, sew up, close

stitching *n* **sewing**, stitches, seam, needlework, embroidery

stock *n* **1 supply**, stockpile, hoard, reserve, accumulation **2 livestock**, farm animals, domestic animals, cattle, sheep ■ *adj* **standard**, typical, routine, run-of-the-mill, ordinary ■ *v* **keep**, have a supply of, have available, carry, supply

stockade *n* **1 barrier**, fence, enclosure, palisade, paling **2 enclosure**, fort, pen, fenced area, enclosed area

stockbroker *n* **securities broker**, broker, investment analyst, financial adviser, trader

stock car *n* **racing car**, dragster, hot rod *(slang)*

stock exchange *n* **stock market**, trading,

bourse, exchange, money market

stockholder n investor, shareholder, stakeholder, bondholder

stockings n leg coverings, nylons, hose, pantyhose, leggings

stocking stuffer n Christmas present, Christmas gift, small present, small gift, trinket

stock-in-trade n 1 basic resource, staple, commodity 2 goods, equipment, stock, merchandise, wares

stock market n financial market, stock exchange, exchange, market, bourse

stockpile n supply, hoard, accumulation, store, stock ■ v store up, stock up on, store, squirrel away, collect. See COMPARE AND CONTRAST at collect.

stockroom n storeroom, storehouse, store, warehouse

stocks n shares, bonds, holdings

stock-still adv motionless, completely still, absolutely still, immobile, without moving Opposite: moving

stocktaking n 1 evaluation, assessment, appraisal, reassessment, reappraisal 2 inventory, listing, itemizing, counting, checking

stock up v stockpile, hoard, save up, collect, lay in Opposite: finish off

stocky adj thickset, sturdy, solid, stout, squat Opposite: slight

stockyard n yard, enclosure, farmyard, farm, enclosed yard

stodgy (infml) adj 1 heavy, filling, starchy, indigestible, hard to digest Opposite: light 2 dull, turgid, uninteresting, unexciting, stuffy Opposite: lively

stoic n impassive person, patient person, fatalist, ascetic, unfeeling person ■ adj long-suffering, impassive, resigned, enduring, tolerant Opposite: excitable. See COMPARE AND CONTRAST at impassive.

stoical see stoic

stoicism n impassiveness, endurance, patience, indifference, fortitude Opposite: excitability

stoke v 1 put fuel on, add fuel to, fuel, stoke up 2 strengthen, intensify, stir up, stoke up, encourage

stoke up see stoke

stole n garment, shawl, wrap, scarf, pashmina

stolid adj impassive, unresponsive, dull, emotionless, insensitive Opposite: emotional. See COMPARE AND CONTRAST at impassive.

stomachache n stomach pain, colic, indigestion, cramp, stitch

stomach-churning see stomach-turning

stomach pump (infml) n suction pump, suction device, aspirator, siphon, syringe

stomach-turning adj sickening, nauseating, revolting, disgusting, repulsive

stomp v tread heavily, stamp, tramp, clump, plod

stone-broke (infml) adj penniless, impoverished, poor, bankrupt, broke (infml) Opposite: rich

stone-cold adj very cold, chilly, icy, frozen, freezing Opposite: boiling ■ adv (infml) completely, absolutely, utterly, totally, dead

stone-dead adj lifeless, cold, dead as a dodo, dead as a doornail, deceased (fml) Opposite: alive

stoneground adj ground, milled, crushed, powdered

stone's throw n short distance, no distance, short way, hop, skip, and jump, striking distance

stonewall (infml) v 1 evade, obstruct, avoid, refuse, rebuff Opposite: cooperate 2 delay, hold off, hold back, stall

stonewashed adj faded, worn, distressed, washed-out, acid-washed

stonework n masonry, brickwork, walls

stony adj 1 rocky, flinty, pebbly, rock-strewn, shingly 2 pitiless, unfeeling, unsympathetic, unyielding, flinty Opposite: compassionate

stony-faced adj expressionless, unemotional, unfriendly, blank, cold Opposite: smiling

stony-hearted adj hardhearted, unfeeling, pitiless, unsympathetic, hard Opposite: soft-hearted

stooge n straight partner, comic actor, comedian, butt, foil

stool n seat, chair, footrest, ottoman, hassock

stoop v 1 bend down, bend forward, bend over, bend, lean forward Opposite: straighten up 2 lower yourself, condescend, deign, debase yourself, patronize

stop v 1 discontinue, end, bring to an end, bring to a close, bring to a standstill Opposite: begin 2 prevent, impede, hinder, prohibit, obstruct Opposite: permit 3 end, finish, come to an end, be over, break off Opposite: begin 4 pause, interrupt, break off, stop off, take a break Opposite: continue 5 block, block up, block off, obstruct, plug ■ n halt, break, rest, stopover, stay

stop by v drop in, call by, call, visit, stop off

stopcock n valve, faucet, cock, spigot, stopper

stopgap n temporary solution, substitute, makeshift, expedient, temporary measure

stop off v call, stop by, stop, drop in, visit

stopover n break in your journey, stop, halt, pause, stop-off

stoppage n 1 strike, work stoppage, wildcat strike, walkout, slowdown 2 blockage, obstruction, obstacle, barrier

stopped adj 1 stationary, still, at a standstill, immobile, motionless Opposite: moving 2 clogged, blocked, congested, backed up, stopped up *Opposite*: open **3 not working**, out of order, out of commission, worn-out, crashed *Opposite*: working

stopper *n* plug, bung, cork, top, lid

stop up *v* plug, plug up, block, block up, block off

stop working *v* break down, break, fail, seize up *Opposite*: function

storage *n* **1 storing**, stowage, stowing, packing, loading **2 storage space**, storage capacity, storage area, stowage, room

WORD BANK
❏ **types of storage spaces** arms depot, arsenal, attic, barn, basement, bunker, cellar, depository, depot, dump, elevator, garage, garbage dump, gasometer, grain elevator, granary, hangar, hayloft, hold, landfill, larder, loft, luggage compartment, magazine, morgue, mortuary, pantry, shed, silo, strongroom, treasury, warehouse, water tower, weapon store, woodshed

store *v* put away, stow, keep, deposit, put in storage ■ *n* **1 supply**, stockpile, hoard, accumulation, collection **2 shop**, outlet, emporium, showroom **3 warehouse**, depository, depot, stockroom, repository

WORD BANK
❏ **types of food outlets** bakery, bodega, butcher's, candy store, deli, delicatessen, drive-through, farmers' market, grocer's, grocery store, refreshment stand, supermarket, takeout
❏ **types of retail outlets** bazaar, beauty parlor, big-box store, bookstore, boutique, chain store, convenience store, corner store, covered market, department store, dime store, discount store, dispensary, druggist, drugstore, duty-free, filling station, flea market, garden center, gas station, general store, hair salon, hardware store, hypermarket, kiosk, mall, mart, mom-and-pop store, newsstand, nursery, pharmacy, post office, salesroom, service station, supercenter, superstore, thrift shop, warehouse

storekeeper *n* retailer, seller, salesperson, merchant, trader

stores *n* supplies, provisions, equipment, goods, food

store up *v* amass, hoard, save, accumulate, stockpile

storm *n* **1 tempest**, squall, gale, hurricane, tornado **2 outburst**, outbreak, explosion, eruption, wave ■ *v* **1 capture**, carry, take by storm, take, overmaster *(literary)* **2 rage**, fume, rant and rave, thunder, bluster **3 stamp**, stomp, stalk, flounce, march

stormbound *adj* housebound, confined, isolated, cut off, snowed in

storm cloud *n* sign of violence, omen, herald, harbinger, danger signal

stormproof *adj* storm-resistant, protected, strong, tough, waterproof

storm sewer *n* storm drain, drain, gutter, channel, drainage system

storm-tossed *adj* choppy, stormy, rough, battered, wild *Opposite*: calm

stormy *adj* **1 squally**, rainy, thundery, blustery, windy *Opposite*: calm **2 tempestuous**, violent, turbulent, unsettled, volatile *Opposite*: placid

story *n* **1 floor**, level, section, division, landing **2 tale**, narrative, account, legend, chronicle **3 account**, report, version, statement, description **4** *(infml)* lie, untruth, falsehood, baldfaced lie, fib *(infml)* **5 article**, piece, feature, report, item

storybook *adj* fairy-tale, fictional, make-believe, mythical, fanciful *Opposite*: real

story line *n* plot, narrative, story, theme, scenario

storyteller *n* **1 narrator**, teller of tales, teller, relater, raconteur **2** *(infml)* liar, prevaricator, deceiver, fabricator, fibber *(infml)*

stoup *n* basin, vessel, bowl, receptacle, chalice

stout *adj* **1 thickset**, heavy, solid, plump, chubby *Opposite*: slender **2 brave**, firm, stalwart, determined, resolute *Opposite*: faint-hearted **3 sturdy**, strong, solid, substantial, tough *Opposite*: flimsy

stouthearted *adj* courageous, brave, resolute, bold, valiant *Opposite*: cowardly

stoutness *n* **1 fatness**, heaviness, solidity, plumpness, chubbiness *Opposite*: slenderness **2 bravery**, firmness, stalwartness, determination, resoluteness **3 sturdiness**, solidity, strength, heftiness, toughness *Opposite*: flimsiness

stow *v* put away, put, pack, store, deposit

stowage *n* stowing, storage, packing, loading, putting away

stowaway *n* runaway, escapee, escaper, fugitive refugee

straddle *v* **1 be astride**, bestride, sit astride, stand astride **2 span**, include, overlap, link, connect

strafe *v* bombard, attack, fire at, shell, blitz ■ *n* aerial attack, bombardment, air attack, blitz, shelling

straggle *v* **1 stray**, ramble, maunder, meander, rove *Opposite*: keep up **2 lag**, lag behind, trail, trail behind, fall behind **3 spread untidily**, spread out, sprawl, extend, spread

straggler *n* dawdler, laggard, loiterer, lingerer, slowpoke *(infml)* *Opposite*: leader

straggly *adj* untidy, unkempt, messy, disheveled, tousled *Opposite*: tidy

straight *adj* **1 candid**, frank, direct, open, honest *Opposite*: devious **2 level**, upright, horizontal, vertical, perpendicular *Opposite*: askew **3 honest**, straightforward, fair, law-abiding, aboveboard *Opposite*: dishonest **4 consecutive**, successive, uninterrupted, in a row, running **5 undiluted**, neat, plain, unmixed, unadulterated *Opposite*:

diluted **6 tidy**, neat, in order, orderly, organized *Opposite*: untidy ∎ *adv* **1 as the crow flies**, in a straight line, directly, from A to B, by the shortest possible route *Opposite*: indirectly **2 directly**, without delay, immediately, at once, instantly *Opposite*: later

straightaway .*adv* **immediately**, at once, without delay, right away, promptly *Opposite*: later

straighten *v* **1 make straight**, straighten out, unbend, uncurl, flatten *Opposite*: bend **2 make level**, level, set straight, straighten up, adjust **3 tidy**, tidy up, order, arrange, organize

straighten out *v* **1 make straight**, straighten, unbend, uncurl, flatten *Opposite*: bend **2 put right**, sort out, set right, settle, rectify *Opposite*: confuse

straighten up *v* **align**, justify, straighten, level, make flush

straight-faced *adj* **deadpan**, poker-faced, expressionless, blank, serious *Opposite*: smiling

straightforward *adj* **1 frank**, forthright, candid, direct, honest *Opposite*: devious **2 easy**, simple, facile, uncomplicated, clear-cut *Opposite*: complicated

straightforwardness *n* **1 frankness**, candor, honesty, truthfulness, openness *Opposite*: deviousness **2 ease**, facility, simplicity, clarity, easiness *Opposite*: difficulty

straight off *(infml)* *adv* **at once**, right away, straightaway, immediately, without delay *Opposite*: later

straight out *adv* **unhesitatingly**, without hesitation, directly, straight, without beating around the bush

straight-out *(infml)* *adj* **1 blunt**, unrestrained, direct, frank, honest *Opposite*: restrained **2 total**, complete, utter, out-and-out, thorough

straight-talking *adj* **blunt**, direct, frank, candid, forthright *Opposite*: evasive

strain *v* **1 make a great effort**, try hard, struggle, labor, strive **2 damage**, injure, hurt, pull, sprain **3 drain**, sieve, filter, sift, separate **4 tax**, overburden, overload, burden, overtax ∎ *n* **1 nervous tension**, tension, stress, worry, anxiety **2 exertion**, effort, tension, struggle, force **3 injury**, sprain, wrench, crick **4 breed**, species, type, form, sort

strained *adj* **1 stressed**, tense, worried, nervous, anxious *Opposite*: calm **2 tense**, forced, artificial, awkward, labored *Opposite*: natural

strait *n* **passage**, channel, canal, sound

straitened *adj* **impoverished**, severe, distressed, difficult, pinched *Opposite*: comfortable

straitjacket *n* **restriction**, limitation, restraint, shackles, constraint *Opposite*: freedom

strait-laced *adj* **prudish**, puritanical, prim, moralistic, strict *Opposite*: broad-minded

strand *n* **1 thread**, filament, fiber, string, wire **2 lock**, tress, wisp, curl **3 element**, component, constituent, aspect, feature ∎ *v* **cut off**, maroon, trap, leave high and dry, abandon *Opposite*: rescue

strange *adj* **1 odd**, bizarre, outlandish, eccentric, weird *Opposite*: normal **2 unfamiliar**, foreign, alien, unknown, mysterious *Opposite*: familiar **3 inexplicable**, surprising, funny, astonishing, perplexing *Opposite*: unsurprising

strangely *adv* **1 oddly**, bizarrely, outlandishly, eccentrically, weirdly *Opposite*: normally **2 inexplicably**, surprisingly, funnily, astonishingly, perplexingly *Opposite*: unsurprisingly

strangeness *n* **1 weirdness**, peculiarity, eccentricity, abnormality, incongruity *Opposite*: normality **2 lack of familiarity**, newness, foreignness, mysteriousness

stranger *n* **foreigner**, alien, outsider, visitor, guest *Opposite*: acquaintance

strangle *v* **1 choke**, strangulate, throttle, garrote, asphyxiate **2 stifle**, repress, suppress, inhibit, smother *Opposite*: express

stranglehold *n* **1 power**, dominion, control, sway, domination **2 strong hold**, throttlehold, iron grip, vicelike grip, grip

strangulate *v* **strangle**, throttle, choke, smother, asphyxiate

strangulation *n* **strangling**, throttling, choking, smothering, asphyxiation

strap *n* **band**, fastening, belt, strip, leash ∎ *v* **fasten**, belt, secure, lash, buckle

straphanger *(infml)* *n* **passenger**, commuter, traveler, rider

strapped *(infml)* *adj* **needy**, wanting, short of money, impecunious, impoverished *Opposite*: flush *(infml)*

strapping *(infml)* *adj* **robust**, broad-shouldered, burly, well-built, sturdy *Opposite*: delicate

stratagem *n* **trick**, ruse, ploy, wile, subterfuge

strategic *adj* **planned**, tactical, calculated, deliberate, premeditated *Opposite*: unplanned

strategist *n* **tactician**, planner, policymaker, plotter, schemer

strategy *n* **plan**, scheme, policy, approach, tactic

stratum *(fml)* *n* **layer**, band, level, division, section

straw *n* **grass**, hay, stubble, chaff

straw-hat *adj* **summer**, seasonal, temporary, traveling, summer stock

straw poll *n* **poll**, opinion poll, show of hands, referendum, questionnaire

stray *v* **wander away**, wander off, go astray, get lost, drift ∎ *adj* **lost**, wandering, abandoned, homeless, vagrant

streak n 1 **line**, band, strip, stripe, vein 2 **run**, stretch, roll 3 **element**, side, trait, characteristic, quality ■ v 1 **mark**, stripe, stain, line, fleck 2 **move fast**, fly, flash, zoom, whiz

streaky adj **stripy**, striped, striated, banded, lined

stream n 1 **watercourse**, river, torrent, rivulet, tributary 2 **jet**, spurt, torrent, cascade Opposite: drip 3 **flood**, torrent, barrage, onslaught ■ v **flow**, pour out, flood, gush, spill

streamer n **flag**, banner, bunting, ribbon, decoration

streamline v **rationalize**, modernize, update, reorganize, restructure

streamlined adj 1 **sleek**, smooth, slick, aerodynamic 2 **efficient**, rationalized, modernized, updated, reorganized Opposite: cumbersome

street credibility n **coolness**, credibility, sophistication, fashionableness, street cred (infml)

streetwise (infml) adj **astute**, quick-witted, sharp-witted, smart, sharp Opposite: inexperienced

strength n 1 **power**, force, might, potency, muscle Opposite: weakness 2 **strong point**, strong suit, forte, asset, métier Opposite: weakness 3 **intensity**, concentration, dilution, depth, potency

strengthen v **make stronger**, reinforce, fortify, brace, toughen Opposite: weaken

strength of mind n **resolve**, determination, strength, fortitude, willpower Opposite: weakness

strenuous adj 1 **taxing**, arduous, exhausting, demanding, hard Opposite: light 2 **active**, energetic, determined, spirited, tireless Opposite: half-hearted. See COMPARE AND CONTRAST at hard.

stress n 1 **strain**, anxiety, worry, tension, trauma 2 **emphasis**, importance, weight, accent, urgency ■ v **emphasize**, lay emphasis on, underline, underscore, accentuate. See COMPARE AND CONTRAST at worry.

stressed adj **harassed**, worried, strained, tense, anxious Opposite: relaxed

stressed out (infml) see **stressed**

stressful adj **demanding**, taxing, worrying, traumatic, tense Opposite: relaxing

stress out (infml) v **worry**, bother, get to, harass, perturb Opposite: relax

stretch v 1 **extend**, elongate, enlarge, widen, broaden Opposite: shrink 2 **spread out**, extend, unfold, spread, unroll 3 **be elastic**, give, expand, yield ■ n 1 **give**, bounce, spring, elasticity Opposite: rigidity 2 **section**, expanse, bit, area, sweep 3 **spell**, period, stint, time, run

stretch a point v 1 **make allowances**, bend the rules, turn a blind eye, make an exception 2 **exaggerate**, overstate, inflate, amplify,

embroider Opposite: understate

stretched adj 1 **extended**, outstretched, elongated, expanded, lengthened Opposite: contracted 2 **strained**, overextended, pushed, fraught, busy Opposite: relaxed

stretch out v **recline**, lie back, bask, lounge, sprawl

stretchy adj **elastic**, flexible, springy, pliable Opposite: rigid

strew v 1 **scatter**, throw, disperse, distribute, spread Opposite: gather 2 **litter**, cover, fill, sprinkle, dot

striation n **pattern**, marking, corrugation, incision, ridge

stricken adj 1 **troubled**, tormented, wracked, disturbed, traumatized 2 **laid low**, afflicted, suffering, affected, wracked Opposite: well 3 **injured**, damaged, wounded, hurt, struck

strict adj 1 **severe**, firm, stern, harsh, stringent Opposite: lenient 2 **exact**, precise, accurate, narrow, meticulous Opposite: inaccurate

strictness n 1 **severity**, firmness, sternness, harshness, stringency Opposite: leniency 2 **exactitude**, precision, accuracy, narrowness, meticulousness Opposite: inaccuracy

stricture (fml) n 1 **criticism**, attack, rebuke, telling off, censure 2 **restriction**, restraint, limit, constraint, limitation

stride v **step**, walk, pace, tread, march ■ n 1 **pace**, step, tread, gait, walk 2 **advance**, progress, development, improvement, headway

strident adj 1 **loud**, harsh, grating, shrill, raucous Opposite: soft 2 **vociferous**, forceful, persuasive, clamorous, baying Opposite: gentle

strife n **trouble**, conflict, discord, contention, fighting Opposite: harmony

strike v 1 **hit**, beat, smack, thump, clout 2 **collide with**, hit, crash into, smash into, bump into Opposite: miss 3 **occur to**, come to mind, dawn on, hit, come to 4 **attack**, launch an attack, fall on, set on, hit 5 **take industrial action**, stop work, walk out 6 **discover**, hit upon, light on, stumble across, chance upon 7 **reach**, arrive at, attain, achieve, arrange ■ n 1 **raid**, attack, assault, foray, air strike 2 **slowdown**, walkout, work stoppage

strike down v 1 **knock down**, floor, fell, bring down, knock out 2 **afflict**, lay low, infect, affect, make ill 3 **kill**, bring down, murder, assassinate, slaughter

strike it rich v **hit the jackpot**, come into money, make your fortune, laugh all the way to the bank, rake it in (infml)

strike off v **delete**, cross off, remove, withdraw Opposite: include

strike out v 1 (infml) **fail**, fall short, miss the boat, mismanage, bomb (infml) 2 **set out**, leave, depart, go, move off *Opposite*: arrive **3 attack**, lash out, set on, assail **4 cross out**, delete, score out, strike through, cancel

striker *n* **1 picket**, picketer, demonstrator, protester **2 soccer player**, forward, attacker, winger

strike up *v* **start**, begin, commence, initiate, make a start *Opposite*: stop

strike while the iron's hot *v* **take the opportunity**, grab the chance, make the most of it, make hay while the sun shines *(infml)*

striking *adj* **1 conspicuous**, noticeable, marked, remarkable, salient *Opposite*: inconspicuous **2 good-looking**, handsome, attractive, eye-catching, beautiful

striking distance *n* **stone's throw**, short distance, a hairsbreadth, hop, skip, and jump, spitting distance *(infml)*

string *n* **1 cord**, thread, filament, twine, rope **2 sequence**, series, run, chain, succession

string along *(infml)* *v* **1 deceive**, mislead, lead on, lead down the garden path, send on a wild-goose chase **2 tag along**, hang around, go along, go along for the ride, join in **3 agree**, go along with, be of one mind, concur, approve *Opposite*: disagree

stringency *n* **severity**, strictness, rigor, harshness, inflexibility *Opposite*: flexibility

stringent *adj* **severe**, strict, rigorous, stern, harsh *Opposite*: lax

stringer *n* **journalist**, reporter, correspondent, columnist, writer

stringy *adj* **tough**, chewy, sinewy, gristly, fibrous *Opposite*: tender

strip *v* **1 undress**, strip off, doff, shed, peel off *Opposite*: dress **2 deprive**, take away, divest, deny, rid *Opposite*: furnish *(fml)* ▪ *n* **band**, sliver, shred, ribbon, slip

stripe *n* **band of color**, strip, band, line, streak

stripped *adj* **bare**, exposed, unprotected, uncovered, unvarnished *Opposite*: coated

stripped-down *adj* **lean**, spare, sparse, minimalist, utilitarian

strive *v* **struggle**, go all out, do your best, do your utmost, make every effort

stroke *n* **1 hit**, blow, knock, rap, lash **2 rub**, caress, fondle, pat ▪ *v* **caress**, fondle, pat, rub

stroll *v* **walk**, amble, saunter, ramble, go for a constitutional ▪ *n* **saunter**, walk, amble, turn, wander

stroller *n* **buggy**, baby carriage, baby buggy

strong *adj* **1 powerful**, burly, brawny, muscular, sturdy *Opposite*: weak **2 robust**, sturdy, stout, solid, durable *Opposite*: fragile **3 intense**, concentrated, pungent, piquant, spicy *Opposite*: insipid **4 glaring**, dazzling, bright, stark, brilliant *Opposite*: dim **5 convincing**, sound, clear, clear-cut, persuasive *Opposite*: weak **6 fervent**, great, intense, deep, deep-seated *Opposite*: weak **7 keen**, staunch, dedicated, firm, fanatical *Opposite*: indifferent

strong-arm *(infml)* *adj* **coercive**, forcible, violent, physical, forceful *Opposite*: peaceable ▪ *v* **coerce**, compel, force, frighten, bully

strongbox *n* **safe-deposit box**, cash box, safe, coffer, vault

stronghold *n* **fortress**, refuge, bastion, citadel, sanctuary

strong-minded *adj* **1 determined**, dogged, persevering, persistent, resolute *Opposite*: weak-willed **2 confident**, clear-thinking, certain, intelligent, decisive

strong-mindedness *n* **1 determination**, doggedness, perseverance, persistence, resoluteness *Opposite*: vacillation **2 confidence**, strength, strength of character, character, clarity *Opposite*: weakness

strong point *n* **strength**, forte, asset, métier, strong suit *Opposite*: weakness

strong suit *see* **strong point**

strong-willed *adj* **resolute**, determined, strong-minded, iron-willed, unbending *Opposite*: weak

structural *adj* **1 physical**, mechanical, organizational, operational **2 basic**, important, essential, fundamental, underlying

structure *n* **1 construction**, assembly, building, edifice, erection *(fml)* **2 arrangement**, organization, construction, configuration, makeup ▪ *v* **arrange**, construct, configure, put together, make up

structured *adj* **1 organized**, planned, controlled, designed, arranged *Opposite*: unstructured **2 defined**, coordinated, well-defined, designed, formal *Opposite*: amorphous

struggle *v* **1 writhe**, wriggle, thrash, brawl, scuffle **2 fight**, grapple, tussle, wrestle, battle **3 strive**, try, strain, fight, labor *Opposite*: coast ▪ *n* **1 tussle**, fight, brawl, scuffle, skirmish **2 effort**, exertion, labor, toil, work

strum *v* **play**, thrum, improvise, jam, twang

strut *v* **swagger**, march, parade, prance, walk ▪ *n* **support**, rod, brace, crosspiece, girder

stub *n* **stump**, end, remains, remnant, counterfoil ▪ *v* **hit**, bump, bang, knock, bash *(infml)*

stubble *n* **1 whiskers**, five o'clock shadow, growth, beard, mustache **2 stalks**, stems, debris, refuse, leavings

stubborn *adj* **1 obstinate**, immovable, inflexible, willful, mulish *Opposite*: flexible **2 persistent**, dogged, tenacious, persevering, determined *Opposite*: half-hearted

stubbornness *n* **1 obstinacy**, inflexibility, obduracy, pigheadedness, mulishness *Opposite*: flexibility **2 persistence**, tenacity, perseverance, doggedness, stalwartness

stubby *adj* **short**, broad, thick, stumpy, squat *Opposite*: slender

stub out *v* **extinguish**, put out, snuff

stuck adj 1 **wedged**, fixed, trapped, caught, jammed Opposite: loose 2 **baffled**, mystified, puzzled, without an answer, at a complete loss

stuck-up (infml) adj **snobbish**, arrogant, conceited, superior, self-important Opposite: unassuming

stud n **knob**, boss, rivet, nail, screw ■ v 1 **dot**, pepper, sprinkle, scatter, speckle 2 **emboss**, fit with studs, decorate, fasten, rivet

student n **scholar**, pupil, schoolboy, schoolgirl, schoolchild Opposite: teacher

student loan n **loan**, government loan, educational loan, subsidized loan

studied adj **deliberate**, intentional, calculated, considered, premeditated Opposite: spontaneous

studio n 1 **workplace**, workshop, workroom, atelier, pottery 2 **academy**, conservatory, dance school, ballet school, dance academy

studious adj 1 **thoughtful**, serious, reflective, bookish, scholarly Opposite: frivolous 2 **diligent**, painstaking, careful, assiduous, industrious Opposite: careless

study v 1 **learn**, take in, review, read, hit the books (infml) 2 **investigate**, research, experiment, examine, consider ■ n 1 **learning**, education, training, schoolwork, lessons 2 **report**, findings, conclusions, research paper, analysis 3 **investigation**, examination, survey, review, inquiry

stuff v fill, pack, cram, ram, jam ■ n 1 **material**, substance, matter, raw material 2 **things**, objects, paraphernalia, articles, mess 3 **possessions**, belongings, things, kit, tackle

stuffed adj 1 **filled**, lined, packed, jammed, crammed 2 (infml) **full**, fit to burst, replete, sated, satiated Opposite: hungry

stuffed shirt (infml) n **fogy**, old fogy, killjoy, spoilsport, fuddy-duddy (infml)

stuffiness n 1 **airlessness**, staleness, closeness, mugginess, fug Opposite: freshness 2 **formality**, conventionality, staidness, standoffishness, pomposity Opposite: informality

stuffy adj 1 **airless**, stale, smelly, hot, warm Opposite: fresh 2 **strait-laced**, old-fashioned, conventional, formal, pompous Opposite: informal 3 **congested**, blocked up, stuffed up, clogged up Opposite: clear

stultify v 1 **bore**, dull, numb, deaden, put off Opposite: stimulate 2 **make a fool of**, belittle, ridicule, humiliate, set up (infml) 3 **cancel out**, block, render useless, preempt, vitiate Opposite: advance

stumble v 1 **trip**, trip up, lose your footing, lose your balance, falter 2 **stagger**, lurch, sway, blunder, roll 3 **hesitate**, stop and start, hem and haw, falter, stammer 4 **come across**, find, discover, happen on, chance on ■ n 1 **blunder**, trip, stagger, false step, mishap 2 **mistake**, hesitation, slip, blunder,

slip-up (infml). See COMPARE AND CONTRAST at hesitate.

stumbling block n **obstacle**, problem, difficulty, sticking point, obstruction Opposite: aid

stump n **base**, stub, butt, end, remains ■ v **baffle**, puzzle, perplex, mystify, nonplus Opposite: enlighten

stumpy adj **squat**, stubby, short, thickset, broad Opposite: lanky

stun v 1 **shock**, upset, dumbfound, daze, amaze 2 **knock out**, paralyse, numb, daze, put out of action Opposite: bring around

stunner (infml) n **star**, smash, sensation, hit, triumph

stunning adj **spectacular**, striking, fabulous, splendid, superb Opposite: unimpressive

stunningly adv **extremely**, spectacularly, strikingly, fabulously, remarkably Opposite: moderately

stunt v **inhibit**, restrict, arrest, hold back, impede Opposite: assist ■ n **feat**, exploit, act, deed, show

stunted adj **underdeveloped**, undersized, small, short, little

stupefaction n 1 (literary) **amazement**, astonishment, wonder, surprise, awe 2 **confusion**, befuddlement, bemusement, perplexity, bewilderment

stupefied adj 1 **confused**, fuddled, punch-drunk, stunned, befuddled Opposite: clear-headed 2 **amazed**, astonished, astounded, stunned, dazed

stupefy v 1 **amaze**, astonish, astound, surprise, stagger 2 **confuse**, befuddle, bewilder, stun, perplex Opposite: enlighten

stupendous adj 1 **astonishing**, astounding, amazing, surprising, stunning Opposite: unremarkable 2 **fantastic**, wonderful, out of this world, marvelous, great Opposite: awful 3 **huge**, vast, large, colossal, enormous Opposite: tiny

stupendously adv **tremendously**, impressively, amazingly, exceptionally, remarkably Opposite: slightly

stupid adj 1 **unintelligent**, dull, brainless, obtuse, witless Opposite: intelligent 2 **unwise**, senseless, ill-advised, imprudent, injudicious Opposite: wise 3 **foolish**, fatuous, inane, nonsensical, silly Opposite: sensible

stupidity n **foolishness**, foolhardiness, silliness, inanity, folly Opposite: sense

stupor n 1 **torpor**, lethargy, inertness, limpness, blankness Opposite: activeness 2 **daze**, dream, trance, shock, numbness Opposite: consciousness

sturdiness n **strength**, solidity, durability, toughness, hardiness Opposite: weakness

sturdy adj 1 **well-made**, durable, robust, tough, strong Opposite: rickety 2 **well-built**, strong, robust, powerful, muscular Opposite: frail 3 **resolute**, decisive, determined, strenuous, enthusiastic *Opposite*: feeble

stutter *v* **stammer**, trip over your tongue, falter, stumble, hesitate *Opposite*: enunciate ■ *n* **stammer**, speech disorder, impediment, impairment, speech impediment

sty *n* **cyst**, swelling, lump, boil, sore

style *n* 1 **method**, approach, way, manner, fashion 2 **flair**, panache, chic, bravura, stylishness *Opposite*: gracelessness 3 **design**, type, sort, form, variety 4 **luxury**, luxuriousness, extravagance, lavishness, opulence ■ *v* 1 **fashion**, design, shape, cut, adapt 2 *(fml)* **name**, call, nickname, label, term

stylish *adj* **fashionable**, sophisticated, chic, modish, smart *Opposite*: unfashionable

stylishness *n* **style**, flair, chic, panache, smartness *Opposite*: dowdiness

stylistic *adj* **formal**, technical, literary, musical, artistic *Opposite*: spontaneous

stylize *v* **formalize**, abstract, schematize, systematize, outline

stylized *adj* **conventional**, artificial, formalized, formal, unnatural *Opposite*: natural

stymie *v* **hinder**, prevent, block, thwart, confound *Opposite*: enable ■ *n* **impasse**, dead end, stalemate, standstill, deadlock *Opposite*: breakthrough

suave *adj* **urbane**, smooth, polished, polite, sophisticated *Opposite*: awkward

subcategory *n* **subsection**, subclass, subgroup, subdivision

subconscious *adj* **unconscious**, intuitive, hidden, unintentional, involuntary *Opposite*: deliberate

subcontract *v* **delegate**, farm out, contract out, commission, mandate

subculture *n* **subgroup**, culture, grouping, group, subdivision

subcutaneous *adj* **hypodermic**, hypodermal, intravenous, internal, dermatological

subdirectory *n* **division**, subdivision, directory, file, storage space

subdivide *v* **divide**, section, segment, split, cut *Opposite*: unify

subdivision *n* 1 **section**, part, division, sector, tract 2 **division**, sectioning, segmenting, separation, splitting up *Opposite*: unification

subdue *v* 1 **restrain**, suppress, hold back, control, discipline 2 **pacify**, calm, calm down, soothe, mollify 3 **subjugate**, conquer, vanquish, defeat, overpower

subdued *adj* 1 **gentle**, low, restrained, muted, subtle *Opposite*: loud 2 **passive**, cowed, submissive, quiet, unresponsive *Opposite*: uplifted

subgroup *n* **subcategory**, subsection, subclass, subdivision, smaller group

subhuman *adj* **bestial**, animal, inhuman, inhumane, wicked

subject *n* 1 **topic**, theme, focus, subject matter, area under discussion 2 **specialty**, field, study, discipline, area 3 **subordinate**, vassal, liege, dependent, citizen *Opposite*: sovereign

---

COMPARE AND CONTRAST CORE MEANING: what is under discussion

subject a matter that is under discussion or investigation; **topic** a matter dealt with in a text or discussion; **subject matter** the material dealt with in a movie, discussion, or other medium; **matter** the material that is dealt with in speech or writing, as opposed to its presentation; **theme** a distinct, recurring, and unifying idea in music, literature, art, or film; **burden** (*literary*) the main argument or recurrent theme in music or literature.

---

subjection *n* **domination**, subjugation, overpowering, enslavement, oppression

subjective *adj* 1 **slanted**, biased, prejudiced, skewed, one-sided *Opposite*: objective 2 **individual**, particular, idiosyncratic, independent, personal *Opposite*: general

subjectively *adv* **personally**, individually, instinctively, intuitively, emotionally *Opposite*: objectively

subjectivity *n* **bias**, prejudice, partisanship, partiality *Opposite*: objectivity

subject matter *n* **topic**, theme, subject, focus, question. *See* COMPARE AND CONTRAST *at* **subject**.

subject to *v* **cause to experience**, cause to undergo, expose to, put through, make susceptible ■ *adj* **conditional on**, dependent on, depending on, bound by, answerable to *Opposite*: unrelated

subjugate *v* **conquer**, vanquish, subdue, defeat, overpower *Opposite*: liberate

sublimate *v* **channel**, redirect, transfer, direct, reroute

sublimation *n* **redirection**, transferal, direction, rerouting, division

sublime *adj* 1 **inspiring**, inspirational, uplifting, awe-inspiring, moving *Opposite*: ridiculous 2 *(infml)* **excellent**, superb, splendid, marvelous, wonderful

subliminal *adj* **subconscious**, unconscious, hidden, concealed, unintentional *Opposite*: conscious

submerge *v* 1 **plunge**, immerse, dip, sink, duck 2 **suppress**, conceal, hide, stifle *Opposite*: reveal

submerged *adj* **underwater**, flooded, inundated, waterlogged, sunken

submission *n* 1 **obedience**, compliance, capitulation, surrender, acquiescence *Opposite*: resistance 2 **proposal**, suggestion, plan, tender, offer

submissive *adj* **obedient**, passive, compliant, acquiescent, subservient *Opposite*: assertive

submit *v* 1 **present**, propose, tender, offer,

suggest *Opposite*: withdraw **2 give in**, yield, agree to, acquiesce, resign yourself to *Opposite*: resist. *See* COMPARE AND CONTRAST *at* yield.

subnormal *adj* substandard, second-rate, poor, inferior, below average *Opposite*: superior

subordinate *adj* **secondary**, lesser, subsidiary, inferior, lower *Opposite*: main ■ *n* **assistant**, junior, underling, minion, aide *Opposite*: boss

subordination *n* **relegation**, demotion, reduction, subservience

suborn *v* incite, bribe, induce, entice, corrupt

subpoena *n* summons, order, call ■ *v* **summon**, compel, require, order, command

subscribe *v* **1 donate to**, give to, pledge, promise, contribute **2 agree with**, approve of, support, condone, hold with *Opposite*: disagree

subscription *n* **payment**, donation, contribution

subsequent *adj* **following**, succeeding, ensuing, successive, consequent *Opposite*: preceding

subservient *adj* **obedient**, compliant, acquiescent, docile, deferential *Opposite*: assertive

subset *n* subsection, subdivision, subgroup, subcategory, subclass

subside *v* **1 diminish**, lessen, decrease, dwindle, wane *Opposite*: build up **2 collapse**, cave in, fall down, drop, sink *Opposite*: rise

subsidence *n* subsiding, sinking, settling, dropping, collapsing

subsidiary *adj* **1 subordinate**, lesser, secondary, junior, lower *Opposite*: major **2 supplementary**, auxiliary, ancillary, additional, contributory *Opposite*: main ■ *n* **branch**, division, holding, company, firm

subsidize *v* **finance**, fund, sponsor, back, support

subsidy *n* **funding**, financial backing, grant, support, aid

subsist *v* exist, survive, live, make ends meet, keep going

subsistence *n* **survival**, existence, maintenance, sustenance

subspecies *n* **category**, strain, genus, sort, class

substance *n* **1 material**, matter, stuff, ingredient, body **2 core**, essence, import, gist, nub **3 affluence**, property, money, means, wealth *Opposite*: poverty

substandard *adj* inferior, second-rate, poor, subnormal, below average *Opposite*: superior

substantial *adj* considerable, large, extensive, significant, important *Opposite*: small

substantially *adv* **considerably**, significantly,

noticeably, markedly, greatly *Opposite*: insignificantly

substantiate *v* **validate**, authenticate, verify, corroborate, prove *Opposite*: disprove

substantiation *n* **corroboration**, confirmation, validation, authentication, support

substantive *adj* **1 practical**, applicable, functional, utilitarian *Opposite*: impractical **2 essential**, fundamental, basic, central, elementary *Opposite*: secondary **3 independent**, autonomous, separate, individual *Opposite*: dependent **4 substantial**, decent, considerable, respectable, significant *Opposite*: insignificant

substantively *adv* **1 practically**, functionally, applicably **2 essentially**, fundamentally, basically, centrally, elementarily **3 independently**, autonomously, individually, separately **4 substantially**, considerably, significantly, noticeably, markedly *Opposite*: insignificantly

substitute *v* **1 replace with**, exchange, use instead, switch, swap *(infml)* **2 stand in for**, fill in for, take the place of, relieve, deputize for ■ *n* **alternative**, alternate, replacement, stand-in, locum

substitution *n* **replacement**, switch, exchange, changeover, change

subsume *v* include, incorporate, count, list, consider

subterfuge *n* trick, ploy, ruse, stratagem, maneuver

subterranean *adj* **1 underground**, deep, below ground, buried, hidden **2 secret**, clandestine, underground, covert, arcane *Opposite*: open

subtext *n* **implication**, hidden agenda, suggestion, connotation, intimation

subtitle *n* caption, legend, surtitle, supertitle

subtle *adj* **1 slight**, faint, fine, thin, imperceptible *Opposite*: coarse **2 understated**, delicate, indirect, elusive, refined *Opposite*: blunt **3 intelligent**, experienced, sensitive, shrewd, perceptive *Opposite*: obtuse **4 cunning**, sly, crafty, devious, tricky *Opposite*: ingenuous

subtleness *n* **1 delicacy**, subtlety, refinement, intricacy, elusiveness *Opposite*: bluntness **2 intelligence**, experience, sensitivity, shrewdness, perceptiveness **3 cunning**, deviousness, slyness, craftiness, trickiness *Opposite*: ingenuousness **4 slightness**, faintness, fineness

subtlety *n* **1 delicacy**, subtleness, refinement, intricacy, elusiveness *Opposite*: blatancy **2 detail**, nicety, fine point, nuance **3 sensitivity**, delicacy, tact, discernment, finesse

subtract *v* **take away**, take from, take off, deduct, withdraw *Opposite*: add

subtraction *n* **deduction**, removal, withdrawal, debit, deletion *Opposite*: addition

suburb *n* conurbation, district, bedroom community, environs, development *Opposite*: downtown

suburban *adj* **outlying**, peripheral, out-of-town, outer, residential *Opposite*: central

suburbia *n* **suburbs**, conurbation, greenbelt, environs, exurbia *Opposite*: downtown

subvention *(fml)* *n* **1 grant**, subsidy, payment, donation, endowment **2 aid**, support, backing, sponsorship, funding

subversion *n* **rebellion**, sedition, treason, mutiny, insurrection *Opposite*: compliance

subversive *adj* **dissident**, rebellious, revolutionary, insubordinate, seditious *Opposite*: law-abiding ■ *n* **traitor**, collaborator, mutineer, revolutionary, insubordinate *Opposite*: patriot

subvert *v* **undermine**, overthrow, destabilize, sabotage, disrupt *Opposite*: support

subway *n* **underground railroad**, metro, underground, tube

subzero *adj* **freezing**, bitter, icy, ice-cold, glacial *Opposite*: tropical

succeed *v* **1 do well**, get ahead, prosper, be successful, thrive *Opposite*: fail **2 achieve**, accomplish, hit the target, turn out well, be successful *Opposite*: fail **3 follow**, come after, replace, supersede, supplant *Opposite*: precede

succeeding *adj* **following**, subsequent, ensuing, next, successive *Opposite*: preceding

success *n* **1 achievement**, accomplishment, victory, triumph, feat *Opposite*: failure **2 hit**, winner, sensation, star, triumph *Opposite*: failure

successful *adj* **1 fruitful**, positive, effective, efficacious *(fml)* *Opposite*: unsuccessful **2 prosperous**, up-and-coming, well-off, wealthy, rich *Opposite*: poor **3 flourishing**, thriving, booming, profitable, lucrative *Opposite*: ailing

succession *n* **series**, sequence, chain, run, string *Opposite*: individual

successive *adj* **consecutive**, succeeding, following, sequential, uninterrupted *Opposite*: single

successor *n* **heir**, inheritor, replacement, beneficiary *Opposite*: predecessor

success story *n* **success**, winner, sensation, hit, triumph

succinct *adj* **concise**, pithy, brief, to the point, laconic *Opposite*: long-winded

succinctness *n* **concision**, pithiness, conciseness, brevity, briefness *Opposite*: verbosity

succor *(literary)* *n* **1 help**, relief, aid, support, assistance **2 benefactor**, support, rescuer, provider, helpmate *Opposite*: enemy ■ *v* **assist**, support, rescue, relieve, aid *Opposite*: abandon

succulence *n* **juiciness**, lusciousness, tenderness, moistness, tastiness *Opposite*: dryness

succulent *adj* **juicy**, moist, tender, luscious, delicious *Opposite*: dry

succumb *v* **1 give way**, yield, give in, submit, surrender *Opposite*: withstand **2 die**, pass away, perish, depart, expire *(fml)*. *See* COMPARE AND CONTRAST *at* yield.

suck *v* **1 draw**, pull on, lap, slurp, drink **2 extract**, draw, pull, force, take out **3 pull**, draw, force, sweep, bear ■ *n* **slurp**, draw, pull, drink, taste

sucker *(infml)* *n* **gull**, dupe, pushover *(infml)*, chump *(infml)*, fall guy *(slang)* ■ *v* **trick**, con, fool, gull, dupe

suck in *v* **1 breathe in**, inhale, draw in, take in, pull in **2 involve**, implicate, entangle, embroil, draw in *Opposite*: exclude

suck up *v* **1 absorb**, soak up, take up, sop up *Opposite*: exude **2** *(infml)* **ingratiate yourself**, flatter, grovel, toady, crawl *(infml)*

suction *n* **force**, pressure, pull, draw, drag

sudden *adj* **unexpected**, abrupt, rapid, swift, hasty *Opposite*: gradual

suddenly *adv* **unexpectedly**, abruptly, rapidly, swiftly, all of a sudden *Opposite*: gradually

suddenness *n* **unexpectedness**, quickness, abruptness, rapidity, swiftness

suds *n* **lather**, bubbles, foam, froth, spume *(literary)*

sue *v* **1** *(fml)* **petition**, beg, plead, appeal, implore *(fml)* **2 litigate**, prosecute, indict, file a suit, charge

suffer *v* **1 feel pain**, hurt, agonize, ache, smart **2 undergo**, experience, bear, endure, go through **3 tolerate**, endure, bear, put up with, stand **4 deteriorate**, fall off, be impaired, drop off *(infml)*

sufferance *n* **1 tolerance**, toleration, acquiescence, allowance, permission *Opposite*: prohibition **2 endurance**, stamina, staying power, stoicism, fortitude

sufferer *n* **invalid**, victim, patient, case, martyr

suffering *n* **1 pain**, distress, agony, torment, affliction **2 sorrow**, grief, misery, woe, anguish

suffice *(fml)* *v* **be sufficient**, do, serve, suit

sufficiency *n* **right amount**, adequacy, abundance, plenty *Opposite*: insufficiency

sufficient *adj* **adequate**, enough, satisfactory, necessary, appropriate *Opposite*: inadequate

suffocate *v* **smother**, choke, stifle, throttle, asphyxiate

suffuse *v* **spread through**, pervade, fill, saturate, flood

sugar *n* *(infml)* **honey**, sweetheart, darling, dearest, precious ■ *v* **sweeten**, dress up, disguise, titivate, improve

sugary adj **1 sweet**, syrupy, sickly, sugared, sweetened Opposite: bitter **2 sentimental**, mawkish, gushy, mushy, syrupy Opposite: dry

suggest v **1 propose**, put forward, advise, recommend, advocate Opposite: veto **2 remind**, bring to mind, call to mind, evoke, conjure up **3 imply**, insinuate, intimate, indicate, hint Opposite: state. See COMPARE AND CONTRAST at **recommend**.

suggestibility n **susceptibility**, openness, vulnerability, credulousness, credulity Opposite: strong-mindedness

suggestible adj **susceptible**, impressionable, gullible, credulous, malleable Opposite: strong-minded

suggestion n **1 proposal**, proposition, submission, recommendation, idea Opposite: order **2 evocation**, air, aura, hint, trace **3 implication**, hint, insinuation, intimation, indication Opposite: statement

suggestive adj **1 evocative**, redolent, reminiscent, indicative, expressive **2 improper**, indelicate, indecent, lewd, risqué

suicidal adj **1** (infml) **desperate**, cheerless, hopeless, unhappy, miserable **2 dangerous**, treacherous, perilous, reckless, madcap Opposite: sensible

suicide n **1 death**, self-destruction, self-immolation **2 recklessness**, rashness, perversity, irresponsibility, madness

suit n **costume**, ensemble, dress suit, trouser suit, uniform ■ v **1 go with**, match, fit, be fitting, agree with Opposite: clash **2 flatter**, become, show up, enhance

WORD BANK

❑ **types of suit** all-in-one, black tie, boiler suit, business suit, catsuit, dress suit, jump suit, overalls, pantsuit, pinstripe suit, trouser suit, white tie, zoot suit

suitability n **appropriateness**, aptness, fittingness, fitness, correctness Opposite: unsuitability

suitable adj **appropriate**, apposite, fit, apt, right Opposite: inappropriate

suitcase n **case**, luggage, baggage, bag, valise

suite n **set**, collection, group, complement

suited adj **right**, matched, well-matched, appropriate, apposite Opposite: wrong

sulfurous adj **acrid**, reeking, stinking, foul, bitter

sulk v **mope**, be in a mood, feel sorry for yourself, be in a huff, pout Opposite: rejoice (literary) ■ n **bad temper**, mood, temper, huff, bad mood

sulkiness n **moodiness**, resentfulness, temper, bad temper, moroseness Opposite: joviality

sulky adj **morose**, angry, resentful, sullen, unsociable Opposite: jovial

sullen adj **1 surly**, morose, hostile, bad-tempered, dour Opposite: friendly **2** (literary) **leaden**, cloudy, dull, gray, brooding Opposite: bright

sullenness n **surliness**, hostility, bad temper, moodiness, moroseness Opposite: friendliness

sullied adj **1 tainted**, dishonoured, discredited, corrupt, disgraced **2** (literary) **polluted**, contaminated, dirty, soiled, foul

sully v **1 tarnish**, taint, smear, denigrate, spoil Opposite: praise **2** (literary) **pollute**, contaminate, dirty, soil, foul Opposite: clean

sultry adj **hot**, humid, muggy, stifling, oppressive Opposite: fresh

sum n **1 calculation**, addition, computation, summation **2 figure**, amount, quantity, entirety, totality

summarily adv **instantly**, immediately, instantaneously, abruptly, suddenly Opposite: eventually

summarize v **sum up**, précis, abridge, recap, go over Opposite: elaborate

summary n **précis**, synopsis, digest, sum-up, outline Opposite: exposition ■ adj **1 swift**, rapid, instant, immediate, instantaneous Opposite: considered **2 short**, brief, concise, abridged, succinct

summation n **1 summary**, summing up, synopsis, outline, précis **2 sum total**, total, sum, final total, grand total **3 addition**, calculation, computation, sum

summer n **1 summertime**, dog days, midsummer, solstice Opposite: winter **2 warm weather**, sun, sunshine, warmth, heat **3 prime**, best time, summertime, best years, golden age

summerhouse n **gazebo**, pagoda, hut, shed, shelter

summertime see **summer**

summery adj **warm**, balmy, sunny, hot Opposite: wintry

summit n **1 peak**, top, pinnacle, apex, acme Opposite: base **2 conference**, meeting, summit meeting, talks

summon v **1 call**, send for, call for, call upon, beckon Opposite: dismiss **2 convene**, call together, get together, gather, assemble Opposite: dismiss **3 muster**, rouse, find, activate, rally Opposite: demobilize

summons n **order**, writ, directive, command, subpoena

sumptuous adj **costly**, lavish, splendid, opulent, spectacular Opposite: meager

sumptuousness n **luxuriousness**, luxury, lavishness, splendor, opulence

sum total n **whole**, totality, entirety, aggregate, summation

sum up v **summarize**, recap, synopsize, encapsulate, abridge Opposite: elaborate

sunbaked adj **hardened**, dried, sun-dried, heated, cracked

sunbathe v **sun yourself**, bask, tan, catch some rays (slang)

sunbeam n **ray**, beam, shaft, sunlight, sunshine Opposite: moonbeam

Sunday best n **finery**, formal wear, best clothes, best bib and tucker (infml)

sunder (literary) v **separate**, divide, split, sever, cut

sundown n **sunset**, nightfall, twilight, dusk, evening Opposite: sunrise

sun-dried adj **dried**, preserved, dried up, dehydrated, jerked Opposite: fresh

sundries n **miscellany**, hodgepodge, miscellanea, assortment, odds and ends

sundry adj **various**, miscellaneous, assorted, varied, different Opposite: uniform

sunglasses n **dark glasses**, sunspecs (infml), shades (infml)

sunk adj **1 ruined**, dashed, in trouble, defeated, destroyed Opposite: successful **2 depressed**, downcast, downhearted, dejected, in the dumps Opposite: happy

sunken adj **1 submerged**, underwater, immersed **2 hollow**, gaunt, deep-set, cadaverous, pinched **3 recessed**, lower, settled, dipped, depressed Opposite: raised

sunless adj **dark**, cloudy, overcast, murky, gloomy Opposite: sunny

sunlight n **sunshine**, daylight, light, rays, sunbeams

sunlit adj **sunny**, bright, light, sundrenched, bathed in light Opposite: dark

sunnily adv **cheerfully**, cheerily, happily, genially, gaily Opposite: gloomily

sunny adj **1 sunlit**, bright, luminous, brilliant, cloudless Opposite: dark **2 cheerful**, cheery, bright, positive, optimistic Opposite: gloomy

sunrise n **dawn**, daybreak, break of day, first light, sunup Opposite: sunset

sunscreen see suntan lotion

sunset n **sundown**, dusk, evening, night, nightfall Opposite: sunrise

sunshade n **parasol**, umbrella, garden umbrella, beach umbrella, awning

sunshine n **sunlight**, light, rays, sunbeams, brightness Opposite: rainfall

suntan lotion n **sunscreen**, sunblock, tanning lotion, suntan oil, sun protection

suntanned adj **brown**, tanned, bronzed, sunburned Opposite: pale

suntan oil see suntan lotion

sunup n **dawn**, sunrise, daybreak, break of day, morning Opposite: nightfall

sup v **spoon**, sip, drink, partake of, lap Opposite: gulp ■ n **mouthful**, sip, swallow, drink, draft Opposite: gulp

super adj **1** (infml) **wonderful**, fantastic, great, marvelous, fabulous Opposite: awful **2 superior**, better, enhanced, improved, outstanding Opposite: inferior

superabundant adj **overabundant**, in excess, excessive, extra, abounding Opposite: insufficient

superannuated adj **1 retired**, pensioned off, discharged, elderly, aged Opposite: working **2 worn out**, worn, unusable, used up, useless Opposite: new **3 out-of-date**, antiquated, out of fashion, outmoded, passé Opposite: fashionable

superb adj **excellent**, outstanding, wonderful, splendid, fabulous Opposite: abysmal

superbug n **supergerm**, germ, microorganism, pathogen, bug (infml)

supercharge v **1 boost**, modify, charge, power up, amplify Opposite: downgrade **2 charge**, overdo, load, overload, hype Opposite: understate

supercilious adj **arrogant**, contemptuous, disdainful, pompous, superior Opposite: humble

superciliousness n **arrogance**, contemptuousness, contempt, condescension, haughtiness Opposite: humility

supercool (infml) adj **cool**, modern, contemporary, fashionable, trendy (infml) Opposite: passé

super-duper (infml) adj **excellent**, colossal, impressive, pleasing, wonderful Opposite: inferior

superego n **conscience**, integrity, scruples, sense of propriety, sense of judgment

superficial adj **1 surface**, shallow, external, exterior, on the surface Opposite: deep **2 insincere**, shallow, artificial, phony, apparent Opposite: sincere **3 cursory**, sketchy, rapid, hasty, quick Opposite: thorough **4 shallow**, trivial, trifling, unimportant, paltry Opposite: profound

superficiality n **shallowness**, triviality, frivolity, levity, paltriness Opposite: profundity

superficially adv **1 apparently**, seemingly, supposedly, outwardly, ostensibly Opposite: wholly **2 cursorily**, sketchily, rapidly, hastily, casually Opposite: thoroughly

superfine adj **1 delicate**, fine, light, sheer, fragile Opposite: coarse **2 superior**, first-class, first-rate, high-quality, best Opposite: inferior

superfluity n **1 luxury**, extra, frill, trifle, indulgence Opposite: necessity **2 oversupply**, excess, overabundance, surfeit, surplus Opposite: insufficiency

superfluous adj **extra**, surplus, redundant, unnecessary, unessential Opposite: basic

superhero n **champion**, crusader, rescuer, fighter, protector

superhuman adj **phenomenal**, prodigious, staggering, heroic, exceptional Opposite: normal

superimpose v **place over**, overlay, lay over, apply to, cover

superintend v **supervise**, manage, oversee,

administer, control *Opposite*: ignore

superintendent *n* **manager**, supervisor, administrator, officer, controller *Opposite*: underling

superior *adj* **1 better**, better-quality, advanced, improved, enhanced *Opposite*: inferior **2 larger**, greater, bigger, higher, more *Opposite*: smaller **3 excellent**, high-class, top-quality, exclusive, first-class *Opposite*: second-rate **4 higher**, upper, over, above *Opposite*: lower **5 condescending**, arrogant, disdainful, supercilious, aloof *Opposite*: humble ■ *n* **boss**, manager, chief, elder, better *Opposite*: inferior

superiority *n* **1 advantage**, dominance, lead, preeminence, power *Opposite*: inferiority **2 condescension**, arrogance, haughtiness, disdain, aloofness *Opposite*: humility

superiority complex *n* **superiority**, inflated ego, self-importance, pride, superciliousness *Opposite*: inferiority complex

superlative *adj* **excellent**, unmatched, unbeatable, untouchable, best *Opposite*: unremarkable

supernatural *adj* **paranormal**, mystic, mystical, ghostly, ghostlike *Opposite*: natural

WORD BANK
❑ **types of supernatural beings** banshee, brownie, elf, fairy, fairy godmother, fay (*literary*), genie, imp, jinni, pixie, poltergeist, sprite

supernumerary *adj* **1 extra**, excessive, superfluous, spare, surplus *Opposite*: necessary **2 substitute**, extra, auxiliary, ancillary, additional *Opposite*: permanent

superpower *n* **world power**, giant, power bloc, global force, global influence

supersaver *n* **discount**, special offer, concession

supersede *v* **succeed**, take over, overtake, supplant, replace *Opposite*: precede

superstar *n* **star**, megastar, celebrity, icon, luminary *Opposite*: nobody

superstition *n* **fallacy**, false notion, delusion, misconception, fantasy

superstitious *adj* **credulous**, gullible, illogical, irrational, delusory *Opposite*: rational

superstructure *n* **1 structure**, construction, elevation, frame, framework *Opposite*: foundation **2 idea**, concept, system, structure, argument *Opposite*: premise

supertitle *n* **surtitle**, caption, legend

supervene (*fml*) *v* **1 interrupt**, charge in, butt in, appear, turn up **2 ensue**, follow, supersede, succeed, pursue

supervise *v* **oversee**, manage, administer, control, run *Opposite*: neglect

supervision *n* **1 management**, direction, administration, regulation, command *Opposite*: neglect **2 care**, custody, guardianship, protection, charge

supervisor *n* **manager**, administrator, superintendent, controller, overseer *Opposite*: underling

supervisory *adj* **managerial**, administrative, superintendent, managing, controlling *Opposite*: subordinate

supine *adj* **1 flat**, horizontal, flat on one's back, prostrate, prone *Opposite*: standing **2 lethargic**, passive, inactive, apathetic, listless *Opposite*: vigorous

supplant *v* **oust**, displace, succeed, replace, unseat *Opposite*: install

supple *adj* **1 lithe**, agile, mobile, double-jointed, sinuous *Opposite*: stiff **2 bendable**, elastic, plastic, pliant, pliable *Opposite*: rigid

supplement *n* **1 addition**, extra, complement, enhancement, increase *Opposite*: deduction **2 section**, insert, appendix, attachment, rider ■ *v* **add**, complement, accompany, enhance, improve *Opposite*: deduct

supplemental *see* **supplementary**

supplementary *adj* **extra**, additional, added, add-on, supplemental *Opposite*: deducted

suppleness *n* **litheness**, agility, mobility, flexibility, limberness *Opposite*: stiffness

suppliant (*fml*) *adj* **prayerful**, petitionary, begging, pleading, supplicant (*fml*) *Opposite*: beneficent ■ *n* **petitioner**, applicant, aspirant, suitor, beggar *Opposite*: benefactor

supplicant (*fml*) *n* **petitioner**, applicant, suitor, aspirant, beggar *Opposite*: donor

supplicate (*fml*) *v* **appeal**, petition, request, beg, entreat *Opposite*: grant

supplication (*fml*) *n* **appeal**, request, entreaty, petition, plea *Opposite*: concession

supplier *n* **provider**, trader, seller, dealer, contractor *Opposite*: consumer

supplies *n* **provisions**, materials, goods, food, stores

supply *v* **provide**, give, make available, sell, bring *Opposite*: receive ■ *n* **amount**, quantity, fund, reserve, stock *Opposite*: dearth

support *v* **1 hold up**, reinforce, prop up, maintain, shore up *Opposite*: weaken **2 sustain**, provide for, keep, take care of, look after *Opposite*: neglect **3 help**, encourage, back up, aid, be there for *Opposite*: abandon **4 champion**, back, follow, espouse, be in favor of *Opposite*: oppose **5 corroborate**, confirm, verify, bear witness, prove *Opposite*: deny **6** (*literary*) **bear**, hold, carry, sustain, take ■ *n* **1 prop**, foundation, scaffold, brace, stanchion **2 sustenance**, provision, care, funding, funds *Opposite*: abandonment **3 assistance**, encouragement, backing, help, aid **4 corroboration**, confirmation, verification, authentication, substantiation *Opposite*: denial

supportable *(literary) adj* **tolerable**, bearable, acceptable, manageable, sustainable *Opposite*: insupportable

supporter *n* **follower**, fan, enthusiast, devotee, ally *Opposite*: detractor

support group *n* **encounter group**, forum, self-help group, therapy group, circle

support hose *n* **stockings**, nylons, pantyhose, tights, legwear

supporting *adj* **secondary**, backup, subsidiary, supportive, auxiliary *Opposite*: primary

supportive *adj* **helpful**, caring, sympathetic, compassionate, reassuring *Opposite*: unhelpful

support system *n* **friends**, network, helpers, group, support

suppose *v* **1 presume**, assume, understand, believe, expect **2 imagine**, pretend, consider, theorize, hypothesize

supposed *adj* **1 hypothetical**, theoretical, imaginary, fictional, made-up *Opposite*: actual **2 thought**, believed, assumed, alleged, understood *Opposite*: known

supposedly *adv* **allegedly**, evidently, apparently, theoretically, hypothetically *Opposite*: actually

supposing *conj* **assuming**, suppose, let's say, let's assume, say

supposition *n* **1 belief**, guess, idea, theory, possibility *Opposite*: fact **2 guesswork**, inference, hypothesis, speculation, conjecture *Opposite*: knowledge

suppress *v* **1 hold back**, repress, stifle, restrain, contain *Opposite*: express **2 overpower**, overwhelm, overturn, conquer, defeat *Opposite*: submit **3 muffle**, withhold, censor, smother, quash *Opposite*: publicize

suppression *n* **1 repression**, containment, control, restraint, inhibition *Opposite*: expression **2 conquest**, defeat, destruction, overthrow, clampdown **3 withholding**, cover-up, concealment, censorship, veil of secrecy *Opposite*: revelation

suppurate *v* **discharge pus**, fester, weep, ooze, seep

supranational *adj* **multinational**, international, cosmopolitan, worldwide, universal *Opposite*: local

supremacist *n* **chauvinist**, racist, xenophobe, bigot, sexist

supremacy *n* **1 preeminence**, ascendancy, primacy, superiority, domination *Opposite*: inferiority **2 reign**, sovereignty, rule, authority, power

supreme *adj* **1 highest**, best, ultimate, superlative, utmost *Opposite*: worst **2 sovereign**, dominant, uppermost, first, highest

supremely *adv* **extremely**, completely, enormously, absolutely, superlatively

supremo *(infml) n* **leader**, head, chief, authority, expert

surcharge *v* **charge extra**, charge again, charge more, tack on, levy again ■ *n* **extra charge**, supplement, extra, price, hidden extra

sure *adj* **1 unquestionable**, undisputable, certain, definite, guaranteed *Opposite*: uncertain **2 certain**, in no doubt, convinced, positive, confident *Opposite*: uncertain **3 dependable**, reliable, effective, trustworthy, trusty *Opposite*: unreliable ■ *adv* **1** *(infml)* **really**, certainly, surely, definitely, positively *Opposite*: doubtfully **2** *(infml)* **of course**, yes, certainly, by all means, yes indeed

sure-fire *(infml) adj* **guaranteed**, dependable, safe, assured, foolproof *Opposite*: doubtful

sure-footed *adj* **1 agile**, skilled, skillful, confident, nimble *Opposite*: clumsy **2 confident**, competent, unerring, capable, infallible

surely *adv* **1 confidently**, assuredly, with conviction, with confidence, with assurance *Opposite*: insecurely **2 certainly**, definitely, of course, without doubt, unquestionably *Opposite*: doubtfully

sureness *n* **certainty**, certitude, confidence, assurance, firm belief *Opposite*: uncertainty

sure thing *(infml) n* **certainty**, safe bet, odds-on chance, winner, cinch *(infml)*

surety *n* **security**, indemnity, guarantee, warranty, bond

surf *n* **waves**, breakers, rollers, whitecaps, spray

surface *n* **outside**, top, exterior, façade, side *Opposite*: inside ■ *adj* **superficial**, shallow, external, exterior, outward *Opposite*: inner ■ *v* **1 rise**, float up, come up, go up, emerge *Opposite*: sink **2 appear**, reappear, turn up, show up, pop up **3 become known**, come to light, come out, come out in the open, emerge **4 coat**, cover, skim, overlay, resurface

surface mail *n* **overland mail**, regular mail, first-class mail, registered mail, special delivery *Opposite*: airmail

surfeit *n* **excess**, surplus, glut, flood, oversupply *Opposite*: deficit

surge *v* **rush**, rush forward, flow, pour, gush ■ *n* **flow**, outpouring, gush, rush, heave

surgeon *n* **doctor**, physician, medical practitioner, specialist, neurosurgeon

surgical *adj* **1 medical**, clinical, operating, invasive **2 precise**, exact, accurate, definite, meticulous *Opposite*: imprecise

surly *adj* **gruff**, brusque, abrupt, short, curt *Opposite*: friendly

surmise *v* **guess**, deduce, infer, construe, gather *Opposite*: know ■ *n* **guesswork**, deduction, inference, conclusion, assumption *Opposite*: knowledge

surmount *v* **1 overcome**, prevail, conquer,

triumph, get through *Opposite*: fail 2 *(fml)*
scale, climb, top, clear, ascend *Opposite*:
descend

surmountable *adj* **manageable**, conquerable,
resolvable, controllable, winnable *Opposite*: intractable

surname *n* **last name**, family name, cognomen *Opposite*: first name

surpass *v* **exceed**, better, outdo, outshine,
improve on *Opposite*: trail

surpassing *(literary) adj* **outstanding**, superior, exceptional, greater, better *Opposite*:
inferior

surplus *n* **excess**, extra, spare, leftovers,
remainder *Opposite*: shortfall ■ *adj* **extra**,
excess, spare, remaining, additional *Opposite*: essential

surprise *v* **1 startle**, alarm, astonish,
astound, amaze **2 catch unawares**, catch
napping, take by surprise, burst in on,
intrude on ■ *n* **1 shock**, revelation, bolt
from the blue, disclosure, bombshell
(infml) **2 astonishment**, amazement,
wonder, disbelief, shock

surprised *adj* **astonished**, astounded,
amazed, taken aback, staggered

surprising *adj* **astonishing**, astounding,
amazing, shocking, startling *Opposite*:
expected

surprisingly *adv* **1 astonishingly**, astoundingly, amazingly, unexpectedly, unpredictably **2 to my surprise**, to my amazement, out of the blue, without warning,
without prior notice

surreal *adj* **strange**, weird, odd, unreal,
dreamlike *Opposite*: ordinary

surrender *v* **1 give in**, give up, admit defeat,
lay down your arms, yield *Opposite*: hold
out **2 relinquish**, give up, hand over, part
with, forfeit *Opposite*: retain ■ *n* **admission
of defeat**, submission, laying down of
arms, capitulation, renunciation *Opposite*:
perseverance. *See* COMPARE AND CONTRAST *at*
yield.

surreptitious *adj* **furtive**, secret, sneaky, sly,
covert *Opposite*: open. *See* COMPARE AND CONTRAST *at* secret.

surreptitiousness *n* **secrecy**, covertness, discretion, concealment, stealth *Opposite*:
openness

surrogacy *n* **substitution**, proxy, standing in,
surrogateship, replacement

surrogate *n* **substitute**, replacement, proxy,
stand-in, deputy

surround *v* **1 enclose**, encircle, encase,
enfold, envelop **2 besiege**, lay siege to,
encircle, hem in ■ *n* **border**, mount, edge,
edging, frame

surrounding *adj* **nearby**, close, adjacent,
neighboring, immediate *Opposite*: distant

surroundings *n* **environs**, surrounds, setting,
environment, background

surtax *n* **surcharge**, tax, levy, extra, supplement *Opposite*: relief

surtitle *n* **supertitle**, caption, legend

surveillance *n* **observation**, investigation,
scrutiny, reconnaissance, shadowing

survey *n* **1 inspection**, examination, investigation, review, inquiry **2 analysis**,
appraisal, scrutiny, evaluation, assessment ■ *v* **1 examine**, study, inspect, assess,
analyze **2 look at**, consider, peruse, regard,
think about **3 plot**, chart, map out,
measure, graph *Opposite*: sketch

surveyor *n* **inspector**, assessor, examiner,
reviewer, evaluator

survival *n* **existence**, endurance, being, subsistence, persistence *Opposite*: death

survive *v* **1 live**, live on, endure, carry on,
go on *Opposite*: perish **2 outlive**, outlast,
live through *Opposite*: die

surviving *adj* **living**, alive, enduring, persisting, remaining *Opposite*: gone

survivor *n* **fighter**, stayer, sticker, toughie
(infml)

susceptibility *n* **1 vulnerability**, defenselessness, weakness, exposure, predisposition *Opposite*: imperviousness
2 sensitivity, receptiveness, openness,
touchiness, impressionableness *Opposite*:
hardness

susceptible *adj* **1 vulnerable**, at risk, liable,
prone, disposed *Opposite*: invulnerable
2 sensitive, receptive, open, impressionable, swayable *Opposite*: impervious

suspect *v* **1 think**, believe, suppose, imagine,
guess **2 doubt**, distrust, mistrust, have
doubts, disbelieve *Opposite*: trust ■
n **accused**, defendant, respondent ■
adj **suspicious**, doubtful, dubious, unsure,
questionable *Opposite*: trustworthy

suspend *v* **1 hang**, hang up, dangle, swing,
string up **2 interrupt**, check, break off,
adjourn, hold *Opposite*: resume **3 postpone**, put on hold, defer, delay, stay *Opposite*: bring forward

suspended *adj* **1 hanging**, floating, hovering,
dangling, strung up **2 postponed**, put off,
deferred, adjourned, held over *Opposite*:
advanced **3 barred**, banned, proscribed,
excluded *Opposite*: allowed

suspended sentence *n* **deferred sentence**,
deferment, sentence, punishment, judgment

suspense *n* **1 uncertainty**, unsureness, doubt,
insecurity, confusion *Opposite*: knowledge **2 anticipation**, expectation, expectancy, excitement, tension *Opposite*:
flatness **3 anxiety**, apprehension, tension,
fear, nervousness *Opposite*: calm

suspension *n* **interruption**, holdup, check,
postponement, delay *Opposite*: resumption

suspicion *n* **1 mistrust**, apprehension, distrust, disbelief, wariness *Opposite*: trust
2 doubt, question, inkling, misgiving,
feeling *Opposite*: certainty **3 hint**, suggestion, trace, touch, tinge

suspicious *adj* **1 suspect**, dubious, shady, shifty, untrustworthy *Opposite*: trustworthy **2 doubtful**, distrustful, mistrustful, apprehensive, wary *Opposite*: sure

sustain *v* **1 withstand**, bear, tolerate, endure, weather *Opposite*: buckle **2 experience**, undergo, suffer, incur, contract **3 maintain**, continue, carry on, keep up, keep going *Opposite*: quit **4 nourish**, keep going, feed, nurture *Opposite*: deplete **5 support**, hold up, prop up, keep up, maintain

sustainable *adj* **1 maintainable**, bearable, justifiable, workable, defensible **2 ecological**, environmental, green, natural, balanced *Opposite*: unsustainable

sustained *adj* **continued**, constant, continual, continuous, nonstop *Opposite*: temporary

sustenance *n* **nourishment**, food, nutrition, provisions, rations *Opposite*: deprivation

susurrate *v* **rustle**, whisper, murmur, breathe

suture *n* **seam**, join, junction, joint, closure ■ *v* **sew**, sew up, stitch, stitch up, close *Opposite*: cut

suzerain *n* **superpower**, colonial power, ruling nation

svelte *adj* **lithe**, graceful, slender, willowy, sylphlike *Opposite*: stocky

Svengali *n* **manipulator**, controller, guru, charmer, guide

swab *n* **gauze**, lint, cloth, wipe, pad ■ *v* **wipe**, clean, cleanse, moisten, wash

swaddle *v* **wrap**, bandage, wrap up, swathe, envelop *Opposite*: unwrap

swag *n* **1 curtain**, drape, hanging, drapery **2 festoon**, garland, chain

swagger *v* **strut**, parade, flounce, prance, sweep *Opposite*: creep ■ *n* **boastfulness**, arrogance, bluster, conceit, boasting *Opposite*: timidity

swaggering *adj* **1 self-important**, self-satisfied, strutting, smug, arrogant *Opposite*: self-effacing **2 boastful**, boasting, blustering, bragging, vaunting *Opposite*: modest

swain *(literary) n* **admirer**, boyfriend, young man, lover, suitor *(fml)*

swallow *v* **1 ingest**, consume, take in, down, eat *Opposite*: vomit **2 gulp**, sip, gulp down, gobble up *Opposite*: regurgitate **3 destroy**, engulf, swallow up, take over, gobble up **4 suppress**, repress, choke back, hold back, hide *Opposite*: express **5 retract**, take back, back down, recant, eat your words **6** *(infml)* **believe**, accept, fall for, credit, buy *(infml)* *Opposite*: reject ■ *n* **gulp**, sip, nip, mouthful, swig *(infml)*

swamp *n* **wetland**, marsh, bog, mire, fen ■ *v* **1 overwhelm**, snow under, overload, inundate, flood **2 flood**, inundate, deluge, engulf, drown *Opposite*: drain

swampland *n* **swamps**, marshes, marshland, bog, everglade

swampy *adj* **marshy**, boggy, muddy, slushy, squelchy *Opposite*: dry

swank *v* *(slang)* **show off**, boast, brag, strut, swagger ■ *n* *(infml)* **ostentation**, show, affectation, exhibitionism ■ *adj* *(infml)* **upmarket**, glamorous, smart, high-class, swanky *(infml) Opposite*: downmarket

swanky *(infml) adj* **upmarket**, glamorous, high-class, stylish, elegant *Opposite*: downmarket

swan song *n* **farewell**, final act, last act, curtain, finale *Opposite*: debut

swap *(infml) v* **exchange**, trade, barter, do a deal, change ■ *n* **changeover**, substitution, exchange, switch, interchange

sward *n* **turf**, grass, grassland, green, lawn

swarm *n* **1 group**, cloud, flight **2 horde**, crowd, throng, flock, bevy ■ *v* **1 group**, hover, circle, fly, rise **2 teem**, be overrun, bristle, be alive with, be full **3 crowd**, throng, mass, flock, pile

swarming *adj* **crawling**, teeming, brimming, overrun, crowded *Opposite*: empty

swarthy *adj* **dark**, weather-beaten, dark-complexioned, leathery, tanned *Opposite*: pale

swashbuckler *n* **1 adventurer**, daredevil, swash, buccaneer, pirate **2 action movie**, period film, action film, adventure movie, actioner *(infml)*

swashbuckling *adj* **1 daring**, adventurous, heroic, exciting, cavalier *Opposite*: timid **2 strutting**, swaggering, boasting, blustery, blustering *Opposite*: modest

swat *v* **swipe**, slap, hit, smack, thwack

swatch *n* **sample**, batch, strip, snip, piece

swathe *v* **1 wrap**, cover, bandage, bind, entwine *Opposite*: unwrap **2 enfold**, envelop, drape, cloak, shroud *Opposite*: expose ■ *n* **strip**, ribbon, band, wrapping, bandage

sway *v* **1 swing**, waver, oscillate, move to and fro, rock **2 bend**, lean, veer, slant, tilt **3 influence**, bias, affect, control, persuade ■ *n* **power**, influence, control, authority, command *Opposite*: subjection

swear *v* **1 vow**, pledge, promise, give your word, attest **2 curse**, blaspheme, damn, utter profanities, cuss *(infml) Opposite*: bless **3 affirm**, assert, declare, claim, maintain

swear by *v* **trust**, rely on, depend on, have faith in, put your faith in *Opposite*: doubt

swear in *v* **inaugurate**, install, initiate, induct, administer an oath to *Opposite*: discharge

swear off *v* **give up**, renounce, abstain from, desist from, stop

swear-word *n* **expletive**, four-letter word, curse, bad language, profanity

sweat *v* **1** *(infml)* **worry**, fret, panic, be anxious, be concerned *Opposite*: relax **2 perspire**, swelter, wilt, drip

sweat out v **wait out**, see through, endure, see out, stick out *Opposite*: give up on

sweaty adj **1 perspiring**, covered with sweat, clammy, damp, sticky *Opposite*: dry **2 hot**, boiling, warm, sticky, sultry *Opposite*: cool

sweep v **1 brush**, clean up, tidy up, clear away, brush off **2 speed**, zoom, race, fly, dash *Opposite*: creep **3 carry**, move, seize, grab, take **4 arc**, arch, bend, bow, curve ■ n **1 arc**, arch, bend, bow, swing **2 scope**, range, extent, stretch, span

sweep aside v **dismiss**, ignore, brush aside, have done with, reject *Opposite*: consider

sweep away v **1 bowl over**, astonish, carry away, astound, overwhelm **2 brush**, sweep up, clean up, clear up, remove

sweeping adj **1 far-reaching**, comprehensive, all-encompassing, extensive, across-the-board *Opposite*: restricted **2 indiscriminate**, generalized, general, broad, blanket *Opposite*: specific

sweep somebody off his/her feet v **attract**, enchant, charm, allure, beguile *Opposite*: turn off *(infml)*

sweepstakes n **lottery**, draw, raffle, game of chance, prize drawing

sweep up v **brush**, tidy up, clean, pick up, clean up

sweet adj **1 sugary**, syrupy, saccharine, sweetened, honeyed *Opposite*: bitter **2 fresh**, pure, wholesome *Opposite*: foul **3 sweet-smelling**, fragrant, perfumed, scented, odorous *(literary)* *Opposite*: smelly **4 melodious**, melodic, harmonious, musical, tuneful *Opposite*: harsh **5 satisfying**, gratifying, enjoyable, rewarding, pleasing *Opposite*: unrewarding **6 kind**, thoughtful, considerate, pleasant, amiable *Opposite*: inconsiderate **7 lovable**, charming, engaging, appealing, attractive *Opposite*: unappealing

sweeten v **1 make sweeter**, add sugar to, sugar-coat, candy-coat, sugar **2 enhance**, improve, better, intensify, heighten **3 pacify**, mollify, appease, soothe, soften up *Opposite*: aggravate

sweetener n **1 sweet substance**, sugar, saccharine, aspartame **2** *(infml)* **bribe**, inducement, carrot, honey, molasses

sweetening n **sweet substance**, sweetener, sugar, saccharine, aspartame

sweetheart n **darling**, dear, dearest, beloved, precious

sweetie *(infml)* see **sweetheart**

sweetie pie *(infml)* see **sweetheart**

sweetness n **1 sugariness**, syrupiness, saccharinity *Opposite*: sourness **2 melodiousness**, harmony, pleasantness, mellifluousness *Opposite*: harshness **3 freshness**, pureness, purity, wholesomeness **4 charm**, cuteness, appeal, attractiveness,

delightfulness **5 kindness**, thoughtfulness, consideration, pleasantness, amiability *Opposite*: unkindness **6 fragrance**, sweet smell, perfume **7 lovableness**, charm, appeal, attraction

sweetness and light n **pleasantness**, harmony, peace, friendliness, concord *Opposite*: unpleasantness

sweet nothings n **romantic words**, romantic phrases, loving words, endearments, pillow talk

sweet-smelling adj **aromatic**, perfumed, fragrant, sweet-scented, fresh *Opposite*: smelly

sweet talk *(infml)* n **flattery**, smooth talk, cajolery, blarney *(infml)*, soft soap *(infml)*

sweet-talk *(infml)* v **charm**, flatter, smooth-talk, persuade, cajole *Opposite*: bully

sweet tooth n **craving**, taste, fondness, liking, relish

swell v **1 puff up**, puff out, swell up, bulge, bloat *Opposite*: deflate **2 increase**, grow, enlarge, inflate, expand *Opposite*: decrease **3 add to**, increase, enhance, improve, expand *Opposite*: diminish ■ n **1 wave**, undulation, billow, breaker, surge **2** *(dated infml)* **fop**, fashion plate, clotheshorse *(infml)*, dude *(slang)*, dandy *(dated)* ■ adj *(dated infml)* **really nice**, fantastic, wonderful, marvelous, fabulous *Opposite*: awful

swellheaded *(infml)* adj **conceited**, full of yourself, vain, self-important, puffed up *Opposite*: modest

swelling n **bulge**, bump, puffiness, inflammation, distension

swelter v **feel hot**, sweat, perspire, overheat, burn *Opposite*: shiver

sweltering adj **boiling**, baking, burning up, red-hot, blistering *Opposite*: freezing

swerve v **veer**, veer off, turn sharply, swing over, change direction

swift adj **quick**, speedy, fast, rapid, prompt

swiftness n **rapidity**, quickness, fastness, pace, speed *Opposite*: slowness

swig *(infml)* v **drink**, swill, toss off, take a drop, guzzle *(infml)* ■ n **mouthful**, nip, draft, drink

swill v **1 rinse**, sluice, wash out, wash down, swab **2 gulp down**, swig *(infml)*, guzzle *(infml)*, knock back *(infml)*, quaff *(literary)* ■ n **pig food**, slops, mash, scraps

swim v **1 bathe**, go for a dip, go swimming **2 spin**, whirl, reel, sway

swimmingly adv **successfully**, well, smoothly, easily, like a house on fire *Opposite*: laboriously

swindle v **cheat**, con, dupe, trick, double-cross ■ n **fraud**, hoax, embezzlement, con, confidence game

swindler n **cheat**, trickster, charlatan, fraud, embezzler

swine n **hog**, boar, pig

swing v **1 dangle**, hang, hang down, be suspended, sway **2 swerve**, veer, reel, pivot, rotate **3 rock**, fluctuate, move back and forth, sway, move backward and forward **4** (infml) **manage**, succeed in, accomplish, arrange, bring off ■ n **swipe**, smack, slap, thump, blow

swing around v **turn around**, spin around, whirl around, twirl around, wheel around

swing at v **hit**, hit out at, lash out, strike, thump

swipe v **1 hit**, swing at, lash out, hit out at, strike **2** (infml) **steal**, pilfer, make off with, walk off with, run off with ■ n **1 blow**, hit, swing, slap, smack **2** (infml) **critical remark**, cutting remark, dig, putdown (infml) Opposite: compliment

swipe card n **plastic card**, magnetic card, smart card, key card, credit card

swirl v **whirl**, twirl, spin, eddy, churn ■ n **twirl**, whirl, spin, eddy

swish v **hiss**, whoosh, whistle, whisper, rustle

switch n **1 control**, lever, button, knob, key **2 change**, shift, adjustment, difference, modification **3 exchange**, substitution, changeover, replacement, trade **4 whip**, lash, crop, cat-o'-nine-tails

switchback n **bend**, twist, zigzag, hairpin, turn

switch off v **1 shut down**, stop, deactivate, disconnect, cut Opposite: switch on **2** (infml) **relax**, unwind, stop worrying, stop paying attention, chill out (infml)

switch on v **turn on**, start, start up, activate, connect Opposite: switch off

swivel v **spin**, rotate, revolve, pivot, turn around

swollen adj **distended**, inflamed, engorged, puffy, puffed-up

swoon v **pass out**, faint, black out, lose consciousness, faint away ■ n **faint**, blackout, loss of consciousness, unconsciousness

swoop v **pounce**, jump, leap, dive, fly down

swoosh v **rustle**, swish, rush, swirl, whiz

swordplay n **sword fighting**, fencing, dueling, foil fencing, combat

sworn adj **confirmed**, affirmed, avowed (fml)

sybarite n **voluptuary**, sensualist, hedonist, epicurean, pleasure-lover Opposite: spartan

sycophancy n **servility**, obsequiousness, flattery, fawning, toadying

sycophant n **toady**, flatterer, minion, yes man, bootlicker (infml)

sycophantic adj **ingratiating**, flattering, kowtowing, obsequious, apple-polishing (slang)

syllabus n **course outline**, curriculum, program, program of study, prospectus

sylph n **nymph**, sprite, fairy, dryad, naiad

sylphlike adj **slender**, willowy, lithe, slim, graceful Opposite: hefty

symbiosis n **cooperation**, interdependence, relationship, association, synergy Opposite: independence

symbiotic adj **mutually beneficial**, interdependent, synergetic, cooperative, reciprocal Opposite: independent

symbol n **1 sign**, representation, character, figure, mark **2 emblem**, image, badge, logo

symbolic adj **representative**, figurative, emblematic, representational

symbolism n **imagery**, allegory, representation

symbolize v **represent**, be a symbol of, be a sign of, signify, stand for

symmetrical adj **balanced**, even, equal, proportioned, regular Opposite: asymmetric

symmetry n **regularity**, balance, equilibrium, evenness, proportion Opposite: asymmetry

sympathetic adj **1 understanding**, concerned, kind, kindly, compassionate Opposite: unfeeling **2 approving**, in agreement, in accord, supportive, well-disposed Opposite: against **3 agreeable**, congenial, likable, friendly, amiable Opposite: disagreeable

sympathize v **empathize**, feel sorry for, commiserate, express sympathy, understand

sympathizer n **partisan**, backer, follower, adherent, well-wisher Opposite: opponent

sympathy n **1 understanding**, compassion, kindness, consideration, empathy Opposite: incomprehension **2 pity**, commiseration, condolences **3 approval**, agreement, support, backing

symphonic adj **musical**, orchestral, instrumental, classical, philharmonic

symposium n **conference**, seminar, meeting, convention

symptom n **indication**, sign, warning sign, indicator

symptomatic adj **indicative**, suggestive, characteristic

synchronize v **harmonize**, coordinate, orchestrate, bring into line, match

synchronized adj **coordinated**, harmonized, corresponding, matched, in time

syncopate v **modify**, play, shift, swing, stress

syncopation n **shift of accent**, modification, accent, stress, rhythm

syndicate n **association**, collective, consortium, organization, group

syndrome n **condition**, disease, pattern, set of symptoms, disorder

synergy n **working together**, interaction, cooperation, combined effect, collaboration

synonym n **alternative word**, alternative expression, other word, substitute, replacement

synonymous *adj* identical, the same, one and the same, equal, tantamount *Opposite*: different

synopsis *n* outline, rundown, précis, summing up, summary

syntax *n* grammar, sentence structure, language rules, composition, word order

synthesis *n* 1 mixture, amalgamation, combination, blend, fusion *Opposite*: separation 2 **production**, creation, making, manufacture

synthesize *v* 1 manufacture, create, make, produce 2 **fuse**, blend, combine, amalgamate, integrate *Opposite*: separate

synthetic *adj* 1 **artificial**, fake, mock, imitation, faux *Opposite*: real 2 insincere, sham, bogus, put on, phony *Opposite*: genuine

syrup *n* maple syrup, corn syrup, molasses, sauce

syrupy *adj* 1 sugary, thick, sweet 2 sentimental, sickly, mawkish, cloying, schmaltzy (*infml*)

system *n* 1 scheme, arrangement, classification, structure, organism 2 **method**, technique, procedure, routine, approach 3 **orderliness**, regularity, method, logic *Opposite*: disorder

systematic *adj* **methodical** orderly, organized, efficient, logical *Opposite*: disorganized

systematize *v* arrange, order, regulate, sort, classify

systemic *adj* universal, complete, general

T

tab *n* 1 flap, label, ticket, stub, strip 2 (*infml*) bill, check, account, running total

tabernacle *n* chest, cabinet, container, case, box

table *n* 1 bench, board, desk, counter, stand 2 **food**, fare, diet, provision, menu 3 **chart**, graph, diagram, spreadsheet, record ■ *v* postpone, shelve, defer, put on the back burner, put on ice *Opposite*: bring forward

WORD BANK

❏ **types of tables** bedside table, card table, coffee table, console, davenport, desk, dining table, dressing table, end table, escritoire, gateleg table, night table, Pembroke table, picnic table, roll-top desk, tea table, trestle table, vanity table, worktable, writing desk

tableau *n* display, picture, montage, scene, representation

tablecloth *n* cover, cloth, covering

tableland *n* plain, flatland, prairie, plateau, upland *Opposite*: lowland

table mat *n* place mat, coaster, mat, pad, trivet

tablet *n* 1 pill, capsule, lozenge 2 slab, block, bar, cake, lump

tableware *n* crockery, plates, dishes, dinner service, tea service

tabloid *adj* sensationalist, shocking, lurid, scandalous, yellow

taboo *adj* 1 **offensive**, unmentionable, unthinkable, distasteful, off-limits 2 **forbidden**, banned, prohibited, barred, proscribed *Opposite*: acceptable ■ *n* ban, prohibition, bar, restriction, interdict ■ *v* forbid, ban, prohibit, bar, proscribe *Opposite*: allow

tabular *adj* flat, level, smooth, even, horizontal

tabulate *v* tabularize, chart, arrange, organize, present

tabulation *n* tabularization, arrangement, organization, presentation, formulation

tacit *adj* unspoken, implicit, inferred, implied, understood *Opposite*: explicit

taciturn *adj* reserved, uncommunicative, reticent, silent, quiet *Opposite*: garrulous. *See* COMPARE *and* CONTRAST *at* silent.

taciturnity *n* reserve, uncommunicativeness, reticence, silence, quietness *Opposite*: garrulousness

tack *n* 1 nail, pin, screw, staple, clip 2 **approach**, tactic, line, method, policy 3 **direction**, path, bearing, course, way ■ *v* 1 pin, nail, fasten, attach, affix *Opposite*: unfasten 2 **append**, add on, tag on, stick on, attach *Opposite*: remove

tackiness (*infml*) *n* tastelessness, bad taste, vulgarity, cheapness, nastiness *Opposite*: tastefulness

tackle *n* 1 **challenge**, attack, block, confrontation, throw 2 **equipment**, apparatus, kit, outfit, tools ■ *v* 1 **undertake**, begin, embark upon, attempt, engage in 2 **confront**, challenge, face, speak to, collar 3 **block**, stop, throw, seize, grab

tacky *adj* 1 **sticky**, messy, gluey, gummy, adhesive *Opposite*: dry 2 (*infml*) **tasteless**, in bad taste, vulgar, cheap, nasty *Opposite*: tasteful

tact *n* **diplomacy**, discretion, sensitivity, delicacy, thoughtfulness *Opposite*: tactlessness

tactful *adj* diplomatic, discreet, sensitive, delicate, thoughtful *Opposite*: tactless

tactic *n* method, approach, course, ploy, policy

tactical *adj* **strategic**, planned, premeditated, preemptive, psychological *Opposite*: accidental

tactician *n* **strategist**, negotiator, planner, schemer, diplomat

tactics *n* **strategy**, planning, campaign, maneuvers, devices

tactile *adj* **1 tangible**, palpable, perceptible, physical, concrete *Opposite*: intangible **2 demonstrative**, physical, affectionate, touchy-feely *(infml) Opposite*: reserved

tactless *adj* **insensitive**, undiplomatic, indiscreet, indelicate, thoughtless *Opposite*: tactful

tactlessness *n* **insensitivity**, indiscretion, indelicacy, thoughtlessness, inconsiderateness *Opposite*: tact

tad *(infml) n* **bit**, little, touch, mite, dash *Opposite*: lot

tag *n* **label**, ticket, tab, docket, identifier ■ *v* **1 mark**, label, ticket, docket, identify **2 append**, tack on, add on, attach, stick on *Opposite*: remove

tag along *v* **link up**, join in, follow, accompany, go with

tail *(infml) n* **follower**, shadow, stalker, pursuer, tracker ■ *v* **follow**, trail, track, shadow, stalk

tail end *n* **end**, close, ending, conclusion, finish *Opposite*: start

tailgate *v* **dog**, hound, be hard on the heels of, follow, pursue

tail off *v* **fade**, peter out, dwindle, decrease, fall away *Opposite*: build up

tailor *v* **1 make**, make to measure, cut, fashion, mold **2 adapt**, customize, custom-build, modify, fit

tailored *adj* **1 custom-made**, made-to-order, made-to-measure, tailor-made, handmade *Opposite*: off-the-rack **2 fitted**, shaped, well-cut, figure-hugging, close-fitting *Opposite*: casual **3 adapted**, customized, custom-built, modified, altered

tailor-made *adj* **1 perfect**, ideal, right, suitable, appropriate *Opposite*: wrong **2 made-to-measure**, made-to-order, custom-made, tailored, handmade *Opposite*: off-the-rack

tailpiece *n* **end**, end piece, finale, finial, coda

tailspin *n* **1 nosedive**, dive, spin, spiral, descent **2** *(infml)* **panic**, flap, turmoil, flat spin, whirl

taint *v* **contaminate**, pollute, stain, spoil, infect *Opposite*: enhance ■ *n* **stain**, blemish, blot, defect, fault

tainted *adj* **contaminated**, polluted, stained, spoiled, soiled *Opposite*: pure

take *v* **1 remove**, appropriate, acquire, grab, seize *Opposite*: give **2 grasp**, grab, seize, catch, catch on to *Opposite*: drop **3 carry**, transfer, fetch, bring, transport *Opposite*: leave **4 conquer**, capture, win, seize, secure *Opposite*: lose **5 choose**, select, procure, receive, buy *Opposite*: leave **6 accompany**, bring, escort, guide, lead **7 undertake**, adopt, accept, take on, assume *Opposite*: refuse **8 bear**, stand, endure, tolerate, suffer *Opposite*: reject **9 support**, hold up, hold, bear, manage **10 contain**, hold, accept, accommodate, house **11 study**, learn, read, do, take up *Opposite*: teach **12 consider**, look at, discuss, examine, think about *Opposite*: disregard **13 require**, need, demand, use, accept *Opposite*: reject **14 derive**, draw, experience, feel, extract **15 presume**, assume, believe, consider, perceive **16 succeed**, work, stick, root *Opposite*: fail **17 subtract**, deduct, take away, take off, remove *Opposite*: add ■ *n* **1 receipts**, takings, earnings, income, revenue *Opposite*: expenditure **2 shot**, sequence, scene **3 impression**, interpretation, opinion, view, point of view

take aback *v* **surprise**, stun, shock, nonplus, bowl over

take a back seat *v* **hold back**, restrain yourself, rein back, stay out of it

take a break *v* **rest**, relax, take time out, come up for air, pause *Opposite*: press on

take a breather *(infml) see* **take a break**

take account of *v* **allow for**, take into consideration, bear in mind, make allowances for, keep in mind *Opposite*: ignore

take a chance *v* **gamble**, venture, risk it, chance it, stick your neck out *Opposite*: play safe

take action *v* **act**, do something, take the plunge, take the bull by the horns, take steps

take a dim view of *v* **disapprove of**, not think much of, frown on, object to, dislike *Opposite*: approve

take advantage of somebody *v* **exploit**, use, mistreat, abuse, take for a ride

take advantage of something *v* **make the most of**, cash in on, profit from, exploit, make use of

take a fancy to *v* **like**, approve of, take a liking to, be fond of, love *Opposite*: dislike

take after *v* **resemble**, act like, imitate, look like, bear a resemblance to *Opposite*: differ

take a gamble *v* **gamble**, venture, risk it, chance it, stick your neck out *Opposite*: play safe

take amiss *v* **take the wrong way**, take exception, take umbrage, take offense, be put out *Opposite*: understand

take an oath *v* **promise**, swear, pledge, vow, give your word

take apart *v* **1 dismantle**, take to pieces, break up, pull apart, undo *Opposite*: assemble **2** *(infml)* **criticize**, censure, condemn, lash, pan *(infml) Opposite*: praise

take at face value *v* **believe**, accept, take for granted, rely on, not read the small print *Opposite*: question

take a turn for the worse *v* **go from bad to**

worse, deteriorate, decline, slip, relapse *Opposite*: improve

take away v 1 **remove**, cart off, carry off, carry away, take off *Opposite*: bring 2 **subtract**, deduct, take, take off *Opposite*: add

take back v 1 **withdraw**, retract, recant, renounce, disclaim *Opposite*: stick to 2 **regain**, recapture, retake, recover, retrieve *Opposite*: give back 3 **return**, exchange, refund, redeem, trade in *Opposite*: keep 4 **reinstate**, reaccept, bring back, welcome back, have back *Opposite*: dismiss 5 **remind**, transport, jog your memory, put you in mind of, make you think of

take by storm v 1 **capture**, overwhelm, storm, seize, conquer 2 **captivate**, bowl over, impress, charm, enthrall

take by surprise v **surprise**, burst in on, catch napping, take unawares, catch unawares

take care v 1 **be careful**, pay attention, look out, watch out, watch your step 2 **make sure**, ensure, make certain, confirm, check *Opposite*: neglect

take care of v 1 **look after**, care for, nurse, tend, support *Opposite*: neglect 2 **deal with**, see to, handle, manage, do *Opposite*: neglect

take charge v **assume responsibility**, take over, hold the fort, take the reins, take up the baton *Opposite*: step down

take control *see* **take charge**

take cover v **hide**, take shelter, shelter, take refuge, conceal yourself *Opposite*: emerge

take down v 1 **note**, jot down, write down, make a note of, record 2 **dismantle**, demolish, knock down, pull down, take apart *Opposite*: put up 3 **humiliate**, humble, deflate, embarrass, mortify *Opposite*: puff up

take effect v **happen**, function, work, operate, succeed

take exception v **take offense**, take umbrage, be put out, object, disapprove *Opposite*: welcome

take five (*infml*) v **take a break**, take time out, take a rest, rest, relax *Opposite*: keep on

take flight v **run away**, run off, flee, take off, decamp *Opposite*: stay put

take for a ride v **cheat**, deceive, swindle, trick, con

take for granted v 1 **assume**, presume, expect, count on, presuppose 2 **undervalue**, underrate, hold cheap, hold in contempt, disregard *Opposite*: appreciate

take heart v **cheer up**, perk up, brighten up, take comfort, snap out of it *Opposite*: lose heart

take home v **make**, be paid, net, earn, get

take-home pay n **net income**, after-tax income, net salary, net wages, net pay

take in v 1 **absorb**, understand, comprehend, grasp, assimilate *Opposite*: ignore 2 **include**, contain, comprise, encompass, cover *Opposite*: exclude 3 **deceive**, dupe, fool, mislead, trick 4 **let in**, receive, admit, entertain, accommodate *Opposite*: bar 5 **reduce**, alter, shrink, shorten, draw in *Opposite*: let out

take in hand v **deal with**, cope with, tackle, get to grips with, take on

take in one's stride v **deal with**, cope with, accept, take on board, manage

take into consideration v **allow for**, take into account, bear in mind, make allowances for, keep in mind *Opposite*: ignore

take into custody v **arrest**, detain, imprison, confine, hold *Opposite*: release

take issue with v **disagree**, differ, beg to differ, oppose, challenge *Opposite*: agree

take it easy v 1 **relax**, unwind, put your feet up, laze around, lounge around *Opposite*: toil 2 **calm down**, relax, simmer down, keep your shirt on, lighten up (*infml*) *Opposite*: explode

take legal action v **go to court**, sue, press charges, prosecute, litigate

taken adj **occupied**, in use, engaged, spoken for, busy *Opposite*: free

taken aback adj **stunned**, shocked, dumbfounded, speechless, bowled over *Opposite*: unimpressed

take no notice of v **ignore**, disregard, pay no attention, pay no heed, close your eyes *Opposite*: notice

take off v 1 **launch**, depart, leave, lift off, fly off *Opposite*: land 2 **remove**, discard, strip off, slip out of, peel off *Opposite*: put on 3 **deduct**, subtract, take away, take, remove *Opposite*: add 4 **cancel**, suspend, discontinue, abolish, do away with *Opposite*: reinstate 5 (*infml*) **succeed**, flourish, bloom, boom, prosper *Opposite*: flop (*infml*) 6 (*infml*) **leave**, go, depart, disappear, set out *Opposite*: stay 7 (*infml*) **parody**, imitate, mimic, impersonate, satirize. *See* COMPARE AND CONTRAST *at* **imitate**.

takeoff n 1 **departure**, ascent, launch, lift off, start *Opposite*: touchdown 2 (*infml*) **imitation**, impersonation, impression, parody, skit

take offense v **take exception**, take umbrage, take amiss, take the wrong way, be put out

take on v 1 **undertake**, assume, deal with, accept, adopt *Opposite*: refuse 2 **employ**, hire, engage, sign, bring on board *Opposite*: fire 3 **adopt**, acquire, gain, display, show *Opposite*: lose 4 **face**, confront, oppose, fight, vie with *Opposite*: avoid

take on board v **understand**, grasp, comprehend, realize, absorb *Opposite*: deny

take out v 1 **ask out**, invite out, accompany, treat, take *Opposite*: stand up 2 **arrange**, organize, set up, obtain, acquire *Opposite*: cancel 3 **vent**, direct, aim, express, relieve 4 **remove**, extract, pull out, bring out, fish out *Opposite*: insert

takeout *adj* **ready-made**, precooked, prepared, carryout, to go ■ *n* **carryout**, fast food, ready meal

take over *v* **1 take possession of**, annex, capture, hijack, seize *Opposite*: cede *(fml)* **2 take control**, take charge, take the reins, step in, assume responsibility *Opposite*: step down

takeover *n* **coup**, overthrow, seizure, appropriation, occupation *Opposite*: secession

take part *v* **join in**, participate, play, play a part, cooperate *Opposite*: opt out *(infml)*

take place *v* **happen**, occur, have effect, go on, come about

take pleasure in *v* **delight in**, enjoy, be taken with, love, take great delight in *Opposite*: hate

take possession of *v* **take over**, take control of, sequester, impound, occupy *Opposite*: abandon

take precedence *v* **have priority**, outweigh, come first, come before, predominate

take prisoner *v* **capture**, take captive, take hostage, seize, imprison *Opposite*: release

taker *n* **customer**, client, patron, purchaser, buyer

take root *v* **set in**, develop, start, grow, settle in *Opposite*: die off

take shape *v* **form**, develop, crystallize, take form, shape up *Opposite*: dissolve

take steps *v* **make a start**, proceed, start, take action, do something

take stock *v* **reflect**, sum up, think over, count your blessings, contemplate

take the blame *v* **take responsibility**, face the music, own up, take the rap *(slang)* *Opposite*: get away with

take the bull by the horns *v* **take the plunge**, bite the bullet, take the initiative, jump in, plunge in *Opposite*: hold back

take the edge off *v* **dampen**, blunt, dilute, relieve, mitigate *Opposite*: heighten

take the lead *v* **blaze a trail**, set a trend, originate, break new ground, break through *Opposite*: fall behind

take the place of *v* **replace**, succeed, displace, supersede, take over from

take the plunge *v* **dive in**, jump in, throw caution to the wind, take the bull by the horns, bite the bullet *Opposite*: hold back

take the rough with the smooth *v* **take the bad with the good**, make the best of things, look on the bright side, keep your chin up, go with the flow *Opposite*: crack up *(infml)*

take to *v* **1 warm to**, take a fancy to, take a liking to, fall for, befriend *Opposite*: dislike **2 begin**, start, commence, take up, go in for *Opposite*: stop

take to court *v* **prosecute**, sue, take legal action, press charges, file a suit

take to pieces *v* **take apart**, dismantle, disassemble, strip down, break up *Opposite*: put together

take to task *v* **reprimand**, scold, rebuke, reprove, criticize *Opposite*: praise

take to your heels *v* **run away**, run off, flee, run, fly *Opposite*: stay put

take unawares *v* **surprise**, sneak up on, catch off guard, take by surprise, startle

take under advisement *v* **consider**, weigh up, mull over, reflect, ponder

take up *v* **1 start**, go in for, adopt, engage in, assume *Opposite*: give up **2 continue**, resume, go on, pick up, carry on *Opposite*: leave off **3 raise**, lift, pick up, gather up, hoist *Opposite*: put down **4 shorten**, raise, lift, pin up, gather up *Opposite*: let down **5 occupy**, fill, cover. absorb, consume

take-up *n* **acceptance**, reception, use, participation, response

take up the baton *v* **take control**, take charge, take over, take the reins, step in *Opposite*: step down

take up the gauntlet *v* **accept a challenge**, take on, confront, stand up to *Opposite*: run away

taking *adj* **captivating**, attractive, enchanting, pleasing, winning *Opposite*: unattractive

takings *n* **earnings**, income, proceeds, profits, receipts *Opposite*: expenditure

tale *n* **1 account**, fiction, romance, anecdote, legend **2 lie**, untruth, rumor, falsehood, story *Opposite*: truth

talent *n* **aptitude**, flair, gift, bent, knack

COMPARE AND CONTRAST CORE MEANING: the natural ability to do something well

talent a natural ability to do something well that can be developed by training; **gift** a natural ability, especially an artistic ability, or a social skill; **aptitude** a natural ability to do or learn something, especially one that is not yet fully developed; **flair** a natural ability to do something well, especially creative or artistic ability; **bent** a natural ability, inclination, or liking for something; **knack** an intuitive ability to do something well, especially one that might not be developed by training; **genius** exceptional intellectual or creative ability.

---

talented *adj* **gifted**, accomplished, able, brilliant, artistic

taleteller *n* **informer**, turncoat, tattletale, snitch *(slang)*, stool pigeon *(slang)*

talisman *n* **stone**, jewel, amulet, charm, trinket

talk *v* **1 communicate**, speak, chat, gossip, chatter **2 converse**, debate, compare notes, have a discussion, discuss **3 confess**, betray, turn over, inform, crack ■ *n* **1 conversation**, exchange, dialogue, tête-à-tête, heart-to-heart **2 lecture**, speech, address, discourse, oration **3 gossip**, conversation, rumor, chatter, speculation **4 language**, words, vocabulary, jargon, speech

talkative *adj* **chatty**, verbose, garrulous, voluble, fluent *Opposite*: reticent

COMPARE AND CONTRAST CORE MEANING: talking a lot
talkative willing to talk readily and at length; **chatty** talking freely about unimportant things in a friendly way; **gossipy** talking with relish about other people and their lives, often unkindly or maliciously; **garrulous** excessively or pointlessly talkative; **loquacious** tending to talk a great deal.

talkativeness n **chattiness**, verbosity, garrulousness, volubility, fluency Opposite: reticence

talk back v argue, answer back, defy, retort, quibble

talker n **communicator**, conversationalist, speaker, gossip, chatterer

talking n 1 **speaking**, conversation, chat, chatting, gossip 2 **debate**, words, discussion, negotiation, conference

talking point n topic of conversation, debating point, issue, question, hot topic

talking-to (infml) n **dressing-down**, reprimand, lecture, tongue-lashing, scolding

talk into v persuade, coax, induce, convince, move Opposite: talk out of

talk out of v dissuade, sway, discourage, deter, advise against Opposite: talk into

talk over v discuss, negotiate, debate, review, go into

talks n negotiations, discussions, summit, dialogue, conference

talk turkey (infml) v open up, put your cards on the table, get down to brass tacks, get to the point, get to the nitty-gritty Opposite: equivocate

tall adj 1 **high**, big, giant, lofty, lanky Opposite: short 2 **difficult**, hard, complicated, demanding, trying Opposite: easy 3 **incredible**, unbelievable, unlikely, farfetched, exaggerated Opposite: likely

tallness n **height**, loftiness, size, lankiness, stature Opposite: shortness

tall story see tall tale

tall tale n **cock-and-bull story**, unlikely story, tale, tall story, fairy tale

tally v 1 **match**, correspond, agree, check, equate Opposite: clash 2 **compute**, count, reckon, score, total ■ n **score**, count, total, reckoning, calculation

talon n claw, nail, fingernail, hook, spur

tame adj 1 **domestic**, domesticated, broken, trained, disciplined Opposite: wild 2 **docile**, meek, compliant, subdued, unresisting Opposite: rebellious 3 **bland**, dull, insipid, boring, unexciting Opposite: exciting ■ v 1 **domesticate**, break in, train, discipline, pacify 2 **repress**, suppress, overcome, subjugate, subdue

tameness n 1 **docility**, meekness, compliance, submissiveness, obedience Opposite: rebelliousness 2 **blandness**, dullness, insipidness, flatness, tedium Opposite: excitement

tamp v fill, pack, stuff, cram, compress

tamper v 1 **interfere**, meddle, monkey with, fool with, tinker 2 **corrupt**, r.g, influence, manipulate, bribe

tampon n plug, pad, wad, swab, compress

tan n suntan, sunburn, color, bronze, brownness ■ v 1 **bronze**, brown, toast, burn 2 **treat**, preserve, process, dye, wash ■ adj **bronzed**, sunburned, dark, suntanned, tanned

tang n trace, hint, smack, suggestion, flavor

tangent n **line**, curve, angle, refraction, curvature

tangential adj **peripheral**, lateral, oblique, divergent, indirect Opposite: central

tangibility n 1 **palpability**, perceptibility, physicality, reality, solidity Opposite: intangibility 2 **actuality**, reality, clarity, plainness, obviousness Opposite: intangibility

tangible adj 1 **palpable**, touchable, perceptible, concrete, physical Opposite: intangible 2 **actual**, substantial, real, certain, evident Opposite: intangible

tangle v 1 **knot**, twist, snarl, interweave, intertwine Opposite: untangle 2 **snag**, catch, snarl, snare, hook Opposite: undo 3 **trap**, catch, ensnare, entangle, enmesh Opposite: release ■ **come up against**, confront, mess with, square up, oppose Opposite: avoid ■ n 1 **mass**, jumble, knot, mesh, web 2 **mess**, jam, difficulty, mix-up, complication

tangled adj 1 **knotted**, twisted, snarled, interwoven, intertwined Opposite: straight 2 **complicated**, confused, knotty, complex, messy Opposite: straightforward

tangy adj **pungent**, sharp, strong, piquant, tasty Opposite: bland

tank n cistern, boiler, reservoir, container, chamber

tankard n mug, beer mug, jug, stein, toby jug

tanker n transporter, freighter, truck

tanned adj **brown**, bronzed, suntanned, dark, sunburned Opposite: pale

tantalize v **tease**, entice, torment, torture, tempt Opposite: turn off (infml)

tantalizing adj **teasing**, enticing, tormenting, tempting, provocative Opposite: boring

tantamount adj **equal**, equivalent, the same as, synonymous, as good as Opposite: different

tantrum n **outburst**, fit of temper, fit, frenzy, fret

tap n 1 **blow**, rap, knock, bang, beat 2 **stopper**, plug, bung, cork 3 **spigot**, valve, spout, faucet, stopcock ■ v 1 **rap**, knock, bang, beat, strike 2 **appoint**, select, nominate, commission, recruit Opposite: pass over 3 **draw off**, draw out, extract, run off, release Opposite: block up 4 **bug**, listen in on, record, monitor, intercept 5 (infml) **use**, utilize, draw on, draw off, exploit

tape *n* **1 ribbon**, strip, string, tie, band **2 adhesive tape**, duct tape, masking tape, friction tape, packing tape **3 cassette**, cassette tape, video, videotape, videocassette **4 tape measure**, measuring tape, measure, tapeline ■ *v* **1 record**, tape-record, copy, save, videotape *Opposite*: erase **2 stick**, fasten, attach, secure, bind *Opposite*: detach

tape measure *n* **tape**, measuring tape, measure, rule, ruler

taper *v* **1 narrow**, come to a point, thin down, dwindle, elongate *Opposite*: widen **2 reduce**, phase out, taper off, tail off, diminish *Opposite*: increase ■ *n* **1 candle**, torch, light, flame **2 narrowing**, point, thinning down, dwindling, elongation

tape-record *v* **tape**, record, copy, save, video

tapered *adj* **1 tapering**, narrowing, pointed, elongated, shaped *Opposite*: flared **2 gradually reduced**, phased out, tailed off, diminished, decreased

tapering *adj* **tapered**, narrowing, pointed, elongated, shaped *Opposite*: widening

tapestry *n* **wall hanging**, drapery, arras

tar *n* **asphalt**, tarmac, pitch, blacktop, macadam

tardiness *n* **lateness**, delay, belatedness, unpunctuality *Opposite*: punctuality

tardy *adj* **late**, delayed, overdue, belated, unpunctual *Opposite*: punctual

target *n* **1 board**, mark, bull's eye, bull, goal **2 aim**, objective, object, focus, end **3 butt**, victim, scapegoat, foil, recipient ■ *v* **1 aim at**, aim for, focus on, home in on, seek out **2 direct**, aim, point, level, train

tariff *n* **1 tax**, duty, due, excise, levy **2 price**, price list, rate, charge, cost

tarmac *n* **tar**, asphalt, pitch, blacktop, macadam

tarn *n* **lake**, pool, pond, lagoon, water

tarnish *v* **1 dull**, discolor, stain, smear, smudge *Opposite*: clean **2 sully**, damage, stain, taint, blot *Opposite*: enhance

tarnished *adj* **1 dull**, discolored, stained, smeared, smudged *Opposite*: shiny **2 sullied**, damaged, stained, tainted, blotted *Opposite*: enhanced

tarpaulin *n* **canvas**, cover, sheet, sheeting, tarp *(infml)*

tarry *v* **1 remain**, stay, stay put, visit, sojourn *(literary)* **2 linger**, loiter, dawdle, hang around, hesitate

tart *adj* **1 sharp**, acid, acidic, sour, bitter *Opposite*: sweet **2 acerbic**, biting, sharp, sour, acid *Opposite*: kind ■ *n* **pie**, tartlet, pastry, quiche, flan

tartan *n* **pattern**, plaid, check

tartar *n* **plaque**, deposit, residue, coating, scale

tartness *n* **1 sharpness**, acidity, sourness, bitterness *Opposite*: sweetness **2 acerbity**,

sharpness, sourness, acidity, bitterness *Opposite*: kindness

task *n* **job**, chore, duty, mission, commission

task force *n* **team**, unit, squad, detail, crew

tassel *n* **bobble**, tuft, fringe, braid, edging

taste *n* **1 sense of taste**, palate, discrimination, sensitivity, perception **2 flavor**, tang, savor, hint, smack **3 try**, sample, test, bite, nibble **4 liking**, preference, leaning, penchant, fondness *Opposite*: dislike **5 discrimination**, discernment, judgment, tastefulness, good taste ■ *v* **1 discern**, pick up, recognize, get, feel **2 sample**, try, test, eat, bite *Opposite*: devour **3 experience**, sample, preview, get a taste of, get a hint of

tasteful *adj* **discerning**, discriminating, sophisticated, refined, stylish *Opposite*: tasteless

tastefulness *n* **discernment**, discrimination, judgment, taste, sophistication *Opposite*: tastelessness

tasteless *adj* **1 bland**, flavorless, flat, insipid, weak *Opposite*: tasty **2 in bad taste**, in poor taste, cheap, flashy, loud *Opposite*: tasteful **3 vulgar**, crude, foul-mouthed, boorish, gross

tastelessness *n* **1 blandness**, flavorlessness, flatness, insipidness, weakness *Opposite*: tastiness **2 bad taste**, poor taste, cheapness, flashiness, loudness *Opposite*: tastefulness

taster *n* **analyst**, sampler, buyer, specialist, connoisseur

tastiness *n* **deliciousness**, flavor, yumminess, juiciness, succulence *Opposite*: tastelessness

tasty *adj* **delicious**, flavorsome, mouthwatering, appetizing, succulent *Opposite*: tasteless

tater *(infml)* *n* **potato**, spud *(slang)*, murphy *(dated infml)*

tattered *adj* **torn**, ragged, tatty, dilapidated, frayed *Opposite*: smart

tatters *n* **rags**, shreds, bits, pieces, strips

tattiness *n* **shabbiness**, scruffiness, raggedness, dilapidation, untidiness *Opposite*: smartness

tattle *v* **gossip**, tittle-tattle, prattle, chat, chatter *Opposite*: keep secret ■ *n* **1 gossip**, tattler, telltale, tattletale, informer **2 tittle-tattle**, gossip, prattle, chat, chatter *Opposite*: fact

tattler *n* **gossip**, tattle, telltale, tattletale, informer

tattletale *n* **talebearer**, telltale, tattler, informer, snitch *(slang)*

tattoo *n* **1 design**, pattern, picture, decoration, mark **2 signal**, summons, call, recall, order **3 parade**, display, tournament, show, pageant

tatty *adj* **shabby**, worn, scruffy, dog-eared, down-at-heel *Opposite*: smart

taunt v **mock**, tease, jeer, sneer, goad *Opposite*: compliment ■ n **insult**, gibe, sneer, affront, criticism *Opposite*: compliment

taunting adj **mocking**, provocative, provoking, teasing, spiteful *Opposite*: kind

taut adj 1 **tight**, stretched, rigid, stiff, tense *Opposite*: slack 2 **worried**, anxious, stressed, tense, nervous *Opposite*: calm

tauten v **tighten**, stretch, stiffen, pull tight, tense *Opposite*: slacken

tautness n **tightness**, tension, pull, stretch, rigidity *Opposite*: slackness

tautological adj **repetitious**, repetitive, inelegant, reiterative, redundant

tautology n **repetition**, reiteration, duplication, redundancy, superfluity

tavern n **bar**, inn, watering hole (*infml*), roadhouse (*dated*)

tawdriness n **cheapness**, gaudiness, flashiness, showiness, tastelessness *Opposite*: tastefulness

tawdry adj **cheap**, gaudy, flashy, showy, tasteless *Opposite*: tasteful

tax n **duty**, levy, toll, excise, tariff ■ v 1 **strain**, overtax, overstretch, stretch, overload *Opposite*: relieve 2 **charge**, hit, burden, cream off, deduct *Opposite*: exempt 3 **accuse**, reproach, blame, confront, present

taxable adj **chargeable**, assessable, dutiable, rateable, payable *Opposite*: tax-exempt

taxation n 1 **fiscal policy**, tax policy, tax system, revenue system, taxes 2 **duty**, levy, toll, dues, excise

tax-exempt adj **exempt from taxation**, exempt, untaxed, tax-free, duty-free *Opposite*: taxable

taxing adj **demanding**, tough, difficult, strenuous, challenging *Opposite*: effortless

taxonomy n **classification**, nomenclature, taxonomic system, catalog, categorization

tea n **drink**, infusion, tisane, brew, decoction

teach v 1 **impart**, communicate, show, explain, clarify *Opposite*: learn 2 **educate**, tutor, train, instruct, coach *Oppos te*: learn

COMPARE AND CONTRAST CORE MEANING: impart knowledge or skill in something
teach impart knowledge or skill to somebody by instruction or example; **educate** increase the knowledge or develop the abilities of somebody by formal teaching or training, especially in a school or college context; **train** teach the skills necessary for a particular task or job by means of instruction, observation, and practice; **instruct** teach somebody a subject methodology, or skill, not necessarily in a school or college context; **coach** give special tuition to one person or a small group of people, especially in preparation for an exam, or to teach sports, artistic, or life skills; **tutor** give somebody individual tuition in a particular subject or skill; **school** train somebody in a particular skill or area of expertise in a thorough and detailed way; **drill** teach something by means of repeated exercises and practice.

teacher n **educator**, tutor, instructor, coach, trainer *Opposite*: student

teaching n 1 **education**, lessons, instruction, coaching, training *Opposite*: learning 2 **philosophy**, ideas, principles, beliefs, thinking

team n 1 **side**, squad, players, lineup, crew 2 **group**, band, crew, gang, panel

teammate n **colleague**, co-player, partner, captain, fellow player

teamster n 1 **trucker**, driver, truck driver, hauler 2 **driver**, carter, charioteer, handler, trainer

team up v **join forces**, collaborate, cooperate, work together, get together *Opposite*: split up

teamwork n **cooperation**, collaboration, joint effort, solidarity, communication

tear v 1 **rip**, rend, split, gash, slash *Opposite*: join 2 **snatch**, rip, grab, wrench, pluck *Opposite*: coax 3 **dash**, rush, hurry, rip, streak *Opposite*: saunter 4 **sprain**, rip, pull, injure, damage ■ n 1 **slit**, rip, split, slash, gash *Opposite*: join 2 **binge**, spree, orgy, rampage, splurge (*infml*) 3 **teardrop**, drop, droplet, drip, bead

COMPARE AND CONTRAST CORE MEANING: pull apart forcibly
tear pull something apart, either by accident or on purpose, leaving jagged edges; **rend** pull something apart violently; **rip** tear something with a sudden rough splitting action, accompanied by a distinctive noise, especially accidentally; **split** divide something into two parts with a single movement, usually by force.

tear apart v 1 **destroy**, fragment, wreck, separate, dismantle *Opposite*: reunite 2 **distress**, disturb, devastate, pain, hurt *Opposite*: reassure

tear away v **drag away**, pull away, haul away, depart, leave *Opposite*: linger

tear down v **demolish**, rip down, pull down, destroy, remove *Opposite*: construct

teardrop n **tear**, drop, droplet, drip, bead

tearful adj 1 **in tears**, crying, weeping, sobbing, howling 2 **sad**, emotional, unhappy, mournful, melancholy *Opposite*: cheerful

tear into v **lay into**, attack, go for, round on, set on *Opposite*: praise

tearjerker (*infml*) n **sentimental story**, drama, tragedy, sad story, weepie (*infml*) *Opposite*: comedy

tear up v **rip up**, shred, destroy, rip to pieces, rip to shreds

tease v 1 **torment**, harass, pester, bother, annoy *Opposite*: pet 2 **joke**, laugh, mock, kid, taunt 3 **tantalize**, arouse, lead somebody on, encourage, excite *Opposite*:

satisfy **4 brush**, comb, style, coif (fml) ■
n **joker**, clown, mocker, teaser, tormentor

teaser n **1 tease**, joker, clown, mocker, josher
(infml) **2 puzzle**, puzzler, brainteaser, tough
one, mystery

tea service n **tea set**, cups and saucers,
china, porcelain, crockery

tea set see **tea service**

teasing adj **1 playful**, mocking, tongue-in-
cheek, mischievous, jokey Opposite:
serious **2 provocative**, coy, flirtatious, suggestive, tempting Opposite: straightforward ■ n **playfulness**, banter, repartee,
raillery, ribbing (infml) Opposite: seriousness

technical adj **1 technological**, scientific,
industrial, mechanical **2 practical**, mechanical, procedural, methodological, methodical **3 nominal**, official, strict, narrow,
literal Opposite: loose **4 specialized**,
precise, official, professional, specialist
Opposite: general

technicality n **detail**, small point, trifle

technician n **specialist**, expert, operator,
mechanic, engineer

technique n **method**, system, practice,
modus operandi, procedure

technological adj **technical**, scientific,
industrial, high-tech

technologist n **scientist**, engineer, technician, maven

technology n **1 equipment**, machinery, tools
2 skill, knowledge, expertise, know-how
(infml)

tedious adj **boring**, dull, dreary, monotonous, mind-numbing Opposite: interesting

tediousness n **boredom**, dullness, dreariness, monotony, tedium Opposite: excitement

tedium see **tediousness**

teed off (infml) adj **angry**, annoyed, irritated, furious, fuming Opposite: calm

teem v **swarm**, crowd, abound, be full, be
stuffed

teeming adj **swarming**, packed, crowded,
crawling, seething Opposite: empty

teen (infml) adj **teenage**, adolescent, youth,
young, juvenile ■ n **teenager**, adolescent,
young person, youth, youngster

teenage adj **adolescent**, young, youth,
juvenile, teen (infml)

teenager n **adolescent**, young person, youth,
youngster, young adult. See COMPARE AND
CONTRAST at **youth**.

teens n **adolescence**, youth, young adulthood

teeny (infml) adj **tiny**, small, little, minute,
wee Opposite: enormous

tee off v **drive off**, start, begin, commence,
initiate

teeter v **totter**, stagger, wobble, shake,
dodder

teetotal adj **dry**, nondrinking, abstemious,
abstinent, sober

telecaster n **broadcaster**, announcer, commentator, newscaster, anchor

telegram n **wire**, cable, message, telegraph,
telex

telegraph v **send by wire**, send a message,
cable, wire, transmit

telegraphic adj **concise**, abbreviated, condensed, truncated, succinct Opposite:
verbose

telepathic adj **clairvoyant**, psychic, tele-
kinetic, extrasensory, subconscious

telepathy n **thought transference**, ESP, extrasensory perception, mind-reading, sixth
sense

telephone v **phone**, call, give somebody a
call, buzz (infml)

telephone call n **call**, phone call, buzz
(infml)

telescopic adj **1 magnifying**, enlarging, telephoto, zoom **2 collapsible**, retractable,
foldaway, foldup, compactible

telethon n **fundraiser**, charity appeal, broadcast appeal, solicitation, benefit

televise v **broadcast**, emit, relay, put out,
put on

television n **TV** (infml), small screen (infml),
tube (infml), boob tube (infml)

tell v **1 relate**, narrate, recount, describe,
report **2 inform**, let know, say, advise,
notify Opposite: keep in the dark **3 express**,
say, voice, communicate, state **4 instruct**,
order, direct, command, charge **5 distinguish**, recognize, differentiate, identify,
discriminate Opposite: confuse **6 divulge**,
disclose, expose, reveal, inform Opposite:
keep secret

tell against v **count against**, go against,
work against, weigh against

tell apart v **distinguish**, differentiate, tell one
from another, identify, tell the difference
between

teller n **cashier**, banker, bank clerk

telling adj **1 revealing**, informative, significant, telltale, indicative Opposite:
uninformative **2 effective**, expressive,
important, significant, influential Opposite: ineffective

telling-off (infml) n **reprimand**, scolding,
dressing-down, lecture, tongue-lashing
Opposite: praise

tell lies v **lie**, tell untruths, tell stories, dissemble, perjure yourself Opposite: tell the
truth

tell off (infml) v **reprimand**, scold, rebuke,
rake over the coals, take to task Opposite:
commend

tell stories v **tell lies**, lie, tell untruths, prevaricate, fabricate

telltale adj **revealing**, informative, betray-
ing, significant, divulging Opposite:
uninformative

tell the truth v be honest, give your word, be straight with, be open, be truthful Opposite: lie

temerity n nerve, audacity, gall, boldness, impudence Opposite: reticence

temp n temporary worker, office temporary, fill-in, stand-in, temporary secretary ■ v do temporary work, fill in, stand in

temper n 1 disposition, temperament, state of mind, frame of mind, humor 2 anger, rage, bad mood, bad humor, mood ■ v moderate, mitigate, alleviate, soften, lighten Opposite: intensify

temperament n nature, character, personality, disposition, temper

temperamental adj unpredictable, erratic, unreliable, undependable, up and down Opposite: consistent

temperance n 1 teetotalism, sobriety, abstinence, abstemiousness, soberness Opposite: intemperance 2 self-control, restraint, self-restraint, moderation, self-denial Opposite: indulgence

temperate adj 1 restrained, self-controlled, controlled, measured, reasonable Opposite: intemperate 2 moderate, mild, clement, pleasant, comfortable Opposite: extreme

tempered adj hardened, toughened, hard, annealed, strengthened

tempest n 1 uproar, commotion, tumult, upheaval, disturbance 2 (literary) storm, gale, thunderstorm, hurricane, cyclone Opposite: calm

tempestuous adj 1 emotional, passionate, intense, hysterical, violent Opposite: relaxed 2 stormy, rough, turbulent, intemperate, inclement Opposite: calm

template n pattern, master, stencil, model, prototype

tempo n beat, speed, pulse, rhythm, measure

temporal adj 1 chronological, time-based, sequential, progressive, historical Opposite: spatial 2 worldly, earthly, secular, lay, profane Opposite: spiritual

temporary adj passing, transitory, short-lived, fleeting, ephemeral Opposite: permanent

---

COMPARE AND CONTRAST CORE MEANING: lasting only a short time

temporary lasting or designed to last for a short time; **fleeting** very brief or rapid; **passing** superficial and not long-lasting; **transitory** existing only for a short time; **ephemeral** lasting for a short time and leaving no permanent trace; **evanescent** (literary) disappearing after a short time and soon forgotten; **short-lived** lasting only for a short time.

---

temporize v delay, defer, procrastinate, take your time, hesitate Opposite: set to

tempt v 1 lure, allure, entice, attract, excite

Opposite: repel 2 invite, attract, appeal, draw, move Opposite: put off

temptation n 1 lure, enticement, attraction, offer, invitation 2 desire, craving, urge, impulse, compulsion Opposite: repulsion 3 persuasion, coaxing, inducement, enticement, invitation Opposite: repulsion

tempted adj of a mind to, attracted, interested, curious, drawn Opposite: uninterested

tempting adj alluring, enticing, attractive, appealing, inviting Opposite: unappealing

tenable adj reasonable, acceptable, defensible, plausible, rational Opposite: untenable

tenacious adj stubborn, obstinate, resolute, firm, persistent Opposite: irresolute

tenacity n stubbornness, obstinacy, resolve, firmness, persistence Opposite: irresolution

tenancy n occupancy, rental, contract, lease, tenure Opposite: ownership

tenant n renter, occupier, occupant, resident, lodger Opposite: landlord

tend v 1 have a habit of, have a tendency to, incline, lean toward, be disposed 2 incline, veer, lean, bend, verge 3 look after, care for, take care of, cultivate, attend to Opposite: neglect 4 be in charge of, manage, keep an eye on, watch over, watch

tendency n 1 propensity, bent, leaning, inclination, predisposition 2 trend, drift, movement, bias, current

tendentious adj provocative, opinionated, biased, partisan, subjective Opposite: impartial

tender adj 1 sensitive, delicate, sore, raw, painful 2 loving, caring, affectionate, fond, kind Opposite: rough 3 young, youthful, immature, inexperienced, impressionable Opposite: seasoned ■ n proposal, proposition, bid, offer, submission ■ v offer, proffer, present, give, hand in Opposite: withdraw

tenderfoot (infml) n novice, recruit, raw recruit, newcomer, beginner Opposite: old hand

tenderhearted adj soft-hearted, compassionate, sympathetic, kind, soft Opposite: hardhearted

tenderheartedness n soft-heartedness, compassion, sympathy, tenderness, kindness Opposite: hardheartedness

tenderize v beat, smash, hit, soak, steep

tenderness n 1 sensitivity, soreness, rawness, painfulness, inflammation 2 sympathy, gentleness, kindness, kindheartedness, fondness Opposite: unkindness

tendril n 1 stem, vine, shoot, frond, branch 2 (literary) twist, coil, wisp, lock, curl

tenement n apartment building, apartment house, high-rise, housing project

tenet n **principle**, theory, idea, assumption, belief

tenor n **mood**, tone, gist, drift, meaning

tense adj **1 anxious**, nervous, stressed, worried, edgy Opposite: relaxed **2 taut**, tight, rigid, stiff, strained Opposite: loose

tensile adj **ductile**, stretchy, stretchable, workable, malleable Opposite: rigid

tension n **1 worry**, nervousness, anxiety, stress, strain Opposite: relaxation **2 tautness**, tightness, stiffness, strain, pressure Opposite: relaxation **3 conflict**, ill feeling, friction, hostility, mistrust Opposite: ease

tent n **shelter**, marquee, bivouac, camp, pavilion

tentacle n **limb**, organ, appendage, feeler, antenna

tentative adj **1 hesitant**, cautious, faltering, unsure, timid Opposite: sure **2 provisional**, exploratory, speculative, unconfirmed, indefinite Opposite: definite

tenuous adj **weak**, shaky, unsubstantiated, questionable, feeble Opposite: convincing

tenure n **1 tenancy**, freehold, occupancy, occupation, lease Opposite: ownership **2** (fml) **term**, duration, span, period, time

tepid adj **1 lukewarm**, blood hot, warmish, warm, barely warm Opposite: icy **2 unenthusiastic**, half-hearted, lukewarm, indifferent, apathetic Opposite: enthusiastic

tercentenary n **300th anniversary**, anniversary, commemoration, celebration, festival

tercentennial see tercentenary

term n **1 word**, expression, phrase, name, idiom **2** (fml) **period**, time, stretch, tenure, span ■ v **call**, name, label, dub, designate

terminal adj **fatal**, incurable, deadly, mortal, lethal Opposite: curable ■ n **1 workstation**, computer, monitor **2 station**, airport, rail terminal, passenger terminal, terminus. See COMPARE AND CONTRAST at deadly.

terminally adv **fatally**, incurably, mortally, lethally, critically

terminate v **1 end**, finish, come to an end, conclude, stop Opposite: start **2 dismiss**, let go, lay off, fire (infml), sack (infml) Opposite: hire

termination (fml) n **end**, finish, close, expiry, conclusion Opposite: start

terminology n **terms**, language, expressions, vocabulary, jargon

terminus n **last stop**, station, end of the line, depot, garage

terms n **1 conditions**, stipulations, provisos, provisions, requisites **2 footing**, rapport, relations, relationship, standing **3 language**, expressions, vocabulary, terminology, jargon

terrace n **walkway**, patio, porch, veranda, promenade

terraced adj **1 adjoining**, attached, joined

Opposite: detached **2 in terraces**, stepped, ridged, tiered, split-level

terrain n **land**, topography, territory, ground, landscape

terrestrial adj **1 earthly**, worldly, global, telluric Opposite: extraterrestrial **2 land-dwelling**, surface-dwelling, land, earth-bound

terrible adj **1 extreme**, severe, serious, grave, intense Opposite: mild **2 awful**, dreadful, rotten, appalling, poor Opposite: wonderful **3 horrible**, horrifying, horrific, horrendous, frightful Opposite: pleasant

terribly adv **1 awfully**, appallingly, offensively, intolerably, horribly Opposite: pleasantly **2 very**, extremely, tremendously, exceedingly, incredibly Opposite: slightly

terrific adj **1 enormous**, great, huge, massive, tremendous Opposite: insignificant **2** (infml) **wonderful**, marvelous, excellent, remarkable, superb Opposite: awful

terrifically adv **very**, extremely, tremendously, exceedingly, incredibly Opposite: slightly

terrified adj **frightened**, horrified, scared, scared stiff, petrified Opposite: unafraid

terrify v **frighten**, horrify, scare, petrify, shock Opposite: comfort

terrifying adj **frightening**, petrifying, chilling, startling, alarming Opposite: reassuring

territorial adj **1 regional**, local, land, provincial, national **2 defensive**, protective, possessive, assertive, jealous

territory n **1 land**, terrain, ground, area, region **2 country**, land, state, province, region **3 field**, subject, specialty, area, terrain **4 patch**, beat, domain, pitch, property

terror n **1 fear**, horror, dread, fright, alarm Opposite: security **2** (infml) **nuisance**, troublemaker, imp, pest (infml), ruffian (dated)

terrorism n **intimidation**, terror, resistance, guerrilla warfare, sabotage

terrorist n **guerrilla**, partisan, freedom fighter, saboteur, nonstate actor

terrorize v **terrify**, frighten, scare, threaten, intimidate Opposite: reassure

terror-stricken adj **terrified**, petrified, scared to death, scared stiff, frightened out of your wits Opposite: calm

terse adj **1 abrupt**, curt, short, brusque, clipped Opposite: expansive **2 concise**, brief, succinct, pithy, short and sweet Opposite: wordy

terseness n **1 abruptness**, curtness, shortness, brusqueness, snappishness Opposite: expansiveness **2 concision**, brevity, succinctness, pithiness, economy Opposite: verbosity

test n **1 examination**, exam, quiz, trial, assessment **2 trial run**, trial, test drive, run-through, practice **3 proof**, evidence, sign, criterion, yardstick **4 ordeal**, hardship, tribulation, torment, difficulty ◼ *v* **try**, try out, put to the test, examine, quiz

testament *n* **evidence**, witness, testimony, proof, demonstration

test drive *n* **trial run**, trial, drive, run, spin

test-drive *v* **try out**, try, take for a spin, put something through its paces, drive

tested *adj* **verified**, tried, confirmed, established, experienced *Opposite*: untried

tester *n* **sample**, trial size, free sample, free gift

testify *v* **1 give evidence**, bear witness, appear, swear, state **2** *(fml)* **prove**, show, confirm, bear out, indicate *Opposite*: disprove

testimonial *n* **1 recommendation**, reference, endorsement, confirmation, statement **2 tribute**, honor, reward, celebration, acknowledgment

testimony *n* **1 evidence**, statement, declaration, deposition, affidavit **2 indication**, demonstration, testament, evidence, witness

testiness *(infml)* *n* **irritability**, grumpiness, impatience, touchiness, crabbiness

testing *adj* **challenging**, difficult, taxing, tough, trying *Opposite*: easy

testy *(infml)* *adj* **irritable**, grumpy, impatient, touchy, crabby *Opposite*: even-tempered

tetchiness *(infml)* *see* **testiness**

tetchy *(infml)* *see* **testy**

tether *n* **rope**, chain, lead, rein, tie ◼ *v* **tie up**, tie, hitch, fasten, secure *Opposite*: release

text *n* **1 manuscript**, transcript, typescript, writing, script **2 passage**, piece, article, extract, content **3 textbook**, schoolbook, reader, primer, manual ◼ *v* **communicate**, contact, correspond, send a text message, write

textbook *n* **text**, schoolbook, reader, primer, manual ◼ *adj* **model**, classic, typical, prime, definitive *Opposite*: atypical

textile *n* **fabric**, cloth, material, piece goods, yard goods

textual *adj* **written**, word-based, documented, documentary, stylistic

texture *n* **feel**, touch, surface, consistency, quality

textured *adj* **surfaced**, raised, rough, coarse, bumpy *Opposite*: smooth

thank *v* **express thanks**, show gratitude, express appreciation, show appreciation, be grateful

thankful *adj* **1 grateful**, appreciative, gratified, obliged, beholden *Opposite*: ungrateful **2 pleased**, glad, relieved, happy, satisfied *Opposite*: dissatisfied

thankfully *adv* **1 gratefully**, appreciatively, with gratitude, with thanks *Opposite*: ungratefully **2** *(infml)* **luckily**, happily, mer-

cifully, fortunately, as luck would have it

thankfulness *n* **gratitude**, thanks, appreciation, appreciativeness, recognition *Opposite*: ingratitude

thankless *adj* **unappreciated**, unrewarding, unacknowledged, taken for granted, difficult *Opposite*: rewarding

thanks *n* **gratitude**, appreciation, thankfulness, appreciativeness, recognition *Opposite*: ingratitude

thanks to *prep* **because of**, on account of, due to, owing to, as a result of

thatch *n* **1 roofing**, roof, straw, rushes, reeds **2 thick hair**, hair, shock, mop, tresses

thaw *v* **melt**, defrost, soften, liquefy, warm up *Opposite*: freeze

theater *n* **1 playhouse**, auditorium, moviehouse, lecture theater, hall **2 drama**, plays, dramatic art, the stage, acting **3 sphere**, focus, realm, scene, site

theatergoer *n* **playgoer**, drama-lover, spectator

theatrical *adj* **1 dramatic**, acting, stage, dramaturgical **2 melodramatic**, dramatic, histrionic, exaggerated, affected *Opposite*: restrained

theft *n* **robbery**, stealing, burglary, shoplifting, holdup

theism *n* **faith**, belief, religion, piety *Opposite*: atheism

theme *n* **1 subject**, topic, idea, subject matter, matter **2 melody**, music, refrain, leitmotif, theme tune. *See* COMPARE AND CONTRAST *at* subject.

then *adv* **1 at that time**, at that moment, at that point, at that juncture, then and there *Opposite*: now **2 next**, afterward, subsequently, later, and **3 in that case**, so, therefore **4 on the other hand**, but then, then again, but then again, nonetheless **5 and**, in addition, too, also, besides

thence *(fml or literary)* *adv* **1 from there**, on, onward, forward, thereafter **2 therefore**, so, then, thus *(fml)* **3 from that time on**, thereafter, thenceforth, then, from then on *Opposite*: hitherto

thenceforth, thenceforward *see* **thence**

theological *adj* **religious**, scriptural, doctrinal, dogmatic, spiritual

theology *n* **divinity**, religion, religious studies, doctrine, dogmatics

theorem *n* **proposition**, formula, deduction, statement, proposal

theoretical *adj* **theoretic**, hypothetical, academic, notional, imaginary *Opposite*: concrete

theorist *n* **philosopher**, thinker, theoretician, theorizer, academic

theorize *v* **hypothesize**, conjecture, imagine, conceive, put forward

theory *n* **1 philosophy**, model, concept, system, scheme **2 hypothesis**, premise, presumption, conjecture, supposition

therapeutic *adj* **1 healing**, relaxing, calming, satisfying, helpful *Opposite*: stressful **2 curative**, remedial, corrective, restorative, medicinal *Opposite*: preventive

therapist *n* **psychoanalyst**, psychotherapist, analyst, psychiatrist, counselor

therapy *n* **treatment**, rehabilitation, healing, help, remedy

thereabout *see* **thereabouts**

thereabouts *adv* **around there**, around then, near there, in that area, or so

thereafter *adv* **after that**, from that time on, afterward, subsequently, then *Opposite*: previously

the real McCoy *(infml)* *n* **the real thing**, the genuine article, the very thing, the real deal

thereby *adv* **so**, in that way, by this means, in so doing, in this manner

therefore *adv* **consequently**, so, and so, then, as a result

thereupon *(fml)* *adv* **immediately**, directly, consequently, subsequently, accordingly

thermal *adj* **warm**, hot, tepid, volcanic *Opposite*: cool ■ *n* **warm air**, current, updraft

thermostat *n* **regulator**, control, device, bimetallic strip, sensor

thesaurus *n* **vocabulary list**, word list, lexicon

thesis *n* **1 proposition**, theory, notion, hypothesis, idea *Opposite*: antithesis **2 dissertation**, paper, essay, composition, treatise

thespian *n* **actor**, actress, player, artiste, personality ■ *adj* *(literary)* **theatrical**, dramatic, melodramatic, histrionic, stagy

thick *adj* **1 deep**, broad, fat, wide, chunky *Opposite*: thin **2 dense**, profuse, bushy, impenetrable, copious *Opposite*: thin **3 viscous**, syrupy, gooey, glutinous, heavy *Opposite*: runny **4 filled**, full, covered, crowded, teeming *Opposite*: empty **5 indistinct**, slurred, muffled, hoarse, gruff *Opposite*: clear **6 pronounced**, impenetrable, distinct, extreme, marked *Opposite*: slight

thicken *v* **congeal**, stiffen, set, solidify, clot *Opposite*: thin

thicket *n* **copse**, coppice, grove, covert, undergrowth *Opposite*: clearing

thickness *n* **1 width**, breadth, depth, wideness, chunkiness *Opposite*: thinness **2 viscosity**, stiffness, body, texture, stodginess *Opposite*: fluidity

thickset *adj* **stocky**, heavy, hefty, bulky, solid *Opposite*: slight

thick-skinned *adj* **1 unsympathetic**, insensitive, callous, unfeeling, tactless *Opposite*: sensitive **2 impervious**, unconcerned, unmoved, tough, hardened *Opposite*: thin-skinned

thief *n* **robber**, burglar, shoplifter, pickpocket, bandit

thieve *v* **steal**, rob, shoplift, raid, burgle *Opposite*: return

thimble *n* **cover**, cap, protector

thin *adj* **1 narrow**, fine, slim, threadlike, slender *Opposite*: thick **2 skinny**, slim, slender, bony, lean *Opposite*: fat **3 watery**, weak, dilute, diluted, runny *Opposite*: thick **4 sheer**, gauzy, diaphanous, light, fine *Opposite*: thick **5 reedy**, high, tinny, shrill, squeaky *Opposite*: resonant ■ *v* **water down**, dilute, thin out, weaken, disperse *Opposite*: condense

---

COMPARE AND CONTRAST CORE MEANING: without much flesh, the opposite of fat **thin** having little body fat; **lean** muscular and fit-looking, without excess fat; **slim** pleasingly thin and well-proportioned; **slender** gracefully and attractively thin; **emaciated** unhealthily thin, usually because of illness or starvation; **scraggy** or **scrawny** unpleasantly or unhealthily thin and bony; **skinny** extremely thin.

---

thing *n* **1 object**, article, item, entity, gadget **2 detail**, point, idea, issue, feature **3 occurrence**, event, incident, phenomenon, matter **4** *(infml)* **obsession**, fixation, mania, craze, preoccupation

thingamabob *(infml)* *n* **thing**, whatsit *(infml)*, thingamajig *(infml)*, thingummy *(infml)*, thingy *(infml)*

thingamajig *(infml)* *see* **thingamabob**

things *n* **belongings**, clothes, possessions, equipment, stuff

thingumabob *(infml)* *see* **thingamabob**

thingumajig *(infml)* *see* **thingamabob**

thingummy *(infml)* *see* **thingamabob**

thingy *(infml)* *see* **thingamabob**

think *v* **1 reason**, contemplate, reflect, ponder, deliberate *Opposite*: act **2 believe**, feel, consider, judge, agree *Opposite*: doubt

thinker *n* **philosopher**, theorist, intellectual, academic, scholar *Opposite*: doer

thinking *adj* **rational**, thoughtful, intelligent, discerning, intellectual *Opposite*: unthinking ■ *n* **thoughts**, philosophy, idea, theory, accepted wisdom

think over *v* **reflect**, deliberate, ponder, chew over, contemplate *Opposite*: forget

think tank *n* **committee**, body, advisory board, group of experts, commission

think the world of *v* **have a high regard for**, think highly of, like, have a high opinion of, look up to

think through *v* **consider**, contemplate, ponder, mull over

think twice *v* **think carefully**, be careful, be wary, take heed, consider

think up *v* **invent**, devise, come up with, create, dream up

thinner *n* solvent, diluent, diluter, stripper, cleaner

thinness *n* **1 narrowness**, fineness, slenderness, slimness, shallowness *Opposite*: thickness **2 skinniness**, emaciation, leanness, boniness, lankiness *Opposite*: fatness

thin-skinned *adj* **sensitive**, hypersensitive, easily upset, emotional, touchy *Opposite*: thick-skinned

third party *n* **intermediary**, go-between, arbitrator

third-rate *adj* **poor quality**, inferior, mediocre, poor, shoddy *Opposite*: first-class

thirst *n* **1 dehydration**, dryness, thirstiness, thirsting **2 craving**, desire, longing, hunger, eagerness *Opposite*: apathy ▪ *v* desire, crave, want, ache, pine

thirsty *adj* **1 dehydrated**, dry, parched, thirsting **2 desiring**, craving, eager, keen, hungry *Opposite*: apathetic

thong *n* string, cord, band, strap, belt

thorn *n* prickle, barb, spike, spine, point

thorny *adj* **1 prickly**, barbed, spiky, spiny, pointed **2 tricky**, problematic, awkward, controversial, knotty *Opposite*: uncontroversial

thorough *adj* **1 methodical**, careful, systematic, painstaking, meticulous *Opposite*: careless **2 full**, detailed, systematic, exhaustive, in-depth *Opposite*: careless **3 absolute**, complete, total, out-and-out, utter *Opposite*: partial. *See* COMPARE AND CONTRAST *at* **careful**.

thoroughbred *adj* pedigree, purebred, pure

thoroughfare *n* main road, through street, street, road, way *Opposite*: backstreet

thoroughgoing *adj* **1 full**, detailed, systematic, exhaustive, in-depth *Opposite*: careless **2 complete**, thorough, absolute, total, out-and-out *Opposite*: partial

thoroughly *adv* **1 methodically**, carefully, systematically, painstakingly, meticulously *Opposite*: carelessly **2 completely**, absolutely, totally, utterly, from top to bottom *Opposite*: partially

thoroughness *n* care, attention to detail, meticulousness, scrupulousness, diligence *Opposite*: carelessness

though *conj* although, while, even if, even though, despite the fact that ▪ *adv* however, and yet, yet, nevertheless, nonetheless

thought *n* **1 consideration**, contemplation, thinking, attention, reflection **2 idea**, notion, brain wave, inspiration, concept **3 ideas**, philosophy, thinking, notions, accepted wisdom

thoughtful *adj* **1 considerate**, kind, caring, unselfish, selfless *Opposite*: thoughtless **2 pensive**, meditative, contemplative, brooding, reflective **3 careful**, meticulous, painstaking, thorough, deep *Opposite*: superficial

thoughtfulness *n* **1 consideration**, kindness, care, unselfishness, selflessness *Opposite*: thoughtlessness **2 pensiveness**, meditation, contemplation, reflection, thought **3 care**, attention to detail, attention, thought, carefulness *Opposite*: superficiality

thoughtless *adj* **1 inconsiderate**, unkind, uncaring, selfish, insensitive *Opposite*: thoughtful **2 careless**, heedless, reckless, negligent, unthinking *Opposite*: prudent

thoughtlessness *n* **1 inconsideration**, unkindness, selfishness, insensitivity, tactlessness *Opposite*: thoughtfulness **2 carelessness**, heedlessness, recklessness, negligence, inattention *Opposite*: prudence

thought-provoking *adj* **stimulating**, challenging, provocative, interesting, inspiring *Opposite*: dull

thoughts *n* opinion, view, point of view, feelings, judgment

thrash *v* **1 beat**, whip, give a hiding, spank, smack **2 defeat**, beat, trounce, whip, paste *Opposite*: lose **3 toss** writhe, flail, squirm, roll

thrashing *n* **1 beating** whipping, spanking, battering, lashing **2 defeat**, rout, downfall, conquest, beating *Opposite*: victory

thread *n* **1 cotton**, cord, yarn, strand, fiber **2 idea**, drift, gist, sequence, story line ▪ *v* **1 string**, wind, loop, lace, pass through **2 make your way** pick your way, edge through, squeeze through, negotiate

threadbare *adj* **1 worn**, worn-out, shabby, ragged, thin *Opposite*: new **2 well-worn**, trite, hackneyed clichéd, banal *Opposite*: original

threat *n* **1 warning**, menace, intimidation **2 danger**, risk, hazard, menace, peril *Opposite*: promise

threaten *v* **1 intimidate**, bully, menace, warn, terrorize *Opposite*: reassure **2 endanger**, jeopardize, menace, compromise, cloud *Opposite*: guard **3 loom**, lurk, hover, portend, creep up

threatened *adj* **endangered**, at risk, in peril, vulnerable, dying out *Opposite*: safe

threatening *adj* **1 intimidating**, bullying, menacing, hostile, aggressive *Opposite*: reassuring **2 ominous**, menacing, foreboding, inauspicious, sinister *Opposite*: reassuring

three-dimensional *adj* **1 three-D**, solid, deep *Opposite*: two-dimensional **2 believable**, realistic, convincing, lifelike, true-to-life *Opposite*: two-dimensional

thresh *v* winnow, flail, separate, beat, rub

threshold *n* **1 doorway**, door, doorstep, entrance, entry **2 starting point**, verge, brink, edge, dawn *Opposite*: end **3 level**, limit, maximum, ceiling, outside

thrift *n* **frugality**, economy, carefulness, caution, prudence *Opposite*: extravagance

thrifty *adj* frugal, economical, careful, cautious, prudent Opposite: extravagant

thrill v **excite**, electrify, exhilarate, delight, inspire Opposite: bore ■ n **adventure**, delight, joy, pleasure, quiver Opposite: bore

thrilled adj **excited**, electrified, exhilarated, ecstatic, elated Opposite: disappointed

thriller n **whodunit**, murder mystery, crime novel, detective story, page-turner

thrilling adj **exciting**, electrifying, exhilarating, delightful, inspiring Opposite: boring

thrive v **1 be healthy**, grow well, flourish, bloom, blossom Opposite: decline **2 be successful**, flourish, prosper, boom, bloom Opposite: fail

thriving adj **flourishing**, prosperous, booming, blooming, blossoming Opposite: failing

throaty adj **husky**, hoarse, croaky, gruff, guttural Opposite: piping

throb v **pound**, thump, pulsate, pulse, thud ■ n **pounding**, thump, pulsation, pulse, rhythm

thrombosis n **coagulation**, clotting, blockage, occlusion

throne n **1 seat**, chair, cathedra **2 power**, authority, sovereignty, command, rule

throng n **multitude**, mass, crowd, horde, swarm Opposite: few ■ v **crowd**, pack, jam, cram, inundate Opposite: disperse

throttle v **1 regulate**, control, adjust, correct, check **2 strangle**, choke, garrote, strangulate, suffocate **3 silence**, gag, muzzle, stifle, subdue

through prep **1 across**, past, throughout, within, around **2 during**, throughout, during the course of, in **3 via**, out of, by way of, by means of **4 because of**, owing to, due to, as a result of

through and through adv **completely**, totally, entirely, utterly, at heart Opposite: partially

throughout prep **through**, during, all over, during the course of, in

throughput n **amount**, quantity, data, material, output

throw v **1 fling**, toss, hurl, pitch, lob Opposite: catch **2 drop**, leave, put, cast, toss **3 project**, cast, direct, send out, beam **4 move**, flick, switch, connect, disconnect **5 organize**, arrange, host, give, hold **6** (infml) **confuse**, puzzle, bewilder, perplex, baffle ■ n **1 toss**, lob, heave, pitch, fling **2 rug**, cover, blanket, shawl, coverlet

COMPARE AND CONTRAST CORE MEANING: send something through the air

throw cause something to go through the air using a physical movement; **chuck** (infml) throw something in a reckless or aimless way; **fling** throw something fast using a lot of force; **heave** (infml) throw something large or heavy with

effort in a particular direction; **hurl** throw something with great force; **toss** throw something small or light in a casual or careless way; **cast** throw something to a particular place or into a particular thing, or throw a fishing line or net.

throw away v **1 discard**, throw out, get rid of, dispose of, dump Opposite: keep **2 waste**, squander, fritter away, ruin, spoil Opposite: make the most of

throwaway adj **1 off-the-cuff**, casual, offhand, passing, spontaneous Opposite: intended **2 disposable**, paper, plastic **3 wasteful**, profligate, extravagant, careless, improvident Opposite: frugal

throwback n **reversion**, regression, resemblance, relic, retrogression

throw in v **1 add**, drop in, include, mention, refer to **2 include**, add, give, add on, give away

throw in the towel (infml) v **give in**, surrender, give up, admit defeat, concede Opposite: stand firm

throw off v **1 shake off**, shed, shrug off, get rid of, discard Opposite: keep **2 elude**, evade, escape, give somebody the slip, shake off

throw out v **1 discard**, throw away, get rid of, dispose of, dump Opposite: keep **2 expel**, eject, show the door, dismiss, kick out (infml) Opposite: welcome **3 dismiss**, reject, disallow, turn down, refuse Opposite: pass

throw up v **1 cause**, create, produce, bring to light, pose Opposite: conceal **2** (infml) **abandon**, give up, relinquish, resign, throw away Opposite: keep **3** (infml) **vomit**, be sick, gag, retch, spew

throw yourself into v **engross yourself in**, immerse yourself in, bury yourself in, devote yourself to, commit to

thrum v **strum**, pluck, twang, play, brush

thrust v **1 push**, shove, force, propel, prod **2 stretch**, extend, stretch out, reach, reach out ■ n **1 shove**, push, prod, lunge, drive **2 attack**, assault, offensive, push, drive **3 point**, gist, meaning, focus, direction **4 power**, force, propulsion, momentum, impetus

thug n **brute**, criminal, mugger, hoodlum, gangster

thumb v **flick through**, flip through, leaf through, skim, browse through Opposite: pore over

thumbs down (infml) n **disapproval**, rejection, denial, no, veto Opposite: thumbs up (infml)

thumbs up (infml) n **approval**, acceptance, agreement, endorsement, ratification Opposite: thumbs down (infml)

thump v **punch**, hit, whack, pummel

thumping (infml) adj **large**, huge, enormous, impressive ■ adv **very**, exceptionally, extremely, inordinately, really

thunder n din, boom, rumble, roar, clap ■
v **1 boom**, roar, resound, rumble, clap
2 shout, bellow, boom, roar, yell *Opposite*:
whisper

thunderbolt n **1 thunderclap**, clap of thunder,
thunder, crash of thunder **2 shock**, surprise, bolt from the blue, eye opener, kick
in the face

thunderclap *see* **thunderbolt**

thunderous adj **deafening**, loud, roaring,
booming, crashing

thunderstorm n storm, downpour, deluge,
rainstorm, cloudburst

thunderstruck adj **incredulous**, amazed,
taken aback, stunned, shocked

thus (fml) adv **1 therefore**, consequently, as a
result, so, accordingly **2 like this**, in this
way, in this manner, as follows, like so

thus far adv **up till now**, up to now, yet, so
far, hitherto

thwack n **smack**, clap, knock, rap, whack ■
v **hit**, strike, whack, smack, slap

thwart v **frustrate**, spoil, prevent, foil, ruin
Opposite: aid

tic n **twitch**, spasm, convulsion, fit, paroxysm

ticket n **1 permit**, travel document, voucher,
receipt, coupon **2 label**, tag, tab, marker,
sticker

tickle v **1 prickle**, irritate, scratch, itch
2 amuse, entertain, delight, please, make
somebody laugh

tickler n **reminder**, prompt, follow-up,
chaser

ticklish adj **tricky**, delicate, thorny,
awkward, problematic *Opposite*: straightforward

tickly adj **prickly**, itchy, irritating, scratchy

tick off (infml) v **annoy**, irritate, bother, get
on your nerves, bug (infml)

tidal wave n **1 tsunami**, bore, eagre **2 surge**,
wave, swell, deluge

tidbit n **1 morsel**, taste, bite, delicacy, goody
2 gossip, news, scandal, latest, scrap

tide n **current**, flow, surge, wave, drift

tidiness n **neatness**, trimness, orderliness,
order, regulation

tidings (literary) n **news**, notification, intelligence, information, word

tidy adj **1 neat**, orderly, shipshape, in order,
organized *Opposite*: untidy **2 smart**,
immaculate, well-groomed, dapper,
spruce *Opposite*: untidy **3 large**, fair considerable, sizable, reasonable *Opposite*:
small ■ v **neaten**, tidy up, clear up,
straighten, arrange

tie v **1 bind**, fasten, secure, attach, lash *Opposite*: untie **2 be equal**, draw, finish equal,
finish even, be neck and neck (infml) ■
n **1 bond**, link, connection, relation, join
2 draw, dead heat, equal finish, stalemate

tiebreaker n **deciding game**, tie-break,
decider

tied up adj **unavailable**, engaged, occupied,
busy, otherwise engaged *Opposite*: available

tie in v **connect**, associate, relate, link, join
Opposite: disconnect

tie-in n **link**, relationship, connection,
linkup, association

tie in knots v **confuse**, muddle, mix up,
baffle, bewilder

tier n **row**, level, layer, stage, rank

tie the knot (infml) v **get married**, marry, wed,
walk down the aisle, get hitched (infml)

tie up v **1 lash**, truss, fasten, lace, tie *Opposite*: untie **2 complete**, clinch, finalize,
resolve, end

tie-up n **1 delay**, holdup, stoppage, obstruction, hitch **2 link** connection, linkup, association, relationship

tiff n **quarrel**, argument, falling-out, squabble, disagreement

tight adj **1 taut**, stretched, tense, firm, stiff
Opposite: loose **2 close-fitting**, body-
hugging, skintight, snug, fitted *Opposite*:
baggy **3 firm**, fixed, strong, unyielding,
tough *Opposite*: weak **4 strict**, stringent,
harsh, firm, tough *Opposite*: lax **5 mean**,
stingy, tightfisted, parsimonious, niggardly *Opposite*: generous **6 difficult**, problematic, awkward, tricky, tough *Opposite*:
easy

tighten v **make tighter**, tauten, constrict,
stiffen, squeeze *Opposite*: loosen

tighten your belt v **cut back**, economize,
retrench, pull in your horns

tightfisted adj **mean**, stingy, tight, grasping,
miserly *Opposite*: generous

tightfistedness n **scrimping**, meanness,
stinginess, tightness, miserliness *Opposite*: generosity

tightfitting adj **tight**, close-fitting, snug,
figure-hugging, skintight *Opposite*: baggy

tightknit adj **closely connected**, integrated,
united, interwoven, intertwined

tight-lipped adj **silent**, uncommunicative,
reticent, withdrawn, taciturn *Opposite*:
loquacious

tightness n **tension**, tautness, stiffness, rigidity *Opposite*: looseness

tight spot n **tight corner**, difficult position,
tricky situation, predicament, quandary

till n **cash register**, cash box, box, drawer,
tray ■ v **plow**, dig, cultivate, turn over, rake

tilt v **tip**, slope, slant, lean, list *Opposite*:
straighten up ■ n **slope**, slant, angle, gradient, incline

tilted adj **slanted**, slanting, sloping, sloped,
lopsided *Opposite*: level

timber n **trees**, woods, timberland, woodland

timbre n **tone**, pitch, resonance, sound,
quality

time *n* **1 period**, while, spell, stretch, stint **2 occasion**, instance, moment, point, instant **3 era**, age, epoch, period, season **4 tempo**, speed, rhythm, beat, measure ■ *v* **1 count**, measure, clock, calculate, record **2 schedule**, program, timetable, plan, arrange

---

WORD BANK
❑ **types of time periods** calendar month, fortnight, leap year, lunar month, midweek, month, quarter, semester, trimester, week, weekend, year

---

time bomb *n* tinderbox, volcano, accident waiting to happen, flashpoint

time-consuming *adj* laborious, slow, inefficient, long, onerous *Opposite*: time-saving

time-honored *adj* traditional, customary, habitual, age-old, respected *Opposite*: recent

time lag *n* lapse, interlude, gap, interval, pause

timeless *adj* eternal, ageless, enduring, undying, everlasting *Opposite*: ephemeral

timelessness *n* agelessness, endurance, endlessness, changelessness, immutability *Opposite*: transience

timely *adj* opportune, well-timed, appropriate, apt, judicious *Opposite*: untimely

time off *n* leisure, free time, spare time, leave, time out

time out *n* rest, breathing space, respite, break, leave

timepiece *n* chronometer, timer, clock

timesaving *adj* quick, streamlined, efficient, effective, improved *Opposite*: time-consuming

timescale *n* timetable, schedule, time, period, span

timeserver *n* opportunist, weathercock, waverer, equivocator, vacillator *Opposite*: stalwart

timespan *n* duration, period, extent, length, span

timetable *n* schedule, agenda, plan, program, calendar

timeworn *adj* **1 shabby**, tattered, threadbare, worn, well-worn *Opposite*: brand-new **2 hackneyed**, overworked, stale, trite, stock *Opposite*: original

timid *adj* nervous, shy, fearful, timorous, diffident *Opposite*: bold

timidity *n* nervousness, shyness, fearfulness, timorousness, diffidence *Opposite*: boldness

timing *n* judgment, effectiveness, control, mastery, technique

timorous *adj* nervous, fearful, timid, frightened, scared *Opposite*: brave

timorousness *n* nervousness, fearfulness, timicity, shyness, fear *Opposite*: bravery

tin *n* box, container, caddy, cake tin, cookie tin

tincture *n* **1 solution**, essence, distillate, extract, distillation **2 tinge**, tint, hint, nuance, tone

tinder *n* kindling, firewood, brushwood, sticks, twigs

tinderbox *n* flashpoint, crucible, volcano, no-go area, accident waiting to happen

ting *v* ding, ting-a-ling, ring, ping, tinkle

tinge *n* hint, touch, dash, drop, trace ■ *v* tint, color, stain, shade, mix

tingle *v* prickle, sting, itch, tickle, prick ■ *n* sting, prickle, itch, tickle, prick

tingling *adj* prickly, itchy, scratchy, burning, stinging

tinker *v* **1 fiddle**, tamper, interfere, fool around, play **2 repair**, mend, fix, put right

tinkle *v* ring, jingle, clink, chink, ding

tinny *adj* **1 thin**, high, metallic, shrill, ringing *Opposite*: resonant **2 shoddy**, cheap, worthless, inferior, poor

tinsel *n* **1 metallic thread**, glitter, streamer, spangle, decoration **2 showiness**, glitz, flashiness, pretentiousness, glitter

tint *n* **1 shade**, color, hue, touch, trace **2 rinse**, dye, colorant, streak, highlight ■ *v* dye, color, shade, streak, rinse

tiny *adj* minute, miniature, minuscule, small, little *Opposite*: enormous

tip *v* **1 tilt**, slope, slant, lean, list *Opposite*: straighten **2 knock over**, pour, empty, spill, knock **3 give**, slip, reward, pay, bribe ■ *n* **1 slope**, slant, angle, gradient, incline **2 gratuity**, gift, reward, bonus, extra **3 warning**, clue, pointer, prompt, hint **4 hint**, suggestion, idea, pointer

tip off *v* warn, inform, advise, forewarn, tell

tip-off *(infml)* *n* warning, clue, hint, pointer, prompt

tipster *n* adviser, consultant, analyst, informant, informer

tiptoe *v* creep, sneak, steal, skulk, glide *Opposite*: stamp

tiptop *(infml)* *adj* first-rate, excellent, superb, first-class, superlative *Opposite*: dreadful

tirade *n* outburst, rant, diatribe, harangue, lecture

tire *v* exhaust, wear out, drain, fatigue, enervate

tired *adj* **1 weary**, sleepy, drowsy, fatigued, exhausted *Opposite*: energetic **2 bored**, weary, sick, jaded, dissatisfied **3 overused**, trite, hackneyed, clichéd, old *Opposite*: fresh

tiredness *n* weariness, sleepiness, fatigue, drowsiness, exhaustion *Opposite*: energy

tireless *adj* untiring, diligent, determined, unstinting, assiduous *Opposite*: weary

tirelessness *n* diligence, determination, assiduousness, indefatigability, industriousness *Opposite*: weariness

tiresome adj **annoying**, irritating, tedious, wearisome, dull

tiring adj **exhausting**, strenuous, arduous, wearing, demanding

tissue n 1 **soft tissue**, fleshy tissue, flesh, matter, material 2 **web**, net, network, mass, series

titan n **giant**, superman, superwoman, genius Opposite: nobody

titanic adj **colossal**, monumental, immense, gigantic, massive Opposite: insignificant

tit for tat n **retaliation**, revenge, reprisal, vengeance, retribution

tithe n **church tax**, tax, duty, contribution, portion

titivate v **do up**, dress up, adorn, decorate, beautify

titivation n **adornment**, embellishment, beautification, prettification, enhancement

title n 1 **name**, heading, label, designation 2 **championship**, trophy, cup, award 3 **ownership**, entitlement, deed, right, claim ■ v **call**, name, label, designate, refer to

titled adj **noble**, aristocratic, patrician, blue-blooded, upper-class

title deed n **title**, deed, document, proof of ownership, ownership

titleholder n 1 **champion**, winner, reigning champion, cupholder 2 **owner**, proprietor, possessor, vendor, holder

title page n **front page**, title, opening page, frontispiece

tittle-tattle n **gossip**, scandal, rumor, hearsay, tale ■ v **gossip**, chatter, prattle, yak (infml), blather (infml)

titular adj **nominal**, in name only, supposed, ostensible, so-called Opposite: actual

tizzy (infml) n **panic**, dither, flap (infml), lather (infml), state (infml)

T-junction n **junction**, intersection, fork, road junction

toady n **flatterer**, sycophant, groveler, brown-noser (slang) ■ v **grovel**, fawn, flatter, kowtow, crawl (infml)

toadying n **obsequiousness**, sycophancy, servility, flattery, fawning ■ adj **obsequious**, sycophantic, servile, flattering, fawning

to all intents and purposes adv **practically**, in practice, virtually, as good as, pretty much (infml)

toast n 1 **salute**, tribute, pledge, health 2 **darling**, favorite, delight, sweetheart ■ v 1 **grill**, brown, crisp, heat, cook 2 **drink to**, pledge, salute, drink the health of

toasty adj **warm**, snug, cozy, pleasant Opposite: chilly

toboggan n **sled**, sleigh, bobsled, luge ■ v 1 **sled**, sleigh, luge 2 **slip**, slide, hurtle, tumble

tocsin n **alarm**, warning, bell, siren, signal

to date adv **up to the present time**, so far, up to now, as yet, thus far

today adv **nowadays**, these days, currently, now, at the moment Opposite: yesteryear

toddle v 1 **totter**, patter, pad, waddle 2 (infml) **walk**, stroll, amble

toddler n **child**, baby, tot (infml), kid (infml)

to-do (infml) n **fuss**, commotion, bother, scene, ado

toehold n **start**, advantage, starting point, jumping-off place, beginning

together adv 1 **jointly**, as one, mutually, in concert, collectively Opposite: alone 2 **simultaneously**, at once, at the same time, concurrently all together Opposite: separately ■ adj (infml) **composed**, calm, collected, organized, cool Opposite: flustered

togetherness n **closeness**, intimacy, devotedness, friendship, inseparability Opposite: estrangement

together with prep **as well as**, accompanied by, with, alongside, in addition to

toggle n 1 **fastener**, peg, button, buckle, clasp 2 **switch**, key, command, button, lever ■ v **change**, change over, switch, move, transfer

togs (infml) n **clothes**, outfit, dress, clothing, rig out (infml)

toil n **work**, labor, drudgery, slog, hard work Opposite: relaxation ■ v **labor**, strive, work, slog, slave Opposite: take it easy

toilet n 1 **lavatory**, chamber pot, urinal, latrine, water closet 2 **bathroom**, powder room, restroom, washroom, comfort station 3 (fml) **washing**, dressing, grooming, bathing, toilette

toiletry n **beauty product**, skincare product, cosmetic product

WORD BANK

☐ **types of toiletries** aftershave, bath salts, body scrub, body wash, bubble bath, cleanser, cleansing cream, cologne, conditioner, cotton balls, dental floss, deodorant, eau de cologne, eau de toilette, face cream, facial mask, facial scrub, foam bath, hair gel, hair mousse, hair spray, hand cream, moisturizer, mouthwash, night cream, perfume, shampoo, shaving cream, shower gel, soap, talcum powder, toilet water, toner, toothpaste

toilette (literary) n **dressing**, grooming, bathing, getting dressed, preparations

toilet water n **cologne**, eau de cologne, eau de toilette, scent, aftershave

token n 1 **voucher**, coupon, slip, coin 2 **mark**, demonstration, sign, symbol, indication 3 **keepsake**, remembrance, souvenir, reminder, memento ■ adj **symbolic**, nominal, perfunctory, empty

tolerable adj 1 **bearable**, acceptable, endurable, supportable (literary) Opposite: unbearable 2 **reasonable**, average, passable, fair, adequate Opposite: intolerable

tolerance n **broad-mindedness**, acceptance, open-mindedness, lenience, charity Opposite: intolerance

tolerant *adj* **accepting,** easygoing, lenient, broad-minded, open-minded *Opposite*: intolerant

tolerate *v* **stand,** bear, abide, put up with, endure *Opposite*: forbid

toleration *n* **allowance,** acceptance, open-mindedness, broad-mindedness, liberality *Opposite*: prejudice

toll *n* **1 fee,** tax, levy, payment, duty **2 peal,** ring, ding-dong, clang, ding-a-ling

tollbooth *n* **barrier,** gate, kiosk, booth, ticket office

toll-free *adj* **free,** complimentary, gratis, costless

tollgate *n* **barrier,** gate, entrance, exit

tomb *n* **burial chamber,** catacomb, grave, burial place, crypt

tomboyish *adj* **boyish,** unladylike, mannish, boisterous, unruly

tombstone *n* **headstone,** gravestone, monument

tome *n* **book,** volume, digest, work

tomfoolery *(infml)* *n* **silliness,** horseplay, mischief, clowning, fooling around *Opposite*: sensibleness

ton *(infml)* *n* **mass,** mountain, lot, ocean, stack *(infml)*

tonality *n* **tone,** timbre, pitch, sound, sound quality *Opposite*: atonality

tone *n* **1 quality,** manner, character, attitude, tendency **2 sound,** pitch, quality, timbre **3 character,** atmosphere, feel, ambiance **4 color,** hue, tint, tinge, shade

tone down *v* **dilute,** moderate, soften, restrain, modulate *Opposite*: intensify

toneless *adj* **colorless,** expressionless, monotonous, neutral, monochrome *Opposite*: vibrant

tone up *v* **firm up,** strengthen, get in shape, exercise

tongue *n* **language,** patois, dialect, speech, idiom. *See* COMPARE AND CONTRAST *at* **language.**

tongue-in-cheek *adj* **lighthearted,** ironic, insincere, flippant, whimsical *Opposite*: serious

tongue-tied *adj* **speechless,** shy, awkward, silent, inarticulate *Opposite*: talkative

tonic *n* **boost,** fillip, stimulant, shot in the arm, livener

tonnage *n* **weight,** heaviness, capacity, size

tons *adv* **a lot,** a great deal, lots, loads *(infml)* ■ *n (infml)* **lots,** plenty, oodles *(infml)*, loads *(infml)*, piles *(infml)*

tony *(infml)* *adj* **elegant,** expensive, stylish, fashionable, posh *(infml)*

too *adv* **1 also,** as well, in addition, besides, moreover **2 excessively,** overly, extremely, exceedingly, overmuch *Opposite*: insufficiently

tool *n* **instrument,** implement, device, means, utensil

WORD BANK

❑ **types of carpentry tools** awl, bradawl, drill, hammer, jigsaw, mallet, plane, sander, saw, vise

❑ **types of cosmetic tools** comb, curling iron, emery board, hairbrush, hair dryer, nailbrush, nail clippers, nail file, nail scissors, razor, shaving brush, tweezers

❑ **types of general tools** bellows, blowtorch, crowbar, file, grease gun, jack, jimmy, lathe, machine tool, pincers, pliers, plumb line, plunger, poker, pump, punch, rasp, screwdriver, socket wrench, soldering iron, spade, tongs, trowel, wrench

❑ **types of medical instruments** forceps, lancet, probe, scalpel, speculum, stethoscope, syringe

tooth *n* **1 fang,** tusk, chopper *(slang)*, chomper *(slang)* **2 indentation,** projection, tine, cog, prong

WORD BANK

❑ **types of teeth** baby tooth, bucktooth *(infml)*, canine, chopper, cuspid, denture, eyetooth, fang, incisor, milk tooth, molar, premolar, wisdom tooth

toothless *adj* **powerless,** useless, impotent, ineffective, ineffectual *Opposite*: effective

toothsome *adj* **delicious,** palatable, tasty, appetizing, mouthwatering *Opposite*: unappetizing

tootle *(infml)* *v* **1 drive slowly,** go slowly, meander, wend your way, crawl *Opposite*: dash **2 hoot,** sound, honk, beep, sound the horn ■ *n* **drive,** meander, crawl *Opposite*: dash

top *n* **1 pinnacle,** summit, peak, apex, crown *Opposite*: bottom **2 cork,** lid, cap, cover, stopper ■ *adj* **1 highest,** topmost, maximum, uppermost *Opposite*: bottom **2 best,** first, chief, principal, important ■ *v* **outdo,** surpass, better, improve on, cap

WORD BANK

❑ **types of sweaters** cardigan, crew neck, jersey, mock turtle, pullover, sweater, turtleneck, twin set, V neck

❑ **types of tops** basque, blouse, bodice, body warmer, bolero, bustier, gilet, halter, jerkin, polo shirt, shirt, smock, surplice, sweatshirt, T-shirt, tabard, tank top, tee, tube top, tunic, vest, vestment

top-class *adj* **best,** world-class, first-class, first-rate, topflight

top drawer *n* **1 cream,** crème de la crème, elite, pick, best **2 aristocracy,** nobility, high society, gentry, upper class

top-drawer *adj* **1 topflight,** best, first-rate, first-class, premium **2 upper class,** high class, noble, titled, aristocratic

topflight *adj* **top-drawer,** best, first-rate, first-class, premium

top-heavy *adj* **unbalanced,** unstable, uneven, disproportionate, lopsided

topic *n* theme, subject, matter, issue, subject matter. *See* COMPARE AND CONTRAST *at* **subject**.

topical *adj* up-to-date, interesting, current, newsworthy, contemporary

topicality *n* interest, relevance, newsworthiness, current interest, contemporaneity

top-level *adj* highest, most senior, most important, most powerful

topmost *adj* highest, uppermost, top, peak *Opposite*: bottommost

topnotch *(infml) adj* top-class, first-rate, superior, first-class, excellent *Opposite*: inferior

top-of-the-range *adj* best, most expensive, exclusive, premium, premier *Opposite*: basic

topographical *adj* geographic, structural, natural, landscape, environmental

topography *n* features, landscape, geography, structure, countryside

topping *n* top layer, coating, glaze, garnish, frosting *Opposite*: filling

topple *v* 1 fall over, tip over, collapse, fall, tumble 2 bring down, overthrow, depose, oust, remove

top-quality *adj* choice, select, fine, rare

top-ranking *adj* high-ranking, senior, important, powerful, high-level

top-rated *adj* popular, well-liked, top, top ten, number one *Opposite*: unpopular

tops *(infml) adv* at most, as a maximum, at the most, max *(slang)*

top-secret *adj* undercover, covert, secret, clandestine, restricted

topsoil *n* soil, earth, loam, dirt, peat

topspin *n* forward spin, spin, momentum, force, impetus

topsy-turvy *adj* confused, disordered, chaotic, in disarray, upside down *Opposite*: orderly

top up *v* 1 refill, replenish, refuel, freshen 2 make up, augment, complete, chip in *(infml)*

tor *n* peak, crag, outcrop, rock face

torchlight *n* beam, light, illumination, lamplight

torment *v* annoy, tease, plague, persecute, taunt *Opposite*: comfort ■ *n* 1 anguish, suffering, agony, distress, pain *Opposite*: pleasure 2 nuisance, bane, plague, annoyance, irritation *Opposite*: delight

tormented *adj* anguished, tortured, distressed, grief-stricken, plagued

tormenter *see* **tormentor**

tormentor *n* oppressor, tyrant, persecutor, bully, teaser

torn *adj* 1 ripped, frayed, ragged, tattered, shabby 2 undecided, of two minds, uncertain, in a quandary, in a dilemma *Opposite*: decided

tornado *n* hurricane, whirlwind, cyclone, storm, windstorm

torpedo *(infml) v* ruin, destroy, wreck, spoil, thwart

torpid *adj* lazy, languorous, listless, sluggish, apathetic *Opposite*: energetic

torpor *n* inactivity, inertia, indolence, languor, lethargy *Opposite*: excitement

torque *n* rotating force, rotation, twisting, turning, turning force

torrent *n* 1 rush, flood, flow, deluge, gush *Opposite*: trickle 2 outburst, flood, flow, tide, stream

torrential *adj* heavy, pouring, driving, lashing, drenching *Opposite*: light

torrid *adj* 1 hot, stifling, sweltering, boiling, burning *Opposite*: cool 2 passionate, amorous, impassioned, erotic, steamy *(infml)*

torsion *n* twisting, turning, turning force, rotation, spin

tort *n* wrongful act, unlawful act, illegal act, offense, misdemeanor

tortuous *adj* 1 twisting, winding, convoluted, circuitous, indirect *Opposite*: direct 2 complex, complicated, intricate, difficult, involved *Opposite*: simple 3 devious, deceitful, crafty, sly, artful *Opposite*: straightforward

torture *v* torment, afflict, persecute, brutalize, punish ■ *n* agony, torment, anguish, pain, suffering

torturer *n* intimidator, bully, pesterer, harasser, teaser

toss *v* 1 throw, pitch, fling, lob, hurl 2 mix, stir, blend, mix up ■ *v* 1 lob, throw, pitch, heave, fling. *See* COMPARE AND CONTRAST *at* **throw**.

toss-up *n* even chance, chance, risk, fifty-fifty, luck of the draw

tot *n* 1 dram, finger, thimbleful, snifter *(infml)* 2 *(infml)* toddler, child, baby, small child, kid *(infml)*

total *n* sum, whole, entirety, full amount, totality ■ *adj* 1 entire, whole, full, complete, aggregate *Opposite*: partial 2 absolute, unmitigated, complete, unreserved, out-and-out ■ *v* 1 add up, count up, tot up, calculate, sum 2 amount to, add up to, come to, equal, make

totalitarian *adj* authoritarian, tyrannous, one-party, oppressive, autocratic *Opposite*: democratic

totalitarianism *n* despotism, absolutism, tyranny, autocracy, authoritarianism

totality *n* entirety, whole, total, sum, full amount *Opposite*: part

totally *adv* completely, entirely, absolutely, wholly, fully *Opposite*: partly

tote *(infml) v* 1 carry, cart, lug, haul, heave 2 brandish, carry, hold, wield, bear

totem *n* 1 ritual object, sacred symbol, icon, charm, talisman 2 symbol, representation, emblem, image, icon

totemic adj **symbolic**, emblematic, iconic, representative

to the letter adv **exactly**, precisely, literally, word for word, accurately

to the point adj **relevant**, apt, apposite, pertinent, germane *Opposite*: irrelevant

totter v **walk unsteadily**, stagger, wobble, teeter, stumble

tot up v **add up**, total, count up, add together, calculate

touch n 1 **pat**, tap, stroke, fondle, feel 2 **trace**, bit, dash, drop, hint 3 **style**, facility, gift, knack, ability ■ v 1 **handle**, feel, finger, tap, stroke 2 **converge**, meet, come into contact, join, contact *Opposite*: separate 3 **move**, affect, upset, stir, touch a chord 4 **match**, come close to, meet, rival, equal

touch-and-go adj **uncertain**, unpredictable, doubtful, unknown, risky *Opposite*: certain

touch down v **land**, alight, come down, set down, arrive *Opposite*: take off

touchdown n 1 **landing**, descent, arrival *Opposite*: blastoff 2 **score**, try, point

touched adj 1 **affected**, moved, warmed, heartened, impressed *Opposite*: unmoved 2 *(literary)* **tinged**, tinted, shaded, marked, streaked

touchiness n **irritability**, impatience, grumpiness, cantankerousness, moodiness *Opposite*: composure

touching adj **moving**, poignant, stirring, tender, pitiful. *See* COMPARE AND CONTRAST *at* moving.

touch on v **deal with**, refer to, mention, treat, allude to

touchstone n **criterion**, standard, benchmark, yardstick, hallmark

touch up v **retouch**, restore, freshen, freshen up, refurbish

touchy adj 1 **sensitive**, quick-tempered, impatient, petulant, cantankerous *Opposite*: even-tempered 2 **delicate**, sensitive, tricky, awkward, ticklish

touchy-feely *(infml)* adj **demonstrative**, expressive, effusive, unreserved, emotional *Opposite*: undemonstrative

tough adj 1 **threatening**, rough, hard, harsh, dangerous *Opposite*: pleasant 2 **durable**, strong, sturdy, robust, hardy *Opposite*: weak 3 **difficult**, hard, demanding, exacting, arduous *Opposite*: easy 4 **severe**, strict, rigid, inflexible, stern *Opposite*: lenient 5 **hard**, chewy, stringy, stiff, leathery *Opposite*: tender. *See* COMPARE AND CONTRAST *at* hard.

toughen v **strengthen**, harden, build up, reinforce, fortify *Opposite*: weaken

toughened adj **hardened**, reinforced, strengthened, fortified, unbreakable

tough-minded adj **realistic**, determined, tough, single-minded, resilient *Opposite*: weak-willed

toughness n 1 **durability**, hardiness, robustness, roughness, stoutness *Opposite*: flimsiness 2 **hardness**, chewiness, stringiness, stiffness *Opposite*: tenderness 3 **roughness**, harshness, hardness, danger *Opposite*: pleasantness 4 **difficulty**, arduousness, strenuousness, challenge, trickiness *Opposite*: ease 5 **severity**, strictness, rigidity, inflexibility, firmness *Opposite*: leniency

toupee n **wig**, hairpiece, hair extension

tour n **trip**, excursion, expedition, outing, journey ■ v **sightsee**, explore, visit, travel around, go around

tourism n **travel**, travel industry, leisure industry, service sector

tourist n **traveler**, sightseer, visitor, vacationer, day tripper

touristy adj **crowded**, busy, much-frequented, popular, overvisited *Opposite*: quiet

tournament n **contest**, competition, event, tourney, game

tourniquet n **band**, strap, bandage

tousle v **tangle**, ruffle, rumple, dishevel, disorder *Opposite*: tidy

tousled adj **disheveled**, messy, tangled, ruffled, windswept *Opposite*: tidy

tout v **advertise**, hype, flaunt, push, publicize *Opposite*: understate ■ n **seller**, hawker, peddler, vendor

tow v **pull**, drag, draw, haul, lug. *See* COMPARE AND CONTRAST *at* pull.

toward prep 1 **in the direction of**, to, near, just before 2 **regarding**, concerning, for, about, on

towel n **cloth**, bath towel, hand towel, guest towel, dishtowel ■ v **dry**, rub down, rub, wipe, dab

tower v 1 **loom**, overlook, be head and shoulders above, soar, rise 2 **surpass**, exceed, excel, top, transcend

towering adj **high**, tall, soaring, lofty, immense *Opposite*: short

tower of strength *(infml)* n **rock**, mainstay, anchor, helper, advocate

town n **municipality**, city, settlement, township, metropolis. *See* COMPARE AND CONTRAST *at* city.

townie *(infml)* n **town dweller**, city dweller, urbanite, city slicker

townsfolk n **townspeople**, populace, residents, inhabitants

township n **small town**, urban area, settlement, town, hamlet

townspeople n **townsfolk**, populace, residents, inhabitants

towpath n **path**, footpath, canal path, track, pathway

towrope n **towline**, rope, line, cable, cord

toxic adj **poisonous**, deadly, lethal, noxious, contaminated *Opposite*: harmless

toxicity n **poisonousness**, venomousness, deadliness, noxiousness, harmfulness Opposite: harmlessness

toxin n **poison**, pollutant, contaminant, venom

toy with v 1 **flirt with**, tease, philander 2 **think about**, consider, ponder, contemplate, entertain Opposite: dismiss 3 **play with**, fiddle with, fidget with, handle, finger

trace v 1 **draw**, outline, copy, mark out, sketch 2 **find**, locate, discover, hunt down, track down ■ n 1 **sign**, indication, evidence, remnant, residue 2 **suggestion**, hint, dash, drop, touch

tracery n **decoration**, pattern, design, interlacing, ornamentation

track n 1 **path**, pathway, road, way, footpath 2 **trail**, footprints, footsteps, path, trace ■ v **follow**, hunt down, chase, pursue, stalk

track down v **find**, hunt down, catch, capture, discover

tracker n **trailer**, follower, chaser, hunter, shadow

tract n 1 **area**, territory, zone, region, expanse 2 **pamphlet**, article, treatise, leaflet

tractability n 1 **docility**, controllability, manageability, obedience, manipulability Opposite: intractability 2 **malleability**, pliability, workability, ductility, elasticity Opposite: intractability

tractable adj 1 **docile**, controllable, manageable, obedient, manipulable Opposite: intractable 2 **malleable**, pliable, workable, ductile, elastic Opposite: intractable

traction n 1 **adhesive friction**, grip, purchase, adhesion 2 **power**, tractive force, pull, tow, tug

trade n 1 **commerce**, business, industry, market, dealings 2 **occupation**, job, employment, line of work, profession 3 **customers**, public, patrons, custom, clientele ■ v 1 **deal**, buy and sell, do business, operate, traffic 2 **exchange**, barter, negotiate, swap (infml), dicker (infml)

trade fair n **exhibition**, exposition, fair, display, show

trade in v **exchange**, redeem, give in part payment, barter, swap (infml)

trade-in n **part exchange**, exchange, deal, transaction, swap (infml)

trademark n 1 **symbol**, logo, emblem, brand 2 **characteristic**, feature, trait, attribute, facet

trade name n **brand name**, brand, trademark, name, registered trademark

tradeoff n **compromise**, adjustment, interchange, transaction, balance

trader n **dealer**, buyer, seller, broker, agent

tradition n **custom**, institution, ritual, habit, convention Opposite: innovation. See COMPARE AND CONTRAST at **habit**.

traditional adj **usual**, conventional, customary, established, fixed Opposite: progressive

traditionalism n **conventionalism**, conservatism, conformity, orthodoxy, fundamentalism Opposite: progressivism

traditionalist n **conservative**, purist, fundamentalist, conformist Opposite: progressive ■ adj **traditional**, conservative, purist, orthodox, conventional Opposite: progressive

traditionalistic see **traditionalist**

traduce v **criticize**, disparage, malign, run down, defame Opposite: praise

traffic n 1 **road traffic**, traffic flow, circulation, stream of traffic, rush-hour traffic 2 **transportation**, movement, passage, toing and froing, travel 3 **trade**, business, commerce, dealings, transactions ■ v 1 **have dealings**, deal in, trade, trade in, transfer 2 **smuggle**, run, handle

traffic jam n **bottleneck**, gridlock, tie-up, holdup

tragedy n **disaster**, calamity, catastrophe, misfortune, heartbreak Opposite: joy

tragic adj **sad**, disastrous, catastrophic, heartbreaking, heartrending Opposite: joyous

tragicomic adj **bittersweet**, poignant, affecting, moving

trail v 1 **follow**, track, tail, shadow, trace 2 **tug**, drag, pull, draw, tow Opposite: push 3 **drop back**, lag behind, fall behind, straggle, follow on Opposite: lead ■ n 1 **path**, track, way, road, footpath 2 **track**, footprints, footsteps, paw marks, paw prints

trail away v **fade**, disappear, grow faint, die away, diminish Opposite: intensify

trailblazer n **pioneer**, leader, innovator, entrepreneur, architect

trailer n **clip**, preview, ad (infml), promo (infml)

train n 1 **procession**, file, convoy, line 2 **sequence**, chain, succession, string, series ■ v 1 **teach**, coach, educate, instruct, tutor 2 **exercise**, work out, stay fit, stay in shape 3 **aim**, direct, focus, line up, point. See COMPARE AND CONTRAST at **teach**.

trained adj **skilled**, qualified, proficient, accomplished, competent

trainee n **apprentice**, learner, novice, beginner Opposite: trainer

trainer n **coach**, teacher, guide, instructor, mentor Opposite: trainee

training n 1 **education**, schooling, teaching, guidance, tuition 2 **exercise**, working out, physical activity, drill

traipse v **walk**, roam, rove, wander, ramble

trait n **mannerism**, peculiarity, attribute, characteristic, feature

traitor n **conspirator**, collaborator, turncoat, defector, deserter Opposite: loyalist

traitorous adj **disloyal**, faithless, duplicitous, deceitful, treacherous Opposite: loyal

trajectory n **route**, course, flight, path, line

trammel n **restriction**, limitation, hindrance, curb, constraint ■ v 1 **confine**, limit, restrain, restrict, hinder 2 **ensnare**, snare, catch, net, entangle

tramp n 1 **vagrant**, homeless person, beggar, vagabond, hobo 2 **traipse**, march, trek, hike, trudge ■ v **trudge**, trek, hike, traipse, march

trample v **crush**, flatten, walk on, stamp on, step on

trance n **dream**, daze, spell, stupor, reverie *Opposite*: alertness

tranquil adj 1 **calm**, serene, peaceful, still, relaxing *Opposite*: noisy 2 **composed**, calm, cool, unruffled, unperturbed *Opposite*: agitated

tranquility see tranquillity

tranquilize v **sedate**, calm, put out, put under, knock out

tranquillity n 1 **composure**, calmness, coolness, self-possession, serenity *Opposite*: panic 2 **calm**, serenity, stillness, peacefulness, hush *Opposite*: turmoil

transact v **carry out**, conduct, manage, handle, perform

transaction n **deal**, business, contract, matter, operation

transatlantic adj **transoceanic**, intercontinental, long-haul

transcend v **rise above**, go beyond, exceed, go above, excel

transcendence n 1 **divine existence**, otherworldliness, state of grace, perfection, wholeness *Opposite*: mundaneness 2 **superiority**, greatness, excellence, preeminence, loftiness *Opposite*: inferiority

transcendent adj 1 **superior**, excellent, supreme, great, unequalled *Opposite*: inferior 2 **divine**, perfect, heavenly, supernatural, otherworldly *Opposite*: earthy 3 **mystical**, awe-inspiring, uplifting, inspirational, inspiring

transcendental adj 1 **mystical**, awe-inspiring, uplifting, inspirational, inspiring 2 **divine**, perfect, heavenly, supernatural, otherworldly

transcontinental adj **pancontinental**, coast-to-coast, continent-wide

transcribe v **copy out**, write out, copy, set down, write down

transcript n **record**, copy, text, transcription

transcription see transcript

transect v **divide**, bisect, cut, split, cut across

transfer v 1 **move**, transport, relocate, remove, shift 2 **transmit**, convey, hand on, hand over, turn over ■ n 1 **transmission**, handover, assignment, allocation, transference 2 **relocation**, removal, move, resettlement, displacement

transference n **transfer**, transferal, conversion, devolution, conveyance

transfiguration n **metamorphosis**, transformation, makeover, change, conversion

transfigure v **change**, metamorphose, transform, convert, transmute

transfix v 1 **fascinate**, mesmerize, engross, spellbind, hypnotize 2 **stab**, spike, gore, run through, pierce

transform v **alter**, convert, change, transmute, renovate. *See* COMPARE AND CONTRAST *at* **change**.

transformation n **alteration**, conversion, revolution, renovation, makeover

transgress v **misbehave**, disobey, go astray, lapse, sin *Opposite*: behave

transgression n **wrongdoing**, misbehavior, disobedience, lapse, sin

transgressor n **wrongdoer**, lawbreaker, sinner, offender, criminal

transience n **briefness**, brevity, impermanence, transitoriness, shortness *Opposite*: permanence

transient adj **fleeting**, brief, passing, transitory, temporary *Opposite*: permanent

transit n **transportation**, transfer, transport, travel, shipment

transition n **changeover**, shift, change, alteration, move

transitional adj **intermediate**, in-between, interim, provisional, temporary *Opposite*: permanent

transitory adj **fleeting**, passing, brief, temporary, momentary *Opposite*: permanent. *See* COMPARE AND CONTRAST *at* **temporary**.

translate v 1 **interpret**, decode, decipher, explain, render *(fml)* 2 **convert**, transform, transmute, turn, change

translation n **conversion**, paraphrase, version, rendition, interpretation

translator n **interpreter**, decoder, decipherer, converter

transliterate v **transcribe**, convert, translate, transmute, transform

transliteration n **transcription**, conversion, translation, transformation, rendering

translucence n 1 **transparency**, sheerness, filminess, limpidity, translucency *Opposite*: opacity 2 **glow**, luminosity, brightness, luminescence, luminousness *Opposite*: dullness

translucent adj 1 **transparent**, semi-transparent, see-through, lucid, clear *Opposite*: opaque 2 **glowing**, luminous, radiant, shining, lustrous *Opposite*: dull

transmigrate v **wander**, migrate, travel, shift, drift *Opposite*: settle

transmigration n **migration**, wandering, traveling, movement, shifting

transmissible adj **communicable**, infectious, contagious, catching

transmission n 1 **show**, broadcast, program 2 **spread**, communication, diffusion, conduction

transmit v 1 **put on the air**, send out, put

out, broadcast 2 **convey**, hand on, spread, communicate, diffuse

transmittable adj **communicable**, infectious, catching, contagious

transmittance n **transmission**, diffusion, conduction, transfer, transferal

transmutation n **transfiguration**, transmogrification, change, transformation, alteration

transmute v **transfigure**, transmogrify, transform, alter, change. See COMPARE AND CONTRAST at **change**.

transnational adj **international**, multinational, transcontinental, intercontinental, global ■ n **multinational**, conglomerate, corporation

transparency n 1 **slide**, photograph, photo, shot Opposite: print 2 **clearness**, limpidity, translucence, filminess, sheerness Opposite: opacity 3 **clarity**, plainness, obviousness, directness, unambiguousness Opposite: ambiguousness

transparent adj 1 **see-through**, clear, translucent, crystal clear Opposite: opaque 2 **obvious**, apparent, plain, evident Opposite: unclear

transpire v **happen**, occur, take place, come about, go on

transplant v **remove**, relocate, move, transfer, shift

transplantation n **relocation**, movement, transfer, replacement, uprooting

transport v **convey**, move, bring, carry, transfer ■ n 1 **conveyance**, carriage, transportation, transference, passage 2 **vehicle**, transportation, conveyance, means of transport

transportable adj **mobile**, portable, movable, travel, transferable

transportation n **transport**, conveyance, carriage, transference, passage

transporter n **carrier**, hauler, courier, shipper, delivery service

transpose v 1 **invert**, switch, reverse, exchange, swap (infml) 2 **move**, transfer, rearrange, alter, reorder

transposition n 1 **reversal**, inversion, switch, exchange, substitution 2 **rearrangement**, reordering, recasting, relocation, shuffle

transubstantiation (fml) n **conversion**, transformation, metamorphosis, mutation, alteration

transverse adj **crosswise**, at right angles, sloping, oblique, slanting

trap n **ruse**, trick, snare, deception, con ■ v 1 **catch**, ensnare, entrap, ambush, corner Opposite: release 2 **trick**, deceive, dupe, con, ensnare

trap door n **hatch**, flap, small door, entrance, doorway

trapped adj 1 **shut in**, locked in, stuck, surrounded, hemmed in Opposite: released 2 **stuck**, caught, jammed, stuck fast, wedged Opposite: free

trappings n **accessories**, accouterments, paraphernalia, trimmings, frills

trash n 1 **nonsense**, drivel, gibberish, double talk, rubbish 2 **garbage**, waste, refuse, litter, debris ■ v 1 (infml) **wreck**, destroy, ruin, damage, smash 2 (infml) **condemn**, criticize, censure, pan (infml), knock (slang) Opposite: praise

trashy adj **cheap**, worthless, tasteless, shabby, poor quality Opposite: quality

trauma n **shock**, upset, disturbance, ordeal, suffering

traumatic adj **shocking**, disturbing, upsetting, distressing, harrowing

traumatize v **shock**, upset, distress, devastate, disturb

traumatized adj **disturbed**, shocked, upset, troubled, distressed Opposite: unaffected

travail n **hard work**, toil, effort, exertion, labor

travel v **journey**, tour, take a trip, voyage, trek ■ adj **portable**, lightweight, foldaway, collapsible, transportable

traveler n 1 **tourist**, vacationer, passenger, sightseer, visitor 2 **itinerant**, traveling worker, nomad, rover, wanderer

travelog see **travelogue**

travelogue n **travel piece**, talk, lecture, travel program

travels n **voyage**, journey, trip, exploration, trekking

travel-sick adj **queasy**, nauseous, unwell, ill, seasick

traverse v **cross**, pass through, negotiate, navigate, go across

travesty n **charade**, caricature, sham, parody, pretense

trawl v **fish**, catch fish, go fishing

tray n 1 **salver**, platter, serving dish, plate, oven tray 2 **receptacle**, container, in-box, out-box

treacherous adj 1 **unfaithful**, traitorous, disloyal, deceitful, false Opposite: loyal 2 **dangerous**, hazardous, precarious, unsafe, perilous Opposite: safe

treachery n **deceit**, treason, deceitfulness, sedition, disloyalty Opposite: loyalty

treacly adj **sentimental**, mawkish, romanticized, romantic, slushy

tread v 1 **trample**, crush, squash, flatten, stomp 2 **walk**, step, stride, tramp, pace ■ n **step**, footstep, footfall, tramp, stamp

treadle n **foot pedal**, lever, control

treadmill n **daily grind**, routine, drudgery, toil, slog

treason n **sedition**, treachery, disloyalty, subversion, betrayal Opposite: allegiance

treasonable adj **traitorous**, treacherous, subversive, disloyal, rebellious

treasure n 1 **wealth**, riches, money, valuables, cache 2 **star**, paragon, pearl, prize, gem (infml) ■ v **cherish**, value, prize, adore, hold dear *Opposite*: neglect

treasured *adj* **dear**, precious, loved, cherished, beloved

treasurer *n* **banker**, bursar, bookkeeper, accountant, financial officer

treat *v* **1 regard**, behave toward, consider, act toward, think of **2 care for**, take care of, doctor, cure, nurse **3 pay for**, pick up the check, pick up the tab, pay the bill, give **4 indulge**, spoil, pamper, make a fuss of **5 deal with**, go into, discuss, handle, touch on ■ *n* **luxury**, extravagance, indulgence, delight, pleasure *Opposite*: necessity

treatise *n* **dissertation**, discourse, essay, thesis, paper

treatment *n* **1 cure**, healing, care, therapy, medicine *Opposite*: placebo **2 handling**, behavior, conduct, dealing, management

treaty *n* **agreement**, accord, contract, pact, truce

treble *adj* **1 triple**, three times, thrice, threefold **2 high-pitched**, high, shrill, piping ■ *v* **increase**, triple, increase threefold, increase by three, multiply

tree *n* **1 sapling**, bush, shrub **2 diagram**, tree diagram, family tree, hierarchy, pyramid

treetop *n* **crown**, canopy, foliage

trek *v* **hike**, walk, ramble, march, tramp ■ *n* **walk**, hike, ramble, journey, march

trellis *n* **lattice**, grille, fence, fencing, frame

tremble *v* **shiver**, shake, shudder, quiver, quaver ■ *n* **shake**, shiver, shudder, quake, quiver

trembling *n* **shaking**, vibrating, quivering, shuddering, wobbling ■ *adj* **1 unsteady**, vibrating, quivering, shuddering, quaking *Opposite*: still **2 timorous**, tremulous, nervous, terrified, fearful *Opposite*: confident

tremendous *adj* **1 great**, incredible, fabulous, terrific, marvelous *Opposite*: awful **2 huge**, great, enormous, vast, immense *Opposite*: tiny

tremendously *adv* **very**, extremely, greatly, enormously, vastly *Opposite*: slightly

tremor *n* **1 shake**, tremble, vibration, quiver, shiver **2 earthquake**, shock, quake *(infml)*

tremulous *adj* **1 unsteady**, quivering, trembling, quavering, shaky *Opposite*: steady **2 timid**, timorous, trembling, shy, fearful *Opposite*: confident

trench *n* **ditch**, channel, drain, dugout, trough

trenchancy *n* **incisiveness**, forcefulness, acerbity, brutality, directness *Opposite*: gentleness

trenchant *adj* **incisive**, cutting, sharp, biting, acerbic *Opposite*: mild

trend *n* **1 tendency**, drift, leaning, inclination, movement **2 fashion**, style, look, craze, vogue

trendsetter *n* **innovator**, pacesetter, modernizer, leader, leading light *Opposite*: imitator

trendsetting *adj* **influential**, innovative, cutting-edge, leading, new *Opposite*: conventional

trendy *(infml) adj* **fashionable**, in, up-to-the-minute, cool, stylish *Opposite*: unfashionable

trepidation *n* **fear**, anxiety, unease, nervousness, apprehension *Opposite*: equanimity *(fml)*

trespass *v* **intrude**, infringe, encroach, invade, interlope

trespasser *n* **intruder**, squatter, interloper, snooper *(infml) Opposite*: guest

tress *n* **lock**, strand, curl, tuft, wisp

tresses *n* **hair**, curls, ringlets, locks *(literary)*

trestle *n* **support**, bracket, stand, frame, framework

triad *n* **trio**, threesome, triangle, troika, triumvirate

trial *n* **1 test**, examination, experiment, tryout, audition **2 hearing**, court case, court-martial, prosecution, legal proceedings **3 ordeal**, hardship, suffering, trouble, misery ■ *adj* **experimental**, probationary, pilot, provisional, test

triangle *n* **threesome**, trio, three-way relationship, triad, trinity

triangular *adj* **three-sided**, trilateral, three-cornered, wedge-shaped, deltoid

tribal *adj* **ethnic**, family, ancestral, familial, group

tribe *n* **1 people**, ethnic group, community, society, population **2** *(infml)* **family**, clan, kinfolk, people *(infml)*

tribulation *n* **misfortune**, trial, suffering, ordeal, distress

tribunal *n* **1 court**, court of law, law court **2 board**, panel, committee, body

tributary *n* **branch**, arm, offshoot, river, stream

tribute *n* **1 compliment**, mark of respect, honor, praise, acknowledgment **2 tax**, duty, excise, toll, payment

trice *n* **instant**, flash, moment, twinkling, no time

trick *n* **1 deception**, ploy, ruse, hoax, dodge **2 joke**, prank, stunt, caper **3 knack**, technique, skill, secret **4 habit**, mannerism, trait, characteristic, way ■ *v* **deceive**, cheat, mislead, trap, fool ■ *adj* **fake**, false, artificial, bogus, hoax *Opposite*: real

trickery *n* **1 deception**, deceit, fraud, scam *(slang)*, sting *(slang)* **2 dishonesty**, deception, deceit, fraudulence, chicanery

trickiness *n* **1 difficulty**, complication, delicacy, awkwardness, intricacy *Opposite*: simplicity **2 craftiness**, slipperiness, deviousness, slyness, duplicity *Opposite*: honesty

trickle *v* **drip**, drop, seep, dribble, ooze

Opposite: flood ■ *n* **dribble**, drop, drip
Opposite: flood

trickster *n* cheat, swindler, charlatan, fraud,
slippery customer

tricky *adj* **1 complicated**, delicate, awkward,
thorny, problematic *Opposite*: simple
2 devious, sly, deceitful, crafty, cunning
Opposite: straight

trier *n* **1 tester**, experimenter, taster, volunteer, guinea pig **2 sticker**, fighter, striver,
struggler, stayer *Opposite*: defeatist

trifle *n* **1 nothing**, frippery, triviality
2 smidgen, bit, little, drop, touch

trifling *adj* trivial, petty, small, tiny, silly
Opposite: significant

trigger *v* **activate**, set off, cause, generate,
start *Opposite*: halt

trigger-happy *(infml)* *adj* **rash**, violent, dangerous, wild, unpredictable

trigger off *v* **activate**, set off, cause, generate,
start *Opposite*: halt

trill *v* warble, quaver, shrill, tweet, vibrate

trillion *(infml)* *n* **lots**, tons *(infml)*, loads
(infml), stacks *(infml)*, heaps *(infml)*

trilogy *n* series, sequence, set, cycle, trio

trim *v* **1 clip**, cut, shear, pare, prune *Opposite*: lengthen **2 cut back**, prune, decrease,
lower, shave *Opposite*: augment *(fml)*
3 decorate, adorn, embroider, embellish,
edge ■ *adj* **1 tidy**, orderly, smart, spruce,
dapper *Opposite*: messy **2 slim**, fit,
shapely, sleek, slender *Opposite*: bulky ■
n **decoration**, adornment, frill, edge,
border

trimming *n* **decoration**, adornment, frill,
garnish, extra

trimmings *n* **1 side dishes**, extras, accompaniments, fixings *(infml)* **2 extras**, accompaniments, add-ons, accessories, embellishments **3 clippings**, parings, bits, pieces,
nail clippings

trimness *n* **1 neatness**, tidiness, smartness,
spruceness, orderliness **2 slenderness**,
slimness, compactness, sleekness, thinness

trinity *n* threesome, trio, triad, troika, triplet

trinket *n* ornament, charm, knickknack,
bauble, gewgaw

trio *n* threesome, triad, troika, trinity, triangle

trip *n* **1 journey**, tour, excursion, expedition,
outing **2 slip**, stumble, tumble, fall ■
v **1 stumble**, trip up, slip, tumble, falter
2 skip, hop, prance, caper, dance

tripartite *adj* **three-way**, three-party, multilateral, triple

tripe *(infml)* *n* **rubbish**, nonsense, garbage,
drivel, trash *Opposite*: fact

triple *adj* **1 tripartite**, three-way, three-
layered, triple-decker *Opposite*: single
2 treble, threefold, multiple *Opposite*:
single ■ *v* **treble**, triplicate, multiply by
three, increase, boost *Opposite*: reduce

triplet *n* trio, triad, threesome, troika

trip up *v* **1 stumble**, trip, slip, tumble, fall
2 trap, trick, confuse, disconcert, unsettle

trite *adj* **commonplace**, stale, tired, pedestrian, worn *Opposite*: original

triteness *n* **dullness**, tiredness, staleness,
corniness, banality *Opposite*: originality

triumph *n* **1 victory**, achievement, conquest,
accomplishment, coup *Opposite*: failure
2 rejoicing, pride, elation, delight, satisfaction *Opposite*: sorrow ■ *v* **succeed**,
prevail, win, overcome, be victorious
Opposite: lose

triumphal *adj* ceremonial, commemorative,
victory, heroic, celebratory

triumphant *adj* **1 winning**, victorious, glorious, dominant, proud **2 exultant**, celebratory, jubilant, elated, delighted
Opposite: sorrowful

triumph over *v* **overcome**, defeat, beat,
prevail over, get the better of

triumvirate *n* trio, threesome, triad, troika,
triplet

trivet *n* **stand**, support, rest, tripod

trivia *n* minutiae, trivialities, froth, nonsense,
trifles *Opposite*: essentials

trivial *adj* **unimportant**, small, inconsequential, slight, trifling *Opposite*: crucial

triviality *n* **1 unimportance**, inconsequence,
worthlessness, insignificance, pettiness
Opposite: importance **2 trifle**, nothing,
frippery

trivialize *v* **play down**, belittle, underestimate, make light of, tone down *Opposite*: highlight

troika *n* trio, triumvirate, threesome, triad,
triplet

troll *v* **1 fish**, angle, trail, spin, lure **2 amble**,
wander, saunter, drift, walk ■ *n* **giant**, ogre,
hobgoblin, goblin, monster

troop *n* **crowd**, horde, throng, multitude,
herd ■ *v* **1 move**, gather, rally, come
together, get together **2 march**, parade,
stream, trudge, traipse

trophy *n* cup, award, medal, crown, title

tropical *adj* **hot**, steamy, humid, sultry,
stifling *Opposite*: temperate

trot *v* jog, run, hurry, scurry, scamper *Opposite*: saunter

troubadour *n* minstrel, musician, poet, wandering minstrel, bard *(literary)*

trouble *n* **1 worry**, concern, distress, anxiety,
care **2 problem**, difficulty, dilemma, nuisance, snag *Opposite*: ease **3 complaint**,
ailment, disease, illness, malady *Opposite*:
good health **4 effort**, bother, inconvenience, work, thought **5 strife**, unrest,
disorder, disturbance, discontent *Opposite*: accord ■ *v* **1 concern**, worry, distress,
agitate, harass **2 bother**, put out, inconvenience, disturb, burden **3 make an effort**,
take pains, exert yourself, bother *Opposite*: hang back. *See* COMPARE AND CONTRAST *at*
bother.

troubled adj 1 **anxious**, concerned, bothered, worried, disturbed Opposite: calm 2 **problematic**, tricky, awkward, difficult Opposite: easy

trouble-free adj **easy**, simple, painless, straightforward, uncomplicated Opposite: troublesome

troublemaker n **mischief-maker**, menace, agitator, firebrand, rabble-rouser Opposite: conciliator

troubleshooter n 1 **technician**, engineer, mechanic, problem solver, expert 2 **mediator**, consultant, ombudsman, adviser, problem solver

troublesome adj 1 **disorderly**, rowdy, unruly, uncooperative, undisciplined Opposite: well-behaved 2 **worrying**, upsetting, bothersome, wearisome, difficult Opposite: trouble-free

trough n 1 **manger**, crib, rack, holder 2 **channel**, furrow, trench, gutter, ditch 3 **depression**, low, low pressure area Opposite: ridge

trounce v **beat**, thrash, rout, crush, overwhelm. See COMPARE AND CONTRAST at defeat.

trouncing n **routing**, thrashing, crushing, drubbing, beating

troupe n **company**, cast, band, ensemble, group

truancy n **absence**, nonattendance, absenteeism, malingering Opposite: attendance

truant n **absentee**, malingerer, shirker ■ v **shirk**, malinger, go AWOL, play hooky (infml)

truce n **ceasefire**, armistice, treaty, peace, respite

truculence n **defiance**, belligerence, sullenness, insolence, impertinence Opposite: enthusiasm

truculent adj **hostile**, belligerent, defiant, quarrelsome, argumentative Opposite: easygoing

trudge v **tramp**, traipse, slog, plod, trek ■ n **slog**, trek, hike, march, haul

true adj 1 **factual**, accurate, right, correct, proper Opposite: false 2 **real**, genuine, actual, valid, authentic Opposite: fake 3 **faithful**, dedicated, constant, loyal, sincere Opposite: unfaithful

true-blue adj **loyal**, incorruptible, faithful, honest, staunch Opposite: disloyal

true-life adj **genuine**, realistic, real-life, real, true

true to life adj **realistic**, convincing, accurate, authentic, lifelike Opposite: unrealistic

truism n **axiom**, cliché, maxim, adage, saying

truly adv 1 **sincerely**, faithfully, honestly, in all honesty, genuinely Opposite: insincerely 2 **very**, greatly, really, indeed, exceptionally 3 **really**, in fact, beyond doubt, actually, indeed

trump v **outdo**, go one better, call somebody's bluff, undermine, outmaneuver

trumped-up adj **false**, fake, invented, made-up, fabricated Opposite: genuine

truncate v **shorten**, abbreviate, trim, cut, prune Opposite: lengthen

trundle v 1 **roll** along, rattle, labor, wheel 2 **traipse**, trail, saunter, lumber, wander

trunk n **stem**, bole, stalk

trunks n **swimming trunks**, bathing trunks, shorts

truss v **bind**, tie up, tie, tether, string

trust n 1 **faith**, belief, hope, conviction, confidence Opposite: distrust 2 **consortium**, cartel, syndicate, group, organization 3 **custody**, care, protection, responsibility, guard ■ v 1 **have faith in**, believe, rely on, depend on, confide in Opposite: distrust 2 **hope**, believe, expect, assume, suppose Opposite: despair 3 **entrust**, confide, assign, consign, commit

trustee n 1 **representative**, deputy, agent, executor, guardian 2 **fund manager**, fund administrator, director

trustfulness n **unwariness**, credulity, innocence, lack of caution, trustingness Opposite: wariness

trusting adj **gullible**, credulous, unquestioning, believing, naïve Opposite: suspicious

trustworthiness n **honesty**, dependability, reliability, fidelity, constancy Opposite: dishonesty

trustworthy adj **dependable**, reliable, responsible, truthful, honest Opposite: corrupt

trusty adj **faithful**, dependable, reliable, constant, loyal Opposite: unreliable

truth n 1 **fact**, certainty, reality, actuality, veracity Opposite: untruth 2 **honesty**, integrity, fidelity, sincerity

truthful adj 1 **honest**, straight, frank, open, straightforward Opposite: dishonest 2 **correct**, true, reliable, accurate, exact Opposite: false

truthfulness n 1 **honesty**, truth, candor, frankness, openness Opposite: dishonesty 2 **accuracy**, reliability, correctness, exactitude, faithfulness Opposite: inaccuracy

try v 1 **attempt**, strive, aim, seek, undertake 2 **test**, sample, taste, appraise, evaluate 3 **strain**, vex, tax, exasperate, annoy Opposite: soothe 4 **judge**, put on trial, hear, take to court ■ n **attempt**, effort, go, stab (infml), crack (infml)

trying adj **annoying**, tiresome, irritating, wearisome, frustrating Opposite: soothing

try out v **test**, sample, check out, experiment with, appraise

tryout n **practice**, run through, trial, rehearsal, preparation

tryst n **assignation**, rendezvous, meeting, date, encounter

try your hand v **experiment**, try out, take a shot, make an attempt, take a stab (infml)

tub n 1 **container**, carton, pot, drum, barrel 2 **hot tub**, plunge bath, bathtub

tubby (infml) adj **plump**, chubby, portly, overweight, heavy Opposite: skinny

tube n **pipe**, cylinder, hose, conduit, duct

tuber n **storage organ**, rhizome, root, underground stem

tubing n **tubes**, pipes, plumbing

tubular adj **tube-shaped**, cylindrical, tubelike, hollow

tuck v 1 **insert**, put, push, slip, place Opposite: remove 2 **pleat**, fold, dart, gather, pucker ∎ n **pleat**, fold, dart, gather, pucker

tuft n **clump**, tussock, cluster, bunch, truss

tug v **pull**, tow, haul, heave, jerk Opposite: push ∎ n 1 **yank**, heave, pull, jerk, haul Opposite: push 2 see **tugboat**. See COMPARE AND CONTRAST at pull.

tug of war n **tussle**, power struggle, struggle, battle, wrangle Opposite: agreement

tuition n **instruction**, teaching, schooling, training, education

tumble v 1 **fall over**, fall down, stumble, trip up, topple Opposite: stand up 2 **plummet**, drop, nose-dive, plunge, dive Opposite: rise

tumbledown adj **ramshackle**, rickety, rundown, derelict, dilapidated

tumbler n 1 **glass**, tall glass, whiskey glass, highball glass, beaker 2 **acrobat**, gymnast, aerialist, trapeze artist, entertainer

tummy (infml) n **stomach**, abdomen, paunch, pot, gut

tumor n **growth**, lump, malignant tumor, benign tumor, cancer

tumult n **uproar**, commotion, clamor, hubbub, hullabaloo Opposite: peace

tumultuous adj 1 **turbulent**, confused, chaotic, agitated Opposite: calm 2 **unrestrained**, unbridled, riotous, boisterous, rowdy Opposite: restrained

tune n **melody**, song, air, jingle, harmony ∎ v **adjust**, fine-tune, change, alter, modify

tuneful adj **melodic**, melodious, harmonious, musical, pleasant Opposite: discordant

tuneless adj **unmusical**, droning, monotone, atonal, monotonous Opposite: tuneful

tune-up n **service**, overhaul, fine-tune, check, maintenance

tunnel n 1 **channel**, passageway, subway, shaft, underpass Opposite: bridge 2 **burrow**, hole, warren, earth, sett ∎ v **excavate**, burrow, dig, mine, channel

turbid adj 1 **muddy**, cloudy, opaque, dirty, murky Opposite: clear 2 **confused**, muddled, disorganized, scrambled, chaotic Opposite: clear

turbulence n 1 **commotion**, confusion, turmoil, disorder, unrest Opposite: calm 2 **violence**, rowdiness, unruliness, riotousness, restlessness 3 **storminess**, tempestuousness, choppiness, blusteriness

turbulent adj 1 **confused**, unstable, chaotic, tumultuous, in turmoil Opposite: orderly 2 **stormy**, tempestuous, raging, choppy, blustery Opposite: settled 3 **violent**, rowdy, unruly, riotous, quarrelsome Opposite: peaceful

tureen n **bowl**, serving dish, dish, casserole

turf n 1 **lawn**, grass, pasture, meadow, verdure 2 (infml) **area of expertise**, sphere of influence, field, territory, orbit 3 (infml) **territory**, patch, beat, home turf, neighborhood

turgid adj **pompous**, boring, dull, hard going, stilted Opposite: amusing

turmoil n **chaos**, disorder, confusion, uproar, tumult Opposite: order

turn v 1 **twist**, revolve, rotate, go around, spin 2 **bend**, change direction, bear, veer, meander 3 **direct**, aim, point, focus, set 4 **go**, become, alter, convert, transform 5 **curdle**, go sour, sour, spoil, go bad ∎ n 1 **go**, try, chance, opportunity, shot (infml) 2 **rotation**, revolution, twist, spin, twirl 3 **bend**, corner, junction, fork, curve 4 **errand**, favor, good turn, service, good deed 5 **ride**, spin, jaunt, trip, outing 6 **fit**, seizure, attack, funny turn, spasm 7 **fright**, scare, shock, start, jolt 8 **performance**, act, skit, sketch, recitation

turn a blind eye to v **overlook**, ignore, take no notice of, disregard, excuse Opposite: condemn

turnabout n **reversal**, sea change, U-turn, change, shift

turn against v **turn on**, reject, rebuff, spurn, exclude

turn around v 1 **complete**, finish, accomplish, process 2 **improve**, boost, increase, bump up (infml)

turnaround n 1 **reversal**, U-turn, improvement, change, shift 2 **dispatch**, processing, completion

turn away v **dismiss**, reject, repel, rebuff, refuse Opposite: welcome

turn away from v **reject**, give up, abandon, abjure, relinquish Opposite: take up

turn back v 1 **go back**, retrace your steps, return Opposite: continue 2 **fold back**, fold down, fold over, turn down, turn over

turncoat n **traitor**, deserter, defector, collaborator, double agent

turn down v 1 **refuse**, decline, reject, disallow, veto Opposite: accept 2 **lessen**, lower, decrease, reduce, muffle Opposite: turn up

turned-out adj **groomed**, dressed, presented, clad, got up (infml)

turn in v 1 **inform on**, blow the whistle on, betray, report, turn over 2 **hand in**, hand over, give in, remit, submit 3 (infml) **go to bed**, go to sleep, hit the sack (infml), hit the hay (infml) Opposite: rise

turning n **joinery**, carpentry, woodworking, carving, cabinetmaking

turning point *n* **crossroads**, defining moment, decisive moment, crisis, watershed

turn off *v* **1 switch off**, deactivate, shut down, disable, stop *Opposite*: turn on **2 relax**, unwind, switch off, wind down, take it easy *Opposite*: gear up **3** *(infml)* **disgust**, irritate, bore, deter, displease *Opposite*: attract

turnoff *n* **turn**, exit, junction, minor road

turn of phrase *n* **way with words**, way of putting things, way of speaking, style, manner

turn on *v* **1 switch on**, start, activate, get going, set in motion *Opposite*: turn off **2 depend on**, rest on, hinge on, center on, hang on **3 attack**, go for, round on, lay into, set upon *Opposite*: defend **4** *(infml)* **arouse**, excite, interest, enthuse, stimulate *Opposite*: turn off

turn out *v* **1 produce**, make, manufacture, churn out, assemble **2 end up**, work out, come out, transpire, result **3 evict**, throw out, empty, eject, expel *Opposite*: welcome **4 turn off**, switch off, deactivate, shut down, disable *Opposite*: turn on **5 attend**, turn up, show up, appear, put in an appearance

turnout *n* **crowd**, audience, attendance, gathering

turn over *v* **1 capsize**, flip over, overturn, upturn, turn turtle **2 mull over**, think about, go over, consider, reflect on **3 hand over**, hand in, give in, remit, submit *Opposite*: hold onto

turnover *n* **1 incomings**, income, gross revenue, business, revenue *Opposite*: costs **2 throughput**, sales, trade, business, buying and selling **3 staff renewal rate**, hiring and firing rate, staff resignation rate, staff resignations, staff turnover

turnstile *n* **gate**, barrier, entrance, park entrance

turn the corner *v* **get better**, start to improve, look up, be on the turn, be out of danger

turn to *v* **consult**, refer to, fall back on, resort to, rely on

turn turtle *v* **capsize**, flip over, turn over, overturn, upturn

turn up *v* **1 find**, uncover, unearth, dig up, discover *Opposite*: conceal **2 increase**, amplify, intensify, boost, step up *Opposite*: turn down **3 come to light**, surface, appear, reappear, materialize *Opposite*: disappear **4 arrive**, appear, attend, put in an appearance, come

turn your back on *v* **ignore**, abandon, leave behind, put behind you, forsake *Opposite*: take care of

turn your nose up at *v* **scorn**, disdain, sneer at, sniff at, reject *Opposite*: accept

turn your stomach *v* **sicken**, disgust, repel, revolt, nauseate *Opposite*: attract

turpitude *(fml)* *n* **immorality**, wickedness, depravity, baseness, improbity

turret *n* **tower**, battlement, steeple, bartizan

tussle *v* **fight**, brawl, scuffle, clash, struggle ■ *n* **brawl**, fight, struggle, scuffle, clash

tutelage *n* **instruction**, guidance, teaching, coaching, expert hand

tutor *n* **teacher**, instructor, professor, lecturer, trainer ■ *v* **teach**, educate, instruct, school, coach. *See* COMPARE AND CONTRAST *at* teach.

tutorial *n* **class**, lesson, seminar, lecture, discussion group

TV *(infml)* *n* **television**, tube *(infml)*, small screen *(infml)*, boob tube *(infml)*

twaddle *(infml)* *n* **nonsense**, balderdash, rubbish, drivel, garbage *Opposite*: sense

twang *n* **accent**, drawl, intonation, inflection, resonance ■ *v* **reverberate**, vibrate, ping, plunk

tweak *v* **1 pinch**, nip, jerk, twist, tug **2** *(infml)* **fine-tune**, correct, adjust, modify, regulate ■ *n* **nip**, pinch, twist, jerk, tug

tweedy *adj* **casual**, informal, sporty, horsy, outdoor

tweet *v* **chirp**, peep, chirrup, twitter, cheep

twenty-four/seven *adv* **around the clock**, all the time, constantly, always

twice *adv* **two times**, double, twofold

twiddle *v* **fidget**, fiddle, play, toy, handle

twig *n* **branch**, shoot, stem, stick

twilight *n* **dusk**, nightfall, evening, sunset, sundown *Opposite*: dawn

twilit *adj* **dusky**, shady, shadowy, moonlit, crepuscular *(literary)* *Opposite*: sunlit

twin *n* **double**, doppelgänger, clone, identical twin, Siamese twin ■ *adj* **1 identical**, matching, alike, indistinguishable, like *Opposite*: different **2 dual**, double, twofold, paired *Opposite*: single ■ *v* **pair**, link, join, match, associate

twine *n* **string**, thread, cord, yarn ■ *v* **coil**, twist, wind, loop, snake

twinge *n* **pang**, pain, stitch, ache, wrench

twinkle *v* **shine**, sparkle, glimmer, gleam, flicker ■ *n* **sparkle**, gleam, glimmer, flicker, shine

twinkling *n* **flash**, second, moment, split second, instant

twirl *v* **1 wind**, coil, twist, curl, bend **2 spin**, rotate, whirl, turn, revolve ■ *n* **1 coil**, spiral, twist, loop **2 whirl**, spin, revolution, rotation, turn

twist *v* **1 wind**, coil, curl, bend, twirl **2 rotate**, turn, screw, unscrew, wind **3 sprain**, pull, hurt, injure, turn **4 distort**, misrepresent, alter, manipulate, warp *Opposite*: clarify **5 meander**, snake, wind, curve, bend **6 contort**, screw up, grimace, crumple, writhe ■ *n* **1 rotation**, screw, wind, turn **2 spiral**, coil, kink, curl, bend **3 development**, change, turn, incident, event

twisted *adj* **1 warped**, perverse, sick, perverted, abnormal *Opposite*: wholesome **2 misshapen**, distorted, warped, bent, deformed *Opposite*: straight

twisting *adj* **winding**, meandering, twisty, windy, snaking

twist somebody's arm *v* **compel**, force, pressure, coerce, persuade

twisty *adj* **winding**, tortuous, meandering, snaking, twisting *Opposite*: straight

twitch *v* **jerk**, jolt, shudder, yank, convulse ■ *n* **tic**, spasm, jerk, jolt, convulsion

twitchiness *n* **jitteriness**, jumpiness, restlessness, uneasiness, nervousness

twitchy *adj* **nervous**, fidgety, on edge, agitated, jumpy *Opposite*: still

two-dimensional *adj* **1 flat**, flattened, plane, smooth, level *Opposite*: three-dimensional **2 superficial**, shallow, oversimplified, formulaic, cardboard *Opposite*: complex

two-faced *adj* **hypocritical**, false, insincere, deceitful, double dealing *Opposite*: genuine

twofold *adj* **double**, dual, twin

twosome *n* **pair**, duo, couple, two of a kind

two-time *v* **1 be unfaithful**, cheat, deceive, cuckold (*archaic*) **2 betray**, mislead, deceive, double-cross, take in

two-tone *adj* **striped**, two-color, light-and-dark, two-toned, stripy

two-way *adj* **reciprocal**, cooperative, shared, mutual, collaborative

tycoon *n* **magnate**, mogul, business person, industrialist

tyke *n* **child**, imp, urchin, monkey (*infml*), scamp (*infml*)

type *n* **1 kind**, sort, category, class, genre **2 font**, typeface, lettering, print, style ■ *v* **key**, input, enter, key in ■ *n* (*infml*) **character**, individual, person, sort

COMPARE AND CONTRAST CORE MEANING: a group having a common quality or qualities

type a group of individuals or items with strongly marked and readily defined similarities; **kind** a group of individuals or items connected by shared characteristics; **sort** a general word used in the same way as *kind*; **category** a set of things that are classified together because of common characteristics; **class** used in the same way as *category*; **species** a specific group of animals, plants, insects, or other organisms, used in formal taxonomic classification; **genre** a particular style of painting, writing, dance, or other art form.

Type A *adj* **dynamic**, driven, ambitious, energetic, efficient

typecast *v* **stereotype**, pigeonhole, categorize, limit, restrict

typeface *n* **script**, type, font, lettering, print

typhoon *n* **storm**, cyclone, tornado, hurricane, tropical storm

typical *adj* **1 characteristic**, archetypal, distinctive, representative, emblematic *Opposite*: uncharacteristic **2 usual**, normal, standard, mainstream, average *Opposite*: unusual

typify *v* **characterize**, epitomize, symbolize, exemplify, personify

typo (*infml*) *n* **misprint**, typographical error, keyboarding error, error, mistake *Opposite*: correction

typography *n* **1 design**, typesetting, formatting, layout, composition **2 print style**, font, type, lettering, script

tyrannical *adj* **oppressive**, dictatorial, autocratic, despotic, authoritarian

tyrannize *v* **oppress**, dictate, bully, domineer, intimidate

tyranny *n* **oppression**, dictatorship, autocracy, domination, despotism

tyrant *n* **oppressor**, dictator, bully, autocrat, despot

tyro *n* **novice**, beginner, learner, newcomer, trainee *Opposite*: veteran. *See* COMPARE AND CONTRAST *at* beginner.

U

ubiquitous *adj* **omnipresent**, universal, pervasive, global, abundant

UFO *n* **flying saucer**, spaceship, spacecraft

ugliness *n* **1 unattractiveness**, unsightliness, hideousness, repulsiveness *Opposite*: attractiveness **2 violence**, hostility, cruelty, viciousness, malice *Opposite*: friendliness **3 unpleasantness**, dreadfulness, horridness, obnoxiousness, foulness

ugly *adj* **1 unattractive**, hideous, unsightly, revolting, repulsive *Opposite*: attractive **2 unpleasant**, horrible, dreadful, horrid, obnoxious *Opposite*: nice **3 nasty**, threat-

ening, dangerous, intimidating, menacing *Opposite*: friendly. *See* COMPARE AND CONTRAST *at* unattractive.

ulcer *n* **boil**, abscess, pustule, carbuncle, sore

ulterior *adj* **hidden**, concealed, secret, underhand, unknown *Opposite*: transparent

ulterior motive *n* **hidden agenda**, hidden intention, design, scheme

ultimate *adj* **1 final**, last, eventual, decisive, definitive *Opposite*: first **2 fundamental**, basic, essential, supreme, extreme *Opposite*: superficial

ultimately *adv* **in the end**, eventually, in due course, finally, at last *Opposite*: initially

ultimatum *n* **challenge**, demand, requirement, petition, stipulation

ultra *adj* **extreme**, radical, revolutionary, excessive, extremist *Opposite*: mainstream

ultramodern *adj* **avant-garde**, progressive, modernistic, radical, futuristic *Opposite*: old-fashioned

umbrage *n* **offense**, exception, resentment, affront, slight

umbrella *n* **aegis**, auspices, authority, protection, support

umpire *n* **referee**, adjudicator, arbitrator, arbiter, mediator ■ *v* **adjudicate**, referee, arbitrate, judge, mediate

umpteen *(infml)* *adj* **countless**, numerous, innumerable, millions of, myriad

unabashed *adj* **unashamed**, unembarrassed, shameless, bold, brazen *Opposite*: abashed

unabated *adj* **persistent**, undiminished, relentless, unrelieved, unrelenting *Opposite*: reduced

unable *adj* **powerless**, incapable, impotent, inept, incompetent *Opposite*: able

unabridged *adj* **full-length**, complete, whole, entire, uncut *Opposite*: abridged

unacceptable *adj* **intolerable**, insupportable, undesirable, objectionable, deplorable *Opposite*: acceptable

unaccommodating *adj* **unhelpful**, awkward, uncooperative, difficult, disobliging *Opposite*: helpful

unaccompanied *adj* **alone**, by yourself, on your own, lone, solitary

unaccomplished *adj* **1 unfinished**, incomplete, uncompleted, unfulfilled, undone *Opposite*: accomplished **2 unskillful**, amateurish, unpolished, inexpert, untalented *Opposite*: accomplished

unaccountable *adj* **inexplicable**, puzzling, strange, unfathomable, baffling *Opposite*: explicable

unaccounted-for *adj* **missing**, lost, absent, gone, disappeared

unaccustomed *adj* **1 unused**, not used, inexperienced, unfamiliar, unacquainted *Opposite*: accustomed **2 unfamiliar**, unusual, different, new, strange *Opposite*: accustomed

unachievable *adj* **unattainable**, impracticable, impossible, unfeasible, inaccessible *Opposite*: achievable

unacquainted *adj* **ignorant**, unaccustomed, unaware, uninformed, unknowledgeable *Opposite*: knowledgeable

unadorned *adj* **plain**, bare, austere, simple, unembellished *Opposite*: ornate

unadulterated *adj* **pure**, untouched, untainted, complete, unmodified *Opposite*: tainted

unadventurous *adj* **cautious**, conservative, careful, timid, shy *Opposite*: daredevil

unaffected *adj* **1 unchanged**, unaltered, unmoved, impervious, impassive *Opposite*: different **2 genuine**, natural, unpretentious, sincere, modest *Opposite*: pretentious

unafraid *adj* **fearless**, bold, confident, brave, courageous *Opposite*: afraid

unaided *adv* **unassisted**, independently, by yourself, of your own accord, on your own *Opposite*: jointly

unalleviated *adj* **constant**, unrelieved, unremitting, unmitigated, inexorable *Opposite*: intermittent

unalloyed *adj* **pure**, sheer, absolute, total, utter *Opposite*: partial

unalterable *adj* **unchangeable**, fixed, irreversible, final, set *Opposite*: impermanent

unambiguous *adj* **unmistakable**, clear-cut, explicit, definite, decided *Opposite*: vague

unambitious *adj* **apathetic**, unaspiring, unenterprising, unassertive, lazy *Opposite*: ambitious

unanimous *adj* **common**, agreed, undisputed, undivided, united *Opposite*: undecided

unannounced *adj* **unexpected**, impromptu, spontaneous, surprise *Opposite*: arranged

unanswerable *adj* **unfathomable**, insoluble, unresolvable, unsolvable, inexplicable

unanticipated *adj* **surprising**, unexpected, unlooked-for, unforeseen, unsuspected *Opposite*: expected

unapologetic *adj* **impenitent**, unrepentant, unreformed, unremorseful, without regret *Opposite*: penitent

unappealing *adj* **unattractive**, unpleasant, disagreeable, uninviting, unlikable *Opposite*: appealing. *See* COMPARE AND CONTRAST *at* unattractive.

unappetizing *adj* **unattractive**, unpleasant, unenticing, uninviting, unpalatable *Opposite*: appetizing

unapproachable *adj* **distant**, unfriendly, aloof, cold, standoffish *Opposite*: approachable

unarguable *adj* **beyond doubt**, incontestable, incontrovertible, indisputable, beyond question *Opposite*: arguable

unarmed *adj* **unprotected**, defenseless, exposed, vulnerable, weaponless *Opposite*: armed

unashamed *adj* **unembarrassed**, unapologetic, blatant, brazen, barefaced *Opposite*: ashamed

unasked *adj* **1 unsolicited**, uninvited, unsought, unexpected, unimaginable *Opposite*: expected **2 uninvited**, unwelcome, excluded, unexpected, left out

unassailable *adj* **1 incontrovertible**, unquestionable, impregnable, irrefutable, indisputable *Opposite*: tenuous **2 invincible**, unbeatable, impregnable, indomitable, invulnerable *Opposite*: vulnerable

unassisted *adj* **unaided**, single-handed, solo, lone *Opposite*: assisted

unassuming *adj* **modest**, humble, self-effacing, unassertive, meek *Opposite*: arrogant

unattached *adj* **free**, uncommitted, single, unmarried, separated *Opposite*: attached

unattainable *adj* **unachievable**, impossible, unfeasible, inaccessible, unreachable *Opposite*: attainable

unattractive *adj* **unappealing**, ugly, nasty, unpleasant, distasteful *Opposite*: attractive

COMPARE AND CONTRAST CORE MEANING: not pleasant to look at

unattractive not pleasant in appearance; **unsightly** spoiling an appearance which would otherwise be quite attractive; **ugly** very unpleasant to look at; **hideous** extremely unpleasant to look at; **homely** describes somebody who is not attractive; **plain** describes somebody, especially a woman, who is not attractive.

unattractiveness *n* **ugliness**, unpleasantness, unsightliness, distastefulness, repulsiveness *Opposite*: attractiveness

unauthorized *adj* **illegal**, unlawful, unofficial, unsanctioned, unlicensed *Opposite*: legitimate

unavailability *n* **unobtainability**, inaccessibility, unattainability, unreachability, absence *Opposite*: availability

unavailable *adj* **1 unobtainable**, inaccessible, unattainable, unreachable, absent *Opposite*: available **2 engaged**, busy, occupied, unobtainable *Opposite*: available

unavailing *adj* **vain**, unsuccessful, futile, failed, ineffective *Opposite*: successful

unavoidability *n* **inevitability**, inescapability, certainty, necessity, obligation

unavoidable *adj* **inevitable**, inescapable, obvious, manifest, obligatory *Opposite*: avoidable

unaware *adj* **ignorant**, uninformed, oblivious, unconscious, unmindful *Opposite*: conscious

unawares *adv* **by surprise**, off guard, unexpectedly

unbalance *v* **disturb**, unhinge, derange, distort, destabilize *Opposite*: stabilize

unbalanced *adj* **1 unstable**, disturbed, unhinged, deranged *Opposite*: well-balanced **2 uneven**, lopsided, unequal, crooked, top-heavy *Opposite*: even **3 biased**, one-sided, inequitable, prejudiced, unfair *Opposite*: impartial

unbearable *adj* **intolerable**, agonizing, excruciating, awful, insufferable *Opposite*: tolerable

unbeatable *adj* **invincible**, supreme, unassailable, unconquerable, peerless *Opposite*: vulnerable

unbeaten *adj* **undefeated**, unsurpassed, successful, triumphant, victorious

unbecoming *adj* **improper**, inappropriate, incorrect, unsuitable, unflattering *Opposite*: fitting

unbelief *n* **nonbelief**, skepticism, incredulity, agnosticism, atheism *Opposite*: faith

unbelievable *adj* **1 incredible**, amazing, extraordinary, astonishing, great *Opposite*: ordinary **2 implausible**, incredible, far-fetched, fantastic, unlikely *Opposite*: plausible

unbelievably *adv* **extraordinarily**, incredibly, extremely, very, exceptionally *Opposite*: unremarkably

unbeliever *n* **nonbeliever**, skeptic, atheist, agnostic, freethinker *Opposite*: believer

unbelieving *adj* **incredulous**, skeptical, doubting, suspicious, questioning *Opposite*: credulous

unbend *v* **straighten**, release, free, relax, loosen *Opposite*: bend

unbending *adj* **inflexible**, fixed, rigid, adamant, obdurate *Opposite*: flexible

unbiased *adj* **impartial**, balanced, dispassionate, neutral, unprejudiced *Opposite*: partial

unbind *v* **untie**, release, free, undo, liberate *Opposite*: bind

unblemished *adj* **flawless**, perfect, untarnished, pure, blameless *Opposite*: flawed

unblock *v* **clear**, unclog, free, clear out, clean out *Opposite*: block

unbolt *v* **unfasten**, unlock, open, unscrew, release *Opposite*: lock

unbounded *adj* **limitless**, unrestrained, abundant, boundless, uncontrolled *Opposite*: limited

unbowed *adj* **undefeated**, defiant, stubborn, determined, relentless *Opposite*: defeated

unbreakable *adj* **indestructible**, strong, permanent, indissoluble, firm *Opposite*: fragile

unbridled *adj* **unrestrained**, uncontrolled, uninhibited, unconcealed, unchecked *Opposite*: contained

unbroken *adj* **continuous**, constant, uninterrupted, steady, complete *Opposite*: intermittent

unburden *(fml)* *v* **relieve**, divest, free, release, let go *Opposite*: brood

unbutton *v* **undo**, open, unfasten *Opposite*: fasten

uncalled-for *adj* **unjustified**, unwarranted, undeserved, unprovoked, gratuitous *Opposite*: justifiable

uncanny *adj* **eerie**, weird, strange, mysterious, supernatural

uncared-for *adj* **neglected**, unloved, untended, unkempt, unattended *Opposite*: cherished

uncaring *adj* **hardhearted**, unfeeling, heartless, indifferent, cold Opposite: caring

unceasing adj **constant**, continuous, interminable, never-ending, perpetual Opposite: sporadic

unceremonious adj **abrupt**, hasty, rushed, terse, rude Opposite: gracious

uncertain adj **1 unsure**, vague, doubtful, hesitant, undecided Opposite: sure **2 indeterminate**, inexact, undefined, indefinite, ambiguous Opposite: exact. See COMPARE AND CONTRAST at doubtful.

uncertainty n **doubt**, indecision, hesitation, vagueness, ambiguity Opposite: confidence

unchain v **release**, unlock, unfetter, unshackle, liberate Opposite: chain

unchangeable adj **fixed**, unalterable, unvarying, constant, unchanged Opposite: changeable

unchanged adj **unaffected**, unmoved, untouched Opposite: affected

unchanging adj **static**, fixed, invariable, unchangeable, rigid Opposite: flexible

uncharacteristic adj **unusual**, atypical, abnormal, out of character, unexpected Opposite: typical

uncharitable adj **mean**, unkind, hurtful, spiteful, cruel Opposite: generous

uncharted adj **unexplored**, new, unfamiliar, unmapped, unknown Opposite: familiar

unchecked adj **unimpeded**, unrestrained, unhindered, unrestricted, unconstrained Opposite: restricted

uncivil adj **rude**, discourteous, impolite, insulting, bad-mannered Opposite: courteous

uncivilized adj **1 primitive**, barbaric, uncultured, unsophisticated, crude Opposite: civilized **2 remote**, distant, far-off, isolated, unreachable Opposite: reachable **3 coarse**, impolite, discourteous, unrefined, vulgar Opposite: polite

unclasp v **unfasten**, undo, open, unbuckle, untie Opposite: fasten

unclassified adj **1 random**, unsystematic, disorganized, unorganized, uncategorized Opposite: organized **2 open**, public, released, unconcealed, accessible Opposite: secret

unclean adj **1 impure**, dirty, contaminated, polluted, infected Opposite: pure **2 unchaste**, sinful, impure, unworthy, immoral Opposite: chaste. See COMPARE AND CONTRAST at dirty.

uncleanness n **1 dirtiness**, filthiness, impurity, griminess, squalor Opposite: cleanness **2 unchasteness**, sinfulness, impurity, unworthiness, immorality Opposite: chasteness

unclear adj **1 indistinct**, hazy, indeterminate, blurred, indistinguishable Opposite: clear **2 uncertain**, doubtful, undecided, unsure, in doubt Opposite: definite. See COMPARE AND CONTRAST at obscure.

unclench v **relax**, release, open, let go, slacken Opposite: tighten

unclog v **unblock**, clear, free, release, clean out Opposite: block

unclothe v **undress**, strip, uncover, disrobe (fml) Opposite: dress

unclothed adj **bare**, naked, uncovered, undressed, nude Opposite: dressed

uncoil v **unravel**, unwind, undo, untwist, release Opposite: twist

uncomfortable adj **1 painful**, tight, rough, scratchy, itchy Opposite: comfortable **2 embarrassing**, awkward, difficult, tricky, unpleasant Opposite: enjoyable **3 uneasy**, awkward, ill at ease, embarrassed, tense Opposite: relaxed

uncommitted adj **casual**, uninterested, indifferent, unattached, free Opposite: committed

uncommon adj **rare**, unusual, infrequent, scarce, special Opposite: common

uncommunicative adj **reserved**, reticent, taciturn, silent, withdrawn Opposite: talkative. See COMPARE AND CONTRAST at silent.

uncomplaining adj **accepting**, tolerant, long-suffering, patient, accommodating Opposite: intolerant

uncomplicated adj **simple**, straightforward, unfussy, basic, unsophisticated Opposite: complex

uncomplimentary adj **disparaging**, derogatory, unflattering, negative, rude Opposite: complimentary

uncompromising adj **inflexible**, rigid, adamant, unbending, obdurate Opposite: flexible

unconcealed adj **obvious**, open, evident, apparent, blatant Opposite: hidden

unconcern n **indifference**, apathy, disregard, nonchalance, disinterest Opposite: anxiety

unconcerned adj **indifferent**, unworried, nonchalant, undaunted, undisturbed Opposite: anxious

unconditional adj **unqualified**, total, categorical, absolute, unrestricted Opposite: qualified

unconditioned adj **unrestricted**, limitless, undefined, unlimited, open-ended Opposite: restricted

unconfident adj **insecure**, unsure, nervous, apprehensive, self-doubting Opposite: self-assured

unconfined adj **free**, liberated, released, loose, at large Opposite: restricted

unconfirmed adj **unverified**, unsubstantiated, unproven, unofficial, unsupported Opposite: verified

uncongenial adj **disagreeable**, unfriendly, unwelcoming, unpleasant, inhospitable Opposite: friendly

unconnected adj **separate**, unrelated, independent, distinct, isolated Opposite: linked

unconquerable *adj* **unbeatable**, unassailable, unattainable, insurmountable, indomitable *Opposite*: vulnerable

unconscionable *adj* **1 unacceptable**, shocking, horrifying, immoral, reprehensible *Opposite*: acceptable **2 unreasonable**, beyond the pale, irrational, ridiculous, illogical *Opposite*: reasonable

unconscious *adj* **1 comatose**, insentient, insensible, out cold, cataleptic *Opposite*: awake **2 unaware**, oblivious, ignorant, unwitting, insensible *Opposite*: aware **3 unintentional**, automatic, mechanical, instinctive, involuntary *Opposite*: deliberate ■ *n* **id**, superego, ego, self, psyche

unconsciousness *n* oblivion, sleep, nothingness, insentience, catalepsy *Opposite*: consciousness

unconsidered *adj* **hasty**, unthinking, impulsive, reactive, imprudent *Opposite*: considered

unconstitutional *adj* **illegal**, unauthorized, unlawful, undemocratic, unofficial *Opposite*: lawful

unconstrained *adj* **unimpeded**, free, unrestrained, unrestricted, unhindered *Opposite*: restricted

unconstructive *adj* **unhelpful**, negative, unenthusiastic, uncooperative, ineffectual *Opposite*: constructive

uncontaminated *adj* **pure**, clean, unadulterated, antiseptic, sterilized *Opposite*: contaminated

uncontrollable *adj* **1 irrepressible**, uncontainable, overpowering, wild, overwhelming **2 unruly**, disobedient, out of control, unmanageable, disorderly *Opposite*: well-behaved

uncontrolled *adj* **unrestrained**, abandoned, wild, hysterical, uninhibited *Opposite*: restrained

uncontroversial *adj* **undisputed**, uncontentious, uncontended, unquestionable, indisputable *Opposite*: controversial

unconventional *adj* **eccentric**, unusual, alternative, avant-garde, strange *Opposite*: conventional

unconventionality *n* **eccentricity**, originality, nonconformity, oddness, quirkiness *Opposite*: conventionality

unconvinced *adj* **skeptical**, incredulous, disbelieving, unimpressed, unmoved *Opposite*: convinced

unconvincing *adj* **implausible**, unimpressive, weak, feeble, unsuccessful *Opposite*: persuasive

uncooked *adj* **raw**, rare, fresh, unprepared *Opposite*: cooked

uncooperative *adj* **unhelpful**, disobliging, awkward, obstinate, contrary *Opposite*: amenable

uncoordinated *adj* **clumsy**, ungainly, awkward, ungraceful, inept *Opposite*: graceful

uncork *v* **1 open**, break open, unplug, break into, pop open *Opposite*: plug **2 unleash**, release, give vent to, pour out, set free *Opposite*: hold in

uncorrupted *adj* **unadulterated**, unspoiled, uncontaminated, chaste, pure *Opposite*: corrupted

uncounted *adj* **innumerable**, countless, numerous, myriad, incalculable *Opposite*: few

uncouple *v* **undo**, disengage, separate, detach, unyoke *Opposite*: join

uncouth *adj* **rude**, uncivilized, bad-mannered, ill-mannered, foul-mouthed *Opposite*: polite

uncouthness *n* **rudeness**, vulgarity, bad manners, crudeness, coarseness *Opposite*: politeness

uncover *v* **expose**, discover, reveal, unearth, find out *Opposite*: conceal

uncovered *adj* **exposed**, bare, open, naked, revealed *Opposite*: concealed

uncovering *n* **exposure**, discovery, disclosure, revelation *Opposite*: concealment

uncritical *adj* **indiscriminating**, accepting, credulous, naive, gullible *Opposite*: discriminating

unction *n* **1 balm**, ointment, salve, oil, lotion **2 earnestness**, fervor, zeal, passion, enthusiasm

unctuous *adj* **1 ingratiating**, sycophantic, slimy, smarmy, obsequious *Opposite*: arrogant **2 oily**, greasy, fatty, slippery, slimy

uncultivated *adj* **1 unrefined**, unsophisticated, coarse, uncultured, unpolished *Opposite*: refined **2 fallow**, untilled, unplanted, unfarmed *Opposite*: cultivated

uncultured *adj* **unrefined**, philistine, boorish, unsophisticated, uncultivated *Opposite*: refined

uncurl *v* **straighten**, straighten out, uncoil, flatten, unwind *Opposite*: curl

uncut *adj* **unabridged**, complete, full-length, unedited, uncensored *Opposite*: abridged

undamaged *adj* **unspoiled**, untouched, unharmed, unhurt, intact *Opposite*: spoiled

undaunted *adj* **fearless**, unconcerned, unworried, carefree, undisturbed *Opposite*: scared

undeceive *v* **inform**, tell, notify, enlighten, disabuse *Opposite*: deceive

undecided *adj* **1 of two minds**, in doubt, dithering, vacillating, uncertain *Opposite*: decided **2 in doubt**, unresolved, open, unclear, vague *Opposite*: certain

undecipherable *adj* **illegible**, unreadable, inexplicable, mysterious, unfathomable *Opposite*: clear

undecorated *adj* **plain**, simple, unornamented, austere, spartan *Opposite*: ornate

undefeated *adj* **unbeaten**, reigning, unvanquished, unconquered, unbowed *Opposite*: defeated

undefended *adj* **unguarded**, unprotected, unfortified, deserted, defenseless *Opposite*: defended

undefiled *adj* **unsullied**, pure, unpolluted, unblemished, unstained *Opposite*: defiled *(fml)*

undefined *adj* **indeterminate**, vague, approximate, open-ended, indefinite *Opposite*: defined

undemanding *adj* **easy**, straightforward, light, simple, unchallenging *Opposite*: demanding

undemocratic *adj* **inequitable**, unfair, autocratic, high-handed, dictatorial *Opposite*: democratic

undemonstrative *adj* **unemotional**, restrained, phlegmatic, stoical, impassive *Opposite*: demonstrative

undeniable *adj* **irrefutable**, indisputable, incontestable, incontrovertible, unquestionable *Opposite*: questionable

undependable *adj* **unreliable**, unpredictable, variable, erratic, fickle *Opposite*: dependable

under *prep* **1 beneath**, below, in, underneath *Opposite*: above **2 below**, less than *Opposite*: over

underachieve *v* **disappoint**, flounder, drift, drop out, underperform *Opposite*: excel

underage *adj* **juvenile**, immature, youthful, young, callow

underclothes *n* **underwear**, underclothing, underthings, undies *(infml)*

underclothing *see* underclothes

undercover *adj* **secret**, hidden, covert, disguised, clandestine *Opposite*: open

undercurrent *n* **1 current**, tide, undertow, pull, stream **2 feeling**, hint, undertow, suggestion, connotation

undercut *v* **undermine**, destabilize, detract, weaken, damage *Opposite*: strengthen

underdeveloped *adj* **immature**, small, undersized, weak, unused

underdog *n* **loser**, small fry, runner up, second best, little guy

underdone *adj* **rare**, bloody, pink, undercooked *Opposite*: overdone

underemphasize *v* **play down**, understate, underplay, minimize, underrate *Opposite*: overemphasize

underestimate *v* **undervalue**, underrate, misjudge, miscalculate *Opposite*: overestimate

underfed *adj* **malnourished**, starving, frail, weak, undernourished *Opposite*: well-fed

undergo *v* **experience**, feel, suffer, endure, undertake *Opposite*: avoid

underground *adj* **1 subterranean**, below ground, covered, buried, deep **2 subversive**, secretive, dissident, alternative, covert *Opposite*: open

undergrowth *n* **bushes**, scrub, brushwood, vegetation, understory

underhand *adj* **deceitful**, dishonest, sneaky, mean, sly *Opposite*: open ■ *adv* **deceitfully**, dishonestly, sneakily, slyly, craftily *Opposite*: openly

underhanded *see* underhand

underlie *v* **lie beneath**, lie behind, motivate, cause, inspire

underline *v* **underscore**, emphasize, highlight, feature, stress *Opposite*: ignore

underling *n* **minion**, inferior, subject, junior, subordinate *Opposite*: superior

underlying *adj* **fundamental**, original, causal, primary, basic

undermine *v* **weaken**, dent, chip away at, challenge, destabilize *Opposite*: bolster

underneath *prep* **under**, beneath, below *Opposite*: on top of ■ *n* **base**, bottom, underside, footing, foundation *Opposite*: top

under no circumstances *adv* **by no means**, on no account, not at all, in no way, never

undernourished *adj* **malnourished**, underfed, starved, hungry, famished *Opposite*: well-fed

undernourishment *n* **malnutrition**, starvation, hunger, famine

underperform *v* **fail**, underachieve, disappoint, flounder, drift *Opposite*: excel

underpin *v* **1 shore up**, prop up, reinforce, support, buttress *Opposite*: undermine **2 support**, lie beneath, underlie, give support to, bolster *Opposite*: weaken

underpinning *n* **foundation**, reinforcement, groundwork, keystone, bedrock

underplay *v* **make light of**, minimize, understate, play down, talk down *Opposite*: overplay

underprice *v* **cheapen**, undersell, underrepresent, understate *Opposite*: overprice

underprivileged *adj* **disadvantaged**, deprived, poor, needy, neglected *Opposite*: well-off

underprop *v* **underpin**, shore up, prop up, jack up, reinforce *Opposite*: undermine

underrate *v* **undervalue**, underestimate, think little of, devalue, misjudge *Opposite*: overrate

underrated *adj* **undervalued**, underestimated, unappreciated, unrecognized, misunderstood *Opposite*: overrated

underrepresent *v* **understate**, undersell, lessen, play down, make light of *Opposite*: overemphasize

underscore *v* **underline**, highlight, emphasize, accentuate, call attention to *Opposite*: ignore

undersea *adj* **submarine**, underwater, bathyal, bathypelagic

undersell v understate, play down, make light of, denigrate, cheapen *Opposite*: oversell

undershrub n subshrub, bush, plant

underside n base, bottom, underneath, basement, foundation

undersized adj puny, underdeveloped, small, short, stunted *Opposite*: extra-large

understand v 1 comprehend, appreciate, know, recognize, realize 2 sympathize, empathize, identify, appreciate

understandable adj comprehensible, clear, logical, reasonable, fathomable *Opposite*: incomprehensible

understanding n agreement, arrangement, deal, contract, settlement ■ adj sympathetic, empathetic, considerate, thoughtful, kind *Opposite*: unsympathetic ■ n 1 sympathy, empathy, identification, consideration, kindness *Opposite*: indifference 2 grasp, perception, intellect, mind, wit *Opposite*: ignorance 3 interpretation, construction, personal feeling, estimation, perception

understate v play down, minimize, devalue, belittle, make little of *Opposite*: exaggerate

understated adj modest, inconspicuous, discreet, unfussy, minimalist *Opposite*: exaggerated

understatement n irony, dryness, sarcasm, underestimation *Opposite*: exaggeration

understood adj unspoken, tacit, silent, unstated, unwritten *Opposite*: explicit

understory n forest floor, bushes, undergrowth, underwood, brush

understrength adj 1 understaffed, shorthanded, short-staffed, short, down 2 dilute, weak, thin, diluted, watered down

understudy n substitute, cover, standby, stand-in, replacement

undertake v take on, assume, start, commence, embark on *Opposite*: relinquish

undertaker n funeral director, mortician, embalmer

undertaking n responsibility, task, job, enterprise, commission

under-the-counter adj illegal, unofficial, illicit, wrongful, criminal *Opposite*: aboveboard

under-the-table adj underhand, unofficial, secret, surreptitious, sneaky *Opposite*: aboveboard

under the weather adj ill, unwell, sick, run-down *Opposite*: well

underthings n underwear, underclothes, underclothing, undies *(infml)*

undertone n hint, suggestion, trace, tinge, undercurrent *Opposite*: overtone

undertow n current, undercurrent, tide, pull, stream

undervalue v underrate, underestimate, play down, devalue, belittle *Opposite*: overrate

underwater adj 1 submerged, sunken, flooded, subaquatic, subsurface *Opposite*: dry 2 undersea, submarine, sunken, submerged, marine

underway adj happening, in progress, ongoing, on the go, proceeding

underwear n underclothes, underclothing, underthings, undies *(infml)*

WORD BANK
❑ types of lower-body underwear bloomers *(dated)*, boxer shorts, briefs, corset, crinoline, drawers, foundation garment, garter, girdle, G-string, jockstrap, knee-highs, legwarmer, long johns, nylons, panties, pantyhose, petticoat, slip, sock, stockings, string, support hose, thigh-highs, thong, underpants, underskirt
❑ types of upper body underwear basque, body stocking, body suit, bra, camisole, chemise, teddy, undershirt, union suit

underweight adj skinny, skin-and-bone, scrawny, half-starved, underfed *Opposite*: overweight

underworld n gangland, criminal world, netherworld *(fml)* ■ adj criminal, gangland, illicit, illegal, unlawful *Opposite*: legal

under wraps *(infml)* adj hidden, secret, confidential, private, buried *Opposite*: open

underwrite v guarantee, countersign, back, endorse, fund

underwriter n sponsor, backer, supporter, guarantor, financier

undeserved adj unwarranted, unmerited, unearned, unfair, unjustifiable *Opposite*: deserved

undesirable adj unwanted, unwelcome, uninvited, objectionable, disagreeable *Opposite*: desirable

undetectable adj untraceable, indiscernible, unnoticeable, imperceptible, invisible *Opposite*: obvious

undetermined adj 1 unresolved, indeterminate, indefinite, undecided, incalculable *Opposite*: definite 2 unknown, undiscovered, unidentified, unheard of, unfamiliar *Opposite*: known 3 hesitating, undecided, irresolute, unsettled, vacillating *Opposite*: decided

undeveloped adj immature, young, embryonic, unripe, emergent *Opposite*: mature

undeviating adj unswerving, firm, solid, absolute, total *Opposite*: shaky

undies *(infml)* n underwear, underclothes, underclothing, underthings

undignified adj unseemly, unbecoming, indecorous, improper, humiliating *Opposite*: dignified

undiluted adj straight, neat, unadulterated, unmixed, full-strength *Opposite*: diluted

undiplomatic adj tactless, crass, thoughtless, indiscreet, inconsiderate *Opposite*: diplomatic

undirected adj purposeless, aimless, directionless, pointless, wandering *Opposite*: purposeful

undisciplined *adj* **unmanageable**, out of control, wild, unruly, disobedient *Opposite*: well-behaved

undisclosed *adj* **secret**, unnamed, hidden, unrevealed, unidentified *Opposite*: known

undisguised *adj* **unconcealed**, plain, straightforward, open, public *Opposite*: concealed

undisposed *adj* **unwilling**, loath, reluctant, unprepared, hesitant *Opposite*: disposed

undisputed *adj* **acknowledged**, undoubted, certain, undeniable, unquestionable *Opposite*: questionable

undistinguished *adj* **ordinary**, everyday, run-of-the-mill, commonplace, nothing special *Opposite*: unusual

undistorted *adj* **factual**, truthful, exact, accurate, straight *Opposite*: inaccurate

undisturbed *adj* **1 uninterrupted**, in peace, unbroken, unobstructed *Opposite*: interrupted **2 untouched**, intact, whole, flawless, undamaged *Opposite*: damaged **3 peaceful**, serene, composed, at peace, at ease *Opposite*: anxious

undivided *adj* **complete**, entire, whole, total, full *Opposite*: partial

undo *v* **1 unfasten**, untie, unbutton, loosen, disengage *Opposite*: fasten **2 cancel out**, cancel, nullify, invalidate, render null and void

undoing *n* **downfall**, ruin, ruination, collapse, destruction *Opposite*: making

undone *adj* **1 uncompleted**, unfinished, incomplete, half-done, unconcluded *Opposite*: done **2 unfastened**, open, gaping, unzipped, unbuttoned **3 ruined**, in trouble, lost, in deep water, destroyed *Opposite*: fine

undoubted *adj* **certain**, sure, absolute, definite, indubitable *Opposite*: doubtful

undreamed-of *adj* **unexpected**, unhoped-for, unimaginable, unanticipated, unlooked-for *Opposite*: anticipated

undress *v* **strip off**, strip, unclothe, remove your clothes, bare *Opposite*: dress

undressed *adj* **naked**, bare, nude, stripped, with nothing on *Opposite*: dressed. *See* COMPARE AND CONTRAST *at* naked.

undue *adj* **unwarranted**, excessive, unnecessary, unjustified, unjustifiable *Opposite*: justified

undulant *(fml) see* undulating

undulate *v* **roll**, ripple, rise and fall, swell, heave

undulating *adj* **rolling**, rising and falling, swelling, heaving, surging

undulation *n* **wave**, ripple, furrow, crinkle, wrinkle

unduly *adv* **excessively**, overly, disproportionately, unjustifiably, undeservedly *Opposite*: justifiably

undying *adj* **unending**, never-ending, endless, perpetual, eternal *Opposite*: inconstant

unearned *adj* **undeserved**, unwarranted, unmerited, unjustified, uncalled-for

unearth *v* **1 disclose**, reveal, expose, publicize, bring to light *Opposite*: cover up **2 dig up**, exhume, disinter, excavate, extract *Opposite*: bury

unearthly *adj* **1 unreasonable**, inappropriate, outrageous, ridiculous, absurd *Opposite*: acceptable **2 eerie**, weird, bizarre, strange, macabre *Opposite*: normal

unease *n* **anxiety**, nervousness, restlessness, awkwardness, uneasiness *Opposite*: calm. *See* COMPARE AND CONTRAST *at* worry.

uneasiness *n* **anxiety**, nervousness, restlessness, awkwardness, unease *Opposite*: calmness

uneasy *adj* **anxious**, nervous, troubled, uncomfortable, ill at ease *Opposite*: calm

uneconomic *adj* **1 unprofitable**, not viable, profitless *Opposite*: profitable **2 inefficient**, wasteful, uneconomical, improvident, extravagant *Opposite*: efficient

uneconomical *adj* **inefficient**, wasteful, extravagant, uneconomic, profligate *Opposite*: efficient

unedited *adj* **complete**, unabridged, unexpurgated, uncut, full-length *Opposite*: edited

uneducated *adj* **unschooled**, untaught, ignorant, illiterate, uninformed *Opposite*: educated

unembellished *adj* **1 unadorned**, plain, without ornamentation, simple, straightforward *Opposite*: fancy **2 factual**, unembroidered, undistorted, truthful, straightforward *Opposite*: fictional

unembroidered *adj* **factual**, unembellished, undistorted, truthful, unvarnished *Opposite*: florid

unemotional *adj* **impassive**, dispassionate, undemonstrative, unresponsive, detached *Opposite*: emotional

unemployed *adj* **jobless**, out of work, out of a job, laid off, on unemployment *Opposite*: employed

unemployment *n* **joblessness**, job loss, idleness *Opposite*: employment

unending *adj* **endless**, never-ending, eternal, everlasting, interminable *Opposite*: finite

unendurable *adj* **insufferable**, unbearable, intolerable, insupportable, excruciating *Opposite*: bearable

unenlightened *adj* **1 prejudiced**, ignorant, narrow, narrow-minded, closed-minded *Opposite*: enlightened **2 unaware**, uninformed, ignorant, oblivious, unacquainted *Opposite*: informed

unenthusiastic *adj* **apathetic**, indifferent, unresponsive, lukewarm, half-hearted *Opposite*: enthusiastic

unenviable *adj* **undesirable**, disagreeable, unpleasant, uninviting, objectionable *Opposite*: enviable

unequal *adj* **1 uneven**, unbalanced, lopsided, asymmetrical, disproportionate *Opposite*: equal **2 unfair**, inequitable, one-sided, mismatched, unbalanced *Opposite*: fair **3 unsatisfactory**, unfit, unable, incapable, inadequate

unequaled *adj* **unrivaled**, unique, unmatched, unchallenged, superior *Opposite*: ordinary

unequivocal *adj* **clear**, plain, unambiguous, unmistakable, explicit

unerring *adj* **certain**, sure, absolute, positive, definite *Opposite*: faulty

unessential *adj* **dispensable**, superfluous, unnecessary, inessential, replaceable *Opposite*: essential

unethical *adj* **unprincipled**, immoral, wrong, bad, unscrupulous *Opposite*: ethical

uneven *adj* **1 rough**, jagged, bumpy, patchy, irregular *Opposite*: level **2 unequal**, unbalanced, lopsided, asymmetrical, disproportionate *Opposite*: equal **3 mismatched**, one-sided, unfair, unbalanced, disproportionate *Opposite*: fair

unevenness *n* **1 roughness**, jaggedness, bumpiness, patchiness *Opposite*: evenness **2 inequality**, one-sidedness, disparity *Opposite*: equality **3 asymmetry**, disproportion, irregularity *Opposite*: symmetry

uneventful *adj* **boring**, monotonous, ordinary, humdrum, dull *Opposite*: exciting

unexceptionable *adj* **inoffensive**, unobjectionable, faultless, irreproachable, acceptable *Opposite*: exceptionable *(fml)*

unexceptional *adj* **undistinguished**, nondescript, anonymous, modest, indifferent *Opposite*: extraordinary

unexcited *adj* **calm**, restrained, subdued, unresponsive, impassive *Opposite*: excited

unexciting *adj* **dull**, boring, tedious, monotonous, humdrum *Opposite*: exciting

unexpected *adj* **unforeseen**, unanticipated, unpredicted, surprising, startling *Opposite*: expected

unexplained *adj* **mysterious**, unsolved, inexplicable, impenetrable, arcane *Opposite*: apparent

unexpressed *adj* **unstated**, unspoken, unsaid, unknown *Opposite*: articulated

unfailing *adj* **reliable**, certain, dependable, trustworthy, constant *Opposite*: erratic

unfair *adj* **1 unjust**, inequitable, iniquitous, unwarranted, unmerited *Opposite*: fair **2 unethical**, dishonest, dishonorable, deceitful, underhand *Opposite*: honest **3 partial**, one-sided, biased, prejudicial, discriminating *Opposite*: fair

unfairness *n* **1 injustice**, wrongness, wrong, iniquitousness, unreasonableness *Opposite*: fairness **2 underhandedness**, dishonesty, dishonorableness, deceitfulness, fraudulence *Opposite*: honesty **3 partiality**, one-sidedness, bias, prejudice, discrimination *Opposite*: fairness

unfaithful *adj* **disloyal**, false, untrue, adulterous, treacherous *Opposite*: faithful

unfaithfulness *n* **disloyalty**, infidelity, falseness, adultery, treachery *Opposite*: faithfulness

unfaltering *adj* **untiring**, indefatigable, tireless, unflagging, persistent *Opposite*: faltering

unfamiliar *adj* **1 unknown**, new, untried, strange, alien *Opposite*: familiar **2 unacquainted**, unaccustomed, unaware, unversed, unskilled *Opposite*: familiar

unfamiliarity *n* **1 newness**, strangeness, unusualness, foreignness, exoticism *Opposite*: familiarity **2 unaccustomedness**, inexperience, ignorance, unawareness, lack of experience *Opposite*: familiarity

unfashionable *adj* **out-of-date**, outmoded, dated, old-fashioned, behind the times *Opposite*: trendy *(infml)*

unfasten *v* **undo**, unhook, unlock, disengage, detach *Opposite*: fasten

unfastened *adj* **undone**, loosened, untied, unbuttoned, unzipped *Opposite*: fastened

unfathomable *adj* **1 deep**, profound, bottomless, unsounded, unplumbed *Opposite*: shallow **2 incomprehensible**, impenetrable, inscrutable, unknowable, indecipherable *Opposite*: straightforward

unfavorable *adj* **1 disapproving**, negative, uncomplimentary, opposed, hostile *Opposite*: approving **2 harmful**, adverse, bad, detrimental, disadvantageous *Opposite*: beneficial

unfeasible *adj* **impracticable**, impractical, unworkable, unachievable, out of the question *Opposite*: feasible

unfeeling *adj* **unsympathetic**, hardhearted, callous, cruel, heartless *Opposite*: sympathetic

unfetter *v* **release**, liberate, free, unchain, unshackle *Opposite*: fetter

unfettered *adj* **freed**, unencumbered, unconstrained, unregulated, autonomous *Opposite*: constrained

unfilled *adj* **empty**, vacant, void, unoccupied, untaken *Opposite*: full

unfinished *adj* **incomplete**, uncompleted, fragmentary, partial, ongoing *Opposite*: finished

unfit *adj* **1 unsuitable**, inappropriate, unsuited, inapt, unacceptable *Opposite*: suitable **2 unqualified**, incompetent, inept, useless, incapable *Opposite*: competent **3 out of shape**, out of condition, unhealthy, weak, puny *Opposite*: fit

unfitted *adj* **unsuited**, unequipped, unprepared, unsuitable, unqualified *Opposite*: fitted

unfitting *adj* **unsuitable**, inappropriate, unbecoming, out of place, unseemly *Opposite*: fitting

unfix *v* **detach**, loosen, disengage, separate, undo *Opposite*: attach

unflagging *adj* **untiring**, indefatigable, tireless, unfaltering, persistent *Opposite*: weak

unflappability *n* **calmness**, coolness, patience, composure, control *Opposite*: excitability

unflappable *adj* **composed**, calm, unflustered, collected, imperturbable *Opposite*: anxious

unflattering *adj* **1 unbecoming**, unattractive, unappealing, ugly *Opposite*: becoming **2 critical**, uncomplimentary, faultfinding, unfavorable *Opposite*: complimentary

unfledged *adj* **inexperienced**, naive, innocent, fresh, immature *Opposite*: experienced

unflinching *adj* **unwavering**, constant, steady, undaunted, persistent *Opposite*: wavering

unflustered *adj* **composed**, calm, unflappable, collected, imperturbable *Opposite*: agitated

unfocused *adj* **1 blurred**, unclear, fuzzy, indistinct, bleary *Opposite*: clear **2 ill-defined**, nonspecific, imprecise, woolly, vague *Opposite*: focused

unfold *v* **1 open out**, open up, unfurl, spread out, display *Opposite*: fold up **2 explain**, clarify, make known, disclose, reveal *Opposite*: conceal **3 develop**, evolve, grow, progress, advance *Opposite*: deteriorate

unforced *adj* **voluntary**, natural, spontaneous, unwitting, unprompted *Opposite*: forced

unforeseeable *adj* **unexpected**, unanticipated, undreamed-of, unpredictable, surprise *Opposite*: predictable

unforeseen *adj* **unexpected**, unanticipated, unpredicted, surprising, startling *Opposite*: expected

unforgettable *adj* **memorable**, remarkable, treasured, cherished, haunting *Opposite*: unremarkable

unforgivable *adj* **unpardonable**, inexcusable, indefensible, unjustifiable, intolerable *Opposite*: understandable

unforgiving *adj* **1 intolerant**, merciless, pitiless, remorseless, vindictive *Opposite*: tolerant **2 demanding**, exacting, taxing, challenging, hard *Opposite*: easy

unformed *adj* **1 shapeless**, formless, indistinct, imprecise, amorphous *Opposite*: distinct **2 undeveloped**, immature, green, callow, underdeveloped *Opposite*: mature

unformulated *adj* **vague**, indistinct, unclear, hazy, nebulous *Opposite*: clear

unforthcoming *adj* **uncommunicative**, reticent, taciturn, standoffish, distant *Opposite*: voluble

unfortunate *adj* **1 unlucky**, luckless, unsuccessful, unhappy, ill-fated *Opposite*: lucky **2 disastrous**, calamitous, doomed, hopeless, fateful *Opposite*: fortunate **3 inappropriate**, inopportune, ill-timed, tactless, untimely *Opposite*: timely ■ *n* **wretch**, underdog, loser, lame duck, weakling

unfortunately *adv* **1 unluckily**, unhappily, regrettably, sadly, alas *Opposite*: fortunately **2 inappropriately**, inopportunely, tactlessly, ill-advisedly, regrettably *Opposite*: appropriately

unfounded *adj* **groundless**, unsupported, baseless, unsubstantiated, speculative *Opposite*: proven

unfreeze *v* **relax**, rescind, repeal, release, liberate *Opposite*: freeze

unfrequented *adj* **lonely**, neglected, isolated, quiet, desolate *Opposite*: busy

unfriendliness *n* **aloofness**, surliness, coldness, coolness, frostiness *Opposite*: friendliness

unfriendly *adj* **1 aloof**, distant, surly, cold, frosty *Opposite*: friendly **2 unfavorable**, illdisposed, inimical, hostile, inauspicious *Opposite*: well-disposed

unfruitful *adj* **1 unsuccessful**, unprofitable, unproductive, unrewarding, fruitless *Opposite*: profitable **2 infertile**, sterile, barren, bare, fruitless *Opposite*: fertile

unfurl *v* **open out**, open up, unfold, spread out, expand *Opposite*: fold up

unfurnished *adj* **bare**, empty, unequipped, unfitted *Opposite*: furnished

unfussy *adj* **understated**, simple, uncomplicated, modest, plain *Opposite*: fussy

ungainliness *n* **1 gracelessness**, awkwardness, clumsiness, inelegance, gaucheness *Opposite*: gracefulness **2 awkwardness**, unwieldiness, cumbersomeness, heaviness, clumsiness *Opposite*: convenience

ungainly *adj* **1 graceless**, awkward, clumsy, inelegant, ungraceful *Opposite*: graceful **2 awkward**, unwieldy, cumbersome, inconvenient, heavy *Opposite*: convenient

ungenerous *adj* **1 stingy**, miserly, tightfisted, parsimonious, grudging *Opposite*: generous **2 mean-spirited**, nasty, mean, unkind, cruel *Opposite*: kind

unglued *adj* **1 separated**, detached, parted, disconnected, divided *Opposite*: whole **2** *(infml)* **upset**, angry, disconcerted, hysterical, unnerved *Opposite*: calm

ungodly *adj* **1 impious**, irreligious, irreverent, blasphemous, disrespectful *Opposite*: pious **2 wicked**, sinful, immoral, corrupt, depraved *Opposite*: virtuous **3** *(infml)* **unreasonable**, unearthly, late, unsocial, ridiculous *Opposite*: reasonable

ungovernable *adj* **uncontrollable**, out of control, unmanageable, unruly, anarchic *Opposite*: controllable

ungraceful adj 1 **clumsy**, ungainly, graceless, uncoordinated, lumbering Opposite: elegant 2 **rude**, impolite, discourteous, gruff, brusque Opposite: polite

ungracious adj **ill-mannered**, discourteous, rude, impolite, bad-mannered Opposite: gracious

ungrateful adj 1 **unappreciative**, thankless, churlish, unmindful, ungracious Opposite: grateful 2 **unpleasant**, unrewarding, thankless, unsatisfying Opposite: rewarding

ungratefully adv **unappreciatively**, churlishly, thanklessly, ungraciously Opposite: gratefully

ungratefulness n unappreciativeness, ingratitude, churlishness, thanklessness, ungraciousness Opposite: gratitude

unguarded adj 1 **unwary**, careless, indiscreet, thoughtless, imprudent Opposite: guarded 2 **unprotected**, undefended, unshielded, unfortified, defenseless Opposite: guarded

unguent n ointment, salve, balm, lotion, oil

unhampered adj **unrestricted**, unimpeded, unhindered, unconstrained, free Opposite: restricted

unhappily adv 1 **sadly**, miserably, discontentedly, despondently, dejectedly Opposite: happily 2 **unfortunately**, unluckily, regrettably, alas, sadly Opposite: luckily

unhappiness n **sadness**, sorrow, grief, misery, discontent Opposite: happiness

unhappy adj 1 **sad**, miserable, discontented, despondent, dejected Opposite: happy 2 **unfortunate**, ill-fated, hopeless, doomed, fateful Opposite: fortunate 3 **inappropriate**, ill-chosen, infelicitous, tactless, unfortunate Opposite: well-chosen 4 **displeased** annoyed, upset, angry, disappointed Opposite: pleased

unharmed adj **uninjured**, unhurt, unscathed, undamaged, unscratched Opposite: harmed

unhealthy adj 1 **harmful**, detrimental, injurious, damaging, unwholesome Opposite: healthy 2 **sick**, unfit, out of condition, out of shape, sickly Opposite: well 3 **corrupt**, unwholesome, morbid, unnatural, ghoulish Opposite: wholesome

unheard adj **unheeded**, disregarded, ignored, overlooked, unnoticed

unheard-of adj 1 **unknown**, unfamiliar, new, obscure, undiscovered Opposite: well-known 2 **unprecedented**, exceptional, extraordinary, novel, unusual Opposite: ordinary 3 **offensive**, rude, disgusting, repulsive, shocking Opposite: inoffensive

unhelpful adj 1 **uncooperative**, contrary, awkward, unaccommodating, obstructive Opposite: helpful 2 **useless**, unconstructive, impractical, unnecessary, negative Opposite: useful

unhelpfulness n 1 **uncooperativeness**, unsupportiveness, contrariness, impracticality Opposite: helpfulness 2 **uselessness**, negativity, pointlessness, needlessness, worthlessness Opposite: usefulness

unhesitating adj prompt, unreserved, wholehearted, confident, forthright Opposite: tentative

unhindered adj unimpeded, unconstrained, unrestricted, unobstructed, unchecked

unhinge v unbalance, derange, madden, drive insane, disturb

unhinged adj **unbalanced**, deranged, disturbed, irrational Opposite: sane

unhitch v unfasten, untie, undo, uncouple, detach Opposite: fasten

unholy adj 1 **unconsecrated**, unhallowed, unblessed, profane, secular Opposite: consecrated 2 **ungodly**, blasphemous, secular, immoral, evil Opposite: holy 3 **outrageous**, ungodly, disgraceful, scandalous, shocking

unhook v undo, release, uncouple, detach, disengage Opposite: hook

unhoped-for adj unexpected, unanticipated, surprising, undreamed-of, unforeseen Opposite: expected

unhopeful adj **doubtful**, despondent, gloomy, dejected, pessimistic Opposite: hopeful

unhurried adj slow, easygoing, dawdling, calm, deliberate Opposite: hurried

unhurt adj **uninjured**, unharmed, undamaged, unscathed, safe Opposite: hurt

unhygienic adj **insanitary**, unclean, polluted, unhealthy, foul Opposite: hygienic

unidentified adj nameless, anonymous, faceless, unnamed, unknown Opposite: known

unidentified flying object see **UFO**

unification n amalgamation, union, merger, alliance, association Opposite: split

unified adj united, combined, amalgamated, incorporated, integrated Opposite: disjointed

uniform n livery, dress, costume, garb, attire (fml) Opposite: mufti ■ adj 1 **unchanging**, unvarying, even, unbroken, undeviating Opposite: uneven 2 **consistent**, standardized, homogeneous, harmonized, regular Opposite: inconsistent 3 **identical**, like, alike, similar, equal Opposite: different

uniformity n **consistency**, regularity, standardization, homogeneity, evenness Opposite: inconsistency

unify v unite, join, amalgamate, merge, combine Opposite: separate

unilateral adj one-sided, independent, autonomous, autarchic, individual Opposite: joint

unimaginable adj **inconceivable**, unbelievable, incredible, unthinkable, indescribable Opposite: conceivable

unimaginative *adj* dull, boring, insipid, bland, uninspired *Opposite*: imaginative

unimpaired *adj* undamaged, unaffected, unhindered, perfect, operational *Opposite*: impaired

unimpassioned *adj* **unemotional**, cool, detached, sober, calm *Opposite*: impassioned

unimpeachable *adj* **faultless**, flawless, impeccable, irreproachable, blameless *Opposite*: blameworthy

unimpeded *adj* **without hindrance**, unhindered, unhampered, unchecked, unconstrained *Opposite*: hindered

unimportance *n* **insignificance**, inconsequentiality, irrelevance, slightness, triviality *Opposite*: importance

unimportant *adj* **inconsequential**, slight, insignificant, trivial, trifling *Opposite*: important

unimpressed *adj* **unenthusiastic**, uninspired, unconvinced, unmoved, indifferent *Opposite*: enthusiastic

unimpressive *adj* **uninspiring**, indifferent, mediocre, unimposing, insignificant *Opposite*: impressive

unimproved *adj* **unchanged**, unaltered, natural, original, unworked *Opposite*: improved

unincorporated *adj* **independent**, separate, distinct, stand-alone, autonomous *Opposite*: incorporated

unindustrialized *adj* **undeveloped**, farming, agricultural, rural *Opposite*: industrialized

uninformative *adj* **unhelpful**, vague, uncommunicative, unproductive, useless *Opposite*: informative

uninformed *adj* **ignorant**, uneducated, unaware, unacquainted, unfamiliar *Opposite*: informed

uninhabitable *adj* **derelict**, dilapidated, ramshackle, tumbledown, run-down *Opposite*: habitable

uninhabited *adj* **unoccupied**, unpopulated, deserted, abandoned, unpeopled *Opposite*: inhabited

uninhibited *adj* **1 unrestrained**, outgoing, unconstrained, candid, open *Opposite*: shy **2 wanton**, abandoned, dissolute, licentious, immodest *Opposite*: restrained

uninitiated *adj* * **inexperienced**, unskilled, unversed, unqualified, untrained *Opposite*: experienced

uninjured *adj* **unhurt**, unharmed, undamaged, intact, safe *Opposite*: hurt

uninspired *adj* **bland**, insipid, boring, dull, unimaginative *Opposite*: inspired

uninspiring *adj* **dull**, lackluster, lifeless, boring, tame *Opposite*: inspiring

uninstructed *adj* **untaught**, unschooled, uneducated, uninformed, untutored *Opposite*: educated

unintelligent *adj* **stupid**, foolish, silly, inane *Opposite*: clever

unintelligible *adj* **incomprehensible**, inarticulate, incoherent, garbled, jumbled *Opposite*: intelligible

unintended *see* unintentional

unintentional *adj* **accidental**, inadvertent, unplanned, chance, involuntary *Opposite*: intentional

uninterested *adj* **indifferent**, apathetic, blasé, impassive, unconcerned *Opposite*: concerned

uninteresting *adj* **boring**, dull, unexciting, tedious, monotonous *Opposite*: interesting

uninterrupted *adj* **continuous**, continual, nonstop, incessant never-ending *Opposite*: sporadic

uninvited *adj* **unwelcome**, unwanted, undesirable, unsought, unsolicited *Opposite*: welcome

uninviting *adj* **unappealing**, unattractive, bleak, unpalatable, disgusting *Opposite*: attractive

uninvolved *adj* **1 detached**, removed, aloof, unconcerned, indifferent *Opposite*: involved **2 uncomplicated**, straightforward, easy, simple, plain *Opposite*: convoluted **3 single**, footloose and fancy free, unmarried, unattached, free *Opposite*: attached *(infml)*

union *n* **1 amalgamation**, combination, blending, coming together, joining together *Opposite*: separation **2 coalition**, alliance, association, confederacy, confederation **3 agreement**, harmony, accord, unity, unison *Opposite*: discord **4 marriage**, matrimony, wedlock, bond, wedding *Opposite*: divorce

unique *adj* **sole**, single, exclusive, exceptional, inimitable *Opposite*: common

uniqueness *n* **individuality**, exclusivity, exceptionality, inimitability, distinctiveness *Opposite*: commonness

unison *n* **agreement**, harmony, accord, unity, union *Opposite*: discord

unit *n* **1 component**, element, part, piece, item **2 corps**, detachment, group, company, troop

unite *v* **1 join**, fuse, mix, bond, come together *Opposite*: separate **2 marry**, wed, hitch, bond, tie

united *adj* **joint**, combined, amalgamated, unified, cohesive *Opposite*: separated

unitize *v* **1 bring together**, unite, combine, centralize, condense *Opposite*: separate **2 separate**, take apart, break up, divide up, disassemble *Opposite*: join

unity *n* **agreement**, harmony, accord, unison, union *Opposite*: disarray

universal *adj* **worldwide**, widespread, general, common, collective *Opposite*: local. *See* COMPARE AND CONTRAST *at* **widespread**.

universalism n **breadth**, amplitude, diversity, gamut, spectrum

universe n **cosmos**, world, creation, life, space

university n **institution of higher education**, college, academia, academy, school

unjust adj **unfair**, undue, undeserved, unmerited, unwarranted Opposite: just

unjustifiable adj **indefensible**, unwarrantable, inexcusable, unforgivable, unpardonable Opposite: justifiable

unjustified adj **unfounded**, baseless, unfair, unwarranted, unpardonable Opposite: justified

unjustly adv **unfairly**, unreasonably, partially, one-sidedly, discriminatorily Opposite: fairly

unkempt adj **disheveled**, untidy, rumpled, tousled, messy Opposite: tidy

unkind adj **nasty**, mean, cruel, callous, heartless Opposite: kind

unkindness n **nastiness**, meanness, cruelty callousness, heartlessness Opposite: kindness

unknot v **untie**, undo, unpick, disentangle, unstitch Opposite: knot

unknowable adj **incomprehensible**, enigmatic, mysterious, indecipherable, arcane Opposite: comprehensible

unknowing adj 1 **unwitting**, ingenuous, naive, innocent, ignorant Opposite: knowing 2 **unintentional**, accidental, inadvertent, unintended, unplanned Opposite: deliberate

unknown adj 1 **unidentified**, indefinite, mysterious, unheard of, nameless Opposite: known 2 **unfamiliar**, strange, foreign, alien, undiscovered Opposite: familiar ■ n **nonentity**, nobody, newcomer, beginner, stranger Opposite: celebrity

unlabored adj **effortless**, easy, painless, trouble-free, carefree Opposite: labored

unlace v **undo**, unfasten, unthread, unknot, untie Opposite: lace

unlatch v **open**, undo, unfasten, unlock, unbolt Opposite: latch

unlawful adj **illegal**, illicit, illegitimate, wrongful, nonlegal Opposite: lawful

---

COMPARE AND CONTRAST CORE MEANING: not in accordance with laws or rules

unlawful not permitted by the law or by the rules of an organization or religion, or not recognized as valid by those laws or rules; **illegal** contravening a specific written statute, rule, or law, especially a criminal law; **illicit** not permitted by the law, suggesting especialy that something is considered morally wrong or unacceptable; **wrongful** (often used in civil lawsuits) unjust, unfair, or against conscience, but not punishable by criminal law.

---

unlearned adj **uneducated**, illiterate, unschooled, unlettered, untutored Opposite: educated

unleash v **set free**, give a free rein to, allow to run free, allow to run riot, uncheck Opposite: control

unless prep **if not**, if, except, save, but for

unlettered adj **uneducated**, illiterate, unschooled, untaught, untutored Opposite: educated

unlicensed adj **uninhibited**, unrestricted, unrestrained, abandoned, immoral Opposite: inhibited

unlike adj **different**, dissimilar, nothing like, distinct, contrasting Opposite: like

unlikelihood n **improbability**, doubtfulness, implausibility, dubiousness, questionability Opposite: likelihood

unlikely adj 1 **improbable**, doubtful, dubious, questionable Opposite: likely 2 **implausible**, dubious, doubtful, suspect, incongruous Opposite: credible

unlimited adj **limitless**, infinite, unrestricted, unrestrained, boundless Opposite: limited

unlisted adj **private**, unpublished, confidential, unpublicized, secret Opposite: listed

unlit adj **dark**, darkened, dim, pitch-black, murky Opposite: bright

unload v **unpack**, drop off, drop, deliver, empty Opposite: load

unlock v 1 **undo**, release, unchain, open, unbolt Opposite: lock 2 **solve**, reveal, answer, expose, get to the bottom of

unlooked-for adj **unexpected**, undreamed-of, unanticipated, uninvited, unsolicited Opposite: expected

unloose v **set free**, release, let out, unleash, let off the leash Opposite: tie up

unlovely adj **unattractive**, objectionable, obnoxious, nasty, ugly Opposite: attractive

unluckiness n **bad luck**, misfortune, ill luck, mishap Opposite: luck

unlucky adj 1 **unsuccessful**, wretched, hapless, unfortunate, tragic Opposite: lucky 2 **inauspicious**, fateful, ill-fated, doomed, star-crossed Opposite: fortunate

unmake v 1 **undo**, take apart, reverse, deconstruct, dismantle Opposite: put back 2 **demote**, fire, sack, replace, expel

unmanageable adj **uncontrollable**, unruly, riotous, out of control, out of hand Opposite: manageable

unmanliness n **weakness**, cowardliness, timidity, fearfulness, apprehension Opposite: manliness

unmanly adj **weak**, cowardly, timid, fearful, apprehensive Opposite: manly

unmannered adj 1 **rude**, boorish, impolite, crude, coarse Opposite: well-mannered 2 **unaffected**, easy, natural, genuine, simple Opposite: affected

unmannerly adj **rude**, impolite, ill-mannered, bad-mannered, disrespectful Opposite: polite

unmarked *adj* **spotless**, unblemished, pristine, immaculate, perfect *Opposite*: marked

unmarried *adj* **single**, unattached, bachelor, spinster, free *Opposite*: married

unmask *v* **expose**, blow the whistle on, reveal, unveil, debunk *Opposite*: conceal

unmatched *adj* **supreme**, matchless, unrivaled, consummate, unparalleled

unmeant *adj* **unintended**, accidental, inadvertent, unplanned, unintentional *Opposite*: deliberate

unmentionable *adj* **taboo**, offensive, prohibited, forbidden, restricted *Opposite*: respectable ■ *n* **taboo**, no-go area, anathema, no-no *(infml)*

unmerciful *adj* **1 cruel**, severe, harsh, hard, unsparing *Opposite*: merciful **2 excessive**, unrelenting, extreme, remorseless, unremitting

unmerited *adj* **undeserved**, unwarranted, unjustified, unearned, unjust *Opposite*: fair

unmindful *adj* **unaware**, oblivious, unconscious, careless, heedless *Opposite*: mindful

unmistakable *adj* **obvious**, definite, distinctive, unambiguous, unique *Opposite*: ambiguous

unmitigated *adj* **sheer**, pure, absolute, unadulterated, unalloyed

unmodified *adj* **original**, unchanged, basic, untouched *Opposite*: modified

unmotivated *adj* **apathetic**, unenthusiastic, indifferent, shiftless, uninterested *Opposite*: keen

unmovable *adj* **inflexible**, rigid, stubborn, obstinate, obdurate *Opposite*: flexible

unmoved *adj* **indifferent**, unaffected, unresponsive, insensitive, impassive *Opposite*: touched *See* COMPARE AND CONTRAST *at* **impassive**.

unmoving *adj* **still**, motionless, inactive, lifeless, inert *Opposite*: moving

unmusical *adj* **unmelodic**, dissonant, discordant, jarring, harsh *Opposite*: musical

unnamed *adj* **unidentified**, anonymous, unspecified, nameless, unknown *Opposite*: named

unnatural *adj* **1 abnormal**, aberrant, atypical, unusual, perverted *Opposite*: normal **2 strange**, odd, peculiar, atypical, irregular *Opposite*: typical **3 supernatural**, weird, bizarre, paranormal, uncanny *Opposite*: ordinary **4 artificial**, contrived, affected, insincere, pretend *Opposite*: natural

unnecessary *adj* **needless**, pointless, redundant, superfluous, gratuitous *Opposite*: necessary

unneeded *adj* **extra**, superfluous, unnecessary, surplus, unwanted *Opposite*: necessary

unnerve *v* **alarm**, frighten, scare, upset, nonplus *Opposite*: calm

unnerved *adj* **frightened**, scared, alarmed, unsettled, anxious *Opposite*: calm

unnerving *adj* **frightening**, unsettling, demoralizing, intimidating, upsetting *Opposite*: comforting

unnoticeable *adj* **invisible**, imperceptible, unremarkable, inconspicuous, hidden *Opposite*: conspicuous

unnoticed *adj* **unobserved**, overlooked, ignored, unseen, disregarded

unnumbered *adj* **1 numberless**, numerous, myriad, countless, many *Opposite*: few **2 unidentified**, unmarked, untagged, uncounted

unobjectionable *adj* **inoffensive**, agreeable, pleasant, innocuous, harmless *Opposite*: unpleasant

unobservant *adj* **inattentive**, unperceptive, incurious, negligent, careless *Opposite*: observant

unobserved *adj* **unnoticed**, ignored, overlooked, unseen, disregarded *Opposite*: evident

unobstructed *adj* **clear**, free, unhindered, passable, open *Opposite*: barred

unobtainable *adj* **unavailable**, unattainable, inaccessible, out of stock *Opposite*: available

unobtrusive *adj* **inconspicuous**, unremarkable, modest, bland, discreet *Opposite*: conspicuous

unoccupied *adj* **1 inactive**, idle, out of work, unemployed, at loose ends *(infml)* *Opposite*: busy **2 vacant**, free, untenanted, empty, disused *Opposite*: occupied. *See* COMPARE AND CONTRAST *at* **vacant**.

unofficial *adj* **unauthorized**, unsanctioned, informal, unendorsed, private *Opposite*: official

unopposed *adj* **unchallenged**, unobstructed, unrestricted, unhampered, unimpeded *Opposite*: challenged

unorganized *adj* **1 chaotic**, disorganized, muddled, messy, disorderly *Opposite*: well-organized **2 careless**, disorganized, unprepared, sloppy, slapdash *Opposite*: methodical

unoriginal *adj* **derivative**, copied, imitative, clichéd, banal *Opposite*: original

unoriginality *n* **derivativeness**, triteness, staleness, imitativeness, banality *Opposite*: originality

unorthodox *adj* **unconventional**, nonconformist, untraditional, unusual, eccentric *Opposite*: orthodox

unpack *v* **unload**, take out, empty, undo, empty out *Opposite*: pack up

unpaid *adj* **1 unsettled**, outstanding, overdue, due, owed *Opposite*: paid **2 voluntary**, amateur, honorary, free *Opposite*: paid

unpalatable adj **1 inedible**, indigestible, disgusting, revolting, foul-tasting Opposite: tasty **2 unacceptable**, unpleasant, painful, disagreeable, harsh Opposite: acceptable

unparalleled adj **unmatched**, supreme, matchless, beyond compare, unequaled Opposite: mediocre

unpardonable adj **unforgivable**, indefensible, inexcusable, deplorable, reprehensible Opposite: understandable

unpeg v **undo**, unfasten, untie, detach, release Opposite: fasten

unperceptive adj **undiscerning**, unobservant, insensitive, obtuse, indiscriminate Opposite: perceptive

unperturbed adj **calm**, at peace, tranquil, collected, composed Opposite: anxious

unpick v **unravel**, untangle, untie, undo, disentangle

unplanned adj **1 unintended**, accidental, unintentional, unexpected, inadvertent Opposite: planned **2 spontaneous**, impromptu, ad hoc, unprepared, spur-of-the-moment Opposite: planned

unpleasant adj **1 disagreeable**, nasty, unlikable, horrible, horrid Opposite: pleasant **2 unfriendly**, hostile, cold, unkind, spiteful Opposite: friendly

unpleasantness n **1 disagreeableness**, nastiness, horribleness, horridness, distastefulness Opposite: pleasantness **2 ill feeling**, trouble, fuss, bother, upset Opposite: harmony **3 unfriendliness**, spitefulness, nastiness, unkindness, offensiveness Opposite: friendliness **4 disagreement**, conflict, argument, quarrel, dispute Opposite: agreement

unplug v **1 unblock**, clear, free, clean, release **2 disconnect**, switch off, undo, take out, remove Opposite: plug in

unplumbed adj **mysterious**, unfathomable, enigmatic, unexplored, unknowable Opposite: known

unpolluted adj **clean**, pure, uncontaminated, untainted, fresh Opposite: contaminated

unpopular adj **disliked**, hated, out of favor, shunned, detested Opposite: popular

unpopulated adj **abandoned**, deserted, depopulated, uninhabited, empty Opposite: overcrowded

unpracticed adj **inexperienced**, unrehearsed, unschooled, untrained, unfamiliar Opposite: practiced

unprecedented adj **unparalleled**, extraordinary, record, first-time, unique Opposite: ordinary

unpredictability n **randomness**, impulsiveness, volatility, fickleness, changeableness Opposite: predictability

unpredictable adj **random**, erratic, changeable, impulsive, volatile Opposite: predictable

unpredicted adj **surprising**, unexpected, shocking, astonishing, unforeseen Opposite: predicted

unprejudiced adj **fair**, neutral, tolerant, unbiased, evenhanded Opposite: biased

unpremeditated adj **unplanned**, unintended, impulsive, spur-of-the-moment, sudden Opposite: premeditated

unprepared adj **1 unready**, unsuspecting, ill-equipped, unqualified, untrained Opposite: prepared **2 improvised**, unrehearsed, ad hoc, impromptu, spontaneous Opposite: rehearsed

unprepossessing adj **ugly**, unattractive, plain, unpleasant, uninviting Opposite: attractive

unpretentious adj **modest**, unassuming, unaffected, natural, self-effacing Opposite: pretentious

unpretentiousness n **modesty**, humility, humbleness, simplicity, artlessness Opposite: grandiosity

unprincipled adj **dishonest**, corrupt, amoral, immoral, devious Opposite: honest

unprintable adj **rude**, foul, offensive, shocking, coarse Opposite: inoffensive

unproblematic adj **easy**, smooth, straightforward, trouble-free, simple Opposite: tricky

unprocessed adj **natural**, whole, unrefined, untreated, crude

unproductive adj **1 fruitless**, infertile, barren, sterile, blocked Opposite: fertile **2 idle**, lazy, slow, wasteful, inefficient Opposite: productive

unprofessional adj **1 unethical**, unprincipled, immoral, dishonorable, wrong Opposite: ethical **2 amateurish**, amateur, slack, inexpert, shoddy Opposite: expert

unprofitable adj **1 unsuccessful**, running at a loss, nonpaying, insolvent, nonprofit Opposite: profitable **2 unhelpful**, useless, pointless, futile, fruitless Opposite: helpful

unpromising adj **gloomy**, bleak, discouraging, doubtful, off-putting Opposite: encouraging

unprompted adj **spontaneous**, unforced, impulsive, willing, voluntary Opposite: forced

unpronounceable adj **unsayable**, difficult, impossible

unpronounced adj **silent**, mute, unvoiced, unspoken, unsaid Opposite: voiced

unprotected adj **defenseless**, undefended, open to attack, insecure, vulnerable Opposite: secure

unproven adj **unverified**, unconfirmed, untried, untested, undocumented Opposite: proven

unprovoked adj **gratuitous**, wanton, senseless, motiveless, uncalled-for Opposite: provoked

unqualified adj 1 **untrained**, unprofessional, ill-equipped, inexpert, untaught Opposite: trained 2 **definite**, unreserved, absolute, complete, utter Opposite: qualified

unquantifiable adj **immeasurable**, uncountable, unidentifiable, indefinable, indeterminate Opposite: quantifiable

unquestionable adj **indisputable**, incontestable, absolute, undeniable, categorical Opposite: arguable

unquestioned adj **undisputed**, accepted, unchallenged, automatic, logical Opposite: questionable

unquestioning adj **unthinking**, wholehearted, obedient, absolute, automatic Opposite: reluctant

unquiet adj 1 **noisy**, turbulent, loud, rowdy, boisterous Opposite: quiet 2 **anxious**, unsettled, restless, agitated, fidgety Opposite: calm

unravel v 1 **undo**, untie, unknot, loosen, disentangle Opposite: tie 2 **solve**, clear up, resolve, sort out, get to the bottom of 3 **fail**, go wrong, fall apart, collapse, crumble Opposite: come together

unreadable adj 1 **illegible**, incomprehensible, indecipherable, scrawled, scribbled Opposite: legible 2 **impenetrable**, dense, tedious, turgid, boring Opposite: readable 3 **blank**, expressionless, impassive, poker-faced, inscrutable

unreal adj 1 **imaginary**, dreamlike, illusory, fantastic, weird Opposite: real 2 **false**, artificial, imitation, fake, pretend Opposite: genuine

unrealistic adj **impractical**, idealistic, impractical, improbable, unlikely Opposite: practical

unreality n 1 **strangeness**, incongruity, oddness, weirdness, abnormality Opposite: reality 2 **fantasy**, delusion, fancy, self-delusion, illusion Opposite: reality

unreasonable adj 1 **irrational**, perverse, arbitrary, unreasoning, awkward Opposite: rational 2 **excessive**, exorbitant, immoderate, extravagant, extreme Opposite: reasonable

unreasonableness n 1 **irrationality**, arbitrariness, awkwardness, perverseness, difficultness Opposite: rationality 2 **excessiveness**, injustice, exorbitance, extravagance, unfairness Opposite: reasonableness

unreceptive adj **disinclined**, ill-disposed, unwilling, resistant, unteachable Opposite: receptive

unreconstructed adj 1 **old-fashioned**, unchanging, unrepentant, dyed-in-the-wool, traditional 2 **unchanged**, unaltered, unvaried, unmodified, original

unrefined adj 1 **unprocessed**, untreated, raw, crude, untouched Opposite: refined 2 **vulgar**, unsophisticated, uncultured, crude, coarse Opposite: sophisticated

unreformed adj **unapologetic**, unrepentant, dyed-in-the-wool, inveterate, diehard Opposite: reformed

unrehearsed adj **unprepared**, impromptu, off-the-cuff, spontaneous, impulsive Opposite: prepared

unrelated adj 1 **unconnected**, separate, distinct, dissimilar, disparate Opposite: linked 2 **irrelevant**, beside the point, extraneous, unconnected, impertinent (fml) Opposite: relevant

unrelenting adj **remorseless**, relentless, insistent, merciless, pitiless Opposite: yielding

unreliability n 1 **undependability**, untrustworthiness, unpredictability, changeableness, irregularity Opposite: dependability 2 **inaccuracy**, fallibility, untrustworthiness, flimsiness, dubiousness Opposite: reliability

unreliable adj 1 **undependable**, fly-by-night, variable, unpredictable, changeable Opposite: dependable 2 **inaccurate**, fallacious, flimsy, threadbare, untrue Opposite: reliable

unrelieved adj **constant**, unbroken, chronic, unmitigated, unalleviated Opposite: intermittent

unremarkable adj **ordinary**, everyday, commonplace, average, typical Opposite: remarkable

unremitting adj **constant**, incessant, continuous, chronic, unrelenting Opposite: intermittent

unremorseful adj **unrepentant**, unapologetic, impenitent, unashamed, shameless Opposite: apologetic

unrepentant adj **impenitent**, unapologetic, unashamed, shameless, unremorseful Opposite: remorseful

unreserved adj 1 **unqualified**, total, complete, utter, absolute Opposite: qualified 2 **open**, demonstrative, candid, frank, extrovert Opposite: reserved

unresolved adj **unsettled**, unanswered, uncertain, vague, pending Opposite: settled

unresponsive adj **unfeeling**, insensitive, indifferent, impassive, uncaring Opposite: responsive

unresponsiveness n **unfeelingness**, insensitivity, indifference, impassiveness, coldness Opposite: responsiveness

unrest n 1 **discontent**, turbulence, strife, conflict, disturbance Opposite: calm 2 **anxiousness**, anxiety, disquiet, worry, uneasiness Opposite: peace

unrestrained adj **uncontrolled**, wild, unrestricted, abandoned, uninhibited Opposite: restrained

unrestricted adj **open**, unobstructed, unhindered, unlimited, unhampered Opposite: restricted

unrevealed *adj* **secret**, hidden, unknown, mysterious, clandestine *Opposite*: known

unrewarding *adj* **thankless**, fruitless, unfulfilling, unsatisfactory, difficult *Opposite*: satisfying

unrighteous *adj* **1 sinful**, wicked, evil, irreligious, unholy *Opposite*: righteous **2 unjust**, unfair, ill-deserved, unkind, wrong *Opposite*: just

unripe *adj* **immature**, green, young, fresh, undeveloped *Opposite*: ripe

unrivaled *adj* **unequaled**, unchallenged, unsurpassed, unbeatable, unparalleled *Opposite*: ordinary

unroll *v* **open**, unfurl, stretch out, spread out, unfold *Opposite*: roll up

unruffled *adj* **calm**, tranquil, unmoved, in control, at ease *Opposite*: flustered

unruliness *n* **boisterousness**, disruptiveness, disorderliness, rowdiness, recalcitrance *Opposite*: orderliness

unruly *adj* **boisterous**, disruptive, disorderly, rowdy, wild *Opposite*: orderly

---

COMPARE AND CONTRAST CORE MEANING: not submitting to control

unruly boisterous, disruptive, and difficult to control or discipline; **intractable** (*fml*) strong-willed and rebellious, refusing to be controlled or to submit to discipline; **recalcitrant** obstinate and defiant in refusing to submit to discipline or control; **obstreperous** noisy, difficult to control, and uncooperative; **willful** stubbornly disregarding the opinions or advice of others; **wild** showing a general lack of control or restraint; **wayward** disobedient and uncontrollable.

---

unrushed *adj* **unhurried**, slow, leisurely, calm, gentle *Opposite*: hurried

unsafe *adj* **dangerous**, insecure, hazardous, risky, perilous *Opposite*: secure

unsaid *adj* **tacit**, unspoken, implicit, silent, unstated *Opposite*: spoken

unsatisfactory *adj* **inadequate**, unacceptable, substandard, disappointing, insufficient *Opposite*: acceptable

unsatisfied *adj* **displeased**, discontented, unhappy, unfulfilled, disgruntled *Opposite*: pleased

unsavory *adj* **1 unpleasant**, disagreeable, revolting, disgusting, nasty *Opposite*: pleasant **2 immoral**, unpleasant, villainous, shady, unacceptable *Opposite*: wholesome

unscathed *adj* **unharmed**, intact, unhurt, untouched, safe *Opposite*: injured

unschooled *adj* **uneducated**, untaught, untutored, untrained, illiterate *Opposite*: educated

unscientific *adj* **intuitive**, instinctive, irrational, unempirical, seat-of-the-pants (*infml*) *Opposite*: systematic

unscramble *v* **decode**, sort out, decipher, work out, make out *Opposite*: encode

unscrew *v* **take off**, remove, detach, loosen, undo *Opposite*: tighten

unscripted *adj* **unplanned**, unexpected, impromptu, impulsive, unscheduled

unscrupulous *adj* **dishonest**, unprincipled, corrupt, immoral, deceitful *Opposite*: honest

unscrupulousness *n* **dishonesty**, corruptness, crookedness, immorality, deviousness *Opposite*: honesty

unseal *v* **open**, uncap, unstop, break open, unscrew *Opposite*: seal

unseasonable *adj* **1 unusual**, abnormal, unexpected, odd, strange *Opposite*: seasonable **2 untimely**, inopportune, ill-timed, inconvenient, unwelcome *Opposite*: seasonable

unseat *v* **depose**, oust, overthrow, dethrone, remove *Opposite*: enthrone (*fml*)

unseemliness *n* **impropriety**, tastelessness, uncouthness, loutishness, rudeness *Opposite*: propriety

unseemly *adj* **inappropriate**, rude, uncouth, improper, indecorous *Opposite*: proper

unseen *adj* **hidden**, unnoticed, unobserved, invisible, concealed *Opposite*: noticeable

unselective *adj* **indiscriminating**, undiscerning, blanket, haphazard, random *Opposite*: discerning

unselfish *adj* **selfless**, generous, noble, magnanimous, liberal *Opposite*: selfish

unselfishness *n* **selflessness**, generosity, magnanimity, kindness, consideration *Opposite*: selfishness

unsentimental *adj* **unemotional**, impassive, unfeeling, hard-bitten, tough *Opposite*: sentimental

unsettle *v* **worry**, disturb, upset, disconcert, unnerve *Opposite*: soothe

unsettled *adj* **1 anxious**, worried, disturbed, upset, disconcerted *Opposite*: calm **2 changeable**, variable, unpredictable, uncertain, changing *Opposite*: settled **3 undecided**, unresolved, undetermined, open-ended, arguable *Opposite*: decided

unsettling *adj* **upsetting**, worrying, disturbing, disconcerting, disquieting *Opposite*: soothing

unshackle *v* **release**, unchain, let loose, set free, liberate *Opposite*: chain

unshakable *adj* **steadfast**, resolute, constant, unwavering, entrenched *Opposite*: wavering

unshaped *adj* **unformed**, formless, shapeless, amorphous, indistinct *Opposite*: shaped

unsheathe *v* **draw**, pull, remove, extract, uncover

unsightliness *n* **ugliness**, hideousness, horridness, unpleasantness, nastiness *Opposite*: attractiveness

unsightly *adj* **unattractive**, ugly, hideous, unpleasant, unprepossessing *Opposite*:

attractive. *See* COMPARE AND CONTRAST *at* **unattractive.**

unskilled *adj* **inexpert**, amateurish, untrained, uneducated, unqualified *Opposite*: trained

unskillful *adj* **inept**, unskilled, untrained, untalented, incompetent *Opposite*: skillful

unsmiling *adj* **stern**, severe, serious, dour, grim-faced *Opposite*: cordial

unsnag *v* **disentangle**, clear, free, untangle, release *Opposite*: snag

unsnarl *v* **disentangle**, clear, free, untangle, unblock *Opposite*: tangle

unsociable *adj* **unfriendly**, antisocial, aloof, shy, standoffish *Opposite*: friendly

unsolicited *adj* **unwelcome**, unwanted, uninvited, unsought, spontaneous *Opposite*: requested

unsolvable *adj* **impenetrable**, unknowable, impossible, unfathomable, insoluble *Opposite*: soluble

unsolved *adj* **unexplained**, unresolved, mysterious, baffling *Opposite*: resolved

unsophisticated *adj* **1 unworldly**, naive, inexperienced, ingenuous, simple *Opposite*: sophisticated **2 crude**, simple, unrefined, basic, primitive *Opposite*: advanced

unsought *adj* **unsolicited**, spontaneous, uninvited, uncalled-for, unwanted

unsound *adj* **1 ill**, frail, unwell, unhealthy, sick *Opposite*: well **2 unsafe**, unstable, rickety, in poor condition, ramshackle *Opposite*: secure **3 illogical**, specious, flawed, fallacious, erroneous *Opposite*: logical

unsparing *adj* **1 merciless**, harsh, cruel, unforgiving, severe *Opposite*: merciful **2 generous**, munificent, openhanded, liberal, charitable *Opposite*: frugal

unspeakable *adj* **1 indescribable**, inexpressible, unutterable, undefinable, overwhelming **2 awful**, disgusting, appalling, foul, revolting

unspeakably *adv* **1 indescribably**, inexpressibly, unutterably, undefinably, unbelievably **2 terribly**, awfully, appallingly, horribly, horrendously

unspeaking *adj* **silent**, mute, wordless, still, speechless *Opposite*: verbose

unspecified *adj* **unnamed**, indefinite, vague, indeterminate, undetermined *Opposite*: specific

unspiritual *adj* **earthly**, worldly, mundane, material, irreligious *Opposite*: spiritual

unspoiled *adj* **1 pristine**, pure, perfect, untouched, unharmed *Opposite*: marred **2 uncorrupted**, natural, innocent, pure, wholesome *Opposite*: spoiled

unspoken *adj* **tacit**, understood, silent, implicit, undeclared *Opposite*: explicit

unsporting *adj* **dishonest**, unfair, dishonorable, disreputable, mean-spirited *Opposite*: sporting

unsportsmanlike *adj* **dirty**, dishonest, nasty, foul, unethical *Opposite*: exemplary

unspotted *adj* **1 unstained**, clean, spotless, unblemished, pristine *Opposite*: spotted **2 pure**, moral, unblemished, faultless, righteous *Opposite*: impure **3 unobserved**, unseen, unnoticed, unperceived, undiscovered *Opposite*: seen

unstable *adj* **1 unbalanced**, uneven, wobbly, rickety, ramshackle *Opposite*: steady **2 volatile**, unpredictable, unsteady, erratic, unhinged *Opposite*: stable

unstated *adj* **unspecified**, unspoken, tacit, understood, implicit *Opposite*: specified

unsteadiness *n* **1 tremulousness**, instability, shakiness, precariousness, treacherousness *Opposite*: stability **2 changeability**, erraticism, variability, unreliability, irregularity *Opposite*: constancy

unsteady *adj* **1 wobbly**, shaky, unstable, uneven, rickety *Opposite*: stable **2 changeable**, erratic, variable, unreliable, irregular *Opposite*: constant

unstick *v* **release**, pry, free, take off, take down *Opposite*: stick

unstinting *adj* **generous**, charitable, openhanded, liberal, unsparing *Opposite*: stingy

unstipulated *adj* **unspecified**, unstated, unmentioned, undeclared *Opposite*: specified

unstop *v* **unblock**, free, clear, unplug, open up *Opposite*: stop

unstoppable *adj* **irresistible**, overwhelming, overpowering, persistent, unrelenting *Opposite*: avoidable

unstrained *adj* **cloudy**, milky, opaque, murky *Opposite*: clear

unstrap *v* **undo**, remove, unbuckle, unshackle, unleash *Opposite*: tie up

unstressed *adj* **relaxed**, carefree, at ease, cool, calm *Opposite*: stressed

unstructured *adj* **formless**, shapeless, amorphous, free *Opposite*: structured

unstudied *adj* **unaffected**, natural, genuine, sincere, relaxed *Opposite*: affected

unsubstantiated *adj* **unconfirmed**, unproven, unsupported, uncorroborated *Opposite*: proven

unsuccessful *adj* **ineffective**, failed, vain, unproductive, abortive *Opposite*: successful

unsuitability *n* **inappropriateness**, inaptness, unbecomingness, incongruity, incompatibility *Opposite*: appropriateness

unsuitable *adj* **inappropriate**, unbecoming, unfitting, inapt, unbefitting *Opposite*: appropriate

unsullied *adj* **pure**, clean, unblemished, faultless, untarnished *Opposite*: tarnished

unsung *adj* **unacknowledged**, silent, unrecognized, anonymous, nameless *Opposite*: renowned

unsupported adj **uncorroborated**, unconfirmed, unsubstantiated, unverified, unfounded Opposite: supported

unsure adj **1 uncertain**, doubtful, unconvinced, dubious, suspicious Opposite: certain **2 unconfident**, hesitant, shy, insecure, irresolute Opposite: confident. See COMPARE AND CONTRAST at doubtful.

unsurpassed adj **unrivaled**, unmatched, supreme, incomparable, unequaled Opposite: ordinary

unsurprising adj **predictable**, foreseeable, expected, anticipated, foreseen Opposite: surprising

unsurprisingly adv **of course**, naturally, obviously, expectedly, predictably Opposite: surprisingly

unsuspected adj **unanticipated**, unpredicted, unknown, unimagined, surprise Opposite: known

unsuspecting adj **unwary**, gullible, credulous, innocent, unsuspicious Opposite: wary

unsustainable adj **unjustifiable**, unmaintainable, unverifiable, untenable, indefensible Opposite: sustainable

unswerving adj **unwavering**, staunch, reliable, trusty, solid Opposite: wavering

unsymmetrical adj **asymmetrical**, uneven, irregular, lopsided Opposite: symmetrical

unsympathetic adj **unfeeling**, uncaring, insensitive, cold, indifferent Opposite: caring

unsystematic adj **haphazard**, random, chaotic, disorganized, disorderly Opposite: organized

untainted adj **unpolluted**, undamaged, unblemished, unspoiled, pure Opposite: tainted

untaken adj **available**, unclaimed, unoccupied, free, spare Opposite: taken

untangle v **unravel**, disentangle, untie, unpick, straighten out Opposite: tangle

untapped adj **unused**, unexploited, untouched, available, intact Opposite: used

untarnished adj **unblemished**, clean, spotless, shining, unsullied Opposite: blemished

untaught adj **untutored**, uneducated, untrained, natural, born Opposite: trained

untenable adj **indefensible**, unsustainable, weak, unsound, shaky Opposite: watertight

untested adj **1 inexperienced**, unproven, inexpert, new, raw Opposite: experienced **2 experimental**, untried, unapproved, unverified, unproven Opposite: reliable

untether v **release**, untie, unstrap, unchain, free Opposite: tie up

unthinkable adj **1 absurd**, ridiculous, unlikely, impossible, improbable Opposite: likely **2 unimaginable**, impossible, fantastic, unbelievable, incredible Opposite: conceivable

unthinking adj **1 careless**, thoughtless, tactless, undiplomatic, inconsiderate Opposite: thoughtful **2 instinctive**, automatic, mechanical, intuitive, impulsive Opposite: calculated

unthreatened adj **secure**, safe, safe and sound, protected, impregnable Opposite: threatened

untidiness n **1 mess**, disorder, muddle, disarray, jumble Opposite: order **2 shabbiness**, scruffiness, raggedness Opposite: smartness

untidy adj **1 messy**, in a mess, disorderly, muddled, jumbled Opposite: neat **2 unkempt**, ragged, shabby, scruffy, bedraggled Opposite: smart

untie v **1 unknot**, unfasten, loosen, undo, unravel Opposite: fasten **2 release**, free, set free, unleash, let loose Opposite: tie up

until prep **up until**, while waiting for, pending, till, up to

untimely adj **1 ill-timed**, inconvenient, inappropriate, unfortunate, inopportune Opposite: timely **2 premature**, early, precocious, advance Opposite: late

untiring adj **tireless**, determined, dogged, indefatigable, constant Opposite: faltering

untold adj **1 indescribable**, inexpressible, indefinable, ineffable (fml) **2 uncountable**, countless, innumerable, myriad, numberless Opposite: few

untouchable adj **unattainable**, matchless, superlative, superior, unrivaled Opposite: ordinary

untouched adj **1 unhurt**, intact, unharmed, undamaged, safe and sound Opposite: injured **2 unaffected**, indifferent, unmoved, unimpressed, unconcerned Opposite: affected

untoward adj **1 annoying**, unpleasant, inconvenient, troublesome, awkward Opposite: pleasant **2 inappropriate**, unfitting, unseemly, improper, unbecoming Opposite: appropriate

untrained adj **untaught**, inexpert, untutored, unqualified, inexperienced Opposite: trained

untrammeled adj **unrestricted**, free, unhindered, unimpeded, liberated Opposite: restrained

untreated adj **unprocessed**, unrefined, natural, raw, crude Opposite: treated

untried adj **untested**, inexperienced, unproven, new, novel Opposite: tested

untroubled adj **peaceful**, calm, tranquil, undisturbed, unflustered Opposite: troubled

untrue adj **1 false**, incorrect, wrong, fallacious, untruthful Opposite: true **2 cheating**, unfaithful, disloyal, treacherous, two-faced Opposite: faithful

untrustworthiness n **unreliability**, dishonesty, deceitfulness, disloyalty, treachery Opposite: dependability

untrustworthy adj **unreliable**, dishonest, deceitful, disloyal, treacherous Opposite: dependable

untruth n **lie**, falsehood, fiction, fabrication, deceit Opposite: truth. See COMPARE AND CONTRAST at **lie**.

untruthful adj **lying**, mendacious, dishonest, deceitful, false Opposite: truthful

untruthfulness n **dishonesty**, deceit, lies, falsehood, fabrication Opposite: truthfulness

untutored adj **untaught**, uneducated, untrained, unschooled, unqualified Opposite: educated

unusable adj **useless**, out of commission, unworkable, inoperative, broken Opposite: usable

unused adj **1 new**, brand-new, fresh, pristine Opposite: used **2 idle**, vacant, unemployed, unexploited, fallow **3 unaccustomed**, unfamiliar, unacquainted, inexperienced Opposite: familiar

unusual adj **1 uncommon**, rare, infrequent, scarce, unfamiliar Opposite: common **2 strange**, odd, curious, extraordinary, abnormal Opposite: ordinary

unutterable adj **unspeakable**, indescribable, inexpressible, indefinable, ineffable (fml)

unvarnished adj **plain**, straight, honest, unembellished, literal Opposite: embellished

unvarying adj **unwavering**, constant, unchanging, consistent, inflexible Opposite: varying

unveil v **1 uncover**, unwrap, bare, expose Opposite: cover **2 reveal**, expose, make public, divulge, show Opposite: conceal

unveiling n **1 opening**, launch, presentation, inauguration, debut Opposite: closure **2 revelation**, disclosure, exposure, uncovering, release Opposite: cover-up

unventilated adj **airless**, stuffy, unaired, close, stale Opposite: airy

unverified adj **unconfirmed**, unsupported, unsubstantiated, uncorroborated, unproven Opposite: verified

unvoiced adj **unspoken**, silent, secret, hidden, mute Opposite: spoken

unwanted adj **1 surplus**, superfluous, unnecessary, discarded, redundant Opposite: necessary **2 unwelcome**, unsolicited, annoying, undesirable, uninvited Opposite: welcome

unwariness n **incautiousness**, unguardedness, rashness, carelessness, gullibility Opposite: wariness

unwarrantable adj **uncalled-for**, indefensible, unjustifiable, unforgivable, inexcusable

unwarranted adj **unjustified**, undeserved, unnecessary, gratuitous, needless Opposite: justified

unwary adj **imprudent**, unguarded, rash, careless, unsuspecting Opposite: wary

unwashed adj **dirty**, grubby, grimy, sordid, squalid Opposite: clean

unwavering adj **firm**, staunch, solid, steadfast, untiring Opposite: irresolute

unwearied adj **unflagging**, tireless, indefatigable, uncomplaining, unceasing

unwelcome adj **unwanted**, undesirable, annoying, unsolicited, uninvited Opposite: welcome

unwelcoming adj **hostile**, unfriendly, standoffish, unreceptive, inhospitable Opposite: friendly

unwell adj **ill**, sick, under the weather, out of sorts, indisposed (fml) Opposite: well

unwholesome adj **unpleasant**, distasteful, objectionable, nasty, disagreeable Opposite: pleasant

unwholesomeness n **1 foulness**, insalubriousness, noxiousness, unhealthiness, harmfulness Opposite: wholesomeness **2 coarseness**, indecency, vulgarity, foulness, profanity Opposite: wholesomeness

unwieldy adj **awkward**, heavy, bulky, cumbersome, clumsy Opposite: manageable

unwilling adj **reluctant**, disinclined, grudging, loath, unenthusiastic Opposite: willing

COMPARE AND CONTRAST CORE MEANING: lacking the desire to do something
unwilling not prepared to do something; **reluctant** showing no enthusiasm for doing something and only doing it if forced; **disinclined** showing a lack of enthusiasm for something rather than a strong objection to it; **averse** (fml) strongly opposed to or disliking something; **hesitant** not eager to do something because of uncertainty or lack of confidence; **loath** having reservations about doing something.

unwillingness n **reluctance**, disinclination, refusal, indisposition, opposition Opposite: willingness

unwind v **1 undo**, loosen, unravel, untwist, disentangle Opposite: wind **2 relax**, wind down, slow down, calm down, kick back Opposite: work up

unwise adj **foolish**, imprudent, rash, ill-advised, injudicious Opposite: prudent

unwitting adj **1 unaware**, unsuspecting, ignorant, innocent, unconscious Opposite: knowing **2 accidental**, involuntary, unintentional, coincidental, inadvertent Opposite: deliberate

unwonted (literary) adj **unusual**, atypical, uncharacteristic, singular, unexpected Opposite: customary

unworkable adj **impracticable**, unusable, unfeasible, ineffectual, impractical Opposite: viable

unworldliness n **innocence**, naiveté, simplicity, ingenuousness, callowness *Opposite*: worldliness

unworldly adj **inexperienced**, callow, green, ingenuous, artless *Opposite*: experienced

unworried adj **calm**, untroubled, at ease, unruffled, unflustered *Opposite*: perturbed

unworthiness n 1 **worthlessness**, contemptibility, pitifulness, unfitness 2 **shamefulness**, dishonor, discredit, shame, disgrace

unworthy adj 1 **undeserving**, worthless, contemptible, pitiful, unfit *Opposite*: deserving 2 **shameful**, degrading, dishonorable, disgraceful, disreputable *Opposite*: reputable

unwrap v **undo**, unpack, remove, open, tear open *Opposite*: wrap

unwritten adj 1 **spoken**, oral, unrecorded, vocal, unprinted *Opposite*: written 2 **understood**, accepted, traditional, tacit, known

unyielding adj 1 **firm**, unbending, obstinate, steadfast, obdurate *Opposite*: acquiescent 2 **inflexible**, rigid, stiff, unbending, solid *Opposite*: flexible

unyoke v **untie**, separate, disjoin, unhook, loose *Opposite*: join

unzip v 1 **undo**, unfasten, open, disengage, free 2 **open**, expand, access, decompress *Opposite*: compress

up adj 1 **awake**, out of bed, up and about, active, up and around *Opposite*: asleep 2 **happy**, positive, optimistic, hopeful, cheerful *Opposite*: down 3 **winning**, in the lead, ahead, leading *Opposite*: behind

up-and-coming adj **emerging**, rising, budding, promising, talented *Opposite*: over-the-hill

up-and-down adj 1 **moody**, temperamental, changeable, tempestuous, turbulent *Opposite*: equable 2 **rising and falling**, bobbing, bouncing

upbeat (*infml*) adj **optimistic**, cheerful, positive, buoyant, bubbly *Opposite*: downbeat (*infml*)

upbraid v **scold**, reproach, chastise, reprimand, rebuke *Opposite*: praise

upbringing n **education**, childhood, background, rearing, nurture

upcoming adj **future**, imminent, forthcoming, impending, approaching *Opposite*: past

update v 1 **inform**, bring up-to-date, keep informed, keep posted, fill in 2 **modernize**, revise, renew, bring up-to-date, renovate

upend v **turn over**, tip over, upset, topple, flip over *Opposite*: right

up-front (*infml*) adj **straightforward**, honest, frank, plain-spoken, open *Opposite*: coy

upgrade v 1 **promote**, advance, elevate, raise, move up *Opposite*: demote 2 **improve**,

update, renew, modernize, renovate *Opposite*: downgrade ■ n 1 **promotion**, advancement, elevation, exaltation *Opposite*: demotion 2 **improvement**, upgrading, renovation, modernization, enhancement

upgrading n 1 **promotion**, advancement, step up, advance, progression *Opposite*: demotion 2 **improvement**, renovation, modernization, transformation, enhancement

upheaval n **disturbance**, turmoil, disorder, confusion, cataclysm *Opposite*: peace

upheave v **lift up**, raise, thrust up, elevate, lift *Opposite*: drop

uphill adj 1 **climbing**, ascending, rising, mounting *Opposite*: downhill 2 **difficult**, hard, arduous, demanding, tough *Opposite*: easy

uphold v **support**, sustain, maintain, defend, endorse

upholster v **cover**, pad, stuff, fill, decorate

upholstery n **fabric**, furnishings, covers, furniture, material

up in arms adj **angry**, indignant, offended, resentful, exasperated *Opposite*: unconcerned

up in the air adj **uncertain**, undecided, vague, in the balance, unsettled *Opposite*: decided

upkeep n **maintenance**, repairs, keep, conservation, preservation

upland n **moorland**, high ground, highland, plateau, tableland *Opposite*: lowland

uplift v 1 **elevate**, raise, hoist, lift *Opposite*: drop 2 **inspire**, enrich, improve, move, hearten *Opposite*: depress

uplifting adj **inspiring**, elevating, improving, enriching, heartening *Opposite*: depressing

upmarket adj **expensive**, high-class, smart, chic, exclusive *Opposite*: downmarket

upper adj **higher**, greater, better, superior *Opposite*: lower

upper circle n **gallery**, loggia, balcony, circle, dress circle

upper class n **aristocracy**, nobility, noblesse, gentry, elite *Opposite*: lower class

upper-class adj **aristocratic**, noble, blueblooded, highborn (*literary*) *Opposite*: lower-class

upper crust *see* **upper class**

uppercut n **blow**, punch, hit, haymaker (*slang*)

upper hand n **advantage**, initiative, ascendancy, edge, control *Opposite*: disadvantage

uppermost adj 1 **highest**, top, topmost, upmost *Opposite*: bottom 2 **primary**, main, principal, chief, greatest *Opposite*: last

uppity (*infml*) adj **presumptuous**, pretentious, snobbish, haughty, bumptious *Opposite*: humble

upright adj 1 **standing**, straight, vertical, erect

Opposite: horizontal **2 righteous**, moral, honorable, decent, honest *Opposite*: immoral

uprightness *n* **righteousness**, morality, honorableness, decency, honesty *Opposite*: immorality

uprising *n* **rebellion**, revolution, revolt, rising, unrest

uproar *n* **disturbance**, noise, chaos, pandemonium, upheaval *Opposite*: quiet

uproarious *adj* **hilarious**, funny, riotous, raucous, boisterous

uproot *v* **pull up**, deracinate, dig up, rip up *Opposite*: plant **2 displace**, evacuate, move on, relocate, deracinate *Opposite*: settle

uprush *n* **rush**, surge, updraft, draft, blast

upscale *adj* **upmarket**, smart, exclusive, expensive, high-class *Opposite*: downmarket

upset *v* **1 spill**, knock over, tip over, overturn, upend *Opposite*: right **2 disturb**, disrupt, reorder, reverse, mix up *Opposite*: order **3 distress**, hurt, disturb, sadden, trouble *Opposite*: please ■ *n* **1 defeat**, disappointment, affront, letdown, shock **2 surprise**, shock, confusion, disarray, disruption ■ *adj* **sad**, disturbed, unhappy, hurt, disappointed *Opposite*: composed

upset stomach *n* **indigestion**, stomachache, heartburn, bellyache *(infml)*, tummy ache *(infml)*

upsetting *adj* **distressing**, disturbing, hurtful, offensive, disappointing *Opposite*: pleasing

upshot *n* **result**, outcome, consequence, effect, end

upside *n* **advantage**, benefit, plus *(infml)*, positive *(infml)* *Opposite*: disadvantage

upside-down *adj* **1 upturned**, wrong way up, wrong side up, overturned, on its head *Opposite*: upright **2 in a mess**, messy, untidy, topsy-turvy, in disorder *Opposite*: orderly

upstage *v* **outdo**, outmaneuver, put somebody's nose out of joint, outshine, surpass

upstanding *adj* **honorable**, virtuous, honest, decent, respectable *Opposite*: degenerate

upstart *n* **nobody**, unknown, parvenu, arriviste, nonentity *Opposite*: grandee

upstretched *adj* **raised**, upraised, upturned, outstretched, extended *Opposite*: hanging down

upsurge *n* **increase**, rise, surge, gain, expansion *Opposite*: decrease

upswing *n* **increase**, improvement, upturn, turnaround, upsurge *Opposite*: downswing

uptake *n* **1 acceptance**, approval, interest, commitment, agreement *Opposite*: refusal **2 understanding**, comprehension, perception, appreciation, apprehension *Opposite*: incomprehension

up-tempo *adj* **exciting**, lively, fast, rapid, frenetic *Opposite*: dull

up the creek *(infml)* *adj* **in trouble**, in dire straits, in difficulty, in a predicament, in hot water *(infml)*

uptight *(infml)* *adj* **tense**, bothered, anxious, wound up, neurotic *Opposite*: calm

up-to-date *adj* **1 informed**, in touch, conversant, in the know, au fait **2 current**, latest, new, brand-new, modern *Opposite*: old-fashioned **3 fashionable**, upscale, cool, chic, trendy *(infml)* *Opposite*: passé

up to speed *adj* **in control**, on top of things, au fait, at home, informed *Opposite*: ignorant

up-to-the-minute *adj* **latest**, current, contemporary, state-of-the-art, contemporaneous *Opposite*: out-of-date

up to your ears *adj* **busy**, snowed under, swamped, flooded, rushed off your feet *Opposite*: idle

upturn *v* **overturn**, capsize, tip over, upset, turn turtle *Opposite*: right ■ *n* **improvement**, recovery, revival, growth, expansion *Opposite*: slump

upward *adv* **up**, uphill, in the air, aloft, higher *Opposite*: downward ■ *adj* **1 ascendant**, mounting, skyward, uphill, ascending *Opposite*: downward **2 rising**, improving, increasing, growing, expanding *Opposite*: downward

upwelling *n* **upsurge**, surge, burst, outburst, outpouring

upwind *adj* **windward**, exposed, open, bare, windy *Opposite*: leeward

up with *adj* **abreast**, up-to-date, familiar, conversant, au fait

urban *adj* **city**, town, built-up, municipal, inner-city *Opposite*: rural

urbane *adj* **sophisticated**, refined, courteous, suave, polished *Opposite*: unsophisticated

urbanite *n* **metropolitan**, cosmopolitan, citizen, resident, townie *(infml)* *Opposite*: rustic

urbanity *n* **sophistication**, refinement, courteousness, courtesy, suaveness *Opposite*: uncouthness

urbanization *n* **development**, suburbanization, expansion, sprawl, spread

urban myth *n* **myth**, folktale, tale, tall story, tall tale

urban sprawl *n* **urbanization**, development, suburbia, sprawl, expansion

urchin *n* **imp**, rascal, tyke, brat, hooligan *(infml)*

urge *v* **1 advise**, recommend, exhort, prevail on, press *Opposite*: dissuade **2 advocate**, commend, promote, back, support *Opposite*: downplay **3 encourage**, drive, push, force, impel *Opposite*: discourage ■ *n* **need**, wish, impulse, desire, inclination *Opposite*: disinclination

urgency n **1 need**, exigency, importance, necessity, hurry *Opposite*: unimportance **2 earnestness**, insistence, perseverance, firmness, resolve *Opposite*: vacillation

urgent adj **1 earnest**, insistent, persuasive, pleading, demanding *Opposite*: half-hearted **2 vital**, crucial, pressing, imperative, burning *Opposite*: trivial

urgently adv **immediately**, straightaway, instantly, at once, directly *Opposite*: whenever

urn n **vase**, container, vessel, pot, jug

usable adj **functional**, practical, serviceable, working, functioning *Opposite*: unusable

usage n **1 treatment**, handling, control, management, running **2 practice**, procedure, custom, norm, tradition

use v **1 employ**, make use of, utilize, exercise, bring into play *Opposite*: forgo **2 consume**, expend, spend, exhaust, use up *Opposite*: conserve **3 manipulate**, exploit, take advantage of, mistreat, abuse **4 behave toward**, handle, treat, manipulate, manage **5 benefit from**, make use of, enjoy, avail yourself of, tap ■ n **1 expenditure**, consumption, wear and tear, wastage, depletion *Opposite*: saving **2 treatment**, handling, manipulation, exploitation, management **3 employment**, application, utilization, exploitation, consumption *Opposite*: disuse **4 purpose**, function, application, service, role **5 usefulness**, help, assistance, benefit, aid *Opposite*: harm **6** *(literary)* **usage**, custom, habit, practice, routine

---

COMPARE AND CONTRAST CORE MEANING: put something to use

use put something into action or service; **employ** make use of something such as a tool or a resource in a particular way; **make use of** use what is readily available, especially in a sensible or economical way; **utilize** find a practical or unintended use for something.

---

used adj **1 secondhand**, castoff, hand-me-down, recycled *Opposite*: new **2 expended**, old, worn, worn out, consumed *Opposite*: remaining **3 exploited**, taken advantage of, misused, manipulated, abused

used to adj **1 accustomed**, hardened, inured, schooled, conditioned *Opposite*: unaccustomed **2 familiar**, at home, au fait, at ease, easy *Opposite*: unfamiliar

useful adj **1 practical**, helpful, serviceable, of use, constructive *Opposite*: useless **2 convenient**, valuable, beneficial, advantageous, expedient *Opposite*: disadvantageous

usefulness n **1 practicality**, helpfulness, worth, utility, convenience *Opposite*: uselessness **2 valuableness**, convenience, advantageousness, expediency, suitability

useless adj **1 unusable**, impractical, unserviceable, inoperable, unworkable *Opposite*: useful **2 unsuccessful**, futile, ineffectual, unavailing, worthless *Opposite*: successful **3** *(infml)* **inept**, hopeless, incompetent, inefficient, ineffectual *Opposite*: effective

uselessness n **1 impracticality**, unusableness, inoperability, unworkability, inadequacy *Opposite*: usefulness **2 unsuccessfulness**, pointlessness, futility, ineffectualness, ineffectiveness *Opposite*: worth **3** *(infml)* **ineptness**, hopelessness, ineffectiveness, incompetence, inefficiency *Opposite*: effectiveness

user n **operator**, worker, employer, manipulator, handler

user-friendliness n **accessibility**, manageability, handiness, manipulability, convenience *Opposite*: inaccessibility

user-friendly adj **accessible**, comprehensible, intelligible, manipulable, manageable *Opposite*: inaccessible

use up v **expend**, consume, exhaust, wear out, deplete *Opposite*: conserve

usher n **attendant**, escort, guide, leader, conductor ■ v **escort**, conduct, guide, steer, pilot

usher in v **herald**, introduce, lead to, announce, signal *Opposite*: see out

usual adj **1 normal**, typical, common, standard, natural *Opposite*: exceptional **2 habitual**, routine, everyday, customary, familiar *Opposite*: irregular

---

COMPARE AND CONTRAST CORE MEANING: often done, used, bought, or consumed

usual normal, common, or typical; **customary** conforming to regular or typical practice; **habitual** done so often or repeatedly that the behavior or practice has become ingrained; **routine** normal, regular, and usual in every way, even predictable, repetitive, and monotonous; **wonted** *(fml)* usual or typical.

---

usually adv **normally**, typically, customarily, generally, by and large *Opposite*: exceptionally

usurp v **seize**, appropriate, take over, assume, commandeer *Opposite*: surrender

usury n **moneylending**, overcharging, extortion, daylight robbery *(infml)*, highway robbery *(infml)*

utensil n **tool**, instrument, implement, appliance, device

WORD BANK
❑ **types of utensils** beater, bottle opener, can opener, corkscrew, drainer, garlic press, grater, grinder, juice extractor, liquidizer, mill, mortar, nutcracker, opener, peeler, pestle, reamer, sieve, soup ladle, spatula, strainer, whisk

utilitarian adj **practical**, useful, serviceable, functional, down-to-earth *Opposite*: useless

utility n **1 usefulness**, practicality, efficiency,

lessness 2 **convenience**, service, benefit,
worth, advantage *Opposite*: worthlessness
utilization *n* **use**, application, employment,
deployment, operation
utilize *v* **use**, apply, employ, operate,
develop *Opposite*: forgo. *See* COMPARE AND
CONTRAST *at* **use**.
utmost *adj* 1 **greatest**, highest, extreme,
chief, supreme *Opposite*: least 2 **farthest**,
extreme, most distant, farthermost, remotest
utopia *n* **ideal**, paradise, never-never land,
heaven, Shangri-la
utopian *adj* 1 **ideal**, perfect, ultimate, best,

model 2 **idealistic**, naive, impracticable,
impractical, unworkable *Opposite*: pragmatic ■ *n* **idealist**, romantic, visionary,
dreamer, purist *Opposite*: pragmatist
utter *v* **say**, speak, pronounce, express, state
■ *adj* **absolute**, total, complete, sheer,
downright *Opposite*: partial
utterance *n* 1 **word**, sound, note, noise,
exclamation *Opposite*: silence 2 **statement**,
speech, remark, declaration, announcement
U-turn *n* 1 **turn**, rotation, revolution, about-
face, volte-face 2 **change**, reversal, volte
face, about-face

V

vacancy *n* **job**, post, position, opening,
opportunity
vacant *adj* 1 **empty**, available, unoccupied,
not in use, void *Opposite*: occupied
2 **blank**, empty, expressionless, indifferent, vacuous *Opposite*: alert

COMPARE AND CONTRAST CORE MEANING:
lacking contents or occupants
vacant without occupants or contents, often
temporarily; **unoccupied** not lived in by anybody,
or currently without occupants; **empty** not containing or holding anything, or without occupants; **void** having no contents, or having no
incumbent, occupant, or holder.

vacate *v* 1 **leave**, relinquish, check out, give
up, depart *Opposite*: occupy 2 **empty**,
evacuate, clear out, free, divest *Opposite*:
fill
vacation *n* **holiday**, break, trip, rest, retreat
vacationer *n* **vacationist**, traveler, tourist,
sightseer, visitor
vaccinate *v* **inoculate**, immunize, protect
Opposite: expose
vaccination *n* **inoculation**, injection, immunization
vaccine *n* **inoculation**, injection, serum,
preparation, shot *(infml)*
vacillate *v* **waver**, hesitate, dither, think
twice, equivocate *Opposite*: decide. *See*
COMPARE AND CONTRAST *at* **hesitate**.
vacillating *adj* **irresolute**, indecisive, of two
minds, hesitant, dithering *Opposite*: resolute
vacillation *n* **indecisiveness**, irresoluteness,
indecision, irresolution, hesitancy *Opposite*: resolution
vacuity *(fml)* *n* **mindlessness**, blankness,
vacantness, inaneness, stupidity *Opposite*:
intelligence

vacuous *adj* **stupid**, unintelligent, inane,
vacant, mindless *Opposite*: intelligent
vacuum *n* **void**, space, emptiness, nothingness, blankness
vagabond *n* **vagrant**, tramp, beggar, drifter,
wanderer *Opposite*: resident
vagary *n* **whim**, fancy, notion, mood, quirk
Opposite: choice
vagrancy *n* **homelessness**, penury, destitution, rootlessness, begging *Opposite*:
residence
vagrant *n* **vagabond**, tramp, beggar, drifter,
hobo *Opposite*: resident ■ *adj* **nomadic**, itinerant, wandering, roaming, roving *Opposite*: settled
vague *adj* 1 **indistinct**, unclear, indistinguishable, hazy, fuzzy *Opposite*: clear
2 **unclear**, imprecise, indefinite, ambiguous, equivocal *Opposite*: definite 3 **absent-
minded**, abstracted, distracted, distant,
unclear *Opposite*: alert
vagueness *n* 1 **nebulousness**, imprecision,
indistinctness, ambiguity, elusiveness
Opposite: precision 2 **abstraction**, absent-
mindedness, pensiveness, dreaminess
Opposite: attentiveness 3 **haziness**, fuzziness, formlessness, imprecision, blur-
redness *Opposite*: clarity
vain *adj* 1 **useless**, ineffective, otiose, unsuccessful, hopeless *Opposite*: successful
2 **empty**, hollow, idle, pointless, futile
Opposite: reliable 3 **proud**, conceited, narcissistic, arrogant, self-important *Opposite*: humble

COMPARE AND CONTRAST CORE MEANING:
without substance or unlikely to be carried
though
vain failing to have or unlikely to have the
intended or desired result; **empty** lacking substance, sincerity, or truthfulness; **hollow** not
sincere or genuine; **idle** unlikely to be carried

out or impossible to put into effect.

vainglorious (literary) adj proud, boastful, self-important, conceited, puffed up

vale (literary) n valley, dale, gorge, dell (literary) Opposite: hill

valediction (fml) n farewell, goodbye, sendoff, adieu (literary), leave-taking (literary)

valedictory (fml) n farewell, goodbye, parting, leave-taking (literary) Opposite: welcome ■ adj parting, farewell, goodbye, final, last Opposite: welcoming

valet v clean, clean out, vacuum, tidy, polish

valetudinarian n 1 convalescent, patient, invalid, valetudinary 2 hypochondriac, neurotic, valetudinary ■ adj sickly, feeble, unhealthy, frail, weak Opposite: healthy

valiant adj brave, courageous, heroic, fearless, noble Opposite: cowardly

valid adj 1 reasonable, sound, rational, justifiable, legitimate Opposite: unjustifiable 2 lawful, legal, binding, effective, in force Opposite: illegal 3 usable, acceptable, authorized, endorsed, official Opposite: unusable 4 convincing, compelling, sound, persuasive, cogent Opposite: unconvincing

COMPARE AND CONTRAST CORE MEANING: worthy of acceptance or credence
valid having a solid foundation or justification; **cogent** forceful and convincing to the intellect and reason; **convincing** likely to overcome doubts and win the support of those who hear it; **reasonable** acceptable and according to common sense; **sound** based on good sense and acceptable reasoning and worthy of approval.

validate v 1 prove, substantiate, confirm, authenticate, corroborate Opposite: disprove 2 authorize, certify, endorse, ratify, legalize Opposite: invalidate

validation n 1 authentication, proof, endorsement, confirmation, corroboration 2 authorization, endorsement, ratification, certification, legalization Opposite: invalidation

validity n 1 cogency, rationality, legitimacy, soundness, strength Opposite: weakness 2 legality, authority, legitimacy, authenticity, lawfulness

valley n gorge, dale, basin, vale (literary), dell (literary) Opposite: hill

valor n courage, bravery, heroism, fearlessness, boldness Opposite: cowardice

valorous adj noble, brave, courageous, heroic, fearless Opposite: cowardly

valuable adj 1 costly, expensive, priceless, dear, important Opposite: inexpensive 2 invaluable, helpful, important, valued, useful Opposite: worthless 3 cherished, valued, appreciated, respected, treasured

valuation n estimate, assessment, evaluation, appraisal, survey

value n 1 worth, price, cost, rate, charge 2 benefit, importance, worth, significance, usefulness Opposite: insignificance ■ v 1 prize, appreciate, respect, esteem, treasure Opposite: scorn 2 rate, assess, estimate, evaluate, appraise

valued adj appreciated, respected, esteemed, treasured, cherished

valueless adj inconsequential, worthless, insignificant, paltry, miserable Opposite: valuable

values n principles, standards, morals, ethics, ideals

valve n regulator, controller, stopcock, tap, faucet

vampire n parasite, hanger-on, predator, sponge, freeloader (infml)

van n forefront, front, lead, head, vanguard

vandal n criminal, trespasser, delinquent, thug, hooligan (infml)

vandalism n damage, destruction, defacement, wreckage, sabotage

vandalize v destroy, damage, deface, wreck, break

vane n blade, slat, fin, plate, strip

vanguard n 1 front line, front, advance guard Opposite: rearguard 2 forefront, front, lead, head, cutting edge

vanilla adj plain, ordinary, boring, unexciting, bland Opposite: interesting

vanish v 1 disappear, evaporate, fade away, peter out, go Opposite: appear 2 become extinct, die out, disappear, cease to exist, be exterminated

vanished adj disappeared, missing, died out, gone, extinct Opposite: present

vanity n 1 pride, narcissism, self-importance, conceit, arrogance Opposite: humility 2 futility, emptiness, uselessness, pointlessness, worthlessness Opposite: value

vanquish v defeat, conquer, subjugate, crush, subdue Opposite: surrender. See COMPARE AND CONTRAST at defeat.

vantage point n 1 viewpoint, viewing platform, belvedere, lookout, crow's nest 2 standpoint, viewpoint, angle, point of view, perspective

vapid adj 1 lifeless, uninteresting, unexciting, vacuous, tame Opposite: lively 2 flavorless, insipid, tasteless, weak, tame Opposite: tasty

vapor n 1 gas, air, ether 2 smoke, fumes, cloud, fog, haze 3 aerosol, spray, mist

vaporize v 1 evaporate, turn to vapor, boil away, boil, heat Opposite: condense 2 vanish, disappear, evaporate, fade away, go away 3 destroy, annihilate, burn, incinerate, decimate Opposite: preserve

vaporizer n nebulizer, atomizer, aerosol, spray, inhaler

vaporous adj 1 gaseous, smoky, misty, steamy, foggy 2 volatile, unstable, unpredictable, explosive, flammable *Opposite*: stable **3 insubstantial**, ephemeral, impermanent, evanescent, nebulous *Opposite*: solid **4 fanciful**, ridiculous, implausible, fantastic, unreal *Opposite*: real **5 murky**, hazy, cloudy, obscure, dim *Opposite*: clear

variability *n* **1 erraticism**, inconsistency, capriciousness, changeability, unpredictability *Opposite*: predictability **2 unevenness**, patchiness, irregularity, inconsistency *Opposite*: consistency **3 flexibility**, adaptability, fickleness, inconstancy, mutability *Opposite*: fixedness

variable *adj* **1 varying**, changing, fluctuating, changeable, erratic *Opposite*: constant **2 uneven**, patchy, up-and-down, irregular, inconsistent *Opposite*: consistent **3 mutable**, adjustable, flexible, capricious, inconstant *Opposite*: fixed

variance *n* **1 divergence**, disparity, difference, discrepancy, inconsistency *Opposite*: consistency **2 alteration**, modification, adjustment, change **3 conflict**, clash, dissent, dispute, difference of opinion *Opposite*: agreement

variant *adj* **irregular**, different, optional, modified, abnormal ■ *n* **variation**, alternate, alternative, deviation, modification

variation *n* **1 difference**, disparity, dissimilarity, distinction, discrepancy *Opposite*: similarity **2 variant**, adaptation, reworking, departure, alteration

varied *adj* **heterogeneous**, diverse, wide-ranging, mixed, different *Opposite*: homogeneous

variegated *adj* **spotted**, mottled, pied, dappled, speckled *Opposite*: uniform

variety *n* **1 collection**, diversity, assortment, selection, multiplicity **2 diversity**, change, variability, variation *Opposite*: monotony **3 type**, kind, form, sort, category

variety show *n* **show**, revue, cabaret, entertainment, performance

various *adj* **1 a variety of**, a range of, an assortment of, a mixture of, different *Opposite*: same **2 numerous**, many, a number of, several, countless *Opposite*: few

varnish *n* **lacquer**, paint, finish, glaze, coating ■ *v* **paint**, glaze, finish, polish, lacquer

vary *v* **1 change**, alter, fluctuate, adjust, adapt *Opposite*: standardize **2 diverge**, differ, be different, contrast, fluctuate *Opposite*: conform. *See* COMPARE AND CONTRAST *at* change.

vase *n* **rose bowl**, urn, jug, pot, container

vast *adj* **massive**, huge, enormous, gigantic, immense *Opposite*: small

vastly *adv* **much**, greatly, infinitely, immensely, immeasurably *Opposite*: slightly

vastness *n* **massiveness**, incalculability, limitlessness, immensity, hugeness

vat *n* **container**, cask, barrel, tank, drum

vaudeville *n* **show**, entertainment, variety show, burlesque, revue

vault *n* **1 arch**, dome, cupola **2 crypt**, cellar, mausoleum, undercroft, burial chamber **3 strongroom**, treasury, safe, treasure house ■ *v* **jump**, leap, spring, hurdle, bound

vaulted *adj* **curved**, domed, arched

vaunt *v* **puff**, boast, brag, show off, hype *Opposite*: play down

vaunted *adj* **hyped**, praised, promoted, advertised, flaunted *Opposite*: downplayed

vector *n* **course**, trajectory, path, flight path, route

veer *v* **change course**, turn, swing, swerve, bend

vegan *n* **fruitarian**, vegetarian, veggie (*infml*)

vegetable *adj* **plant**, herbal, vegetal

WORD BANK

❏ **types of root vegetables** beet, bok choy, carrot, cassava, celeriac, new potato, parsnip, potato, rutabaga, sugar beet, sweet potato, turnip, yam

❏ **types of vegetables** artichoke, asparagus, brassica, broccoli, Brussels sprout, cabbage, cauliflower, collard greens, corn on the cob, eggplant, fennel, garlic, greens, kale, leek, marrow squash, okra, onion, pumpkin, spinach, squash, sweet corn, Swiss chard, zucchini

---

vegetarian *n* **fruitarian**, vegan, lactovegetarian, ovolactovegetarian, veggie (*infml*) ■ *adj* **fruitarian**, vegan, lactovegetarian, ovolactovegetarian, veggie (*infml*)

vegetate *v* **sit around**, stagnate, twiddle your thumbs, kill time, loaf

vegetation *n* **plants**, plant life, flora, ground cover, bedding

veggie (*infml*) *n* **lactovegetarian**, fruitarian, vegetarian, ovolactovegetarian, vegan

vehemence *n* **forcefulness**, intensity, fervor, passion, violence *Opposite*: indifference

vehement *adj* **fervent**, passionate, heated, violent, intense *Opposite*: apathetic

vehicle *n* **1 means of transport**, transport, conveyance **2 medium**, means of expression, channel, means, mouthpiece

---

WORD BANK

❏ **types of commercial or industrial vehicles** backhoe, bulldozer, cab, combine, combine harvester, crane, digger, dump truck, earthmover, hearse, pickup, semitrailer, snowplow, steamroller, tanker, taxi, taxicab, tow truck, tractor, transporter, truck, van, wrecker, yellow cab

❏ **types of leisure vehicles** all-terrain vehicle, bobsled, cablecar, camper, chair lift, dogsled, dune buggy, go-cart, golf cart, land yacht, luge, mobile home, motor home, RV, sled, sleigh, snowmobile, toboggan, trailer

❏ **types of military vehicles** amphibian, armored car, jeep, tank

❏ **types of public service vehicles** ambulance,

bus, firetruck, garbage truck, jitney, minibus, police car, prowl car, shuttle, squad car, trolley

❏ **types of controls** accelerator, brake, choke, clutch, gas gauge, gearshift, horn, odometer, pedal, rev counter, speedometer, steering wheel, wheel

❏ **types of internal features** air bag, back seat, booster seat, cab, car seat, child seat, cup holder, dashboard, driver's seat, glove compartment, headrest, passenger seat, rearview mirror, seat belt, sound system, sun visor

❏ **types of external features** brake light, bumper, exhaust pipe, fog light, hazard light, headlight, high beam, hubcap, kick-start, license plate, luggage rack, mud flap, mudguard, muffler, parking light, plate, side mirror, splashguard, stoplight, taillight, tire, turn signal, wheel, windshield wiper

❏ **parts of an external structure** airfoil, axle, bodywork, chassis, coachwork, fender, fin, grille, hood, hull, side mirror, spoiler, sunroof, tailgate, trunk, windshield

veil *n* mask, blanket, shroud, covering, curtain ■ *v* **cover**, conceal, hide, mask, cloak *Opposite*: reveal

veiled *adj* **1 indirect**, oblique, obscure, covert, roundabout *Opposite*: overt **2 masked**, cloaked, shrouded, covered, hooded *Opposite*: uncovered

vein *n* **1 layer**, seam, lode, stratum, deposit **2 mood**, frame of mind, manner, strain, attitude **3 streak**, strip, stripe, line

veined *adj* **patterned**, marbled, lined, streaked

veld *n* **grassland**, savanna, prairie, plain

veldt *see* **veld**

velocity *n* **speed**, rate, rapidity, swiftness, pace

velvety *adj* **soft**, smooth, silky, downy, furry *Opposite*: rough

venal *adj* **1 corruptible**, mercenary, bribable, bent, unprincipled *Opposite*: honest **2 corrupt**, degenerate, decadent, lawless, amoral *Opposite*: aboveboard

vend *v* **sell**, trade, deal in, hawk, supply

vendetta *n* **1 feud**, blood feud, quarrel, dispute, grudge **2 campaign**, crusade, war, battle, hate campaign

vending machine *n* **coin-operated machine**, dispenser, snack machine, slot machine

vendor *n* **seller**, retailer, dealer, supplier, merchant

veneer *n* **1 covering**, facing, finish, surface, layer **2 appearance**, semblance, pretense, guise, show ■ *v* **cover**, finish, conceal, plate

venerable *adj* **respected**, esteemed, honored, revered, admired *Opposite*: disreputable

venerate *v* **revere**, worship, adore, idolize, esteem *Opposite*: disrespect

veneration *n* **worship**, adoration, reverence, honor, respect *Opposite*: disdain. *See* COMPARE AND CONTRAST *at* **regard**.

vengeance *n* **revenge**, retribution, reprisal, retaliation, punishment

vengeful *adj* **vindictive**, implacable, unforgiving, revengeful, resentful *Opposite*: merciful

venial *adj* **forgivable**, excusable, pardonable, understandable, minor *Opposite*: unforgivable

venom *n* **1 poison**, toxin, bane *Opposite*: antidote **2 malice**, spite, rancor, spleen, acrimony *Opposite*: affection

venomous *adj* **1 poisonous**, deadly, toxic, noxious lethal *Opposite*: harmless **2 malicious**, spiteful, virulent, bitter, rancorous

vent *n* **opening**, outlet, aperture, escape, exhaust ■ *v* **express**, give vent to, find expression for, voice, release *Opposite*: suppress

ventilate *v* **1 air**, aerate, air out, freshen **2 publicize**, make public, make known, air, express

ventilation *n* **air circulation**, airing, aeration

ventilator *n* **1 fan**, vent, opening, flue, aperture **2 life support machine**, respirator, breathing apparatus, iron lung

venture *n* **1 business enterprise**, undertaking, scheme, project, endeavor **2 undertaking**, course, endeavor, project, mission ■ *v* **1 hazard**, dare, undertake, brave, try **2 offer**, put forward, volunteer, express, say **3 presume**, dare, be so bold, take the liberty, have the audacity

venturesome *(fml) adj* **1 daring**, adventurous, enterprising, bold, brave *Opposite*: cautious **2 hazardous**, chancy, dangerous, risky, perilous *Opposite*: safe

venue *n* **site**, place, location, scene, setting

veracious *adj* **honest**, truthful, genuine, principled, dependable *Opposite*: dishonest

veracity *n* **1 truth**, accuracy, reliability, genuineness, authenticity *Opposite*: falsity **2 truthfulness**, honesty, integrity, uprightness, reliability *Opposite*: dishonesty

veranda *n* **terrace**, balcony, porch, loggia, gallery

verbal *adj* **spoken**, oral, vocal, unwritten, voiced *Opposite*: unspoken

COMPARE AND CONTRAST CORE MEANING: expressed in words

verbal using words, especially spoken words, rather than pictures or physical action; **spoken** expressed with the voice; **oral** expressed in spoken form rather than in writing.

verbalization *n* **articulation**, expression, speech, voicing

verbalize *v* **express**, articulate, voice, put into words, speak

verbatim *adj* **exact**, word for word, precise, literal, letter-perfect *Opposite*: imprecise ■ *adv* **word for word**, exactly, precisely, to the letter, literally *Opposite*: approximately

verbiage *n* empty words, claptrap *(infml)*, waffle *(infml)*, gobbledygook *(infml)*

verbose *adj* wordy, prolix, long-winded, talkative, bombastic *Opposite*: taciturn. *See* COMPARE AND CONTRAST *at* **wordy**.

verbosity *n* long-windedness, garrulousness, wordiness, prolixity, loquaciousness *Opposite*: succinctness

verdant *adj* green, lush, luxuriant, fertile, leafy

verdict *n* decision, judgment, finding, result, outcome

verdigris *n* patina, tarnish, corrosion, greenness, coloration

verdure *n* greenery, lushness, vegetation, flora, plant life

verge *n* edge, border, threshold, approach, limit ■ *v* be near to, approach, border on, come close to, near

verging on *adj* almost, bordering on, close to, tantamount to

verifiable *adj* demonstrable, provable, confirmable, certifiable, showable *Opposite*: moot

verification *n* confirmation, corroboration, proof, substantiation, authentication *Opposite*: contradiction

verified *adj* confirmed, proved, shown, tested, substantiated *Opposite*: unconfirmed

verify *v* confirm, bear out, prove, authenticate, validate *Opposite*: disprove

verisimilitude *(fml)* *n* truth, credibility, authenticity, reliability, plausibility *Opposite*: falsity

veritable *adj* absolute, real, genuine, out-and-out, authentic *Opposite*: false

verity *(fml)* *n* truth, fact, principle, reality, sincerity

verminous *adj* infested, pest-ridden, louse-ridden, rat-infested, crawling

vernacular *n* dialect, language, patois, argot, colloquial speech

versatile *adj* 1 adaptable, flexible, resourceful, multitalented, all-around *Opposite*: inflexible 2 multipurpose, adaptable, handy, useful, nifty *(infml)* *Opposite*: inflexible

versatility *n* 1 adaptability, flexibility, resourcefulness *Opposite*: inflexibility 2 usefulness, handiness, niftiness *(infml)*

verse *n* 1 poetry, rhyme, blank verse, free verse, doggerel *Opposite*: prose 2 stanza, canto, section, unit

versed *adj* experienced, competent, conversant, proficient, knowledgeable *Opposite*: inexperienced

version *n* 1 account, description, report, side, story 2 form, type, variety, kind, sort 3 adaptation, edition, translation, rendering

versus *prep* 1 against, contra, in competition with 2 as opposed to, contrasted with, set against, against, as against

vertebrate *n* animal, mammal, bird, reptile, amphibian *Opposite*: invertebrate

vertex *n* apex, summit, height, pinnacle, apogee *Opposite*: base

vertical *adj* perpendicular, upright, erect, straight up, straight down *Opposite*: horizontal

vertiginous *adj* high, dizzying, tall, lofty, exposed

vertigo *n* dizziness, giddiness, unsteadiness, faintness, lightheadedness

verve *n* vitality, energy, dynamism, vigor, dash *Opposite*: lethargy

very *adv* extremely, incredibly, awfully, exceptionally, exceedingly *Opposite*: a bit *(infml)* ■ *adj* actual, self-same, same, identical, exact

vessel *n* 1 container, pot, bowl, jug, pitcher 2 boat, ship, craft

vest *v* devolve, consign, entrust, assign, lodge

vested interest *n* 1 special interest, interest, concern, stake, investment 2 stakeholder, supporter, shareholder

vestibule *n* entrance hall, foyer, lobby, antechamber, atrium

vestige *n* trace, sign, mark, indication, hint

vestigial *adj* 1 residual, remaining, imperceptible, token 2 nonfunctioning, functionless, stunted, degenerate, atrophic *Opposite*: functional

vestment *n* 1 robe, garment, dress, habit, uniform 2 surplice, chasuble, cope, vesture *(archaic)*

vet *v* examine, check, scrutinize, research, inspect

veteran *n* expert, old hand, past master, trouper, old-timer *Opposite*: novice

veto *n* 1 rejection, refusal, bar, disallowance, prevention *Opposite*: approval 2 prohibition, ban, sanction, embargo, order *Opposite*: release ■ *v* 1 reject, turn down, bar, disallow, refuse *Opposite*: approve 2 prohibit, ban, forbid, outlaw, proscribe *Opposite*: permit

vex *v* 1 annoy, displease, irk, irritate, anger *Opposite*: pacify 2 agitate, distress, trouble, bother, torment *Opposite*: placate 3 confound, confuse, perplex, puzzle, tease *Opposite*: enlighten

vexation *n* annoyance, upset, displeasure, bother, irritation *Opposite*: satisfaction

vexatious *adj* annoying, upsetting, irritating, troublesome, bothersome *Opposite*: placatory

vexed *adj* 1 irritated, provoked, annoyed, upset, angry *Opposite*: calm 2 debated, controversial, contentious, fractious, problematic *Opposite*: uncomplicated

vexing *adj* **annoying**, puzzling, frustrating, worrying, worrisome *Opposite*: easy

via *prep* **by way of**, through, by

viability *n* **practicability**, feasibility, practicality, capability, sustainability *Opposite*: impracticality

viable *adj* **practicable**, worthwhile, feasible, practical, sustainable *Opposite*: impossible

vial *n* **ampoule**, vessel, container, flask, bottle

vibrancy *n* **vitality**, vivacity, animation, enthusiasm, effervescence *Opposite*: lethargy

vibrant *adj* **1 pulsating**, energetic, vibrating, effervescent, alive *Opposite*: listless **2 bright**, dazzling, vivid, brilliant, flamboyant *Opposite*: dull

vibrate *v* **shake**, quiver, tremble, shudder, judder

vibration *n* **shaking**, quivering, trembling, shuddering, juddering *Opposite*: stillness

vicarage *n* **rectory**, manse, church house, parsonage, residence

vicarious *adj* **1 displaced**, secondhand, indirect, remote, removed *Opposite*: direct **2 empathetic**, sympathetic, assumed, imagined, adopted **3 delegated**, surrogate, substitute, proxy, deputized

vice *n* **1 depravity**, iniquity, evil, wickedness, immorality *Opposite*: goodness **2 defect**, failing, flaw, imperfection, fault *Opposite*: strength

vicinal *adj* **1 neighboring**, adjacent, nearby, close, proximate *Opposite*: distant **2 local**, district, municipal, regional, provincial *Opposite*: international

vicinity *n* **neighborhood**, environs, locality, district, area

vicious *adj* **1 ferocious**, savage, wild, brutish, fierce *Opposite*: gentle **2 spiteful**, malicious, mean, rancorous, backbiting *Opposite*: kind

vicious circle *n* **Catch-22**, no-win situation, impasse, stalemate

viciousness *n* **1 ferociousness**, savagery, wildness, brutishness, ferocity *Opposite*: gentleness **2 maliciousness**, meanness, spitefulness, rancorousness, venomousness *Opposite*: kindness

vicissitudes *n* **changes**, variations, vagaries, ups and downs, fluctuations

victim *n* **1 fatality**, casualty, sufferer, injured party **2 dupe**, butt, target, object, prey

victimization *n* **persecution**, discrimination, oppression, ill-treatment, harassment *Opposite*: favoritism

victimize *v* **persecute**, discriminate against, harass, oppress, pick on *Opposite*: favor

victor *n* **winner**, champion, conqueror, medalist, prizewinner *Opposite*: loser

victorious *adj* **winning**, triumphant, champion, prizewinning, successful *Opposite*: losing

victory *n* **conquest**, triumph, win, success *Opposite*: defeat

victuals *n* **food**, provisions, supplies, foodstuffs, food and drink

video *v* **videotape**, record, tape, film, capture

WORD BANK
❏ **types of video equipment** camcorder, DVD, palmcorder, VCR, video camera, videocassette, videocassette recorder, videodisk, video recorder, videotape

video display terminal *n* **screen**, monitor, interface, terminal, viewer

videotape *v* **record**, video, tape, film, capture

vie *v* **compete**, contend, contest, strive, fight *Opposite*: collaborate

view *n* **1 sight**, vision, observation, examination, scrutiny **2 scene**, picture, spectacle, prospect, vista **3 opinion**, interpretation, assessment, understanding ■ *v* **1 consider**, regard, think of, perceive, look on **2 inspect**, examine, look over, look at, observe **3 look at**, see, regard, observe, notice

viewable *adj* **1 available**, on view, on display, accessible **2 fit**, presentable, acceptable, all right, appropriate *Opposite*: inappropriate

viewer *n* **watcher**, spectator, onlooker, ogler, observer

viewing *n* **1 watching**, inspecting, seeing, observing, looking **2 programming**, broadcasts, programs, broadcasting, showing

viewpoint *n* **1 point of view**, view, perspective, standpoint, position **2 vantage point**, viewing platform, belvedere, lookout, crow's nest

vigil *n* **night watch**, watch, wake

vigilance *n* **watchfulness**, attentiveness, observance, care, caution *Opposite*: inattentiveness

vigilant *adj* **watchful**, alert, attentive, on your guard, wary *Opposite*: inattentive. *See* COMPARE AND CONTRAST *at* **cautious**.

vignette *n* **1 design**, decoration, illustration, frontispiece, picture **2 essay**, article, piece, monograph **3 picture**, painting, drawing, photograph, print **4 scene**, extract, clip, fragment, snippet

vigor *n* **1 vitality**, strength, energy, robustness, power *Opposite*: lethargy **2 intensity**, strength, force, ferocity, violence *Opposite*: feebleness **3 potency**, life, robustness, stamina, staying power *Opposite*: weakness

vigorous *adj* **robust**, active, strong, energetic, dynamic *Opposite*: feeble

vile *adj* **1 evil**, wicked, shameful, depraved, base *Opposite*: good **2 unpleasant**, horrid, horrible, dreadful, awful *Opposite*: pleasant **3 disgusting**, loathsome, revolting, repulsive, repellent *Opposite*: admirable. *See* COMPARE AND CONTRAST *at* **mean**.

vileness *n* **1 evil**, depravity, wickedness, lowness, degradation *Opposite*: goodness **2 unpleasantness**, dreadfulness, awfulness, horridness, horribleness *Opposite*: pleasantness **3 repulsiveness**, loathsomeness, hatefulness, despicableness

vilification *n* **maliciousness**, abuse, disparagement, criticism, backbiting *Opposite*: acclaim

vilify *v* **malign**, abuse, denigrate, belittle, disparage *Opposite*: compliment. *See* COMPARE AND CONTRAST *at* malign.

village *n* **hamlet**, rural community, settlement

villager *n* **country dweller**, rustic, country cousin *(dated)*

villain *n* **scoundrel**, rogue, desperado, heavy, baddie *(infml) Opposite*: hero

villainous *adj* **1 wicked**, criminal, heinous, depraved, iniquitous *Opposite*: good **2 unpleasant**, undesirable, obnoxious, offensive, unreliable *Opposite*: pleasant

villainy *n* **wickedness**, wrongdoing, evil, foul play, badness *Opposite*: goodness

vim *(infml)* *n* **vitality**, energy, vigor, exuberance, verve *Opposite*: lethargy

vindicate *v* **1 justify**, maintain, claim, support, defend **2 clear**, exonerate, absolve, acquit, exculpate *(fml) Opposite*: implicate

vindication *n* **1 exoneration**, absolution, acquittal, exculpation *(fml) Opposite*: implication **2 justification**, evidence, proof, assertion

vindictive *adj* **1 spiteful**, malicious, mean, cruel, hurtful *Opposite*: kind **2 vengeful**, unforgiving, revengeful, rancorous, implacable *Opposite*: forgiving

vindictiveness *n* **1 spite**, malice, cruelty, nastiness, unkindness *Opposite*: kindness **2 vengefulness**, bitterness, rancor, resentment

vine *n* **climber**, creeper, liana

vinegary *adj* **1 sour**, astringent, acidic, acid, tart *Opposite*: sweet **2 irritable**, sour, bitter, embittered, unpleasant *Opposite*: pleasant

vintage *n* **era**, time, age, epoch, period ▪ *adj* **1 classic**, typical, traditional, essential, prime *Opposite*: atypical **2 out-of-date**, dated, antique, old, outmoded *Opposite*: new

vinyl *n* **LPs**, records, discs, singles, albums

violate *v* **1 disregard**, infringe, defy, breach, disobey *Opposite*: obey **2 defile**, desecrate, spoil, destroy, ruin *Opposite*: venerate **3 disrupt**, disturb, interrupt, encroach upon, intrude upon *Opposite*: respect

violation *n* **1 infringement**, breach, contravention, defiance, disobedience *Opposite*: obedience **2 defilement**, desecration, destruction, ruin, abuse *Opposite*: veneration **3 disruption**, intrusion, encroachment, disturbance, interruption *Opposite*: respect

violence *n* **1 physical force**, pugnaciousness, pugnacity, aggression, fighting *Opposite*: passivity **2 ferocity**, strength, force, fierceness, viciousness *Opposite*: gentleness

violent *adj* **1 pugnacious**, aggressive, brutal, cruel, sadistic *Opposite*: peaceful **2 fierce**, ferocious, vehement, vicious, forceful *Opposite*: gentle

VIP *n* **dignitary**, name, luminary, star, celebrity

viperish *adj* **malicious**, spiteful, nasty, unkind, malevolent *Opposite*: kind

virtual *adj* **1 near**, practical, effective, fundamental, essential *Opposite*: actual **2 computer-generated**, simulated, cybernetic

virtually *adv* **1 almost**, nearly, near, nigh on to, close to **2 in effect**, effectively, essentially, fundamentally, to all intents and purposes

virtual reality *n* **simulated reality**, computer simulation, simulation, VR, cyberspace

virtue *n* **1 asset**, feature, quality, advantage, benefit *Opposite*: disadvantage **2 goodness**, righteousness, integrity, honesty, morality *Opposite*: wickedness

virtuosity *n* **skill**, technique, brilliance, flair, talent

virtuoso *n* **1 musician**, bravura player, artist, maestro **2 wunderkind**, genius, maven, prodigy, ace *(infml)*

virtuous *adj* **good**, righteous, worthy, honorable, moral *Opposite*: bad

virulent *adj* **1 infectious**, contagious, poisonous, lethal, strong *Opposite*: weak **2 malicious**, bitter, vituperative, venomous, fierce *Opposite*: kind

virus *n* **1 illness**, infection, sickness, disease **2 computer virus**, Trojan horse, worm

visa *n* **endorsement**, pass, entry permit, documents, papers

visage *n* **1** *(literary)* **face**, expression, countenance, features, mug *(slang)* **2 look**, appearance, aspect, form, mien *(fml)*

vis-à-vis *prep* **1 regarding**, in relation to, in respect of, re, with reference to **2 versus**, compared with, contrasted with, in comparison with, opposite to

viscera *n* **internal organs**, intestines, entrails, guts, bowels

visceral *adj* **instinctual**, instinctive, intuitive, gut, primitive *Opposite*: reasoned

viscid *adj* **thick**, sticky, gooey, gluey, gummy *Opposite*: runny

viscosity *n* **viscidness**, thickness, stickiness, gluiness, gooeyness *Opposite*: fluidity

viscous *adj* **viscid**, thick, sticky, glutinous, gelatinous *Opposite*: runny

visibility *n* **1 discernibility**, perceptibility, conspicuousness, luminosity *Opposite*: invisibility **2 prominence**, familiarity, profile, image, high profile

visible *adj* **1 noticeable**, observable, perceptible, evident, in evidence *Opposite*: invisible **2 prominent**, high-profile, familiar, ubiquitous

vision *n* **1 revelation**, prophecy, dream, hallucination, apparition **2 concept**, mental picture, idea, image, visualization **3 foresight**, imagination, forethought, prescience, farsightedness **4 eyesight**, sight, ability to see

visionary *adj* **1 inventive**, creative, farseeing, prescient, original *Opposite*: unimaginative **2 unrealistic**, impracticable, quixotic, fanciful, unworkable *Opposite*: practicable ■ *n* **prophet**, dreamer, thinker, seer

visit *v* **1 go to**, stay in, stay at, stop with, stop at **2 call on**, drop in on, go to see, pay a visit, pop in *(infml)* ■ *n* **1 social call**, official visit, call, duty call **2 stay**, stopover, break, trip, outing

visitation *n* **1 visit**, examination, inspection, check, checkup **2 punishment**, curse, calamity, blight, catastrophe

visitor *n* **caller**, guest, tourist, sightseer

visitor center *n* **tourist center**, information office, information center

visor *n* **screen**, blind, eyeshade

vista *n* **view**, panorama, outlook, scene, landscape

visual *adj* **1 graphic**, pictorial, filmic, painterly, photographic **2 optical**, chromatic, ophthalmic, ocular **3 concrete**, visible, discernible, observable, evident ■ *n* **graphic**, visual aid, illustration, picture, photograph

visual aid *n* **model**, film, video, chart, illustration

visualization *n* **1 imagining**, conjuring up, picturing, conception **2 mental image**, mental picture, vision, hallucination, image **3 positive thinking**, therapy, cognitive therapy, meditation, image creation

visualize *v* **imagine**, envisage, picture, see in your mind's eye, dream of

vital *adj* **1 important**, crucial, fundamental, critical, necessary *Opposite*: unimportant **2 energetic**, vigorous, vivacious, dynamic, vibrant *Opposite*: lifeless. *See* COMPARE AND CONTRAST *at* necessary.

vitality *n* **liveliness**, energy, vivacity, life, animation *Opposite*: lethargy

vitalize *v* **animate**, energize, buoy up, bolster, hearten *Opposite*: deaden

vitally *adv* **extremely**, indispensably, enormously, absolutely, really

vitreous *adj* **enamel**, vitric, vitriform, glasslike, glassy

vitriol *n* **hatred**, bitterness, venom, spleen, sarcasm *Opposite*: love

vitriolic *adj* **spiteful**, venomous, hurtful, acerbic, bitter *Opposite*: kind

vituperation *n* **1 outburst**, attack, criticism, censuring, condemnation **2 abuse**, venom, vitriol, savaging, mauling

vituperative *adj* **insulting**, abusive, offensive, malicious, slanderous

vivacious *adj* **vibrant**, lively, bubbly, cheerful, spirited *Opposite*: languid

vivacity *n* **high-spiritedness**, liveliness, animation, verve, vivaciousness *Opposite*: lethargy

vivid *adj* **1 intense**, rich, gaudy, bright, glowing *Opposite*: dull **2 striking**, powerful, strong, clear, intense *Opposite*: understated **3 active**, lively, creative, ingenious, original *Opposite*: prosaic **4 fresh**, distinct, clear, crystal clear, lucid *Opposite*: vague

vividness *n* **1 richness**, gaudiness, colorfulness, brightness, vibrancy *Opposite*: dullness **2 freshness**, distinctness, clarity, lucidity, clearness *Opposite*: vagueness **3 power**, strength, clarity, intensity **4 liveliness**, creativity, ingeniousness, flamboyance, intensity *Opposite*: banality

vocabulary *n* **1 language**, words, terms, expressions, terminology **2 dictionary**, glossary, lexicon, word list. *See* COMPARE AND CONTRAST *at* language.

vocal *adj* **1 uttered**, verbal, voiced, spoken, unwritten *Opposite*: silent **2 outspoken**, frank, insistent, vociferous, voluble *Opposite*: quiet

vocalist *n* **singer**, lead vocalist, backing vocalist, lead singer, songster

vocalize *v* **express**, voice, articulate, give voice to, put into words

vocals *n* **lyrics**, words, singing, chorus

vocation *n* **1 career**, profession, job, occupation, work **2 aptitude**, inclination, talent, bent, urge

vocational *adj* **occupational**, professional, job-related, career, work

vociferous *adj* **clamorous**, vocal, loud, voluble, raucous *Opposite*: quiet

vogue *n* **fashion**, trend, craze, rage, mode

voguish *adj* **1 fashionable**, elegant, chic, stylish, modish *Opposite*: unfashionable **2 passing**, in vogue, in, up-to-the-minute, popular *Opposite*: unpopular

voice *n* **1 speech**, singing, vocal sound, power of speech **2 opinion**, say, right of speech, expression, declaration ■ *v* **1 express**, assert, declare, proclaim, opine *(fml)* **2 pronounce**, articulate, utter, declare, intone *(fml)*

voiced *adj* **stated**, enunciated, spoken, uttered, expressed

voiceless *adj* **1 silent**, unspeaking, mute, taciturn, wordless *Opposite*: speaking **2 unrepresented**, disenfranchised, invisible, ignored, forgotten *Opposite*: represented

voiceover *n* **narration**, commentary, narrative

void *adj* **1 annulled**, canceled, invalid, null and void, negated *(fml)* *Opposite*: valid **2 empty**, vacant, unoccupied, not in use, occupied ■ *n* **empty space**, emptiness, vacuum, hollowness, abyss ■ *v* **cancel**, annul, render null and void, vacate, reject. *See* COMPARE AND CONTRAST *at* **vacant**.

volatile *adj* 1 **unstable**, precarious, changeable, dangerous, hazardous *Opposite*: stable 2 **unpredictable**, explosive, hot-blooded, impulsive, fickle *Opposite*: placid

volatility *n* 1 **instability**, precariousness, changeability, explosiveness *Opposite*: stability 2 **unpredictability**, explosiveness, hot-bloodedness, impulsiveness, fickleness *Opposite*: placidity

volition *n* **wish**, will, decision, choice, desire *Opposite*: coercion

volley *n* **torrent**, shower, stream, cascade, barrage ■ *v* **lob**, hit, strike, kick

volte-face *n* **U-turn**, reversal, change of direction, about-face, change of heart

voluble *adj* **talkative**, fluent, articulate, verbose, loquacious *Opposite*: taciturn

volume *n* 1 **quantity**, amount, degree, size, level 2 **capacity**, size, dimensions, measurements, bulk 3 **book**, tome, work 4 **part**, section, edition

voluminous *adj* **big**, huge, large, capacious, roomy *Opposite*: small

voluntarily *adv* **willingly**, of your own accord, happily, gladly, freely *Opposite*: reluctantly

voluntary *adj* 1 **unpaid**, charitable, volunteer *Opposite*: professional 2 **intended**, intentional, controlled, deliberate, chosen *Opposite*: involuntary

volunteer *n* **helper**, candy striper, unpaid worker ■ *v* 1 **offer**, come forward, agree, step up, undertake 2 **give**, offer, tell, advise, inform

vomit *v* 1 **be sick**, be nauseous, be nauseated, gag, retch 2 **expel**, spew out, spew forth, eject, send out ■ *n* **sick**, vomitus, barf *(infml)*, puke *(slang)*, bile *(literary)*

voracious *adj* **insatiable**, avid, hungry, ravenous, gluttonous *Opposite*: sated

voraciousness *see* **voracity**

voracity *n* **greed**, greediness, gluttony, hunger, rapaciousness

vortex *n* 1 **whirlpool**, whirlwind, waterspout,

tornado, cyclone 2 **quagmire**, morass, maelstrom, turbulence, whirlwind

vote *n* **ballot**, election, secret ballot, show of hands, poll ■ *v* **choose**, cast your vote, elect, opt for, support *Opposite*: abstain

voter *n* **elector**, constituent, supporter, backer

votive *adj* 1 **ritual**, prayerful, supplicatory *(fml)*, precatory *(fml)* 2 **promised**, pledged, vowed, contractual, agreed

voucher *n* **coupon**, ticket, receipt, check, chit *(dated)*

vouch for *v* **speak for**, support, guarantee, back up, stand up for

vouchsafe *v* 1 **give**, grant, offer, bestow *(fml)* 2 *(fml)* **promise**, agree, allow, permit, consent

vow *n* **promise**, oath, pledge, guarantee, declaration ■ *v* **swear**, promise, guarantee, undertake, declare

voyage *n* **journey**, trip, expedition, passage, crossing ■ *v* **journey**, sail, cruise, travel

voyager *n* **traveler**, explorer, adventurer, tourist, vacationer

vulgar *adj* 1 **rude**, offensive, crude, bad, earthy *Opposite*: decent 2 **tasteless**, brash, common, kitsch, ostentatious *Opposite*: tasteful 3 **bad-mannered**, uncouth, discourteous, unrefined, rude *Opposite*: polite

vulgarism *n* 1 **obscenity**, swear word, four-letter word, expletive, rude word 2 **colloquialism**, popular expression, idiom, common term

vulgarity *n* 1 **rudeness**, offensiveness, crudeness, crudity, earthiness *Opposite*: decency 2 **bad manners**, uncouthness, rudeness, loutishness, boorishness *Opposite*: politeness 3 **tastelessness**, brashness, ostentatiousness, commonness, kitsch *Opposite*: tastefulness 4 **swear word**, curse, bad language, four-letter word, rude word

vulnerability *n* **susceptibility**, weakness, defenselessness, helplessness, exposure *Opposite*: invincibility

vulnerable *adj* **susceptible**, weak, defenseless, helpless, exposed *Opposite*: invincible

vulturine *adj* **opportunistic**, exploitative, greedy, avaricious, grasping

W

wackiness *(infml)* *n* **zaniness**, silliness, wildness, eccentricity, oddness *Opposite*: conventionality

wacky *(infml)* *adj* **silly**, zany, madcap, way out, off the wall *Opposite*: conventional

wad *n* 1 **bundle**, roll, sheaf, stack, pile 2 **lump**, mass, cushion, clump, chunk 3 **twist**, chew, portion, gob *(slang)* ■ *v* 1 **plug**, lag, stuff, fill, pad 2 **compress**, scrunch, squeeze, compact, screw

wadding *n* padding, lining, insulation, lagging, filling

waddle *v* toddle, sway, shuffle, wobble

wade *v* paddle, stride, walk, splash

wade through *v* plow through, struggle through, battle through, tackle, deal with

wafer-thin *adj* thin, paper-thin, slim

waffle (*infml*) *v* equivocate, prevaricate, vacillate, beat around the bush, dither ■ *n* nonsense, drivel, balderdash, rubbish, guff (*infml*)

waft *v* drift, float, glide, sail, fan ■ *n* puff, breath, gust, breeze, draft

wag *v* wave to and fro, move from side to side, flap, wiggle, waggle ■ *n* 1 wiggle, waggle, shake, twitch, wave 2 (*infml*) wit, humorist, comedian, comic, joker

wage *n* salary, pay, earnings, income, take-home pay ■ *v* carry on, conduct, pursue, engage in, fight

---

COMPARE AND CONTRAST CORE MEANING: money given for work done

wage a fixed regular payment made on an hourly, weekly, or daily basis, especially to manual workers; **salary** a fixed regular annual sum, usually paid on a monthly basis, especially to clerical or professional workers; **pay** a wage or salary; **fee** a payment made to a professional person by a client; **remuneration** payment for work, goods, or services; **emolument** (*fml*) any payment for work; **honorarium** money given in exchange for services for which there is normally no fixed charge; **stipend** a regular payment or allowance for living expenses, especially one made to a member of the clergy or a student.

---

wage earner *n* breadwinner, provider, earner, worker, supporter

wager *n* bet, gamble, stake, ante ■ *v* bet, gamble, stake, risk, venture

wages *n* salary, pay, earnings, income, take-home pay

wage war on *v* oppose, combat, resist, fight, do battle

waggish (*nfml*) *adj* humorous, witty, mischievous, droll, jocular

waggishness (*infml*) *n* humorousness, wit, mischievousness, mischief, drollness

waggle *v* wiggle, wag, shake, wave to and fro, move from side to side

waif *n* stray, soul, urchin, orphan, ragamuffin (*dated*)

wail *v* 1 howl, moan, weep, yowl, keen 2 complain, fuss, raise a ruckus, whine, kick up a storm (*infml*) ■ *n* 1 howl, moan, yowl, scream, cry 2 complaint, protest, whine, fuss, scream

wainscot *n* paneling, wainscoting, cladding, lining

waistline *n* waist, middle, midriff

wait *v* 1 stay, remain, hang around, linger, stop 2 delay, pause, hold your fire, postpone, hang on *Opposite*: begin 3 expect,

anticipate, await. **wait on** ■ *n* delay, pause, interval, postponement, gap

waiter *n* server, attendant, maître d', waitperson, maître d'hôtel

waiting area *n* concourse, foyer, meeting point, waiting room, reception

wait on *v* 1 care for, serve, mother, nurse, take care of 2 (*infml*) expect, anticipate, await, wait for

waive *v* surrender, give up, relinquish, put aside, ignore *Opposite*: retain

waiver *n* 1 disclaimer, relinquishment, renunciation, abdication, abandonment 2 contract, agreement, bond

wake *v* 1 wake up, awaken, stir, come around, come to 2 arouse, stir, awaken, rouse, kindle *Opposite*: stifle

wakeful *adj* 1 restless, disturbed, sleepless, unable to sleep, insomniac *Opposite*: drowsy 2 alert, vigilant, on guard, attentive, aware *Opposite*: inattentive

wakefulness *n* 1 restlessness, sleeplessness, insomnia, tossing and turning, restiveness *Opposite*: drowsiness 2 alertness, vigilance, attentiveness, awareness, watchfulness *Opposite*: inattentiveness

waken *see* wake up

wake up *v* 1 wake, awaken, stir, come around, come to *Opposite*: go to sleep 2 liven up, come to life, come alive, revive, animate

walk *v* go on foot, stroll, amble, saunter, march ■ *n* 1 stroll, saunter, march, amble, promenade (*fml*) 2 gait, pace, tread, stride, way of walking

walkabout (*infml*) *n* walk, stroll, saunter, amble, tour

walk a tightrope *v* tread dangerously, invite trouble, ask for trouble, ask for it, skate on thin ice

walk away *v* 1 abandon, leave, withdraw, abdicate, back down from 2 win, triumph, sail through, succeed, walk it (*infml*)

walkaway (*infml*) *n* cinch (*infml*), piece of cake (*infml*), breeze (*infml*), pushover (*infml*), walkover (*infml*) *Opposite*: challenge

walk down the aisle *v* get married, marry, tie the knot (*infml*), get hitched (*infml*), wed (*fml or literary*)

walker *n* hiker, rambler, mall walker, stroller

walking *adj* outdoor, hiking, rambling, cross-country, heavy-duty

walking stick *n* cane, stick, bamboo, staff

walk in on *v* barge in, march in, interrupt, intrude, butt in

walk off *v* turn your back, walk away, leave, go, quit *Opposite*: remain

walk off with *v* steal, embezzle, pocket, appropriate, take

walk-on *n* bit part, cameo, minor part, extra, nonspeaking part

walk out v 1 **leave**, storm out, go off in a huff, flounce out, take yourself off (infml) 2 **go on strike**, take industrial action, stop work

walkout n **strike**, stoppage, protest

walk out on (infml) v **leave**, abandon, leave in the lurch, go, desert

walk over (infml) v **defeat**, beat, overpower, trounce, thrash

walkover (infml) n **easy victory**, child's play, runaway, runaway victory, pushover (infml) Opposite: challenge

walk through v **rehearse**, practice, run through

walkway n 1 **path**, footpath, pathway, sidewalk, alley 2 **aisle**, corridor, passage, passageway

wall n **partition**, divider, screen, panel, bulkhead

wallet n **folder**, file, case, holder

wallop (infml) v 1 **thump**, smack, thwack, strike, hit 2 **defeat**, beat, shut out, trounce, whip ■ n 1 **blow**, thump, bash, smack, thwack 2 **fizz**, punch, clout, pizazz (infml), buzz (infml)

walloping (infml) n 1 **beating**, thrashing, hiding (infml) 2 **defeat**, drubbing, rout, hiding (infml) ■ adj **huge**, enormous, gigantic, stupendous, massive ■ adv **extremely**, very, tremendously, inordinately, stupendously

wallow v **flounder**, stumble, lurch, stagger, welter

wallow in v **enjoy**, bask in, revel in, relish, make the most of

wall-to-wall (infml) adj **omnipresent**, all-pervasive, nonstop, ceaseless, never-ending

waltz n (infml) **snap**, cinch (infml), piece of cake (infml), breeze (infml), pushover (infml) ■ v 1 **walk**, stroll, swan, breeze, saunter 2 **romp**, sail, steam, whizz, cruise

wan adj 1 **pallid**, ashen, ashy, drawn, washed-out 2 **listless**, feeble, weak, down, depressed Opposite: strong

wand n **baton**, stick, rod, pointer

wander v 1 **stroll**, meander, walk, ramble, roam 2 **drift**, stray, digress, lose the point, lose the thread ■ n **walk**, stroll, ramble, mosey (infml), mooch (slang)

wanderer n **nomad**, vagrant, itinerant, traveler, rover

wandering adj **itinerant**, nomadic, peripatetic, traveling, drifting Opposite: settled

wanderlust n **desire to travel**, itchy feet, travel bug

wane v **diminish**, decrease, decline, get smaller, fade Opposite: wax (literary)

wangle (infml) v **engineer**, contrive, obtain, get, fix (infml)

waning adj **fading**, declining, weakening, diminishing, disappearing Opposite: increasing

wannabe (infml) n **hopeful**, aspirant, imitator, clone, camp follower ■ adj **aspiring**, aspirational, would-be, hopeful, budding

want v 1 **desire**, wish for, long for, crave, covet 2 **need**, require, lack, be short of, miss ■ n 1 **lack**, absence, shortage, scarcity, dearth 2 **poverty**, famine, hunger, need, neediness

COMPARE AND CONTRAST CORE MEANING: seek to have, do, or achieve something

want feel a need or desire for something; **desire** want something very strongly; **wish** have a strong, sometimes unrealistic, desire to have or to do something; **long** have a strong desire for somebody or something, especially something difficult to achieve; **yearn** want something very much, especially with a feeling of sadness when it seems unlikely that it can ever be obtained; **covet** have a strong desire to possess something that belongs to somebody else, or (fml) want something very much; **crave** want something very much, especially when this desire is physical.

wanted adj **required**, sought, sought after, hunted, desired

wanting adj **deficient**, inadequate, imperfect, not good enough, not up to standard Opposite: adequate ■ prep **without**, lacking, in need of, short of, minus

wanton adj 1 **gratuitous**, motiveless, meaningless, reckless, needless Opposite: justifiable 2 **immoral**, immodest, abandoned, licentious, lustful Opposite: restrained 3 **malevolent**, malicious, cruel, vicious, nasty Opposite: benign 4 **excessive**, extravagant, unrestrained, heedless, unreasonable Opposite: restrained

wantonness n **depravity**, debauchery, immorality, shamelessness, impiety Opposite: restraint

wants n **needs**, requirements, desires, requests, wishes

war n 1 **warfare**, hostilities, fighting, combat, action Opposite: peace 2 **campaign**, battle, struggle, fight, conflict 3 **competition**, rivalry, feud, battle, struggle. See COMPARE AND CONTRAST at fight.

warble v **sing**, trill, pipe up, chirrup, sing out

war cry n **battle cry**, rallying call, call to arms

warden n **custodian**, curator, keeper, steward, superintendent

ward off v **defend against**, protect against, deflect, hold off, keep at bay

wardrobe n **clothes**, clothing, apparel, gear (infml), attire (fml)

wares n **goods**, merchandise, produce, products, commodities

warfare n 1 **fighting**, conflict, combat, action, hostilities 2 **rivalry**, feud, competition, contest, struggle

warhorse n **campaigner**, warrior, stalwart, old hand, master

wariness n **caution**, suspicion, care, circumspection, guardedness Opposite: carelessness

warlike adj **1 belligerent**, aggressive, bellicose, confrontational, hostile Opposite: friendly **2 martial**, military, militaristic, warring, war

warlock n **sorcerer**, wizard, enchanter, witch, necromancer (literary)

warlord n **military leader**, general, chieftain, guerrilla leader, commander

warm adj **1 temperate**, tepid, balmy, hot, lukewarm Opposite: cool **2 kind**, kindly, warm-hearted, kindhearted, friendly Opposite: unfriendly **3 cozy**, inviting, restful, cheerful, cheery Opposite: unwelcoming **4 sincere**, heartfelt, deep, earnest, wholehearted **5 lively**, passionate, ardent, fiery, enthusiastic Opposite: cool ■ v **1 take to**, become fond of, take a liking to, take a fancy to, get along with Opposite: cool off **2 heat**, heat up, reheat, warm up, melt Opposite: cool **3 become enthusiastic about**, get going on, get fired up about, get excited, become enthused ■ n **warmth**, warmness, heat Opposite: cold

warm-blooded adj **passionate**, impetuous, enthusiastic, ardent, emotional Opposite: cold-blooded

warm-hearted adj **kindly**, tender, kind, sympathetic, affectionate Opposite: cold-hearted

warm-heartedness n **tenderness**, kindness, sympathy, affection, love Opposite: cold-heartedness

warmness see **warmth**

warmonger n **hawk**, belligerent, jingo, jingoist, aggressor Opposite: peacemaker

warmongering n **saber rattling**, belligerence, aggression, jingoism, hawkishness Opposite: peacemaking

warmth n **1 warmness**, heat, hotness Opposite: cold **2 balminess**, temperateness, high temperature, warmness Opposite: coldness **3 friendliness**, cordiality, warm-heartedness, kindheartedness, warmness Opposite: cold-heartedness **4 enthusiasm**, eagerness, earnestness, ardor, fervor Opposite: apathy

warm up v **1 warm**, heat, heat up, reheat, warm over Opposite: cool off **2 limber up**, loosen up, get loose, stretch Opposite: cool off

warm-up n **exercises**, limbering up, loosening up, preparation

warn v **1 caution**, advise, inform, notify, tell **2 alert**, forewarn, advise, tell, notify

warning n **1 notice**, caution, caveat, word of warning, heads-up **2 threat**, indication, portent, wake-up call, forewarning ■ adj **cautionary**, threatening, cautioning

warn off v **deter**, discourage, dissuade, put off, scare off

war of words n **argument**, row, slinging match, disagreement, fight

warp v **1 distort**, twist, deform, bend, buckle Opposite: straighten **2 change**, pervert, damage, distort, misrepresent ■ n **twist**, bend, distortion, deviation, alteration

warped adj **1 misshapen**, distorted, deformed, twisted, bent **2 changed**, damaged, distorted, misrepresented, confused **3 partial**, biased, one-sided, prejudiced, skewed Opposite: impartial

warrant n **authorization**, license, permit, authority, certification ■ v **1 merit**, deserve, necessitate, call for, demand **2 guarantee**, affirm, certify, secure, assure

warranty n **guarantee**, contract, pledge, assurance

warren n **1 hole**, earth, habitat, burrow, lair **2 maze**, labyrinth, catacomb

warring adj **belligerent**, combatant, fighting, sparring, opposing Opposite: friendly

warrior n **soldier**, fighter, combatant, trooper

wart n **lump**, growth, verruca

war-torn adj **war-ravaged**, frontline, battle-weary, war-scarred, battle-scarred Opposite: peaceful

wary adj **watchful**, cautious, suspicious, distrustful, mistrustful Opposite: careless. See COMPARE AND CONTRAST at **cautious**.

wash v **1 clean**, bathe, rinse, sponge down, wash down **2 erode**, wash away, carry away, bear away, sweep away **3 bathe**, clean up, wash up **4 flow over**, splash, lap, swish, pound ■ n **1 stain**, tint, rinse, suffusion, coloring **2 shower**, shampoo, sponge, rinse, wash-down **3 layer**, film, coat, overlay, coating

washable adj **easy-care**, colorfast, preshrunk, unfading, wash-and-wear

washbasin n **hand basin**, basin, bowl, sink, washbowl

washbowl see **washbasin**

wash down v **clean**, rinse, sluice, sponge down, hose down

washed-out adj **1 exhausted**, tired out, used up, drained, all in Opposite: energetic **2 wan**, gray, pallid, ashen, ashy

washed-up (infml) adj **unsuccessful**, finished, defeated, through, failed Opposite: successful

washer n **seal**, gasket, liner, ring, lining

washing n **1 laundry**, dirty linen, dirty clothes, wash **2 wash**, weekly wash, clothes wash **3 coat**, coating, film, layer, overlay

wash out v **wash**, rinse, flush, swill, hose

washout (infml) n **failure**, dead loss, disaster, disappointment, flop (infml) Opposite: success

wash over v **flow over**, engulf, sweep over, overwhelm, come over

washroom n **restroom**, bathroom, toilet, lavatory, powder room

wash your hands of v disown, abandon, refuse to have anything to do with, absolve yourself, ignore

waspish adj 1 irritable, touchy, irascible, cantankerous, peevish Opposite: affable 2 malignant, spiteful, malicious, nasty, vindictive Opposite: friendly

waspishness n 1 irritability, touchiness, irascibility, cantankerousness, peevishness Opposite: affability 2 spitefulness, spite, malice, maliciousness, nastiness Opposite: friendliness

waspy see waspish

wastage n waste, surplus, excess, leftovers

waste v 1 squander, fritter away, misuse, dissipate, throw away Opposite: save 2 ravage, devastate, ruin, spoil, despoil 3 atrophy, wither, become emaciated, waste away, weaken Opposite: strengthen ■ n litter, garbage, trash, gray water, rubbish ■ adj 1 excess, surplus, unwanted, discarded, remaining 2 uncultivated, barren, bare, fallow Opposite: cultivated

waste away v wither, waste, atrophy, become emaciated, weaken Opposite: strengthen

wasted adj 1 missed, misused, lost, unexploited, unused 2 ravaged, withered, shrunken, atrophied, emaciated Opposite: healthy 3 futile, fruitless, unproductive, worthless, useless Opposite: worthwhile

wasteful adj extravagant, careless, uneconomical, profligate, lavish Opposite: frugal

wastefulness n extravagance, carelessness, profligacy, improvidence, lavishness Opposite: frugality

wasteland n wilds, wilderness, desert, badlands, wastes

wastes see wasteland

watch v 1 observe, look at, stare at, gaze at, survey Opposite: ignore 2 pay attention to, beware, mind, be cautious about, consider 3 spy on, stalk, keep under observation, keep an eye on, keep under surveillance 4 look after, keep an eye on, mind, guard, watch over Opposite: neglect ■ n guard, lookout, sentry, sentinel

watchdog n ombudsman, supervisory body, regulator, overseer

watcher n observer, onlooker, spectator, viewer, witness

watchful adj observant, attentive, alert, vigilant, on the alert Opposite: inattentive

watchfulness n alertness, attention, vigilance, caution, care Opposite: inattentiveness

watchman n night watchman, guard, security guard, custodian, caretaker

watch out v 1 be careful, look out, be alert, be wary, take care 2 look out, look, wait, watch, be on the lookout

watch over v supervise, look after, keep an eye on, guard, mind Opposite: neglect

watchtower n lookout tower, lookout post, observation tower, crow's nest

watchword n motto, slogan, maxim, byword, catch phrase

watch your step v be careful, take care, watch out, look out, pay attention

watch your weight v be on a diet, diet, slim, watch what you eat, cut down

water n liquid, rainwater, seawater, mineral water, tap water ■ v 1 soak, spray, irrigate, drench, sprinkle 2 fill with tears, stream, run, fill up, well

water bird n waterfowl, freshwater bird, duck

waterborne adj 1 aquatic, floating, marine, riverine 2 transmissible, contagious, catching

watercourse n 1 ditch, conduit, drain, culvert 2 waterway, channel, stream, river, rivulet

water down v 1 dilute, thin down, weaken, attenuate Opposite: thicken 2 soften, reduce, moderate, mitigate, regulate Opposite: beef up (infml)

watered-down adj 1 diluted, dilute, thin, weak, insipid Opposite: concentrated 2 moderated, weakened, vapid, qualified, toned-down Opposite: unqualified

waterfall n cascade, cataract, falls, weir

waterfowl n water bird, freshwater bird, duck

waterfront n harbor, lakefront, oceanfront, seafront, water's edge

water hole n oasis, pool, pond, water source, spring

watering hole n 1 oasis, pool, pond, water hole, wallow 2 (infml) bar, saloon, club

waterless adj dry, arid, parched, dehydrated

water line n 1 load line, Plimsoll line, Plimsoll mark, watermark 2 tidemark, watermark, high watermark, floodmark, tideline

waterlogged adj sodden, sopping, drenched, wet, soaking Opposite: dry

watermark n 1 mark, imprint, logo, emblem 2 water line, load line, Plimsoll line, Plimsoll mark 3 tidemark, water line, high watermark, floodmark, tideline

waterproof adj water-resistant, rainproof, watertight, impermeable Opposite: permeable

watershed n turning point, defining moment, breaking point, seminal moment, crisis

waterside n riverbank, shore, bank, water's edge, waterfront ■ adj waterfront, beachfront, seaside, lakeside, riverside

watertight adj 1 sealed, waterproof, impermeable, rainproof Opposite: permeable 2 incontrovertible, unassailable, sound, firm, irrefutable Opposite: weak

waterway n watercourse, canal, river, channel, stream

waterworks n tears, crying, weeping, sobbing, blubbering (infml)

watery *adj* 1 **watered-down**, thin, weak, runny, dilute *Opposite*: thick 2 **wet**, soggy, squelchy, boggy, moist *Opposite*: dry 3 **feeble**, weak, faint, wan, hazy *Opposite*: forceful 4 **bland**, tasteless, insipid, weak, diluted *Opposite*: strong

wave *v* 1 **gesticulate**, gesture, signal, beckon 2 **brandish**, flourish, wield, wag, shake 3 **flutter**, flap, sway, undulate, move to and fro ■ *n* 1 **breaker**, roller, bumper, ripple, surge 2 **upsurge**, groundswell, tendency, trend, movement 3 **gesture**, signal, sign 4 **rash**, spate, outbreak, epidemic, series 5 **current**, surge, impulse, oscillation, undulation 6 **curl**, kink, undulation, ringlet

waver *v* 1 **dither**, hesitate, be indecisive, be irresolute, vacillate 2 **tremble**, shake, flutter, flicker, shudder. *See* COMPARE AND CONTRAST *at* **hesitate.**

wavering *n* **fluctuation**, vacillation, indecisiveness, irresolution, uncertainty *Opposite*: resolution ■ *adj* 1 **indecisive**, uncertain, undecided, vacillating, uncommitted *Opposite*: decisive 2 **flickering**, shaky, trembling, quivering, unsteady

waviness *n* **curliness**, unevenness, undulation, corrugation, sinuosity

wavy *adj* **curly**, curvy, crimped, undulating *Opposite*: straight

wax *n* **beeswax**, candle wax, tallow ■ *v* 1 **polish**, shine, buff, put a shine on, buff up 2 (*literary*) **become**, turn, grow, start to be 3 (*literary*) **expand**, increase, enlarge, get bigger, grow *Opposite*: wane

waxen *adj* **pale**, pallid, ashen, ashy, wan

waxiness *n* **greasiness**, fattiness, slipperiness, shininess, slickness

waxwork *n* **figure**, manikin, model, effigy, replica

way *n* 1 **method**, means, technique, mode, system 2 **custom**, style, practice, tradition, discipline 3 **route**, road, direction, path 4 **street**, avenue, lane, path, pathway

wayfarer (*literary*) *n* **traveler**, wanderer, walker, rover, roamer

waylay *v* **accost**, intercept, surprise, ambush, lie in wait for

way of life *n* **lifestyle**, customs, habits, traditions

way of thinking *n* **ideas**, beliefs, opinion, philosophy, position

way-out *adj* 1 (*infml*) **unusual**, peculiar, odd, strange, weird *Opposite*: conventional 2 (*dated infml*) **excellent**, wonderful, terrific, fantastic, great

ways *n* **habits**, conduct, customs, behavior, traditions

ways and means *n* **methods**, approaches, means, devices, systems

wayside *n* **roadside**, curb, edge, shoulder

wayward *adj* **willful**, naughty, unruly, errant, disobedient *Opposite*: well-behaved. *See* COMPARE AND CONTRAST *at* **unruly.**

waywardness *n* **willfulness**, naughtiness, disobedience, unruliness, rebelliousness *Opposite*: obedience

weak *adj* 1 **feeble**, frail, infirm, debilitated, puny *Opposite*: robust 2 **tired**, faint, enervated, exhausted, drained *Opposite*: strong 3 **delicate**, insubstantial, flimsy, wispy, fragile *Opposite*: sturdy 4 **vulnerable**, defenseless, helpless, unprotected, unguarded *Opposite*: invulnerable 5 **powerless**, ineffectual, toothless, inadequate, feeble *Opposite*: powerful 6 **cowardly**, spineless, faint-hearted, timid, weak-willed *Opposite*: bold 7 **faint**, feeble, low, dim, soft *Opposite*: strong 8 **watery**, diluted, insipid, bland, tasteless *Opposite*: strong 9 **unconvincing**, half-hearted, ineffectual, feeble, implausible *Opposite*: convincing

---

COMPARE AND CONTRAST CORE MEANING: lacking physical strength or energy

weak not physically fit or mentally strong; **feeble** lacking physical or mental strength or health; **frail** in a physically weak state as a result of illness or advanced years; **infirm** lacking strength as a result of long illness or advanced years; **debilitated** with strength and energy temporarily diminished as a result of illness or physical exertion; **decrepit** (*infml*) made weak by advanced years; **enervated** made weak and tired by physical or mental exertion.

---

weaken *v* 1 **grow weaker**, deteriorate, fail, decline, wane *Opposite*: strengthen 2 **give in**, cave in, give way, yield, vacillate *Opposite*: stand firm 3 **damage**, destabilize, detract from, shake, undermine *Opposite*: bolster 4 **dilute**, water down, thin, adulterate *Opposite*: strengthen 5 **enfeeble**, exhaust, enervate, debilitate, sap *Opposite*: fortify

weakened *adj* **debilitated**, enfeebled, deteriorated, declining, faded

weakening *n* **deterioration**, decline, damage, destabilization, undermining *Opposite*: strengthening

weak-kneed *adj* **spineless**, cowardly, weak, feeble, submissive *Opposite*: courageous

weakness *n* 1 **flaw**, fault, Achilles heel, weak spot, weak point *Opposite*: strength 2 **frailty**, feebleness, flimsiness, fragility, debility *Opposite*: robustness 3 **powerlessness**, vulnerability, defenselessness, helplessness, impotence *Opposite*: strength 4 **fondness**, liking, taste, soft spot, penchant *Opposite*: dislike 5 **faintness**, softness, dimness, paleness, feebleness *Opposite*: strength 6 **wateriness**, blandness, lack of flavor, insipidness *Opposite*: strong flavor

weak point *n* **weakness**, Achilles heel, failing, fault, limitation *Opposite*: strong point

weak spot *see* **weak point**

weak-willed *adj* irresolute, spineless, vacillating, easily led, spiritless *Opposite*: resolute

weal *see* **wheal**

wealth *n* 1 riches, prosperity, affluence, means, assets *Opposite*: poverty 2 large quantity, abundance, cornucopia, variety, choice *Opposite*: dearth

wealthy *adj* rich, well-off, well-to-do, affluent, prosperous *Opposite*: poor

weapon *n* 1 armament, firearm, missile, gun 2 defense, deterrent, big stick

weaponry *n* arms, armaments, arsenal, weapons, ordnance

weapon store *n* arsenal, armory, storeroom, store, cache

wear *v* 1 be dressed in, dress in, show off, have on, put on 2 display, bear, carry, hold, show 3 rub, fray, scuff, grind, wear out ■ *n* 1 deterioration, wear and tear, friction, abrasion, scuffing 2 dress, clothing, clothes, garments, uniform

wear and tear *n* deterioration, wear, attrition, abrasion, erosion

wear away *v* erode, wear down, wear out, eat at, eat away at

wear down *v* overcome, weaken, erode, wear away, wear out

weariness *n* 1 tiredness, exhaustion, fatigue, lethargy, inertia *Opposite*: energy 2 apathy, disillusionment, jadedness, disenchantment *Opposite*: enthusiasm

wearing *adj* tiring, exhausting, trying, tiresome, wearisome *Opposite*: refreshing

wearisome *adj* tiresome, boring, tedious, trying, thankless *Opposite*: stimulating

wear off *v* weaken, fade, lessen, diminish, disappear *Opposite*: increase

wear out *v* 1 exhaust, tire out, fatigue, sap, drain *Opposite*: invigorate 2 use up, run down, fray, deplete, trash (*infml*) *Opposite*: renovate

weary *adj* 1 tired, tired out, exhausted, worn out, fatigued *Opposite*: fresh 2 disillusioned, disenchanted, jaded, worn down, fed up (*infml*) *Opposite*: enthusiastic ■ *v* drain, sap, exhaust, tire, lose patience

wearying *adj* tiresome, wearisome, tiring, exhausting, wearing

wear yourself out *v* tire yourself out, exhaust yourself, run yourself into the ground, overdo it, burn the candle at both ends

weather *n* climate, meteorological conditions, climatic conditions, elements ■ *v* 1 endure, withstand, sit out, ride out, last out *Opposite*: succumb 2 erode, corrode, season, toughen, harden

weather-beaten *adj* worn, battered, windswept, weathered, gnarled

weather-bound *adj* delayed, held up, fogbound, snowbound, postponed

weathercock *see* **weather vane**

weathered *adj* worn, battered, windswept, weather-beaten, gnarled

weatherproof *adj* watertight, waterproof, rainproof, stormproof, windproof

weather vane *n* wind indicator, wind gauge, weathercock, anemometer, windsock

weave *v* 1 interlace, lace, intertwine, plait, knit *Opposite*: unpick 2 invent, create, compose, construct, fabricate 3 zigzag, stagger, wind, twist, crisscross ■ *n* pile, texture, nap

web *n* network, mesh, net, tissue, grid

webbing *n* lattice, trellis, netting, network, strap work

wed *v* 1 get married, walk down the aisle, say "I do", get hitched (*infml*), tie the knot (*infml*) *Opposite*: split up 2 join in matrimony, marry, join in wedlock, unite 3 join, link, unite, marry, merge *Opposite*: separate 4 (*fml or literary*) marry, take in marriage, espouse (*archaic*) *Opposite*: divorce

wedded *adj* 1 marital, conjugal, married, matrimonial, connubial (*literary*) 2 committed, devoted, linked, connected, attached *Opposite*: unattached

wedding *n* marriage, wedding ceremony, marriage ceremony, nuptials (*fml*)

wedge *n* segment, block, chock, sliver, hunk ■ *v* 1 lodge, hold, fix, jam, block *Opposite*: dislodge 2 cram, pack, jam, ram, stuff

wedlock *n* matrimony, marriage, married state

wee *adj* small, minute, petite, little, tiny *Opposite*: big

weed *v* hoe, tidy, pick over, clear

WORD BANK
❑ **types of weeds** bindweed, burdock, chickweed, dandelion, dock, goldenrod, jimsonweed, nettle, poison ivy, poison oak, ragweed, stinging nettle, thistle, tumbleweed

weed out *v* remove, extract, discard, get rid of, eliminate *Opposite*: select

weedy *adj* weak, puny, thin, scraggy, feeble *Opposite*: strong

weekend *v* stay, vacation, take a break, visit

weekender *n* tourist, vacationer, visitor, sightseer

weensy (*infml*) *see* **weeny**

weeny (*infml*) *adj* tiny, little, small, wee, minute *Opposite*: huge

weep *v* 1 cry, sob, wail, snivel, boohoo 2 leak, suppurate, seep, exude, ooze

weeper (*infml*) *see* **weepie**

weepie (*infml*) *n* movie, film, melodrama, tearjerker (*infml*)

weepy *adj* 1 oversentimental, slushy, mushy, syrupy, overemotional 2 tearful, emotional, sad, miserable, sensitive

weigh *v* consider, ponder, think about, evaluate, meditate on

weigh against v **count against**, tell against, militate against, countervail

weigh down v 1 **worry**, depress, get down, trouble, burden *Opposite*: hearten 2 **overload**, load down, burden, charge, encumber

weight n 1 **heaviness**, mass, bulk, heft, weightiness 2 **burden**, load, encumbrance 3 **influence**, power, substance, significance, import

weighted adj **biased**, prejudiced, slanted, subjective, one-sided *Opposite*: impartial

weightiness n 1 **weight**, heaviness, mass, bulk, heft 2 **gravity**, seriousness, importance, heaviness, import

weighting n **allowance**, premium, increment

weightless adj **light**, feathery, insubstantial, ethereal, airy *Opposite*: heavy

weighty adj 1 **heavy**, big, substantial, hefty, bulky *Opposite*: insubstantial 2 **important**, serious, grave, solemn, momentous *Opposite*: frivolous

weir n **dam**, barrage, dike, barrier, wall

weird adj **strange**, odd, bizarre, peculiar, unusual *Opposite*: normal

welcome adj 1 **at home**, comfortable, at ease, relaxed, comfy *(infml)* *Opposite*: unwelcome 2 **longed-for**, long-awaited, timely, opportune, heaven-sent *Opposite*: untimely 3 **appreciated**, pleasurable, delightful, pleasing, pleasant *Opposite*: unwelcome ■ n **greeting**, reception, salutation, salute, hospitality *Opposite*: farewell ■ v 1 **greet**, receive, hail, meet, salute *Opposite*: snub 2 **accept**, appreciate, approve, jump at, be grateful for *Opposite*: reject

welcoming adj **friendly**, warm, hospitable, convivial, openhearted *Opposite*: unwelcoming

weld v **fuse**, join, repair, solder, link *Opposite*: separate ■ n **repair**, join, link, joint, bond

welfare n 1 **well-being**, interests, happiness, good, safety *Opposite*: harm 2 **benefits**, aid, assistance

well n 1 **shaft**, bore, borehole, pit 2 **spring**, fountain, artesian well, source, water supply ■ v 1 **spring up**, brim, surge, rise, gush *Opposite*: subside 2 **grow**, rise, swell, intensify, increase *Opposite*: subside ■ adv 1 **pleasingly**, splendidly, perfectly, pleasantly, nicely *Opposite*: badly 2 **properly**, ethically, acceptably, correctly, suitably *Opposite*: improperly 3 **competently**, ably, skillfully, capably, satisfactorily *Opposite*: badly 4 **justly**, appropriately, fairly, fittingly, justifiably *Opposite*: unfairly 5 **comfortably**, easily, agreeably 6 **favorably**, highly, admiringly, kindly, positively *Opposite*: unfavorably 7 **thoroughly**, fully, carefully, completely, meticulously *Opposite*: partially 8 **clearly**, precisely, in detail, distinctly, perfectly *Opposite*: poorly 9 **familiarly**, intimately, closely, personally, deeply *Opposite*: slightly 10 **good-naturedly**, good-humoredly, cheerfully, jovially, genially 11 **anyway**, anyhow, in any case, to make a long story short, now then ■ adj 1 **healthy**, glowing, fit, fighting fit, in good health *Opposite*: unwell 2 **satisfactory**, all right, good, lucky, fortunate *Opposite*: unsatisfactory

well-adjusted adj **stable**, normal, level-headed, well-balanced, sane *Opposite*: maladjusted

well-advised adj **sensible**, prudent, wise, judicious, shrewd *Opposite*: ill-advised

well-appointed adj **well-equipped**, well-resourced, fully furnished, well-furnished, luxurious

well-argued adj **clear**, clearly stated, cogent, sensible, lucid *Opposite*: illogical

well-balanced adj 1 **harmonious**, balanced, well-proportioned, proportionate, coordinated *Opposite*: unbalanced 2 **sensible**, rational, stable, judicious, well-adjusted *Opposite*: unstable

well-behaved adj **good**, obedient, dutiful, well-mannered, polite *Opposite*: disobedient

well-being n **happiness**, comfort, security, good, welfare

well-beloved adj 1 **loved**, cherished, desired, beloved, adored *Opposite*: hated 2 **respected**, honored, venerated, revered, esteemed *Opposite*: disgraced

wellborn adj **aristocratic**, blue-blooded, noble, patrician, highborn *(literary)* *Opposite*: lowly

well-bred adj **polite**, well-mannered, mannerly, courteous, refined *Opposite*: common

well-built adj **sturdy**, strong, muscular, muscly, burly *Opposite*: puny

well-chosen adj **choice**, appropriate, apposite, apt, relevant *Opposite*: inappropriate

well-defined adj **distinct**, sharp, definite, clear, precise *Opposite*: vague

well-designed adj 1 **elegant**, stylish, well-made, chic, classy *(infml)* 2 **handy**, ingenious, clever, useful, neat

well-developed adj 1 **well-built**, strong, toned, finely honed, muscular *Opposite*: puny 2 **sophisticated**, well-rounded, strong, mature, acute *Opposite*: underdeveloped

well-disposed adj **approving**, friendly, kindly, sympathetic, benevolent *Opposite*: hostile

well-dressed adj **smart**, chic, stylish, elegant, dapper *Opposite*: scruffy

well-educated adj **cultured**, erudite, knowledgeable, well-read, learned *Opposite*: ignorant

well-endowed adj 1 **affluent**, wealthy, well-

to-do, rich, moneyed *Opposite*: poor
2 gifted, skilled, talented, able, skillful

well-equipped *adj* **well-appointed**, well-resourced, well-furnished, luxurious, lavish *Opposite*: spartan

well-established *adj* firm, deep-rooted, unshakable, fixed, ingrained *Opposite*: shaky

well-expressed *adj* **eloquent**, persuasive, fluent, expressive, articulate *Opposite*: inarticulate

well-fed *adj* **1 healthy**, well-nourished, thriving, flourishing **2 overweight**, fat, obese, bulky, stout *Opposite*: thin

well-fixed *(infml)* *adj* **well-to-do**, wealthy, prosperous, well-off, moneyed *Opposite*: poor

well-founded *adj* **logical**, understandable, justifiable, substantiated, sound *Opposite*: illogical

well-groomed *adj* **well-turned-out**, well-dressed, smart, dapper, spruce *Opposite*: unkempt

well-grounded *adj* **1 knowledgeable**, well-informed, au fait, conversant, well-acquainted *Opposite*: ignorant **2 well-founded**, logical, understandable, justifiable, substantiated *Opposite*: illogical

well-heeled *(infml)* *adj* **wealthy**, well-off, comfortable, rich, affluent *Opposite*: poor

well-informed *adj* **knowledgeable**, informed, in the know, up-to-date, educated *Opposite*: uneducated

well-intentioned *adj* **well-meant**, well-meaning, kindly, goodhearted, benevolent *Opposite*: malicious

well-kept *adj* **1 neat**, tidy, well-maintained, orderly, ordered *Opposite*: untidy **2 preserved**, safe, cherished, treasured, confidential

well-known *adj* **famous**, renowned, eminent, familiar, recognized *Opposite*: unknown

well-mannered *adj* **polite**, mannerly, decent, decorous, courteous *Opposite*: impolite

well-matched *adj* **compatible**, suited, complementary, well-suited, suitable *Opposite*: incompatible

well-meaning *adj* **well-intentioned**, kind, kindly, goodhearted, benevolent *Opposite*: malicious

well-meant *adj* **well-intentioned**, kind, kindly, kind-hearted, goodhearted *Opposite*: malicious

well-nigh *adv* **nearly**, almost, nigh on to, practically, just about *Opposite*: totally

well-off *adj* **1 wealthy**, rich, comfortable, affluent, prosperous *Opposite*: poor **2 lucky**, fortunate, in luck, privileged, blessed *Opposite*: unfortunate

well-oiled *adj* **efficient**, smooth-running, well-organized, effective, well-ordered *Opposite*: inefficient

well-ordered *adj* **tidy**, regimented, disciplined, efficient, well-organized *Opposite*: inefficient

well-organized *adj* **efficient**, disciplined, well-ordered, regimented, ordered *Opposite*: inefficient

well-paid *adj* **lucrative**, profitable, productive, rewarding, remunerative

well-preserved *adj* **youthful**, fresh-looking, young-looking, girlish, boyish *Opposite*: wizened

well-read *adj* **knowledgeable**, educated, cultured, erudite, well-educated *Opposite*: uninformed

well-rounded *adj* **1 experienced**, seasoned, accomplished, well-versed, mature *Opposite*: inexperienced **2 comprehensive**, varied, wide, balanced, broad *Opposite*: narrow **3 shapely**, pleasing, well-formed, attractive, curvaceous *Opposite*: unattractive

well-spoken *adj* **articulate**, eloquent, refined, fluent, coherent *Opposite*: inarticulate ·

well-suited *adj* **compatible**, well-matched, complementary, of a kind, suited *Opposite*: incompatible

well-thought-of *adj* **respected**, esteemed, highly regarded, reputable, admired *Opposite*: despised

well-thought-out *adj* **well-planned**, well-organized, ingenious, elegant, neat *Opposite*: disorganized

well-timed *adj* **timely**, opportune, propitious, felicitous, appropriate *Opposite*: untimely

well-to-do *adj* **wealthy**, rich, well-off, affluent, prosperous *Opposite*: poor

well-tried *adj* **tried and tested**, established, well-founded, tried and true, acknowledged *Opposite*: untried

well-turned *adj* **1 shapely**, graceful, elegant, well-formed, pretty *Opposite*: inelegant **2 eloquent**, well-crafted, well-expressed, articulate, witty *Opposite*: clumsy

well-turned-out *adj* **neat**, smart, spruce, dapper, well-dressed *Opposite*: unkempt

well up *v* **surge**, gush forth, spring up, spill over, emanate *Opposite*: subside

well-versed *adj* **knowledgeable**, familiar, experienced, informed, well-read *Opposite*: ignorant

well-wisher *n* **supporter**, sympathizer, friend, guardian angel *(infml)* *Opposite*: detractor

well-worn *adj* **1 worn**, worn out, ragged, threadbare, frayed *Opposite*: brand-new **2 hackneyed**, timeworn, unoriginal, banal, overworked *Opposite*: original

welt *n* **wheal**, swelling, ridge, wound, mark

welter *n* **flurry**, jumble, mass, confusion, muddle ■ *v* **wallow**, roll, pitch and toss

wend v proceed, go, travel, move, journey Opposite: stay put

western n cowboy movie, spaghetti western, horse opera

wet adj 1 damp, soaked, soaking, drenched, sodden Opposite: dry 2 rainy, showery, drizzly, damp, misty Opposite: dry ■ n 1 wet weather, rain, drizzle, damp, dampness Opposite: dry 2 moisture, wetness, liquid, damp, dampness Opposite: dry ■ v make wet, dampen, moisten, soak, saturate Opposite: dry

wet blanket (infml) n spoilsport, killjoy, party pooper (infml), stick-in-the-mud (infml), stuffed shirt (infml)

wetland n marsh, swamp, fen, bog, marshes Opposite: desert

wetness n dampness, damp, humidity, condensation, moisture Opposite: dryness

whack v hit, thump, slap, strike, clout ■ n thump, blow, slap, thwack, clout

wharf n quay, quayside, jetty, pier, dock

whatchamacallit (infml) n whatnot, thingamabob (infml), thingumajig (infml), thingy (infml), thingummy (infml)

whatever pron anything, everything, all, no matter what, whatsoever ■ adv at all, whatsoever, of any kind

what's more adv besides, moreover, in addition, also, furthermore

whatsoever adj at all, whatever, of any kind

wheal n swelling, welt, wound, mark, contusion (fml)

wheedle v 1 coax, cajole, inveigle, charm, persuade Opposite: bully 2 coax out, get out, draw out, obtain, extract

wheel v 1 roll, trundle, maneuver, move 2 turn, veer, swing, circle, swivel

wheel around v swivel around, swing around, turn around, spin around, turn full circle

wheel clamp n Denver boot, clamp, lock, immobilizer

wheeler-dealer (infml) n fixer, negotiator, dealer, trader

wheeze v 1 breathe heavily, gasp, rasp, pant, rattle 2 speak hoarsely, whisper, hiss, rasp, pant

wheeziness n breathlessness, hoarseness, gasping, puffing, panting

wheezy adj breathless, hoarse, short of breath, out of breath, husky

whelp n cub, pup, puppy, baby, offspring ■ v give birth, bear young, pup, cub, litter

when all's said and done adv all things considered, basically, all in all, altogether, at the end of the day

whenever conj every time, each time, each and every time, on every occasion, when

whereabouts n location, situation, position, site, place

whereas conj while, where, but, however, although

whereupon (fml) conj at which point, at which, as a result of which, so, and so

wherewithal n means, ability, resources, money, finances

whet v 1 sharpen, hone, grind, file Opposite: blunt 2 stimulate, arouse, augment, rouse, kindle Opposite: quell

whiff n 1 smell, aroma, scent, odor, reek 2 trace, vestige, sign, hint, suggestion

while conj 1 as, at the same time as, even as, during which 2 even though, though, although, despite the fact, whereas 3 but, however, in contrast, whereas ■ n time, period, interval, little, bit

while away v pass, spend, idle, fritter away, kill

whim n impulse, urge, notion, quirk, caprice

whimper v cry, whine, sob, snivel, moan

whimsical adj 1 fanciful, quirky, unusual, imaginative, original Opposite: practical 2 amusing, playful, humorous, witty, quaint Opposite: serious 3 erratic, unpredictable, random, impulsive, capricious Opposite: dependable

whimsy n 1 quaintness, oddity, oddness, eccentricity, quirkiness Opposite: seriousness 2 fancy, flight of fancy, whim, caprice, fantasy

whine v 1 whimper, cry, wail, moan, bleat 2 wail, moan, howl, drone, hum 3 grumble, complain, gripe (infml), moan (infml), bellyache (infml) Opposite: accept ■ n complaint, wail, whimper, cry, moan (infml). See COMPARE AND CONTRAST at complain.

whiner n grumbler, complainer, moaner (infml), grouch (infml)

whinny v neigh, whicker, nicker

whip v 1 flog, thrash, beat, lash, flagellate 2 whisk, beat, cream, aerate, stir ■ n lash, crop, cat-o'-nine-tails, switch

whiplash n blow, stroke, lash, hit, impact

whip up v 1 stir up, drum up, incite, provoke, arouse Opposite: pacify 2 (infml) rattle off, prepare, concoct, cook, produce

whir v hum, purr, buzz, whine, drone

whirl v spin, twirl, reel, rotate, turn ■ n 1 rotation, spin, twirl, turn, twizzle 2 flurry, bustle, hustle, commotion, tumult

whirlpool n eddy, vortex, swirl, current, waterspout

whirlwind n tornado, hurricane, cyclone, waterspout, vortex ■ adj rapid, short-lived, tumultuous, brief, swift Opposite: leisurely

whisk v 1 beat, whip, cream, aerate, stir 2 take, bundle, bustle, hustle, whip Opposite: drag

whisker n hairsbreadth, fraction, inch, millimeter

whiskers n facial hair, sideburns, mustache, muttonchops, stubble

whisper v murmur, sigh, mutter, breathe,

utter *Opposite*: shout ■ *n* **rumor**, word, gossip, tale, hint *Opposite*: fact

whistle *v* **screech**, shrill, shriek, hoot

whistle-blower *n* **informer**, mole, telltale, tattletale, snitch *(slang)*

whistle-stop *adj* **barnstorming**, whirlwind, lightning, rapid, speedy *Opposite*: relaxed

whit *(dated)* *n* **iota**, bit, jot, grain, speck

white *adj* **1 snowy**, silver, silvery, bleached, gray *Opposite*: black **2 pale**, pallid, ashen, wan, washed-out *Opposite*: flushed **3 frosty**, snowy, hoary, icy, frozen

---

WORD BANK

❏ **types of white** cream, eggshell, ivory, magnolia, off-white, oyster, pearl, platinum, silver, snow white

---

white-bread *(infml)* *adj* **bland**, dull, conventional, boring, routine *Opposite*: extraordinary

whitecap *n* **crest**, surf, breaker, wave

white-collar *adj* **professional**, managerial, management, salaried, office *Opposite*: blue-collar

white-hot *adj* **1 incandescent**, glowing, white, luminescent, hot *Opposite*: ice-cold **2 intense**, fevered, frenetic, frenzied, excited *Opposite*: lethargic

white-knuckle *adj* **exhilarating**, frightening, terrifying, exciting, roller-coaster *Opposite*: safe

whiten *v* **blanch**, whitewash, bleach, fade, pale *Opposite*: darken

whiteness *n* **paleness**, milkiness, lightness, pallor, wanness *Opposite*: ruddiness

whiteout *n* **blizzard**, snowstorm, storm

whitewash *n* **1 distemper**, lime, whitening, paint **2 cover-up**, deception, conspiracy, plot, concealment *Opposite*: exposure **3** *(infml)* **defeat**, rout, one-horse race, trouncing, beating *Opposite*: triumph ■ *v* **1 paint**, decorate, distemper, cover, smear **2 misrepresent**, cover up, conceal, explain away, gloss over *Opposite*: expose **3 trounce**, defeat, beat, shut out, rout *Opposite*: succumb

white water *n* **1 rapids**, torrents, foam, spray, current **2 shallows**, shoals, sandbanks, sandbar

whittle *v* **carve**, shape, fashion, shave, sculpt

whittle away *v* **eat into**, erode, eat away at, reduce, consume *Opposite*: build up

whittle down *v* **cut down**, trim, pare down, reduce, diminish *Opposite*: increase

whiz *v* **1 whir**, hum, hiss, buzz, rattle **2 dash**, go, pop *(infml)*, zip *(infml)*, zap *(infml)* *Opposite*: dawdle ■ *n* *(infml)* **expert**, prodigy, genius, whiz kid *(infml)*, wizard *(infml)*

whiz kid *(infml)* *n* **prodigy**, expert, genius, wizard *(infml)*, whiz *(infml)*

whodunit *n* **mystery**, thriller, cliffhanger

whole *adj* **1 entire**, complete, full, in one piece, total *Opposite*: partial **2 intact**, in one piece, unbroken, undivided, unspoiled *Opposite*: broken **3 unimpaired**, healthy, sound, fit, well *Opposite*: unhealthy **4 healed**, cured, healthy, restored, rehabilitated *Opposite*: ill ■ *n* **1 sum total**, aggregate, total, unit, entity **2 entirety**, totality, unity, everything, all *Opposite*: part

wholehearted *adj* **enthusiastic**, passionate, unreserved, total, unstinting *Opposite*: grudging

wholeness *n* **completeness**, entirety, totality, unity, fullness

wholesale *adj* **extensive**, comprehensive, across-the-board, indiscriminate, blanket *Opposite*: partial ■ *adv* **indiscriminately**, extensively, comprehensively, generally, broadly *Opposite*: partially

wholesaler *n* **trader**, retailer, supplier, dealer, vendor

wholesome *adj* **1 healthy**, healthful, nutritious, good, nourishing *Opposite*: unwholesome **2 decent**, moral, clean, honest, clean-living *Opposite*: unwholesome **3 sensible**, open, honest, commonsensical, practical *Opposite*: unhelpful **4 fit**, healthy, clean-cut, ruddy, blooming *Opposite*: unhealthy

wholesomeness *n* **1 freshness**, healthiness, healthfulness, naturalness, goodness *Opposite*: unwholesomeness **2 morality**, uprightness, decency, integrity, virtuousness *Opposite*: immorality **3 common sense**, sense, practicality, good sense, openness *Opposite*: impracticality **4 healthiness**, fitness, glow, ruddiness, haleness *Opposite*: unwholesomeness

wholly *adv* **1 completely**, entirely, totally, altogether, utterly *Opposite*: partially **2 solely**, exclusively, only, just, absolutely *Opposite*: generally

whoop *v* **cry out**, shout, scream, howl, hoot

whoosh *n* **dash**, zoom, rush, spurt, surge ■ *v* **1 rush**, zoom, burst, whistle, whiz *Opposite*: dawdle **2 zoom**, whistle, swish, hiss, roar

whopper *(infml)* *n* **1 monster**, giant, elephant, Goliath, leviathan **2 lie**, untruth, tale, fabrication, falsehood *Opposite*: truth

whopping *(infml)* *n* **1 thrashing**, defeat, drubbing, pasting *(infml)*, licking *(infml)* ■ *adj* **enormous**, gigantic, monstrous, huge, big *Opposite*: tiny

whorl *n* **spiral**, coil, curl, twist, swirl

whys and wherefores *n* **reasons**, ins and outs, details, the full picture, motives

wicked *adj* **1 evil**, bad, wrong, depraved, immoral *Opposite*: good **2 mischievous**, naughty, roguish, impish, teasing *Opposite*: respectful **3 mean**, cutting, acerbic, sharp, malicious *Opposite*: gentle **4** *(infml)* **distressing**, dreadful, awful, atrocious, severe *Opposite*: excellent

wickedness n 1 **evil**, badness, iniquity, sin, impiety Opposite: goodness 2 **impishness**, cheekiness, naughtiness, mischievousness

wicker n **cane**, rattan, wickerwork, bamboo

wicket n **gate**, door, opening, aperture, entrance

wide adj 1 **broad**, ample, large, thick, spacious Opposite: narrow 2 **extensive**, varied, widespread, inclusive, eclectic Opposite: narrow 3 **baggy**, roomy, loose, loose-fitting, capacious Opposite: tight ■ adv **off course**, off target, off the mark, wide of the mark, out

wide-awake (infml) adj **fully awake**, alert, bright-eyed and bushy-tailed, perky, watchful Opposite: asleep

wide-eyed adj 1 **amazed**, astonished, open-mouthed, dumbfounded, flabbergasted (infml) Opposite: impassive 2 **naive**, innocent, inexperienced, green, credulous Opposite: knowing

widely adv **extensively**, broadly, generally, far and wide, commonly Opposite: narrowly

widen v **broaden**, extend, expand, enlarge, make wider Opposite: narrow

wide-open adj 1 **open wide**, gaping, yawning, cavernous, agape (literary) 2 **unpredictable**, undecided, anybody's guess, unsettled, in the balance Opposite: settled 3 **vulnerable**, unprotected, exposed, unguarded, at risk Opposite: protected

wide-ranging adj **extensive**, widespread, comprehensive, across-the-board, inclusive Opposite: narrow

widespread adj **extensive**, prevalent, general, common, rife Opposite: limited

COMPARE AND CONTRAST CORE MEANING: occurring over a wide area
widespread existing or happening in many places, or affecting many people; **prevalent** occurring commonly or widely as a dominant feature; **rife** full of or severely affected by something undesirable that occurs frequently or in great numbers over a wide area, especially when it appears to be uncontrollable; **epidemic** spreading more quickly and more extensively than expected; **universal** affecting the whole world or everyone in the world.

width n **breadth**, thickness, girth, size, measurement

wield v 1 **exercise**, exert, use, have, employ 2 **brandish**, manipulate, handle, ply, carry Opposite: conceal

wife n **spouse**, partner, mate, consort Opposite: husband

wig n **toupee**, hairpiece, periwig, extension, rug (infml)

wiggle v **wriggle**, waggle, twist, jiggle, squirm ■ n **jiggle**, shake, wriggle, twist, waggle

wiggly adj **undulating**, wavy, curved, curvy, curving Opposite: straight

wigwam n **tepee**, tent, yurt, hut, lodge

wild adj 1 **untamed**, undomesticated, uncultivated, natural, feral Opposite: tame 2 **rough**, desolate, barren, remote, uninhabited Opposite: gentle 3 **enthusiastic**, eager, mad, excited, thrilled Opposite: unenthusiastic 4 **rowdy**, undisciplined, riotous, unruly, rough Opposite: orderly 5 **stormy**, blustery, squally, tempestuous, windswept Opposite: calm 6 **overwhelmed**, overcome, overpowered, devastated, destroyed 7 **untidy**, disheveled, unkempt, tousled, messy Opposite: tidy 8 (infml) **outrageous** madcap, foolish, unconventional, irrational Opposite: sensible. See COMPARE AND CONTRAST at **unruly**.

wilderness n **wilds**, rough country, wasteland, desert, outback

wildlife n **flora and fauna**, nature, natural world, environment, biota

wildness n 1 **rowdiness**, lack of control, lack of discipline, unruliness, roughness Opposite: orderliness 2 **roughness**, remoteness, desolation, barrenness, harshness 3 **dishevelment**, messiness, scruffiness, untidiness, unruliness Opposite: tidiness 4 (infml) **recklessness**, madness, foolishness, passion, waywardness

wiles n **tricks**, trickery, guile, deceit, artifice (fml)

wiliness n **cunning**, wiles, craftiness, guile, craft Opposite: ingenuousness

will n 1 **mind**, brain, consciousness, thoughts, thought processes 2 **determination**, resolve, willpower, motivation, spirit 3 **desire**, inclination, wish, longing, determination 4 (fml) **bidding**, command, dictate, wish, desire ■ v **want**, wish, yearn, desire, long

willful adj 1 **deliberate**, determined, intentional, conscious, malicious Opposite: unwitting 2 **stubborn**, obstinate, headstrong, perverse, obstreperous Opposite: compliant

willfulness n 1 **premeditation**, consciousness, deliberateness, maliciousness, malevolence 2 **stubbornness**, obstinacy, perverseness, perversity, obstreperousness Opposite: compliance

willies (infml) n **shakes**, goose bumps, jitters (infml), creeps (infml), shivers (infml)

willing adj 1 **eager**, keen, enthusiastic, game, helpful Opposite: reluctant 2 **prepared**, ready, set, agreeable, disposed Opposite: unwilling

willingly adv 1 **freely**, readily, gladly, happily, cheerfully Opposite: unwillingly 2 **eagerly**, enthusiastically, keenly, cooperatively, readily Opposite: reluctantly

willingness n 1 **readiness**, inclination, will, preparedness, disposition Opposite: unwillingness 2 **enthusiasm**, alacrity, motivation, eagerness, keenness Opposite: reluctance

willowy adj 1 **graceful**, slim, elegant, lissome, svelte Opposite: stocky 2 **flexible**, bendable, malleable, springy, supple Opposite: stiff

willpower n **determination**, resolve, resolution, iron will, strength of will Opposite: weakness

willy-nilly adv **regardless**, anyway, in any case, like it or not, unceremoniously ■ adj **haphazard**, random, unsystematic, arbitrary, unselective Opposite: methodical

wilt v **droop**, shrivel, wither, fade, wane Opposite: flourish

wily adj **crafty**, cunning, guileful, sly, devious Opposite: ingenuous

win v 1 **come first**, succeed, triumph, be victorious, be successful Opposite: lose 2 **gain**, earn, secure, attain, collect Opposite: lose ■ n **victory**, success, triumph, landslide, conquest Opposite: defeat

wince n 1 **grimace**, scowl, flinch, gasp, cringe Opposite: smile 2 **recoil**, flinch, cringe, jump, start ■ v 1 **grimace**, scowl, shudder, flinch, gasp Opposite: smile 2 **recoil**, flinch, jump, cringe, shrink. See COMPARE AND CONTRAST at recoil.

winch n **hoist**, windlass, pulley, crane, capstan ■ v **raise**, hoist, lift, lift up, pull

wind n **current of air**, breeze, gale, squall, gust ■ v 1 **coil**, twist, encircle, roll, wrap around Opposite: unwind 2 **snake**, meander, bend, curve, twist

WORD BANK
❑ **types of winds** antitrade, bise, chinook, cyclone, foehn, harmattan, hurricane, khamsin, levanter, mistral, monsoon, northeaster, northwester, Santa Ana, simoom, sirocco, southeaster, southwester, tornado, trade wind, tramontana, typhoon, westerly

windbreak n **shelter**, panel, barrier, screen, fence

wind down v **relax**, unwind, rest, loosen up, hang loose

winded adj **breathless**, out of breath, short of breath, panting, gasping

windfall n **bonus**, handout, bonanza, payout, dividend

winding adj **zigzagging**, snaky, snaking, twisting, curving Opposite: straight

windlass n **winch**, hoist, crane, capstan, pulley

window n 1 **pane**, windowpane, glass, glazing 2 **opportunity**, period, chance, slot, window of opportunity 3 **gap**, space, opening, hole 4 **dialogue box**, box, frame, display, interface

WORD BANK
❑ **types of windows** bay window, casement, dormer window, fanlight, French window, lancet window, picture window, porthole, rose window, sash window, skylight, transom

❑ **parts of a window** ledge, pane, sill, window ledge, windowpane, windowsill

windowpane n **pane**, window, glass, glazing

windowsill n **ledge**, window ledge, sill, shelf

windscreen n **windbreak**, screen, shelter, barrier

windstorm n **storm**, wind, gale, hurricane, cyclone

windswept adj **desolate**, windy, barren, inhospitable, exposed Opposite: sheltered

wind up v 1 **end**, conclude, bring to an end, complete, finish Opposite: start off 2 **prepare**, get ready, take aim, pitch

windup adj **clockwork**, mechanical, spring-operated, manual

windy adj 1 **blustery**, breezy, stormy, gusty, squally Opposite: still 2 (infml) **wordy**, voluble, verbose, pompous, bombastic Opposite: meek

winery n **vineyard**, wine producer, wine grower, estate, chateau

wing n 1 **annex**, extension, part, arm, section 2 **division**, subdivision, arm, section, department ■ v 1 **fly**, head, speed, race, whiz 2 **injure**, wound, hurt, maim, shoot

wink v **flash**, twinkle, sparkle, glitter, glint

winner n 1 **victor**, champion, conqueror, leader, frontrunner (infml) Opposite: loser 2 **success**, hit, sensation, triumph, sure thing (infml) Opposite: failure

winning adj 1 **charming**, captivating, endearing, persuasive, engaging Opposite: unprepossessing 2 **successful**, triumphant, victorious, best, champion

winnings n **prize money**, prize, money, earnings, receipts

winnow v **examine**, go through, sort through, pick over, inspect

win over v **convince**, persuade, convert, win around, bring around

winsome adj **charming**, fetching, sweet, lovely, attractive

winter n 1 **wintertime**, midwinter, depth of winter Opposite: summer 2 **end**, twilight, close, closing, ending

wintriness n **chilliness**, coldness, bitterness, iciness, bleakness Opposite: warmth

wintry adj **chilly**, cold, bracing, freezing, nippy Opposite: summery

wipe v 1 **rub**, polish, mop, swab, clean 2 **smear**, spread, rub, distribute, streak 3 **erase**, remove, delete, obliterate, destroy

wipe out (infml) v **annihilate**, destroy, eradicate, obliterate, exterminate Opposite: protect

wipe the floor with (infml) v **defeat**, beat hollow, thrash, trounce, outclass

wipe the slate clean (infml) v **make a fresh start**, start over, start afresh, forgive and forget, bury the hatchet

wire n **cable**, lead, line, filament, cord ■ v **connect**, hook up, install, equip

wired adj **1 strengthened**, supported, reinforced, held together, bound **2** (infml) **online**, on the Net, on the Web, connected **3** (infml) **energetic**, excited, wound up, hyperactive

wiretap v **tap**, bug, monitor, listen in on, eavesdrop ■ n **tap**, monitor, bug (infml)

wiriness n **1 leanness**, slimness, thinness, muscularity, strength Opposite: fatness **2 coarseness**, stiffness, bristliness, roughness, scratchiness Opposite: softness

wiry adj **1 lean**, slim, thin, muscular, sinewy Opposite: fat **2 coarse**, stiff, bristly, rough, scratchy Opposite: soft

wisdom n **understanding**, sense, knowledge, insight, perception Opposite: foolishness

wise adj **1 astute**, intelligent, clever, prudent, sensible Opposite: foolish **2 knowledgeable**, learned, informed, erudite, aware Opposite: ignorant **3 shrewd**, cunning, crafty, devious, wily

wisecrack (infml) n **witticism**, quip, riposte, gibe, retort ■ v **joke**, quip, gibe, retort, gag

wish v **1 want**, desire, crave, require, covet **2 demand**, ask, request, ask for, bid ■ n **1 desire**, aspiration, hope, yearning, longing Opposite: disinclination **2 request**, demand, bidding, command, requirement. See COMPARE AND CONTRAST at want.

wishful thinking n **delusion**, fantasy, self-delusion, self-deception, idealism Opposite: reality

wishy-washy (infml) adj **1 indecisive**, irresolute, weak, feeble, spineless Opposite: decisive **2 watery**, insipid, bland, tasteless, weak Opposite: strong

wisp n **strand**, scrap, tendril, thread, lock

wispy adj **flimsy**, fine, thin, light, slight Opposite: substantial

wistful adj **pensive**, melancholy, thoughtful, reflective, contemplative Opposite: satisfied

wistfulness n **melancholy**, pensiveness, reminiscence, nostalgia, dreaminess Opposite: contentment

wit n **1 wittiness**, jocularity, facetiousness, fun, humor Opposite: seriousness **2 intelligence**, smartness, cleverness, intellect, keenness Opposite: stupidity **3 comedian**, humorist, comic, joker, satirist

witch n **enchantress**, sorceress, magician, occultist, necromancer (literary)

witch doctor n **shaman**, healer, soothsayer, medium, druid

with prep **1 together with**, along with, in conjunction with, beside, alongside Opposite: without **2 in addition to**, plus, including, as well as, and Opposite: without

with bated breath adv **expectantly**, in anticipation, on the edge of your seat, anxiously, hopefully

withdraw v **1 remove**, take out, extract, pull out, draw Opposite: insert **2 retract**, renounce, disavow, revoke, take back Opposite: confirm **3 leave**, depart, retire, pull out, retreat Opposite: remain

withdrawal n **1 removal**, extraction, drawing, taking out, taking away Opposite: insertion **2 retreat**, departure, leaving, abandonment, retirement Opposite: arrival **3 retraction**, renunciation, revocation, disclaimer, abjuration Opposite: confirmation **4 alienation**, depression, isolation, detachment

withdrawn adj **reserved**, inhibited, solitary, introverted, introvert Opposite: outgoing

with ease adv **easily**, effortlessly, confidently, efficiently, smoothly

wither v **1 shrivel**, wilt, dry up, shrink, droop Opposite: bloom **2 weaken**, waste away, decline, fade, wane Opposite: strengthen **3 crush**, mortify, humiliate, abash, put down

withering adj **contemptuous**, scornful, sarcastic, sneering, arrogant Opposite: complimentary

with hindsight adv **in retrospect**, retrospectively, looking back, from experience

withhold v **hold back**, keep back, refuse, deny, suppress Opposite: give

within adv **inside**, in, indoors, in the interior Opposite: outside

within an ace of prep **within reach of**, a hairsbreadth from, a stone's throw from, on the verge of

within reach adv **within your grasp**, reachable, accessible at hand, at your fingertips

with-it (dated infml) adj **cool**, fashionable, up-to-date, modern, modish

with one voice adv **unanimously**, simultaneously, as one, all together, in unison

without prep **devoid of**, lacking, minus, in default of, sans (literary) Opposite: with

without fail adv **for certain**, reliably, like clockwork, unfailingly, dependably

without further ado adv **immediately**, at once, straightaway, forthwith, on the double

with reason adv **rightly**, with good cause, justifiably, justly, properly Opposite: unjustifiably

with reference to see with regard to

with regard to prep **regarding**, as regards, relating to, in connection with, concerning

with respect to see with regard to

withstand v **endure**, survive, resist, bear, weather Opposite: succumb

with your back to the wall adj **in trouble**, in difficulties, in a tight corner, in a tight spot, in dire straits

witless adj **foolish**, stupid, mindless, unintelligent, silly Opposite: sensible

witness n **observer**, spectator, bystander, onlooker, watcher ■ v **1 see**, observe, view, perceive, watch **2 countersign**, endorse, sign, attest, authenticate

wits *n* reason, shrewdness, acumen, faculties, mind

witticism *n* quip, joke, riposte, gibe, one-liner

wittiness *n* cleverness, sharpness, keenness, comedy, sense of humor *Opposite*: dullness

wittingly *adv* knowingly, consciously, purposely, on purpose, intentionally *Opposite*: unwittingly

witty *adj* amusing, droll, humorous, funny, entertaining *Opposite*: dull

wiz *(infml)* *n* expert, prodigy, genius, wizard *(infml)*, ace *(infml)*

wizard *n* 1 sorcerer, warlock, magician, shaman, witch doctor 2 *(infml)* expert, prodigy, genius, virtuoso, ace *(infml)*

wizardry *n* 1 sorcery, magic, divination, shamanism, spells 2 skill, expertise, genius, brilliance, accomplishment

wizened *adj* wrinkled, lined, shriveled, wrinkly, withered *Opposite*: smooth

wobble *v* 1 shake, vibrate, tremble, bob, quiver 2 quaver, wave, shake, vary, oscillate 3 dither, waver, vacillate, shilly-shally, hesitate *Opposite*: take the plunge

wobbliness *n* 1 shakiness, unsteadiness, instability, ricketiness, rockiness *Opposite*: steadiness 2 *(infml)* weakness, unsteadiness, shakiness, trembling, reeling *Opposite*: steadiness

wobbly *adj* 1 unstable, unsteady, rickety, rocky, shaky *Opposite*: steady 2 *(infml)* weak, trembling, woozy, dizzy, unsteady *Opposite*: fit

woe *n* 1 grief, distress, anguish, affliction, sadness *Opposite*: happiness 2 affliction, misfortune, calamity, disaster, trouble *Opposite*: joy

woebegone *adj* miserable, anguished, despairing, sad, wretched *Opposite*: cheerful

woeful *adj* 1 unhappy, doleful, sad, sorrowful, mournful *Opposite*: cheerful 2 distressing, traumatic, harrowing, tragic, unpleasant 3 pathetic, pitiful, regrettable, bad, inadequate *Opposite*: wonderful

wok *n* pan, frying pan, skillet

wolf *n* *(infml)* Casanova, Don Juan, Romeo, womanizer, Lothario *(literary)* ■ *v* gobble, bolt, gulp down, devour, gorge *Opposite*: nibble

woman *n* female, lady, matron *Opposite*: man

womanhood *n* 1 adulthood, maturity, independence *Opposite*: manhood 2 women, womankind, females, womenfolk *Opposite*: mankind

womankind *n* women, womanhood, females, womenfolk *Opposite*: mankind

womanly *adj* female, feminine *Opposite*: manly

wonder *n* 1 surprise, astonishment, awe, amazement, admiration 2 miracle, phenomenon, marvel, sensation, curiosity ■ *v* 1 speculate, doubt, question, conjecture, ponder 2 marvel, admire, gaze at, be amazed

wonderful *adj* 1 magnificent, superb, amazing, astonishing, fantastic *Opposite*: awful 2 delightful, pleasing, great, brilliant, perfect

wonderland *n* utopia, paradise, heaven, never-never land, nirvana

wonderment *n* amazement, astonishment, awe, surprise, bewilderment

wondrous *(literary)* *adj* wonderful, astounding, incredible, astonishing, marvelous *Opposite*: mediocre

wont *(fml)* *adj* accustomed, used, in the habit of, inclined, liable *Opposite*: unaccustomed ■ *n* habit, custom, tendency, preference, practice. *See* COMPARE AND CONTRAST *at* habit.

wonted *(literary)* *adj* usual, typical, customary, preferred, chosen *Opposite*: unaccustomed. *See* COMPARE AND CONTRAST *at* usual.

woo *(literary)* *v* court, persuade, encourage, entice, pursue *Opposite*: discourage

wood *n* 1 lumber, firewood, logs, planks, kindling 2 forest, woodland, copse, covert, coppice

woodcarving *n* 1 carving, sculpture, woodworking, art, craft 2 sculpture, figure, embellishment, adornment, feature

woodcut *n* 1 block, carving, design, matrix 2 print, engraving, picture, illustration, portrait

wooded *adj* forested, woody, timbered, arboreal, sylvan *(literary)*

wooden *adj* 1 wood, woody, ligneous, timber 2 stilted, inexpressive, stiff, emotionless, deadpan *Opposite*: expressive 3 dull, toneless, flat *Opposite*: resonant

woodland *n* forest, wood, woods, timberland

woods *n* wood, forest, woodland, copse, covert

woodshed *n* shed, outbuilding, outhouse, garden shed, lean-to

woodwork *n* fixtures, doors, window frames, paneling, skirting

woodworking *n* carpentry, joinery, cabinetmaking, turning

WORD BANK

❏ types of woodworking cabinetmaking, carpentry, carving, joinery, marquetry, woodcarving

---

woody *adj* forested, wooded, timbered, woodland, arboreal

woof *v* bark, yap, yelp

woolen *adj* knitted, woven, wool, woolly, crocheted

woolens *n* clothing, sweaters, cardigans

woolgather *v* daydream, dream, be miles

away, fantasize, be lost in thought

woollen *see* **woolen**

woollens *see* **woolens**

woolly *adj* **1 woolen**, knitted, woven, wool, crocheted **2 vague**, confused, unfocused, unclear, ill-defined *Opposite*: clear

woozy *adj* **dizzy**, faint, lightheaded, unsteady, nauseous *Opposite*: clear-headed

word *n* **1 term**, expression, name **2 chat**, conversation, talk, discussion, announcement **3 information**, news, communication, info *(infml)*, skinny *(slang)* **4 rumor**, report, whisper, gossip, tittle-tattle **5 promise**, assurance, guarantee, oath, pledge **6 command**, order, authorization, say-so *(infml)*, go-ahead *(infml)* **7 password**, code word, magic word, keyword ■ *v* **express**, phrase, couch, utter, articulate

word for word *adv* **verbatim**, in the same words, faithfully, exactly, precisely *Opposite*: loosely

word-for-word *adj* **verbatim**, faithful, exact, precise, accurate *Opposite*: loose

wordiness *n* **long-windedness**, verbosity, loquaciousness, prolixity *Opposite*: succinctness

wording *n* **phrasing**, words, language, phraseology, diction

wordless *adj* **silent**, mute, nonverbal, mimed, gestured

word list *n* **vocabulary**, glossary, dictionary, thesaurus, lexicon

word-perfect *adj* **correct**, accurate, exact, precise, literal

wordplay *n* **punning**, puns, repartee, wit, banter

WORD BANK

❏ **types of wordplay** acrostic, anagram, logogram, malapropism, palindrome, pun, spoonerism, telestich

---

words *n* **1 argument**, disagreement, difference of opinion, dispute, confrontation **2 lyrics**, verses, chorus, libretto, text

wordy *adj* **verbose**, long-winded, rambling, loquacious, prolix *Opposite*: concise

---

COMPARE AND CONTRAST CORE MEANING: too long or not concisely expressed

wordy using an excessive number of words in writing or speech; **verbose** expressed in language that is wordy and not precise; **long-winded** tediously wordy in speech or writing; **rambling** excessively long with many changes of subject, making it difficult to follow; **prolix** tiresomely wordy; **diffuse** lacking organization and conciseness.

---

work *n* **1 labor**, employment, job, vocation, occupation *Opposite*: unemployment **2 effort**, exertion, labor, toil, slog *Opposite*: leisure **3 composition**, design, creation, opus, masterpiece ■ *v* **1 toil**, labor, slog,

drudge **2 perform**, bring about, produce, effect *(fml)* **3 succeed**, be successful, work out, thrive **4 operate**, control, drive, run, function

workable *adj* **practical**, practicable, feasible, doable *Opposite*: impracticable

workaday *adj* **everyday**, ordinary, plain, homespun, commonplace *Opposite*: extraordinary

work against *v* **counteract**, cancel out, oppose, run counter to, interfere with *Opposite*: support

workaholic *n* **overachiever**, type A, workhorse *(infml)* *Opposite*: idler

workbench *n* **bench**, worktop, work surface, worktable

workbook *n* **exercise book**, schoolbook, notebook, notepad, book

worked up *(infml)* *adj* **agitated**, upset, excited, worried, hot and bothered *Opposite*: calm

worker *n* **employee**, member of staff, hand, operative, wage earner

work force *n* **personnel**, staff, employees, workers, human resources

workhorse *(infml)* *n* **hard worker**, good worker, rock, mainstay, pillar

working *adj* **1 operational**, functioning, effective, running *Opposite*: broken **2 employed**, occupied, at work, salaried *Opposite*: unemployed

working class *n* **manual workers**, hoi polloi, the masses, proletariat, wage-earners *Opposite*: aristocracy

working group *n* **task force**, team, committee, unit

working out *n* **exercising**, physical exercise, exercise, training, physical training

workings *n* **mechanism**, machinery, works, moving parts

workload *n* **amount of work**, assignment, job, load, capacity

workmate *n* **colleague**, coworker, fellow worker

work of art *n* **1 objet d'art**, creation, painting, sculpture, picture **2 masterpiece**, beauty, tour de force, pièce de résistance, work of genius *Opposite*: disaster *(infml)*

work on *v* **1 develop**, hone, build up, work up, perfect **2 influence**, sway, persuade, pressure

work out *v* **1 exercise**, train, drill **2 solve**, figure out, decipher, resolve, deduce **3 understand**, comprehend, make sense of, fathom, conceive **4 plan**, devise, outline, sketch, arrange. *See* COMPARE AND CONTRAST *at* **deduce**.

workout *n* **1 exercise session**, exercises, training, aerobics, calisthenics **2 test**, road test, trial, run

workplace *n* **place of work**, workshop, workstation, work, office

workroom *n* room, workshop, study, office, studio

works *n* **1 factory**, plant, installation, industrial unit, manufacturing plant **2 mechanism**, workings, machinery, moving parts **3** *(infml)* **everything**, the whole thing, the lot, all of it, the whole kit and caboodle *(infml)*

worksheet *n* **1 homework sheet**, handout, test, quiz, question sheet **2 schedule**, job sheet, log, record

workspace *n* **working area**, workstation, workplace, booth, cubicle

workstation *n* **workplace**, workspace, computer terminal

work surface *n* **surface**, worktop, workbench, workspace, work unit

worktop *n* **counter**, bench, work surface

work up *v* **1 develop**, work on, hone, improve, refine **2 agitate**, upset, disturb, provoke, irritate *Opposite*: calm

workup *n* **diagnosis**, examination, checkup, medical

world *n* **1 Earth**, planet, globe **2 biosphere**, ecosphere, creation, all God's creatures, flora and fauna **3 humankind**, humanity, the human race **4 domain**, realm, sphere, circle, area

world-beater *n* **champion**, superstar, one in a million, star, classic

world-class *adj* **first-rate**, first-class, superlative, outstanding, topnotch *(infml)*

world-famous *adj* **famous**, renowned, popular, acclaimed, notorious *Opposite*: unknown

worldliness *n* **1 materialism**, consumerism, acquisitiveness, greed, secularism **2 experience**, knowledge, sophistication, worldly wisdom

worldly *adj* **1 material**, temporal, earthly, materialistic, human **2 experienced**, sophisticated, mature, knowing, worldly wise *Opposite*: naive

worldly goods *n* **possessions**, belongings, assets, property

worldly-wise *adj* **sophisticated**, experienced, mature, knowing, worldly *Opposite*: naive

world-weariness *n* **discontent**, melancholy, boredom, ennui

world-weary *adj* **jaded**, discontented, bored, melancholic

worldwide *adj* **universal**, international, all-inclusive, wide-reaching, global *Opposite*: local

worm-eaten *adj* **1 wormy**, worm-infested, holey, rotten, decaying **2 dilapidated**, ramshackle, tumbledown, rickety

worm out *v* **elicit**, find out, coax out, ferret out, inveigle

worn *adj* **damaged**, shabby, tatty, dog-eared, dilapidated

worn out *adj* **1 exhausted**, tired, done in *(infml)*, done for *(infml)*, wiped out *(infml)* **2 tatty**, tattered, shabby, dilapidated, battered

worried *adj* **concerned**, anxious, apprehensive, nervous, bothered *Opposite*: unconcerned

worrier *n* **pessimist**, neurotic, fidget, worrywart *(infml)*, fussbudget *(infml)*

worrisome *adj* **troublesome**, worrying, annoying, irritating, bothersome

worry *v* **1 be anxious**, fret, be troubled, be concerned, be bothered **2 annoy**, pester, bother, trouble, disturb **3 touch**, pick, interfere with, claw at, tear at ■ *n* **anxiety**, unease, disquiet, discomfort, care

---

COMPARE AND CONTRAST CORE MEANING: a troubled mind

worry a troubled state of mind resulting from concern about current or potential difficulties; **unease** a feeling of anxiousness or lack of satisfaction with a situation; **care** a state of troubled anxiety; **anxiety** nervous apprehension about a future event or a general fear of possible misfortune; **angst** nonspecific chronic anxiety about the human condition or the state of the world; **stress** the worry and nervous apprehension related to a particular situation or event, for example, a job or the process of moving house.

---

worrying *adj* **perturbing**, disturbing, upsetting, disquieting, nerve-racking *Opposite*: reassuring

worse *adj* **not as good as**, inferior, of inferior quality, poorer, of poorer quality *Opposite*: better

worsen *v* **1 get worse**, deteriorate, degenerate, go downhill, degrade *Opposite*: improve **2 make something worse**, exacerbate, aggravate, impair, inflame *Opposite*: improve

worsening *n* **deterioration**, aggravation, degeneration, decline *Opposite*: improvement

worship *v* **adore**, love, revere, adulate, deify ■ *n* **adoration**, love, reverence, respect, devotion

worshiper *n* **celebrant**, participant, member of congregation, believer, convert

worshipful *adj* **reverential**, respectful, reverent, deferential, adoring

worst *adj* **nastiest**, vilest, poorest, wickedest, foulest *Opposite*: best

worth *n* **1 value**, price, cost, rate **2 merit**, appeal, significance, attraction, importance **3 wealth**, means, assets, value, substance

worthiness *n* **1 merit**, value, worth, praiseworthiness **2 dullness**, earnestness, boringness

worthless *adj* **1 valueless**, of no value, of little worth, insignificant, useless *Opposite*: valuable **2 empty**, hollow, meaningless, futile, pointless

worthlessness n 1 **insignificance**, unimportance, irrelevance, triviality Opposite: value 2 **pointlessness**, meaninglessness, futility, emptiness, hollowness

worthwhile adj **valuable**, useful, meaningful, sensible, advisable Opposite: worthless

worthy adj 1 **commendable**, praiseworthy, laudable, admirable, valuable 2 **well-intentioned**, well-meaning, earnest, pedestrian, dull

would-be adj **hopeful**, aspiring, prospective, budding, potential

wound n **injury**, lesion, cut, gash, sore ■ v 1 **injure**, hurt, harm, damage, mutilate 2 **offend**, upset, hurt, injure, distress

wounded adj 1 **injured**, hurt, suffering 2 **offended**, hurt, upset, distressed, aggrieved

wounding adj **hurtful**, cutting, acerbic, sharp Opposite: kind

wound up (infml) adj **stressed**, upset, tense, infuriated, exasperated Opposite: relaxed

wow (infml) n **winner**, smash, triumph, sensation, knockout (infml) Opposite: flop (infml)

wraith n **ghost**, phantom, apparition, spirit, specter

wrangle v **argue**, dispute, quarrel, bicker, squabble ■ n **dispute**, argument, quarrel, squabble, disagreement

wrangler n **ranch hand**, farm hand, cowboy, cowgirl, cowpoke (infml)

wrap v 1 **enfold**, drape, swathe, cover, envelop 2 **wrap up**, gift wrap, package Opposite: unwrap ■ n 1 **shawl**, cloak, stole, cape 2 **wrapping**, packaging, casing, covering

wrapped up adj **engrossed**, absorbed, preoccupied, obsessed, fascinated

wrapper n **covering**, wrapping, wrap, cover, packaging

wrapping n **packaging**, covering, casing, wrap, cover

wrap up v 1 **wrap**, gift wrap, parcel, package Opposite: unwrap 2 **dress warmly**, muffle up, bundle up (infml) 3 (infml) **conclude**, complete, finish, finish off, end Opposite: begin

wrath n **anger**, rage, fury, madness, ire (fml). See COMPARE AND CONTRAST at anger.

wrathful adj **furious**, angry, irate enraged, fuming

wreak v **cause**, do, inflict, create, bring about

wreath n **garland**, circlet, headdress, laurel

wreathe v 1 **adorn**, cover, garland, swathe, festoon 2 **twist**, writhe, coil, wind

wreck v **destroy**, ruin, demolish, break, shatter ■ n 1 **ruin**, remains, wreckage, shell, hulk 2 **crash**, collision, accident, smashup, fender bender (infml)

wreckage n **ruins**, remains, debris, wreck, rubble

wrecked adj 1 **broken**, smashed, damaged, ruined, cracked 2 (infml) **exhausted**, worn-out, bushed (infml), done in (infml)

wrench v 1 **strain**, injure, hurt, pull, sprain 2 **pull**, tug, haul, heave, jerk ■ n 1 **injury**, sprain, strain, crick 2 **pull**, tug, haul, heave, jerk

wrest v 1 **gain**, take, seize, grasp 2 **grab**, snatch, tug, pull

wrestle v **struggle**, fight, grapple, tussle, brawl

wretch n 1 **unfortunate**, victim, languisher, sufferer, poor thing 2 **rogue**, rascal, imp, scalawag (dated infml) 3 (fml) **scoundrel**, rascal, rogue, villain, blackguard

wretched adj 1 **miserable**, desolate, heartbroken, pitiful, dejected Opposite: happy 2 **harsh**, hard, deprived, inferior, grim Opposite: comfortable 3 **worthless**, base, despicable, inadequate, inferior Opposite: noble 4 **irritating**, annoying, infuriating, frustrating, exasperating

wriggle v **wiggle**, writhe, turn, squirm, twist

wring v **squeeze**, twist, mangle, press, compress

wrinkle n **crease**, crinkle, line, fold, furrow ■ v **screw**, crumple, crinkle, crease, fold Opposite: smooth

wrinkled adj 1 **crumpled**, creased, crinkly, rucked, rumpled Opposite: smooth 2 **wrinkly**, wizened, weathered, lined, furrowed Opposite: smooth

wrinkly see wrinkled

writ n **summons**, court order, injunction, restraining order, TRO

write v 1 **inscribe**, put pen to paper, transcribe, engrave, carve 2 **write down**, put in writing, note down, enter, record 3 **compose**, create, script, author, devise 4 **send a letter to**, drop a line to, correspond with, contact, get in touch with

write down v **record**, note down, jot down, set down, put in writing

write off (infml) v **cancel**, forget, disregard, set aside, abandon

writer n **author**, novelist, playwright, poet, journalist

write-up n **report**, article, piece, review, critique

writhe v **squirm**, wriggle, twist, struggle, thrash

writing n 1 **script**, symbols, inscription, marks, characters 2 **text**, literature, prose, journalism, copy

written adj **on paper**, printed, in black and white, in print

wrong adj 1 **incorrect**, mistaken, erroneous, off beam, wide of the mark Opposite: right 2 **immoral**, wicked, dishonest, illegal, sinful Opposite: right 3 **amiss**, not right, unsuitable, improper, inappropriate Opposite: suitable ■ n **sin**, crime, injury, harm, damage ■ v **insult**, injure, wound, harm, ill-treat

wrongdoer n criminal, offender, sinner, reprobate, outlaw

wrongdoing n bad behavior, unlawful activity, crime, offense, misconduct

wrong-foot v catch out, surprise, take unawares, take by surprise, trip up

wrongful adj illegal, unlawful, unfair, unjust, criminal Opposite: rightful. See COMPARE AND CONTRAST at **unlawful**.

wrong-headed adj 1 unreasonable, obstinate, stubborn, perverse 2 irrational, unreasoning, unthinking, ill-considered, ill-conceived

wrought-up adj tense, nervous, agitated, excited, on edge

wry adj ironic, cynical, sardonic, dry, droll

wryness n humor, irony, satire, dryness, drollness

XYZ

xenophobia n chauvinism, racial intolerance, dislike of foreigners, nationalism, prejudice Opposite: tolerance

xenophobic adj chauvinistic, intolerant, nationalistic, prejudiced, racist Opposite: tolerant

yak (infml) v chatter, chat, talk, gossip, natter

yammer v (infml) chatter, chat, talk, gossip, natter

yank v pull, tug, jerk, wrench, snatch ■ n tug, pull, jerk, wrench, heave. See COMPARE AND CONTRAST at **pull**.

yap v 1 bark, yelp, bay, woof 2 (infml) chatter, chat, talk, gossip

yard n 1 plot, patch, grass, lawn 2 patio, courtyard, terrace, back yard 3 enclosure, work area, storage area

yardstick n measure, index, gauge, benchmark, standard

yarn n 1 thread, fiber, wool 2 (infml) story, tale, tall story, tall tale, shaggy-dog story

yawn v 1 stretch, stretch yourself, rub your eyes, sigh, nod 2 gape, split, fly open, gap, crack Opposite: close up ■ n bore, nonevent, waste of time, mind-numbing experience, drag (infml) Opposite: laugh

yawning adj deep, cavernous, gaping, wide, open Opposite: narrow

yearbook n annual, annual report, almanac

yearly adv annually, every year, once a year

yearn v desire, long, crave, ache, hanker. See COMPARE AND CONTRAST at **want**.

yearning n desire, longing, yen, hunger, thirst

year-round adj constant, continual, continuous, perennial Opposite: seasonal

years n an age, an inordinate length of time, eons, ages (infml), centuries (infml)

yell v shout, scream, shriek, roar, bellow ■ n shriek, shout, scream, roar, bellow

yell at v scold, shout at, rebuke, lash, chew out (infml)

yelp v bark, yap, cry, squeal, squeak

yen n urge, desire, wish, longing, yearning

yes adv affirmative, sure, certainly, absolutely, of course Opposite: no ■ n affirmative, positive response, nod, aye, thumbs up (infml) Opposite: no

yesteryear n past, long ago, former times, days gone by, olden days Opposite: today

yet adv 1 up to now, so far, thus far, hitherto, until now 2 however, nevertheless, nonetheless, still, in spite of that

yield v 1 produce, bear, generate, bring in, return 2 give in, submit, surrender, succumb, capitulate Opposite: resist 3 give up, concede, grant, relinquish, resign Opposite: keep ■ n 1 harvest, crop, produce, vintage 2 profit, earnings, income, revenue, return

---

COMPARE AND CONTRAST CORE MEANING: give way

yield give way to something such as force, pressure, entreaty, or persuasion; **capitulate** cease to resist a superior force, especially one that seems invincible, sometimes without having offered strong opposition; **submit** accept somebody else's authority or will, especially reluctantly or under pressure; **succumb** give in to something due to weakness or the failure to offer effective opposition; **surrender** give way to the power of another person and stop offering resistance, usually after active opposition.

---

yielding adj 1 soft, elastic, springy, squashy, resilient Opposite: firm 2 compliant, acquiescent, docile, accommodating, tractable Opposite: stubborn

yoke n repression, oppression, burden, bondage, encumbrance

young adj 1 youthful, little, juvenile, adolescent, immature Opposite: old 2 new, early, undeveloped, fledgling, beginning Opposite: established ■ n offspring, children, babies, litter, brood

---

WORD BANK

❏ types of young animals bullock, calf, colt, cub, fawn, foal, heifer, joey, kid, kitten, lamb, leveret, piglet, pup, puppy, whelp, yearling

❏ types of young birds chick, cygnet, duckling, eaglet, eyas, fledgling, gosling, nestling, owlet, pullet, squab

younger generation *n* young people, youth, teenagers, adolescents, youngsters

young person *n* teenager, adolescent, youngster, juvenile, child *Opposite*: adult

youngster *n* child, young person, teenager, youth, adolescent *Opposite*: adult. See COMPARE AND CONTRAST *at* youth.

youth *n* **1** childhood, adolescence, formative years, infancy, early life *Opposite*: adulthood **2** child, teenager, youngster, minor, young person *Opposite*: adult

COMPARE AND CONTRAST CORE MEANING: somebody who is young
youth a man or boy who is in his teens or early twenties; **child** a young person between birth and the onset of puberty; **kid** (*infml*) a child or young person; **teenager** somebody between the ages of thirteen and nineteen; **youngster** somebody who is young, or somebody younger than others mentioned or present.

youthful *adj* **1** young, childlike, childish, boyish, girlish *Opposite*: old **2** vigorous, energetic, lively, enthusiastic, active *Opposite*: sluggish

youthfulness *n* **1** youth, freshness, newness, childishness, first flush of youth *Opposite*: age **2** enthusiasm, energy, radiance, vigor, liveliness *Opposite*: sluggishness

yowl *v* howl, squall, squeal, wail, caterwaul

yucky (*infml*) *adj* nasty, revolting, horrid, unpleasant, disgusting *Opposite*: yummy (*infml*)

yummy (*infml*) *adj* delicious, tasty, mouthwatering, delectable, luscious *Opposite*: yucky (*infml*)

zany *adj* unconventional, madcap, crazy (*infml*), wacky (*infml*)

zap (*infml*) *v* **1** destroy, kill, annihilate, exterminate, delete **2** change channels, switch channels, flick through, cruise, surf **3** whiz, zoom, tear, rip, shoot *Opposite*: dawdle

zappy (*infml*) *adj* lively, forceful, striking, eye-catching, energetic

zeal *n* enthusiasm, passion, fanaticism, fervor, ardor *Opposite*: apathy

zealot *n* extremist, fanatic, bigot, evangelist, dogmatist *Opposite*: moderate

zealous *adj* enthusiastic, keen, passionate, fervent, ardent *Opposite*: apathetic

zenith *n* peak, summit, pinnacle, top, acme *Opposite*: nadir

zeppelin *n* airship, dirigible, blimp, aircraft, balloon

zero *n* nothing, nil, naught, zip (*infml*), zilch (*infml*)

zest *n* **1** enthusiasm, keenness, gusto, relish, appetite *Opposite*: apathy **2** taste, tang, piquancy, bite, spice

zestful *adj* enthusiastic, keen, passionate, dynamic, energetic *Opposite*: apathetic

zigzag *v* wind, meander, crisscross, weave, snake

zilch (*infml*) *n* nothing, zero, nil, naught, zip (*infml*)

zillion (*infml*) *n* million, billion, truckload, mountain, gazillion (*slang*)

zing (*infml*) *n* vitality, dynamism, energy, punch, vigor *Opposite*: apathy

zip *n* **1** (*infml*) energy, vigor, vitality, dynamism, punch *Opposite*: apathy **2** (*infml*) nothing, nil, zero, zilch (*infml*), zippo (*infml*) ■ *v* **1** compact, compress, condense **2** (*infml*) go fast, whiz, zoom, rocket, whoosh *Opposite*: dawdle

zodiac *n* astrologer's chart, astrological diagram, astrological calendar

zodiacal *adj* astrological, horoscopic, celestial

zombie (*infml*) *n* automaton, robot, machine, sleepwalker (*infml*)

zonal *adj* regional, territorial, area, district, zone-specific

zone *n* area, region, district, sector, neighborhood

zoo *n* zoological gardens, menagerie, safari park, wildlife refuge, game reserve

zoom *v* **1** go fast, whiz, whoosh, rocket, go like a bullet *Opposite*: dawdle **2** increase, shoot up, rise, rocket, take off *Opposite*: plummet

zoom in *v* home in, pinpoint, focus, narrow down, concentrate